The Cacti of the United States and Canada

THE Cacti OF THE
UNITED STATES AND CANADA

LYMAN BENSON

With line drawings by Lucretia Breazeale Hamilton

STANFORD UNIVERSITY PRESS, Stanford, California

This material is based upon work supported
by the National Science Foundation under
Grant Numbers GS-1056C2, G9089, GB2925,
and GN-37323. Any opinions, findings,
conclusions, or recommendations expressed
in this work are those of the author and do not
necessarily reflect the views of the Foundation.

For illustration sources not given in the figure
legends, see Illustration Credits, p. 1009.

To the memory of
EVELYN LINDERHOLM BENSON
1907-1980

Preface

This book is intended to make available to the public the results of 48 years of research upon the genera and species of cacti native or introduced in the United States and Canada. The term "public" is used here in the broadest sense to include all who are interested in cactus plants—from botanical specialists and ecologists to naturalists, horticulturists, hobbyists, ranchers, and those with only a casual interest in recognizing a species or two. Basically, this is a technical monograph, but background information is extensive and illustration is profuse. Moreover, scientific terminology is restricted to that really necessary, and the more esoteric supporting data are gathered into a section following the main body of text. Thus, in a single volume there is something for everyone with an interest in cacti.

The first part of the book takes up a variety of topics related to the classification, structure, physiology, evolution, ecology, history, uses, and conservation of cacti; the second part is a comprehensive, systematic treatment of all members of the cactus family occurring naturally in North America north of Mexico, and the main outline of the formal arrangement is a description of the family and of each of its component genera, species, and varieties. This part also includes certain hybrid populations and all introduced species persisting without the intentional aid of man. The identification of any individual cactus plant may be made superficially from the pictures and descriptions but more accurately by use of the keys, tables, and maps.

Support for the research presented here has come from several sources. During the early stages, several research grants were received from the Claremont Graduate School, and a grant was made for 1950 by the Society of Sigma Xi. Three larger grants were made by the National Science Foundation for the periods 1956-59, 1959-64, and 1965-67. Research grants were awarded by Pomona College during the period 1968-71. Pomona College also granted sabbatical leaves primarily for the study of cacti during 1950-51, 1957-58, 1964-65, and the spring of 1970. Finally, the National Science Foundation awarded the publisher a generous grant in partial support of publication, and a grant was also made by Mrs. Gordon A. Alles of Pasadena. This aid in all phases of the work is acknowledged with gratitude.

The U.S. National Herbarium (Smithsonian Institution: Division of Plants, National Museum) has been particularly helpful. A debt of gratitude is owed that institution for a cooperative arrangement under which the very large collection of *Opuntia* made by David Griffiths of the U.S. Department of Agriculture during the period from about 1905 to 1916 was studied and curated at Pomona College by the writer and the first set of duplicate material was given to the Herbarium of Pomona College. The almost identical basic set was returned to the National Herbarium late in 1970.

Special appreciation is extended to the Missouri Botanical Garden, which made the all-important cactus collection of George Engelmann available on loan from 1951 through 1970 for constant study in connection with the literature, the Herbarium of Pomona College, other collections on loan, and the manuscript for this book. The availability of this collection has provided an insight not otherwise obtainable into the astute works of Engelmann.

Gratitude is expressed to the directors and curators of more than 60 other herbaria (see Documentation) for opportunities to study specimens and for many special courtesies.

The author is grateful for four special sections of the text contributed by others. These sections, the results of their research, are as follows:

Dr. F. W. Went, Desert Research Institute, University of Nevada System: physiology of cacti.

Dr. Edward F. Anderson, Department of Biological Sciences, Whitman College, Walla Walla, Washington: history and uses of peyote, *Lophophora williamsii*.

Dr. David L. Walkington, Department of Botany, Division of Science, California State University, Fullerton: chemical characters of the introduced fruit tree *Opuntia ficus-indica*, the native species, and the spontaneously growing hybrids, as well as the local rapid evolution of prickly pears.

Second Lieutenant Brian S. Bean, U.S. Marine Corps: analysis of the soils upon which *Pediocactus sileri* grows, deviation from them forming an absolute barrier to the migration of the species.

Unless otherwise stated, the photographs in this book are by the author. However, a great many people and institutions have made additional illustrations available, and various journals and publishing houses have been generous in giving permission to include material published previously. This help is appreciated deeply. Credit for illustrations published previously is given under "Illustration Credits," back of the book.

The U.S. National Herbarium has made available the photographs taken by the late David Griffiths and the paintings prepared by L. C. C. Krieger for Griffiths's projected book on the species of *Opuntia*, for use in the writer's publications on the cacti and especially for this book. The writer is grateful for this courtesy.

Dr. Charles T. Mason, Jr., Director of the University of Arizona Herbarium, has made photographs taken by the late Homer L. Shantz and Robert H. Peebles available for use; his help is appreciated deeply. The Peebles plant specimens and photographs are now the property of the University of Arizona Herbarium, under an arrangement made by the writer in 1944 with Dr. Peebles and the U.S. Department of Agriculture Field Station at Sacaton for transfer of the Kearney and Peebles plant collections and photographs to the University.

Mr. Charles E. Glass, Editor of the *Cactus and Succulent Journal*, has granted permission to use text material and photographs that have illustrated the publications of the writer and others in that journal. His courtesies are appreciated.

The Missouri Botanical Garden has made available about 20 photographs of cacti that were filed as herbarium specimens. These were taken in the 1890's and early 1900's, but the name of the photographer and usually the place of origin of the garden specimen are not indicated. The excellent pencil illustrations of Paulus Roetter are acknowledged by Engelmann as follows: "I take great pleasure to acknowledge my indebtedness to the modest and faithful artist, *Mr. Paulus Roetter*, who has adorned this memoir by his skillful pencil . . ." (cf. p. 33, Engelmann, in W. H. Emory, *Report of the United States and Mexican Boundary Survey* 2: 1-78, *pl. 1-75*, 1859). These illustrations have been made available through the courtesy of the Missouri Botanical Garden for use in this book. Those appearing here represent taxa not readily available as living plants with flowers and fruits. The numerous courtesies of the Garden are acknowledged with gratitude.

The many useful photographs taken by others are acknowledged in the legends. The excellent conversions of some from Kodachrome to black-and-white are by Dr. Frank P. McWhorter or Mr. Donald W. Dimock. The fine developing and printing of many black-and-white photographs is by Mr. Russell V. Lapp, who has converted some Kodachromes to black-and-white, as well.

Special gratitude is extended to Mrs. Lucretia Breazeale Hamilton of Tucson, who has prepared, from live material and to superb effect, most of the line drawings for this book, as well as for the three editions of *The Cacti of Arizona,* for the two (and a third in preparation) of *The Trees and Shrubs of the Southwestern Deserts,* for *The Native Cacti of California,* and for the treatment of the Cactaceae in C. L. Lundell's *Flora of Texas* (three of which are used here through the courtesy of Dr. Lundell and the Texas Research Foundation). The line drawings by Mrs. Hamilton are indicated by the initials L.B.H. Necessarily, drawing has been restricted to the plants available and in flower, as well as (usually) in fruit. Although they have been secured from many places, they have been the taxa available in nature or in cultivation near Tucson, because all have been drawn from living material.

Line drawings of a few species have been added by the author (designated by L.B.), but the chief source of drawings of species occurring farther away, especially in Texas, is the work of Paulus Roetter for George Engelmann, as acknowledged above.

The topographic-and-political basemap used for the many distributional maps in the text was prepared by the author and Albert P. Burkhardt. Mr. Burkhardt designed also the typography of the book and the layout of the color illustrations.

Page layouts for the text are the work of Patricia Brito. The book was set by Linotype, in Sabon type, chiefly at Stanford University Press.

Through 50 years many typists have contributed to the preparation of the manuscript for this book. During recent years the major contributions have been by Mrs. Orvil H. Huling, Miss Nancy Phillips, and Miss Vivienne Becky (Mrs. Brian S. Bean). Mrs. Huling typed the material for the Documentation section to specification, for direct use in publication, with amazing accuracy and precision, and with perception of the meaning and composition of this difficult and extensive material. The help of these three and many earlier typists is acknowledged with gratitude and with appreciation of their excellent work.

Mrs. Helen Speck, Secretary of the Department of Botany of Pomona College, has been helpful in innumerable ways, and her efforts are much appreciated.

LYMAN BENSON

Contents

*Forty-eight pages of color illustrations, in three sixteen-page groups,
   follow pages 468, 596, and 788*

Introduction

Cacti are the most popular succulent plants in cultivation. There are hundreds of national, regional, and local societies devoted to succulents, and there are more than 20 journals concerning these plants. The Cactaceae, or cactus family, and the Crassulaceae, or stonecrop family, are composed wholly of succulents, but the other plants of this type are scattered through many other families composed mostly of nonsucculent plants. The cacti—bizarre in appearance, their flowers large and beautiful—are the succulents of greatest interest. Their preeminence in public interest is reflected in the wording "cactus and succulent" that so often appears in the names of societies.

Even though cacti are common in nature only in parts of the Western Hemisphere, and probably none (not even *Rhipsalis*, pp. 537-38) are native outside the Americas, cultivated cacti are enjoyed both indoors and out, throughout the world. Because most species are frost-sensitive, in temperate regions they must be grown indoors, and in North America or Eurasia they are planted in the open only from the southernmost temperate areas to the Tropics. Indoors, the plants are curiosities throughout the year and objects of wonder and delight when the disproportionately large flowers appear. Where cacti can be grown outdoors (see Figs. 1-5), often they are the most striking or even the dominant feature of gardens or landscaping.

In popular language the word "cactus" is often corrupted to mean any plant with "stickers" or with thick, swollen stems or leaves.* These features are significant, but the real distinctions are

precise. The spines of cacti are produced in clusters at regular intervals on the stem, in the positions normal for buds, i.e. just above the usual positions of leaves, though leaves are visible in only a few cacti. Each spine cluster (this sometimes represented by a single spine) is within a clearly defined area also bearing felt, wool, or other structures shorter than the spines. This area is known as an *areole* (diminutive of area), and it occurs in no other plants (see Fig. 6).

All cacti are *stem succulents*, and, except for a few tropical species mostly of *Pereskia*, none has permanent visible leaves. Most other stem succulents do not resemble the cacti, and there is little danger of confusion. Some African species of the unrelated spurges (*Euphorbia*) (Figs. 29-31, pp.

Fig. 1. *Cereus peruvianus* planted as a fruit tree beside a house in southern California. The fruit is edible and delicately perfumed (see Fig. 567). A California fan palm, *Washingtonia filifera*, is on the right, a hybrid *Hibiscus* on the left.

*The word "cactus" was originally the Latin name (derived from the Greek *kaktos*) for the cardoon, a prickly plant found in southern Europe and North Africa. Among the first cacti known to Europeans was one they called *Echinomelocactus*, abridged by Tournefort to *Melocactus*. Later, Linnaeus, whose book *Species Plantarum* (1753) is the official beginning of botanical nomenclature, shortened the name still further to *Cactus*. However, Linnaeus included several genera under *Cactus*, and application is a moot point. Link and Otto published the name *Melocactus* in 1827, and it is in general use today, though Britton and Rose placed its species under *Cactus*.

Fig. 2. Cactus planting in the Huntington Botanical Gardens, San Marino, California. (See also Figs. 3–5.)

Fig. 3. Lefthand section of the planting in Fig. 2: *Cereus* (*Rathbunia*) *alamosensis*, southern Sonora to Tepic, Mexico, sprawling above the smaller cacti; *Mammillaria compressa*, central Mexico, covering the rocks in the foreground, the plants variable; *Yucca elephantipes* in the background at left.

Fig. 4. Center section, with species of *Cereus* in the background: *C. (Cleistocactus) straussii*, Bolivia, middle and at left; *C. (Cephalocereus) chrysacanthus*, Puebla and Oaxaca, Mexico, left of center; *C. (Cephalocereus) palmeri*, eastern Mexico, right of center; *C. (Neobuxbaumia) euphorbioides*, Tamaulipas and perhaps Veracruz, Mexico, extreme right. The paper bags are concerned with the protection of fruits and seeds from birds until the seeds can be collected for experimental studies. Species of *Mammillaria* in the fore- and middleground: *M. compressa*, central Mexico, lower left and most prominent in the planting (see Fig. 3); *M. zuccariniana,* San Luis Potosí, Mexico, the *Mammillaria* at the extreme upper left and on the right at midlevel; *M. candida*, central Mexico, the plant with white spines and large stems at the top, just below the large *Cereus*; *M. geminispina*, north-central Mexico, the white-spined plant next to *C. compressa* in the lower right corner.

3

Fig. 5. Righthand section, featuring the golden barrel cactus, *Echinocactus grusonii*, central Mexico from San Luis Potosí to Hidalgo, top of embankment at the right. Species of *Cereus* in the background: C. (*Cephalocereus*) *palmeri*, eastern Mexico, left; C. (*Neobuxbaumia*) *euphorbioides*, Tamaulipas and perhaps Veracruz, Mexico, next to left and center; a hybrid, named as *Pachgerocereus orcuttii*, a cross of *Cereus emoryi* and C. *pringlei*, northwestern Baja California, right, among the barrel cacti. Species of *Mammillaria* in the fore- and middleground: *M. geminispina*, north-central Mexico, forming several white-spined mounds especially in the lower left corner and at middle left; *M. elongata*, eastern Mexico, the slender-stemmed darker (yellow-spined) plant between the two white mounds at the lower left and other plants near the barrel cacti; *M. zuccariniana*, San Luis Potosí, Mexico, above the boulder at lower left; *M. spinosissima*, central Mexico, the large, seemingly banded stem in front of the clusters of barrel cacti.

27-28) are stem succulents seemingly like cacti, but their stiff, pointed structures are not produced in areoles and the juice is not acrid (a few cacti have milky juice, but it is bland and of a different chemical nature).

The *leaf succulents* may be distinguished from the cacti at a glance; they have conspicuous fleshy leaves and usually inconspicuous stems. They include notably the ice plants (*Mesembryanthemum*) (Fig. 71), the living stones (*Lithops*) (Figs. 72 and 73), and the many relatives of these plants native in southern Africa; the stonecrop family (Crassulaceae, notably *Sedum*); the century plants (*Agave*); the aloes (*Aloë*, Figs. 7 and 8; and even some members of the grape family, e.g. *Cissus* (Fig. 9).

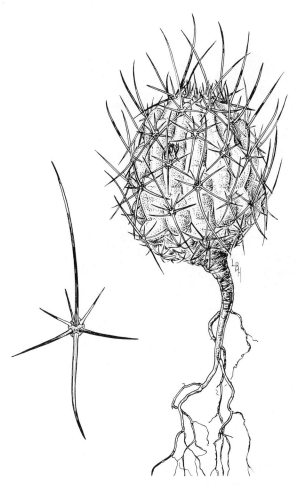

Fig. 6. *Echinocereus fendleri* var. *fendleri*, a succulent stem bearing spines in areoles; and a single areole bearing spines emerging from the feltlike wool covering the areole surface.

In the United States, cacti are sold in great numbers for cultivation in gardens, greenhouses, and homes, but otherwise they are of little economic value. However, in Mexico and other Latin American countries the fruits of cacti and even the stems and the ephemeral leaves of prickly pears and chollas are of major importance in the diets of local residents. In the United States and Latin America the stems of prickly pears and chollas and sometimes of other cacti are also an important source of food and water for range livestock during drought periods. The peyote (*Lophophora*), an obscure cactus containing hallucinogenic alkaloids, is an important element of Indian Christian religious ceremonies. These subjects are discussed under "The Uses of Cacti" (pp. 216-41).

Cacti occur nearly throughout North and South America, from Peace River in far northern British Columbia and Alberta to the Strait of Magellan. Some hardy plants grow within 4° of the Arctic Circle and others within 10° of the Antarctic Circle. In the United States cacti are abundant mostly in areas with warm winters; near large population centers, they are dominant or significant only in the Southwest and in Florida. A large number of native cacti would very likely be known only to those living in the immediate areas of distribution, were it not that these are the places attracting winter visitors. Many vacationers are fascinated by the amazing forms of the cacti, and those who stay on into the spring are enthralled by the beauty of the flowers.

Many genera and species of cacti occur in the horse latitudes of North and South America—i.e. from 23° to 34° north or south of the Equator. In North America this vast region lies along the southern edge of the United States and across northern Mexico. According to a conservative interpretation of species, there are more than twice as many taxa of cacti in Mexico as in the United States. Cold ocean currents and the high Andes have striking effects on the dry regions in the horse latitudes of South America, extending the deserts and adjacent areas of dry climate northward along the Pacific Coast and both northward and southward in the lee of the cordillera of Argentina. Thus, great numbers of cacti occur from Peru to Chile and from Brazil to Argentina. Most of these are in dry areas, but some occur even in rain forests. The numbers of genera, species, and varieties of cacti occurring in Latin America are large but unknown, and an estimate is impossible because of the chaotic classification of the family as a whole, the paucity of information, and the fine and artificial division commonly applied to the genera and species of the family. Understanding the taxa of cacti in Latin America will require many decades of thorough and meticulous work in the field and laboratory.

The early studies of cacti in the United States were stimulated by the occasional discovery of an exciting, bizarre plant resembling those earlier described and figured in the literature. Cacti had been brought to European gardens from Latin America since shortly after the expeditions of Columbus, but they were few and rare in the British colonies along the Atlantic coast of North America. Aside from *Opuntia humifusa*, which reached Linnaeus with the Clayton collections from Virginia, little was known of the cacti of temperate North America when *Species Plan-*

Fig. 7. *Aloë* growing on the floor of the Namib Desert, South West Africa (Namibia), between Swakopmund and the Kahn River; in gravel and sand near a quartz outcrop. The permanent feature of each plant is a rosette of succulent leaves much like those of an American century plant (*Agave*). The flowering stems arise after a rain, which is rare. Lily family (Liliaceae).

Fig. 8. The kokerboom (quiver tree), *Aloë dichotoma*, in the inner (eastern and upland) Namib Desert, South West Africa (Namibia); actually in a dry grassland just above the desert. The Bushmen use the branches to hold arrows or darts; a section is cut, and the soft pith is hollowed out to make the quiver. Both the stems and the leaves are succulent. Lily family (Liliaceae).

Fig. 9. A dicotyledonous stem succulent, *Cissus*, growing in a dry grassland in the inner (eastern and upland) Namib Desert, South West Africa (Namibia). During the almost perpetual dry season, the leaves and twigs fall away, but, as with the related grapes cultivated in dry regions, rapid growth occurs whenever there is sufficient rainfall. Grape family (Vitaceae).

6

tarum appeared in 1753. Florida was a Spanish possession, and it was explored with the other North American colonies of Spain, but early collections of cacti from the peninsula were of little importance in comparison with those from possessions of Spain farther south.

In 1811, Thomas Nuttall of Philadelphia (Fig. 10), later of Harvard University, travelled by canoe up the Missouri River to the Mandan Sioux villages and Ft. Manuel Lisa in North Dakota (see Fig. 11). There he collected *Opuntia polyacantha*, *O. fragilis*, *Coryphantha vivipara*, and *C. missouriensis*, the only four species of cacti in the area, and the names of all four were based on his collections, doubtless of living plants. The specimens were not preserved, however, and neotypes have been collected specially by Larry W. Mitich (Mitich & Benson, 1977). In 1836, after crossing the continent to the mouth of the Columbia River, Nuttall visited California by ship and collected cacti at San Diego, then continued around the Horn on the ship of Dana's *Two Years Before the Mast*. However, his observations and collections of cacti in the regions that became parts of the United States were overshadowed by the more abundant specimens brought from Mexico, Central America, the Caribbean, and South America, some of which had become prominent in the gardens of the Old World.

The cacti of the southwestern United States occur mostly in the interior, and few early botanists could have reached any but those in southern and central Texas, which were collected by Jean Louis Berlandier (Switzerland), Ferdinand Lindheimer (Texas), and Heinrich Poselger (Prussia) during the 1840's. Many cactus collections were taken to Europe, but Berlandier's and Lindheimer's extensive collections of plants from Texas are preserved in various American herbaria, primarily the Missouri Botanical Garden. The species introduced into horticulture in the early period appear in various old books covering the flora of a region or locality or describing cacti as garden plants.

The great age of discovery of species of cacti in the United States—from 1845 to 1883—was the time of George Engelmann of St. Louis, whose research on the cactus family is by far the best, matched in bulk but not approached in quality. Although he was a practicing physician pursuing botany as a spare-time project, Engelmann (Fig. 12) devoted much effort to several groups of plants and especially the Cactaceae. Other plants in which he took a particular interest include the dodders (*Cuscuta*), the rushes (*Juncus*), the yuc-

Fig. 10. Thomas Nuttall (1786–1859), great explorer and botanist; born in England, lived for a time in Philadelphia, served for many years on the faculty at Harvard University, and later returned to England. Nuttall explored the United States from coast to coast; in 1811 he collected the four species of cacti occurring in North Dakota, the first species collected in the United States other than the eastern *Opuntia humifusa*, sent to Linnaeus from Virginia. Nuttall was a collector and student of birds and minerals, as well, as witness the ubiquitous technical reference "Nutt." (See Credits)

cas (*Yucca*), the century plants (*Agave*), the cone-bearing trees (*Pinales*), the oaks (*Quercus*), the grapes (*Vitis*), the spurge family (*Euphorbiaceae*), and the quillworts (*Isoëtes*). Engelmann was one of the quadrumvirate who founded and developed botany in North America, the others being John Torrey of Columbia College (now Columbia University), Thomas Nuttall of Philadelphia and later Harvard University, and Asa Gray of Harvard. Each of these four provided the stimulus not only for the development of a science but also for the founding of a world-renowned institution—the New York Botanical Garden and especially its herbarium (including that of Columbia), the Gray Herbarium of Harvard University and its botanical garden, and the Missouri Botanical Garden and especially its herbarium.

Engelmann's work was the product of a keen, enquiring, well-trained mind and of a sound, balanced judgment. As with Nuttall, Torrey, and Gray, he published remarkably sound work on the basis of only meager plant material. He was born in Frankfurt-am-Main, and he received his

Fig. 11. Mandan Indians and their village of earth houses on the bank of the Missouri River in North Dakota. The Mandans are considered to have been the most advanced tribe of the upper Missouri. Nuttall collected the four North Dakota cacti near the "Mandan Towns," and stayed at Fort Manuel Lisa (later Ft. Vanderburgh) near these towns in 1811. The four species he collected were (except for *Opuntia humifusa*) the first from the United States. (Carl Bodmer; see Credits)

training in botany at Heidelberg, Berlin, and Wurzburg at a time when Germany led the world in this field. When he emigrated to the United States in 1832, he brought not only the best medical training but also the finest of botanical backgrounds to the frontier outpost of St. Louis, where he established a medical practice in 1835.

Torrey and Gray did not claim to understand the cacti, and they referred all cactus collections to Engelmann, probably with relief. Engelmann had many friends in the German settlements in the West, and among them was Ferdinand Lindheimer in New Braunfels, Texas. Engelmann based several new species on the many cactus specimens that Lindheimer sent him. Other cacti were sent from central Texas by another of his

Fig. 12. George Engelmann (1809–84), St. Louis physician; born in Germany and educated at Heidelberg, Berlin, and Wurzburg; astute botanist and the most outstanding student of cacti of all time. This photograph was a gift to Dr. John Torrey, another of the leading botanists of America. (Courtesy of the New York Botanical Garden)

friends, Dr. F. Roemer, geologist of the University of Bonn. Plants from the vicinity of Santa Fe, New Mexico, came from August Fendler.

St. Louis was the base for the launching of a number of U.S. Government exploring and surveying expeditions to the West. Partly through the influence of the instigator of these expeditions, Senator Thomas Hart Benton of Missouri, the collections of cacti made along the way by naturalists and surgeons were sent to Engelmann. He studied the notes of William H. Emory (Fig. 13) and the drawings of the artist, J. M. Stanly, from the Military Reconnaissance Expedition from Ft. Leavenworth, Kansas, to San Diego in 1846. Among the nine species of cacti named from the notes and illustrations was the saguaro, *Cereus giganteus* (see Fig. 568). There were no specimens of the cacti of the Emory Expedition, but 120 years later the writer collected cacti at the various Emory campsites, and neotypes were designated from them. In 1846-47, Dr. A. Wislizenus, a surgeon attached to the U.S. Army during the war with Mexico, collected cacti in New Mexico, Texas, and northeastern Mexico, and at about the same time Josiah Gregg was collecting in the same areas of Texas and Mexico. All the specimens came to Engelmann. The survey of the international boundary between the United States and Mexico, 1851-53, brought collections by Charles Wright, C. C. Parry, J. M. Bigelow, George Thurber, and Arthur Schott. Earlier collections by Wright, in 1849, and later ones by Schott during the exploration of the Gadsden Purchase, in 1854-55, also brought large numbers of cacti to St. Louis. Bigelow became the surgeon and botanist for the Whipple Expedition, which in 1853-54 explored the approximate route of the Santa Fe Railroad along the 35th parallel; and with Engelmann he was co-author of the text on the cacti in the Pacific Railroad Report. Cacti were added to Engelmann's collection by the Ives Expedition to the Colorado River of the West (1857-58); the King Expedition along the 40th parallel through Utah and Nevada (1868), along the route selected for the Union Pacific and Southern Pacific railroads; the Simpson Expedition (1859), exploring for a new wagon route from Provo, Utah, to Carson Valley, Nevada; the Geological Survey of California, with botanical reports by Brewer and Watson (1876-80); and the Wheeler Expedition, which undertook a number of geographical surveys (account published in 1878).

Engelmann, like Torrey and Gray, was a genius who could piece together scattered fragments of

Fig. 13. Gen. William H. Emory (1811–87), U.S. Army Corps of Topographical Engineers, one of the principal explorers of the American West; in charge of the United States and Mexican Boundary Survey; collector of many species of cacti on the earliest expeditions for the United States through the Southwest. In 1846, Emory led a military reconnaissance from Ft. Leavenworth, Kansas, to San Diego, California; the campsites where cacti were reported were visited during the preparation of this book, and specimens (neotypes) were collected 120 years after the expedition. Thus, the species described as new could be evaluated; they had not been collected during the reconnaissance but only illustrated by quick sketches and described briefly.

information into an amazingly well-organized whole. His insight has not been matched in later studies of the Cactaceae. Since Engelmann, students of the family have been preoccupied with discovery of new entities, real or otherwise, and their concern with organization has been restricted to cataloging and description. The interrelationships among individual plants and among the taxa they compose have received little attention, and each species has been assumed to be represented sufficiently by one or more garden plants. For the early days of botany, this was to be expected, because discovery must precede organization. During the nineteenth century a number of able European botanists and horticulturists prepared books cataloging the known cacti of their times, and these have served as a basis for studying the family, despite being based wholly on garden plants with no precise records of origin.

An exception to the domination of cactus study by amateurs after the death of Engelmann (1809-84) was the research of John Merle Coulter (1851-

1928), U.S. National Herbarium, Washington, D.C., who brought together much information from the scattered literature and carried out field studies on the cacti. His work in organization must have been a great aid to Joseph Nelson Rose (see below), later in charge of the specimens of the Cactaceae at the same institution. Coulter and Rose published papers together on various groups of plants, especially the parsley family, or Umbelliferae. Coulter was engaged in other botanical projects, including preparation of his *Botany of Western Texas* (1891-94) and *Manual of Botany of the Rocky Mountain Region* (1885), revised by Aven Nelson as the well-known *New Manual of Rocky Mountain Botany* (1909).

The research efforts of Coulter and of David Griffiths (1867-1935) were bright spots during a long, dull period of the taxonomy of cacti. The meticulous research of Griffiths, who traveled widely in the United States and Mexico, brought cuttings of innumerable plants of *Opuntia* into the experimental gardens of the U.S.D.A., kept complete records of the plants, and assembled thousands of herbarium specimens from them, represented something new to cactus study, including methods long neglected or ignored afterward. Unfortunately, neither Coulter nor Griffiths remained long in the study of cacti. Coulter became a morphologist, which was then a new field, and chairman of the Botany Department of the University of Chicago, and he promoted his new field by downgrading the old. His own work had been rapid and not meticulous, and he accordingly misjudged taxonomy. Griffiths, having started outstanding research in one field, was transferred to another before it was completed, as so often happens in government work. However, despite his boundless energy and vast background in plant breeding and other fields, somehow he could not correlate his enormous mass of taxonomic data but merely multiplied the number of named species, and only a few of the newly named ones have proved to be acceptable as taxa.

Beginning about 1920, interest in the cacti burgeoned, but until recently the family has engaged the interest of only a few trained botanical taxonomists. Research institutions and universities and colleges were infrequent in the cactus country until about the last two or three decades. Inasmuch as cacti are more difficult than other plants to make into herbarium specimens, nearly all the preliminary work had to be done in the field, and this restricted taking part in extensive field research to those living nearby. The advent of the automobile and the airplane made travel easier, and more research workers were able to study cacti in their natural habitats, to learn something of the complex population systems occurring in the field, and to apply new methods of study to the evolution and classification of the taxa. From 1920 to 1965 many books and journal papers were written by people who, though intelligent enough, lacked formal training in botany, and these works have been useful, if limited, contributions to basic research. During this period the work of two technical botanists was of special value. Dr. Robert H. Peebles (1900-1956), U.S. Department of Agriculture cotton-breeding station, Sacaton, Arizona, contributed the section on the Cactaceae for Kearney and Peebles, *Arizona Flora* (University of California Press, 1960, really a revision of a 1942 publication). This was a meticulous piece of research based on extensive field work. Dr. Ira L. Wiggins (1899-) of Stanford University prepared (*Opuntia* with Carl B. Wolf) the treatment of the Cactaceae in L. R. Abrams, *Illustrated Flora of the Pacific States* (Stanford University Press, vol. 3, 1951) and that in Shreve and Wiggins, *Vegetation and Flora of the Sonoran Desert* (Stanford University Press, 1964). Although, in both cases, the work on the cacti was included in volumes dealing with a broader subject, it was sound taxonomic research readily available to all but discovered mostly by those with botanical training or with an interest in all groups of plants. Dr. Wiggins was also of great aid to the layman studying cacti through his help as informal technical adviser for the Cactus and Succulent Society of America and its *Cactus and Succulent Journal*.

The most extensive works on cacti are those of the twentieth century by Britton and Rose (1919-23; Figs. 14 and 15) and Backeberg (1958-62). Like their nineteenth-century predecessors, these are essentially descriptive catalogs representing attempts to bring together the existing literature and to add to it the results of recent exploration. Britton and Rose based their studies to a considerable extent on Rose's exploration in both North and South America; Backeberg also travelled in South America but without preserving specimens. However, in both instances fieldwork was directed largely toward discovery of new plants to be described as species, and little effort was directed toward understanding and organizing them. The emphasis was on differences, not on similarities indicating relationships, and the result was large numbers of newly named species, some

Fig. 14. Dr. Nathaniel Lord Britton (1859–1934), founder and Director of the New York Botanical Garden and Professor of Botany at Columbia University; author of numerous botanical works; senior author of *The Cactaceae* (1919–23). His best-known botanical publications are *Manual of the Flora of the Northern States and Canada*, 1907, and (with Addison Brown) *An Illustrated Flora of the Northern United States, Canada, . . .* (ed. 2), 1913 (revised as *The New Britton and Brown, Illustrated Flora, . . .* , by Henry A. Gleason, 1952). Britton published extensive revisions of many groups of plants in *The North American Flora*, New York Botanical Garden, a series of monographs by specialists integrated toward a flora of the continent.

classification. We need to know more of the evolutionary relationships of taxa and of their ecological relationships with the plant and animal communities in which they are members. A definitive monograph of the family is needed, but the underlying research may require a century or more. This book is intended to be a beginning in this direction, but it is only a first step.

My own interest in cacti began in 1929 with the collection of specimens of two species in the state of Washington. Interest in the family increased, and my study of the species developed from 1931 to 1938 as a member of the faculty of Bakersfield Junior College, in reach of the deserts of California and Arizona. The first edition of *The Cacti of Arizona* (1940) was written at Tucson during a period on the faculty of the University of Arizona from 1938 to 1944. Since then, the

Fig. 15. Dr. Joseph Nelson Rose (1862–1928), Associate Botanist of the United States National Herbarium (Smithsonian Institution) for the Cactaceae, Crassulaceae, and Umbelliferae. Drs. Britton and Rose were associated in numerous publications concerning these and other plant families, including especially the subfamilies Mimosoideae and Caesalpinioideae of the Leguminosae, or pea family. Photograph taken in Argentina in 1915, when Rose was about 53. (See Credits)

valid, most not. Britton and Rose worked with herbarium specimens to the extent they were available in America and Europe, and Rose added many collections to the U.S. National Herbarium and the New York Botanical Garden. Backeberg, for his part, scorned herbarium specimens and swore he would never make one; he worked largely from the literature published by others. The keys in the books of Britton and Rose and of Backeberg reflect the orientation of the authors toward finding, listing, and describing but not evaluating or organizing taxa; they cannot be used effectively. Past emphasis on discovery, cataloging, and description is understandable, but most, though not all, taxa have been through these procedures and have been named, most of them several times by different authors. Emphasis ought now to shift to more mature phases of

Botany Department and the Herbarium of Pomona College have provided a vantage point on the edge of the deserts and other dry country. During the course of preparing this book, all 50 states and most of Canada have been explored for cacti. Specimens in the herbaria of more than 60 institutions in North America, Europe, Venezuela, and Trinidad have been studied, and thousands of living plants from which new herbarium specimens were obtained have been placed in cultivation for study. Libraries in a number of countries have been consulted. Altogether, parts of 48 years have been devoted to research on the cacti, most of which has found its way into the preparation of this book.

The text of the book is made up of two parts, the first a discussion of a broad range of topics underlying the formal classification and descriptions presented in Part II.

Part I begins by describing the plant characters used commonly for the identification of cacti by means of the keys and descriptions in Part II. This discussion is intended as preparation to implement the immediate process of pigeonholing plants, as one might identify coins or postage stamps, but, above and beyond this, it is intended to call attention to the place of each taxon in nature and its relationship not only to other cacti but also to other plants and animals. In the background is the basis for delimitation of taxa and assessing their degree of interrelationships.

The characters assessed most thoroughly in the research basic to this book are necessarily those most readily studied in the field and the herbaria. Fortunately, these are also the features most easily determined and most practical to use in identification. Other characters are too little known and too obscure and difficult to determine to have been employed up to this time in the study of as many as 269 native taxa. Their study requires so much time, expense, and equipment that research is feasible for only small groups of species. Consequently, knowledge of them will accumulate slowly, and for the near future it will not be of much direct use to most people trying to identify cacti. The value of the more obscure characters is great, if indirect; studies of them increase the information on which the system of classification is based, and make it more natural and more usable.

Thus, necessarily, such a book as this may solve only some of the problems of classification, and one of its major objectives is to put what is known into order and perspective. This approach also points up what is unknown, and it provides a basis for recognition of problems and their study by many investigators. The great hope is that from here on small groups of taxa may be studied more intensively and that problems concerning them may be solved by more thorough field studies combined with the application of new techniques and many approaches. These may include anatomical, cytological, pollen, and seed character studies; investigation of fine structures with the scanning electron microscope; research on chemical characters; and experimental studies of ecological and genetic features. To be of real value, all these investigations of characters must involve more than studies that merely record and catalog the results of a survey of occurrence of one character. Often such investigations have been based on garden plants of unknown relationships to natural populations. To be significant in classification, each minute or obscure character observed must be correlated in combination with the other known characters of the same plant and with still others in the same or different natural populations. Furthermore, any interpretation must be kept in perspective. Merely adding knowledge of a newly studied character to the pool does not, by itself, call for a new classification. Any taxonomic system based on overemphasis of a single character is artificial, whether the knowledge concerning the character is new or old. However, if new elements are woven into the character combinations to be considered, the study of new characters and chemical processes should yield exciting new information and viewpoints. We may hope also that research will take some wholly new pathways and that these will bring still further refinement of classification. Thus, any type of new research may implement the immediate process of determining the accepted name of a cactus and at the same time help to indicate its place in nature and in the higher units of plant classification.

Despite minimizing the number of recognized taxa through conservatism in their interpretation, the process of remodeling genera, species, and varieties has led inevitably to naming some new ones and to shifting the names of others. A quick count indicates that eight new species and 17 new varieties have been named during the course of research, and that 22 species and 76 varieties have been given new nomenclatural combinations, as the unavoidable result of a new study of the basis for their classification. Altogether, the text treats 137 species, and there are 132 varieties beyond one per species (usually the nomenclaturally typical one). Thus, fortunately, despite the thorough overhauling of both classification and nomenclature, most of the taxa still retain epithets by which they have been known in the past. However, many epithets appear in new combinations, and the internal structure or varietal composition of most species has been rearranged.

Sections of Part I are devoted to the structure and physiology of cacti, the investigation of chemical characters, the relationships of the family to higher and lower taxa, the research methods employed in preparing this volume, and the geographical, geological, ecological, and climatic factors having impact on the distribution of taxa and on the relationships of taxa to floristic associations. The concluding chapters are concerned with the uses of cacti by man and with the endangered cactus species occurring in the United States.

Part II, which begins with a brief discussion of the methods of treatment employed in the text, is designed to promote two scientific processes: identification and classification of cacti. *Identification* is the matching of an object such as a cactus with its proper position in an established system of classification (or taxonomic system). It involves using the characters described and discussed in Part I (and defined in the Glossary) to compare a particular cactus with the keys, tables, descriptions, illustrations, and maps in Part II. This procedure should bring the reader by stages to the treatment of a taxon and to the name determined by the author to be the correct one. *Classification* is the process of constructing the taxonomic system itself. Systems of classification are always subject to change, and any author worth his salt must have reservations about his own system. In devising it he will have evaluated many fragments of data and often wished more information were available. More than anyone else, he is in a position to point out the shortcomings of his taxonomic conclusions. The hope of any taxonomic author is to point the way to further research that may solve some of the remaining problems and others not yet known—and thus improve the taxonomic system.

Part II concludes with a section documenting the underlying research on classification through reference to herbarium specimens by collector and field number, using the symbols of the herbaria in which the collections are housed. It documents the choice of scientific names through reference to original publications and type specimens or their substitutes (isotypes, lectotypes, and neotypes).

The reference matter (at the back of the book) includes Glossary, Bibliography, Illustration Credits, and Indexes.

Part One

BIOLOGY, TAXONOMY, AND ECOLOGY

1. The Structure of Cacti

In desert plants, water loss must be minimal, and there must be protection from animals seeking water. The cacti can survive in arid regions primarily because they present a combination of essentially *leafless, succulent stems; spines in areoles;* and *shallow, wide-spreading root systems.* The form and character of the *flowers, pollen, fruits,* and *seeds* of cacti, also discussed in the following pages, may represent less obvious adaptations to dry environments.

Leafless, Succulent Stems

The conspicuous feature of a cactus is the stem. In all but a few genera of the family, the mature stems bear no leaves, and most cacti do not have leaves at any time. In temperate regions only the chollas and the prickly pears (*Opuntia*) develop leaves, and even these are small, succulent, and ephemeral (see Figs. 16 and 17). They appear each year on the newly developed *joints,* or stem segments, but fall away after about one to three months. The members of only two subtropical and tropical genera, *Pereskia* (Fig. 18) and *Pereskiopsis,* have broad persistent leaves. In both genera the leaves resemble those of other dicotyledons, but they are clearly succulent. In the cacti of dry regions the surface exposed to drying is reduced by the elimination of leaves, and food manufacture is taken over by the stems.

The stems of cacti are thick and succulent. Thus, the ratio of surface to volume is low, and water loss is at a minimum. A large quantity of soft living tissue in the outer and inner parts of the stem (the cortex and pith) provides a great reservoir in which food materials and especially water are stored (see Fig. 19). The water is used sparingly during periods of drought, which in the desert occur through much of every year and all of some years. In cactus stems the development of the cortex and pith is remarkable, and there is only a little woody tissue between them providing support and conduction.

Cactus stems have a thick waxy *cuticle* enabling the plants to withstand long periods of drought. The effectiveness of the protective cuticle (Fig. 20) may be demonstrated by peeling off the surface layer of cells, or *epidermis,* which has secreted the cuticle, from a detached stem joint of a prickly pear. An unpeeled joint will remain alive for months or even years, but a peeled one will dry out and shrivel to a small volume in less than a day.

The stems of cacti may be simple, unbranched, and columnar, as in the barrel cacti (Fig. 21), or they may be branched either near ground level (Fig. 22) or far above it. In some genera, series of cylindroid or flattened stem joints may be formed, as for example in the chollas and prickly pears. The stem surface may be smooth, as in the prickly pears, but more commonly, as in *Mammillaria* (Fig. 941) and *Coryphantha,* it is covered with mounds, or *tubercles;* fundamentally, these are enlarged leaf bases (Boke, 1952, 1953, 1955b), each bearing an *areole,* or spine-bearing area. In some genera (including *Cereus, Echinocereus, Ferocactus,* and *Echinocactus*) the tubercles are borne on ridges, or *ribs,* running vertically or spirally along the stem. Sometimes, as in the saguaro, the spiral pattern occurs only in the areoles; i.e., the ribs bearing the areoles are obviously vertical on the stem. In most cacti, if ribs are present, their course is spiral, and the tubercles and areoles occur along the ribs.

In many families of flowering plants, it occasionally happens that a stem and its branches are parallel and grown together, i.e., *fasciated.* This occurs sometimes in cacti, and the resulting plants may have weird shapes. The plant or a branch may form a symmetrical "crest" (see Fig. 23). The more fantastic and irregular types are described as "monstrose." There are many theories concerning the basis for the phenomenon, but the cause is unknown.

Text continued on p. 23

Fig. 16. Tree cholla, *Opuntia imbricata*, showing the leaves and their gradual disappearance as the stem joint matures, and also the gradual maturing of spines in the areoles. *Group above*: left, relatively young joint with immature spines and a few persisting leaves (near the apex, which develops later than the lower part of the joint) and with two emerging new joints at the apex, these with a leaf below each areole and with only small, bristle-like spines; other joints of varying degrees of leaf retention and maturity of spines; and maturing fruits, with few persistent leaves. *Group at right*: middle, a young stem joint bearing a cylindroid-tapering leaf just below each areole, the leaves falling away after 1 to 3 months; right, older joint with no leaves and with fully developed spines; left, young fruits with a leaf below each areole. (David Griffiths)

Fig. 17. A hybrid prickly pear, intermediate between *Opuntia littoralis* vars. *vaseyi* and *austrocalifornica*, the former variety spiny and the latter spineless, the latter variety and the hybrid glaucous, i.e. with a dense powdery layer of wax on the stem, the wax removed by the thumb mark in the picture; an old joint with no leaves and the few spines mature; and a young joint with a leaf below each areole and the spines not yet visible. (David Griffiths)

Fig. 18. *Pereskia grandifolia*, a cactus with leafy mature stems, the leaves mostly one below each areole, but some growing among the spines within the areole; fruits, showing the scars where leaves were attached during early development.

Fig. 20. The stem cuticle and water retention: four photographs of a joint of the stem of a prickly pear, *Opuntia ficus-indica. Above left*, The joint with half of its epidermis and the covering cuticle of wax peeled away. *Above right*, The same joint 5 hours later. *Below left*, After 48 hours. *Below right*, After one week. The unpeeled half of the joint has callused over the area next to the peeled half and will remain alive indefinitely.

20

Fig. 19 (*above*). Cross section of the stem of a barrel cactus, *Ferocactus acanthodes* var. *lecontei*. The relatively small soft central pith is surrounded by a cylindroid network of vascular, or conducting, tissue, but the bulk of the stem consists of soft cortical tissue (surrounding the conducting tissue) that serves for the storage of reserve food and water. The external ribs of the stem bear areoles with spines (spreading radial spines and hooked central spines, as shown at the right), and the rib surface is covered by a thick cuticle and a layer of wax. (From *The Native Cacti of California*)

Fig. 21 (*left*). The cylindroid, un-branched stem of a barrel cactus, *Ferocactus acanthodes* var. ***lecontei***, growing in the Mojavean Desert near the Santa Maria River in Yavapai Co., Arizona. There are no leaves, and the stem carries on all the photosynthesis, or food manufacture. The low ratio of surface to volume favors water retention in the succulent stem, which has ample storage capacity for both food and water; and the accordion pleating of the ribs and grooves allows for expansion or contraction according to the amount of water stored. The spines protect the stem against rodents and other animals seeking a water supply (see Fig. 19).

Fig. 22. The many branches of the stem of a hedgehog cactus, *Echinocereus fasciculatus* var. *bonkerae*, the plant forming a mound. By contrast, in the saguaro, *Cereus giganteus* (Figs. 568–85), branching occurs far above ground. (A. A. Nichol)

Fig. 23. Fasciation: a saguaro bearing a crest of abnormal branches, these parallel and grown together into a crest. (David Griffiths; see Credits)

Spines in Areoles

Only in the cacti do *the stems bear spines in areoles*. A *spine*, in the strict sense of the term, is a structure developed from a leaf or a part of one, and in nearly all cacti it is the only vestige of the leaf from which it was derived. The *areole*, or diminutive area, in which the spines are borne is a derivative of the bud formed in the angle (*axil*) above the fleshy leaf or above the normal position of a leaf on the stem (Boke, 1944, 1951, 1952). In all but a few cacti the original leaf at the base of the areole is represented by only a minute hump of tissue, discernible through the microscope in a thin-cut section of the young stem. The leaves of all flowering plants have *axillary buds*, but only the cacti have areoles enclosing the buds from which the spines and other structures develop. The areoles, being developed in the leaf axils, follow the characteristic spiral pattern on the stem for *alternately* (actually spirally) arranged leaves, rather than the arrangement in *opposite* pairs or in *whorls* of three or more that characterize some other plant groups. The axillary bud within the areole may or may not remain active; in the relatively primitive genus *Pereskia* the bud continues to be active, and in *P. grandifolia* it may produce foliage leaves (Fig. 18).

New information (Mauseth, 1977) indicates the foliar nature of spines. Buds in the areoles of the plains prickly pear, *Opuntia polyacantha* var. *polyacantha*, may develop either leaves or spines. Leaf primordia treated with cytokinin develop into normal leaves; those to which gibberellic acid has been applied become spines.

In a few species of cacti, spines are present only in juvenile plants, and they are not developed on older stems. In addition to spines, the areoles usually bear bristles or masses of hairs, and in the prickly pears and chollas there are also short, sharp, barbed structures known as *glochids*, which to humans may be more troublesome than the spines (see Figs. 24-27). Usually, spininess or spinelessness is constant within a species or some of its members, but sometimes spiny prickly pears brought into cultivation produce spineless joints bearing only glochids (see Fig. 28).

In part, the spines of cacti are a mechanism of defense, particularly of stored water, against the inroads of thirsty animals. Especially during dry periods, rodents try to eat the plants, mostly for the water, and although some may force entrance between the spine clusters guarding the surface, most are deterred. Other desert succulents have different defenses. For example, in *Euphorbia* (Euphorbiales, Figs. 29-31), including the succulent cactuslike African species, the water reserve is protected primarily by the acrid nature of the juice. Some euphorbias are protected also by spines (usually less effectively than by the acridity); such spines are of a different type than those of the Cactaceae and are not borne in areoles.

In some species of cacti the spines, or at least the principal spines, are directed downward. During a light rain or a mist, water droplets accumulate on the tip of each spine and fall to the ground (see Fig. 32). Thus, the spines concentrate atmospheric water and deposit it on the soil; and just beneath the surface of the soil lie the roots. Often, also, the curvature of the stems and especially of the joints of prickly pears or chollas aids in concentration of rainwater into large drops or small "streams" that soak the ground beneath the plant.

Spines and the other structures borne in areoles are of many types, mostly correlated with obvious or obscure functions, though commonly the values of the spines to the cactus have been determined only superficially. The spines in an areole may be all alike or remarkably diverse and specialized: long or short; slender or stout; straight, curving, or recurved; cylindroid or needlelike or flattened; smooth, rough, cross-ribbed, or channeled-and-ridged; white, gray, black, or various other colors, or of more than one color; apically straight, curved, or hooked; smooth or barbed (Fig. 33) in various degrees; and basally tapering to bulbous. Along with the spines, there may or may not be hairs of several types and glochids (see Fig. 34). Glochids are rarely absent in the chollas and prickly pears (*Opuntia*), and they do not occur in the other genera of the Cactaceae.

In some cacti, the spines of an areole are not all alike, and often there is a distinction of *central* and *radial* spines (see Fig. 35). The central spines are more or less in the center of the areole, or at least they form a circle or two; the radial spines radiate from the margins of the areole, and there may be more than one series. This distinction may be obvious or obscure, and often classification is a matter of individual interpretation. Often a striking geometrical pattern is produced by the regular, usually spiral, pattern of the many areoles and the regular positioning of the central and radial spines in each areole.

The fine structure of the surface and the external features of cactus spines are only beginning to be studied in detail. Research has become

Text continued on p. 31

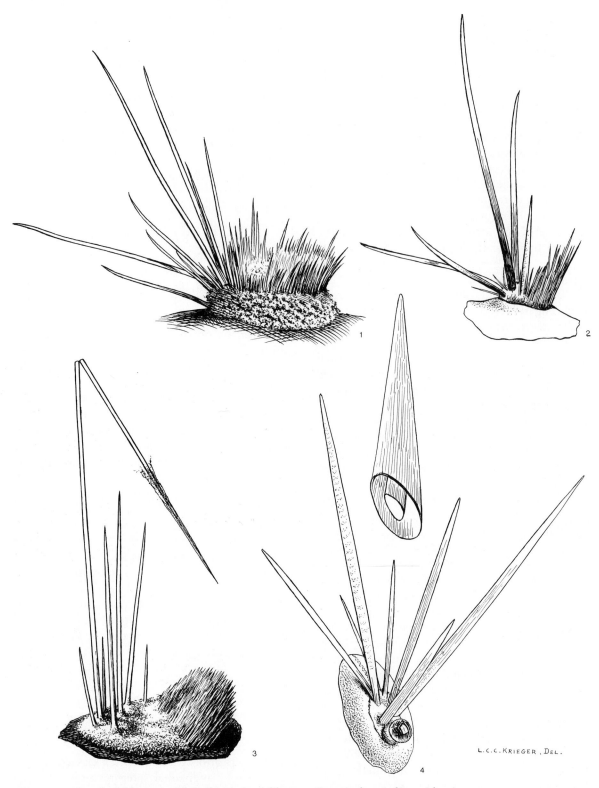

Fig. 24. Areoles of prickly pears and chollas. *1*, A prickly pear, *Opuntia ficus-indica*, with spines, glochids, and wool, ×2.25. *2*, A prickly pear, *O. phaeacantha* var. *major*, with spines and glochids, ×3.5. *3*, A cholla, *O. imbricata*, with spines and glochids, one of the spines showing (at its tip) the separation of the outer layers of cells as a sheath, characteristic of the chollas but not the prickly pears, ×3.5. *4*, A cholla, *O. tunicata*, showing the detached and enlarged papery sheath of the spine, natural size; a globule of nectar almost covers the tuft of glochids. Nectar glands in the areoles of *Opuntia* secrete a sugar solution that may dry into a mass of crystalline sugar, which is then gathered by bees and wasps. (L. C. C. Krieger for David Griffiths)

Fig. 25. A prickly pear, *Opuntia basilaris* var. *treleasei*, with prominent glochids and few and rather small spines (seen most clearly at lower right); Rancho Santa Ana Botanic Garden.

Fig. 26 (*below*). Prickly pear with only glochids, some of these having fallen from the areoles and showing on the joint surface; *Opuntia microdasys* (Mexico). (Frank P. McWhorter)

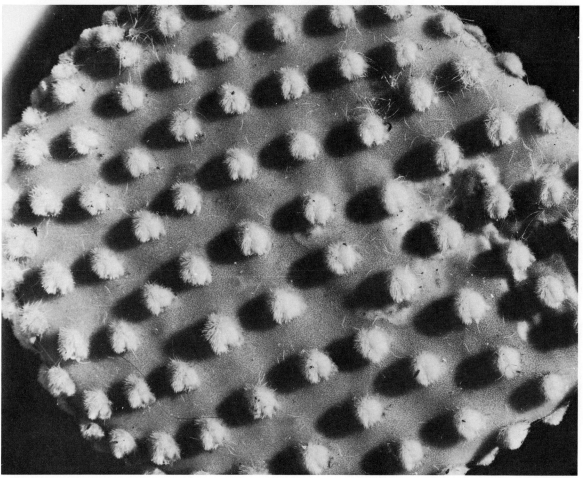

L.C.C.KRIEGER DEL.

Fig. 27. The barbs of prickly pear glochids, ×475. *1, Opuntia phaeacantha* var. *major* 2, *O. macrocalyx* Griffiths (status undetermined, named from cultivated material): *a*, middle portion of glochid: *b*, tip of glochid. (L. C. C. Krieger for David Griffiths)

Fig. 28. Change in spininess after transfer from the field to cultivation, *Opuntia macrorhiza*: the dead portion of the spiny original joint from which the plant was propagated remains (just right of center); the more recently grown joints that developed in cultivation are spineless, even those that clearly have reached maturity. This phenomenon is uncommon.

Fig. 29. Plants superficially resembling cacti (see also Figs. 30 & 31): here, a succulent species of *Euphorbia* growing in dry grassland just above the Namib Desert (inland, eastward from the desert), South West Africa (Namibia). The plant could be mistaken, on the basis of appearance, for a species of *Cereus*. The succulent euphorbias are restricted to the Old World, the cacti to the New.

Fig. 30. Comparison of the appearance of *Euphorbia horrida* and *Thelocactus neglance*. (Frank P. McWhorter)

Fig. 31. *Euphorbia ingens*, a succulent tree of a type occurring in southern Africa, as in Natal, South Africa, where this species is native; Huntington Botanical Gardens. In the garden, the surrounding plants are the California fan palm, *Washingtonia filifera*, upper left, the trunk and a skirt of dead leaves showing; Canary Island date palm, *Phoenix canariensis*, leaves of three trees; *Crassula portulacea*, lower left; *Aloë berhana*, the leaf rosette at lower center; *Aloë arborescens* hybrid, leaves at lower right.

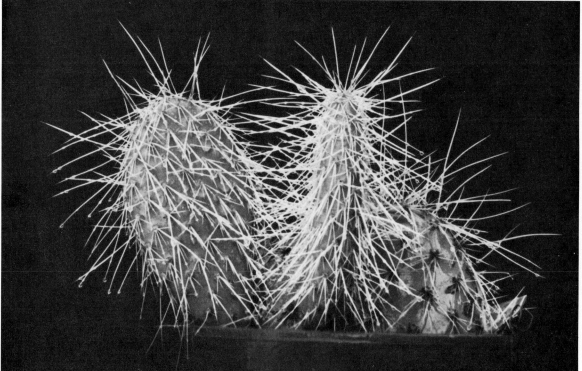

Fig. 32. Water concentration by cactus spines. Most cacti live in regions of low rainfall, and many concentrate water from heavy mists into drops that fall from the tips of the spines and soak the soil beneath. Species with some spines directed downward, and collecting water droplets, are shown here. *Above, Echinocereus,* natural hybrid from the Franklin Mts., near El Paso, Texas. *Below, Opuntia nicholii,* a prickly pear from the Navajo Bridge, Coconino Co., Arizona. (From *Plant Taxonomy, Methods and Principles*)

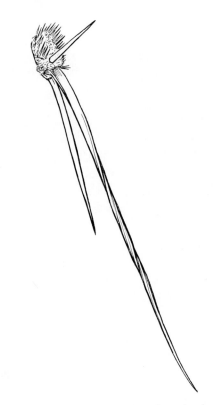

Fig. 33. Enlarged tip of a spine of *Opuntia phaeacantha* var. *major*, showing the retrorse barbs characteristic of *Opuntia* and much larger than these in some species. (L. C. C. Krieger for David Griffiths; see Credits)

Fig. 34. An areole of a prickly pear, *Opuntia phaeacantha* var. *major*; with three spines of varying lengths, glochids, and fine wool.

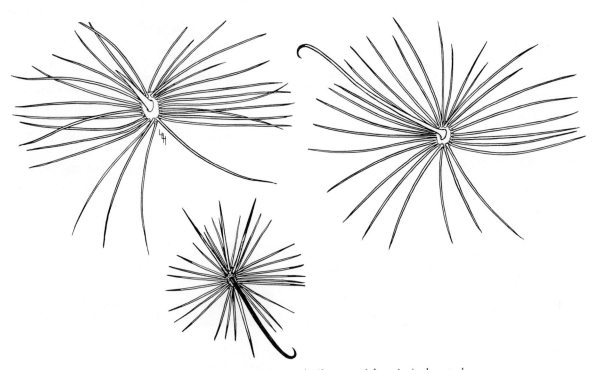

Fig. 35. Central and radial spines, *Mammillaria grahamii*: *Left*, Short, straight principal central spine of var. *oliviae*, the two upper central spines similar to the radial spines and inconspicuous. *Right*, Long, hooked principal central spine of var. *grahamii*, in this plant the upper centrals again similar to the radials. *Below*, The usual differentiation of central and radial spines in var. *grahamii*, the upper centrals stouter than the radials.

possible recently as the scanning electron microscope has become available (see Fig. 36). This instrument has revealed a wide variety of surface patterns, some related to prevention of withdrawal of the spine, some doubtless of significance in other ways as yet undetermined. According to Schill et al. (1973), the cells of the spine surface break more or less regularly into separate sections, exposing submicroscopic sugar crystals within the cells. The authors (1973, f. *17, 20*) illustrate these in *Epithelantha*. The greatly magnified surface structure of some cactus spines has been illustrated by Schill (*loc. cit.*), Franke (1974), and Robinson (1974). Although, so far, the fine structure has not been correlated well with classification, it is certain to be of significance in refining the taxonomy of the cacti.

The spines of young cacti may differ markedly from those of adult plants of the same species (see Figs. 37 and 38). In a species with strongly differentiated central and radial spines on mature stems, the young stems may have few or no central spines. Consequently, the juvenile plants may differ so much from the adults that they seem to be of a different species. For example, in the same publication in 1828, DeCandolle named *Mammillaria cornifera* and *M. radians*. In 1923 Britton and Rose transferred both of the proposed species to another genus as *Coryphantha cornifera* and *C. radians*. However, *C. radians* is synonymous with *C. cornifera*, because it was based merely upon juvenile plants of that species. Similarly, *M. pectinata*, described by Engelmann in 1859 and recombined by Britton and Rose in 1923 as *C. pectinata*, was based upon a juvenile form of *C. cornifera* var. *echinus*. Instances of this sort are not uncommon, and the confusion often persists in the botanical literature for a century or more. The descriptions and keys in this book are based upon the adult plants, *and the keys are not necessarily applicable to seedlings.*

The Shallow, Widely Spreading Root System

The roots of cacti (see Figs. 39 and 40) spread widely just beneath the surface of the soil. Cannon (1911) found the roots of a large barrel cactus (*Ferocactus wislizenii*) to occur at an average depth of 3 cm (about 1-1/4 inches). They spread horizontally, dipping under rocks, then resuming their normal depth. The roots of a relatively small plant, 6 dm (2 feet) high and 3.5 dm (14 inches) in diameter, spread outward into a circle with about a 3.5 m (11.5 feet) radius. The outermost and other absorbing roots were only about 1.5 cm

(3/5 inch) below the surface. The root system of a young saguaro (*Cereus giganteus*) only 12 cm (under 5 inches) high filled a circle 10 m (33 feet) in diameter and about 1 dm (4 inches) beneath the surface. Even during long drought periods, the distal portions of the roots remain receptive to some water (Cannon, *loc. cit.*), and rapid growth of the root hairs makes much more available. Consequently, after a relatively light rain, that may penetrate only a short distance into the soil, the plant can absorb water quickly. Furthermore, the shallow-rooted cacti do not compete with their deeper-rooted neighbors, such as the shrubs *Menodora* and *Acacia*, which Cannon found to have almost no surface roots.

Fallen joints of chollas or prickly pears and fragments or uprooted stems of other cacti root rapidly (see Fig. 41). In certain genera, this may result in asexual reproduction, and therefore in survival through periods unfavorable to sexual reproduction. Thus, some species are not wholly dependent upon the optimal combinations of temperature, soil, and temporarily available moisture necessary for the germination and establishment of seedlings. Even during years when rainfall is restricted to cool periods, when seeds do not germinate, branches or even fruits (Figs. 42 and 43) of some species may root and grow. A cactus stem is likely to develop roots even if it is in contact not with the soil but only with dry air. Rooting can also proceed within a stem cavity caused by injury, as shown in Fig. 44.

Thus, the combination of vegetative characters that gives dry-land or desert cacti their characteristic appearance—and which is not duplicated in any other family of plants—provides features important to drought resistance and to protection from thirsty animals. This subject is developed further in the next chapter, "The Physiology of Cacti." We proceed now to the reproductive features, the flowers and fruits, and to the characters of the structures they produce, pollen and seeds.

Flowers

The flowers of most cacti arise within or near the areoles of the stem (see Fig. 45). In such genera as *Pereskia*, *Opuntia*, and *Cereus*, they are among or beside the spines but in any case within the edge of the spine-bearing areole. In *Echinocereus* (Fig. 46), the flower bud bursts through the epidermis of the stem above the spine-bearing areole, in a separate areole of its own. In *Mammillaria* (Fig. 47), the flower develops deep be-

Text continued on p. 39

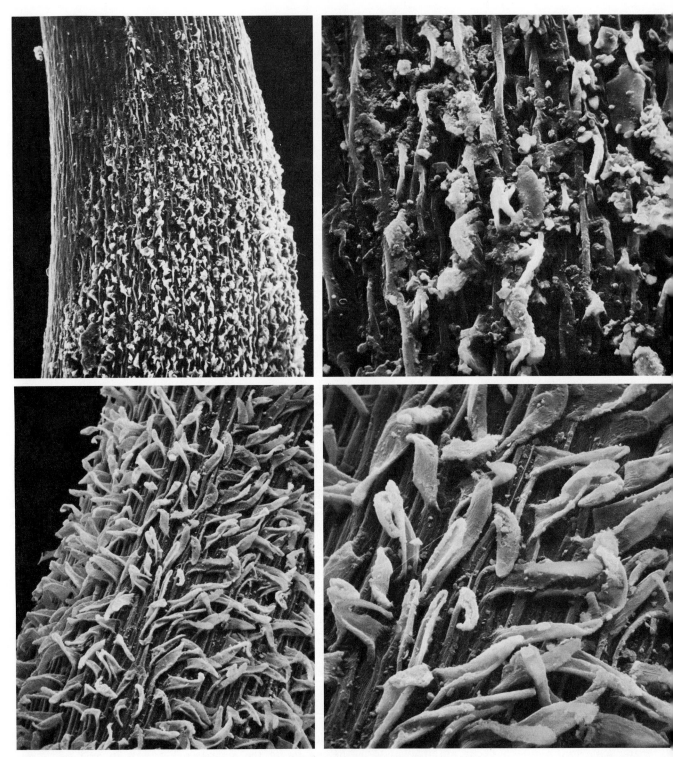

Fig. 36. Fine structure of the surfaces of spines; photographs obtained with the scanning electron microscope. *Two above*, spine of *Ferocactus latispinus* var. *latispinus*, ×200 and ×500; *two below*, spine of *Ferocactus hystrix*, ×185 and ×460. (Photographs courtesy of Herbert W. Franke, based on the research of Hans Till; see Credits)

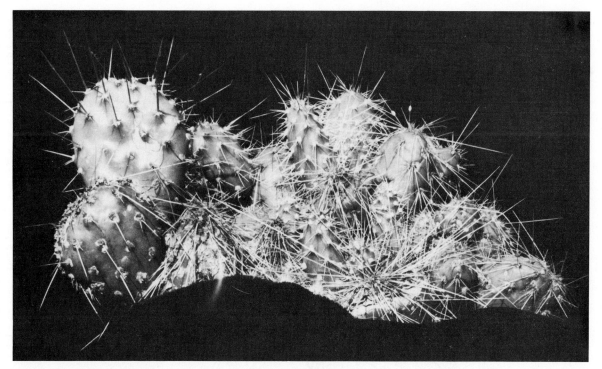

Fig. 37. Young cactus plants may differ markedly in spine and other characters from the adults of the same species. This plant was collected at the Four Corners of Utah, Colorado, Arizona, and New Mexico in 1962 and grown in a pot. The juvenile joints (at the right) bore long, slender, pale gray, mostly deflexed spines and gave the impression during several years that this might be a new species or variety; the adult joints (left) appeared in 1971 and produced the shorter, stouter, reddish-brown, upward-directed to spreading or deflexed spines that are characteristic of *Opuntia polyacantha* var. *rufispina*.

Fig. 38. Reproduction by mature and juvenile plants of the same species, *Neolloydia erectocentra* var. *erectocentra*, both bearing fruits. The characteristic single erect central spine is evident in all but the lowest areoles (the first formed) of the older plant; in the areoles of the younger plant (probably 2–4 years old) there are no centrals. In the field (between Willcox and San Pedro Valley, Cochise Co., Arizona), a series of plants evidently of intermediate ages showed the stages of development between those in the picture. Thus, sexual reproduction may begin before the vegetative part of the plant is mature; seeds from the plant at the right presumably would produce plants that in time would take on the characters of the plant at the left.

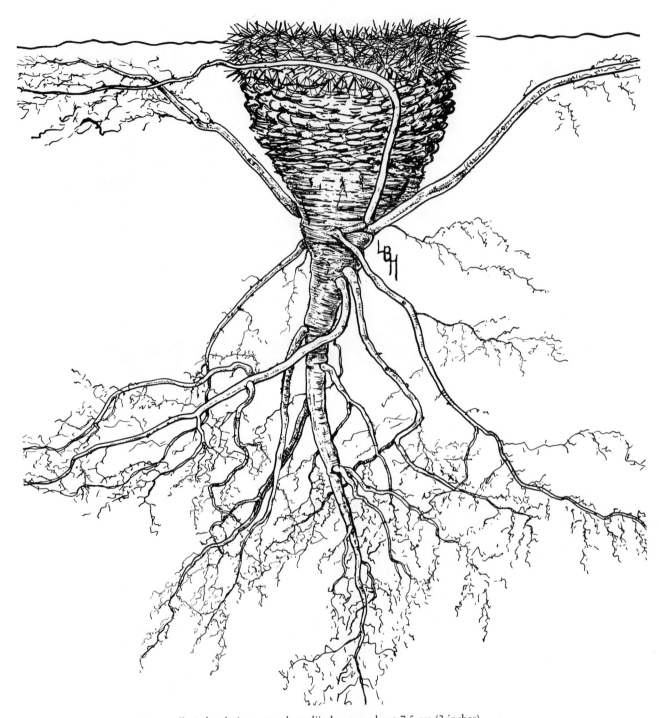

Fig. 39. Root system of *Mammillaria heyderi* var. *macdougalii*, the stem about 7.5 cm (3 inches) in height and diameter, all but the uppermost surface below ground level (see wavy line), the tap root tapering rapidly and only about 1.5 dm (6 inches) long, the branch roots spreading widely at 1–2 dm (4–8 inches) beneath the soil surface. Natural size.

Fig. 40. Roots of a cholla, *Opuntia echinocarpa*, in the Mojavean Desert. Although the stem was only 6 dm (2 feet) tall and only about 4 cm (1.5+ inches) in diameter, one root was followed for nearly 11 m (35 feet), and at its deepest descent it was only about 7.5 cm (3 inches) beneath the surface. (Scott E. Haselton; see Credits)

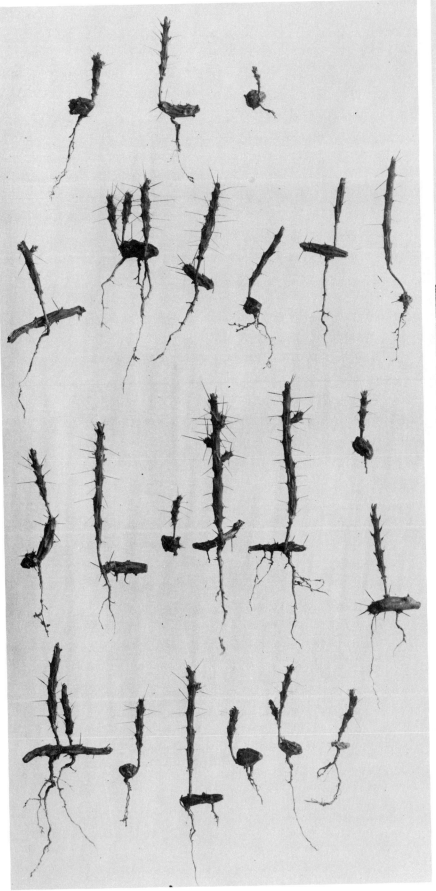

Fig. 42 (*above*). Regeneration of a cholla, *Opuntia kelvinensis*, from a fallen fruit. The new plant was about 3 or 4 years old. (From *Plant Taxonomy, Methods and Principles*)

Fig. 41. Regeneration of a pencil cholla, *Opuntia leptocaulis*, from fallen very slender (pencil-like) joints of the stem (e.g. the left plant in the lower row) and from fallen fruits (the others in that row). (David Griffiths)

Fig. 44. Longitudinal section of the stem of a pincushion cactus (*Coryphantha*), showing the very thick cortex and pith and between them the thin layer of vascular tissue (xylem and phloem). The lower part of the stem has a cavity due to injury, and roots are growing into the cavity from the cambium between the xylem (wood) and phloem in the vascular tissue above. (Robert H. Peebles; see Credits)

Fig. 43. Growth of a joint and a fertile fruit from the sterile fruits of a prickly pear. (David Griffiths)

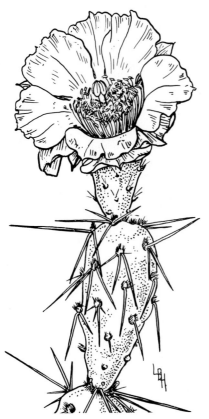

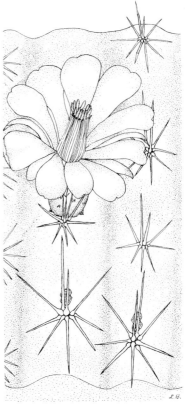

Fig. 45. Flower developed from within a spine-bearing areole; a prickly pear, *Opuntia fragilis*.

Fig. 46. Flower above the spine-bearing areole, but on the same rib of the stem, the flower bud having burst through the epidermis of the stem but actually in an areole of its own; a red-flowered hedgehog cactus, *Echinocereus triglochidiatus* var. *gurneyi*.

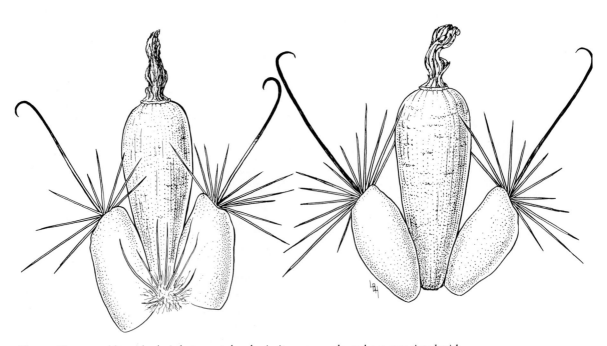

Fig. 47. Flower and later the fruit between tubercles in its own areole and not associated with the spine-bearing areoles at the summits of the tubercles. *Left*, Fruit between tubercles and surrounded by wool and spines from the flower-bearing areole; *Mammillaria dioica*. *Right*, Flower between tubercles, but the flower-bearing areole not developing wool or spines; *M. microcarpa*.

tween a pair of tubercles of the stem, far from the spine-bearing areoles, which occupy the summits of the tubercles. In some species of the genus, such as *M. dioica*, there are spines around the flower, between the tubercles, indicating perhaps that the flower has been produced by an areolar structure. In *Lophophora, Ferocactus, Echinocactus, Sclerocactus, Pediocactus, Epithelantha,* and *Thelocactus* the flowers are in a differentiated area at the ventral edge of the areole (i.e. toward the stem apex), but this area (see Fig. 48) merges into the rest of the areole with no isthmus between the spine- and flower-bearing sections. In *Neolloydia, Ancistrocactus,* and *Coryphantha* the spiniferous and floriferous sections of the areole are separated by a wide interval, but they are connected by a narrow, felted *isthmus*, which may form an elongate groove (see Fig. 49). The earliest flowers on the young stem in at least some species of *Ancistrocactus* and *Coryphantha* (and perhaps *Neolloydia*) are produced high on the tubercle (which is separate and not part of a rib). From then on, as during later seasons flowers appear on new crops of tubercles, the flowers develop lower and lower on the ventral surface of the tubercle, and the connecting groove becomes longer and longer (see Fig. 50). Finally, in some subsequent year, the flower emerges from the base of the tubercle, the groove extending full length. This phenomenon has been observed in

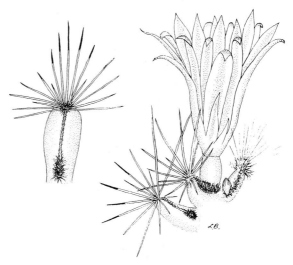

Fig. 49. Flower in a part of the areole separate from the spines, and the parts joined by a narrow to rather broad isthmus; *Coryphantha robertii. Left,* tubercle with an areole, showing the isthmus and the flower- and fruit-bearing part after fall of the fruit. *Right,* flower, showing its position on the tubercle; on the tubercle at the right of the flower, a flower bud.

Ancistrocactus (Benson, 1966a) and in *Coryphantha* (Boke, 1952), but it has not been observed sufficiently in *Neolloydia*.

The cactus flower (see Figs. 51-55) is of a special type best understood by beginning with the lower parts and working upward. The flower is characterized by an *inferior ovary*, so named because it appears to be attached below the other flower parts. The ovary is enclosed by and ordinarily joined with the inferior part of the *floral tube* or *cup*, which seemingly forms an outer coat of the ovary. Above the ovary for a few millimeters to 1 dm (1/4 to 4 inches) or more, the superior part of the floral tube or cup is free from the ovary, and the other flower parts arise from its inner surface or its margin. A flower having a floral tube or cup joined with the ovary is described as *epigynous*, and, with one exception, this is the only flower type occurring in the cactus family. Some species of the relatively primitive genus *Pereskia* have *perigynous* flowers, which differ only in having the floral cup not joined with the ovary. The floral tube or cup of a cactus is a complex structure formed by joining of the bases of the stamens, the bases of the sepal-like and petal-like structures, and the upper part of the stem branch bearing the flower. In nearly all cacti almost the entire lower part of the floral cup is developed from the upper part, or *receptacle*, of the small branch bearing the flower; and the

Fig. 48. Flower (in this case, fruit) in a differentiated part of the areole (this hairy) directly above and adjoining the spine-bearing part of the areole; *Ferocactus wislizenii.*

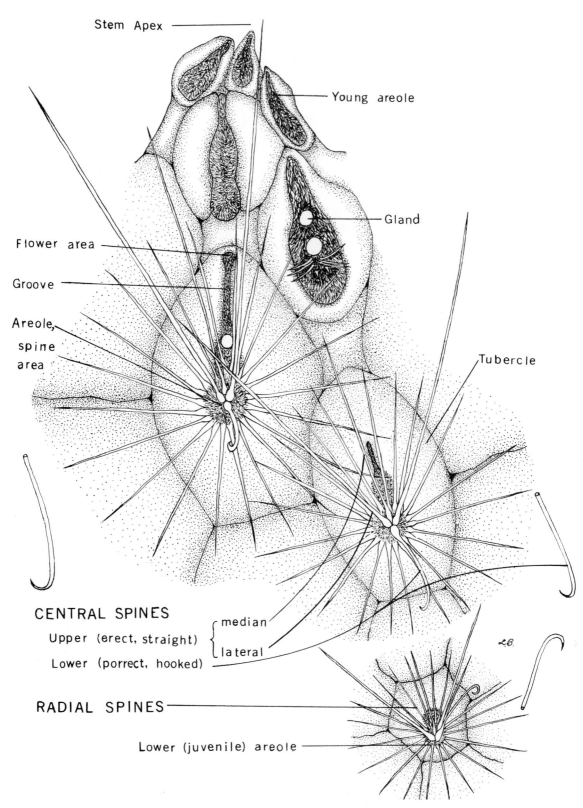

Stem Apex

Young areole

Gland

Flower area

Groove

Areole,
spine
area

Tubercle

CENTRAL SPINES
Upper (erect, straight)
Lower (porrect, hooked)

median
lateral

RADIAL SPINES

Lower (juvenile) areole

Fig. 50. Transition of flower position in *Ancistrocactus*: enlargement of a few tubercles of various ages showing the developmental stages of the areoles they bear, several tubercles from the upper part of the plant and one from the lower part, the latter produced when the plant was in a juvenile vegetative stage. From the base to the apex of the stem, there is a gradual development of the groove between the spine-bearing and the flowering and fruiting parts of the areole (shown here after fall of the fruits). The first areoles produced are like those of a barrel cactus, the later ones like the mature areoles of *Coryphantha*, which, so far as studied, goes through a similar transition. (See Credits)

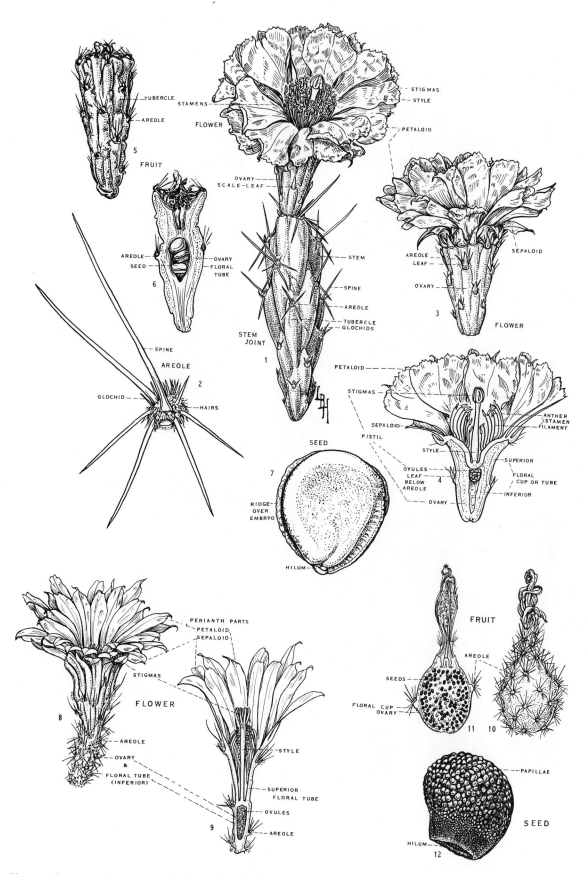

Fig. 51. The parts of a cactus, as labeled: *1–7*, a cholla, *Opuntia schottii* var. *grahamii*; *8–11*, *Cereus poselgeri*.

Figs. 52–55. Flower structure in *Cereus peruvianus* (for labels of flower parts, see Fig. 51). In Fig. 52 (*above left*), open flowers and young fruits, the style persistent on the young fruit and the stigmas remaining on the style. Fig. 53 (*above right*). Side view of the flower, showing the ovary at the very base, this of no greater diameter than the floral tube above it (for inside view, see Fig. 51), the tube bearing scale-leaves, these being most prominent and largest above, and there shading into the sepaloids, which shade on upward into the petaloids. Fig. 54 (*below left*). Longitudinal section of the flower, showing the ovary (below) adnate with the investing inferior floral tube, which continues into the superior floral tube above (the part free from the ovary). The style and stigmas are in the center of the floral tube. Numerous stamens, with their long stalks (the filaments) and pollen-bearing anthers, cover the upper part of the inside of the superior floral tube. Fig. 55 (*below right*). The sepaloids, petaloids, stamens, and stigmas. At the right the dried stigmas of an older flower are lodged on the petaloids.

surface, like that of an ordinary stem, bears leaves. However, the leaves are small and fleshy, and they are called *scale-leaves*. There is an areole in the axil or angle above each scale-leaf. The areoles of the tube may bear spines, glochids, or hairs. On the upper part of the floral tube the scale-leaves are longer, and they shade off into structures resembling the sepals of other flowers. These are the *sepaloid perianth parts,* or, simply, *sepaloids.** Near the apex of the floral tube the sepaloids grade into *petaloid perianth parts,* or *petaloids.* These appear to be derived from the same sources as the sepaloids (not from stamens, as the petals of most flowers do).

Numerous *stamens* arise on the inside of the upper portion of the floral tube. These produce pollen, and each consists of a *filament,* or stalk, and an *anther* composed of four *pollen sacs* arising from a *connective* by which they are attached to the filament. The *pistil* is made up of the *ovary* and a usually elongate *style* bearing several *stigmas,* each receptive to pollen. Pollination is effected mostly by bees or beetles, though sometimes by moths, birds, bats, or other agencies. The *pollen grain* germinates in the sugar solution on the stigma, then grows down through the hollow style into the ovary, where fertilization occurs and the seed is developed. The ovary and its contents are discussed below, under "Fruits."

The *pistil* of a cactus is composed of three to many *carpels,* each of which is a specialized leaf bearing *placentae,* which in turn bear the *ovules,* each of which develops, after fertilization, into a *seed.* The carpels form a hollow cylinder, being joined edge-to-edge through their entire length, except apically. The tip of each carpel forms a separate *stigma,* receptive to pollen; the next portion below is the style; and the larger basal portion is the ovary, which is hollow (i.e. lacking crosswalls). Along each margin of each carpel in the ovary there is a vertical placenta bearing a row of ovules. When the pollen grain is deposited on the stigma, it grows into an elongate tube enclosing two male gamete nuclei. When the pollen tube reaches an ovule, it bursts, and one gamete nucleus joins with the female gamete cell, or egg, effecting fertilization and the ultimate formation of a new individual plant embryo within the seed. Thus, the cactus fruit, whatever its shape at maturity, is a development from a hollow cylinder formed from the carpels and the investing and adnate inferior floral tube, and it

bears seeds in vertical, though commonly not easily distinguishable, rows over the entire inner surface.

Pollen

The pollen grains of *Opuntia* differ from those of the other Cactaceae and other flowering plants (Kurtz, 1948, 1949, 1963). Species of *Cereus, Echinocactus,* and *Mammillaria* produce the small, spheroidal, *tricolpate* pollen grains typical of dicotyledons (Fig. 56, *1*; in a tricolpate pollen grain there are characteristically three germinal furrows concerned with emergence of the pollen tube, which carries the male gamete cell to the egg or female gamete cell). The species of *Opuntia* have a remarkable series of pollen-grain forms that occur in only the Cactaceae. The basic form is a cube-and-dodecahedron configuration, as illustrated in Fig. 56, *2.* This a solid figure with 18 faces, including six smaller squares and 12 larger hexagons. Each hexagonal face includes a *germinal furrow.* Although the pollen grains of the chollas (Fig. 56, *7 & 8*) appear to have essentially this pattern, it is not clear, and the grains are nearly spheroidal. In the prickly pears the special pattern is obvious, but the degree of emphasis varies. For example, it is elaborate in *Opuntia erinacea* var. *ursina* (Fig. 56, *5*) but relatively faint in *Opuntia violacea* var. *macrocentra* (Fig. 56, *3*).

According to Kurtz (1963, tables), pollen grains with 12 or more furrows occur primarily in *Opuntia* and its segregates and in some members of the complexes to which *Epiphyllum* and *Rhipsalis* belong. They occur here and there in other groups of genera, but they are uncommon in *Cereus.*

Some of the characters of pollen grains are distinctive for species. These include the surface sculpturing of the *exine,* or outer wall, the grain size, and the proportionate area covered by each germinal furrow. The surface of the pollen grain may be smooth, pitted, or covered with spinules, and the spinules may bear a reticulate, or netlike, surface pattern. To some extent the surface markings or protrusions tend to be correlated with genera or species.

References (pollen): Erdtman, 1952, *Pollen morphology and plant taxonomy;* Kurtz, 1948, 1949, *Pollen grain characters of certain Cactaceae,* 1963, *Pollen morphology of the Cactaceae;* Tsukada, 1964, *Pollen morphology and identification II. Cactaceae;* Anderson & Stone, 1971, *Pollen analysis of Lophophora.*

*The ending "-oid" means "with the appearance of." "Sepaloid" and "petaloid" are adjectives, but used here as nouns, for convenience, as with "asteroid" and "thyroid."

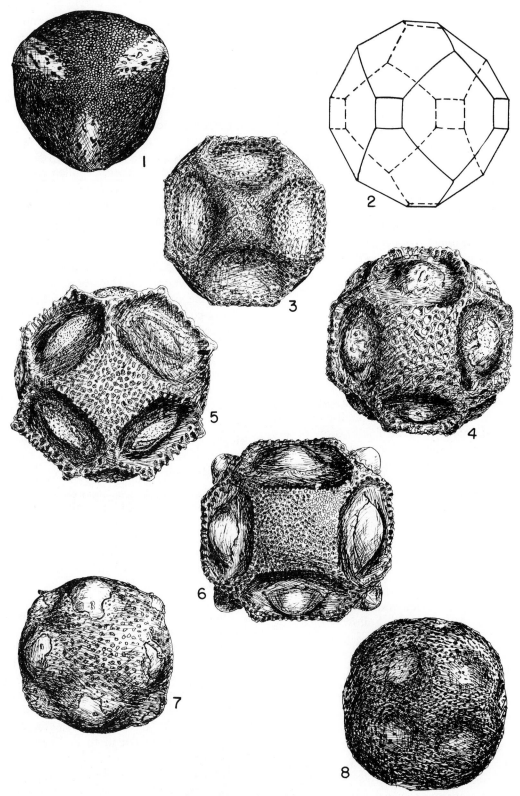

Fig. 56. Types of pollen grains. *1*, Saguaro, *Cereus giganteus*, the pollen grain small and nearly a spheroid, unspecialized. *2*, The typical idealized cube-and-dodecahedron shape of the pollen grains of chollas and prickly pears (*Opuntia*). *3–6*, Prickly pears. *3*, *O. violacea* var. *macrocentra*. *4*, Beavertail cactus, *O. basilaris*. *5*, Grizzly-bear cactus, *O. erinacea* var. *ursina*. *6*, Little prickly pear, *O. fragilis*. *7*, *8*, Chollas, the grains nearly spheroidal and not showing the cube-and-dodecahedron shape very well. *7*, Staghorn cholla, *O. acanthocarpa*. *8*, Jumping cholla, *O. fulgida* var. *mamillata*. (Edwin B. Kurtz, Jr.; see Credits)

Fruits

Strictly speaking, the fruit of a cactus is the ovary wall and all it encloses, but the ovary wall is joined with the lower part of the floral tube, which surrounds it, and the fruit is thus composed of two parts. Most cactus fruits are fleshy (see Fig. 57), and the juicy outer portion forming the wall is composed of two layers, the inner derived from the ovary and the outer from the floral tube. In some species of various genera the fruit does not become fleshy (Fig. 58), and it becomes dry just at maturity of the enclosed seeds.

Most but not all dry fruits and a few fleshy ones split lengthwise along one or more regular lines; that is, they are *dehiscent* (Fig. 59). In other species the dry fruit may remain *indehiscent*, or it may open along a circular horizontal line at any level or by formation of a basal or apical *pore* or by a combination of methods.

The surface of the fruit is basically a stem, the greater part of the lower portion of the floral tube being derived from the apical part of the small stem (receptacle) that gives rise to the parts of the flower, whether these are joined to each other basally or not. Like any other stem, this one may bear leaves (these being reduced to scale-leaves, as described for the flower) and areoles. Each areole may be subtended by a scale-leaf, and sometimes by an elaborate, fringed one, and it may or may not bear spines (see Fig. 60), hairs, or bristles. In some fruits the areoles are vestigial and not visible to the naked eye, as in *Coryphantha* and *Mammillaria*. Ordinarily, each fruit produces a large number of seeds; smaller numbers, like 10-20, are rare.

Fig. 58. Mature dry fruits of a prickly pear, *Opuntia nicholii*, the surface tan and dry, the spine clusters of the areoles coming off (two shown detached); at lower left, three seeds. (From *The Cacti of Arizona*)

Fig. 57. Mature fleshy fruits of a prickly pear, *Opuntia phaeacantha* var. *major*, showing the smooth, red surface and the areoles (especially the upper ones) with glochids; the thin layer of waxy powder partly rubbed off the left fruit. (David Griffiths)

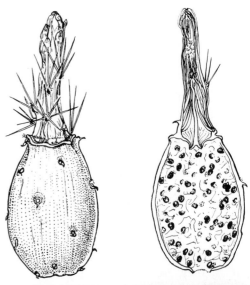

Fig. 60. Fruit of a red-flowered hedgehog cactus, *Echinocereus triglochidiatus* var. *melanacanthus*: left, the fruit now mature and the spine clusters fallen, the red ovary fleshy at first but now drying, the superior floral cup and the flower parts (enclosed) persistent; right, longitudinal section of the fruit, showing the black seeds embedded in the pulp of the fleshy stalks (funiculi), the style and the stamens dried but persistent in the superior floral tube.

Fig. 59. Mature fleshy, red, dehiscent fruit (and younger fruits) of *Cereus peruvianus*, the fruit opened, revealing the edible, delicately aromatic, white pulp (stalks of the seeds) and the embedded black seeds; the styles and stigmas (dark lines running downward) are still attached.

Seeds

The seed of a cactus consists of a hard protective outer *seed coat*; the *embryo*, which in due course becomes the new plant; and a mass of *storage tissue* with reserve food, which becomes available to the seedling when it starts to grow and before it can produce much food of its own.

The seed coat. The hard outer layer protects the embryo and the storage tissue from water loss, from being eaten readily by most insects, and from digestion by microscopic organisms or some larger animals. It may be of various colors, such as gray, brown, tan, white, red or reddish, bone-color, or straw-color. It may be smooth and dull or shiny, or roughened with projections such as *papillae*, or with pits, ridges, or a network of ridges or grooves. These features may be detected with a dissecting microscope or a hand lens. The microscopic structure of the coat, which may be studied with prepared slides and the use of a compound microscope, also varies greatly.

The examination of the external and internal features of the seed coat with the powerful electron microscope offers an intriguing new opportunity for study, providing the ability to see minute characters hitherto unknown and to correlate their presence with the occurrence of other characters of the plants. Herbert W. Franke (1971) presented an excellent group of illustrations (see Fig. 61) of the seed coats of four taxa of *Gymnocalycium* (Cactaceae), showing marked variation from species to species in the material studied.

The embryo. Fundamentally, the embryo of a cactus is a cylinder, though in most genera it is curved. The larger part of the axis of the cylinder consists of the *hypocotyl*, which ends (ultimately below) in the root tip and is continuous (ultimately above) with the almost microscopic *epicotyl*, which develops later into the stem and gives rise to leaves. In the Cactaceae, as in the other dicotyledons, the first two leaves of the new plant are present in the seed, and they are known as *cotyledons*, or seed leaves. Thus, the embryo is a continuous, usually curving, axis ending above in a minute growing region that becomes the terminal bud of the stem. In this embryonic stage, the epicotyl is flanked by the cotyledons, which continue beyond it, usually for some distance. When the seed germinates and grows into a seedling, the cotyledons of *Opuntia* are somewhat leaflike and visible above ground (Fig. 80), but those of other genera, such as *Cereus* (Fig. 66), remain minute or microscopic, and the seedling appears to be a spiny mass of undifferentiated tissue. At least in the genera with curving embryos, the curvature usually is correlated with development from the *usually, but not always, campylotropous* ovule.

In some genera the embryo within the seed is *incumbent* (Fig. 64), in others *accumbent* (Fig. 66). The embryo types in the various genera are indicated in the Key to the Genera of Cactaceae, pp. 260-63.

Storage tissue. The food reserve of a cactus seed is formed for the most part from the *perisperm*, originally a tissue (*megasporangium* or *nucellus*) of the female parent plant, which enclosed the cells that gave rise to the *egg* or *female gamete* cell. The egg, after being joined with one of the two *male gamete* cells of the pollen tube, divided repeatedly and became the embryo. In most flowering plants, the reserve food is stored in the *endosperm*, a tissue from a large cell adjoining the egg. In this cell, two nuclei fused and then joined with the other male gamete from the pollen tube. Subsequently, the resulting cell, unique in having *3n* chromosomes, divided and formed a tissue, the *endosperm*, used at least temporarily for food storage and never reproducing. In only a few flowering plants, like the Cactales, the food is stored in the perisperm, instead. In other orders it is absorbed into the cotyledons for storage.

Seed shape and the hilum. The seeds of cacti may be circular to ovate, elliptic, or elongate, and either longer than broad or broader than long, or they may be irregular. The *hilum*, or scar at the point where the stalk, or *funiculus*, was attached, is prominent.

The hilum is the only fixed point on the outside of the seed. Regardless of whether the seed is longer than broad or of any particular shape, the hilum is, *per se*, the base of the seed, and it is the starting point in determining shape and proportions. Failure to note this point has led many authors to refer to the hilum as "basal" when the seed was simply longer than broad and "lateral" when actually the seed was broader than long, the hilum merely appearing to be on one side. If the seed were made of putty, it could be reshaped into any of the seed forms, and the hilum would *appear* to be at the base or the side, according to proportion of length and breadth of the mass.

Types of seeds. The seeds of *Pereskia,* the genus of the Cactaceae retaining the greatest number of primitive characters, are of a relatively simple form and external coat structure. They

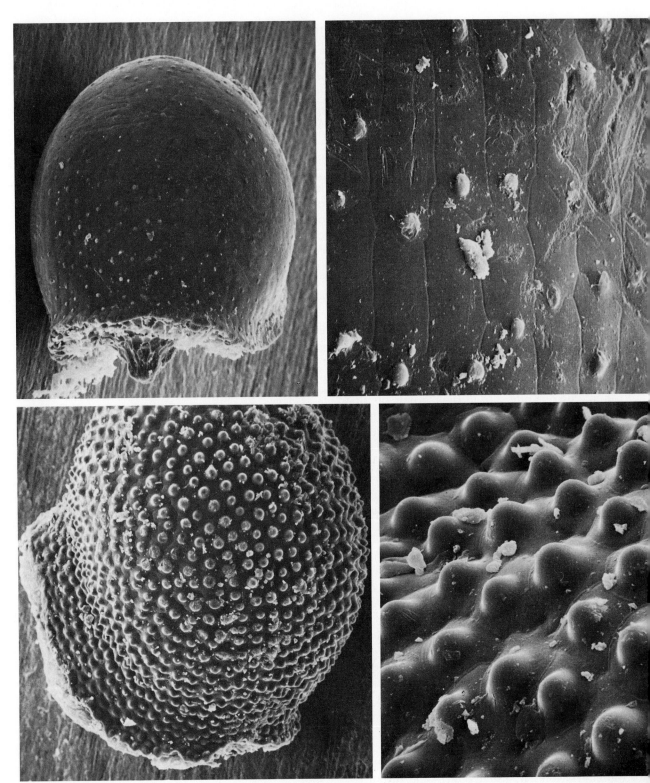

Fig. 61. Fine structure of the seed coats of four taxa of *Gymnocalycium* (Cactaceae); photo-graphs obtained with the scanning electron microscope. *Two above left,* Seed coat of *G. manzanense* var. *breviflorum,* ×90 and ×420. *Two above right, G. hypopleurum,* × 92 and ×460. *Two below left, G. manzanense* var. *manzanense,* ×90 and ×450. *Two below right, kossei,* ×90 and ×450. (Photographs courtesy of Herbert W. Franke, based on the research o Hans Till; see Credits)

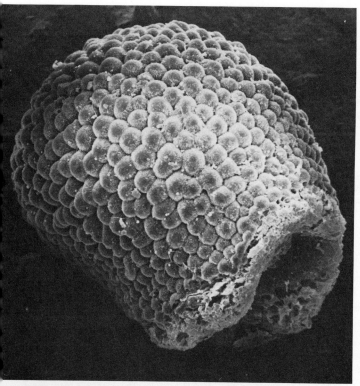 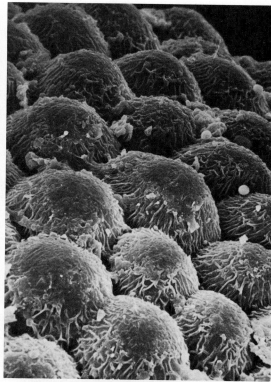

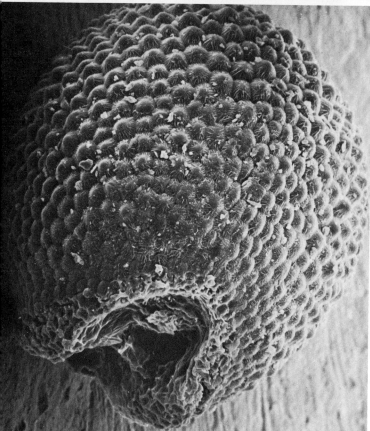 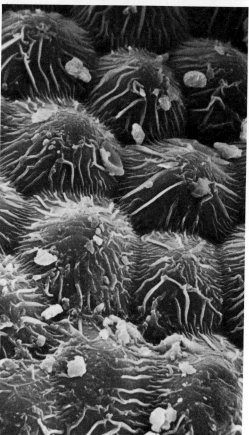

Fig. 62. Seed of *Pereskia grandifolia*, the seed broader than long but contorted so that the hilum (the truly basal structure) appears to be toward one side and on the diagonal. The surface appears smooth to the naked eye, but actually it is minutely and faintly reticulate.

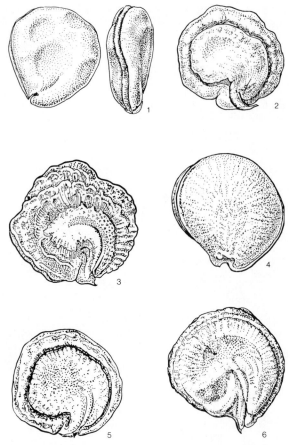

Fig. 63. Seeds of the *Opuntia* type. 1, A cholla, *Opuntia spinosior*, the rim not clearly differentiated in side view, but clear in the edge view of the seed; an unspecialized type. 2–6, Prickly pears. 2, 3, Dry-fruited prickly pears. 2, *O. polyacantha* var. *juniperina*, showing the broad, corky-appearing rim, characteristic of the dry-fruited prickly pears. 3, Yellow-flowered beavertail cactus, *O. basilaris* var. *aurea*, with a broad and even more elaborate rim. 4–7, Fleshy-fruited prickly pears. 4, The Eastern prickly pear, *O. humifusa*, with the narrow rim of the extreme type in the fleshy-fruited prickly pears. 5, *O. macrorhiza*, a closely related Western species, the rim broader but not as broad as in the dry-fruited prickly pears. 6, The common and widespread large prickly pear, *O. phaeacantha* var. *major*, the rim relatively broad for a fleshy-fruited species.

may represent an ancestral type or one slightly modified from that occurring in the forerunners of the family, but this is a matter of conjecture. Externally, seeds of *Pereskia* (Fig. 62) are not unlike those of some genera having less specialized seeds of the *Cereus* type, discussed below.

According to external form and structure, there are two principal types of seeds among the cacti occurring in the United States and Canada—the *Opuntia* type (Figs. 51, 7; 62; and 63) and the *Cereus* type (Figs. 51, 12; 65; and 66).

Opuntia type. The seeds of chollas and prickly pears (Figs. 63 and 64), are basically disklike, but the "disk" may be angular or very irregular, as in some chollas, such as *Opuntia imbricata* and *O. fulgida*. There is an outer rim, beyond the area enclosing the embryo and the stored food, and often it is differentiated strongly from the central part of the seed coat. Inside the seed, the embryo curves or even recurves like a hook at the cotyledon end.

Cereus type. The seeds of the other genera include many modifications of form. The basic form occurs in *Cereus, Echinocereus,* and *Mammillaria* and in all or some species of other genera, as illustrated here (Figs. 65 and 66) and in many figures in Part II. The extreme form resembles a German helmet of World War I, and the more common type is similar but deeper.

Seed characters and classification. Seed characters are useful in the combinations of features making distinctions between many genera and species of Cactaceae. For example, in *Opuntia* the surface of the seed coat is smooth, as seen with minor magnification, but in the other genera it may vary from smooth to rough through the presence of any of the surface markings mentioned above. Similarly, the differentiated rim of the seed beyond the area covering the embryo is

a feature of only *Opuntia*. However, the rim is much more strongly developed in most prickly pears than in the chollas, though there is some overlap in degree of the character.

The great variability of the seeds of the *Cereus* type makes them helpful in classification, provided they are studied in sufficient detail in many individuals and they are correlated with other characters. For example, in the literature one distinction of *Mammillaria* and *Coryphantha* is based on the occurrence of seeds that are longer than broad in the former and the reverse in the latter. However, this distinction breaks down, as

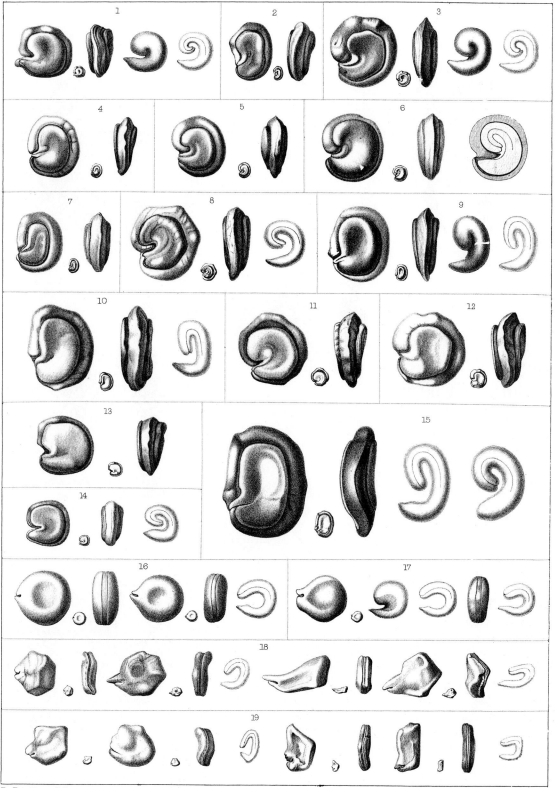

P. Roetter del.

Picart sc.

Fig. 64. Seeds and embryos of *Opuntia*; note the large incumbent cotyledons (with the back of one curving toward the hypocotyl, or axis). *1–15*, Prickly pears. *1, O. ficus-indica* (type of *O. engelmannii* from Chihuahua). *2–4, O. phaeacantha* var. *discata. 5–7, 9–13, O. phaeacantha* var. *major. 8, O. violacea* var. *macrocentra. 14, O. macrorhiza* var. *pottsii. 15, O. arenaria,* the only dry-fruited prickly pear in the figure; note the very broad rim of the seed. *16–19,* Chollas, the rim narrow and inconspicuous, the body of the seed drawn out (at least in these species) into a sort of stalk and a pair of lips around the mouthlike hilum (scar where the seed was attached). *16–17, O. imbricata. 18, O. fulgida* var. *fulgida. 19, O. fulgida* var. *mamillata.* Note the fantastic seed shapes in *18* and *19.* (Paulus Roetter in Engelmann/Emory, *pl. 75*)

51

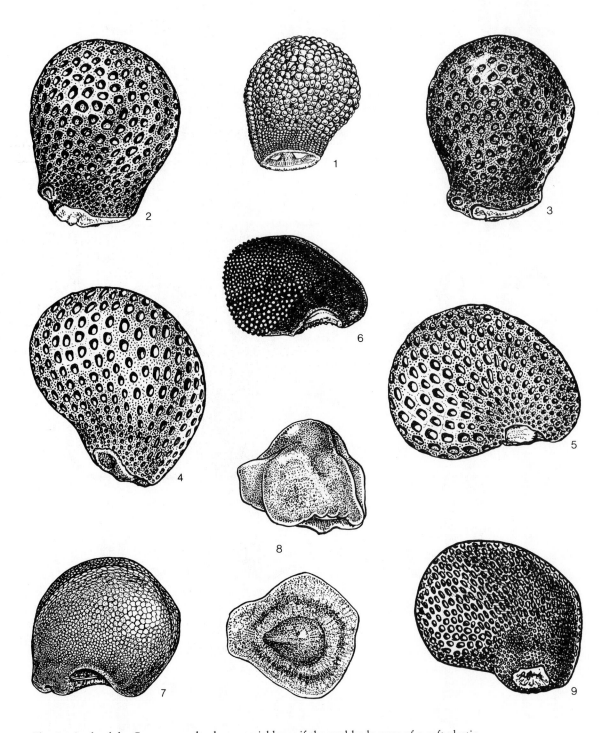

Fig. 65. Seeds of the *Cereus* type, the shapes variable, as if the seed body were of a soft plastic material molded in one way or another above the fundamental basal point, the hilum. The chief variation is from longer than broad, as in *1–3*, to broader than long, as in *5–7*; intermediate forms are common. The surface of the seed coat varies from papillate (*1*) to pitted (*4*) to reticulate (*7*). *1, Echinocereus triglochidiatus* var. *melanacanthus. 2, Mammillaria mainiae. 3–5, Coryphantha* (note the wide range of seed types within the genus; the shape in *5* is prevalent). *3, C. missouriensis. 4, C. robertii. 5, C. sneedii. 6, Sclerocactus parviflorus* var. *intermedius. 7, Echinocactus texensis. 8, E. asterias,* external side view (above), at least half the height being due to the enlargement of a chamber from the seed coat encircling the hilum and the micropyle through which the pollen tube enters; view from beneath (below), showing the chamber around the hilum and micropyle and the recessed opening. *9, Ferocactus viridescens,* the seed often described as longer than broad, a characterization open to interpretation because of distortion on the diagonal, as is so to a slightly lesser degree in *4.*

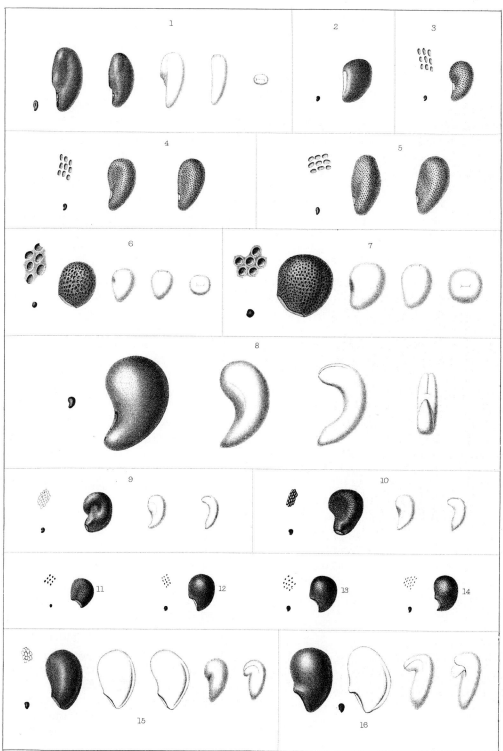

P. Roetter del.

Picart sc.

Fig. 66. Seeds of the *Cereus* type, in some cases showing embryos. The basic shape of the seed is longer than broad, but in *Coryphantha* and some other genera it may be broader than long (*1–5, 8*), though *C. missouriensis*, in the same genus, has seeds of the basic shape. In the other genera, the seeds shown here are longer than broad or of transitional types in which the hilum is on the diagonal. The seed coat may have a pattern of pits or dots, or a network, as shown by the enlargements of small portions of the surfaces. The cotyledons are accumbent (with one edge of each toward the axis of the embryo) in *Coryphantha* (*1–8*, except *1, 6*, and *7*, in which they are minute and the embryo is nearly straight). In *Ancistrocactus, 9–10*, the cotyledons are accumbent. In *Cereus, 15* and *16*, they are incumbent (with the back of one toward the axis, the back of the other away from it). *1, Coryphantha sulcata. 2, C. compacta* (Mexico). *3, 4, C. vivipara* var. *vivipara. 5, C. vivipara* var. *radiosa. 6, C. missouriensis* var. *missouriensis. 7, C. missouriensis* var. *caespitosa. 8, C. scheeri* var. *robustispina. 9, Ancistrocactus uncinatus. 10, A. uncinatus* var. *wrightii. 11–13, Ferocactus hamatacanthus* var. *sinuatus. 14,* "the form sent by Poselger under the name *Echinocactus robustus.*" *15, Cereus thurberi. 16, C. schottii.* (Paulus Roetter in Engelmann/Emory, *pl. 74*)

shown in the accompanying illustrations. *Coryphantha dasyacantha, C. robertii,* and *C. duncanii* have seeds like those of *Mammillaria* (longer than broad), and so does *C. missouriensis,* a species obviously only distantly related to them. However, the near relatives of these species, *C. strobiliformis* and *C. sneedii,* have seeds of the common type for *Coryphantha,* not only in greater breadth than length but also in proportionate size of the hilum and in coat texture. In the barrel cacti there are similar extreme types of seed shape; in *Ferocactus* the seeds are longer than broad and in *Echinocactus* broader than long. However, in *Ferocactus* there are many transitional types between the extremes. The intermediate types range from clearly longer than broad to only doubtfully so, and the hilum may be obviously basal or seemingly "sub-basal" or "diagonal."

The seed characters of the cacti are in need of a thorough review for correlation with all other features of the plants. After a careful study of *Mammillaria,* Shurly (1956) found no consistent correlation of the characters of the seeds with other structures, but correlations doubtless do occur in some groups of species of the cacti. The study of the seeds is not a separate field, as some have assumed, but merely one facet of investigation of the whole plant, individual-by-individual and for species after species. The consideration of seed characters is deficient in all works, including this one, but the use of seeds in classification is limited by the relatively small number of herbarium collections showing the seeds *together with the other characters of the individual that produced them.* A collection of seeds not correlated with full herbarium specimens is of little value for taxonomic purposes, because the relationship to other characters is unknown. Even the name of the species from which the seeds came represents no more than an individual's unverifiable opinion. Moreover, one sampling of seeds does not necessarily represent those typical of a species, variety, or genus. There is still much hard work to be done in accumulating *numerous documented specimens with seeds* before seed characters can be given due consideration. The same is true, of course, for other obscure characters, including pollen characters, chromosome counts, and chemical characters.

References (anatomy; for *Pereskia, cf.* pp. 264-67): Boke, 1941, *Zonation in the shoot apices of Trichocereus spachianus and Opuntia cylindrica,* 1944, *Histogenesis of the leaf and areole in* *Opuntia cylindrica,* 1951, *Histogenesis of the vegetative shoot in Echinocereus,* 1952, *Leaf and areole development in Coryphantha,* 1953, *Tubercle development in Mammillaria heyderi,* 1955a, *Development of the vegetative shoot in Rhipsalis cassytha,* 1955b, *Dimorphic areoles of Epithelantha,* 1956, *Developmental anatomy and the validity of the genus Bartschella,* 1957a, *Comparative histogenesis of the areoles in Homalocephala and Echinocactus,* 1957b, *Structure and development of the shoot in Toumeya,* 1958, *Areole histogenesis in Mammillaria lasiacantha,* 1959, *Endomorphic and ectomorphic characters in Pelecyphora and Encephalocarpus,* 1960, *Anatomy and development in Solisia,* 1961, *Structure and development of the shoot in Dolicothele,* 1963b, *Anatomy and development of the flower and fruit of Pereskia pititache,* 1964, *The cactus gynoecium: a new interpretation;* Buxbaum, 1944, *Untersuchungen zur Morphologie der Kakteenblüte,* 1. *Teil: Das Gynoecium,* 1950, *Morphology of cacti,* I. *Roots and stems,* 1953, *Morphology of cacti,* II. *Flower,* 1957, *Morphologie der Kakteen.* II. *Blüte. Die Kakteen* (ed. H. Krainz); Freeman, 1969, *The developmental anatomy of Opuntia basilaris,* I. *Embryo, root, transition zone,* 1970, *The developmental anatomy of Opuntia basilaris,* II. *Apical meristem, leaves, areoles, glochids;* Poindexter, 1951, *The cactus spine and related structures;* Tiagi, 1955, *Studies in floral morphology,* II. *Vascular anatomy of the flower of certain species of the Cactaceae,* 1957, *Studies in floral morphology,* III. *A contribution to the floral morphology of Mammillaria tenuis.*

Chromosomes

The basic chromosome number, x, for the cacti is 11. Usually this is also the reduced number, n, occurring in the sexual or gametophyte generation. (However, the reduced number, n, is not necessarily basic; sometimes it may be $2x$, $3x$, or some other number, representing a multiple or a modification of the basic number.) In most of the genera and species of cacti so far investigated the basic number (11) is repeated with monotonous regularity. In some genera, e.g. *Mammillaria* (Remski, 1954) and *Opuntia* (Katagiri, 1953; Pinkava & McLeod, 1971; Pinkava, McLeod, McGill & Brown, 1973), polyploidy has been shown in certain species. This includes tetraploidy, hexaploidy, octoploidy, and even up to 24-ploidy (in *Mammillaria capensis* var. *pallida*). Thus far, ploidy has been of help in the interpretation of some species, but study has only begun. Additional studies (such as those of Pinkava et al. in progress) are needed to correlate chromosome numbers with other characters and their combinations in living natural populations.

Remski (1954) points out that the same basic chromosome number occurs in at least some of the Myrtaceae, which have been suggested as relatives of the Cactaceae, but any such relationship probably is far removed.

References (chromosomes): Anderson, 1962, *A revision of Ariocarpus II. The status of the proposed genus Neogomesia;* Beard, 1937, *Some chromosome complements in the Cactaceae and a study of meiosis in Echinocereus papillosus;* Diers, 1961, *Der Anteil an Polyploiden in den Vegetationsgürtein der WestKordillere Perus;* Johansen, 1933, *Recent work on the cytology of the cacti;* Katagiri, 1953, *Chromosome numbers and polyploidy in certain Cactaceae;* Megata, 1941, *Eine Liste von Chromosomen bei Kakteen und anderen Sukkulenten;* Moore, 1967, *The Echinocereus enneacanthus-dubius-stramineus complex;* Pinkava & McLeod, 1971, *Chromosome numbers in some cacti of western North America;* Pinkava, McLeod, McGill, & Brown, 1973, same title—II; Remski, 1954, *Cytological investigations in Mammillaria and some associated genera;* Sato, 1958, *The chromosome[s] of the Cactaceae;* Spencer, 1955, *A cytological study of the Cactaceae of Puerto Rico;* Stockwell, 1935, *Chromosome numbers of some of the Cactaceae.*

2. The Physiology of Cacti

Contributed by **Frits W. Went**[*]

The physiology of the cacti is to some extent that of most flowering plants, but some patterns of physiological processes are characteristic of the Cactaceae (and often of other succulent plants) and rare in other plant families. Cactus physiology is discussed here in terms of the following topics: seeds and germination, metabolism, growth, water relations, flowering, temperature tolerance, and habitats.

Seeds and Germination

By far the most common method of reproduction in the cactus family is by seeds. The fruits of most species are fleshy, and the rather small seeds are distributed evenly through a soft, sweet-tasting pulp consisting mainly of the water-swollen (deliquescent) funiculi, or stalks, by which the seeds are attached to the placentas on the ovary wall. Although this fruit pulp would seem to be an ideal medium for seed germination, the seeds do not grow in the fruit, probably because the pulp contains germination inhibitors. The presence of such chemicals has been demonstrated in other pulpy fruits, like tomatoes and melons.

After cactus seeds have been washed free from the pulp, they retain their viability for a long time. Because germination occurs only at higher temperatures, in nature cactus seedlings develop during the summer. In cultivation, the seeds of most species germinate readily when sown in moist soil at about 21°C (70°F). In some species the seed coat is very hard, and before such seeds are planted they must be scarified, either by rubbing with sand, by filing, or by treatment with sulfuric acid. The appearance of the embryo and of the seedling during germination varies. In *Opuntia* the two cotyledons, or seed leaves (developed in the embryo in the seed), become large and fleshy. The cotyledons of *Cereus* and its rela-

tives are microscopic in the seed, and they do not enlarge in proportion to the growing embryo. In these plants the germinating embryo appears like a tiny blob, which soon starts to form spines at its apex.

Some cacti reproduce not only sexually by seeds but also asexually from detached joints, which produce roots after they separate from the parent plant (see p. 31). In some species, e.g. *Opuntia bigelovii*, reproduction proceeds exclusively from the readily detached joints. These root with ease, and then produce new plants. Unrooted joints die eventually, partly because they are unable to absorb water from the soil. Since the detached joints remain close to the parent plant, *O. bigelovii* grows typically in dense circular stands. This pattern is quite different from the distributional arrangements of other cacti, which propagate through seeds dispersed by various methods and grow at random wherever conditions are best.

Remarkably, the detached joints of *Opuntia bigelovii,* despite the numerous sharp spines with their retrorse barbs, often are carried by woodrats, or packrats, and are used to protect the entrance to the nest. How the packrats avoid injury by the spines of these joints is difficult to understand, but the protection the joints provide the nest is effective (see p. 93).

In cultivation, cacti may be reproduced by grafting portions of one plant on another. Although the partners selected must both be members of this family, they need not be close relatives. In this respect, the Cactaceae resemble some other families or subfamilies, like the Solanaceae, the Cucurbitaceae, and the subfamily Pomoideae of the Rosaceae, in which almost any species can be grafted successfully on any other member of the group. According to occasional claims, plants of other families can be grafted successfully on the cacti, but investigation of a number of such cases has shown that the graft merely rooted in the suc-

[*]Desert Research Institute, University of Nevada System, Reno.

culent tissue of the cactus, using the soft parenchyma as a soil substitute. Growers of monstrosities graft crested or other fasciated forms (see p. 17) on normal cacti, because such abnormal forms do not reproduce through seeds and they are difficult to propagate as cuttings.

Metabolism

All succulents, and the cacti in particular, are sealed off from their environment by a thick and essentially impermeable outer coat, or cuticle. Thus, they lose very little water by transpiration, and they can live under conditions where minimal liquid water is available. However, the enclosure of the tissues so that almost no water vapor diffuses outward has a corollary—no CO_2 can diffuse through the cuticle from the outside air into the body of the cactus.

Retention of water without excluding CO_2 is complicated by the fact that no plant membrane is differentially permeable to CO_2 and H_2O molecules. If anything, a water molecule (molecular weight, 18), being lighter, diffuses faster than a CO_2 molecule (molecular weight, 44), and the diffusion gradient for H_2O is much greater than that for CO_2. Thus, water may leave even faster than CO_2 enters.

In the dry regions where most succulents occur, day temperatures are high, and water evaporates rapidly. Consequently, the stomata, or pores, of the stem must be closed during the day, but they may be open during the cool night, permitting CO_2 to enter. Although at that time photosynthesis cannot occur for lack of light, the carbon dioxide is retained by being combined chemically into compounds from which it may dissociate the next day. This holding over of CO_2 from night to day is a special feature of succulent plants called "succulent metabolism," or CAM (Crassulacean acid metabolism).

In the usual process of photosynthesis, CO_2, absorbed from the air through the open stomata of the leaves or young stems, is reduced at once to carbohydrates through the use of light energy from the sun. In succulents the absorbed CO_2 is incorporated first into malic or isocitric acid, by a reversible process occurring in darkness. At low temperatures the equilibrium lies toward the acid side; but at higher temperatures CO_2 is released. Since the stomata of cacti are closed during the day and open at night, when the temperature is lower, acid is formed during the night—the cooler the night the more acid. Production of malic acid

during the night causes acidification of the cactus tissues from the late afternoon on. Thus, in the morning cacti contain two to four times as much free acid as in the evening. This they have in common with almost all succulents, including such plants as miner's lettuce (*Montia perfoliata*) and purslane (*Portulaca oleracea*), which taste much more acid in the morning than in the evening.

One of the most important aspects of succulent metabolism is that the lower the temperature the more CO_2 can be fixed as an organic acid and the more will be available the next day for photosynthesis. At high night temperatures, CO_2, instead of being fixed, is released, leaving no acid for photosynthesis. For this reason, the cacti and other succulents need a pronounced thermoperiodicity in their environment, and this condition is at the maximum in arid climates. Relatively few cacti do well in regions where the day-and-night temperature range is small, though some species are adapted even to tropical rainforests.

In addition to these other limitations, the amount of CO_2 that can be absorbed each night is limited severely by the quantity of acid that can be formed. Consequently, the rate of photosynthesis in cacti is slow, and in turn the growth rate is low.

Growth

Basically, the growth of cacti is the same as that of other plants. An apical meristem continues to produce new cells, which slowly differentiate into mature stem tissues. In a barrel cactus the tissues around the stem tip may grow for one year, but once maturity is reached, no further growth occurs, and the diameter of the stem remains constant, subject only to fluctuations in the water balance. Beyond maturity, no further cell divisions occur in the soft parenchyma, and the fleshy parts of the cactus stem disintegrate after the limited lifespan of each cell is exceeded. Generally, each cell type has a definite lifespan: leaf cells 6 months to a year, stem cells 1 to several years, and parenchyma cells in wood 5 to 10 years. During mitosis each cell renews its lease on life, and therefore meristems, as long as they retain their function of forming new cells, have an indefinite lifespan. Thus, through cambial activity forming new wood and phloem, the stems of *Opuntia* and *Cereus* may become very old. In age they are no longer surrounded by the cortex of fleshy parenchyma, because this layer has been sloughed off. However, other parenchyma cells of cacti ap parently can live for decades, and probably they are among the longest-lived cells in the plant kingdom.

In some cacti, stems continue to grow in girth long after meristematic growth has ceased. In these species the epidermal and cortical cells must divide, and the plant retains a living, smooth surface for a very long time. Examples include *Lophophora williamsii* and *Echinocactus* (*Astrophytum*) *myriostigma.*

In most Cereae, stem growth is monopodial, i.e., the apical growing point continues cell divisions. If this apical meristem is injured, a lateral bud takes over its function, producing, for example, the candelabrumlike growth form of the saguaro, *Cereus giganteus.*

In *Rhipsalis* and *Opuntia*, typically growth is sympodial, one joint being developed from another, the axis not necessarily continuing in a straight line. This pattern is followed even in the fruiting of *Opuntia fulgida,* in which a new flower may be produced from an areole of a fruit of the preceding year. Continuation of this process year after year results in zigzag branched chains of fruits of as many as 23 age groups hanging down from the older joints. Since this species never or rarely reproduces through seeds, ordinarily it makes little or no difference whether or not the seeds are dispersed.

Because the special metabolism of succulents allows them to carry over carbon dioxide absorbed at night, when evaporation of water is low, to be used in photosynthesis the next day, the highest rate of carbohydrate synthesis occurs after cool nights. For this reason, succulents grow best when cool nights are followed by warm days, a sequence typical of arid climates. Thus, cacti and other succulents are adapted ideally in growth response, as well as special metabolism, to their usual dry environment.

Because cacti, like succulents in general, grow during the warm season of the year, they are good house and greenhouse plants, provided they are kept cool and well ventilated at night. Knowledge of the growth requirements and unusual metabolism of cacti can be translated into practical hints for the succulent grower. Whereas during the day cacti may be kept in a warm greenhouse without much ventilation, during the night ventilation is important. Then the ventilators in the greenhouse should be kept open for both air circulation and cooling.

Water Relations

As indicated above, all cacti have numerous structures and responses that tend to decrease water loss by transpiration. In addition to the water-retaining surface layer, the ratio of surface to volume is low, because most genera have no leaves and the stems are mostly thick and compact. Only *Pereskia* and *Pereskiopsis* have permanent leaves, and even they are rather succulent. In *Opuntia* the leaves are reduced to small, mostly elongate, succulent green structures that are shed soon after emergence, and in *Cereus* and nearly all the other genera there is no macroscopic vestige of a leaf in the mature plant. As noted under "Seeds and Germination" above, cotyledon development in *Pereskia* and *Opuntia* is much greater than that in other genera, paralleling the degree of development of foliage leaves.

Inasmuch as the succulent stems of all cacti have a very high ratio of surface to volume, the area of transpiration is minute in proportion to the very large water-storage capacity. Almost the entire inside of the stem of the cactus is taken up by parenchymatous water-storage tissue, and a typical cactus plant consists of 80-90 percent water. Consequently, a cactus plant will lose less than one-thousandth as much water as a mesophytic plant of the same weight, and it does not need to replenish its water continuously.

As in the younger stems of all plants, the epidermis of even a mature cactus stem includes many stomata, about 15-18 per square millimeter. At least in the few cases investigated so far, the most important property of the cactus stomata is their being closed during the day and open at night. During daylight, when the relative humidity of the air is low (down to 10-20 percent), hardly any water vapor is lost by transpiration through the stomata. In contrast, at night, when the water-vapor gradient between cactus and air is steep, the stomata are open, and CO_2 can be absorbed without much loss of water.

A further adaptation of cacti to arid growing conditions is their slime content. Normally, if a plant is cut or wounded, the exposed tissues dry out rapidly, because there is no check on excessive transpiration. Because of the wound, a leaf, a branch, or even the entire plant may dry out gradually and wither, unless enough water can be supplied by the root system to make up for the unusual water loss. Except after a rain, little water is available to a cactus root system, and, but for the presence of slime, a wound or cut might be fatal. The slime, a polysaccharide present in all the cactus cells, or in special slime cells, soon covers the cut surface and dries into a horny, impermeable layer over the wound. This seal prevents further water loss, just as a dry gelatin surface layer covers certain pills, though the centers remain liquid. The cell wall of an ordinary plant cell does not check the movement of water, but in a cactus, once an injury is covered with dried slime, evaporation stops.

Cacti have another defense against water loss through wounds, a procedure that is most pronounced in the saguaro. In this plant the tissues around any wound—for example, around the nest holes made by woodpeckers and used later by owls—soon produce a layer of cork. This layer can become quite thick, and it may seal off the plant tissues around the nest cavity with a water-resistant cover.

The root systems of cacti also are adapted to their special life habits. Most young cacti form penetrating anchor roots with which they are fastened securely to the ground. Most of the later-developed root system, however, is very shallow. The long lateral roots spread around the adult plant in all directions, mostly only a few centimeters below the soil surface. These roots are fleshy, and except on new distal ones, they are covered with a thick, irregular, cork layer that prevents water loss to the bone-dry upper soil layers. Within two days after a summer rain, myriads of tiny hair roots penetrate through the cork layers of the old roots, absorbing the available soil water and quickly resaturating the cactus tissues with water. As soon as the upper soil layers about the cactus roots are dry again, the root hairs dry up, and again the cactus retreats within its safe cork layer. Thus, the root hairs act as a valve mechanism, allowing water to pass in but not out. And with its shallow, spreading root system the cactus can take advantage of even minor rains and replenish its stored water supply, whereas most other desert perennials can utilize only the heavier rains penetrating as far as their deeper root systems.

Still another adaptation of cacti to arid conditions is their ability to withstand considerable water loss. Whereas most mesophytes wilt or even die when they lose even 10-20 percent of their water, cacti can lose 60 percent with impunity. In prickly pears the joints shrink, causing crinkling of the flat surfaces of the stems. The cylindroid stems of barrel cacti shrink only laterally, along the deeper grooves and narrower ridges running lengthwise.

Flowering

The flower physiology of cacti is interesting, but it has been neglected by botanists. Most cactus flowers last for only one or a few days, and they are not long available for study. The large flower size is often out of proportion to the size of the plant, and obviously much metabolic energy is expended in flower bud growth and in blooming. It has been found that the wilting of the flower at the end of the blooming is due to exhaustion of the proteins (rather than of the carbohydrates) in the petaloids and stamens, which causes cell collapse. This physiology contrasts with that of most other flowers, which either abscise the old flower parts before their cells collapse or exhaust the supply of sugars. Such flowers can be kept fresh longer simply by supplying them with sugar, but this expedient is ineffective with cactus flowers.

The night-blooming cacti, some species of which occur in Arizona, have large, often very fragrant, flowers that open after sunset and wilt the next day, usually in the morning. Being mostly moth-pollinated, the flowers are white or pale yellow; they do not need the brilliant colors of the bird-, bee-, and butterfly-pollinated day-bloomers. In *Cereus (Selenicereus) grandiflorus,* sometimes called Queen-of-the-Night, the trigger for the opening of the flower is provided 24 hours earlier: i.e., the darkening associated with sunset on the previous day provides the stimulus for opening the bud. If one wishes to have the flowers of his Queen-of-the-Night cactus open in the afternoon, he must place the plant in darkness the preceding noon. Any bud ready to open the next evening will do so at noon rather than at sunset. This delayed triggering of flowering is known in other plants, as well: the California poppy (*Eschscholtzia californica*) closes its flowers 20 hours after the sunset of the preceding day, and it is possible to prevent their closing by keeping the plants in artificial light during the preceding night.

The opening of a cactus flower, and particularly of a Queen-of-the-Night, is a fascinating spectacle. For the bud to open fully requires about half an hour. In a bud the numerous sepaloids are closed tightly around the petaloids. In the late afternoon of the day of flowering the tips of the outer sepaloids loosen, and at sunset they start to unfold so rapidly that one can *see* the sepaloids, then the petaloids, spreading with slightly jerking movements. In succession, first the outer sepaloids and then those farther inward unfold and spread, until finally the petaloids are uncovered, and they, too, begin to spread.

In some cacti the stamens are sensitive to touch. In certain species of *Opuntia*, insects crawling between the filaments stimulate them to move inward, bringing the anthers closer to the stigmas and narrowing the passage the insect commonly follows (see p. 269). However, this is not a mechanism favoring self-pollination, because most cacti are protandrous—i.e., the anthers in a given flower shed pollen before the stigmatic surfaces of the same flower are receptive—and because they are self-sterile.

The westernmost North American cacti tend to flower during the spring. This is true of nearly all perennials, including succulents, living in summer-dry climates with cool winters, particularly of plants having large, slow-ripening fruits. Especially for succulents, the urgency for completion of flowering and fruiting before real drought sets in is less than for most perennials. Thus, the desert cacti usually flower a month later than most other desert plants. Whereas in the Colorado River basin the herbs, especially the desert annuals, reach their peak of flowering during late March and in April, the height of cactus flowering is during May. Most of the species of cacti occurring in dry areas near the deserts flower during May and June, and many Arizona cacti flower even later, during the period of summer rains. The few cacti growing high up in the mountains also flower later (into July).

In tropical and semitropical regions, cacti tend toward strictly seasonal flowering. Thus, the Brazilian Christmas cactus (*Schlumbergera*, known also as *Zygocactus*), frequently grown as a house plant, flowers in the United States in late December, apparently in response to the short winter days. Another Brazilian cactus grown as a houseplant, *Phyllocactus*, flowers in the North Temperate Zone during April, and it is therefore sometimes called Easter cactus. Although there is no experimental evidence, presumably the response is conditioned photoperiodically. If so, the flowering behavior of the Brazilian cacti must be analogous to the flowering of Brazilian orchids cultivated in the Northern Hemisphere: *Cattleya trianae* is a short-day plant that flowers in early winter, whereas *C. mossiae* flowers during early spring.

Temperature Tolerance

Since most cacti grow in warm sub-arid regions, where air and soil temperatures can reach high levels—over 49°C (120°F) air temperature and over 65°C (150°F) soil temperature—they must be able to avoid or tolerate great heat. For most plants, even tropical ones, temperatures over 54°C (130°F) lasting for even short periods are lethal (see Fig. 67). Consequently, we find in many plants mechanisms enabling them to avoid or counteract high temperatures. One common method of lowering temperatures is by means of evaporative cooling. However, cacti must preserve water; they and other succulents cannot avail themselves of this method. Many plants have a thick cork layer insulating them from excessively hot air or soil. This we find in cacti, especially at the surface of the soil, which, because of strong insolation, can be 5.5-11°C (10-20°F) warmer than the air just above or the soil just beneath.

But no mechanism can prevent the insides of the thick stems or joints of cacti from overheating. Inside the joints of *Opuntia* a temperature of 59°C (138°F) has been measured while the air temperature was 43°C (110°F). The massive bodies of other cacti, never shaded by leaves, also must overheat. Very likely the thick layer of spines of a barrel cactus reduces overheating, but nevertheless cactus cells must be able to tolerate much higher temperatures than those of most other plants.

Plants as full of water as cacti are usually very frost-sensitive. Actually, the great majority of cacti are killed by frost, and most can be cultivated out-of-doors only in nearly frost-free areas. However, cacti able to grow in northern areas or higher up in the mountains are able to resist frost. Most of the frost-resistant cacti are species of *Opuntia*, although there are some Cereae among them.

Habitats

Contrary to common belief, the cacti are not primarily extreme desert plants, and many species of North American cacti grow outside the deserts. They do not grow necessarily in the most extreme deserts, and in the center of Death Valley there are no cacti at all. The same is true of the most extreme desert in South America, the

Fig. 67. Relative effects of temperature on cacti and other plants. *Top, Opuntia fragilis* with *Oxalis corniculata* as a weed in the pot: the weed had almost hidden the small prickly pear until the pot was placed for three days against a south-facing wall in hot, dry weather during the summer; the *Oxalis* was then killed by the high temperature and resulting drying, but the cactus was not injured. *Middle two,* Similar treatment of a small spineless prickly pear: *middle left,* after 1 day against the wall; *middle right,* after 3 days. *Bottom two,* Similar treatment of a young freely branching plant of *Echinocereus triglochidiatus*: *bottom left,* before treatment, the *Oxalis* nearly covering the cactus; *bottom right,* after 3 days against the wall, the *Oxalis* dead and the cactus exposed to the light.

Atacama Desert of Chile. *Cereus atacamensis* occurs only along the borders of this desert, because cacti do need water to replenish their losses, and it is available only where there are occasional rains. These rains need not penetrate deeply into the soil; an occasional superficial wetting is enough. Some South American species of *Cereus* can even subsist under fog-drip in the rainless areas near Antofagasta, Chile, and around Lima, Peru, where precipitation is less than 2.5 cm (1 inch) per year. But there the air is so moist that, even though no other flowering plants can exist, the epiphyte *Tillandsia* grows on the cactus stems.

Cacti also are not well adapted to living in saline areas. Thus, one never finds them in dry lakes. Their absence there also may be related to the fact that they cannot grow in heavy clay, but grow best in loose sandy or rocky soils. Actually, many species of cacti grow best on rock faces, where their roots follow fissures in the rock and they are wetted each time rainwater seeps in.

Tree trunks and branches provide a major habitat of some cacti, but outside the tropics there are few of these epiphytes, or "air plants." Such plants live on branches of trees without parasitizing them, deriving from this habitat only a preferred location nearer the light and out of the competition for space and light on the forest floor. But even in a moist rain forest the epiphytic mode of life poses problems of water balance, because epiphytes have no roots reaching the ever-moist soil, and they must derive their water from that trickling down the branches or settling in crevices of the branches and bark during a rain. Thus, the succulent habit, which restricts water loss between rains to a minimum, is a distinct advantage to an epiphyte. Consequently, many epiphytic orchids and other plants are succulents, and many cacti are epiphytic. The whole genus *Rhipsalis* (including a species occurring in Florida), all species of *Epiphyllum*, and many species of *Cereus* are epiphytes, growing on the branches and trunks of tropical forest trees. One of the requirements for the epiphytic mode of living is that seeds be deposited on branches by wind or by birds. Thus, it is not surprising that *Rhipsalis* produces its seeds in white berries eaten by birds that leave the seeds in their droppings on tree branches.

Rock outcroppings, pine barrens, and other infertile spots with very shallow soil, so common in the southeastern United States, are also favored locations for cacti. Thus, many kinds of environments unfavorable to most plants are the best locations for some cacti, chiefly because of their succulence.

3. Chemical Characters of Cacti

The chemical characters of plants are fundamental but elusive. They are difficult to investigate for more than a few individuals of a species, and they are meaningless unless their association with other characters is assessed at the same time. Most studies of chemical characters of the Cactaceae have been applied to the family as a whole, and these characters are not included in this section, which concerns variability from species to species or variety to variety. Two examples of such studies are presented, by David L. Walkington and Brian S. Bean. (Cf. McLaughlin, 1966–.)

Chemical Characters of the Cell Content of Prickly Pears

David L. Walkington has studied various aspects of chemical characters of a group of presumably hybridizing prickly pears occurring in southern California. His chemical research was related to the advent of the Indian fig (locally called mission cactus), *Opuntia ficus-indica*, from Mexico, its remarkable hybridization with native species, and the consequent production of gigantic hybrid swarms (Benson & Walkington, 1965; Benson, 1969c). The following research essay by Dr. Walkington is given as an example of the value of studying chemical characters for taxonomic purposes, with the hope that many similar studies will be undertaken.

A CHEMOTAXONOMIC STUDY OF SOME SPECIES OF OPUNTIA OCCURRING IN SOUTHERN CALIFORNIA
Contributed by David L. Walkington*

The prickly pears growing west of the mountains in southern California are of a wide variety of forms exhibiting variable combinations of morphological characters. Some forms have become segregated and have maintained relatively consistent combinations of characters. Others cannot be categorized satisfactorily, and they

*Department of Botany, California State University, Fullerton, California.

seem to represent intermediates in hybrid swarms.

As has been recounted by Benson and Walkington (1965), cultivars of the fruit-tree prickly pear of Mexico, *Opuntia ficus-indica*, were introduced by the Franciscan Fathers as they established their missions along the coast of California during the eighteenth century. In the course of time, these cultivars, now known as mission cacti, were planted extensively in other areas, and some escaped and became established in moister, deeper soils along washes in valleys or at the mouths of canyons. Hybridization was postulated (Benson & Walkington, 1965; Benson, 1969c) to occur between these plants and varieties of the smaller native species, especially varieties of *O. littoralis* and more rarely varieties of *O. phaeacantha*. Many local hillside populations include plants with character combinations ranging from those of the mission cacti to those of the native species.

The investigation described here was undertaken in an attempt to circumscribe more accurately those taxa that may represent naturally occurring or introduced species or varieties and to determine the origins and relationships of these taxa and the possible hybrid forms.

Methods of investigation. The basic approach in making this study was correlation of detailed morphological studies with chemical analyses of the plants, the assumption being that the more closely related the plants, the more similar they will be in physical and chemical makeup. Collections and observations were made from Santa Barbara, California, south to 6.5 km (4 miles) below Ensenada, Baja California, Mexico, and east to the edges of the Mojave and Sonoran deserts. Collection trips were made also into central and southern Arizona, New Mexico, Texas, and Mexico as far south as Querétaro. The collections were processed by observing and measuring stem joints, spines, flowers, fruits, and seeds, paying particular attention to lengths and widths of parts, distribution of parts, and such characteristics as color and markings.

Chemical analysis involved extraction of water-soluble chemicals called flavonoids along with similar compounds from one-year-old stem joints followed by separation and comparison of these compounds, using a method known as two-dimensional paper chromatography. This technique has been of remarkable value to chemists interested in separating mixtures of organic chemicals into pure, isolated compounds. Botanists have found it useful particularly in separating chemicals extracted from plants. The technique is based on the phenomenon that occurs when ink is spilled on cloth or paper and the various pigments making up the ink separate as distinct bands or rings of color around the original location. An extract of a plant is placed near one corner of a large rectangular piece of filter paper, and the paper is suspended from a trough containing a solvent such as water or alcohol. The solvent is soaked up by the paper, and the fluid moves through the sheet downward. The chemicals contained within the original area are carried down the paper with the solvent; however, not all the chemicals move at the same rate or for the same distance, resulting in their separation in discrete spots. The paper then is dried and hung again in the trough so that all the spots are distributed in a horizontal direction along the trough, i.e. at right angles to the original direction of solvent flow. This time the solvent, which is usually different from the first one, carries the spots down the surface of the paper perpendicularly to the original direction of flow. Any spots that may have overlapped in the first direction usually are separated in this second direction. This, then, completes the development of a two-dimensional chromatogram upon which each spot concludes its flow in a specific position relative to the others. The positions are always consistent from one trial to the next for the particular chemicals separated if the same paper and solvent system are used.

The details of the extraction procedure and the two-dimensional chromatographic development used in this study are given in the boxed explanation. The following discussion presents, in general, how chemical comparisons were made and correlated with morphological data.

Chromatograms from each collection were compared, and an index of relationship was calculated for each collection in comparison with all others (see Figs. 68 and 69). Chromatograms from different plants were analyzed in pairs and a value of 1 was assigned to each spot in both

chromatograms. The index of relationship (I.R.) for the pair then was calculated by the following formula:

$$\text{I.R.} = \frac{\text{number of matching spots}}{\text{total number of spots}} \times 100$$

In the analyses of the indices of relationship, chemical types were developed by grouping collections exhibiting similar chromatographic patterns. These chemical types were then correlated with consistent morphological types. The indices from all collections of each chemical type were averaged and compared. These collections were then compared with those not morphologically or chemically consistent to determine possible relationships.

An additional analysis of the indices of relationship was made in an attempt to determine the possible origin of certain chemical types and unclassified local collections. This analysis was based on the assumption that the chemicals in a hybrid should approach the sum of the chemicals present in the parents. As an arbitrary standard for means of attaining consistency in comparison, an I.R. of below 50 was considered to represent little chemical affinity, and an I.R. above 60 was thought to be an indication of similar chemical makeup. Pairs of chromatograms exhibiting indices of less than 50 were chosen, and then chromatograms from each pair were compared with all the others for indices of relationship of above 60. The two chromatograms having the mutual I.R. of below 50 and the third chromatogram exhibiting an I.R. of above 60 to each of the other two were considered a triangle that had the potentialities for demonstrating possible hybrid origin. The chromatograms were examined for the occurrence of different chemical constituents in each of the putative parents and for a summation of these compounds in the possible hybrid (Figs. 68 & 69).

Results and conclusions. According to the collections and observations, in grassland and open chaparral habitats of the cismontane region of southern California (i.e. west of the mountain axis) many populations include prickly pears exhibiting a wide variety of forms, many of which compose large thickets. The combinations of characters range from those of the introduced mission cactus, *Opuntia ficus-indica* and its cultivars, to those of the low-growing native species, *O. littoralis* vars. (Benson & Walkington, 1965; Benson, 1969c). A nearly consistent combination of characters was observed in plants growing in

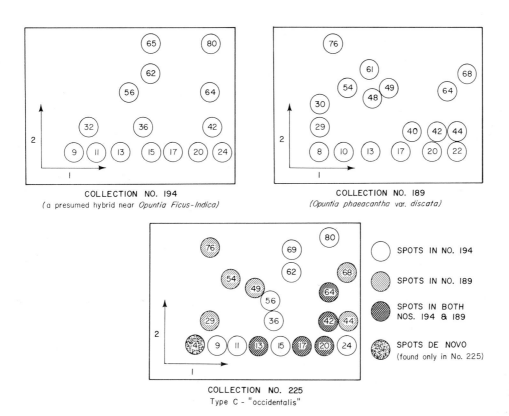

Fig. 68. Representations of two-dimensional chromatograms illustrating a summation of chemicals in a collection of a presumed hybrid (no. 225, Type C, "hybrid population occidentalis") from those of *Opuntia ficus-indica* (no. 194) and *O. phaeacantha* var. *discata* (no. 189). (David L. Walkington)

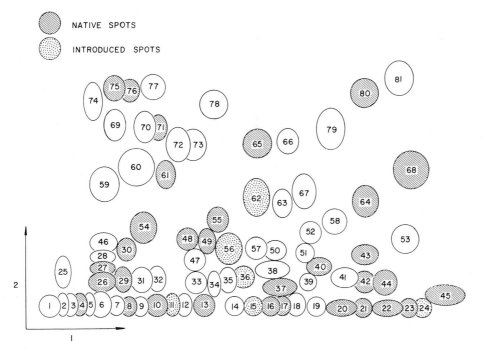

Fig. 69. A composite of two-dimensional chromatograms of chemical constituents of prickly pear stem joints, including an indication of the spots representing compounds occurring in native plants of coastal southern California and those characteristic of the introduced Indian fig or mission cactus, *Opuntia ficus-indica*. (David L. Walkington)

the mountains and along the western edge of the desert.

Analysis of the morphological data revealed ten basic, more or less distinct morphological types among the variety of forms in cismontane habitats. The following are the names applied to these types:

1. *Opuntia ficus-indica* (spineless)
2. *O. ficus-indica* (spiny; sometimes referred to as *O. megacantha*)
3. Type C *"occidentalis"*
4. Type D *"occidentalis"*
5. *O. oricola*
6. *O. phaeacantha* var. *discata*
7. *O. littoralis* var. *austrocalifornica*
8. *O. littoralis* var. *piercei*
9. *O. littoralis* var. *vaseyi*
10. Type I *"demissa"*

In determining chemical relationships, the results of chromatographic data indicated the most dependable and taxonomically significant chemical constituents to be the flavonoids and related compounds found in the de-spined stem-joint extracts. A total of 81 different compounds was observed, with as many as 47 found in a single extract. *O. ficus-indica* cultivars contained up to seven unique chemical constituents. In comparison, a total of 34 chemicals was found to be characteristic of the native species of the peripheral cismontane and transmontane collections. The first eight of the ten established morphological types listed above could be delineated as chemical types based on the similarities in chemical patterns between individual collections within a morphological type. The first five contained chemical constituents found in the introduced mission cactus. The remaining three (of the first eight) exhibited close chemical affinities with the native plants occurring in the deserts of California, Arizona, and New Mexico. One, *O. phaeacantha* var. *discata,* is a shrubby local coastal form with large subulate spines. Another, *O. littoralis* var. *austrocalifornica,* is a low-growing inland form with a few very small acicular spines or usually none. The third, *O. littoralis* var. *piercei,* is a clumpy form, with long decurrent acicular spines, found at higher elevations, up to 2,175 m (7,250 ft). The first two in the list above constituted collections of escaped cultivars of the mission cactus. The next three types also contained native chemical constituents. Of these, Type C *"occidentalis"* and Type D *"occidentalis"* exhibited close chemical indices of relationship to both the introduced mission cactus and the native species. Also, the occurrence of chemical summation could be demonstrated in the extracts of these two types. In this study they are classified as hybrids, and they are given the name Hybrid Population *"occidentalis"* because of the common usage of this epithet for plants of this type. The third type, *O. oricola,* showed some morphological similarity to the introduced mission cactus as well as to a native coastal element. However, no close chemical indices of relationship or chemical summation could be determined. All the cismontane populations studied included escaped mission cacti along with a number of unclassified forms that revealed morphological and chemical similarities to both the introduced mission cactus and the native species.

The following interpretation is made in an attempt to explain, on the basis of this study, the origins and relationships of the cismontane taxa. As explained above and on pp. 517-18, native populations consisting of low-growing shrubby prickly pears have hybridized freely with the introduced Mexican cactus, *Opuntia ficus-indica,* and its cultivars. At about the time of introduction of the Mexican species, weeds, including many Mediterranean grasses, were brought inadvertently by the white man, and these formed a dense cover in the lowlands and on hillsides. Fires became frequent and increasingly intense. Plants of the native species could not survive these fires, and they became reduced in number, but the larger hybrid plants that formed rather tall, dense, spreading thickets were burned only around the edges (Benson & Walkington, 1965; Benson, 1969c). The resistant centers, therefore, continued to grow outward and to occupy more and more space after each grass fire. Selection by fire has favored these hybrid types, leaving only a few clones of the unadulterated native species persisting in the more protected areas. An examination of the lectotype of the first described southern California prickly pear, *O. occidentalis,* and a study of the plants growing in the type locality suggest that the name was based on a collection from either an escaped cultivar of *O. ficus-indica* or a hybrid. Consequently, the name *O. occidentalis* is a synonym or near synonym for *O. ficus-indica,* and the epithet *littoralis,* having priority in time of publication, is the valid one for the small coastal and inland species and its varieties. Of the four recognized cismontane Californian varieties of *O. littoralis,* namely vars. *littoralis, vaseyi, austrocalifornica,*

CHEMICAL ANALYSIS BY TWO-DIMENSIONAL CHROMATOGRAPHY

By David L. Walkington (see text)

For this study three to five one-year-old stem joints from each clone were de-spined, washed with distilled water, sectioned into thin slices, and dried in an oven at 70°C for 4 to 5 days. The dried sections were then mixed and stored for future use. In order to extract the chemical constituents, the dried stem material was pounded into a powder and weighed. A 1:10 w/v ratio of the powder to a solvent of acidified methanol (methyl alcohol; 1 percent hydrochloric acid in pure methanol v/v) was mixed in a Waring blender for 2 minutes. The mixture was then allowed to sit at room temperature for 24 hours for further extraction. At the end of this period, the extract was poured through cheesecloth to remove the pulp and filtered through a Buchner funnel using Whatman #1 filter paper. The filtrate was then poured into previously weighed dishes and evaporated to dryness during 24 to 48 hours in a fuming hood. The evaporated residue was redissolved in the acidified methanol solvent in the ratio of 1:5 w/v and centrifuged for 15 minutes at 2,000 × g. The resulting supernatant was ready for chromatographic separation. Duplicate extractions were prepared for each clone tested. Because one chromatography chamber (chromatocab) will hold eight chromatography papers (chromatograms), four clones could be tested each time. Chromatograms were prepared by spotting approximately 20 lambda of the extract at one corner of a 46 cm × 57 cm sheet of Whatman #1 filter paper. The chromatocab was sealed and the system allowed to equilibrate for at least 6 hours. After this period the mobile solvent of

n-butanol, acetic acid, and water in the ratio of 6:1:2 was poured into the troughs, and a descending chromatographic separation occurred. After approximately 15 hours, the chromatograms were removed, hung in a fuming hood, and dried. Each chromatogram was then scanned under both long-wave (3,660 Å) and short-wave (2,537 Å) ultraviolet light for fluorescing and absorbing spots. Subsequently the chromatograms were hung in another chromatocab at right angles to the direction of flow to the first solvent system and allowed to equilibrate in the presence of ammoniated ethyl alcohol for at least 6 hours. At the end of the equilibration period, the second-dimension mobile solvent of ethyl alcohol, ammonium hydroxide (reagent strength or 58 percent) and water in the ratio of 18:1:1 was added to the troughs (the ratio using 100-percent ammonium hydroxide would be expressed as 90:3:7). After approximately 7 hours of descending separation, the chromatograms were removed, dried, and again examined under long-wave and short-wave ultraviolet light for fluorescing and absorbing spots. Ammonia vapors were used to develop these spots, and in many cases a particular color characteristic could be noted and recorded. The chromatograms then were placed in an oven for 24 hours at 85°C, this being a modification of the technique used by Riley and Bryant (1959, 1961). This heat treatment altered or "toasted" certain invisible chemical constituents and rendered them fluorescent under ultraviolet light, permitting them to be circled and recorded.

---

and *piercei*, only the last two could be identified chemically in this study. The varieties *littoralis* and *vaseyi* are assumed to have been more or less swamped out through hybridization in most of the areas where they occurred.

Relationship of a Cactus to a Special Soil Type

The genus *Pediocactus* is known to include seven species, six of them confined to the Colorado Plateau or to adjacent similar regions and the seventh occurring from eastern Washington to the Rocky Mountains and southward to the Colorado Plateau. Though the relationship of the genus to certain taxa in Mexico is not known (now under study by Edward F. Anderson), the species group in the United States is distinctive in its own right, regardless of whether species occurring farther south may or may not be included in the same genus. Each species of the Colorado Plateau is localized and restricted to a particular underlying rock and a particular soil type.

One species, *P. sileri*, is restricted to a narrow

and intermittent area about 64-80 km (40-50 mi) long, stretching along the Arizona side of the Utah-Arizona border. The plant occurs on an improbable white, fine, powdery soil that has been reported as "gypsum," though no evidence for this has been published (see Fig. 70). Soil samples were obtained from the vicinity of Pipe Spring, Arizona, along with material for cultivation and for an herbarium specimen, through the courtesy of Mr. Tom Bill, Chairman of the Navajo Tribal Council (*Benson & Bean et al. 16733, Pom*). The analysis indicates an amazing complex of internal physiological relationships with the bizarre soil and its chemical makeup. The species is difficult to cultivate in ordinary potting soils, but so far it is growing better in its own soil from northern Arizona.

Mr. Bean's analysis of the soil at various levels at the collection site indicates the possibilities for studies of the relationships of the species of *Pediocactus* to special soil types and their chemical compositions, and it emphasizes the need for at-

Fig. 70. *Pediocactus sileri* in its natural habitat near Pipe Spring, Arizona, on the Navajo Indian Reservation, the soil heavily encrusted with material brought up from beneath by water that has evaporated. In much popular literature the soil has been described as "gypsum," but not analyzed. Low contrast with the soil is a protection to the cactus. The plants do not live long in cultivation.

tention to soil and rock preferences and tolerances as one factor in the classification of taxa. The analysis presented here, with its tentative conclusions, is only the first step in a projected series.

SOIL ANALYSIS FOR PEDIOCACTUS SILERI
Contributed by Brian S. Bean*

Samples from the root stratum, surface layer, and gully bottom of the *Pediocactus sileri* habitat were analyzed. (Owing to the nature of the soil-testing apparatus used, the numerical data must be evaluated on a relative basis.)

*Department of Botany, Pomona College, Claremont, California; now Second Lieutenant, U.S. Marine Corps.

Root-stratum soil constituency. Nine tests were undertaken.

Carbonate test: Highly positive; when a single drop of dilute HCl was added to the sample, a great deal of gas evolution was observed. No activity occurred, however, when a *filtered* sample was treated with dilute acid.

Calcium test: Highly positive; a precipitate formed immediately. The test indicates *at least* 200 ppm CA^{+2}, which is equivalent to 2,140 lbs/acre in a stratum 7.87 inches thick, or 50 lbs/1,000 ft² in a stratum of that thickness. Blackboard chalk was assayed at 400 ppm Ca^{+2}.

Sulphates test: Highly positive; the test indicates SO_4^{-2} *in excess of* 800 ppm in the soil sample. The same result was obtained when 1 ml distilled H_2O was added for dilution purposes. The precipitate thus formed persisted when 1 ml of HCl was added to the test solution.

Magnesium test: The test indicates more than 6 ppm, which corresponds to 64.2 lbs/acre, or 1.5 lbs/1,000 ft². The same result was obtained when the sample solution was diluted with 1 ml distilled H_2O.

Chlorides test: This test, performed twice, indicates less than 20 ppm chlorides, even after excess testing reagent was added.

Ammonium test: Less than 2 ppm, corresponding to 21.4 lbs/acre, or 0.50 lb/1,000 ft².

Manganese test: Less than 1 ppm, corresponding to 10.7 lbs/acre, or 0.25 lb/1,000 ft².

Phosphorus test: The procedure indicates a phosphorus concentration of 1-2.5 ppm, corresponding to 10.7-26.7 lbs/acre, or 0.25-0.63 lb/1,000 ft². I estimate a concentration of about 2 ppm.

Nitrate test: More than 25 ppm and probably between 50 and 100 ppm (NO_{3-}). If 50 ppm is the actual value, the NO_{3-} concentration of this sample is 500 lbs/acre.

In view of the high concentration of both Ca^{+2} and SO_4^{-2}, a predominant mineral constituent must be gypsum ($CaSO_4 \cdot 2H_2O$). Anhydrite ($CaSO_4$) probably does not occur in large surface concentrations in the Pipe Spring region. The relatively low concentration of Mg^{+2} (<6 ppm) indicates that epsomite ($MgSO_4 \cdot 7H_2O$) is an insignificant constituent. Further, epsomite, which occurs as a white efflorescence on cave walls or as salt-spring deposits, is probably lacking from the sample area.

The heretofore undetected high-carbonate concentration is an interesting result. It should be noted that "gypsum will not bubble in acid like [marble]" (Pough, 1960). The fact that the filtered sample exhibited no acid reactivity indicates that the carbonate mineral(s) is (are) present in macroparticulate form. Surface-water leaching, however, should make this easily soluble constituent seasonally available for root-hair absorption. Because of the previously cited relative Mg^{+2} deficiency, both magnesite ($MgCO_3$) and dolomite ($CaMg(CO_3)_2$) are unlikely major carbonate constituents. It appears, then, that calcite or caliche ($CaCO_3$) is the probable carbonate mineral present.

Interestingly, chlorides are deemphasized. Manganese is similarly present in low concentrations. Phosphorus appears to be available in low to moderate concentrations at 2 ppm. Although the ammonium (NH_4^+) test indicates low availability (<2 ppm), nitrate (NO_{3-}) is present in moderately high concentrations (perhaps in excess of 50 ppm).

We conclude that the mineral root environment consists primarily of gypsum and calcite, whose respective anions, SO_4^{-2} and CO_3^{-2}, will associate with hydrogen ions present in rain-derived surface waters to produce an acidic environment.

Surface-layer soil constituency. Five tests of this more or less pure white material were made.

Sulphates test: The sulphates assay revealed a very high concentration of SO_4^{-2}.

Calcium test: Less than 40 ppm Ca^{+2} indicated.

Magnesium test: 0.5 ppm Mg^{+2} indicated.

Potassium test: 50 ppm K^+ indicated.

Flame tests: Neither wet nor dry flame tests yielded characteristic colors.

Magnesium is again unimportant. The high (SO_4^{-2}) would indicate the predominance of gypsum in the sample, but the (Ca^{+2}) is not as high. The negative flame test results preclude the presence of sodium or strontium sulphate. Although flaming did not produce the purple color characteristic of K^+, this cation was present in moderate concentrations. Perhaps the association of K^+, Ca^{+2}, and Mg^{+2} with SO_4^{-2} results collectively in polyhalite ($K_2Ca_2Mg(SO_4)_4 \cdot 2H_2O$). The predominant mineral constituent certainly contains sulphate.

Gully bottom. Rocks collected from gully bottoms in the sample area exhibited no gas evolution when treated with an HCl solution. This indicates an absence of carbonate minerals. A light pure-white powder collected from gully walls exhibited slight gas evolution upon treatment with acid. We may infer that gypsum was the predominant constituent.

General conclusions. Because phosphorus and nitrogen compounds were available in more or less nonstress concentrations, the physiological specialization of the cactus plants probably centers on selective detoxification or exclusion of the harsh inorganic materials of the root substratum.

4. The Family and the Order

The Cactales possess some characters similar to those of each of several other orders of the flowering plants, or Angiospermae (Benson, 1957). Relationship to the orders Myrtales, Guttiferales, and Loasales has been suggested because of some characters in common, but any affinity is not close. There is a relationship to the order Ranales, but the similarities are counterbalanced by marked differences. One point is of particular importance—the similarity of the carpels of *Pereskia pititache* to those of the primitive woody Ranales (cf. Benson, 1957, Chapt. XVII; Boke, 1963b). This may or perhaps may not indicate an independent origin of the Cactales from very primitive flowering plant stock and an early separation in evolutionary development from the lines ancestral to related groups.

Some authors, particularly recent ones, have considered the Cactaceae to be related closely to the Aizoaceae, or carpetweed family, and to be in the same order, Caryophyllales. The Subfamily Ficoideae of the Aizoaceae includes extreme succulent plants, but they are of less bizarre appearance than the Cactaceae. The best known succulent Aizoaceae are the ice plant, or sea fig (see Fig. 71), and other species of the genus *Mesembryanthemum, sensu latu.* Some species of *Lithops,* living rock or living stone (Figs. 72 and 73), are extreme succulents, with only one or two pairs of large, fleshy leaves and insignificant, obscure stems. These plants are cultivated widely for their novel appearance. The Ficoideae include many species in southern Africa and a few introduced or one presumably native on the American Pacific Coast from Oregon to Baja California and in Chile. The number of taxa in South Africa and the adjacent deserts of South West Africa (Namibia) is amazing.

Placing the Cactaceae in the order Caryophyllales, or the same or a modified order, usually as Centrospermae, often with some of the other families excluded, was stimulated first by the ob-vious succulence of both the Cactaceae and the Ficoideae, and additional similarities have been pointed out. The following characters are shared by the Family Cactaceae and the Subfamily Ficoideae of the Aizoaceae:

1. Succulence.

2. Presence of betacyanins. In all but two orders of flowering plants, coloring ranging from near red to near blue (violet to purple) is due to pigments called anthocyanins. These change color from an acid to a basic medium just as litmus paper does. Colors ranging from yellow to orange may be due to the related anthoxanthins. During the last few years, a group of chemically unrelated pigments has been found, so far as investigated, to produce parallel results in most of the families of the Caryophyllales and in the Cactales. These are betalains—betacyanins corresponding in color to anthocyanins and betaxanthins to anthoxanthins. However, the betalains contain nitrogen; the anthocyanins and anthoxanthins do not. Anthoxanthins and betaxanthins often occur in the same species or individual, but the occurrence together of betacyanins and anthocyanins has been reported only once (Gascoigne, Ritchie & White, 1948). The presence of betacyanins rather than anthocyanins is a significant taxonomic character, because it is restricted to the Caryophyllales (except the Caryophyllaceae and the subfamily Molluginoideae of the Aizoaceae) and to the Cactales (Alston & Turner, 1963; Mabry, 1966a, 1966b; Mabry & Dreiding, 1967).

3. Similar structure of the pollen grains. The surface layers are similar, and the grains have three nuclei.

4. Usually campylotropous or amphitropous ovules. In the Caryophyllales the ovules are orthotropous in one family, the Polygonaceae, but campylotropous or amphitropous (between campylotropous and anatropous) in the other families. In the Cactaceae they are usually campylotropous but sometimes amphitropous or ortho-

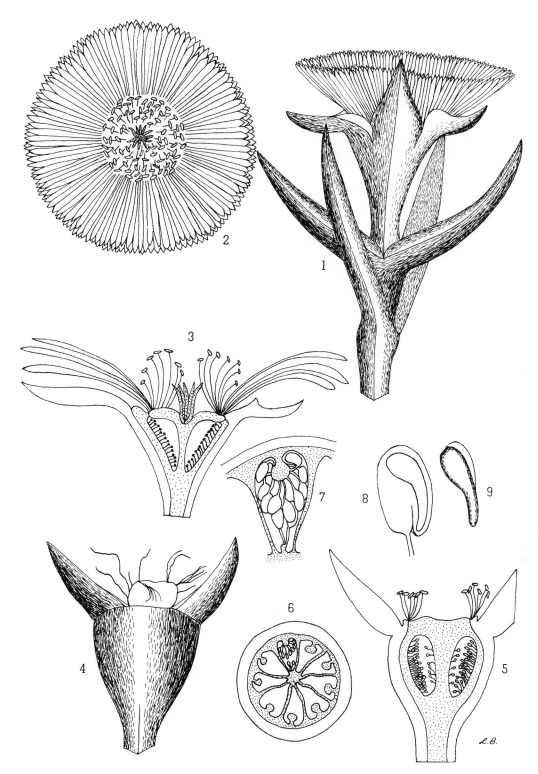

Fig. 71. The ice plant or sea fig, *Mesembryanthemum chilense* (*Carpobrotus aequilaterus*), of the American Pacific Coast (Order Caryophyllales; Family Aizoaceae; Subfamily Ficoideae). *1*, Branch and flower, showing the succulent, opposite leaves, the succulent sepals, and the numerous petal-like staminodia (sterile stamens); the stem relatively small and not very succulent. *2*, Top view of the flower, showing the staminodia, stamens, and stigmas. *3*, Flower in longitudinal section, showing (below) the inferior ovary and the investing inferior floral tube and two of the included seed chambers and the ovules, as well as the sepals and (above) staminodia, stamens, and stigmas. *4*, Fruit, with the persistent sepals. *5*, Fruit in longitudinal section, the stamens and sepals persistent, the ovules borne on both the inner and the outer edges of the ovary. *6*, Fruit in cross section, showing the several seed chambers (there being only one in the cacti). *7*, One chamber enlarged, showing the ovules and placentae. *8*, Longitudinal section of a seed, showing (below) the funiculus and (upper right) the position of the embryo. *9*, Embryo, not curved, showing the two cotyledons. (From *Plant Classification*)

Fig. 73 (*above*). A living stone, *Lithops schwantesii* var. *kunjasensis*, in cultivation, showing two leaves in a pair in each plant. (Ladislaus Cutak)

Fig. 72 (*left*). A living stone, *Lithops* (*sensu latu*) sp., in its native habitat in the Little Karoo, Cape Province, South Africa; there are two pairs of photosynthetic opposite leaves (one aging, one developing) in each plant; the stem is minute.

tropous (Fig. 74). In other flowering plants, ovule types vary, but these are rare; the ovules of most angiosperms are anatropous.

5. *Similar development of the megagametophyte.* The female gametophyte, or megagametophyte generation (with the reduced number of chromosomes in each cell, *n*), which produces the egg, or female gamete, is similar in development.

6. *Storage of reserve food usually in the perisperm* (nucellus or megasporangium) of the seed, instead of in the endosperm (a special tissue of the flowering plants resulting from the fertilization of a diploid cell by one male gamete while the other fertilizes the egg).

7. *Sieve-tube plastid type.* According to Behnke (1971) and Behnke & Turner (1971), fine-structure studies indicate that the plastids in the phloem cells (food-conducting elements, the sieve-tubes) are of S-type (accumulating starch) or P-type (having, with or without starch grains,

protein inclusions). Preliminary studies of 34 species in 23 families of angiosperms seem to indicate similarities within certain groups. Investigation of the Caryophyllales (though of only 33 species in 11 families) indicates the presence in this complex of families of a specific type of plastid having peripheral ring-shaped bundles of proteinaceous filaments and often an additional proteinaceous core. In the Cactaceae only *Pereskia aculeata* and *P. grandifolia* have been investigated, but both have the type of plastid occurring in the small number of species of the Caryophyllales investigated so far.

These similarities, taken alone, seem to indicate a close relationship between the Cactales and at least some of the Caryophyllales, but the differences between the two groups are even more striking.

1. *Succulence and the presence of leaves.* Even the type of succulence in the two plant groups is different: most Cactaceae are stem succulents;

the Ficoideae are extreme leaf succulents. The stems of all but a few cacti are the ultimate in succulence; those of the Ficoideae are not succulent or they are only slightly so. Usually the Cactaceae have no foliage leaves, these being represented by microscopic rudiments; large leaves occur in only such genera as *Pereskia* and *Pereskiopsis* and ephemerally in *Opuntia*. The Ficoideae are noted for succulent leaves of greater bulk than the stems, which may be very small. Although the occurrence of succulence of some kind may or may not be an indication of distant relationship, it is a relatively poor basis for merging the orders.

2. Arrangement of leaves. The leaves (when present) and the areoles of the Cactaceae are alternate (spiral); those of the Ficoideae are opposite.

3. Presence or absence of spines. The cacti always produce spines on the juvenile stems and nearly always on the adult stems. This is another essential character of the group. The Ficoideae are spineless, as are the other Caryophyllales, except the Didiereaceae.

4. The presence of areoles. The cactus areole is possibly a unique feature not duplicated in other flowering plants. In all cacti this structure is developed in the axils of the leaves (or more often of lumps of tissue representing vestiges of leaves). The Aizoaceae and other Caryophyllales do not have areoles. Chorinsky (1931) reported structures in one genus (*Acampseros*) of the Portulacaceae (Caryophyllales) that she considered to be homologous with the areoles of the Cactaceae. The point is a subject for further study, but if Chorinsky is correct her finding supports only a remote relationship, not inclusion in the same order. The possible duplication of a character occurring throughout the Cactales in a single species of the Caryophyllales, a large

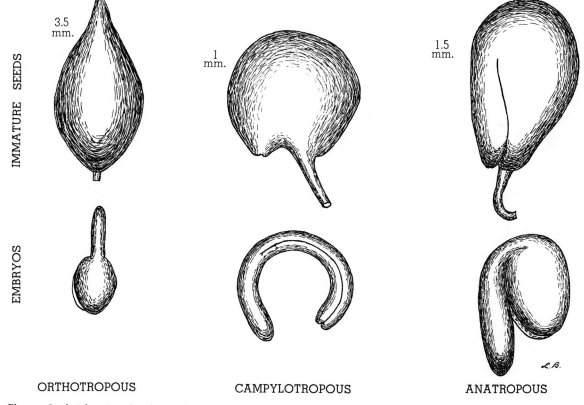

IMMATURE SEEDS

EMBRYOS

3.5 mm.

1 mm.

1.5 mm.

ORTHOTROPOUS   CAMPYLOTROPOUS   ANATROPOUS

Fig. 74. Seeds (above) and embryos (below) developed from different types of ovules. *Left*, from an orthotropous ovule, the ovule straight and the micropyle terminal; a wild buckwheat, *Eriogonum fasciculatum* var. *polifolium. Center*, from a campylotropous ovule, the ovule curved by greater growth on one side and the micropyle relatively near the stalk, or funiculus, the embryo also curved; the common type of ovule and embryo in the cacti, but not the only type; chickweed, *Stellaria media. Right*, from an anatropous ovule, with the ovule body bent back on itself and fused, the micropyle very near the funiculus; the ovule type occurring in the vast majority of flowering plants; shepherd's purse, *Capsella bursa-pastoris*. For embryos in the Cactaceae, see Figs. 64 and 66. (From *Plant Classification*)

order of perhaps 8,000 species, is of almost negligible significance in weakening the limits of the orders.

A far more significant investigation of areoles is by Rauh (1951, 1956, 1961, 1976), whose remarkable studies of the Didiereaceae may indicate relationship of that family to the Cactaceae. According to Rauh, the stems of the Didiereaceae produce areoles similar to those of the Pereskioideae. The spines are specialized leaves, as in the Cactaceae, and the number in the areole is variable—one in *Alluaudia*, two in *Decaryia*, and several in *Didierea*. The later leaves produced within the areole (as sometimes in *Pereskia*) are about usual for dicotyledons. They are deciduous with the approach of the dry season, and more are produced with the onset of another rainy season.

5. Perianth type. In both the Cactales and the Ficoideae, in each flower there are numerous petaloid structures. However, the transition, always present in the cacti, from scale-leaves through sepaloid to petaloid structures is not duplicated in the Ficoideae. In the Ficoideae, as in most other flowering plants, the "petals" have arisen through sterilization and broadening of stamens, that is, the outer stamens have become sterile through loss of anthers and petal-like through broadening of the filaments. These petals are said by Rendle (1925, 2: 112) to have arisen from a fundamental group of five primordia, each of which has given rise to many stamens toward the center and to several to many petals toward the periphery of the flower, a feature occurring in some other orders of flowering plants. In *Mesembryanthemum* and the other Aizoaceae there is no intergradation of sepals and petals.

6. Origin of the stamens. In the Cactaceae each of the many to hundreds or even (as counted by Bessey, up to 3,482) spirally arranged stamens may arise from a separate primordium, as in *Pereskia pititache* (Boke, 1963). In *Mesembryanthemum* (see Rendle, 1925) the stamens and petals, though numerous, are said to arise from a cycle of five primordia (see above).

7. Nodes, leaves, and spines on the floral cup. These structures, present in the Cactaceae, are absent in the Ficoideae. The floral tube or cup in the Cactales is at least partly a hypanthium (a specialized stem tip, or receptacle, with the usual type of stem joints, i.e. nodes and internodes), and the areoles of the floral tube or cup may give rise in some species to flowers and fruits or even vegetative branches or roots.

8. Style(s). In the Cactaceae there is always only a single style terminated by several stigmas; in the Aizoaceae several styles arise from the ovary.

9. Number of chambers in the ovary. In the cacti the ovary at flowering time and the fruit have only one chamber; those of the Aizoaceae have more than one, there being as many partitions as there are carpels.

10. Placentation. The placentae in the Cactaceae begin their development in a central (axile) position in the ovary, but ultimately they are marginal (parietal, or on the ovary wall). Those of the Ficoideae remain in the center at the inner angles of the partitions of the ovary. Each carpel of a cactus ovary is like a pea pod split midway between the dorsal (back) and ventral (front) vascular bundles of the margins and opened with the dorsal segment projecting upward and the ventral segment (to which the ovules are attached) downward. Commonly the external wall of each carpel is adnate with the hypanthium. This is probably unique. (See Boke, 1964.)

11. Type of inferior ovary. The ovary of a cactus is inferior (or pseudoinferior or, according to Boke, actually superior), largely because of its peculiar sunken position in the receptacle, or stem-apex (Boke, 1963b, 1964), a feature occurring in few other plant families and not in the Ficoideae (Eames, 1961). This feature weighs strongly in the decision to maintain the Cactales as a separate order.

Thus, the similarities of the two families, Cactaceae and Aizoaceae (Ficoideae), particularly in certain obscure characters, indicate relationship and an ancient common origin from very primitive ancestors. However, the large number of differences indicates the presumed relationship to be only distant. Probably, divergence from a common ancestry occurred far back in geologic time. The marked and largely consistent differences have been ignored by writers attempting to promote inclusion of the Cactaceae in the Caryophyllales or in a segregated segment of that order.

Werner Rauh of the University of Heidelberg, an outstanding research investigator and an indefatigable explorer, has studied in great detail not only many cacti of both North and South America but also the little known family Didiereaceae of Madagascar (1961, 1976, 1977; Rauh & Reznik, 1961). Usually the family, consisting of four genera, is attributed to the Caryophyllales, and Rauh affirms this relationship, as well as an alliance with the Cactaceae.

In some ways the Didiereaceae resemble the Opuntieae and especially the Pereskieae of the Cactaceae. They are not really succulents, but they are considered woody succulents, because the pith serves for water storage, though the cortex of the stem does not. The spines and leaves are borne in a structure (Kurtztriebe) in most respects fundamentally similar to a cactus areole (p. 23). Both Kurtztrieben and areoles result from lack of elongation of the lateral branches of the stem, the bud not adding cells to the branch but producing appendages, either spines or foliage leaves. In most cacti only spines are developed, but in *Pereskia* foliage leaves are formed also in the areoles (Figs. 18, 236, and 237). Commonly also there are hairs and wool, and, in *Opuntia,* glochids; these features do not occur in the Didiereaceae. In the Didiereaceae the first leaves formed in the Kurtztriebe are specialized as persistent spines, and the later leaves are photosynthetic and deciduous, being replaced in succeeding seasons. The pollen grains are similar to those of some Cactaceae, and the reddish pigments of the plants, when present, are betacyanins.

For plants of dry countries, the Kurtztriebe or an approximation of it is a good device for coping with the alternating wet and dry facets of a desert or other seasonally dry climate. The ocotillo, *Fouquieria splendens,* and other Fouquieriaceae produce essentially the same device; the details, however, are different, even though the results are the same and the plant is similar in appearance to the Didiereaceae (as well as to some cacti). The woody, not really succulent, stem produces a leaf below each node during the first season of growth, but all the soft parts finally fall away, leaving only the midrib and the petiole as a spine. During the succeeding years, the bud of the microscopic branch axillary to the spine does not add to the branch but produces a crop of leaves whenever there is sufficient moisture, these falling away at the onset of dry weather, as in the Didiereaceae. Thus, the combination of a slightly succulent woody stem, spines, and seasonal production of leaves from the bud of a microscopic branch occurring in the Didiereaceae is duplicated in the unrelated Fouquieriaceae of northwestern Mexico and the adjacent deserts of the United States. In the ocotillo the spine is from the leaf to which the areole is axillary; in the Didiereaceae the spines are the first leaves produced within the areole. Similarity of the same features of the Didiereaceae and the Cactaceae may or may not represent parallel development, as in the Didiereaceae and Fouquiereaceae.

The degree of relationship of the Didiereaceae and the Cactaceae cannot be assessed without an intimate knowledge of the Didiereaceae, and no attempt at a complete evaluation is made here. However, the following differences in reproductive structures should be noted. Instead of one or rarely a few flowers from deep within the areole or a special area adjoining it, the Kurtztrieben develop much-branched cymes, each bearing numerous flowers; these are small and unisexual (the plants being dioecious), whereas cactus flowers are bisexual. Furthermore, in the Didiereaceae the flower is hypogynous, and it develops a hypogynous disk; in all the Cactaceae the flower is either perigynous or epigynous. Instead of the numerous intergrading sepaloids and petaloids and the even greater number of stamens of the cactus flower, there are two sepaloid and four petaloid perianth parts and 8-10 stamens. In the pistillate flower of the Didiereaceae, two bracts beneath the perianth ultimately become wings attached indirectly through the pedicel and receptacle to the small, nutlike fruit, thus aiding in its dispersal. There are no nodes, leaves, or spines on the ovary, but of course there is no floral cup covering it. The peculiar placentation of the cacti is not duplicated in the Didiereaceae; instead of the single ovary chamber with numerous seeds universal in the Cactaceae, there are three chambers, only one fertile and this with a solitary seed. Unlike either the Cactaceae or the Aizoaceae, the food reserve in the seed of the Didiereaceae is in the endosperm, rather than the perisperm.

Despite a probable remote relationship to each of the several families and orders mentioned above and a closer one to the Caryophyllales, on the basis of present evidence the Cactales are interpreted as a strongly segregated monotypic order. Probably the Cactales and the Caryophyllales, however circumscribed or named, are composed of surviving endpoints in the evolution of a once considerable group of plants. No doubt the two orders are related, at least distantly, but there is no justification for merging them.

The difficulties of classification of the orders and families lie in the vastness and the complexity of the problem. To establish clearly which characters occur throughout a large order of plants is a tremendous undertaking, and proving nonoccurrence in any particular plant group is impossible, as is proof of *any* negative proposition. Thus, reaching even an approximation of the closeness of relationship of the Cactales and the Caryophyllales will require a long-continued assembling and assessing of the facts.

5. The Family and the Genera

The origin and relationships of taxa within the Cactaceae are no better established than those between the family and other dicotyledonous groups. Evolutionary relationships and contemporary classification are discussed in the following pages.

Evolutionary Relationships within the Family

The interrelationships of plants or animals are similar to those in the human population of a small, stable community in a remote Old World village. During a given year, only a few generations are represented in the village, and almost everyone living there has relatives in the village. There are some grandparents; more parents; many aunts, uncles, sisters, and brothers; and innumerable cousins. Great-grandparents are few, and probably there are no great-great-grandparents. The population systems of plants or animals at a given point in geologic time parallel those in the village; most species within any genus, as with siblings or cousins, are relatives. However, *they were not derived one from another but from a common ancestry most or all of which has disappeared.* Some immediate ancestors may be still present, but most are gone, and the fossil record of the earlier ancestors ranges from fragmentary to none.

The study of the currently living natural population systems of organisms can yield only fragments of an evolutionary tree—mostly the terminal branchlets. Charts supposedly depicting the course of evolution, such as the one by Bessey presented here (Fig. 75), rest on a misconception of the nature of the evidence, being based on the assumption that all or most groups of *living* plants or animals were derived *from each other*. Some small groups of closely related species may be evaluated partly on this basis, because ancestral types may survive as species in particular situations while their modified descendants take over in others, as on individual islands of an archipelago like the Galápagos or Hawaii. However, only a few ancestral types persist through long periods of geologic time, and these few, a minute percentage of those that lived together in the past, are scarcely representative of ancestral pathways of development. The usual course of evolution is one of complex divergence and convergence of complicated natural population systems, as suggested by the accompanying diagrams (Figs. 76-78).

Few preexisting organisms have left satisfactory traces in the form of fossils; only the hard or resistant parts of individuals are likely to be preserved. Usually the fossil series are inadequate for the reconstruction of more than fragments of an evolutionary tree. However, fairly good series of fossils of a few plant groups have been discovered. The gymnosperms (the pines and firs and their relatives) are an example. Fossils are formed readily from the woody roots and stems, tough leaves ("needles"), cones, seeds, and pollen grains. In petrified specimens even minute structural features of the cell walls are shown clearly. Thus, most of the critical parts of a preexisting individual can be matched up with each other, and much of the tree can be reconstructed, often even though the upper parts may have been scattered and the roots may be in a lower layer of rock. Consequently, a fairly satisfactory evolutionary tree for gymnosperms has been worked out. For the same reason, the pteridophytes, which include the ferns, can be analyzed along broad outlines. However, no evolutionary tree can be reconstructed for soft plants, or for those like the angiosperms with soft reproductive parts, and for most plant and animal groups the evidence of the nature of extinct species is slight.

Evolution within the cactus family is a matter of conjecture, partly for lack of fossils. The only known fossil that could conceivably be of a cactus almost certainly does not represent one. The name *Eopuntia douglassii* Chaney (1944) is based on

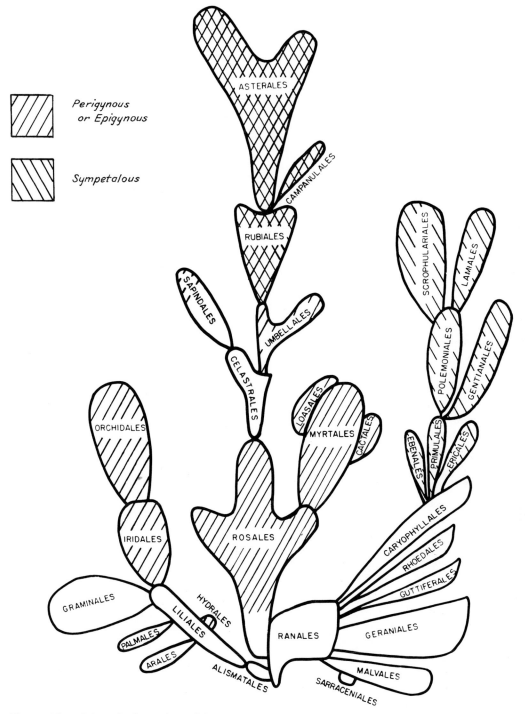

Fig. 75. The origin and relationships of the orders of flowering plants, according to Bessey. This is a modification of the chart known commonly as "Bessey's Cactus" or "Opuntia besseyi," first published in 1915. The left branch represents the orders of monocotyledons, the middle branch the perigynous and epigynous dicotyledons (some flowers with hypogynous discs interpreted by Bessey as perigynous, instead of hypogynous), and the branches at the right the hypogynous dicotyledons. The presumed origin of one order from another is indicated by attachment of the figure representing the order to the one below. The area of each figure is approximately proportional to the number of species in the order. Construction of similar phylogenetic charts is popular, but unless they are based on much evidence, especially from fossils, they have no basis. Furthermore, one living order was not necessarily or likely derived from any other living order; derivation in the vast majority of cases was from a common ancestor, which has disappeared, usually leaving no trace. (From *Plant Classification*; see also Credits)

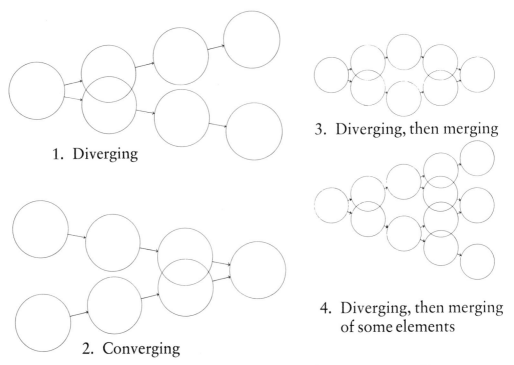

1. Diverging

3. Diverging, then merging

2. Converging

4. Diverging, then merging of some elements

Fig. 76. Evolution of genetically converging and diverging population systems. (From *Plant Taxonomy, Methods and Principles*)

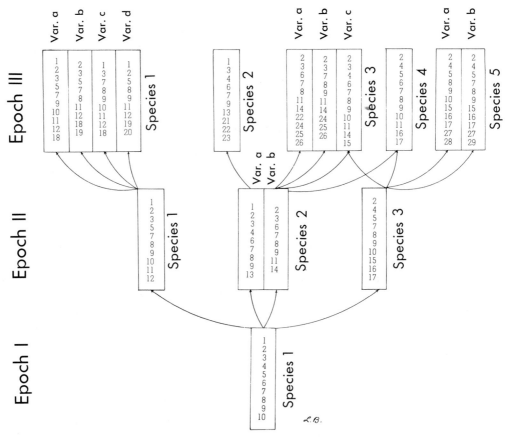

Fig. 77. The usual course of evolution through units of geologic time (in this case epochs). Diagnostic characters of each species or variety are indicated by numbers, and characters may be followed by these numbers from one epoch to another. In the second epoch, three major population systems (one including two minor ones, or varieties) have evolved, and each has retained some of the characters of the single population or taxon of the first epoch, but it has also lost some and gained others, as shown by new numbers. The process is carried still further in the third epoch, and, as indicated by arrows, some of the units of this epoch were derived by hybridization (convergence) of elements that existed during the second epoch, the new gene combinations having undergone further selection as the environment changed from one epoch to the next. (From *Plant Taxonomy, Methods and Principles*)

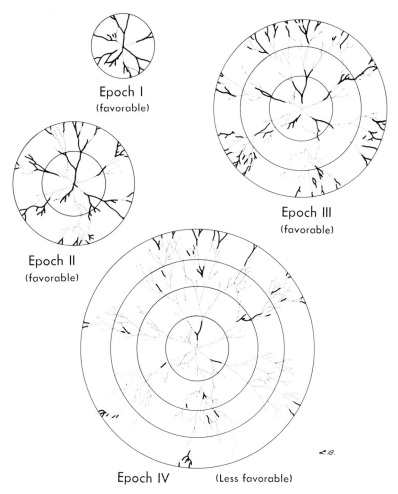

Epoch I
(favorable)

Epoch II
(favorable)

Epoch III
(favorable)

Epoch IV   (Less favorable)

Fig. 78. Chart showing the typical development of taxa during four epochs of geologic time. Conditions during the first three epochs were favorable, those during the fourth unfavorable, to the plant group. Solid dark lines represent natural plant populations living during the particular epoch; broken lines indicate populations that have died out. The true degree of complexity might be indicated with greater accuracy if three dimensions were available. (From *Plant Taxonomy, Methods and Principles*)

specimens from Eocene shales in the Uintah Basin of Utah. The identity of this plant has been debated hotly, and no sure conclusion concerning its nature is at hand (cf. Haselton, 1950; Brown, 1959; and Becker, 1960). The stems, leaves (if any), flowers, and fruits of cacti are soft and more likely to decay than to enter into formation of fossils. The harder spines and seeds may be preserved, but divorced from the rest of the plant they can do no more than to indicate the possible presence of members of a genus or of a generic group of cacti in a particular place and time.

The first question concerning an evolutionary series is, "Where does it start?" Sometimes, an organism has certain features clearly not specialized and possibly primitive, that is, retained from types ancestral to both the taxon and related living taxa. Rarely, the plant or animal may include many such features, and then the organism may be considered primitive. However, usually the putative primitive characters occur in combination with others that are specialized and probably of recent evolutionary origin. Even determination of which characters are to be considered primitive is difficult and subject to unsuspected errors. Frequently, the features that are cited by one author as primitive and basic are shown by another to be advanced and even to have been derived from presumably *more* "advanced" characters. Characters may be considered advanced if they are adapted to the time and place. Obviously, the environments to which plants must adapt do not remain static over the millennia, and an apparently "regressive" shift in the characters of a taxon may be actually adaptive.

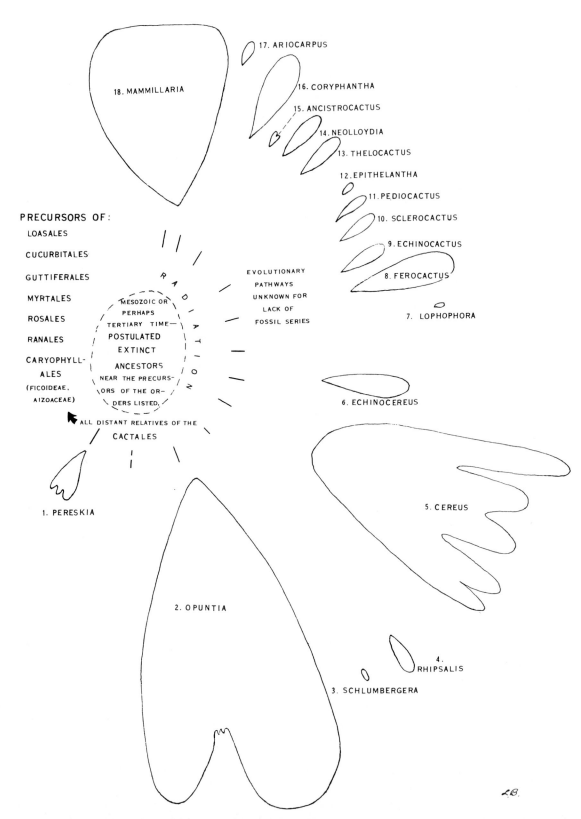

Fig. 79. Chart of relationships of the genera of cacti of the United States and Canada. This chart does not depict evolutionary series of development, because these are unknown and because few living groups of organisms were derived one from another but from now extinct and unknown common ancestors. Nearness of the figures representing two or more genera indicates their approximate degree of relationship, as indicated by proportionate numbers of characters in common.

The living species and the genera of the Cactaceae cannot be arranged on any solid basis into an evolutionary tree like that in Fig. 75. In some instances a twig or a branch of the family tree of the cacti may be made out, but these fragments of knowledge are not adequate to reveal even the rough outlines of the total course of evolution within the family. Occasionally, one taxon may appear to have been derived from a still unmodified living member of another, but in most cases this is unlikely, and for a major taxon, like a genus, it is usually impossible to prove.

Among closely related species or groups of species, sometimes evolutionary pathways may be traced through the study of chromosomes, provided the taxa (or some of them) have distinctive chromosome sets, such as those of some polyploids and especially of some amphiploids. So far, this method has not been productive in studying the evolution of the cacti. The basic chromosome number (x) for the family is 11, and, although polyploids are known, no major pattern of their formation has appeared.

For the simple objective of indicating degrees of relationship, another type of chart is valid: the affinities of organisms are indicated by their possessing many characters in common but few differences. Characters are unequally stable in the combinations in taxa. Consequently, no precise indicator of degree of relationship is possible, but the numbers or percentages of characters in common may be taken as rough indices. For the Cactaceae of the United States and Canada, the relationships of the genera, as thus determined, are indicated in Fig. 79. *This chart shows only relationships; it carries no implication that one living taxon was derived from another existing one.* There is much to be said for this expedient. Parallel evolution may account for the duplication of one or two characters in unrelated or remotely related organisms, but it is unlikely to account for more. The likelihood of chance coincidence of characters decreases in geometric proportion to the number of character pairs considered—entire constellations of similarities almost certainly indicate close affinities. However, the necessity to adapt—perhaps at different points in geologic time—to a similar environment may produce remarkable (if superficial) similarities, as for example in the swordfish, dolphin, and ichthyosaur.

Few plant or animal groups retain only primitive characters through long periods of geologic time. Most or all have some more recently ac-

quired and specialized features in combination with others that have been either advantageous or at least not particularly detrimental and have remained the same or little changed through millions of years. In the Cactaceae the group having retained the greatest percentage of probably primitive characters is the genus *Pereskia* (pp. 264-69 and included figures), but along with the primitive characters there are specialized and probably advanced features. The presumably relatively primitive characters of *Pereskia* include: (1) less succulent stems than those of the other Cactaceae; (2) broad, flat leaves, which, though succulent, are reminiscent of those of other dicotyledons (leaves are reduced and ephemeral in *Opuntia* and eliminated or microscopic in the rest of the family); (3) anatomical features, such as pinnate leaf venation and special cellular structures in the leaves and stems (see I. W. Bailey, 1968, 374-75); (4) perigynous flowers in some species, as opposed to a specialized type of epigynous flowers in the rest of the family; (5) in *P. pititache,* the primitive, incompletely sealed carpels, or seed-bearing leaves (each forming a unit of the compound pistil), each lacking a definite stigma, and the short style unsealed and lined with stigmatic tissue (Boke, 1963b).

References (*Pereskia*): I. W. Bailey (see Bibliography); Boke, 1954, 1963a, 1963b, 1964, 1966, 1968.

Major Subdivisions of the Family

The cactus family is a coherent unit, and there have been no major attempts to subdivide it into families of lesser scope. Even though the most extremely differentiated members of the family vary markedly from each other, there are transitions ranging from one peripheral member of the group to each of the others, and the discontinuities of the major groupings are not broad. Division into subfamilies probably is not warranted. Usually the family is subdivided into three tribes, as follows:

1. Pereskieae. Stems slender and elongate, not jointed; leaves broad and flat, succulent, but resembling those of other dicotyledons; flowers perigynous or epigynous, each with a pedicel, though this may be very short; glochids none. *Pereskia.*

2. Opuntieae. Stems composed of series of slender or broad and flattened joints; leaves circular or elliptic in cross section, usually small, deciduous after 1-3 months from formation of the joints; flowers epigynous, sessile; floral tube short and obconical, with the stamen-bearing area beginning just above the ovary; glochids present in the areoles. *Opuntia* and its allies.

3. Cereae. Stems various; leaves on the mature stems none or vestigial, represented only by humps of tissue present during the early development of the stem; flowers epigynous, sessile; floral tube funnelform to elongate, the stamen-bearing area beginning well above the ovary. All other genera.

Even the characters listed above are not infallibly diagnostic; in any given case, some characters usually present in the combination may be lacking. For example, the genus *Pereskiopsis,* related more closely to *Opuntia* than to *Pereskia,* strongly resembles the latter in stems and foliage.

Segregating the Genera

The interpretation adopted here for the genera is conservative. As with all other works concerning questions of classification, this book represents not the ultimate result of investigation but merely a step toward development of a better classification system. Some tentative conclusions will require modification as more evidence becomes available, and some realignment of genera will be necessary. Some genera, including *Opuntia, Echinocereus, Sclerocactus,* and *Pediocactus,* have been studied in considerable detail; others, such as *Cereus* (in the broad sense in which it is treated here), are not well enough known for the world as a whole to be evaluated thoroughly.

In particular, any attempt at a realignment of *Cereus* into lesser genera would be premature from the viewpoint of classification—and disastrous from that of nomenclature. *Cereus* in the broad sense, ranging from California to Florida and southward through much of Latin America, is an enormous and complex group of species not understood by anyone and much in need of a thorough and comprehensive study. Various schemes for organizing *Cereus* into a number of new genera have been proposed, but each of these, on the basis of the evidence available, has crippling weaknesses. Each of several attempts by the writer to realign the segments of *Cereus* appearing in this book into genera of lesser scope has ended in frustration and the conclusion that too little is known. At first sight, the "genera" appearing under various proposed classification systems may seem plausible, but all attempts to analyze the consistency of associations of characters and to write workable keys lead to floundering. There are glaring gaps in the information available, and the groupings and segregations of the proposed taxa tend to be arbitrary. At best they are only partly natural and largely artificial, because they overemphasize the predetermined "importance" of certain characters. The construction of a natural classification system requires many years of patient investigation of the group to be studied throughout its natural geographic range. The complexes of characters tending to appear in combination must be determined, and the degree of consistency of their association must be assessed across the board. Treatments of *Cereus* thus far have been based chiefly on cultivated plants, or on their study supplemented by a few field observations, and all have been weakened by dependence on single characters, each thought to be *the marker* of a group. This circumstance recalls the artificial "sexual" system of Linnaeus, in which classification of plants (after several anomalous groups were segregated) was based primarily upon number of stamens. Linnaeus, himself, adopted the artificial system, not as the ultimate in classification, but as an interim practical expedient, to be used only until a better natural system than his own "fragment" of one could be worked out for grouping natural orders (families) according to relationships. Almost alone in his time, he recognized the limitations of his system. Recent authors have proposed similarly artificial systems for classifying *Cereus* (as well as other cacti), presumably without realizing the nature of their conclusions.

No proposal made so far offers a reasonable prospect for a solution to the problem of classifying *Cereus.* As more data become available, clearer lines of segregation into genera may appear, but for the time being the classical interpretation as an inclusive genus is retained. Even this conservative decision has required a few nomenclatural changes, but any other course would have required many, many more.

The status of *Echinocereus* presents no problem. It is segregated clearly from *Cereus*—most obviously by the position of the flower bud, which bursts through the stem-epidermis above a spine-bearing areole. This character, a part of a combination characterizing *Echinocereus,* is not known to be duplicated in *Cereus* or any other genus of the Cactaceae.

Several other genera are not well enough represented in the United States to warrant an attempt at reclassification. Only one or two species in each of *Pereskia, Schlumbergera,* and *Rhipsalis* occur within the range of this book, and in two of the genera the species are introduced rather than native.

Lophophora and *Ariocarpus* are represented each by a single native species. However, the two genera have been studied intensively as complete units by Edward F. Anderson (for *Lophophora*, see Anderson, 1969; for *Ariocarpus*, see Anderson, 1960, 1962, 1963, 1964).

Opuntia is a distinctive unit clearly different from the other genera occurring in the United States. The chief question in the classification of this genus is the status of internal units proposed by some as separate genera. The chollas (subgenus *Cylindropuntia*) and the prickly pears (subgenus *Opuntia*) are distinctive in their extreme forms, but the characters really distinguishing them are few and not wholly consistent. Usually the cylindroid joints of the stems of the chollas and the flattened joints of the prickly pears are in marked contrast. However, the initial joints of the seedlings of prickly pears are cylindroid; the genetic mechanism producing flattening of the stems does not become effective until the formation of the second and succeeding joints (Figs. 80-82). Joints almost like the initial one may continue to be produced in forms of *O. fragilis* and *O. basilaris* var. *brachyclada*, the flattening being only slight. Moreover, in *Opuntia*, Section *Consolea*, the main trunks are cylindroid and not jointed, whereas the small branches are flat and like those of other prickly pears. According to Britton and Rose (1919), "Some [species of *Opuntia*] with round stems have flowers which suggest a closer relationship with the species with flattened stems."

In most but not all chollas the joints of the stem are indeterminate, i.e., they continue to elongate by growth of the terminal bud for an indefinite period. In most but not all prickly pears the joints are determinate, i.e., they cease growth because the terminal bud becomes inactive. However, in Subgenus *Cylindropuntia*, Section *Clavatae*, and in Subgenus *Opuntia*, Section *Consolea*, this relationship is reversed.

In the Subgenus *Cylindropuntia* the epidermis of the spine usually separates into a thin, paper-like sheath, which slips off, and this does not occur in the Subgenus *Opuntia*. However, in Subgenus *Cylindropuntia*, Section *Clavatae*, the sheath separates only at the extreme tip of the spine. Moreover, the glochids are usually larger and much more effective in the prickly pears than in the chollas, but some of the largest and most

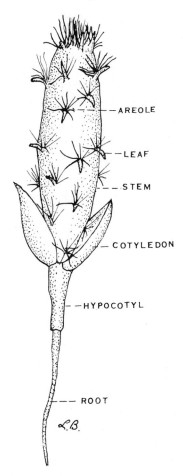

Fig. 80. Seedling of a very young prickly pear, as labeled. The stem is only 4 mm (1/6 inch) long.

troublesome occur in the chollas of the Section *Clavatae*.

These distinctions and one other—the seeds of prickly pears have more strongly developed rims—are the only ones available so far offering sufficient stability to be used in a key to the two subgenera. Because of their instability, distinction of *Cylindropuntia* as a genus is not justified at this time.

In 1849 Prince Salm-Dyck, a European cultivator and student of cacti, proposed the genus *Nopalea*, which has been interpreted to include several species of prickly pears occurring primarily in Mexico and Central America. Some of these are cultivated throughout the Tropics and adjacent frost-free regions as ornamentals, and *Opuntia cochenillifera* once was used extensively as a host plant for the cochineal insect, which produces a formerly important dye (see p. 236). The basis for segregating these species is the relative shortness of the perianth parts, combined with the elongation of the style and the stamens,

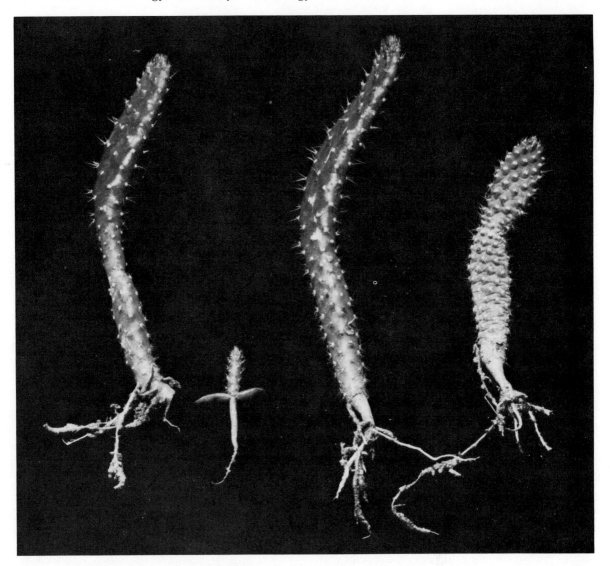

Fig. 81. Stem development in prickly pears. Very small seedling of a prickly pear, *Opuntia tomentosa*, still bearing the cotyledons, as in Fig. 80, and older seedlings showing transitions from the first, cylindroid stem joint to the later, flattened joints.

which protrude beyond the perianth. This seems to be the only distinctive characteristic consistently appearing in this group of species, otherwise simply a group of prickly pears; hence *Nopalea* is an even less likely candidate for generic status than *Cylindropuntia*. In this book O. *cochenillifera* appears among the prickly pears.

The status of the proposed genera *Consolea* and *Brasiliopuntia* is little stronger. Their segregation is based primarily upon the presence of cylindroid, unjointed trunks in both and the fact that in *Brasiliopuntia* only the ultimate branches are flattened, the main branches as well as the trunk being cylindroid. In both proposed genera the joints are indeterminate; however, this feature is duplicated in an otherwise typical prickly pear, *Opuntia lindheimeri* var. *linguiformis*.

The distinction of *Mammillaria* and *Coryphantha* is difficult, because there are transitional species, and in some of them the usually reliable characters tend sometimes to be in unusual alliances. This is a borderline case of distinction of genera, even though many characters run through nearly all of one group and none of the other. For this reason, in several earlier works by the writer they were considered as a single genus, *Mammillaria*. For keying purposes, three characters are particularly useful:

1. In *Mammillaria* the flowers emerge between tubercles in special areoles of their own (these rarely with vestigial spines), and they are separated completely from the apical spine-bearing areoles of the tubercles. In *Coryphantha* the flower is borne on the ventral side of the tubercle,

and, except in the earliest flowers of the plant, the flower-bearing part of the areole is joined by an isthmus to the spine-bearing part of the areole at the apex of the tubercle. So far as found, there are no exceptions in the two genera.

2. In *Mammillaria* the flowers and fruits are produced *among* tubercles of previous seasons on the side of the stem, or at least away from the apical area in which new tubercles are being formed. In *Coryphantha* the flowers and fruits are produced *upon* the newly developing tubercles of the season, at the apex of the stem. Some cases may be transitional, but these have not been studied fully.

Fig. 82. Stem development. Prickly pear seedling with a cylindroid joint formed the first year and a flattened one formed the second year. In the chollas, cylindroid stem joints are produced every year, indefinitely; there is never a change to flattened joints. (From *The Native Cacti of California*)

3. In *Mammillaria* the seeds are longer than broad. In *Coryphantha* the seeds are usually broader than long, so much so that the hilum appears to be on the "side of the seed." In a few species, however, the seed is longer than broad, as in *Mammillaria*, and this character is completely reliable only when the seed is broader than long, as it is nearly always in *Coryphantha* and never in *Mammillaria*.

The segregation of some groups of species into separate genera, instead of their inclusion in the once large genus *Echinocactus* was proposed first as a matter of atomization, which was supposed by some to solve all problems of classification. However, intensive study of the groups described as *Pediocactus* and *Sclerocactus* has indicated these to be distinctive genera fairly well separated by several characters in combination, as is indicated in the keys. Intensive work on these two genera was carried out especially during the 1950's and 1960's (Benson: for *Pediocactus*, 1961-62; for *Sclerocactus*, 1966b). The thorough morphological study of *Epithelantha* by Boke (1969) is reflected taxonomically in the published work of the writer (1969b).

The distinction of *Ferocactus* and *Echinocactus* is only moderately clear. The most consistently occurring key characters of *Echinocactus* appear to be the spinose or aristate tips of the sepaloids and the shape of the seed, which is broader than long—the craterlike hilum, as a consequence, appearing as if it were on the side. In *Ferocactus* the hilum usually is obviously basal, but in some species it may appear to be "sub-basal" or "diagonal." The fruits of *Ferocactus* remain fleshy long after maturity; those of *Echinocactus* tend to become dry at or shortly after maturity.

In 1839 Lemaire proposed segregation of a genus *Astrophytum* from *Echinocactus*, basing the genus on species occurring in Mexico. One of these (*E. asterias*) grows also near the Rio Grande in Texas. The generic status of *Astrophytum* has gone more or less unchallenged for a long time, probably because two spineless species common in cultivation are distinctive in appearance. However, the other two species have spines. Perhaps a significant character is the depressed hilum, the margins of which may be raised into a collar (a fantastic one in *E. asterias*), but this tendency may occur in other species. A character perhaps restricted to *Astrophytum* is the presence of white scales on the surface of the stem. The flower structure of *Astrophytum* is that of *Echinocactus*. Only the single Texan species is involved in this study, and it is retained in *Echinocactus*, pending a more thorough review of the proposed genus.

6. Species, Varieties, and Hybrids

Species, as well as all the lesser taxa or hybrids included in them, are composed of many similar but differing individuals. In the populations constituting a given species, there are many combinations of genes, and this variability promotes adaptability to minor environmental niches or even to more than one major one. Seeds of flowering plants are produced in great profusion, and the hundreds of ovules in even a single ovary of a cactus are likely to have received pollen from many different individuals. Consequently, among the hundreds or thousands of potential offspring of a single individual, some will very likely be adapted to any of a host of slightly differing habitats.

The Nature of Species and Other Taxa

From one geological epoch to another there are considerable changes of the environment, and all plants and animals adaptable to the new conditions are altered in an irregular fashion. New gene combinations are adapted to one phase or another of the new set of ecological factors, but the plants with some combinations must migrate to a different area if they are to survive. Those with other combinations cannot cope with the new ecological conditions, and they die. Thus the pool of genes of a given taxon loses some elements, and it gains others through mutation or through hybridizing with other taxa. As genes are lost or gained, the various genetic combinations are stirred around, and the taxon changes—imperceptibly in the short term, but markedly over a longer period. At any point in time the many gene combinations occurring in the taxon are those modified from others that survived preceding epochs, but they are always in flux and they never continue for long, geologically speaking, without change.

The units of biological classification, such as species, constitute groups of living organisms each with groups of associated characters that tend to remain together through successive generations. These character groupings represent underlying combinations of genes, and the number of genes in common (as opposed to those differing) between groups of organisms is the basis for determining degrees of relationships and the outlines of species and other taxa. However, the index is rough. Some of the characters having the greatest effect on adaptation to the environment are physiological and invisible, and, although some characters are the product of single gene pairs, many others appear because of the interaction of the genes of two or several pairs. Although the observable association of characters is only a sample of the underlying character-and-gene combination, it is useful, and it is generally the only index of relationship or classification of taxa available.

The occurrence of characters in clusters is due to isolation by any of many kinds of breeding barriers between the plants or animals composing the different groupings, and to features of the environment to which some groups are adapted and others are not. If there were no barriers to interbreeding and no differences in relationship to ecology, there would be little or no differentiation into taxa. The effectiveness of the factors controlling interbreeding varies, and the combinations of ecological factors may differ within a few meters or even less, with the clusters of genes adaptable to environmental niches varying accordingly. Consequently, the lines of segregation of clusters or of the groupings of clusters to be designated as taxa rarely are sharp.

The problem of the taxonomist is to classify living organisms into recognizable groups of related individuals and to name the more significant groups as taxa. Despite the complex variation of the character combinations and the infinite degrees of difference between the plants or animals having them, only a few ranks of distinction are practical. Thus, assigning of organisms to taxa of various ranks is a matter of judgment of many complexly interlocking factors, and the problems of classification have no simple solutions.

A taxonomic system, or system of classification, is developed by evaluating the degrees of clustering of characters and drawing lines between taxa according to the patterning of the clusters. No single character occurs necessarily throughout a taxon or in only one taxon and not others, but some features may be abundant in one taxonomic grouping and rare in all or some others. Because no two individuals are alike and the numbers of character recombinations usually separating taxa are infinite, any classification system can follow only the broad outlines of character association.

If classification proceeds according to the relative stability of the associations of characters, obviously differing in a single character is not a defensible basis for the segregation of species or other taxa. Furthermore, no one character can be the marker of a species; the marker is the combination. In books on the cacti, much difficulty has arisen through naming of each presumably new plant on the basis of a single character appearing in a cultivated individual, or one dried and placed in an herbarium, on the assumption that this character, unknown in other specimens, indicated a new species. Often plants differing in a single striking character may have been derived from only a few of the seeds in a single fruit, even though the rest of the seeds produced plants with different characters. A brown-eyed man may have a blue-eyed brother, but no one would argue that the two were of different species. Nevertheless, this type of argument is not uncommon in the designation of species of the Cactaceae.

The distinction of species from varieties is one of degree. Species are differentiated from each other by more characters, and these are more stable in the combinations; varieties are segregated by fewer characters, and the clusters tend to separate more readily. Thus, classification of species and varieties or of any other taxa requires a balancing of complex patterns of degrees of difference and of stability of combinations.

Definition of Taxa

As shown above, the fundamental nature of taxa is basic to all problems of classifying species and lower (infraspecific) taxa. In their fundamental nature all taxa may be defined in essentially the same way (Benson, 1962, 281-90).

Briefly, *a living natural taxon is a reproducing population or system of populations of genetically related individuals*. The definition is the same for species or any higher or lower taxon, except for adding a word like "closely" before "related." The question is how closely? Obviously, the degrees of relationship and of similarity vary with the rank of the taxon. Certainly higher taxa like orders, families, and genera must be less closely related than the species they include. Likewise, subspecies must be more closely related than the species they compose and less closely related than the varieties they include.

The definition above, with the addition of "closely," applies to species. This is a tangible entity, and we know something of its nature; consequently we can write a workable definition, so long as we do not attempt to build into the definition some formula by which to separate one species from another. Attempts to incorporate criteria for distinguishing species into the definition have been disastrous. An example is any definition based on the notion that species may be separated according to inability to interbreed and produce fertile offspring. Actually, intersterility or interfertility of natural populations may occur in any level of taxa from subforma up. Thus, the definition of a species or other taxon is one subject; the distinction of taxa from each other is another.

Taxa Below the Rank of Species

A species is composed of subspecies, which are composed of varieties, which may be made up of lesser infraspecific taxa, such as subvarieties, formae, and subformae. However, in this study only one named taxon below the rank of species is employed. This is *variety*; subspecies, subvarieties, formae, and subformae are not distinguished.

Through most of the world even the classification of plant species is not far along or it is spotty. In such countries as the United States, the flora is better known than in most other areas, but it has not had the intensive study given to the flora of most parts of western Europe. Thus, an attempt to organize the components of any but a few intensively studied species into categories of various ranks would be futile; not enough is known.

Even though (1) for the Cactaceae information is not nearly adequate for classifying the taxa of even the United States into both subspecies and varieties; (2) the other members of the floras of North America ordinarily are too little known to justify a similar classification; and (3) the floras of much of the world, especially those of the Horse Latitudes and the Tropics, are much less known than those of North America, and for many plant groups classification even into species is still in a primitive stage, this does not preclude the use of subspecies and variety in cases in which information is available for the fine distinctions and they are considered to be worthwhile. The usage of "sub-" taxa is accepted under the Code at other hierarchical levels: subclasses, suborders, subfamilies, and subgenera. Except for its level in the hierarchy, each of these taxa is no different from the ones of the usual basic sequence: kingdom, class, order, family, genus, species, variety. The standard taxa differ in that their usage is mandatory, except that use of infraspecific taxa is optional, at least in practice. Thus, after a very thorough monographic study covering all the species in such a group as a genus, an author may be justified in organizing the lesser taxa into both subspecies and varieties (or perhaps into even lesser taxa, as well). This may be done regardless of the state of knowledge of other genera or higher taxa in the region in which the components of a special group have been studied. Certainly a fine-grained statement of relationships is justified if the data on which it is based are abundant and similarly fine-grained. The possibility of using subspecies as an extra category when it is needed and when its distinction can be justified has been overlooked. This sensible procedure is suggested by Ira L. Wiggins.

Since too little is known of the flora of the New World (to which the cacti are confined) to justify the organization of more than one level of infraspecific category, the common expedient for all plants is to use only one—either subspecies or variety. Which one to employ is a question surrounded by controversy—controversy revolving around attempts during the twentieth century to substitute subspecies for the established use of variety. Two uses of the term have arisen—one in Europe and one primarily in the United States.

In Europe, the common interpretation of subspecies is the correct one sanctioned by the International Code of Botanical Nomenclature—as a taxon between the ranks of species and variety. A species is composed of subspecies, which are composed of varieties, which may be composed of lesser infraspecific taxa, such as subvarieties, formae, and subformae. Thus, there is a place in the system for each taxonomic level if data are adequate for making the fine distinctions and if the distinctions are considered to be worthwhile. In Europe elaborate arrangements of infraspecific taxa are employed for study of the local flora. In the British Isles there are fewer than 2,000 species of native vascular plants (ferns and seed plants), and innumerable botanists and other sorts have studied them for centuries. A system of taxa including species, subspecies, and varieties—and even subvarieties, formae, and subformae, as well—is possible, and perhaps understandable. The flora is limited not only in total number of species but also in most cases to relatively few species within a genus. The relief is modest, and local variation in both climates and habitats is relatively minor; consequently, differentiation within one species tends to be much less than in a complex mountainous region with great variation in altitude and with coastal to alpine to desert areas within a few miles, as in the western part of North America or South America or in eastern Asia or on the small islands of Hawaii. Thus, in the British Isles, accurate distinctions of minor taxa are possible and perhaps feasible, and in some countries of Europe the possibilities are parallel.

In the United States, the interpretation of subspecies has been different. About 1900, the local American liberal school of plant taxonomy began adopting subspecies as the only infraspecific taxon. This category was thought to represent a new concept. Most of those employing it argued that a subspecies was basically different from a variety—being a geographical entity. This placed the emphasis upon only one of a number of possible isolating mechanisms to the exclusion of others, which can operate just as effectively or more so in keeping taxa more or less separate. For example, genetic, ecological, physiological, and ethological factors were ignored. This notion passed, but it was replaced by another, that in some mystical way subspecies were of a different "biological" nature from varieties. Somehow subspecies were real biological entities; varieties were not.

If subspecies is to be the only category below the rank of species, organization should be truly at that level, as interpreted in Europe; if variety, the traditional rank, is to be maintained, organization should be at that level. If subspecies is chosen for use, there should be fewer taxa than if variety is employed, because subspecies are made up of varieties and obviously there are more varieties. Unless this is so, there is no point to the substitution of subspecies for the long-prevailing use of variety.

Most authors who have used only subspecies have degraded the category and made it a catch-all for all ranks from subspecies to forma, producing not very convincing systems of classification. Other authors have misused variety in the same way. In practice, the varieties of one author frequently become the subspecies of another, and the new name combination is published with the new author's name following. The overwhelming majority of known infraspecific taxa have been named as varieties. Few, except those in the small number of groups revised by investigators preferring subspecies, have been given epithets of subspecific rank. The chief obstacle to the use of subspecies is the necessity for formal nomenclatural recombinations and, in each case, the substitution of a new author's name after the plant name combination.

A stock argument for preferring subspecies is that variety has been used in more than one way, and consequently the term is ambiguous and must be dropped. In the English-speaking countries, variety has been used in horticulture to designate a minor race of practical or esthetic importance, and for a time this did cause confusion. However, the actual term used for technical names is not the English word "variety" but the Latin designation *varietas* sanctioned by the *International Code of Botanical Nomenclature* (Stafleu et al., e.g. 1972). Furthermore, for two decades the difficulty has been resolved (Article 28) as follows: "Variants of infraspecific rank, which arise in cultivation through hybridization, mutation, selection, or other processes, and which are of sufficient interest to be distinguished by a name, receive cultivar epithets preferably in common language (i.e. fancy epithets) markedly different from the Latin epithets of species and varieties. . . . Detailed regulations for the nomenclature of plants in cultivation . . . appear in the International Code of Nomenclature for Cultivated Plants." Thus, the ambiguity attending the use of variety has been cleared up; that of the use of subspecies remains.

There are two reasons for choosing variety instead of subspecies: (1) this taxon is of lower rank, and it permits recognition of a wider range of clearly defined infraspecific taxa, perhaps in time to be organized into subspecies in the true sense, but for now of sufficient differentiation and degree of distinctness to be categorized and recorded; and (2) epithets of varietal rank exist

in abundance and often they are already in the accepted combinations, little recombining being necessary, whereas almost every subspecies would require a new name or a new combination.

In the Cactaceae the substitution of subspecies for variety would require literally thousands of status changes, because the category has not been used much. Information is meager, and one seldom has enough to justify an organization into *both* subspecies and varieties. Consequently, the only course open—if variety is to be eschewed—would be nomenclatural changes of varieties to subspecies, accompanied by the appending of a new author's name to each infraspecific taxon. Such a procedure would be a disgrace to its author.

Hybrids

Hybrids are common among the cacti, as they are in nearly all plant and animal groups. The popular image of a hybrid is a single rare, conspicuously intermediate, and usually sterile F_1 hybrid, such as the mule. However, in most cases hybridization is much more subtle, and its study requires the correlation of the character combinations of many individuals. Commonly the F_1 may breed back to one or both of its parents besides breeding with itself. Usually this is followed by the interbreeding of whatever genetic types may survive, and often the result is a hybrid swarm composed of many individuals that combine in various ways and percentages the characters of the original species, varieties, or other taxa entering into the cross. The existence of such a hybrid swarm is detected by careful inspection of character combinations of many individuals. Hybrid swarms are everywhere, but few see them because few look for them.

Similar populations may exist because the ancestral taxa never have diverged completely, as with two structurally and ecologically different Californian black oaks—the California black oak, *Quercus kelloggii*, and the interior live oak, *Q. wislizenii*. All over California these two plants intergrade, and individuals with character combinations ranging from those of one species to those of the other are abundant (see Figs. 83-85). In fact, a "pure" population of either species is rare (less so for the black oak), except near the upper extreme of altitude for the black oak and the lower for the live oak. Visible characters in the combinations vary among local ecological pockets, and the sensitivity of the gene combina-

Fig. 83. The California black oak, *Quercus kelloggii* (left), and the interior live oak of California, *Q. wislizenii* (right). The black oak is a tree of the upper part of the California Oak Woodland and of much of the Pacific Montane Forest (yellow-pine forest); the interior live oak occurs in the California Oak Woodland and the California Chaparral, at mostly lower altitudes than the black oak, though there is a considerable area of altitudinal overlap and of complex intergradation of the species.

Fig. 85. Intergradation (across both photographs) of the California black oak, *Quercus kelloggii*, and the interior live oak, *Q. wislizenii*, at Hospital Rock, Sequoia National Park, in a presumed hybrid swarm; a leaf or a twig from each of a group of individuals growing in an intermediate habitat between the habitats occupied by the two species. *Q. wislizenii* is abundant on south-facing slopes all through the area; *Q. kelloggii* occurs nearby on very steep north-facing slopes above Kaweah River, and it is rare at this altitude, about 900 m (3,000 feet). (From *Plant Taxonomy, Methods and Principles*)

Fig. 84. The oracle oak, named *Quercus morehus* before its hybrid nature and origin were understood. Its selection of characters is approximately that of the Expected F$_1$ generation of a natural cross of the California black oak, *Q. kelloggii*, and the interior live oak, *Q. wislizenii*. Trees with this character combination are occasional throughout California, where the two species occur together. (From *Plant Classification*; and from *Plant Taxonomy, Methods and Principles*)

tions to the environment is amazing. All that comes to public attention is an occasional plant approximating the hypothetical F_1 generation; this is quickly tabbed as "*Quercus morehus*," the oracle oak, and the many individuals shading into both species are overlooked. (The English name for the approximate F_1 hybrid was coined by Jepson to reflect the oracular certainty of those who thought the plant was or was not a hybrid.) More recently the heterozygous nature of the trees has been shown experimentally (Wolf, 1938).

Similarly, most cacti hybridize with related species or varieties. *Echinocereus fendleri, E. fasciculatus,* and *E. engelmannii* are composed of an irregular network of 15 varieties ranging from New Mexico to California. *E. fendleri* var. *fendleri* occurs mostly through the higher grasslands in and near New Mexico and east-central Arizona; in central New Mexico it intergrades with var. *kuenzleri,* a local variety; in southwestern New Mexico and southeastern Arizona it shades into var. *rectispinus.* In the same area var. *rectispinus* is not always distinguishable from *E. fasciculatus* var. *fasciculatus,* which shades into *E. fasciculatus* vars. *boyce-thompsonii* and *bonkerae,* occurring a little north and west in Arizona. In the foothills along the Mogollon Rim in central Arizona, var. *boyce-thompsonii* and var. *fasciculatus* intergrade with *E. engelmannii* vars. *engelmannii* and *acicularis.* The last two varieties occur westward across the Arizona Desert, but var. *acicularis* is much more common. On Papago Indian lands along the southern border of Arizona both of the last two varieties intergrade with the local and very striking var. *nicholii.* In California, only var. *engelmannii* continues westward across the Colorado and the southern Mojavean deserts to the Cascade-Sierra Nevada axis, where the deserts end. In the southern Mojavean Desert this variety intergrades with the localized var. *howei.* Northward it hybridizes with var. *chrysocentrus* of the eastern Mojavean Desert in Nevada and Utah, and that variety intergrades with var. *variegatus,* which follows up the Colorado River watershed to the Navajoan Desert in southern Utah and to the Little Colorado in northern Arizona. Probably var. *variegatus* intergrades with the closely related var. *purpureus,* local near St. George, Utah, but observation is not complete. Finally, var. *engelmannii* shades into local varieties—var. *armatus* here and there across the central Mojavean Desert in California and Nevada and var. *munzii,* a mountain variety ranging

up to about 2,400 m (8,000 ft) in the San Bernardino and San Jacinto Mountains at the western edges of the deserts. Thus, there is a branching chain of varieties through a large area, and those of the three species intergrade wherever they come into contact. However, each is adapted through most of its range to areas with particular environmental conditions. Where these overlap, hybridizing occurs, and there is intergradation through hybrid swarms.

Similar examples of intergradation based presumably on hybridization (or incomplete divergence from a common ancestor) are abundant. The eight varieties of *Echinocereus triglochidiatus* intergrade through even a little greater geographical range than the 15 of the *E. fendleri* complex discussed above. The seven varieties of *Coryphantha vivipara* occupy different geographical and ecological niches ranging from eastern Oregon to Alberta and southward to the Californian deserts and Texas, and their intergradation is as bewildering as that of the species and varieties of *Echinocereus.* Examples from the other genera are numerous; hybridization and intergradation are the rule, not the exception. One of the most intensively studied examples of hybridization and of natural selection among the hybrids of cacti followed the introduction of the Indian fig or mission cactus (*Opuntia ficus-indica*) into southern California by the Franciscan Fathers, who founded the chain of California missions (Benson & Walkington, 1965; Benson, 1969d). This case is described in relation to the analysis of chemical characters (pp. 63-69) and in the descriptive text (pp. 517-18).

Preservation of Hybrids through Asexual Reproduction

Among the chollas and prickly pears, the survival of hybrids is promoted by asexual reproduction. Vegetative multiplication preserves many gene combinations otherwise unlikely to be reproduced quickly or in large numbers by the normal sexual sorting and recombining processes. The teddy-bear cholla, *Opuntia bigelovii* var. *bigelovii,* reproduces primarily, if not wholly, by the abscission of vegetative joints, which fall readily from the plant and immediately root and grow (Fig. 86). Thus, there are dense thickets or even forests of plants of this species, showing little or no variation in characters, and none or practically none within the range of the variety in the United States. Through asexual reproduction,

Fig. 86. Asexual reproduction from fallen joints of the stems; teddy-bear cholla, *Opuntia bigelovii* var. *bigelovii*. The upper joints of the plant form short side branches, which are detached readily and carried by passing large mammals or which fall to the ground directly. The joints in due course produce roots, and each joint becomes a new plant, genetically identical with the parent plant.

perhaps a single clone or a few similar clones may have spread over both the Colorado and the Arizona deserts during the 10,000 years since the close of Pleistocene. During the last pluvial period of Pleistocene time (see p. 142), the occurrence of vegetation types and floristic associations in western Arizona was lower by about 300 m (1,000 ft) or more likely 600 m (2,000 ft) in elevation than at present (as determined by the evidence of woodrat middens, Van Devender & King, 1971). Thus, the more frost-sensitive species of the Colorado and Arizona deserts must have survived in areas farther south near the Gulf of California or perhaps in a few refugia barely within the United States. The desert ironwood, *Olneya tesota*, is characteristic of these two deserts, and it grows no higher than 750 m (2,500 ft). Whenever there is a severe frost, the ironwoods lose all their outer twigs and smaller branches. Similarly, *Opuntia bigelovii* var. *bigelovii* requires high temperatures, and it is restricted to areas below 600 m (2,000 ft) or rarely 900 m (3,000 ft). During the Pleistocene, very likely neither of these species occurred north of

Mexico, and probably both have migrated northward since then, especially during the very warm period of 8,000 to 4,000 years ago. In view of the lack of variability in the teddy-bear cholla, its rapid reproduction by fallen joints, and the ease with which these joints are detached from the plant and attached to animals by the dense, sharp, barbed spines, the present population in the United States may be a single vegetative strain (or a few of them). This must represent a well-adapted gene combination occurring in the possibly more variable populations near the Gulf of California (a point to be determined). Inasmuch as woodrats make large middens of teddy-bear cholla joints (see Fig. 87), these serving as a protection to the nests, study of the migration of the cactus during the Pleistocene is possible. The flora of an area is preserved in the middens over the nests of woodrats or packrats, and the age of the plants in the nests may be determined by carbon dating. Thus, the migrations of *Opuntia bigelovii* may be ascertained through their presence or absence in woodrat nests of different ages.

One other gene combination of *O. bigelovii*,

Fig. 87. Teddy-bear cholla, *Opuntia bigelovii* var. *bigelovii*, and a woodrat midden and dwelling built with and protected by joints of the cactus. Woodrat middens are built of plant parts and other objects from within a short distance of the nest. By carbon dating, the plant fragments can be associated with a particular time, as, for example, 1,000 years ago, especially so if the nests have been built in dry caves or recesses in rocks, where they have been preserved. Thus the character of the vegetation and the floristic association present at each time can be determined.

that of var. *hoffmanii* (Fig. 322), occurs in the United States. This distinctive variety occurs only near the mountains of the Colorado Desert in southern San Diego County, California. Probably its history has been parallel to that of var. *bigelovii*.

The two varieties of *Opuntia bigelovii* (Figs. 322 and 86) present a classification problem with no solution in sight. If seedlings of the species should show a great degree of heterozygosity and, if each of the two varieties should prove to be a clone or group of clones capable of maintaining its integrity only through asexual reproduction, should the two be recognized as separate taxa? There is no simple answer. In some plant groups, such as some buttercups (*Ranunculus*) or plants of the dandelion group in the sunflower family (e.g., *Taraxacum* and *Crepis*), there may be hundreds or thousands of races that reproduce asexually, though more subtly. In these cases, the plants reproduce by *apomixis*, a deceptive form of asexual reproduction that appears to be normal sexual reproduction. Seeds develop, but there is

no joining of male and female gametes, and diploid cells of the female parent grow into a false embryo with identical genetic characters—like a cutting from the mother plant. Thus, there may be innumerable apomictic races, each perpetuating a different heterozygous clone formed by hybridizing and not reproducible sexually. These do not intergrade, and some authors with a simple view of taxa have considered each to be a species. If the suspected nature of vars. *bigelovii* and *hoffmanii* is correct, they are essentially similar—in the effect of their method of reproduction—to such apomictic races, and their status as varieties is dubious. At present, all we know with certainty is that there is a strikingly clear and consistent distinction between the two geographically and apparently reproductively segregated races.

Opuntia prolifera (Fig. 305) of the southern California coast and *O. fulgida* of the Arizona Desert reproduce both by dropping joints and by a type of apomixis. *O. fulgida* var. *fulgida* (Fig. 88), like *O. bigelovii* var. *bigelovii* (see Figs. 324–26), has occupied an enormous territory probably by the rapid spreading of a few clones, these showing only slight local variability. Var. *mamillata* (Figs. 315–17) has a somewhat disjunct and more restricted range wholly within the area of var. *fulgida*. The plants of each variety are distinctive and distinguishable from far off, but their character combinations seem to be maintained only through asexual reproduction. Thus, the two recognized varieties of O. *fulgida* have the same shaky taxonomic status as those of O. *bigelovii*.

Opuntia munzii (Fig. 320) is a rare and local race also maintained largely by asexual reproduc-

Fig. 88. Sterile fruits of *Opuntia fulgida* var. *fulgida*, each producing one or more buds that grow into flower(s), or in one case a spiny branch; these arise from the areoles of the floral cup investing and adnate with the ovary. If the fruits are detached and they fall on the ground, each one grows like a vegetative branch into a new plant. Thus, sexual reproduction is simulated but not carried out.

tion. Again, the species may consist of a single clone or a few localized but similar clones. However, in this case there is no existing pair of taxa of a sufficient degree of similarity to be likely forebears of O. *munzii*. If the species is of hybrid origin and highly heterozygous (a point still to be proved), probably it was derived from preexisting and now extinct taxa or from the cross of a species similar to O. *bigelovii* with an unknown population system. Thus, the species as it exists now is probably distinct from other living types, whatever its origin or genetic and reproductive nature.

Opuntia bigelovii, O. *prolifera*, O. *fulgida*, and O. *munzii* and their varieties probably represent surviving remnants and reinvaders derived from perhaps larger and more complex pre-Pleistocene or interglacial-period population systems. Likely the only survivors in the United States, if any, were restricted to favorable localities; otherwise all must have been forced south of the present international boundary for a time. If so, the present representatives in California, Nevada, and Arizona must have moved northward at various rates and with different degrees of facility during the last 10,000 years.

For these and other chollas and for many prickly pears (e.g. *Opuntia nicholii*), there are similar problems of genetic make-up, reproductive mechanisms, and taxonomic status. The simplest (but not really simple) method of clarifying some of the problems is to grow seedlings from all the viable seeds of various individual plants. The results should indicate whether relatively slightly variable plants are highly heterozygous, with many genes unexpressed because of the suppression of sexual reproduction. However, if the plants grown from seeds are no more variable than those occurring in nature, either they are homozygous, or nearly so, or there is an apomictic mechanism at work. The final step is the investigation of fertilization and the development of the embryo to determine whether apomixis occurs.

7. Policy in Classification

The genera and species of cacti occurring in the United States and Canada are defined differently by the authors of various books and papers. In this book only 18 genera are recognized, whereas, in their four-volume work on the Cactaceae, Britton and Rose (1919-23) applied 33 generic names to the cacti of the same area. Discrepancies like this do not reflect necessarily errors or mistakes in judgment but, rather, differences of opinion concerning policy in classification. Some botanists ("liberals") prefer to include a narrow range of forms within a taxon; others ("conservatives") prefer including a broader group of variants in each taxon.

Considerations in the Choice of Policy

Each botanist attempts to classify plants in a uniform manner, and no system is necessarily "right" or "wrong," provided that the organisms are grouped according to natural relationships and the arrangement is essentially consistent (see Benson, 1962, Chapters 1-10). On purely logical grounds, if the population systems accorded scientific names are natural, then all policies ranging from conservative to liberal must be of equal value. The choice of policy should be based on (1) an attempt at *conformity with the prevailing practice* of botanists in classifying the plant kingdom as a whole, insofar as this prevalence can be determined, and (2) *practical considerations*.

Conformity with prevailing practice. The policy basic to the research adopted for this book is conservative, partly because this is most nearly in harmony with worldwide prevailing botanical practice.

The work of Britton and Rose included books and numerous papers on a number of families of the floras of North America and to a lesser extent the floras of other regions, especially of South America. Their research was carried out according to a policy representing the height of influence of a local liberal school in the United States. This group, led by Britton, flourished from about 1900 to 1930. Most, though not all, of its policies have been abandoned or modified by the great majority of later botanists.

There is no comprehensive coverage of the cactus family according to conservative policy, and recent classification of this special group has taken the opposite direction. Unfortunately, the useful volumes on the Cactaceae by Britton and Rose have not been matched by any recent usable botanical treatment of the family. Still more unfortunately, the authors of numerous popular, semitechnical, and even some technical books and journal papers have tended to increase the number of microgenera and microspecies of cacti far beyond even the number recognized by Britton and Rose. This has been done not by an orderly, logical division of taxa into smaller natural units, but by splitting them arbitrarily and transferring irregular segments into unnatural groups, each of which is held together by the presence of only a single striking character, regardless of other features. A classification of the entire plant kingdom along the policy lines favored by Britton and Rose would require at least one million changes of plant names. A similar extension to all plants of the policies of some recent authors of works on the cactus family would require an astronomical number of changes.

Practical considerations. The importance of a conservative policy with respect to recognition of species is illustrated by the following points:

1. Treatment of less stable taxa. Many fairly well-marked population systems lack character combinations of sufficient stability to make their segregation by keys practical. According to a conservative policy, these systems are considered more effectively as varieties than as species, and consequently they are not included in the keys used to separate major population systems classified in the rank of species. Taxa to be accorded specific rank should be marked by relatively clear and stable diagnostic characters, and their identification by keys is facilitated by the elimination of the minor, less stable population systems from this rank. In this book, when a species is represented by two or more varieties, they are distinguished by a table of characters and not by a key (see *Opuntia acanthocarpa*, p. 292). This policy places the burden of differentiation upon a complex of characters to be compared in the table rather than upon a single feature. Most keys tend to place the emphasis for each decision upon one or two characters; comparing whole complexes of not wholly stable characters across several leads of a key is more difficult.

2. Correlation of geographical units. If local units are organized as separate species rather than as varieties within species, carrying a knowledge of the flora of one region to another region is difficult. Each area then appears as a local, independent unit and not as a phase of the general flora of a continent or other large geographical unit. For example, a fern, the common bracken or brake (*Pteridium aquilinum*), is nearly cosmopolitan, but somewhat different population systems occur on different continents or parts of them. These have been named as species, but the character alliances marking the taxa are unstable, and even the most significant local character combinations represent only phases of a worldwide complex. The populations intergrade, and many plants do not fit clearly into any of the prevailing types. Considering the only slightly differing groups to be varieties of a single species emphasizes their interrelationships without obscuring their somewhat inconsistent differences; considering them to be species obscures or obliterates the similarities and emphasizes only the differences. With knowledge of a conservative classification system, a person traveling from one part of the world to another can carry some of what he has learned in one region to the next. Otherwise, confusion is likely, because essentially the same plant has a different name in each place.

Similarly, a person who is familiar with the box-elder (a type of maple, *Acer negundo*), common through the East, Middle West, and South, would be amazed to find the similar box-elder of California listed in books as *A. californicum*—a different species. In the Rocky Mountains his experience might be similar, for the box-elder occurring there has been named *A. interius*. Still another box-elder occurring in the southern states has appeared as *A. texanum*. The box-elders of different regions do have some differences, but over large intervening geographical areas the combinations of characters that supposedly mark species are inconsistent, and in many plants some diagnostic characters of one taxon may occur with some of those of another. If all four box-elders mentioned above are to be considered to be varieties of a single species, *A. negundo*, as vars. *negundo, californicum, interius,* and *texanum* (the last of doubtful status), the interrelationships are understood readily. Thus, if a single box-elder is mentioned in a book concerned with the plants of one region, it falls immediately into place as part of a transcontinental system of minor populations. If it is named as a species, the relationship is lost.

Thus, under a conservative system "variety" becomes a strong and useful category, and its use improves organization.

Policy Employed in This Book

The policy underlying classification of the taxa described in this book is conservative, but the use of the research presented here is not limited to a single interpretation. Within the limits set by restriction to natural units of classification, there is still room for difference of opinion concerning grouped or divided taxa. For those who prefer, other interpretations are possible, and the treatment of every genus, species, and variety is supplemented under "Documentation" (pp. 911ff) by a complete list of published synonyms, some of which are used by other authors. Thus, other interpretations are facilitated, provided they can be justified on the basis of the nature of the living populations of plants composing the proposed taxa.

The introduction to the second edition of *The Cacti of Arizona* (Benson, ed. 2, 1950) pointed out the need for a better scheme of classification of the Cactaceae, a scheme based on new information and providing a re-evaluation and realignment of all the taxa. The system of classification adopted then was taken up tentatively and without future commitment, because it provided a more satisfactory organization of taxa than the exceedingly liberal and partly artificial interpretation of Britton and Rose (1919-23), then still dominant.

Since that statement was published 30 years ago, continuous research has been applied to the cactus family, and particularly to the genera and species occurring in the United States and Canada. Many problems remain to be solved, but the present classification is at least a step toward understanding the relationships of taxa and their delimitation according to natural boundaries. Despite the extensive investigation of field populations and of the specimens in many herbaria, numerous decisions must be tentative until more data become available. In all research there is forever an approach to the truth, but a complete grasp of the truth is unattainable. Much remains to be learned about the cacti of the United States and Canada, but this book is hoped to put their classification into better order and to facilitate future studies. Classification of most of the rest of the family, occurring in Latin America, is in various stages of progress, and it ranges from fairly well understood to chaotic, according to the genus or the area or region.

On theoretical grounds, both conservative and liberal interpretations are tenable, and they are of equal value, but the position of a "lumper" or a "splitter" cannot be justified. These epithets refer to taxonomists who group living population systems into "taxa" that are not natural units. These merely artificial assemblages of plants or animals are made up either by "lumping" together large, incoherent groups or by "splitting" off smaller groups according to the presence or absence of one or two characters to which arbitrary "importance" is attached. Splitting of taxa has been unusually common in treatments of the Cactaceae, as it has been with most other plants and animals that catch the public fancy—for example, the birds or the butterflies. Almost always in these cases the splitting of species or other taxa has been based on an arbitrary choice of one character considered to be *the mark* of the species and thus so important that its presence or absence replaces all other considerations. However, no character is *per se* more significant than another, and its importance in marking a taxon is merely in proportion to its degree of consistency in association with other characters.

8. Field and Herbarium Study

The judgments necessary for classification of plants are based on data from both living individuals and preserved specimens. Living plant populations in the field are the best source of information, and collections from these populations may be brought into gardens for temporary propagation, observation, and experimentation. Ordinarily, plants known only from gardens are of minor use in research, because they are usually without data and there is no way of ascertaining their relationships to population systems occurring in nature. Dried or sometimes fluid-preserved specimens are important both for original data and for preservation of permanent records of the plants studied. Unfortunately, most herbaria do not have large collections of pressed cactus specimens. Consequently, data from this source are less readily available than for other families, and we must rely primarily—and disproportionately—upon the natural populations in the field.

Refinements in classification can benefit from more detailed research, through the use of statistical, cytological, and microscopic technical methods; data secured from paleobotany; and experimental data accumulated from chemistry, plant physiology, and genetics. However, these methods are adapted mostly to intensive study of small groups of species, and they can be applied only sparingly to parts of an organizational research study involving many taxa. Such a reorganization of a large group paves the way for innumerable detailed studies of the special problems it reveals and makes accessible for subsequent research.

Field Studies

The field studies supporting the preparation of this book have occupied 49 years (see pp. 11f and 110), and they include investigation in all 50 states (see Fig. 89), the Canadian provinces where cacti occur, and some parts of Latin America. Emphasis has been on the internal variations and the intergradations of natural population systems and their relationship to the ecological factors of the environment. The number of herbarium specimens of cacti resulting from this travel and research has not been counted, but it runs into the thousands.

The species occurring in adjacent Mexico have been observed in relationship to those occurring in the United States, both to determine the limits and ramifications of species and varieties and to work out more accurately the scopes of genera. Cacti in the Caribbean region have been considered in the herbarium and the field for the same purpose and particularly to gain a better insight into the nature and relationships of the tropical cacti native in southern Florida and (sparingly) near Brownsville, Texas, or introduced in Hawaii.

Herbarium Studies

Any large herbarium is a depository for materials used in taxonomic research. The specimens provide both evidence for studies of the past and a basis for present and future investigation. However, in most herbaria pressed specimens of the cacti are few and inadequate, because specimens of these plants are not made as frequently or as well as are those of most other plant groups.

Succulent, spiny plants such as the cacti can be made into excellent herbarium specimens (see Figs. 90-92), but this requires a knowledge of special methods of preparation and more than the usual amount of effort. Consequently, the relatively few specimens of cacti that have come into herbaria from either the field or gardens are commonly meager in content and poorly preserved. Often a specimen is composed of only some collapsed remains of a plant that died in cultivation or of a single flower or fruit or some seeds or a cluster of spines. Unfortunately, in many instances the information used by former students of the Cactaceae cannot be evaluated critically, because the living material they studied was not retained or it was poorly and incompletely preserved.

Because the normal accumulation of evidence from the past is lacking, the specimens in any one herbarium or group of several herbaria are inadequate for preliminary studies. It was not possible to begin research on the cacti by going to the herbaria to determine the main outlines of taxa, to discover taxonomic problems, or to learn their nature.

The burden of beginning research on the cacti of the United States and Canada rested almost wholly on an analysis of populations occurring naturally in the field—a much more difficult and time-consuming process than working out the main outlines in the herbarium first. As field studies have progressed, new specimens have been added to the herbarium, and much information has been added both in the plant specimens themselves and on their labels. However, the mechanical task of preparing herbarium specimens to

represent the character combinations in each of, for example, 100 or more individuals examined at any one point in the field is excessive. The effort is beyond the limits of time and endurance of the investigator or of space for field transportation. Necessarily, much of the burden of correlation of data has depended on notes and memory, aided by specimens brought to the herbarium and the garden.

Dependence upon comparison of mental images of growing plants composing field populations has been supplemented considerably during the later phases of study by visiting more than 60 herbaria. Although no herbarium can supply a beginning for taxonomic study of the cacti, the total number of specimens in all the herbaria is considerable. Taken as a whole, the accumulation of specimens forms a significant body of raw data indicating the basis for delimitation of species and other taxa. Unfortunately, it cannot be examined all at once, and the scattering of

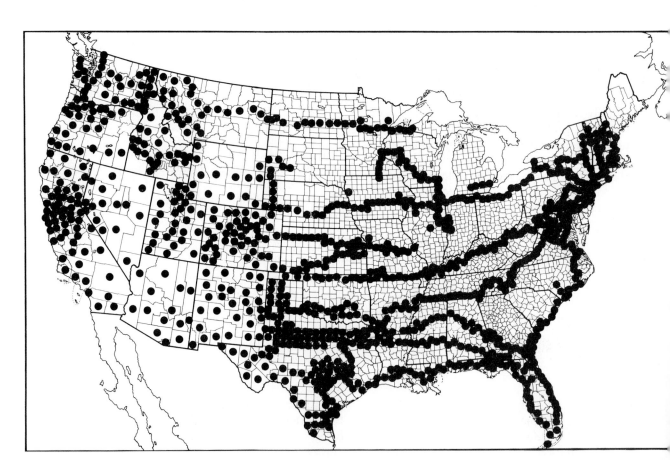

Fig. 89. Map of the 48 contiguous states of the United States, showing the areas visited for field studies of the cacti, but not showing those in Alaska, Hawaii, Canada, Mexico, or the Caribbean region. Each county in which these investigations proceeded is marked by a dot; however, this dot may cover completely a small eastern county but take up only a part of a western county larger than some eastern states. The map does not indicate the much more thorough study in the western counties.

Fig. 90. Herbarium specimen of a prickly pear, *Opuntia macrorhiza*, showing the essential features of the plant, these reinforced by flowers, fruits, and (not labeled) seeds in the paper-fragment folders on the sheet.

specimens does not mean much until a background is developed in the field. Thus, research has required carrying mental impressions from the field to each of many herbaria, visited one at a time during several decades. Some herbaria have been studied a number of times as correlations developed and were modified, but many collections could be seen only once. Nevertheless, the contribution of herbarium specimens to research on the cacti has been enormous, because, despite the handicap of scattered information, the study of these specimens in many herbaria provided the opportunity to put together fragments of information about the ramifications of taxa and their distribution. Ultimately this provided a helpful and workable basis for the reconsideration of

Fig. 91. An herbarium, the plants housed in steel cabinets, the one at the right with the door open, showing the folders containing pressed specimens. Combined herbaria of Pomona College and the Rancho Santa Ana Botanic Garden, Claremont, California.

Fig. 92. Specimens in folders in the pigeonholes of a steel herbarium cabinet.

taxa and the formulation of ideas concerning their classification.

When a system of classification has been formulated, the choice of names to be applied to the accepted taxa must be worked out according to the *International Code of Botanical Nomenclature* (Lanjouw [Stafleu] et al., 1972), and this procedure centers in the herbaria, where *type specimens* and other authentic materials are preserved. Nearly all the existing *types* of the taxa occurring in the United States have been investigated, and these and the other specimens cited in the literature have been studied for their bearing on nomenclature as well as classification. When no type was designated, as was frequently the case in the older literature, it has been necessary to determine as nearly as possible the plants on which names were based. Whenever a reasonable decision could be made concerning the plants an author had in mind but did not preserve, a substitute for a type has been designated in order to end uncertainty. If any of the material studied by the author of the taxon is available, selection of a *lectotype* is required, providing the extant specimen fits the original description. If no original material is known to exist, a *neotype* must be chosen from other collections or collected in the field. In many cases a neotype has been collected at the source of the original plants. Sometimes this has involved numerous or ex-

tended trips, such as following out the route of the Emory military reconnaissance expedition of 1846 and collecting specimens at the campsites of the expedition. Thus, the plants described and illustrated (but not collected) at each point along the way, usually the campground for the night, from Kansas to southern California are represented now by neotypes from the original sites. A similar method was used in the study of the cacti of the Simpson Expedition undertaken in 1858-59 between Utah Lake, Utah, and Carson Valley, Nevada, in search of a new wagon route. Many other type localities have been visited so as to study the natural populations from which type specimens were collected.

The addition of specimens of the Cactaceae to the herbaria is a great need, because the paucity of collections is a handicap to further research. The primary factor in the scarcity of specimens is the collectors' lack of familiarity with the special methods of making specimens of cacti, compounded by a supposition that the procedures are much more difficult than they really are. For this reason, a discussion of the significance of specimens and of methods of making them follows.

Herbarium Specimens as Permanent Records

Need for a permanent record. No matter how carefully a plant may be described in the literature, the ultimate authority concerning its characters is the plant itself. For centuries an herbarium specimen will show the exact basis for an author's description of the plant and for his conclusions concerning its classification and nomenclature. Consequently, every author is obliged to preserve specimens as a record of the basis for his publications. This includes type specimens and such plants as may have been employed in statistical or experimental research. Thus, it is necessary to preserve plants to document the exact meaning of what is published, and the lack of such records makes much of the literature on the cacti essentially useless for research purposes. Innumerable books must be nearly discounted, because there is no way to check the bases on which they rest.

The herbarium record not only documents the literature but also provides data fundamental to classification and nomenclature, as indicated above. Study of specimens reveals the makeup of species and other taxa and their intergradation, and it indicates which other plants approach the character combinations of the type plants or essentially match them. In addition, the data on the specimen labels indicate the relationship of the plant to the environment in which it lived and the geographical distribution of the taxon.

Use of the record. Under the universally accepted *International Code of Botanical Nomenclature* (Lanjouw [Stafleu], 1972), whenever a new species or variety is described, a type specimen must be designated and must be preserved in a permanent collection to show the nature of the plant. Since January 1, 1958, no newly described species or variety will be accepted in botany unless a type (*holotype*) is designated. A name not based on a type specimen is considered a *nomen nudum* or bare name: officially, it is unpublished; it has no status insofar as priority is concerned, and later names published validly must supersede it.

The connection of type specimens with recent botanical literature is precise. The published description of each new taxon normally includes a reference to the name and field number or serial specimen number of the collector of the type, and usually references to the collectors of other specimens as well. A serial number in the sequence for the specimens in the herbarium as a whole usually is stamped on each specimen sheet. Thus, the type specimen is designated in the literature not only by collector and field number but also by an herbarium sheet number. This eliminates the likelihood of confusion.

However, an herbarium is much more than a depository for type specimens; it is the basis for much of the complicated literature of systematic botany. At one time the Southern California room of the Herbarium of Pomona College was essentially the late P. A. Munz's *Manual of Southern California Botany* (1935) preserved in herbarium form. Although the herbarium has grown and it has been rearranged, the Californian specimens still serve this function. Any qualified person may determine there exactly what the author had in mind with respect to nearly any species appearing in the *Manual* and, now, what he had in mind concerning many of those in *A California Flora* (1959) and in *A Flora of Southern California* (1974). In the U.S. National Herbarium, Smithsonian Institution, Washington, D.C., numerous cactus collections by J. N. Rose document the writings of Britton and Rose. The exact meaning and the basis for published papers and books, such as *The Cactaceae* (1919-23), by these men, as well as works by many others, may be determined from these collections and from duplicates in the Herbarium of the New York Botanical Garden. The primary function of any large herbarium, then, is to preserve records of the material upon which botanical literature has been based and *most important of all to provide a body of raw data upon which to form the basis for further studies and to enable old records and judgments to be correlated with new.*

Preparation of Specimens

Collections of dried specimens forming herbaria are far better actuarial risks than gardens, because well-prepared specimens will last for an indefinite period. The herbarium of Caesalpino, preserved since about 1583 in Florence, Italy, is still in good condition. The herbarium of the great eighteenth-century Swedish botanist, Linnaeus, is in London, and many other Linnaean specimens are at Stockholm. These collections are an all but indelible record of the meaning of many of the descriptions in Linnaeus's *Species Plantarum, Genera Plantarum,* and other works.

The quality of specimens is determined largely by their preparation for pressing*; almost always after drying there is only slight change. However, a few plants go through a predictable process of losing flower color after pressing, e.g. the California poppy, *Eschscholtzia californica* and many

*Detailed methods of preparing cactus specimens have been published: see Peebles, 1942; Wiggins, 1950; Benson, 1950, 1957b.

buttercups (*Ranunculus*). If the pressing has been done well, the pressed specimens of most plants will retain the original colors of stems, leaves, and flowers, and they will last as long as they are kept dry, in the dark, and at a reasonable temperature. Certain colors like the green of chlorophyll and the mostly reds and yellows of other insoluble pigments are not much changed in pressing and drying. The water-soluble pigments, anthocyanins in most plants but betacyanins in cacti, produce colors in the magenta series, and these are altered according to the acidity or alkalinity of the cell sap. Thus, they tend toward red in an acid medium and toward blue in an alkaline one. No matter how the pressing of a specimen has been done, these dissolved pigments will not retain the original color; they turn to a dull blue. However, the presence of these pigments is indicated by the blue, even though it is altered from the original color.

Selection of material for specimens. Ideally, the material selected for specimens should include all the significant parts of the plant. Specimens of smaller cacti should include *at least* the halves of a stem cut vertically; those of larger species should be made partly from representative portions of the stem. Both young joints with leaves and older ones with mature spines are needed for a prickly pear or a cholla specimen. For a barrel cactus at least a portion of the stem showing ribs is necessary, and it should exhibit all types of spines. The angles of spreading of the spines of any cactus should be preserved for some areoles. If it is practical, the characters of the root system also should be shown. The flowers, fruits, and seeds are of primary importance, and they should be represented if they are obtainable. Good photographs of the plant are an excellent supplement to a specimen. However, they are not in themselves a specimen, because they cannot be dissected, and no photographs can show all the features of a given plant. Ideally, the specimen will include both plant and photographs.

Preparing material for specimens. Medium-sized cacti are prepared for pressing by splitting the stems with a knife and fork and often by hollowing out the interiors. If the cut surfaces are covered very heavily with table salt or borax, after one to several hours an amazing quantity of water may be blotted up or even poured off before the stems are pressed. Just as the specimen starts to curl, it should be pressed.

Ordinarily, the preparation of specimens for mounting on herbarium sheets is more desirable than the preservation of the plants in boxes or jars, because the plants may be filed with the others of the same kind. However, bulky material may be difficult to prepare for herbarium sheets. Large segments, as, for example, several ribs from the stem of a barrel cactus, may be salted and then dried in the open air for storage in cartons or they may be preserved in jars with 5-10 percent formaldehyde or one of various formalin-alcohol solutions as a preservative.

Flowers are split lengthwise and not hollowed out, but they should be salted heavily on the cut surfaces. Not only does the salt aid in the removal of water from the specimen, but also it prevents or reduces the growth of molds. Because the salt is applied only to the cuts, it will not show on the herbarium specimen. However, for specimens showing the inside of the flower, the salt may be removed after drying, by careful brushing or by washing with water followed by a brief redrying process.

Salt is a deliquescent substance, and in humid climates it absorbs water from the air, making specimens wet. Consequently, in humid regions the cells of the plant specimen must be killed in some other way. Killing the cells of the plant by dipping the material in boiling water or treating it with formaldehyde may be substituted for the use of salt. In the tropics, where the humidity is very high, drying even nonsucculent specimens is difficult, and special drying methods must be used. Freeze drying is a new method.

Pressing specimens. Cactus specimens should be dry within two to four days. This may be accomplished with a simple plant press (Fig. 93) consisting, for example, of two pieces of half-inch (1.25 cm) plywood cut to standard herbarium mounting-sheet size, 16-1/2 × 11-1/2 inches (roughly 4.1 × 2.9 dm) or a little larger, perhaps 18 × 12 inches (4.5 × 3 dm). The two pieces of wood and the enclosed materials are tied into a bundle by two straps or by ropes, such as window-sash cords, about 7 feet (2 m) long.

Cardboards and blotters used as driers are cut to fit the press. The best cardboard for the purpose is the corrugated type used for cartons. The corrugations should run crosswise in the press to decrease the length of the air channels, and they should be large, so that air currents may pass through the press. The blotting paper should be nearly as thick as the cardboard.

Specimens are placed in folders, each fashioned by folding a standard-size American newspaper page once. Such a folder is about the size of the press and the cardboards and blotters. The sequence in the press (Fig. 94) is as follows: blotter, specimen folded in newspaper, cardboard, specimen folded in newspaper, blotter, etc. Thus, the specimens fill in the spaces between the alternating cardboards and blotters. The newspaper is absorbent and close-fitting, as is the blotter on one side of the specimen; the cardboard presents a smooth, flat surface on the other side. For thick specimens like those of cacti, extra blotters are necessary.

A recent development in plant-pressing technique used by Pomona College students is the substitution of sheets of non-inflammable foam for cardboards and blotters. These have not been tried extensively for cactus specimens, but they work well for other plants.

The press should be placed in a cabinet supplying an air current from an electric fan-and-heater combination. It should be aligned so that the air current passes through the corrugations of the cardboards; and for cactus specimens the drying materials should be changed every day.

Placing the cut stems of large or medium-sized cacti between heavy iron gratings without paper and arranging them above a fan-heater combination for three or four days produces good specimens without the necessity for changing driers (see Fig. 95).

Fig. 93 (*left*). A plant press made from two pieces of half-inch plywood, tied with window-sash cord. The press contains alternating sheets of cardboard and blotting paper, the specimens in folded newspaper sheets between them.

Fig. 95 (*above*). Split and salted joints of a cholla and of a prickly pear on a grating of expanded steel. The other heavy grating will be placed on top of the specimens, and a current of warm, dry air will be directed through the gratings.

Fig. 94 (*left*). An open plant press with the halves of a stem joint of a prickly pear split and salted and ready for pressing. The sheets of corrugated cardboard allow air to pass through the press, promoting drying; the blotters absorb water from the plant and fit closely around it. If cacti are dried in this way, the driers must be changed daily.

Mounting Specimens

Standard herbarium mounting paper is cut to 16-1/2 × 11-1/2 inch (41 × 29 cm) sheets of special heavy stock obtainable from botanical-supply companies or, with custom cutting, from paper manufacturers. The labels as well as the sheets must be printed on all-rag paper, because other papers disintegrate during the passage of time, whereas rag papers last for centuries. Unfortunately, all-rag paper is becoming difficult to find.

Specimens of cacti are mounted by covering the high points of the lower (cut) surfaces of the stems or the lower sides of flowers or fruits with some heavy adhesive material. A mounting-plastic preparation (for formula, see Benson, 1957b, p. 396) has been used widely until recently, but unfortunately it contains toluene, and except perhaps in the open air its extensive use in mounting is questionable because of the possible harmful effect on human health. A satisfactory substitute is being sought. Certain glues have been tried, but they are not as satisfactory as plastic. The plastic and the best glues adhere strongly to both the plant and the paper, and cactus specimens have only to be allowed to stand until the adhesive is set. Additional sewing and taping are unnecessary.

A split cactus flower is mounted properly with the half bearing the style and stigma on the cut side turned upward to show the inner flower structures. The other half of the flower is mounted cut-side-down to display the outer structures. Similarly, half of each fruit is mounted to show the internal structures, such as the seeds, and the other half to show the external features.

Recording Data for Specimen Labels

Specimens intended for research should include the data specified by the label shown in Fig. 96. The selection of data categories for the label is based on 50 years of field collecting and research on herbarium specimens. The categories are those that have been found to be most needed in research.

First line of the label. The scientific name of the plant, the genus and species, occupies the top line of the label (the variety, if any, the second). The name of the plant is followed by the name of the author of the species, as furnished in technical publications. Authors' names (often supplied as abbreviations) are given partly for precision, because the same name combination may have been applied by different authors to two or more taxa,

or the same taxon may have received more than one name. An example of name duplication may be taken from the last century: *Cactus ferox* Willd. (1813) was applied later, without knowledge of duplication, to another species as *Cactus ferox* Nutt. (1818). The name combination can be used, then, only for the species to which it was applied first. Sometimes, duplicating names may appear in publications on the floras of mutually distant areas, and both names may be in use for a long time before the duplication of the name combination is discovered. In such cases, the citation of authors' names may avoid confusion, because placing the name of the author after each plant name limits application to the taxon intended, excluding any other, unintended, use of the same name.

The name of a species may be followed by the name of only one author, as in the examples above, or there may be more than one. In some cases there will be two names or abbreviations because of joint authorship, e.g. Bentham & Hooker, but in others one name appears in parentheses and another (or more than one) follows, e.g. *Ferocactus acanthodes* (Lemaire) Britton & Rose. In such cases, the author whose name appears in parentheses supplied the epithet for the species (here, *acanthodes*) but in a different name combination (in this instance, *Echinocactus acanthodes* Lemaire). The later authors, Britton and Rose, published the name now accepted for the plant, *Ferocactus acanthodes*, recombining the original epithet under another genus.

Authors' names or their abbreviations are really brief literature references. If the genus, the species, and the author's name, for example *Cactus ferox* Willd., are known, the *Index Kewensis* or the *Gray Herbarium Card Index* will provide the rest of the reference to the original place of publication of the name of the taxon, and usually this provides the information needed for determination of the *type specimen*. Type specimens do not appear in the older literature, but often there is information facilitating the choice of a substitute (lectotype or neotype). In the recent literature, internationally sanctioned practice requires that a type specimen be designated, and this is accompanied by an indication of the place of collection or *type locality*. Study of plants growing in the type locality reveals the nature of the population of which the plant was a part, and study in different areas may show whether the described taxon really is segregated from others.

Variety. On the next line of the label, "var."

Herbarium of Pomona College

var...

State.. County...

Locality..

....

Mt. range..Alt..................................

Drainage area...

Soil..

Floristic association..

Slope...Date...............................19...........

Collector..No................................

....

Fig. 96. Example of a specimen label designed to include the usual data needed for a plant specimen, for use either at the time the specimen is identified or later, as the basis for research. Here, the data entered are those corresponding to the numbered record of one of the plants recorded in the field book in Fig. 97. Many specimens collected for the purposes of the collector are later deposited in large herbaria, where they become part of the data used in botanical research; the data required by this label make the specimen much more valuable for such ultimate purposes. (In the context of this book, the wording of one item should be changed: for "Veg. type" read "Floristic Association"; see Chapter 10.)

stands for *varietas* or "variety." The required author references parallel those discussed above. The transfer of a variety from one species to another or of a species to varietal status or the reverse results in similar citation of the names of both the original publishing author and the author who transferred the epithet to its present combination. For example, *Mammillaria desertii* Engelm. was the basis for *Coryphantha vivipara* (Nuttall) Britton & Rose var. *desertii* (Engelm.) W. T. Marshall.

State, county, and locality. The next three parts of the label relate to the place of collection, and the data entered opposite "locality" should be specific and linked to an unchanging geographic feature. This may be a valley or a mountain or an established town (i.e. a town not dependent on an unstable income like that from a mine, and therefore prone ultimately to a ghost-town fate). Ordinarily the collection locality is an undistinguished point in a broad area, and it should therefore be linked by a measurement of distance to the nearest stable and easily located reference point.

Mountain range. The mountain range is important not only as a permanent geographic feature but also as research information in its own right. The flora of a mountain differs from that of surrounding valleys and often from that of other mountain ranges, especially those composed of different rocks. Thus, occurrence in a particular mountain range may indicate certain ecological relationships of a taxon, and this may provide evidence bearing upon the general geographical distribution and ecology of its members. Ecologically, mountain ranges are like islands in the sky, and many of them support endemic species developed in isolation.

Altitude. The zonation of plants according to altitude in the mountains is of major significance. Less than 10 airline miles (16 km) from the low-lying Colorado Desert at Palm Springs, the summit of Mt. San Jacinto rises to 10,805 feet (3,266 m) elevation. Within this local 10,000-foot (3,023 m) range of altitude there are three obvious floristic associations, each composing an obvious zone of vegetation, and few species overlap these divisions through a significant altitudinal range. During a summer day at Palm Springs the temperature may reach 43-49°C (110-120°F), but on Mt. San Jacinto only 18-24°C (65-75°F). During the winter, Palm Springs may be at 7°C (45°F) and Mt. San Jacinto at −18°C (0°F). Thus, the occurrence of species includes correlation with altitude as well as with localities and general ranges of distribution.

Drainage area. The two sides of a mountain

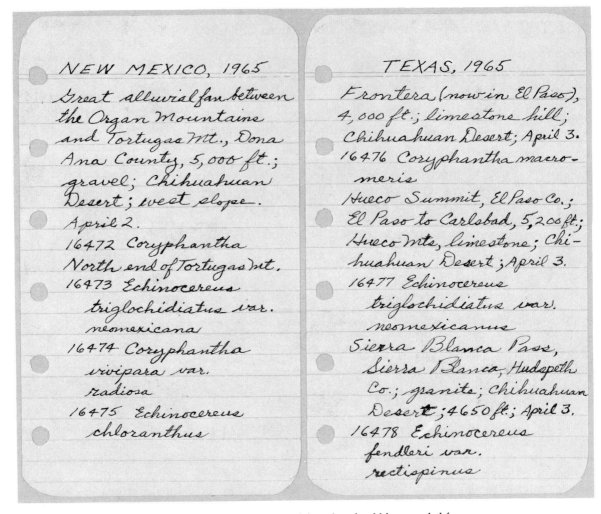

NEW MEXICO, 1965

Great alluvial fan between the Organ Mountains and Tortugas Mt., Dona Ana County, 5,000 ft.; gravel; Chihuahuan Desert; west slope. April 2.
16472 Coryphantha
North end of Tortugas Mt.
16473 Echinocereus triglochidiatus var. neomexicana
16474 Coryphantha vivipara var. radiosa
16475 Echinocereus chloranthus

TEXAS, 1965

Frontera (now in El Paso), 4,000 ft.; limestone hill; Chihuahuan Desert; April 3.
16476 Coryphantha macromeris
Hueco Summit, El Paso Co.; El Paso to Carlsbad, 5,200 ft.; Hueco Mts., limestone; Chihuahuan Desert; April 3.
16477 Echinocereus triglochidiatus var. neomexicanus
Sierra Blanca Pass, Sierra Blanca, Hudspeth Co.; granite; Chihuahuan Desert; 4650 ft.; April 3.
16478 Echinocereus fendleri var. rectispinus

Fig. 97. Pages of a field record book, indicating the types of data that should be recorded for each specimen collected in the field. Specimens are numbered serially. The specimen label resulting from one of the records here is shown in Fig. 96. Provided that at least the key points are recorded, some other items may be added readily from maps or other sources, and these may or may not be recorded in the field book.

range may have great environmental differences. The drainage area on one side of the range may be wet if it is upwind and toward the ocean; the area on the leeward side away from the ocean may be dry (Figs. 127, 195). For example, at Vancouver, just west of the high mountains of southern British Columbia, the average rainfall is several times as great as that on the eastern side of the mountains near Okanagan Lake. For this reason the floristic associations on the two sides of the range are far different—Pacific Lowland Forest on the west and patches of Sagebrush Desert on the east. Often these differences are implied by the "drainage area" appearing on the label. Vancouver is on the forested coastal drainage area of Puget Sound, and Okanagan Lake is on the drier inland drainage of the Columbia

River. Drainage areas are indicated by terms often designating regions of differing floras and vegetation, e.g. Atlantic Coastal Plain, Gulf Coastal Plain, Colorado River, Missouri River, Rio Grande, San Joaquin Valley, Pacific Slope, Mojave Desert, Colorado Desert, Columbia Basin, Great Basin, Great Plains.

Soil. The data significant for the space marked "soil" vary according to the background of the collector. A soil chemist will use special terms unfamiliar to most botanists. Many botanists will record such terms as "clay," "sandy," "alluvial," "volcanic," "acid," "alkaline," "gypsum," "calcareous," "porous," "peat," "red," "fine," or "gravelly" soil. Any point that can be determined accurately should be recorded, and this should include derivation of the soil from some recognizable special kind of rock, such as basalt, granite, limestone, or serpentine, because many plants occur on soil arising from only one or a few rock types.

Floristic association. Data concerning floristic associations (see pp. 136-215) will vary with the background of the collector. For example, such locally equivalent terms as "brush" and "chaparral" will be adopted by different people. A specific designation for the floristic association is best, but names differ according to the various available systems of classification of floras or vegetation. Even if no system is known to the collector, a description in ordinary terms is helpful. Such a designation as "piney woods," "swamp forest," "hardwood forest," "north woods," "yellow-pine forest," "woodland," "brushland," "desert," "prairie," or "plains" may provide some of the information needed for research.

Slope. The occurrence of a plant on a north-facing or south-facing ("north" or "south") slope of a mountain may be as significant as a variation of 300-600 m (1,000-2,000 ft) in altitude. The south face is in the direct rays of the sun; the north is not. Hence, the temperature is markedly lower on the north slope, and evaporation is slower. The lush vegetation resulting from greater moisture retention produces more leaf mold and a better soil.

Number. The specimens of the collector are numbered serially. Many variations of numbering systems are possible, but the universal use of one system is more important than any improvement to be gained by devising an original system that others may not understand.

The common use of a serial field number is understood by all botanists. As it is collected in the field, each plant is given a number recorded in a notebook or "field book" (Fig. 97) with the essential data concerning the habitat. The plants of each collector are numbered consecutively, beginning with 1 and continuing from year to year without a break. The data for each locality in which specimens are collected on a given date need be entered in the field book only once, with the numbers of the specimens collected there following in a list that leaves room for the scientific name of each plant to be entered later, after the specimens have been identified. Duplicates of a specimen are given the same field number. Only the field number needs to be written on the newspaper sheet on which the plant is pressed; this number links the specimen with the data for the label. Because it is not duplicated, in the botanical literature this number facilitates reference to the specimens collected by an individual. For example, reference to *Rose 11741* is definitive, and it covers both the specimen retained by the collector and duplicate specimens sent elsewhere. A symbol following the field number indicates in the literature the herbarium in which the specimen has been examined, e.g. *NY* for New York Botanical Garden or *Mo* for Missouri Botanical Garden. A series of symbols indicates the presence of duplicate specimens in several herbaria. (See Documentation, following main text.)

Lack of data. In some instances a space on the label may be left blank for lack of information. Although all the data indicated on the sample label are useful, even previously collected specimens with labels bearing only the locality may be valuable. An experienced botanist familiar with the area of collection often may be able to provide much information beyond that on the label. For example, "Ft. Collins, Colorado," carries connotations concerning the floristic association of the Great Plains, and such information as the elevation of a flat area can be supplied from maps.

9. Geographic Distribution and the Environment

Not all the research for this book has been taxonomic; part of it has been concerned with plant distribution and with the relationships of species to the physical environment and to their neighbors, both plants and animals. Cactus research and the study of plant geography both began for the writer during the spring of 1929, with a transfer for one quarter from Stanford University to the University of Washington. In the main, the purpose of the transfer was to see another university and another part of the country, as well as the plants in the field, especially *Ranunculus*. The lowlands and the mountains of western Washington were far different in aspect and flora from most of California, though the lowland forests resemble the redwood belt of California. The eye-opener was a trip across the Cascades to central Washington on May 4 and 5. The country was Sagebrush Desert in full bloom, and there was a cactus in flower! The trip brought fascination with the cacti and with the contrasts of plant communities of vastly different sorts within a day's travel.

During the following years, trips to moist, cold places were associated with studies of *Ranunculus*, and travel to hot, dry places accompanied research on the Cactaceae. General fieldwork in all parts of North America and research on both groups of plants brought first-hand experience with a host of species of different environments, as did studies on other plant families. All of this work, however, brought dissatisfaction, as far as taxonomic purposes are concerned, with extant ecological systems for the classification of vegetation. For taxonomic studies, the composition of the flora and the tendency of certain species to occur in mutual association are of primary importance. Over the years, a system of classification has evolved, a system employing *floras* as basic units, with secondary groupings of subdivisions into *floristic associations*, which correspond locally with the various formations described by the ecologists—forests, woodlands, brushlands, grasslands, and deserts. However, these *ecological formations*, or *vegetation types*, occur around the world in broad climatic belts or zones, generally in both hemispheres, whereas the floras and floristic associations occur within one or more of these zones for only the distance the species composing them have been able to migrate. Across an ocean or other barrier, a formation such as rain forest resumes, but though it is of similar appearance it is developed from a different flora—most or all of its species derive from a different ancestral stock. This chapter is an elaboration of this principle and its application to the floras and floristic associations of North America and to the occurrence of cacti according to their environmental relationships.

The system of classification of floras and floristic associations set forth here is, in its present form, new. Earlier publications on the subject* were steps along the way in its development, and there have been many revisions as research proceeded, partly as this monograph on the cacti of the United States and Canada has been carried forward. The floristic associations, taken up systematically in Chapter 10, are an integral part of the book, and throughout the text each species or variety is related to its association or associations.

The cacti are specialized ecologically; most species are adapted to dry climates, many to deserts. However, some are able to live in almost any association of plant and animal species occurring in North America. This chapter is designed to define and describe the floras and floristic associations of North America and to present the basic relationships of the cacti to the floristic associations in which they occur. The chapter discusses the changing environmental factors that

---

*The following are earlier publications dealing with this subject: Benson, 1942, *The Relationship of Ranunculus to the North American Floras*; 1948, *A Treatise on the North American Ranunculi*; 1957b, *Plant Classification*; 1962, *Plant Taxonomy, Methods and Principles*; 1969, *The Cacti of Arizona*, ed. 3; 1969c, *The Native Cacti of California*.

have stimulated the evolution of both the floristic associations and the species within them, including cacti; and it explains the present geographical distribution of the species in the light of ecological relationships.

The Occurrence of Cacti in the Americas

The Cactaceae are at least essentially an American family occurring almost throughout the New World, from Peace River in northern Canada to Patagonia. They are native probably only in the Americas (see pp. 114-16), and "cactus country" occurs primarily in the Horse Latitudes,* the two belts of calm between the Temperate and Tropical zones. Primarily, cacti occur in deserts and adjacent dry areas, especially grasslands and woodlands, but some live in moist tropical or some temperate places. In southern Florida a few species occur even where the water table is within 10-20 cm (4-8 in) of the soil surface. Some species grow in the relatively moist eastern parts of the United States and Canada, but usually they are restricted to well-drained sandy or rocky soil. There are of course vast numbers of cactus species in Mexico, Central and South America, and the West Indies, their relationships often poorly understood.

In the deserts of southern Arizona the giant cactus or saguaro towers above all else, and large chollas and prickly pears are predominant among the shrubs and small trees of the desert floor and alluvial fans. To one with a northern background the landscape and the plants of the desert do not seem real or even possible. Yet they are characteristic of much of the Horse Latitudes, which occupy more than one-ninth of the latitudinal distance from pole to pole, and, because of the relatively large diameter of the Earth between 23° and 34°, much more than that fraction of the surface of the planet.

Cacti are known to be native in all the states except Hawaii, Alaska, Vermont, New Hampshire, and Maine. In Canada they occur in British Columbia, Alberta, Saskatchewan, Manitoba, and Ontario. They are most abundant in the desert or arid regions from southern California

*Such names as Horse Latitudes, Temperate Zone, Arctic Zone, and Tropical Zone are used formally with initial capitals, because they are part of the system of classification of climates and of floras presented in this chapter and the next. The origin of the term "horse latitudes" is unknown. Sailing vessels were becalmed there, and, according to speculation, seafarers were forced to heave overboard large animals like horses, because they consumed too much precious water.

across Arizona to New Mexico and central and southern Texas, but they are significant in the floras of Nevada, Utah, Colorado, and Florida and less so in the Columbia Basin, in the northern Rocky Mountains, and on the Great Plains (see Table 1). The most spectacular stands are on the low hills and mountain ranges of the deserts in southern Arizona; the plants are equally abundant but less conspicuous in the vicinity of the Rio Grande in southern New Mexico and Texas. In other states the number of species is smaller, but one or more taxa may be abundant. In Hawaii, where there are no native cacti, a few introduced species have escaped from cultivation; the spiny form of the Indian fig, *Opuntia ficus-indica,* is conspicuous on the dry southwestern sides of the islands.

A few cacti occur far to the northward. Along the northern fringe of its range, *Opuntia fragilis* grows on sand and rocks about northern Puget Sound in British Columbia and Washington, near the 150 Mile House on the Caribou Highway in British Columbia, along Peace River in far northeastern British Columbia and northwestern Alberta, on plains and hills in Saskatchewan, near Lake of the Woods in Manitoba, and near Kaladar in eastern Ontario. The range of *O. polyacantha* extends into the southern halves of Alberta and Saskatchewan. *O. humifusa,* almost alone, occurs across the Middle West and the East as far north as Wisconsin, southernmost Ontario, and the coast of Massachusetts. *Opuntia erinacea* var. *columbiana* is endemic in the Columbia Basin. *Pediocactus simpsonii* var. *robustior* grows in eastern Washington, eastern Oregon, southern Idaho, and northwestern Nevada. *Coryphantha vivipara* var. *vivipara* and *C. missouriensis* var. *missouriensis* extend northward as far as central Idaho and North Dakota, var. *vivipara* into Alberta. In the Rocky Mountains *Pediocactus simpsonii* var. *minor* ascends the mountains into grasslands (Rocky Mountain Parkland) and even into dry, open places in the Rocky Mountain Subalpine Forest (spruce-fir) up to 2,850 or even 3,300 m (9,500 or 11,000 ft). Of course, these species do not represent the evolutionary or ecological mainstream of the Cactaceae; they are types that have become specialized, particularly in resistance to cold.

In the continental United States, the species of cacti fall into the following major geographical groupings, which are nearly, though not wholly, mutually exclusive:

1. Coastal California.

TABLE I

Occurrence of Cacti in the Principal Cactus States and in Groups of Other States

The species and varieties occurring in the various states are listed under each genus by the numbers and letters assigned to them in the text Part II. Preceding each listing, the numbers of species and varieties are added to indicate the total number of taxa of that genus in that sta[?] e.g. "13 + 4 = 17". The number to the left of the plus sign stands for the species; the number to the right, for the varieties (beyond t[?] minimum number of one per species). The introduced taxa are indicated by a superscript above the number of native species or varieties, e[?] "$21^2 + 14^1 = 35^3$" (35 taxa, 3 introduced); in the listings beneath the state totals, introduced taxa are indicated by italic type.

GENUS	CANADA	PACIFIC NORTH-WEST[a]	CALIFORNIA	NORTHERN ROCKIES[b]	NEVADA	UTAH	COLORADO	NEW MEXICO
1. PERESKIA $0^2 + 0 = 0^2$								
2. OPUNTIA $44^6 + 54^1 = 98^7$	3 + 0 = 3 23a; 24a; 34a	3 + 0 = 3 23a; 24a; 26b	$19^2 + 16 = 35^2$ 1a, b; 2; 3a, b; 4a, b, c; 11; 13; 14a, b; 18; 19c(?), d; 22(?); 23b; 24a; 26a, c, d; 28a, b, e; 35a; 36a, b, c, d, e; 39e, f, i; 43; 44; 46; 47	5 + 1 = 6 23a, c; 24a; 26b; 34a; 35a	13 + 4 = 17 3a; 4a; 6b; 18; 19d; 22; 23a, b; 24a; 26a, c, d; 28a; 36e; 39e, f(?); 44	13 + 10 = 23 3a; 4a, d; 6a, b; 22; 23a, b, c, d; 24a; 26a, c, d; 27; 28a, d; 35a; 36e; 39a, e, f; 44	7 + 6 = 13 6a; 8a; 23a, b, c, d; 24a, b; 26a, d; 35a; 39a, e	$20^1 + 15 = 35^1$ 5b; 6a, c; 7; 8a; 1[?] 15; 17a; 19a; 20b; 23a, b, c, d; 24a, b 26a, d, e; 34a; 35a 38a, c, d, e; 39a, b, e, f, g; 40a[?] 46
3. SCHLUMBERGERA $0^1 + 0 = 0^1$								
4. RHIPSALIS $1 + 0 = 1$								
5. CEREUS $12^5 + 3^1 = 15^6$			2 + 0 = 2 2; 13					1 + 0 = 1 15a
6. ECHINOCEREUS $13^0 + 37^0 = 50^0$			2 + 6 = 8 1a, b; 7a, b, c, d, e, i	1 + 0 = 1 12a	2 + 3 = 5 1a, b; 7a, c, e	2 + 3 = 5 1a, b; 7e, f, g	4 + 2 = 6 1a, g, h; 4a; 11b; 12a	9 + 10 = 19 1a, c, d, g, h; 4a, [?] 5a; 8a, c; 9; 10a, [?] 11b, d; 12a, d; 13[?]
7. LOPHOPHORA $1 + 0 = 1$								
8. FEROCACTUS $6 + 3 = 9$			2 + 1 = 3 1a, b; 4		1 + 0 = 1 1b	1 + 0 = 1 1b		2 + 0 = 2 2; 5a
9. ECHINOCACTUS $4 + 2 = 6$			1 + 0 = 1 1a		1 + 1 = 2 1a, b	1 + 0 = 1 1b		2 + 0 = 2 2a; 3
10. SCLEROCACTUS $8 + 1 = 9$			1 + 0 = 1 8		2 + 0 = 2 4; 8	5 + 1 = 6 1; 3; 4; 5; 7a, b	3 + 1 = 4 1; 2; 7a, b	2 + 0 = 2 2; 7b
11. PEDIOCACTUS $7 + 3 = 10$		1 + 1 = 2 1a, c		1 + 0 = 1 1a	1 + 1 = 2 1a, c	2 + 1 = 3 1a, b; 5	1 + 1 = 2 1a, b	3 + 1 = 4 1a, b; 3; 7
12. EPITHELANTHA $2 + 0 = 2$								1 + 0 = 1 1
13. THELOCACTUS $1 + 1 = 2$								
14. NEOLLOYDIA $7 + 2 = 9$			1 + 0 = 1 7		1 + 0 = 1 7	1 + 0 = 1 7		1 + 1 = 2 5a, b
15. ANCISTROCACTUS $3 + 0 = 3$								1 + 0 = 1 3a
16. CORYPHANTHA $15 + 17 = 32$	1 + 0 = 1 4a	1 + 0 = 1 4a	1 + 2 = 3 4e, f, g	2 + 0 = 2 4a; 15a	1 + 2 = 3 4d, e, g	2 + 2 = 4 4a, d, e; 15b	2 + 1 = 3 4a, d; 15a	7 + 6 = 13 2a; 3a, b; 4a, b, c, 10a, c; 11a, b; 14;
17. ARIOCARPUS $1 + 0 = 1$								
18. MAMMILLARIA $13 + 5 = 18$			3 + 0 = 3 6; 8; 13		1 + 0 = 1 13	1 + 0 = 1 13		4 + 2 = 6 2a, c; 4; 10; 11a; 12a, b
ALL GENERA $138^{14} + 127^2 = 265^{16}$	4 + 0 = 4	5 + 1 = 6	$32^2 + 25 = 57^2$	9 + 1 = 10	23 + 11 = 34	28 + 17 = 45	17 + 11 = 28	$53^1 + 35 = 88^1$
STATE RANKING			4		6	5	7	3

[a]Washington, Oregon, northern Idaho
[b]Montana, Wyoming, and southern and eastern Idaho

ARIZONA	N. GREAT PLAINS[c]	OKLAHOMA	TEXAS	MIDWEST AND EAST	SOUTHERN STATES[d]	FLORIDA	HAWAII
						0[2] + 0 = 0[2] *1, 2*	
27 + 28 = 55 8a; 4a, b, d, e; 6a, b; 7; 8a; 9; 12a, b; 14b; 15; 16; 17b; 18; , b, c, d; 21; 22(?); 23a, b, c, d; b; 26a, c, d, e; 27; 28a, c, d, e; , b; 36b, e; 38a, b, c, d; d, e, f, h, i, j; 44	5 + 0 = 5 8a; 23a; 24a; 35a; 39e	10 + 2 = 12 5b; 8a; 15; 17a; 23a, d; 24a; 34a; 35a; 39b, e; 40a	19[1] + 19 = 38[1] 5a, b; 8a, b; 15; 17a; 19a; 20a, b; 23a, b, d; 24a; 25; 29; 32; 34a, c; 35a, b; 37; 38a, c, d, e; 39a, b, c, e, f; 40a, b, c, e; 41a, b; 45a, b; 46	4 + 0 = 4 23a; 24a; 34a; 35a;	5 + 2[1] = 7[1] 32; 34a, c; 35a; 40a, *d*(?); 41a, b	6[5] + 3 = 9[5] 30, 31; 32; *33*; 34a, b, c; 41a, b; *42*; *46*(?); 48; 49; *50*	0[3] + 0 = 0[3] *33; 42*(?); *46*
							0[1] + 0 = 0[1] *1*
						1 + 0 = 1 1	
5 + 1 = 6 2; 14; 15a, b; 17			4 + 0 = 4 6; 9(?); 15a; 16			4[3] + 2[1] = 6[4] 3a; 4a, b; 6; *7a, b; 8; 10*; 11a, b	0[2] + 0 = 0[2] *1; 5*
6 + 14 = 20 b(?), c, f, g, h; 4a, b; 5a, b, c; a, b, e, f, h; 10a, b, e	2 + 0 = 2 11a(?); 12a	2 + 1 = 3 11a, f; 12a	10 + 21 = 31 1a, c, d, e; 2a, b, c; 3; 4a, b; 8a, b, c, d; 9; 10b, c, d, e; 11a, b, c, d, e, f; 12a, b, c, d; 13a, b				
			1 + 0 = 1 1				
3 + 2 = 5 b, c; 2; 3			3 + 1 = 4 2; 5a				
2 + 1 = 3 b; 2b			3 + 0 = 3 2a; 3; 4				
3 + 1 = 4 7a, b							
6 + 1 = 7 ; 4; 5; 6a, b; 7	1 + 0 = 1 1a						
1 + 0 = 1			2 + 0 = 2 1; 2				
			1 + 1 = 2 1a, b				
3 + 1 = 4 a, b; 7			5 + 1 = 6 1; 2; 3; 4; 5a, b				
			3 + 0 = 3 1; 2; 3a				
5 + 7 = 12 4c, d, e, f, g; 9; 10a, c; b	2 + 1 = 3 4a; 15a, b	2 + 1 = 3 4a, b; 15b	14 + 8 = 22 1; 2a, b; 3a, b, c; 4a, b; 5; 6; 7a, b; 8a; 10a, b; 11a, b; 12a, b; 13; 14; 15c, d	1 + 0 = 1 4a	1 + 0 = 1 15b		
			1 + 0 = 1 1				
9 + 4 = 13 d; 4; 7; 8; 9; 10; 11a, b; b; 13		1 + 0 = 1 2a	7 + 2 = 9 1a; 2a, b, c; 3a; 4; 5; 11a; 12a				
70 + 60 = 130	10 + 1 = 11	15 + 4 = 19	73[1] + 53 = 126[1]	5 + 0 = 5	6 + 2[1] = 8[1]	11[10] + 5[1] = 16[11]	0[6] + 0 = 0[6]
2 (species), 1 (taxa)		8	1 (species), 2 (taxa)			9	

h and South Dakota, Nebraska, Kansas
pt Florida

113

2. The Inland Basins (Columbia Basin, Great Basin, and Colorado Basin) west of the Continental Divide.

3. The midcontinental plains and hills east of the Continental Divide, especially in southern New Mexico and in western and southern Texas.

4. Florida and the adjacent Gulf and Atlantic coasts.

The areas of greatest concentration of species are in Arizona and Texas. As shown in Table 1, 70 species are native in Arizona and 73 in Texas, but 60 additional varieties (beyond the nomenclaturally typical one in each species) occur in Arizona and only 53 in Texas. Thus, there are 130 native taxa in Arizona and 126 in Texas. The Arizona species include many that are large and spectacular, such as the saguaro, the organ pipe cactus, the senita, the big barrel cacti, the treelike chollas, and the large prickly pears.

The Occurrence of Cacti in the World

The occurrence of the single genus *Rhipsalis* (Fig. 98) in the Old World tropics in Africa, Madagascar, and Ceylon (Sri Lanka) has been explained in terms of three possibilities: (1) *persistence* since the Mesozoic Era, when South America and Africa were probably parts of a single continent, Gondwanaland (or an earlier all-inclusive continent, Pangaea); (2) *pre-Columbian introduction,* at an unknown time during the Cenozoic Era, by some method of natural long-distance dispersal; (3) *post-Columbian introduction* by man. When data are few, theories are numerous.

Persistence. This postulate depends on the theory of continental drift (advocated by Camp, 1948) and plate tectonics. Recently this theory has moved from the realm of speculation to become an apparently sound explanation of many of the geographical-distribution problems relating to living organisms. According to new evidence, South America and Africa have been wedged apart during the last 160 million years by an upward movement of molten rock through a fissure along the underwater Midatlantic Ridge. Movement of 1-10 cm (up to 4 inches) a year is indicated by: (1) the matching contours of the opposite coastlines and the similar fossil beds on and near the two shores of the Atlantic; (2) a gradient from newer and thinner to older and thicker deposits of sediments on the ocean floor from the ridge toward each continent; (3) the mirror-image series of magnetic patterns in the lava deposits from the ridge to the two shores

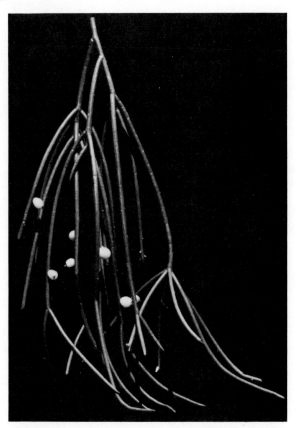

Fig. 98. *Rhipsalis baccifera* (long known as *R. cassutha*), a branch with fruits (small, white, very fleshy berries). The flexible, slender branches dangle from trees, forming dense clusters sometimes as much as 9 m (30 feet) long. The berries are eaten by birds, which deposit the seeds on tree branches and other objects where birds perch or roost.

(these being due to periodic reversals of the north and south poles of the Earth with consequent shifts in the orientations of the iron oxide particles in the lavas that cooled at different times); (4) the ages of volcanoes and volcanic remnants in the ocean, these being older and older from the ridge toward either shore; and (5) the presence of similar or the same plants and animals on the two continents.

If the genus *Rhipsalis* or an immediate forebear did occur in Gondwanaland before its separation into South America and Africa, and if the genus has persisted since Mesozoic time on both continents, one might expect the cacti present during the Mesozoic to have been near the evolutionary starting point of the Cactaceae, and the present members of the family to have diverged considerably on the two continents. Also, one would suppose that the living members of the family on both continents would include some less specialized types, and that some genera occurring on one continent and not on the other would be more specialized. However, *Rhipsalis* is a highly specialized genus, unlikely to have developed during the Mesozoic and certainly neither ancestral to the rest of the family nor even related closely to the ancestral stock. If the genus occurring in both hemispheres were *Pereskia* instead of *Rhipsalis*, persistence since the Mesozoic would be more plausible.

If *Rhipsalis* had occurred on both sides of the Atlantic Ocean for more than 100 million years, almost certainly the species on the separated continents would differ, if not the genus itself. Although eight Old World species of *Rhipsalis* had been named, in 1923 Britton and Rose recognized only one species occurring in Africa (on Mt. Kilimanjaro), two in Madagascar, and one in tropical Africa and Ceylon. They pointed out, furthermore, that after considerable study Roland-Gosselin (1912) had considered all four to be species also occurring in Latin America, and they accepted his interpretation. This interpretation still has not been revised.

Thus, continuous occupation of both continents by *Rhipsalis* since Mesozoic time is possible but unlikely. Introduction into the Old World is more plausible; the question is when and by what means.

Pre-Columbian introduction. If there was an ancient natural introduction, it must have resulted from one or more of the common means of long-distance dispersal of plants: by birds, wind, floating, or rafting. Let us examine each.

The fruits of *Rhipsalis* are small, fleshy, and mucilaginous, and commonly they are eaten by birds. Thus, the seeds may have been carried across the ocean in the digestive tracts or stuck to the bodies of migratory birds (Anthony, 1948). Most routes of bird migration are north-south rather than east-west, but others do occur. The Old World and the New World have been separated by a significant distance for millions of years, but as few as four successful flights could have sufficed to introduce four species from Latin America into Africa, Madagascar, and Ceylon. Transportation by birds is a somewhat plausible explanation, though there is no evidence that it is the correct one.

The species of plants dispersed by air currents are necessarily those with light, readily transported reproductive parts. The seeds of *Rhipsalis* are too large and heavy for this means of travel.

No information is available concerning the buoyancy of the branches, fruits, or seeds of *Rhip-* *salis* in salt water, or their resistance to it. However, transportation across such a distance by this means does not seem likely. Movement across short distances, e.g., between islands of the Caribbean and Florida, is more plausible.

Debris washed into the ocean by storms sometimes floats for a considerable distance as a raft before breaking up or sinking. The epiphytic plants of *Rhipsalis*, already attached to tree branches or trunks, could be carried readily, even above water, in this way. The distance across the Atlantic alone is great, and there are many buffeting waves, but *Rhipsalis* would be more likely than most plants to cling to a tree trunk or to its branches, above water. A warm ocean current of the Atlantic moves from the coast of Brazil to western Africa, but not to eastern Africa and beyond (Fig. 116).

Post-Columbian introduction. Recent transportation by a human agency is a clear possibility. Ship captains and other travelers of early days were fascinated by tropical plants, and they carried them to various places where they were introduced into horticulture. *Rhipsalis* is both a beautiful plant and a curiosity, as a succulent, leafless epiphyte living upon and dangling gracefully from tree branches, logs, or cliffs. It was among the first plants to capture the attention of explorers of the tropics.

Tropical climates around the world are enough alike that many cultivated plants have escaped and joined the native vegetation or competed with it and replaced it, especially in disturbed areas. For example, in the lowlands of Oahu, Hawaii, there are almost no native plants remaining (see Fig. 197). Migrants from other parts of the world, aided by human disturbance of the native species, have crowded out the original taxa and supplanted them. This is true in many parts of the tropics, especially those affected by agriculture, fire, lumbering, and overgrazing.

The principal species of *Rhipsalis* in the Old World is *R. baccifera,* occurring in tropical Africa and Ceylon (see Fig. 99). Since it is also the most widespread and abundant species in Latin America and the one universally cultivated, its escape from cultivation in two widely separated parts of the Eastern Hemisphere tropics, and its rapid dispersal there, seem likely. *R. baccifera* could have invaded disturbed areas or even native forests with ease. The small, fleshy, mucilaginous fruits of *Rhipsalis* are eaten or carried on the bills, shanks, feet, and feathers of nonmigratory as well as migratory birds, and the escape of this genus from cultivation to the surrounding forests is likely. There have been nearly five centuries during which this could have occurred.

The occurrence of *R. lindbergiana* only in the mountains of Rio de Janeiro Province in Brazil and on Mt. Kilimanjaro in equatorial East Africa is either a first-rate case of disjunct distribution or the result of introduction into East Africa by man. Occurrence in Africa far from the ocean and on the distant side of the continent is difficult to explain by the expected movements of migratory birds or water currents. More needs to be learned of the distribution of the species on Mt. Kilimanjaro, especially concerning altitude and nearness to human trails or habitations.

R. fasciculata and *R. prismatica* occur in Madagascar, and the Madagascar specimen of *R. fasciculata* seen by Britton and Rose differed from the Brazilian plant they examined only in having a few hairs in the areoles. This case, too, can be explained more readily by human introduction than by long-distance dispersal. Although Madagascar is an island in the ocean, it is far up the distant side of Africa from South America, and it is 115° of longitude from the nearest part of the American tropics. No ocean currents or bird-migration routes connect these places.

In summary, introduction of some kind is a better explanation of the presence of *Rhipsalis* in the Eastern Hemisphere than persistence as a relic since Mesozoic time. Natural or human-assisted migration may have occurred during either pre- or post-Columbian time, or there may have been separate introductions during both periods. Populations of *Rhipsalis* on both sides of the Atlantic must undergo a thorough taxonomic and ecological study before any firm conclusions can be reached. Herbarium research, extensive field studies, as well as experimental investigations are needed, because the species of the genus, and their interrelationships, are known only sketchily. Until more information permitting a precise classification of the taxa is available, ideas about the geographical distribution of *Rhipsalis* and its relationship to geographical history are mostly speculation.

The occurrence of *Rhipsalis* in the Old World, then, is not evidence of the origin of the Cactaceae in Pangaea, Gondwanaland, or Africa. Because there are no fossils, the only evidence of the place of origin of the cacti available is the current distribution of the genera and species, and their abundance in the Americas and probable absence as native plants in the Eastern Hemisphere indicate a New World origin. We cannot, however, rule out origin in Gondwanaland followed by extinction in the Old World and survival in the New, even though there is no evidence of this and none is likely to be found.

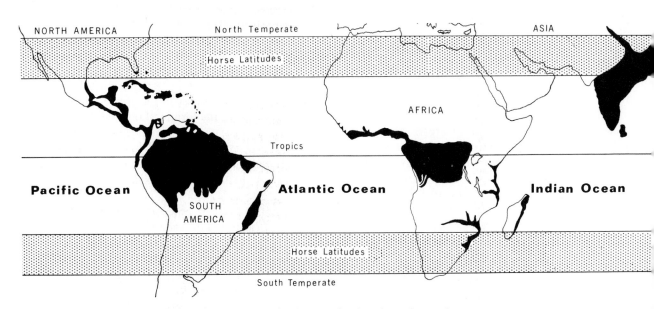

Fig. 99. Distribution of tropical rain forest (interpreted rather strictly, there being large adjacent areas transitional to woodland savanna). *Rhipsalis baccifera* is native throughout the tropical rain forests of the Americas and introduced or possibly native in Africa (areas undetermined) and Ceylon, or Sri Lanka; *R. lindbergiana* occurs also in tropical rain forests in the mountains of Rio de Janeiro Province of Brazil and on Mt. Kilimanjaro near the border of Kenya and Tanzania; *R. fasciculata* and *R. prismatica* occur in southeastern Brazil and in Madagascar.

Association of Organisms

Plants, like people, do not live alone, but associate with others of their kind and still others unlike them. An individual plant or its offspring cannot do well alone for long. There must be enough of its kind to compete with other species, to absorb the loss of some individuals while others survive, and to provide the genetic variability necessary to survival of at least some individuals when the climate and the environment change. Each species is affected directly by the physical factors of the environment, and it is interrelated with many other organisms. It benefits from some and competes with others in a complex ecological pattern.

One of the best examples of direct interdependence of species is that between the ant acacias and the acacia ants of tropical America (Janzen, 1966). The ants live in cavities they hollow out in the spines of the acacia (see Fig. 100). They are fierce in defense, driving away deer and other browsing animals, and they protect the plant from nibbling by various insects and even clear away all competing or fire-carrying plants from the ground beneath the tree. In return, the ant acacias produce nectars and special nutritious Beltian bodies on the leaflets, which the ants use as food. Without this species of acacia the ants would starve; without the acacia ants the acacia would be vulnerable to the browsing animals, to fire, and to competition. Similarly, there are countless close interrelationships of plants and animals in which a special food or shelter is exchanged for pollination.

Most plants are dependent upon other species of plants—for the humus necessary to the seedbed, for shade at all or critical stages of their life history, or for presenting a windbreak or a barrier to browsing or grazing animals. For example, the saguaro (*Cereus giganteus*) is restricted in occurrence to areas where the dead leaves of trees or shrubs and the stems and leaves of herbaceous plants provide sufficient humus to form a relatively rich water-retaining soil in which the saguaro seeds may germinate. Surrounding leafy plants protect the seedling from the intense rays of the desert sun and from the wind, reducing the rate of evaporation. As the young saguaro grows taller, it is likely to be successful only if there is a nurse tree or perhaps a rock providing shade and, for a time at least, some protection from the movements of large mammals (see Figs. 583-85).

Competition among plants is intense everywhere, both for light above ground and for water

and salts beneath the surface. This may be observed in any lawn of temperate regions, where such weeds as plantains, dandelions, clovers, and daisies shade out the grass with their broad leaves. Daisies (*Bellis perennis*) take over large areas by growing out a few centimeters or inches each year, covering the grass and shutting off the light (see Fig. 101). Underground, dandelions establish elaborate root systems not easily pulled up, and a new plant may develop from each remaining broken branch root. There the dandelions and other weeds compete with the grass for water and salts. The same relationships obtain in a forest, where some trees overtop others and kill them. When fir or spruce-fir forest in the high Sierra Nevada or the Rockies is burned, fir or spruce seedlings may not reappear for many decades or even a century or two. First come weeds, then lodgepole pines. The pine seedlings do well in the soil disturbed by the fire, as they do also along road embankments. The lodgepoles become fairly tall, and the trunks reach 3-6 dm (1-2 ft) in diameter. After a century or so, the soil is altered sufficiently that fir and spruce seedlings may grow in it, but pine seedlings cannot. In time, the other trees overtop the pines and shade out nearly all of them (see Fig. 102). When the fir and spruce canopy returns, many smaller species dependent on its shade and on the better character of the mature forest soil return to the association. Thus the aerial and subterranean environment in which plants live is dependent on a complex set of interlocking physical and biological factors. The lodgepole pine forest is a subclimax stage in secondary succession, as discussed below.

Succession occurs under the climatic conditions of an area: the floristic association and the vegetation type tend toward an ecological *climax*—a state in which there is a mature soil and in which the associated species of plants and animals can hold their own indefinitely, being replaced only by their own offspring and those of their associates in the climax. On bare new land, as in the wake of volcanic activity (Fig. 103) or on a new island arising in the ocean, the rocks, gravel, sand, or dust gradually will be covered by various organisms, at first by *pioneers* including algae, lichens, some ferns, and small seed plants. This pioneering may proceed slowly or rapidly, according to local conditions. For example, on one part of the dry side of the island of Hawaii, the footpaths worn across lava during hundreds of years of travel by barefooted natives are still bare, lacking even pio-

Fig. 100. Acacias inhabited by ants, to the mutual benefit of plant and animal. *a, Acacia collinsii* in a heavily grazed pasture in southeastern Nicaragua, the vegetation beneath the plant cleared away by ants living in the acacia, thus reducing competition from other plants and danger from fire. *b, A. cornigera,* two types of spines (*1, 2*) produced on the same tree, Veracruz, Mexico; the spines of the acacias are hollowed out and inhabited by acacia ants. *c, A. hindsii,* two types of spines on the same tree, Nayarit, Mexico. *d,* Bipinnate leaf of *A. hindsii. e, A. cornigera,* nectar gland with a raised border, at the summit of the petiole below the leaflets; from a seedling, the seeds from Guanacaste, Costa Rica. *f,* Same, a gland near the base of the petiole. *g,* Same, Beltian bodies on the tips of the secondary leaflets. Both the nectaries and the Beltian bodies are sources of food for the acacia ants. (Daniel H. Janzen; see Credits)

Fig. 101. A daisy, *Bellis perennis*, encroaching on the territory of the grasses in a lawn. The daisy spreads gradually, and its dense rosettes of basal leaves cover the grasses and shade them out.

Fig. 102. Lodgepole pine, *Pinus contorta* var. *latifolia*, forming a mature stand in the Pacific Subalpine Forest at Mammoth Lakes, Sierra Nevada, California, following a fire of perhaps a century ago. The young trees (with the storied or layered effect of leafy branches) are not lodgepole pine but red fir, *Abies magnifica*, the dominant tree of the climax forest of the area. The lodgepole pines, with trunks up to 6 dm (2 feet) in diameter, and their associates represent a subclimax in secondary succession following the fire.

119

Fig. 103. Formation of new land available for primary succession; in 1958 this area in the southeastern part of the "Big Island" of Hawaii was occupied by a village; when this picture was taken in 1961 a new mountain had arisen. A few remains of habitations flank the embattled tree in the foreground.

Fig. 104. Primary succession on relatively recent flows of rough lava (aa type) from Mauna Loa on the dry west coast of the Island of Hawaii, south of Kailua, in 1958: *above*, more recent flow not coated with lichens or other plants; *below*, older flow with a yellowish crust (white in the picture) of pioneer lichens. On the dry side of the island, succession is slow.

Fig. 105. Primary succession: plants on a 1959 aa lava flow on the wet southeastern part of the Island of Hawaii, in 1961; lichens and algae coating the rough rocks, and ferns already starting in the rock crevices.

neers (see Fig. 104). However, a few miles away on the wet side of the island, two years after an eruption in 1959 a thick cover of algae and lichens had begun developing on the lava flow, and there were ferns in the crevices of the rocks (Fig. 105). The pioneers alter the rocks chemically, contributing to their disintegration, and after death and decay they add humus to the incipient soil. In time, another set of plants, benefiting from effects of the pioneers, takes over the area, and another stage of succession, a *subclimax,* is reached and maintained for a time before giving way to one or more further subclimax stages, for which it has prepared the way. Some centuries or millennia after the advent of the pioneers, the end of the series, the *climax,* is reached, and it remains stable until the climate changes, the mountains are worn down by erosion, the land is denuded by glaciers (p. 142), or some temporary disturbance occurs.

Temporary disturbance results from a natural phenomenon like a flood or hurricane or light-

ning-set fires, or from the activities of man or his animals—man induces fires, or permits overgrazing. Ordinarily such a disturbance does not require repeating of the entire *succession,* from pioneers to climax. The process can begin farther along, because there is still soil with some humus. Usually some seeds and rhizomes or other underground parts of plants are present in the soil, or seeds or spores of climax or subclimax plants are blown or carried in from nearby. Succession beginning beyond the pioneer stage is called *secondary succession* (Figs. 106-8), and the slow reestablishment of a burned-over forest or an overgrazed hillside (Figs. 109 and 110) is of this type.

Because they are dependent on the same chemical and physical factors and upon each other for existence, some species of plants and associated animals tend to live together. For example, the saguaro (pp. 546-58; Figs. 569-85) and a host of other species require a particular type of desert

Fig. 106. Secondary succession, following fire in a Rocky Mountain Subalpine Forest at 2,550 m (8,500 feet) elevation on San Francisco Peaks, northern Arizona: dense stand of quaking aspen, *Populus tremuloides*, forming a subclimax on the site of an old fire; the volcanic soil retains much of the water from winter rain and snow, and growth is rapid; summer, the trees leafy.

Fig. 107. Secondary succession, a later stage than in Fig. 106, in the same area, at about 2,700 m (9,000 feet): young Colorado blue spruces, *Picea pungens*, and Engelmann spruces, *Picea engelmannii*, growing up under the aspens; winter, the aspens bare.

Fig. 108. Secondary succession, same area as Fig. 107: transition toward the climax Rocky Mountain Subalpine Forest of spruces and firs (as dominants); the spruces now overtopping and shading out the aspens.

122

Fig. 109. Overgrazing, interfering with the Arizona Desert climax vegetation and floristic association, east of Lukeville, near the Mexican boundary but on the Organ Pipe Cactus National Monument, Arizona, April 1972. The area behind the fence is a small exclosure for comparison of the effects of grazing and the lack of it in the Monument. The effect of overgrazing is obvious.

Fig. 110. Various degrees of overgrazing in Great Plains Grassland, near Miles City, Wyoming. The grass has disappeared from most of the area, though a little remains in the foreground and at left. Inside the fence, there is little but invading sagebrush, *Artemisia tridentata*, here a weed from the Great Basin. Outside the fence, in the distance at the left, there is sagebrush, but the ground between bushes has not been laid entirely bare and beaten to dust, as at the right. By careful management a similar area in Desert Grassland near Oracle, Pinal Co., Arizona, had been brought back to grassland when it was given to the University of Arizona about 1940.

climate with both winter and summer rain. For the saguaro the stored water from the winter rains promotes growth during the spring months, especially March and April, and flowering during the relatively dry month of May. Even during the extreme drought of June the stored water supply is sufficient for fruit and seed development. The thundershowers of July and August make the desert moist and green again, and because of the high temperature and moist soil a few of the thousands of seeds may germinate. The seedlings then grow if the humus and the shade provided by the other desert plants are adequate. Ultimately, the saguaro relies on a variety of desert animals for pollination—by day, the whitewing doves and various insects; by night, the bats and night-flying insects. In turn, because of its spines and its height, the giant cactus provides protection for many creatures. Woodpeckers and flickers drill holes in its high branches and nest there, and they are succeeded in the nest holes by other birds. The whitewing dove visits the flowers and later, during the early summer, lives on the fruits and seeds.

Where the Arizona Desert stops, so does the saguaro, because other ecological conditions are not right for it or for its associates. West of the Colorado River in California there are only a few saguaros, these on hills near the river. At this longitude, summer rain vanishes, and at the lower altitudes characteristic of the Colorado Desert of southeastern California the climate is very hot and dry. The extreme drought during July and August rules out the possibility of germination and growth of saguaro seeds and seedlings, as well as of those of other plants depending on summer rainfall. The area is desert, but not the right desert for the giant cactus or its associates; another association of desert species is at home there.

Floras, Floristic Associations, and Vegetation

A *historic natural flora* is a more or less stable unit of plants associated with each other (and with certain animals). Usually the species or their forerunners have remained together through a considerable amount of geologic time—for example, since Miocene or Pliocene time, though some floras are newer or still only incipient. Each flora is characterized and marked by a distinctive selection of native taxa, including varieties, species, and even genera endemic to the area occupied by the flora or its subdivisions.

The genetic makeup of each taxon in a flora is forever subject to change, especially so if the environment changes. Consequently, its relationship to physical and chemical ecological factors and to its associates may be altered with the passage of time and with trends of climatic change. For example, during the last million years (see Table 2), the north-temperate climate has shifted at least four times between cold, wet glacial periods and warmer and, on the whole, much drier interglacial times similar to the present. The last two thousand years have been relatively warm, and the preceding seven thousand warmer, but the long glacial period ending prior to them was much colder and wetter. With the coming of each new climatic period, the species associated in each flora have had to evolve or perish. As natural selection shifted one way or the other, each surviving species, or some of its members, adapted to the new environment. Consequently, the survivors in each association are not exactly like their forebears, though they retain some characters of their ancestry together with new ones or new combinations permitting persistence in the climate of the moment.

At any time, especially as the environment changes, some taxa associated with Flora A may leave the group (or simply extend their range), taking up new alliances in new habitats in Flora B; others may invade from floras B and C, in time becoming, perhaps, established or even dominant members of Flora A; and still others will fare poorly in the altered pattern of environment and competition, and will decline to extinction. No two taxa have identical ecological requirements. Those living together are evidently able to tolerate the present conditions, though any of them might be better adapted to a somewhat different environment if one were available. The taxa live together because their tolerances overlap. Some species or their ecological phases occur also in other floras, where they are able to adapt to the conditions of other communities.

Periods of disequilibrium do not necessarily conclude with the outright rejection of certain competitors. Members of different floras, brought into contact as conditions change, may *hybridize*, producing new gene combinations. Some of the offspring may be better adapted to the environment of the time and place than either parent, or they may survive in an environment intermediate between those of the hybridizing species, or in that of one or both ancestors. Sometimes the new assortments of genes are augmented by gene mutations.

During the Pleistocene (p. 142 and Table 2), all living organisms migrated on a grand scale. The oscillations of climate, not only near the ice sheets but also all through the temperate zones and to a lesser extent even into the tropics, kept taxa struggling for survival in changing environments. As the ecological conditions were altered, often species migrated to areas with new climates, climates that either were somewhat like the climates to which they had been accustomed or were in other ways suitable for exploitation. These shifts brought taxa together under unstable conditions to which none were preadapted by long-continued natural selection. Consequently, hybrids, ordinarily at a disadvantage through lack of preselection in a stable environment, fared better in competition under these conditions than they would in a stabilized flora, and some of them replaced the parental species. This migration and mixing of taxa resulted in the alteration of floras, and often the changes were irreversible, even when the climatic trend was reversed.

The validity of historic floras as a part of the basis for classifying plant associations is derived from the fact that some members of each flora, or their modified descendants, do remain together through millions of years. As the environment changes, species must change, but those living in the same area encounter the same trend of ecological changes. If the various species are to persist, some of their adaptations must be essentially parallel; at least they must enable all of the species to cope with the same climate. This pressure tends to keep most of the association together, even though some members may survive through one combination of adaptive characters and others through different combinations.

Vegetation is composed of all the plants occurring in one place, regardless of the taxa included or of their relationships or history. The units of vegetation are *formations (ecological formations)* based upon the prevailing *form* of the plants in the community—thus forest, woodland, brushland or chaparral, grassland, desert. A formation of vegetation occurring in one part of the world may be ecologically similar to one in another, even though not one species, or even one genus, may be the same and some of the families may be different. The chaparral of California, for example, has counterparts in the Mediterranean countries, western Cape Province of South Africa,

Chile, and southwestern Australia, as well as on the high peaks above the trade winds in Hawaii. The dry climates of all these areas favor plants of similar form and adaptations to drought. However, none of the plant species living in any of these places has had an opportunity during more than 100 million years to move naturally from one chaparral region to another. Thus, even though—from the standpoint of ecological formations—the vegetations of two areas may seem interchangeable, it becomes apparent, upon inspection, that the species composition or floristic association of each is derived from its own distinct flora.

Because each flora tends to be restricted to a particular zone or region where it has developed, or to an adjacent one it has captured in the past, it tends to evolve into the ecological formations that are appropriate to the region. For example, the Southwestern Woodland Flora is historically an oak woodland, but today, although woodlands remain predominant, the area is also marked by derived chaparrals and grasslands. Under local conditions some plants in a woodland may be adaptable to occurrence in open places among the trees. As conditions change, the openings may enlarge until they form considerable areas of grassland, as in the numerous small, grassy openings in the California Oak Woodland of northern California. With change toward a drier climate, as occurred at the close of the Pleistocene, a new grassland vegetation may evolve. For example, the Pacific Grassland of the Sacramento and San Joaquin valleys is really a highly modified large, dry opening in the surrounding oak woodland on the moister hills around the combined valleys. Except for the invasion of a few species from other floras, the Pacific Grassland is a derivative of the same flora as the oak woodland.

Commonly a floristic association coincides with a part of an ecological formation, the two being identical through a certain geographical range. Within such an area the species composition and the formation tend to form a coherent unit. However, in a similar climate in an area remote and shielded by some geographic barrier like an ocean or a high mountain range, or even in an area of somewhat different climate, an equivalent vegetation formation may be expressed with different species of plants, often derived from a different flora and composing a different floristic association.

For ecological purposes, assemblages of plants

TABLE 2
Geologic Time

(Time approximate, indicated in millions of years before the present, myBP)

Era	Period	Epoch	Historical event, North America	Plants	Animals
CENOZOIC 70 myBP	Quaternary 1 (1-3?) myBP	Recent and Pleistocene (Separation not convincing) 1 (1-3?) myBP	Alteration of cold and wet glacial and warm and dry (or wet) interglacial periods; retreat of ice only 10,000 yBP, perhaps not permanent; migration of coniferous forests across volcanic Atlantic islands between North America and Europe no longer possible; rapid rise of western North American mountains	Continued dominance of flowering plants; migrations and countermigrations of floras and floristic associations according to climatic changes; consequent scrambling of genetic combinations and natural populations and rapid evolution of taxa and floristic units	Rise of man; extinction of most large mammals
	Tertiary 70myBP (Under an alternative system of classification, all before the Miocene is known as the Paleogene Period, and the Miocene to the present as the Neogene Period)	Pliocene 11 myBP	At 5.7 myBP, land connection of North and South America completed	Dominance of flowering plants; forerunners of present floras and floristic associations recognizable during the Miocene, but changed in many ways during ensuing epochs (see text) Lowland climates and floras of North America tending to be tropical or subtropical, Cretaceous through Oligocene; temperate climates and floras becoming predominant through area of United States and Canada during Miocene (Note: the ecological category "coniferous forest" constitutes one to five dominant conifer species plus hundreds of taxa of flowering plants)	Dominance of mammals, birds, and insects, the latter with more species than all other organisms together
		Miocene 25 myBP	Beginning of minor uplift of the Cascade–Sierra Nevada axis and of reconstitution of the Rocky Mountains		
		Oligocene 40 myBP	Rocky Mountains worn to a peneplane, through Oligocene and most of Miocene		
		Eocene 60 myBP	At 50 myBP, direct migration between North America and Europe still possible; South America separated from North America (Yucatan) by 3,000 km (1,860 mi)		
		Paleocene 70 myBP	Rocky Mountains uplifted from the Triassic through the Eocene (first generation)		

Throughout the Cenozoic, rainfall and snowfall have been reduced erratically in western North America, and summer rain has disappeared on the Pacific Coast and in the inland basins

Era	Period		Continents	Plants	Animals
MESOZOIC 250 myBP	Cretaceous 135 myBP	The epochs of the Mesozoic not significant to study of the present North American Floras, whose Cretaceous forerunners were only distant relatives	At 81 myBP, last direct migration of North American and European plants; opening of South Atlantic Ocean between South America and Africa	Ascendancy of flowering plants, the time of their origin during the Mesozoic debated	Ascendancy of mammals, birds, and insects; extinction of dinosaurs at end of period
	Jurassic 180 myBP		Continents beginning to separate; Laurasia (Eurasia and North America) divided from Gondwanaland (Southern Hemisphere continents) from the Mediterranean eastward	Dominance of cone-bearing trees, cycads, and other gymnosperms over spore-bearing vascular plants (pteridophytes)	Dominance of reptiles, including dinosaurs
	Triassic 250 myBP		Pangaea includes all the present continents and large islands as one unit	Ascendancy of gymnosperms over pteridophytes	Maximum development of amphibians; rise of dinosaurs
PALEOZOIC 600 myBP	Six periods, but these not relevant to the modern floras	The epochs not significant for this work	Pangaea, but with changes over the continent	Predominance of pteridophytes (psilophytes, ferns, club mosses, and horsetails) and of early gymnosperms, mostly seed ferns and Cordaitales; preserved mostly in coal beds	Dominance of invertebrates, chordates, fishes, and amphibians; reptiles developing
PRECAMBRIAN	4.5 billion yBP; few organisms hard enough to leave fossils, but some soft ones leaving traces; the record meager				

usually are classified according to vegetation types (formations), but for taxonomic purposes a classification by floras and floristic associations is more useful in interpreting the nature and distinctions of species and varieties. The method of classification may shift in primary emphasis according to the objectives of the investigator.

The Relationship of Floras and Vegetation to World Climate

The primary distribution of the world's vegetation is determined by climatic zones around the Earth from west to east, and these zones are distributed chiefly according to the global, or planetary, winds and calms. Within each of these zones, differing floras, cut off from each other by oceans, tend to produce similar ecological formations around the world.

A prevailing climate and a corresponding formation occur at each level of latitude in the Northern or Southern Hemisphere. For example,

all the major deserts of the world (see Fig. 111) occur in or extend into the belt of calms known as the Horse Latitudes, between 23° and 34° north or south latitude. In the Northern Hemisphere, they are in North America, North Africa, and Asia; in the Southern Hemisphere, they are in South America, southern Africa (Fig. 112), and Australia. Although the deserts of these continents have a similar appearance, their vegetation is derived from different floras, with no overlap of species.

The climates of the different levels of latitude are determined, in broad outline, by the *global winds and calms,* patterns of air movement that are fundamental for sailing vessels and for the navigation of ships and planes. In botany, as indicated above, they are also of primary significance, because they determine the zones of climate and environment in which plants grow. The principal zones of the Earth are shown in Fig. 113.

The pattern of the global, or planetary, winds and of the calms is determined chiefly by unequal

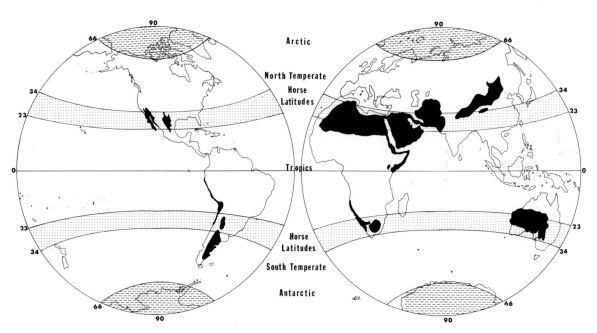

Fig. 111. The larger, drier deserts of the world, which tend to be in or near the Horse Latitudes. Some, as in the lee of the high Andes of South America, occur in the extreme rainshadows of temperate or tropical regions. In tropical South America, the deserts are west of the Andes, in the lee of the tradewinds; in southern South America, they are east of the same range, in the lee of the prevailing westerlies; and between the tropical and southern reaches, they are on both sides of the Andes, in the Horse Latitudes. Others, as in the tropics of Africa or South America, are affected wholly or partly by cold adjacent ocean currents, the land being nearly always warmer than the ocean and little moisture being deposited. The Gobi Desert in Asia extends northward to 50° latitude because it is cut off completely from warm water and consequent moisture-laden winds (a great land mass is westward, the Himalaya Mountains stand to the south, the Arctic is to the north, and the prevailing westerlies block any moisture otherwise available from the east). Lesser desert areas occur in rainshadows on the continents and oceanic islands; or on "desert islands," as in the Galápagos, surrounded by cold currents; or on islands on their headlands too low to lift the air mass passing over them.

Fig. 112. The Namib Desert in South West Africa (Namibia), the dry wash, or omuramba, of the Kahn River; the area closely resembles the more extreme deserts of the southwestern United States in both physiography and vegetation, but with not even one native plant species the same and with few of the same genera.

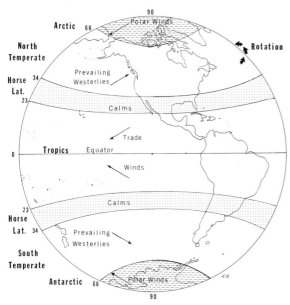

Fig. 113. The major wind systems and climatic zones of the Western Hemisphere. The Arctic and Antarctic zones are cold, and the dense air tends to expand and to form the polar winds radiating from the poles toward the equator. Air also moves toward both poles and the equator from the mass descending over the Horse Latitudes in the Northern and Southern hemispheres, the latitudes of calms. Each wind system is associated closely with the cold, intermediate, or hot climate of a major region. For deflection of the winds to the east or west, see Fig. 114.

solar heating of the atmosphere and of the surface of the Earth at different latitudes and at various altitudes. The direction of the winds is affected also by both the convection and subsidence of the air masses, the development of low or high pressures within them, and the direction of rotation of the Earth. The movement of the air masses is affected by seasonal factors based on tilting of the planet's axis, factors that are responsible for the extreme seasons near the poles and for seasons even at the *geographic equator*. There the *heat equator*, with its accompanying downpours of rain, passes twice each year, as the sun appears to go north and south.

In the Horse Latitudes, near the 30th parallel in either the Northern or Southern Hemisphere, the air mass is descending. As the atmosphere reaches lower altitudes, it comes under greater pressure from the air above; consequently, it becomes compressed and warmer, and its moisture-holding capacity increases. If the air descends over a large land mass, the area is likely to be a desert, because the tendency of the air is to take up rather than to deposit moisture. However, some areas in the Horse Latitudes are not deserts, especially if the land masses are small or maritime. In such cases the descending air encounters adjacent warm seas, absorbs moisture, and deposits this on the nearby land, as in Florida and along the Gulf Coast.

Because the descending air mass near the 30th parallel is under high pressure, it spreads out over the surface from the east-west zone of descent, some moving south and some north. Thus, in each hemisphere there is a constant flow of air—the *trade winds*—from the Horse Latitudes across the tropics toward the low-pressure area of warm, expanded air at the heat equator. The meeting of the two air streams, or trade winds, from the north and south forces the combined air mass upward, reinforcing the tendency of the light, warm air at the heat equator to rise through convection. The upward air movement replaces surface movement, and this results in the belt of *tropical calms,* or *doldrums.* Whenever air rises, the weight of the atmospheric mass still above it is reduced, and the ascending air, under lower pressure, expands and cools, losing some of its moisture-holding capacity. In the vicinity of the heat equator the warm, rising air is nearly saturated with water. Consequently, as the moisture condenses at higher altitudes, there is frequent heavy rain in that portion of the tropics.

Air movement from the two zones of the Horse Latitudes toward the equator is not directly from north to south or south to north. In both hemispheres it is deflected to the westward by the rotation of the Earth* (see Fig. 114). The circumference of the planet is about 24,000 (24,901) miles, and it rotates once in 24 hours; consequently any point on the equator moves eastward at about 1,000 miles an hour. (Metric measurements are 38,400 km and 1,600 kph.) If the air along the surface were not also moving, the effects would be disastrous. A 1,000-mph gale would be far more intense than any recorded wind velocity. Hurricane winds reach 160 mph (250 kph); tornado winds are stronger. Fortunately, the air mass at any given point on the Earth tends to assume about the same speed as the ground beneath it. However, air moving from one latitude to another encounters a new ground speed, and it is deflected according to whether the new rate of ground movement is faster or slower. Toward either pole the speed of rotation decreases in proportion to the lesser circumference of the Earth at higher latitudes, and as the pole is approached the rate of ground movement tends toward zero.

The air mass descending at or near the 30th

*The relative gain or loss of speed due to inertia of substances or bodies with respect to the Earth's surface is called the *Coriolis effect.*

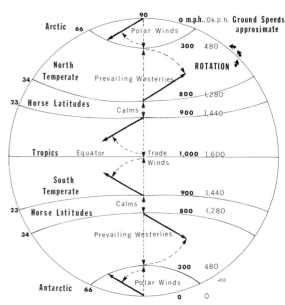

Fig. 114. Deflection of the winds by relative rotation speeds of the Earth (see also Fig. 115); rough approximations of rotation velocities (ground speeds) in miles per hour and km per hour are shown in the two right columns. The direction of wind deflection in various zones is indicated by arrows. Air moving toward the equator goes from an area where the ground speed of rotation is lesser to one where it is greater; thus the air mass tends to be left behind to the westward, and the wind is easterly (from the east; actually northeast or southeast, as with the trade winds). Air moving toward the poles moves from areas of greater ground speed to lesser; the air is thus deflected eastward because the air is moving faster than the ground beneath it, and the wind is westerly (more or less from the west).

parallel tends to assume the rotation speed of the Earth at that latitude—approximately 900 mph (1,440 kph). In both hemispheres the portion of the air mass moving toward the equator tends through inertia to be left behind to the westward by the increasingly rapid eastward motion of the land. For this reason the trade winds in the Northern Hemisphere blow more or less from northeast to southwest, and those in the Southern Hemisphere from southeast to northwest.

By contrast, the air masses moving poleward from the Horse Latitudes encounter lower surface speeds—only roughly 800 mph (1,280 kph) at the 40th parallel and 700 mph (1,120 kph) at the 48th. Because the relative speed of the incoming air exceeds that of the surface, the air moves eastward faster than the land or water beneath. This produces the *prevailing westerly winds,* blowing eastward and northward in the Northern Hemisphere. The wind velocity increases as the air mass moves northward, and the regions between 40° and 50° long have been known to sailors as the "roaring forties," especially in the Southern Hemisphere, where there is less interference from land and the winds are stronger.

The *polar winds* result from movement of air toward the equator from the high-pressure areas around either pole, where the cold, contracted air tends to expand. In the Northern Hemisphere, the air mass is deflected to the west as it moves southward, because it is moving from an area of less ground speed to one of greater. Through inertia, it is left behind. In the Northern Hemisphere the polar winds blow from northeast to southwest, in the Southern Hemisphere from southeast to northwest.

The deflection of the winds above the surface of the Earth occurs also at higher altitudes, affecting, for example, the *jet streams*. A similar de-

flection produces a westward or eastward movement of the ocean currents. In all such instances the lag or forging ahead of the gas or liquid occurs because its speed is different from that of the ground or sea bottom over which it is traveling.

The three great wind systems in each hemisphere correspond to the surface positions of three idealized lower-atmosphere circulation systems or cells—the *tradewind* or *Hadley cell*, the *midlatitude* or *Ferrel cell*, and the *polar cell* (see Fig. 115). In the tradewind cell of the Northern Hemisphere tropics, the air from the Horse Latitudes moves toward the heat equator, then rises to 16-19 km (10-12 mi) and moves northward at about that level. Finally it descends over the Horse Latitudes, completing the cycle. In the midlatitude cell, the zone of prevailing westerlies,

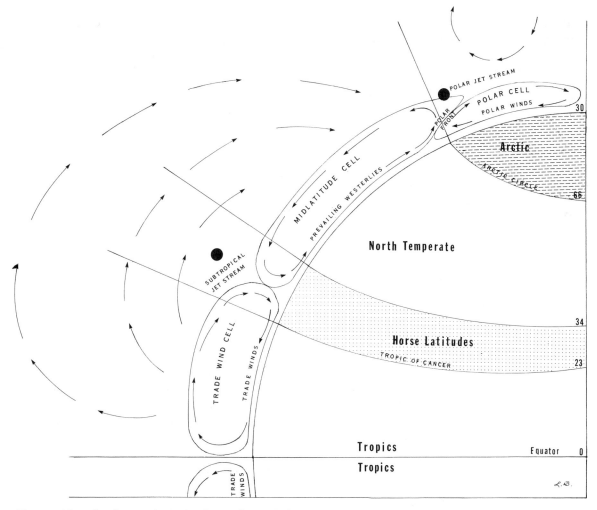

Fig. 115. The cells of atmospheric circulation above a little more than one-fourth the surface of the Earth, showing the circulation of air within cells above major climatic zones. In the diagram only the movements to north or south are shown; deflection of each surface wind eastward or westward is shown in Fig. 114.

the air moves northeastward to about 50° north latitude, then rises at a low angle, overlying the southern part of the cold polar cell through a meandering belt known as the *polar front*. The air of the midlatitude cell rises to about 16 km (10 mi), where it moves southward to the Horse Latitudes and descends. The air of the northern polar cell moves along the surface toward the southwest, then returns to the north at a higher level (up to 10 km, or 6 mi), where it descends.

The slanting layer of the polar front is the site of great disturbance, because the warm air moving from the southwest and the cold air coming from the northeast meet. At higher levels above the turbulent belt of contact, the *polar jet stream* is generated. The presence of this narrow, intense current of air at the upper level of the midlatitude cell above the polar front was calculated mathematically during World War II from data based on the gradient of temperature relationships of the atmospheric masses and the expected deflection of the air mass to the westward. Soon afterward the actual existence of the winds was demonstrated by the difficulties of flying United States military planes from the Marianas westward toward Japan in the face of the jet stream. The energy causing the polar jet stream comes from the eddies or cyclones (not tornados) and anticyclones along the polar front, and the stream is associated with the rising of warm air and the sinking of cold air in the cyclones or storm centers of middle latitudes.

In the Northern Hemisphere, the *subtropical jet stream* flows northeastward above the area of atmospheric subsidence in the Horse Latitudes. Its direction is determined by the northward movement of the upper air of the trade-wind cell and deflection westward as the air moves poleward. The two jet streams are inconsistent in occurrence around the world, and they meander, at times merging in some places. Thus, the polar jet stream is associated with turbulence and storms beneath, but ordinarily the subtropical jet stream is connected with the fair weather of the Horse Latitudes.

Effects of Water and Land Masses on Patterns of Climate

The broad outline of world weather patterns given in the discussion above is essential background for an understanding of the distribution of plants, but it is oversimplified. The areas of land and sea, the altitudes of the land masses, and the unequal heating and cooling determined by the types of surface of various regions may deflect the global winds or modify their local effects.

The Earth is not a simple, perfect sphere with a smooth surface, or even one covered wholly by water; continents and large islands modify the climates of all zones. Because the surface varies, there is unequal heating and cooling, not only at different latitudes but also according to surface type. Heat from the sun penetrates much farther into the transparent water of the oceans than into land, and diffusion and water currents carry the heat to lower levels. Thus, heat does not accumulate at the surface. Consequently, and because more heat is required to raise the temperature of water than to raise that of any other substance, the oceans remain relatively cool during the summer. At the same time the land becomes hot, because solar heat cannot be absorbed deeply, and the temperature at and near the surface builds up, except for radiation at night. During the winter, the ocean does not cool rapidly, because water requires more heat loss in lowering its temperature than does any other substance, and because circulation of water tends to stabilize the temperature of the great oceanic mass.

The pattern of ocean currents modifies the climatic zones by carrying warm or cold water into different parts of the zones and from one zone to another. The forces resulting in ocean currents are (1) winds, (2) the varying speeds of rotation of the surface of the Earth at different latitudes, and (3) vertical and horizontal differences in the density of the sea water. Through friction on the surface of the ocean, the global and local winds induce ocean currents that tend to be similar to the major air movements. Ocean currents are deflected to the west or east in the same way as the global winds. Water moving toward the equator moves also westward; water approaching the poles moves eastward, as well. Temperature differences due to evaporation, exposure of the upper water to the sun, and dilution of dissolved salts by rain or snow affect the density of sea water near the surface, making it different from that in the depths of the ocean. Because of differing density, there is overturning and redistributing of masses of water, producing vertical and also horizontal movement, and currents are induced at all levels. Thus, the ocean is not static, but a dynamic mass of moving water.

If all the world were ocean, the currents would assume a pattern based on the factors discussed above, and their major movements would parallel more or less those of the planetary winds. However, the continents and large islands are barriers deflecting the currents and containing them within oceans or parts of oceans (see Fig 116). The climates of the land masses are affected according to the temperatures of the adjacent oceans and their currents or to upwellings of cold water. The temperature of the adjacent water has a stabilizing influence on the climate of the land, reducing the severity of both winter and summer. Because, also, winds blowing across water absorb moisture (the warmer the water the greater the quantity), an area downwind from a warm ocean current tends to be both warm and moist. For example, currents continuing the Gulf Stream from the American tropics carry warm water to the European coast, and the prevailing westerlies transfer heat and moisture to the land. Consequently, even the Scandinavian Peninsula is much warmer than the corresponding latitude in eastern North America, which is upwind from the ocean. Similar currents bring warm water from tropical eastern Asia to western North America.

Even a warm wind moistened as it blows across a warm sea will not necessarily relinquish water over the land. On the coast of California, rain occurs in the lowlands only during the winter when the land is colder than the ocean and the moisture of the prevailing westerlies is precipitated. During the summer the land is warmer than the ocean, and no rain falls. For the same reason a similar winter-wet, summer-dry climate occurs also at the equatorial edge of the temperate zone along the Mediterranean Sea, in central Chile, in western Cape Province of South Africa, and in southwestern Australia. However, Curaçao, in the Caribbean off the Venezuelan coast, is in the path of the trade winds and within the tropics, but it receives so little rainfall that drinking water for 130,000 people must be obtained by desalting sea water, and there is no water for yards or gardens. The land surface is low, and it gives no lift to the trade winds, which usually blow across without precipitation. The entire island is dry, and cacti are abundant. Higher islands in the

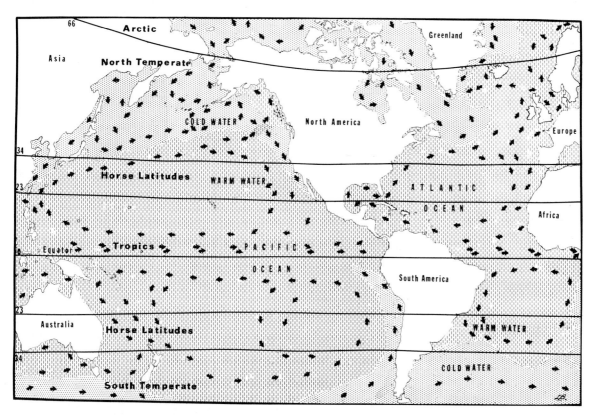

Fig. 116. Diagram of the ocean currents affecting North and South America. At each level of latitude, the currents are contained within the areas of ocean confined by continents and large islands. Areas of warm water centering about the equator are shown by vertical broken lines; those of cold water centering toward the poles are indicated by dots. The currents occur within the areas of temperature (in the Gulf of Alaska two currents cross, presumably the lighter warm current above and the heavier cold current below). The climate of the land is affected profoundly by the adjacent ocean currents, especially by those upwind.

Caribbean, like Jamaica and Puerto Rico, have abundant rainfall on their windward sides, because the air of the trade winds is elevated as it passes over. As it rises, the air expands, cools, and loses moisture. On the same islands or those of the Hawaiian Chain, the air descending on the leeward sides of the mountains is compressed and consequently warmed, and it tends to take up water instead of releasing it. The result is desiccation, and each island has a dry or desert side as well as a wet one. On continents like North or South America, where a short distance inland a major mountain chain runs north and south athwart a global wind like the prevailing westerlies, there is similar formation of deserts and dry grasslands in the lee of the mountains. The dry area downwind from a mountain is known as a *rain shadow* (see Figs. 127, 195).

Whenever an air mass rises in crossing over mountains, the precipitation is greater at higher altitudes on the windward sides of the mountains, because the moving air is forced to higher and higher levels. The only exception occurs on high volcanic islands like those of Hawaii, where the airstream divides below the narrow summit of each high volcanic cone and does not pass over the top, leaving it dry.

Because of interference with the normal movement of the global winds, deserts or arid areas may occur far north or south of the Horse Latitudes. In western North America, the Sagebrush Desert extends in the lee of the Cascade-Sierra Nevada mountain axis for 200 miles (320 km) north of the Canadian boundary to Thompson River. In South America the deserts of Argentina occur in the rain shadow of the Andes far south of the Horse Latitudes. There the Andes lie across the southeastward course of the prevailing westerlies; and the desert is therefore on the east.

Cold currents or upwelling of cold water near a shore in either the tropics or the Horse Latitudes may lead to the formation of deserts, or at least intensify the forces tending to produce deserts. The Namib Desert in South West Africa (or Namibia) continues well north of the Tropic of Capricorn partly because of cold water offshore, the land temperature being usually higher than the water temperature. The result is an extreme desert. Similar exceedingly dry deserts occur north of the Tropic of Capricorn along the western coast of South America adjacent to cold water, as they do also in Baja California in North America. Here there is, as well, a great rain shadow from the Andes, which run counter, at this latitude, to the trade winds blowing toward the northwest. Here the desert is on the west.

Thus, the major floral and vegetational zones and subordinate regions of the Earth, and hence the distributional patterns of taxa, are correlated with climates governed primarily by the global or planetary winds and calms. However, within each major climatic or vegetation zone local conditions may produce a great variety of climates, floristic associations, and vegetation formations.

The Cacti and the Major Climatic Zones

Like other plant groups, the Cactaceae are distributed according to the patterns of the global zones of winds and calms, but with only those of the Western Hemisphere. The cacti have not been able to cross the oceans; accordingly they are members of only the New World floras. Doubtless they could survive in the Old World, and in fact some chollas and prickly pears have escaped there from cultivation—as, probably, has *Rhipsalis* (p. 537). Some species of *Opuntia* have even become pests in a number of areas, notably in Australia and South Africa, where much time and money have been put into efforts to eradicate them. However, the niches in the ecological formations of the Eastern Hemisphere that might have been most favorable to cacti usually have been taken naturally by other families associated with Old World floras. Invasion by cacti usually has been in disturbed areas, where they are crowded out or crowded into a subclimax.

The following are the major climatic zones of North America, arranged according to the global winds and calms:

The Polar Winds and the Arctic Zone. Beyond timberline in the far north. The climate is matched in severity of the winters in the Alpine Areas above timberline in the mountains to the southward, and there is a relationship between the alpine and arctic species, as well as a similarity of the ecological formations. The Subarctic Zone occurs near but south of timberline in the far north in a belt transitional with the Temperate Zone. This is the great area of spruce-fir forest extending across central Alaska and covering much of Canada.

The Prevailing Westerlies and the Temperate Zone. A median band across the continent, including the southern edge of Canada and all but the southern fringe of the 48 contiguous states;

intermediate between the cold north and the hot south, but the local climates various and remarkably variable during the year. During the winter all areas have frost at times, and in some the temperature is far below freezing, often for long periods, preventing the occurrence of most tropical plants.

The Horse Latitudes and the Desert Zone. At lower altitudes on the great land masses in this zone there is a predisposition to formation of deserts. In both hemispheres the Desert Zone is the center of cactus distribution. In maritime areas, such as the Gulf Coast and Florida, deserts are not formed, because moisture is locally abundant.

The Trade Winds, the Tropical Calms, and the Torrid Zone. The tropical climate is moist, but there are wet and dry seasons according to the cycle of changing position of the heat equator or belt of convergence of the trade winds.

Special factors affecting the floras of North America within each climatic zone or included region are discussed in the next chapter, in conjunction with the description of particular floras and floristic associations.

10. The Floras and Floristic Associations of North America

In North America north of Mexico there are eight major *floras*, each composed of one or more subdivisions, or *floristic associations* (see Table 3). Each flora tends to dominate either an entire climatic zone or a large region within one. However, within each zone or region occupied *primarily* by one particular flora, there may be a representation of other floras in special habitats, as in the rain shadow of a mountain range or on the mountains themselves. For example, in Arizona between the desert north of Phoenix at 330 m elevation (1,082 ft) and the summit of the San Francisco Peaks at 3,557 m (11,670 ft), there are floristic associations characteristic of all the climates from the Horse Latitudes to the Alpine Areas. This occurs within a distance of only 160 km (100 mi) but in an altitudinal range of 3,227 m (10,588 ft). Usually, the prevailing flora is the one occurring at low to moderate elevations over most of a zone or region. However, the same flora may occur in some localities in other zones or regions, wherever the local climate is similar to that where the flora is dominant. Often this may be at a different altitude or in a different relationship to the mountains or the sea.

The North American floras and their subordinate floristic associations are listed in Table 3 (Hawaii is included because it is part of the United States), and they are correlated with the major climatic zones and their subdivisions occurring in North America north of Mexico. In the text following, each flora and floristic region is described, and each group of descriptions is accompanied by a brief characterization (in smaller type) of the climates affecting the flora and its subdivisions. In the descriptive text (Part II of this book), the description of each species and variety is followed by a statement of geographical distribution and of the relationship of the taxon to one or more floristic associations.

The lists of "marker species" under the floristic associations include only the woody plants, because these are present and readily visible during the whole year. Every association includes a far greater number of taxa of characteristic herbaceous plants, but these are present or evident during only the brief season favoring their growth. Most of the lists of marker species do not include the cacti, which are correlated separately in Table 4 (pp. 210-15) with the floristic associations. However, the cacti are listed in text in instances where they are of special importance, particularly if their presence is the chief evidence available supporting the status of a given floristic association within the classification of the units of the flora.

The material in Chapter 9 is essential background to what follows.

THE ARCTIC ZONE AND THE ALPINE AREAS
(Climatic Zones for Flora I)

The Arctic Zone lies north of timberline from Nome and the Brooks Range in Alaska to southern Hudson Bay and the Arctic and Atlantic oceans. The Alpine Areas occur above timberline in the western mountains from the Aleutian Islands and mainland Alaska south of the Brooks Range to California and New Mexico.

I. THE TUNDRA FLORA

Around the world in northern regions—beyond timberline in the far north and above timberline in the mountains of the temperate zone. **Markers:** numerous species of low-growing perennial herbs. The few woody plants are matted shrubs, such as dwarf willows (*Salix* spp.). (Fig. 117.)

The subdivisions of the flora of the tundra occur not only in the Arctic Zone but also at high altitudes in the Temperate Zone. In the areas of occurrence, the dominant factor is the winter climate, with its low temperature and high winds. However, there are great differences in other factors, and consequently the arctic and alpine manifestations of the Tundra Flora are different in many ways, though similar in others.

Winter cold, commonly accompanied by high

winds, is the factor binding the elements of the Tundra Flora together. All plants are low-growing, because tall species protruding above the snow would be unable to cope with the wind, and especially with the wind-driven ice particles, during the physiologically dry winter when all is frozen. The few plants with woody stems do not use them for support but for storage of food and water, and they lie flat on the tundra. Even though in the arctic day and night the sun appears to move constantly in a tilted circle above the horizon, the summer temperatures are only slightly above freezing, and the growing season lasts for only a month or six weeks. All the tundra plants are perennials; annuals would have no opportunity to complete their life cycles during one brief growing season.

In North America the Arctic Zone and the Alpine Areas are inhabited by phases of the Tundra Flora. The Arctic Tundra is circumpolar, and a clear division of American and Eurasian floristic associations is not possible. In the mountains of western North America a special floristic association, the West American Alpine Tundra, has de-

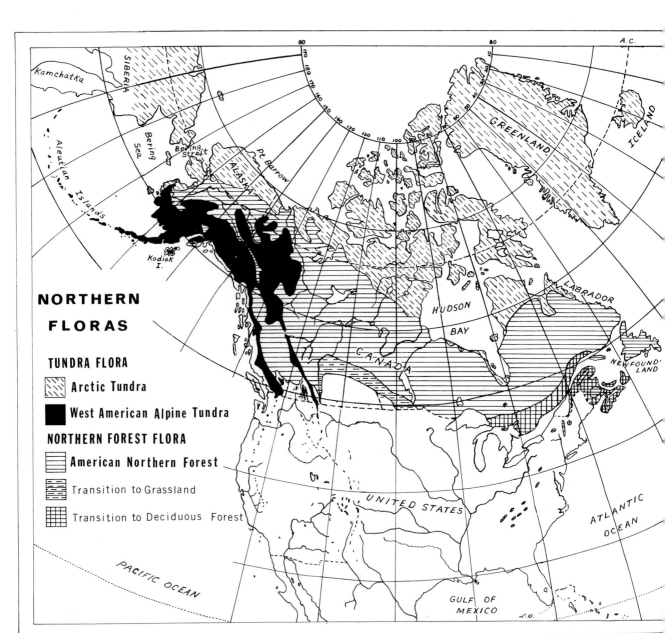

Fig. 117. Distribution of the northern floras, the Tundra Flora and the Northern Forest Flora, in North America. (From *Plant Classification*)

Fig. 118. Arctic Tundra: Southampton Island in the mouth (north end) of Hudson Bay, Canada. A densely sodded grassland supporting only perennials, few of which, like prostrate willows, are woody. Low stature is a protection from the wind-driven ice particles of the subzero winter. The conspicuous plant is a cotton grass, actually a sedge, *Eriophorum*.

veloped above timberline. The Eurasian alpine floristic associations are different but related; an extension of one of these occupies the western Aleutian Islands, extending there from Kamchatka in Siberia and intergrading with the West American Alpine Tundra extending westward from mainland Alaska. The alpine floras of New Zealand and South America bear little or no floristic relationship to those of the Northern Hemisphere. The African alpine floras are partly unique and partly allied to northern floras.

Cacti. Partly because of the severe cold, the Arctic Zone and the Alpine Tundra support no cacti. However, a few species occurring farther south are able to endure climates as cold or colder (see p. 143).

I.1. The Arctic Tundra

Beyond timberline near sea level and on the lower and the few high arctic mountains, such

The American Arctic Region
(Climatic Region for Association I.1)

The winter climate of the arctic is governed by the disappearance of the sun during most of the period (for three months at Point Barrow, Alaska) and by the consequent cold arctic air mass and the polar winds emanating from it. During the summer, the sun does not set for three months, and only parts of this period, when the temperature is just above freezing, are suitable for plant activity. The precipitation in the arctic is low—the average per year north of 75-80° is only 10 cm (4 in). If water were not retained by freezing until its release during the four to six weeks of the growing season, the arctic would be a desert.

as the Brooks Range in Alaska; on the mountains of the subarctic and of E North America as far s as Mt. Washington in New Hampshire. (Fig. 118.)

The winter cold rules out all but a relatively small number of well-adapted plants and animals—a few hundred in North America, others in Eurasia.

The Alpine Areas
(Climatic Region for Associations I.2 & I.3)
These areas occur, except in the Aleutian Islands, only at high altitudes on mountain summits and ridges, where the atmospheric blanket is thin and evaporation is rapid. Day and night lengths are those of the Temperate Region.

I.2. The West American Alpine Tundra

Mountains of w North America from Alaska to California, Arizona, and New Mexico; w Aleutian Islands. Above timberline at relatively low elevations in the subarctic and at higher elevations southward; 600 m (2,000 ft) in c Alaska; 1,500 m (5,000 ft) on Mt. Baker, Washington; 3,300 m (11,000 ft) in s California, Arizona, and New Mexico. (Figs. 119 and 120.)

The conditions under which the Tundra Flora of the Alpine Areas must grow are similar to those of the arctic in severity of the cold and wind, but they differ in other respects because of latitude and altitude. During the summer growing season, there is alternation of day and night,

limiting the flora to relatively short-day plants, and often the sunshine is intense because of the thin atmospheric blanket and the high angle of the sun. The total and daily ranges of temperature, slight in the arctic, are great in alpine areas of the southern mountains because of high insolation during the day and rapid radiation into the thin air cover at night. In the Alpine Areas there is much more ultraviolet light. At high altitudes the evaporation rate is high and the soil dries quickly, producing even desert conditions in some spots. (Fig. 121.)

I.3. The Siberian Alpine Tundra

Mountains of the Aleutian Islands mostly from Adak westward (a majority of the species on that island being of this floristic association, a minority from the Alaskan mainland). The association occurs down to the coast, but there it is diluted by a few subalpine or coastal species. Mountains of n Asia.

The Aleutian Islands are rain- and fog-drenched

Fig. 119. West American Alpine Tundra, an alpine meadow among cliffs; the Garden Wall near Logan Pass, Glacier National Park, Montana. The knife-edge at the right is an arrete resulting from the gouging of enormous back-to-back glaciers during the Pleistocene, the glaciation having ceased just before the thin wall might have crumbled. (From *Plant Taxonomy, Methods and Principles*)

Fig. 120. Timberline, transition from West American Alpine Tundra to Rocky Mountain Subalpine Forest; Glacier National Park near Logan Pass, Mt. Clements in the background. A small glacier stands against the mountain, showing its lateral moraine; stunted Engelmann spruce, *Picea engelmannii*, in the foreground.

Fig. 121 (*below*). Siberian Alpine Tundra, the thin layer characteristic of mountain tundra: here, freezing is not continuous through the year, as in the arctic, and some plant and animal remains decay; thus there is no build-up of organic matter beyond about 20 cm (8 inches) in depth. The upper layer is tundra composed of herbaceous perennials growing in a mixture of organic remains and some soil; below the tundra, volcanic ash and sand. The waterfall is the visible beginning of a little stream, covered over beyond this point by the overgrowth of tundra. The picture was taken in dense fog on Mt. Moffat, Adak, Aleutian Islands, with visibility only 3 m (10 feet); the stream was used as a guide in climbing the mountain, and the ascent necessarily stopped at this point.

through most of the year, and only the period from June until early August may include some "warm" days with the temperature at 4.5-9°C (40-50°F). However, the extreme cold and the snows of the arctic are not matched. Tundra does not accumulate to great depths, being mostly 2-3 dm (8-12 in) thick. Even the most evident species during the brief summer flowering season are of genera characteristic of mountain regions, e.g. *Lupinus* and *Anemone*.

THE SUBARCTIC ZONE
(Climatic Zone for Flora II)

The spruce-fir forest areas of extreme winter cold, south of timberline above and below the Actic Circle. Timberline marks the boundary between the Tundra Flora and the Northern Forest Flora, as well as between the Arctic Zone and the Subarctic Zone. According to topography and interference with the global winds, in the far north the Subarctic Zone ranges from 320 km (200+mi) south of timberline to several hundred kilometers south. Middle Alaska to much of Canada and the Atlantic coast; northeastern United States at some elevated points near the Canadian border; in modified form in the Appalachian chain.

As in the arctic, the climate is affected during the winter by the low angle and ultimately the almost complete disappearance of the sun. During the winter the cold polar continental air mass enlarges greatly, covering the entire Subarctic Zone and extending irregularly southward over the Temperate Zone. In the far north, precipitation is not great, and most of it is snow, which persists late into the time when spring or early summer occurs farther south. As in the arctic, permafrost is present, but usually the ground thaws in the upper 2-3 m (6-10 ft), whereas in the northernmost arctic land areas only a surface layer of 3-4 dm (12-16 in) thaws, as at Point Barrow, Alaska.

II. THE NORTHERN FOREST FLORA

The present flora of the forests of the far north (see Fig. 123) is not fully mature, and it is best seen as an incipient or developing flora. The forest present before the Pleistocene glacial periods was not necessarily like the present forest, but a forerunner of some sort must have been developing in the north during the long and gradual cooling and drying of the North American climate during the Tertiary Period. The subarctic forest of North America appears similar to the taiga of northern Eurasia, and doubtless both are derivatives of floras occurring on the great northern continent, Laurasia (a contemporary of Gondwanaland in the south). During Cretaceous and Cenozoic time North America and Eurasia have drifted slowly apart. The only stepping stones were volcanic. The related species of the northern forests of the two land masses have had a long, eventful, largely independent history, and they have evolved in different ways.

The coming of the Pleistocene ice sheets (see Fig. 122) was the great event in the history of the subarctic forests. The forerunner of the American Northern Forest was partly wiped out by the advance of the ice, and the surviving species were those able to move southward before the ice. The Pleistocene scenery in North America must have been magnificent. All the northern land was covered by a sheet of ice as much as 3.2 km (2 mi) thick, stretching from ocean to ocean and southward as far as the sites of Olympia, Washington; Flathead Lake, Montana; St. Louis; Cincinnati; and Long Island. As its own great weight caused the ice sheet to flow outward from the center, it scoured the plains and even enveloped mountains.

Whenever the ice melted, as it did four or more times, the plants and animals of the subarctic returned northward, each time migrating into the disturbed soil of areas otherwise devoid of plants. The species migrating northward were necessarily those capable of rapid movement and able to thrive on disturbed soil over permafrost in areas of severe winter climate. In both North America and Eurasia the species most likely to meet the requirements of the areas just freed from ice tended to be those previously in the north or their modified descendants. This circumstance preserved some similarity between the northern forests of the two hemispheres. However, on both land masses other plants have joined the migrations, and the species compositions of the two forests have diverged through both evolution of some included species and replacement of many others by invaders from other floras.

The number of plant species in the subarctic is small, and there are relatively few endemic species. Mobile species, like those of the northern forests, do not tend to be endemics of particular localities. For example, in *Ranunculus*, a genus with many species easily adaptable to the subarctic and with many endemics in both the Arctic and Alpine divisions of the Tundra Flora and in the Rocky Mountain Montane and Subalpine forests (Benson, 1942, 1962), there are no endemics in the American Northern Forest—only wide-ranging aquatic and marsh or stream-bank species distributed widely by waterfowl.

The present northern forests have developed under unstable conditions; at least in many areas, they have not reached a climax (see p. 121), and they are still in stages of succession. During the course of time, the present forest species, forming a subclimax, may be expected to be replaced at least to some extent by species able to travel less rapidly but better adapted to the subarctic environment.

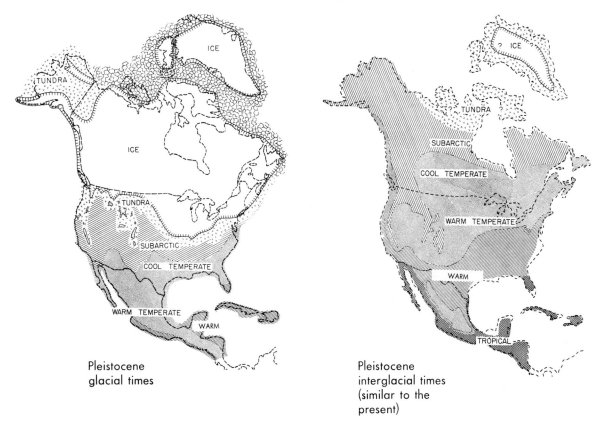

Pleistocene
glacial times

Pleistocene
interglacial times
(similar to the
present)

Fig. 122. Glacial and interglacial times during the Pleistocene: maps indicating in a generalized way the change of temperature during the 1 (to 3) billion years of the epoch. The ice sheet covering the area of Canada and the northern United States was up to 3.3 km (2 miles) thick. During the glacial periods, the temperatures were lower, the precipitation higher, south of the area under ice. (Erling Dorf, see Credits; also from *Plant Taxonomy, Methods and Principles*)

The instability of the Subarctic Zone is illustrated by great areas not yet fully recovered from the glaciations. For example, under the great weight of the ice, the ground level was lowered by hundreds of meters, and in places it is estimated that the surface has still about 270 m (850 ft) to rise. This would be enough to shrink the Gulf of St. Lawrence and almost to drain Hudson Bay. The rise of the land is tilting the Great Lakes about 3-5 dm (1-1.7 ft) per century. Thus, the hastily assembled hodgepodge of both transitory and permanent elements composing the northern forest is likely to undergo further modification.

II.1. The American Northern Forest

The northernmost forest belt, lying s of timberline from Matanuska Valley, Alaska, to Labrador and Newfoundland, curving s around s end of Hudson Bay. At low altitudes in the N and at relatively low elevations in the mountains to the s. **Markers:** white spruce, *Picea glauca*; black spruce, *P. mariana*; balsam fir, *Abies balsamea*;

black larch or tamarack, *Larix laricina*; white cedar, *Thuja occidentalis*. (Figs. 123 and 124.)

Cacti. A single species of cactus occurs in the far north under the rigorous conditions of the American Northern Forest, which is, as indicated above, still subclimax in ecological succession, occupying an area under ice until only about 10,000 years ago. The species is native in far northern British Columbia and Alberta along Peace River. It does not occur in the shade of the subclimax forest but in open places with rocky, gravelly, or sandy soil, where there is more sunshine and competing plants are fewer. Often the prickly pear occurs in areas of old river floods now in various early subclimax stages.

Certainly the presence of *Opuntia fragilis* only 4 degrees from the Arctic Circle is due in part to its ability to withstand cold, but other cacti not occurring so far north also can endure extreme low temperatures. This feat is accomplished by a number of species of cacti, in part by unknown physiological mechanisms and in part by virtue of various dissolved substances in the cell sap,

Fig. 123. American Northern Forest, from a boat on the Tanana River near Fairbanks, Alaska. The dominant forest tree is white spruce, *Picea glauca*.

Fig. 124. Same locality, showing succession in three stages on the river bank: climax spruce forest (white spruce, *Picea glauca*, predominating) in the background on areas not flooded recently; birches *(Betula)*, quaking aspen *(Populus tremuloides)*, and willows *(Salix)* on the less-stable middle ground; and young plants of the same species coming up in the recently flooded foreground above the bank.

144

Fig. 125. A prickly pear, *Opuntia littoralis* var. *martiniana*, at about 2,100 m (7,000 feet) elevation in northern Arizona, the snow beginning to melt. The blanket of snow protects northern and high-mountain cacti from the extreme low winter temperatures by excluding the much colder air and by retaining the heat of the ground and the heat from the low metabolism of the plant. (A. A. Nichol)

which yield a freezing point lower than that of water. An important factor is very low stature, and, in the northern prickly pears, during the approach of winter, the stems become flabby and lie almost flat against the ground. Thus, the plants are covered quickly by the snow, which forms a blanket protecting the stems from the lower temperature of the air and from the high winds of winter (Fig. 125). The low winter metabolism of the plant maintains a higher temperature inside the cells, and the low ratio of surface to volume reduces the heat exchange with the soil and snow. In this respect, *O. fragilis* must have a slight advantage over the other prickly pears, because the joints of the stem are proportionately much thicker than those in the other species, and consequently the ratio of surface to volume is reduced. At the same time, this thickness may be necessary, because the small size of the joints has the opposite effect, smaller objects having a greater ratio of surface to volume than larger ones.

A boyhood memory is of a Chautauqua lecture by Roald Amundsen, who, on the basis of his extensive travels in the arctic by dogsled, suggested that the lowest temperatures occurring in North America were not in the arctic, but in the dry continental interior where there is much more fluctuation than elsewhere. This includes the lower interior parts of British Columbia and the southern Yukon, Alberta, Saskatchewan, Manitoba, Ontario, eastern Montana, and the Dako-

tas. The lowest temperatures recorded for Canada, at least before 1977, were as follows: Snag, southwestern Yukon, –63°C (–81°F), the lowest for North America; Smith River, British Columbia, –59°C (–74°F); Fort Vermilion, Alberta, –61°C (–78°F); and Iroquois Falls, Ontario, –58°C (–73°F). The temperatures of the Northwest Territories of Canada and of the arctic do not reach these low minima. The lowest reading at Point Barrow, Alaska, the extreme northern tip of North America, is –49°C (–56°F). The lowest temperature recorded in the United States, –62°C (–80°F), was in the interior of Alaska farther south, at Prospect Creek. The lowest in the 48 contiguous states, –57°C (–70°F), was at Rogers Pass, Montana, at an elevation somewhat higher than that of the adjacent Great Plains. Thus, the region in which cacti occur in southern Canada and the northern edge of the United States is the site of almost the lowest minimum temperatures on the continent, and therefore cold alone cannot be the major limiting factor of the northern distribution of these species. However, both winters and summers with long-continued cold weather may produce marginal or submarginal habitats, as may dampness, which favors competing plants and restricts the cacti to well-drained soils.

Four native species of cacti occur commonly on the plains of Montana and North Dakota. These are represented by *Opuntia fragilis* var.

fragilis, O. polyacantha var. *polyacantha, Coryphantha vivipara* var. *vivipara,* and *C. missouriensis* var. *missouriensis.* Each is the northernmost variety of a wide-ranging variable species. Each is the nomenclaturally typical variety because it was part of a population named long before any other from collections by the hardy botanical collector Thomas Nuttall, who spent part of 1811 at Ft. Manuel Lisa (now Ft. Vanderburgh) on the Missouri River in North Dakota (Mitich & Benson, 1977; p. 7). Each of these plants is specialized in resistance to cold; other varieties of some of the species occur in cold areas in the mountains farther south and southwest.

All four species, in large numbers, have invaded the areas denuded by ice during the Pleistocene. As these areas proceed toward climax, certain slower-moving species become dominant, replacing some of those that had been in the vanguard as the ice retreated. Each of the cacti is relatively mobile and able to spread by seeds. The two prickly pears are members of a group with dry fruits rimmed by several subapical spirals of very sharp and strongly barbed spines. The fruits form little burs that readily attach to the skin or catch in the hair or fur of mammals, and thus they are carried for considerable distances. The two coryphanthas, or pincushion cacti, have smooth, fleshy fruits eaten by small mammals and birds that then distribute the undigested seeds. The fruits of *Coryphantha vivipara* are green and obscure and perhaps eaten by small mammals, which do not see color, but those of *C. missouriensis* are bright red, conspicuous, and attractive, and they are eaten by birds, which do see color. For example, obtaining a color photograph of *C. missouriensis* var. *missouriensis* in fruit for this book was delayed for several years because a plant to be photographed was left outdoors unguarded when the telephone rang. Just as the conversation ended, a house finch was making off with the last fruit. Thus, all four species are mobile through sexual reproduction, and this has facilitated the invasion of the nearer, southerly, glaciated areas.

The prickly pears have the added advantage of asexual reproduction by growth from detached vegetative joints, thus bypassing the difficulties—especially severe in a marginal habitat—of forming new plants from seeds. The flowering and fruiting processes require time, and they are restricted to a sequence of favorable seasons. Seeds must have a good seedbed and water at the right time for germination, and there must be more water soon afterward if the small and easily desiccated seedlings are to grow. The young plants are vulnerable not only to drought but also to the attacks of insects and larger animals. Few survive. At the same time, a prickly pear joint is already essentially an adult in being, containing a far larger reserve of water and food than does a seed, and a fully developed photosynthetic tissue, as well. An epidermis with a thick, waxy cuticle is a defense against drought, and the spines fend off mammals. The joint produces roots rapidly, and this occurs whether there is water or not, even on a joint placed on a shelf or in a paper bag.

For a plant advancing into a new habit of marginal suitability—in this case a relatively cold, wet area—vegetative reproduction is ideal, provided the sections of the stem are mobile. The joints of *Opuntia polyacantha* are medium-sized and firmly attached, and their spines are sharp but unbarbed. They are carried by animals, but less frequently than are those of *O. fragilis.* The joints in this species are very small, only 2-5 cm (mostly 1-2 in) long, and readily detached (hence the specific epithet), and their spines are effectively barbed. The joints of *O. fragilis* cling to animals in a way anyone who has walked through a patch of this cactus will remember, because the spines penetrate even heavy leather boots and they cannot be pulled out. The species is widespread in the United States, and from British Columbia to Ontario it occurs in the formerly glaciated country farther north than any other cactus.

The mobility of the joints probably is the chief reason for the occurrence of *Opuntia fragilis* farther north than its relatives. On the Great Plains of Alberta and Saskatchewan there were numerous large grazing mammals like deer, antelope, and bison, or buffalo. When these animals grazed or lay down in grass where *O. fragilis* grew, and then moved on, they must have carried away joints of the cactus, the joints clinging to their legs and bodies, or even to their muzzles, as so often happens with cattle today. The plains buffalo occurred in enormous herds, and their great hairy bodies would have been ideal for transporting the small cactus joints. The places where buffalo lay down probably included many plants of *O. fragilis.* According to Jack E. Schmautz, U.S. Forest Service (personal communication, 1976), the cactus is common at the edges of "slick spots" formed on solodized solonetz soils* in eastern Montana and western North Dakota. These areas, known as "buffalo wallows," may have been frequented by buffalo in the past, though this has not been proved. However, they are often good places to look for arrowheads, stone knives, and scrapers, and the presence of the artifacts has led to the inference that the spots were actually buffalo wallows.

The plains buffalo, *Bison bison bison,* did not occur in the far northern woods or in the forests of the Rocky Mountains, but it was replaced there by the wood buffalo, *B. bison athabascae.* The wood buffalo occurred even farther north than Peace River, into the present Northwest Territories, as at Wood Buffalo Park (where many of the animals now stocking the park are said to be hybrids of the two subspecies).

There is some indication that *Opuntia fragilis* depends wholly or largely on asexual reproduction in the north, and that this has favored an altered food economy. According to Larry W. Mitich (personal communication), the species flowers only sparingly in North Dakota. Elimination of sexual reproduction, if it is ineffective anyhow at that or higher latitudes, could conserve food, permitting its use in other ways.

Occurrence of Cacti Within the Temperate Zone

Cacti occur through nearly all of the temperate United States, but they are both abundant and varied mostly along the southern edge of the country near the Horse Latitudes, where there is warmth. The moist, cool lowlands of the temperate Pacific Coast support no cacti, with one exception: *Opuntia fragilis* occurs along northern Puget Sound in the rain shadows of the Olympic Mountains in Washington and the mountains of Vancouver Island, British Columbia. Otherwise, on the Pacific Slope the family is restricted to the southern San Joaquin Valley and southern California. Similarly, cacti are rare east of the Mississippi River. Except in the far south or near the

Great Lakes, there is only one species, *O. humifusa,* occurring in all the states of the area, except the three of northern New England. However, it is restricted to partly disturbed sand or to rocky areas, where excess water drains away rapidly and where most other plants do not compete well. The dry areas in the inland basins between the Cascade-Sierra Nevada Axis (p. 148) and the Rocky Mountains, in the Rockies, and on the Great Plains support a considerable number of species of Cactaceae, and often there are extensive populations. These species have adapted to severe winter cold, and, as with *O. fragilis* in the far north, some of the prickly pears tend to lose water, become limp, and flatten out on the ground during the winter, when often they are covered with snow. When spring comes they become turgid and upright again.

THE TEMPERATE ZONE
(Climatic Zone for Floras III through VI)

In North America, essentially the 48 contiguous states and most of the southern edge of Canada, but excluding the southern fringe of the United States, which is in the Horse Latitudes.

The Temperate Zone is characterized by climatic variability from day to day, season to season, and year to year. The changes during a single day may be greater than those during a whole year in the tropics. The prevailing westerlies carry air picked up under a variety of conditions from above hot or cold land or warm or cold ocean currents in the northern Horse Latitudes and in the Temperate Zone. The polar winds bring cold air from the north, especially from the arctic. The area of meeting of the winds is also the zone of contact of the Northern Hemisphere midlatitude cell and the polar cell. There the warmer air from the south overlies the colder air from the north along the polar front, and both are overlain by the polar jet stream and the great wavelike meanderings of the upper atmosphere. The ridges and troughs of the upper air of the zone of contact and of the Temperate Zone reflect the presence of warm and cold surface areas beneath, as well as the interference of the great mountain ranges with the wind system. The zone is one of great irregularity of atmospheric masses and of turbulence and disturbance, and the inconsistencies of climate arise from this condition.

Along the unstable polar front, low- and high-pressure areas form, and these move eastward. The swirling low-pressure areas, or cyclones, are composed of both warm and cold air, and they yield rain, snow, and wind. The low pressure in a cyclonic area promotes the movement of air inward from every direction, and the turbulent mass rises, expands, cools, and loses moisture. Many cyclones follow recognizable storm tracks from west to east, their frequency and strength fluctuating with the seasons. The anticyclones, or high-pressure areas, act in the opposite way, i.e., the air moves away from them in all directions along the surface, the sky clears, and the weather is fair.

The Temperate Zone includes four major climatic regions, each of these inhabited primarily by a different historic natural flora.

---

*A solonetz clay is high in sodium, and, because sodium clay is readily dispersible, ordinarily it would be transported to greater depth. However, the swelling of the clay when wet inhibits its movement downward, and the sodium-clay level is formed near the surface. If leaching is activated by decaying vegetation, the production of organic acids results in the movement of calcium from lower layers into the upper, and the calcium replaces the sodium. The soil then becomes a solod or planasol, with calcium clay near the surface. Where such a clay lies in a depression, the spot is likely to have been, at some time, a buffalo wallow.

The Western Temperate Region
(Climatic Region for Associations III.1 through III.7)

Moister areas of the valleys, plains, and lower mountains from south-central Alaska and the Yukon to the redwood belt of coastal northern California and the intermountain valleys of eastern British Columbia; at middle elevations in the mountains of the same area and at higher elevations through the 11 contiguous Western States and thence disjunctly to the Sierra San Pedro Martir, Baja California; the Black Hills, South Dakota; and the Chisos Mountains, western Texas.

The principal physiographic features of the western part of North America are two great mountain chains, the Cascade-Sierra Nevada Axis and the Rocky Mountain System (Fig. 126). Both mountain systems affect climate, but the effect of the axis near the coast is much greater. The Cascade-Sierra Nevada Axis stretches like a great stone wall from central coastal Alaska to Baja California. The part in Washington, Oregon, and California consists of (1) the volcanic Cascade Mountains, extending from just north of the Canadian border to Mt. Lassen in California; (2) the fault block of the Sierra Nevada, now worn away and exposing the underlying granite, ending at Walker Pass and in the Greenhorn Mountains in Kern County; (3) connecting granitic ranges in and just north of southern California —the Piute, Tehachapi, Liebre, San Gabriel, and San Bernardino mountains; and (4) the granitic Peninsular Ranges—the San Jacinto, Palomar, Cuyamaca, and Laguna mountains in southern California, these continuing into the Sierra San Pedro Martir and other ranges to the tip of Baja California. This great wall stands crosswise to the prevailing westerly winds, and it is the most important terrestrial physical feature affecting climate in the contiguous Western States. The Rocky Mountain System does not form a continuous axis; it is composed of many short ranges, mostly running parallel and more or less north-and-south and connecting with each other at various points. There are two major breaks, one across southern Wyoming and another across southeastern Arizona and southern New Mexico where the network of mountains levels out and the continental divide is difficult to find in the plains and hilly country.

Between the two great mountain systems there are four major basins, or more or less flat areas—the Columbia (River) Basin, the Columbia Plateau (essentially a basin), the Great Basin, and the Colorado (River) Basin. With one exception, each is drained by a major river system; the Great Basin has no outlet, and the present amount of excess water is contained in various playas, dry lakes, and a few like Walker Lake, Pyramid Lake, Great Salt Lake, Utah Lake, and Sevier Lake with water. The Columbia River and its tributary, the Snake River, drain both the Columbia Basin and the Columbia Plateau. The Colorado River flows through the Colorado Basin on its lower course, but nearly all of its water comes from the headwaters in the Rocky Mountains or, to some extent, from the Colorado Plateau (Fig. 126). The four basins will be referred to as the Inland Basins.

The Pacific Coast of North America is an area of summer drought and winter rain, and this climate occurs not only on the coast but also, in modified versions, inland. As explained earlier, during all seasons the prevailing westerly winds are moisture-laden from their passage over warm seas. However, during the summer the land along the coast is warmer than the ocean. Consequently, when the wind reaches the low coastal area, there is little or no precipitation. During the winter the land is generally colder than the ocean, and often there is rain then along the coastal lowlands.

As the prevailing westerlies move inland from the Pacific, they are deflected upward over the hills and mountains, especially those forming the Cascade-Sierra Nevada Axis (see Fig. 127). As the air mass rises there is heavy precipitation, during the winter, on the western sides and the summits of the mountains.

In the rain shadow east of the mountain axis, there are arid lands in the Inland Basins. Much of the area to the northward (the Columbia Basin and the Great Basin) is occupied by Sagebrush Desert (Southwestern Woodland Flora) and much to the southward by the creosote bush deserts (Mexican Desert Flora). The areas lying east of the lesser mountains near the coast, e.g. the Sacramento and San Joaquin valleys of California, also may be very dry.

The climate of the Rocky Mountains combines features of the weather of the Pacific Coast and the Inland Basins with that of the Eastern Temperate Region (p. 160). The prevailing westerly air mass is given another lift in passing over the Rockies, but by then the air is often drier. However, winter storms pass along a storm track over the northern Cascades into the northern part of the Columbia Basin and then often veer southward along the Rocky Mountain System, especially when a blocking high pressure area over California does not extend that far eastward. The cold north winds of the eastern winter also may blow through the Rocky Mountain area, and this makes the climate more severe than that in the Cascade-Sierra Nevada Axis. During the summer the warm, humid mass of air from the Gulf of Mexico lying over eastern North America reaches the Rockies, bringing thundershowers.

At higher elevations in the Rocky Mountains, both the winter and the summer rains are heavier. During the winter the prevailing westerlies lose moisture in greater proportion at the upper altitudes. During the summer the rays of the sun, passing through a relatively thin atmospheric shield, heat the ground high in the mountains, and the warmed surface air rises. This triggers convection showers, mostly during the afternoon and evening.

III. THE WESTERN FOREST FLORA

The area described for the Western Temperate Region. Mostly forests, in some cases grasslands. Various altitudes, as described for each floristic association. (Figs. 128 and 129.)

The outlines of the Western Temperate Region are complex. Through all 11 Western States and southern British Columbia this region and the Southwestern Temperate Region interdigitate. The floristic associations of the Southwestern region occur primarily in areas of lower rainfall, mostly at lower elevations—the Inland Basins and most of the lowlands of California, together with extensive areas at moderate altitudes in Arizona, New Mexico, and westernmost Texas. No single state is wholly within the region of the western forests or of the southwestern woodlands. In addition, the southern portions of California, Arizona, and New Mexico include the edges of the Horse Latitudes and their characteristic deserts marked by the creosote bush, *Larrea divaricata*.

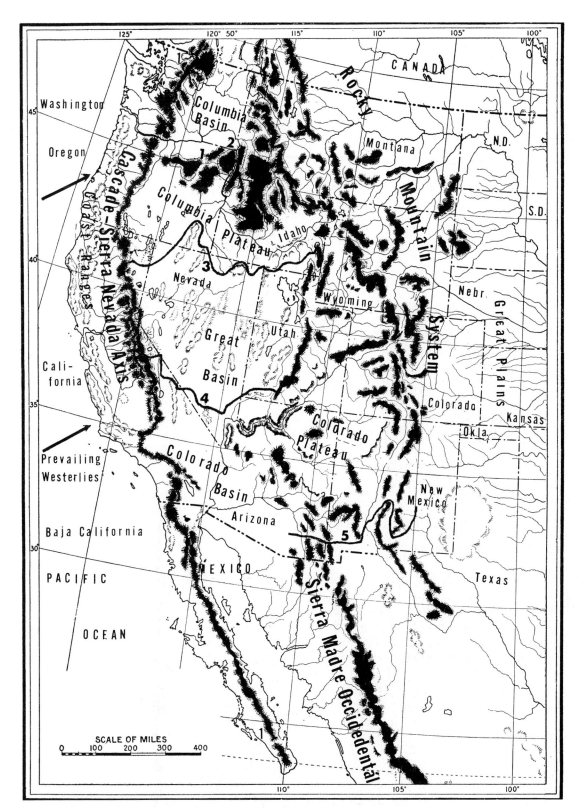

Fig. 126. Map of all but the northern part of western North America, showing the two great mountain systems: the Cascade–Sierra Nevada Axis in the United States and its extension into Baja California; and the Rocky Mountain System and the southern continuation of the continental divide as the Sierra Madre Occidental in Mexico. The Cascade–Sierra Nevada Axis is the physiographic feature of North America having the greatest effect on climate, because it stands like a great stone wall running from central Alaska to Baja California. When the prevailing westerlies cross it, they lose moisture on the west side and the summit; but on the east side, from the southern Yukon to Baja California, there is a rain shadow and the interior is dry. This effect is repeated as the winds cross the Rocky Mountains, but the air is already relatively dry and the Rockies do not form a continuous axis; thus the effect there is less.

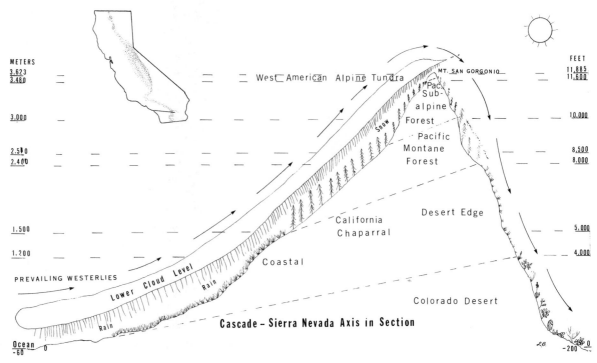

Fig. 127. Diagram of the Cascade–Sierra Nevada Axis in cross section through the San Bernardino Mts. of southern California, from the coast to the Salton Sea basin. (The section has had to be bent slightly to include these features in a single slice; and the low, nearly flat areas along the coast have been much shortened to reduce the width of the map.) During the winter the prevailing westerlies, bringing moisture from the ocean, deposit some on the coastal lowlands, then often colder than the ocean. As the air mass crosses the mountain axis, it is lifted, and the air expands, cools, and drops more moisture as rain or, at higher levels, snow. As it descends on the east, it comes under greater pressure and is compressed and warmed; it gains in moisture-holding capacity, and therefore little water is deposited as rain. This pattern occurs through almost the entire length of the mountain axis, from Alaska to northern Baja California.

Different versions of the Western Forest Flora occur in the three climatic regions of the Western Temperate Region: (1) the lowlands of the Pacific Coast, from middle coastal Alaska to Santa Cruz and the Big Sur, California; (2) all but the summits of the mountains of the Cascade-Sierra Nevada Axis and nearby ranges; and (3) all but the summits of the Rockies.

During middle Miocene a great system of temperate forests occurred from northern China and Japan along the continental shelves to western North America, where it continued from Alaska to the approximate latitudes of San Francisco, Salt Lake City, and Denver. At that time there was neither a Cascade-Sierra Nevada Axis nor a significant Rocky Mountain System. The former had not yet risen, and the latter had been worn to a peneplane between generations of the mountain system. The entire western part of the continent was characterized by plains, rolling hills, and small mountain ranges. The northern half of this plains region was occupied by the system of

temperate forests, the southern half by the oak woodland ancestral to the Southwestern Woodland Flora.

Since middle Miocene the two great north-south mountain axes have arisen: the Cascade-Sierra Nevada Axis, the Cascades arising through volcanic action, the continuing Sierra Nevada as a gigantic fault block sloping gently westward and steeply eastward (along the fault), and the granitic ranges in southern California uplifting only recently; the Rocky Mountain System, arising through a general uplift of the area, accompanied by washing away of the debris from the valleys and exposure of the old hard-rock pattern of the first generation of the mountain system. The rising of the mountains threw up barriers across the prevailing westerly wind system, creating new habitats at various altitudes in the mountains and giving rise to a rain shadow east of each range. This divided the generalized forerunner of the Western Forest Flora into coastal, montane (middle altitude), and subalpine floristic associations, and it provided new cold habitats available to the Alpine Tundra and new dry ones taken over by the new floristic associations derived from the oak woodland. Across the north in British Columbia today there remains much intergradation of the Cascade-Sierra Nevada and Rocky Mountain versions of the forests, but below Canada they are differentiated, strongly so at the latitude of California and Colorado.

Since the Miocene, in the entire area west of the Rockies there has been slow, erratic reduction of precipitation, and summer rainfall has ceased almost altogether except for some convection showers in the high mountains. The Miocene forests of the West included a wide variety of broad-leaved deciduous trees (dicotyledons) together with numerous individuals of a smaller number of coniferous species. Reduction of total

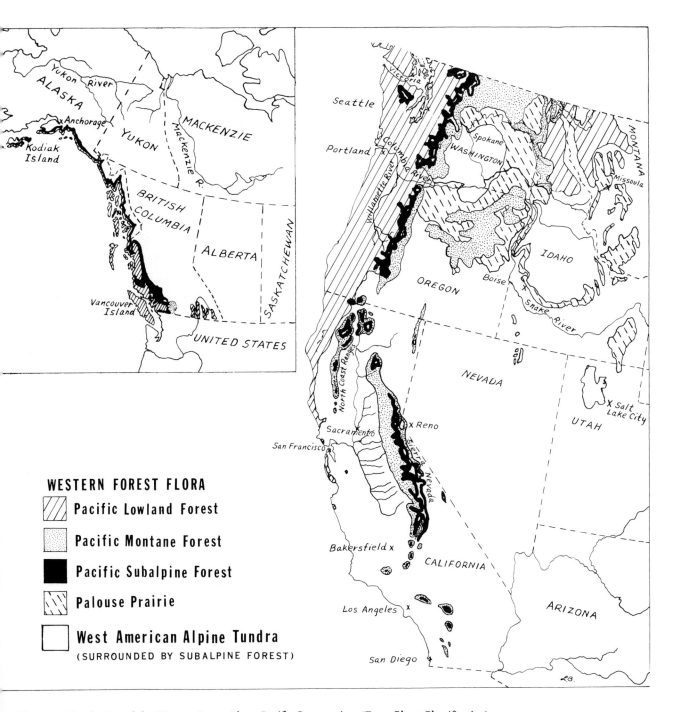

WESTERN FOREST FLORA

- /// Pacific Lowland Forest
- ▦ Pacific Montane Forest
- ■ Pacific Subalpine Forest
- ▨ Palouse Prairie
- ☐ West American Alpine Tundra
  (SURROUNDED BY SUBALPINE FOREST)

Fig. 128. Distribution of the Western Forest Flora, Pacific Coast region. (From *Plant Classification*)

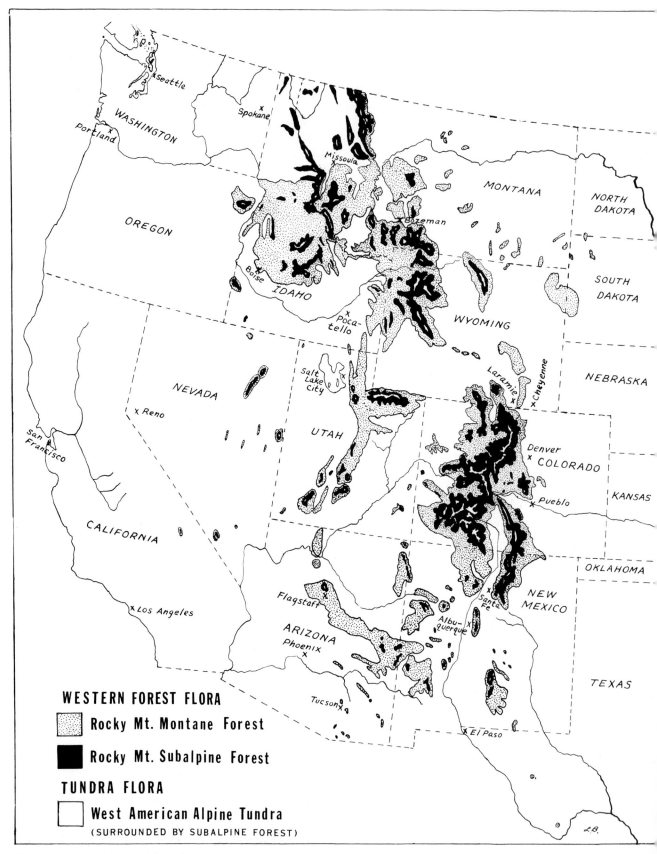

WESTERN FOREST FLORA

Rocky Mt. Montane Forest

Rocky Mt. Subalpine Forest

TUNDRA FLORA

West American Alpine Tundra
(SURROUNDED BY SUBALPINE FOREST)

Fig. 129. Distribution of the Western Forest Flora, Rocky Mountain region. Rocky Mountain Parkland occurs in patches within (or next to) the two forest associations. (From *Plant Classification*)

rainfall, and especially of summer rain, changed the character of the forests. The broad-leaved dicotyledons require water during the summer; and they may endure winter cold, as well as the resulting physiological drought occurring when the water supply is frozen, by shedding their leaves during the autumn. In the West there is not enough summer water, even in the mountains, to support a general cover of broad-leaved trees. Consequently, the more drought-resistant conifers dominate all the western forests ecologically, while all but a few of the deciduous trees and shrubs are restricted to low ground near streams, lakes, and ponds or to springy spots or to places where there is subsurface water. They occur also in the coastal fog belt or in deeper soils of north-facing slopes, where drying is less rapid. Consequently, the forests of the West are classified according to ecological formations as coniferous, those of the East mostly as deciduous. The original Miocene forests from which they were derived were "mixed" forests of both coniferous and deciduous trees.

With the uplift of the Cascades in Washington, Oregon, and northernmost California, a rain shadow was formed to the eastward in the Columbia Basin in Washington, northeastern Oregon, northern Idaho, and the edge of Montana. The lower levels near the Columbia and Snake rivers have been invaded since the Pleistocene by Sagebrush Desert from the Great Basin, as the Southwestern Woodland Flora was modified in the rain shadow of the Cascade-Sierra Nevada Axis. The upper levels of the Columbia Basin floor are the Palouse country, and the present floristic association is the Palouse Prairie, a grassland formed as the area became drier and as the Indians set fires to improve hunting grounds or to drive game into ambush. The Palouse Prairie, like other floristic associations, was derived from several sources, the major contribution being from the Miocene forest.

As the second generation of the Rockies arose slowly and irregularly to the present level, new habitats developed in the mountains and their rain shadows. The floristic associations on the mountain system are Rocky Mountain forests at montane and subalpine levels and a puzzling grassland high in mountain valleys (see p. 160).

Cacti. The Cactaceae occur sparingly in dry habitats in all the floristic associations of the Western Forest Flora, except the Pacific Subalpine Forest. On the northern Pacific Slope, *Opuntia fragilis* occurs on sandy or rocky soils in the Pacific Lowland Forest on the northern shores and

the drier islands of Puget Sound. Prickly pears occur on the desert sides of the mountains, some in the lower, drier parts of the Pacific Montane Forest. A cholla, *O. parryi*, grows in this forest at 1,890 m (6,200 ft) in the San Bernardino Mountains in southern California. In the same mountain range a hedgehog cactus, *Echinocereus engelmannii* var. *munzii*, occurs at 2,100 m (7,000 ft). Cacti occur abundantly in some parts of the Palouse Prairie, and they are occasional in the lower parts of the Rocky Mountain Montane Forest and in the Rocky Mountain Parkland. Their presence in the Rocky Mountain Subalpine Forest has not been established directly, but specimens have been collected at 3,300 m (11,000 ft) at La Veta Pass, Colorado, almost certainly within this forest. In the adjoining Rocky Mountain Parkland, cacti have been collected within 3 m (10 ft) of the forest.

III.1. The Pacific Lowland Forest

Coastal Alaska to Santa Cruz, Monterey Bay, and the Big Sur, California; inland N to the Canadian Rockies and W Glacier National Park, Montana. Low elevations. **Markers:** Douglas fir, *Pseudotsuga menziesii* var. *menziesii*; western hemlock, *Tsuga heterophylla*; giant cedar, *Thuja plicata*; coast redwood, *Sequoia sempervirens*; lowland fir, *Abies grandis*; tideland, or Sitka, spruce, *Picea sitchensis*; tan oak, *Lithocarpus densiflorus*; Garry oak, *Quercus garryana*; red elderberry, *Sambucus racemosa* var. *callicarpa*; madrone, *Arbutus menziesii*; salal, *Gaultheria shallon*; coffeeberry or cascara sagrada, *Rhamnus purshiana*; Oregon grape, *Berberis nervosa*; barberry, *Berberis aquifolium*; vine maple, *Acer circinatum*; and many others. (Figs. 130 and 131.)

Cacti. One prickly pear, *Opuntia fragilis*, occurs on Vancouver Island and along Puget Sound in British Columbia and Washington.

III.2. The Pacific Montane Forest

Mountains from E Washington and E Oregon to N Baja California. The lower forest belt. Extending down the mountains to the beginning of the Palouse Prairie, Sagebrush Desert, California Oak Woodland, or California Chaparral. The lowest levels in s California at about 1,500-1,800 m (5,000-6,000 ft), but occurring down to 900 m (3,000 ft) or lower in N California and the Pacific Northwest. **Markers:** Western yellow pine, *Pinus ponderosa* var. *ponderosa*; sugar pine, *P. lambertiana*; white fir, *Abies concolor*; incense cedar, *Libocedrus (Calocedrus) decurrens*; big tree or

Fig. 130. Pacific Lowland Forest in northern California, dominated by coast redwoods, *Sequoia sempervirens*, and to a lesser extent by Douglas fir; sword ferns, *Polystichum munitum*, are abundant on the forest floor. (Frank P. McWhorter)

154

Sierra redwood, *Sequoiadendron giganteum*; California black oak, *Quercus kelloggii* (also in the upper edge of the California Oak Woodland).

Cacti. A few species occur along the edge of the forest or in dry places within the forest on the desert sides of the mountains along the Cascade-Sierra Nevada Axis from Mono County, California, southward. (Fig. 132.)

III.3. The Pacific Subalpine Forest

Mountains of the Pacific coastal region and the Cascade-Sierra Nevada Axis and those of the w Columbia and Great basins. The upper forest belt. Extending to timberline and N and s for about 4,800 km (3,000 mi). In Alaska at 60-600 m (200-2,000 ft); in the Pacific Northwest at 900-1,500 m (3,000-5,000 ft); in s California at 2,200-3,300 m (7,500-11,000 ft). **Markers:** Mountain hemlock, *Tsuga mertensiana*; Alaska cedar, *Chamaecyparis nootkatensis*; firs, *Abies nobilis* and

amabilis; red fir, *A. magnifica*; alpine larch, *Larix lyallii*; western white pine, *Pinus monticola*; white bark pine, *P. albicaulis*; Jeffrey pine, *P. ponderosa* var. *jeffreyi*; foxtail pine, *P. balfouriana*; huckleberry oak, *Quercus vaccinifolia*; Sierra chinquapin, *Castanopsis sempervirens*. (Fig. 133.)

Cacti. None at this altitude on the Pacific Coast.

III.4. The Palouse Prairie

A grassland area of winter rainfall, now scattered in occurrence because the area has been reduced to spots untouched by the plow; E Washington, E Oregon, Idaho, NE Utah, and w edge of Wyoming. Except in the SE mostly 600-700 m (2,000-2,500 ft); in SE Idaho, Utah, and Wyoming, 1,200-1,500 m (4,000-5,000 ft). **Markers:** Idaho fescue or blue bunch grass, *Festuca idahoensis*; wheat grass or bunch grass, *Agropyron spicatum*. (Fig. 134.)

Cacti. Prickly pears are abundant in the sandy

Fig. 131. Pacific Lowland Forest, dominated by Douglas fir, *Pseudotsuga menziesii* var. *menziesii* (trunk diameter nearly 3 m, or 8 feet); giant cedar, *Thuja plicata*; western hemlock, *Tsuga heterophylla*; and lowland fir, *Abies grandis*; and with many broad-leaved shrubs in the understory. Near Tacoma, Washington, in 1926. (Homer L. Shantz)

Fig. 132. Pacific Montane Forest, dominated by western yellow pine, *Pinus ponderosa* var. *ponderosa* (center); sugar pine, *P. lambertiana* (not showing); incense cedar, *Libocedrus* (*Calocedrus*) *decurrens* (right); and white fir, *Abies concolor* (not showing). Rim-of-the-World Drive, San Bernardino Mts., San Bernardino Co., California.

Fig. 133. Pacific Subalpine Forest, dominated by red fir, *Abies magnifica*, and mountain hemlock, *Tsuga mertensiana*. South side of Mt. Lassen, California.

Fig. 134. Palouse Prairie, with dense stands of bunch grasses, *Agropyron spicatum* and *Festuca idahoensis*; 8 km (5 miles) west of Colton, Whitman Co., Washington. (Robert L. Benson)

or rocky areas of the canyons flanking the larger rivers. The common cactus here is an endemic variety of prickly pear, *Opuntia erinacea* var. *columbiana*, and *O. fragilis* occurs in the area and hybridizes with var. *columbiana*. The best development of *Pediocactus simpsonii* var. *robustior* is in the Sagebrush Desert along the western side of the Columbia River Valley and in the western part of the Palouse Prairie.

III.5. The Rocky Mountain Montane Forest

The lower forest belt. Extending from the level of intergradation with the subalpine forest down the mountains to the beginning of woodland, brushland, grassland, Sagebrush Desert, or Navajoan Desert. Mountains of north-central Idaho to the Black Hills, Arizona, and trans-Pecos Texas. Northward, 600-1,200 m (2,000-4,000 ft); southward, about 1,800-2,400 m (6,000-8,000 ft). **Markers:** Rocky Mountain Douglas fir, *Pseudotsuga menziesii* var. *glauca*; Rocky Mountain yellow pine, *Pinus ponderosa* var. *scopulorum*; western yellow pine, *P. ponderosa* var. *ponderosa*; Arizona yellow pine, *P. ponderosa* var. *arizonica* (five-needled); Apache pine, *P. ponderosa*

var. *mayriana* (known as *P. apacheca*); white fir, *Abies concolor*; Rocky Mountain juniper or red cedar, *Juniperus scopulorum*; Gambel oak, *Quercus gambelii*. (Figs. 135 and 136.)

Cacti. Although several species of cacti occur within the lower margin of the forest, only *Pediocactus simpsonii* var. *minor* occurs through any considerable portion of the forest, chiefly in Colorado and New Mexico.

III.6. The Rocky Mountain Subalpine Forest

The upper forest belt, extending from the montane forest to timberline. Throughout the Rocky Mountain System from w Canada southward. In E Nevada, Arizona, and New Mexico beginning at 2,250-2,700 m (7,500-9,000 ft), but lower northward. **Markers:** Alpine fir, *Abies lasiocarpa*; Engelmann spruce, *Picea engelmannii*; Colorado blue spruce, *P. pungens*; bristlecone pine, *Pinus aristata*; limber pine, *P. flexilis* (sometimes in the montane forest, as well). (Figs. 137 and 138.)

Cacti. The only cactus occurring clearly in this forest is *Pediocactus simpsonii* var. *minor*, which ascends to 2,700 m (9,000 ft) or rarely 3,300 m (11,000 ft).

Fig. 135. Rocky Mountain Montane Forest, dominated by western yellow pine, *Pinus ponderosa* var. *ponderosa*; Williams Valley, White Mts., Apache National Forest, Arizona. (Daniel O. Todd, U.S. Forest Service)

Fig. 136. Rocky Mountain Montane Forest, dominated by western yellow pine, *Pinus ponderosa* var. *ponderosa*, the trees mostly small in this rocky and gravelly lower portion of the forest. The cacti of the forest occur mostly in this type of habitat. Just southeast of San Francisco Peaks (at left), Coconino Co., northern Arizona.

Fig. 137. Rocky Mountain Subalpine Forest in winter; southeastern side of Grand Mesa, Delta Co., Colorado. The narrowly conical trees with short, flexible branches are characteristic of subalpine forests around the world; the snow accumulating on the branches slides off when the weight bends the branches downward. Engelmann spruce and Colorado blue spruce, *Picea engelmannii* and *P. pungens*; alpine fir, *Abies lasiocarpa*.

Fig. 138. Rocky Mountain Subalpine Forest in summer; small lake in a Pleistocene glacial cirque just north of the summit of Mt. Aeneas, Mission Mts., Flathead Co., Montana. Again, Engelmann spruce and alpine fir.

159

Fig. 139. Rocky Mountain Parkland, a grassland at high elevations in the southern Rockies, here at 2,850 m (9,500 feet); between Glentivar and Hartsel, Park Co., Colorado. The mountains in the background are from 13,000 to 14,000 feet high.

III.7. The Rocky Mountain Parkland

High, open, grassy valleys known as "parks." The c and s part of the Rocky Mountain System, at 2,100-2,850 m (7,000-9,500 ft). **Markers:** Grasses and other herbaceous plants. (Fig. 139.)

The status of this grassland as a floristic association is uncertain; probably it was derived from the neighboring forests, likely with the aid of fire, which kills the seedlings of trees and shrubs, but its floristic composition and relationships are much in need of study. The primary purpose is to call the problem to attention.

Cacti. Small species occur among the grasses on the hillsides up to the edge of the Rocky Mountain Subalpine Forest.

The Eastern Temperate Region
(Climatic Region for Association IV.1)

A narrow fringe of southeastern Canada in the St. Lawrence Valley and near the eastern Great Lakes; the United States east of the Great Plains. Actually, near the Gulf of Mexico, on the southern Atlantic Coastal Plain, and in Florida this region includes a moist segment of the Horse Latitudes.

In eastern temperate North America the range of temperature is great, the seasons change abruptly, and precipitation occurs the year around. The average temperatures of the warmest and coldest months differ by usually 28-33°C (50-60°F) and sometimes 50°C (90°F). These great differences are responsible for the "four seasons" of the region —two extremes and two transitional periods.

The winter climate is governed in part by the great system of storms of the Temperate Zone, developed from the prevailing westerlies, the polar front, and the upper winds such as the polar jet stream above the front.

Because land far from the ocean cools rapidly, during the winter the interior of the continent is affected by a great mass of cold air, the polar continental air mass, centering over most of eastern Canada. With the onset of winter, this air mass merges with the arctic air mass over Greenland, forming an enormous dome of cold air. In an open system, cold air is contracted and dense, and it exerts pressure. For this reason cold winds sweep southward at least into the Great Plains, the Middle West, and New England. Commonly this air system may extend from the arctic to Arkansas and eastward or westward, but at times it crosses the Rockies, altering the climate there, and rarely it may reach even northern California or Florida.

Another great mass of air under high pressure centers over the Gulf of Mexico, where the air from above is descending in the Horse Latitudes. This air, warmed by compression during its descent, picks up moisture over the Gulf. When spring comes, the land in the north becomes warmer, and, in an open system lacking the addition of descending air, the air mass is expanded and under low pressure. As the remainder of the continental polar air mass shrinks back to the north, warm air under high pressure moves north from the Gulf region of the Horse Latitudes, and eastern North America is covered by an unstable, warm, wet air mass that stays all summer. Consequently, the summer climate is characteristically humid and wet, and thunderstorms are frequent. The summer rainfall is augmented sometimes, especially near the Gulf and Atlantic coasts, by hurricanes formed in the Caribbean.

IV. THE EASTERN FOREST FLORA

Along the SE edge of Canada and covering the eastern two-thirds of the United States, i.e. the Middle West, East, and South. Low elevations from sea level to 300 or 600 m (1,000 or 2,000 ft) but reaching higher levels in the Appalachian system. (Fig. 140.)

The Eastern Forest Flora is composed mostly of deciduous forests representing the remnants and modifications of old floras present in the region since Eocene or Cretaceous time. They have been affected by a general trend of the climate from more or less tropical to temperate; changes of altitude of some areas through uplift and erosion cycles, especially in the Appalachian system; development of minor drought areas; and glaciation and its influence on the temperature and moisture of the climate southward.

Cacti. The summer rainfall of the eastern third of the continent is favorable to most cacti, as long as they are on well-drained soil, but its large quantity also favors competitors, and the winter cold is devastating to all but a few species of cacti. In the Middle West, the East, and the temperate part of the South, sandy or rocky soils support cacti, though in most areas only *Opuntia humifusa*. Near the Great Lakes, where the water exerts a local temperature-stabilizing influence, O. *macrorhiza* and O. *fragilis* grow in the sandy areas of shores and dunes and on rock outcrops. As indicated earlier, a few species of cacti are not limited by cold alone, and probably in cold areas, as well as moist, competition with better-adapted plants is a major factor in limiting the cacti. Southward, toward the Horse Latitudes, the number of cacti increases rapidly in the well-drained areas, even though the climate near the Gulf of Mexico is moist.

IV.1. The Deciduous Forests

The Great Lakes region and the valley of the St. Lawrence River to the Gulf of Mexico and the Atlantic Coast. **Markers:** Many deciduous trees and shrubs and some conifers (not given in the list below), especially the following, selected from a long list: sweet gum, *Liquidambar styraciflua*; flowering dogwood, *Cornus florida*; hop hornbeam, *Carpinus caroliniana*; beech, *Fagus grandifolia* (with locally segregated races); American chestnut, *Castanea dentata* (now nearly extinct because of blight); white oak, *Quercus alba*; red oak, *Q. rubra*; chinquapin oak, *Q. prinoides*; shingle oak, *Q. imbricaria*; scarlet oak, *Q. coccinea*; willow oak, *Q. phellos*; chestnut oak, *Q. prinus*; black oak, *Q. velutina*; post oak, *Q. stel-*

lata; bur oak, *Q. macrocarpa*; overcup oak, *Q. lyrata*; butternut, *Juglans cinerea*; black walnut, *J. nigra*; pecan, *Carya illinoensis*; shagbark hickory, *C. ovata*; butternut or pignut, *C. cordiformis*; big shellbark, *C. laciniosa*; mockernut, *C. tomentosa*; pignut, *C. glabra*; sweet pignut, *C. ovalis*; magnolias, *Magnolia virginiana, acuminata, macrophylla, tripetala, grandiflora,* and *fraseri*; Carolina allspice, *Calycanthus fertilis*; tulip tree, *Liriodendron tulipifera*; pawpaws, *Asimina triloba* and *parviflora*; sassafras, *Sassafras albidum*; red bay, *Persea borbonia*; pond spice, *Litsea aestivalis*; spice bush, *Lindera benzoin*; basswoods, *Tilia floridana, americana, heterophylla,* and *neglecta*; burning bushes, *Euonymus atropurpureus* and *americanus*; buckeyes or horse chestnuts, *Aesculus* (several species); maples, *Acer saccharum* (sugar maple), *rubrum, nigrum,* etc.; elms, *Ulmus americana, rubra, alata, thomasii,* and *serotina*; hackberries, *Celtis occidentalis, tenuifolia,* and *laevigata*; mulberry, *Morus rubra*; persimmon, *Diospyros virginiana*; ashes, *Fraxinus americana, tomentosa, caroliniana, pennsylvanica,* and *quadrangulata*; sycamore, *Platanus occidentalis*; and a host of others. (Figs. 141-45.)

The several floristic associations of the Deciduous Forests are complex in character, and they shade into one another; their floristic classification is in need of further study. As indicated by the numerous markers of the forest, the communities of plants are rich from a floristic point of view. Because of the low topography and the great extent of areas with similar climate, many of the species occur through a high percentage of the Eastern Temperate Region.

The two most distinctive, and most confusing, phases of the Eastern Deciduous Forests are subclimaxes maintained for only so long as there are, in one case, frequent fires and, in the other, frequent flooding, as follows:

Southern Pine Forest. Relatively low elevations on the plains and hills of the Atlantic and Gulf coastal plains from Long Island, New York, and E Texas to Florida. Once the pine trees reach a substantial height, they stand above the frequent grass fires, which destroy not only their own seedlings but also those of deciduous trees, which otherwise would overtop and shade out the relatively small pine species. Characteristic species include the scrub pine, *Pinus virginiana*; loblolly pine, *P. taeda*; longleaf pine, *P. australis*; shortleaf pine, *P. echinata*; and pond pine, *P. serotina*. The open forest and the relatively warm climate, drier than average for eastern North America, are favorable to a few species of cacti. (Fig. 146.)

Southern Riverbottom Forest. Very low eleva-

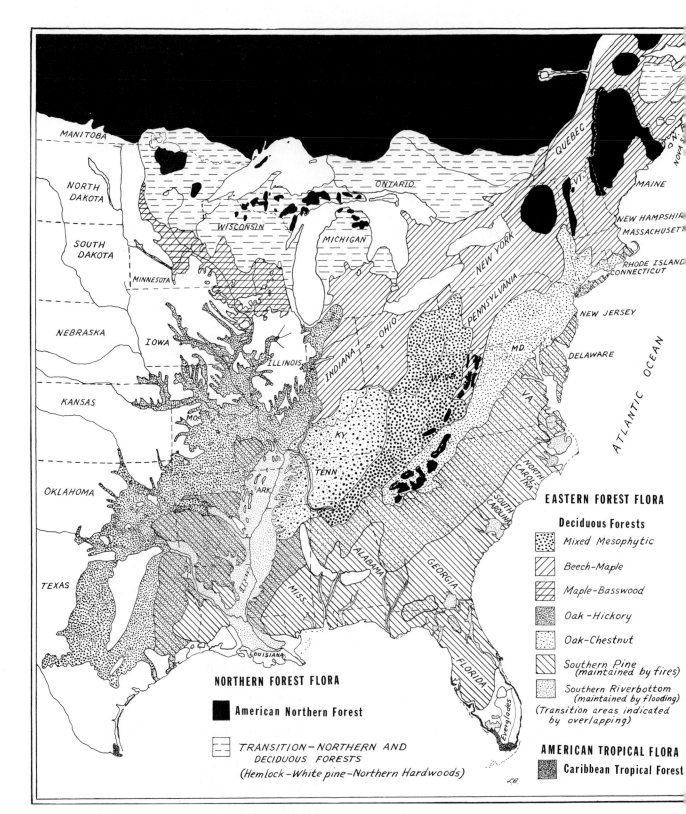

EASTERN FOREST FLORA

Deciduous Forests

- Mixed Mesophytic
- Beech-Maple
- Maple-Basswood
- Oak-Hickory
- Oak-Chestnut
- Southern Pine *(maintained by fires)*
- Southern Riverbottom *(maintained by flooding)*
(Transition areas indicated by overlapping)

AMERICAN TROPICAL FLORA

- Caribbean Tropical Forest

NORTHERN FOREST FLORA

- American Northern Forest
- TRANSITION—NORTHERN AND DECIDUOUS FORESTS *(Hemlock–White pine–Northern Hardwoods)*

Fig. 140. Map emphasizing the Deciduous Forests of eastern North America, but indicating the adjacent parts of the American Northern Forest and the Caribbean Tropical Forest. The subdivisions of the Deciduous Forests are still under study; for this book they are not significant, because only one cactus, *Opuntia humifusa*, occurs in more than a little of the region, except in Florida and along the Gulf Coast. (From *Plant Classification*)

162

Fig. 141. Aerial view of Eastern Deciduous Forest; looking northeast at the St. François Mts., near Arcadia, Missouri. (John S. Shelton)

Fig. 142. Deciduous Forest in summer; the large trees are white oaks, *Quercus alba*. Virgin forest in Spring Mill State Park, Hoosier National Forest, Indiana. (Leland J. Prater, U.S. Forest Service; from *Plant Classification*)

163

Fig. 144 (*above*). Deciduous Forest in the early spring, after the snow has melted but before much growth is visible; at the left a dogwood, *Cornus florida*, is just starting to bloom. Forest about 40 years old and in succession, following both clearing and the eradication of chestnuts by a blight introduced from the Old World, the American chestnut having little immunity. The original climax Oak-Chestnut Forest cannot be restored; the dominant trees are oaks. High ridge in the Shenandoah National Park, Virginia.

Fig. 145 (*right*). Deciduous Forest similar to that in Fig. 144, but at about 300 m (1,000 feet) less elevation; the dogwoods in full bloom on the same day, but not yet in leaf; other trees still bare.

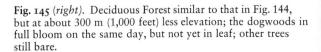

Fig. 146. Southern Pine Forest, a successional phase of an Eastern Deciduous Forest maintained by frequent fires, which do not harm the larger pine trees standing high above the grass, but kill seedlings of all trees, preventing return of the climax Deciduous Forest. An open forest like this is favorable to the few species of cacti inhabiting the Gulf and Atlantic coastal plains. Longleaf pine, *Pinus australis*; forest of the Crosby Lumber Company, Mississippi. (Paul S. Carter, U.S. Forest Service from *Plant Classification*)

tions throughout the Southern States; maintained where drainage is poor and water stays the year around, drowning out the usual plants of the Deciduous Forests. The most characteristic tree is the bald cypress or swamp cypress, *Taxodium distichum,* and common associates are cotton gum, *Nyssa aquatica,* and *N. aquatica* var. *biflora.* In shallow swamps of especially southern Georgia, South Carolina, and Florida, the swamp cypress is replaced by the pond cypress, *Taxodium ascendens,* in association with the pond pine, *Pinus serotina.* Specialized cacti occur on the margins or the higher ground (hammocks), and some vinelike jungle cacti become introduced. (Fig. 147.)

Fig. 147. Southern Riverbottom Forest, a successional phase of an Eastern Deciduous Forest maintained by flooding; the water is now low, exposing the great basal swellings of the trunks, these important as buttresses for support in the wet soil, and, by virtue of internal passages, as aerating organs for the submerged roots. (U.S. Forest Service; from *Plant Classification*)

V. THE PLAINS AND PRAIRIE FLORA

The Plains and Prairie Flora of the Great Plains (Fig. 148) is not fully formed, and it must be considered a developing or incipient flora. The grasslands have been formed on the dry central plains east of the Rocky Mountains probably only since the Pleistocene, though earlier versions may have existed during the interglacial periods. According to Wells (1970a, 1970b), the Great Plains would be covered with a dryland type of forest if fire had not been an important factor. Fire not only burns the mature trees but also eliminates the seedlings of woody plants, and it may prevent a forest from developing. However, it does not injure the rhizomes of the perennial grasses dominating the plains. Since the Pleistocene both natural fires set by lightning and others set annually by Indians to improve the grassland for grazing and to round up game have restricted the

The Midcontinent Temperate Region
(Climatic Region for Associations V.1 & V.2)

The great treeless region between the Rocky Mountain System and the beginning of forest at varying distances west of the Mississippi River; high plains and valleys in the southern parts of the Rocky Mountain region in Colorado, Arizona, and New Mexico.

The ground in the interior of the continent becomes very cold during the winter and very hot during the summer. *During the winter* the polar continental air mass covers the area, and the high pressure within the mass tends to make the air move away over the surface instead of rising. This reduces winter precipitation. The Midcontinent Temperate Region is also in the rain shadow of the Rockies. Nevertheless, the area is affected by the storms originating along the polar front. *During the summer* the warm, moist air from the Gulf of Mexico brings thundershowers, as it does in the Eastern Temperate Region, but Midcontinent precipitation is less than Eastern in both summer and winter. The southern Great Plains and the southernmost Rocky Mountain region, where there are grasslands, are near and within the Horse Latitudes, and total precipitation there is low, though higher than in the deserts nearby at lower altitudes.

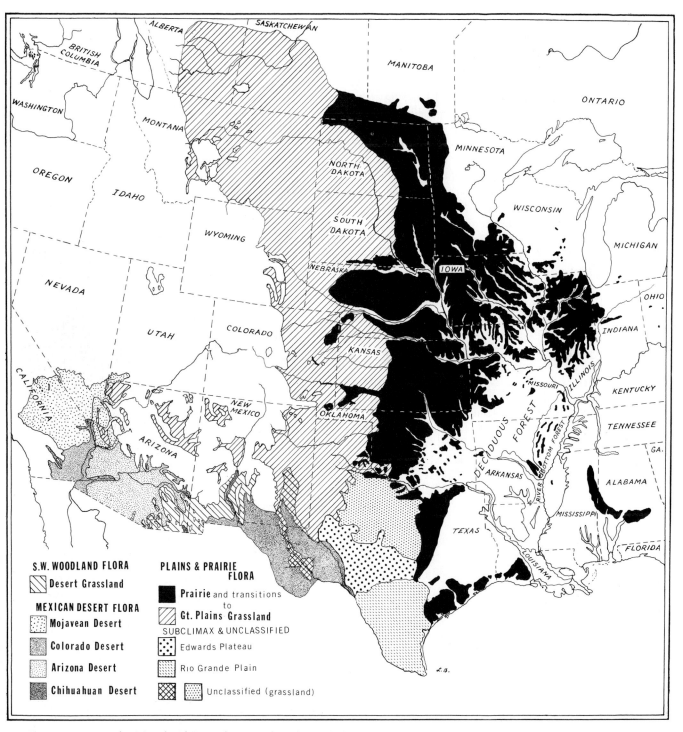

Fig. 148. Map emphasizing the Plains and Prairie Flora, but including, as well, the related Desert Grassland (Southwestern Woodland Flora) and the interfingering elements of Mexican Desert Flora of the Southwest. The Closed-Cone Pine and Insular Endemic associations, both very restricted in extent, are not indicated. (From *Plant Classification*)

167

trees to rough escarpments and areas downwind from water barriers to fire. Otherwise, the great prairie fires were free to spread over the whole region. Since the coming of the white man, some areas where there is more water, as in the Middle West and parts of eastern Texas, have become Deciduous Forests, and some, like the Edwards Plateau and the Rio Grande Plain of Texas, have become brushland and woodland of a mixed, uncertain floristic derivation.

Some elements of the floristic associations of the Plains and Prairie Flora are interrelated and restricted to this flora, but most species occur also in the nearest adjacent floras. There are few endemic taxa of either plants or animals. Furthermore, grasslands everywhere have been overgrazed or put to the plow more quickly than has any other ecological formation. Consequently, the floristic associations have been destroyed, reduced, or modified, and evidence concerning the nature of the original assemblage of species is scanty. The evidence available indicates a not very distinctive grouping of plants not necessarily characteristic of a flora, and the status of the Plains and Prairie Flora is doubtful.

Cacti. Several species are abundant in the drier grasslands. They occur far to the northward, even in Canada on the northern Great Plains in Alberta, Saskatchewan, and Manitoba, and their variety and abundance increase southward. Low-growing, mat-forming prickly pears and solitary or mound-forming coryphanthas are abundant even on the northern Great Plains, and larger species of cacti appear from Colorado southward. Thus, the larger juicy-fruited prickly pears, including the varieties of *Opuntia phaeacantha*, and smaller ones, such as *O. macrorhiza*, become prominent as lumps protruding above or among the grasses. The treelike cholla, *O. imbricata*, forms extensive patches, and other cacti occur on the low hills and the bluffs along the rivers. In the extension of the grasslands of the Horse Latitudes into New Mexico and Texas there are numerous species of cacti, and they are a major part of both the flora and the vegetation.

V.1. The Prairie

The tall-grass Prairie of the Middle West, occurring just W of the Deciduous Forests and in open places surrounded by forest. Low elevations, mostly 300-450 m (1,000-1,500 ft). Originally the Prairie occurred in extensive areas near the Mississippi River and E to parts of the Ohio Valley. **Markers:** Numerous grasses and herbs. The larg-

Fig. 149. Prairie, with big bluestem, *Andropogon gerardii*, predominating; the grasses about 3 m (10 feet) high. Near Brownfield Woods, University of Illinois, Urbana. (Robert L. Benson)

est is big bluestem, *Andropogon gerardii*; others are little bluestem, *A. scoparius*; porcupine grass, *Stipa spartea*; Indian grass or wood grass, *Sorghastrum nutans*. These plants are considered indicators of the Prairie, but actually each is a wide-ranging species occurring over a vast part of North America. This is typical of the species occurring in the Plains and Prairie Flora. (Fig. 149.)

The Prairie was brought into cultivation with relative ease, and nearly all of it has been plowed. Other areas reverted to forest when the annual burning by Indians ceased and the seedlings of trees and shrubs could grow. There are only scattered remnants now—in old cemeteries, on sandy or rocky or otherwise poor land, along the rights-of-way of old or abandoned railroads, or in some private reserves. Some remaining Prairie is preserved by educational institutions, as at Brownfield Woods of the University of Illinois, or they are included in parks or nature preserves.

Some of the grasses are as much as 2-3 m (6-10 ft) tall, and in the few areas preserved they indicate that travel through some parts of the original Prairie was not as easy as in other grasslands. Rainfall is higher than on the Great Plains, and westward the grasses become gradually shorter.

Cacti. Except in disturbed or sandy places, the dense sod prevents the occurrence of cacti.

V.2. The Great Plains Grassland

The Great Plains and the lower valleys of the Rocky Mountains, especially southward into N Arizona and New Mexico. Mostly about 1,050-1,500(1,800) m (3,500-5,000 or 6,000 ft) or s to 2,100-2,700 m (7,000-9,000 ft). **Markers:** Numerous grasses and other herbaceous plants; plains yucca, *Yucca glauca.* (Fig. 150.)

Cacti. Cacti are common on both the northern and southern Great Plains, but they are more abundant southward, and more genera and species are represented there. (Figs. 151 and 152.)

Several unclassified grasslands or probably grassland derivatives occur in Texas and adjacent southern New Mexico. Two major ones are modified from the original grassland by the presence of woody and other species that have grown since the annual fires set by the Indians have stopped. Some local grasslands are transitional between the Great Plains Grassland and the Desert Grassland, and classification is difficult. The major unclassified types are as follows:

The Edwards Plateau. Basically an extension of the Great Plains Grassland; modified by the invasion of trees and shrubs since the start of grazing and the cessation of Indian fires. The central plateau of Texas. Mostly at about 600-900 m (2,000-3,000 ft). The vegetation is of mixed origin, some elements, especially the conspicuous woody plants, being derived from adjacent floristic associations. Prominent invading woody species include honey mesquite, *Prosopis juliflora* var. *glandulosa;* shinnery oak, *Quercus havardii;* live oak, *Q. virginiana;* and junipers ("cedars"), *Juniperus pinchotii* and *ashei.* There are few endemic species. Cacti are abundant, but there is only one local species, a rare endemic, *Ancistrocactus tobuschii.*

Fig. 150. Great Plains Grassland on the sandhills of western Nebraska, in Morrill Co. south of Alliance (Butte Co.); plains species of cacti abundant.

Fig. 151. Overgrazed open spot in the Great Plains Grassland in southeastern New Mexico, about 1910, with typical species of cacti: middle foreground, *Opuntia macrorhiza* var. *pottsii*; left foreground, *O. polyacantha* var. *trichophora* (probably this variety, though the characteristic long threadlike spines of the lower part of the plant do not show in the picture); above, tree cholla, *O. imbricata*; middle right (the low domelike plant), horse crippler, *Echinocactus texensis*. These taxa are characteristic of the southern part of the Great Plains, mostly within the Horse Latitudes. (David Griffiths)

Fig. 152. Grazed Great Plains Grassland in southeastern New Mexico or western Texas; blue grama grass, *Bouteloua gracilis*, with tree cholla, *Opuntia imbricata*, the latter affected by drought. (David Griffiths)

170

The Rio Grande Plain. The Rio Grande Valley in Texas from Val Verde and Webb Cos. to the mouth of the river and the plains s of the Edwards Plateau and E to the Gulf of Mexico and s into adjacent Mexico. Low elevations; mostly under 200 m (660 ft). The area lies wholly within the Horse Latitudes. The flora is of mixed origin, and it includes not only species related to those in the other grasslands but also some derived from the Chihuahuan Desert and other floras in Mexico. According to Gould (1962), the original vegetation was a grassland or a savannah (grassland with scattered trees). Under long continued overgrazing and other disturbances and reduction of fire, trees and shrubs have taken over much of the area. Particularly prominent are honey mesquite, *Prosopis juliflora* var. *glandulosa*; the post oak, *Quercus stellata*; and the live oak, *Q. virginiana*. Field study has been devoted largely to the cacti and the trees and shrubs, and the total aggregation of species has not been evaluated. The solution to the problem must come partly or largely from studies in Mexico. The case for consideration as an independent floristic association is supported by the presence of a number of endemic cacti. Other characteristic species have not been evaluated. **Markers** (cacti only): *Echinocereus pentalophus*; *E. berlandieri* vars. *berlandieri*, *papillosus*, and *angusticeps*; *E. enneacanthus* var. *brevispinus*; *E. reichenbachii* vars. *albertii* and *fitchii*; *Mammillaria longimamma* var. *sphaerica*; *M. prolifera* var. *texana*; *Ferocactus setispinus*; *F. hamatacanthus* var. *sinuatus*; *Echinocactus asterias*; *Ancistrocactus scheeri*; *Coryphantha robertii*; *C. macromeris* var. *runyonii*. As indicated by the list, this plain is one of the most important areas for cacti in the United States, and there are many endemic species. (Fig. 153.)

Fig. 153. The Rio Grande Plain near the Rio Grande in southern Texas. The area was once grassland, when it was burned annually by the Indians and the seedlings of trees and shrubs were kept down; now, much of the area is mesquite thicket or woodland. Grass is sparse (as here) to dense, according to the intensity of grazing. Where the mesquites are not dense, the grasses and other plants under them are available to cattle, as are the pods and young shoots of the mesquites; when the thickets become dense, they exclude cattle. Because the mesquites also absorb much of the water needed for a really good stand of grass, the ranchers try to eliminate them, as well as cacti, which also exclude cattle. But because the cacti grow from fragments, most mechanical means of removal merely increase their number. The cacti include prickly pears (like *Opuntia lindheimeri*, shown here) and chollas (like *O. leptocaulis*, which becomes a large bush in southern Texas). (David Griffiths)

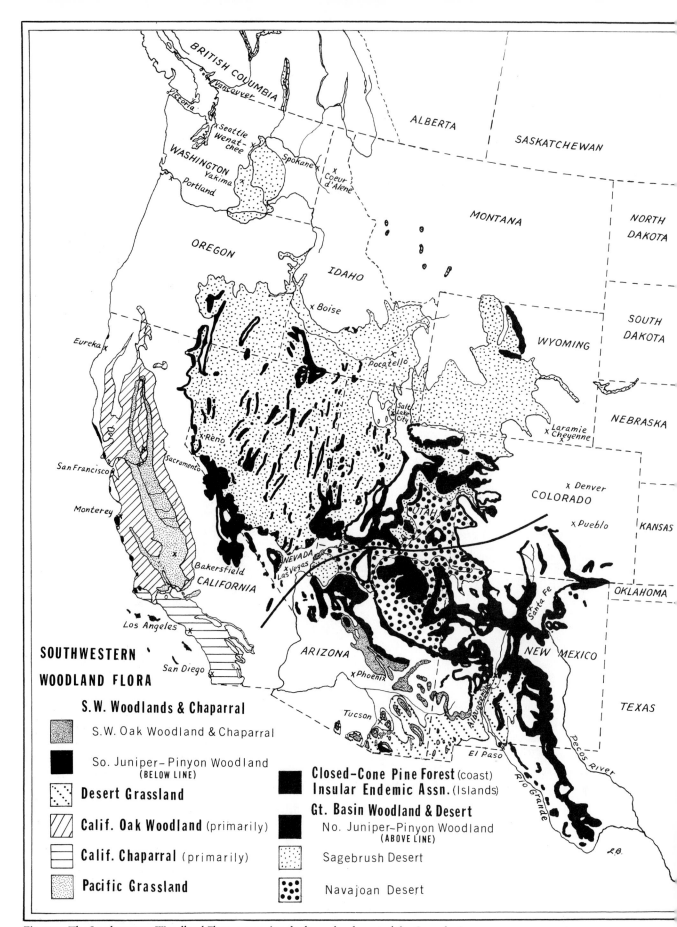

BRITISH COLUMBIA

ALBERTA
SASKATCHEWAN

Victoria
Vancouver

Seattle
Wenat-
chee
Spokane

WASHINGTON
Yakima
Portland

x Coeur
d'Alene

MONTANA

NORTH
DAKOTA

OREGON

IDAHO

x Boise

SOUTH
DAKOTA

Eureka x

x Pocatello

WYOMING

San Francisco

Salt
Lake
City

Laramie
x Cheyenne

NEBRASKA

Monterey

x Reno

Sacramento

UTAH

x Denver

COLORADO

KANSAS

Bakersfield

CALIFORNIA

NEVADA
Las Vegas

x Pueblo

Los Angeles

Santa Fe

OKLAHOMA

San Diego

ARIZONA

x Phoenix

NEW MEXICO

TEXAS

SOUTHWESTERN

Tucson

Albuquerque

WOODLAND FLORA

El Paso

Pecos River

S.W. Woodlands & Chaparral

Rio Grande

S.W. Oak Woodland & Chaparral

L.B.

So. Juniper–Pinyon Woodland
(BELOW LINE)

Closed-Cone Pine Forest (coast)
Insular Endemic Assn. (Islands)

Desert Grassland

Gt. Basin Woodland & Desert

Calif. Oak Woodland (primarily)

No. Juniper–Pinyon Woodland
(ABOVE LINE)

Calif. Chaparral (primarily)

Sagebrush Desert

Pacific Grassland

Navajoan Desert

Fig. 154. The Southwestern Woodland Flora, occupying the lower levels east of the Cascades in the Pacific Northwest and west of the Cascade–Sierra Nevada Axis in most of California, as well as the middle altitudes through the Southwest from eastern California to Wyoming, south-central Colorado, and parts of trans-Pecos Texas. (From *Plant Classification*)

172

The Southwestern Temperate Region
(Climatic Region for Associations VI.1 through VI.8)

The topographic and climatic pattern of the West is complex, and the ramifications of the climatic regions resemble a jigsaw puzzle. The Southwestern Temperate Region includes three climatic areas. These are as follows: the *coastal area*—on the Pacific Slope at low to moderate elevations from the Rogue River in southwestern Oregon to northwestern Baja California; the *Inland Basins*—from Thompson River, British Columbia, to the lowest altitudes in the Columbia Basin and all of the Great Basin; the *far-inland areas*—in the uplands from the Colorado Plateau to southern-middle Colorado, N & E Arizona, and to trans-Pecos Texas. The position and the climate of this region are intermediate between those of the Western Temperate Region in the north and the Desert Zone in the south.

The climates vary in temperatures and in quantity and timing of precipitation. The *coastal area* has a Mediterranean climate with mild, irregularly rainy winters and relatively hot, almost completely dry summers. The *Inland Basins* are in the rain shadow of the Cascade-Sierra Nevada Axis, and the climate is much drier than that on the Pacific Slope. The winter precipitation consists of light rain and snow, and there is no summer rain. The *far-inland areas* receive relatively light winter rain and snow, and the weather remains cold so far into the spring that often the moisture has evaporated before plant growth can begin. The rains during July and August are much more significant in quantity and timing; the water can be used immediately without much loss to the atmosphere. During the summer the vegetation becomes lush.

VI. THE SOUTHWESTERN WOODLAND FLORA

The present woodlands, chaparrals, and grasslands of this flora (Fig. 154) are derivatives of the Madrotertiary Geoflora. This was an oak woodland that migrated northward and westward from the present area of the Sierra Madre Occidental in northwestern Mexico during the Miocene (Axelrod, 1940, 1944, 1950a, 1956, 1957, 1958). It occupied the southern half of the western plains and hills extending from the latitude of San Francisco, Salt Lake City, and Colorado Springs southward to the present Mexican boundary. There were only low or disconnected mountains at the time (p. 150). The northern half of the plain extending over the present Western States was covered by the temperate forest ancestral to the Western Forest Flora.

Since the Miocene the floras of the West have been affected not only by the continuation of the Cenozoic trend toward drier and colder climates and the cessation of summer rainfall west of the Rockies but also by mountain-building. Uplift of the Cascade-Sierra Nevada Axis divided the region. This orogeny began during late Miocene and became more and more significant during the Pliocene and Pleistocene, when the major uplifts occurred. The new climatic patterns forced evolu-

tion of both the Western Forest Flora and the Southwestern Woodland Flora, the two often occupying different levels of altitude in the same area, and both of them today composed of various floristic associations adapted to the climates of different areas. The coniferous woodlands, chaparrals, and grasslands of the Southwestern Woodland Flora have developed in response to the alteration of climate.

In the far-inland area of southeastern Utah, southern Colorado, Arizona, New Mexico, and trans-Pecos Texas, there has been climatic alteration, but it has been within the pattern of dominant summer rain, and in most areas the flora has changed less since the Miocene than has that farther west. The Southwestern Oak Woodland of Arizona and southwestern New Mexico is the nearest modern approach to the woodland of the Miocene. However, through most of the area the Southwestern Woodland Flora has been modified by the uplift of the second generation of the Rockies, and this has altered the simpler patterns of the topography of the Miocene plains and changed the flora and the ecological formations.

VI.1. The Southwestern Woodland and Chaparral

Southernmost Utah to s Colorado, SE Arizona, and w New Mexico, 1,350-2,100 m (4,500-7,000 ft); just above the deserts or usually above the Desert Grassland. A similar unclassified woodland occurs in w Texas.

This is an area of predominant summer rainfall and less significant winter precipitation. Usually, by the time the spring weather is warm enough for much growth to occur, the ground dries up, though during rainy years there may be a good vernal growing season.

Cacti. Cacti are present and in some areas varied and abundant.

The floristic association is composed of three only partly differentiated phases.

1a. The Southwestern Oak Woodland Phase. An often more or less parklike woodland. Arizona at middle altitudes below the Mogollon Rim and from Pinal and Pima Cos. to Cochise Co.; sw New Mexico in Hidalgo and Grant Cos. Mexico in Sonora. About (1,200)1,500-1,800 m (4,000 or 5,000-6,000 ft). **Markers:** Emory oak or bellota, *Quercus emoryi*; Mexican blue oak, *Q. oblongifolia*; Arizona oak, *Q. arizonica*; whiteleaf oak, *Q. hypoleucoides*; Arizona madrone, *Arbutus arizonica*; Arizona cypresses, *Cypressus*

Fig. 155. Southwestern Oak Woodland in the Coronado National Forest, southern Arizona; the characteristic scattered oaks give an open parklike appearance. Many perennial grasses grow between and under the trees, many of these and the other herbaceous plants growing also in the related Desert Grassland. "This cover absorbs like a blotter the water from rains and melting snows." (E. O. Buhler, U.S. Forest Service; from *Plant Classification*)

arizonica vars. *arizonica* and *glabra*; three-leaf pinyon, *Pinus cembroides* var. *cembroides*; Chihuahua pine, *P. leiophylla* var. *chihuahuana*. (Fig. 155.)

Cacti: Several species of Cactaceae occur within or along the lower edge of the Southwestern Oak Woodland.

1b. The Southwestern Chaparral Phase. Brushland dispersed through the area of oak woodland; not a distinctive floristic association like the California Chaparral, and characterized by only a few shrubby species that occur also in the Southwestern Oak Woodland. **Markers:** Mountain lilac, *Ceanothus greggii*; manzanitas, *Arctostaphylos pungens* and *pringlei*; redberry, *Rhamnus crocea* var. *ilicifolia*. The same taxa occur also in the California Chaparral, and they are among a group of species of this flora that occurred across the northern end of the Colorado Basin during the Pleistocene. (Fig. 156.)

Cacti. The cacti here are species occurring also in the Southwestern Oak Woodland Phase.

1c. The Southern Juniper-Pinyon Woodland Phase. A somewhat parklike woodland. Southernmost Utah, where it intergrades with the Northern Juniper-Pinyon Woodland, to the foothills of the Rocky Mountains from s Colorado to E central Arizona, New Mexico, and westernmost Texas. About 1,500-2,100 m (5,000-7,000 ft). **Markers:** Alligator bark juniper, *Juniperus deppeana*; one-seeded juniper, *J. monosperma*; two-leaf pinyon, *Pinus cembroides* var. *edulis*. (Fig. 157.)

This is an area primarily of summer rain. The species are mostly different from those occurring in the Northern Juniper-Pinyon Woodland Phase of the Great Basin Woodland and Desert (p. 185), which has primarily winter precipitation.

Cacti: Most species occur also in the Southwestern Oak Woodland Phase, but some do not.

Fig. 156. Southwestern Chaparral on Hualpai Mountain, south of Kingman, Mohave Co., Arizona, at about 2,400 m (6,000 feet) elevation. The chaparral looks much like that in California, but it is composed of only a few woody species occurring also in the adjacent Southwestern Oak Woodland and in the California Chaparral. The formation is distinctive; the phase of the floristic association is not.

Fig. 157 (below). Southern Juniper-Pinyon Woodland on the hills and bluffs, with Great Plains Grassland on the valley soils at lower elevations, near Grants, New Mexico; a typical relationship in the transition between these floristic associations. (From *Plant Taxonomy, Methods and Principles*)

Fig. 158. Desert Grassland near Rimrock, Yavapai Co., Arizona, typical of the rolling hills below the Mogollon Rim region and in southern Arizona; in the foreground, Engelmann prickly pear, *Opuntia phaeacantha* var. *discata*, and banana yucca, *Yucca baccata*.

Fig. 159. Desert Grassland with the typical presence of soapweed, *Yucca elata*; north of Elgin, Santa Cruz Co., Arizona; Southwestern Oak Woodland at the summit of the higher hill.

Fig. 160. Desert Grassland with large cane chollas, *Opuntia spinosior*, and smaller cacti (not showing); near the Santa Rita Mts. in Pima Co., Arizona. (David Griffiths)

Fig. 161. Desert Grassland with large prickly pears, *Opuntia phaeacantha* var. *major* (foreground), var. *discata*, and a hybrid swarm; near the Santa Rita Mts., Pima Co., Arizona. (David Griffiths)

VI.2. The Desert Grassland

Arizona, near and within the Horse Latitudes, in the hills below the Mogollon Rim and in the SE highlands; s New Mexico and the higher parts of trans-Pecos Texas. Moderate elevations: (750) 900-1,500 m (2,500 or 3,000-5,000 ft). **Markers:** Numerous characteristic grasses, including a dozen species of grama grass (*Bouteloua*) and many of *Aristida* (*Muhlenbergia*), and numerous other genera of Gramineae. Several shrubs and trees occur in the grassland, but probably most are invaders from the oak woodland above or the desert below. (Figs. 158 and 159.)

Since the cessation of Indian-set fires and the advent of overgrazing by cattle, the areas of Desert Grassland have been reduced. The seedlings of trees and shrubs of both higher and lower elevations have been able to grow, instead of being killed by fire, and the areas of grass cover have been reduced drastically by the overabundance of range animals. The seeds of the velvet mesquite, *Prosopis juliflora* var. *velutina*, have been carried in the digestive tracts of cattle grazing and browsing in the bottomlands into the grass-land and deposited with both fertilizer and water-retaining humus, enabling seedlings to become established. The mesquites compete with the grasses for water, and they tend to aid the encroachment of desert plants from lower elevations.

The Desert Grassland is related floristically to the Great Plains Grassland and to the Arizona and Chihuahuan deserts, and in some areas classification is difficult.

Cacti. The Desert Grassland is an important area of occurrence of cacti. Presence within the edge of the Horse Latitudes yields a warm, relatively dry climate with summer and some winter rain, which is favorable to many species. The area is a little higher and moister than the deserts below, and this is suitable for a different group of species. (Figs. 160 and 161.)

VI.3. The California Oak Woodland

An open, parklike woodland. Rogue River Valley in sw Oregon; dominating the lowlands of N California and occurring as "islands" in the California Chaparral of s California. Northward

Fig. 162. California Oak Woodland with scattered blue oaks, *Quercus douglasii*, typical of the foothills of northern California, these forming an open, parklike woodland; eastern base of the Hopland Grade, west of Lakeport, Lake Co., California. The white bark is characteristic of the species, and except in books the plant is known as white oak.

Fig. 163. California Oak Woodland as it appears in the valleys, in the few areas where the deep soils have not been converted to agriculture; valley oak, *Quercus lobata*. The excellent soil supports a dense undergrowth of underbrush and herbaceous plants. Near Lakeside Park, Clear Lake, Lake Co., California.

at 30-600 m (100-2,000 ft); southward to 1,350 m (4,500 ft). **Markers:** blue oak, or white oak, *Quercus douglasii*; valley oak, *Q. lobata*; Engelmann oak, *Q. engelmannii*; southern California black walnut, *Juglans californica*; California buckeye, *Aesculus californica*; and a host of herbaceous species. (Figs. 162 and 163.)

The California Oak Woodland is the characteristic lowland feature of northern California. In its original form the trees were well spaced, and there was a carpet of grasses and other herbs beneath and between them. Grass-fire suppression has permitted an overabundance of young trees, favoring an eventual hot fire and an ultimate change to chaparral. The winter rains begin usually in October and last until April or May, and the hills and valleys turn green in the early fall. During the winter the herbs grow slowly, but they develop rapidly during March and April and bloom profusely in April and May. Near the coast the growing and flowering seasons are earlier by about one month than they are farther inland. During late May and early June the hills dry, and they remain dry through the summer and until the first fall rains.

Cacti. The climate of northern California appears unfavorable for cacti, but almost the same climatic cycle supports them in southern California, where the dominant floristic association is California Chaparral. However, in the south the average temperature is about 6°C (10°F) higher, and the rainfall is about 15 cm (6 in) less. *Opuntia basilaris* var. *basilaris* is rare among the oaks in Tulare and Kern counties, California.

VI.4. The California Chaparral

Brushland with many species of fire-resistant shrubs, these surviving the common and intense brushfires mostly by crown-sprouting from thickened underground parts. Mostly on the mountainsides of s California, including the slopes above the deserts, and occurring in "islands" in the oak woodland of N California. Mostly 150-1,500 m (500-5,000 ft). **Markers:** mountain lilacs, *Ceanothus foliosus, spinosus, divaricatus, tomentosus, oliganthus, verrucosus, megacarpus, crassifolius, cuneatus,* and *jepsonii*; bush poppy, *Dendromecon rigida*; barberries, *Berberis dictyota* and *nevinii*; California styrax, *Styrax officinalis* var. *californica*; some manzanitas, *Arctostaphylos glauca, stanfordiana, canescens, glandulosa,* and *tomentosa*; foothill ash, *Fraxinus dipetala*; chaparral pea, *Pickeringia montana*; mountain mahoganies, *Cercocarpus montanus* var. *glaber* (known as *C. betuloides*) and *minutiflorus*; chamise brush, *Adenostoma fasciculatum*; red shanks, *A. sparsifolium*; flowering currants, *Ribes malvaceum* vars. *viridiflorum* and *indecorum*; chaparral honeysuckles, *Lonicera subspicata* and *interrupta*; scrub oaks, *Quercus dumosa, durata,* etc.; silk tassel bushes, *Garrya veatchii, fremontii,* and *flavescens*; knobcone pine, *Pinus attenuata*; Sargent cypress, *Cupressus sargentii*; McNab cypress, *C. macnabiana*; and many other shrubs and some herbaceous plants. (Fig. 164.)

The length of the list of endemic woody species indicates the stability and the unique character of this floristic association, as well as its distinction from the California Oak Woodland. This is in strong contrast with the Southwestern Chaparral of Arizona, in which the few characteristic species occur also in the Southwestern Oak Woodland and the California Chaparral.

The California Chaparral once dominated some parts of the lowland valleys of southern California, as well as the hills and lower mountainsides, but clearing for agriculture, grazing land, and other human activities destroyed it in some places and enabled it to spread into others once occupied by a little-known grassland now essentially extinct. From place to place the area is either greatly disturbed and now covered primarily with introduced Mediterranean weeds, mostly annual grasses, or in transitional climax phases of invasion by or return to chaparral. These are the coastal sagebrush subclimax, characterized by coastal sagebrush, *Artemisia californica*; a shrubby wild buckwheat, *Eriogonum fasciculatum* var. *polifolium*; a yerba santa or yerba mansa, either *Eriodictyon trichocalyx* or *E. crassifolium*; black sage, *Salvia mellifera* (mostly along the edges of the hills); bee sage, or white sage, *S. apiana*; scale broom, *Lepidospartum*

Fig. 164. California Chaparral; numerous densely grown shrubs of many species, these mostly endemic to the chaparral and all fire-resistant, mostly by crown-sprouting from storage parts under ground. The plant in flower in the foreground is chamise brush, *Adenostoma fasciculatum*; the large one on the right is the scrub oak, *Quercus dumosa*. The grassy, cleared area at the right is along a road; this clearing is supposed to reduce fire danger, but it has the opposite effect because the annual, summer-dry grasses are excellent tinder for starting a fire and igniting the shrubs of the chaparral. Near Highland Springs, Lake Co., California.

Fig. 165. Desert-edge California Chaparral between Castaic and Gorman, Los Angeles Co., where the dominant shrub is the desert scrub oak of California, *Quercus turbinella* var. *californica*. Here, toward the coast near a low gap from the desert, the chaparral is more dense than along the edge of the desert, where it is open, with considerable space between shrubs, except in the more favorable locations like this one.

squamatum; and *Haplopappus pinifolius*. The second subclimax is dominated by chamise brush, *Adenostoma fasciculatum*. The transitional or subclimax manifestations of California Chaparral are so distinctive in appearance that under systems of classification emphasizing vegetation formations rather than floristic associations they have been considered to be separate formations apart from the chaparral.

Cacti. Most of the Cactaceae of coastal southern California are prickly pears, but chollas, *Opuntia prolifera* and *O. parryi* (two varieties) occur west of the mountains. In coastal San Diego County, one species each of *Cereus*, *Ferocactus*, and *Mammillaria* occurs on the hills, bluffs, and flats.

Although the coastal side of the mountain axis in southern California is a natural distribution center for cacti, their occurrence there is limited by the intensity of the fires running through the shrub of the chaparral. Cacti cannot endure really hot fires, and many are killed by even the flash fires in the high, dry grass of summer. Some occur on rocky or sandy banks, where the vegetation, including grasses, is sparse, or in the sandy or gravelly flood areas of dry washes. Some large, sprawling hybrids survive the occasional grass fires by forming dense thickets that exclude the grasses (see Figs. 535-41).

Cacti are more abundant in brushland on the desert side of the mountains of southern California (on the eastern side of the Cascade-Sierra Nevada Axis), where there is a local, more open, desert-edge version of the California Chaparral with species selected in accordance with the drier climate (see Fig. 165). Often the nature of this phase of the floristic association is obscured by the presence of junipers and pinyons among the shrubs, and it has been confused with the Northern Juniper-Pinyon Woodland. However, the common juniper in the association is the California juniper, *Juniperus californica* var. *californica*, a chaparral species occurring in the California Coast Ranges as far north as Lake County. The Utah juniper, *Juniperus californica* var. *osteosperma*, is rare. The four-needle pinyon, *Pinus cembroides* var. *parryana,* is also a chaparral plant. This variety grows from the Santa Rosa Mountains in Riverside County southward into Baja California. The one-leaf pinyon, var. *monophylla,* occurring mostly from the Palms-to-Pines Highway north, is actually the one dominant in the Northern Juniper-Pinyon Woodland of the Great Basin; its range extends southward in the rain shadow above the edge of the Mojavean Desert from the eastern side of the Sierra Nevada. This phase of the California Chaparral is fairly rich in cacti. It is rocky and relatively dry, and the shrubs tend to be spaced widely, leaving rocky or sandy places where the heat of brushfires does not become too intense for the survival of cacti.

VI.5. The Pacific Grassland

In the Sacramento Valley of California, occurring in patches among areas of oak woodland and of chaparral; the prevailing floristic association of the San Joaquin Valley and the surrounding foothills up to the beginning of blue oaks and extending into neighboring small valleys of the South Coast Ranges; in s California, in w Antelope Valley, adjoining the Mojavean Desert.

Mostly at 30-480 m (100-1,600 ft), but in Antelope Valley (extreme rain shadow) at 900-1,200 m (3,000-4,000 ft). **Markers:** Numerous herbaceous species, these now partly crowded out by Mediterranean weeds, especially weedy grasses. The valley floors have been disturbed for agriculture, and the hills by overgrazing. (Fig. 166.)

Nearly all the native species are related to those in the California Oak Woodland or the California Chaparral. A few have invaded from the deserts, following along the Pitt River into the Sacramento Valley or migrating across Walker Pass into the San Joaquin. Originally the northern part of the grassland was maintained by a combination of drought and Indian fires that killed the seedlings of woody plants. In the southern part, drought alone was probably enough.

In rare years of adequate, well-distributed rainfall, the margins of the southern San Joaquin Valley become an unbelievable mass of many colors when the wildflowers bloom at the end of March and the beginning of April. The color display (see Fig. 167) is more magnificent than any in the North American deserts or on the Texas

Fig. 166. Pacific Grassland during the dry summer, a season of little or usually no rainfall in California, the average total for the year being less than 10 cm (4 inches) at this point; northeast of Soda Lake, Carissa Plains, San Luis Obispo Co., California. The bushy shrub is *Haplopappus acradenius.*

Fig. 167. Pacific Grassland during a moist, rainy spring with the rains coming at regular intervals, a rare phenomenon; the hillside is dominated by California poppies, *Eschscholzia californica* var. *crocea*, but supports many other flowering species, in this case obscured by the mass of orange-yellow poppies. (Frasher Collection, Pomona Public Library)

plains, and it is equal even to that in the flower fields of Namaqualand in South Africa. Good years are rare, and recently they have occurred only in 1932, 1935, 1937, 1941, 1952, 1958, and 1973. Before World War II the floor of the southern end of the valley was a flower field, but then it was plowed, and now the flowers are restricted to the great alluvial fans and the lower hills.

Cacti. In the southern San Joaquin Valley and the adjacent foothills of the Greenhorn and Tehachapi ranges, *Opuntia basilaris* var. *treleasei* still forms extensive patches, though they have been reduced by human activities. These become flower gardens during May, when the cactus mats may be covered with beautiful cerise flowers about 10 cm (4 in) in diameter.

VI.6. The Closed-Cone Pine Forest

Forest, but the small coniferous trees of types more often associated with and probably derived from the Madrotertiary Geoflora (Axelrod, 1967a), which gave rise probably to the Southwestern Woodland Flora. California near sea level from Trinidad, Humboldt Co., to N Sonoma Co.; intermittent s along the coast to Santa Barbara Co.; Santa Cruz and Santa Rosa Is. **Markers:**

Monterey pine, *Pinus radiata*; Bishop pine, *P. muricata*; beach pine, *Pinus contorta* var. *contorta* (but this variety occurring also farther northward along the coast); pygmy beach pine, *P. contorta* var. *bolanderi*; Monterey cypress, *Cupressus macrocarpa*; Gowen cypress, *C. goveniana*; pygmy cypress, *C. goveniana* var. *pygmaea*; manzanitas, *Arctostaphylos hookeri, pumila, nummularia,* and others. (Fig. 168.)

The maritime climate, with nearly frost-free winters and summer fogs, has enabled many species to persist near the ocean. The fogs accompanying seasonal upwelling of cold water along the shore provide some water for the closed-cone pines and the smaller plants growing beneath them. The fog condenses on the needles (leaves), and the water is concentrated into drops on the "drip tips," the drops then falling to the ground.

The Closed-Cone Pine Forest is not a completely differentiated floristic association. Even in the continuous strip along the Mendocino Coast and in the "island" at Monterey, the association occurs mostly on stabilized sand, steep hills, or ocean bluffs, primarily in areas of recent or old disturbance. Often the forest is a successional phase on unstable land, and ultimately it gives

Fig. 168. Closed-Cone Pine Forest on unstable ground above an ocean inlet; mouth of Russian Gulch, Russian Gulch State Park, south of Ft. Bragg, Mendocino Co., California. The dominant trees are Bishop pine, *Pinus muricata,* and beach pine, *P. contorta* var. *contorta.*

way to the redwood version of the Pacific Lowland Forest. In part, though, the association is dependent on coastal conditions not necessarily favorable to the redwood forest.

Cacti: The Closed-Cone Pine Forest is one of the few floristic associations in North America with no native cacti. The winter climate is mild and lacks killing frost, and the soil tends to be sandy and well-drained. However, the winter rainfall is high, and many plants better adapted than cacti are favored.

VI.7. The California Insular Association

Islands off the coast of s California and Baja California; a few small areas on the coastal mainland. **Markers:** Island bush poppy, *Dendromecon harfordii;* island oak, *Quercus dumosa* var. *macdonaldii;* Catalina ironwood, *Lyonothamnus floribundus* vars. *floribundus* and *asplenifolius;* mountain mahoganies, *Cercocarpus montanus*

vars. *traskiae* and *alnifolia;* Catalina cherry, *Prunus ilicifolia* var. *occidentalis;* redberry, *Rhamnus crocea* var. *pirifolia;* mountain lilacs, *Ceanothus insularis* and *arboreus;* tree mallow, *Lavatera assurgentiflora.*

The species endemic to the islands and a few coastal bluffs have been confined there primarily by sensitivity to the frosts occurring on the interior mainland. The endemics have been present since the Oligocene (Axelrod, 1967a, 1967b), though during the Tertiary some occurred on the mainland, even far inland beyond the site of the present Cascade-Sierra Nevada Axis. During all of Cenozoic time there has been a general trend of cooling and drying, and near the Pacific Coast summer rainfall has ceased. These changes have restricted species to the islands or to the Closed-Cone Pine Forest, i.e. to places where there are no killing frosts and where there is also summer fog.

The floristic association is not wholly distinct from the California Chaparral; the relict endemic species mingle with others occurring commonly also on the mainland. The island endemics are dominant in some areas but less so in others, and the association varies on the two major groups of islands. On the northern group—San Miguel, Santa Rosa, Santa Cruz, and Anacapa—the chaparral both resembles and differs from that of the adjacent mainland in Santa Barbara and Ventura counties. On the southern group—San Nicolas, Santa Catalina, Santa Barbara, and San Clemente—the chaparral is partly similar to that of southern Los Angeles, Orange, and San Diego counties. Ancient land connections are indicated.

Cacti. Cacti occur on all the islands, but they are more numerous and varied on the southern ones. The same species also occur on the adjacent mainland. There are several taxa of prickly pears, and *Cereus emoryi* occurs on the southern islands.

VI.8. The Great Basin Woodland and Desert

Columbia Basin; the dominant floristic association of the Great Basin; overlapping into adjacent areas. Altitude is indicated under the three phases.

Winter rain or snow is predominant, but light. Summer rainfall is slight and irregular, except in the Navajoan Desert Phase.

The floristic association is of diverse origin. It includes elements from both the Madrotertiary Geoflora and the Miocene forests. It has evolved into two Great Basin phases occurring at different levels of altitude, one on rocky mountainsides, the other on deep valley soils. The third phase occurs on the Colorado Plateau.

8a. The Northern Juniper-Pinyon Woodland Phase. A more or less parklike woodland occupying higher altitudes and more rocky soils than the Sagebrush Desert. Mostly 1,500-2,100 m (5,000-7,000 ft). **Markers:** One-leaf pinyon, *Pinus cembroides* var. *monophylla*; Utah juniper, *Juni-*

Fig. 169. Northern Juniper-Pinyon Woodland near the mouth of Zion Canyon, Zion National Park, Washington Co., Utah; Utah juniper, *Juniperus californica* var. *osteosperma*; two-leaf pinyon, *Pinus cembroides* var. *edulis*; shrubs, including desert scrub oak, *Quercus turbinella* var. *turbinella*; at lower left, a young Fremont cottonwood, *Populus fremontii*, not yet in leaf.

perus californica var. *osteosperma* (*Juniperus osteosperma*); rabbit brush, *Chrysothamnus nauseosus* vars. (several, similar in appearance). (Fig. 169.)

This is an area of relatively light winter precipitation, including both rain and snow.

Cacti. A number of species occur, and some taxa are common.

8b. The Sagebrush Desert Phase. A desert characterized by the gray-green sagebrush, *Artemisia tridentata,* and in some areas by light gray shadscales, or saltbushes, *Atriplex.* Thompson River, British Columbia, to the lower elevations of the Columbia Basin and the Great Basin; represented by some (probably introduced) elements, including the sagebrush, occurring on overgrazed land E of the Continental Divide in Wyoming and even farther E on the Great Plains. Mostly

1,200-1,800 m (4,000-6,000 ft). In the valleys, occupying deeper soils, at lower altitudes, than the Northern Juniper-Pinyon Woodland. **Markers:** Sagebrush, *Artemisia tridentata*; black sage, *Artemisia arbuscula*; shadscale, *Atriplex confertifolia*; salt sage, *Atriplex nuttallii*; purple sage, *Salvia dorrii* var. *carnosa*; antelope brush, *Purshia tridentata*; desert peach, *Prunus andersonii*. (Fig. 170.)

Cacti. Common, some species abundant.

8c. The Navajoan Desert Phase. Colorado Plateau in S Utah to SW Colorado, N Arizona, and NW New Mexico. Commonly 1,200-1,500 m (4,000-5,000 ft). **Markers:** nearly all the species of *Pediocactus,* except *P. simpsonii*; most of the species of *Sclerocactus.* (Fig. 171.)

This desert is in need of further study and evaluation as a floristic unit. The localized and eco-

Fig. 170. Sagebrush Desert on a flat with deep soil; Ruby Mts., Elko Co., Nevada. Sagebrush, *Artemisia tridentata,* dominates. Northern Juniper-Pinyon Woodland on the lower hills in the background; Rocky Mountain Montane and Subalpine forests above; and West American Alpine Tundra on the highest peak. (Frank P. McWhorter)

Fig. 171. Navajoan Desert, showing the wind sculpturing of the soft, fine-grained, reddish-tan sandstone of the Navajo country, the sculpturing accomplished by blowing sand. Great open spaces are covered with widely dispersed low shrubs like those in both pictures, no one shrub being dominant through the whole desert; cacti are numerous. The Arches National Park, north of Moab, Grand Co., Utah.

logically specialized species of endemic cacti indicate floristic coherence. According to Stanley L. Welsh (Intermountain Biogeography Symposium, Univ. of Montana, June 15, 1976), 182 endemic plant taxa occur on the Colorado Plateau below 1,950 m (6,500 ft). Thus, the study of other plant groups may confirm the floristic unit indicated by the Cactaceae.

The Navajo country is distinctive in topography and scenery, and it is one of the most beautiful areas on Earth. It is noted for colored rock formations in a delightful setting of peaceful, gray-green, shrubby mountain- and rock-studded plains stretching seemingly to eternity. Many special places have been set aside as National Parks and National Monuments; thousands of others would be if they occurred anywhere else.

Cacti. In addition to the cacti mentioned above, there are many others. The area is rich in small species with beautiful flowers.

THE HORSE LATITUDES — THE DESERT ZONE
(Climatic Zone for Flora VII)

The low-altitude deserts near the international boundary from southeastern California (east of the mountain axis) to southern Arizona (below the Mogollon Rim), southern New Mexico, and trans-Pecos Texas; grasslands at the next higher level of elevation, and with greater rainfall, from central and southeastern Arizona to southern New Mexico and western and southern Texas; forest areas in the mountains and in the maritime region of the Gulf and Atlantic coasts and in Florida.

The 30th parallel of latitude extends across the northern part of western Mexico and through Texas between Austin and San Antonio, Louisiana near New Orleans, and Florida near St. Augustine. Northward the Horse Latitudes give way gradually to the zone of prevailing westerlies, but their influence, especially during the summer, may extend as far as about the 34th parallel, which runs near Los Angeles, Phoenix, Wichita Falls, Birmingham, and Wilmington (North Carolina). In the west the descending air mass of the Horse Latitudes encounters only land, and this tends to be occupied by mountains with intervening deserts and high, dry grasslands. Eastward the corresponding air mass picks up moisture over the warm Gulf of Mexico and the Atlantic Ocean; consequently, there are no deserts in the Horse Latitudes of eastern North America. The maritime areas along the Gulf of Mexico, on the Atlantic Coast, and in Florida have a moist climate.

The Horse Latitudes have no sharp boundaries. At the north, the prevailing westerlies begin imperceptibly. At the south, the tradewinds begin similarly. The generally accepted southern limit is at the Tropic of Cancer, 23°N, extending through the tip of Baja California, Mazatlán, Ciudad Victoria, and Havana. However, in some areas the Horse Latitudes are interpreted as running farther south, to 20° or even 15°, where local climatic conditions produce deserts. The Florida Keys reach only 24.5°N, but their climate is more of the tropics than of the Horse Latitudes, because of proximity to warm seas.

The deserts are characterized by sunshine, clear skies, low rainfall, and often strong local winds. The variation in temperature between day and night is extreme, commonly about 28°C (50°F), and the average temperature shifts greatly with the seasons. Usually the desert summer is hot, but in some deserts the winter is cold. Temperature instability is promoted by the lack of water as a stabilizing influence, the uninhibited high-angle sunshine falling directly on the mostly bare ground, and the resulting convection and the rapid radiation at night.

According to Axelrod (1967c), fully formed deserts are a new phenomenon of late Cenozoic time; nevertheless, they cover about 20 percent of the land of the world. The deserts of the United States have reached their present degree of development rapidly since the Pleistocene glacial periods, though at least semideserts must have been forming and receding during the interglacial periods, as well, since these times were similar to the present time. In the United States the uplift of the Cascade-Sierra Nevada Axis —slightly during the Miocene, more during the Pliocene, mostly during Pleistocene—triggered the formation of real deserts, following the general drying trend of the Cenozoic and the return of warmth and dryness after the Pleistocene. The beginnings of desert conditions occurred by middle Cenozoic time, but development has been gradual.

The deserts include a wide range of soil types derived from a great range of parent rocks. Some of the more bizarre types include sand dunes, like those in the vicinity of the Colorado River in California across from Yuma, Arizona (see Fig. 172); alkali flats occurring about dry lakes (Fig. 173); completely barren rock formations, as in some areas adjacent to Death Valley, California (Fig. 174); and desert pavement, covering large areas of the desert floor. Desert pavement (Fig. 175) consists of a layer of rock fragments covering a very fine, flourlike soil. This is deceptively firm, and many an automobile has sunk to the hubs of its wheels following an attempt to start too quickly. Originally the mixture of rock, gravel, and soil rose several meters higher, but the fine soil has been washed away by rain and blown away by the desert winds. Ultimately the remaining rock fragments and gravel have formed a mosaiclike pattern over the surface, protecting the fine soil beneath from further erosion.

VII. THE MEXICAN DESERT FLORA

The Southwestern Deserts of the United States and their extensions s into Mexico. The Mojavean and Colorado Deserts of California to s Arizona below the Mogollon Rim; New Mexico s of Socorro and the Sacramento Mountains; trans-Pecos Texas. Mexico from Baja California to Coahuila, Zacatecas, San Luis Potosí, and Querétaro. From below sea level near the Salton Sea and in Death Valley to 1,050 m (3,500 ft) or, in extreme rain shadows, even 1,500 m (5,000 ft); mostly 1,200-1,800 m (4,000-6,000 ft) in the Chihuahuan Desert.

The Mexican Desert Flora has essentially the same geographic range as the creosote bush, *Larrea tridentata,* of North America. This dark-green shrub, 1-2(3) m (3-6 or 10 ft) tall, forms an in-

Fig. 172. Desert sand dunes, formed by the wind; Imperial Co., California, west of the Colorado River and Yuma, Arizona.

Fig. 173. Desert alkali flat below sea level, supporting only specialized plants of the Chenopodiaceae—*Suaeda* and *Allenrolfea*—and, along the borders, *Atriplex*. Near Bad Water, Death Valley, California; Black Mts. in the background.

Fig. 174. An area with no vegetation, the various rocks differently colored and exposed; Zabriskie Point, Black Mts., Death Valley National Park, California.

Fig. 175. Desert pavement. *Left*, undisturbed, the rock fragments interlocking in a mosaic retarding erosion by wind or water. *Right*, the same spot (note rock positions) after a flick with the toe of a boot, exposing the fine, powdery soil beneath the rock fragments. The rocks are an accumulation from those originally dispersed in soil above, the soil carried away until only the rocks were left, forming a continuous layer.

190

verted cone or a lump supported by lead-colored basal branches. The plants are spaced widely, sometimes giving the impression of being planted. (Fig. 176.) In most open areas they dominate the landscape, but they may be overtopped by larger species, like the saguaro, *Cereus giganteus*; the foothill palo verde, *Cercidium microphyllum*; or the ocotillo, *Fouquieria splendens*. Along washes the creosote bushes are larger, but they are more or less lost among still larger trees and shrubs, like the mesquites, *Prosopis*; the blue palo verde, *Cercidium floridum*; the desert ironwood, *Olneya tesota*; and many others.

All desert plants must conserve water during the dry seasons, and there are many adaptations directed to this end. Water retention by cacti is discussed on p. 58. Mature desert cacti have no leaves, and the leaves of most other desert plants are small; thus, the area of potential water loss is reduced. Some desert species have deep root systems, reaching water far below the surface. At the beginning of the dry season, many shrubs lose their leaves or the leaves dry up, and perennials die down to ground level, living over as rhizomes or stem bases, usually with roots. Annual plants, abundant in the deserts, die at about the time the seeds mature, and only the seeds live through the drought period.

Although the deserts are new, plants adapted to dry habitats have been developing at least

Fig. 176. Mexican Desert Flora, specifically Arizona Desert; Papago Indian Reservation, Pima Co., Arizona. The ubiquitous creosote bush, *Larrea tridentata* var. *tridentata*, is an amazingly accurate indicator of this flora. Characteristically, the plants are widely spaced, as here, reducing competition; the spacing is attributed to secretion of growth inhibitors into the soil, reducing competition from young plants. Young saguaros, *Cereus giganteus*, are on the hills in the background.

through all of Cenozoic time. This is indicated by the fossil record, which shows woodlands, chaparrals, and thorn forests far back in the Tertiary. These formations must have occupied relatively dry habitats. The antiquity of the major desert taxa and their long separation from their relatives of moister habitats is indicated by special genera and families (Axelrod, 1967c). For example, three monotypic or small genera endemic to the North American deserts have no or few close relatives within their families: an elephant tree, *Pachycormus discolor*; a crucifixion thorn, *Castela emoryi*; and the goat nut, *Simmondsia chinensis* (from North America, the scientific name inappropriate). The relationships of four families of mostly desert or dryland plants are unknown and not close: Cactaceae, Fouquieriaceae (ocotillo, cirio), Crossosomataceae (*Crossosoma*), and Koeberliniaceae (crucifixion thorns). All these taxa must have evolved under drought conditions during a long period of isolation from their relatives.

The present genera and families of drought-resistant plants did not necessarily evolve in large areas of xerophytic vegetation similar to the present deserts. Many dry habitats are local, e.g. the rain-shadow pockets in the lees of mountains or high islands or on exposed ridges of granite or gneiss with very little soil. Examples occur on Stone Mountain, Georgia; on Sugarloaf at Rio de Janeiro; and in the Catinga in Brazil. In such pockets, which occur even in tropical forests, the forerunners of plants of the desert floras may have been developing since the Mesozoic (Axelrod, 1972b).

Most of the species in the deserts of the United States are derivatives of floristic elements of the dry regions of northern Mexico or of plants that during the Tertiary occupied dry pockets in the local rain shadows of discontinuous mountain ranges formerly near or within the areas of the present deserts. According to Axelrod (1940, 1948, 1950, 1957, 1967c), the deserts just east of the Cascade-Sierra Nevada Axis were formed largely during and since the Pleistocene. During this period the mountain axis was rising, and the rain shadows were developing. Consequently, many present desert species migrated northward from the Horse Latitudes, and others spread out into the large new area of rain shadow from the dry pockets they had occupied earlier. In both groups of migrants there must have been much hybridizing and natural selection in the new environments.

The Mexican Desert Flora varies regionally, and the individual deserts have different aspects. The Mojavean Desert is covered with low, gray-green shrubs, and in the upper levels the Joshua trees, *Yucca brevifolia* vars., rise conspicuously above them. The Colorado Desert features lighter green shrubs against light-colored soils or gravels, and tall shrubs or trees only along watercourses or in bottomlands. The Arizona Desert supports conspicuous large cacti and often many shrubs, these dense enough to be confused with chaparral. The Chihuahuan Desert, as it occurs in the United States, has a low and relatively sparse cover of shrubs, except in washes and at higher levels, and the creosote bushes are small.

According to ecological classifications, the Colorado and Arizona deserts are part of the Sonoran Deserts, a category apart from the Mojavean Desert and the Chihuahuan Desert. However, recent checking of species of woody plants in preparation of the third edition of *The Trees and Shrubs of the Southwestern Deserts* (Benson & Darrow, 1945, 1954) shows that all four deserts —Mojavean, Colorado, Arizona, and Chihuahuan—are about equally interrelated floristically. Consequently, each is presented here as a floristic association in its own right. One or more other floristic associations may be included in the remainder of the Sonoran Desert area in Mexico, as defined ecologically.

Cacti: The Horse Latitudes of North and South America are the chief centers of distribution of the cactus family, and the cacti are among the most outstanding members of the characteristic desert floras, in some cases the dominant feature of the vegetation. In the Northern Hemisphere they are clustered in Mexico and along the southern fringe of the western United States. In the Southern Hemisphere they occur primarily in the deserts and other dry areas along the bases of the Andes. The present connections between the deserts of the two continents are chiefly through intermittent tropical dry areas, such as rain shadows, coastal dunes, and headlands.

All the deserts of the United States are rich in cacti (see Table 4, pp. 210-15), and many species are markers of the individual deserts. In all four creosote-bush-desert floristic associations, the cacti are conspicuous in at least some places, and in the Arizona Desert they are the outstanding feature of the landscapes of most areas.

VII.1. The Mojavean Desert

The Mojave Desert (a geographic, not botanical, term) in California and similar deserts E to Washington Co., Utah, and to just beyond the

Bill Williams and Santa Maria rivers in NW Arizona. Mostly 600-1,200 m (2,000-4,000 ft), but rarely to 1,500 m (5,000 ft) in the extreme rain shadows of high mountains. **Markers:** Joshua trees, *Yucca brevifolia* vars. *brevifolia* and *jaegeriana*; Parry saltbush, *Atriplex parryi*; *Mortonia scabrella* var. *utahensis*; *Menodora spinescens*; desert crucifixion thorn, *Canotia holacantha*; *Lycium parishii*; *L. pallidum* var. *oligospermum*; Death Valley sage, *Salvia funerea*; Mojave sage, *S. mohavensis*; spiny senna, *Cassia armata*; indigo bushes, *Dalea arborescens* and *fremontii* vars. *pubescens*, *saundersii*, and *minutifolia*; *Amphiachyris fremontii*; *Acamptopappus schockleyi*; *Haplopappus linearifolius* var. *interior*; *Chrysothamnus teretifolius*; horse brush, *Tetradymia stenolepis*; *Viguiera reticulata*; woolly bur sage, *Ambrosia* (*Franseria*) *eriocentra*; Mormon or Mexican teas, *Ephedra viridis* and *californica* var. *funerea*. (Figs. 177-79).

Fig. 177. Mojavean Desert, dominated by the Joshua tree, *Yucca brevifolia*, at the higher levels of elevation, mostly above 900 m (3,000 feet). Other plants here are the Engelmann prickly pear, *Opuntia phaeacantha* var. *discata*; staghorn cholla, *O. acanthocarpa* var. *coloradensis*; several plants of the creosote bush, *Larrea tridentata* var. *tridentata*; and a young barrel cactus, *Ferocactus acanthodes* var. *lecontei* (in the center). Near Santa Maria River, southwestern Yavapai Co., Arizona. This spot is at the southern edge of the Mojavean Desert, and a single ocotillo, *Fouquieria splendens*, an Arizona Desert species, stands on the horizon at the right.

Fig. 178. Mojavean Desert near Walker Pass, Kern Co., California. The Joshua tree here is a form that is common in the hills at the western edge of the Mojavean Desert, the plants producing numerous stems in a dense cluster from shorter than usual underground stems, or rhizomes. (Frank P. McWhorter)

Winter temperatures may be relatively low, and freezing is common. There are about 20-30 cm (8-12 in) of rain or snow, nearly all during the winter. Summer rain is rare, deriving, when it does occur, from unusual meanderings of tropical storms from the west coast of Mexico.

The upper levels of the Mojavean Desert, above 900 m (3,000 ft), are characterized by the Joshua tree, *Yucca brevifolia,* which occurs on both alluvial fans and hills or mountainsides. (Other species of trees occur only along watercourses.)

Except at the western edge of the desert, the Joshua trees stand well apart, like trees in an orchard, except that they are not in rows. Along the western hills of the Mojavean Desert a local form of the tree sends up many shoots from under ground, and there are dense clumps of trees. From the eastern edge of California to Utah the hills are covered by a dwarf Joshua tree, var. *jaegeriana,* having shorter and narrower leaves.

Cacti. Several species are abundant in the Mojavean Desert.

Fig. 179. Mojavean Desert a little below the level of Joshua trees, which in most areas appear at about 900 m (3,000 feet) elevation and above. A barrel cactus, *Echinocactus polycephalus*, characteristic of this desert, is in the foreground; other plants (distinguished with difficulty) are creosote bush, *Larrea tridentata* var. *tridentata*, in left middle ground, and Death Valley ephedra, *Ephedra californica* var. *funerea*, at the right. Pass in the Funeral Mts. between Furnace Creek and Death Valley Junction, California.

VII.2. The Colorado Desert

California and Arizona in the low areas of the Salton Sea Basin and along and near the Colorado and Gila rivers; adjacent NE Baja California and NW Sonora. Mostly below 450-600 m (1,500-2,000 ft) but rarely to 1,200 m (4,000 ft) in the extreme rain shadows of high mountains like the San Jacinto range. **Markers:** Species occurring mostly along watercourses or in subirrigated places: smoke tree, *Dalea spinosa*; California fan palm, *Washingtonia filifera*. Species occurring in drier areas: diamond cholla, *Opuntia ramosissima*; *Ayenia compacta*; *Tetracoccus hallii*; desert crucifixion thorn, *Castela emoryi*; *Condalia parryi*; desert milkweeds, *Asclepias subulata* and *albicans*; *Lycium brevipes* and *L. andersonii* var. *deserticola*; sages, *Salvia greatae* and *eremostachya*; *Justicia (Beloperone) californica*; *Hoff-*

manseggia microphylla; indigo bushes, *Dalea schottii* and *emoryi*; desert apricot, *Prunus fremontii*; *Brickellia frutescens*; *Haplopappus propinquus*; holly-leaf bur sage, *Ambrosia* (*Franseria*) *ilicifolia*; desert century plant, *Agave desertii*. (Figs. 180 and 181.) (See also the discussion of the Arizona Desert, concluding paragraph.)

The elevations are lower, and the temperatures higher, than those of the Mojavean Desert, and heavy frost occurs only rarely. The rainfall is less, only 5-12.5 cm (2-5 in) during the winter.

During the summer or early fall, in some years, one or more tropical storms may continue northward into the deserts, bringing rare summer rainfall. Some trees and shrubs common in Arizona are rare or local in the Colorado Desert in California, because their seeds can germinate only at high temperature after the unusual summer rains. Thus, young plants occur in distinct age classes,

according to the occasional years of significant summer rain during which seeds could have germinated.

Cacti. The Cactaceae are a major part of the floristic association of the Colorado Desert, and often they are conspicuous. The teddy bear chollas, *Opuntia bigelovii*, are prominent on the lower gravelly or rocky slopes. Var. *hoffmanii* may form miniature forests, as in Mason Valley, San Diego Co., California. Var. *bigelovii* forms more extensive forests, as at Pinto Basin, Joshua Tree National Monument, and northwest of Needles in California. *O. ramosissima* is prominent as either a mat-forming plant or a shrub in many areas, especially sandy areas. *O. wigginsii* is inconspicuous and rare, but it occurs only in the Colorado Desert; the same is true of the large chollas, *O. echinocarpa* var. *wolfii*, *O. acanthocarpa* var. *ganderi*, and *O. munzii*. The following

Fig. 180. Colorado Desert just south of Palm Springs, Riverside Co., California. A sandy area supporting silver cholla, *Opuntia echinocarpa* var. *echinocarpa*; creosote bush, *Larrea tridentata* var. *tridentata*; and blue palo verde, *Cercidium floridum*. Granitic hills in the background.

Fig. 181. Colorado Desert, Mason Valley, San Diego Co., California. A barrel cactus, *Ferocactus acanthodes* var. *acanthodes*; young teddy-bear chollas, *Opuntia bigelovii* var. *hoffmanii*; a smaller cholla, *O. echinocarpa* var. *wolfii*, at lower right; an ocotillo, *Fouquieria splendens*, center; and desert century plant, *Agave desertii*.

occur mostly in the Colorado Desert, but they overlap slightly into adjacent floristic associations: *Echinocereus engelmannii* var. *engelmannii*, *Ferocactus acanthodes* var. *acanthodes*, *Coryphantha vivipara* var. *alversonii*, and *Mammillaria tetrancistra*.

VII.3. The Arizona Desert

The principal s area of Arizona and the one with the most striking plants. Arizona s of the Mogollon Rim, except at the higher or the very lowest elevations. About 550-1,050 m (1,800-3,500 ft) or rarely 300 m (1,000 ft), as at Phoenix. **Markers:** Saguaro or giant cactus, *Cereus giganteus*, and many other cacti (Table 4, pp. 210-15); desert cotton, *Gossypium thurberi*; desert olive, *Forestiera shrevei*; blue palo verde, *Cercidium floridum*; foothill palo verde, *C. microphyllum*; *Sophora arizonica* and *formosa*; *Coursetia glandulosa*; *Brickellia coulteri*; burro weed, *Haplopappus tenuisectus*; desert broom, *Baccharis sarothroides*; canyon ragweed, *Ambrosia (Fran-*

Fig. 182. Arizona Desert in bloom, northwest of Tucson, Pima Co., Arizona. The conspicuous flowering annuals are a variety of the California poppy, *Eschscholzia californica*, known locally as *E. mexicana*; also saguaros, *Cereus giganteus*; low bushy chollas, *Opuntia acanthocarpa* var. *major*; foothill palos verdes, *Cercidium microphyllum*; and in the distance, many creosote bushes, *Larrea tridentata* var. *tridentata*. (Homer L. Shantz)

Fig. 183. Arizona Desert, the upper part adjoining the Desert Grassland and therefore with patches of perennial grasses. Saguaro, *Cereus giganteus*; Engelmann prickly pear, *Opuntia phaeacantha* var. *discata*; velvet mesquite, *Prosopis juliflora* var. *velutina* (right); and a young Thornber yucca, *Yucca baccata* var. *brevifolia* (center, obscured). Colossal Cave, Rincon Mts., Pima Co., Arizona.

Fig. 184. Arizona Desert: young saguaros, *Cereus giganteus*; organ pipe cacti, *Cereus thurberi*; foothill palos verdes, *Cercidium microphyllum*; *cat claw, Acacia greggii* (left foreground, now leafless); and prickly pear, *Opuntia phaeacantha* var. *flavispina*. Ajo Mts., Organ Pipe Cactus National Monument, Pima Co., Arizona.

Fig. 185. Arizona Desert: organ pipe cacti, *Cereus thurberi*; ocotillo, *Fouquieria splendens* (right foreground); foothill palo verde, *Cercidium microphyllum* (behind organ pipe cacti); and at the left a saguaro, *Cereus giganteus*, branching at the top following injury to the terminal bud. Ajo Mts., Organ Pipe Cactus National Monument, Pima Co., Arizona.

199

seria) ambrosioides; bur sages, *Ambrosia (Franseria) deltoidea* and *cordifolia*; Thornber yucca, *Yucca baccata* var. *brevifolia*. (Figs. 182-85.)

This desert receives both winter rain (at Tucson 10-15 cm, or 4-6 in, spread out between October and March or April) and summer rain (at Tucson 12.5-17.5 cm, or 5-7 in, concentrated in July and August). The two seasons of rainfall produce nearly independent vernal and aestival herbaceous floras, and different annual plants flower during the spring and summer seasons. Perennials may grow at both times, but usually they flower during only one season, as do the woody plants and cacti. The spring flowering season is chiefly in March, extending in wet years into early April. Most cacti and many woody plants flower during May, using residual stored water.

Cacti. The Arizona Desert is the most striking in the United States, and the large cacti are its principal feature. They provide the unique character of the desert flats, hills, and low mountains. Species are numerous.

A number of woody species occur in both the Colorado Desert and the Arizona Desert, especially the following: desert ironwood, *Olneya tesota*; ocotillo, *Fouquieria splendens*; jojoba or goat nut, *Simmondsia chinensis*; desert willow, *Chilopsis linearis* var. *arcuata*; *Lycium cooperi*, *macrodon*, and *fremontii*; desert lavender, *Hyptis emoryi*; cat claw, *Acacia greggii*; blue palo verde, *Cercidium floridum*; teddy bear cholla, *Opuntia bigelovii*; *Trixis californica*; *Peucephyllum schottii*; burrobrush, *Hymenoclea salsola* var. *pentalepis*.

VII.4. The Chihuahuan Desert

From s New Mexico to trans-Pecos Texas; a few characteristic species occurring in Cochise

Fig. 186. Chihuahuan Desert: lechuguilla, a century plant, *Agave lechuguilla*, conspicuous among the limestone slabs, one of the markers of this desert. Tornillo Creek, Big Bend National Park, Brewster Co., Texas. (Edward F. Anderson)

Fig. 187. Chihuahuan Desert in northern Mexico: a dense stand of tree cholla, *Opuntia imbricata*; a large century plant, *Agave*; a prickly pear, undetermined species of *Opuntia*. (David Griffiths)

Co., Arizona. Mexico on the Mexican Plateau s as far as San Luis Potosí and disjunctly in Querétaro. Mostly 1,200-1,800 m (4,000-6,000 ft). **Markers:** Lechuguilla, *Agave lechuguilla*; *Dasylirion leiophyllum*; Spanish dagger, *Yucca carnerosana*; Torrey yucca, *Yucca torreyi*; red barberry, *Berberis trifoliolata*; chittam wood, *Bumelia lanuginosa* var. *rigida*; desert willows, *Chilopsis linearis* vars. *linearis* and *glutinosa*; yellow trumpet flower, *Tecoma stans* var. *angustatum*; chuparosa, *Anisacanthus thurberi*; *Acacia constricta* var. *vernicosa*; shrubby senna, *Cassia wislizenii*; crucifixion thorn, *Koeberlinia spinosa*; numerous cacti (see Table 4, pp. 210-15); tar brush or black brush, *Flourensia cernua*; mariola, *Parthenium incanum*; and many other woody species. (Fig. 186.)

The Chihuahuan Desert is developed best in Mexico, and only the northern fringe occurs in the United States. Here, on its periphery, the desert seems drier than the deserts west of the continental divide, and the creosote bushes are mostly scraggly and yellow-green. Large yuccas and the lechuguilla and many large shrubs add character to the desert.

Cacti. The cacti are small, but they are numerous and they include many exquisite and interesting species. The finest representation of both the Chihuahuan Desert and its cacti in the United States is in the Big Bend country of the Rio Grande in Brewster Co., Texas. (Fig. 187.)

VIII. THE AMERICAN TROPICAL FLORA

The American tropics stretch from central Mexico and the tip of Florida to northern Chile, southern Bolivia, central Paraguay, and the edge of southern Brazil, and within this area there is great local variation in climate and topography. Consequently, the American Tropical Flora is varied and composed of a number of regional floristic associations, all but one beyond the territory covered in this book. In the continental United States that lone floristic association, the Caribbean Tropical Forest, is represented chiefly in southern Florida and slightly near Brownsville, at the southern tip of Texas. (Fig. 188.)

VIII.1. The Caribbean Tropical Forest

Islands of the Caribbean Sea; s tips of Florida and Texas. Near sea level. **Markers:** Pawpaw or custard apple, *Annona glabra*; sugar apple, *A. squamosa*; strangler fig, *Ficus aurea*; wild fig or banyan, *F. citrifolia*; nettle tree, *Trema micrantha*; West Indian nettle tree, *T. lamarckiana*; Joe wood, *Jacquinia keyensis*; myrsine, *Myrsine guaiensis*; satin leaf, *Chrysophyllum olivaeforme*; mastic, *Mastichodendron foetidissimum*; bustic or cassada, *Dipholis salicifolia*; antwood, *Bumelia celastrina* var. *angustifolia*; wild sapodilla, *Manilkara bahamensis*; black mangrove, *Avicenna germinans*; wild tamarind, *Lysiloma latisiliqua*; cat claw, *Pithecellobium unguis-cati*;

THE TORRID ZONE
(Climate Zone for Flora VIII)

The tropics include the two belts of trade winds and the intervening belt of tropical calms, or doldrums; they run roughly from the Tropic of Cancer to the Tropic of Capricorn. The heat equator is the belt of convergence or of rising air, where the trade winds of the north and south meet and the ascending moist air loses great quantities of water. With the tilting of the axis of the Earth, the rainy belt of the heat equator shifts north and south, crossing the geographical equator twice each year. Thus, there are wet and dry seasons, two of each every year at the equator and one of each at the northern and southern extremities of the climatic migration. At the limits of movement of the heat equator into either hemisphere, a dry season during the winter alternates with a wet one during the summer, as near Delhi, India. During the winter, the edges of the tropical zone shift into the Horse Latitudes.

Often the upwind and downwind sides of tropical land masses have remarkably dissimilar climates and vegetation. The windward sides of many islands or continents have remarkably high precipitation. For example, on the northeast side of Kauai in Hawaii, the annual rainfall averages 15 m (50 ft, or 600 inches). In contrast, near Waimea Canyon, only a few miles away and across a plateau only 1,200 m (4,000 ft) high, the average is perhaps 25-40 cm (10-16 in). Some areas in Hawaii are reminiscent of the deserts of Arizona. This phenomenon occurs on the leeward sides of all the main islands of the Hawaiian group, on the higher islands of the Caribbean, in southern Mexico, and in many other tropical parts of the world.

The warm, moist tropical climate is favorable to many plant taxa, and the origin of land plants and of their major taxa may have occurred in the tropics, most likely in the tropical uplands (Axelrod, 1952). More specialized plants, adapted to the severe dry conditions of the Horse Latitudes, the winter frost of the temperate zones, or the extreme winter cold of the arctic, probably are offshoots from major plant groups that occurred first in the tropics.

Because the Torrid Zone has a favorable climate, through Cenozoic time it has been a reservoir of plants of many families, genera, and species. The numbers of species are enormous. For example, Barro Colorado, a small island in the Canal Zone, supports about 1,400 native species, a number approaching that in the flora of the British Isles.

Other, mostly small, areas in the tropics are very dry. Over many low-lying tropical islands, such as Curaçao, the trade winds are not elevated sufficiently to cause much precipitation. The low windward headlands of even the higher islands exposed to the trade winds may be dry, because the winds meet no high obstacle where they first encounter the islands. Examples are on St. Croix and St. Thomas in the Virgin Islands, where the headlands support a number of cacti. Some species, for example *Opuntia rubescens*, a semaphore cactus, are conspicuous. The desert islands in the central and eastern Pacific Ocean are surrounded by the Humboldt (Peru) Current, which is always colder than the land, and, although they are near the geographical equator, the heat equator is almost always diverted north of them. The Galapagos Islands, for example, lie on the equator, but at lower altitudes they are very dry and they support many large cacti.

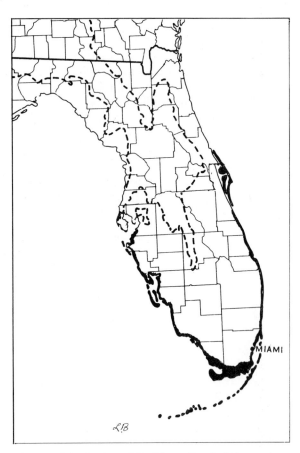

Fig. 188. Distribution of Caribbean Tropical Forest along the coasts of Florida.

Caesalpinia pauciflora; buttonwood, *Conocarpus erecta*; black olive, *Bucida buceras*; white mangrove, *Laguncularia racemosa*; spanish stopper, *Eugenia myrtoides*; white stopper, *E. axillaris*; red stopper, *E. rhombea*; ironwood, *E. confusa*; lideflower, *Calyptranthes pallens*; myrtle-of-the-river, *C. zuzygium*; mangrove, *Rhizophora mangle*; princewood, *Exostema caribaeum*; seven-year apple, *Casasia clusifolia*; wild coffee, *Psychotria undata*; Bahaman wild coffee, *P. lingustrifolia* and *P. sulzneri*; cherry cabbage palm, *Pseudophoenix sargentii*; Florida royal palm, *Roystonea elata*; Florida thatch palm, *Thrinax parviflora*; silver palm, *Coccothrinax argentata*; saw cabbage, *A. coeloraphe* var. *wrightii*; Caribbean pine, *Pinus caribaea*; and many others. (Figs. 189-92.)

The Caribbean Region
(Climatic Region for Flora VIII)
(as it occurs in the continental United States)

The tropical areas of the continental United States are typical of the fringe of the trade-wind belt, having a dry winter and a very wet summer. The tropical areas of Florida include a southern coastal fringe, the Everglades (flooded during the summer and sometimes dry during the winter), and the Keys or small islands. The fluctuations of topography are so slight that a meter or even a few decimeters may make the difference between shallow sea or embayment, marsh, hammocks (nearly but not quite islands), and keys—the whole series occurring within this difference of elevation.

Fig. 189. Caribbean Tropical Forest, a dense rain forest. The few cacti occurring in the undisturbed forest are epiphytes, like *Rhipsalis*, or clambering climbing plants. Northern Martinique, West Indies, a Department of France.

Fig. 190 (*above*). Caribbean Tropical Forest, disturbed by a hurricane, and only a few trees left standing. The palm is encircled by the roots of the strangler fig, *Ficus aurea*, which started as an epiphyte, then developed aerial roots that have enveloped the palm trunk, and eventually will support the fig when the palm dies. The only known locality for *Rhipsalis baccifera* in the continental United States is on a log in the devastated forest just beyond this spot. Everglades National Park, Cape Sable, Florida.

Fig. 191 (*left*). Edge of the Caribbean Tropical Forest on open, sandy land on Merritt Island, eastern coast of Florida. A tropical species of pine, *Pinus caribaea*, and the saw palmetto, *Serenoa serrulata*, glaucous coastal form, predominate; cacti abound.

Fig. 192. Caribbean Tropical Forest, Big Pine Key, Monroe Co., Florida. Mangroves, *Rhizophora mangle*, spread along the shallow water of the seashore, supporting themselves by producing adventitious roots from the branches; the coconut palm, *Cocos nucifera*, occurs on sandy tropical shores throughout the world. Several species of cacti, including four not known otherwise from the continental United States (but occurring also in the West Indies) grow in the sandy soil at the edge of the woods behind beaches of this type.

Forests grow on the coast, hammocks, and keys. As the list shows, they are rich in native species characteristic of the Caribbean Tropical Forest. Only about 9 percent of the flora of tropical Florida as a whole is endemic, and the endemics are mostly herbaceous dicotyledons. Southern Florida has been open to colonization by plants and for their subsequent evolution for only a short time. During the Pleistocene the state was submerged in the ocean, and the present tropical flora has migrated across the Caribbean since then. Most of the tropical species in Florida are those readily transported over water.

The present occurrence of tropical plant species near Brownsville, Texas, is minor. During Cenozoic time the distance of extension of the tropical flora northward along the western shore of the Gulf of Mexico has varied. The trend of movement has been mostly southward in response to the general trend toward a cooler and in most places drier climate. Probably the few tropical species at the southern tip of Texas are relict.

They include *Cereus spinulosus* (at least reportedly collected there) and *C. pentagonus*.

Cacti. Cacti occur in tropical Florida mostly on sandy flats; on coastal shell mounds, a little better drained than their surroundings; and in disturbed forest areas. A few species, including some of *Opuntia* and *Cereus*, and *Rhipsalis baccifera*, are native in the jungles. Several taxa of *Cereus* are endemic.

THE HAWAIIAN FLORA

The Hawaiian series of islands and atolls is independent physically, but floristically it is part of the vast tropical region of southeastern Asia and the islands of the southwestern Pacific Ocean. The region includes a great series of Old World, basically tropical, floras, with phases adapted to the wet and dry sides of the islands and to the temperate conditions at higher altitudes. These floras have no connection with the North American Floras; they are discussed here as a separate unit because Hawaii is one of the United States, because many people from the mainland visit there, and because some cacti have been introduced on the dry sides of the islands.

The Hawaiian Flora is composed of the plants that have been able to migrate there during the 5 million years of the island chain's existence. Plants arriving by one means or another in Hawaii found competition only from each other, because their former competitors occurring elsewhere had been excluded—they were free to occupy any untaken environmental niche.

There were many niches. The range of altitude is about 4,200 m (14,000 ft), and this provided both tropical-lowland and temperate-highland habitats. One side of each mountain is toward the trade winds and wet (Fig. 194), the other away from them and amazingly dry (Fig. 195). Around the mountain, between these extremes, there are many deep, gashlike canyons (Fig. 196), each with a somewhat different combination of ecological factors.

The Hawaiian Region
(Climatic Region for the Hawaiian Flora)

The islands of the Hawaiian chain, stretching from Midway southeastward to the island of Hawaii. The region, of course, is not a part of North America, but it is discussed because it is part of the United States. (Fig. 193.)

The islands are in a permanently isolated series 3,200 km (2,000 mi) long, the younger islands lying toward the southeast and the older to the northwest. According to the theory of continental drift, the islands originate in an opening in the Earth's crust under the southeastern edge of the island of Hawaii, where there are active volcanoes. The older islands have been wedged westward, and there is a sequence of ages. The youngest island, Hawaii, includes peaks like Mauna Loa (active, nearly 4,200 m, or 13,680 ft, high) in the south and Mauna Kea (inactive, about 36 m higher, 13,796 ft) in the older northern part of the island. The southeastern part of the next island, Maui, includes Haleakala, an extinct volcano about 3,000 m (10,025 ft) high. The older western segment of Maui rises to only about 1,200 m (4,000 ft), and the rest of the islands in the main group are about the same height, having been eroded during a long period. The islands west of Kauai, stretching to Midway, are only slightly above sea level, and there is little exposed volcanic rock, the surface of nearly every island being covered with coral sand.

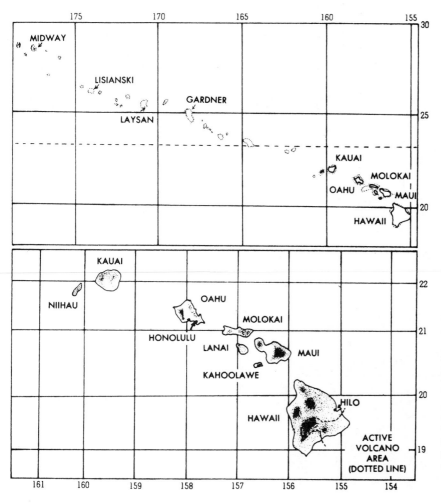

Fig. 193. The Hawaiian chain of islands. *Above,* the entire chain, including minor islands and remnants of islands (atolls), stretching westward across the Pacific as far as Midway. *Below,* the Hawaiian Islands proper. According to recent studies of continental drift, new islands are formed above an opening in the crust of the Earth under the southeastern part of the Island of Hawaii, where there are active volcanoes, such as Mauna Loa and Kilauea. As islands have been formed, they have been wedged northwestward through seafloor spreading. Thus, the younger islands, less eroded, are at the southeastern end of the chain, and the older at the northwestern. The latter are eroded almost or completely to sea level, and coral sand replaces lava. (From *Plant Taxonomy, Methods and Principles*)

Fig. 194. Rain forest in Iao Canyon on the windward side of western Maui, Hawaii; rainfall about 10 m or 1,000 cm (400 inches or 33 feet) per year.

Fig. 195 (*below*). Desert-like hillsides and irrigated sugarcane fields on the leeward side of the mountain shown in Fig. 194, east of Lahaina. Rainfall here is low; rain clouds cover the other side of the mountain and the crest, but the sky is clear here in the rain shadow.

Fig. 196. Southeastern Molokai, Hawaii: deep, gashlike canyons and flat-topped ridges formed by erosion of a plain or slope.

Since there were many habitats available for the taking, the individuals of each species best adapted to the environment of each place and best equipped to meet whatever competition was developing evolved as much as might be necessary. Thus, as in the Galapagos Islands, a relatively small number of invading genera and species populated the islands with many diverse species derived from them. The resulting number of closely related species in Hawaii is large, and all but a few ubiquitous tropical strand species are endemic. They are in compact groups in various families and genera, indicating only a few original invaders. Genera with large numbers of species include: *Cyrtandra* (more than 100), *Astelia, Schiedea, Pelea, Fagara, Hibiscus, Viola, Labordia, Haplostachys, Phyllostegia, Stenogyne, Coprosma, Hedyotis, Clermontia, Cyanea, Delissa, Lobelia, Bidens, Dubautia,* and *Lipochaeta* (St. John, 1946).

Unfortunately, most of the native flora of the lowlands of Hawaii is gone, replaced by invading plants from other parts of the tropics (Fig. 197). In many places, as through the tropics in general, all plants are introduced. Division of the native

Hawaiian Flora into natural floristic associations will require further study; the tentative associations include the following, but these intergrade with each other through innumerable intermediate pockets.

Cacti. The dry sides of the Hawaiian Islands (Leeward Association) are favorable to cacti, but the Cactaceae have not been able to cross the ocean from the Americas by natural means. Through the intervention of man, however, the spiny form of the Indian fig, or mission cactus, of California has become established on the dry sides of all the islands of the main group, and a few other species have been introduced locally on the drier parts of Oahu and Kauai. (Fig. 198.)

The Ohia-Fern Forest. Tropical windward, wet lowlands, the native taxa mostly crowded out by introduced species on Oahu and parts of other islands, but beautiful in out-of-the-way places and even near Hilo on Hawaii. Various tree ferns form a canopy mostly 3-6 m (10-20 ft) above the forest floor, and the Ohia, *Metrosideros polymorpha* complex, rises above it, the trunks like posts supporting a roof. (Fig. 199.)

The Koa Forest. At middle elevations. The

Fig. 197. Dense tropical vegetation of the lowlands of Oahu, Hawaii. All the plants here are introduced from other parts of the tropics, replacing the native species since the coming of the European and American explorers.

Fig. 198 (*below*). Spiny form of the Indian fig or mission cactus, *Opuntia ficus-indica*, growing at the base of the road to Waimea Canyon and Kokee, on the dry side of Kauai, Hawaii. These cacti are abundant on the dry sides of all of the main islands.

Fig. 199 (*left*). Native Hawaiian Flora: Ohia-Fern Forest on Kilauea, Island of Hawaii, dominated by the ohia, *Metrosideros* spp., and various tree ferns, the ohias rising far above the ferns and the wealth of smaller species on tree fern trunks or on the ground.

Fig. 201 (*above*). Native Hawaiian Flora: Summit Association. The vegetation, silversword, *Agyroxiphium* sp., and associated shrubs, is reminiscent of the chaparral in California and elsewhere. The trade winds pass around, instead of over, the high peaks and ridges, leaving the summits with little precipitation. Haleakala, eastern Maui, Hawaii, at about 2,400 m (8,000 feet) elevation.

Fig. 200 (*left*). Native Hawaiian Flora: Koa Forest near Waimea Canyon, Kauai, dominated by the koa, *Acacia koa*, a species with flattened petioles instead of leaf blades.

209

characteristic tree is the koa, *Acacia koa,* a species with flattened petioles (phyllodes) instead of complete bipinnate leaves. (Fig. 200.)

The Leeward Association. Dry areas at low altitudes away from the trade winds. Some of these are reminiscent of the deserts of the Southwest.

The Summit Association. Dry areas supporting shrubs and reminiscent of chaparral. These occur on the highest mountains of Maui and Hawaii, which are left without much moisture toward the summits because the trade winds divide around the summits instead of going over them. This is known as "parting the clouds." On Haleakala, Maui, beginning at about 2,550 m (8,500 ft). (Fig. 201.)

The Strand Association. The smaller islands to the west of the main group are composed almost wholly of limestone formed as the lava was eroded away. This was derived chiefly from marine organisms, like corals and mollusks, which lived and died along the shore of the coral island or atoll, but both plants and animals secreting carbonates contributed to the formation of the limestone. The present islands are close to sea level, though some have been uplifted a little or the water level has risen or receded as water has been released from the polar icecaps or taken into them. Only a few species compose the land vegetation of the strand, but the species composition varies from place to place and with local ecology.

Distribution of Cacti in Floristic Associations

The chart that follows (Table 4) places all of the cactus species and varieties treated in the body of this work in their respective North American floras and floristic associations. Occurrences of native species are given as primary (P), secondary (S), or minor (m); occurrences of introduced species are given as common (I) or minor (i). (Two of the associations given, the Edwards Plateau and the Rio Grande Plain, both in Texas, are of uncertain, subclimax origin and mixed floristic composition, and they are not to be considered formally classified.)

TABLE 4

Distribution of Species and Varieties of Cacti According to Natural Floras and Floristic Associations

Native species or varieties:
P primary occurrence   m minor occurrence
S secondary occurrence   r rare and disjunct occurrence

Introduced species or varieties:
I common occurrence
i minor occurrence

(Arabic numbers and letters in column heads follow the plan of Table 3, p. 137)

Genus, species, or variety	II Nor. For. 1	III 1	III 2	III 4	III 5	III 6	III 7	IV East For. 1	V 1	V 2	V EPRG	VI 1a	VI 1b	VI 1c	VI 2	VI 3	VI 4	VI 5	VI 7	VI 8a	VI 8b	VI 8c	VII 1	VII 2	VII 3	VII 4	VIII Amer. Trop. 1	Hawaii LA
1. PERESKIA																												
1. *P. aculeata* (W. Indies & S. America)																											i	
2. *P. grandifolia* (Brazil)																											i	
2. OPUNTIA																												
1a. *O. parryi* var. *parryi*		m												P	m								m	m				
b. var. *serpentina*														P														
2. *O. wigginsii*																								P				
3a. *O. echinocarpa* var. *echinocarpa*																							P	S				
b. var. *wolfii*																							P					
4a. *O. acanthocarpa* var. *coloradensis*																	P						m	m				
b. var. *major*																								m	P			
c. var. *ganderi*														m										P				
d. var. *acanthocarpa*															m								P					
e. var. *thornberi*																							m		P			
5a. *O. tunicata* var. *tunicata*																										P		
b. var. *davisii*									P																			
6a. *O. whipplei* var. *whipplei*					m				P			P								m	m		m					
b. var. *multigeniculata*																					P							
c. var. *viridiflora*									P			P																
7. *O. spinosior*					m						S	S	S	P										P				P
8a. *O. imbricata* var. *imbricata*					m				P			S		S														P
b. var. *argentea*																												P

TABLE 4 (cont.)

Flora and floristic association

Genus, species, or variety	II Nor. For.	III Western Forest						IV East For.	V Plains and Prairie						VI Southwestern Woodland											VII Mexican Desert				VIII Amer. Trop.	Hawaii
	1	1	2	4	5	6	7	1	1	2	E	P	R	G	1a	1b	1c	2	3	4	5	7	8a	8b	8c	1	2	3	4	1	LA
9. *O. versicolor*																													P			
10. *O. kelvinensis*																													P			
11. *O. prolifera*																			P	P											
12a. *O. fulgida* var. *fulgida*																	S												P			
b. var. *mamillata*																	S												P			
13. *O. munzii*																										P						
14a. *O. bigelovii* var. *hoffmannii*																										P						
b. var. *bigelovii*																										P	P					
15. *O. leptocaulis*											S	S	P													m		P		P	
16. *O. arbuscula*																												P				
17a. *O. kleiniae* var. *kleiniae*									P								S											P		P	
b. var. *tetracantha*																	P											P		m	
18. *O. ramosissima*																										m	P					
19a. *O. stanlyi* var. *stanlyi*																	P											S	m		
b. var. *peeblesiana*																												P			
c. var. *kunzei*																											P	m			
d. var. *parishii*																										P					
20a. *O. schottii* var. *schottii*										P																			P		
b. var. *grahamii*																													P		
21. *O. clavata*									P																						
22. *O. pulchella*																						P									
23a. *O. polyacantha* var. *polyacantha*			m					m	P						m								m	m							
b. var. *rufispina*			m		m				m						P								P	P						m	
c. var. *juniperina*									m						P								m								
d. var. *trichophora*									m						P																
24a. *O. fragilis* var. *fragilis*	m	m		m	m			m	m	P					m								P	P							
b. var. *brachyarthra*									P						P								m	m							
25. *O. arenaria*																													P		
26a. *O. erinacea* var. *erinacea*																		m					m	m	S	P	m				
b. var. *columbiana*				P																				P							
c. var. *ursina*																										P					
d. var. *utahensis*					m													m					P	m							
e. var. *hystricina*									m									m					P	m							
27. *O. nicholii*																									P						
28a. *O. basilaris* var. *basilaris*				m														m	m	m			m	m		P	P				
b. var. *brachyclada*																			P												
c. var. *longiareolata*																										P					
d. var. *aurea*																						P			m						
e. var. *treleasei*																					P					m					
29. *O. rufida*																													P		
30. *O. cubensis*																														P	
31. *O. triacantha*																														P	
32. *O. pusilla*								P																						m	
33. *O. vulgaris* (Paraguay & Braz. to Arg.)																														i	i
34a. *O. humifusa* var. *humifusa*								P	P	r		m																			
b. var. *ammophila*								P																							
c. var. *austrina*								P																						m	
35a. *O. macrorhiza* var. *macrorhiza*						m		m	m	P	P	m			S	m	P	m				m									
b. var. *pottsii*										m								P											m		
36a. *O. littoralis* var. *littoralis*																				P	P										
b. var. *vaseyi*																				P											
c. var. *austrocalifornica*																				P											
d. var. *piercei*			P																	m											
e. var. *martiniana*				m																		P				S					
37. *O. atrispina*												P	P																P		
38a. *O. violacea* var. *violacea*																		P										m			
b. var. *gosseliniana*																		P										m			

TABLE 4 (cont.)

Flora and floristic association

Genus, species, or variety	II Nor. For.	III Western Forest						IV East For.	V Plains and Prairie			VI Southwestern Woodland											VII Mexican Desert				VIII Amer. Trop.	Hawaii
	1	1	2	4	5	6	7	1	1	2	EPRG	1a	1b	1c	2	3	4	5	7	8a	8b	8c	1	2	3	4	1	LA
c. var. *santa-rita*												m		P											m	m		
d. var. *macrocentra*														S											m	P		
e. var. *castetteri*																										P		
39a. O. *phaeacantha* var. *phaeacantha*				m					S				P															
b. var *camanchica*									S P																			
c. var. *spinosibacca*																										P		
d. var. *laevis*												S		P											S	P		
e. var. *major*		m	m						S	m	m	S		P		S			S				m	m	P	P		
f. var. *discata*									S	m	m	m		m	P	P		S	S			m	S	S	P	P		
g. var. *wootonii*														P														
h. var. *superbospina*																							P					
i. var. *mojavensis*																							P					
j. var. *flavispina*																										P		
40a. O. *lindheimeri* var. *lindheimeri*									P	P	P																m	
b. var. *tricolor*										P	P																	
c. var. *lehmannii*											P																	
d. var. *cuija* (Mexico)								i?																				
e. var. *linguiformis*									P																			
41a. O. *stricta* var. *stricta*								P																			S	
b. var. *dillenii*								S																			P	i
42. O. *cochenillifera* (Mexico)																											i	i
43. O. *oricola*																P		P										
44. O. *chlorotica*												m		m	S		m				m		P	m	m	P		
45a. O. *strigil* var. *strigil*																										P		
b. var. *flexospina*											P																	
46. O. *ficus-indica* (Mexico)									i					i								i					i	i
47. O. *tomentosa* (Mexico)																					i							
48. O. *leucotricha* (Mexico)																											i	
49. O. *spinosissima*																											P	
50. O. *brasiliensis* (South America)																											i	
3. SCHLUMBERGERA																												
1. S. *truncata* (Brazil)																												i
4. RHIPSALIS																												
1. R. *baccifera*																											P	
5. CEREUS																												
1. C. *peruvianus* (s. e. South America)																												i
2. C. *giganteus*																							m	P				
3a. C. *eriophorus* var. *fragrans*																											P	
4a. C. *gracilis* var. *simpsonii*																											P	
b. var. *aboriginum*																											P	
5. C. *martinii* (Argentina)																												i
6. C. *pentagonus*											m																P	i
7a. C. *grandiflorus* var. *grandiflorus* (W. Ind.)																											P	i
b. var. *armatus* (e. coast of Mexico)																											i	i
8. C. *pteranthus* (Mexico)																											i	i
9. C. *spinulosus*																											P	i
10. C. *undatus* (Tropical America)																											P	i
11a. C. *robinii* var. *robinii*																											P	
b. var. *deeringii*																											P	
12. C. *thurberi*																								P				
13. C. *emoryi*																			P	P								
14. C. *schottii*																								P				
15a. C. *greggii* var. *greggii*																									P			
b. var. *transmontanus*																								P				
16. C. *poselgeri*											P																	
17. C. *striatus*																							P	m				

TABLE 4 (cont.)

Flora and floristic association

Genus, species, or variety	II Nor. For. 1	III 1	III 2	III 4	III 5	III 6	III 7	IV East For. 1	V 1	V 2	V EPRG	VI 1a	VI 1b	VI 1c	VI 2	VI 3	VI 4	VI 5	VI 7	VI 8a	VI 8b	VI 8c	VII 1	VII 2	VII 3	VII 4	VIII 1	Hawaii LA
6. ECHINOCEREUS																												
1a. *E. triglochidiatus* var. *melanacanthus*					S				m	S		P	m	P	m		m			P	m	P						
b. var. *mojavensis*					m											m					P		P					
c. var. *neomexicanus*												P		S	S													
d. var. *gurneyi*															P											P		
e. var. *paucispinus*									m						m											P		
f. var. *arizonicus*												P	S															
g. var. *gonacanthus*															P													
h. var. *triglochidiatus*															P													
2a. *E. berlandieri* var. *berlandieri*											P																	
b. var. *papillosus*											P																	
c. var. *angusticeps*											P																	
3. *E. pentalophus*											P																	
4a. *E. fendleri* var. *fendleri*					m				P						P													
b. var. *rectispinus*																P									m	m		
c. var. *kuenzleri*									P						P	m												
5a. *E. fasciculatus* var. *fasciculatus*															m								P					
b. var. *boyce-thompsonii*																							P					
c. var. *bonkerae*																P												
6. *E. ledingii*												P	m			m												
7a. *E. engelmannii* var. *engelmannii*																				m			P	m				
b. var. *acicularis*																				m			m	P				
c. var. *armatus*																							P					
d. var. *munzii*		P															P											
e. var. *chrysocentrus*																				m			P					
f. var. *variegatus*									S					P								P	P					
g. var. *purpureus*																				P			P					
h. var. *nicholii*																							S	P				
i. var. *howei*																							P					
8a. *E. enneacanthus* var. *enneacanthus*									P	P																P		
b. var. *brevispinus*										P																		
c. var. *stramineus*																										P		
d. var. *dubius*																										P		
9. *E. lloydii*																										P		
10a. *E. pectinatus* var. *rigidissimus*															m		P									P		
b. var. *pectinatus*																	P									P		
c. var. *wenigeri*																										P		
d. var. *minor*																										P		
e. var. *neomexicanus*																	P									P		
11a. *E. reichenbachii* var. *reichenbachii*									P	P																		
b. var. *perbellus*									P																			
c. var. *albertii*										P	P																	
d. var. *fitchii*										P	P																	
e. var. *chisosensis*																										P		
f. var. *albispinus*									P	P																		
12a. *E. viridiflorus* var. *viridiflorus*							P		P	P				S														
b. var. *davisii*																P												
c. var. *correllii*															P	P												
d. var. *cylindricus*									m								m									P		
13a. *E. chloranthus* var. *chloranthus*											m				m											P		
b. var. *neocapillus*															P											P		
7. LOPHOPHORA																												
1. *L. williamsii*											P															P		
8. FEROCACTUS																												
1a. *F. acanthodes* var. *acanthodes*																									P			
b. var. *lecontei*																							P	m	P			
c. var. *eastwoodiae*																									P			

TABLE 4 (cont.)

Flora and floristic association. Column groups: **II** Nor. For.; **III** Western Forest; **IV** East For.; **V** Plains and Prairie; **VI** Southwestern Woodland; **VII** Mexican Desert; **VIII** Amer. Trop.; Hawaii.

Genus, species, or variety	II·1	III·1	III·2	III·4	III·5	III·6	III·7	IV·1	V·1	V·2	V·E	V·P	V·R	V·G	VI·1a	VI·1b	VI·1c	VI·2	VI·3	VI·4	VI·5	VI·7	VI·8a	VI·8b	VI·8c	VII·1	VII·2	VII·3	VII·4	VIII·1	Hawaii·LA
2. F. wislizenii																		P										P	P		
3. F. covillei																											m	P			
4. F. viridescens																				P											
5a. F. hamatacanthus var. hamatacanthus												m						S											P		
b. var. sinuatus												P																			
6. F. setispinus										S		P																			
9. ECHINOCACTUS																															
1a. E. polycephalus var. polycephalus																										P					
b. var. xeranthemoides																							m		P						
2a. E. horizonthalonius var. horizonthalonius																													P		
b. var. nicholii																												P			
3. E. texensis									P	P		P																			
4. E. asterias												P																			
10. SCLEROCACTUS																															
1. S. glaucus																								P							
2. S. mesae-verdae																								P							
3. S. wrightiae																								P							
4. S. pubispinus																						P									
5. S. spinosior																						P		P							
6. S. whipplei																							P	P							
7a. S. parviflorus var. parviflorus																							P	P							
b. var. intermedius																							P	P							
8. S. polyancistrus																										P					
11. PEDIOCACTUS																															
1a. P. simpsonii var. simpsonii					m																		P	P							
b. var. minor					P			P									S						S								
c. var. robustior																								P							
2. P. bradyi																									P						
3. P. knowltonii																	P														
4. P. paradinei									m														m	P							
5. P. sileri																							m	P		m					
6a. P. peeblesianus var. fickeiseniae									m															P							
b. var. peeblesianus																								P							
7. P. papyracanthus									P								S														
12. EPITHELANTHA																															
1. E. micromeris																		P											P		
2. E. bokei																													P		
13. THELOCACTUS																															
1a. T. bicolor var. schottii												P						m										P			
b. var. flavidispinus												P						P													
14. NEOLLOYDIA																															
1. N. conoidea																													P		
2. N. warnockii																													P		
3. N. gautii								P																							
4. N. mariposensis																													P		
5a. N. intertexta var. intertexta																		P											m		
b. var. dasyacantha																		m											P		
6a. N. erectocentra var. erectocentra																		P										m			
b. var. acunensis																											P	P			
7. N. johnsonii																										P		m			
15. ANCISTROCACTUS																															
1. A. tobuschii										P																					
2. A. scheeri												P																			
3a. A. uncinatus var. wrightii																													P		

TABLE 4 (cont.)

Genus, species, or variety	II Nor. For.	III Western Forest						IV East For.	V Plains and Prairie						VI Southwestern Woodland											VII Mexican Desert				VIII Amer. Trop.	Hawaii
	1	1	2	4	5	6	7	1	1	2	E	P	R	G	1a	1b	1c	2	3	4	5	7	8a	8b	8c	1	2	3	4	1	LA
16. CORYPHANTHA																															
1. C. minima																	P															
2a. C. macromeris var. macromeris																														P		
b. var. runyonii											P																					
3a. C. scheeri var. scheeri																														P		
b. var. valida																	S													P		
c. var. uncinata																														P		
d. var. robustispina															m		P											m				
4a. C. vivipara var. vivipara									P									m									m					
b. var. radiosa									P	S								m												m		
c. var. bisbeeana																	P															
d. var. arizonica					S													P			P											
e. var. desertii																							m	m		P						
f. var. alversonii																							P	P	P							
g. var. rosea																					P					m						
5. C. hesteri																	P															
6. C. ramillosa																														P		
7a. C. sulcata var. sulcata											P																					
b. var. nickelsiae											P																					
8a. C. cornifera var. echinus										S								S												P		
9. C. recurvata															P			P														
10a. C. strobiliformis var. strobiliformis																		S												P		
b. var. durispina																	P													P		
c. var. orcuttii																	P															
11a. C. sneedii var. sneedii																														P		
b. var. leei																														P		
12a. C. dasyacantha var. dasyacantha															P		P													S		
b. var. varicolor																	P															
13. C. robertii											P																		m			
14. C. duncanii																	P													P		
15a. C. missouriensis var. missouriensis									P						S							S										
b. var. marstonii					S										P																	
c. var. caespitosa									P																							
d. var. robustior									P	P																						
17. ARIOCARPUS																															
1. A. fissuratus																													P		
18. MAMMILLARIA																															
1a. M. longimamma var. sphaerica										P																						
2a. M. heyderi var. heyderi										P	P																		P		
b. var. hemisphaerica											P																					
c. var. meiacantha									P									P											P			
d. var. macdougalii																		P											P			
3a. M. prolifera var. texana											P																					
4. M. lasiacantha																		S											P			
5. M. pottsii																													P			
6. M. dioica																				P						P						
7. M. mainiae															m			P									S					
8. M. microcarpa																										m	P					
9. M. thornberi																										m	P					
10. M. viridiflora					m						P	P	P													m						
11a. M. grahamii var. grahamii																		P										m	m			
b. var. oliviae																		P											m			
12a. M. wrightii var. wrightii									P						S		S	S														
b. var. wilcoxii																		P										m	m			
13. M. tetrancistra																										m	P	m				

11. The Uses of Cacti

To most inhabitants of the temperate regions, a cactus is a fat, spiny little plant in a pot, or a large one seen in a picture of an exotic desert landscape in the Southwest or in Latin America. Often Northern windowsills are decorated with cacti, and those who happen by are invariably amazed by their proportionately large, beautifully colored flowers. Having a few plants brings about a creeping addiction to cultivating cacti. Soon the windowsill is not large enough, and the collection spreads to other windows and wherever else members of the family will permit. Ultimately a greenhouse becomes a necessity.

Where cacti grow out-of-doors, as in the Southwest or the Southern States or other warm areas, they are planted in gardens as ornamentals, and

Suggested Books on the Culture of Cacti

These books (with one addition) are those recommended by Charles E. Glass, Editor, and Robert Foster, Assistant Editor, of the *Cactus and Succulent Journal*.

Borg, John. 1937, 1951, 1959. *Cacti*. Blandford Press, London.

Brooklyn Botanic Garden. 1963, 1966. *Handbook of Succulent Plants*. Reprinted from *Plants and Gardens* 19 (3).

Chidamian, Claude. 1958. *The Book of Cacti, and Other Succulents*. American Garden Guild, Garden City, N.Y.

Dawson, E. Yale. 1963. *How to Know the Cacti*. Wm. C. Brown Co., Dubuque, Iowa.

Glass, Charles E., and Robert Foster. 1976. *Cacti and Succulents for the Amateur*. Obtainable from the authors, Box 3010, Santa Barbara, California 93105.

Haage, Walther. Translated and revised by E. E. Kemp. 1963. *Cacti and Succulents: A Practical Handbook*. Dutton, New York.

Haselton, Scott E. 1944. *Cacti and Succulents and How to Grow Them*. Desert Botanical Garden in Papago Park, Phoenix.

Lamb, Edgar, and Brian M. Lamb. 1959-63. *The Illustrated Reference on Cacti and Other Succulents*. 4 vols. Blandford Press, London.

————. 1969. *The Pocket Encyclopedia of Cacti in Color*. Blandford Press, London.

Subick, Randolph, and Jirina Kaplicka. 1971. *Decorative Cacti*. Hamlyn Publishing Group, London.

Cactus and Succulent Journals and Societies

NORTH AMERICA

The Cactus & Succulent Journal. Cactus and Succulent Society of America. Box 3010, Santa Barbara, California. Many local affiliated societies.

Saguaroland Bulletin. Arizona Cactus and Native Flora Society. Desert Botanical Garden of Arizona, Phoenix.

Cactaceas y Suculentas Méxicanas. La Sociedad Méxicana de Cactologia, A.C. México, D.F.

GREAT BRITAIN

The Cactus and Succulent Journal of Great Britain. The Cactus and Succulent Society of Great Britain. Surrey. Branch societies.

National Cactus and Succulent Journal. The National Cactus and Succulent Society, Yorkshire. Branch societies.

Journal of the Mammillaria Society. Surrey.

CONTINENTAL EUROPE

Cactus. L'Association Française des Amateurs de Cactées et Plantes Grasses. Paris, France. (Probably ceased publication.)

Cactus. Willebroek, Belgium.

Cactusvrieden. Hoboken, Belgium.

Succulenta. Nederlands-Belgische Vereiniging von Liefhebbers van Cactussen en andere Vetplanten. Netherlands.

I. O. S. Bulletin. International Organization for Succulent Plant Study. Wageningen, Netherlands.

Kakteen und Andere Sukkulenten. Deutsche Kakteen-Gesellschaft. West Germany. Gesellschaft Österreichischer Kakteenfreunde. Austria. Schweizerische Kakteen-Gesellschaft. Switzerland.

Stackelpost. Mainz-Kostheim, West Germany.

Kakteen/Succulenten. Dresden, East Germany.

Sukkulentenkunde. Schweizerische Kakteen-Gesellschaft. Zürich, Switzerland.

Kaktusy. Czechoslovakian journal, obtainable from D. Neumann, 3066 Georgia Street, Oakland, California 94602.

JAPAN

Succulentarum Japonica. Japanese Section of the International Organization for Succulent Plant Study. Tokyo.

Journal of the Cactus and Succulent Society of Japan. Kyoto University.

The Study of Cacti. Desert Plant Society of Japan, Kanagawaken.

Shaboten-sha. Kanagawa.

AUSTRALIA AND NEW ZEALAND

The Spine. Cactus and Succulent Society of Australia. Victoria.

Cactus and Succulent Journal. Cactus and Succulent Society of New South Wales.

New Zealand Cactus and Succulent Journal. Auckland.

often they are used as hedges, the spiny types making effective boundary markers (see Fig. 202). The larger cacti are planted as fruit trees or specimen plants, often set off against the side of a house or a garden wall.

Cultivation of cacti is a growing hobby of temperate regions, and currently the Cactus and Succulent Society of America has a worldwide direct membership of 6,000 and over 60 affiliated local societies in the United States. Interest in growing cacti is ubiquitous, and there are more than 20 cactus and succulent journals, each published by a national society or a regional one, as for German-speaking Europe. These organizations reflect the intense interest in the bizarre plants with the beautiful flowers.

Besides their extensive use in horticulture throughout the world, cacti have a variety of other uses. An unusual case is the use of the wood of some species of *Cereus* and of the larger

Fig. 202. *Cereus (Pachycereus) marginatus* as a hedge plant, a use common in central and southern Mexico; the fruit not very fleshy or of much use for food. (Photograph by David Griffiths, about 1910, the hairline mark from a crack in the glass-plate negative)

chollas, especially the jumping cholla, *Opuntia fulgida,* for making novelties. The major uses of cacti are (or have been) *for food* for man or his livestock, as a host plant for *production of cochineal dye* by the cochineal insect, perhaps as an *emergency source of water* in the desert, and as an *adjunct to religion.*

As Food for Man

In many parts of the American Horse Latitudes, the fruits or other parts of cacti are staple foods.* The fruits are even more important than such temperate ones as apples, because for some residents of Latin America, including Mexico, they are the main or virtually the only article of food for as much as two months of the year. In the United States and Mexico, the cacti most frequently used for food are prickly pears, *Opuntia;* species of *Cereus;* and barrel cacti, *Ferocactus* and *Echinocactus.*

Prickly pears. In Mexico and in parts of the states along the border the fruits or tunas of prickly pears are a major food commonly sold in the markets. There are many more local and widespread strains than of such fruits as apples or peaches, and the tunas can be had in many sizes, colors, and flavors. Hybridizing of species of prickly pears is so common that new strains, or cultivars, arise frequently. The cultivars are not necessarily standardized, and any desirable seedling is propagated immediately because doing so is quite easy. A joint of the stem is cut off, and after a week or two during which the cut calluses, the joint is planted. Single plants or hedges of many plants yield fruits for home use or sale, and in many areas there are small orchards or more often random plantations. A planting may consist of a single species or strains of several.

The tunas are used for prepared foods as well as fresh fruit. Special varieties are cooked, made into pickles, or processed in any of several other ways (see Figs. 203-7). The fruits may be dried in the sun as are figs, grapes, pears, peaches, and apricots. The peeled fruit may be put through colanders to remove the seeds, following which the resulting juice is evaporated to the proper consistency and puddled, stirred, or worked into products such as "*queso,*" which resembles cheese and keeps for a long time. According to Nicker-

---

*Recipes for the use of cacti and other succulent plants as food have been compiled and edited by Joyce L. Tate in *Cactus Cookbook* (Cactus and Succulent Society of America, 1971).

Fig. 203. Elderly Mexican gentleman with prickly pears grown in his back yard at La Verne, California; plants brought from Zacatecas, Mexico, the nearest one xoconostle, *Opuntia chaveña* Griffiths (status undetermined). Settlers from Mexico in the U.S. Southwest have introduced a wide variety of species and cultivars of prickly pears into cultivation about their homes. (Léia Scheinvar)

Fig. 204. Joint of a spineless prickly pear, *Opuntia ficus-indica*, bearing edible fruits about the size of tennis balls, these ranging in external and internal color from red through orange to yellow. (David Griffiths)

Fig. 205. Wagon and team hauling tunas, the fruits of prickly pears, to a home; a large species of *Opuntia* in cultivation near the house; Mexico, about 1905. (David Griffiths)

Fig. 206. A factory for *miel de tuna* and *queso*, showing the fireplaces outside heating the cooking vats inside; Montesa, Mexico, about 1905. Tools for controlling the fire are leaning against the wall of the building. (David Griffiths)

Fig. 207. The same factory, showing the large troughs and vats inside, these heated from the fireplaces on the other side of the wall. (David Griffiths)

219

Fig. 208. Peeling the tunas, or fruits, of prickly pears in the factory of Fig. 207. (David Griffiths, the glass-plate negative broken at upper right; see Credits)

Fig. 209. Carrying out a barrel of the thickened juice of tunas; factory of Fig. 207. (David Griffiths)

son (1929, used with permission), *miel de tuna* . . . is made from the crushed pulp, after the seeds have been extracted, by slowly boiling it down to a thick syrup, which is then stirred or ladled in a special way while it cools. It gradually crystallizes and has a very pleasing flavor, somewhat like maple sugar, only finer grained. Long sticks of this can be purchased in the better Mexican markets in the cities of Southern California, and doubtless in all cities of the southwestern states. . . .

The tunas are considered a blessing, especially to the poor, who are dependent on them not only during the season when they are fresh and among the few foods available, but also later when the preserves are a staple food. Individuals are reported to eat as many as 100 fresh fruits during a day. However, the flesh, like that of a watermelon, contains a large percentage of water along with the sugar and other nutritive materials. The numerous relatively large seeds are eaten with the flesh, and they seem not to be injurious.

The fruits are collected for processing (see Figs. 208 and 209) as follows: "Workmen use a sharp knife in the right hand to make a cut across the top and down one side of the fruit. . . . Then with the thumb and index finger of the left hand they

Fig. 210. A cholla, *Opuntia subulata*, the species of *Opuntia* having the largest leaves, these used for food; widely cultivated in South America, especially on the western coast, but its origin not established. (David Griffiths)

Fig. 211. A joint of *Opuntia subulata*, showing the elongate leaves and the felt and spines of the areoles. (David Griffiths)

push apart the rind of the fruit and pick out the pulp ball, placing it usually in earthenware ollas strapped on their backs" (Griffiths and Thompson, 1930). The chief problem is the removal of the surface covering, or epidermis, of the fruit without dislodging the small barbed spines, or glochids, onto the flesh of the fruit or into the fingers or palms. Careful peeling with a knife and fork is a good method for beginners.

According to Nickerson (1929, quoted with permission):

The tuna market in the highland cities of Mexico is a very distinctive feature. The business is . . . carried on in a most simple . . . way. During the greater part of the season purchasers come to the booths, separated only by the size of the individual awnings or the length and number of the benches and stools, where they may purchase one or more varieties of fresh tunas at a very low price. The purchaser is supplied with a stool upon which he can sit, and a knife with which to peel the tuna he has purchased.

During the height of the season, when the fruit is plentiful, women appear at the market each morning with huge baskets of ready-peeled tunas, which are placed on earthen saucers and disposed of at one cent each. Each purchaser is furnished with the tip of a maguey [century plant] leaf or a thorn of the mesquite with which to hold the pulp while eating.

In Mexico the vegetative parts of the prickly pears are used also for food. The flat young stem joints are eaten as vegetables, after being peeled, cut up, and either boiled with water changes or

Fig. 212. Cardón or candebobe, *Cereus (Lemaireocereus) weberi*, a species used for fruit in Puebla and Oaxaca, Mexico; plants near Tomellín, 1909. The fruits are spiny, but the spine clusters fall away at maturity. (David Griffiths; see Credits)

fried in batter like eggplant. The leaves, succulent cylinders or cones appearing on the young joints, also those of various chollas, for only a month or two, are cooked like string beans. However, the far longer leaves, as well as the young joints, of some species of the related chollas are used much more commonly in this way (see Figs. 210 and 211).

Species of Cereus. The Papago Indians of southwestern Arizona gather large quantities of the fruits of the saguaro and the organ pipe cactus. They have retained the rights to these fruits in the Organ Pipe Cactus National Monument, which was derived from Papago lands. The following is quoted with permission from George Lindsay (1940):

The fruit is gathered by the natives with the aid of a strong pole tipped with a spike or hook. With this the ripened fruits (or pitahayas) are wrenched from the tall branches, and are deftly caught in a soft net or basket to avoid bruising by striking the ground. Spine-bearing areoles are easily brushed off with a twig or bunch of grass, and the perishable pitahayas are packed in a basket to be carried back to the village or ranchito. To be eaten, the outer rind, some quarter-inch in thickness, is split with a knife and peeled back, exposing the crimson pulp with tiny shining black seeds. The seeds are eaten with the pulp, but are small and not objectionable as are those of the tuna cactus fruit. The flesh seems always to be crisp and cool, even

if picked from the sunny side of a plant on a very hot day. The flavor is bland and refreshing. Once while looking for plants on Coronado Island in the Gulf of California, near Loreto, my guides picked two five-gallon cans of pitahayas in little over an hour.

In Latin America there are many large species of *Cereus* (in the broad sense), and the fruits are used in various countries, especially in Mexico, as food in much the same way as are those of prickly pears (see Fig. 212).

Barrel cacti. Cactus candy is made from the stems of the larger species of barrel cacti, which contain much soft tissue in both the (outer) cortex and the (inner) pith. Chunks or strips are boiled, and the water is replaced several times, removing the mucilage. Candy is made by adding sugar, coloring, and flavoring.

As Food for Livestock

Cactus plants are important as range food for deer and other native animals and for livestock, because they provide water and some nutritive value.

Even the large barrel cacti (*Ferocactus*) are used at times for stock feed. George Lindsay (1952) reports their use during the frequent drought periods in Baja California. The barrel-cactus populations near towns have been reduced toward zero, and even islands have lost large numbers of these cacti because fishermen have sold them on the mainland. The spines are cut off, leaving the soft interior of the plant available to stock.

The more slender stems of chollas and the flat joints of prickly pears are edible without treatment, though burning off the spines makes them more readily available.

Chollas. Many range livestock do not touch chollas, but some do. Cattle, having once started to eat them, continue to do so, and their addiction to chollas is sometimes amazing. In 1941, near the Camino del Diablo in the exceedingly dry and remote area of southwestern Arizona along the Mexican boundary, the writer saw a bull whose face was almost completely covered with clinging joints of the teddy bear cholla, *Opuntia bigelovii.* Nevertheless, he was busily eating the cholla, which is covered by dense masses of sharp, effectively barbed spines. The spines apparently do not harm the cattle, as indicated by James Manson (1933, quoted with permission):

Between Cajeme, Sonora, and the Gulf of . . . California lies a region that is arid during nine months of the year. Patches of salt grass, a few mesquite trees, clusters of a green reed and large quantities of cactus of all species spot the country. I have crossed this plain many times on hunting and fishing expeditions to the coast and on many occasions have observed cattle and deer feasting on cholla. Not only have I made this observation during the dry season but also when there was water available nearby, and never have I heard of stock dying because of the spines.

So emphatic . . . is the . . . [contention] that the spines are harmful that I began a systematic check-up among the many cattlemen of Arizona and Sonora, receiving only their vigorous denials of any casualties among cattle from a cholla diet. Indeed, my very question incited broad grins and at times raucous laughter. . . . [According to S. H. Parsons,] . . . who lived many years in the Kino Bay country of Sonora: "My own cattle in Sonora would come in with their mouths and muzzles covered with joints of the cactus and the spines. I have noticed that in a day or so, if the cattle are kept in the corral, the joints drop off without any apparent harm. We have slaughtered many cattle but never found cholla spines having injured them internally. Another thing, even the milk cows that are fed every day in the corrals, when allowed to go out where the cholla is abundant, eat the joints because they like them, not because they are starving. I did not know that anyone familiar with our Southwest did not know that cattle, as well as many wild animals, eat cholla."

. . . In summing up, the general consensus is that the spines that for a day or so cling to [the cattle's] . . . mouths and muzzles are eliminated by suppuration or absorption. The spines that are swallowed are so well crushed and ground by chewing that the action of the gastric juices disposes of their viciousness, thus preventing intestinal perforation.

Prickly Pears. Cattle and other desert range animals use native prickly pears in much the same way as chollas, with about the same, mostly emergency, values and similar limitations.

A great controversy once raged about the potential commercial value of prickly pears for livestock food (see Figs. 213-15), as well as for other purposes, and the degree of their value is still open to some debate. To understand the real significance of prickly pears on the cattle ranges, we shall review and examine this controversy and the concurrent great cactus boom and bust of about 1900 to 1917.

At the start of the twentieth century, Luther Burbank caught the public imagination with advertising of his new horticultural varieties of plants. A childhood memory is of Thomas A. Edison, Henry Ford, Harvey S. Firestone, and Luther Burbank being honored as the four heroes of the modern era at the 1915 Panama-Pacific International Exposition in San Francisco. This was early in the great period of science, technology, invention, and new methods.

Burbank was not a scientist but an imaginative practical plant breeder. During the first years of the twentieth century, genetics as a science was unknown to the public and something new to biologists. The work of Mendel in Austria at about the time of the American Civil War had been ignored or lost and had been rediscovered only in 1901. However, the groundwork for the study of heredity moved forward rapidly during the next decade and from then on. It did not affect Burbank, who represented the last great flowering of pregenetic plant breeding. His goals were practical; his method was trial-and-error; his results were not understood and not repeatable. He developed large numbers of improved types of commercial and ornamental plants, many being of practical value, and for this he is justly famous. He also gave an enormous impetus to the field of plant breeding, which soon afterward came to be placed upon a more precise scientific basis.

The unfortunate cactus-boom fiasco may have resulted from, at least primarily, the work of promoters. As will be seen below, Burbank's involvement in the enterprise is difficult to determine (see Figs. 216-18).

At times Burbank disclaimed interest in the exploitation of his productions. For example, in a statement "By the Friends and Relatives of Luther Burbank, Approved by Luther Burbank,

Fig. 213. Burning the spines from a prickly pear plant, *Opuntia lindheimeri*, to aid cattle in eating the stem joints. The flame thrower probably was an elaboration of a gasoline blowtorch. Texas, about 1910 to 1915. (David Griffiths)

Fig. 214. Cattle eating joints just after the spines have been burned away. (David Griffiths)

Fig. 215. Cattle eating joints scattered on the ground in a feed lot. (David Griffiths)

224

BURBANK OFFERS CACTUS FOR MEAT

SAN FRANCISCO, Jan. 28.—The demand for a cheap and satisfying substitute for meat gives Luther Burbank, the plant wizard, an opportunity to educate the public taste for spineless cactus.

Burbank himself prefers his cactus fruit to peaches. It appears on his table variously, boiled as greens, fried like eggplant, sliced in a salad or sweet pickled as dessert. Some months ago he gave a banquet, at which nothing was served but spineless cactus.

Dr. F. N. Doud, president of a thornless cactus farming company, is a cactus food enthusiast, finding it rich in the salts needed to keep the human system in repair. They neutralize, he says, the acids that tear down and destroy the nerve cells. Being absolutely starchless, the food is also an ideal diet for the overstout. Dr. Doud thinks the cactus will solve the food problem of the future.

BURBANK DISCLOSES NEW PLANT WONDER

San Francisco, Dec. 22.—Luther Burbank, the plant "wizard," made the astonishing statement to-day of his discovery that the spineless cactus makes fine whitewash. One leaf is said to make ten gallons, and it also makes fine paint. The cost of manufacture is said to be less than one-fifth of what is used at present.

The fibre of the plant is said to be an excellent substitute for rubber and a superior article for automobile tires.

Fig. 216. Claims made for Burbank's spineless cactus; newspaper clippings, the upper one from the Washington *Times*, January 29, 1910, the source of the other unknown. (Clippings ex David Griffiths)

"THE BLUNDERBERRY."

In "The Country Gentleman" "Ananias B. Good" writes the following, in which he certainly "makes good":

"Some years ago I was trying to cross the rattlesnake plantain on the rum cherry, with a view to securing an antidote for delirium tremens. But my assistants became so inebriated working with these materials that they did many strange and unexpected things. They got several of my best kinds of crossing stock all mixed together, including my Scotch whisky vine and my German sausage tree. From these mixtures came all sorts of odd and useless results, many of which had no advertising value whatever; but amongst the lot was this Blunderberry.

"The plant is something between a vine and a tree, and is very prolific when it blossoms. But as it blooms, in this country at least, only on the 29th of February, we get a crop only in presidential years. I offered it privately to two very gullible seedsmen to be brought out as the Leap-Year Fruit, or Presidential Manna; but neither man had the ready money; and I find that in this plant creating business it is best always to do business on a cash basis. In my failure to make an immediate sale, however, I committed the second and most serious blunder connected with the Blunderberry.

"Some question has been raised as to whether my Blunderberry is a genuine creation or only a newspaper fake. I have decided, however, to dispose of this innuendo once for all by offering a prize of a farm in California and an Ingersoll watch to anyone who will prove that anything like what I have described ever existed before. Furthermore, I am willing to outdo the original creator of such advertising specialties and will offer ten thousand dollars ($10,000) cash, cold coin, to anyone who will prove that the Blunderberry has any earthly use.

"It has always been my misfortune to wake up too late when anything especially good was to come off. Had I got out my Blunderberry a few years earlier, or had I promptly introduced my seedless apple, I might have made a good thing. Now, however, the field has been taken up by very similar, but really quite inferior, varieties."
                                        ANANIAS B. GOOD.

Fig. 217. Excerpt from the *Country Gentleman*, about 1910. One of Burbank's much publicized creations was the wonderberry, derived in whole or in part from the black nightshade, *Solanum nigrum*, a weed distributed widely in warm parts of the world. Although the berries of this species are poisonous when green, they become edible when ripe, and are used for pies and preserves. The weed is common in grainfields, as in the Dakotas, where it grows after the cutting of the field crop, hence the name stubbleberry. A cultivated form is known as the garden huckleberry; and "Solanum burbankii" is said to be a hybrid between the garden huckleberry and *S. nigrum*. (Clippings ex David Griffiths)

Santa Rosa, California, U.S.A., August, 1907," there is an appeal to people not to waste Mr. Burbank's time with unnecessary letters and questions, which had bogged him down, and a notice to the public to stay off his property, which had been overrun by crowds. The paper asks that the following points be observed: (1) Mr. Burbank has nothing for sale; (2) he is not a nurseryman, florist, seedsman, or raiser of seeds or plants for sale; (3) he is the originator of new kinds of useful plants; (4) these are sold through dealers, many of them listed.

However, other pamphlets issued in Burbank's name tell a different story. For example, Burbank's "*The Gold Medal Newest Agricultural-Horticultural Opuntias*, Santa Rosa, Sonoma Co., Cal., U.S.A., June 1st, 1911," states the virtues of

prickly pears for (1) food for all kinds of stock including poultry; (2) fresh fruit ("far superior to the banana in flavor"); (3) jams, jellies, syrups, and candies; (4) pickles (from the young leaves); (5) mixing material for whitewash (juice of the stems); (6) poultices and a substitute for hot water bags; (7) coloring (from the fruits) for ices, jellies, and confectionery; (8) "various other forms of food" (from the fruits and leaves); (9) alcohol and paper pulp; and (10) soil binding and water preservation ("moreover the cactus facili-

Fig. 218. Field of Burbank's "Improved Thornless Cactus": "3 year old plants. fruit about ½ grown." Production is stated to be 198,637 pounds (99 tons) of fruit per acre. Santa Rosa, California, October 1, 1908. (Photographer unknown; see Credits)

tates the penetration of the earth by waters which reappear below in the form of springs"). Above Burbank's name on the first page is a statement of production of ". . . Sixty to One Hundred tons [of fruit] per acre. . . ." On the fifth page there is a picture of sheep in Australia eating prickly pear joints and the caption: "AN AUSTRALIAN VIEW. Feeding Sheep on Cactus Where Severe Droughts Have Caused the Death of Many Millions of Sheep and Other Stock." The ninth and eleventh pages (all pages unnumbered) are devoted to reproduction of newspaper clippings praising Burbank and deriding the scientists, like David Griffiths, who did not accept his claims. Cacti are said to be inexpensive to plant, to require no cultivation, and to be brought into production for only ". . . $60.00 per acre, which would amply cover all expenses, except the cost of the plants, until the third year when the planta-

tion would be in full bearing." Rich land is said not to be necessarily required, and land available at $50.00 per acre (very satisfactory) or as low as $5.00 (feasible) is suggested, but it is thought that even white alkali probably could be withstood. The land should yield a ". . . crop worth nearly or quite $400.00 per acre on the third and every succeeding year. . . ." (And money, then, was made of gold. To find the modern monetary equivalents, multiplication by at least 8 is necessary.) In Burbank's *"Prices for the Summer of 1911,"* enclosed in the pamphlet, cuttings (joints) of the varieties El Dorado, Competent, Signal, and Titania were offered for $3.00 each. "Sixty tons of the common type of so-called 'spineless' cactus so often sold as 'Burbank's' or 'just as good as Burbank's,' price: *Cuttings* each 2¢. . . ." This seems to have come from Burbank or his own sales organization, but it does not coincide with the first paper mentioned above. This is true of a similar earlier promotional booklet, *The New Agricultural-Horticultural Opuntias*, Santa Rosa, June 1, 1907, with similar laudatory statements quoted from the press and from "intellectuals."

A pamphlet (undated) entitled *Luther Burbank's Opuntia or Thornless Cactus, His Greatest Achievement*, was issued by the Thornless Cactus Farming Company, Merchants Trust Company Building, Los Angeles, California. On page 26, a facsimile of a letter from Burbank dated September 20, 1907, certifies sale of all interest, right, and title to certain named creations in cacti to the Company. These are stated to be ". . . all the best varieties which I have so far offered of my productions of cacti." On page 15, prospective production had advanced to 200 tons per acre; on page 16 deserts were about to bloom; on page 27 Burbank was quoted as saying, "Every plant of the new varieties of Thornless Cactus is worth $500.00"; on page 27 was a statement that in lots of at least 10, plants could be had by sending in $2.00 for each one; and on pages 23 and 29 were indications that the Thornless Cactus Farming Company had stock and that an investment in the Company would pay.

In a booklet entitled *Luther Burbank's Spineless Cactus*, 1913, an undated letter from Luther Burbank designates The Luther Burbank Company (General Offices, Exposition Building, Pine and Battery Streets, San Francisco) as the ". . . sole distributor of the Luther Burbank Horticultural productions, and from no other source can anyone be positively assured of obtaining genuine Luther Burbank Production."

Thus Burbank's connection with cactus promotion is not clear, and a reading of these documents leaves the question confused and clearly a subject for further research rather than opinion. The story of the promotional side of the boom is long and complex.

The main scientific points revolve about the research of David Griffiths, U.S. Department of Agriculture, who, with others, undertook during the spineless cactus boom extensive scientific investigations of the available kinds of prickly pears, of the value of the fruits for human food, and of the joints for stock feed. In the United States, human use of the fruits still is limited, and the claimed value as a crop plant for this country has not been confirmed by time. Extensive use as forage was negated by the investigations of Grif-

Fig. 219. The pest prickly pear of Australia, the spiny form of the Indian fig, *Opuntia ficus-indica*, known as *O. megacantha*. (J. H. Maiden, Botanic Garden, Sydney; collection of David Griffiths)

Fig. 220. A large prickly pear species, *Opuntia lindheimeri*, killed by cochineal insects; U.S.D.A. Plant Introduction Garden, Chico, California, 1916. The insects were nonetheless unimportant in controlling prickly pears in Australia. (David Griffiths)

fiths, Hare, and others and then by widespread horticultural trial. The spineless varieties originated in warm countries, and they turned out to be vulnerable to cold, present every winter in the deserts; to rabbits and rodents, against which effective protection from spines was lacking; and to shortage of sustained enthusiasm, when, as predicted by Griffiths, good, well-watered land was found to be necessary and to be more valuable for other, more nutritious crops. In Australia, South Africa, and elsewhere the spineless plants went wild and reproduced some spiny plants by seeds, some spineless ones being heterozygous and therefore yielding both spiny and spineless progeny, and became pests as the spiny ones persisted (see Fig. 219). Much valuable land became worthless, and enormous sums were spent upon cactus eradication. However, much of this can be traced to earlier introductions. For example, in Australia *Opuntia inermis* [*O. stricta*], introduced through a single plant in 1839, was a dreaded pest, and there was legislation against it as early as 1883.

The following excerpts from early volumes of the *Cactus & Succulent Journal* and an agricultural bulletin document the principal features of the cactus boom and its results in the words of

individuals who were adult contemporaries of the prickly-pear excitement.

The following is quoted with permission from Lawrence (1931):

Popularly, Luther Burbank is credited with the development of spineless cactus. He certainly got more notoriety out of his experiments along that line than in anything else he ever did.

But he never claimed the discovery of spineless cactus, and he never claimed much merit for his development of the species. All the claiming was done by glib stock-salesmen who saw the chance to lure the credulous into purchases of shares in companies to promote the cultivation of spineless cactus. It was highly embarrassing to Luther, who was a scientific experimentalist and not a promoter of get-rich-quick schemes.

He proved that cactus could be bred with large fleshy joints, devoid of spines. Having done that he was through.

The fakers now stepped in and tried to induce nice old ladies of both sexes to embark in the business of raising Burbank spineless cactus. As a result there sprang up acres upon acres of this hybrid Opuntia all over the southland.

Even now one may ride about Los Angeles and see abandoned acreage given over about twenty years ago to raising spineless cactus. Of course the tenderfeet were successful in raising the crop, but of what good was it, after they had raised it?

The promoters had painted vivid pictures of untold wealth to be derived from selling spineless cactus in bales by the ton to feed to cattle in lieu of hay. The suckers didn't stop to investigate. They never even so much as offered a slab to a cow.

The claims of the promoters aroused scientific interest, as well. The following is quoted with permission from E. O. Orpet (1939):

[The spineless horticultural varieties] . . . revert readily by seeds to their normal spiny species. This was discovered in Australia, where tons were sent to supply forage in their great desert spaces. The cacti flowered, the fruits were devoured by birds, seeds scattered broadcast, and [some of] the seedlings came back spiny and were the worst pest they had ever had to contend with until our Government sent out the larvae of the Cochineal Mealy-Bug, which soon devastated the opuntias. [See Fig. 220; a moth larva, of *Cactoblastis cactorum*, has been used much more effectively than the cochineal insects, which have not given the expected results.]

At the time of the Burbank exploitation, the men in charge at Washington decided to find out how much value this plant had as forage about 1915 [1905]. The late Dr. David Griffiths was put on the job, and as always, he did it well [see Figs. 221 and 222], getting together 600 kinds of *Opuntia* from their native habitat and some from one of the French colonies where an eminent Frenchman had produced seedlings of certain types that as variants proved promising, as often happens by selection. These with all others were grown at the Plant Introduction Garden at Chico, California, and there was another station and planting in Texas [two, at San Antonio and Brownsville]. After years of trial, and descriptions of many . . . [thought] to be new to science, Dr. Griffiths wrote a Government Bulletin with great care, and summed up the whole situation in a sentence which I will quote from memory, "The spineless cactus must have water, and, where this is obtained, a better forage food than cactus may be grown."

It was estimated that a cow would have to eat 200 pounds [at a time] to get the same nourishment that [a normal amount of] a feed of other forage would furnish. . . .

It is commonly supposed that Burbank originated these spineless opuntias. We have the authority of Mr. Ernest Braunton that he had sent them as curios, which they were, but Burbank seemed to vision value and proceeded to publicize this. . . .

David Fairchild reported in his book *The World Is My Garden* that he learned that Dr. Carlos Spegazzini, an Italian botanist, had brought from the dry plains of (Gran Chaco) Argentina a spineless Opuntia, where it served as a cattle fodder. In 1899 Mr. Fairchild sent material to the Department of Agriculture and it was much later that Burbank publicized the "spineless cactus" as his own creation.

Actually, there are many kinds of spineless or nearly spineless prickly pears, as shown in the key to even the species of *Opuntia* occurring in the United States (pp. 381-82). Some species or botanical varieties may be always spineless, but commonly the spineless types are local or cultivated strains. Burbank's plants were mostly spineless types of *Opuntia ficus-indica*, the Indian fig, and perhaps other species, taken from Mexico to many warm, dry parts of the world soon after the arrival of the Spanish conquerors. Burbank's new strains may have been obtained by breeding various cultivars or species with each other and retaining the desirable progeny. Also, however, he may have planted the seeds of spineless types and merely selected the offspring he wanted. The progeny of such heterozygous plants are highly variable, and any new form can be reproduced rapidly and without variation by planting its stem joints as cuttings. The nature of the areole and the degree of spininess vary (see Fig. 223).

The most useful prickly pears for livestock are those native on the cattle ranges, adapted to the conditions there. Their greatest value is associated with drought periods when both food and water are scarce. The following is quoted from J. J. Thornber (1911):

It is not intended by this to advocate the use of cactus and other roughage as general feed, but rather as valuable emergency forage to fall back upon during times of drought. Having studied carefully for years the part that cactus forage has played on many ranges in southern Arizona, and knowing its importance as a feed in parts of southern and southwestern Texas, it is impossible for the writer to escape the conclusion that large numbers of stock on our ranges owe their existence to the much despised cactus [see Fig. 224]. When there is little else on the ranges, cattle turn to cacti for feed and water; and, while the animals suffer evident discomfort in grazing the unsinged joints of chollas and other cacti, nevertheless, by so doing they escape death from starvation and thirst. Thus they are enabled to pass over periods of drought to seasons and years of plenty. This being possible under open range conditions, we may reasonably expect more from cacti when planted systematically on the ranges.

For various reasons, the writer has never considered practicable the growing of cactus . . . as a major forage for stock. With the limited rainfall at lower altitudes where cacti would of necessity have to be grown, these plants make slow progress, as shown under both natural and cultivated conditions. The most serious objection to cactus forage is its tendency to cause digestive disturbances when eaten in large quantities. Practical stockmen who advocate the use of cactus forage state that cattle cannot live on it exclusively for an indefinite time; and that when driven to eat it as a principal diet they suffer from scouring. This is all the more pronounced when stock are in a run-down and half-starved condition previous to being given this feed. These objections to cactus forage are met in Texas by feeding singed or chopped pear along with

EXPERTS OF U.S. PINHEADS, SAYS PLANT SAGE

Burbank Scores, Denounces and Satirizes Agricultural Department

CLAIMS IT HAS DERIDED HIM

Denominates Federal Spineless Cactus 'Trash,' as Old as Pyramids

SAN FRANCISCO. July 19.—Charges that experts in the United States Department of Agriculture, through ignorance or worse, are this season sending out tons of "just as good as Burbank" spineless cactus which in reality is "ancient trash, such as the builders of the pyramids in Egypt might have cultivated," are made by Luther Burbank in a pamphlet just published by the plant sage of Santa Rosa.

Burbank writes in the first person about his work and fires a whole broadside of sarcasm and scorn at the government experts in the Department of Agriculture.

His opinion of his own achievements is disclosed in an introduction in which he speaks of them as "the most valuable improvements in vegetable life during the centuries, fully equal in importance to the discovery of a new continent."

'Pinheads,' Says Sage

Experts in the government service at Washington are called "low-browed, narrow-gauged and pin-headed employes, who have to keep shouting to hold their places and who are largely responsible for the trash free seed and the trash so-called spineless cactus distribution."

"Only nine years required to wake up the experts," is the caption placed by Burbank over his chapter telling how reluctant the Washington authorities have been to recognize his work.

"The existence of the United States Department of Agriculture has been supposed, among other things, for the purpose of fostering and encouraging improved methods," writes the famous plant wizard.

"That the cause of agriculture and horticulture would receive a lasting benefit by the prompt dismissal of the low-browed, narrow-gauged, pin-headed employes is too well known to need further comment."

After telling how he finally succeeded in developing a seedless and spineless cactus, Burbank says the department at Washington at last became ludicrously earnest in its interest in my experiments.

Two Kinds of Experts

"The employes of the Department of Agriculture," he writes, "are with few exceptions upright and honorable gentlemen with whom I am on the most friendly terms. Sometimes, however, one of the 'other kind' gets a job.

"One of the 'other kind' of Government 'experts,' a certain David Griffiths, after visiting my grounds on several occasions, awoke at last with a shock and took occasion to publish a bulletin on the 'spineless prickly pear,' its whole end and aim and too evident purpose being only to deride and belittle the long and very expensive experiments which had been made here, before he or the department had awakened from its drowsy indifference to the great value of this long-neglected gift of nature, which now promises to be of as great or even greater value to the human race than the discovery of steam."

After reprinting a large number of newspaper editorials praising his work, Burbank returns to the attack by declaring that his spineless cactus will produce fifteen to one as compared with the best "expert" Government cactus.

WHY BURBANK HAS BECOME PEEVISH ABOUT GOVERNMENT'S CACTUS WORK

Found Plant That Infringes on His Spineless Invention

Cuts Into His Business But Works to Advantage of the Public

Luther Burbank has so far forgotten his knowledge of propriety that recently he broke into public print and assailed officials connected with the National Bureau of Plant Industry as being "low-browed pinheads," his estimate of their brain power being drawn from their claims that there is no such plant as an absolutely spineless cactus.

A news dispatch from Washington says:

"Burbank, huh! If you claimed to be the inventor of the only spineless cactus known to man, and were selling cuts of it all over the country at from $2 to $5 a cut, and someone wrote a pamphlet declaring that there is no such thing as a spineless cactus at all, wouldn't it make you mad? That's what's the matter with Burbank.

"If you were selling the cuts and the pamphlets said that there was a near-spineless cactus, but that the field for its culture was exceedingly limited, and that anyway the cactus that has outgrown most of its spines is an ancient plant that grows all the way from Malta to Mexico and is unpatentable, it would make you still madder,

wouldn't it? Well, that's some more of what's the matter with Burbank."

With this kind of words and a few more the Agricultural Department to-day dismissed the charges made by Luther Burbank that the scientificos of the department were low-browed pinheads.

Far from it taking nine years to wake them up, the department officials declare they have been publishing cactus bulletins at the rate of at least one annually for many years, and even now Professor David Griffiths, whom Professor Burbank classes as a pinhead, is writing another bulletin.

The last cactus bulletin from the department brought an angry snort of disdain from Burbank, and what the forthcoming bulletin may do must be left to the future. The bulletin says:

"Four spineless varieties are common in this country and have been cultivated for so long a time that their origin is not known. Some of these are as spineless as any known to science today."

In referring to these varieties and their distribution by the department, the bulletin says:

"There is a great range of varieties to select from, the spiniest to the least spiny that are known. The so-called spineless ones vary in the number of spines. Like all material known to science today, none of them is entirely spineless, and there is none perfectly spineless anywhere.

"There are a number of nurserymen who have on hand stocks of some varieties of prickly pears, and are offering them for sale, usually under the name of 'spineless cactus.' Farmers who desire to grow this crop should consult the map on page 15.

"If located outside of the area shown

no one will be justified in spending either time or money in the expectation of making either an economic crop out of 'spineless' prickly pears. Outside the shaded area of the map, attention should be given only to shiny, hardy varieties."

The "shaded area" on the map limits the field for the spineless cactus to a portion of the California coast, Southern California and Arizona, the extreme south of Texas, and the coast line of Florida.

In the forthcoming new bulletin it is understood the area that the government officials designate as fit for the cultivation of the spineless variety of cactus will be much further limited.

The controversy is of considerable interest locally for the reason that about fifteen tons of cactus pads were shipped this spring from the National Plant Introduction Garden at Chico, under the personal supervision of Dr. Griffiths, to various parts of the United States for the purpose of propagation with a view to increasing the fodder supply in stock growing sections. These plants were for free distribution, and only distributed after their worth had been proven. In the line of breeding with a view to ridding plants of their spines, the government has made no effort, and Burbank may have all the glory on that score. The Bureau of Plant Industry has simply gathered cactus plants from many parts of the world, and in its search, perhaps unfortunately for Burbank's cactus business, has found some cacti which are almost without spines, or as nearly so as Burbank's. Proven of value for fodder, the government places them in the hands of people willing to make the most of them for themselves and the productiveness of the nation, regardless of the private business of Mr. Burbank.

As a matter of fact, the largest growers of cactus for fodder prefer certain varieties of the spiny cactus,

---

Fig. 222 (*above*). A reply to Burbank's attack, *Chico Record*, Chico, California, July 22, 1911. (Clipping ex David Griffiths)

Fig. 221 (*facing page*). Burbank's attack on the United States Department of Agriculture Bureau of Plant Industry and David Griffiths; Los Angeles *Examiner*, July 30, 1911. (Clipping ex David Griffiths)

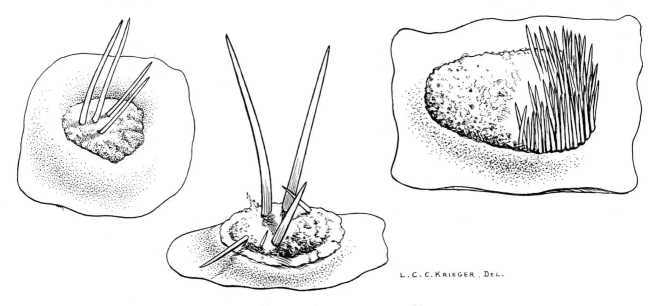

Fig. 223. The areoles of spineless prickly pears, roughly ×6. *Left,* From a one-year-old joint of the commercial cultivar "Anacantha" (Burbank), with four glochids. *Center,* from a one-year-old joint of another commercial cultivar, "Santa Rosa" (Burbank), showing four spines and two glochids. *Right,* Plant from the highlands of Mexico (*Griffiths 8,145*) introduced by the Department of Agriculture, the least spiny of 2,400 plants from as many sources. However, at about four years of age, the areoles develop short glochids, as shown in the areole. (L. C. C. Krieger for David Griffiths)

TEXAS HAD IT ALWAYS

The recent hair-pulling, eye-gouging bout between Luther Burbank, the creator of floral freaks, and the Agricultural Department, to which allusion is made in the editorial columns of the New York Times, July 21, serves as gratuitous advertisement for Texas.

The verbal altercation, intimates the Times, grew out of a spineless cactus, leaving the specious inference that the noted botanist is indeed a man of parts. During recent years, says the editorial, Mr. Burbank has been trying to produce a thornless cactus to be used as food for stock. Just about the time that his efforts met with success, the Agricultural Department stepped into the ring as a claimant for the cactus grafting honors, which, up to that time, had been monopolized by the Californian. Whereupon, the Times states, Mr. Burbank became filled with wrath, declaring that the government's goods would not pass pure food inspection because of "degeneracy."

Now, from the time that La Salle landed at Matagorda bay, and the Indians gathered around and told him that he was in "Tejas," this state has been growing spineless cactus. Back in the old cowboy days, when the grass became scant on the prairies the cowboys fed their herds of cattle on the spineless cacti. The product has been grown by the Mexicans along the Rio Grande river for many years—"in Texas, down by the Rio Grande," the land that tradition says was forgotten the day after the creation and given to the devil for the marshalling and maneuvering of his legions. Verily, on such TEXAS land has the spineless cactus been successfully grown for years, but only in small quantities.

That the Texas product is not "degenerate" is known to every ranchman between San Antonio and the Gulf of Mexico. It is only recently, however, that an attempt has been made to grow this species of cactus in sufficient quantities to serve as winter food for cattle. Experiments now being carried forward in the Brownsville country and near San Antonio give promise that the growing of the indigenous spineless cactus will soon be added to the long list of agricultural industries of the state. Its growth, however, is restricted to southern latitudes; San Antonio is the geographical northern limit in Texas.

So, while Mr. Burbank and the Agricultural Department are pulling hair and making faces and performing their digito-nasal feats in their own peculiar fashion, Texas smiles at the show—and continues to grow spineless cacti without the fashionable process of grafting.

Fig. 224. The antiquity of prickly pears as forage plants. San Antonio *Light,* San Antonio, Texas, July 28, 1911. (Clipping ex David Griffiths)

232

inexpensive concentrates like cotton-seed meal. A ration of this kind has been found to be not only life-sustaining, but actually fattening to range stock. In this connection the Texan stockman is fortunate in having at hand almost unlimited quantities of inexpensive cotton-seed meal, which is rich in protein content, to feed along with prickly pear forage of well-known low nutritive value. In Arizona it will be found financially advantageous to use alfalfa hay in place of cotton-seed meal. [Arizona now has cotton.]"

Thus, during the Burbank "thornless cactus" boom, early in the twentieth century, spineless horticultural varieties of *Opuntia ficus-indica*, the Indian fig, were pushed for various uses (see Fig. 225). However, this plant requires good soil and water. Like other cacti, it can survive drought, but water must be available at times or there is little growth. *O. ficus-indica* is not a desert plant, but one native in moist but mild tropical uplands. Furthermore, it is frost-sensitive, and deserts have cold winter nights. Spinelessness, however, proved an even more serious deficiency: the plants were unprotected from rabbits and rodents, and they did not last long in fields or on ranges.

The controversy over uses of prickly pears for stock feed and other purposes died before it was fully resolved—the First World War had diverted public attention to other matters, the great claims were not substantiated, and the Age of Science changed technologies and needs. I have been impressed, in various parts of the western world, by how little the ways of human life changed during the several centuries preceding the time of my grandparents or during even my own early life, prior to 1920. They were not profoundly different from those of earlier civilizations, and the world of Burbank was simply an extension of the world of the nineteenth century. Although such innovations as gas lights, kerosene, railroads, steamboats, the repeating rifle, and something of the machine age had had an impact upon the way of life, the changes for most individuals had not been profound. During Burbank's time electricity was a discovery with possibilities and already some uses, the telephone and indoor plumbing were available in the cities and just invading the country, the "tin lizzy" started by a crank activated by elbow grease was here but not yet available to the masses, and the practice of medicine was still learned in rural areas by a sort of apprentice system concerned with the administration of physic and various pink pills. Against this background, the ten virtues of cacti listed by Burbank (p. 225) seemed important. However, the tenth was obviously fanciful; some, like a basis for food coloring or for hot-water bags or for ingredients for whitewash and poultices, were to be swamped during the scientific age to come; some, like the production of alcohol or paper pulp, were not practical; and others, including food for livestock, were of value only during emergency and at restricted times and places. Thus, in the light of his time, Burbank's contribution seemed of more value than it does now, but his time was not to last.

Despite the failure of the massive attempt to introduce cacti into the United States as multipurpose plants, we shall do well now to reassess their potential value. In Mexico, cacti, especially prickly pears, are a staple source of food, and their value there and in many other parts of the world is unquestionable (see Figs. 226 and 227). That the fruits have not become popular in the United States may be due primarily to the large seeds and the numerous barbed glochids in the areoles. Application of the new methods of plant breeding, based on the principles of genetics, to the best varieties could yield new strains with larger fruits having even better flavor, few or small glochids, and higher nutritional value, and perhaps lacking seeds and stem spines. The pool of genes in Mexico is rich, and strains cultivated there include the necessary features for highly improved plants. A great service to the people of much of the warmer parts of the world can be performed by the application of new background knowledge and new research tools and methods to the study of the prickly pears. They are grown easily, without fertilizer or special horticultural methods, about houses in countries where such a source of food is needed. The crop plant in this case has been proved already by centuries of use to be practical for growing in tropical uplands, the Horse Latitudes, and the southern margin of the Temperate Zone. Strains resistant to cold might extend cultivation a little farther into temperate areas, and resistance to diseases and pests would improve the effectiveness of cultivation in all regions.

References (uses of prickly pears): Dodd, 1927, *Biological control of prickly pear in Australia*, 1940, *The biological campaign against prickly pear*; Ewart, 1910, *Prickly pear. A fodder plant for cultivation?*; Griffiths, 1905, *The prickly pear and other cacti as stock food*, 1908, *The prickly pear as a farm crop*, 1909, *The "spineless" prickly pears*, 1912, *The thornless prickly pears*, 1913, *Behavior, under cultural conditions, of species of cacti known as Opuntia*, 1915a, *Hardier spineless cactus*, 1915b, *Yields of native prickly pear in southern Texas*, 1929, *El nopal como alimento*

Fig. 225. The cactus cycle of boom and bust. Plants of Burbank's spineless prickly pears; these covered many thousands of acres through much of the southern parts of the United States. *Top*, New planting by J. C. Thurman, Waldo, Texas, 1915. *Middle*, Older planting by C. C. Molby, Browns Valley, California, 1915. *Bottom*, Planting abandoned at Waldo, Texas; photographed one year later. (David Griffiths)

Fig. 226. A present-day plantation of the Indian fig, *Opuntia ficus-indica*, on a commercial cactus farm near San Jose, California. (Walter S. Phillips; from *The Native Cacti of California*)

Fig. 227. Plants cultivated by the United States Department of Agriculture in 1916, showing the profuse production of large, edible fruits. What is needed is scientific experiment designed to produce highly improved strains for use as garden and crop plants, especially where machinery, fertilizers, and "modern methods" of agriculture are not available. Cacti of this type can be grown with little effort in warm, dry countries. (David Griffiths; from *The Native Cacti of California*)

235

del ganado; Griffiths & Hare, 1907a, *Summary of recent investigations of the value of cacti as stock food*, 1907b, *The tuna as food for man*, 1908, *The prickly pear and other cacti as food for stock*; Hare, 1908, *Experiments on digestibility of prickly pear by cattle*, 1911, *A study of carbohydrates in the prickly pear and its fruits*; Horn, 1913, *Prickly pear experiments*; Howard, 1945, *Luther Burbank's plant contributions*; Lindsay, 1952, *The use of cactus as stock food*; Lumholz, 1912, *New trails in Mexico*; Maiden, 1898, *A preliminary study of the prickly pears naturalized in New South Wales*, 1911-17, *The prickly pears of interest to Australians*; Petty, 1935, *Cactoblastis cactorum*; Prickly Pear Destruction Commission; Moree, 1927, 1967, *Prickly pear destruction in New South Wales*; Ruggles, 1956, *Insect heroes [Cactoblastis] not welcome in Sydney*; Sinclair, 1928, *Prickly pear as stock food and some of its other uses*; Thornber, 1910, *The grazing ranges of Arizona*, 1911, *Native cacti as emergency forage plants*; Uphof, 1916, *Cold resistance in spineless cacti*; Tichermak, 1910, *Stachellose*

Kakteen als Viehfutter; Turpin & Gill, 1928, *Insurance against drought*; *Drought resistant fodders: with special reference to cactus*; Woodward, Turner & Griffiths, 1915, *Prickly pears as feed for dairy cows*.

Production of Cochineal Dye

In pre-Columbian times the culture of the cochineal was important to the Aztecs, who used the pigment to dye the robes of their emperor and annually demanded bags of the insects as tribute from their vassals. The Indians of Mexico cultivated cacti on plantations devoted to producing the dye. The insects were preserved through the rainy season on prickly pear joints stored in dry places, and then were used to furnish an enhanced supply of insects for the plantations when the dry season came in November.

The female insect, which furnishes the dye, is black-purple, large, and stationary. The bright red males are small and short-lived, and they make up less than 0.5 percent of the population.

Fig. 228. Prickly pears parasitized by cochineal insects at the Plant Introduction Garden at Chico, California; a Texas hybrid of *Opuntia ficus-indica* and *O. lindheimeri* parasitized by a Californian cochineal insect. (David Griffiths)

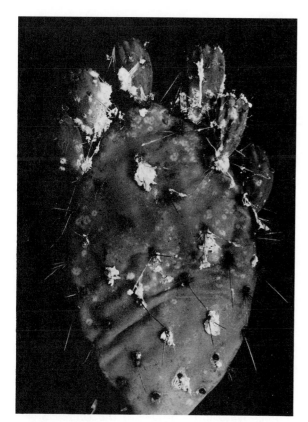

Fig. 229. *Opuntia littoralis* var. *vaseyi* parasitized by a native Californian cochineal insect; southern California. (Robert S. Woods)

Even the female is only 1-2 mm in diameter; but the cottonlike fibrous material she secretes about herself is easily visible on the plants.

Europe had no good or reliable source of bright red dye for fabrics, and the colorful Aztec robes were of great interest to the Spanish conquerors. The dye soon was produced commercially on cactus plantations in the warm parts of the Spanish New World and sold in Europe, but its source remained a secret until Leeuwenhoek studied the dye material under his microscope. Eventually, live insects and cactus plants were introduced on plantations in the Mediterranean countries and the Canary Islands. The use of cochineal declined with the advent of twentieth-century synthetic colorings, but it still provides the carmine used in preparing microscope slides, as well as crimson lake and a variety of other dyes used mostly in small quantities.

Evans (1967) has written a particularly good paper on the cochineal insect and its history and uses.

Other cochineal insects attack various species of prickly pears, including those native to southern California and the introduced *Opuntia ficus-indica* (see Figs. 228 and 229).

As an Emergency Source of Water

The barrel cacti (*Ferocactus, Echinocactus,* and their relatives) have been hailed as the saviors of desert travelers by virtue of providing drinking water. If the top of the stem is cut off and the pulp is beaten, water is extracted. The quantity available and the flavor depend on the kind of cactus, the recency of rain, and perhaps (for flavor; see p. 57) the time of day. The writer found the fluid of *F. acanthodes* var. *acanthodes* bland and insipid. Whether it would quench thirst is uncertain; it has not been tried under conditions of pronounced thirst. Frits Went found barrel-cactus juice to be unpleasant and slimy, and not a thirst-quencher. Some fleshy cacti like the saguaro, *Cereus giganteus,* have a very unpleasant flavor; the various barrel cacti have different flavors, but there has been little study of their juice.

Perhaps the most extensive investigation was by Cutak (1943, 1946), who, with Robert H. Peebles and a number of others, found the juice of *Ferocactus acanthodes* var. *lecontei* refreshing even during drought season (see Fig. 230), and the

Fig. 230. The flesh of a barrel cactus, *Ferocactus acanthodes* var. *lecontei.* Pounding or chewing yields a considerable amount of bland juice; the flavor varies in other species. The juice has been suggested as an emergency source of drinking water (see text). (Ladislaus Cutak; courtesy of the Missouri Botanical Garden)

pulp of *F. wislizenii* similar to watermelon rind in water content and flavor. According to Cutak, the fluid of *F. acanthodes* var. *acanthodes* puckered his lips, and it was reminiscent of a half-ripe persimmon. However, he did not find the juice to be slimy or nauseous as claimed by others.

Cutak cites two cases of lives saved by chewing barrel cactus flesh—one a Marine flier downed during desert training for World War II, the other a geologist stranded on a ledge in the Grand Canyon. He suggests the plant as only an emergency water source.

Unfortunately, no really thorough study of the juice of various cactus species has been published. The problem is important, and both practical and biochemical studies are needed. The results could save lives, especially if particular species were shown to be useful, others dangerous.

References: Coville, 1904, *Desert plants as a source of drinking water*; Cutak, 1943, *The life-saving barrel cactus—myth or fact?*, 1946, *Is there palatable water in the barrel cactus?*; Frick, 1932, *Water, water, everywhere!*; Marshall, 1956a, *The barrel cactus as a source of water*.

As an Adjunct to Religion

In the southern Rocky Mountain region, cacti are important in Indian religious ceremonies and in the training and testing of young warriors through a partly religious rite. The current Easter ceremonial beating with stems of chollas derives from the ceremonial use of these plants during prehistoric times. During the ceremonies in which the young men of some tribes, like the Zuñi, became warriors, the initiates would grind the stems of *Opuntia imbricata* under their armpits. According to Lucile Housely (thesis, Claremont Graduate School, 1974), centuries ago the Jemez Indians cultivated this plant for food, protection of villages on the mesas, and ceremonial purposes. She has found chollas persisting today on the obscured sites of Jemez habitations in yellow pine forest (Rocky Mountain Montane Forest) above the normal altitude range for the species.

A much more widely used cactus is the peyote (see Figs. 231-33), as described below:

THE HISTORY AND USES OF PEYOTE
Contributed by Edward F. Anderson*

Lophophora williamsii has many common names: peyote, peyotl, peyotillo, mescal button (not to be confused with mescal from *Agave* spp.

*Department of Biological Sciences, Whitman College, Walla Walla, Washington.

or with mescal beans from *Sophora secundifolia*), *raíz diabólica*, dumpling cactus, and many others in various Indian languages.

This plant has been used ceremonially since pre-Columbian times primarily because of its hallucinogenic properties. The Spanish conquistadores, when they arrived in Mexico in the sixteenth century, found it in use by the Aztecs and other Mexican Indian tribes for both therapeutic and religious purposes, and in many tribes the plant was revered as a god or the prophet of a god. After the Spanish conquest, Roman Catholic priests made a determined effort to discourage the use of peyote and other pagan religious symbols. Religious documents state that the eating of peyote is as serious a sin as murder or the eating of human flesh, and they designate the plant by such terms as raíz diabólica (devil's root). Despite the strenuous efforts of church leaders to discourage the use of peyote, it continued to have important religious significance for many Indian groups in Mexico, including the Lipan, Tamaulipan, Carrizo, Aztec, Tarahumara, and Cora-Huichol tribes.

During the nineteenth century the peyote ceremonies were introduced into the United States from Mexico primarily by the Mescalero Apache and Tonkawa Indians. From these tribes peyotism radiated rapidly throughout the plains states, and by the early twentieth century it had been introduced to most Indian tribes of the United States and southern Canada. Today peyotism is probably the most widespread religious belief among the Indians, involving about a quarter-million believers. In many states it is incorporated as the Native American Church, recognized as a legitimate Christian sect.

In Mexico, the religious ceremonies involving peyote emphasize agriculture, hunting, curing, and divination. Following ritualistic pilgrimages to the regions where peyote grows in northern Mexico, elaborate festivals are held, these involving singing, dancing, praying, and curing. The visions induced by eating the plant are believed to foretell future events.

In the plains regions of the United States, the peyote ceremony is more of a social affair involving White Christian beliefs as well as many traditional aboriginal customs, rituals, and implements. The ceremony consists primarily of eating peyote "buttons" (the top part of the plant, usually dried), singing, praying, and meditating. The ceremony usually starts at dusk and lasts through the night, often with curing of the sick as the final ritual. In some tribes women are pro-

Fig. 232 (*above*). Peyote in flower, showing the raised areoles of the stem, each bearing a dense tuft of long, woolly hairs. Spines are present only in juvenile plants.

Fig. 231 (*left*). Peyote, *Lophophora williamsii*, growing among grasses. (Edward F. Anderson)

Fig. 233. Peyote, relatively young plants, one with its first branch. The small branches like this (or the main stem) are cut off, and are known as "peyote buttons." The plant is stimulated to branch from the base, and in later years it yields many buttons.

hibited from participating fully in the services. Anthropologists point out that the Native American Church is a combination of aboriginal religious beliefs and certain Christian ones. For example, some tribes use the Bible, believe in the Trinity, and take peyote as the sacrament of the Lord's Supper. Many also believe that Jesus Christ personally gave them peyote so that they might better see God and the true way of life.

Since the introduction of peyotism into the United States, both White religious leaders and the Bureau of Indian Affairs have tried to discourage the eating of the plant and have urged adoption of Federal legislation to prohibit its use. Nonetheless, the Federal Government has never passed a regulation prohibiting its ceremonial use, probably because such an action would violate the First Amendment to the Constitution. However, certain states have declared its use illegal. White officials, in their campaigns to persuade or force the Indians to discredit peyote, have circulated statements some of which were inaccurate and misleading. Anthropologists claim there was a federally directed effort during the latter part of the nineteenth century to eradicate the Indian culture and to replace it with White social organization, language, customs, religion, and mores. One result of this effort was an almost fanatical religious persecution of the native religious groups by both White religious leaders and government officials. However, the aboriginal Indian religious beliefs and traditions were not completely eradicated, and in many tribes the peyote religion has been a successful method of bridging the two cultures by incorporating certain Christian dogmas with traditional aboriginal ceremonies. Most Indians defend the use of peyote, stating that it is of spiritual benefit to the persons involved, that it strengthens their social ties with the tribe, and that it tends to reduce alcoholism (most peyote churches specifically prohibit the use of alcohol by their members).

Peyote has been described by some as a narcotic plant. However, pharmacological data indicate that it is not physiologically addicting or habit-forming and that it has no narcotic (sleep-producing) effect on man. Nevertheless, some persons may become psychologically dependent on peyote, if they let their life's activities become centered around its religious use. Most pharmacologists classify peyote as a hallucinogenic or psychomimetic plant similar to teo-nanacatyl, or the sacred mushroom of the Aztecs (*Psilocybe mexicana* and certain other agarics), the Aztec

ololiuqui (*Datura* spp.), and lysergic acid diethylamide (LSD-25). The hallucinogenic chemical in peyote is the alkaloid mescaline, one of at least 15 naturally occurring alkaloids in *Lophophora*. Apparently, *Lophophora williamsii* is the only species used for ceremonial purposes, partly because of its greater geographic distribution and ready availability, but also because it contains much more mescaline than does the southern species, *L. diffusa*, which occurs only in Querétaro, Mexico.

Mescaline, a beta-phenylethylamine, has an indole ring structure similar to that of certain naturally occurring neurohumors (serotonin, for example) and some other hallucinogenic drugs such as psilocybin, psilocin, and LSD-25. The effects of mescaline on human beings are relatively minor when compared to those of the true narcotics such as opium and its derivatives, which become physiologically addicting. The user never loses consciousness because of the influence of mescaline, although his senses are greatly altered. Visual sensitivity is affected most, and both actual and imagined images are seen in vivid colors—hence the reference to peyote visions as "technicolor hallucinations." Visions with the eyes open usually involve a changed perception of light and space, and often a person is aware of greater physical beauty, especially with regard to visual harmony, color, and detail. Sometimes he becomes unable to distinguish between subject and object, and he reaches an almost mystical state during which he is unable to differentiate himself from his surroundings. Even greater visual effects are produced with the eyes closed, and images varying from abstract forms to imaginary animals or people occur in brilliant color and with dramatic intensity. On occasion the visions may be unpleasant or even terrifying. The type of visual experience apparently depends on the dosage of mescaline, the personality traits and mood of the subject, and the social and psychological context in which the substance is taken.

The actual physiological action of mescaline is a mild excitement of the sympathetic nervous system, producing such effects as the dilation of the pupils, an increase of systolic blood pressure, the constriction of peripheral arterioles, and a slight increase in the excitability of certain spinal reflexes, such as the knee jerk. The brain waves exhibit a more or less nonspecific "arousal" pattern. The most noticeable side effects on the subject are an intense nausea during the early stages (less so with pure mescaline than with peyote "buttons") and a relatively prolonged period of insomnia following the period of visions. There is no indication that peyote affects sex drive. Traditionally, peyote is taken either by eating the green or dried top of the plant or by drinking a tea (made by boiling dried or fresh plant tops in water). Some modern innovations include enclosing the powdered plant material in large gelatine capsules, which are taken orally, and hypodermic injection of a solution of mescaline from peyote.

Little research has been carried out to determine the validity of the claims of Indians regarding the curative powers of peyote. In psychiatric studies and therapy, for the most part mescaline has been replaced by LSD-25. The physiological effects of the two substances are similar, although LSD-25 is about 1,000 times as potent.

References: Anderson, 1969, *The biogeography, ecology and taxonomy of Lophophora (Cactaceae)*; Block, 1958, *Pharmacological aspects of mescaline*; Boke and Anderson, 1970, *Structure, development, and taxonomy in the genus Lophophora*; De Ropp, 1957, *Drugs and the mind*; Division of Narcotic Drugs, United Nations, 1959, *Peyotl bulletin on narcotics*; Fischer, 1958, *Pharmacology and metabolism of mescaline*; Himwich, 1958, *Psychopharmacologic drugs*; Kluver, 1966, *Mescal and mechanisms of hallucinations*; La Barre, 1938, *The peyote cult*, 1960, *Twenty years of peyote studies*; Lanternari, 1965, *The religions of the oppressed*; Lundstrom and Agurell, 1967, *Thin-layer chromatography of the peyote alkaloids*, 1968, *Biosynthesis of mescaline and anhalamine in peyote*; Neff and Rossi, 1963, *Mescaline*; Prentiss and Morgan, 1896, *Therapeutic uses of mescal buttons (Anhalonium lewinni)*; Rouhier, 1927, *Le peyotl*; Schultes, 1940, *The aboriginal therapeutic uses of Lophophora williamsii*; Slotkin, 1956, *The peyote religion*; Slotkin and McAllester, 1952, *Menomini peyotism*; Smythies, 1963, *The mescaline phenomena*.

A more recent work is Anderson, 1980, *Peyote: The Divine Cactus.*

12. The Conservation of Cacti

Before measures to protect the native cacti can be devised, it is necessary to understand the forces threatening their survival. This chapter* discusses both.

The Vulnerability of Cacti

The cactus family may be the most vulnerable of all to the extinction of species. In the United States there are 268 taxa of native Cactaceae. About 72, or 26 percent, of these are either so rare or so restricted in occurrence as to be vulnerable to extinction.

Some cacti are wide-ranging, adaptable, and tenacious, and they are only here and there subject to much disturbance by man; some even thrive on it. *Opuntia fragilis* (Figs. 389-92) occurs mostly on sandy, nonagricultural lands; hence man may reduce the populations of the species, but he does not eradicate them. The species is propagated readily not only by seeds but also because its easily detached joints are carried some distance away when their barbed spines hook into the flesh of mammals, and it is more likely to spread into new habitats and territory than to be eliminated in old habitats (see p. 146). The eastern *O. humifusa* is saved from extinction in competition with other plants better adapted to moist areas because it grows on rock outcrops or sandy land not suitable for competitors and of low agricultural value. *O. macrorhiza*, a western close relative, is also in little danger, because it occurs on a variety of nonagricultural lands and because it is not large enough or sufficiently abundant on cattle ranges to be considered a pest. The varieties of *O. phaeacantha* are large plants occurring from California to Colorado and Texas, but most varieties cover desert space not critical for grazing animals, and the plants are left alone. Other varie-

*Much the same material has been published—in *National Parks & Conservation Magazine* 49: 17-21, 1975, and in a pamphlet, *Help Save Our Endangered Plants*, Nat. Parks & Conserv. Assn. 17-21, 1976. It is used by prearrangement and slightly revised.

ties occurring in grassland form masses where one individual may exclude cattle and sheep from an area as much as 6 m (20 ft) in diameter. However, often removal is not practical, and in some places the plants are tolerated as an emergency food during drought. Then, the spines are burned off, and cattle may eat the flat stem joints, which are poor but usable food with some water. The similar *O. lindheimeri*, growing through most of Texas, is used in the same way, but it is considered mostly a pest, because it excludes range animals from grass. Tremendous efforts to eradicate the plant have produced only a reduction of numbers in some places. Attempts at mechanical removal may result in even more plants, because the fragments regenerate rapidly in the disturbed soil and often competitors of the cactus are killed or set back by the efforts to remove the prickly pear.

Most species of wide-ranging cacti are prickly pears, like those listed above, and only a few smaller cacti are of similar broad distributional patterns. Nearly all require stable conditions, and they rarely invade disturbed areas. An example is a pincushion cactus, *Coryphantha vivipara*, a species composed of several varieties with different ecological requirements occurring from California to North Dakota and Texas. Another is *C. missouriensis*, occurring from central Idaho to North Dakota, Kansas, northern Arizona, and New Mexico and represented by disjunct local varieties in parts of Texas. The coryphanthas bear little or no relationship to range management, and man does not destroy a significant percentage of each population, taken as a whole. However, the flowers are attractive, and the removal of plants for cultivation may reduce local abundance. The red-flowered hedgehog cacti (*Echinocereus triglochidiatus*, several varieties) include plants adapted to a wide range of upland, mountain, and desert habitats occurring from California to Colorado and Texas and southward into Mexico. For the most part, like the coryphanthas, most hedgehog cacti are not vulnerable to immediate extermination, though some rare local varieties are.

Most species of cacti, however, are neither so variable nor so well adapted to a wide range of environments as these. They are restricted to a few areas of regions with severe climates, mostly in the deserts or in dry grasslands or woodlands near them. Within these areas of special climates the cacti are restricted each to a particular selection of environmental factors related to precipitation, prevailing temperature, direction of slope, amount of drainage, and soil chemistry and texture. Each is restricted further to a particular habitat niche.

Within its niche, each cactus must compete with other plants that may shade it out or take away water near the surface of the soil, the only level at which cacti have absorbing roots. Some species may be dependent on the composition of the soil forming a seedbed beneath other plants, mostly shrubs or trees, or they may require the shade of larger species, mostly during the seedling stage but in some cases later as well.

Many of the cacti (other than most chollas or prickly pears) are restricted to special soil types. Restrictions may be determined both by soil texture and soil chemical content, and in part by derivation from such rocks as limestone or igneous types. Some species are spared from extermination by man because they grow in out-of-the-way places and on limited outcrops of a particular rock, in pockets of a special soil poor for agriculture, or in a dry area impractical to irrigate. Some of the soils are so extreme in their composition as to be passed up by collectors as impossible habitats for cacti. Even when these plants are located, often they do not become popular in cultivation, because they do not live long in ordinary soils or potting mixtures. Each of the species of *Pediocactus* except one occurs almost wholly on a special and often unusual soil (see pp. 67-69), and this poses a problem for the botanist. For scientific accuracy these soils should be described in detail, but if all the information concerning the habitats of these rare species were released to the public some species might soon disappear.

Factors Threatening Cacti

The chief threats to the cacti are *commercial exploitation, overzealous collecting, housing developments, agriculture, grazing,* and *fire.*

Commercial exploitation. Rarity increases the commercial demand for a species or a variety. Several of the new very small species of cacti described and named by the writer have appeared almost instantaneously in commercial catalogs in various parts of the world, and the prices have ranged from $25 to $50 a plant. This has occurred despite considerable caution about revealing the exact location of collection. For scientific accuracy, there must be some kind of a reasonably specific statement, but this has been restricted to designating the general area rather than an exact locality. The wording has been designed to make finding the plant possible but to avoid promoting its extermination at the type locality, which was either the only actual site of occurrence or one of the few known. Thus, at least collecting has been dispersed to a wider area, and in most cases the plants first known are still there. Despite all this, each new taxon has appeared soon in collections and the trade, and obviously the plants for sale were not grown from seeds but taken directly from the field.

Overzealous collecting. Adding to private collections in greenhouses and gardens is a relatively minor cause of the reduction of numbers of a species. However, it has led to decimation of some rare plants in at least the few localities in which they are known to occur. In one Southwestern state a new variety of *Echinocereus* or hedgehog cactus has been reported to have been exterminated at the type locality simply because its existence and its whereabouts were known to too many people. Probably each individual took only a few plants for his garden, but there were not very many there. Fortunately, according to a recent report, a few undisturbed plants have been found. In northern Arizona a low-growing cactus, *Pediocactus peeblesianus* var. *peeblesianus,* ranging in diameter from that of a quarter to that of a fifty-cent piece, has been known for about 40 years to occur through an area only 8-10 km (5 to 6 mi) long, and there it is rare and obscure. Each of a number of scientists has spent many days in the field on hands and knees looking for this plant. After a number of years it was found by an enthusiastic group of amateurs most of whom were concerned deeply about the rarity of the species and its possible disappearance from nature. For this reason, many were shocked to see one lady at a meeting with a number of the plants sewn to the brim of her hat. Perhaps thoughtlessness is the number one enemy.

Housing developments. Rare cacti are found mostly on the hills; housing developments are mostly in the valleys. However, there are exceptions, and in some areas housing projects are so extensive as to blot out everything else. For example, near Albuquerque local cactus enthusiasts removed plants of the rare and obscure *Pediocactus papyracanthus* to cultivation to save them before housing-development bulldozers arrived. In the vicinity of San Diego several rare, localized species occur on relatively flat land or on low, rolling hills. In the course of time the whole area from at least Del Mar to the Mexican boundary appears due to become one great city, and the outlook for the native cacti is bleak. In Florida most cacti occur in the stabilized sandy land back of the beach. Along both the Gulf and Atlantic coasts and on many of the keys this area is being bulldozed in preparation for houses. With the fantastic growth of cities and urban areas in Florida, the cacti and many other native plants may be eliminated. Some are of restricted occurrence, and even a little commercial development of their habitats will eliminate them. In the state, four species of cacti of special interest—three prickly pears, *Opuntia cubensis*, *O. triacantha*, and *O. spinosissima*, and a columnar or treelike plant, *Cereus robinii*—grow on one part of a single key. All these species occur on the limited dry areas of some islands of the Caribbean, but in the continental United States the three prickly pears are known to occur only on the one key. *Cereus robinii* is known from two other localities on the keys and a limited area in Cuba. There is already housing on the two keys, as well as on the adjacent ones. Thus, one small development would wipe out three of the species and limit the other to the two additional areas in which it was collected long ago and in which even now it may not persist.

Agriculture. For the most part, agriculture is at peace with cacti in much the same way Sitting Bull was at peace with his enemies—he had killed them all. All but an infinitesimal amount of the good agricultural land in the United States is farmed or it has become urban. Much of the poor valley land has been converted to agriculture and then allowed to start the long road of succession back toward a natural area only to have this interrupted by several more trials at agriculture. This has tended to eliminate the smaller species of cacti, but frequently the prickly pears have been able to invade the disturbed areas and often they have benefited by the removal of competition. However, if they ever occurred naturally in the deep good soils of the valleys, the smaller species of cacti are gone. Probably they were not numerous, because the mostly deep soils were occupied originally by competitors better adapted than cacti.

Grazing. Usually grazing is unfavorable to cacti, especially to small ones or to the seedlings of large ones. Some of the plants are eaten for water; some are kicked out by the animals' hooves; and some are no longer able to reproduce effectively, because the native plants that provide the humus in their seedbed have been killed out. An example of a cactus whose seedbed has been obliterated in many areas is the saguaro, *Cereus giganteus* (p. 117). On the whole, however, grazing does not eliminate the smaller cacti or the seedlings but tends to restrict them to favorable spots, where some individuals may persist despite range animals. At least this is true if goats are not included among the grazing and browsing animals—where goats are present, not much else survives. Some aggressive cacti, including prickly pears and chollas, may gain from grazing, because many competitors are eliminated.

Fire. Fire is the enemy of many plants and the friend of others. Hot fires kill forests and convert the landscape to an early stage of a secondary ecological succession process requiring many years or even centuries before the normal climax vegetation is restored. At the same time, fire maintains grasslands by killing out seedlings of shrubs and trees; for grassland, it is a benefactor. In a given area, the presence or absence of fire affects the ultimate character of its vegetation.

Many cacti are exceedingly vulnerable to fire, but mostly they live in places where fires do not sweep through. In the deserts, commonly, the combustible plants are spaced too widely for fire to be carried readily from one to the next. Along the edges of the deserts and in the chaparrals and grasslands adjoining them, fire is a major threat, and the cacti can persist only in areas where a fire does not become particularly hot, as, for example, on rock outcrops or sandy flats or on hillsides without a dense cover of brush.

In southern California, fire excludes cacti from the climax chaparral, and they are restricted to dry, gravelly washes or to grassy, disturbed areas. Here the nature of the cactus populations has been altered gradually since the coming of the Mission Fathers in 1769. The padres brought the mission cactus, a Mexican fruit tree, *Opuntia ficus-indica*, and their livestock brought the seeds of weedy, summer-dry, Mediterranean grasses, as discussed on pp. 63-67 and 517-18. The pollen of the introduced cactus was carried by insects to the native plants (O. *littoralis* vars.), producing vast hybrid swarms. Neither parental species is able to withstand the hot summer fires running through the dry grass, but some of the hybrids combine the sprawling habit of the native species with the larger size of the mission cactus, and they form thickets that partly exclude grass and therefore fire. For 200 years selection has favored these hybrids. Evolutionary selection in the direction of an ultimate new species has all but eliminated the original native cacti. It has made O. *littoralis* vars. *covillei* and *austrocalifornica* relative rarities. These plants still exist in their extreme form in areas like the dry, gravelly washes where they have been protected somewhat from fire, but the number of plants not hybridized is diminishing, and gradually the native taxa are losing out to hybrids able to cope with fire. Obviously, no ordinary protective measures can save the native species. It is being absorbed into a new genetic system brought about by large-scale environmental changes due to a new and burgeoning human population living over the whole geographic range of the cactus species.

In the perennial grasslands occurring from Arizona to Texas, fire merely burns off the dry, dead tops of the grasses, and after the next rain regeneration from underground is rapid. Most of the cacti occur either in areas disturbed by overgrazing or in those shielded from fire by rocky or thin, sandy soils not supporting a dense growth of grass. The recent reduction of fire, originally set annually by the Indians to make better pasture for game, has altered the character of many grasslands. Some have become forests or dry woodlands because seedlings of trees or shrubs no longer are eliminated by fire. The Desert Grassland of Arizona is being invaded by desert woody plants. This change of the plant communities has affected the cacti in several ways: by upsetting the ecosystem and thereby eliminating some competitors, substituting others, and removing some of the plants that had aided in the survival of cacti or their seedlings; by altering the character of the soil and its moisture-holding capacity; and by altering exposure to the sun.

Preservation of Cacti

Because the effects of housing developments, agriculture, grazing, and fire are difficult to combat except in limited areas, usually the feasible method of preserving the small, rare species of cacti is the prevention or at least reduction of commercial exploitation and overzealous collecting.

There is an important place for cactus dealers and the sale of cacti, and reasonable propagation and marketing of plants are desirable. These plants are of interest to many people, and their enjoyment throughout the world is important. The unscrupulous commercial dealer is probably uncommon; most dealers are people of conscience, and they follow reasonable procedures. The crux of the problem is the method of obtaining plants for sale. If they are taken directly from the field, the drain on the native population is severe; if the seeds are collected and plants are propagated from them, sale is desirable and legitimate. The capacity of plants in the field to produce seeds so far outstrips actual reproduction that removal of some is virtually inconsequential. If all the cactus seeds produced in the desert during even one year were to grow into plants, the desert would become an impenetrable thicket. Thus, any attempts to save the rare species of cacti should concentrate primarily on preventing the removal of living plants from the field for direct sale. Projected laws should be aimed in this direction.

Overzealous collecting for home propagation is intended to come under the same laws. However, regardless of the laws, an educational campaign should bring some direct results and enlist the support of the garden enthusiasts and of the better commercial dealers, as well. Whatever laws are to be drawn up will not be enforced unless they have the support of the public, and the greatest care must be taken to make them fair and equitable, and neither too severe nor too mild.

For some species, salvation may be secured in protected areas. Many cacti occur, at least principally, within National Parks and National Monuments such as the Organ Pipe Cactus National Monument or the Saguaro National Monument in Arizona or the Big Bend National Park in Texas. Thus they have the built-in protection of the National Park Service.

Some species occur on only a few outcrops of a particular rock scattered over a few to many kilometers or miles. These rocky places are practically worthless to the cattle or sheep ranges around them, and their cost should be relatively small. They are no asset to the range lands, and often these are public lands, anyhow. The Federal Government is not likely to set up a separate administration for a few hills harboring one lone

TABLE 5.
Endangered, Threatened, or Possibly Extinct Cactaceae of the United States

Taxon	Status	States
Ancistrocactus tobuschii	End, B	Tex
Cereus eriophorus var. *fragrans*	End, B	Fla
Cereus gracilis var. *aboriginum*	End, B	Fla
Cereus gracilis var. *simpsonii*	End, B	Fla
Cereus robinii var. *deeringii*	End, B	Fla
Cereus robinii var. *robinii*	End, B	Fla
Coryphantha dasyacantha var. *varicolor*	Thr, B	Tex
Coryphantha duncanii	Thr, B	Tex
Coryphantha hesteri	Thr, B	Tex
Coryphantha minima	End, B	Tex
Coryphantha ramillosa	End, A	Tex, Mex
Coryphantha recurvata	Thr, A	Ariz, Mex
Coryphantha scheeri var. *robustispina*	Thr, B	Ariz, Mex
Coryphantha scheeri var. *uncinata*		Tex
Coryphantha sneedii var. *leei*	Thr, B	N Mex
Coryphantha sneedii var. *sneedii*	Thr, B	Tex, N Mex
Coryphantha strobiliformis var. *durispina*	End, A	Tex
Coryphantha sulcata var. *nickelsiae*	Thr, C	Tex, Mex
Coryphantha vivipara var. *alversonii*	Thr, A	Ariz, Cal
Coryphantha vivipara var. *rosea*	Thr, B	Ariz, Nev, Cal
Echinocactus horizonthalonius var. *nicholii*	End, B	Ariz
Echinocereus berlandieri var. *angusticeps*	Ext? (1934), C	Tex
Echinocereus chloranthus var. *neocapillus*	End, C	Tex
Echinocereus engelmannii var. *howei*	End, C	Cal
Echinocereus engelmannii var. *munzii*	Thr, C	Cal, Mex
Echinocereus engelmannii var. *purpureus*	End, C	Utah
Echinocereus fendleri var. *kuenzleri*	Ext, A	N Mex, Mex
Echinocereus ledingii	Thr, B	Ariz
Echinocereus lloydii	End, B	Tex, N Mex
Echinocereus reichenbachii var. *albertii*	End, B	Tex
Echinocereus reichenbachii var. *chisosensis*	Thr, B	Tex
Echinocereus reichenbachii var. *fitchii*	Thr, B	Tex
Echinocereus triglochidiatus var. *triglochidiatus*	End, B	N Mex
Echinocereus viridiflorus var. *correllii*	Thr, A	Tex
Echinocereus viridiflorus var. *davisii*	End, A	Tex
Epithelantha bokei	Thr, A	Tex, Mex
Ferocactus viridescens	End, B	Cal, Mex
Ferocactus acanthodes var. *eastwoodiae*	Thr, C	Ariz
Mammillaria orestera	Thr, B	Ariz
Mammillaria thornberi	Thr, B	Ariz, Mex
Neolloydia erectocentra var. *acunensis*	Thr, B	Ariz, Mex
Neolloydia erectocentra var. *erectocentra*	Thr, B	Ariz
Neolloydia gautii	End, C	Tex
Neolloydia mariposensis	End, B	Tex, Mex
Neolloydia warnockii	Thr, B	Tex
Opuntia arenaria	Thr, C	Tex, Mex
Opuntia basilaris var. *brachyclada*	Thr, C	Cal
Opuntia basilaris var. *longiareolata*	Thr, C	Ariz
Opuntia basilaris var. *treleasei*	Thr, C	Cal, Ariz
Opuntia imbricata var. *argentea*	Thr, C	Tex
Opuntia munzii	Thr, C	Cal
Opuntia parryi var. *serpentina*	Thr, C	Cal, Mex
Opuntia phaeacantha var. *flavispina*	Thr, C	Ariz
Opuntia phaeacantha var. *mojavensis*	Thr, C	Cal, Ariz
Opuntia phaeacantha var. *superbospina*	Thr, C	Ariz
Opuntia spinosissima	Thr, C	Fla, W.I.
Opuntia strigil var. *flexospina*	Ext? (1911), C	Tex
Opuntia triacantha	Thr, C	Fla, W.I., Guade-loupe, Puerto Rico, Virgin Islands

(cont.)

TABLE 5 (cont.)

Taxon	Status	States
Opuntia whipplei var. *multigeniculata*	Thr, C	Ariz, Nev, Utah
Pediocactus bradyi	End, A	Ariz
Pediocactus knowltonii	End, A	N Mex
Pediocactus papyracanthus	Thr, A	N Mex, Ariz, Mex
Pediocactus paradinei	Thr, A	Ariz
Pediocactus peeblesianus var. *fickeiseniae*	Thr, A	Ariz
Pediocactus peeblesianus var. *peeblesianus*	End, A	Ariz
Pediocactus sileri	End, B	Ariz
Sclerocactus glaucus	End, A	Utah, Col
Sclerocactus mesae-verdae	Thr, A	Col, N Mex
Sclerocactus pubispinus	Thr, C	Nev, Utah
Sclerocactus spinosior	Thr, A	Utah, Ariz
Sclerocactus wrightiae	Thr, B	Utah
Thelocactus bicolor var. *flavidispinus*	Thr, B	Tex, Mex

An explanation of the notation is given below.

species of cactus, but often areas with rare and endangered cacti can be linked with an existing facility, as developed in the next paragraph.

There are instances in which extension of a National Park or Monument to include even a relatively small tract of land now just outside the boundaries of the preserved area could save a rare cactus. A very rare localized species occurring in northern Arizona on the edge of a small National Monument comes to mind. The plant is restricted to a peculiar soil of no agricultural or grazing value. Almost the entire known range of the species is on a single fantastic soil outcrop no more than 400 m (a quarter-mile) wide though perhaps 32 km (20 miles) long. The area is a part of Indian lands, but inasmuch as it has no value for grazing, an arrangement to include it in the National Monument may be feasible. Fortunately, the tribe is aware of the rarity of the cactus and concerned about its preservation, and this may be helpful. As another example, *Pediocactus peeblesianus* var. *fickeiseniae* occupies hills not far from the Grand Canyon National Park, and perhaps some of the hills could be added to the Park.

A study of individual hills occupied by unusual cacti may reveal that there are other plants of special interest sharing the peculiarities of the soil, and these may strengthen the case for area preservation.

Thus, the Cactaceae include not only a high percentage of rare local species, but also a great many species particularly vulnerable to destruction by man because of the public and commercial interest in these amazing plants with their beautiful flowers. The obvious methods of protection are through requiring the propagation of plants from seeds, rather than the removal of living plants for sale; through adding some areas—in which rare cacti occur—to existing neighboring National Parks and National Monuments and state and county parks; and through the encouragement of such organizations as the Nature Conservancy to set aside small areas for preservation. In most cases preservation of the cacti will have to be combined with the saving of other endangered plants and animals and with the setting aside of areas that are also of geological or archaeological interest.

Table 5 lists the endangered, threatened, and in a few cases possibly extinct taxa of Cactaceae of the United States. The list was prepared by Dr. Dale Jenkins of the Smithsonian Institution, as Chairman of the Regional Threatened Plants Committee, International Convention, United Nations, during consultation with the author and from a check of the galley proofs for this book. It is the basis for the list of endangered and threatened species of cacti protected by Federal law.

An endangered species is one in immediate peril of extinction. Almost always it is rare and of restricted distribution, or in the pathway of great environmental change. Definitions of threatened species vary, but the degree of danger to them is less or it is not immediate. The following letters are used in the table to represent the degree of human exploitation of the taxa:

A: Commercially collected and sold

B: Collector's item

C: Not collected; too rare to be found readily, or unsuitable for growing.

Part Two

THE CACTI

Notes on Use of the Text

The following discussion covers subjects necessary to a proper understanding of the treatment of taxa in the main text. Additional background material, some of it of direct relevance to the treatment in text, is given in the twelve chapters of Part I; specific data supporting matters of nomenclature and distribution in the text are given in the Documentation section, following the text.

The Taxa Treated

The taxa of cacti treated in this book are those occurring as native plants in the United States and Canada and those introduced there and established without the intentional aid of man. Extraterritorial taxa of Mexico or the Caribbean region are mentioned or discussed briefly only when their inclusion aids in understanding the related taxa occurring in the United States. Usually those mentioned are varieties of a species represented by other varieties within the area of the book. Often the variety growing farther south is the nomenclaturally typical one, because the area of common occurrence in Mexico was reached by European explorers earlier than the parts of the United States where cacti are most abundant. Typically, the Mexican variety was collected before the others, and it is accordingly the one on which the name of the species was based. It may be typical only in the sense of including the type specimen of the species, but often the most common and most widespread variety was also the first collected and named, because it was more likely to be encountered than a less common plant of restricted occurrence. Thus, knowing the characters of the typical variety is often essential to understanding the other varieties and the species as a whole.

Identification of Cacti by Keys and Tables

The identity of a plant, animal, or other object may be determined by the use of a series of keys.

Like an outline, each key is designed to facilitate a process of elimination of all but the taxon to which the object belongs.

No key to families of the order Cactales is necessary, because the order is currently thought to embrace only the Cactaceae. However, the Cactaceae include many genera, and the key to them (in the text for the family) enables the reader to eliminate all but one. The key to the species in that genus is used similarly, to determine the correct taxon of that rank. None of the keys in this book includes taxa that occur only outside of the United States and Canada.

Each key is made up of a series of pairs of opposed *leads* (for an example, see p. 685). The members of the primary pair begin at the left margin, and each is preceded by the number 1. One will fit the plant being identified; the other will not, and it is eliminated. Under the correct lead, *either* the correct taxon is named *or* a subordinate pair of leads numbered 2 appears. The indentation is like that of a secondary element in an outline. The next choice is between these two leads. One is ruled out, and unless the name of the taxon appears at the end of the lead remaining, the next choice is between two still lower-ranking leads numbered 3 and indented farther. The process continues until no more choices are available. At this point, one lead of the pair does not describe the plant, but the alternate lead does, giving at the righthand margin the name of the taxon, preceded by a number indicating its relative position in the text following.

The key to the genera of cacti described in this book begins on p. 260, with the primary opposed leads numbered 1. Identification of a particular plant—for example, the desert night-blooming cereus—begins with a choice between these leads. This plant "fits" the lower lead 1, because there are no leaves on the adult plant, the stems are markedly succulent, and the flowers are epigynous and without stalks. The next step is a choice between the upper and lower leads 2, which begin a little farther from the left margin than leads 1. The plant fits lower lead 2, because there are no glochids, the mature stem is always leafless, the floral tube is elongated above the ovary, the seeds are not bony, the cotyledons are not leaflike, etc. It also fits the lower lead 3 (beneath lower lead 2), because there are small spines on the stem (which is composed of joints), the plants do not grow on other plants, the stems do not produce aerial roots, and the upper floral tube is tubular but not bent and not saucerlike.

The number 4A is used for the next pair of opposed leads, because 4 has been used above for a pair of leads subordinate to upper lead 3. These leads are indented the same distance as leads 4, and the letter "A" is merely an identification tag to prevent confusion with leads 4 and to ensure matching of the correct leads, even though the members of the pair may appear on different pages. The desert night-blooming cereus fits upper lead 4A, and under it upper lead 5, which places the plant under the genus *Cereus,* discussed on p. 539.

The treatment of *Cereus,* a good deal farther along in the book, begins with a description of the genus, a statement of the number of species included, a broad outline of geographical distribution, and a list of the species. The key to the species (p. 541) is used like the previous key. Since the desert night-blooming cereus has an enormous tap root and the other characters given in lower lead 1, it fits upper lead 2A, and the species is *Cereus greggii,* or number 15 under the genus, described on p. 588.

The description and discussion pertain to the species as a whole, and the two varieties composing *Cereus greggii* are discussed in paragraphs under numbers 15a and 15b. They are segregated by a table of characters (p. 589) rather than by a key. The combinations of characters marking varieties are less dependable in occurrence in each individual plant than are those separating species or genera. A table, contrasting entire clusters of characters at a glance, is more practical than a key in the identification of varieties, because the character groups are less stable. Fortunately, the number of varieties usually is small. The characters appearing in the table constitute the description of the variety, that is, its special combination of characters as opposed to those of other varieties of the species. This information is not repeated in the text.

Var. *greggii* bears the same epithet, or adjective used as a noun, as the species as a whole. It is known as the typical variety for the reason discussed above (p. 251), but it is not necessarily typical (or representative) of the species in the ordinary sense of the word. The two varieties occupy different areas—east and west of the continental divide.

Keys and tables must be used with caution, because they can reflect only the characters ordinarily present in a taxon, and these may be only an approximation of those of any one plant. Because the associations of characters are complex, effective use of a key requires consideration of the whole complex of characters described in each pair of leads. The characters in each lead are arranged in order of the degree in which they are present in the vast majority of members of the taxa included in the lead. Sometimes any of them may be absent from the character combination of a given plant, but the first ones in the series are less frequently lacking than the last. (The characters given in the tables to varieties are *not* arranged according to frequency of occurrence.)

Identification of plants is a difficult process, and patience is necessary. No matter how well keys are constructed or how effectively they may be used, there will be some false starts and failures. This is inevitable, because the underlying problems of classification are complex, and writing a key requires an attempt to simplify them. The only possible result is some oversimplification.

In some instances one lead of a pair in a key may include characters not appearing in the opposed lead. Usually these characters appear in parentheses. To be used effectively, keys must be dichotomous (with pairs of forks), but three or more elements sometimes cannot be divided readily on that basis. For example, suppose plants numbered arbitrarily 1, 2, and 3 can be distinguished on the basis of three characters, and suppose further that the distribution of characters is as follows:

Plant 1: erect, yellow, spineless
Plant 2: erect, green, spiny
Plant 3: prostrate, yellow, spiny

Here, no matter how a key is written, not all the characters can be opposed directly. Consequently, an expedient like that shown (see key, next page) may be necessary. In lower lead 1, leaf color and spine presence are important for checking, but they cannot be opposed directly to

HYPOTHETICAL KEY, THREE CHARACTERS (SEE TEXT)

1. Plant erect.
    2. Leaves yellow; stems spineless ....**Plant 1**
    2. Leaves green; stems spiny...**Plant 2**
1. Plant prostrate; leaves yellow; stems spineless.........................**Plant 3**

upper lead 1, unless the statement there reads "leaves yellow or green; stems spined or spineless." Sometimes this expedient is adopted, but it is somewhat awkward and not wholly satisfactory.

When it will be helpful, the geographical distribution of a taxon or group of taxa is given in a key lead, but the leads in a pair do not necessarily match in this respect.

In popular books, commonly there are simple keys employing a single character pair in each lead. Use of these keys is chiefly a frustration, except in dealing with a very small number of plants or animals, few of which have close relationship. Such an exception might be the flora of a limited geographical unit such as a county in flat country, where there are only a few species altogether and where a genus is likely to be represented by a single species or two or three distantly related species. Here, simple keys may be adequate.

The Naming of Cacti

Scientific names. Frequently, various authors have assigned a variety of scientific names to the same plant. Usually this reflects an underlying difference in interpretation of classification. In one book or paper a particular taxon may appear as a genus, in another as a subgenus, and in still another as a section of a subgenus. Similarly, a lesser taxon may be presented in one work as a species, in another as a variety, and in another as a minor form not formally segregated from other populations of a species interpreted more broadly. Thus, the same plant may appear as *Opuntia fulgida* var. *mamillata* in one book, *Opuntia mamillata* in a second, and *Cylindropuntia fulgida* var. *mamillata* in a third. In due course it may appear as a species of *Cylindropuntia,* but to date this combination has not been published.

Other differences in naming may reflect problems of nomenclature. Some names appearing in the literature of botany are invalid; consequently they must be replaced by valid names. The selection of the proper scientific name for a taxon is automatic, once it is classified in a particular rank (e.g., species), through application of the *International Code of Botanical Nomenclature* (Lanjouw [Stafleu] et al., 1972). Stated simply, the Code embodies the following principles: (1) a taxon may have only one correct name; (2) the same name is not correct for two or more taxa; (3) if more than one scientific name has been applied to a taxon, the choice is determined by priority in time of publication; and (4) the identity of a plant given a scientific name is determined by a type specimen designated by its author. The Code is far more complex than this; it is similar to a code of law. (For a fuller explanation, see Benson, 1962, Chapters 9-13.)

Capitalization or decapitalization of epithets. Specific and varietal epithets are decapitalized in this book for the following reason (quoted from Benson, 1974a): "The editors of Stanford University Press prefer decapitalization of specific and varietal epithets, and [this book] follows the usage the writer has adopted [tentatively], after some investigation. . . . Since 1950, either decapitalization of all epithets or capitalization of those formed from personal, vernacular, or generic names has been permitted under the International Code of Botanical Nomenclature. In 1954, the writer submitted to the International Botanical Congress meeting in Paris two proposals, one for capitals and one for decapitalization, requesting that one or the other be adopted as a rule, not [simply] a recommendation. Neither was adopted, and the confusion of practice has continued. A hoped-for strong trend one way or the other has not developed, [though] if anything, there has been a slow drift in the world as a whole in the direction of decapitalization. The present status of the problem is difficult to assess, and many of the most important works, including most of the primary ones in the United States, employ capitals. The problem is minor; . . . [but] opinions are strong and . . . [the] perpetuation [of the problem] may be assumed. However, it seems to be time to try again with the proposals of 1954." The question was considered at the International Botanical Congress at Leningrad in 1975, but no changes were made, a circumstance reflecting the lack of a strong trend in either direction. In the meantime, decapitalization has been adopted only for this book, and the question remains open for the future.

Popular names. The common-language names of plants (for cacti, mostly in English, Spanish, or an Indian language) are by nature irregular in formation, origin, and application. Because they are vernacular names, there are no established rules to be followed in selecting them. Not uncommonly, several plants may have the same English or other names or a single plant may have several. In this book, much-used vernacular names commonly are given if they are available. However, most cacti lack popular names other than those applied to large groups, such as barrel cacti, prickly pears, chollas, or hedgehog cacti, or those applied to whole genera. In a few cases, appropriate names have been included even though usage of them in the past has been slight.

The Treatments of Taxa

Headings. The genera of the Cactaceae are numbered consecutively, to facilitate reference from the "Key to the Genera" to the text. There the number of each genus appears at the beginning of the text for that genus and in the running heads (top of page). The various species in each genus are numbered in similar fashion, and they, too, appear in the text in numerical order. Varieties each bear the species number and a lowercase letter distinguishing that variety from the others. For example, species 10 may include varieties 10a, 10b, and 10c. Usually, one of these is the nomenclaturally typical variety, and its epithet repeats that of the species. The authors' names following the names of the species and varieties are explained on p. 106. The typical variety carries no author references; it exists automatically, and its epithet did not need to be published officially. Data on the year and place of original publication, for all taxa, are given in the Documentation section, which follows the same sequence as the main text.

The three sections of color plates are also arranged in text sequence and keyed to the text by genus and species numbers (at the bases of the pages in the color sections). The color plates are not referred to specifically in the text, but comparison of these "running feet" (in the color sections) with the text running heads, and with the species numbers given in the boldface headings

within the text, allows rapid location of corresponding material. The running heads in the Documentation section are similarly keyed to text.

Descriptions. The descriptions of taxa follow a consistent sequence of arrangement: (1) matters pertaining to the plant as a whole; (2) vegetative parts (the roots, if an unusual feature is known and they are not, as usual, all of the common fibrous type); stems and their appendages (general features, including any of the following that may be present: ribs, tubercles, leaves, areoles, and spines); (3) flowers, including the areas in which they are produced, the floral tube, epigyny or rarely perigyny, general features of size, and individual parts, including the sepaloids, petaloids, stamens (anthers and filaments), and pistils (styles, stigmas, and ovaries); (4) fruits; (5) seeds. Not all the features listed are described for every taxon. For example, not all are variable between genera, and only the varying characters are included in the generic descriptions. The same is true of the descriptions of species, in which only the characters varying from species to species in the genus are included. Under the species, the varieties are described in tables of their varying characters.

The descriptions may not include characters that are taxonomically trivial or those that are unavailable in the pressed or preserved materials at hand or the living plants within reach. Some taxa have been seen (or some parts have been examined) in only pressed specimens, and these may not include all the characters or those such as colors of some parts, which may be distorted. Each description is a composite drawn from the sources available—in some cases numerous herbarium specimens and living plants, in others few of either. Although the approximation of characters is likely to be accurate, the limitations of materials make it necessarily so. The herbarium specimens of cacti are few and poor compared with those of other plants more frequently pressed and preserved. Because of size and the difficulty of pressing, commonly only fragments of a cactus are represented. Often these may be restricted to a single part of the plant, such as a flower, a cluster of spines, or some seeds.

In some cases a known feature has been omitted or stated with reservation because it has been seen in too few specimens or living plants. For example, in the only flower for which data are available the filaments of the stamens may be pink. However, if this is stated in the description for the taxon, confusion may result, because other colors may occur in different individuals. A parallel case would be description of the hair of human beings as nearly black, as a Japanese of the fifteenth century might have supposed.

In the descriptions a single new pair of terms is employed. The perianth parts of cacti are of a different derivation from those of most flowering plants. The outer series shades from scale leaves to sepaloid structures, or sepaloid perianth parts, which may be homologous with the specialized leaves forming the sepals of other flowering plants. Because of the complexity of the entire series and the uncertainties of the homologies, as well as for simplicity, these structures are called *sepaloids*. This is an adjective used as a noun, as with "asteroid" or "thyroid." Similarly, the inner, or petaloid perianth parts are called *petaloids*, because they resemble petals, though their origin is different from that of the petals of other flowering plants.

The descriptions are based on the characters of mature plants, because the characters of the seedlings of most species are not well known, except to growers, who do not record them. Most cactus plants in the field are either several years old or fully mature. Seedlings of cacti rarely survive in abundance in nature unless there is a disturbance of the balance of organisms in their habitat. The competition of older plants of both their own species and many others usually eliminates them. As long as the community remains undisturbed, there is little need for the addition of new individuals, as the species can continue without the incorporation of more than a few from time to time. If very many were added, the population would become too dense to be supported, and thinning would follow. Thus, few new individuals survive the rigors of natural selection, though many may have germinated.

Juvenile plants usually differ from adults in a number of characters, and this may cause confusion in classification and even lead to the describing and naming of supposed new taxa based on the juvenile forms. These plants may flower and fruit for several years during the period of development and gradual changing of their vegetative characters before the appearance of the ultimate features marking mature individuals. Thus, a young but apparently mature, reproducing plant may be quite different from older plants of its species. The study of juvenile sequences of characters and the tracing of development from seedling to adult is a complex subject for future research.

Distribution of species and varieties. The statements in the text concerning the relationship of taxa to the environment are based on observations of nearly all the species and varieties in the field. They include assessing the types of soils, the terrain, and the altitudes in which the taxa occur. Each species or variety is linked to occurrence as part of one or more floristic associations (pp. 136-215), and often it is one of the marker species of an association, as indicated by its restriction or near restriction to that association. The statements of geographical range of occurrence are based on observation, notes, and specimens.

The spots or symbols of occurrence on the distribution maps are restricted to areas from which there are specimens in an herbarium. This approach is taken in the name of promoting gradual progress toward precise knowledge of distribution. There are enough herbarium specimens to give some degree of accuracy to the outlines of distribution, but not enough to fill in all the details. Field observation could add much to what is on the maps, but this is not recorded because it depends too much on memory and judgment and because it is not subject to a direct check by another individual. In time, enough specimens may accumulate to permit a degree of precision not possible now.

In one instance the documented distribution on the map is extended considerably (in crosshatching) by field observation (p. 546). The enormous saguaro (*Cereus giganteus*) is represented poorly in herbarium specimens, but it is so conspicuous and unmistakable in identity in the field that its distribution record can be augmented greatly from observation. The extant specimens alone would give only a fragmentary representation of the occurrence of this important species.

All taxa have been mapped unless, as with a few, data were inadequate. For a small number of species or varieties the distributional ranges are known but not shown precisely, and the text covers them only in broad outline. These exceptions are rare, threatened, or endangered taxa likely to become extinct if they are collected too zealously in the field for commercial purposes or for cultivation by individuals. In such cases a statement of the single or few specific local area(s) known has been withheld, but the general range is given. This approach has been taken to prevent the few discovered populations from being eradicated by the overly eager, and at least to make collecting more diffuse. As indicated on pp. 245-46, a cornerstone of the conservation of cacti and other plants is the practice of obtaining them for sale by propagation from seeds rather than by taking plants directly from the field. Seed loss is almost negligible for most species, because under natural conditions the sexual-reproduction potential far outstrips the actual germination and production of new plants from seeds. If the native populations are not disturbed, only a few seedlings need to be added to the population each year, and only a very small number can develop in competition with other plants.

For the same reason, some remarkably interesting information concerning the relationship of taxa to soils and other environmental factors has been withheld if the knowledge would endanger the species. The dilemma is an exasperating one: scientific information should become public knowledge, but if it is available to everyone some unscrupulous collectors will be guided to the plants concerned, which then may become extinct.

The base map by Albert Burkhardt underlying the distribution maps was prepared especially for this book. It is not merely a broad approximation of vast regions: the physiographic features have been produced from careful study of more detailed maps; county and state lines and national boundaries have been produced with care and correlated with rivers, mountain ranges, and other physiographic features. Thus, the distribution of each taxon can be related, insofar as the evidence available permits, to geography, topography, and floristic association(s).

The individual maps are not numbered, and only where the map for a given species falls more than two or three pages away from the text for that species—because for simplicity it is included on the map for another species—is a reference given in text to the place where it may be found.

Citation of specimens. In the text following there are a few citations of herbarium specimens documenting the principles of classification, the distribution of species or varieties, the occurrence of hybrid swarms, or the occurrence of taxa in unexpected places. Additional citations are to be found in the Documentation section, which lists some of the formal evidence for statements made in the text, and which follows the same sequence as the text. Only a small number of the specimens examined in about 65 herbaria has been cited, and for many the reader must refer to the so far unpublished records made in the herbaria consulted. However, the most important examples are given in each case, and each has been evaluated carefully for inclusion.

A typical citation is as follows: *NEW MEXICO. GUADALUPE CO.* Anton Chico, *Griffiths 10329, US, Pom.* This citation, given in the Documentation under *Opuntia phaeacantha* var. *camanchica* includes the state, county, place of collection (often also a mountain range, the altitude, and other features, if these were recorded on the label, as in this case they were not), the name of the collector, his field number, and the herbaria in which the specimens are located. The symbols appearing in the example are as follows: *US*, United States National Herbarium, Smithsonian Institution, Washington, D.C.; *Pom*, Herbarium of Pomona College, Claremont, California. A full list of symbols appears in the Documentation section, following the text.

Capsule characterizations. In a paragraph under each species and variety, except the few not known well or unknown in the field, a brief statement of the general appearance or striking features of the plant is included. This is intended to emphasize the characters that catch the eye and to convey a sense of the impression made by the taxon when it is encountered in the field.

Illustrations. Although the illustration of taxa in this volume is profuse, and although there are both colored and black-and-white photographs, as well as line drawings, the coverage of species and varieties is necessarily irregular. Photography is limited necessarily to what is available, and securing good photographs of field plants in flower or fruit requires being in the right part of a vast continent at the right time. Flowers are present only a few days of each year, and no one can predict exactly when. Fruits are not likely to be available at the same time. However, studies of the cacti have involved not only much research in the field but also bringing plants into temporary cultivation. Many hundreds have been grown in pots, and these have been propagated from parts of the plants made into specimens for the Herbarium of Pomona College, all parts of the specimen being identifiable by the field number during all stages of research. Flowers and fruits have been collected from the propagated fragments and added to the herbarium specimens, and at the same time data from them have been supplied for the description of taxa. These plants also have been the subjects for color and black-

and-white photography of flowering and fruiting stems, and many of the illustrations are from this source. Nevertheless, there is a disproportionate representation of species occurring in more frequently visited areas, even though the entire area covered in the book has been visited several times for the study of cacti.

As stated in the Preface, unless specified otherwise, the photographs and drawings in this book are by the author. A great many people and institutions have made additional illustrations available, however, and many journals and publishing houses have been generous in giving permission to include previously published material. The contributions of individuals and the use of material published previously are acknowledged in the legends of the illustrations, in the Preface, or in the Illustration Credits (back of the book).

Measurements. Finer measurements are given only in the metric system. The greater ones are given in both kilometers and miles or in both meters and yards (or feet). The original manuscript presented all measurements in equivalents under both the metric and English systems, but the cost of publication rendered the retention of both prohibitive. The following are some equivalents:

1 millimeter (mm) equals 1/25 (0.04) inch
1 centimeter (cm) equals 10 mm or 2/5 (0.4) inch
1 decimeter (dm) equals 10 cm or 4 inches
1 meter (m) equals 1,000 m, 100 cm, 10 dm, or 39.37 inches, thus 3.37 inches more than 1 yard
1 kilometer (km) equals 1,000 m or 3/5 (0.6) mile
1 kilogram (kg) equals 2.2 pounds

The key to beginning use of the metric system for reading plant descriptions and keys is knowing a few important equivalents and making their use become automatic through applying them. For understanding the larger measurements such as those of stems, the decimeter (dm) and the meter (m) are basic, and, fortunately, each of these has a readily understandable English equivalent:

1 dm is almost exactly 4 inches, and 3 make 1 foot
1 m is a little more than a yard (39.37 inches)

The equivalents for the finer measurements do not have as readily comprehensible English equivalents, but the following will help:

One cm is 2/5 inch (there are 2.5 cm per inch); it is equal to the space for a four-letter word on a standard typewriter or for five letters on an elite machine. It is equal to a six-letter word in the larger type used in the descriptions in this book or to a seven- or eight-letter word in the small type used in the keys and tables. It is the width of the tip of a man's little finger, but of course such a measurement varies from one individual to the next.

One mm is about 1/25 inch. If this is interpreted as 1/24, it falls midway between 1/16 and 1/32 inch, the width of a small letter s in the larger type used in this book, in the descriptions.

The most significant contribution of the metric system is that the units progress in size as multiples of 10, and this can be applied to the English equivalents:

10 mm equal 1 cm; 1 mm equals 0.04 inch; 1 cm equals 0.4 inch
10 cm equal 1 dm; 1 dm equals 4 inches
10 dm equal 1 m; 1 m equals about 40 (39.37) inches

Measurements of altitude are translated from the metric to the English system on the basic approximation of 300 m equal 1,000 ft. This is very nearly correct and is convenient. Thus, 900 m will be considered to be 3,000 feet. (The actual equivalent of 300 m is 984.25 ft., but this precision is not required, and exact field data based on surveyor's work seldom are available.)

Metric weights are expressed in kilograms (kg), and 1 kg equals 2.2 lbs.; 1 lb. equals 0.45 kg.

Measurements taken from specimen labels or from the literature have been left in the original systems of measurement, usually the English system, to avoid compromising the accuracy of the original data.

Order Cactales / Family Cactaceae

Plants of various forms, from small and simple to erect or sprawling shrubs, vines, or trees. Stems 1 to many, simple or branching, succulent (sometimes with woody "skeleton"), minute to 16 m long, to nearly 1 m diam; trunk lacking or to (2)17 m high, nearly 1 m diam; ribs none to many; tubercles (if present) separate or through various fractions of their height coalescent and merging with stem ribs. Roots sometimes tuberous. Leaves usually not discernible in adult plant; when present, from persistent, large, and flat to ephemeral, small, and conical or cylindroid. Areoles produced in leaf-axils or morphological equivalents, bearing spines in at least the juvenile stages of stem. Spines exceedingly variable, sometimes lacking. Flowers and fruits produced on either new or old growth and accordingly located near or below apex of stem or branch, developed either at apex or on upper side of a tubercle or between tubercles within, near, or distant from spine-bearing part of areole, usually either merging with it or connected by an isthmus; flower-bearing area persisting for many years after fall of fruit and forming circular, irregular, oblong, or elongate and often narrow scar. Flower usually epigynous, but epigyny of a different origin than in other flowering plants (Boke, 1964; Johnson, 1918); in *Pereskia* often perigynous; floral tube a hypanthium developed from receptacle, bare or bearing areoles and often small leaves; superior floral tube (above junction with ovary) from almost obsolete to elongate and tubular; leaves or scale-leaves of floral tube around ovary shading off into outer sepaloids, these shading into petaloids (the usually highly colored inner parts); sepaloids and petaloids few to numerous; stamens numerous, sometimes more than 1,000 (highest count 3,482), arranged spirally; carpels cyclic, 3-20+ (to at least 24); stigmas separate; style 1; ovary with a single chamber and numerous ovules on (as seen at maturity) parietal placentae (on ovary wall, the placentation actually complex but fundamentally axile); ovules usually campylotropous but sometimes amphitropous or orthotropous. Fruits fleshy or dry at maturity, without surface appendages or with tubercles, scales, spines, hairs, or glochids of various shapes and sizes; fruits early or late deciduous or long persistent. Seeds black, brown, gray, reddish, white, or bone-white, usually numerous, of various shapes, from longer than broad to broader than long (length being hilum to opposite side), mostly 1-5 mm greatest dimension; hilum either obviously basal or appearing "lateral" (actually by definition basal); cotyledons either accumbent or incumbent (sometimes oblique).

An undetermined number of valid species (perhaps 800 to 1,500 or more) occurring from Canada to southern South America; *Rhipsalis* native or introduced in tropical Africa and Ceylon. About 151 species and 133 varieties (other than the nomenclaturally typical varieties) occurring as native or in a few cases introduced plants in Canada and the U.S. A few prickly pears have escaped in the warm parts of the world; in some regions they have become pests.

Cactaceae, from Gr. *kaktos*, a prickly plant.

Classification of the family Cactaceae as a whole is little understood. At any level of taxonomy from variety to genus, the taxa have been investigated only slightly. A reasonably thorough study of the taxonomic problems of the family, including those of relationships, generic limits, and nomenclature, will require many years. For this book, study of the cacti of Latin America and the West Indies has been pursued largely with respect to understanding the taxa of the United States and Canada, and presentation of a consistent classification of the family as a whole has not been attempted. Two expedients are employed:

1. With the list of species and varieties given under each of the recognized genera occurring in North America north of Mexico, the proposed related genera (and, for that matter, species) occurring to the southward are mentioned for reference purposes and to indicate the general scope

of the family. However, most of the genera remain unevaluated, and the dubious status of many is indicated. Commonly, the treatment of the Cactaceae by Britton and Rose (1919-23) forms all or most of the basis for these references, because the book is well known and is the primary source for many other works. Thus, reference to the genera proposed by Britton and Rose should be helpful to many readers.

2. The list of genera of the Cactaceae assembled by David R. Hunt (1967) is given below. It was not intended by its author to be a complete solution to the many problems of classifying the genera of the family, but rather to be an interim attempt to introduce some order into what is known, to facilitate further attacks upon the problems of taxonomy. It is presented here for the same purpose and to provide an overall view of the family. However, the system of classification proposed by Hunt does not appear in any comprehensive taxonomic book devoted to the cacti; thus, it does not facilitate reference to other works, and Britton and Rose's names are of more use for that purpose. Nevertheless, Hunt's list, which follows, indicates some of the points to be considered in future research, and for the present it is the best-considered overall list of genera available for the classification of the family. Genera listed by number and by page number are those treated in this volume.

Tribe 1. PERESKIEAE
1. *Pereskia* (N. & S. America), p. 264
   Maihuenia (Argentina, Chile)

Tribe 2. OPUNTIEAE
   Quiabentia (Bolivia, Brazil, Argentina)
   Pereskiopsis (Mexico, Guatemala)
   Pterocactus (Argentina)
   Tacinga (Brazil)
2. *Opuntia* (N. & S. America), p. 269

Tribe 3. CACTEAE (CEREAE)
Subtribe 1. CEREINAE (proposed segregates from *Cereus*)
Group A
5. *Cereus* (West Indies to Argentina), p. 539
   Monvillea (West Indies, South America)
   Cephalocereus (=*Cereus*; tropical and subtropical America)
   Jasminocereus (Galápagos Is.)
   Stetsonia (Argentina)
   Browningia (Peru, Bolivia, Chile)
   Escontria (Mexico)
   Carnegiea (=*Cereus*; U.S., Mexico)

Pachycereus (Mexico)
Lophocereus (=*Cereus*; U.S., Mexico)
Myrtillocactus (Mexico, Guatemala)
Lemaireocereus (=*Cereus*; U.S. to Colombia & Venezuela)
Corryocactus (Peru, Chile)
Eulychnia (Peru, Bolivia, Chile)
Neoraimondia (Peru, Bolivia, Chile)
6. *Echinocereus* (U.S., Mexico), p. 601
   Rathbunia (Mexico)
   Neoabbottia (Hispaniola)
   Armatocereus (Ecuador)
   Leptocereus (West Indies)
   Brachycereus (Galápagos Is.)
   Calymmanthium (Peru)
   Dendrocereus (Cuba)
   Acanthocereus (=*Cereus*; U.S. intermittently to Brazil)
   Harrisia (=*Cereus*; Florida to Argentina)
   Peniocereus (=*Cereus*; U.S., Mexico)
   Nyctocereus (Mexico, Guatemala)

Group B
   Hylocereus (=*Cereus*; Central America to West Indies & Venezuela)
   Selenicereus (=*Cereus*; West Indies to tropical America)
   Heliocereus (Mexico to El Salvador)
   Weberocereus (Central America to Ecuador)
   Aporocactus (Mexico)
   Epiphyllum (West Indies to tropical America)
   Disocactus (West Indies to tropical America)
3. *Schlumbergera* (Brazil; introduced in U.S.), p. 534
4. *Rhipsalis* (Florida to tropical America; southeast Africa; Madagascar; Ceylon), p. 537

Group C
   Espostoa (Ecuador, Bolivia, Peru, Brazil)
   Leocereus (Brazil)
   Borzicactus (Ecuador, Bolivia, Peru, Chile)
   Cleistocactus (Bolivia, Peru, Paraguay, Uruguay)
   Denmoza (Argentina)
   Zehntnerella (Brazil)
   Oroya (Peru)
   Trichocereus (Ecuador to Chile)
   Echinopsis (Bolivia, southern Brazil, Paraguay, Uruguay, Argentina)
   Arthrocereus (Brazil, Argentina)
   Lobivia (Bolivia, Peru, Argentina)
   Rebutia (Argentina)
   Mila (Peru)

Subtribe 2. CACTINEAE
Group A
   Erisyce (Chile)
   Neoporteria (southern Peru, Chile)
   Notocactus (Brazil, Uruguay, Argentina)
   Frailea (Colombia to Uruguay)
   Austrocactus (Patagonia)
   Parodia (Bolivia, Chile, Brazil, Paraguay)
   Blossfeldia (Argentina)

Group B
   Melocactus (Central America, West Indies,
     tropical America)
   Discocactus (Brazil, Paraguay)

Group C
  9. *Echinocactus* (U.S., Mexico, p. 711
   Astrophytum (=*Cereus*; U.S., Mexico)
   Copiapoa (Chile)
   Gymnocalycium (South America)

10. *Sclerocactus* (U.S.; not listed by Hunt), p. 726
11. *Pediocactus* (U.S.), p. 749
13. *Thelocactus* (U.S., Mexico; Hunt's
   interpretation more inclusive), p. 780
 8. *Ferocactus* (U.S., Mexico), p. 684
   Echinofossulocactus (Mexico)
   Leuchtenbergia (Mexico)
   Aztekium (Mexico)
 7. *Lophophora* (U.S., Mexico), p. 680
17. *Ariocarpus* (U.S., Mexico), p. 861
12. *Epithelantha* (U.S., Mexico), p. 772
   Strombocactus (Mexico)
14. *Neolloydia* (U.S., Mexico), p. 784
15. *Ancistrocactus* (U.S., Mexico); not listed
   by Hunt), p. 798
16. *Coryphantha* (U.S., Mexico), p. 809
   Pelecephora (Mexico)
   Escobaria (=*Coryphantha*; U.S., Mexico)
18. *Mammillaria* (U.S. to Colombia &
   West Indies), p. 865

KEY TO THE GENERA OF CACTACEAE

1. Leaves broad and flat, only moderately succulent, resembling those of other dicotyledons, persistent; stems only moderately succulent, slender; flowers perigynous or epigynous, pedicelled; plants much-branched tropical or subtropical clambering shrubs, shrubby vines, or trees...........................**1. Pereskia**, p. 264
1. Leaves none or rudimentary and not discernible to the eye or, if present (in *Opuntia*), nearly terete and usually small, sometimes long and narrow and early deciduous; stems markedly succulent; flowers epigynous, sessile; plants of a variety of forms.
  2. Areoles bearing small or minute, sharp-pointed, barbed bristles (glochids) as well as usually longer and stouter spines; stem when young bearing a fleshy leaf at the base of each areole; floral tube barely developed above the ovary; seeds bony, often discoid; cotyledons large, leaflike, usually incumbent but rarely oblique or accumbent; stems composed of series of cylindroid or flattened joints, *not* ribbed (slightly so in *O. stanlyi* var. *kunzei*); flowers and fruits occurring on stem joints produced the preceding year, the joint flowering only once; flowers and fruits produced within or on the edge of the areole, all of which is spine-bearing; fruit *not* bearing scale-leaves, indehiscent................................**2. Opuntia**, p. 269
  2. Areoles *not* bearing glochids; stem leafless or with only minute (commonly microscopic) bulges or scales representing leaves; floral tube developed into a deep cup or tube above the ovary and below the perianth; seeds *not* bony, of various shapes; cotyledons small or minute, *not* leaflike, variable; stems with or without series of joints; flowers potentially on all stems or branches, new crops commonly appearing year after year on the same branch; flowers and fruits within or outside the areole; fruit with or without scale-leaves; dehiscent or indehiscent.
    3. Stems of mature plants *both* spineless *and* many-jointed; plants growing upon trees or shrubs or rocks or sometimes occurring in humus, the stems frequently producing aerial roots; fruit naked or with a few scales; floral tube *either* funnelform-tubular and sharply bent *or* saucerlike.
      4. Perianth tubular-funnelform, with a sharp bend above the ovary, the sepaloids and petaloids numerous; stem-joints flat, thin, leaflike, the margins toothed or lobed; branches (in U.S. species) arranged dichotomously..............
      ·...**3. Schlumbergera**, p. 534
      4. Perianth saucer-shaped, not bent, the sepaloids and petaloids few; stem-joints cylindroid, elongate, in U.S. species very slender (like lead pencils); branches alternate or in whorls................................**4. Rhipsalis**, p. 537
    3. Stems of mature plants *not both* spineless *and* many-jointed (though sometimes one or the other); plants growing in soil; stems usually *not* producing aerial

roots; fruit with or without scales; floral tube *neither* funnelform to tubular and bent *nor* saucerlike.

4A. Flowers and fruits (as shown on the stem by either their presence or their scars) produced *either* (1) at least within the margin of the spine-bearing areole *or* (2) in a disconnected area above the spine-bearing areole where earlier the flower bud burst through the stem-epidermis, the flower buds appearing always on stem areas at least 1 and often several years old and therefore usually clearly below the current growing point at the apex of the stem or branch; cotyledons incumbent or the embryo similarly oriented but straight; stem with ribs, the tubercles merging into the ribs beneath them; seeds longer than broad, the hilum therefore obviously basal.

5. Flower bud growing within at least the edge of a mature spine-bearing areole; plant never depressed or caespitose, the branches commonly few; stem length 15-100 times diameter, the mature stem(s) 30 cm to 16 m long, when shorter than 60 cm, less than 2.5 cm in diameter; embryo curved . . . .**5. Cereus, p. 539**

5. Flower bud bursting an irregular opening through the epidermis and later leaving a scar just above a mature spine-bearing areole; plant depressed or caespitose, the stems solitary or several or in old plants of some species numerous and forming a mound; stem length (1)2-5(10) times diameter, mature stems 5-30(60) cm long, those of maximum length 5-10 cm in diameter; embryo nearly straight . . . .**6. Echinocereus, p. 601**

4A. Flowers and fruits produced *either* (1) in a specialized, felted, spineless part of the areole on the upper (ventral) side of the tubercle, this either merging into the spine-bearing part of the areole or connected by a sometimes elongate and narrow isthmus, *or* (2) in special obscure (rarely spine-bearing) areoles deep between the tubercles, the flower buds appearing *either* on the new growth of the current season at the apex of the stem or branch *or* on the older areas beneath; cotyledons accumbent; stems with or without ribs, often with only tubercles; seeds of various shapes, the hilum either obviously basal or appearing "lateral."

5A. Flowers and fruits in a felted, adjacent or remote part of the areole on the upper side of the tubercle, this connected with the main spine-bearing portion of the areole directly or by an isthmus, the flowering portion and the isthmus persisting for many years as a circular to jagged scar, the flower buds appearing on new growth of the current season and each developing as the tubercle bearing it grows, the flowers and fruits therefore in 1 or more turns of a spiral at the growing apex of the stem or branch; stem *either* ribbed *or* bearing only tubercles; seeds various.

6. Areoles of the mature plant *not* bearing spines, these appearing on only the seedlings, the areoles bearing tufts of hair; hilum obviously basal (except in *Echinocactus asterias*, in which it is obscured by a special membranous outgrowth of the seed).

7. Stem ribs present; tubercles of the stem merging into the ribs beneath them, smooth, not deeply fissured (except along lines of joining of tubercles and in areolar regions); fruit with or without scale-leaves; petaloids *either* pink *or* yellow and red.

8. Ribs of the stem *not* covered with scales; ovary of the flower and later of the fruit *not* bearing scale-leaves; petaloids pink or tinged with pink. . . . .**7. Lophophora, p. 680**

8. Ribs of the stem covered with radiating white hairy scales; ovary bearing brown scale-leaves, these overlapping like shingles, thin and membranous; petaloids yellow, but the bases red. . . . .**9.4. Echinocactus asterias, p. 725**

7. Stem ribs none; tubercles of the stem separate, in U.S. species each markedly flattened and strongly roughened and fissured on the upper side; fruit *not* bearing scale-leaves; petaloids *either* pink to magenta *or* white . . . .**17. Ariocarpus, p. 861**

6. Areoles of the mature plant bearing spines; hilum variable in apparent position.

7A. Flower-bearing part of the areole adjacent to the spine-bearing part and along 1 edge merging with it, the flower or fruit crowded against the edge of the spine-cluster, the scar marking the former position of the fruit connected directly with and merging into the spine-bearing portion of the areole, extending one-eighth to one-half or rarely (sometimes in *Sclerocactus*) the full length of the tubercle; stems with either ribs or separate tubercles.

8A. Mature fruit *either* retaining the seeds *or* releasing them, but *neither* (1) by separating crosswise at the middle or above the base *nor* (2) by opening along more than 1 vertical slit; ovary (i.e. the inferior floral cup covering the ovary) with or without scales, the scales with or without axillary hairs; seeds of various shapes and dimensions; central spines, if present, straight or hooked; flower-bearing portion of the areole circular to elongate.

9. Flower-bearing portion of the areole broad, nearly circular, the scar marking the former position of the fruit broad and circular to rectangular or irregular; ovary with or without scales or hairs; seeds various.

10. Stems (except in young plants) strongly ribbed, the ribs coalescent with the bases of the tubercles, the length of the free upper portion of the tubercle from one-quarter of height to equal the height; ovary (i.e. the inferior floral cup covering the ovary) with numerous scale-leaves, the areoles axillary to these with or without wool; fruit thick-walled, indehiscent, fleshy.

11. Sepaloids *not* spinose or aristate; seed longer than broad, the hilum either obviously basal or "sub-basal" or sometimes "diagonal"; fruit remaining fleshy for several months after reaching maturity, the upper areoles and those of the inferior floral cup covering the fruit *not* bearing long wool........
.............................**8. Ferocactus**, p. 684

11. Sepaloids with spinose or aristate tips; seed broader than long, the hilum appearing "lateral"; fruit becoming dry soon after reaching maturity, in some species the upper areoles and those of the inferior floral cup (adherent with the mature fruit) bearing long woolly hairs obscuring the fruit....
......................**9. Echinocactus** (in part), p. 711

10. Stems *not* ribbed, bearing separate tubercles; ovary and fruit with few or no scales, the surface never obscured by hairs from the areoles; seed broader than long, the hilum appearing "lateral"; fruit thin-walled, dehiscent or indehiscent, dry or fleshy.

11A. Fruit dry and green or brown at maturity, bearing 1 to several scale-leaves, the length 1 to 1.5 times diameter, the capsule at maturity *both* splitting open along the back (dorsal) side *and* the top and the dried floral parts lifting off like a lid (circumscissile); spines *not* disarticulating crosswise....
.............................**11. Pediocactus**, p. 749

11A. Fruit fleshy but the wall thin and a brilliant red at maturity, with no scale-leaves, the length several times diameter, indehiscent, the superior floral cup deciduous or nearly so; spines ultimately disarticulating crosswise at the middles.........
.............................**12. Epithelantha**, p. 772

9. Flower-bearing portion of the areole narrow, the length 3 to several times the breadth, the scar marking the former position of the fruit similarly elongate, extending along as much as half or more of the length of the tubercle; ovary bearing a few scale-leaves, the areoles axillary to these *not* bearing hairs; seeds longer than broad, with the hilum obviously basal, 1.75 mm long.........
.............................**13. Thelocactus**, p. 780

8A. Mature (dry) fruit releasing the seeds by *either* (1) separating crosswise at some level above the base to near the middle *or* (2) opening along 2-3(4) vertical slits; ovary either without scales or with only a few scales, the areoles axillary to these bearing inconspicuous tufts of short hairs; seeds broader than long and the hilum therefore appearing "lateral," (2)3-4(5) mm broad; central spines commonly hooked but in 1 rare species (*S. glaucus*) not hooked and in another (*S. mesae-verdae*) almost always wanting; flower-bearing portion of the areole sometimes elongate with the length 2 to several times the breadth, the scar sometimes extending even the full length of the tubercle.......................**10. Sclerocactus**, p. 726

7A. Flower-bearing part of the areole distant from the spine-bearing portion, the flower or fruit standing apart from the spine cluster, the scar marking the former position of the fruit at the end of a very narrow felted and usually linelike groove extending to the base of the tubercle (but not on a juvenile stem or on its persistent areoles, and not on rib-segments or tubercles borne on the base of an older stem [see text, p. 39]); stems *not* ribbed, the tubercles separate.

    8B. Fruit dry and green to tan at maturity, opening *either* lengthwise *or* diagonally at the base and releasing the seeds; ovary in flower and in fruit bearing 1 to many scale-leaves; spines all straight or curved, *none hooked* (in U.S., but hooked in a Mexican species) . . . .
. . . . **14. Neolloydia**, p. 784

    8B. Fruit fleshy and green to red at maturity, indehiscent; ovary with or without scale-leaves; spines straight, curved, or hooked.

        9A. Flower and fruit developed (except on juvenile stems) at the base of the upper side of the tubercle, the groove running the full length of the tubercle; ovary with or without scale-leaves; fruit red or green; tubercles coalescent or not.

            10A. Spines, either only the principal central or the lower radials or both, *hooked*; tubercles of the stems *of mature plants* coalescent or adnate basally into or with the ribs, the tops remaining free; ovary in flower and fruit bearing 1 or commonly 2-13 or many scale-leaves . . . . **15. Ancistrocactus**, p. 798

            10A. Spines all straight or curved, *none hooked* (except in *C. scheeri* var. *uncinata*, a rare variety occurring near El Paso, Texas, and having all 4 centrals curved and apically hooked); tubercles of the stems not coalescent, ribs none; ovary *not* bearing scale-leaves . . . . **16. Coryphantha** (in part), p. 809

        9A. Flower and fruit developed at midlevel on the tubercle, the groove only half as long as the tubercle; ovary in flower and fruit bearing a few scale-leaves; fruit green; tubercles *never* coalescent . . . .
. . . . **16.2. Coryphantha macromeris**, p. 812

5A. Flowers and fruits in obscure areoles deep between and not connected with the tubercles, rarely accompanied by spines, the flower buds appearing on the side of the stem in areas developed at least 1, usually several, years earlier and therefore usually remote from the growing stem apex; stem bearing only tubercles; seeds longer than broad, the hilum therefore obviously basal or rarely "oblique" . . . . **18. Mammillaria**, p. 865

1. Pereskia

Clambering shrubs or vines, sometimes trees, often intricately branched, the cylindroid branches only slightly succulent, the ultimate branches up to several m long, 3-6 mm diam; trunk usually lacking; ribs none; tubercles separate and distant, knoblike. Leaves broad and flat, the blades somewhat to markedly succulent, clearly netted-veined, petioled or subsessile. Areoles nearly circular, 1.5-4.5 mm diam. Spines smooth, without sheaths or barbs, usually gray, brown, or yellow; central spines not differentiated; spines 1-6(12), straight, the larger 1.2-5(7.5) cm long, basally 0.5-1 mm diam, commonly acicular, broadly elliptic in cross section. Glochids none. Flowers and fruits produced on new growth of current season, therefore located near apex of new branch. Flower perigynous or epigynous, pedicelled, usually 2.5-4.5 cm diam; in epigynous species superior floral tube above its junction with ovary very short. Fruit usually obovoid to nearly orbiculate, fleshy at maturity, persistent, indehiscent; inferior floral tube also fleshy and at first bearing moderate-sized foliage leaves and sometimes spines, both ultimately deciduous; combined fleshy structure (floral cup and fruit) 1.2-4(5.5) cm long, 1.2-4 cm diam. Seeds black, longer than broad (length being hilum to opposite side), 3-5 mm long; hilum obviously basal; cotyledons accumbent.

About 15 species native in the American tropics. Two species introduced in southern Florida.

The genus is named for the French scientist N. C. F. de Peiresc (1580-1637).

The extraterritorial species of *Pereskia* have received no special study. The following list, which is incomplete, is included for reference purposes, and it reflects only minimal evaluation of the problems of classification, relationships, and nomenclature. The two numbered species are those treated in this volume.

1. *P. aculeata*
   P. sacharosa (Paraguay & Argentina)
   P. moorei (Brazil)
   P. bahiensis (Brazil)
   P. humboldtii (Peru)
   P. vargasii (Peru)
   P. weberiana (Bolivia)
   P. díaz-roemeriana (Bolivia)
   P. autumnalis (Guatemala & El Salvador)
   P. pititache (Oaxaca; perhaps not distinct from *P. autumnalis*)
   P. nicoyana (Costa Rica; perhaps not distinct from *P. autumnalis*)
   P. guamacho (Venezuela)
   P. colombiana (Colombia)
   P. bleo (Colombia)
2. *P. grandifolia*
   P. cubensis (Cuba)
   P. portulacifolia (Haiti)

1. Pereskia aculeata Miller
West Indian or Barbados gooseberry;
Lemon vine

Vine; young main branches erect, later clambering, to 9 m long; larger leaves ovate, oblong, lanceolate, or obovate, the bases acute to rounded, the apices short-acuminate, undulate, the blades to ±7 cm long, ±4 cm broad; spines yellow

---

KEY TO THE SPECIES OF PERESKIA

1. Vines; flower perigynous; spines of the twigs deflexed; twigs ±3 mm in diameter; leaves to 7 cm long; filaments white; flowers many, the inflorescence a panicle or a corymb..1. **P. aculeata**
1. Trees or shrubs; flower epigynous; spines spreading; twigs ±4.5-6 mm in diameter; leaves 7.5-15 cm long; filaments red; flowers few, in a terminal cluster...........
....2. **P. grandifolia**

to gray, on twigs 1 or 2(3) per areole, on main branches 1-3 per areole, to 2.5-4 cm long, acicular and straight, the others, including all on young branches, short, very broad-based, and reflexed; flowers perigynous, 2.5-4.5 cm diam; larger sepaloids pale green, similar to petaloids; petaloids white to pale yellow or light pink, oblanceolate-oblong, 20-25 mm long, 9 mm broad, acute to slightly acuminate, entire; filaments white, 6-9 mm long; style white, 12 mm long, 1.5-2 mm diam; stigmas 5, white, lanceolate, ±4.5 mm long; fruit light yellow, smooth, the leaves and spines of young ovary eventually deciduous, obovoid to orbiculate, ±12 mm long; seeds slightly flattened, ±4.5 mm long; hilum depressed.

Junglelike woods and thickets just above sea level. Caribbean Tropical Forest. Escaped from cultivation in peninsular Florida in Manatee, Highlands, St. Lucie, and Palm Beach Cos.

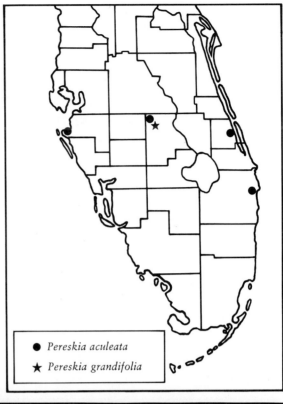

● *Pereskia aculeata*
★ *Pereskia grandifolia*

Fig. 234. Lemon vine or Barbados gooseberry, *Pereskia aculeata*, vegetative plants in the Huntington Botanical Gardens.

Fig. 235. Lemon vine or Barbados gooseberry, *Pereskia aculeata*. (See Credits)

266

2. Pereskia grandifolia Haworth

Tree or shrub 3-6 m high; trunk to 10 cm diam, strongly spiny; larger green branches fleshy, 7.5-12 mm diam; leaves narrowly obovate-oblanceolate, 7.5-15 cm long, 2.5-4 cm broad, apically rounded and mucronate; areoles producing leaves as well as spines; spines dark gray, 4-6 per areole (sometimes 1 or 2), developing slowly, spreading, straight, the longer ones of mature stems 4-6 cm long, 1-1.25 mm diam, acicular, nearly circular in cross section; flowers in small cymes, epigynous, 4-6 cm diam; sepaloids green or reddish with the middles green, to 20 mm long, ±5 mm broad, acute, entire, slightly mucronate, with tufts of white hairs in axils, most conspicuous in bud; petaloids rose, the largest cuneate-obovate, entire, cuspidate, 20-45 mm long, to ±9 mm broad, mucronate or short-acuminate, entire; filaments white, 6-9 mm long; anthers yellow, ±1 mm long; style white, ±12 mm long, 1.5 mm greatest diam; stigmas ±10, white, 2 mm long; ovary in anthesis with a very shallow cup, leafy, leaves to 12+ mm long; fruit fleshy, green or yellowish-green, smooth, obovoid with apex slightly flattened and base somewhat acute, the leaves early deciduous, the stalk nearly 12 mm long, the ovary at this stage obviously inferior, the fruit ± 4 cm long, ±3 cm diam; seeds slightly flattened, asymmetrically obovate, very dark brown to black, smooth and shiny but striate with minute vertical bands of pits, 4 mm long, 3 mm broad, 2 mm thick; hilum appearing "oblique."

Cultivated widely in the tropics; often escaping. Caribbean Tropical Forest. Common in Brazil and the West Indies and collected near Avon Park, Highlands Co., Florida (presumably as an escape).

Fig. 236. *Pereskia grandifolia*, a cactus with leafy, slender stems resembling those of other dicotyledons. The leaves appear one below each areole, but some emerge among the spines within the areole, a pattern not occurring in other cacti. The fruits show the scars where leaves were attached early in their development.

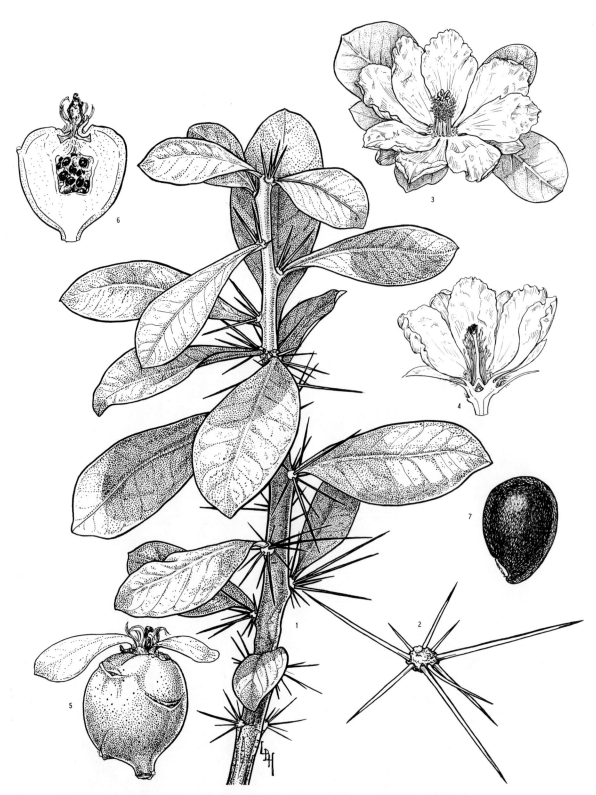

Fig. 237. *Pereskia grandifolia*, ×1.1, except as indicated. *1*, Vegetative branch with large leaves, ×.6; note that some leaves subtend the spine-bearing areoles, whereas others are within areoles (not so in other cacti). *2*, Areole with spines and felt. *3*, Flower; note the leaflike perianth parts, these persistent on the fruit. *4*, Flower in longitudinal section. *5*, Fruit, three leaf scars appearing on the ovary. *6*, Fruit in longitudinal section, showing the epigynous nature of the fruit (as well as the flower); other species of *Pereskia*, e.g. *P. aculeata*, have perigynous flowers and fruits, whereas epigynous fruits are universal in the other cacti. *7*, Seed, ×7.

2. Opuntia

Shrubs, trees, or creeping plants, 5 cm to 8 m high or spreading over as much as 40 m on the ground; stems each a series of joints, the larger joints cylindroid or flattened, 5-30(60) cm long, if cylindroid 0.6-5 cm diam, if flattened 2.5-30 cm broad; trunk lacking or to 1 m high, to 3 cm diam; ribs none; tubercles (when present) separate. Leaves (in U.S. present only in this genus and in *Pereskia*) cylindroid, acicular, or subulate, mostly 5-25(50) mm long, usually not discernible in adult plant. Areoles mostly circular or nearly so. Spines smooth, white, gray, yellow, brown, red, pink, or purplish, commonly 1-10(15) per areole but sometimes none, straight or curved, mostly 0.25-1 mm diam, acicular or subulate, narrowly to broadly elliptic in cross section, sometimes with basal sheaths; glochids (found only in this genus) produced in areoles, adjacent to the longer spines. Flowers and fruits produced on joints of preceding season, near apices of joints, within spine-bearing areoles. Flower usually 1-10 cm diam; floral tube above junction with ovary very short, deciduous after flowering, bearing stamens just above ovary (longer in other genera, except *Pereskia*, and not bearing stamens just above ovary), green or tinged with other colors. Stamens sensitive to touch.* Fruit fleshy or dry at maturity, with or without spines or hairs from areoles, spheroidal to obovoid or elongate, usually 1.2-5 cm long, 1.2-4 cm diam, indehiscent. Seeds gray, tan, brown, white, or tinged with other colors, flat and bony, smooth or irregularly angled and indented; either longer than broad or approximately discoid, usually 1.5-4.5(6) mm in greatest dimension; seed enveloped in aril developed from funiculus; hilum sometimes obviously basal but usually appearing "lateral"; cotyledons incumbent, foliaceous.

Many species, all in the Western Hemisphere, the number uncertain and grossly overestimated in nearly all publications. Fifty native or introduced species occurring from (perhaps) southern Alaska, Br. Columbia, Alberta, and Ontario south throughout the U.S. (except Vermont, New Hampshire, and Maine); introduced in Hawaii. Nearly all these species occur from southern California across the Southwest to southern Colorado and western and southern Texas, a few northward or in Florida. Some of these and many other species are native in Mexico, Central America, the West Indies, and South America, including the Galápagos Islands.

The name *Opuntia* is of uncertain origin, but is said by some to be based on the name of a town in Greece where a cactuslike plant was thought to occur.

Classification of the genus as a whole is in a chaotic state, and the extraterritorial "species" included in the following list are those most likely to prove worthy of retention. Most Latin American and West Indian taxa of *Opuntia* have received limited study, and those included below—being based mainly on Britton & Rose (1919-23)—are mentioned only for reference purposes without benefit of careful evaluation of the problems of classification, relationships, and nomenclature. Their positions in the list indicate supposed relationships with the species occurring north of the Rio Grande. Many more recently described extraterritorial species are not included because their status is uncertain. The numbered species and other numbered infrageneric taxa and the lettered varieties in the list are those treated in this volume.

Subgenus 1. CYLINDROPUNTIA (p. 275)

Section 1. CYLINDRACEAE (N. & S. America)

Series 1. ECHINOCARPAE (North America)

* According to Henslow (1837), "The flowers [of *Opuntia darwinii* Henslow, in Patagonia] had one day arrested [Darwin's] attention by the great irritability which their stamens manifested upon his inserting a piece of straw into the tube, when they immediately collapsed around the pistil, and the segments of the perianth soon after closed also."

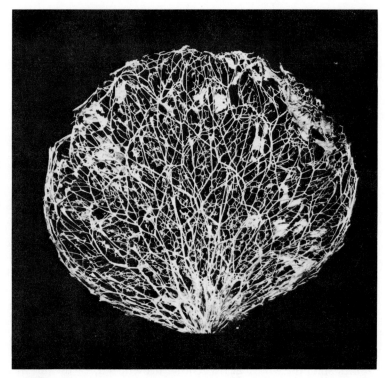

Fig. 239. The woody skeleton of a prickly pear stem joint. (Photograph from a preparation by Ted Hutchison)

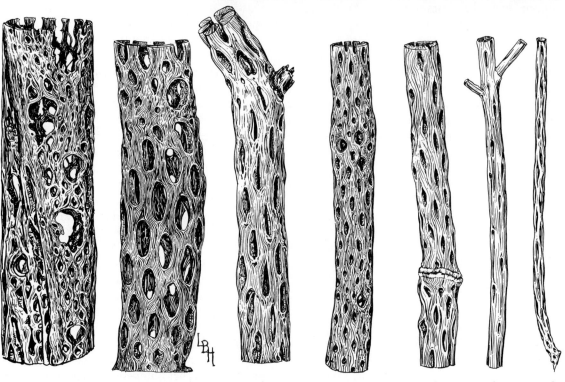

1 2 3 4 5 6 7

Fig. 238. The woods of chollas: *1, O. bigelovii; 2, O. fulgida; 3, O. acanthocarpa; 4, O. spinosior; 5, O. versicolor; 6, O. arbuscula; 7, O. leptocaulis.* The woody portion of the stem is a perforated hollow cylinder (technically the wood of a eustele) typical of the dicotyledons. After the soft tissues both outside and inside the stem disintegrate, the wood is left. This is excellent class material for demonstrating the arrangement of woody tissues. The idea of "vascular bundles" is a misconception; instead, the bundles are parts of the network of the cylinder. Woods of several cholla species are used in the manufacture of desert novelties.

1. *O. parryi*
    vars. a. *parryi*
        b. *serpentina*
    O. rosarica (Baja California)
2. *O. wigginsii*
3. *O. echinocarpa*
    vars. a. *echinocarpa*
        b. *wolfii*
            nuda (Baja California)
4. *O. acanthocarpa*
    vars. a. *coloradensis*
        b. *major*
        c. *ganderi*
        d. *acanthocarpa*
        e. *thornberi*

Series 2. IMBRICATAE (North America)
5. *O. tunicata*
    vars. a. *tunicata*
        b. *davisii*
    O. molesta (Baja California)
6. *O. whipplei*
    vars. a. *whipplei*
        b. *multigeniculata*
        c. *viridiflora*
7. *O. spinosior*
    O. cholla (Baja California)
8. *O. imbricata*
    vars. a. *imbricata*
        b. *argentea*
9. *O. versicolor*
    O. lloydii (Zacatecas)
10. *O. kelvinensis*

Series 3. BIGELOVIANAE (North America)
11. *O. prolifera*
    O. alcahes (Baja California)
    O. burrageana (s Baja California)
12. *O. fulgida*
    vars. a. *fulgida*
        b. *mamillata*
13. *O. munzii*
14. *O. bigelovii*
    vars. a. *hoffmannii*
        b. *bigelovii*
    O. ciribe (Baja California)

Series 4. LEPTOCAULES (N. America & Venezuela)
15. *O. leptocaulis*
    O. caribaea (West Indies & Venezuela)
16. *O. arbuscula*
17. *O. kleiniae*
    vars. a. *kleiniae*
        b. *tetracantha*

O. thurberi (Sonora & Sinaloa; status uncertain)
O. tesajo (Baja California)
O. cineracea (*O. tesajo* var. *cineracea*; Baja California)

Series 5. RAMOSISSIMAE (North America)
18. *O. ramosissima*

[Series undetermined]
    O. marenae (Sonora)

Series VESTITAE (South America)
    O. vestita (Bolivia)
    O. shaferi (Argentina)
    O. verschaffeltii (Bolivia)
    Austrocylindropuntia haematacantha (Bolivia; status uncertain)
    Austrocylindropuntia steiniana (Bolivia; status uncertain)
    O. weingartiana (Bolivia; status uncertain)
    O. humahuacana (Argentina; status uncertain)
    O. hypsophila (Argentina)

Series EUTUBERCULATAE (South America)
    O. clavarioides (Chile)

Series SALMIANAE (South America)
    O. salmiana (Brazil, Paraguay, Argentina)

Series SUBULATAE (South America)
    O. subulata (s Peru; cultivated for the persistent leaves, 5-12 cm long)
    O. exaltata (Peru; cultivated and escaped, Ecuador to N Chile)
    O. pachypus (Peru)
    O. cylindrica (Ecuador & Peru)
    Austrocylindropuntia intermedia (Peru & s Ecuador; status uncertain)
    Austrocylindropuntia tephrocactoides (s Peru; status uncertain)
    O. bradleyi (status uncertain)

Series MIQUELIANAE (South America)
    O. miquelii (Chile)

Section 2. CLAVATAE (N. & S. America)
Series 1. CLAVATAE (North America)
    O. invicta (Baja California)
19. *O. stanlyi*
    vars. a. *stanlyi*
        b. *peeblesiana*
        c. *kunzei*
        d. *parishii*
    O. bradtiana (Coahuila; known also as *Grusonia*)

20. *O. schottii*
    vars. a. *schottii*
        b. *grahamii*
    O. vilis (Zacatecas to San Luis Potosí)
    O. bulbispina (Coahuila)
    O. santamaria (Baja California)
    O. reflexispina (Sonora)
    O. moelleri (Coahuila)
21. *O. clavata*
    O. agglomerata (Coahuila)
    O. dumetorum (Tamaulipas)
22. *O. pulchella*

[The following series are those described in Britton & Rose (1919-23) as composing a proposed South American subgenus *Tephrocactus*, which "is hardly to be distinguished from the North American series *Clavatae*." Perhaps these proposed series should be reclassified under the section *Clavatae*, as one or more series. Numerous species have been proposed by later authors, but no attempt is made here to evaluate them or to assess various proposed rearrangements of taxa and their nomenclature. The species listed are mostly those recognized by Britton and Rose.]

Series WEBERIANAE (South America)
    O. weberi (N Argentina)

Series FLOCCOSAE (South America)
    O. floccosa (Peru & Bolivia)
    O. lagopus (Peru & Bolivia; may be var. of
        O. floccosa)
    O. atroviridis (Peru; may be var. of
        O. floccosa)

Series GLOMERATAE (South America)
    O. australis (Argentina)
    O. platyacantha (Chile & s Argentina;
        status uncertain)

Series PENTLANDIANAE (South America)
    O. aoracantha (w Argentina)
    O. rauppiana (Bolivia)
    O. subterranea (Bolivia & Argentina)
    O. hickenii (Argentina)
    O. darwinii (Argentina)
    O. wetmorei (Argentina)
    O. tarapacana (Chile)
    O. atacamensis (Chile)
    O. russellii (Argentina)
    O. corrugata (Argentina)
    O. ovata (w Argentina)
    O. sphaerica (Peru to Chile)
    O. skottsbergii (Argentina)
    O. nigrispina (s Bolivia & w Argentina)

O. pentlandii (Peru, Bolivia, Argentina)
O. ignescens (Peru)
O. campestris (Peru)
O. alexanderi (Argentina)

[Status uncertain]
    O. chaffeyi (Zacatecas; not studied; has been classified in both subgenera, though recently in *Opuntia*)

Subgenus 2. OPUNTIA (p. 377)
Section 1. OPUNTIA (N. & S. America)

Series 1. POLYACANTHAE (North America)
23. *O. polyacantha*
    vars. a. *polyacantha*
        b. *rufispina*
        c. *juniperina*
        d. *trichophora*
24. *O. fragilis*
    vars. a. *fragilis*
        b. *brachyarthra*
25. *O. arenaria*
26. *O. erinacea*
    vars. a. *erinacea*
        b. *columbiana*
        c. *ursina*
        d. *utahensis*
        e. *hystricina*
27. *O. nicholii*

Series 2. BASILARES (North America)
28. *O. basilaris*
    vars. a. *basilaris*
        b. *brachyclada*
        c. *longiareolata*
        d. *aurea*
        e. *treleasei*
    O. microdasys (N Mexico)
29. *O. rufida*
    O. pycnantha (Baja California; relationship undetermined)

Series 3. OPUNTIAE (N. & S. America)
[This series is composed of many complex and variable species, nearly all those outside the U.S. in need of much study. The first three species are transitional between the subgenera *Cylindropuntia* and *Opuntia*.]
    O. pumila (central & s Mexico)
    O. pubescens (central & s Mexico, Guatemala)
    O. pascoensis (Peru)
    O. curassavica (West Indies)
    O. taylorii (Hispaniola)

O. repens (West Indies)
O. aurantiaca (Uruguay & Argentina)
O. schickendantzii (Argentina)
O. kiska-loro (w Argentina)
O. canina (w Argentina)
O. montevidensis (Uruguay)
O. stenarthra (Argentina & Paraguay)
    (=*O. retrorsa*)
O. utkilio (Argentina)
O. anacantha (Argentina)
O. grosseiana (Paraguay)
30. *O. cubensis*
31. *O. triacantha*
32. *O. pusilla*
  O. bella (Colombia)
  O. tuna (Jamaica)
  O. wentiana (Curaçao & Venezuela)
  O. decumbens (Mexico & Guatemala)
  O. inamoena (Brazil)
33. *O. vulgaris*
  O. elata (Brazil & Paraguay)
  O. cardiosperma (Paraguay)
  O. arechavaletai (Uruguay & Argentina)
  O. mieckleyi (Paraguay)
  O. bonaerensis (Argentina)
  O. echios (Galápagos Is.)
  vars. *echios* (several islands)
    barringtonensis (I. Santa Fé)
    gigantea (I. Santa Cruz)
    inermis (I. Isabela)
    zacana (I. Seymour)
  O. galapageia (Galápagos Is.)
  vars. *galapageia* (Is. Bartolomé, Pinta, San
    Salvador)
    macrocarpa (I. Pinzón)
    profusa (I. Rábida)
  O. helleri (Galápagos Is.)
  O. insularis (Galápagos Is.)
  O. megasperma (Galápagos Is.)
  vars. *megasperma* (Is. Champion, Santa
    María)
    mesophytica (I. San Cristóbal)
    orientalis (I. San Cristóbal)
  O. saxicola (Galápagos Is.: I. Isabela)
  O. delaetiana (Paraguay)
  O. bergeriana (known only from cultivation)
  O. elatior (Curaçao; Panama to Venezuela)
  O. hanburyana (known only from
    cultivation)
  O. quitensis (Ecuador)
  O. schumannii (N South America)
  O. boldinghii (Curaçao, Trinidad, Venezuela)
  O. distans (Argentina)
34. *O. humifusa*

  vars. a. *humifusa*
    b. *ammophila*
    c. *austrina*
35. *O. macrorhiza*
  vars. a. *macrorhiza*
    b. *pottsii*
36. *O. littoralis*
  vars. a. *littoralis*
    b. *vaseyi*
    c. *austrocalifornica*
    d. *piercei*
    e. *martiniana*
37. *O. atrispina*
38. *O. violacea*
  vars. a. *violacea*
    b. *gosseliniana*
    c. *santa-rita*
    d. *macrocentra*
    e. *castetteri*
  O. azurea (NE Zacatecas)
39. *O. phaeacantha*
  vars. a. *phaeacantha*
    b. *camanchica*
    c. *spinosibacca*
    d. *laevis*
    e. *major*
    f. *discata*
    g. *wootonii*
    h. *superbospina*
    i. *mojavensis*
    j. *flavispina*
40. *O. lindheimeri*
  vars. a. *lindheimeri*
    b. *tricolor*
    c. *lehmannii*
    d. *cuija*
    e. *linguiformis*
41. *O. stricta*
  vars. a. *stricta*
    b. *dillenii*
  O. tapona (Baja California)
  O. bravoana (s Baja California)
  O. velutina (s Mexico)
  O. macdougaliana (s Mexico)
  O. durangensis (central Mexico)
  O. sulphurea (Chile & w Argentina)
  O. soehrensii (s Peru, Bolivia, N Argentina)
  O. microdisca (Argentina)
  O. scheeri (Mexico)

[The next eight proposed species often have been segregated under the untenable genera *Nopalea* and *Tacinga*, because the stamens are longer than the petals. The other characters are essentially those of prickly pears.]

42. *O. cochenillifera*
    Nopalea guatemalensis (Guatemala; status uncertain)
    Nopalea brittonii (cultivation; status uncertain)
    O. auberi (Mexico)
    O. dejecta (origin unknown)
    O. karwinskiana (Mexico)
    Nopalea inaperta (Yucatan)
    Tacinga funalis (Brazil; status undetermined)
43. *O. oricola*
44. *O. chlorotica*
45. *O. strigil*
    vars. a. *strigil*
         b. *flexospina*
46. *O. ficus-indica*
    Hybrid population "*occidentalis*" (treated herein)
    Hybrid population "*demissa*" (treated herein)
    Hybrid population "*dillei*" (treated herein)
    Hybrid population "*subarmata*" (treated herein)
    O. quimilo (N Argentina)
    O. robusta (central Mexico)
47. *O. tomentosa*
    O. tomentella
48. *O. leucotricha*
    O. stenopetala (Coahuila to Querétaro & Hidalgo)
    O. glaucescens (Mexico)
    O. grandis (Mexico)
    O. palmadora (Bahia, Brazil)
    O. catingicola (Brazil)
    O. orbiculata (N Mexico)
    O. pilifera (Puebla)

Section 2. CONSOLEA (N. & S. America)

Series 1. SPINOSISSIMAE (U.S. & West Indies)
49. *O. spinosissima*
    O. millspaughii (Cuba & Bahamas; status doubtful)
    O. macrantha (Cuba)
    O. falcata (Haiti)
    O. moniliformis (Hispaniola & Puerto Rico)
    O. rubescens (West Indies)

Series 2. BRASILIENSES (S. America)
50. *O. brasiliensis*
    O. argentina (Argentina)

KEY TO THE SUBGENERA OF OPUNTIA

1. Joints of the stem cylindroid or at least circular in cross section; spine (in North American species) with the epidermis separating either completely or incompletely during the first year of development, forming a thin, paperlike sheath, sometimes (in low, mat-forming species) with the sheath separating at only the tip; glochids *usually but not always* small and inconsequential, except on mostly the underground stems and the fruits of the mat-forming species............Subgenus **Cylindropuntia**, p. 275
1. Joints of the stem, after those developed by seedlings during the first year, flattened or at least *not circular* in cross section (except for some joints in Section CONSOLEA, *O. spinosissima* and *O. brasiliensis*); spine with *no* sheath; glochids *usually but not always* large, well-developed, barbed and effective.......Subgenus **Opuntia**, p. 377

Subgenus Cylindropuntia

Joints of stem cylindroid, or at least circular in cross section, in most species bearing tubercles. Spine during first year of development with the epidermis either completely or partly separating into a thin, paperlike sheath, sometimes (in low, mat-forming species) with the sheath separating only at tip; glochids small and inconsequential, except on underground stems and on fruits of mat-forming species.

Twenty-two species occurring in the U.S. from coastal southern California to Colorado and western and southern Texas. Some of these species range into Mexico; others are native in Mexico, the West Indies, and Central and South America.

Sexual reproduction is uncommon in the Bigelovianae (*O. prolifera, fulgida, munzii,* and *bigelovii*), and it is replaced mostly by the asexual rooting of detached joints or sterile fruits. Thus, through bypassing sexual reproduction, special combinations of genes have become standardized. This guarantees the continuation of patterns of hereditary characters selected by adaptation to the existing environment. Sexual reproduction would yield a variety of forms in every generation, and most of these would be too poorly adapted to survive. However, once a well-adapted gene combination has arisen through sexual reproduction, asexual reproduction can reproduce it very quickly. This is essentially the method used in horticulture—for example, the cultivation of a new apple by cuttings or grafts, which multiply the exact gene combination of the original plant.

In *O. prolifera* and *O. fulgida* there are two forms of asexual reproduction: the rooting of single joints, which are attached weakly and which fall to the ground, and similar rooting of the mostly sterile fruits. However, in both species,

and especially in *O. fulgida,* falling may be delayed for many years because the fruits persist and produce new flowers and fruits from their areoles, thus forming chains. The formation of fruits simulates sexual reproduction; but it does not form an embryo by joining male and female cells, and the individuals produced from the fruits are genetically identical with the female parent and with each other. This type of asexual reproduction, called apomixis, is very common in the plant kingdom, and it serves to make many races of species quickly available to fill new or special environmental niches. The distribution of races into niches occurs with sexual reproduction, but the process is much slower, because most genetic combinations are unsuitable and in every generation they must be eliminated by natural selection.

Either vegetative multiplication or apomixis is an excellent means of distributing quickly and maintaining indefinitely a winning combination of genes, but climatic and other environmental conditions are not permanent. If a gene combination like the one prevailing in *O. bigelovii* is outmoded, either the whole species will become extinct or new combinations produced by sexual reproduction will supplant the parental type and continue to multiply asexually. Thus, even if a species spreads rapidly by asexual means, it must still retain some sexual reproduction or it cannot survive change.

The two varieties of *O. fulgida* reproduce both vegetatively and apomictically. Thus they can exist side-by-side without intergradation. Both have adaptive genetic combinations, but var. *fulgida* is the more widespread and is probably adapted to all the situations favorable to var. *mamillata* and to others as well.

KEY TO THE SPECIES OF THE SUBGENUS CYLINDROPUNTIA

1. Epidermis of the spine separating during the first year of development into a thin, paperlike sheath, the spine slender, not papillate or striate; glochids usually all small and harmless; joints cylindroid, usually uniformly spiny, of varying lengths on differ-

ent parts of the plant, new spines developing from any areole of an older joint, the terminal bud continuing to grow and the joint to elongate for an indefinite period, the plant therefore usually shrubby, arborescent, or treelike (Section 1. CYLINDRA-CEAE).

2. Stem either smooth or with simple tubercles, the areole apical on the tubercle; fruits dry or fleshy, the surface, appendages, and color various; joints usually not woody the first year; spine tips plain or barbed.

3. Fruits dry (drying as the seeds mature), spiny (sometimes only sparsely so), *the spines of the fruit strongly barbed* (Series 1. ECHINOCARPAE).

4. Spines of the fruit few, mostly solitary in the areoles of the 2 uppermost nearly horizontal series; plant with no main trunk, the branches prostrate to erect, obviously green and not obscured by spines; tubercle length 2.5-7 times the width; chaparral areas inland and nearly always w of the mountain axis of s California, except NE San Diego Co. . . . . .1. **O. parryi**

4. Spines of the fruit numerous, several per areole of the 1 or 2 uppermost nearly horizontal series; plant form variable; tubercle length-width ratio variable; deserts from California to sw Utah and Arizona.

5. Terminal joints 6-12 mm in diameter; central spine 1 (or sometimes also 1 or 2 shorter ones), the radial spines 6-8 and much smaller, the fruits, however, with several spines per areole; SE California and sw Arizona. . . . . .2. **O. wigginsii**

5. Terminal joints or some of them at least 15 mm in diameter; central and radial spines indistinguishable.

6. Tubercle length 1-2 times the breadth; longer terminal joints 5-15(38) cm long; main trunk distinctly developed, often one-third to one-half the height of the plant. . . . . .3. **O. echinocarpa**

6. Tubercle length 3 to several times the breadth; longer terminal joints (12)15-50 cm long; main trunk none or, when present, rarely more than one-fifth the height of the plant. . . . . .4. **O. acanthocarpa**

3. Fruits *fleshy* at maturity (sometimes drying later during long persistence on the plant), *spineless* or rarely slightly spiny and the spines not strongly barbed.

4A. Terminal joints or at least some not less than 1.5 cm in diameter.

5A. Larger terminal branches mostly 1.5-2.5(3) cm in diameter at maturity, attached relatively firmly, often elongate; spines of various colors, often dark (Series 2. IMBRICATAE).

6A. Flowers and fruits *not* formed in the areoles of persistent fruits of previous seasons, the fruits thus *not* forming series; mature fruit yellow, sometimes tinged with red or purple, strongly tuberculate, with a deep, cuplike cavity at the apex; leaves *either* all very short *or* the longer (upper) ones slender, not more than 15 mm long or 1.5 mm in diameter.

7. Longer spines 3.8-5 cm long; sheaths of much greater diameter than the spines, 1.5-4 mm in diameter; petaloids yellow or yellowish-green; E New Mexico to w Oklahoma and w Texas. . . . . .5. **O. tunicata**

7. Longer spines 1-3(5) cm long; sheaths of only a little greater diameter than the spines, usually 1-2 mm in diameter; petaloids of various colors.

8. Sheaths of young spines conspicuously white, silvery, or light tan, usually persistent after the first year of growth; larger terminal joints 1-2 cm in diameter; leaves conical, 1.5 mm long, petaloids yellow; s Nevada and Utah and N Arizona to sw Colorado and NW New Mexico . . . . .6. **O. whipplei**

8. Sheaths of young spines *not* conspicuously white or silvery or light tan (except in O. imbricata var. *argentea*, Big Bend National Park, Texas), usually deciduous after the first year of growth; larger terminal joints 1.5-3 cm in diameter; leaves nearly cylindroid, the largest 9-15 mm long, petaloids mostly reddish-purple, sometimes yellow.

9. Tubercles 9-15(19) mm long, of moderate height, about 5 vertical rows visible from the side of the stem; spines ±6-15 mm long, strongly barbed, the sheaths soon deciduous; SE Arizona and sw New Mexico. . . . . .7. **O. spinosior**

9. Tubercles 20-35 mm long, raised, narrow, 3 or 4 vertical rows visible from the side of the stem; spines 12-30 mm long, very strongly barbed, the sheaths persistent about 1 year; Colorado to Kansas (rare), SE Arizona (rare), w Texas, and central Mexico. . . . . 8. **O. imbricata**

6A. Flowers and fruits formed in the areoles of the persistent (usually sterile) fruits of previous seasons, thus forming short series (proliferous); mature fruit green or sometimes merely tinged with red, purple, or yellow, sometimes tuberculate but not strongly so, the apical cuplike cavity usually very shallow; leaves (known only in *O. versicolor*) elongate but not slender, to 19 mm long, to 3 mm in diameter.

    7A. Terminal joints mostly 12.5-35 cm long, 1.5-2 cm in diameter; tubercles 3-5 times as long as broad; spines 6-15 mm long; fruits green with a tinge of purple, lavender, or red.............9. **O. versicolor**

    7A. Terminal joints 6-10 cm long, 2.5-3.8 cm in diameter; tubercles twice as long as broad; spines 19-25 mm long (a single spine in the areole this long); fruits green or tinged with yellow.......**10. O. kelvinensis**

5A. Larger terminal branches (2.5)3-6 cm in diameter at maturity, usually short, readily detached, and abundantly vegetatively reproductive; spines usually straw-colored (Series 3. BIGELOVIANAE).

    6B. Fruits smooth or only slightly tuberculate and with the apical cuplike depression shallow, long-persistent and proliferous; spines barbed but not strongly so; tubercles of the terminal joints distinctly longer than broad; stem branched below and usually several times rebranched above, some main branches at least as long as the usually short main trunk, this 0.3-0.7 m long.

        7B. Fruits forming short chains only 2-4 individuals long; spines not obscuring the stem-joint; coast of s California and Baja California.........
....**11. O. prolifera**

        7B. Fruits forming long branching chains to 10-22 individuals long; spines (except in var. *mamillata*) obscuring the stem-joint; Arizona to Sinaloa
....**12. O. fulgida**

    6B. Fruits markedly tuberculate and with the apical cuplike depression deep, persisting only 1 season, *not* proliferous; spines effectively and strongly barbed; tubercles of the terminal joints (of the common taxon, *O. bigelovii* var. *bigelovii*) nearly as broad as long (twice as long in *O. munzii*, and slightly longer than broad in *O. bigelovii* var. *hoffmannii*); stem erect, forming a column, branching various.

        7C. Tree 2-5 m high, the trunk usually less than half the height of the plant, the major branches elongate, rebranched several times; larger terminal joints 2.5 cm in diameter; tubercles twice as long as broad, *not* hexagonal, ±12-16 mm long, 6-9 mm broad, 3 mm high, abruptly protruding above the stem surface; mountains NE of the Salton Sea, California
....**13. O. munzii**

        7C. Tree in miniature, ±1-1.5(2.5) m high, the trunk (in the common var. *bigelovii*) running like a post almost to the apex of the plant, stout, bearing usually much shorter branches; larger terminal joints 3(4-6) cm in diameter; tubercles less than twice as long as broad, more or less hexagonal, 6-9 mm long, only slightly raised from the stem surface.

            8A. Branches usually simple or only once or twice rebranched; tubercles 1(1.5) times as long as broad; deserts of California, Arizona, and NW Mexico.............................**14. O. bigelovii** (in part)

            8A. Branching somewhat more diffuse; tubercle length 1.5 times breadth; deserts of San Diego Co., California........................
.......................**14a. O. bigelovii** var. **hoffmannii**

4A. Terminal joints not more than 1.2 cm in diameter; spines *not* strongly barbed as in the similar *O. ramosissima* (below) (Series 4. LEPTOCAULES).

    5B. Larger terminal branches ±3-4.5 mm in diameter; fruits red, *not* tuberculate; trunk none or poorly developed....................**15. O. leptocaulis**

    5B. Larger terminal branches 6-12 mm in diameter; fruits of various colors, tuberculate or not; trunk present or absent.

        6C. Trunk 5-10 cm in diameter; fruits 20-40 mm long, green tinged with purple, lavender, or red, not markedly tuberculate (except in sterile or nearly sterile fruits); branches nearly smooth or with low tubercles 2-4(5) cm long......................................**16. O. arbuscula**

        6C. Stem without a large trunk; fruits 15-20 mm long, red or mostly so, strongly tuberculate; branches with strongly raised tubercles 1.2-1.5(2.5) cm long.......................................**17. O. kleiniae**

2. Stem nearly covered with flattened, platelike, diamond-shaped to obovate tubercles, the areole in an apical notch or groove of the tubercle plate; fruits dry at maturity,

tuberculate, spiny or sometimes spineless, brown; joints becoming woody during the first year; spine points with strong barbs (Series 5. RAMOSISSIMAE) . . . .
. . . . **18. O. ramosissima**

1. Epidermis of the spine separating into a sheath at only the extreme apex, the larger spines at least basally flattened and with either rough cross bands of papillae or longitudinal ridges and grooves; glochids (especially on underground stems and often on fruits) large and strongly barbed; joints enlarged upward, all of about the same length, developing only from basal areoles of older joints, the plant therefore tending to form a mat, the terminal bud ceasing to grow when the joint reaches a particular size (Section 2. CLAVATAE).

2A. Petaloids yellow or very rarely reddish; larger spines rigid, papillate and rough to touch, ridged-and-grooved or not so.

3A. Larger spines *not* longitudinally ridged-and-grooved or only very faintly so (at least, on old disintegrating spines appearing so), basally somewhat broader than apically, subulate.

4B. Ovary and fruit *either* spiny in at least some areoles *or* with glochids radiating in all directions; w of Continental Divide from California to s Nevada and sw New Mexico . . . . **19. O. stanlyi**

4B. Ovary and fruit not spiny, the glochids radiating from all but the lower side of the areole; E of Continental Divide in s central New Mexico E of the Rio Grande and in Texas southeastward near the Rio Grande to Cameron Co. and on the adjacent plains . . . . **20. O. schottii**

3A. Larger spines clearly longitudinally ridged-and-grooved, basally proportionately very broad, rather broadly subulate and daggerlike; NE Arizona and E of Continental Divide in N and central New Mexico . . . . **21. O. clavata**

2A. Petaloids purple to rose; spines flexible, *not* papillate or rough to touch, the larger ones usually with longitudinal basal ridges and grooves; Nevada and w Utah . . . .
. . . . **22. O. pulchella**

Fig. 240. A cane cholla, *Opuntia parryi* var. *parryi,* growing in a wash near Claremont, Los Angeles Co., California.

Fig. 241. *Opuntia parryi* var. *parryi,* mature and young joints of the stem, the older joints with spines, the younger ones and the buds with leaves that soon fall away as the spines grow.

Fig. 242. *Opuntia parryi* var. *parryi*, mature joints of a plant with few spines (a condition uncommon in almost any species) and a flower; and a young joint with leaves and developing spines. (David Griffiths)

Fig. 243. *Opuntia parryi* var. *parryi*, a joint with almost mature green fruits and detached mature fruits, the latter spiny and having become dry at maturity. (David Griffiths)

1. Opuntia parryi Engelmann
Cane cholla

Shrubs; stems prostrate, assurgent, or erect; larger terminal joints 0.75-1.5(3) cm long, 1.5-2.5 cm diam; tubercles prominent, length 2.5-7 times width, 12-20(25) mm long vertically, 3-4.5(6) mm wide, protruding 4.5-6 mm; leaves lanceolate in outline but circular in cross section, 4.5-7.5 mm long, 3 mm diam; areoles 6-7.5 mm diam, typically 9 mm apart; spines distributed uniformly on joint, grayish- to reddish-brown or brown (sheaths sometimes lighter), the principal spines 7-20 per areole, most slightly declined, straight, the larger 0.9-1.5(3) cm long, basally 0.8 mm broad, subulate, narrowly elliptic in cross section, barbed; glochids tan to reddish-brown, restricted to upper part of areole, 2-4 mm long; flowers clustered, each 3-4 cm diam, 3-3.5 cm long; sepaloids greenish-yellow (green to nearly yellow) with a purple tinge (often strong), narrowly to clearly obovate-oblong, 0.7-1.6 cm long, 4-10 mm broad, apically rounded but mucronate or mucronulate; petaloids yellow or greenish-yellow, the outer with purplish to reddish tinge, narrowly obovate, 15-20 mm long, 7-10 mm broad, apically rounded but mucronulate, sparsely denticulate, with a few shallow sinuses; filaments 3-6 mm long; anthers 1.2-2 mm long; style purplish-red, stout, ribbed, 1.5-2 mm long, 3-4.5 mm diam; stigmas purplish-red, probably 6 or 7, 2-2.5 mm long, deltoid; ovary in anthesis strongly tuberculate; fruit greenish, turning to tan or brown, dry at maturity, obovoid-turbinate, ±1.2 cm long, ±1 cm diam, with deep cuplike umbilicus, with prominent tubercles, and with relatively few spines, these ±6 mm long, the fruit deciduous in late summer or fall; seeds whitish-tan, flat, nearly circular to irregular in outline, ±6 mm long, ±5 mm broad, 2 mm thick; hilum area with a notch.

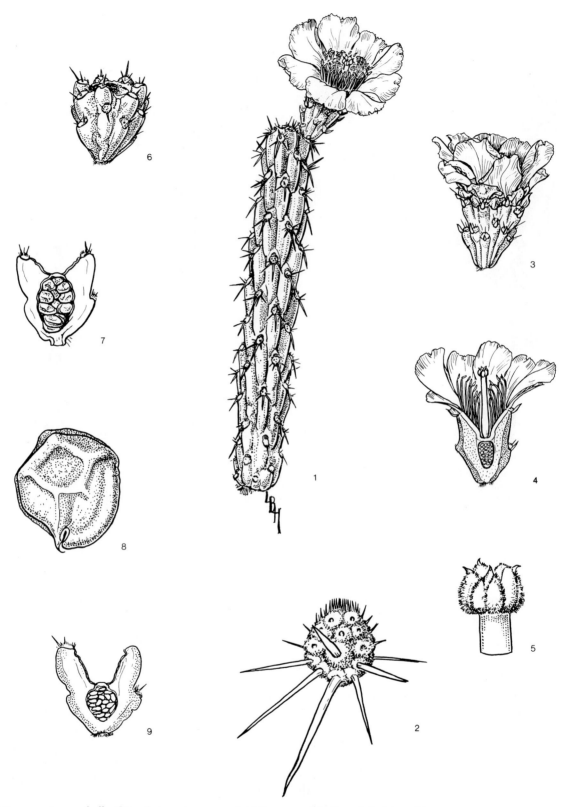

Fig. 244. A cane cholla, *Opuntia parryi* var. *parryi*, ×.8, except as indicated. *1*, Joint with a flower. *2*, Areole with spines, glochids, and short wool, ×5. *3*, Flower. *4*, Flower in longitudinal section. *5*, Stigmas and the upper part of the style, ×6. *6*, Fruit before maturity and drying, tuberculate and with short spines, ×1.1. *7*, Fruit in longitudinal section, showing the seeds. *8*, Seed, ×3.5. *9*, Sterile fruit, showing the undeveloped seeds.

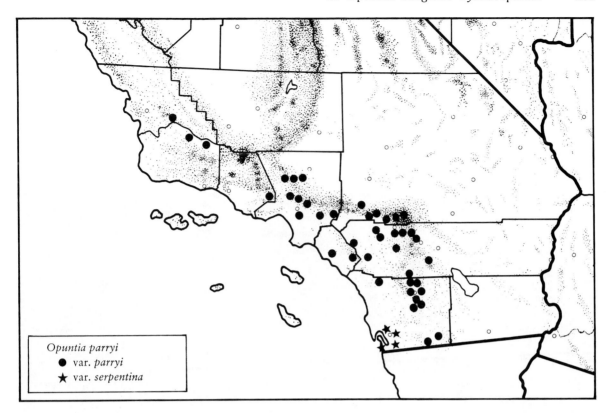

Opuntia parryi
● var. *parryi*
★ var. *serpentina*

Distinctive Characters of the Varieties of **Opuntia parryi**

Character	a. var. **parryi**	b. var. **serpentina**
Habit	Bushy or shrubby; main branches several to many, erect	Prostrate, or stems assurgent or suberect
Larger terminal joints	1.5-2(2.5) cm diam	1.5-2 cm diam
Tubercles	Strongly raised and laterally compressed	Strongly raised but usually not laterally compressed
Tubercle length	4-7 times width	(2.5)3(4) times width
Altitude	Commonly 150-900 m (500-3,000 ft)	To 150 m (500 ft)
Floristic association	California Chaparral (rare above or on desert margin)	California Chaparral (only southern coastal phase)

1a. Opuntia parryi var. parryi. On gravelly or sandy soils of washes, alluvial fans, and canyon bottoms or valleys; almost strictly on coastal side of mountains at 150-900 m (500-3,000 ft). On disturbed land normally covered by California Chaparral. California in Cuyama Valley at N edge of Santa Barbara Co. and from SE Ventura Co., San Fernando Valley, and E Los Angeles Co. to vicinity of San Bernardino; thence s through interior valleys to San Diego Co.; occurring at about 1,900 m (6,200 ft) near Barton Flats, San

Bernardino Mts. (*Benson, Baker, & Adams 16-645, Pom*), barely reaching edge of Mojave Desert at Rock Creek and of Colorado Desert E of Banning and in San Felipe Valley. Occurrence in Pacific Grassland (Cuyama Valley) and in Pacific Montane Forest (Barton Flats) is minor. Probably in NW Baja California.

These dark green shrubs form small, compact colonies among the scattered patches of other shrubs occurring in washes, and they suddenly confront one as little islands apart from the surrounding vegetation. The few colonies along Cuyama Valley are not competing with other shrubs, and they have become dense and as much as 20 m in diameter.

1b. Opuntia parryi var. **serpentina** (Engelmann) L. Benson. Snake cholla. Sandy soils or sandy loam of slopes and valleys in coastal bluff and hill region, usually at less than 150 m (500

ft). Disturbed open places in California Chaparral (south coastal phase). California around San Diego and E to Tecate region. Pacific coast of N Baja California.

The plants form dense mats several meters in diameter, or the elongate individual stems seem to crawl like snakes through shrubs and across open places.

Hybridizes at San Diego with *O. prolifera*.

Fig. 245. Snake cholla, *Opuntia parryi* var. *serpentina*, a snakelike plant sprawling through shrubs in disturbed California Chaparral; near Chula Vista, San Diego Co., California. (*The Native Cacti of California*)

Fig. 246. *Opuntia parryi* var. *serpentina*, bearing flowers and young fruits and showing the weak, drooping joints and their relatively short tubercles; plant from San Diego, California.

Fig. 247. *Opuntia parryi* var. *serpentina* in the Rancho Santa Ana Botanic Garden; tubercles of the stem shorter than those in var. *parryi*.

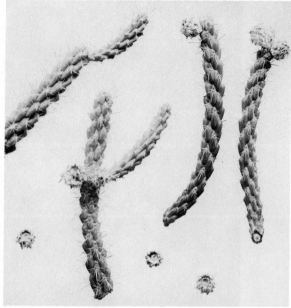

Fig. 249. *Opuntia parryi* var. *serpentina*, mature branches with mature, dry fruits, the detached fruits showing in each case the umbilicus, or apical attachment point of the floral cup that bore the flower parts. (David Griffiths)

Fig. 248 *(left).* *Opuntia parryi* var. *serpentina,* young branches, but these of two ages, the lower one with only a few leaves at the summit, the newer three with leaves their full length. (David Griffiths)

2. Opuntia wigginsii L. Benson

Shrub or treelike, 30-60 cm tall, ±30 cm diam; trunk short, 2-4 cm diam; terminal joints somewhat clavate, gradually expanded upward, 5-10 cm long, basally 6-9 mm diam, apically 9-12 mm diam; tubercles prominent, to 4.5 mm long vertically, 3mm broad, protruding 2 mm; areoles circular, 2-3 mm diam, 3 mm apart; all spines straight, acicular, not markedly barbed, moderately dense but not obscuring joint, red or pink but with straw-colored sheaths, 6-8 per areole, those on terminal part of joint larger, the central spine in areole far larger than others, sometimes accompanied by 1 or 2 (rarely 3) shorter upper centrals, 2-4.5 cm long, basally 0.25-0.5 mm diam, radials almost hairlike, to 3 cm long, basally perhaps 0.1 mm diam; glochids reddish-tan, prominent, 2 mm long; flower 3.5-4 cm diam, ±4 cm long; sepaloids with green and purple middles and greenish-yellow margins, obovate, 10-15 mm long, 7-8 mm broad, short-acuminate; petaloids greenish-yellow, the midribs with purple tinge, cuneate-obovate, 18-22 mm long, 10-13 mm broad, retuse, the margins entire; filaments yellowish-green, 5 mm long; anthers yellow, 2 mm long; style pale greenish-yellow, 12-15 mm long, 1.5 mm diam, not swollen basally; stigmas 5, 1.3 mm long, not lobed, only slightly widened apically; ovary in anthesis tuberculate and spiny, 1.5-2 cm long, the leaves prominent, slender, 15-25 mm long; fruit green, dry at maturity, with all spines of each areole well developed, strongly barbed, the longer 1-2.5 cm long, the fruit 1.5-2 cm long, 1.2-2 cm diam, the umbilicus deep; seeds tan, nearly discoid, 4.5 mm long, 4 mm broad, 1.5 mm thick.

Sandy soils of small washes and flats in the lower desert at less than 300 m (1,000 ft). Colorado Desert. California in Carrizo Desert, E San Diego Co., and in NE Imperial Co.; Arizona in Yuma Co. from Quartzsite area to Gila R. as far E as W Maricopa Co.

This obscure little cholla, growing in out-of-the-way sandy areas where cacti are not expected, is usually a beautiful little silvery-tan tree less than knee-high. It blends with the small patches of sand along washes or occurring as islands in the desert pavement. Commonly it has been passed by as a young *O. echinocarpa.*

See map for *O. echinocarpa* (next species).

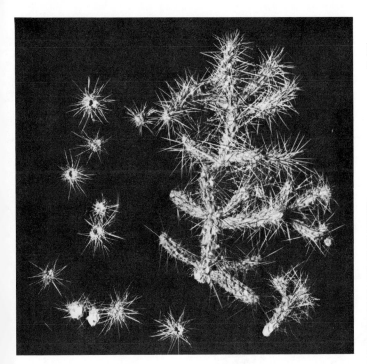

Fig. 252. *Opuntia wigginsii*, branches and detached mature, dry fruits.

Fig. 250. *Opuntia wigginsii*, plant about 3 dm (1 foot) high, on the border between the Colorado and Arizona deserts in western Yuma Co., Arizona.

Fig. 251. *Opuntia wigginsii*, plant in cultivation, showing detail of the stems, tubercles, areoles, and spines. (*The Native Cacti of California*)

285

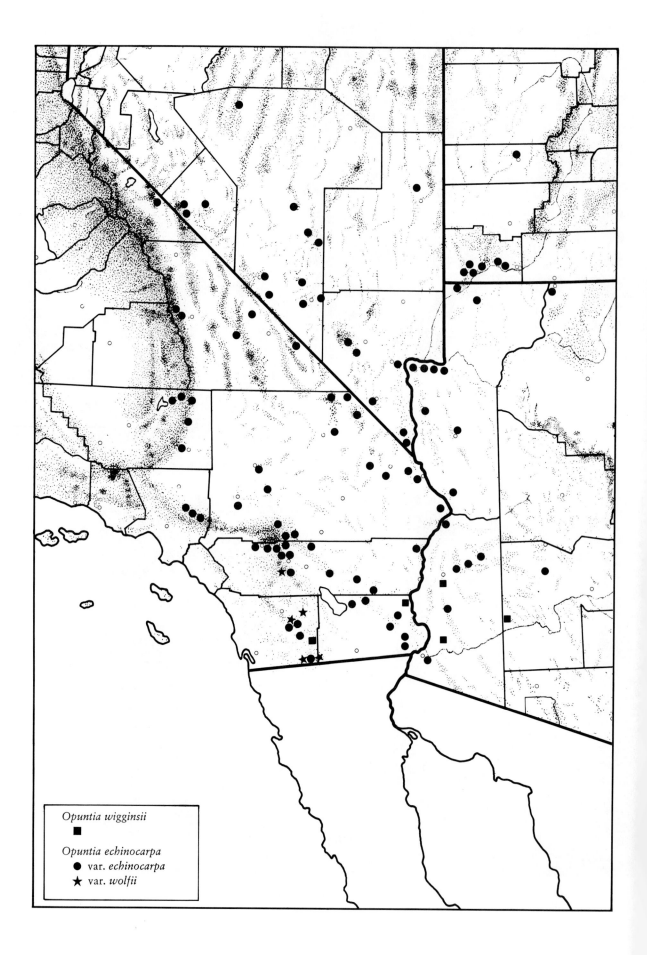

Opuntia wigginsii
■

Opuntia echinocarpa
● var. *echinocarpa*
★ var. *wolfii*

3. Opuntia echinocarpa Engelmann & Bigelow
Silver or golden cholla

Much-branched shrub, usually 1-1.5 m high; trunk often one-third to one-half height of plant, usually 5-7.5 cm diam; larger terminal joints bluish-green, 5-15(38) cm long, rarely (w edge of Colorado Desert) 25-40 cm long, usually ±2 cm diam (rarely 4 cm); tubercles conspicuous, mammillate, length 1-2 times width, 6-10(20) mm long vertically, 5(10) mm broad, protruding 6(10) mm; areoles circular, 4-5 mm diam, 1-2 cm apart; spines straw-colored, silvery, or golden or lower half of each spine pinkish (sheaths similar color, conspicuous, persistent), dense on branches, 3-12 per areole, spreading in all directions, straight, the longer 2-3.8 cm long, basally to 0.8 mm broad, subulate, nearly linear in cross section, not barbed; glochids yellow, minute, to 3 mm long; flower usually 3-6 cm diam, 3-4.5 cm long; sepaloids greenish-yellow, obovate-oblong or obovate-cuneate, to 15 mm long and 12 mm broad, rounded or truncate, but mucronulate; petaloids greenish-yellow, the outer usually with tinge or streak of red, a few obovate-oblanceolate, to 25 mm long, 9-12 mm broad, rounded and mucronulate, essentially entire; filaments ±9 mm long; anthers 2.5-3 mm long; style greenish-yellow, 15-20 mm long, 1.5-2 mm greatest diam (in basal swelling); stigmas apparently 5, nearly 3 mm long, widened upward and lobed; ovary in anthesis strongly tuberculate and spiny; fruit green, turning to light tan or straw, dry at maturity, weakly to strongly tuberculate, with dense spreading spines on upper half, obovoid-turbinate or nearly hemispheric, when mature 1.2-2.5(3) cm long, 1.2-2 cm diam, the umbilicus strongly developed but shallow, the top of ovary flat, the fruit deciduous in late summer or fall; seeds light tan, flat, nearly circular, ±6 mm diam, 2 mm thick; hilum with only a slight notch; cotyledons incumbent.

3a. Opuntia echinocarpa var. echinocarpa. Silver or golden cholla. On sandy or gravelly soil of benches, slopes, mesas, flats, and washes in the desert at 300-1,200(1,700) m (1,000-4,000 or 5,600 ft). Mojavean Desert and (less commonly) Colorado Desert. California at Benton Station, Mono Co., and in Mojave and Colorado Deserts and South Fork Valley, Kern Co.; Nevada from Esmeralda, Nye, and Lincoln Cos. southward; sw Utah near Milford, Beaver Co., and in Washington Co.; Arizona in Mohave, NW Coconino, Yuma, and Maricopa Cos. Mexico in NE Baja California and NW Sonora.

The frequently treelike silvery or golden plants are a distinctive feature of the higher deserts of the western lower basin of the Colorado River. They form conspicuous gray spots above the lower-growing shrubs, and their intricate system of branches stands out in relief.

According to A. A. Nichol, plants of the silver and golden forms remain distinct after being transplanted to a uniform environment.

A preparation by the late John Poindexter indicates the chromosome number (n or 2n) of a specimen (Clark Mt., California, *Wolf 8293*) to be 43 or 44, twice the number found in a similar count of *O. acanthocarpa* var. *coloradensis* from the same place.

Distinctive Characters of the Varieties of **Opuntia echinocarpa**

Character	a. var. **echinocarpa**	b. var. **wolfii**
Stem branching	Intricate	Simple
Larger terminal joints	Not robust, 5-7.5(15) cm long, (1.5)2(2.5) cm diam	Robust, 10-25(38) cm long, 3-4 cm diam
Tubercles	6-9 mm long, ±3-6 mm broad and high	To 20 mm long, 9 mm broad and high
Flower diameter	3-4(6) cm	3.8-5 cm
Fruits	1.2-2.5 cm long, weakly tuberculate	2.5-3 cm long, strongly tuberculate
Altitude	300-1,200(1,700) m (1,000-4,000[5,600] ft)	300-1,200 m (1,000-4,000 ft)
Floristic association	Mojavean Desert (mostly) and Colorado Desert	Colorado Desert (western)

Fig. 255. *Opuntia echinocarpa* var. *echinocarpa*, a branch and two of the characteristic mature, dry fruits. (Robert H. Peebles)

Fig. 254. *Opuntia echinocarpa* var. *echinocarpa* in the Arizona Desert, near Aguila, Maricopa Co., Arizona, showing the occasional miniature tree form of the plant, which tends usually to be shrubby. (*The Native Cacti of California*; and *The Cacti of Arizona*, ed. 3)

Fig. 253. Silver or golden cholla, *Opuntia echinocarpa* var. *echinocarpa*, essentially a shrub, but with a very short trunk, in the Arizona Desert near Aguila, Maricopa Co., Arizona. The plant in the foreground is tobosa grass, *Hilaria mutica*; that in the background is the creosote bush, *Larrea divaricata*.

288

3b. Opuntia echinocarpa var. **wolfii** L. Benson. Sandy or gravelly places or rocky hillsides in the desert and sometimes above, 300-1,200 m (1,000-4,000 ft). On w edge of Colorado Desert. California in Riverside, San Diego, and Imperial Cos. Probably in N Baja California.

The plants are formidable, and each one appears to be a small fortress of thick, strongly spiny branches. The shrub is as big as var. *echinocarpa*, but so much more dense as to seem a different species.

This plant has been confused with O. *echinocarpa* Engelm. & Bigel. var. *parkeri* (Engelm.) Coulter. However, the type specimen of that proposed variety is O. *parryi* Engelm., not this variety, as assumed by Wolf.

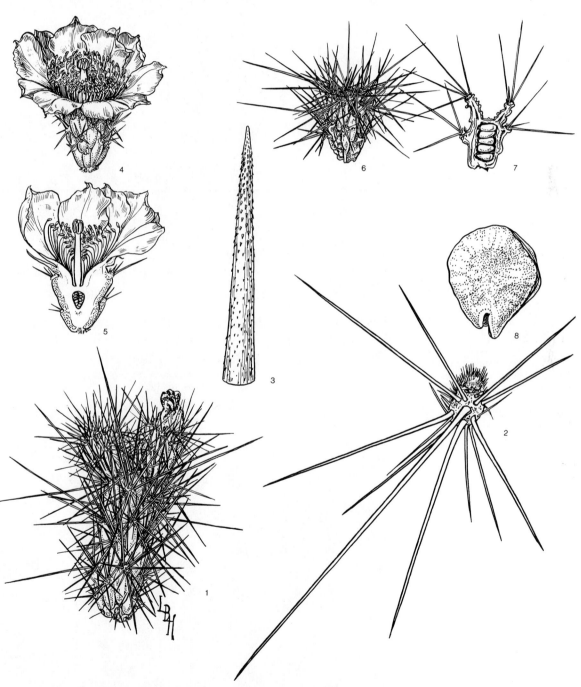

Fig. 256. Silver or golden cholla, *Opuntia echinocarpa* var. *echinocarpa*, ×1.1, except as indicated. *1*, Joint with two immature fruits, ×.9. *2*, Areole with spines, glochids, and felty wool, ×1.7. *3*, Enlarged spine tip, showing the minute barbs, ×7. *4*, Flower. *5*, Flower in longitudinal section. *6*, Fruit, dry at maturity. *7*, Longitudinal section of the mature, dry fruit. *8*, Seed, ×6.

Fig. 257. Silver or golden cholla, *Opuntia echinocarpa* var. *wolfii*, in its natural habitat in the Colorado Desert; Mason Valley, San Diego Co., California. The plant (or plants) branches profusely at ground level but relatively little above. The outlying stems perhaps are fallen ones that have rooted and grown. The barrel cactus is *Ferocactus acanthodes* var. *acanthodes*; the bases of a century plant, *Agave desertii*, and an ocotillo, *Fouquieria splendens*, are at the upper left; the plant in the foreground is brittle bush, *Encelia farinosa*.

Fig. 258. *Opuntia echinocarpa* var. *wolfii*, Rancho Santa Ana Botanic Garden. The very spiny, thickened joints are characteristic of this variety; the short tubercles are characteristic of the species.

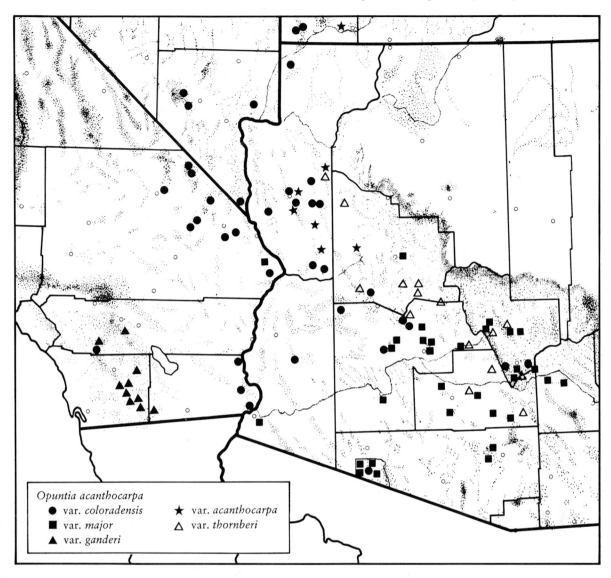

Opuntia acanthocarpa
● var. *coloradensis*   ★ var. *acanthocarpa*
■ var. *major*   △ var. *thornberi*
▲ var. *ganderi*

4. **Opuntia acanthocarpa** Engelmann & Bigelow
Buckhorn cholla

Shrub, arborescent plant, or small tree, 1-3(4) m high; trunk short, usually much less than one-fifth height of plant, to 10-15 cm diam; larger terminal joints 12-50 cm long, 2-3(4) cm diam; tubercles conspicuous, sharply raised and laterally compressed, length 3 to several times width, (12)20-25(50) mm long vertically, ±4.5 mm broad and high; leaves slender, tapering, about as thick as broad, ±12 mm long, ±1.5 mm diam; areoles circular, 5-6 mm diam, 2-4 cm apart; spines tan to reddish-tan or straw-colored or whitish, turning to brown, then to black in age (sheaths conspicuous, straw-colored or rarely silvery, persistent ±1 year), 6-25 per areole, spreading in all directions, straight, the longer 1.2-2.5(4) cm long, basally 0.8-1.2 mm broad, subulate, narrowly linear in cross section, not

strongly barbed; glochids minute; flower 4-5.5 cm diam, 4-6 cm long; sepaloids greenish-yellow or greenish-red, broadly spathulate, to 20 mm long, in upper (expanded area) to 20 mm broad, rounded; petaloids variable in color, usually red, purplish, or yellow, narrowly obovate, 25-40 mm long, to 15 mm broad, rounded, mucronulate, with a few shallow sinuses; filaments 9-12 mm long; anthers to 3 mm long; style 15-20 mm long, 2-3 mm diam; stigmas 5, broad, 3-4.5 mm long; ovary in anthesis spiny; fruit turning to tan or brown, dry at maturity, tuberculate, with (except basally) numerous spreading spines, obovoid-turbinate, 2.5-4 cm long, 1.5-2 cm diam, with deep, cuplike umbilicus, the fruit deciduous in late summer or fall; seeds pale tan or whitish, flattened but irregularly angular (owing to space constraint during development), 5-8 mm long, 3-5 mm broad, 2-3 mm thick.

Distinctive Characters of the Varieties of **Opuntia acanthocarpa**

Character	a. var. coloradensis	b. var. major	c. var. ganderi	d. var. acanthocarpa	e. var. thornberi
Habit	Treelike or sometimes shrubby	Shrubby, sprawling, diffuse	Shrubby or arborescent, robust	Shrubby or arborescent	Shrubby, much-branched, diffuse
Height	1.2-1.8(4) m	0.9-1.5 m	0.9-1.2 m	1.2-1.8 m	0.9-1.5 m
Joints	Relatively few, forming acute angles	Numerous, with many obtuse angles	Few, forming acute angles	Relatively few, forming acute angles	Relatively few, forming acute and obtuse angles
Joint size	15-30 cm long, 2-2.5 cm diam	12-25 cm long, 2-2.5 cm diam	20-50 cm long, 3-4 cm diam	20-50 cm long, ±3 cm diam	25-50 cm long, ±2 cm diam
Tubercles	20-23 mm long, narrow	20-25 mm long, narrow	12-16 mm long, narrow	30-38 mm long, broad	30-50 mm long, narrow
Spine density	Moderate, not obscuring stem	Moderate, not obscuring stem	Dense, obscuring stem	Moderate, not obscuring stem	Sparse, not obscuring stem
Spines per areole	10-12	10-15	15-25	12-20	6-11
Spine length	2.5-4 cm	±2.5 cm	1.2-3 cm	±2.5 cm	1.2-2.5 cm
Spines on fruits	Dense	Dense	Dense	Dense	Dense to sparse or none
Altitude	600-1,300 m (2,000-4,200 ft)	300-900 m (1,000-3,000 ft)	300-900 m (1,000-3,000 ft)	±1,200 m (4,000 ft)	750-1,050 m (2,500-3,500 ft)
Floristic association	Mostly Mojavean Desert (also Sonoran Deserts)	Arizona Desert	Colorado Desert (western) and edge of California Chaparral	Mojavean Desert	Arizona and Mojavean deserts (upper levels)

4a. Opuntia acanthocarpa var. **coloradensis** L. Benson. Buckhorn cholla. On sandy or gravelly soils of benches, slopes of mountains, mesas, flats, and washes in the desert at 600-1,300 m (2,000-4,200 ft). Mojavean (primarily) and Sonoran Deserts. California near Inyokern and occasional in E Mojave Desert and s to E Colorado Desert near Colorado R.; s Nevada in Clark Co.; sw Utah in w Washington Co.; Arizona from Mohave Co. to N Yuma Co. and E in the desert mountains to Yavapai, Gila, w Graham, and sw Pima Cos.

The buckhorn cholla is commonly arborescent or with a very short trunk, and it towers above the lower surrounding desert shrubs. Its long wands tend to be parallel, in contrast to the more divergent branches of O. *echinocarpa*, and the plant is larger. Between Aguila and Congress Junction, Arizona, it forms extensive forests—an attraction for any traveller.

A chromosome preparation by the late John Poindexter indicates the chromosome number (not reduced) of a specimen (Clark Mt., California, *Wolf 8294*) to be 21 or 22, half the number obtained in a similar count of chromosomes in O. *echinocarpa* from the same place.

The variety is named for its habitat, the basin of the lower Colorado River.

Fig. 259. Buckhorn cholla, *Opuntia acanthocarpa* var. *coloradensis,* a typical arborescent plant with flower buds, about 3 m (10 feet) tall; Arizona Desert near Aguila, northwestern Maricopa Co., Arizona. (*The Native Cacti of California*)

Fig. 261. *Opuntia acanthocarpa* var. *coloradensis*, branches showing the elongate tubercles characteristic of the species.

Fig. 262. *Opuntia acanthocarpa* var. *coloradensis*, branch with a flower bud, a flower, and immature fruits. (Robert H. Peebles)

Fig. 260. *Opuntia acanthocarpa* var. *coloradensis*, a shrubby, more spreading plant in the same area as that in Fig. 259, but in the Desert Grassland at the edge of the Arizona Desert.

4b. Opuntia acanthocarpa var. **major** (Engelmann & Bigelow) L. Benson. Sandy soils of flats and washes in the desert at 300-900 m (1,000-3,000 ft). Chiefly Arizona Desert. California near Vidal Junction, Riverside Co.; Arizona from s Yuma Co. to Maricopa, Gila, N Graham, and N Pima Cos. Adjacent N Sonora.

This small variety tends to spread widely, and the branches are more divergent than in var. *coloradensis*. The relatively large shrubs of the Arizona Desert tend to obscure this cholla, and it blends into the vegetation.

The Pima Indians steamed and ate the flower buds.

Fig. 264. *Opuntia acanthocarpa* var. *major*, joints with the characteristic elongate tubercles and a flower, mature dry fruits, and seeds. (Robert H. Peebles)

Fig. 263. Buckhorn cholla, *Opuntia acanthocarpa* var. *major*, about 40 km (25 miles) north of Phoenix, Maricopa Co., Arizona. Despite the name, this is the smallest variety and the one with the most slender joints. The barrel cactus in the distance (right) is *Ferocactus acanthodes* var. *lecontei*; saguaros, *Cereus giganteus*, are at the left.

4c. Opuntia acanthocarpa var. **ganderi** (C. B. Wolf) L. Benson. Gander cholla. Sand and gravel of flats and hillsides in the desert at 300-900 m (1,000-3,000 ft). Colorado Desert and adjacent desert-edge phase of California Chaparral. California along w edge of the desert from Riverside Co. to San Diego and Imperial Cos. Perhaps in adjacent N Baja California.

The plants draw attention from a distance. The compact masses of robust branches with stout brown to gray spines form dense globules among the shrubs of desert hillsides and washes.

Fig. 266. *Opuntia acanthocarpa* var. *ganderi*, young joints still elongating, and bearing leaves beneath the upper tubercles, the leaves on the lower parts of the young joints and on the older joint having fallen away.

Fig. 265. Gander cholla, *Opuntia acanthocarpa* var. *ganderi*, in cultivation in the Rancho Santa Ana Botanic Garden.

4d. Opuntia acanthocarpa var. **acanthocarpa.** Gravelly or sandy soils at upper edge of the desert and in woodland and brush at about 1,200 m (4,000 ft). Mojavean Desert. Utah near Virgin, Washington Co.; Arizona in central and E central Mohave Co. and in sw Yavapai Co. from Hualpai and Cottonwood Mts. to McCloud Mts.

Mature plants are visible from afar. The large arborescent shrubs are thick-branched and formidable even as spiny desert species go. However, they are much larger and more open than those of var. *ganderi* or *O. echinocarpa* var. *wolfii.* More daylight can be seen through them.

A collection from Nevada by J. P. Hester ("just one area in So. Nevada," April 25, 1942, *UC 901707*) is possibly this variety or perhaps a large form of *O. echinocarpa.*

Fig. 268. *Opuntia acanthocarpa* var. *acanthocarpa*, a relatively young plant in the Mojavean Desert at the summit between Burro Creek and Big Sandy Wash, Mohave Co., Arizona.

Fig. 267. Buckhorn cholla, *Opuntia acanthocarpa* var. *acanthocarpa*, relatively young plants in the Mojavean Desert on the lower slopes of Hualpai Mountain, south of Kingman, Mohave Co., Arizona. The large shrubs are one of the desert crucifixion thorns, *Canotia holacantha*, characteristic of the Mojavean Desert.

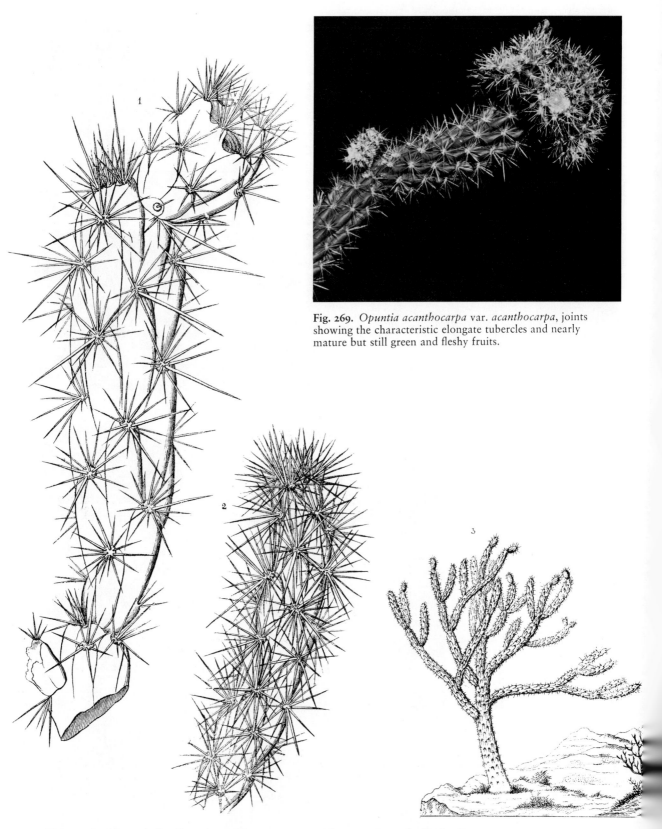

Fig. 269. *Opuntia acanthocarpa* var. *acanthocarpa*, joints showing the characteristic elongate tubercles and nearly mature but still green and fleshy fruits.

Fig. 270. Buckhorn cholla, *Opuntia acanthocarpa* var. *acanthocarpa*, drawn by Paulus Roetter for George Engelmann. After the first collection in 1854, the typical variety of the species was not encountered again in the field until 1941, and for nearly a century the epithet was applied to var. *coloradensis*, which was assumed to be the plant collected at Cactus Pass by J. M. Bigelow on the Pacific Railroad surveying expedition along the present route of the Santa Fe. (See Credits)

4e. Opuntia acanthocarpa var. thornberi

(Thornber & Bonker) L. Benson. Thornber cholla. Rocky or gravelly soils of hillsides and ridges in upper part of the desert, 750-1,050 m (2,500-3,500 ft). Upper edges of Mojavean and (primarily) Arizona Deserts. Arizona in hills of the escarpment below Mogollon Rim from Mohave Co. to Pinal, Gila, and Graham Cos.

The low shrubs are erect to spreading, and a first impression includes this, the greenness of the long joints, and the conspicuous, elongate tubercles not at all obscured by spines.

Fig. 272. *Opuntia acanthocarpa* var. *thornberi*, joints from the plant in Fig. 271, the spines much longer than usual for this variety and probably representing introgression of genes from var. *coloradensis* or var. *major*, both of which occur within a few kilometers of this locality.

Fig. 271. Thornber cholla, *Opuntia acanthocarpa* var. *thornberi*, in the Arizona Desert near Lake Pleasant, north of Phoenix, Maricopa Co., Arizona. Most of the large shrubs in the background are foothill palos verdes, *Cercidium microphyllum*; also in the background are relatively young saguaros, *Cereus giganteus*, and teddy-bear chollas, *Opuntia bigelovii* var. *bigelovii*.

Fig. 273. *Opuntia acanthocarpa* var. *thornberi*, joint with the typical remarkably elongate tubercles and the relatively few and short spines of this variety. The conspicuous feature of most plants of var. *thornberi* is the exposed green of the stems, rather than the masses of spines of the other varieties.

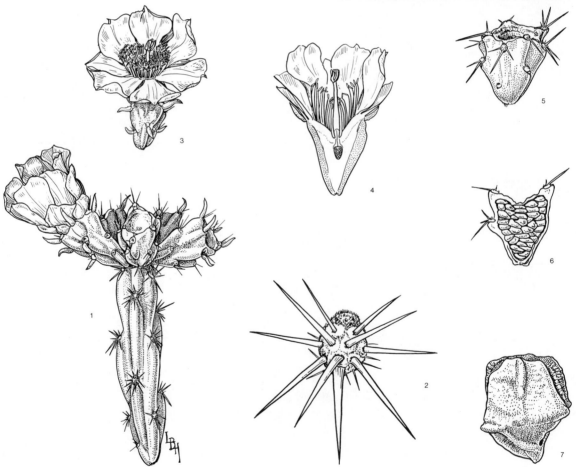

Fig. 274. Thornber cholla, *Opuntia acanthocarpa* var. *thornberi*, ×.75, except as indicated. *1*, Joint with flowers and immature fruits, these still bearing leaves, the spines usually relatively short and not numerous, as here. *2*, Areole with spines, glochids, and wool, ×4.5. *3*, Flower. *4*, Flower in longitudinal section. *5*, Fruit, dry at maturity. *6*, Mature, dry fruit in longitudinal section. *7*, Seed, ×4.

300

5. **Opuntia tunicata** (Lehmann) Link & Otto

Bushy or mat-forming and creeping, 30-60 cm high; trunk ordinarily lacking; main stems numerous and densely branched, the joints either strongly woody or (unlike those of other species in this series) readily detached; larger terminal joints 5-25 cm long, 0.9-3 cm diam; tubercles strongly raised, those on mature joints 12-30 mm long, 4.5-6 mm broad, protruding 3-19 mm; leaves elongate, ovate-acute, 2-3 mm long; areoles ±4.5 mm diam, typically ±2.5 cm apart; spines reddish-brown (the more conspicuous sheaths golden- or yellowish-tan, yellow, or nearly white, thin and papery), about 6-10 per areole, spreading in all directions, straight, the longer 3.8-5 cm long, the largest basally 1-1.5 mm broad (sheaths 1.5-4 mm broad), nearly acicular but somewhat flattened (sheaths flat), barbed; glochids in a small tuft, yellow or brownish, ±1 mm long; flower ±3 cm diam, 4.5-5.5 cm long; sepaloids greenish with yellow border or tinged with red, broader than long to cuneate-oblong or broadly cuneate, 3-12 mm long, 6-9(12) mm broad, truncate or rounded, mucronate, undulate; petaloids yellow, greenish-yellow, or tinged with red, cuneate, apically rounded, 12-20 mm long, 9-12 mm broad, mucronate, undulate; filaments 6 mm long; anthers yellow, ±1.5 mm long; style green to red, 15-20 mm long, 3 mm diam; stigmas 5, 3 mm long, thick; ovary in anthesis tuberculate, with prominent areoles and with glochids ±1.5 mm long, sometimes with spines to 2 cm long; fruit ±3 cm long, ±2.5 cm diam, the umbilicus forming a cup; seeds light tan, irregularly obovate, less than 2.5 mm long, ±2 mm broad, ±1 mm thick.

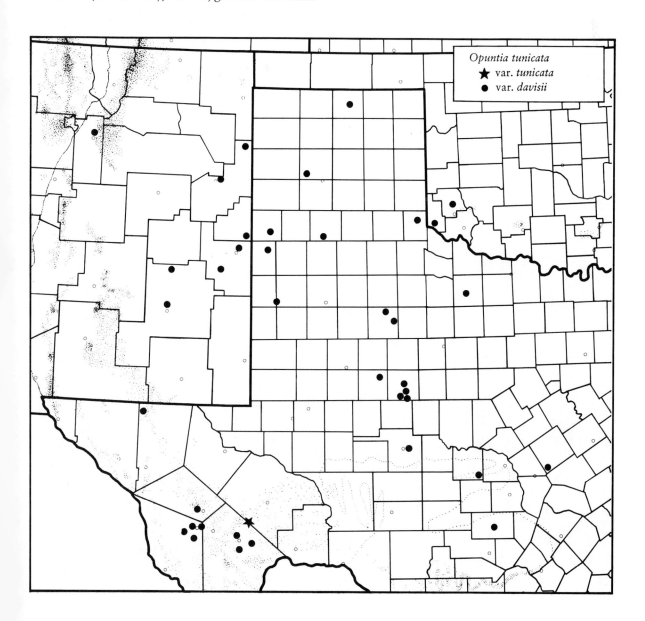

Opuntia tunicata
★ var. *tunicata*
● var. *davisii*

5a. Opuntia tunicata var. **tunicata.** Sheathed cholla, abrojo. Sandy or gravelly soils of hillsides and alluvial fans in the desert at about 1,500 m (5,000 ft) in the U.S. Chihuahuan Desert (in the U.S.). Texas in Glass Mts., Pecos and Brewster Cos., sw of Ft. Stockton. Also Mexico, Cuba, Ecuador, Peru, and Chile.

From a distance the plants in the Glass Mts. look like giant biscuits a meter or more in diameter, and they are conspicuous among the grasses and low shrubs on the hillsides. These are the most compact chollas in the United States, and their barbed spines are among the most effective.

Distinctive Characters of the Varieties of **Opuntia tunicata**

Character	a. var. **tunicata**	b. var. **davisii**
Joints	Not strongly woody, readily detached	Strongly woody, not readily detached
Size of larger terminal joints	Mostly 5-25 cm long, 2.5-3 cm diam	5-15 cm long, 0.9-1.2 cm diam
Tubercles of mature terminal joints	20-30 mm long, ±6 mm broad, protruding 9-19 mm	Mostly 12-15 mm long, 4.5 mm broad, protruding 3 mm
Average length of longest spines	4.4-5 cm	±3.8 cm, some to 5 cm
Spine sheaths	2-4 mm diam, far exceeding diam of spine and therefore loose	1.5-2 mm diam, exceeding diam of spine but less loose
Sheath color	Whitish-tan	Golden-tan
Altitude	±1,500 m (5,000 ft)	600-1,500 m (2,000-5,000 ft)
Floristic association	Chihuahuan Desert	Mostly Great Plains Grassland

Fig. 275. *Opuntia tunicata* var. *tunicata* growing in clumps on an alluvial fan in the Chihuahuan Desert in Mexico. (David Griffiths)

Fig. 276. *Opuntia tunicata* var. *tunicata* in a clump or mat in the Chihuahuan Desert in northern Mexico, the plant with abundant fertile fruits. (David Griffiths)

Fig. 277. *Opuntia tunicata* var. *tunicata* in fruit, showing the large, sheathed spines; outlier of the Glass Mts., Brewster Co., Texas, the only known area of occurrence in the United States.

5b. Opuntia tunicata var. **davisii** (Engelmann & Bigelow) L. Benson. Sandy soils of plains and hills at 600-1,500 m (2,000-5,000 ft). Great Plains Grassland and other grasslands. In E New Mexico on the Llano Estacado; W Texas to Harmon and Greer Cos., Oklahoma, and as far E as hills of E escarpment of Edwards Plateau.

Rare except on the westernmost plains, and not common even there.

These small golden shrubs are conspicuous among the rangeland grasses, where they reach knee or hip height. The barbed spines are both beautiful and memorable.

The roots may be intermittently tuberous (Roswell, New Mexico, *Castetter & Pierce 562, UNM, 2212, UNM, 2212A, UNM*). Cf. Hester, 1939.

6. Opuntia whipplei Engelmann & Bigelow

Bushy, mat-forming, or sometimes erect and shrubby, 30-60 cm (rarely 1.5-2 m) high; stems numerous, erect, arranged compactly, the longer with numerous short lateral branches; larger terminal joints (2.5)7.5-15 cm long, to 1-2 cm diam; tubercles clearly raised, length 1.5-3 times breadth, 2.5-9 mm long, 3-4.5 mm broad, protruding 3-4.5 mm; leaves conical, ±1.5 mm long;

areoles 1.5-2.25 mm diam; spines whitish-pink or pinkish-tan at maturity (sheaths becoming loose and flattening out, conspicuous, white, silvery, light tan, or yellow, usually persistent for a season), spines 4-14 per areole, mostly horizontal or deflexed, straight, the longer 2-2.5(5) cm long, basally to 0.8 mm diam, acicular, elliptic to nearly circular in cross section, not strongly barbed; glochids yellow, more prominent than those of most chollas, 1.5-2.25 mm long; flower 2-3 cm diam, 3-4 cm long; sepaloids yellowish-green, cuneate-obovate, 6-9 mm long, 6-8 mm broad, rounded to nearly truncate, crenate; petaloids pale- or lemon-yellow, narrowly obovate, 10-15 mm long, 6-8 mm broad, acute or obtuse and mucronate, somewhat crenate; filaments ±6 mm long; anthers yellow, 3 mm long; style green or yellowish, 9-12 mm long, 1.5-2 mm diam; stigmas apparently 5, 1.5 mm long; ovary in anthesis with a few slender spines; fruit yellow, fleshy at maturity, strongly tuberculate (except in parasitized fruits), spineless but at first with glochids, obovoid or subglobose, 2-3 cm long, 1.2-1.9(2.2) cm diam, with a deep, cuplike umbilicus (except in parasitized fruits), fruit persistent through winter, not proliferous; seeds pale tan, flattened, ±3 mm long, 2.5-3 mm broad, ±2 mm thick.

Fig. 278. *Opuntia tunicata* var. *davisii* in overgrazed grassland in western Texas or adjacent Mexico. The slender stems contrast with the stout stems of var. *tunicata.* (David Griffiths)

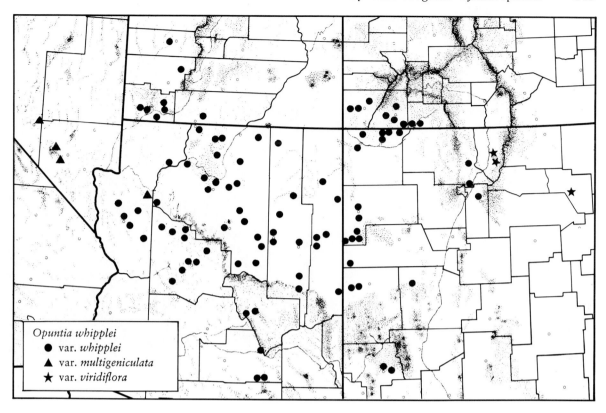

Distinctive Characters of the Varieties of **Opuntia whipplei**

Character	a. var. **whipplei**	b. var. **multigeniculata**	c. var. **viridiflora**
Larger terminal joints	7.5-15 cm long	2.5-5 cm long	5-7 cm long
Tubercle length	3-9 mm, 2-3 times breadth	4.5-6 mm, 1-5 times breadth	±2.5 mm, 3 times breadth
Spine density	Sparse to moderate	Crowded	Moderate
Spines per areole	4-7	10-14	5-7
Color of spine sheaths	White to silvery or sometimes light tan or yellow	Tan to yellowish-pink	Brown
Petaloid color	Pale yellow to lemon-yellow	Light greenish-yellow	Green tinged with red
Altitude	1,350-2,400 m (4,500-8,000 ft)	1,000-1,400 m (3,300-4,700 ft)	1,800-2,100 m (6,000-7,000 ft)
Floristic association	Various deserts, grasslands, and woodlands and edge of forest	Mojavean Desert	Grasslands and Southern Juniper-Pinyon Woodland

6a. Opuntia whipplei var. **whipplei.** Often in deep soils of flats, valleys, plains, and gentle slopes. Chiefly in grasslands at 1,350-2,400 m (4,500-8,000 ft). Great Plains Grassland and edges of Rocky Mountain Montane Forest, Southern Juniper-Pinyon Woodland (fairly common), Navajoan Desert, Mojavean Desert, and Sagebrush Desert. Utah from central Beaver Co. to Washington Co.; sw Colorado from Montezuma Co. to w Archuleta Co.; Arizona from Mohave Co. to Apache Co. and s to Yavapai and Gila Cos. and near Oracle in E Pinal Co.; w New Mexico from San Juan Co. to Rio Arriba and Grant Cos. and collected once in Santa Fe Co.

In most areas this variety is low and mat-forming, making conspicuous cushions 1-2 m in diameter. Elsewhere it is erect, and in rich valley lands it may be 2 m or more in height.

Antelope eat the fruit and young branches.

Fig. 279. *Opuntia whipplei* var. *whipplei,* erect form, which may be as much as 2 m (over 6 feet) high; Mojavean Desert in northern Arizona. (David Griffiths)

Fig. 280. *Opuntia whipplei* var. *whipplei,* evidently a low, spreading plant, but actually one around which sand has collected; the plant has grown as the dune formed, its lower parts being engulfed in the sand and only the tips of the branches receiving light. As the plant grows, sand can be bound at higher and higher levels. Thus, the only exposed joints of the cholla are the new, leafy ones. (Robert H. Peebles)

Fig. 281. *Opuntia whipplei* var. *whipplei,* low, spreading form making large mats in modified Great Plains Grassland on the Navajo Indian Reservation north of The Gap, Coconino Co., Arizona, at about 1,950 m (6,500 feet) elevation. A few of the tuberculate fruits are visible. Often the cacti are nearly covered by grasses, as is the case with the plant in the background, at the left.

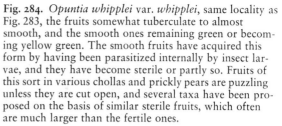

Fig. 284. *Opuntia whipplei* var. *whipplei*, same locality as Fig. 283, the fruits somewhat tuberculate to almost smooth, and the smooth ones remaining green or becoming yellow green. The smooth fruits have acquired this form by having been parasitized internally by insect larvae, and they have become sterile or partly so. Fruits of this sort in various chollas and prickly pears are puzzling unless they are cut open, and several taxa have been proposed on the basis of similar sterile fruits, which often are much larger than the fertile ones.

Fig. 282. *Opuntia whipplei* var. *whipplei*, joints of the plant in Fig. 281, showing the long spines composing conspicuous masses in this form of the species. The tuberculate fruits are characteristic of the species.

Fig. 283. *Opuntia whipplei* var. *whipplei*, sprawling and densely branching plant in the Mojavean Desert at about 1,500 m (5,000 feet) elevation, on the lower slopes of Hualpai Mountain, near Kingman, Mohave Co., Arizona. The plant shows the usual, rather small number of spines per areole and the relatively short tubercles. The tuberculate fruits, normal in this species, turn yellow at maturity. Behind the cactus are banana yuccas, *Yucca baccata*.

Fig. 285. *Opuntia whipplei* var. *whipplei*, ×.6, except as indicated. *1*, Flowering branch. *2*, Fruiting branch. *3*, Areole with spines and glochids, ×1.8. *4*, Flower in longitudinal section. *5*, Stigmas and top of the style enlarged, ×6. *6*, Fruit, this strongly tuberculate and becoming yellow at maturity, ×.9. *7*, Longitudinal section of a fertile fruit, showing the seeds. *8*, Seed enlarged, ×7. *9*, Sterile fruit.

6b. Opuntia whipplei var. **multigeniculata** (Clokey) L. Benson. Rocky and sandy soils of desert slopes at 1,000-1,400 m (3,300-4,700 ft). Mojavean Desert. Nevada on Nevada Test Site in Nye Co. and Charleston (Spring) Mts. NW of Las Vegas, Clark Co.; Utah in Washington Co. (plants perhaps approaching this variety); Arizona in Peach Springs Canyon, Mohave Co.

From a distance the shrubs are inconspicuous among the other low shrubs of the Mojavean Desert hillsides, but from nearby each one is a striking, spiny, irregular mass. It is low and compact, and the very short, thick, spiny joints are crowded into dense clusters.

6c. Opuntia whipplei var. **viridiflora** (Britton & Rose) L. Benson. Hills in grassland or woodland at about 1,800-2,100 m (6,000-7,000 ft).

New Mexico near Santa Fe and in Harding Co.

Probably derived from past interbreeding of *O. whipplei* var. *whipplei* and *O. imbricata*. Currently, var. *whipplei* is known from only one collection in the region where var. *viridiflora* occurs.

New information indicates an unstable population near Santa Fe, and the status of the variety may be dubious.

7. Opuntia spinosior (Engelmann) Toumey
Cane cholla

Shrubs or small trees 1-2(2.5) m high; trunk short, sometimes 22.5 cm diam well above ground level, the branches much longer; larger terminal joints 12.5-30 cm long, 1.5-2.2 cm diam; tubercles remarkably numerous, not more than 10 mm apart, about 5 rows visible from 1 side of stem,

Fig. 286. *Opuntia whipplei* var. *multigeniculata* in the Mojavean Desert at the base of the Charleston Mts., Clark Co., Nevada. This plant exhibits the short, very stout, strongly tuberculate stems and dense spines characteristic of the variety, which is rare and local; a cluster of budding joints, with leaves, grows at the apex of each older joint.

Fig. 287. *Opuntia whipplei* var. *multigeniculata*, another view of the joints.

sharply raised, 9-16(19) mm long, 3 mm broad, protruding 3-6 mm; leaves acicular, slender, nearly terete, somewhat attenuate, 9-12 mm long, to 1.5 mm diam; areoles orbiculate to elliptic, 3-4.5 mm long and broad, typically 6-9 mm apart; spines gray basally, pink toward apices (sheaths dull tan, not conspicuous, falling away during first year), about 10-20 per areole, spreading in all directions, straight, the longer 0.6-1.5 cm long, basally to 0.5 mm diam, acicular, broadly elliptic to circular in cross section, barbed; glochids at first yellowish-tan, minute, ±1 mm long; flower 4.5-5 cm diam, 0.5-6 cm long; sepaloids green with borders the color of petaloids, 4.5-20 mm long, 6-12 mm broad, truncate and mucronate; petaloids usually purple, sometimes red or yellow (rarely white), cuneate, 20-25 mm long, 12-20 mm broad, emarginate with a tooth in notch, crenate-undulate; filaments usually purple, 4.5-6 mm long; anthers yellow, slender, 2.25 mm long; style usually purplish, 12-15 mm long, 3 mm diam; stigmas 5, 3 mm long; ovary in anthesis sparsely short-spiny; fruit bright lemon-yellow, fleshy at maturity, strongly tuberculate, spineless, obovoid, 2.5-4.5 cm long, 2-2.5 cm diam, the umbilicus deep and cuplike, the fruit persistent through winter, not proliferous; seeds light tan, lenticular,

but longer than broad, averaging 4-5 mm long, 3-4 mm broad, 1.5 mm thick.

Deeper soils of flats, valleys, and plains; occasional on hillsides and mountainsides; mostly in grasslands at 600-2,000 m (2,000-6,500 ft). Southwestern Woodland and Chaparral, and occasional at lower edge of Rocky Mountain Montane Forest; typical of Desert Grassland; occurring and sometimes abundant in upper parts of Arizona Desert (especially near Tucson). Arizona from E Maricopa and Gila Cos., s and E to Pima, Santa Cruz, and Cochise Cos.; New Mexico from Valencia Co. to Hidalgo and Luna Cos. and rare eastward to w parts of Socorro, Sierra, and Dona Ana Cos. Mexico in N Sonora and N Chihuahua, but probably not common.

The characteristic mass of gray spines (in winter, after the sheaths have fallen, purplish-gray or purplish-green) sets this plant off from other species. The production of whorls of short joints diverging at right angles from each elongate section of one of the several main stems is also distinctive. The variation of flower color is a temptation to photographers.

Decay of the softer tissues in dead branches of chollas of this type commonly leaves netted hollow cylinders of wood, which are sometimes used

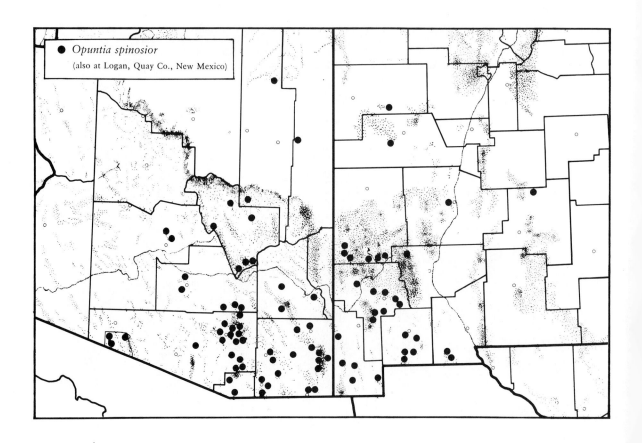

Opuntia spinosior
(also at Logan, Quay Co., New Mexico)

for making canes and other carved novelties.

The fruits turn yellow during the winter, and they may fall away during March. However, usually cattle or native animals have eaten them before then.

Plants growing in New Mexico (e.g., s of Tyrone, Grant Co.) intergrade with *O. imbricata* var. *imbricata*. A plant reported by Peebles from Graham Co., Arizona, was intermediate between *O. spinosior* and *O. imbricata*, differing from the former in having the spines usually fewer than 10 per areole and up to almost 25 mm long and the sheaths conspicuous, basally white, and usually brown apically.

Hybrids between *O. spinosior* and *O. versicolor* are common, especially in the eastern parts of the range of *O. versicolor* (Benson, 1940/50/69); these have been studied intensively by Grant and Grant (1971a, b).

Fig. 288. Cane cholla, *Opuntia spinosior,* in the transition from Arizona Desert to Desert Grassland at the base of the Graham (Pinaleno) Mts., Graham Co., Arizona. Wood (pack) rats have constructed a maximum-security nest from branches of the cholla.

Fig. 289. *Opuntia spinosior,* an arborescent individual in the area of Fig. 288, short trunks being common. Young plants of the soapweed or palmilla, *Yucca elata,* are at left and right.

Fig. 291. *Opuntia spinosior*, old and young joints, the latter with leaves. (David Griffiths)

Fig. 292. *Opuntia spinosior*, relatively young plant with the strongly tuberculate, yellow, mature fruits. (Homer L. Shantz)

Fig. 290. *Opuntia spinosior*, with the spreading and pendulous joints characteristic of the species but more apparent in some plants than in others. (Homer L. Shantz; from *The Cacti of Arizona*; and from *Arizona Cacti*)

312

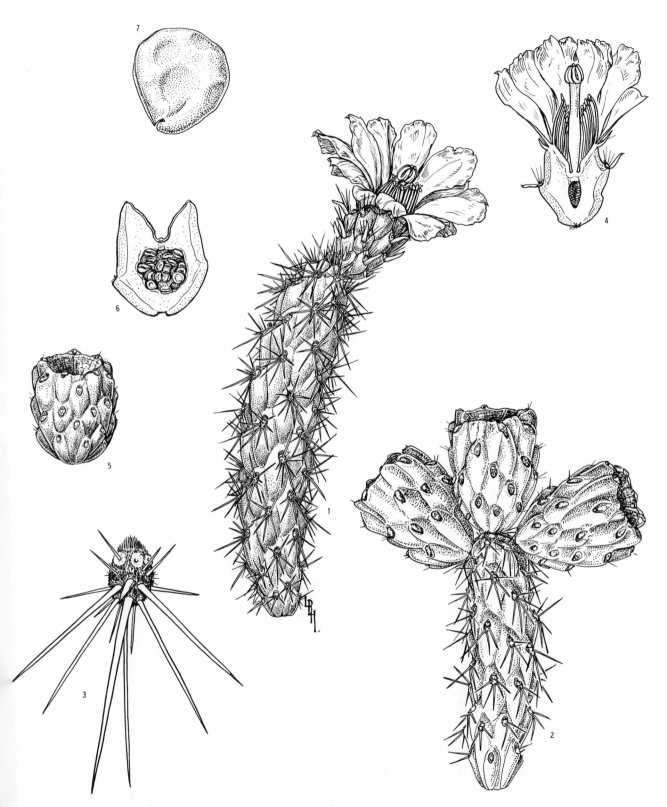

Fig. 293. Cane cholla, *Opuntia spinosior*, ×.9, except as indicated. *1*, Mature joint with a flower. *2*, Joint with tuberculate, yellow fruits. *3*, Areole with spines, glochids, and woolly felt, ×5. *4*, Flower in longitudinal section. *5*, Fruit, showing the tubercles and the deep cup or umbilicus at the apex. *6*, Fruit in longitudinal section. *7*, Seeds, ×5; the seed at the left shows the cordlike ridge along the margin, beyond the embryo.

313

8. Opuntia imbricata (Haworth) DeCandolle
Tree cholla, coyonostole

Arborescent plant, small tree, or (sometimes) thicket-forming shrub, usually 1-2 m high; trunk short, the branches much longer; larger terminal joints commonly 12.5-38 cm long, 2-3 cm diam; tubercles few (compared with *O. spinosior*) but exceedingly prominent, very sharply raised, 3-4 rows visible from 1 side of stem, 2-3.5 cm long, to 4.5-9 mm broad, protruding 6 mm; leaves conical-cylindroid, to 15 mm long, 1.5 mm diam; areoles elliptic, 4.5-6 mm long, typically 12-20 mm apart; spines red or pink (silvery in var. *argentea* of the Big Bend region, Texas), the sheaths dull tan, papery, persistent ±1 year, the spines ±10-30 per areole, spreading in all directions, straight, the longer 1.2-3 cm long, basally ±0.5 mm broad, nearly acicular but somewhat flattened, narrowly elliptic in cross section, strongly barbed (less so in *O. spinosior* and only slightly so in other species of this series); glochids yellow, minute, ±1 mm long; flower 5-7.5 cm diam, to 5-6 cm long; sepaloids green with reddish-purple edges, cuneate to cuneate-oblong, 5-20 mm long, 5-15 mm broad, truncate to somewhat rounded; petaloids reddish-purple, narrowly obovate, 25-40 mm long, 12-20 mm broad, apically broadly rounded, entire to somewhat crenate-undulate; filaments purplish-green, ±6 mm long; anthers yellow, 2 mm long; style green and purple, usually 15-25 mm long, to 3 mm diam; stigmas 7-8, 3-3.5 mm long, rather slender; ovary in anthesis bearing long, slender, deciduous spines; fruit yellow, fleshy at maturity, strongly tuberculate, the tubercles raised as much as 5.5 mm, spineless, obovoid, 2.5-4.5 cm long, 2-3 cm diam,

Fig. 295. *Opuntia imbricata* var. *imbricata*, with the strongly tuberculate fruits, these yellow at maturity. (David Griffiths; see Credits)

Fig. 294. Tree cholla, *Opuntia imbricata* var. *imbricata*, in cultivation, showing the massive, elongate tubercles of the joints. (David Griffiths)

the umbilicus deep and cuplike, the fruit persistent through winter, only rarely proliferous; seeds light tan, lenticular to somewhat irregular, 3 mm diam, 1.5 mm thick.

The plant is usually a miniature tree with an openly branched, rounded crown. The purple or reddish suffusion of the basically dark green branches is striking, especially in cold weather or during drought.

In southwestern New Mexico, flower color is variable, and forms may have perianth colors intermediate between those of this species and those of *O. spinosior*, with which *O. imbricata* intergrades.

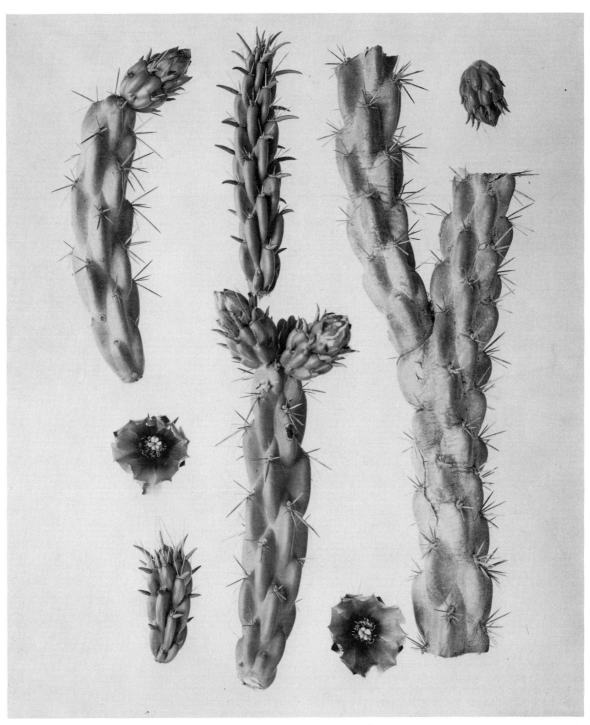

Fig. 296. *Opuntia imbricata* var. *imbricata*, older joints and young ones with leaves, flower buds, and flowers. (David Griffiths)

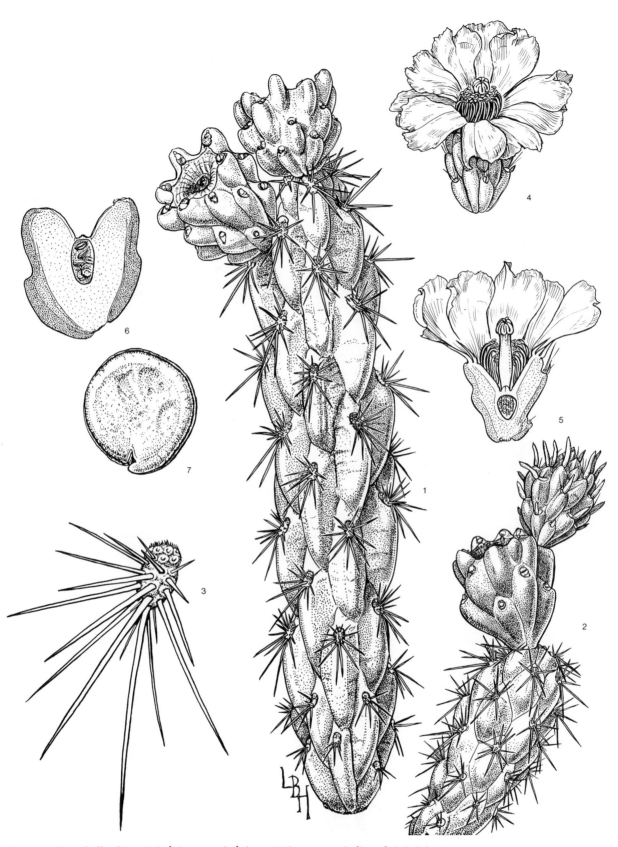

Fig. 297. Tree cholla, *Opuntia imbricata* var. *imbricata*, ×.9, except as indicated. *1, 2,* Joints with fruits, the apical cup or umbilicus of each deep, the sides strongly tuberculate, the surface yellow; the branch of 2 bears a proliferous fruit (one growing from another, a rare occurrence in this species), and the flower bud growing from it bears leaves. *3,* Areole with spines, minute glochids, and felty wool, ×3.5. *4,* Flower. *5,* Flower in longitudinal section. *6,* Fruit in longitudinal section, this one with relatively few seeds. *7,* Seed, ×6.

316

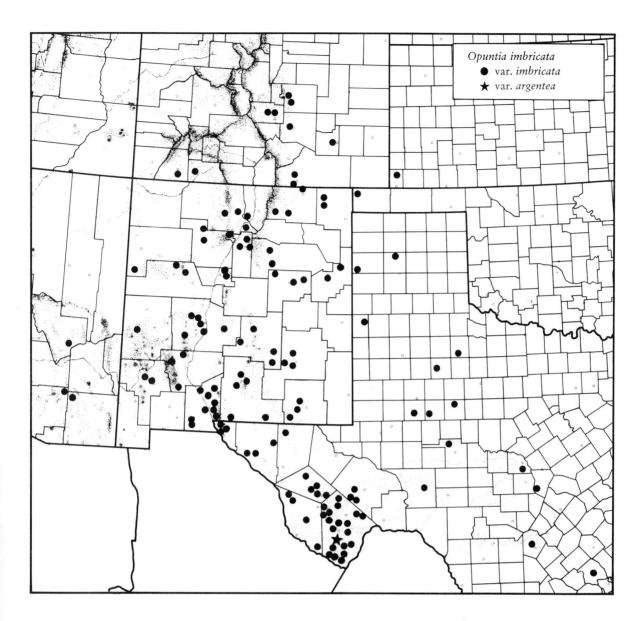

Distinctive Characters of the Varieties of **Opuntia imbricata**

Character	a. var. **imbricata**	b. var. **argentea**
Habit	Arborescent plant or tree, or rarely shrubby and forming thickets	Small erect shrub, often forming thickets
Height	1-2(3) m	To 1.2 m, but usually less
Larger terminal joints	12-38 cm long, ±2-3 cm diam, not glaucous	10-20 cm long, 1.5-3.8 cm diam, relatively more stout, glaucous
Tubercles	2-3.5 cm long, set moderately close together	±2 cm long, set close together
Spines per areole	10-30	10-20
Spine color	Red or pink	Silvery at maturity
Altitude	1,200-1,800 m (4,000-6,000 ft)	600-700 m (2,000-2,400 ft)
Floristic association	Great Plains Grassland; Southwestern Oak Woodland and Chaparral; higher Chihuahuan Desert	Chihuahuan Desert

8a. Opuntia imbricata var. imbricata. Gravelly or sandy soils of hills, flats, valleys, plains, and washes, mostly in grassland at 1,200-1,800 m (4,000-6,000 ft). Great Plains Grassland, Southwestern Woodland and Chaparral, and higher parts of Chihuahuan Desert. Colorado along Front Range and foothills of Rocky Mts. and on w portion of the plains from Colorado Springs s, rare w of Continental Divide in La Plata and Archuleta Cos.; Arizona in se Gila Co. and along San Pedro R. in ne Pima and nw Cochise Cos.; New Mexico, common from Rio Arriba Co. to Union Co. and s to Grant, Luna, and Eddy Cos.; Kansas at Richfield; Oklahoma near Kenton in Cimarron Co.; w Texas and e of Edwards Plateau. In n and central Mexico.

Disjunct occurrence west of the Rio Grande Valley on the southern edge of Colorado, in northwestern New Mexico (new evidence, Housely, 1974), and along the eastern edge of Arizona is due to cultivation by some Indian tribes for blocking access to cliff dwellings; for food from the fruits, buds, and young branches; and for ceremonial purposes in hardening warriors. The plants have persisted for two to several centuries on old ruins of the mountain retreats and habitations of the Jemez Indians, even though the abandoned sites occur in the Rocky Mountain Montane Forest at 1,800-2,400 m (6,200-7,950 ft), well above the normal altitudes for the cholla and for the more xeric floristic and ecological associations normal for the cactus. The areas of habitation have remained as disturbed sandy spots with basic soils unlike the acid types in the surrounding yellow-pine forest and unfavorable to forest plants, including the seedlings of *Pinus ponderosa* (Housely, *ibid.*).

The small trees stand high above the rangeland grasses, and frequently they may form an open miniature woodland an acre or more in extent. Contact with the spines of this plant is particularly painful.

8b. Opuntia imbricata var. argentea Anthony. Deep soils of mesquite thickets of bottomlands and washes in the desert at 600-700 m (2,000-2,400 ft). Chihuahuan Desert. Texas in Brewster Co. on n and e slopes of Mariscal Mt. and w of Solis Ranch, Big Bend National Park, near the Rio Grande s of Chisos Mts. Perhaps in adjacent Mexico.

9. Opuntia versicolor Engelmann
Staghorn cholla

Arborescent plant or small tree, or sometimes a widely spreading low shrub, 1-2.5(4.5) m high; trunk short, the branches much longer; larger terminal joints dull- or lead-green, often elongate, mostly 12.5-35 cm long, 1.5-2 cm diam; tubercles fairly prominent, length 3-5 times breadth, 15-25 mm long, ±4.5 mm broad, protruding 1.5-3(4.5) mm; leaves conic-cylindroid, stout, to 19 mm long, to 3 mm diam; areoles elliptic, 3 mm long, typically 12-15 mm apart; spines reddish or basally gray or apically yellow (sheaths inconspicuous, grayish or yellowish, deciduous within a few months), spines 7-10 per areole, spreading in all directions, straight, the longer 0.6-1.5 cm long, basally ±0.4 mm diam, acicular, broadly elliptic to orbiculate in cross section, not strongly barbed; glochids yellowish-tan, ±1 mm long; flower 3-5.5 cm diam, 3-4 cm long; sepaloids obovate-acuminate, 3-20 mm long, 6-12 mm broad, truncate, mucronulate, undulate; petaloids red, lavender to magenta or rose-purple, yellow, green, bronze, brown, or orange (hence the name of the species), 20-25 mm long, 10-15 mm broad, truncate to rounded, mucronate, undulate; filaments 6 mm long, green to red, lavender, purple, or chocolate; anthers 1.5 mm long, yellow; style white or colored like perianth, 12-15 mm long, 3 mm diam; stigmas 6-10, 3 mm long, stout; ovary in anthesis sometimes with a few spines; fruit green, usually tinged with purple, lavender, or red, fleshy at maturity, not strongly tuberculate, usually spineless, obovoid, (2)2.5-4(4.5) cm long, ±2 cm diam, the umbilicus shallow, the fruit persistent more than 1 year, some fruits proliferous (i.e., with flowers and fruits of later seasons developed from fruit areoles, thus forming short chains of 2 or 3 fruits); seeds light tan, obovate to irregular, 3-5 mm long, 2.5-4 mm broad, 3 mm thick. Note: According to Johnson (1918), fruit proliferation in this species is due at least sometimes and perhaps always to parasitism by the cactus fly.

Deeper sandy soils of canyons, washes, and well-watered areas of flats and valleys in the desert at 600-900 m (2,000-3,000 ft). Arizona Desert. Arizona in Gila Co. and in Pinal and e Pima Cos. (Baboquivari Valley to Santa Cruz R. Valley); most abundant in Comobabi Mts. on Papago Indian Reservation and in foothills near Tucson; near Benson, Cochise Co. Common in adjacent N Sonora.

Opuntia versicolor is a miniature lead-gray-green and purple tree. The trunk is gray, and the slender branches are striking for the purple tinge. During the spring the bright flowers are like roses on the spiny branches.

Hybridizes with *O. spinosior.*

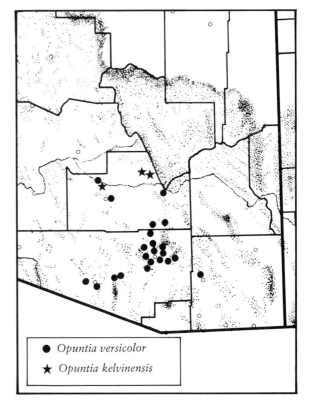

● *Opuntia versicolor*
★ *Opuntia kelvinensis*

Fig. 298. Staghorn cholla, *Opuntia versicolor*, an arborescent plant growing near Tucson, Pima Co., Arizona.

Fig. 299. *Opuntia versicolor*, old joints, flower buds, flowers, and (at upper left) young joints with leaves. (David Griffiths)

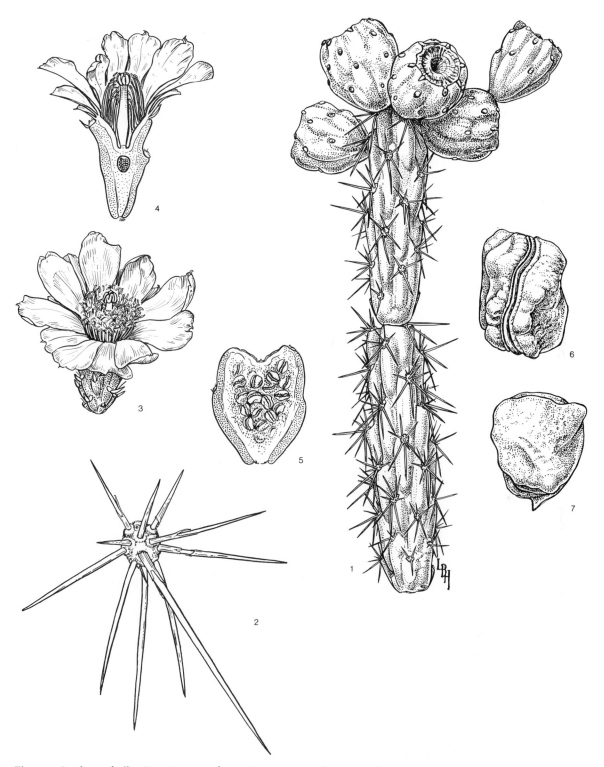

Fig. 300. Staghorn cholla, *Opuntia versicolor*, ×.9, except as indicated. *1*, Mature joints with fruits, the fruits becoming proliferous because new ones develop from the sides of older ones. *2*, Areole with spines, only minute glochids, and wool, ×3.5; the sheaths of the spines visible in various states of separation. *3*, Flower. *4*, Flower in longitudinal section. *5*, Fruit in longitudinal section. *6*, Seed in edge view, showing the cordlike margin beyond the area covering the embryo, ×6. *7*, Seed in side view, ×6.

10. Opuntia kelvinensis V. & K. Grant

Shrub with ±3 stems or with short basal trunk, usually 1.25-2 m high, intricately branched; larger terminal joints rather stout, 6-10 cm long, 2.5-3.8(5) cm diam; tubercles ± twice as long as broad, 12-20 mm long, 6-9 mm broad, protruding 6-9 mm; spines moderately dense on joint, pale pink to gray, (4)5-9 per areole, length variable, the longest 1.9-2.5 cm long; flower ±5 cm diam; petaloids few, usually pink or pale purple; stigma yellow; other flower characters not available; fruit green or green tinged with yellow, fleshy at maturity, somewhat tuberculate, the umbilicus relatively shallow, some fruits proliferous but forming chains of only 2 or 3; seeds few, the ovules mostly abortive.

Hills, ridges, and washes in the desert at 400-925 m (1,300-2,100 ft). Arizona Desert. Arizona in Pinal Co. along Gila R. near Sacaton and from below Kelvin E to above Kearney; Pima Co. near Tucson.

The characters of these populations are intermediate between those of *O. spinosior* and those of *O. fulgida,* either or both of which may occur intermingled with *O. kelvinensis.* A hybrid origin for the species was suggested by Peebles (1936), who pointed out that the tuberculate fruits and the apical cup or umbilicus of the fruit resembled the characters of *O. spinosior,* whereas the small number of petaloids, the compact crown of the plant, and the stoutness of the branches of some plants are characters similar to those of *O. fulgida* var. *mamillata* (cf. Benson, 1940/50/69).

Plants of this type were collected first near Tucson (*Toumey,* Nov. 20, 1899, *US*). Photographs of others were obtained by Peebles from the area along the Gila R. in Pinal Co., Arizona, near Sacaton (*SF 342, Ariz, Pom,* an unnumbered collection, *Pom,* both Pomona College specimens from the garden of the U.S. Field Station at Sacaton; *Peebles SF 8725, Ariz*). The Sacaton plants are intermediate in joint diameter, spine length and

Fig. 301. *Opuntia kelvinensis,* a name applied to natural populations selected from hybrid swarms derived from interbreeding of *O. versicolor* and *O. fulgida* and forming an incipient species. Note the drooping fruit-bearing branches, a character probably derived from *O. fulgida,* and the only slightly proliferous fruits, showing the genetic influence of *O. versicolor.* (Robert H. Peebles; see Credits)

color, fruit color, and ability to produce chains of fruits (of the type found in O. *fulgida*). After Peebles's death, the writer pressed specimens (mentioned above, *Pom*) from the garden at Sacaton in order to preserve additional material of this hybrid population.

The recent extensive studies of V. & K. Grant, "Dynamics of Clonal Microspecies in Cholla Cactus" (1971a), indicate several clonal microspecies, each composed of sterile interspecific hybrids maintained chiefly by asexual reproduction but probably with some sexual reproduction. These are derivatives of O. *spinosior* and O. *fulgida*. Two clones are thought to be F_1 hybrids; others appear to have been derived from later generations. Grant and Grant recognized that not all minor phenomena of population biology can be recognized in formal plant taxonomy by naming species, and that the procedure to be followed is a matter of individual judgment. O. *kelvinensis*, the name for the population series as a species, was applied to the complex of clones as a group. This, of course, raises the question of the status of the species. The problem applies to other cases, *e.g.* that of O. *nicholii* (sp. 27), whose status is of about the same degree of certainty.

Fig. 304. *Opuntia kelvinensis*, joint with proliferous fruits. (Robert H. Peebles; see Credits)

Fig. 302. *Opuntia kelvinensis*, a young plant grown from an areole of a fallen fruit (at bottom), the areole being a vegetative bud in the wall or floral cup investing and adnate with ovary. This is an example of apomixis, or asexual reproduction simulating sexual reproduction. (*Plant Taxonomy, Methods and Principles*)

Fig. 303. *Opuntia kelvinensis*, joints bearing fruits; at the right, a flower and flower bud. The joints are tuberculate, as in O. *spinosior*, and proliferous, as in O. *fulgida* var. *fulgida*. (Robert H. Peebles; see Credits)

11. Opuntia prolifera Engelmann
Coastal cholla

Small trees or arborescent chollas, usually 1-2.5 m high, the crown irregular, dense or open; trunk 30-60 cm long, 5-10 cm diam, branched and re-branched several times, the branches longer than trunk; larger terminal joints dark green, elongate-ellipsoid, 7.5-14 cm long, (3)4-5 cm diam, readily detached, then rooting (the principal method of reproduction), not woody during first year of growth; tubercles mammillate, remarkably large, 12-20 mm long, 4.5-6 mm broad, protruding ±4.5 mm; leaves narrowly conical, 3 mm long; areoles nearly circular, 3-4 mm diam, typically 5-9 mm apart; spines moderately dense on joints, reddish-brown or in age dark gray with yellow-ish tips (sheaths yellowish to tannish or rust-colored, separating during first year of development), (2)6-12 spines per areole, spreading in all directions, straight, the longer 1.2-3 cm long, basally 0.5 mm diam, acicular, elliptic in cross section, not barbed; glochids yellow to tan, in upper part of areole, 1.5-3 mm long; flower ±2.5 cm diam, 2.5-3 cm long; sepaloids green with magenta to reddish-purple borders, nearly square or a little broader than long, to ±6 mm long, slightly broader apically, truncate and mucronate; petal-oids magenta to reddish-purple, narrowly obo-vate, ±12 mm long, ±6 mm broad, rounded, and mucronate or mucronulate, slightly deltoid-cren-ulate; filaments to 6 mm long; anthers yellow, 1.5 mm long; style narrowly obconic, ±12 mm long, 3 mm diam; stigmas 5, 2 mm long, thick; ovary in anthesis sometimes spiny (1 to several spines per areole); fruit green, usually sterile, fleshy at ma-turity, smooth or somewhat tuberculate, globose or broadly obovoid, 2-3 cm diam and length (in later years obovoid, to 5.5 cm long, 4.5 cm diam), the umbilicus rather shallow, fruit persistent for 2 to several years, proliferous, forming branched

Fig. 305. Coastal cholla, *Opuntia prolifera*, many young and a few older plants growing in a disturbed phase of the California Chaparral that has not been burned for a number of years.

chains 2-4 fruits long; seeds (rarely present) ellipsoid, ±5 mm long, ±4 mm broad, ±2.5 mm thick, with raised caruncles.

Fine soils of hills and flats along seacoast at low elevations. Insular Association and California Chaparral. California on Santa Rosa, Santa Cruz, Anacapa, San Nicolas, Santa Catalina, and San Clemente islands (cf. Hoffman, 1932), and on s mainland near ocean from Ventura southward; rarely inland as far as San Fernando and Fallbrook. Mexico on Baja California coast at least as far s as Rosario; Guadalupe Island.

The species forms dense lead-gray-green thickets on ocean bluffs or in valleys or on low hills along the coast. Sometimes large individuals form solitary trees, but usually they are surrounded by younger plants grown from detached joints.

In 1876 J. C. Parker opened 100 fruits, finding only two seeds, both in one fruit (specimen at Missouri Botanical Garden). For a discussion of vegetative and apomictic reproduction in this species, see pp. 94-95.

At San Diego this species hybridizes with O. *parryi* var. *serpentina*.

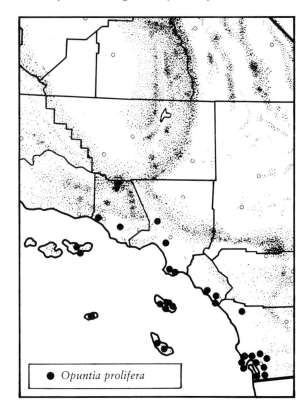

● *Opuntia prolifera*

Fig. 306. *Opuntia prolifera*, joints and fruits, these usually proliferous and forming chains of two to four fruits through growth of new flowers, then fruits, in the areoles of the old fruits. Young flower buds are emerging from several of the fruits at the lower right.

Fig. 307. *Opuntia prolifera*, joints with fruits, the latter becoming proliferous during later years and forming short chains of up to three or four fruits. (David Griffiths)

Fig. 308. *Opuntia prolifera*, old and young joints, the latter with leaves. (David Griffiths)

12. Opuntia fulgida Engelmann
Jumping cholla

Small trees or sometimes arborescent plants, usually 1-3.5(4.5) m high; trunk 30-60(90) cm high, branched and rebranched several times, the branches longer than trunk; larger terminal joints light green, cylindroid or narrowly ellipsoid, 5-15 cm long, 3-5 cm diam, easily detached, then rooting (the principal method of reproduction), not woody during first year of growth; tubercles mammillate, large, 12-22 mm long, 6-9 mm broad, protruding 4.5-9 mm; areoles elliptic, ±4.5 mm long, typically 9-12 mm apart; spines either dense and conspicuous and tending to obscure joint or more rarely (var. *mamillata*) sparse, pink or reddish-brown (the sheaths in both varieties loose, of markedly greater diameter than spines, conspicuous, deciduous after about 1 year), spines (2)6-12 per areole, spreading in all directions, straight, the longer (0.6)2-3 cm long, basally 0.5-0.7 mm broad, acicular to somewhat subulate, elliptic to subtriangular in cross section, barbed; glochids straw-colored, few, to 2 mm long; flower ±2 cm diam, 2-2.5 cm long; sepaloids green, marginally tinged with pink, oblong-semicircular to narrowly oblong, 3-6 mm long, 3 mm broad, obtuse or rounded and mucronate, marginally scarious and minutely toothed; petaloids pink or sometimes white with lavender streaks, few (±5-8), cuneate or cuneate-oblong, 6-9 mm long, 6-9 mm broad, apically rounded and minutely denticulate; filaments white to pink, 4.5 mm long; anthers 1 mm long; style 9 mm long, 1.5 mm diam; stigmas 5, 1.5 mm long; ovary in anthesis large, usually 1.2-2 cm diam, spineless; fruit green (usually sterile), fleshy at maturity, smooth, obovoid, without spines, 2.5-3 cm long the first year but continuing to grow, 2-2.5 cm diam, the umbilicus not deep, the fruit persisting to 22+ years, proliferous, forming long branched chains (adding 1 new fruit each year); seeds light tan or yellowish, irregular to obovate, ±4.5 mm long, 3 mm broad, 1.5-3 mm thick.

The small branches are attached lightly, and they fall readily. On the ground they root and propagate the species vegetatively. Asexual reproduction may arise similarly from either sterile or fertile fallen fruits. However, fruits fall less frequently. The fruit tends to remain attached to the plant, and the next flowering season new flowers develop from the areoles of the floral cup.

As a result, the new fruit or fruits will remain attached to the old. This is repeated many times until the branching chains represent many flowering seasons. The fruits in the chains often are sterile, but they may be fertile. According to Johnson (1918), the seeds remain viable no matter how many years the fruits persist on the plants, and even after the fruits have fallen and taken root. The number of seeds in a fruit may be as many as 100-200. The seeds do not germinate in the fruit, and, according to Johnson, even seeds with chipped coats do not germinate in a medium obtained from the fruits as frequently as they do on moist soil or filter paper; hence he inferred that an inhibiting substance is present. The fruit on the plant enlarges by additions from the cambium of the floral cup. Occasionally a bud of the attached fruit develops into a vegetative branch. For a discussion of vegetative and apomictic reproduction in this species, see pp. 94-95.

12a. Opuntia fulgida var. fulgida. Sandy soils of valleys, plains, mesas, washes, and low hills (sometimes on steeper and more rocky hillsides) in the desert at 300-900(1,350) m (1,000-3,000 or 4,500 ft). Arizona Desert and common almost throughout the Desert Grassland. In s Arizona from Bill Williams R. in N Yuma Co. and from Maricopa Co. SE to lower parts of Gila Co. and s to Pima and NW Cochise Cos.; near upper Gila R. in Graham Co., Arizona, and Hidalgo Co., New Mexico. Mexico in Sonoran Desert as far s as Sinaloa.

The jumping cholla is a magnificent feature of the Arizona Desert. The weird yellowish-straw-colored trees are, as described originally by Schott for Engelmann, ". . . often visible for several miles when the sun strikes the glistening sheaths of their spines." From a distance each plant looks like a haystack on a post. From nearby the dangling clusters of proliferous fruits are reminiscent of clusters of large lumpy grapes.

This variety once formed extensive orchardlike forests. The best stand still remaining is on U.S. 80 between Florence and Tucson north of the Santa Catalina Mts.; but unfortunately, large parts of it were destroyed by fire some years ago. Another forest, along Wilmot Rd. in Tucson, was destroyed in 1940 to make room for a military airfield.

12b. Opuntia fulgida var. **mamillata** (Schott) Coulter. Sandy or gravelly soils of plains, hills, and washes at 300-750 m (1,000-2,500 ft). Arizona Desert and Desert Grassland. Arizona in Pinal and Pima Cos. Mexico in adjacent Sonora.

Var. *mamillata* is a predominantly green, low, squatty tree, much lower and spreading proportionately much farther than var. *fulgida*. The most obvious feature is the green, tuberculate branches, and the spines are not conspicuous.

This variety often occurs with var. *fulgida*, and the few individuals are maintained as separate populations by the asexual reproduction of both. In some areas the dominant or exclusive type. In Arizona the range of this variety is discontinuous but within the range of var. *fulgida*.

Distinctive Characters of the Varieties of **Opuntia fulgida**

Character	a. var. **fulgida**	b. var. **mamillata**
Height	2-3.5(4.5) m	1-1.5 m
Younger joints	Not markedly weak or drooping, with considerable woody tissue after first year	Weak and drooping, with almost no woody tissue for several years
Tubercles	12-16 mm long, 6 mm broad, protruding ±4.5-6 mm	15-22 mm long, 6-9 mm broad, protruding 6-9 mm
Spines per areole	±6-12	2-6
Spine form	Stout and conspicuous, dense and obscuring joint	Slender and inconspicuous, sparse and not obscuring joint
Spine length	2-3 cm	±0.6-1.2(3) cm
Altitude	300-900(1,350) m (1,000-3,000 or 4,500 ft)	300-750 m (1,000-2,500 ft)
Floristic association	Arizona Desert, Desert Grassland	Arizona Desert, Desert Grassland

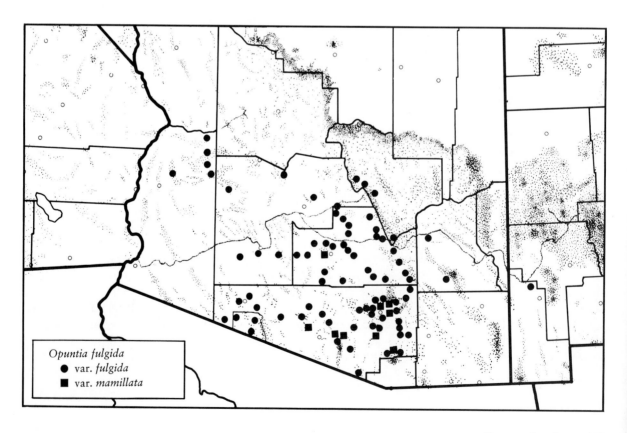

Opuntia fulgida
● var. *fulgida*
■ var. *mamillata*

Text continued on p. 335

Fig. 309. Jumping cholla, *Opuntia fulgida* var. *fulgida*, portion of a forest in miniature, once covering many acres of the Arizona Desert on the site of Davis-Monthan airfield near Tucson, Pima Co., Arizona; photograph taken prior to 1940. (R. B. Streets; from *The Cacti of Arizona*)

Fig. 310. *Opuntia fulgida* var. *fulgida*, a parent tree in the Arizona Desert near Tucson, Pima Co., Arizona, surrounded by young plants that have sprouted from fallen joints. (J. G. Brown; from *The Cacti of Arizona*)

Fig. 312. *Opuntia fulgida* var. *fulgida*, the branch tips weighted heavily with great clusters of proliferous fruits formed by a number of years of growth of new flowers and fruits from the areoles of the older ones; southeast of Florence, Pinal Co., Arizona.

Fig. 311. *Opuntia fulgida* var. *fulgida*, trunk, showing persistent areoles and spines of many years earlier. (Frank P. McWhorter)

Fig. 313. *Opuntia fulgida* var. *fulgida*, dangling short branches bent downward with the weight of fruit chains. The branching pattern of the fruit clusters is similar to that formed by the budding of yeast cells. (Frank P. McWhorter)

330

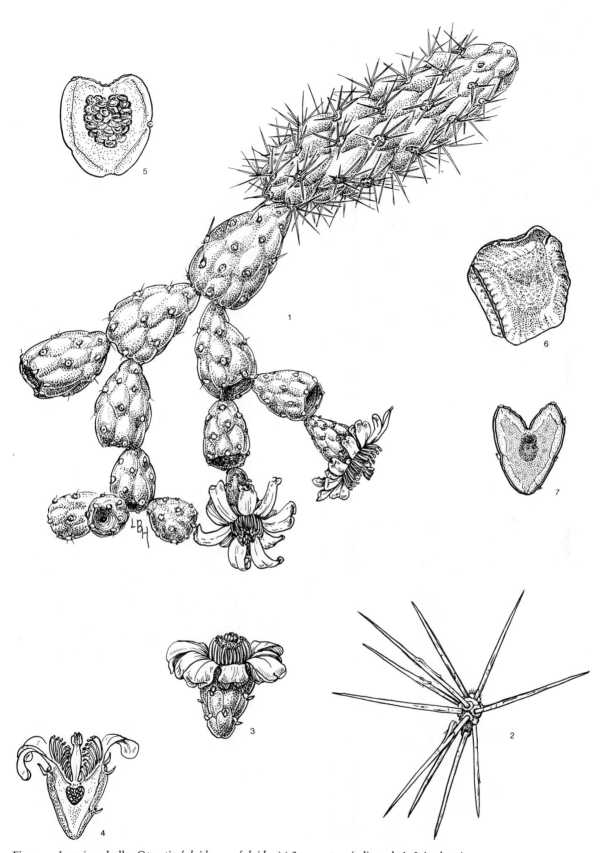

Fig. 314. Jumping cholla, *Opuntia fulgida* var. *fulgida*, ×.3, except as indicated. *1*, Joint bearing a branched chain of fruits and two flowers. *2*, Areole with spines, small glochids, and wool, ×2. *3*, Flower. *4*, Flower in longitudinal section. *5*, Fruit in longitudinal section. *6*, Seed, ×5. *7*, Sterile fruit, the type most common in the branching chains, this ultimately falling to the ground and rooting like a vegetative joint.

Fig. 315. *Opuntia fulgida* var. *mamillata* in Desert Grassland in southeastern Arizona, soon after 1900, with the characteristic low, spreading, partly drooping crown of this variety and with many drooping branches bearing clusters of fruits. The plant was about 3 m (10 feet) high and 5 m (16–17 feet) in diameter, and it obscured all but one rear wheel of a wagon or cart. (David Griffiths; see Credits)

Fig. 316. *Opuntia fulgida* var. *mamillata* on the Papago Indian Reservation east of the Baboquivari (Quinlan) Mts., Pima Co., Arizona. The characteristically weak, thick, drooping branches, prominent tubercles, and relatively inconspicuous spine clusters are characteristic. The plant is not old, and the chains of fruit are only two or three fruits long.

Fig. 317. *Opuntia fulgida* var. *mamillata*, drooping, weak branches with branching chains of fruits, the stems with short, relatively small spines. (David Griffiths)

Fig. 318. *Opuntia fulgida* vars. *fulgida* (lower right) and *mamillata*. The spines of var. *fulgida* are longer, stouter, and more numerous. (David Griffiths)

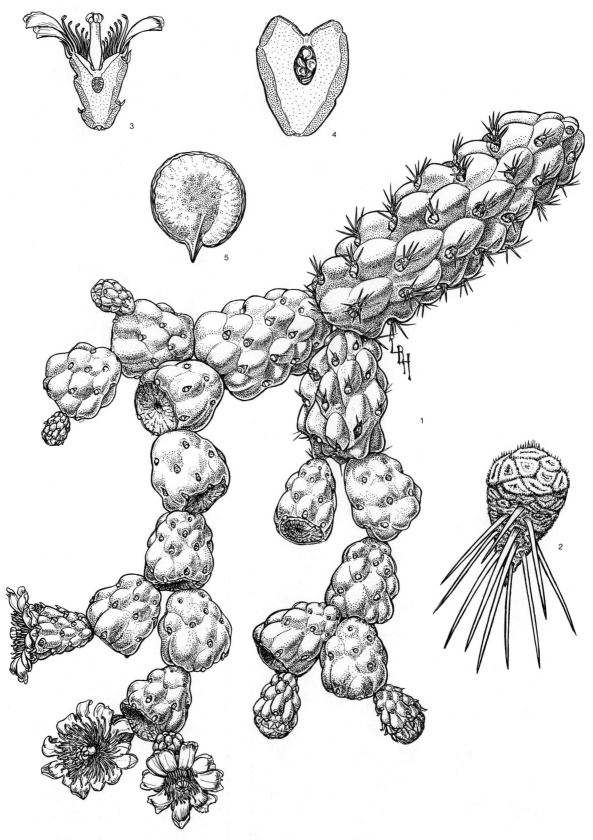

Fig. 319. *Opuntia fulgida* var. *mamillata*, ×.9, except as indicated. *1*, Branch with mature joints and with branched chains of fruits and flowers. *2*, Areole with spines, small glochids, and felty wool, ×6; note the loose sheaths of the spines. *3*, Flower in longitudinal section. *4*, Fruit with a few seeds. *5*, Seed, ×6.

13. Opuntia munzii C. B. Wolf
Munz cholla

Tree, 2-5 m high, with the trunk or the major branches elongate, forming more than half the height of plant, rebranched several times; some larger terminal joints often pendulous or drooping, dark green, cylindroid and mostly 10-25 cm long, ±2.5 cm diam, the older (not necessarily terminal) joints often 4 cm diam; tubercles about twice as long as broad, markedly raised above surface of stem, 12-16 mm long, 6-9 mm broad, protruding 3 mm; areoles 3 mm diam, typically 6-9 mm apart; spines light yellow or straw-colored (sheaths same color, persistent ±1 year), 9-12 per areole, spreading in all directions, straight, the longer 1.2-2 cm long, basally 1 mm diam, acicular, broadly elliptic in cross section, markedly barbed; glochids tan, 1.5 mm long; flower 4-5 cm diam and long; petaloids yellowish-green with tinge of red or lavender; ovary in anthesis with slender spines to 0.9 cm long, these deciduous; other flower details not available; fruit yellow or green (usually sterile and drying without maturing), fleshy at maturity, tuberculate, spineless, ±2 cm long, ±1.5 cm diam, the umbilicus deep and funnel-like, the fruit not persistent or proliferous; seeds light tan, nearly globose, very hard, ±3 mm diam.

Gravelly or sandy soils of washes and canyonsides in the desert at (according to Michael W. Douglas) 330-600 m (1,100-2,000 ft). Colorado Desert. California in Chuckawalla Mts., Riverside Co., and in Chocolate Mts., Imperial Co.

This species has been thought to be a hybrid of *O. bigelovii* and *O. acanthocarpa* var. *coloradensis*. As with the postulated hybrid origin of *O. bigelovii* var. *hoffmannii* (sp. 14a), this may or may not be true, since the evidence is not overwhelming. It is not known whether *O. munzii* is highly heterozygous and incapable of maintaining through sexual reproduction a natural population not overlapping the character combinations of related species. Acceptance of the species is tentative. For a discussion of vegetative reproduction, see p. 31.

See map for *O. bigelovii* (next species).

Fig. 320. Munz cholla, *Opuntia munzii*, small trees in the Rancho Santa Ana Botanic Garden. Note the many branches starting upward from the fallen trunk.

Fig. 321. *Opuntia munzii*, stout branches and trunks, showing the dense array of spines.

14. Opuntia bigelovii Engelmann
Teddy-bear cholla

Miniature trees, usually 1-1.5(2.5) m high, the branches much shorter than trunk, usually re-branched only once or twice; trunk usually full height of plant and bearing only short lateral branches, becoming black as spines turn black; larger terminal joints green or glaucous, narrowly ellipsoid, 7.5-12.5(20) cm long, (3)3.8-6 cm diam, the joints readily detached, mostly deciduous (rooting and reproducing) and leaving main trunk with appearance of a post, usually not markedly woody in first year of growth; tubercles 6-sided, length 1-1.5 times breadth, 6-9 mm long and broad, protruding ±3 mm; areoles 3 mm diam, typically 3-6 mm apart; spines conspicuous and dense, usually obscuring branch (less dense in var. *hoffmannii*), pinkish-tan or reddish-brown (sheaths usually straw-colored, conspicuous, more or less persistent), spines about 6-10 per areole, spreading in all directions, straight, the longer 1.5-2.5 cm long, basally ±1 mm broad, subulate, somewhat flattened in cross section, with many backward-directed microscopic scabrous projections, therefore very strongly barbed, persistent for many years, turning black; glochids straw-colored to reddish-tan, ±1.5 mm long; flower

Distinctive Characters of the Varieties of Opuntia bigelovii

Character	a. var. **hoffmannii**	b. var. **bigelovii**
Branching	More diffuse than in var. *bigelovii*, the main branches longer, more rebranched	Crown compact, the main branches much shorter than main trunk, rebranched only once or twice
Larger terminal joints	±3 cm diam	3.8-6 cm diam
Tubercle size	Length ±1.5 times breadth, usually 9 mm long, 6 mm broad	Length and breadth equal, ±6 mm
Tubercle form	Hexagonal, but elongate	Approximately hexagonal, but sides of irregular length
Spine distribution	Moderately dense, not obscuring stem	Dense, obscuring stem
Spine barbs	Moderate	Strong
Spine color	Pinkish-tan, the sheaths lighter tan or straw-colored	Both spines and sheaths straw-colored
Altitude	300-450 m (1,000-1,500 ft)	30-600(900) m (100-2,000 or 3,000 ft)
Floristic association	Colorado Desert (western)	Colorado Desert

2.5-4 cm diam, 3-4 cm long; sepaloids greenish-yellow, narrowly obovoid, 6-12 mm long, 6 mm broad, rounded and strongly mucronate, denticulate to (in places) sparsely fimbriate; petaloids pale green or yellow streaked with lavender, narrowly cuneate-obovate, 12-20 mm long, to 9 mm broad, truncate, irregularly denticulate; filaments green, to 6 mm long; anthers yellow, ±2 mm long; style greenish-yellow, 20 mm long, 3 mm diam; stigmas 5, 3 mm long, thick, not lobed; ovary in anthesis with slender, deciduous spines to 1.5 cm long; fruit yellow or greenish-yellow (usually sterile), fleshy at maturity, strongly tuberculate, without appendages, 1.2-2 cm long, 0.6-0.9 cm diam, the umbilicus deep and cuplike,

the fruit persistent into or through winter, not proliferous; seeds (when present) broadly obovate, 3 mm long, 2.5 mm broad, 1 mm thick.

For a discussion of vegetative reproduction see pp. 56 and 92-95.

14a. Opuntia bigelovii var. **hoffmannii** Fosberg. Gravelly soils of hillsides and alluvial fans in the desert at 300-450 m (1,000-1,500 ft). Colorado Desert. California in E San Diego Co. from Mason Valley and Vallecitos to Canebrake Canyon, Anza Desert.

The plants are weird small trees with short trunks and longer branches, as in O. *fulgida* var. *fulgida*.

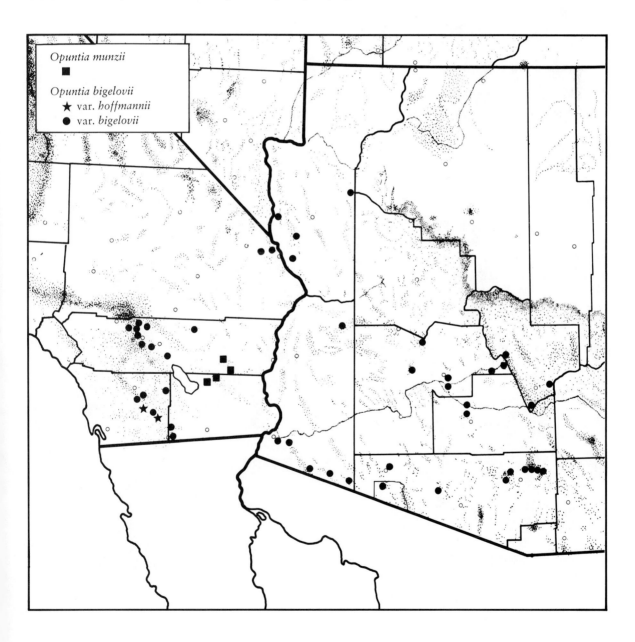

These plants maintain themselves mostly by vegetative reproduction, and they have been suggested as hybrids of var. *bigelovii* and *O. echinocarpa* var. *wolfii*. This may be true, and these plants may be sufficiently heterozygous (variable in their hereditary makeup) that they cannot maintain a distinctive population by sexual reproduction. Flowering, fruiting, and the forming of viable seeds are rare, as in many hybrids; but sexual reproduction is rare also in var. *bigelovii* through much of its range, and is unusual in *O. fulgida*, *O. prolifera*, and other species.

14b. Opuntia bigelovii var. **bigelovii.** Rocky ground or gravelly areas of south-facing hill and mountain slopes (sometimes on flats) in the desert at 30-600(900) m (100-2,000 or 3,000 ft). Colorado Desert in California and Arizona; the lower Arizona Desert in Arizona from Mohave Co. to s Yavapai, and s Gila Cos. and s to Yuma and Pima Cos. In N Baja California and Sonora.

This is a cholla memorable for its weird, postlike to treelike appearance, and still more so for the effectiveness of its spines. These are numerous, sharp, and so strongly barbed that often each

Fig. 322. Teddy-bear cholla or cactus, *Opuntia bigelovii* var. *hoffmanii*, part of a thicket of these plants in the Colorado Desert in Mason Valley, San Diego Co., California. The branching, elongate main trunks are characteristic, and the plants are 2–3 m (6–10 feet) high. Two small plants of *Mammillaria dioica* are just beneath the base of the trunk.

spine must be cut off with scissors before a hand or leg can be freed from a detached joint. Bigelow (U.S. Senate Rept. Expl. & Surv. R.R. Route Pacific Ocean. Botany 4: 13. 1857) wrote as follows:

"We find [February 7] a new species of *Opuntia*, with a reticulated woody stem, very fragile at the joints before hardening into wood, and armed with spines worse than those of a porcupine. It is called by the Mexicans, 'chug.' The plant is the horror of man and beast. Our mules are as fearful of it as ourselves. The barbed spines stick so fast in the flesh that the joint of the plant is separated from the main stem before the spines can be withdrawn. We found this species sometimes ten and twelve feet high, branching very fantastically, in consequence of the fragility and decay of the younger stems and joints."

O. fulgida has a similar appearance, but its spines, though effective, are much less strongly barbed.

Fig. 323. *Opuntia bigelovii* var. *hoffmanii*, young individuals planted in the Rancho Santa Ana Botanic Garden, showing the thick stems and prominent, short tubercles and the less dense spine cover than in var. *bigelovii*.

Text continued on p. 344

Fig. 324. Teddy-bear cholla or cactus, *Opuntia bigelovii* var. *bigelovii*, a forest of these plants and other cacti in the Arizona Desert between Aguila and Congress Junction, in Yavapai Co., Arizona. Relatively young saguaros, *Cereus giganteus*, here near their northern limit of distribution, are confined to south-facing slopes, as are the chollas. Creosote bushes, *Larrea tridentata*, are in the foreground; foothill palos verdes, *Cercidium microphyllum*, are on the hillside.

Fig. 325. *Opuntia bigelovii* var. *bigelovii* in the Colorado Desert, Black Mts., Mohave Co., Arizona, at low elevation near the Colorado River. The ground is littered with fallen joints, and a few of these are beginning to grow into new plants.

340

Fig. 327. *Opuntia bigelovii* var. *bigelovii*, flower, the sensitive stamens curling inward like springs in response to the movements of a bee (right of center), which is kept busy as it forces its way against the resilient stamens to the nectary at the base of the flower. (Robert H. Peebles)

Fig. 326. *Opuntia bigelovii* var. *bigelovii,* plants growing near those of Fig. 325. Here, asexual reproduction is in a later stage, with many young plants coming up from the fallen joints.

341

Fig. 328. *Opuntia bigelovii* var. *bigelovii*, Arizona Desert just north of the Kofa Mts., Yuma Co., Arizona. The plant has the characteristic trunk bearing numerous branches near the apex; most of these can be expected to fall and form new plants, as a few have already. Numerous tuberculate fruits from the preceding season persist, and the young joints are beginning to grow (in April). The spring flowers in the foreground are *Chaenactis*; at the left are saguaros, *Cereus giganteus,* and a creosote bush, *Larrea tridentata*; at the right, behind the saguaro, is a foothill palo verde, *Cercidium microphyllum.*

Fig. 329. *Opuntia bigelovii* var. *bigelovii*, branches with young joints and spineless tuberculate fruits. Commonly the fruits ultimately dry up and fall off; few produce seeds. Most or all of the reproduction of this species in the United States is from fallen joints.

342

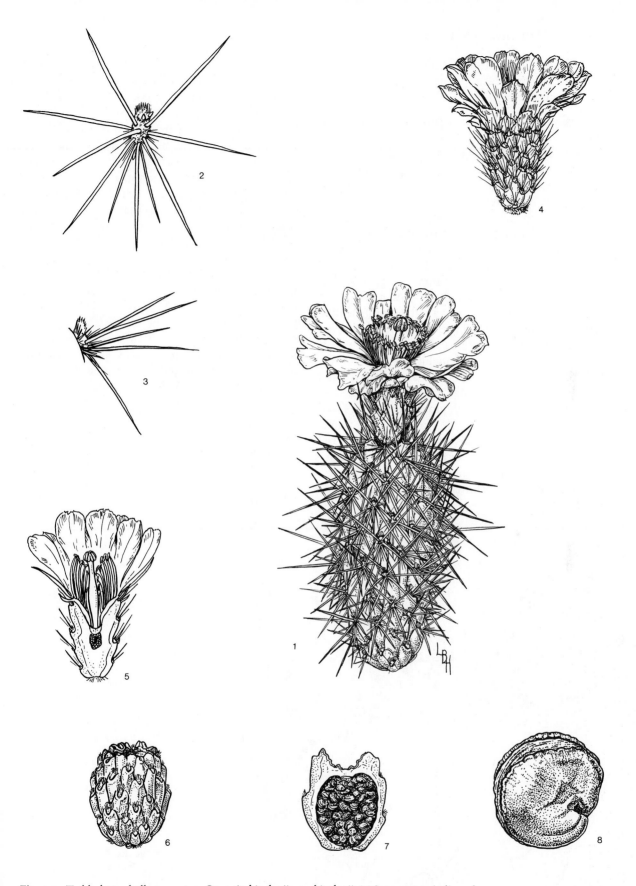

Fig. 330. Teddy-bear cholla or cactus, *Opuntia bigelovii* var. *bigelovii*, ×.9, except as indicated. *1*, Joint in flower. *2, 3*, Areoles, with spines, glochids, and wool, ×1.9. *4*, Flower. *5*, Flower in longitudinal section. *6*, Fruit, this spineless, tuberculate, and yellow. *7*, Fruit in longitudinal section. *8*, Seed, ×6.

15. Opuntia leptocaulis DeCandolle

Desert Christmas cactus, pencil cholla,
    tasajillo, tesajo

Bushes or small erect shrubs mostly 0.5-7 m high, often growing under protection of less brittle larger shrubs; joints of main branches elongate, to 30-40 cm long; internal woody core of older joints nearly solid; larger terminal joints green, much shorter than main branches, cylindroid, usually 2.5-7.5 cm long, 3-4.5 mm diam, the lateral joints short and sometimes spineless (when young); tubercles almost lacking, stem surface nearly smooth; leaves elongate-conical to conical-cylindroid, 3-7.5 mm long; areoles scarcely raised, 1.5 mm diam, 6-9 mm apart; spines gray, sometimes tinged with pink (sheaths tan, conspicuous, persisting ±1 year, loose-fitting, of greater diam than spines), 1 per areole, turned more or less downward, straight, longest 2.5-5 cm long (in one Texas form 0.6-0.9 cm long), basally 0.5 mm diam, acicular, circular in cross section, not markedly barbed; glochids reddish, few, minute, ±1.5 mm long; flower 1-1.5 cm diam, 1.5-2 cm long; sepaloids green with yellow or bronze borders, obovoid or cuneate, 3-6 mm long, 3-4.5 mm broad, apically rounded, undulate; petaloids green to yellow or bronze, obovate or cuneate-obovate, 6-12 mm long, ±6 mm broad, rounded, undulate; filaments ±6 mm long; anthers yellow, 1 mm long; style yellow, 9 mm long, 1.5 mm diam; stigmas 5(?), 1 mm long, proportionately thick; ovary in anthesis tuberculate, not spiny; fruit bright red (in some Texas plants yellow), fleshy at maturity, rather juicy, smooth, spineless but glochids often prominent, obovoid (sterile fruits elongate), ±12 mm long, 9-10.5 mm diam, the umbilicus usually shallow, the fruit persistent through winter, sometimes proliferous; seeds light tan, irregular, 3-4 mm long, ±3 mm broad, 1.5 mm thick.

Heavier soils of mesas, flats, valleys, and plains, and in bottomland soils of washes in the deserts at 60-900 m (200-3,000 ft) or (in New Mexico and w Texas) to 1,500 m (5,000 ft). Mojavean, Arizona, and Chihuahuan Deserts; Great Plains Grassland; and mesquite areas and brushlands of Edwards Plateau and Rio Grande Plain. Arizona from Hualpai Valley in Mohave Co. and Oak Creek Canyon in Coconino Co. s to E Yuma Co. and to Greenlee, Pima, and Cochise Cos.; New Mexico from E Valencia Co. to Quay Co.; s Oklahoma in Arbuckle Mts.; Texas from El Paso to Oldham, Randall, Clay, Johnson, Burnet, Walker, and Victoria Cos. s to Rio Grande. Also N Mexico.

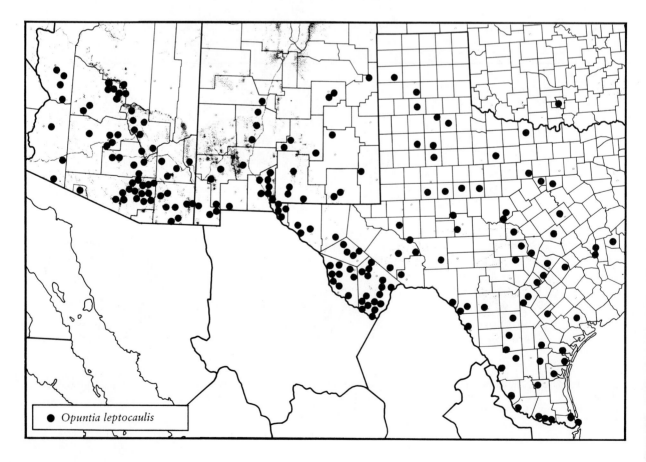

● *Opuntia leptocaulis*

Fig. 331. Desert Christmas cactus or pencil cholla, *Opuntia leptocaulis,* growing in a desert wash. This is the long-spined form. (Homer L. Shantz)

Fig. 332 (*below*). *Opuntia leptocaudis,* nearer view of the long-spined form in cultivation, the most conspicuous structures being the sheaths of the numerous spines. (David Griffiths)

The long- and short-spined forms of the species are strikingly different in appearance, and they have been given various specific name combinations (see Documentation). There may in fact be a correlation between spine length and flower characters. This has been observed, but the chollas do not come into flower quickly in cultivation. Consequently, the flowers of these chollas have been available from too few individuals of either type to afford a solution to the problem. The two major spine types and some intermediate types are found through most of the range of the species.

The plant is often, especially in Texas, a very dense and compact shrub; but among mesquites it may become vinelike, growing upward through shrubbery for as much as 4.5 m.

The bright red fruits are responsible for the localized English name, since they develop in winter, when the desert is relatively drab.

Mr. and Mrs. Orphus C. Bone, collecting in southern Texas on the Rio Grande Plain, have found some plants of *O. leptocaulis* with yellow fruits, which are said to be eaten by birds in preference to the red fruits. Fruit color does not correlate with spine length or other characters.

Fig. 334. *Opuntia leptocaulis,* short-spined form in flower, the branches all young and bearing leaves, as do the flower buds. (David Griffiths)

Fig. 333. *Opuntia leptocaulis,* long-spined form in flower, the branches, flower buds, and young fruits bearing leaves. (David Griffiths)

Fig. 335. *Opuntia leptocaulis,* short-spined form; older joints in the fall or winter, after fall of the leaves that subtended the areoles and after development of the fruits (David Griffiths)

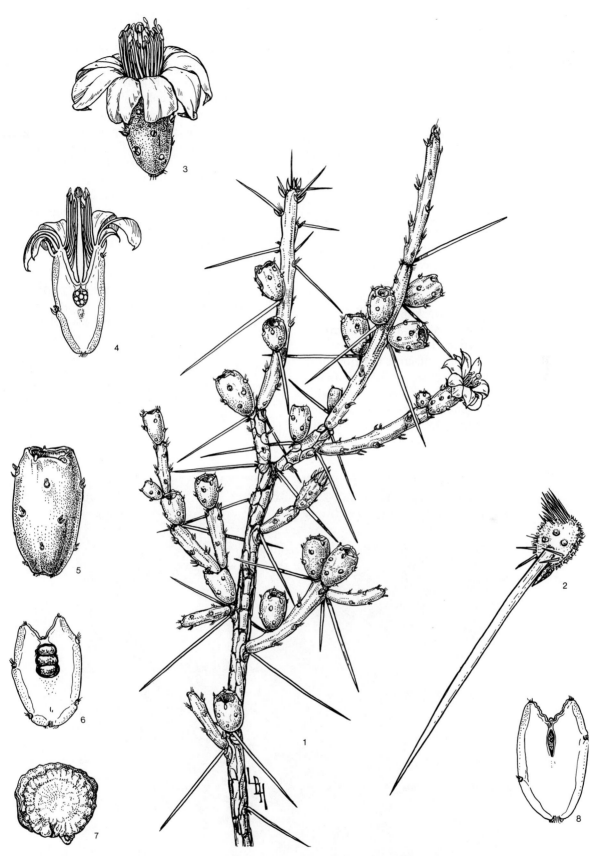

Fig. 336. Desert Christmas cactus or pencil cholla, *Opuntia leptocaulis*. *1*, Long-spined form with a flower and fruits, ×1. *2*, Areole with a spine, glochids, and wool, ×1.6. *3*, Flower, ×2. *4*, Flower in longitudinal section, ×1.3. *5*, Fruit, ×2. *6*, Fruit in longitudinal section, ×2. *7*, Seed, ×6.5. *8*, Sterile fruit, ×2. The proliferous fruits (in *1*) forming chains are uncommon in *O. leptocaulis*; commonly these are sterile.

16. Opuntia arbuscula Engelmann
Pencil cholla

Miniature tree, or sometimes a shrub, 0.6-1.2(3) m high; trunk to 30 cm long, 5-10 cm diam; larger terminal joints green, 5-15 cm long, 6-9(12) mm diam, the surface smooth, the areoles scarcely raised, the woody core of the branch an almost solid cylinder; tubercles low and inconspicuous, 20-40(50) mm long, ±3 mm broad, protruding 1 mm or less; leaves elongate-conical, to 9 mm long; areoles elliptic, 3-4.5 mm long, typically 6-7.5 mm apart; spines reddish- or purplish-tan (sheaths light brown, loose, of markedly greater diam than spines, conspicuous and persistent ±1 year), 1 or sometimes 2-4 per areole, the largest turned more or less downward, straight, the longer 1-4 cm long, basally 0.5-0.7 mm broad, subulate, basally flattened, narrowly elliptic in cross section, not markedly barbed; glochids yellowish, more effective than in most chollas, 2-3 mm long; flower 2-3.5 cm diam, 2.5-4.5 cm long; sepaloids green, edged with color of petaloids, semicircular to cuneate-obovate, 5-20 mm long, 10-15 mm broad, apically rounded, but upper parts mucronulate; petaloids green, yellow, or terra cotta, obovate, 12-15 mm long, 10-15 mm broad, apically rounded, essentially entire; filaments 6-12 mm long; anthers 2 mm long; style the color of petaloids, 10-15 mm long, 1.5-3 mm diam; stigmas 5, 3 mm long, thick; ovary in anthesis spineless; fruit green tinged with purple or red, fleshy at maturity, but not juicy, smooth, spineless, obovoid or narrowly so (more elongate when sterile), 2-4 cm long, 1-2 cm diam, the umbilicus forming only a shallow apical cup, the fruits persistent through winter, not proliferous; seeds light tan, irregular to ellipsoid or obovoid, 4.5 mm long, 3-4 mm broad, 2 mm thick.

Sand and gravel of washes, flats, valleys, and plains in the desert at 300-900 m (1,000-3,000 ft). Arizona Desert. Arizona from s and E Yavapai Co. to Pima, w Santa Cruz, and w Cochise Cos. Mexico in N Sonora and Sinaloa (Culiacán, *Rose, Standley, & Russell 14991, US*).

Usually *Opuntia arbuscula* is a compact dwarf tree about a meter high. Despite the name pencil cholla, the branchlets are more nearly the thickness of a fountain pen. The dark green of these relatively smooth twigs is impressive.

Fig. 337. Pencil cholla, *Opuntia arbuscula*, in the transitional area between Arizona Desert and Desert Grassland, near Colossal Cave, Rincon Mts., Pima Co., Arizona; the plant arborescent, about 1 m (3 feet) high, with some fruits visible. In the background are foothill palos verdes, *Cercidium microphyllum*, the top of a saguaro, *Cereus giganteus*, and (at the right) cat claws, *Acacia greggii*.

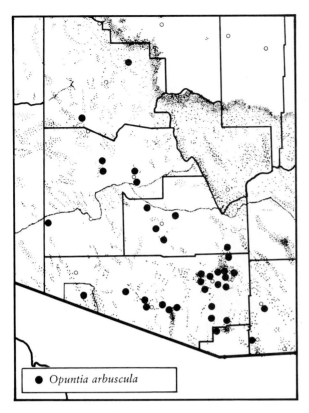

Fig. 339. *Opuntia arbuscula*, joints and flowers, the young joint at the right with leaves, the older one at the left with a flower bud and a flower. (David Griffiths)

● *Opuntia arbuscula*

Fig. 338. *Opuntia arbuscula*, miniature tree in cultivation or on the edge of an old field in the desert. (David Griffiths)

Fig. 341. *Opuntia arbuscula,* branches with spines (usually one per areole) and not quite mature fruits, these smooth at maturity and not proliferous. (David Griffiths)

Fig. 340. *Opuntia arbuscula* growing on the edge of the Desert Grassland in southeastern Arizona (usually occurring in the Arizona Desert), the plant bearing an amazing number of fruits. (David Griffiths; see Credits)

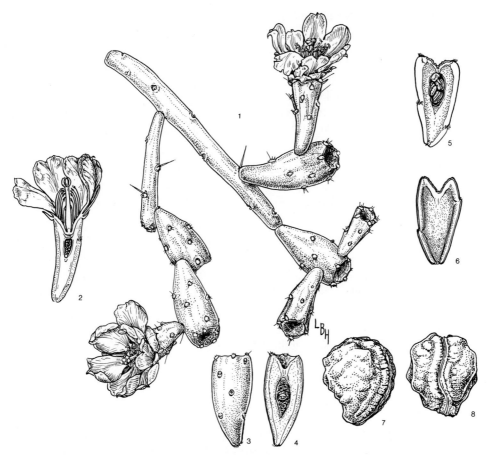

Fig. 342. Pencil cholla, *Opuntia arbuscula*, ×.8, except as indicated. *1*, Branch with chains of fruits and flowers (this very rare). *2*, Flower in longitudinal section. *3*, Fruit. *4, 5*, Fruits in longitudinal section. *6*, Sterile fruit in longitudinal section (the chains of fruits in most species in which they occur are formed by sterile fruits). *7, 8*, Seeds in two views, ×4; the narrow ridge is peripheral to the embryo.

17. **Opuntia kleiniae** DeCandolle
Klein cholla

Bush or shrub 0.3-2 m high; stems branching divergently, upper part of plant open; larger terminal joints with purplish-red cast, 10-30 cm long, 0.5-1 cm diam; central core of branch a nearly solid cylinder of wood, the pith forming only one-fourth to one-third of stem diam; tubercles prominent, 12-25 mm long, 3-4.5 mm broad, protruding ±3 mm; leaves nearly cylindroid, to 12-16.5 mm long; areoles 2-4.5 mm diam, typically 6-12 mm apart; spines distributed uniformly on joint, grayish-pink (sheaths tan, loose, of much greater diam than spines, early deciduous), 1-4 per areole, mostly tending downward, straight, the longer 2-2.5(3) cm long, basally usually 0.5-0.75 mm diam, acicular, slender, broadly elliptic in cross section, markedly barbed; glochids reddish-tan, 1-1.5 mm long; flower 3-5 cm diam, 3-4.5 cm long; sepaloids purple or violet to green, edged with red or brown, ovate-acute or ovate-mucronate to obovate or obovate-cuneate, 6-12 mm long, 6-9 mm broad, apically acute to truncate, entire to undulate, usually mucronate; petaloids reddish-bronze to purple, cuneate to cuneate-obovate, 12-20 mm long, 6-9 mm broad, truncate or rounded, undulate to almost entire; filaments red or greenish, 6-9 mm long; anthers 1-1.5 mm long; style pale green to pinkish orange, 9-12 mm long, 1.5 mm diam; stigmas 5, 3 mm long, thick; ovary in anthesis spineless, 1.2 cm long; fruit red (sometimes green and red), fleshy at maturity but only slightly juicy, tuberculate, spineless, obovoid, 1.5-2 cm long, 1.2-1.5 cm diam, the umbilicus shallow, the fruit persistent through winter, not proliferous; seeds light tan, discoid or obovate-discoid, 3 mm long, 2-3 mm broad, 1-1.5 mm thick.

17a. Opuntia kleiniae var. **kleiniae**. On rocky soils of hillsides and canyons in the deserts and in grasslands at 720-1,200 m (2,400-4,000 ft). Chihuahuan Desert, Desert Grassland, Great Plains Grassland, and intermediate grasslands. New Mexico from Socorro and SE Hidalgo Cos. to Quay and Eddy Cos.; Oklahoma in Kingfisher Co.; W Texas from Hudspeth Co. to Culberson, Jeff Davis, and Brewster Cos.

Collections from Eastland (*L. Benson 11078, Pom*) and Lampasas (*Griffiths 9345, US, Pom*) Cos., Texas, and from Kingfisher Co., Oklahoma (*Weniger* in 1962, *UNM*), probably represent introductions.

According to Fischer (see below), var. *kleiniae* is tetraploid.

Distinctive Characters of the Varieties of **Opuntia kleiniae**

Character	a. var. **kleiniae**	b. var. **tetracantha**
Habit	Suberect	Sprawling or suberect
Height	1.3-2 m	0.3-0.6(1.2) m
Tubercles	Prominent, especially on young joints, 15-25 mm long	Not prominent, 12-15 mm long
Vertical spacing between areoles	3.8-5.6 cm	2-2.5 cm
Spine size	±2 cm long, basally 0.75 mm diam	2.2-3 cm long, basally 0.5 mm diam
Petaloid color	Violet	Green, edged with red or brown
Altitude	720-1,200 m (2,400-4,000 ft)	600-900(1,320) m (2,000-3,000 or 4,500 ft)
Floristic association	Chihuahuan Desert, Desert Grassland, and Great Plains Grassland	Arizona Desert; Desert Grassland; edge of Chihuahuan Desert

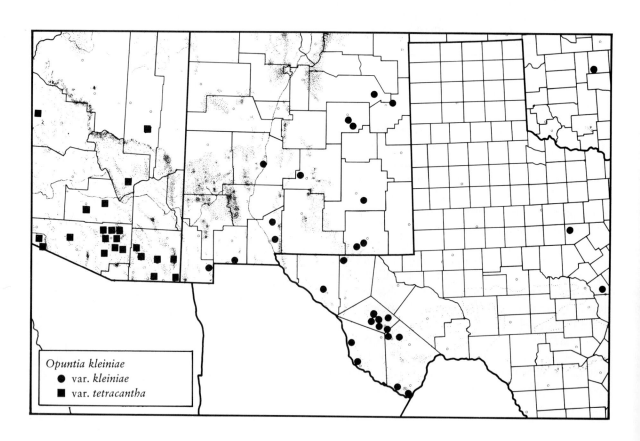

Opuntia kleiniae
● var. *kleiniae*
■ var. *tetracantha*

17b. Opuntia kleiniae var. **tetracantha** (Toumey) W. T. Marshall. Limestone soils of flats, hills, and washes in the desert and in grassland, mostly (in the U.S.) at 600-900(1,320) m (2,000-3,000 or 4,500 ft). Arizona Desert; Desert Grassland; edge of Chihuahuan Desert. Arizona sparingly from s Yavapai Co. and s Navajo Co. to Pima and Cochise Cos. Mexico in Sonora and Sinaloa.

Opuntia kleiniae var. *tetracantha* is an open, widely branching, shrubby pencil cholla. The branchlets, like those of *O. arbuscula*, are of fountain-pen size, but they have much more prominent tubercles and hence a rougher aspect.

The distinctions given here are largely the work of Pierre Fischer (1962: 42, *f. 2*, 9-10). According to his cytological studies, var. *tetracantha* is diploid, var. *kleiniae* tetraploid.

Fig. 343. Klein cholla, *Opuntia kleiniae* var. *kleiniae*, branch with sheathed spines and young fruits bearing leaves, the young branch at the base with a few leaves. (David Griffiths)

Fig. 344. *Opuntia kleiniae* var. *kleiniae*, branches with mature or maturing fruits mostly lacking leaves, but bearing spines from which the sheaths have fallen (there are remnants of sheaths on the younger joint at the upper left). (David Griffiths)

Fig. 345. *Opuntia kleiniae* var. *tetracantha* in the Arizona Desert, west of Vail, Pima Co., Arizona. (David Griffiths)

Fig. 346. *Opuntia kleiniae* var. *tetracantha* in cultivation, showing the characteristic divergent branching. (David Griffiths)

Fig. 347. *Opuntia kleiniae* var. *tetracantha,* young joint with leaves and a flower bud; older joint with flower buds and a flower. (David Griffiths)

Fig. 348. *Opuntia kleiniae* var. *tetracantha,* older joint with fruits, the slender ones above sterile. (David Griffiths)

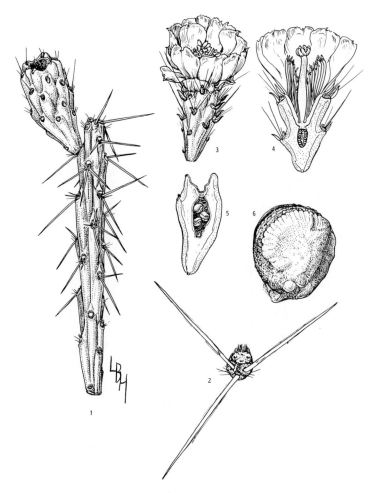

Fig. 349. *Opuntia kleiniae* var. *tetracantha*, ×7.5, except as indicated. *1*, Mature joint with fruits. *2*, Areole with spines, glochids, and felty wool, the spines with sheaths, ×1.5. *3*, Flower. *4*, Flower in longitudinal section. *5*, Fruit in longitudinal section. *6*, Seed, ×5.

18. Opuntia ramosissima Engelmann
Diamond cholla

Bushy, more or less matted, shrubby, or arborescent chollas, 0.15-0.6(1.5) m high; trunk seldom present, the main branches rebranched profusely at or above ground level, some branches equal in length to trunk, when present; larger terminal joints grayish-green, slender, 5-10 cm long, ±6 mm diam; internal core of joint nearly solid, not readily detached, becoming woody first year; tubercles flattened, platelike, diamond-shaped on mature branches, with areole in apical notch or groove, the tubercles 4.5-7.5 mm long, ±4.5 mm broad, protruding 1 mm or less; areoles 2-3 mm long, ±1 mm broad; spines tan (sheath light tan, apically reddish-tan, thin, membranous, conspicuous, persistent ±1 year), spines only in upper areoles of joint, not obscuring branches, at first 1-3 per areole but only 1 developing, spreading or turned slightly downward, straight, the longer

4-5.5 cm long, basally 0.5-0.75 mm diam, acicular, elliptic in cross section, with many minute, strong barbs; young areoles with dense silvery, yellow, or golden wool; glochids (appearing later) same color and ±1.5 mm long; flowers (developed on short lateral branches) ±1.2 cm diam, 3-4.5 cm long, length mostly in ovary; sepaloids mostly green with pink to apricot margins, grading from nearly circular in cross section (e.g., leaves on upper floral cup enclosing ovary) to nearly flat, conic to flattened and ovate, to 6 mm long, 3 mm broad, acuminate; petaloids apricot to brown with some lavender or red, obovate, ±6 mm long, 3-4 mm broad, sharply acute or acuminate, entire; filaments greenish, 3 mm long; anthers yellow, 1.5 mm long; style greenish, 9 mm long, 1.5-2 mm diam; stigmas 7, very thick, 1.5 mm long; ovary in anthesis with spines very short, the pale or white wool prominent in areoles; fruit brown or tan, dry at maturity, usually densely spiny and burlike (with spines to 2 cm long), sometimes spineless, ellipsoid, 2 cm long, 1.2 cm diam, umbilicus deep but not in evidence, the dried perianth normally deciduous but rarely persistent and proliferous (cf. *RSA 110428*); seeds creamy white or very light tannish-gray, nearly circular but irregular, ±3 mm diam, 1-1.5 mm thick; hilum not prominent.

Fine or sandy soils of washes and desert floor, 30-600 (900) m (100-2,000 or 3,000 ft). Colorado Desert. California in s portion of Mojave Desert from Mojave R. to Death Valley and s to Colorado Desert; Nevada in sw Nye Co. and Clark Co.; Arizona from lower areas of Mohave Co. to Yuma Co. and E to w Maricopa Co. and w Pima Co. Mexico in NW Sonora.

The plants become arborescent or large and shrubby in areas along the edge of the Mojavean Desert (e.g., in Joshua Tree National Monument, California, and in southern Nevada); otherwise they tend to be mat-forming or bushy and rarely more than 75cm tall.

The diamond-shaped, cushionlike notched or grooved tubercles are distinctive.

Fig. 350. Diamond cholla, *Opuntia ramosissima*, in the Colorado Desert; photographed with flash illumination, emphasizing the sheathed spines. (Frank P. McWhorter)

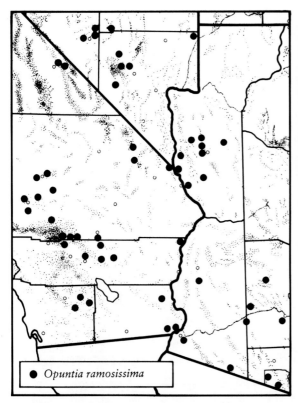

Fig. 352. *Opuntia ramosissima* with the usual type of spiny fruits, these becoming dry, spiny burs. (Homer L. Shantz)

Fig. 351. *Opuntia ramosissima*, joints bearing spineless fruits (which occur occasionally) and showing the diamond-shaped tubercles, each with an apical groove, and the long, sheathed spines. (David Griffiths)

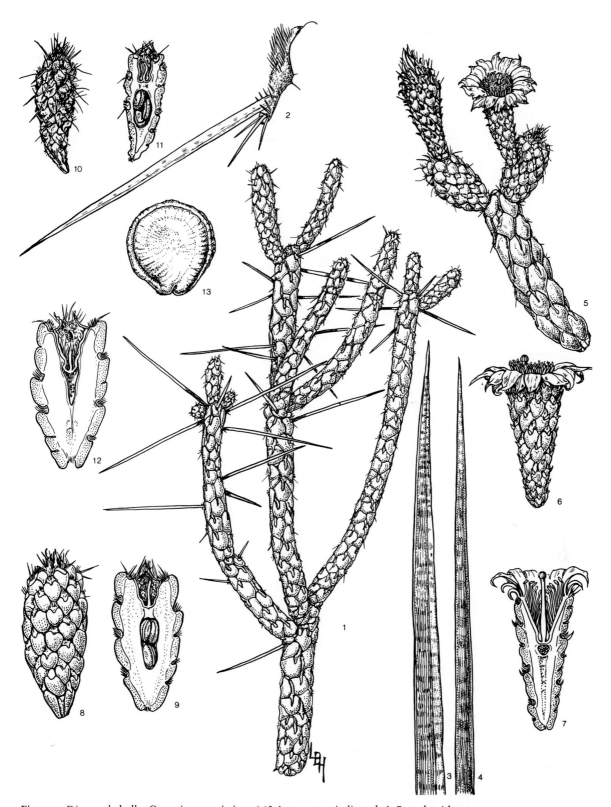

Fig. 353. Diamond cholla, *Opuntia ramosissima*, ×2.4, except as indicated. *1*, Branch with mature joints and spines, showing the diamond-shaped tubercles, the areole in a groove on the tubercle, ×1.2. *2*, Areole with spines, glochids, and felty wool, only one spine becoming large, ×1.8. *3*, Spine enclosed in its papery sheath (epidermis) and visible through the sheath, ×7. *4*, Spine without the sheath, ×7. *5*, Joint with fruits and with a flower bud and a flower growing from these (not usual in this species). *6*, Flower. *7*, Flower in longitudinal section. *8*, Nearly spineless fruit. *9*, Nearly spineless fruit in longitudinal section. *10, 11*, Fruits with short spines (most fruits have long spines). *12*, Sterile fruit in longitudinal section. *13*, Seed, ×3.

359

19. Opuntia stanlyi Engelmann
Devil cholla

Low cholla forming mats or clumps 15(30) cm high, to several meters diam; joints green or dark green, cylindroid to narrowly obovoid, basally gradually or abruptly narrowed, (5)7.5-15(20) cm long, 1.5-4 cm diam, enlarged upward (clavate or clublike), attached firmly; ribs (in var. *kunzei*) formed by coalescence of tubercles, this rare in *Opuntia*; tubercles large and conspicuous, mammillate, 12-30 mm long, 9-12 mm broad, protruding 6-8 mm; leaves succulent, long-triangular, 6 mm long, 2 mm broad; areoles 3-4.5 mm diam, typically 20-25 mm apart; spines mostly on upper portion of joint, tan or straw-colored to brown or red (sheath confined to apical portion of spine), spines with rough papillae in crosswise ranks, not longitudinally ribbed or grooved, 16-33 per areole, the longest turned downward, straight, 5 cm long, basally 1-2.2 mm broad, subulate, linear-elliptic in cross section and not barbed; glochids large (especially those below ground), 6-12 mm long; flower 2.5-5 cm diam, 5-7.5 cm long, sometimes proliferous; sepaloids green with yellow margins, blackening and drying when fruit is young, ovate-acute, to 20 mm long, 12 mm broad, attenuate, entire; petaloids yellow (in var. *parishii* sometimes reddish), narrowly obovate, 15-25 mm long, 9-12 mm broad, attenuate; filaments green, ±6 mm long; anthers yellow, ±1.5 mm long; style green, ±15 mm long, ±2 mm diam; stigmas likely 6-8, ±2 mm long, thick; ovary in anthesis with glochids or slender spines, these deciduous; fruit yellow, fleshy at maturity, smooth, usually densely spiny, with large glochids, slender, enlarged upward, 4.5-8 cm long, 1.2-2 cm diam, with deep umbilicus (this, however, obscured by the persistent perianth), the fruit deciduous; seeds light gray, tan, or yellow, obovate to nearly circular, 3-6 mm long, 3-4.5 mm broad, 1-1.5 mm thick; hilum not prominent; cotyledons oblique or sometimes accumbent.

The mats are formidable, and in some places so extensive or numerous as to turn away horses and riders. The stout, downward-directed spines can yield a severe gash, hence the name devil cholla.

Distinctive Characters of the Varieties of Opuntia stanlyi

Character	a. var. **stanlyi**	b. var. **peeblesiana**	c. var. **kunzei**	d. var. **parishii**
Series of joints above ground	Mostly 1 or 2	Mostly only 1	2 to several	Mostly only 1
Joint shape	Cylindroid, basally abruptly narrowed	Cylindroid, basally gradually narrowed	Cylindroid, basally usually abruptly narrowed	Obovoid or narrowly obovoid, basally gradually narrowed
Size of largest joints	7.5-15+ cm long, 2.5-4 cm diam	7.5-15 cm long, 1.5-4 cm diam	10-15(20) cm long, 2.5-4 cm diam	5-7.5 cm long, 2-3 cm diam
Tubercles	Separate, 25-30 mm long	Separate, 16-25 mm long	In older plants basally coalescent into ribs, 19-30 mm long	Separate, 12-25 mm long
Spines per areole	18-21	23-26	26-33	16-20
Broadest spine	Much broader than others	Slightly broader than others	Slightly broader than others	Much broader than others
Petaloid color	Yellow	Yellow	Yellow	Red or yellow
Fruits	Spiny	Spiny	Spiny	Spineless or weakly spiny
Seed length	4.5-6 mm	4.5 mm	4.5 mm	3-4.5 mm
Altitude	750-1,200 m (2,500-4,000 ft)	300-600 m (1,000-2,000 ft)	90-450 m (300-1,500 ft)	900-1,200 m (3,000-4,000 ft)
Floristic association	Upper Arizona Desert and lower Desert Grassland	Arizona Desert	Colorado Desert and lower Arizona Desert	Mojavean Desert

19a. Opuntia stanlyi var. **stanlyi.** Devil cholla. Sandy or gravelly soils of plains, mesas, washes, and arroyo embankments in the desert, 750-1,200 m (2,500-4,000 ft). Upper portions of Arizona Desert and lower edge of Desert Grassland. Arizona from SE Pinal and s Gila Cos. to s Greenlee and N Cochise Cos.; sw New Mexico mostly near Gila R. in w Grant Co. and N and central Hidalgo Co. Reported in Chihuahua sw of El Paso, Texas, but the identity of the plants needs checking. Collected in 1976 at Candelaria, Presidio Co., Texas (Donald O. Kolle, *Pom*).

19b. Opuntia stanlyi var. **peeblesiana** L. Benson. Peebles cholla. Fine soils of broad valleys in the desert at 300-600 m (1,000-2,000 ft). Arizona Desert. Arizona in Yuma (rare), sw Pinal, and w Pima Cos. from near Bill Williams R. to Papago Indian Reservation s of Casa Grande and s to Quitovaquita and w side of Baboquivari Valley. Adjacent Sonora.

Intergrades completely with var. *kunzei* in some areas.

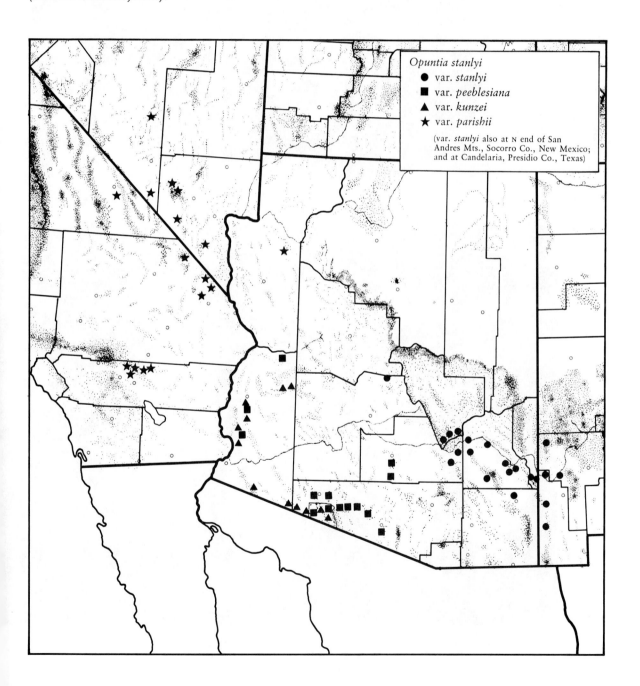

Fig. 354. Devil cholla, *Opuntia stanlyi* var. *stanlyi*, in cultivation, showing the very thick, short stems and the large tubercles. (Robert H. Peebles)

Fig. 355. *Opuntia stanlyi* var. *stanlyi*, part of a joint showing the tubercles and the flattened spines. (That some spines appear broad and some narrow is due to their being seen in flat or edge views.)

362

Fig. 356. *Opuntia stanlyi* var. *peeblesiana* in sand and gravel hillocks built up around the plant by wind in the Arizona Desert near Casa Grande, Pinal Co., Arizona. The numerous deflexed spines are characteristic. (Robert H. Peebles)

Fig. 358 (*left*). *Opuntia stanlyi* var. *peeblesiana*, joints with tubercles and spines and a flower bud and a flower. The long, leafy ovary is characteristic. (David Griffiths)

Fig. 357. *Opuntia stanlyi* var. *peeblesiana* in cultivation, emphasizing the tubercles and spines. (David Griffiths)

363

Fig. 359. *Opuntia stanlyi* var. *kunzei* in the Arizona Desert near Wenden, Yuma Co., Arizona, forming a typical outward-expanding clump. The prominent plants are creosote bushes, *Larrea tridentata*; in the distance is a velvet mesquite, *Prosopis juliflora* var. *velutina*.

Fig. 360. *Opuntia stanlyi* var. *kunzei* forming a dense thicket in the Arizona Desert, southwestern Yuma Co., Arizona. (Robert H. Peebles)

19c. Opuntia stanlyi var. **kunzei** (Rose) L. Benson. Kunze cholla. Sandy or clay soils of broad valleys in the desert at 90-450 m (300-1,500 ft). Colorado Desert and lower edge of Arizona Desert. Reported from SE California; W Arizona in Yuma and W Pima Cos. Mexico in NE Baja California between Mexicali and San Felipe and in Sonora as far S as St. George Bay (Bahía San Jorge).

The occurrence of this variety in California was reported by Baxter (1932, 1935), and the report was accepted by Wiggins (1963). Although the variety does occur just east of the Colorado River in Yuma Co., Arizona, no specimens from across the river in California have been seen. Many other plants, especially those adapted to summer rain (e.g. the saguaro), are very rare west of the river, where summer rain is uncommon.

Former segregation as a species, designated *O. wrightiana*, was based on the differences of the extreme forms; var. *kunzei* and var. *peeblesiana* intergrade completely in at least several areas.

Fig. 362. *Opuntia stanlyi* var. *kunzei*, joints with tubercles, the areoles with many spines. (David Griffiths)

Fig. 361. *Opuntia stanlyi* var. *kunzei*, a single plant showing the typical form of branching from ground level and the flattened spines. (Robert H. Peebles)

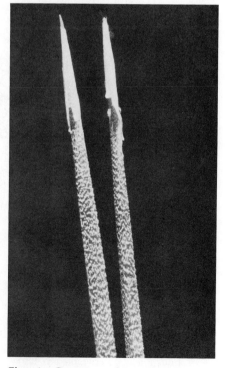

Fig. 363. *Opuntia stanlyi* var. *kunzei*, spine tips enlarged, showing the short sheaths at only the tips, these characteristic of all species of the section *Clavatae*. (Robert H. Peebles)

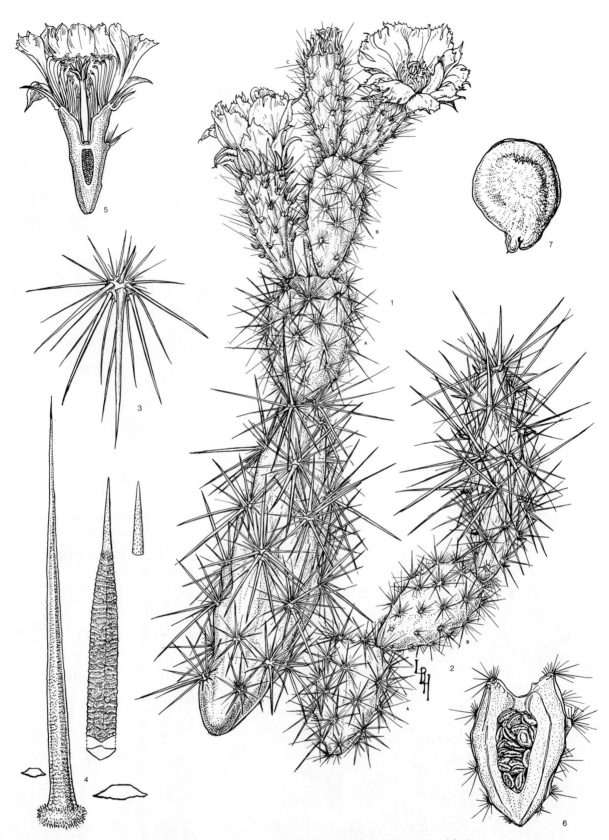

Fig. 364. *Opuntia stanlyi* var. *kunzei*, ×.8, except as indicated. *1*, Joint bearing a chain of fruits, this unusual, the joints not being ordinarily proliferous: fruit *A* fertile (shown in section *6*); fruits *B* and *C* sterile, the proliferous character being associated with sterile, persistent fruits from which new flower buds grow. *2*, A chain of sterile or nearly sterile fruits giving rise to a spiny branch: fruit *A* sterile; fruit *B* with only four seeds. *3*, Spines. *4*, Spine enlarged, the shape of the cross sections in outline: at the left, ×4; at the right, showing the rough, irregular cross ridges and (apex) minute barbs, ×6.5; the additional tip ×13. *5*, Flower in longitudinal section. *6*, Fruit of *1A* in longitudinal section, ×1.1. *7*, Seed, ×5.5.

19d. Opuntia stanlyi var. **parishii** (Orcutt) L. Benson. Parish cholla. Sandy soils of flats, valleys, plains, and mesas in desert at 900-1,200 m (3,000-4,000 ft). Mojavean Desert. California in Death Valley region in Inyo Co. and in E San Bernardino and N Riverside Cos. from Joshua Tree National Monument NE across mountain ranges of E Mojave Desert; S Nevada in SE Nye Co. and in Clark Co. from base of Charleston (Spring) Mts. southward; Arizona in Mohave Co. (rare).

Fig. 366. *Opuntia stanlyi* var. *parishii*, joint with tubercles and spine-bearing areoles, the spines stout and one in each areole broad. (David Griffiths)

Fig. 365. *Opuntia stanlyi* var. *parishii*, the second plant bearing fruits; clumps in the Rancho Santa Ana Botanic Garden.

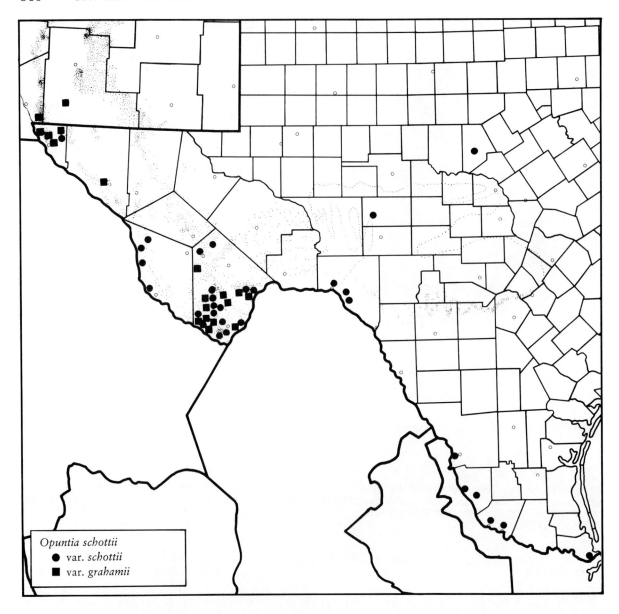

Distinctive Characters of the Varieties of **Opuntia schottii**

Character	a. var. **schottii**	b. var. **grahamii**
Spines per areole	6-10(12)	8-12(15)
Habit and surface of larger spines	Deflexed or spreading, faintly longitudinally ridged-and-grooved, clearly papillate-roughened	Deflexed, not longitudinally ridged-and-grooved, minutely papillate-roughened
Basal breadth of larger spines	1-1.5 mm	1 mm
Spine color	Brownish or yellowish	Tan or gray, tinged with pink or red
Altitude	300-1,200 m (1,000-4,000 ft)	700-1,500 m (2,300-5,000 ft)
Floristic association	Chihuahuan Desert and Rio Grande Plain	Chihuahuan Desert

20. Opuntia schottii Engelmann
Clavellina

Clump- or mat-forming cholla, the clumps low, not more than 7.5-10 cm high, 1-3 m diam; larger terminal joints green, narrowed gradually toward bases, 4-6 cm long, (1)1.5-2.5 cm diam; ribs none, the tubercles not coalescent; tubercles conspicuous, mammillate, 4.5-15 mm long, 3-4.5 mm broad, protruding 3-6 mm; areoles elliptic, 1.5-4.5 mm long, ±6 mm apart; longer spines restricted to uppermost areoles of joint, brownish, yellowish, or tan, or gray tinged with pink or red, clearly papillate-roughened, some with faint longitudinal ridges and grooves, 6-12(15) (of all sizes, some very small) per areole, deflexed or spreading horizontally, straight, the longer 2.5-5 cm long, basally 1-1.5 mm broad, strongly flattened to acicular, narrowly elliptic or nearly circular in section, barbed but not strongly so; glochids tan or pale yellow, 3-6 mm long; flower ±5 cm diam and long; sepaloids yellow, obovate to narrowly obovate, 9-12 mm long, 20-25 mm broad, short, acuminate; petaloids yellow, narrowly obovate, 25-30 mm long, ±12 mm broad, truncate, irregularly shallowly toothed; filaments yellow, ±12 mm long; anthers yellow, narrowly oblong, ±2 mm long; style yellowish, ±15 mm long, 4 mm diam; stigmas ±12, 3 mm long, broad; ovary in anthesis ±1.2 cm long; fruit yellow, fleshy at maturity, not spiny but with persistent glochids, with a short stalk, expanded upward, 4-5.5 cm long, 1.2-4 cm diam, the umbilicus very deep, cuplike, the fruit deciduous; seeds light gray or stained yellow by juice of fruit, nearly circular, flattened, ±4.5 mm diam, 1.5 mm thick; cotyledons oblique to hypocotyl.

Opuntia schottii forms low clumps or mats of small clublike joints. These are much lower than those of the similar *O. stanlyi*.

20a. Opuntia schottii var. schottii. Sandy soils of valleys and plains; in the open or under trees or shrubs in the desert at 300-1,200 m (1,000-4,000 ft); in s Texas at lower elevations. Chihuahuan Desert and Rio Grande Plain. Texas in Rio Grande region near El Paso and from Presidio Co. to Cameron Co. and in Schleicher and Brown Cos. and on s part of coastal plain. Adjacent Mexico.

Intergrades freely with var. *grahamii* in Brewster Co.

Fig. 367. Clavellina, *Opuntia schottii* var. *schottii,* growing in desert pavement, an intricate mass of spines arising from the slender stems; flower buds and a flower; in the Chihuahuan Desert, Lower Tornillo Creek, Big Bend National Park, Brewster Co., Texas.

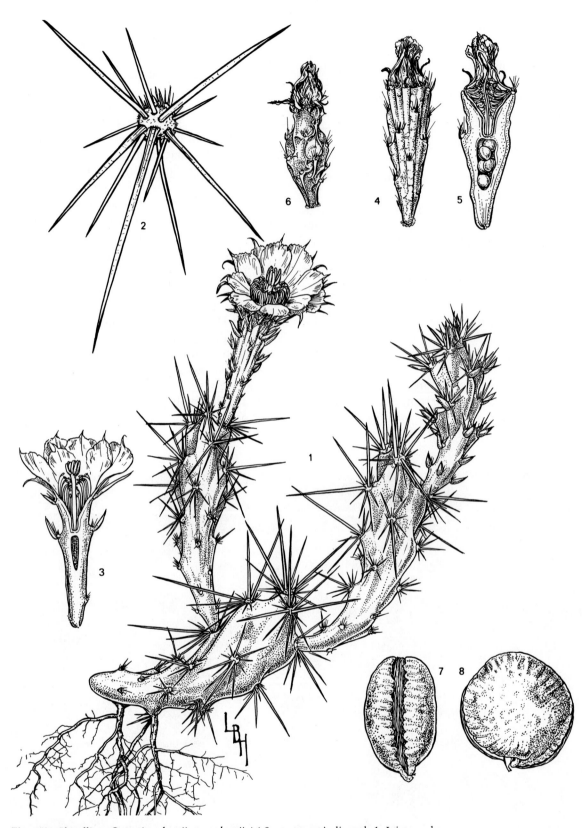

Fig. 368. Clavellina, *Opuntia schottii* var. *schottii*, ×.8, except as indicated. *1*, Joints and a flower. *2*, Areole with spines, glochids, and felty wool, ×1.4. *3*, Flower in longitudinal section. *4*, Fruit, fleshy at maturity. *5*, Fruit in longitudinal section. *6*, Fruit after ultimate drying. *7, 8,* Seed in two views, the cordlike peripheral ridge covered by the embryo, ×6.

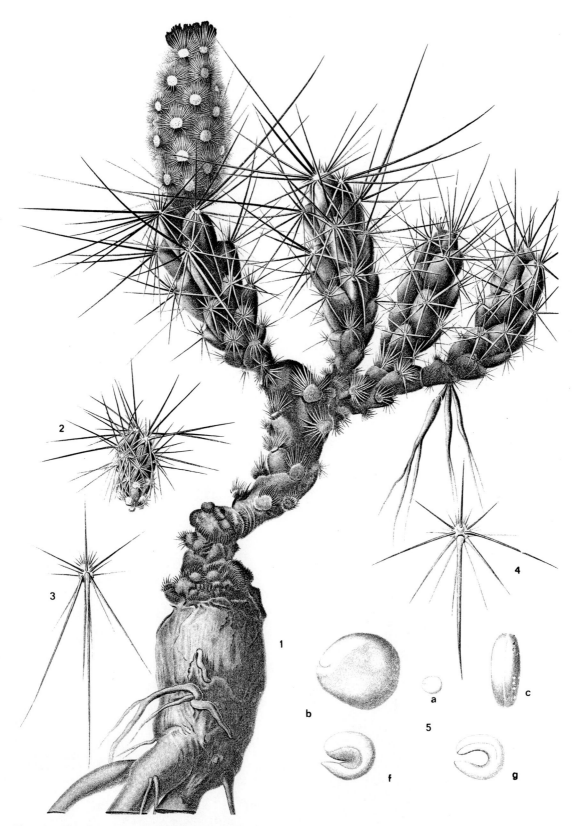

Fig. 369. Clavellina, *Opuntia schottii* var. *grahamii*. *1,* Plant with a fruit; note the somewhat thickened roots. *2,* Small joint. *3, 4,* Areoles with spines, glochids, and felty wool, each with a section of a spine. *5,* Seed: *a, b, c,* entire seed in two views, ×6; *f, g,* embryos, these incumbent (Paulus Roetter in Engelmann/Emory, *pl.* 72)

20b. Opuntia schottii var. **grahamii** (Engelmann) L. Benson. Sand of dunes and flats or alluvial fans in the desert at 700-1,500 m (2,300-5,000 ft). Chihuahuan Desert. New Mexico E of Rio Grande in Organ Mts. and in sw Otero Co.; Texas from El Paso Co. to Brewster Co.

In Brewster Co. this variety intergrades freely with var. *schottii*: e.g., 60 mi. south of Alpine, *L. & R. L. Benson 15496, Pom*; Lower Tornillo Creek near Boquillas, *L. Benson 16502, Pom, 16503, Pom*. Although numerous intermediate plants occurred in both places, these were not collected in an extensive series. Margery S. Anthony listed the following of her collections as "*Opuntia Grahamii × Schottii*," all being from the Big Bend National Park, Brewster Co., Texas: north of Talley Mt., *83, Mich*; south of Nine-Point Mesa, *1267, Mich*; east of Nine-Point Mesa, *909, Mich*; Solis Ranch, *31, Mich, 31b, Mich*; Tornillo Flats, *856, Mich*. From farther west she listed: 15 mi north of Terlingua, *1181, Mich*. These specimens indicate plants intermediate between the two varieties.

21. Opuntia clavata Engelmann
Club cholla

Mat-forming cholla, the mats not more than 7.5-10 cm high, 1-2 m diam; larger terminal joints dark green, clavate, strongly expanded upward from narrow bases, attached firmly, 4-5 cm long, 2-2.5 cm diam, becoming woody during first year; ribs none, the tubercles not coalescent; tubercles conspicuous and relatively large, mammillate, 12 mm long, 3-4 mm broad, protruding 3-4 mm; areoles 2-3 mm diam, typically 6 mm apart; spines mostly toward upper part of joint, ashy-gray, strongly papillate-roughened, clearly ridged and grooved longitudinally (sheath confined to apical portion of spine), spines 10-20 per areole, mostly deflexed, straight, the longer ±2.5 cm long, basally ±2 mm broad, subulate, strongly flattened, the largest daggerlike, broadly linear in cross section, not barbed; glochids yellowish, 6 mm long; flower 3-5 cm diam, 5-6 cm long; sepaloids with green midribs and yellow margins, ovate-attenuate, to 20 mm long, 6 mm broad, bas-

Fig. 370. Club cholla, *Opuntia clavata*, in overgrazed Great Plains Grassland, forming extensive mats. (David Griffiths)

Fig. 371. *Opuntia clavata* in cultivation. Each areole of the old joints bears one very broad-based spine, this far exceeding the others; on each joint, the larger spines appear in only the upper areoles. A young joint stands above the others. (David Griffiths)

Fig. 372. *Opuntia clavata*, plants from between Santa Fe and Los Alamos, New Mexico, the fruits mature or nearly so and turning reddish. The stems run along the ground and produce numerous ascending branches; the apical portion of each joint bears very broad, daggerlike spines, the largest strongly deflexed.

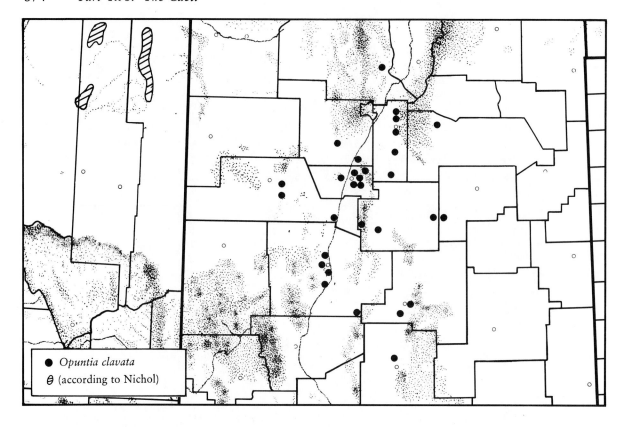

● *Opuntia clavata*
θ (according to Nichol)

ally much narrower in upper attenuate portions; petaloids yellow, apparently cuneate or nearly obdeltoid, ±20 mm long, 12+ mm broad, apparently truncate or rounded, entire; filaments 3-4 mm long; anthers yellow, oblong, ±1.5 mm long; style ±9 mm long, 1.5 mm diam; stigmas about 10, 3 mm long, very broad; ovary in anthesis spineless; fruit yellow, fleshy at maturity, smooth, covered with clusters of yellow or tan glochids, slender, enlarged upward, 4 cm long, 1.9-2.2 cm diam, the umbilicus very deep, the fruit deciduous; seeds yellow, obovate, almost 5 mm long, 4 mm broad, to 1.5 mm thick; cotyledons oblique to hypocotyl.

Sandy soils of valleys and high plains in grassland at 1,800-2,400 m (6,000-8,000 ft). Great Plains Grassland. In NE corner of Arizona (according to A. A. Nichol) in Navajo and Apache Cos.; N and central New Mexico from E Rio Arriba Co. to E Valencia, Socorro, San Miguel, and N Otero Cos.

The species is remarkable for its large white mats of little clubs.

O. clavata is *not* similar to *O. stanlyi* var. *parishii*, as once was suggested.

22. Opuntia pulchella Engelmann
Sand cholla

Low, inconspicuous clump-forming cholla, the clumps usually only a few cm diam; stems arising from glochid-covered tuber 5-7.5 cm diam, the areoles bearing glochids ultimately deciduous; larger terminal joints exceedingly variable, but especially so if plants have been browsed by animals or are in poor health; joints green, gradually expanded upward or narrowly ellipsoid or cylindroid, 2.5-4(10) cm long, 0.5-1.2(2.5) cm diam; ribs none, the tubercles not coalescent; tubercles low and inconspicuous (sometimes projecting and mammillate), 6-9 mm long, ±4 mm broad, protruding 1.5 mm or less; areoles above ground 1.5-3 mm diam, typically (3)6-9 mm apart; longer spines mostly toward top of joint, varying from white to gray, brown, or pink, basally with ridges and grooves, not papillate, bulbous at extreme bases (sheaths apical), spines 8-15 per areole, mostly somewhat deflexed, straight but flexible, the longest one light-colored, to 6 cm long, basally to 1.5 mm broad, subulate, flattened, not barbed; in juvenile plants the spines all alike, white with tan bases, 1.5-3 mm long, very slender, acicular, not ridged or grooved; glochids of tubers yellow to brown, those below ground 10-25 mm long, those of aërial stems yellow, much smaller and either inconspicuous or to 9 mm long; flower (2)3-4 cm diam, (2)3-4.5 cm long; sepaloids green edged with purple or rose, ovate-acute to obovate-acute or broadly lanceolate, 3-20 mm long, 3-12 mm broad, mucronate, minutely undulate; petaloids purple to rose, cuneate or cuneate-obovate, 15-25 mm long, 10-15 mm broad, truncate or retuse, mucronate, marginally undulate; filaments green or yellow, 6 mm long; anthers yellow, 1.5 mm long; style purplish, 10-15 mm long, 1.5-2 mm diam; stigmas 5, 1.5 mm long, thick; ovary in anthesis with long, persistent, bristle-like spines; fruit reddish, fleshy at maturity, smooth, the areoles prominent, each

with 20 or more purplish or brownish soft spines 1.2-1.5 cm long, the fruit 2-3 cm long, 1-1.2 cm diam, the umbilicus very deep and surrounded by flared structure derived from floral cup, the fruit deciduous; seeds bone white, elliptic to irregular, 4.5-6 mm long, 3-4.5 mm broad, 2 mm thick.

Sand of dunes, dry-lake borders, river bottoms, washes, valleys, and plains in the desert at 1,200-1,500 m (4,000-5,000 ft). Sagebrush Desert. Nevada from E central Washoe, Lyon, and Esmeralda Cos. to Lander, Nye, and SE White Pine Cos.; w Utah in Tooele and Millard Cos.; in NW Arizona in (perhaps) Mohave Co. and (according to A. A. Nichol) w edge of Yavapai Co., but occurrence in Arizona is now uncertain. Reported from California by Edwin F. Wiegand.

The species includes several minor forms, but most often these are abnormal types produced

Fig. 373. Sand cholla, *Opuntia pulchella*, forming a dense clump in a sandy flat or playa border in the Sagebrush Desert, near Fallon, Churchill Co., Nevada. The longest spine of each areole, 5 cm (2 inches) or more in length, is conspicuous. The plants, however, are small and inconspicuous, and few see them. (Frank P. McWhorter)

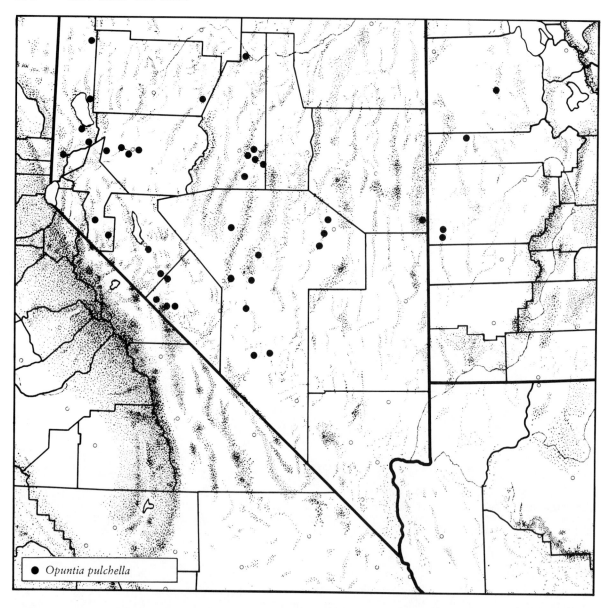

● *Opuntia pulchella*

after injuries, especially those caused by grazing animals. Small or abnormal forms have received names as species (under the proposed genus "*Micropuntia*") on the basis of three characters: (1) the presence of tubers without glochids (these, however, are normally deciduous in older plants, together with the complete areoles); (2) special spine types (but these are highly variable in all populations, and small spines often are produced after injury, disease, or desiccation); and (3) small joints (these, often juvenile, are as variable as spine types) (cf. Benson, 1957a). The ability of the plant to flower and fruit during juvenile stages has given rise to some of the confusion. Specimens collected by Gordon W. Gullion (Smoky Valley, Lander Co., Nevada, in 1958, *Pom*) show transitions from juvenile to adult

plants. After careful and extensive studies in the field, Robert H. Kirkpatrick of Barstow, California, reports (letter of August 11, 1970) as follows: (1) the same plant may have some joints with the characters of "*Micropuntia*" and others with characters of *Opuntia pulchella*; (2) all plants examined had glochids or remnants of them on the underground parts; and (3) joints on the upper part of the stem are often of the current season and are replaced each year, some collected plants having had no branches at one time but having regrown them, with spines up to 25 mm long, in 90 days. Kirkpatrick also reports (letter of June 23, 1971) finding no significant differences in the flowers or fruits of the various forms he has cultivated.

Subgenus Opuntia

Joints of stem strongly flattened (in rare cases only terminal joints or some of them flattened, or joints only elliptic in cross section); tubercles none. Spines never with epidermis or any portion of it separating into deciduous sheaths; glochids well developed and strongly barbed.

Twenty-eight native or introduced species from Br. Columbia to Ontario and Massachusetts and south through the U.S.; a few native in the Southeast, especially in Florida; four or perhaps five species introduced in Hawaii, southern California, Texas, South Carolina, or Florida. Many other species native in Mexico, Central America, the West Indies, and South America.

In five species normally with dry fruit (O. polyacantha, O. fragilis, O. arenaria, O. erinacea, and O. nicholii), sterile fruits and those parasitized by insect larvae may remain fleshy and greenish or slightly purplish instead of becoming dry.

The prickly pears growing on a given hillside commonly include many types. The members of any species vary greatly individually; and frequently, especially on disturbed ground, two or more species may form a hybrid swarm (cf. Benson, 1970b, from which these paragraphs are paraphrased).

On steep hillsides detached prickly-pear joints may roll downhill, root, and form new plants at lower levels, and in a number of places different clones may be traced down a hillside by the color of the joints. For example, on one hillside near Puddingstone Reservoir at Pomona, California, streaks of hybrid cacti with yellow-green, green, or blue-green joints parallel each other down a steep embankment.

In other places the asexually produced descendants of a single plant may crawl away from each other in various directions. Dr. Robert H. Peebles, of the United States Field Station at Sacaton, Arizona, devoted much spare time during his earlier professional career to studying the Arizona cacti and assembled an excellent and technically valuable garden of native species, including a great many prickly pears. During the last 20 years of his life, however, this project was neglected, since his time was taken up with cotton breeding and with administration of the Field Station. In 1957, after the untimely death of Dr. Peebles, I went to Sacaton to see what could be salvaged from the living representatives of his preserved type specimens of cacti, which I had examined in the garden 20 years earlier, when the young plants were well marked by metal stakes bearing numbers. During the many years in which Dr. Peebles had had no time for the study of cacti, the prickly pears had expanded outward, but most of them had died at the centers; each species thus formed a "fairy ring" advancing in all directions. In the usually blank area at the center of the ring the metal stake could be found. Since there were many plants in the garden, the members of each ring had tended to advance through those of the adjacent rings.

My study of the development of prickly pears in this garden, where each one started from a particular numbered stake, prompted the investigation of the same phenomenon in the field, and fairy rings have been found to occur commonly wherever prickly pears are crowded close together. No doubt this explains the occurrence of several plants with no discernible genetic variation growing intermixed with plants of other equally distinct types. Commonly, many types, representing various genetic combinations produced originally by sexual reproduction, are perpetuated and apparently reproduced by the division from time to time of individual plants advancing in all directions.

Parasitism of chollas and prickly pears by insects, and especially of the fruits, is a common phenomenon, often resulting in distorted fruits and the consequent description of "new species." Although such fruits are common in many species, their occurrence seldom has been noted in the literature. An investigation of fruits of this type, and of the insects causing fruit deformities in O. macrorhiza, was published by Martin Ganz (1968).

KEY TO THE SPECIES OF THE SUBGENUS OPUNTIA

1. Trunk (when present) and the main branches composed of flattened joints (these obscure at the bases of the older trunks); terminal bud ceasing growth after the joint reaches a predetermined size (except in *O. lindheimeri* var. *linguiformis*), new joints developing from any of the lateral or usually apical or subapical areoles; flowers of various diameters (Section 1. OPUNTIA).

  2. Fruit becoming tan and dry as the seeds reach maturity (this sometimes delayed until the following spring, and sterile fruits and those parasitized by insect larvae may remain fleshy and greenish or slightly purplish), green or reddish when young (red and fleshy at maturity in only *O. rufida* of w Texas, which has spineless, densely pubescent joints); seeds large, usually (3)5-8 mm long, rough and irregular in outline.

   3. Fruit (except in localized small rare spineless plants of *O. fragilis*, E Great Basin region) with at least an apical rim of divaricately spreading, strongly barbed spines, often spiny all over; joints glabrous, nearly always spiny (Series 1. POLYACANTHAE).

    4. Spines *all* circular to elliptic in cross section, none markedly even basally flattened (the plants rarely spineless, the joints then only 2.5 cm long and the thickness one-half to three-fourths the breadth); British Columbia to the Great Basin, the Rocky Mountain system, the Great Plains, and the Great Lakes, 1 species along the Rio Grande near El Paso.

     5. Larger joints 5-10(12.5) cm long, 3.8-10 cm broad, broadly obovate to orbiculate, to ±1 cm thick, the thickness less than one-quarter the breadth; spines, except those of the fruits, not strongly barbed; joints *not* readily detached
     . . . .**23. O. polyacantha**
     5. Larger joints 2-7.5(10) cm long, to 2.5 cm broad, flattened-obovoid or -ovoid, 0.6-2 cm thick, the thickness one-half to three-quarters the breadth; spines nearly always present, strongly barbed; joints readily detached from the plant and clinging by the barbed spines (these distinctions obliterated by hybridization in parts of the Columbia Basin and the Great Basin).

      6. Roots not bearing areoles or glochids; stigmas 10, oblong, *not* apiculate; fruit obovoid, not constricted, 1.2-1.5 cm long; widely distributed. . . . . .
      . . . . **24. O. fragilis**
      6. Roots (elongate rhizomes?) bearing areoles and masses of glochids; stigmas 5, ovate-acute, apiculate; fruit vaselike, constricted beneath the apex, 2.5-3 cm long; Rio Grande above and below El Paso. . . .**25. O. arenaria**
    4. Spines *all or some* elliptic or narrowly elliptic in cross section, flattened at least basally (this detected by rolling the spine between thumb and finger, the distinction sometimes broken down by hybridization, especially in the Columbia Basin and from s California and s Nevada to N New Mexico); Columbia Basin, Great Basin, and Colorado Basin.

     5A. Spines slender, the larger ones basally 0.25-0.75(1) mm broad, relatively flexible, sometimes slightly twisted; joints 5-12.5 cm long, 2.5-7.5 cm broad, elliptic-oblong to obovate-oblong; California to w New Mexico. . . . .
     . . . . **26. O. erinacea**
     5A. Spines stout, the larger ones basally 1-1.5 mm broad, only slightly flexible, the longer ones markedly twisted; joints (10)12-20 cm long, 7.5-12.5 cm broad, obovate or narrowly so; Colorado River from s Utah to the Navajo Bridge, N Arizona. . . . .**27. O. nicholii**
   3. Fruit *not* with an apical rim of divaricately spreading, strongly barbed spines, spineless or essentially so; joints pubescent (except in some Californian plants), spineless (except *O. basilaris* var. *treleasei*, San Joaquin Valley and near the lower Colorado River, California, and hybrids of *O. basilaris* var. *aurea*, s Utah and N edge of Arizona) (Series 2. BASILARES).

    4A. Fruit dry and greenish to tan at maturity; petaloids cerise, with betacyanin pigments or (in var. *aurea*, s Utah and N edge of Arizona) yellow; plant spreading or prostrate, only 1-3 joints high, rising only 15-30(50) cm; glochids *not* detached without being touched, tan or brown; deserts from California to Utah and N Sonora. . . . .**28. O. basilaris**
    4A. Fruit fleshy and bright red at maturity; petaloids light yellow; plant ascending, large, several joints high, rising 0.9-1.5 m; glochids becoming detached or loose and flying into the air when the joint is jarred, reddish-brown; deserts, Big Bend region, Texas, and adjacent Mexico. . . . .**29. O. rufida**

2. Fruit fleshy and juicy at and long after maturity of the seeds, usually red or reddish-purple but sometimes orange or yellow; seeds small, 2.5-4.5(6) mm in diameter, smooth and regular in outline (Series 3. OPUNTIAE).
3A. Spines present.
   4B. Spines strongly barbed, attaching themselves readily; joints easily detached from the plant and clinging by the barbed spines; plants usually decumbent but sometimes erect, green, *not* bluish-green.
      5B. Spines flattened, at the bases very narrowly elliptic in cross section (as detected by rolling the spine between thumb and finger); joints 10-17.5 cm long, 5-6.2 cm broad, ±1.2 cm thick; Big Pine Key, Florida, and the Caribbean region.................................**30. O. cubensis**
      5B. Spines *not* flattened, broadly elliptic to nearly circular in cross section; joints smaller.
         6A. Joints obovate or elliptic, 5-7.5 cm long, 3-3.8 cm broad, 0.9-1.2 cm thick; spines on mature joints 2-3 per areole; Big Pine Key, Florida, and the Caribbean region.............................**31. O. triacantha**
         6A. Joints slender, narrowly elliptic to narrowly oblong or linear, 2.5-5(6.5) cm long, 1.2-2.5 cm broad (broader and often longer in hybrids, which are common), ±0.5 cm thick; spines 1 or 2 per areole; coastal E Texas to the Carolinas and Florida.........................**32. O. pusilla**
   4B. Spines *not* strongly barbed; joints *not* detached readily from the plant; plants of various habits, green to bluish-green, sometimes tinged with lavender or purple.
      5C. Joints glabrous; prostrate plants, shrubs, or trees.
         6B. Plant 0.5-3 (but in tropical areas, 4-9) m high; trunk, if any, rarely more than 30 cm. long; joints rarely more than 20-30 cm long; spines rarely white; fruit red to purple at maturity; native species.
            7. Spines needle-like, not flattened, elliptic to nearly circular in cross section (sometimes an occasional spine flattened basally or the spines of hybrids of other species with *O. phaeacantha* sometimes flattened), 1-6 (11) per areole (except in some *O. littoralis* vars.), at least some *not* yellow.
               8. Plants low and mat-forming, usually prostrate (in *O. humifusa* var. *ammophila* of Florida sometimes rising the height of 3 or 4 joints), the joints in series of only a few (usually 3-5); largest joints 3.8-10 (in Florida to 17.2) cm long, 4-6(12.5) cm broad; spines white, gray, or brownish.
                  9. Seed margin (covering the embryo) smooth and regular, ±0.5 mm broad; joints dark to light green; petaloids yellow; spines gray or brownish, few and near the upper edge of the joint, 1 per areole (rarely with a second small one), 1.9-3 (to 5.6 in Florida) cm long, 0.5-0.7 (to ±1 in Florida) mm in diameter, spreading; all roots fibrous; E Great Plains to the Atlantic Ocean and the Gulf of Mexico....................**34. O. humifusa** (in part)
                  9. Seed margin irregular, ±1 mm or more broad; joints bluish-green; petaloids yellow to creamy yellow, the bases usually with some red; spines white, pale gray, or rarely brownish or reddish-brown, few to abundant and on mostly the upper part of the joint, 1-6 per areole, 3.8-5.6 cm long, 0.25-0.5 mm in diameter, mostly deflexed; main root tuberous, the others usually fibrous; easternmost California, Utah, and N and E Arizona to the Great Plains.......
                     ....**35. O. macrorhiza**
               8. Plants *not* mat-forming or prostrate, rising the height of several joints, commonly 0.3-2 (in tropical areas, rarely 2-4) m high, but at times some joints forming long series along the ground; largest joints (7.5) 10-30 cm long, (5)7.5-12.5 cm broad; spines tan, brown, pink, gray, black, reddish-brown, or sometimes white or *some but not all* of them yellow.
                  9A. Stem-joints during favorable seasons green, but sometimes during cold or dry weather lavender to reddish-purple (from betacyanin pigments); petaloids commonly yellow or magenta, rarely yellow with red bases (*O. littoralis*, California to N Arizona); spines in each upper areole of the joint (1 or 2)3-11 (occasionally some very small and barely exceeding glochids).
                     10. Largest spines ±1.5 mm in basal diameter; joints green and lus-

trous, thin, basally constricted; each sepaloid with a red mid-stripe; tropical plants introduced in Hawaii and Florida......
.....................................**33. O. vulgaris**

  10. Largest spines ±0.25-1 mm in basal diameter; joints with a bluish caste overlying green, somewhat turgid, *not* basally constricted; each sepaloid green along the midrib, sometimes with additional red or purple pigmentation, especially near the base; native North American plants of Mediterranean climates or deserts.

    11. Spines *not* black-and-yellow, either brown, tan, pink, gray, or rarely white or *some but not all* yellow; petaloids ±10-15, yellow, magenta, or sometimes yellow with magenta bases; flower 5-7.5 cm long; fruit ±3.8(6.2) cm long; s California and Baja California to s Utah and NW and NC Arizona.....
.............................**36. O. littoralis** (in part)

    11. Spines (larger ones) mostly black, near the tips shading rapidly through brown to yellow; petaloids ±7-9, pale yellow; flower 3.8-5 cm long; fruit ±1.2-2 cm long; Texas from Presidio Co. to Nolan and Uvalde Cos. ....**37. O. atrispina**

 9A. Stem-joints at all seasons strongly tinted with lavender or reddish-purple; petaloids pale yellow with red bases and centers; spines in each upper areole of the joint 1 or 2 (in *O. violacea* var. *castetteri*, rarely 3 in some areoles, these whitened); SE Arizona to Texas and adjacent Mexico...........**38. O. violacea** (in part)

7. Spines (at least some of the larger but not necessarily the smaller) at least basally flattened (this detected by rolling the spine between thumb and finger), narrowly elliptic in cross section, tapering, usually 3 or more per areole, if yellow, all yellow (some individuals of an exceptional species, *O. strigil*, Pecos River region, Texas, having narrow, nearly acicular spines, all at first yellow or basally reddish-brown and apically yellow, but dirty dark gray in age or on old herbarium specimens).

 8A. Spines *not all* deflexed, spreading in various directions, the lower spines in the areole *not* markedly longer than the others; spines of various colors; fruit elongate to spheroidal.

  9B. Stamens and style shorter than the perianth; petaloids at least partly yellow, sometimes partly red; joints with a bluish waxy powder on the surfaces, all joints bearing spines; glochids well-developed and troublesome.

   10A. Fruit purple or reddish-purple (with betacyanin pigments, producing a mixture of red and blue), obovoid to elongate; areoles and glochids of the flower bud and the fruit small and inconspicuous; spines 3-6(11) per areole, straight or nearly so; seed irregular, 3-5 mm long or in diameter, the margin enclosing the embryo usually (but not always in plants of hybrid populations "*demissa*" and "*occidentalis*") broad and undulate.

    11. Spines *not* all yellow, *either* (1) at least some gray, tan, brown, reddish, or white, *or* (2), if the spines are yellowish, with reddish or brownish bases; joints bluish-green.

     12. Mature spines *not* (or only a few of them) white or pale gray.

      13. Spines always one color, whether brown or brownish-red or yellow-and-red or sometimes with lighter tips, the longer 2.5-7.5(8.7) cm long; s California almost wholly on the desert sides of the mountains and (rare) from E Mojave Desert to Nevada, Kansas, Oklahoma, and w Texas.................**39. O. phaeacantha** (in part)

      13. Spines not necessarily all the same color, gray, red, brown, or mixtures of these or with yellow, the longest 1.2-3.4 (4.7) cm long; s Californian coastal region..........
..................Hybrid population "**occidentalis**"

     12. Mature spines all white or pale gray, but reddish-brown at the extreme bases, the younger ones sometimes brownish; mountains along the deserts of s California and E to sw Utah, New Mexico, and Texas (mostly w of Pecos River) and adjacent Mexico....**39f. O. phaeacantha** var. **discata**

    11. Spines all yellow, turning to dirty gray or black in age and often so in pressed specimens; joints green.

12A. Seeds discoid, about 3 mm in diameter, the margin enclosing the embryo narrow and smooth; coastal s California
and adjacent Baja California.........................
.......................Hybrid population **"demissa"**

12A. Seeds narrowly asymmetrically elliptic, 3-5 mm long, the
margin enclosing the embryo somewhat irregular; New
Mexico (rare) and Texas to Florida, the Atlantic Coast,
and tropical America.

13A. Fruit obovoid to elongate-obovoid, *not* (except in parasitized fruits) with a basal sterile stalk; seeds 3-4 mm in
diameter; inner sepaloids truncate or emarginate; mostly
Texas and Mexico................**40. O. lindheimeri**

13A. Fruit elongate-obovoid, the base normally constricted
and forming a sterile short stalk; seeds 4-5 mm in diameter; inner sepaloids acute or acuminate; coasts from
Texas to Georgia and Florida and to tropical America
...........................**41. O. stricta** (in part)

10A. Fruit red, subglobose; areoles of the flower bud, including
those on the inferior ovary, bearing conspicuous yellow glochids
to 20 mm long, these persisting on the fruit; spines (4)8-16 per
areole, the lower ones tending to curve and twist gently; seed
discoid, 3 mm in diameter, the margin enclosing the embryo
narrow and smooth; coastal s California, Mexico along the
coast of NW Baja California..................**43. O. oricola**

9B. Stamens and style much longer than the perianth; petaloids red;
joints strictly green; spines (when present) small and weak and
restricted to a few older joints; glochids minute and ineffective;
rare (introduced) in Florida, common in Mexico and cultivated
widely in tropical regions.......**42. O. cochenillifera** (in part)

8A. Spines *all* (1-6 or 8 per areole) deflexed (except sometimes in O. *strigil*
in a few areoles at the top of the joint, the lower spine then markedly
longer than the others and turned upward); spines *either* (1) clearly
yellow *or* (2) reddish-brown basally and shading to yellow apically,
changing (often through white first) to black in age or in herbarium
specimens; fruit spheroidal or nearly so.

9C. Plant 1-2 m high; trunk short but definite; spines yellow, those of
the upper areoles somewhat larger, all deflexed; fruit grayish,
tinged with purple, subglobose to ellipsoid, ±4-6 cm long, the
umbilicus bowl-like; California to sw New Mexico...........
....................................**44. O. chlorotica**

9C. Plant 0.6-1 m high; trunk none; spines reddish-brown with yellow
tips, those of the upper areoles much longer and stouter, some of
these ascending; fruit red, nearly globose, ±1.2-1.9 cm in diameter,
the umbilicus little depressed; Texas w of the Pecos River......
....**45. O. strigil**

6B. Plant at maturity 3-7 m high, usually a tree or arborescent; trunk commonly about 1 m high; larger joints (22.5)30-60 cm long; spines, when
present, nearly white or uncommonly some brownish; fruit (in the local
forms) yellowish to tannish-orange or red; a commonly cultivated species,
escaped in Hawaii and sparingly from s California to Florida........
....................................**46. O. ficus-indica** (in part)

5C. Joints densely hairy or woolly; trees, each with a clearly developed trunk.

6C. Spines usually none, sometimes 1-2 per areole, ±6-9(30) mm long, rigid,
acicular, brown; cultivated species, rarely escaped in California.......
....................................**47. O. tomentosa** (in part)

6C. Spines at first 1-3 per areole, weak, white, but the areoles of the older
joints with additional very long, threadlike, almost filiform, flexible
spines; native of Mexico, introduced along St. Lucie Sound, E coast of
Florida....................................**48. O. leucotricha**

3A. Spines none.

4C. Plant not treelike, *not* with a main trunk; fruits obovoid, 2.5-8.7 cm long, purplish; mostly native plants.

5D. Joints green (lavender- or purple-tinged in winter), *not* bluish-tinged.

6D. Joints orbiculate to obovate, 5-7.5(12.5) cm long, 4-6(7.5) cm broad; scattered western localities and from Minnesota, southern Ontario, and Massachusetts to E Texas and Florida......**34a. O. humifusa** var. **humifusa**

6D. Joints narrowly obovate, narrowly elliptic, or oblong, mostly 12-25(35) cm long, 7.5-10(15 or 20) cm broad; coastal plain, Texas to South Carolina, most abundant in Florida.............**41a. O. stricta** var. **stricta**
5D. Joints blue-green, with at least some pale blue powdered wax masking the chlorophyll (sometimes lavender- or purple-tinged, at least during winter).
6E. Low creeping or sprawling plants to 0.3(0.6) m high; joints mostly narrowly obovate, 5-6.2(8) cm broad, strongly glaucous; s California......
............................**36c. O. littoralis** var. **austrocalifornica**
6E. Large shrubs 0.6-2.4 m or more high; joints broadly obovate to orbiculate, 10-25 cm or more broad.
7A. Joints with a lavender or purple betacyanin pigment conspicuous at all seasons (intensified during cold or drought); SE Arizona to Texas w of Pecos River......................**38c. O. violacea** var. **santa-rita**
7A. Joints green or, during extreme cold or drought, slightly purple.
8B. Sprawling plants growing on rocky ledges of mountains; joints narrowly obovate, 11-15 cm broad; SE Arizona....................
........................**39d. O. phaeacantha** var. **laevis**
8B. Suberect shrubs of hillsides; joints obovate or broader, mostly 15-25 cm broad; SE New Mexico to Texas near the Rio Grande.........
............................Hybrid population **"subarmata"**
4C. Plant usually a tree but sometimes arborescent, at maturity 3-7 m high, the main trunk commonly 1 m high; fruits globular to obovoid, (2.5-3.8, then red) 5-10 cm long; commonly cultivated plants, sometimes escaped about old dwelling sites or in deep soils of valleys or at canyon mouths.
5E. Stamens and style much longer than the perianth parts; petaloids red; glochids few, small, and harmless; joints green; fruits red, ellipsoid, 2.5-3.8 cm long, glabrous.......................**42. O. cochenillifera** (in part)
5E. Stamens and style at maturity shorter than or equaling the perianth parts; petaloids orange or yellow; glochids numerous and effective; joints green to bluish or tannish because of the waxy or hairy covering; fruits as below.
6F. Joints glabrous, (22.5)30-60 cm long; fruit (in the plants introduced in the U.S.) commonly yellowish or tannish-orange but sometimes purple or reddish, globular-obovoid, glabrous, 5-10 cm long.................
....................................**46. O. ficus-indica** (in part)
6F. Joints densely short-woolly, velvety to the touch, mostly 20-30 cm long; fruit red, obovoid, tomentose, 3-4 cm long....**47. O. tomentosa** (in part)
1. Trunk and often the erect main branches cylindroid, *not* clearly jointed; terminal bud active and the joint continuing to elongate for an indefinite period, but all or some of the small lateral joints flattened and reaching approximately a predetermined size, then ceasing growth; flowers 1.2-4 cm in diameter (Section 2. CONSOLEA).
2A. Smaller branches all flattened, relatively thick; spines numerous in all the areoles on some joints, none on other joints (Series 1. SPINOSISSIMAE).................
....**49. O. spinosissima**
2A. Smaller branches of 2 kinds, some cylindroid, some flat and very thin; spines few and only 1 per areole on the flat terminal joints, numerous and several per areole on the trunk and cylindroid joints (Series 2. BRASILIENSES)......**50. O. brasiliensis**

---

23. Opuntia polyacantha Haworth
Plains prickly pear

Clump- or mat-forming prickly pear, with the clumps 0.3 m to several meters diam and 7.5-15 cm high; larger terminal joints bluish-green, orbiculate to broadly obovate, 5-10 (12.5) cm long, 3.8-10 cm broad, ±1 cm thick, glabrous, not detached readily; areoles 1.5-3 mm diam, typically ±6 mm apart; spines distributed variously in different varieties, white to brown or reddish-brown (in age, gray), 6-10 per areole, mostly deflexed, straight or curving slightly downward, the longer 0.6-4.5(8) cm long, basally 0.5-0.75 mm

diam, acicular, circular to elliptic in section, not strongly barbed; glochids yellowish, inconspicuous, ±1.5 mm long; flower 4.5-8 cm diam, 4.5-6 cm long; sepaloids green edged with yellow (rarely with red), ovate-acute or broadly so, 6-25 mm long, 6-15 mm broad, short-acuminate to mucronate, undulate; petaloids yellow, occasionally pale or tinged with pink (rarely red in some varieties), cuneate-obovate, 25-40 mm long, 12-20 mm broad, truncate to rounded, undulate; filaments yellow, 9 mm long; anthers 1.5 mm long; style greenish or yellowish, 12-22 mm long, 1.5 mm diam; stigmas 8-10, 2-3 mm long, thick;

ovary in anthesis with bristly spines and with leaves mostly 3 mm long; fruit dull tan or brown, dry at maturity, spiny (with barbed spines) over entire surface, obovoid, 2-4 cm long, 1.2-2.5 cm diam (larger in sterile fruits parasitized by insect larvae), the umbilicus cuplike, but shallow, the fruit deciduous 2-3 months after flowering; seeds light tan to nearly white, irregular, flattened, the margin usually conspicuous, 3(5-6) mm long, 2-4 mm broad, 1.5 mm thick.

Plants of this species, at least of some varieties, may produce stems from the wide-ranging roots (rhizomes?) (specimens by *Castetter & Pierce, UNM*).

O. polyacantha is lower-growing than *O. erinacea*, and especially the younger plants are less compact (distinctions between the two species are discussed under *O. erinacea*, spp. 26a & 26b.) Eventually, older plants become semiprostrate, often from the weight of snow; in this case they root along the lower edges of the joints.

Hybridizes with *O. fragilis* var. *fragilis* (sp. 24a) and with *O. erinacea* var. *utahensis* (sp. 26d).

23a. Opuntia polyacantha var. **polyacantha.** Sandy soils of plains, flats, and low hills mostly in grassland at 1,000-2,100(2,800) m (3,500-7,000 or 9,300 ft). Great Plains Grassland and borders of Rocky Mountain Montane Forest, Juniper-Pinyon Woodlands, and Sagebrush Desert. Br. Columbia near Cache Creek and Clinton on Caribou Hwy. (reported by Horich, 1960) and in Okanogan Valley; Alberta; Saskatchewan; Idaho to Dakotas and s to NE Nevada, Utah, and New Mexico (Rio Arriba and McKinley Cos. to Union Co. and occasional s to Torrance and Chaves Cos.; Kansas, Missouri (Jasper Co.), and (rare) Oklahoma and Texas panhandles.

The pale gray spiny plants form low clumps or extensive mats sometimes dotting, sometimes covering, the sandy flats and washes and the gentle slopes. During May they become masses of yellow or sometimes pink to red flowers.

O. polyacantha var. *polyacantha* forms hybrid swarms with the fleshy-fruited species *O. phaeacantha* (as does *O. erinacea*). Evidence of this is in photographs by Andrews (C20, C196, C197)

Distinctive Characters of the Varieties of **Opuntia polyacantha**

Character	a. var. **polyacantha**	b. var. **rufispina**	c. var. **juniperina**	d. var. **trichophora**
Spine distribution on joint	In all areoles, but sometimes fewer and shorter in lower areoles	In all areoles	Spines in only the upper areoles	In all areoles
Spines in lower areoles	Rigid, straight, 0.6-1.2 cm long; see color below	Rigid, straight, 1.2-3 cm long; see color below	(No spines in lower areoles)	(Especially on basal joints) threadlike, flexible, curving or undulating, 3.8-7.5 cm long, white or pale gray
Longest spines in upper areoles	2.5-3.8(5.6) cm long	Usually 4.5-8 cm long	2.5-3.8(5) cm long	±2.5(3.8) cm long
Color of larger spines	Reddish-brown or sometimes straw-colored	White, gray or sometimes reddish-brown	Reddish-brown	Reddish-brown or pale gray, except lower ones
Basal diameter of largest spines	To 0.5 mm	0.5-0.75 mm	To 0.5 mm	0.75 mm
Spines on fruits	Dense	Dense	Few, deciduous	Few to many, rather weak
Altitude	1,000-2,100(2,800) m (3,500-7,000 or 9,300 ft)	1,200-2,100(3,000) m (4,000-7,000 or 10,000 ft)	1,400-2,200 m (4,700-7,400 ft)	1,500-2,400 m (5,000-8,000 ft)
Floristic association	Great Plains Grassland; borders of Rocky Mountain Montane Forest, Juniper-Pinyon Woodlands, and Sagebrush Desert	Both the Juniper-Pinyon Woodlands; Sagebrush Desert; Great Plains Grassland; Chihuahuan Desert	Sagebrush Desert; Great Plains Grassland; Southern Juniper-Pinyon Woodland	Mostly Southern Juniper-Pinyon Woodland; also Great Plains Grassland

Text continued on p. 388

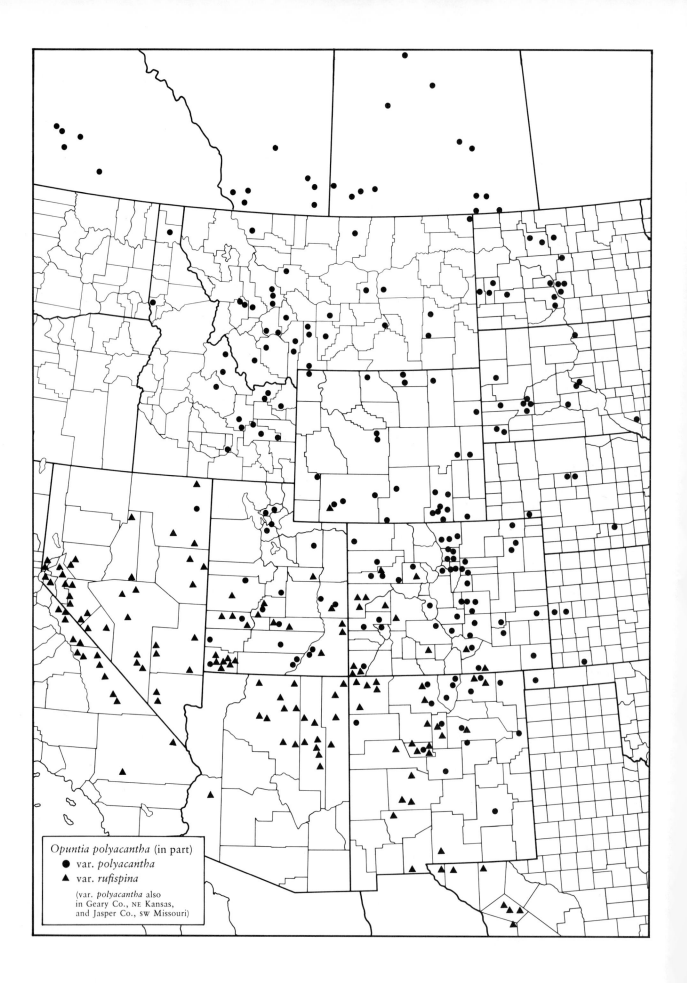

Opuntia polyacantha (in part)
● var. polyacantha
▲ var. rufispina

(var. polyacantha also
in Geary Co., NE Kansas,
and Jasper Co., SW Missouri)

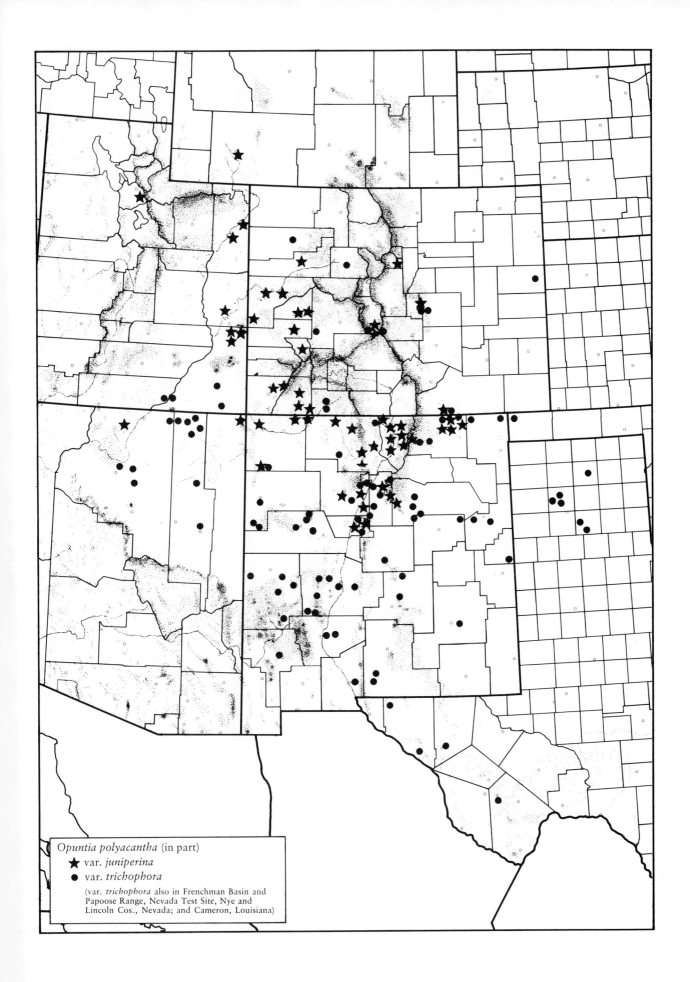

Opuntia polyacantha (in part)
★ var. *juniperina*
● var. *trichophora*

(var. *trichophora* also in Frenchman Basin and
Papoose Range, Nevada Test Site, Nye and
Lincoln Cos., Nevada; and Cameron, Louisiana)

Fig. 375. *Opuntia polyacantha* var. *polyacantha* in flower, near Calgary, Alberta. (W. C. McCalla)

Fig. 374. Plains prickly pear, *Opuntia polyacantha* var. *polyacantha*, in Juniper-Pinyon Woodland near Paria, Kane Co., Utah.

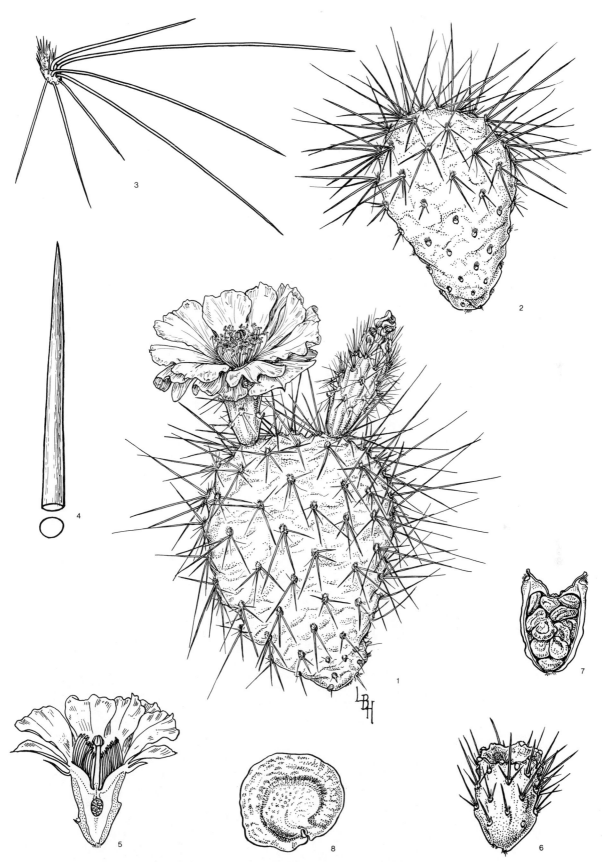

Fig. 376. Plains prickly pear, *Opuntia polyacantha* var. *polyacantha*, ×1.1, except as indicated. *1*, Joint with a flower and a young fruit. *2*, Joint of var. *juniperina* for comparison, the lower part of the joint lacking spines. *3*, Areole with spines, glochids (these larger than the usual type in chollas), and wool. *4*, Spine tip enlarged, ×7; note the lack of barbs. *5*, Flower in longitudinal section. *6*, Fruit. *7*, Fruit in longitudinal section. *8*, Seed, ×3.5.

at the Missouri Botanical Garden. Though these are without locality, they show the two species and an intermediate plant (*C197*). A series of clones representing the two species and various intermediate types was studied 5 mi. north of Trinidad, Las Animas Co., Colorado, in 1950 (*L. & R. L. Benson 14722-14725, Pom*; cf. also *O. phaeacantha*, same station, *L. & R. L. Benson 14718, Pom, 14720, Pom*).

Also intergrades with *O. erinacea* var. *columbiana*, in Br. Columbia, eastern Washington, and Idaho (see sp. 26b).

23b. Opuntia polyacantha var. **rufispina** (Engelmann & Bigelow) L. Benson. Sandy soils in the deserts and woodlands at 1,200-2,100(3,000) m (4,000-7,000 or 10,000 ft). Both Juniper-Pinyon Woodlands; Sagebrush Desert; Great Plains Grassland; Chihuahuan Desert. California along E edge of Sierra Nevada and s to New York Mts. in San Bernardino Co.; almost throughout higher parts of Nevada and (less commonly) Utah; w Colorado; N Arizona from Mohave Co. to Apache Co.; New Mexico from San Juan, Rio Arriba, and Colfax Cos. to Socorro Co. and rare s to Dona Ana Co.; Texas from El Paso Co. to Culberson, Jeff Davis, and NE Presidio Cos.

Var. *rufispina* resembles var. *polyacantha*, but it is taller, and the clumps usually do not spread into mats.

Along the zone of geographical contact with *O. erinacea* var. *erinacea*, distinctions are eroded (see sp. 26a).

Fig. 378. *Opuntia polyacantha* var. *rufispina*, the spines on lower part of the older joint much longer than the lower spines of the two younger joints. (David Griffiths)

Fig. 377. *Opuntia polyacantha* var. *rufispina* in the Sagebrush Desert near Fallon, Churchill Co., Nevada. (Frank P. McWhorter)

Fig. 379. *Opuntia polya-cantha* var. *rufispina* flowering in cultivation. (Robert H. Peebles)

Fig. 380. *Opuntia polyacantha* var. *rufispina*, plant and the mature fruits.

389

23c. Opuntia polyacantha var. **juniperina** (Britton & Rose) L. Benson. Sandy soils of flats, washes, and hillsides in the desert or grassland at 1,400-2,200 m (4,700-7,400 ft). Sagebrush Desert and Great Plains Grassland or open grassy flats in Southern Juniper-Pinyon Woodland. Near Green R., s Wyoming, and s to E Utah and w Colorado and rare in Front Range of Colorado Rocky Mts.; Arizona in NW Coconino Co. and in Carrizo Mts. in Apache Co.; New Mexico from San Juan to Colfax and Bernalillo Cos.

The clumps or mats of stems are greener than those of var. *polyacantha*, because the surface is obscured less by spines. During the winter the lead-green of the stem becomes obscured by reddish purple (betacyanin) pigments.

In New Mexico the variety intergrades with *O. erinacea* var. *utahensis*.

Fig. 382. *Opuntia polyacantha* var. *juniperina*, joints. (David Griffiths)

Fig. 381. *Opuntia polyacantha* var. *juniperina* in Juniper-Pinyon Woodland in northern Arizona.

Fig. 383. *Opuntia polyacantha* var. *juniperina*, plants and the mature dry fruits.

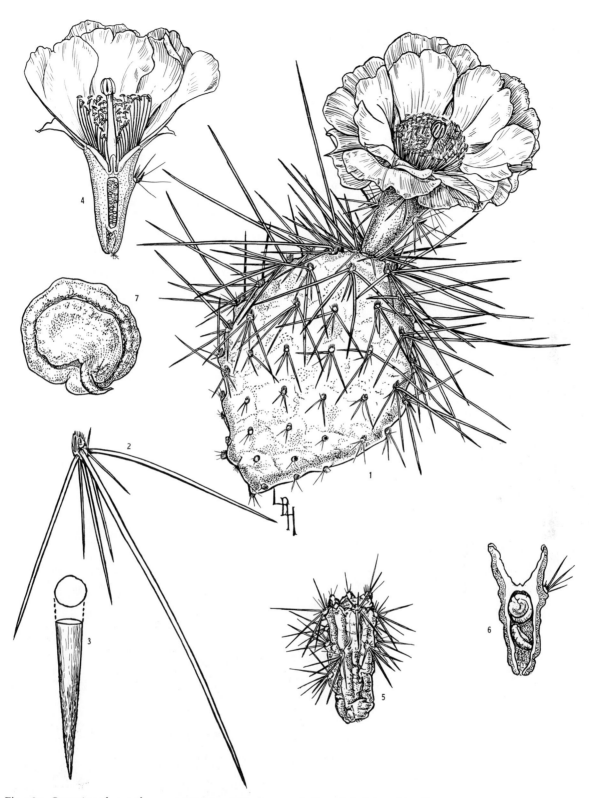

Fig. 384. *Opuntia polyacantha* var. *juniperina*, ×1, except as indicated. *1*, Joint with a flower. *2*, Areole with spines and glochids, ×1.6. *3*, Spine tip, ×8. *4*, Flower in longitudinal section. *5*, Mature, dry fruit. *6*, Fruit in longitudinal section. *7*, Seed, ×5.

23d. Opuntia polyacantha var. **trichophora**
(Engelmann & Bigelow) Coulter. Sandy soils of
plains, hills, or canyonsides in woodland at 1,500-
2,400 m (5,000-8,000 ft); not common at lower
limit. Mostly in Southern Juniper-Pinyon Woodland but also in Great Plains Grassland. SE Utah
and Colorado (uncommon); NE Arizona in N Coconino Co. and in Navajo Co.; New Mexico, almost throughout higher areas; Oklahoma in Cimarron Co.; Texas in the Panhandle in Hutchinson, Potter, and Armstrong Cos. and w of Pecos
R. from E El Paso and Culberson Cos. to Presidio
and Brewster Cos.

Var. *trichophora* is amazing for its shaggy
white-spined joints. The long, flexible spines of
the lower joints are reminiscent of the very long
hair of an Angora goat.

The parallel occurrence of similar, but flattened, spines in *O. erinacea* var. *ursina* is remarkable (see discussion, sp. 26c).

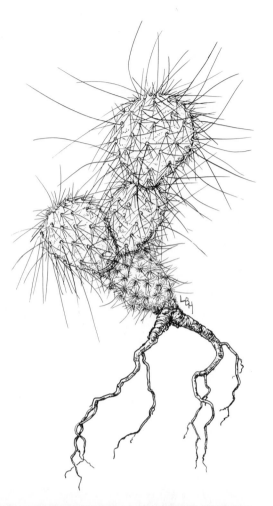

Fig. 385 (*right*). *Opuntia polyacantha* var. *trichophora*,
three-year-old seedling, the first joint cylindroid, ×1.1.

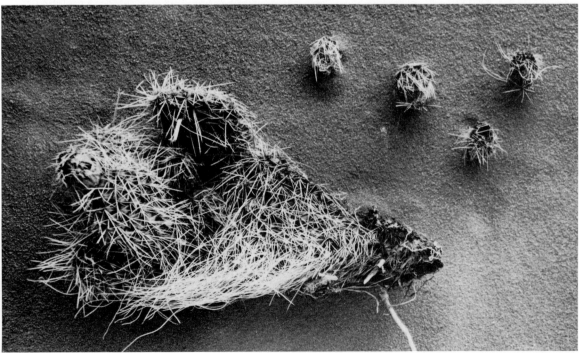

Fig. 386. *Opuntia polyacantha* var. *trichophora* with normal dry fruits.

Fig. 388. *Opuntia polyacantha* var. *trichophora,* plants with the characteristic and numerous elongate, filiform, flexible lower spines.

Fig. 387. *Opuntia polyacantha* var. *trichophora,* a form with only a few flexible lower spines, the plant with the fruits abnormally fleshy, green, and sterile. These result from stimulation by the sting of a parasitic insect at the time it deposited its eggs, the fruits thus galls. One fruit (right) is cut open.

24. **Opuntia fragilis** (Nuttall) Haworth
Little prickly pear

Low, mat-forming plants, usually 5-10 cm high, the clumps often 30+ cm diam; larger terminal joints bluish-green, flattened-obovoid, flattened-ovoid, elliptic, or orbiculate, 2-4.5 cm long, 1.2-2.5(3.8) cm broad, 1.2-2 cm thick, thickness at least one-half breadth, sometimes almost equal, readily detached and often clinging by barbed spines; leaves conical, 1.5-3 mm long; areoles 1.5-3 mm diam, typically 3-6 mm apart; spines usually on most of joint but rarely none, the longest in upper areoles, white or pale gray, 1-6(9) per areole, spreading in all directions, straight, the longer 1.2-1.5(3) cm long, basally 0.7 mm diam, nearly circular to elliptic in cross section, strongly barbed; glochids tan or brownish, 2 mm long; flower 4.5 cm diam, 3-4 cm long; sepaloids green, edged with yellow, the smaller ovate-acute, the intermediate semicircular, the larger nearly orbiculate, 5-15 mm long, 4.5-15 mm broad, acute to broadly rounded and short-acuminate to mucronate, undulate; petaloids yellow or greenish (among hybrids sometimes magenta), cuneate or cuneate-obovate, 15-25 mm long, 12-20 mm broad, truncate to rounded, entire; filaments yellow or greenish, 6 mm long; anthers yellow, 1.5 mm long; style greenish-yellow, 10-15 mm long, ±4 mm diam; stigmas 10, ±2 mm long, thick; fruit green or reddish-green

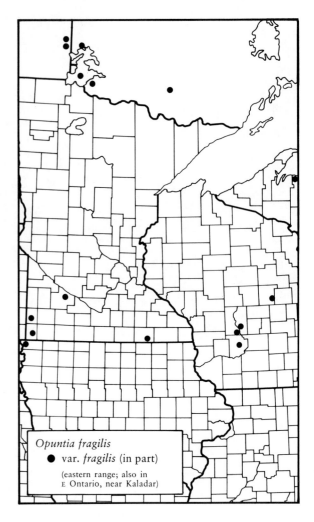

Opuntia fragilis
● var. *fragilis* (in part)
(eastern range; also in E Ontario, near Kaladar)

Distinctive Characters of the Varieties of **Opuntia fragilis**

Character	a. var. **fragilis**	b. var. **brachyarthra**
Larger terminal joints	Elliptic to obovate or orbiculate, 2-3.8(4.4) cm long, 1.2-5 cm broad	(2.5)3.8-4.5 (very rarely 7) cm long, ±2.5 (very rarely to 3.8) cm broad
Longest spines	Gray, tan, brown, or somewhat reddish, 1.2-1.5(2.5) cm long (spines sometimes none)	Red or reddish-brown (1.2)2.5-3 cm long
Altitude	Northward: sea level to 600m (2,000 ft); southward: 900-1,500 (2,400) m (3,000-5,000 or 8,000 ft)	1,350-2,400 m (4,500-8,000 ft)
Floristic association	Chiefly Sagebrush Desert; also sparingly in Pacific Lowland Forest, Palouse Prairie, Rocky Mountain Montane Forest, and Juniper-Pinyon Woodlands; Great Plains Grassland (fairly common); Prairie (rare)	Mostly Southern Juniper-Pinyon Woodland and Great Plains Grassland; also Northern Juniper-Pinyon Woodland and Sagebrush Desert

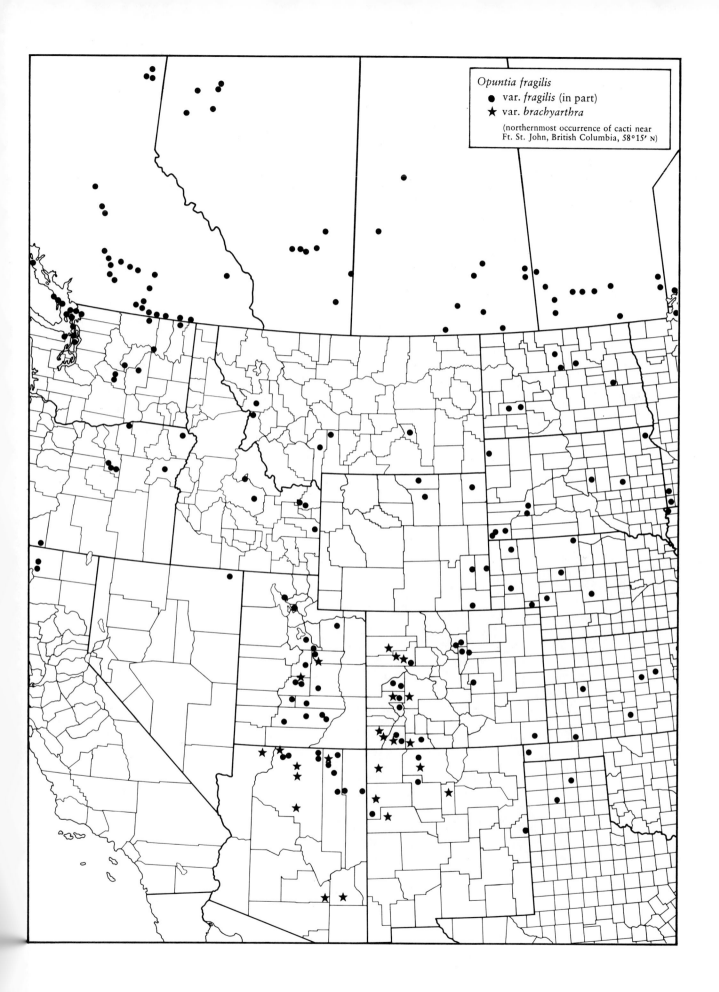

Opuntia fragilis
● var. *fragilis* (in part)
★ var. *brachyarthra*

(northernmost occurrence of cacti near
Ft. St. John, British Columbia, 58°15′ N)

Fig. 389. Little prickly pear, *Opuntia fragilis* var. *fragilis*, in Great Plains Grassland. (Homer L. Shantz)

Fig. 390. *Opuntia fragilis* var. *fragilis* in cultivation. The thick joints are nearly circular in cross section. (David Griffiths)

Fig. 391. *Opuntia fragilis* var. *fragilis*, joints, including a young one with leaves. (David Griffiths)

ward. Chiefly in Sagebrush Desert but also sparingly in Pacific Lowland Forest, Palouse Prairie, Rocky Mountain Montane Forest, Juniper-Pinyon Woodlands; more commonly in Great Plains Grassland, and rarely in the Prairie. Br. Columbia (s Vancouver I. and near Peace R. and Thompson R.) to w Manitoba; near Kaladar, Ontario; drier islands and shores of N Puget Sound, Washington; Columbia Basin and E through Rocky Mts., Great Plains, and Great Lakes region intermittently as far as Michigan (Marquette Co.) and NW Illinois; s and SE to N edge of California, N Nevada, N (mostly NE) Arizona (not common), New Mexico in Sandoval and Curry Cos., Kansas, and Oklahoma and Texas panhandles.

Reportedly on rocky headlands of southernmost Alaskan islands in situations similar to those along Puget Sound, but not found there during a special search in 1959.

Hybrids of this species are common. For example, in the southern reaches of the Columbia Basin in Washington, Oregon, and Idaho it hybridizes freely with *O. erinacea* var. *columbiana* (e.g., a hybrid swarm studied in sandy areas near the Columbia in Umatilla Co., Oregon: 5 mi. northeast of Boardman, *L. Benson 16176, Pom, 16177, Pom*). Several collections from southern Washington (e.g. Pasco, *Griffiths 10041-10044, US, Pom*) and adjacent Oregon and Idaho indicate this type of intergradation to be common.

O. fragilis hybridizes with *O. polyacantha* and *O. erinacea* and the varieties of both, producing numerous combinations of characters, which have been described as representing new species or various species described in the earlier literature. Some plants have joints up to 10 cm long and 2.5-5 cm diam; and in the most striking combinations these are plump, like the much smaller joints of *O. fragilis*. Since the plants can be propagated by cuttings, these types have been distributed widely by nurseries and dealers, appearing under various specific epithets. Hybrids are particularly common in eastern Utah and western Colorado, and they have been studied near La Sal, Utah, and Carbondale, Colorado. (See Documentation section.)

O. fragilis occurs farther north than any other cactus, being known now from several collections from the Peace River drainage in northern Br. Columbia and Alberta. (See Documentation section.)

before maturity, dry and tan at maturity, spiny or spineless (especially in vegetatively spineless plants), obovoid, 1.2-1.5 cm long, 0.9-1.2 cm diam, larger in sterile fruits parasitized by insect larvae, the umbilicus forming a deep cup, the fruit maturing and drying 2-3 months after flowering; seeds bone-colored, very irregularly discoid, the margin conspicuous, ±5-6 mm long, 4-5 mm broad, 1.5 mm thick.

Opuntia fragilis is an almost comical miniature version of a prickly pear. It is an inconspicuous plant, often growing partly beneath shrubs where it is protected from animals. The plump little joints are proportionately much thicker than those of other prickly pears.

24a. Opuntia fragilis var. fragilis. Little prickly pear. Sandy, gravelly, or rocky soils of valleys, low hills, or mountainsides mostly in the desert from sea level to 600 m (2,000 ft) northward, 900-1,500(2,400) m (3,000-5,000 or 8,000 ft) south-

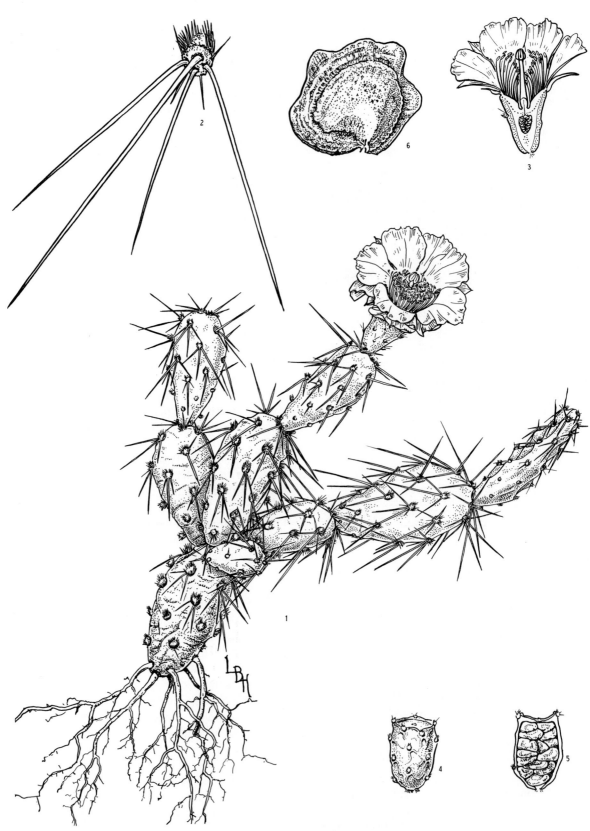

Fig. 392. Little prickly pear, *Opuntia fragilis* var. *fragilis*, ×1.1, except as indicated. *1*, Plant with a flower. *2*, Areole with spines, glochids, and wool. *3*, Flower in longitudinal section. *4*, Fruit, drying at maturity. *5*, Fruit in longitudinal section. *6*, Seed, ×3.

24b. Opuntia fragilis var. **brachyarthra** (Engelmann & Bigelow) Coulter. Sandy or gravelly soils of hills, plains, valleys, and mountainsides at 1,350-2,400 m (4,500-8,000 ft). Mostly in Southern Juniper-Pinyon Woodland and Great Plains Grassland; also along edges of Northern Juniper-Pinyon Woodland and Sagebrush Desert. In w Colorado from Garfield Co. s; Arizona (rare) from NE Mohave Co. to Navajo Co.; New Mexico in San Juan, McKinley, Rio Arriba, Valencia, and perhaps Santa Fe Cos.

Fig. 393. *Opuntia fragilis* var. *brachyarthra*, joints, many mature ones becoming elongate. (David Griffiths)

Fig. 394. *Opuntia fragilis* var. *brachyarthra*, joints with spines, these longer than those of var. *fragilis*. (David Griffiths)

25. Opuntia arenaria Engelmann

Creeping plants forming patches to 15 cm high and to 3 m diam; rhizomelike roots elongate, to 1 m long, these, as well as branches, unexpectedly bearing areoles and glochids; larger terminal joints glaucous, narrowly obovate-oblong, 5-7.5(10.5) cm long, 2-2.5 cm broad, 0.6-1.2 cm thick; areoles above ground ±2 mm diam, below ground to 4.5 mm diam, 4.5-6 mm apart; spines rather dense but not obscuring joint, nearly white to gray, sometimes tan or reddish-tan, 5-7 per areole, usually 1 much larger than others, straight, rigid, the longer 2.5-3.5 cm long, basally 0.5 mm diam, acicular, nearly circular in cross section, not strongly barbed; glochids tan, small in the areoles above ground, larger in those below ground, these ±3 mm long; flower 4-6 cm diam, 4-4.5(6) cm long; sepaloids with midribs green and margins shading off into yellow, the largest ovate-acute, to 12 mm long, 6 mm broad, short-acuminate, entire; petaloids yellow, the largest obovate, ±20-30 mm long, 10-15 mm broad, mucronate, entire; filaments pink-tinged, 6 mm long; anthers yellow, 1.5 mm long; style green, 12-20 mm long, 2-2.5 mm diam at basal swelling; stigmas 5, 2 mm long, ovate-acute, apiculate; ovary in anthesis 1.2 cm long; fruit green, changing toward tan, dry at maturity, with white spines 0.6-0.9 cm long, narrowly obovate-obconical, constricted below apex, 2.5-3 cm long, 0.9-1.2

cm diam, the umbilicus rather deep, the fruit persisting through summer; seeds pale tan, shiny, nearly circular except for indentation at hilum, the margin containing embryo very broad, somewhat irregular, the seeds 7-8 mm diam, 2 mm thick.

The plants usually form small, low mats on the sand. However, despite the small size of the individual joints, the mats are sometimes large and conspicuous.

Sandy areas near the Rio Grande and in adjacent valleys at 1,150-1,350 m (3,800-4,500 ft). Chihuahuan Desert. New Mexico near Rio Grande from Las Cruces s; Texas near Rio Grande from vicinity of El Paso to s edge of Hudspeth Co. and E to Hueco Mts. In Mexico, along Rio Grande near Ciudad Juarez, Chihuahua.

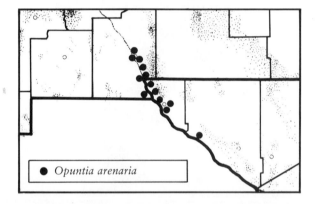

● *Opuntia arenaria*

Fig. 395. *Opuntia arenaria* in cultivation.

Fig. 396. *Opuntia arenaria*, joints, including a young one with leaves; a flower bud. (David Griffiths)

Fig. 397. *Opuntia arenaria*, rhizomelike root; producing joints. (David Griffiths)

26. Opuntia erinacea Engelmann & Bigelow

Low prickly pear, the clumps mostly 15-30 cm high and 1+ m diam; larger terminal joints bluish-green, elongate, elliptic-oblong to obovate-oblong, ±5-12.5 cm long, 2.5-7.5 cm broad, less than 1.2 mm thick, thickness not more than one-fourth breadth; areoles 3 mm diam, typically 4-6 mm apart; spines distributed over entire joint (in var. *utahensis* restricted to upper areoles), white or pale gray, 4-7(9) per areole, deflexed, somewhat but not markedly twisted, flexible, tending to curve irregularly, the longer 3-10 cm long, basally 0.25-0.75(1) mm broad, almost fiiliform but essentially subulate, at least some spines basally elliptic to very narrowly elliptic (clearly flattened) in cross section, not markedly barbed; glochids yellowish or tan, 1.5-6 mm long (longer on underground joints); flower 4.4-7.5 cm diam, 4.5-

7.5 cm long; sepaloids green edged with rose or yellow, ovate-acuminate to obovate, 10-30 mm long, 10-15 mm broad, short-acuminate to mucronate, undulate; petaloids rose to deep pink or yellow, broadly cuneate or cuneate-obovate, 25-35 mm long, 12-15 mm broad, truncate or retuse, mucronate, somewhat undulate; filaments rose or yellow, 3-12 mm long; anthers yellow, 2.25 mm long; style greenish to color of petaloids, 12-20 mm long, 3 mm diam; stigmas 10, 3 mm long, rather slender; ovary in anthesis spiny or usually so; fruit tan to brownish, dry at maturity, densely spiny, the spines spreading (especially around apex) and strongly barbed, fruit obovoid-cylindroid, 2.5-3 cm long, 1.2-2 cm diam, the umbili-

cus deep and cuplike, the fruit deciduous; seeds bone-white, irregularly discoid, 4-6 mm long, slightly less broad, 1.5 mm thick.

26a. Opuntia erinacea var. **erinacea.** Mojave prickly pear. Sandy or gravelly soils of valleys, plains, low hills, or canyonsides in the desert or woodland at 450-1,500(2,250) m (1,500-5,000 or 7,500 ft). Mojavean Desert; Northern Juniper-Pinyon Woodland; Navajoan Desert or occasionally in adjacent parts of Sagebrush Desert, Colorado Desert, or desert-edge phase of California Chaparral. California deserts from s Mono Co. to Mojave Desert and on desert sides of San Gabriel, San Bernardino, San Jacinto, and Santa Rosa

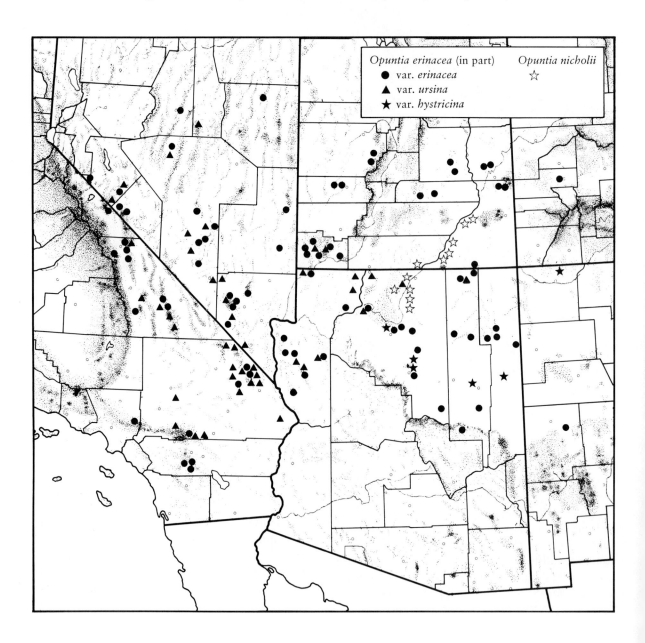

Mts.; Nevada from s Mineral Co. to White Pine Co. and s; Utah from Millard Co. to Grand Co. and s; Colorado at Montrose; Arizona from Mohave Co. to Apache Co.; New Mexico in E Catron Co.

The plants tend to spread widely, forming conspicuous clumps more gray than green and usually of greater diameter than height.

Hybrid swarms formed after interbreeding of *O. erinacea* and *O. phaeacantha* var. *major* (of the fleshy-fruited group of prickly pears) are occasional in southern Utah and northern Arizona. (See Documentation section.)

Distinction of the complex of varieties forming *O. erinacea* from the complex forming *O. polyacantha* is more or less, though not strictly, clearcut on the basis of the flattening (having a narrowly elliptic cross section) of at least the basal portions of the larger spines in *O. erinacea*. This, however, is inconsistent in some instances, and particularly so in zones of geographical overlap from Nevada to northwestern New Mexico. Examples are especially evident along the zone of geographical contact of var. *erinacea* and *O. polyacantha* var. *rufispina*. (See Documentation section.)

Hybridizes also with *O. fragilis* var. *fragilis* (sp. 24a).

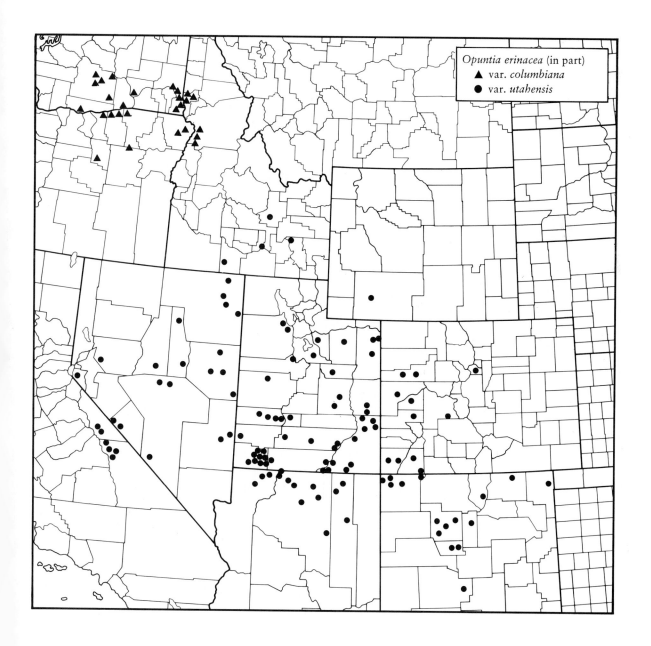

Opuntia erinacea (in part)
▲ var. *columbiana*
● var. *utahensis*

Distinctive Characters of the Varieties of **Opuntia erinacea**

Character	a. var. erinacea	b. var. columbiana	c. var. ursina	d. var. utahensis	e. var. hystricina
Joint shape	Elliptic- to oblong-ovate	Usually elongate-obovate	Elliptic- to oblong obovate	Narrowly to broadly obovate or elliptic	Broadly deltoid-obovate
Joint size	Usually 10-12 cm long, 2.5-5 cm broad	Usually 6.2-12.5 cm long, 2.5-7.5 cm broad	Usually 10-12 cm long, 2.5-5 cm broad	Usually 5-8.7 cm long, 5-7.5 cm broad	±5 cm long and broad
Spine distribution on joint	In all areoles, gradually shorter down joint	In all but a few areoles, abruptly shorter down joint	In all areoles, only slightly shorter down joint, those in lower areoles long and very slender	In all areoles, only slightly shorter down joint	In all areoles, those in upper areoles longest
Longest spines	3-9.5 cm long, 0.5 mm broad, usually recurved or deflexed, somewhat flexuous	3-4.5 cm long, 0.5 mm broad, recurved or deflexed, not markedly flexuous	7.5-10 cm long, 0.25 mm broad, curving, remarkably flexuous	7.5-10 cm long, 0.25 mm broad, curving and deflexed, remarkably flexuous	6-9.5 cm long, 0.5-1 mm broad, spreading, nearly straight, not flexuous
Flower diam	5-7.5 cm	4.4-5 cm	5-7.5 cm	5-7.5 cm	
Spines on fruits	On upper part, abundant	On upper part, fairly numerous	On entire fruit, abundant	On upper part, few and short	On upper part, abundant
Altitude	450-1,500(2,250) m (1,500-5,000 or 7,500 ft)	300-600 m (1,000-2,000 ft) to 1,700 m (5,700 ft) southward	1,200-1,650 m (4,000-5,000 ft)	(900)1,700-2,400 m (3,000 or 5,000 to 8,000 ft)	1,500-2,200 m (5,000-7,300 ft)
Floristic association	Mojavean Desert; Northern Juniper-Pinyon Woodland; Navajoan Desert; occasional in Sagebrush Desert, Colorado Desert and desert-edge California Chaparral	Palouse Prairie; Sagebrush Desert	Upper parts of Mojavean Desert	Juniper-Pinyon Woodlands; upper Sagebrush desert; edge of Rocky Mountain Montane Forest	Sagebrush Desert; Juniper-Pinyon Woodlands; Great Plains Grassland

Unknown

Fig. 398. Mojave prickly pear, *Opuntia erinacea* var. *erinacea*, a creeping plant near Echo Cliffs, Navajo Reservation, Coconino Co., Arizona.

Fig. 399. *Opuntia erinacea* var. *erinacea* near Hackberry, Mohave Co., Arizona. (David Griffiths)

Fig. 400. *Opuntia erinacea* var. *erinacea*, stem joints and a young fruit. (Robert H. Peebles)

405

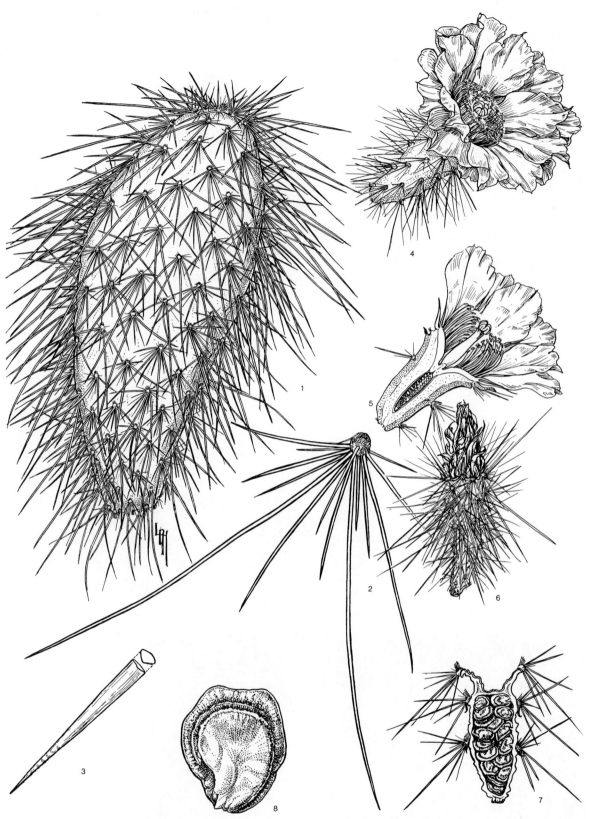

Fig. 401. Mojave prickly pear, *Opuntia erinacea* var. *erinacea*, ×1.1, except as indicated. *1*, Joint. *2*, Areole, showing spines and glochids, ×3. *3*, Spine tip, slightly barbed, ×8. *4*, Flower. *5*, Flower in longitudinal section. *6*, Fruit, dry at maturity. *7*, Fruit in longitudinal section. *8*, Seed, ×6.5.

26b. Opuntia erinacea var. **columbiana** (Griffiths) L. Benson. Rocky soils of hillsides and canyon walls in prairies or desert at 300-600 m (1,000-2,000 ft) northward, southward to 1,700 m (5,700 ft). Palouse Prairie and Sagebrush Desert. Columbia R. Basin in Washington E of Cascade Mts. near Columbia R. and Snake R.; in Oregon along main Columbia R. drainage and in Blue Mt. region; Idaho along Snake R. and near mouths of its larger tributaries, also along Salmon R. as far upstream as Riggins, Idaho Co.

The clumps of this plant are memorable for their narrow joints and sparse, long, deflexed spines from the upper parts of the joints.

This variety has been under observation since it was collected (in flower) at Clarkston, Asotin Co., Washington, in June 1929 (*L. Benson 1642, Pom, DS*). The collection has been kept in cultivation since then, but during 45 years it has not flowered in the climates of California or Tucson.

The variety intergrades, especially in the western part of its range, with *O. fragilis* var. *fragilis* (sp. 24a), and in eastern Washington and in Idaho with *O. polyacantha* var. *polyacantha*. For this reason its normal combinations of characters break down in some localities (particularly the combination of flattened spines with other characters).

Fig. 402. *Opuntia erinacea* var. *columbiana*, joints. (David Griffiths)

Fig. 403. *Opuntia erinacea* var. *columbiana*, on a sand cutbank, Pasco, Franklin Co., Washington. (David Griffiths)

Fig. 404. *Opuntia erinacea* var. *columbiana*, plant collected in flower near Clarkston, eastern Washington, in June 1929. During 48 years of cultivation in northern and southern California and southern Arizona, the plant did not flower again.

Fig. 405. *Opuntia erinacea* var. *columbiana*, plant with flowers and buds. (Robert L. Benson)

26c. Opuntia erinacea var. **ursina** (Weber) Parish. Grizzly bear cactus. Rocky soils of hillsides in the desert mostly at 1,200-1,650 m (4,000-5,500 ft). Upper parts of Mojavean Desert. California in Mojave Desert region from White Mts., Inyo Co., to N Riverside Co.; Nevada in s Mineral, s Eureka, Nye, Clark, and Lincoln Cos.; Utah in Washington Co.; Arizona from Mohave Co. to Navajo Co.

The variety forms large clumps remarkable for their numerous long, flexible, undulating, threadlike, deflexed spines at the bases of the lower joints. This novelty is desirable in cultivation, and consequently the plant has become scarce in the desert.

The parallel occurrence of similar spines in *O. polyacantha* var. *trichophora* (occurring from southwestern Colorado and northeastern Arizona across southern New Mexico to western Oklahoma) is remarkable. The spines of that variety are nearly circular (broadly elliptic) in cross section. The elongate and threadlike character of the spines and their distribution on the plant may represent either parallel development or retention of the character and loss of others derived from a common ancestry.

Fig. 406. Grizzly bear cactus, *Opuntia erinacea* var. *ursina*, in the Rancho Santa Ana Botanic Garden, showing the long, threadlike spines on the lower portions of the lower joints.

Fig. 407. *Opuntia erinacea* var. *ursina*.

26d. Opuntia erinacea var. **utahensis** (Engelmann) L. Benson. Sandy, gravelly, or rocky soils of plains or mountainsides in woodlands at (900) 1,700-2,400 m (3,000 or 5,600-8,000 ft). Juniper-Pinyon Woodlands, upper edge of Sagebrush Desert, and edge of Rocky Mountain Montane Forest. Idaho from Butte Co. to Twin Falls and Bannock Cos., s to California along E side of Sierra Nevada in Mono and Inyo Cos.; middle altitudes in Nevada, Utah, w Colorado and Colorado Rockies (rare); Arizona from Mohave Co. to Apache Co.; New Mexico as far s as E Socorro, Bernalillo, and Union Cos.

The clumps are large and irregular, and often long series of prostrate joints run like boxcars away from the main areas. The green joints are as conspicuous as the gray of the relatively sparse spines.

Var. *utahensis* is the plant known in cultivation as "*O. rhodantha*" and "*O. xanthostemma*."

In New Mexico the variety is represented mostly by forms shading into *O. polyacantha* var. *juniperina*.

Intergradation of var. *utahensis* with var. *erinacea* and with *O. polyacantha* var. *rufispina* is discussed under var. *erinacea* (sp. 26a). Forms recombining its characters with those of other varieties of *O. erinacea* have been studied in the field. Var. *utahensis* also intergrades commonly with the other varieties of *O. polyacantha* and with *O. basilaris* var. *aurea* (especially in and near Zion National Park; see sp. 28d).

Fig. 410. *Opuntia erinacea* var. *utahensis*, mature joint with elongate spines. (David Griffiths)

Fig. 409 (*left*). *Opuntia erinacea* var. *utahensis*, young joint still bearing some leaves, the spines not yet elongate. (David Griffiths)

Fig. 408. *Opuntia erinacea* var. *utahensis* growing near the Virgin River, southern Utah.

Fig. 411. *Opuntia erinacea* var. *utahensis*, prostrate stem, with flower buds and a flower. (Robert H. Peebles)

Fig. 412. *Opuntia erinacea* var. *utahensis*, joints with a flower. The spines are flattened (note the top and edge views, as indicated by arrows). (Robert H. Peebles)

26e. Opuntia erinacea var. **hystricina** (Engelmann & Bigelow) L. Benson. Porcupine prickly pear. Sand or plains, low hills, and washes in deserts, grasslands, or woodlands at 1,500-2,200 m (5,000-7,300 ft). Sagebrush Desert, Juniper-Pinyon Woodlands, and Great Plains Grassland. Arizona on Little Colorado R. watershed and in N Apache Co.; New Mexico in San Juan Co.

The elongate drooping spines from the apex of the joint are the conspicuous feature of the plants. They are more slender than those of *O. nicholii*.

The variety has been misinterpreted by all authors, usually being confused with the long-spined forms of *O. polyacantha* var. *rufispina*. Some specimens of *O. polyacantha* from west central New Mexico as far east as Albuquerque show affinity with this variety.

27. Opuntia nicholii L. Benson
Navajo Bridge prickly pear

Low-growing prickly pear, the clumps 15-22.5 (30) cm high, mostly 1-6 m diam; larger terminal joints bluish-green, narrowly obovate to sometimes obovate, (10)12-20 cm long, (5)7.5-12.5 cm broad, 1.2+ cm thick, thickness not more than one-eighth breadth; areoles 3-4.5 mm diam, typically 1.2-2 cm apart; spines very conspicuous, growing from all areoles, those of lower areoles sometimes shorter, white or very pale gray, often reddish before maturity, 4-7 per areole, deflexed, somewhat flexible, markedly twisting and curving in various directions, the longer spines from upper areoles 7.5-12.5 cm long, basally 1-1.5 mm broad, subulate, very narrowly elliptic in cross section, not barbed; glochids yellowish or tan, short and inconspicuous by comparison with those of other prickly pears, ±3 mm long; flower 6-7.5 cm diam, 6-7 cm long; sepaloids green edged with reddish-purple (rarely with yellow), ovate-acute to broadly cuneate-obovate, 6-30 mm long, 6-20 mm broad, short-acuminate to mucronate, undulate; petaloids magenta to rose (rarely yellow), cuneate-obovate, 35-40 mm long, 25-30 mm broad, rounded or truncate, mucronate, slightly undulate; filaments 15 mm long; anthers yellow, 2.25 mm long; style greenish, 15 mm long, 3 mm diam; stigmas 10, 4.5 mm long, thick; ovary in anthesis moderately to slightly spiny; fruit tan to brownish, dry at maturity, with moderate number of strongly barbed, horizontally spreading or deflexed spines mostly around apices (barbs in a differentiated area at

apex of each spine), 2.5-3.5 cm long, 1.9-2.2 cm diam, the umbilicus shallow, the fruit deciduous 2-3 months after flowering; seeds bone-white, irregular in shape but tending to be elliptic-discoid, 7.5 mm long, 6 mm broad, ±3 mm thick.

Gravelly soils of flats and low ridges in the desert at 1,200-1,500 m (4,000-5,000 ft). Navajoan Desert. Utah in San Juan Co. along and near Glen Canyon of Colorado R. from Ticaboo Canyon to Bridge Canyon; Arizona in Coconino Co. from Utah border near Colorado R. to the broad shelves between Vermilion Cliffs and Echo Cliffs.

The plants suggest a gigantic form of *O. erinacea*. The long, white, deflexed spines curve in a bizarre fashion reminiscent of the horns of Texas longhorn cattle.

The species combines the following characters found in two other species not closely related to each other:

O. erinacea (sp. 26). Spines somewhat flattened, white or very pale gray, deflexed, mark-

Fig. 413. Navajo Bridge prickly pear, *Opuntia nicholii*, growing near Echo Cliffs in the Navajoan Desert south of the Navajo Bridge, Coconino Co., Arizona.

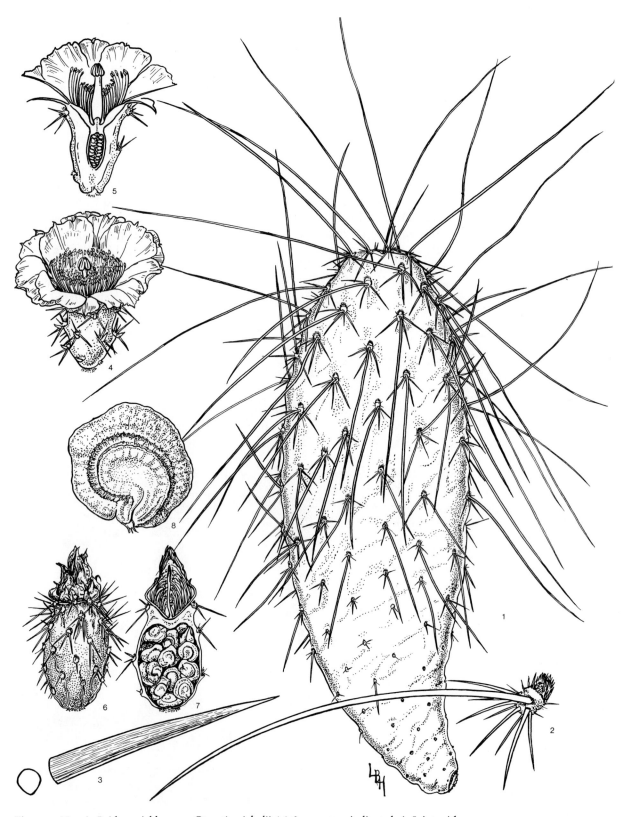

Fig. 414. Navajo Bridge prickly pear, *Opuntia nicholii*, ×.6, except as indicated. *1*, Joint with the characteristic long, deflexed spines. *2*, Areole with spines, glochids, and wool, ×1.7. *3*, Spine tip and cross section, ×5.5. *4*, Flower. *5*, Flower in longitudinal section. *6*, Mature dry fruit, ×8. *7*, Same fruit in longitudinal section. *8*, Seed, ×3.5.

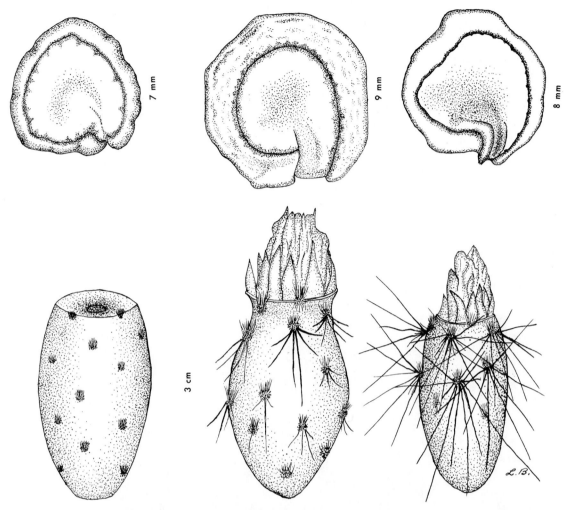

Fig. 415. Comparison of fruits and seeds of *Opuntia nicholii* (center) and its putative parents, *O. phaeacantha* var. *major* (left) and *O. erinacea* var. *erinacea* (right). (*Plant Taxonomy, Methods and Principles*)

edly twisted, relatively flexible; glochids small; flowers nearly always magenta to rose; fruits dry at maturity, with strongly barbed, horizontally spreading spines, especially on upper parts; seeds large.

O. phaeacantha var. *major* (sp. 39e). Joints of similar form but much larger than in *O. erinacea*; spines coarse, stout and stiff, mostly in apical areoles, reddish when young; flowers in rare instances yellow.

The flowers of *O. nicholii* are known only from the collections of Evelyn L. Benson (*318, Pom*), who found only one yellow-flowered plant (*319, Pom*) in a large area.

As prickly-pear populations go, the plants growing at 1,100-1,300 m (3,800-4,200 ft), especially south and east of the Navajo Bridge, have relatively uniform character combinations. How-

ever, despite the stability of the characters that distinguish *O. nicholii* from its relatives, there is still some variation within the species. This variability shows clearly that the plants in a given area are not clones formed by the growth of detached fragments from one original plant.

When *O. nicholii* was named and described in 1950, the writer postulated a hybrid origin in the remote past from *O. erinacea* and *O. phaeacantha* var. *major*, followed by natural selection of a population adapted to the local habitat. This possibility was suggested by the hybridizing of these species observed at Springdale, Utah, and elsewhere. More recently, both species and a hybrid swarm apparently resulting from their interbreeding have been found 10 mi. southeast of the Navajo Bridge at 300 m higher than the usual elevation (*L. & R. L. Benson 15748-15753, Pom*). In other hybrid swarms of the two species, plants similar to O. *nicholii* were not found, but in this area some individuals were identical with it, whereas others graded into O. *erinacea* or O. *phaeacantha* var. *major*.

The status of O. *nicholii* is open to question. It differs from both the probable parental species, and through a considerable area at a particular elevation its rather narrow range of gene combinations is well sorted out. Yet, taken alone, O. *nicholii* is really an incipient species rather than one clearly differentiated. Reduction to varietal status may be a reasonable solution to the problem; but the question, then, is under which species subordinate status should be accorded. Perhaps as much can be said for one as for the other, though if there is any choice it may be in favor of O. *erinacea*.

28. Opuntia basilaris Engelmann & Bigelow
Beavertail cactus

Low-growing prickly pear, the clumps usually 15-30 cm high, 0.3-2 m diam; larger terminal joints blue-green, sometimes (especially in cold weather) also irregularly purplish with a betacyanin pigment, finely papillate, sometimes glabrous but usually minutely canescent (afterwards ashy blue-green and velvety), obovate, sometimes circular, narrowly elongate, or spathulate, 5-20 (32.5) cm long, (2.5)4-10(15) cm broad, ±1.2 cm thick; areoles circular or rarely elongate, 1-3 mm diam, typically 0.9-1.2 cm apart; spines none, except in var. *treleasei*, in that variety yellow to brownish, 1-5 per areole, spreading, straight or rarely curving, the longer 0.5-2.5(3) cm long, basally 0.5 mm (rarely 1 mm) diam, acicular, nearly

Fig. 416. Beavertail cactus, *Opuntia basilaris* var. *basilaris*, between Aguila and Congress Junction, Arizona. The numerous fruits, not quite mature, are still green and fleshy.

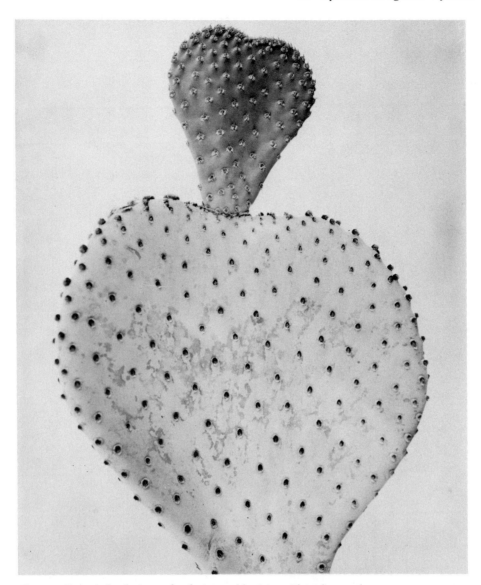

Fig. 417. *Opuntia basilaris* var. *basilaris*, an older joint with no leaves, the areoles small and with minute but strongly barbed glochids; the younger joint with leaves. (David Griffiths; from *The Native Cacti of California*)

circular in cross section, not barbed; glochids brown or brownish-tan, ±3 mm long, troublesome to humans; flower 5-7.5 cm long and in diam; sepaloids greenish, edged with cerise or sometimes yellow, broadly ovate-acute to obovate or cuneate, 5-30 mm long, ±12 mm broad, short-acuminate to cuspidate, nearly entire; petaloids cerise or yellow, obovate or cuneate, 25-40 mm long, 12-25 mm broad, truncate to rounded, cuspidate, undulate-crenate; filaments color of petaloids, 12 mm long; anthers yellow, 2.25 mm long; style the color of perianth, 15-20 mm long, 1.5 mm diam; stigmas 10, 2.25 mm long, thick; ovary in anthesis not spiny; fruit green, changing to tan or gray, dry at maturity, not spiny, except with a few spines in var. *treleasei*, the fruit 2.5-3 cm long, 1.5-2.2 cm diam, the umbilicus of moderate depth, the fruit deciduous within 3-4 months after flowering; seeds bone-white or grayish, nearly circular, smooth or rough and irregular and then the margin conspicuous or corky, the seeds ±6 mm long, slightly less broad, less than 3 mm thick.

28a. Opuntia basilaris var. **basilaris.** Beavertail cactus. Sandy soils and often in gravelly or rocky soils of plains, valleys, washes, or canyons in the desert at 0-1,200 m (sea level to 4,000 ft),

Distinctive Characters of the Varieties of **Opuntia basilaris**

Character	a. var. basilaris	b. var. brachyclada	c. var. longiareolata	d. var. aurea	e. var. treleasei
Joint shape	Obovate, sometimes orbiculate	Elongate, oblong, or spathulate	Spathulate	Elliptic to obovate	Narrowly elliptic or obovate
Joint size	5-17.5 (32.5) cm long, 4-10(15) cm broad	5-7.5(12.5) cm long, 2.5-3(4.5) cm broad	10-12.5 cm long, ±5 cm broad	5-10 cm long, 3-5(6.2) cm broad	7.5-20(25) cm long, 5-10 cm broad
Areoles	Circular, 1.5-3 mm diam	Circular, 1.5 mm diam	Elongate, 3 mm long, 1 mm broad	Circular, 1.5 mm diam	Circular, 3 mm diam
Spines	None	None	None	None	Present (see species description)
Petaloid color	Cerise	Cerise	Cerise	Yellow	Cerise
Seed margin	Inconspicuous	Inconspicuous	Unknown	Large and irregular	Inconspicuous
Altitude	0-1,200 (or to 1,500 or 2,700) m (sea level to 4,000 or sometimes 5,000 or 9,000 ft)	900-1,800 m (3,000-6,000 ft)	600 m (2,000 ft)	1,200-2,100 m (4,000-7,000 ft)	120-300 m (400-1,000 ft)
Floristic association	Mojavean and Colorado deserts; occasional on edges of associations listed below[a]	Desert edge California Chaparral	Mojavean Desert	Juniper-Pinyon Woodlands and upper Mojavean Desert	Pacific Grassland and Mojavean Desert

[a] Sagebrush Desert, California Oak Woodland, California Chaparral, Pacific Grassland, Northern Juniper-Pinyon Woodland, and Pacific Montane Forest.

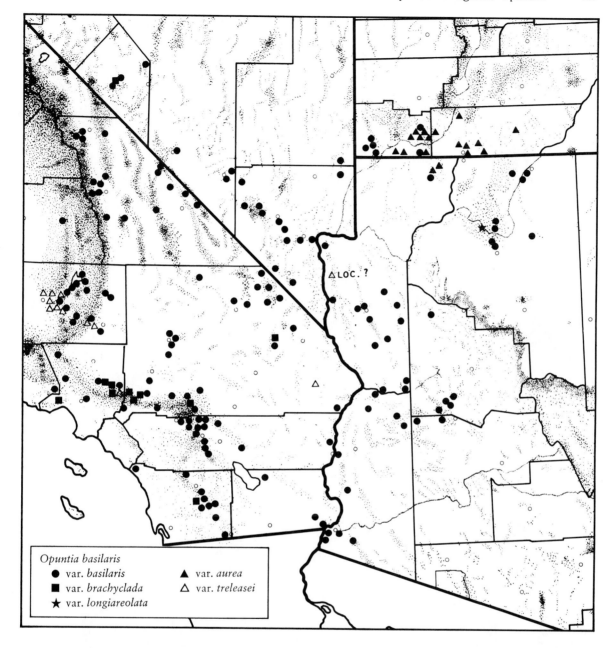

Opuntia basilaris
- ● var. *basilaris*
- ■ var. *brachyclada*
- ★ var. *longiareolata*
- ▲ var. *aurea*
- △ var. *treleasei*

occasionally to 1,500(2,700) m (5,000 or 9,000 ft). Mojavean and Sonoran (Colorado) deserts and along edge of Sagebrush Desert; occasional in California Oak Woodland, California Chaparral, Pacific Grassland, and Northern Juniper-Pinyon Woodland; rare in Pacific Montane Forest. California, occasional at intervals on coastal sides of mountains of the main axis w of the deserts from s Tulare Co. to San Diego Co., common in Inyo Co. and Mojave and Colorado deserts, rare in mountains, but sometimes on E side of Sierra Nevada in Inyo Co. and in San Bernardino Mts.; Nevada from Esmeralda and s Lincoln Cos. to Clark Co.; Utah in sw Washington Co. and (rarely) in Garfield Co.; Arizona from Mohave Co. to Coconino Co. (at low altitudes along Colorado R. system) and to Yavapai, w Yuma, NW Maricopa, and w Pima Cos. Mexico in adjacent N Sonora.

The symmetrical clumps or mounds of purplish spineless joints are the most striking feature of the plants, and the joint does resemble a beaver's tail. The obvious absence of spines commonly leads the unwary to handle the plant and to be stuck with numerous glochids, more irritating than spines.

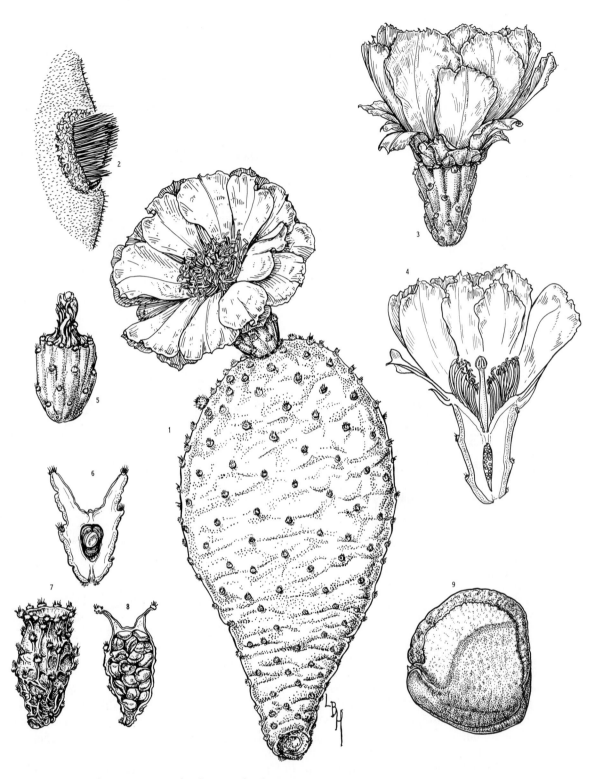

Fig. 418. Beavertail cactus, *Opuntia basilaris* var. *basilaris,* ✕.8, except as indicated. *1,* Joint with a flower. *2,* Areole with only glochids and wool, the surface of the joint pubescent. *3,* Flower. *4,* Flower in longitudinal section. *5,* Fruit, maturing and about to dry. *6,* Fruit in longitudinal section, early stage of drying. *7,* Fruit, after drying. *8,* Dried fruit in longitudinal section, the seeds mature. *9,* Seed, ✕5.5.

28b. Opuntia basilaris var. **brachyclada** (Griffiths) Munz. Little beavertail. Sandy soils of slopes just above the deserts mostly at 900-1,800 m (3,000-6,000 ft). Desert-edge phase of California Chaparral. California on desert sides of San Gabriel and San Bernardino Mts. in Los Angeles and San Bernardino Cos. and, disjunctly, on Vulcan Mt., San Diego Co., and in Providence Mts. (E Mojave Desert region).

This variety is an attractive miniature beavertail.

28c. Opuntia basilaris var. **longiareolata** (Clover & Jotter) L. Benson. Grand Canyon beavertail. Rocky soils at bases of talus slopes in the desert at about 600 m (2,000 ft). Mojavean Desert. Arizona at Granite Rapids, Grand Canyon, Coconino Co.

The validity of this variety is dubious. It is maintained pending field study to determine whether a natural population exists. The plant is known only from the type collection.

28d. Opuntia basilaris var. **aurea** (Baxter) W. T. Marshall. Yellow beavertail. Sand or sandy soils of flats, dunes, and valleys in woodland areas at 1,200-2,100 m (4,000-7,000 ft). Juniper-Pinyon Woodland and upper edge of Navajoan Desert. Utah in SE Washington Co. and in S Kane Co.; Arizona along Utah border N of Pipe Spring, Mohave Co.

This plant is greener than the other varieties, and it is lower and flatter than var. *basilaris.* Often a long series of joints, on edge and rooting, will run out across the sand from the main plant. The clear yellow flowers are a distinctive feature not found in the other varieties.

Intergrades with O. *erinacea* var. *utahensis* (sp. 26d).

Fig. 419. Little beavertail, *Opuntia basilaris* var. *brachyclada*, on the edge of the Mojavean Desert, north face of the San Gabriel Mts., Los Angeles Co., California.

Fig. 420. Yellow beavertail, *Opuntia basilaris* var. *aurea*, in sand dunes at the edge of the Juniper-Pinyon Woodland near Pipe Spring, Mohave Co., Arizona.

Fig. 421. *Opuntia basilaris* var. *aurea* in a sandy area in the edge of the Juniper-Pinyon Woodland, with blue grama grass (*Bouteloua gracilis*) still persisting after disturbance of the sand. In sand, the freight-train-like series of joints are characteristic.

422

Fig. 422. *Opuntia basilaris* var. *aurea* in flower, in sand lodged in cracks of a sandstone ledge above the tunnel in Zion National Park, Washington Co., Utah.

Fig. 423. *Opuntia basilaris* var. *aurea* in flower, with a few spines acquired by hybridization with *O. erinacea* var. *utahensis*. This individual is one of a hybrid swarm at the type locality, just north of Pipe Spring National Monument, Mohave Co., Arizona. (Robert H. Peebles)

423

28e. Opuntia basilaris var. **treleasei** (Coulter) Toumey. Kern cactus. Sandy soils or sand of flats and low hills mostly in grassland at 120-300 m (400-1,000 ft). Pacific Grassland and Mojavean Desert. California in San Joaquin Valley (Kern Co. on plains and foothills NE, E, and SE of Bakersfield) and in Turtle Mts. in E Mojave Desert in San Bernardino Co.; NW Arizona near Colorado R.

A specimen (*E. Wiegand 134* in 1950, *Pom*) collected near Big Pine Recreation Area, San Gabriel Mts., on the border between Los Angeles and San Bernardino Cos., has similar spines, and it appears to represent this variety. The altitude is about 6,500 ft.

This variety is the only cactus other than var. *basilaris* occurring west of the Sierra Nevada crest in central or northern California. (Var. *basilaris* is rare in and near the adjacent California Oak Woodland at about 600-1,050 m (2,000-3,500 ft) in the Greenhorn Mts.) This area, like the rest of western California, has only winter rain, and the seeds of most cacti depend on a moist warm period for germination. The temperatures at which seeds of var. *treleasei* germinate have not been measured, but there is no summer rain at Bakersfield, and there are only 14 cm (5.5 in.) of winter rain.

Fig. 424. Plain dominated by Kern cactus, *Opuntia basilaris* var. *treleasei*, about 1910; since 1931, and perhaps longer, such extensive fields of this species have not been seen. (David Griffiths)

Fig. 425. *Opuntia basi-laris* var. *treleasei* in the Rancho Santa Ana Botanic Garden.

Fig. 426. *Opuntia basi-laris* var. *treleasei*, the young joints (left) bearing leaves beneath the white-woolly areoles, the older joints producing flower buds.

Fig. 427. Blind prickly pear, *Opuntia rufida,* in fruit, in the Chihuahuan Desert. (David Griffiths)

29. Opuntia rufida Engelmann
Blind prickly pear

Shrubby plants mostly 0.9-1.5 m high; trunk none or very short; larger terminal joints blue-green to gray-green, orbiculate, 7.5-15(20) cm diam, ±1.2 cm thick, densely pubescent; leaves conical, 3-4.5 mm long; areoles circular, 3 mm diam, typically 0.5-2 cm apart; spines none; glochids reddish or reddish-brown, conspicuous, readily detached and flying into the air when joint is disturbed, 2.25 mm long; flower 6-7.5 cm diam, 6-7.5 cm long; sepaloids with green centers and yellow edges, lanceolate, to 25 mm long, to ±9 mm broad, acute to truncate and acuminate, marginally or apically sharply denticulate; petaloids pale yellow, changing to orange with withering, broadly cuneate, 30-40 mm long, ±20 mm broad, rounded, somewhat irregularly denticulate or entire; filaments ±7.5 mm long; anthers yellow, slender, ±1.5-2 mm long; style green, ±15-20 mm long, basally 2 mm diam; stigmas ±10, ±4.5 mm long, very stout; ovary in anthesis ±1.2-2 cm long; fruit bright red, fleshy at maturity, slightly tuberculate, ±2.5 cm long, 1.5-2 cm diam, the umbilicus cuplike, not deep, the fruit not long-persistent; seeds gray, elliptic, 3 mm long, a little less broad, 1 mm thick.

Sandy or gravelly soils of rocky hillsides and washes in the desert at 600-1,050 m (2,000-3,500 ft). Chihuahuan Desert. Texas along the Rio Grande in Big Bend region, Presidio and Brewster Cos., and in hills N to within about 70 mi. of Alpine, Brewster Co. Mexico in Chihuahua and Coahuila.

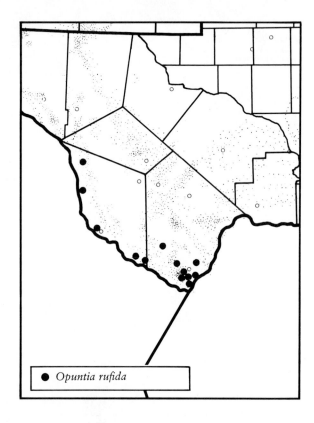

● *Opuntia rufida*

These shrubs form conspicuous, large, blue-green clumps on hillsides of dark, rough boulders. Because spines are absent, the form of the joints is their most striking feature.

The English name derives from the blinding of cattle by the numerous loose, reddish glochids, which sometimes fly into the air when the plants are disturbed. The plant should be handled with caution.

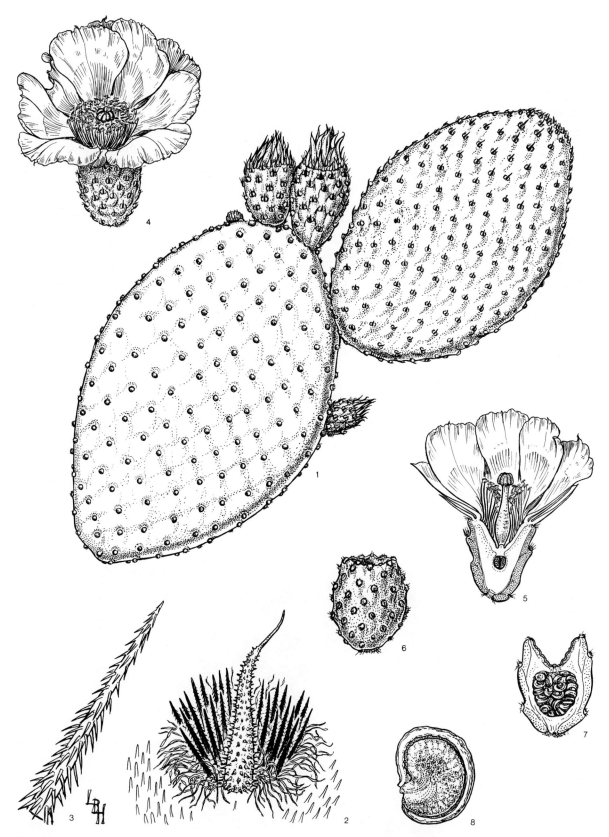

Fig. 428. Blind prickly pear, *Opuntia rufida,* ×.6, except as indicated. *1,* Immature joint with leaves and a mature joint without. *2,* Areole with a leaf (on the near edge), barbed glochids, and hairs (hairs on the joint-surface ×22). *3,* Glochid, showing the barbs, ×60. *4,* Flower. *5,* Flower in longitudinal section. *6,* Fruit, bright red and fleshy at maturity. *7,* Fruit in longitudinal section. *8,* Seed, ×5.

30. Opuntia cubensis Britton & Rose

Bushy plants 30-90 cm high, often forming thickets; larger terminal joints rather dark green, very narrowly elliptic, mostly 10-17.5 cm long, 5-6.2 cm broad, 1.2 cm thick, glabrous; areoles elliptic, 6 mm long, 3 mm broad, typically 1.2 cm apart; spines produced in all or all but lowest areoles, at first partly reddish-brown or yellow, later becoming red and white or gray, ultimately (except at tips) wholly grayish-white, 2 or 3 per areole, spreading in all directions, the lowest the longest, straight, twisted, the longer 2.5-6 cm long, basally 0.5-1 mm diam or breadth, usually acicular or some slightly flattened, elliptic in cross section, clearly barbed; glochids not in evidence, but areoles with grayish-white felt; flower to 6 cm diam, to 7 cm long; sepaloids few (±5), greenish, yellowish, or green and purplish, broadly cuneate to cuneate, 12-25 mm long, 6-9(15) mm broad, broadly truncate and with mucro or cusp ±1.5 mm long, entire; petaloids clear yellow, narrowly obovate to elliptic-obovate or narrowly obcordate, 25-40 mm long, 10-25 mm broad, rounded, truncate, or retuse, cuspidate, entire; filaments pale yellow, 6-15 mm long; anthers pale yellow, slender, 1.5-2 mm long; style light greenish-yellow, 12-20 mm long, 1.5-3 mm diam; stigmas 5, pale cream, ±2 mm long, rather broad; ovary in anthesis slender or obovate, 2-2.5 cm long; fruit reddish or (?) purplish, fleshy at maturity, smooth, with a few spines (these ±9 mm long), to 4 cm long, ±2.5 cm diam, the umbilicus fairly deep; seeds tan or pink (from the juice of the fruit?), nearly circular in outline, ±3 mm diam, 1.5 mm thick.

Sand and brushland flats or near seashore or on disturbed soils of ocean bluffs; occurring only near sea level. Caribbean Tropical Forest. Florida at SE end of Big Pine Key (nearly extinct there, owing to recent road building). West Indies on Cuba, Hispaniola, Puerto Rico, St. Christopher, Tortola, St. Croix, and St. Kitts.

Commonly, the plants are obscured by vegetation, and they are conspicuous only on bluffs or partly cleared areas.

Intergrades with *O. triacantha* (sp. 31).

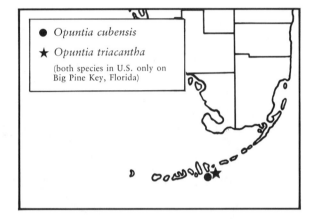

● *Opuntia cubensis*

★ *Opuntia triacantha*

(both species in U.S. only on Big Pine Key, Florida)

Fig. 429. *Opuntia cubensis,* plant from Big Pine Key, Florida, the spines on the sides of the younger joints not yet fully elongated.

Fig. 430. *Opuntia cubensis,* plant from St. Croix, Virgin Islands, with a flower and fruits.

31. Opuntia triacantha (Willdenow) Sweet

Low-growing cactus forming clumps mostly 15-20 cm high, 30-60 cm diam, or the stems sometimes erect, especially when other plants provide support; larger terminal joints green, elliptic, 5-7.5 cm long, 3-3.8 cm broad, 0.9-1.2 cm thick; areoles ±4 mm diam, typically ±1.2 cm apart; spines not dense, pale gray to white, sometimes 1 but on mature joints mostly 2 or 3 per areole, spreading at right angles to joint, straight, the longer 3-4 cm long, basally 0.7-0.8 mm diam, acicular, nearly circular in cross section, not markedly barbed; glochids yellow, becoming brown, 4.5-9 mm long; flower 3-5 cm diam, ±4 cm long; sepaloids green, the margins yellow, obcuneate, to 12 mm long, 6-9 mm broad, acute or acuminate, entire, thin near margins; petaloids clear yellow, 8-10, cuneate-obovate, 20-25 mm long, ±20 mm broad, truncate, slightly emarginate and cuspidate, entire but apically slightly undulate; filaments yellow, ±10 mm long, slender; anthers yellow, ±2 mm long, slender; style pink-tinged, ±12 mm long, ±2 mm diam; stigmas 5-10(?), 3 mm long, thick; ovary in anthesis spineless, with few areoles; fruit red, fleshy at maturity, smooth, obovoid, 2.5-3 cm long, 1.5-2 cm diam, the umbilicus shallow, the fruit not persistent; seeds light tan, thickened-discoid, the rim very narrow, 2.5 mm diam, 1.5 mm thick.

Sandy areas back of beach on old limestone of reefs; just above sea level. Caribbean Tropical Forest. Big Pine Key, Florida. Caribbean Islands from Punta Melones and Desecheo I., Puerto Rico, to Virgin I.; in Lesser Antilles on Guadeloupe.

The clumps of small joints are inconspicuous among the grasses, and stepping on them is disastrous; the spines are long and sharp, like needles.

Intergradation of *O. cubensis* and *O. triacantha* was observed in the field at Big Pine Key in 1954 and 1965, and demonstrated in several specimens at the U.S. National Herbarium, which range from *O. cubensis* (*Killip 31712*) to intermediate (*G. S. Miller 1710*) to *O. triacantha* (*Small,* May 12, 1922).

Fig. 431. *Opuntia triacantha*, plant from Big Pine Key, Florida.

32. **Opuntia pusilla** (Haworth) Haworth

Creeping, often mat-forming plants usually 2.5-7.5 cm high; larger terminal joints green (in winter reddish-purple), narrowly elliptic to elongate and nearly linear, 2.5-5(6.5) cm long, 1.2-2.5 cm broad, ±0.5 cm thick; leaves conical, to 4.5 mm long or ovoid-acute and 2.25 mm long; areoles 1.5-3 mm diam, typically 0.6-0.9 cm apart; spines tending to be in but not necessarily restricted to upper areoles, grayish, whitish, or with a little yellow, 1 (sometimes 2) per areole, spreading at right angles to joint, straight, the longer 2-2.5 cm long, basally ±1 mm diam, acicular, nearly circular in cross section, strongly barbed; glochids tan, becoming gray, 3-4.5 mm long; flower 4-6 cm diam and long; sepaloids green edged with yellow, ovate-acute, 5-25 mm long, 4.5-15 mm broad, acute or mucronate, slightly toothed and undulate; petaloids clear light yellow, few (5-8), cuneate-obovate, 20-30 mm long, 12-20 mm broad, rounded or emarginate, slightly toothed; filaments yellow, 9 mm long; anthers pale yellow, 2.25 mm long; style yellow, 15-20 mm long, 1.5 mm diam; stigmas 5-10(?), 3 mm long, rather thick; ovary in anthesis spineless, with few areoles; fruit purple, fleshy at maturity, smooth, normally 2.5-3 cm long, 1.2-2 cm diam, the umbilicus shallow, the fruit not persistent; seeds grayish, nearly discoid, 4.5 mm long, slightly less broad, 1.5 mm thick.

Sand of mostly coastal dunes, beaches, and woods near sea level. Open areas along edges of deciduous forests and Caribbean Tropical Forest. Texas at Rockport and Anahuac; coastal regions from Mississippi to North Carolina, including N Florida; rare near Ft. Meyers, Florida. A later collection from near Baffle Point on Bolivar Peninsula, Galveston Co., Texas, is reported by Weniger (1970).

This obscure little cactus is a hazard to humans because it occurs in the dunes above the beaches. Its spines are needle-sharp and strongly barbed; the easily detached joints thus become attached to bare feet.

Hybrids of O. *pusilla* and O. *humifusa* var. *humifusa* have been collected at various points from North Carolina to Florida (see sp. 34a).

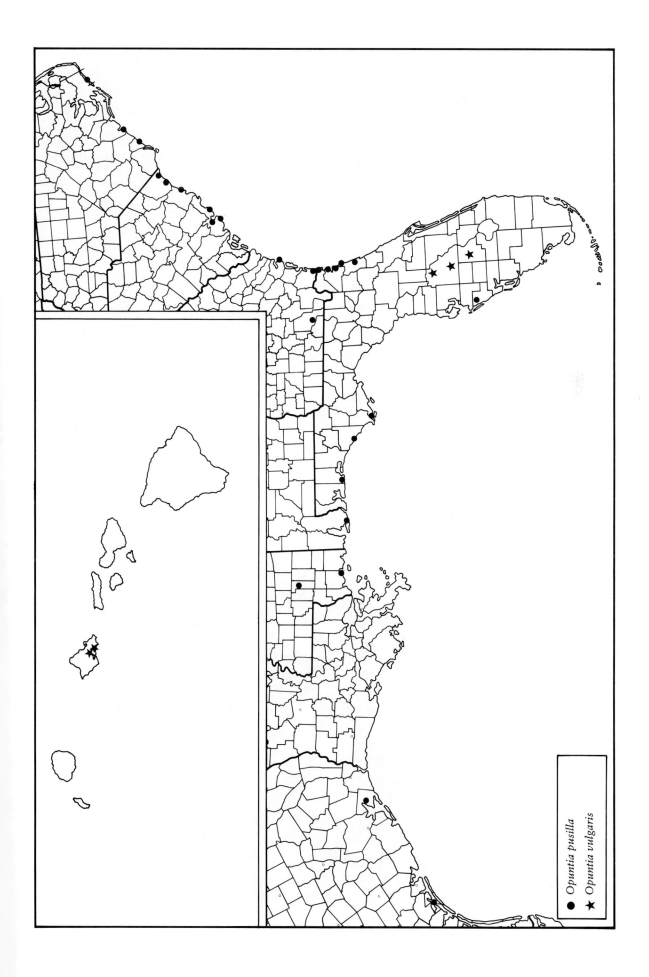

Fig. 433. *Opuntia pusilla*, joints of a plant with fewer than the usual number of spines, the young terminal joints with leaves. The long, sharp, barbed spines are dangerous to bathers along the beaches; the spiny joints cling to bare feet, and the spines even penetrate leather shoes. The elongate fruits are probably sterile. (David Griffiths)

Fig. 432. *Opuntia pusilla*, plant with young joints bearing leaves and an older joint with the long, barbed spines. (David Griffiths)

432

Fig. 434. Plants from a presumed hybrid swarm (*3–10*) formed through interbreeding of *Opuntia pusilla* and *O. humifusa,* the swarm forming a natural population on stabilized sand dunes at Crescent Beach, South Carolina; growing near both parental species. Plants for comparison: *1, O. pusilla,* from Ponte Verde, Florida; *2, O. humifusa,* from Warren, Arkansas. (*Plant Taxonomy, Methods and Principles*)

433

33. Opuntia vulgaris Miller

Shrub or somewhat arborescent, usually 1.3-4 m high; trunk, when present, short, cylindroid, branching profusely above; larger terminal joints lustrous light green, obovate or narrowly so or more or less oblong or lanceolate in outline, markedly narrowed basally, 10-30 cm long, 7.5-12.5 cm broad, thin; leaves short-conical, 2-6 mm long; areoles circular, 3 mm diam, with short wool, typically 2-4 cm apart; spines sparse on joint, gray to reddish- or yellowish-brown, on joints 1 or 2 per areole but on main trunk to 10-12 per areole, spreading in various directions, straight, to 7.5 cm long, basally 1.5 mm diam, acicular, nearly circular in cross section, not markedly barbed; glochids brown or tan, 2-3 mm long; flowers 5-7.5 cm diam, 7.5-10 cm long; sepaloids with midribs red and margins yellow, the largest obovate or broadly cuneate, ±25 mm long, 12-15 mm broad, apically rounded, entire or emarginate; petaloids yellow to orange, rotate, the largest cuneate- to oblanceolate-obovate, 25-40 mm long, 12-40 mm broad, acute, nearly entire; filaments green or white, 12 mm long; anthers pale yellow, ±1 mm long; style green, 12-20 mm long; stigmas 8-10, 4.5-6 mm long, creamy yellow; ovary in anthesis slender, 3-4 cm long; fruit reddish-purple, fleshy at maturity, spineless but with glochids, obovoid, 5-7.5 cm long, 4-5 cm diam, the umbilicus slightly depressed, the fruit edible, long persistent, sometimes proliferous; seeds light tan, irregularly elliptic, 4 mm long, 3 mm broad, 1.5 mm thick.

Native of Brazil, Paraguay, Uruguay, and Argentina; introduced in disturbed areas in the Caribbean Tropical Forest and Asian-Pacific Tropical Forest. Hawaii in Honolulu at Punch Bowl and near Kamehameha School; Florida in Polk Co. at Crooked Lake and Lake Alfred.

In Florida hybridizes in both places with the native *O. humifusa* var. *ammophila*.

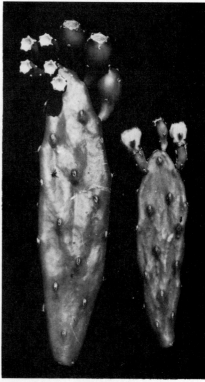

Fig. 436. *Opuntia vulgaris*, spineless joints, one with opening flowers and a young fruit, the other with fruits.

Fig. 435 (*left*). *Opuntia vulgaris*, joints of the spiny type. (David Griffiths)

Fig. 437. *Opuntia vulgaris,* joints of the usual spiny type.

34. Opuntia humifusa (Rafinesque) Rafinesque
Eastern prickly pear

Low clump- or mat-forming prickly pears, usually 7.5-10 cm high, rarely (in Florida) to 30 cm high; roots usually not tuberous; larger terminal joints green or green and lead-colored, in winter reddish-purple, orbiculate to obovate or elliptic, 3.8-10(17.2) cm long, 4-6(12.5) cm broad, 6-9 mm thick; leaves conical or elongate-conical, 4.5-7.5 mm long; areoles few, ±3 mm diam, typically 1-2 cm apart; spines in upper areoles of joint (sometimes none in some varieties), gray or brownish, 1 per areole, spreading at right angles to joint, the longer 1.9-3(5.6) cm long, basally 0.5-1 mm diam, acicular, nearly circular in cross section, not markedly barbed; glochids yellow or brown, 3 mm long; flower 4-6 cm diam and long; sepaloids green edged with yellow, ovate-acute, 5-25 mm long, 4.5-20 mm broad, short-acuminate or acute, undulate; petaloids yellow, cuneate-obovate, 25-40 mm long, 12-20 mm broad, rounded, entire; filaments yellow, 9 mm long; anthers yellow, ±2 mm long; style greenish-yellow, 9-12 mm long, 4.5 mm diam, swollen basally; stigmas 5-10, 3-4.5 mm long, thick; ovary in anthesis smooth, with few areoles; fruit purple or reddish, fleshy at maturity, with some glochids, the fruit 2.5-4 cm long, 2-3 cm diam, the umbilicus somewhat depressed, the fruit persistent until early spring; seed pale tan or gray, nearly circular, 4.5 mm diam, 1.5 mm thick, the margin (covering the embryo) ±0.5 mm broad, smooth and regular.

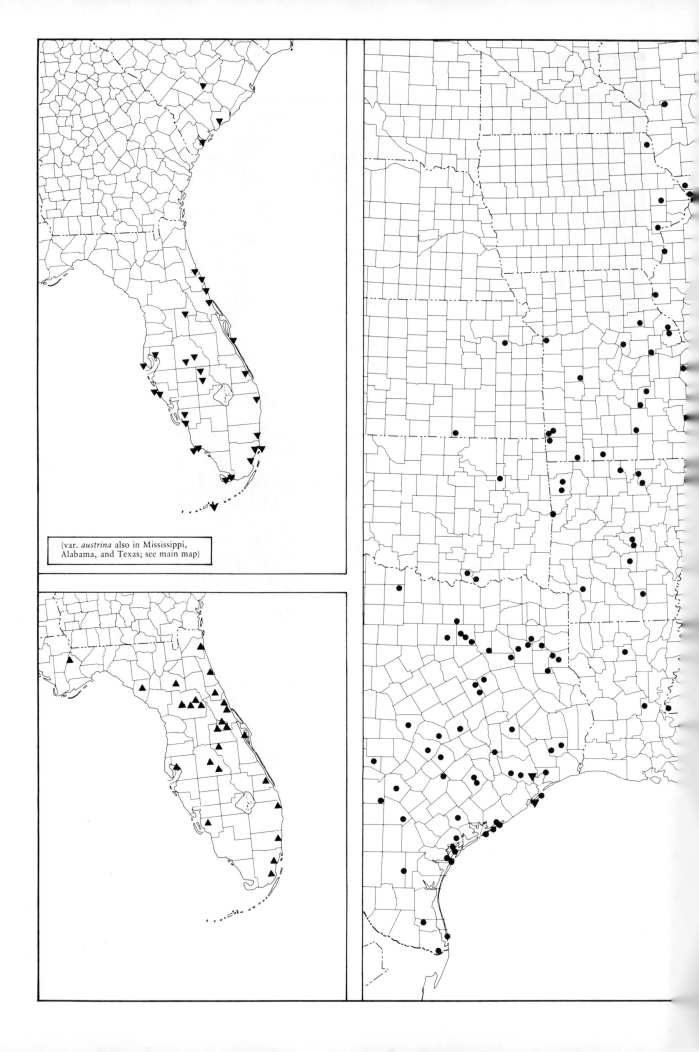

(var. *austrina* also in Mississippi,
Alabama, and Texas; see main map)

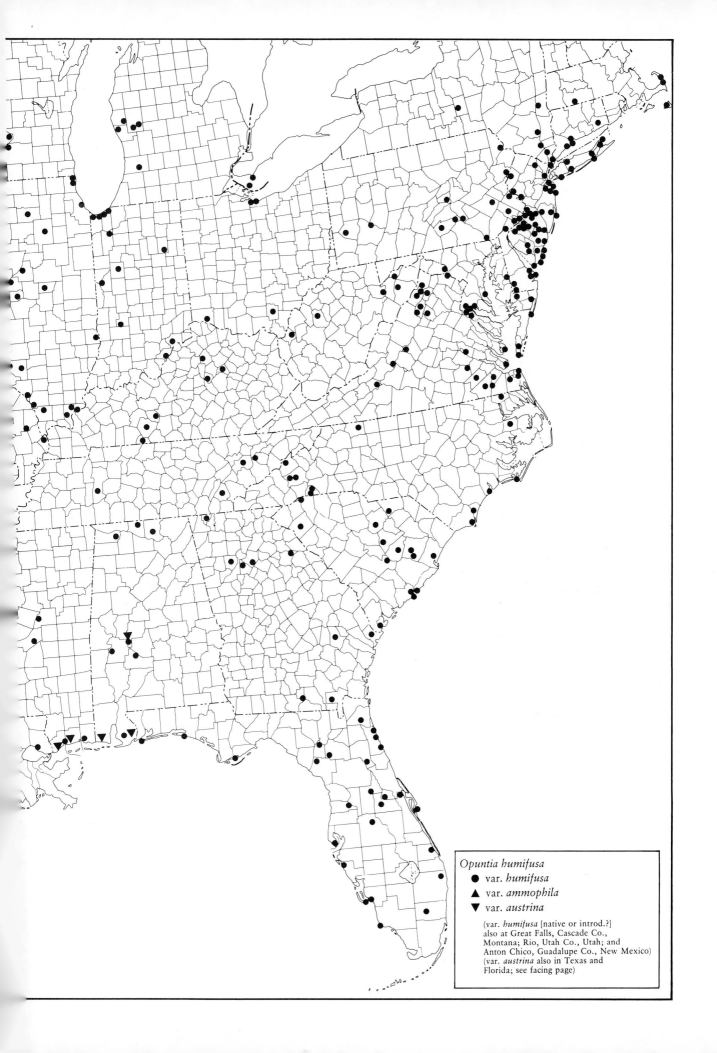

Opuntia humifusa

● var. *humifusa*

▲ var. *ammophila*

▼ var. *austrina*

(var. *humifusa* [native or introd.?]
also at Great Falls, Cascade Co.,
Montana; Rio, Utah Co., Utah; and
Anton Chico, Guadalupe Co., New Mexico)
(var. *austrina* also in Texas and
Florida; see facing page)

Distinctive Characters of the Varieties of **Opuntia humifusa**

Character	a. var. **humifusa**	b. var. **ammophila**	c. var. **austrina**
Habit	Creeping	Often 3 or 4 joints high	Creeping or ascending
Joint color and shape	Dark green, usually orbiculate or broadly obovate	Light green, elongate, narrowly elliptic to narrowly obovate	Dark green, obovate or sometimes elliptic
Joint size	5-7.5(12.5) cm long 4-6.2(7.5) cm broad	Usually 3.8-17.2 cm long, 3.8-6 cm broad	7.5-10(14) cm long, 5-9(12.5) cm broad
Leaves	Conical, to 4.5-6 (in hybrids 22) mm long	Elongate-conical, to 4.5-6(7.5) mm long	Broadly conical, to 6-7.5 mm long
Spines	Usually 2-3 cm long, 0.5-1 mm diam	Usually 2-3(5) cm long, 0.5(0.7) mm diam	Usually 3-5.6 (rarely 8.7) cm long, 1 mm diam
Altitude	1.5-600 m (5-2,000 ft)	1.5-60 m (5-200 ft)	1.5-3 m (5-10 ft)
Floristic association	Prairie; Deciduous Forests	Deciduous Forests	Strand vegetation and Deciduous Forests

34a. Opuntia humifusa var. **humifusa.** Eastern prickly pear. Sandy soil and rock outcrops (ranging from granitic to sandstone or limestone) of hills, valleys, and shores at 1.5-600 m (5-2,000 ft). Prairie and Deciduous Forests (especially south coast). Great Lakes on Point Pelee, Pelee I., and N shore of Lake Erie; Montana at Great Falls; New Mexico at Anton Chico; from E Iowa to sw Wisconsin, w Michigan, and Cape Cod in Massachusetts, s to E Kansas, E Oklahoma, E Texas, and Atlantic and Gulf coasts from Massachusetts to Florida as far s as Collier and Palm Beach Cos.

This small, bluish-green prickly pear forms little patches, astounding mainly for the fact of being cacti far from their expected places. Usually, except on open sand or exposed rock, they tend to be lost among other plants of advancing stages of succession of vegetation surrounding them. These may soon overwhelm the cacti.

Hanks and Fairbrothers (1969) have reviewed ecological and morphological variation in 11 New Jersey populations of *O. humifusa.* Their study indicates that the occurrence of *O. humifusa* is not associated with the presence of any one species or group of species of other plants, except those also occurring in open areas. Soil data indicate no positive correlation between pH or quantities of minerals (Ca, Na, Mg, K) and the occurrence of *O. humifusa.* The species was found either in areas of flat topography or on areas with south-slope exposure up to a 50° slope. The soil type underlying the plants varied from organic detritus over parent rock in rocky depressions to Penn shale-loam, coastal beach-

land, Lakewood sand, or Sassafras sandy loam. In general, the species occurs in open, sunny, dry areas, and the only character common to all sites of occurrence is dryness associated with openness.

In and near northern Florida *O. humifusa* hybridizes with other species. In northeastern Florida, plants intermediate between *O. humifusa* and *O. stricta* var. *stricta* or *dillenii* are common. (See Documentation section.)

At Beaufort, Carteret Co., North Carolina (*L. & R. L. Benson 15684-15686, Pom*) and at Crescent Beach, Horry Co., South Carolina (*L. & R. L. Benson 15671-15672, Pom*), complex populations were found. These populations (specimens in specially prepared series representing hybrid swarms) displayed all conceivable combinations of characters ranging from those of plants clearly of *O. humifusa* var. *humifusa* to those of *O. pusilla.*

Vorsila L. Bohrer, Eastern New Mexico Univ., sent (in 1971) a fruit (*01. C29. 65*) of *O. humifusa* with the characteristic narrow-rimmed seeds, collected in a cave or recess used by prehistoric Indians (Fresnal Shelter, *LA 10101*) near Alamogordo, New Mexico. The fruit was found with remains of other cacti used by the Indians. Currently, only one collection of the species is known from New Mexico (Anton Chico, Guadalupe Co., *Griffiths 10326, US, Pom*). This is about 160 mi. north and slightly east of Alamogordo. The plants at Anton Chico may or may not have been introduced with shipments of livestock. Otherwise, the nearest documented record of occurrence is east of Lake Texoma in Bryan Co., Oklahoma, 560 mi. from Alamogordo and 800 from Anton Chico. *O. humifusa* occurs in areas of higher rainfall than at Alamogordo, and its former occurrence near Fresnal Shelter may indicate a range extending farther westward during and beyond Pleistocene time; this region is occupied now by *O. macrorhiza*, which is characteristic of more xeric environments. According to Dr. Bohrer, a radiocarbon date from the lower cultural deposits at Fresnal Shelter indicates 3,615

±120 years before the present, and archeological evidence suggests dates prior to 300 A.D. for the upper levels.

The next two varieties may have been derived from individuals in the hybrid swarms that develop from crosses involving var. *humifusa*; but of course they could instead be original types from which the present species diverged.

Fig. 438. Eastern prickly pear, *Opuntia humifusa* var. *humifusa*, the more common spiny type; mature joints and young joints with leaves, a flower bud, and flowers. The joints, of the common type, are rounded to broadly elliptic. (David Griffiths)

Fig. 439 (*below*). *Opuntia humifusa,* spineless plant with elongate joints, these features less common in this species. The younger joints bear leaves; one mature joint bears flowers. (David Griffiths)

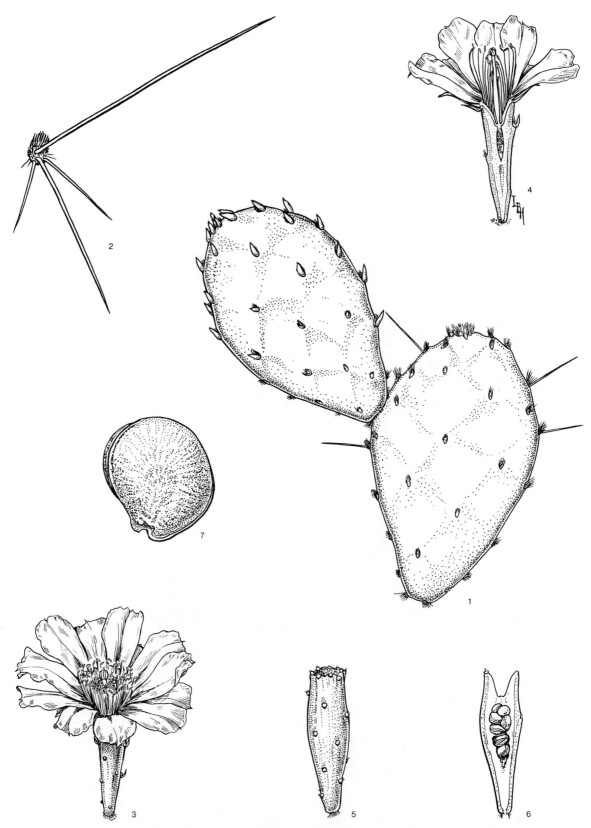

Fig. 440. Eastern prickly pear, *Opuntia humifusa* var. *humifusa*, ×.6, except as indicated. *1*, Young and old joints, the young one with leaves. *2*, Areole with spines, glochids, and wool, ×2.3. *3*, Flower. *4*, Flower in longitudinal section. *5*, Fruit. *6*, Fruit in longitudinal section. *7*, Seed, ×3.5. (In part from *The Cacti of Arizona*, ed. 2)

34b. Opuntia humifusa var. **ammophila** (Small) L. Benson. Sandy soil of beaches and dunes or mostly of interior pinelands and woodlands at 1.5-60 m (5-200 ft). Deciduous Forests of the southeastern coastal plain and adjacent areas. Florida from Liberty and Duval Cos. s to Lee and Dade Cos.

The distinctive feature of the variety is the erect series of three or four elongate joints, giving the clumps a distinctive form different from those of the other varieties and making them visible from across the sandy pinelands.

Hybridizes at Crooked Lake and Lake Alfred, Polk Co., Florida, with *O. vulgaris.*

Fig. 441. *Opuntia humifusa* var. *ammophila,* the young joints with relatively large leaves. (*Plant Taxonomy, Methods and Principles*)

Fig. 442. *Opuntia humifusa* var. *ammophila* in flower, the joints nearly spineless, a feature uncommon in this variety. (*Plant Taxonomy, Methods and Principles*)

34c. Opuntia humifusa var. **austrina** (Small) Dress. Coastal dunes and shell mounds at 1.5-3 m (5-10 ft). Strand vegetation or in Deciduous Forests. Gulf and Atlantic coasts from Houston and Galveston, Texas, to s South Carolina and all of coastal Florida; occasional in sandy soil of interior pinelands of Florida.

The plants form small mounds near or almost upon the shell beaches. The joints are more ascending and larger than in var. *humifusa*, but the colonies are less extensive.

In Texas, near Galveston, intergrades with *O. stricta*; in Florida, hybridizes with other varieties of the species.

Fig. 444. *Opuntia humifusa* var. *austrina* in fruit, the young joints with leaves. (*Plant Taxonomy, Methods and Principles*)

Fig. 443. *Opuntia humifusa* var. *austrina* on Big Pine Key, Florida. (Randy Willich)

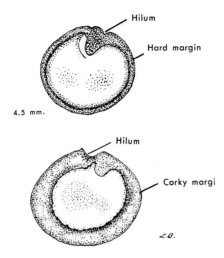

Fig. 445. Comparison of seeds of *Opuntia humifusa* and *O. macrorhiza*. *O. humifusa*, above, occurs in the Middle West, East, and South; *O. macrorhiza*, below, occurs mostly in the Great Plains and the southern Rocky Mountain region. The character of the seed margin, added to other characters known previously, may establish a means of segregating these cacti as species rather than as varieties. This question, like all others in taxonomy, is forever open to investigation. (*Plant Taxonomy, Methods and Principles*)

35. **Opuntia macrorhiza** Engelmann
Plains prickly pear

Low, clump-forming prickly pear, usually 7.5-12.5 cm high, 0.3-1.8 m diam; main root(s) usually tuberous, the other (adventitious) roots along joints often fibrous; larger terminal joints from somewhat to strongly glaucous, therefore bluish-green, orbiculate to obovate, 5-10 cm long, 5-6 (7.5) cm broad, ±12 mm thick; leaves elongate-conical, 7.5 mm long; areoles ±3 mm diam, typically 1-2 cm apart; spines mostly in uppermost areoles, white or gray, rarely brownish or reddish-brown, 1-6 per areole, mostly deflexed, straight or slightly curving, the longer 3.8-5.6 cm long, slender, basally 0.25-0.5 mm diam, acicular, nearly circular or elliptic in cross section, not barbed; glochids yellow or brown, 3 mm long; flower 5-6.2 cm diam and long; sepaloids with midribs green and margins yellow or sometimes reddish, ovate-acute, 5-25 mm long, 5-20 mm broad, short-acuminate or acute, undulate; petaloids yellow or tinged basally with red, cuneate-obovate, 25-40 mm long, 12-25 mm broad, rounded, entire; filaments yellow, 9 mm long; anthers yellow, ±2 mm long; style greenish-yellow, 9-12 mm long, 4.5 mm greatest diam, basally swollen; stigmas 5-10, ±3 mm long, thick; ovary in anthesis smooth, with few areoles; fruit purple or reddish-purple, fleshy at maturity, with some glochids, obovoid, 2.5-4 cm long, 2.5-3 cm diam, the umbilicus somewhat depressed, the fruit persistent for several months; seed pale tan or gray, irregular but basically more or less discoid, ±4.5 mm diam, 1.5-2.25 mm thick, the margin covering the embryo) ±1 mm broad, roughened, irregular.

Distinctive Characters of the Varieties of **Opuntia macrorhiza**

Character	a. var. **macrorhiza**	b. var. **pottsii**
Joints	Moderately glaucous, (6)7.5-10 cm long	Markedly glaucous, 5-6 cm long
Spines	Slender, ±0.5 mm diam	Very slender, ±0.25 mm diam
Perianth color	Yellow, or the centers reddish	Reddish
Altitude	600-2,100(2,400) m (2,000-7,000 or 8,000 ft)	(780)1,200-1,800 m (2,600 or 4,000-6,000 ft)
Floristic association	Great Plains Grassland; Juniper-Pinyon Woodlands; lower Rocky Mountain Montane Forest; Edwards Plateau	Desert Grassland; Great Plains Grassland; Chihuahuan Desert

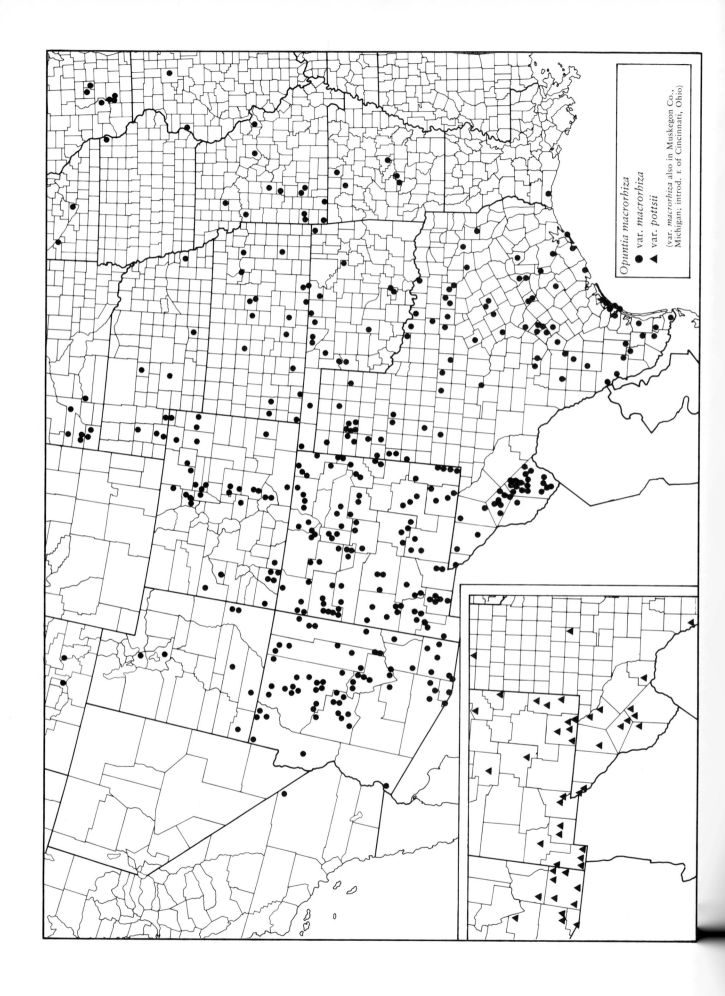

Opuntia macrorhiza

● var. *macrorhiza*
▲ var. *pottsii*

(var. *macrorhiza* also in Muskegon Co., Michigan; introd. E of Cincinnati, Ohio)

35a. Opuntia macrorhiza var. **macrorhiza.**
Sandy, gravelly, or rocky soils of plains and valleys (less commonly on hillsides) at 600-2,100(2,400) m (2,000-7,000 or 8,000 ft). Great Plains Grassland, Juniper-Pinyon Woodlands, Southwestern Oak Woodland, and lower elevations of Rocky Mountain Montane Forest; sometimes in Desert Grassland or the Prairie or along edges of the Deciduous Forests; Rio Grande Plain and remarkably abundant on the Edwards Plateau. California on Clark Mt., San Bernardino Co.; s Idaho (rare); Utah (rare); sw South Dakota; Wyoming near Cheyenne; Colorado; N and E Arizona to s Minnesota, w Michigan, N Illinois, N and w Missouri, w and central Arkansas, Texas (uncommon in E part), and sw Louisiana.

The relatively small dark-green clumps of this variety are conspicuous in woodlands, but in prairies they may be hidden, or partly so, by grasses.

Especially in Arizona and New Mexico, and also in western Texas, this species shades into *O. phaeacantha* vars. Eastward, it intergrades somewhat with *O. humifusa*. Plants with intermediate combinations of characters have received various scientific names on the supposition that they were new species.

Hybridizes also with *O. littoralis* var. *martiniana.*

Fig. 446. Plains prickly pear, *Opuntia macrorhiza* var. *macrorhiza*, on the edge of the Great Plains Grassland. (David Griffiths)

Fig. 447. *Opuntia macrorhiza* var. *macrorhiza* in northern Arizona, the plant with mature fruits. (Robert H. Peebles; from *The Cacti of Arizona*, eds. 1, 2, 3)

Fig. 449. *Opuntia macrorhiza* var. *macrorhiza*, young spineless plant with large glochids and with the tuberous structures characteristic especially of the tap root and the main branch roots but less commonly of the adventitious roots along the stems. These roots are much in need of study; the consistency of their occurrence even in this species has not had thorough investigation. It is not known, for example, (1) whether plants of this species have the genetic capacity to produce such roots, whereas those of other species do not have the capacity, or (2) whether tuberous root formation might be triggered by insect damage or infection. (David Griffiths)

Fig. 448. *Opuntia macrorhiza* var. *macrorhiza*, an older joint; and a younger joint with leaves, a flower bud, and flowers. (David Griffiths)

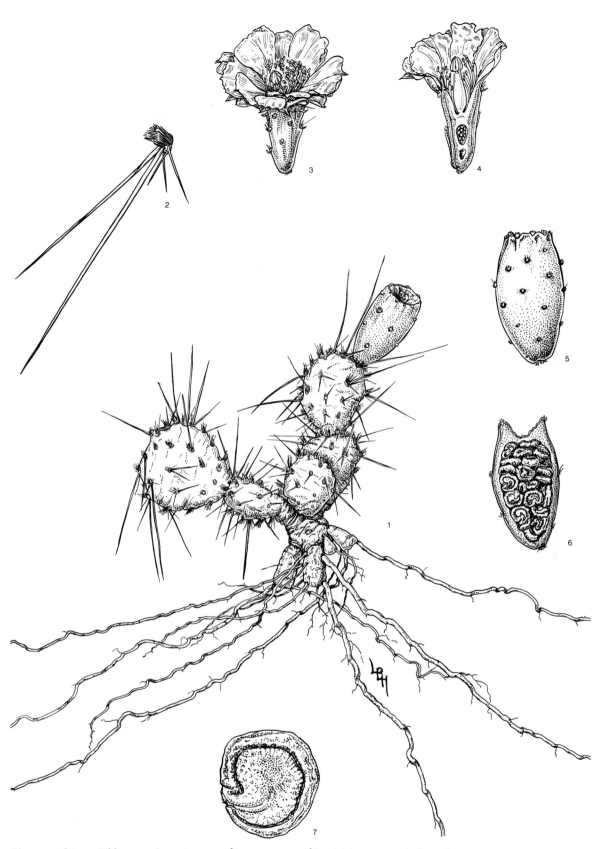

Fig. 450. Plains prickly pear, *Opuntia macrorhiza* var. *macrorhiza*, ×.8, except as indicated. *1*, Four-year-old seedling plant with a fruit, ×.5; but with much smaller joints than those of older plants. *2*, Areole with spines and glochids and a little felt showing, ×1.4. *3*, Flower. *4*, Flower in longitudinal section. *5*, Fruit, this spineless. *6*, Fruit in longitudinal section. *7*, Seed, ×3.2.

Fig. 451. *Opuntia macrorhiza* var. *pottsii*, mature, partly grown, and very young joints (these with leaves), and a flower. For the aspect of the plant and for ecological and floristic relationships, see Fig. 151.

35b. Opuntia macrorhiza var. pottsii (Salm-Dyck) L. Benson.

Sandy or loamy areas of plains and alluvial fans at (780)1,200-1,800 m (2,600 or 4,000-6,000 ft). Desert Grassland and sometimes Great Plains Grassland and Chihuahuan Desert. Arizona in E Pima Co. and Cochise Co.; New Mexico from Grant and Hidalgo Cos. to Torrance, Quay, and Lea Cos.; Texas in Potter Co. in the Panhandle and w of Pecos R. from El Paso Co. to Culberson, Reeves, and Terrell Cos. and in Maverick Co.

The very small bluish clumps of this variety are conspicuous when they occur on the disturbed soil of washes, but elsewhere they are hidden effectively by range grasses, which tend to be of the same color.

According to Anthony (1956), the tuberous roots have milky juice.

36. Opuntia littoralis (Engelmann) Cockerell

Suberect or sprawling shrub, usually 30-60 cm high, 0.6-1.2 m diam; roots fibrous; larger terminal joints green to noticeably (sometimes strongly) glaucous, narrowly obovate or narrowly elliptic to broadly so, sometimes nearly orbiculate, mostly 7.5-25(30) cm long, (5)7.5-10(16) cm broad, 12-20 mm thick; areoles 1.5-3(4.5) mm diam, typically 1.5-3 cm apart; spines distrib-

uted over entire joint or on only upper part (in var. *austrocalifornica*, spines none), brown, tan, pink, gray, or various combinations of these and yellow, 1-11 (or none) per areole, spreading or some deflexed, usually straight, sometimes some curving, the longer 2.5-5(7) cm long, basally to 1 mm diam, circular to elliptic in cross section, not barbed; glochids yellow, tan, or brown, 1.5-4.5 mm long; flower 5-7.5 cm diam and long; sepaloids with midribs green and margins yellow or partly reddish or magenta, lanceolate to ovate-acuminate, obdeltoid-cuneate, or obovate, 5-30 mm long, 3-20 mm broad, acuminate to mucronate, nearly entire; petaloids ±10-15, yellow with red or magenta bases, sometimes magenta or rose-purple, the largest obovate or obovate-cuneate, 25-50 mm long, 15-20 mm broad, rounded and mucronate, nearly entire; filaments yellow, 9-12 mm long; anthers yellow, 2.25 mm long; style yellowish, 12-20 mm long, 3-7 mm greatest diam, basally swollen; stigmas 8-12, 3-4.5 mm long, rather thick; ovary in anthesis spineless or bearing a few small deciduous spines above; fruit reddish to reddish-purple, fleshy at maturity, with only small glochids, obovoid or narrowly so, ±3.8 (rarely 6.2) cm long, 2.5-3.8 cm diam, the umbilicus cuplike, the fruit maturing after several months; seeds light tan or gray, irregular but fundamentally nearly discoid, the margin enclosing the embryo conspicuous and irregular, the size remarkably variable, 3-6 mm long and diam, 1.5 mm thick.

The species, as it occurs today in southern California, consists of remnants persisting in spots somehow protected from disturbance by man or fire. Representative habitats are: (1) in washes or on floodplains where growth of grass on the gravelly soil is irregular and fires do not run for great distances; (2) under trees along foothills where one variety, adapted to deep shade, is away from high grasses (which may be crowded out); and (3) in mountain areas partly shielded from the worst disturbance by man. In hybrid swarms of the "occidentalis" type (O. *littoralis* vars. × O. *ficus-indica*; see under sp. 46), some individuals with almost or exactly the gene combinations of the postulated original native populations still persist.

The nearest relatives of this species are O. *macrorhiza* (southern Rocky Mts. and the Great Plains) and O. *humifusa* (across eastern half of the U.S.). O. *phaeacantha* is less closely related.

The California cochineal insect is common on the joints and fruits of this and other species. The female insect contains a vivid red to royal purple dye (see under sp. 42 and pp. 236-37).

Fig. 452. *Opuntia littoralis* var. *littoralis*, typical sprawling plant near Puddingstone Lake, Pomona, Los Angeles Co., California, the point of occurrence farthest inland. (*The Native Cacti of California*)

Distinctive Characters of the Varieties of **Opuntia littoralis**

Character	a. var. littoralis	b. var. vaseyi	c. var. austrocalifornica	d. var. piercei	e. var. martiniana
Joint surface	Not at all glaucous (notably green)	Somewhat glaucous	Markedly glaucous	Somewhat glaucous	Somewhat glaucous
Joint shape	Narrowly elliptic to narrowly obovate	Narrowly obovate to obovate	Narrowly obovate to almost orbiculate	Narrowly obovate or sometimes elliptic or orbiculate	Obovate to sometimes orbiculate
Joint size	12.5-22 cm long, 7.5-10(12.5) cm broad	10-15(17.5) cm long, 7.5-10(11) cm broad	7.5-12.5(20) cm long, 5-6(8) cm broad	(10)12.5-25(30) cm long; (7)10-16 cm broad	(10)12.5-17.5 cm long, 7.5-14 cm broad
Spine distribution	Covering joint	Covering all but lower part of joint	Spines none or a few along upper edge of joint	Covering upper half to three-fourths of joint	Usually covering all or most of joint
Spines per areole	5-11	1-4(6)	Sometimes 1 or 2 and very small	1-4(6)	1-4(6)
Spine color	Some gray and some yellow or also some red	Brown to dark gray	White, gray, straw-colored or golden; in any case, pale	Reddish basally, the tips yellow or white, becoming gray	Ranging from red-and-yellow to gray
Spine length	3-4.7 cm	2.5-3 cm	0.6-1.2(2) cm (if present)	(2.5)3-5 cm	(2.5)3.8-7 cm
Perianth color	Yellow	Yellow	Red to magenta or flame	Yellow, the center red	Yellow, the center red
Fruit color	Red	Reddish-purple	Reddish-purple	Reddish-purple	Reddish-purple
Altitude	3-150 m (10-500 ft)	300-600(1,350) m (1,000-2,000 or 4,500 ft)	240-600(1,200) m (800-2,000 or rarely 4,000 ft)	1,740-2,175 m (5,800-7,250 ft)	1,350-1,950 m (4,500-6,500 ft)
Floristic association	California Chaparral (disturbed areas)	California Chaparral (disturbed areas)	California Chaparral (disturbed areas)	Lower Pacific Montane Forest; desert edge California Chaparral (area of junipers and pinyons)	Lower Rocky Mountain Montane Forest; Northern Juniper-Pinyon Woodland; Mojavean Desert

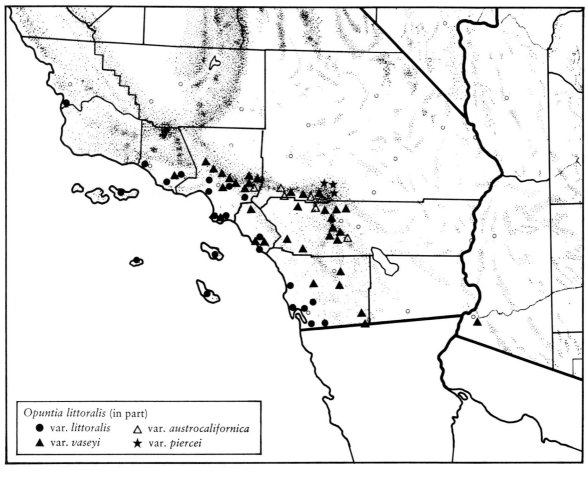

Opuntia littoralis (in part)
● var. littoralis   △ var. austrocalifornica
▲ var. vaseyi   ★ var. piercei

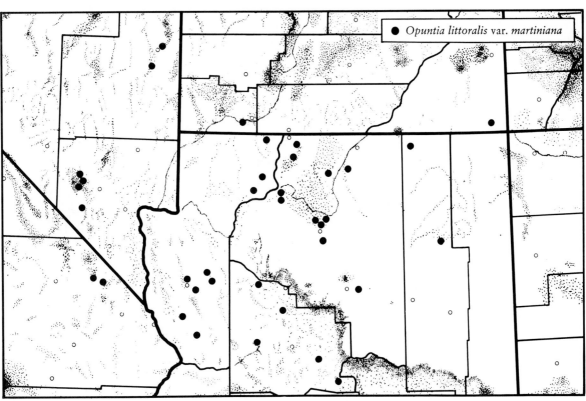

● Opuntia littoralis var. martiniana

36a. Opuntia littoralis var. **littoralis**. Sandy or rocky soils of hills, beaches, and bluffs at 3-150 m (10-500 ft). Disturbed areas of California Chaparral or coastal (natural or induced) grasslands. In s California on islands and along coast and in low valleys to 10-15 mi. inland (as at Fullerton), rarely 40 mi. inland (as at Pomona); Santa Barbara Co. to San Diego Co. Mexico on NW coast of Baja California.

This species forms great colonies a meter or so high and sometimes as much as 0.2 hectare (0.5 acre) in extent. The yellow-green, narrow, densely spiny joints and bright red fruits set the plants off from the other cacti occurring with them.

This is not the *O. littoralis* of most authors, which is usually *O. oricola* Philbrick.

Fig. 453. *Opuntia littoralis* var. *littoralis*, first-year joint with the leaves still present; second-year joint bearing a flower bud and a flower; third-year joint with an increased number of spines per areole.

Fig. 454. *Opuntia littoralis* var. *vaseyi*, an older joint bearing a young joint, a fruit, and a maturing joint with the spines less developed; a separate flower bud and a flower. (David Griffiths)

36b. Opuntia littoralis var. vaseyi (Coulter)
Benson & Walkington. Sandy or gravelly soils of rocky hillsides, alluvial fans, and washes in open areas of chaparral region at 300-600(1,350) m (1,000-2,000 or 4,500 ft). Disturbed areas in California Chaparral. In s California along and near w and s bases of San Gabriel, San Bernardino, and San Jacinto Mts. from Moorpark in s Ventura Co. and Newhall in Los Angeles Co. to w San Bernardino Co., Orange Co., area E of Temecula in Riverside Co., and N San Diego Co.; Arizona at Yuma, Yuma Co. (*Vasey*).

The clumps of this cactus are all but lost in the dense growth of vernal annual weedy grasses introduced from the Mediterranean region. They are in danger of extermination by summer grass fires (see under sp. 46).

Forms hybrid swarms with varieties of O. *phaeacantha* along the Pines-to-Palms Highway in Riverside County.

Fig. 455. *Opuntia littoralis* var. *vaseyi*, mature joint with a flower bud and flowers.

Fig. 456. *Opuntia littoralis* var. *vaseyi*, plant growing at Padua Hills, San Gabriel Mts., near Claremont, Los Angeles Co., California; bearing flower buds, a flower, and a young fruit.

36c. Opuntia littoralis var. **austrocalifornica**
Benson & Walkington. Sandy soils of washes, but
best developed in shade under trees along edges
of foothills and in canyons at 240-600(1,200) m
(800-2,000 or rarely 4,000 ft). California Chaparral. In s California along bases of coastal side of
mountains in Los Angeles and San Bernardino
Cos. from near Glendora to San Bernardino and
Redlands; also on Pines-to-Palms Highway, Riverside Co.

Under the trees this blue-green, spineless cactus forms extensive mats several meters in diameter.

Forms hybrid swarms with O. *littoralis* var.
vaseyi along the Pines-to-Palms Highway.

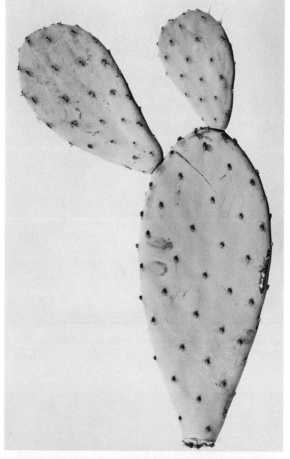

Fig. 458. *Opuntia littoralis* var. *austrocalifornica*, the joints
spineless and glaucous. (David Griffiths)

Fig. 457. *Opuntia littoralis* var.
austrocalifornica near Claremont, Los Angeles Co., California. The plants usually are
spineless, but this one bears a
few spines, as do others intergrading with var. *vaseyi*.

Fig. 459. *Opuntia littoralis* var. *austrocalifornica* in flower, among grasses near Padua Hills, San Gabriel Mts., near Claremont, Los Angeles Co., California.

Fig. 460. *Opuntia littoralis* var. *austrocalifornica*, young joints with leaves and older joints with flowers.

36d. Opuntia littoralis var. **piercei** (Fosberg) Benson & Walkington. Sandy and gravelly soils of flats, washes, and hillsides in forests and woodlands in mountains at 1,740-2,175 m (5,800-7,250 ft). Lower part of Pacific Montane Forest and area of junipers and pinyons in California Chaparral just above the desert. California in San Bernardino Mts., San Bernardino Co.

This green variety occurs on rocky hillsides among junipers and pinyons, but it is most amazing when one comes upon it growing in the disturbed soil of washes or dry hillsides in yellow-pine forest.

Intergrades with *O. phaeacantha* var. *major*.

John Adams has contributed much information for revising the description of this variety. His thorough studies, especially in the San Bernardino Mts., have also provided vital information concerning the geographical distribution and circumscription of the taxon.

36e. Opuntia littoralis var. **martiniana** (L. Benson) L. Benson. On sandy or gravelly soils of valleys, flats, and mountainsides in forests or woodlands, or at edge of the desert at 1,350-1,950 m (4,500-6,500 ft); occasional at extremes of 600 and 2,550 m (2,000 and 8,500 ft). Edge of Rocky Mountain Montane Forest, Northern Juniper-Pinyon Woodland, and Mojavean Desert. California in the region of New York Mts., E San Bernardino Co.; Nevada in Lincoln and Clark Cos.; Utah along Arizona border; Arizona from Mohave Co. to Coconino, N Navajo, and Yavapai Cos.

This relatively large variety is conspicuous on open, lightly wooded or sparsely forested hillsides, where it forms clumps averaging half a meter high and a meter in diameter.

The variety hybridizes with *O. erinacea* (sp. 26), and it shades into *O. phaeacantha* and *O. macrorhiza*. There are also many intermediate forms between it, *O. macrorhiza*, and *O. violacea*. Var. *martiniana* is a connecting link in a five-species complex consisting of *O. littoralis*, *O. violacea*, *O. macrorhiza*, *O. atrispina*, and *O. humifusa*.

Fig. 461. *Opuntia littoralis* var. *martiniana*, upper edge of the Mojavean Desert, Hualpai Mountain, Mohave Co., Arizona.

Fig. 462. *Opuntia littoralis* var. *martiniana*, joints with fruits; Hualpai Mountain.

Fig. 463. *Opuntia atrispina,* Devil's River, Val Verde Co., Texas. (David Griffiths; see Credits)

37. Opuntia atrispina Griffiths

Relatively small, more or less sprawling prickly pears, mostly 0.45-0.6 m high, 0.6-1 m diam; roots fibrous; larger terminal joints green, obovate to nearly orbiculate, 10(15) cm long, 7.5(10) cm broad, ±12 mm thick; areoles 3-4.5 mm diam, typically 1.2-2 cm apart; spines variable, on upper portion of joint, mostly black but toward apices shading rapidly through brown to yellow, mostly 4-7 of greatly differing sizes per areole, the principal one ascending, the next 1 or 2 descending, 1-3 very small and descending, the longer mostly 2.5-4 cm long, basally to 1 mm diam, acicular, nearly circular in cross section, not markedly barbed; glochids yellow, to 6 mm long; flower 5-6 cm diam and 3.8-5 cm long; sepaloids with midribs greenish and otherwise yellow, the largest obovate-cuneate, to 20 mm long, to 12 mm broad, truncate, acuminate, undulate; petaloids ±7-9, pale yellow, the largest broadly cuneate, 25-30 mm long, to 25 mm broad, truncate with short acuminate point in apical notch, undulate; filaments yellow, 6-9 mm long; anthers yellow, nearly 2 mm long; style pale, ±12 mm long, basally 3 mm greatest diam; stigmas 7 or 8, ±3 mm long, relatively broad; ovary in anthesis 1.2-2 cm long; fruit reddish-purple, fleshy at maturity, the flesh greenish-yellow, the fruit with only small areoles on surface, globose to pyriform, 1.2-2 cm long, ±1.2 cm diam; seeds tan or gray, nearly circular, 3 mm diam.

Limestone soils of hills and alluvial fans in desert or grassland at 450-600 m (1,500-2,200 ft). Chihuahuan Desert and to a lesser extent the Edwards Plateau and the Rio Grande Plain. Texas from Presidio Co. to Taylor and Uvalde Cos. and in Bee Co. Apparently rare or intermittent in occurrence.

The dark green clumps are inconspicuous among the shrubs or high grasses.

38. Opuntia violacea Engelmann
Purple prickly pear

Sprawling shrub, usually 0.6-2.4+ m high or sometimes treelike and with short trunk; roots fibrous; larger terminal joints green but at all seasons strongly tinted by betacyanin pigments (reddish-purple), tending to be orbiculate, usually 10-20 cm long and of about equal or somewhat less breadth, ±9 mm thick; areoles small, 1.5 mm diam, typically 1.5-2.5 cm apart; spines few or none, usually restricted to upper portion of joint and often to margin, dark reddish-brown to almost black, sometimes pink or rarely white (var. *castetteri* of westernmost Texas and adjacent New Mexico), 1 (in some areoles 2 or 3) per areole, spreading at right angles to surface of joint or vertically from upper margin, straight or curving, somewhat flexible, the larger 4-10 (17.5) cm long, basally 0.25-1 mm diam, acicular, broadly elliptic or nearly circular in cross section, not barbed; glochids tan, 3-6+ mm long; flower 7.5-9 cm diam and long; sepaloids with green midribs, shading through light red to yellow (at

Distinctive Characters of the Varieties of **Opuntia violacea**

Character	a. var. violacea	b. var. gosseliniana	c. var. santa-rita	d. var. macrocentra	e. var. castetteri
Joint shape	Obovate	Orbicular or broadly obovate	Orbicular	Usually broadly obovate	Mostly broadly obovate
Joint length	10-15 cm	12.5-17.5 cm	15-20 cm	15-17.5 cm	15-17.5 cm
Spine distribution on joint	Abundant near upper margin of joint	On both upper margin and flat sides of joint	None or few, often 2-4 on upper margin of joint	Abundant on and just below upper margin of joint	Abundant on and just below upper margin of joint
Spines per areole	1-3	1 or 2	1	1 or 2	2 or 3
Spine color	Dark reddish-brown	Light reddish-brown to pink or partly yellow	Light reddish-brown to pink or rarely darker	Nearly black	White or mostly so
Spine size	To 4-6 cm long, 0.75 mm diam	To 4-6.2 cm long, 0.5-0.75 mm diam	To 4-6.2 cm long, 0.25-0.7 mm diam	Commonly to (5)7.5-17.5 cm long, 1 mm diam	To 6-12.5 cm long, ±1 mm diam
Altitude	900-1,500 m (3,000-5,000 ft)	900-1,200 m (3,000-4,000 ft)	900-1,500 m (3,000-5,000 ft)	1,500-1,650 m (3,500-5,500 ft)	1,200-1,500 m (4,000-5,000 ft)
Floristic association	Desert Grassland; upper Arizona Desert	Desert Grassland; edges of Sonoran Desert	Desert Grassland; edges of Southwestern Oak Woodland, Arizona Desert, and Chihuahuan Desert	Primarily Chihuahuan Desert; Desert Grassland; rare in Arizona Desert	Chihuahuan Desert

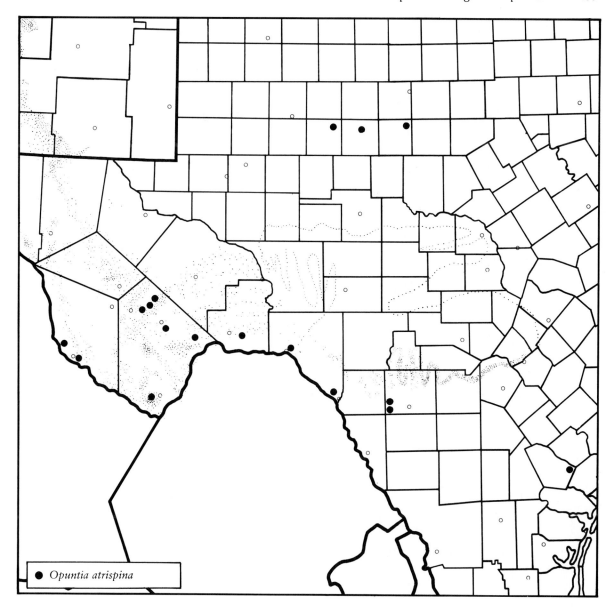

● *Opuntia atrispina*

margins), ovate-acuminate to cuneate-obovate, 5-30 mm long, 10-20 mm broad, short-acuminate to mucronate, undulate; petaloids few, yellow with bright red bases and lower middles, cuneate-obovate, 25-40 mm long, 20-30 mm broad, rounded or truncate, nearly entire; filaments yellow, 9 mm long; anthers yellow, 1.5 mm long; style 12-15 mm long, 3 mm diam; stigmas 5 or more, 4.5 mm long, rather slender; ovary not spiny, about 1 cm long; fruit red or purplish-red, fleshy at maturity, smooth, 2.5-4 cm long, 2 cm diam, the umbilicus cuplike, the fruit persisting until about November; seeds light tan or gray, basally irregularly elliptic, 4.5 mm long, slightly less broad, 1.5 mm thick.

In nature the purplish to lavender color of the joints is characteristic of all varieties at all seasons, but in times of drought or cold the color deepens and may become mahogany red. In the hot, rainy season of July and August the joints become blue-green tinged with purple.

In cultivation, according to R. S. Woods (1933), the color of the joints of var. *santa-rita* may be modified according to the amount of water and light available. And presumably other physiological factors, such as temperature, and genetic factors also affect the color.

Plants intermediate between *O. violacea* (perhaps var. *santa-rita*) and *O. chlorotica* occur in southeastern Arizona (see under sp. 44).

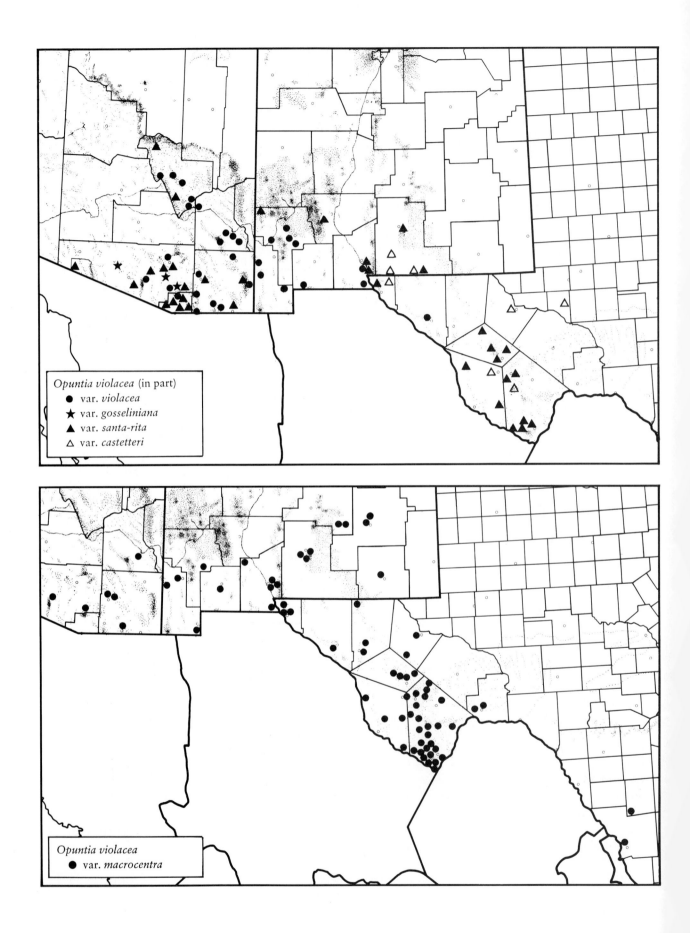

Opuntia violacea (in part)
● var. violacea
★ var. gosseliniana
▲ var. santa-rita
△ var. castetteri

Opuntia violacea
● var. macrocentra

460

38a. Opuntia violacea var. **violacea.** On sandy, gravelly, or rocky soils of hills, slopes, flats, mesas, washes, and canyons in grassland or upper edge of the desert mostly at 900-1,500 m (3,000-5,000 ft). Desert Grassland or upper edge of Arizona Desert. In SE Arizona from Gila Co. to E Pima, Santa Cruz, and Cochise Cos.; SE New Mexico in Grant and Hidalgo Cos. and less common E to Dona Ana Co.; Texas at Sierra Blanca, Hudspeth Co. Mexico in Chihuahua.

The violet-purple color is conspicuous from a distance. This feature was a highlight of the day for Col. Emory, in command of the military expedition that discovered the species in 1846. The same steep hillside he observed is still dotted with the cacti.

Fig. 464. Purple prickly pear, *Opuntia violacea* var. *violacea*, with creosote bushes in the Arizona Desert at Solomon, Graham Co., Arizona, near the type locality.

Fig. 465. *Opuntia violacea* var. *violacea* in fruit in Desert Grassland southwest of Safford, Graham Co., Arizona.

Fig. 466. *Opuntia violacea* var. *violacea*, young joint with leaves and an older joint without; flower bud and flower. (David Griffiths)

Fig. 467. *Opuntia violacea* var. *violacea*, fruits. (David Griffiths)

462

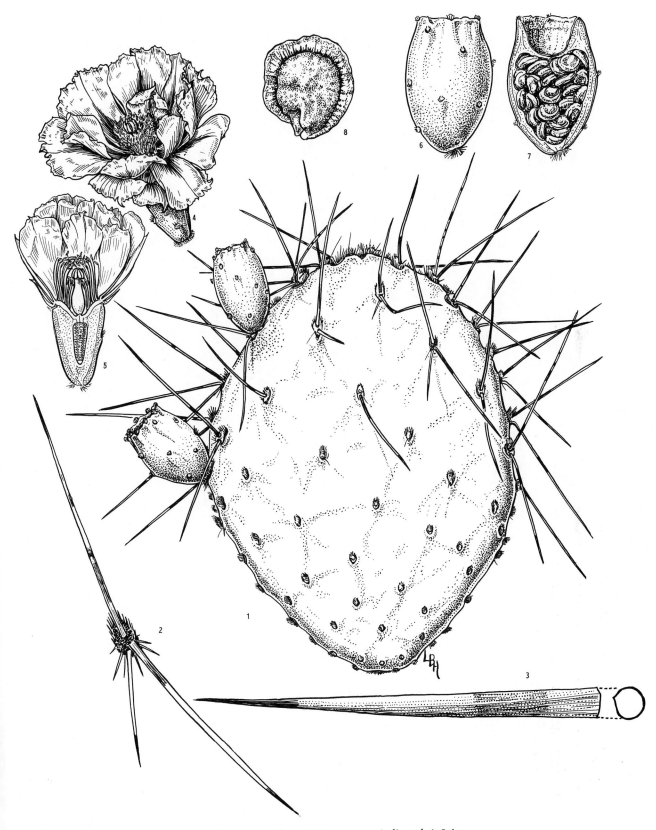

Fig. 468. Purple prickly pear, *Opuntia violacea* var. *violacea*, ✕.8, except as indicated. *1*, Joint with two fruits. *2*, Areole with spines, glochids, and wool, ✕1.5. *3*, Spine tip, ✕5. *4*, Flower. *5*, Flower in longitudinal section. *6*, Fruit. *7*, Fruit in longitudinal section. *8*, Seed, ✕3.

Fig. 469. Purple prickly pear, *Opuntia violacea* var. *gosseliniana*, in Desert Grassland in Sonora, Mexico. (Homer L. Shantz)

38b. Opuntia violacea var. gosseliniana (Weber) L. Benson. Sandy or gravelly soils in grassland and on edges of the desert at 900-1,200 m (3,000-4,000 ft). Desert Grassland or edges of Sonoran Deserts. Arizona in central and s Pima Co. Mexico in Sonora.

This variety is in need of study, especially in Sonora, to determine whether it is distinct from var. *violacea*. The Arizona plants are transitional.

38c. Opuntia violacea var. santa-rita (Griffiths & Hare) L. Benson. Purple prickly pear. Sandy or gravelly soils of plains and sometimes of canyons at 900-1,500 m (3,000-5,000 ft). Desert Grassland or edges of Southwestern Oak Woodland or Arizona and Chihuahuan Deserts. Arizona from Gila and Pima Cos. to Santa Cruz and Cochise Cos.; rare in New Mexico from Grant Co. to Otero Co.; Texas in El Paso, Jeff Davis, Presidio, and Brewster Cos. Mexico in N Sonora.

The violet-purple plants form mounds as much as 2 m high and 3 m in diameter, conspicuous in grassland and especially on gravelly or rocky hillsides. The plants resemble those of var. *violacea*, but they are not spiny.

This variety is cultivated for its attractive purplish color and its almost spineless joints. Large plants may have a short trunk and be almost arborescent. In cultivation in Arizona the plant thrives, but in nature it is not strong in competition because it is not resistant to drought, extreme moisture, or overgrazing. Like other nearly spineless cacti, it is vulnerable to rodents and cattle.

Fig. 470. Purple prickly pear, *Opuntia violacea* var. *santa-rita*, in the Desert Grassland, foothills of the Graham (Pinaleno) Mountains, Graham Co., Arizona. Behind the cactus is velvet mesquite, *Prosopis juliflora* var. *velutina*.

Fig. 471. *Opuntia violacea* var. *santa-rita*, old plant about 2 m (6 ft) high. (David Griffiths)

465

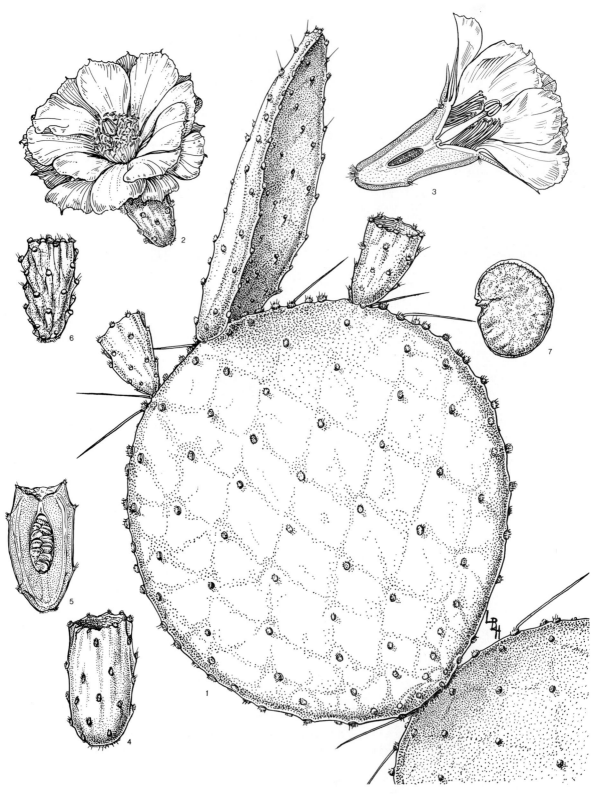

Fig. 472. Purple prickly pear, *Opuntia violacea* var. *santa-rita*, ×.8, except as indicated. *1*, Joints and fruits, the joints spineless or nearly so. *2*, Flower. *3*, Flower in longitudinal section. *4*, Fruit. *5*, Fruit in longitudinal section. *6*, Fruit, this one having dried after maturity. *7*, Seed, ×6.

466

Fig. 473. Black-spined prickly pear, *Opuntia violacea* var. *macrocentra*, in cultivation. The very long, dark spines along the upper edge of the joint are characteristic of the variety. (Homer L. Shantz)

38d. Opuntia violacea var. **macrocentra** (Engelmann) L. Benson. Black-spined prickly pear. Various sandy, gravelly, or other soils of plains, hillsides, and washes at 1,050-1,650 m (3,500-5,500 ft). Primarily in Chihuahuan Desert and Desert Grassland but rare in Arizona Desert. In s Arizona as noted below; New Mexico from Grant and Hidalgo Cos. to Lincoln and Eddy Cos.; Texas w of or near Pecos R. from El Paso Co. to Terrell Co. and in Webb and La Salle Cos. Mexico in Sonora and Chihuahua.

This large variety is conspicuous for the elongate, black, acicular spines on the upper ends of the joints. These are reminiscent of hat pins.

The variety is rare in southern Arizona, or perhaps represented mostly by relics of the introgression of its genes into varieties occurring there. Specimens from west of Tucson and from Benson eastward appear to represent populations with some characters of this variety. A few collections from Cochise County are clearly var. *macrocentra*.

38e. Opuntia violacea var. **castetteri** L. Benson. Limestone soils of rocky hillsides at 1,200-1,500 m (4,000-5,000 ft). Chihuahuan Desert. Arizona in San Pedro Valley, Cochise Co.; New Mexico from Hidalgo Co. to Sierra and Otero Cos.; Texas from El Paso Co. to Crane and Brewster Cos.

The long spines appear to be whitewashed, and this unexpected feature makes the plant stand out among other prickly pears on the hillsides.

Rare throughout range; in some places perhaps not forming consistent populations.

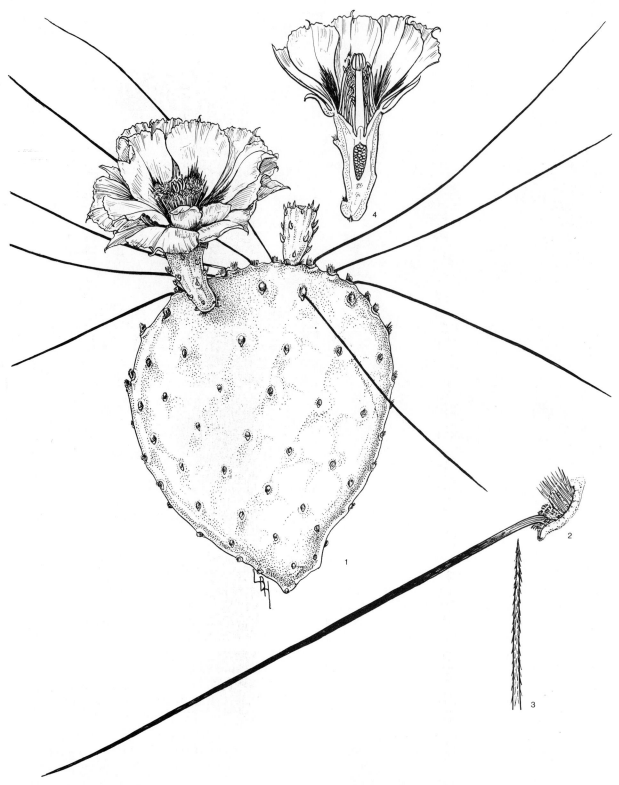

Fig. 474. Black-spined prickly pear, *Opuntia violacea* var. *macrocentra*, ×.6, except as indicated.
1, Joint with a flower and a young fruit. *2*, Areole with a spine, glochids, and wool, ×1.7. *3*,
Tip of a glochid showing the barbs, ×4.5. *4*, Flower in longitudinal section.

1 (*above*). Arizona Desert in summer, west of Superior: saguaros, *Cereus giganteus* (including the tall young plant in foreground); teddy bear chollas, *Opuntia bigelovii*; a barrel cactus, *Ferocactus wislizenii*; fishhook cacti, *Mammillaria microcarpa* (very small cylinders); ocotillo, *Fouquieria splendens* (with the wandlike branches); jojoba, *Simmondsia chinensis* (bright green, large-leafed shrub); and (probably) *Krameria* (the smaller bushes).

2 & 3 (*right*). Silver cholla, *Opuntia echinocarpa* var. *echinocarpa*. 2 (*above right*): mature joints. 3 (*below right*): in flower. (2, R. V. Moran; 3, R. A. Darrow; both from *The Native Cacti of California*)

4. Cane cholla, *Opuntia parryi* var. *parryi*, in flower and with the dry, mature fruits. (L. C. C. Krieger; from *The Native Cacti of California*)

5. Buckhorn cholla, *Opuntia acanthocarpa* var. *major*; the elongate tubercles are characteristic of the species. (From *The Native Cacti of California*)

6. A cane cholla, O. *spinosior*. (W. P. Martin; from *The Cacti of Arizona*)

7 (*above*). The mature fruits of a cane cholla, O. *spinosior*, showing the characteristic deep umbilicus (apical cup) and prominent tubercles.

8. Staghorn cholla, O. *versicolor*. (W. P. Martin; from *The Cacti of Arizona*)

9. A stand of jumping cholla, *Opuntia fulgida* var. *fulgida*, Superstition Mts., Arizona Desert; a saguaro, *Cereus giganteus*, in the background; most of the shrubs here are creosote bushes, *Larrea tridentata*.

10 & 11 (*above right & middle left*). Jumping cholla, *O. fulgida* var. *fulgida*, with characteristic elongate, branching chains of fruits, and with vegetative joints arising from some fruits; the low shrubs, in both figures, are bur sage, *Ambrosia [Franseria] deltoidea*, abundant in the Arizona Desert.

12 & 13 (*below left & below right*). Jumping cholla, *O. fulgida* var. *mamillata*, with fewer and shorter spines, green-appearing joints, lower and more spreading habit, and more drooping branches than var. *fulgida*.

14 (*above*). Forest of teddy bear chollas, *Opuntia bigelovii* var. *bigelovii*, San Tan Mts., Pinal Co., Arizona; on the hill, a few saguaros, *Cereus giganteus*; the larger shrubs are foothill palo verde, *Cercidium microphyllum*.

15. Teddy bear cholla, *O. bigelovii* var. *bigelovii*, the flowers of delicate hue. (R. A. Darrow)

16 (*right*). Teddy bear chollas, *O. bigelovii* var. *bigelovii*, Arizona Desert; nearby are an ocotillo (*Fouquieria splendens*), a saguaro, and a clump of prickly pears, *Opuntia* sp. (From *The Native Cacti of California*)

17. Desert Christmas cactus or pencil cholla, *Opuntia leptocaulis*, in fruit.

18 (*middle right*). Sand cholla, *O. pulchella*, in flower. (G. Tegelberg)

19 (*below left*). *O. pulchella*, juvenile plants in bloom; the stems, spineless or spiny, arise from characteristic underground tubers.

20 (*below right*). Diamond cholla, *O. ramosissima*, emphasizing the yellow sheaths of the spines.

21. Prickly pear, *Opuntia polyacantha* var. *rufispina*,
Colorado National Monument, Mesa Co., Colorado; the
plant at the right is sagebrush, *Artemisia tridentata*.

22 (*left*). Plains prickly pear, *O. polyacantha* var.
polyacantha, the spines long and formidable.

23 (*below*). *O. arenaria*, in flower and bud.

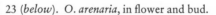

24 (*above left*). Mojave prickly pear, *Opuntia erinacea* var. *erinacea*, at Havasu Falls, near the Colorado River, Arizona. (R. A. Darrow)

25 (*above right*). *O. erinacea* var. *erinacea*, near Chloride, Mohave Co., Arizona. (J. A. Noble)

26. Mojave prickly pear, *O. erinacea* var. *erinacea*, Riverside Co., California. (J. A. Noble)

27. Mojave prickly pear, *O. erinacea* var. *erinacea*, along the Palms-to-Pines Highway, Riverside Co., California. (J. A. Noble)

29 & 30 (*above & below*). *O. erinacea* var. *columbiana*.
29 (*above*): flower buds and flowers. 30 (*below*): west of
Yakima, Washington. (Both by R. L. Benson)

28 (*above*). *Opuntia erinacea* var. *columbiana*,
showing transition from scale-leaves to sepaloids
to petaloids. (R. L. Benson)

31 (*below*). *O. erinacea* var. *utahensis*, in the
Navajo country. (From *The Cacti of Arizona*)

32. Navajo Bridge prickly pear, *Opuntia nicholii*, Coconino Co., Arizona. (E. L. Benson)

33 & 34 (*middle left & lower right*). Beavertail cactus, *O. basilaris* var. *basilaris*. 33 (*middle left*): in flower. 34 (*lower right*): among Joshua trees, *Yucca brevifolia*, in the Ivanpah Mts., Mojave Desert, San Bernardino Co., California. (34, J. A. Noble)

35 (*lower left*). Little beavertail, *O. basilaris* var. *brachyclada*. (J. A. Noble)

36 (*above*). Blind prickly pear,
Opuntia rufida, in the Chihuahuan
Desert, Big Bend National Park, Texas;
the bright-green plant at the right is
Agave lechugilla. (R. Wauer)

37 (*right*). *O. triacantha* in fruit,
Big Pine Key, Florida.

38 (*left*). Eastern prickly pear, *O. compressa*
var. *compressa*, Plummer's Island, Potomac River
above Washington, D.C.

39. *Opuntia littoralis* var. *littoralis*.

40 (*below*). *O. littoralis* var. *littoralis*, with characteristic red fruits.

41 (*below left*). *O. littoralis* var. *austrocalifornica*, a spineless variety with bright reddish flowers; shrubby wild buckwheat, *Eriogonum fasciculatum* var. *foliosum*, at the right.

42 (*below right*). *O. littoralis* var. *martiniana*, Glen Canyon, Utah: at the right, a mature flower; at the left, a flower showing color change after maturity. (D. Wright)

43. *Opuntia atrispina*, Devil's River, Val Verde Co., Texas.

46. *O. phaeacantha* var. *spinosibacca*, with the rare character combination of fleshy, spiny fruits.

44. Purple prickly pear, *O. violacea* var. *santa-rita*, with the extreme coloring produced by betacyanin pigments; the coloring is intensified during drought or cold.

45. Black-spined prickly pear, *O. violacea* var. *macrocentra*. (From *The Cacti of Arizona*)

47. Engelmann prickly pear, *Opuntia phaeacantha* var. *discata*,
long known mistakenly as O. *engelmannii*, in the Arizona Desert.
(W. P. Martin; from *The Cacti of Arizona*)

48. Engelmann prickly pear, O. *phaeacantha* var. *discata*,
in fruit. (From *The Cacti of Arizona*)

49. *O. stricta* var. *dillenii*, on Martinique in the Caribbean;
the remarkably spiny type common in the Antilles.

50 & 51 (*above left & right*). *Opuntia cochenillifera*, collected in Florida and cultivated in California; this species was cultivated for the Aztecs and later the Spanish as a host for the cochineal insect, from which a royal-purple dye was obtained (see text); the relatively long perianth and long stamens and style were the basis for the proposed genus "*Nopalea*."

52 (*lower left*). Pancake pear, O. *chlorotica*, the spines yellow, the joints with a bluish cast.

53 (*lower right*). O. *oricola*, showing the characteristic red fruit; the spines are yellow when young, later turning brownish-gray to black. (From *The Native Cacti of California*)

54. Indian fig or mission cactus, *Opuntia ficus-indica*; a red-fruited, spineless form. (D. L. Walkington; from *The Native Cacti of California*)

56. Indian fig, O. *ficus-indica*, spiny form.

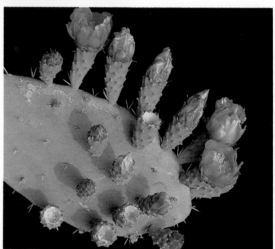

55 (*above & below*). Fruits of O. *ficus-indica*; this form spineless, red to yellow. (L. C. C. Krieger; from *The Native Cacti of California*)

57. Indian fig, O. *ficus-indica*, spiny form (large plant at left), with native prickly pears and a hybrid swarm; Puddingstone Reservoir, Los Angeles Co., California. (From *The Native Cacti of California*)

58. Hybrid prickly pear population "occidentalis," foot-hills of San Gabriel Mts., Los Angeles Co., California.

60. *Opuntia tomentosa*, a Mexican fruit-tree species. (From *The Native Cacti of California*)

59. Hybrid prickly pear population "occidentalis," same locality as above. (From *The Native Cacti of California*)

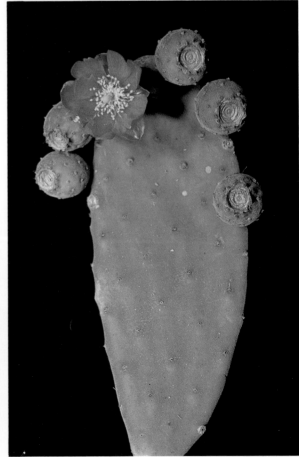

39. Opuntia phaeacantha Engelmann

Large, prostrate or sprawling prickly pears 30-60(90) cm high, in clumps 0.5-2.5 m diam, in some varieties occasionally with chains of several joints on edge along ground; larger terminal joints bluish-green, in cold weather with some lavender to purple betacyanin pigmentation, obovate or sometimes narrowly so or in some varieties orbiculate, 10-34(40) cm long, 7.5-22.5+ cm broad, 12-15 cm thick; leaves elongate-conical, 7.5-9 mm long; areoles elliptic, 6 mm long, typically 2-2.5 cm apart; spines over entire joint or restricted to upper one-third (sometimes one-half or two-thirds) of joint, rarely none, reddish-brown or dark brown, sometimes also with yellow, in some forms grayish or sometimes lighter red or red-and-gray, 1-8(10) per areole, spreading at right angles to joint or some spines deflexed, straight or bent downward, sometimes curved or twisted but usually not strongly so, the longer 2.5-7.5(8.7) cm long, basally 0.7-1.5 mm broad, subulate, some spines clearly flattened, narrowly elliptic in section, not barbed; glochids brown, reddish-tan, or yellowish-tan, 3-12 mm long; flower 6-8 cm diam, 6-7.5 cm long; sepaloids green, bordered with yellow or red, ovate-acuminate to obovate-cuneate or cuneate, 5-30 mm long, 5-20 mm broad, short-acuminate to truncate, mucronate, undulate; petaloids yellow or the bases red, obovate or cuneate-obovate, 25-30 mm long, 20-25 mm broad, truncate or rounded, minutely somewhat denticulate; filaments yellow, 9-12 mm long; anthers yellow, 2.25 mm long; style yellowish or greenish, 20-25 mm long, 4.5-6 mm diam; stigmas 5-10, 6 mm long, rather thick; ovary in anthesis smooth, spineless, the areoles not prominent; fruit wine-color or purplish, fleshy at maturity, smooth (areoles not prominent), usually obovate, sometimes elongate, 3.8-8 cm long, 2-4 cm diam, the umbilicus cuplike but not deep, the fruit persisting until winter; seeds light tan or grayish, irregularly discoid, ±4.5 mm long, a little less broad, 1.5+ mm thick.

O. phaeacantha is a complex species with much internal variation, and it includes several geographical varieties. The varieties are not completely segregated, and often their intergradation is complex. However, they represent strong tendencies in particular geographical areas. Many proposed "new species" have been based on members of this species because of single unusual characters in an individual or because of variation between individuals. Often these specimens have been taken from the hybrid swarms that are produced by interbreeding between the varieties or between *O. phaeacantha* and other species. Hybridizing between all the geographically contiguous varieties and with other species is common, as in the following examples: *O. phaeacantha* var. *major* or var. *discata* with *O. littoralis* (several varieties) in California and with *O. littoralis* var. *martiniana* in Nevada and northwestern Arizona; *O. phaeacantha* vars. *camanchica* and *major* with *O. macrorhiza* on the high plains of northern Arizona and New Mexico and on the Great Plains. Other species with which *O. phaeacantha* hybridizes include *O. polyacantha* and *O. erinacea*.

During the winter the joints of vars. *phaeacantha* and *major* develop bright red borders or facial streaks. During the season of rapid growth the plant is green. Betacyanin pigments, which are reddish to purple, develop at low temperatures. In this species they disappear during warm, moist weather, but in *O. violacea* they are much more persistent.

39a. Opuntia phaeacantha var. phaeacantha.

Sandy or rocky soils of hills, flats, valleys, and canyons in woodlands and grasslands at 1,350-1,800(2,400) m (4,500-6,000 or 8,000 ft). Mostly in Southern Juniper-Pinyon Woodland but also in Great Plains Grassland and lower edge of Rocky Mountain Montane Forest. Utah in La Sal Mts.; w Colorado from vicinity of Grand Junction s and on edge of Great Plains from Boulder Co. s; Arizona along and N of Mogollon Rim and rare along E boundary in Cochise Co.; N New Mexico in Rocky Mountain region and at mostly higher altitudes s to Hidalgo and Lea Cos.; Texas (rare) in Jeff Davis, Brewster, and Terrell Cos.

The plants form large, green, relatively low clumps up to several meters in diameter. Usually they are conspicuous among the shrubs or grasses.

Characters usual in this variety are recognizable in some specimens of other varieties from the deserts of southern Arizona.

Text continued on p. 475

Distinctive Characters of the Varieties of Opuntia phaeacantha

Character	a. var. phaeacantha	b. var. camanchica	c. var. spinosibacca	d. var. laevis	e. var. major
Joint shape	Obovate or nearly so	Broadly obovate to orbiculate	Orbiculate (areoles on small mounds)	Narrowly obovate	Broadly obovate or nearly orbiculate
Joint size	10-15 cm long, 7.5-10 cm broad	14-17.5 cm long, 11-14 cm broad	14-15 cm long and broad	15-25 cm long, 11-15 cm broad	Usually 12.5-25 cm long, 10-20 cm broad
Spine distribution on joint	On upper three-fourths or more of joint	On almost entire joint	On almost entire joint	Spines *none*, except a few in plants intergrading with other varieties	Usually on upper one-half, one-third, or less of joint
Spines per areole	3-5(9) above, 1 or 2 below	5-8 above, 1-4 below	±2-6	(Spines lacking)	Usually 1-3
Spine color	Brown, dark or rarely light	Dark brown	Brownish-red	(Spines lacking)	Dark brown
Spine size	To (3.8)4.5-6.2 cm long, 0.7-1 mm broad	To (4)5-5.6 cm long, 1-1.5 mm broad	To 7.5 cm long, 1 mm broad	(Spines lacking)	To (3)5.6-7 cm long, 1-1.5 mm broad
Fruits	Obovoid, 4.5-7 cm long	Obovoid, 4.5-7 cm long	As in var. *phaeacantha*, but in only this variety spiny at top	Cylindroid, the base narrowed, 6.2-8 cm long	As in var. *phaeacantha*, but a little larger
Altitude	1,350-1,800(2,400) m (4,500-6,000 or 8,000 ft)	900-1,200 m (3,000-4,000 ft)	900 m (3,000 ft)	750-900 m (2,500-3,000 ft)	600-2,100 m (2,000-7,000 ft)
Floristic association	Southern Juniper-Pinyon Woodland; less common in Great Plains Grassland and edge of Rocky Mountain Montane Forest	Great Plains Grassland and adjacent brushlands	Chihuahuan Desert	Upper Arizona Desert; Desert Grassland; lower edge of Southwestern Oak Woodland	Arizona Desert; Chihuahuan Desert; Desert Grassland; less common in Juniper-Pinyon Woodlands, Mojavean Desert, Colorado Desert, and desert-edge California Chaparral; rare in Pacific Montane Forest and Rocky Mountain Montane Forest

Character	f. var. discata	g. var. wootonii	h. var. superbospina	i. var. mojavensis	j. var. flavispina
Joint shape	Orbiculate to elliptic	Narrowly elliptic	Narrowly obovate	Orbiculate or slightly broader than long	Obovate, basally acute
Joint size	Mostly 22.5-30(40) cm long, 17.5-22.5 cm broad	20-34 cm long, 11-15 cm broad	17.5-31 cm long, 10-13.7 cm broad	±21 cm long, ±22.5 cm broad	17.5-27.5 cm long, 12.5-20 cm broad
Spine distribution on joint	In all or all but a few basal areoles of joint	On entire joint	On almost entire joint	In all areoles of joint	On lower edges of all but a few basal areoles, the longer in upper and marginal areoles
Spines per areole	1-4(10)	(2)4-6	(1-5)6-10	5-8, nearly all large, those of all areoles similar	(1)2 or 3 (plus sometimes 1 or 2 smaller ones)
Spine color	White or ashy gray	Dark brown	Dark brown to gray	Dark reddish-brown	Yellow with irregular distribution of red
Spine size	To 2.5-5 (rarely 6-7) cm long, 1-1.5 mm broad	To 7-8.7 cm long, 1.25 mm broad	To 4.5-6.2 cm long, 0.7-1 mm broad	To 5-6.2 cm long, 1 mm broad	To 6.2 cm long, 1.25 mm broad
Fruits	As in var. *phaeacantha*, but a little larger	Unknown	Unknown	Obovoid, 3.8-4.4 cm long	Obovoid, 4-5 cm long
Altitude	600-1,200 m (2,000-4,000 ft)	1,500-1,800 m (5,000-6,000 ft)	760-1,350 m (2,500-4,500 ft)	About 600 m (2,000 ft)	375-1,050 m (1,250-3,500 ft)
Floristic association	Arizona Desert; Desert Grassland; also Mojavean Desert, upper Colorado Desert, Chihuahuan Desert, Juniper-Pinyon Woodlands, and South-western Oak Woodland; rare in California Chaparral	Desert Grassland; Chihuahuan Desert	Mojavean Desert	Mojavean Desert	Arizona Desert; probably upper Colorado Desert

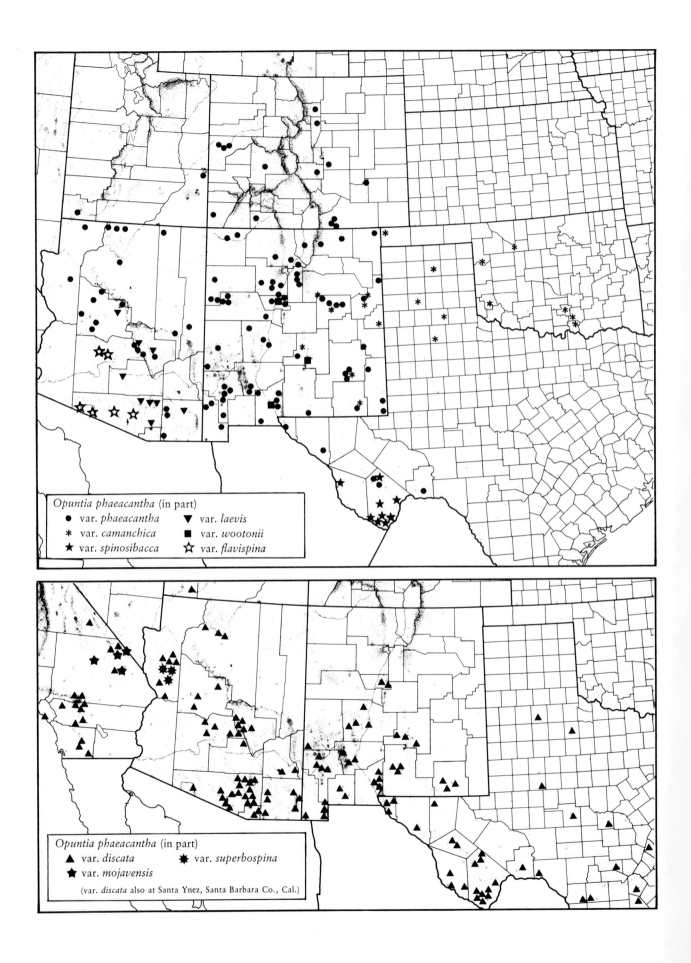

Opuntia phaeacantha (in part)

- var. *phaeacantha*
- ▼ var. *laevis*
- * var. *camanchica*
- ■ var. *wootonii*
- ★ var. *spinosibacca*
- ☆ var. *flavispina*

Opuntia phaeacantha (in part)

- ▲ var. *discata*
- ✳ var. *superbospina*
- ★ var. *mojavensis*

(var. *discata* also at Santa Ynez, Santa Barbara Co., Cal.)

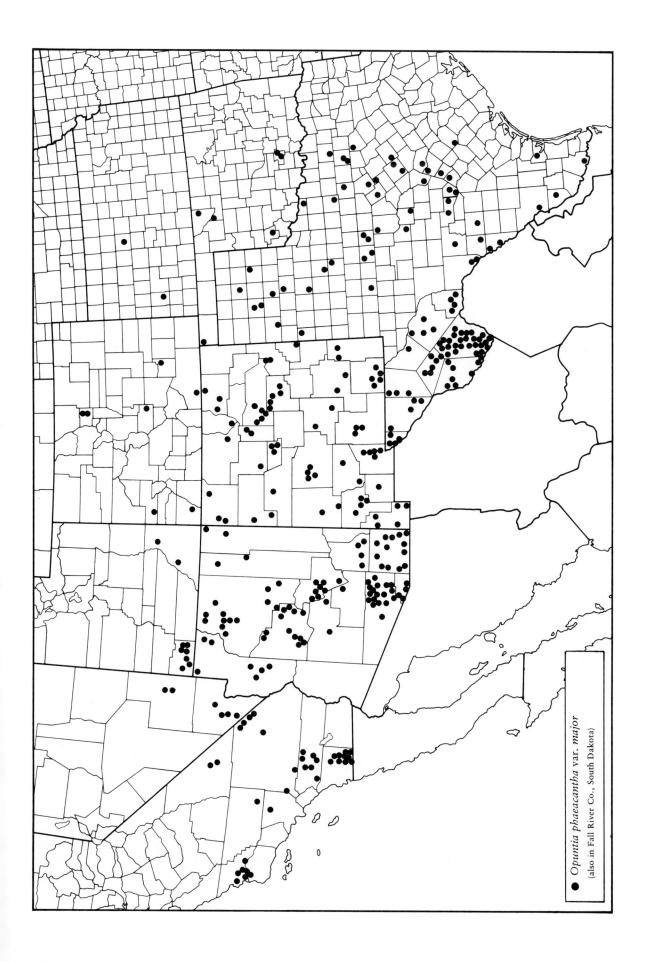

● *Opuntia phaeacantha var. major*
(also in Fall River Co., South Dakota)

Fig. 477. *Opuntia phaeacantha* var. *phaeacantha* with spines characteristically nearly covering the two-year-old joints but the lower spines of the younger joints not yet elongated. (David Griffiths)

Fig. 475. *Opuntia phaeacantha* var. *phaeacantha* near Zuñi, New Mexico, in fruit. (David Griffiths)

Fig. 476. *Opuntia phaeacantha* var. *phaeacantha* in northern Arizona, in flower.

Fig. 478. *Opuntia phaeacantha* var. *camanchica*, two-year-old joint with fruits and with elongate spines in all but the basal areoles; young joint of the current season with the spines of the lower areoles immature. (David Griffiths)

39b. Opuntia phaeacantha var. **camanchica** (Engelmann & Bigelow) L. Benson. Sandy soils, especially those of Llano Estacado and Texas Red Beds at 900-1,200 m (3,000-4,000 ft). Great Plains Grassland and adjacent brushland areas. Uncommon. In E central New Mexico from E San Miguel, Guadalupe, N Lincoln, Chaves, and Eddy Cos. to Quay and Curry Cos.; w half of Oklahoma (as far E as Arbuckle Mts.); Texas in the Panhandle, at Longview in Gregg Co., and at Lampasas in Lampasas Co.; Missouri in Jasper Co.

The variety is low-growing, forming clumps or rosettes of joints conspicuous as little islands in the grasslands.

39c. Opuntia phaeacantha var. **spinosibacca** (Anthony) L. Benson. Gravelly and sandy soils of hills and valleys in the desert at 600-900 m (2,000-3,000 ft). Chihuahuan Desert. Texas in Big Bend region from Ruidosa in Presidio Co. to Brewster Co.

The dominant feature of these large prickly pears, their brownish-red spines, distinguishes them from the other varieties, as does the presence of spines on the fruits.

39d. Opuntia phaeacantha var. **laevis** (Coulter) L. Benson. Rocky ledges of cliffs and very steep canyon walls or sometimes in good soil under trees in canyon bottoms in deserts, grasslands, and woodlands at 750-900 m (2,500-3,000 ft). Upper portion of Arizona Desert, Desert Grassland, and lower edge of Southwestern Oak Woodland. Arizona from Pinal Co. near Sacaton to Gila, Pima, and N Cochise Cos.

Like other spineless cacti, this one is destroyed by cattle, and its survival depends on its ability to grow on inaccessible ledges, in cracks between rocks, or where trees and brush offer some protection. Rodents also feed on the plant, especially during prolonged dry periods, when they depend on it for water.

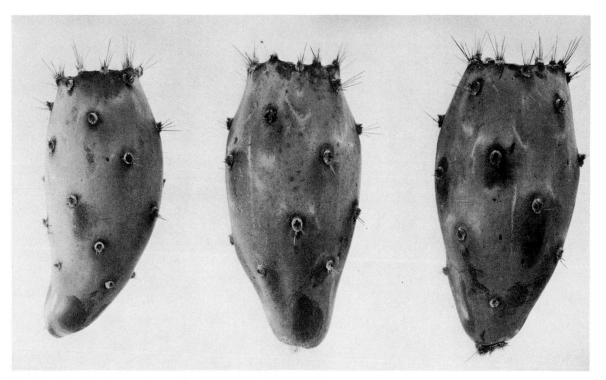

Fig. 480. *Opuntia phaeacantha* var. *laevis*, fruits. (David Griffiths)

Fig. 479. *Opuntia phaeacantha* var. *laevis* in Florida Canyon, Santa Rita Mts., Pima Co., Arizona. The typical habitat on the rocky ledges is a protection to these spineless plants; here, grazing animals cannot usually reach them, but elsewhere they are soon eaten. (David Griffiths)

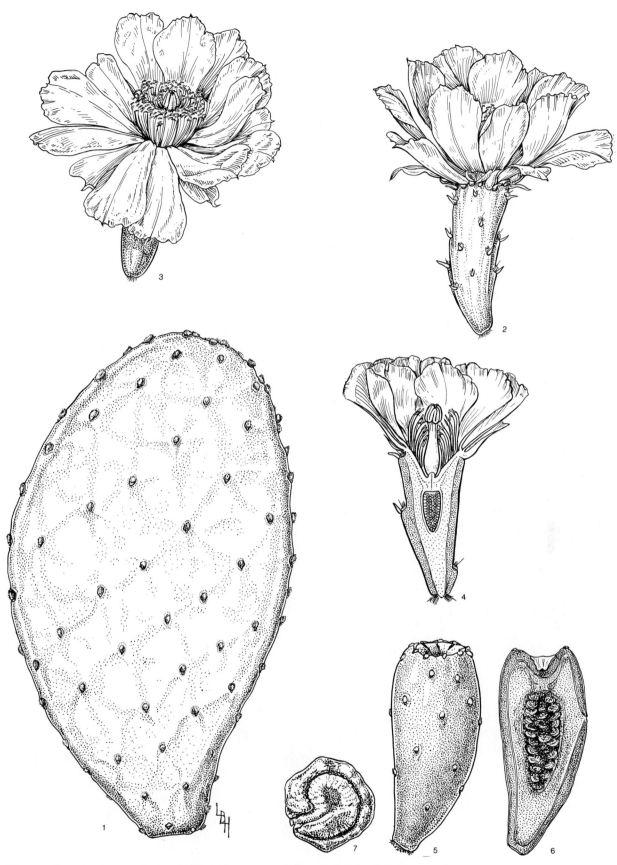

Fig. 481. *Opuntia phaeacantha* var. *laevis*, $\times$.8, except as indicated. *1*, Joint. *2, 3*, Flowers. *4*, Flower in longitudinal section. *5*, Fruit. *6*, Fruit in longitudinal section. *7*, Seed, $\times$4.5.

39e. Opuntia phaeacantha var. **major** Engelmann. Rocky, gravelly, or sandy soils of hillsides (sometimes of valleys or flats) chiefly at 600-2,100 m (2,000-7,000 ft). Mostly in Arizona and Chihuahuan Deserts and Desert Grassland, but also in lower portion of Juniper-Pinyon Woodlands or, in California, also in Mojavean Desert and (rarely) Colorado Desert and in desert-edge phase of California Chaparral (including portions with junipers and pinyons); rare in lower edge of Pacific Montane Forest or Rocky Mountain Montane Forest; here and there in Great Plains Grassland, also on Edwards Plateau and Rio Grande Plain. California near Santa Maria in San Luis Obispo Co. and E through Cuyama Valley; on desert side of mountain axis from Kern Co. (rare) through Los Angeles Co. to San Diego Co., in Death Valley region in Inyo Co., and in E Mojave Desert in San Bernardino Co. (rare); s Nevada in Lincoln and Clark Cos.; s Utah in Washington and San Juan Cos.; sw Colorado (occasional) and rare along Front Range and on Great Plains; Arizona above (not common) and below (common) Mogollon Rim except in and near Yuma Co.; New Mexico, occasional in N and W and common chiefly in s half of state and on s two-thirds of Great Plains area; South Dakota; w Kansas (rare); w half of Oklahoma (rare); Texas in the Panhandle and from El Paso Co. E to Edwards Plateau and uncommon through hill country E and SE; occasional in lower Rio Grande Valley. Mexico in Sonora and Chihuahua.

Though smaller than var. *discata*, this plant is relatively large and is the most abundant prickly pear in the deserts of the Southwest. On the Colorado Plateau and in the southern Rocky Mts., especially in northern New Mexico, it is replaced largely by var. *phaeacantha*, a more localized variety of the highlands.

In California the plant has been in part overlooked and in part confused with other species. It has appeared in some works under *O. mojavensis* (*O. phaeacantha* var. *mojavensis*). Mountain forms have been confused with *O. littoralis* var. *piercei*, with which the variety intergrades.

Occasionally hybridizes with *O. erinacea* var. *erinacea* (sp. 26a) in southern Utah and northern Arizona.

Fig. 483. *Opuntia phaeacantha* var. *major*, mature joint bearing a fruit, and three maturing joints with the lateral spines not fully elongated. The spines, brown, and spreading in all directions, occur on the upper one-third to (in this case) two-thirds of the joint, the longest on the upper margin. (David Griffiths)

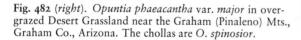

Fig. 482 (*right*). *Opuntia phaeacantha* var. *major* in overgrazed Desert Grassland near the Graham (Pinaleno) Mts., Graham Co., Arizona. The chollas are *O. spinosior*.

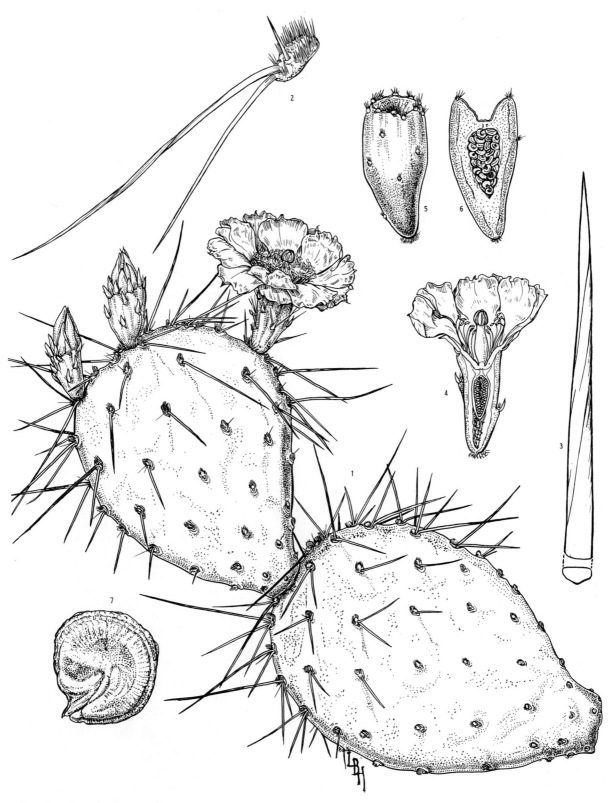

Fig. 484. *Opuntia phaeacantha* var. *major*, ×.6, except as indicated. *1*, Joints with flower buds and a flower, the spines confined to the areoles of the upper one-third to two-thirds of the joint. *2*, Areole with spines, glochids, and wool, ×1.6. *3*, Spine tip, ×6.5. *4*, Flower in longitudinal section. *5*, Fruit. *6*, Fruit in longitudinal section. *7*, Seed, ×6.

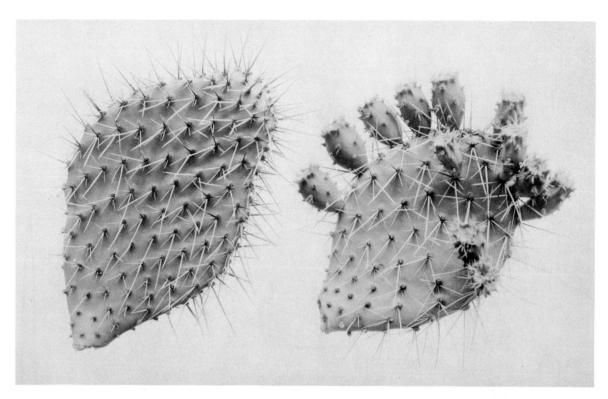

Fig. 485. Character recombinations of *Opuntia phaeacantha* vars. *major* and *discata* (*above*, *right*, and *facing page*). Var. *major* is distributed more widely than var. *discata*. In most places the two occur together, and var. *discata* occurs alone only uncommonly. Where the two are together, commonly there are far more individuals with character recombinations than with the usual combinations of either variety. (David Griffiths)

39f. Opuntia phaeacantha var. **discata** (Griffiths) Benson & Walkington. Engelmann prickly pear. Sandy soils of plains, washes, benches, arroyos, hillsides, valleys, and canyon bottoms in the desert and in grasslands at 600-1,200 m (2,000-4,000 ft), occasionally at extremes of 450 and 1,500 m (1,500 and 5,000 ft). Mostly in Arizona Desert and Desert Grassland, but also in Mojavean Desert, upper edge of Colorado Desert, and Chihuahuan Desert, Juniper-Pinyon Woodlands, Southwestern Oak Woodland. California (in California Chaparral), rare in modified form near coast in s California and (mostly) on desert side of San Bernardino, San Jacinto, and Laguna Mts.; in Mojave Desert in Panamint, Clark, Ivanpah, and Providence Mts.; reported from Nevada in Clark Co.; Utah in Washington Co. near Springdale; Arizona from Mohave Co. SE below Mogollon escarpment to Greenlee Co. and s to Pima and Cochise Cos.; New Mexico usually below 1,500 m (5,000 ft) from Grant and Hidalgo Cos. to Bernalillo and Eddy Cos.; Texas w of Pecos R. and sparingly E to Floyd, King, Travis, and Bexar Cos. Mexico in Sonora, Chihuahua, and Coahuila.

Var. *discata* is the largest and, especially in s Arizona, one of the best-known (as "*Opuntia engelmannii*") native prickly pears of the Southwestern deserts. It is variable in habit of growth, shape and size of joints, and size and distribution of spines.

This variety occurs almost always near or with var. *major*, which has brown spines; these are also longer than those of var. *discata*, and they occur only or largely on the upper part of the joint, which is relatively narrow. Almost everywhere var. *discata* has been investigated most plants are intergrading forms with a host of character combinations. The variety is unstable, and it is commonly a population-fringe extreme occurring with the ubiquitous populations of var. *major*, which has a greater geographical range and is more abundant.

Combinations of the characters of this plant with those of *O. chlorotica* (sp. 44) are shown in plants collected in New Mexico.

Specific rank cannot be defended, and the well-known and much-used name *Opuntia engelmannii* was applied to another taxon (the spiny form of *O. ficus-indica* imported from Mexico). Unfortunately, therefore, the long-established mode of reference is eliminated through reasons of both classification and nomenclature.

Fig. 486. Engelmann prickly pear, *Opuntia phaeacantha* var. *discata*, long known as *O. engelmannii*, a name commonly applied incorrectly, and to plants for which specific rank is untenable. In the plant shown, there are several very stout, white spines in each areole, spreading in various directions. (David Griffiths)

Fig. 487. *Opuntia phaeacantha* var. *discata*, this plant with slender, downward-directed white spines and only one or two in each areole; near the Graham (Pinaleno) Mts., Graham Co., Arizona. A cholla, *O. spinosior*, is in the background.

Fig. 488. *Opuntia phaeacantha* var. *discata*, joints with short, stout, variously spreading white spines; Colossal Cave, Rincon Mts., Pima Co., Arizona.

Fig. 489. *Opuntia phaeacantha* var. *discata*, the spines long and slender, few and white, and especially the lower one deflexed; near Hualpai Mountain, Mohave Co., Arizona.

483

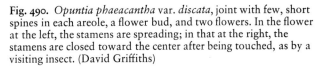

Fig. 491. *Opuntia phaeacantha* var. *discata*, mature fruits (purple). (David Griffiths)

Fig. 490. *Opuntia phaeacantha* var. *discata*, joint with few, short spines in each areole, a flower bud, and two flowers. In the flower at the left, the stamens are spreading; in that at the right, the stamens are closed toward the center after being touched, as by a visiting insect. (David Griffiths)

Fig. 492. A California variant of *Opuntia phaeacantha* var. *discata*, the locally prevailing type with usually rather long, slender white spines, these more or less deflexed. Characters of vars. *major* and *discata* often are combined, yielding a plant like the one in the photograph, the joints of which are of three ages, only the lower one (with the two immature fruits) showing the mature form of the spines. Although the specimen is from the plants at Banning included in the type collection of *O. megacarpa* Griffiths, it is not the extremely long-spined form (with spines in even the lowest areoles) that prompted publication of the proposed species. In books, the name *O. megacarpa* has been misapplied to plants more nearly typical of var. *discata* as it occurs here and there in California and eastward to Texas. (David Griffiths)

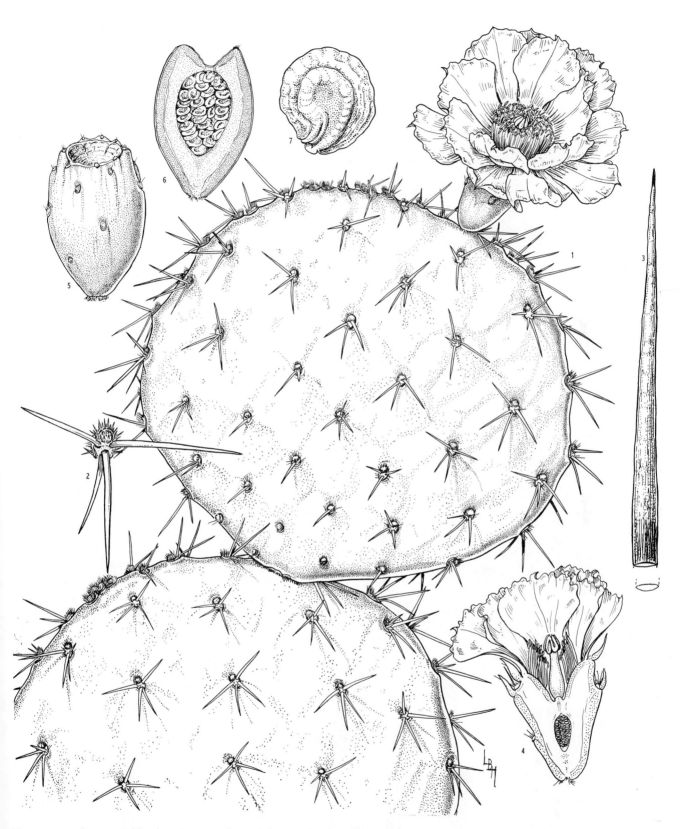

Fig. 493. Engelmann prickly pear, *Opuntia phaeacantha* var. *discata*, ×.9, except as indicated. *1*, Joint with a flower, ×.6. *2*, Areole with spines, glochids, and wool, the principal spine directed downward and the others not spreading widely, ×1.7. *3*, Spine, upper part and cross section, ×7. *4*, Flower in longitudinal section. *5*, Fruit. *6*, Fruit in longitudinal section. *7*, Seed, ×6.

Fig. 494. Wooton prickly pear, *Opuntia phaeacantha* var. *wootonii*, joint, the spines reddish brown and white. (David Griffiths)

39g. Opuntia phaeacantha var. **wootonii** (Griffiths) L. Benson. Wooton prickly pear. Rocky hillsides in the desert or grassland at 1,500-1,800 m (5,000-6,000 ft). Desert Grassland and Chihuahuan Desert. New Mexico in Bernalillo Co., in Organ Mts., Dona Ana Co., and near Hondo in Lincoln Co.

Occupies intermittently a belt on the hills above vars. *major* and *discata*, which occur on the lower slopes.

According to Anthony (1956), the plant occurs in the Big Bend region of Texas as follows: "Scattered in desert shrub vegetation of Tornillo Flats and locally abundant in Christmas Mountains. . . . An extensive population is well established on desert plains within the Christmas Mountains." However, the specimens recorded as var. *wootonii* either are var. *discata* or they exhibit character combinations intermediate between those of vars. *discata* and *major*.

Fig. 495. Big Sandy prickly pear, *Opuntia phaeacantha* var. *superbospina*, in fruit; Mojavean Desert on Hualpai Mountain, Mohave Co., Arizona.

Fig. 496. *Opuntia phaeacantha* var. *superbospina*, showing the long, relatively stout and stiff, white spines, spreading variously from the areole; from the plant of Fig. 495.

39h. Opuntia phaeacantha var. **superbospina** (Griffiths) L. Benson. Big Sandy prickly pear. Desert floor at about 760-1,350 (2,500-4,500 ft). Mojavean Desert. Arizona from Kingman to watershed of Big Sandy Wash, 15-50 mi. SE of Kingman.

The character combinations, including the narrowly obovate joints and the presence of very long, slender spines in all the areoles of the joint, are similar to those of the sporadic combinations in the California plants known as "*O. megacarpa* Griffiths."

39i. Opuntia phaeacantha var. **mojavensis** (Engelman & Bigelow) Fosberg. Desert hills at about 600 m (2,000 ft). Mojavean Desert. California in E Mojave Desert in San Bernardino Co. from near lower Mojave R. to Nevada border and to Kingman, Arizona (Walkington).

39j. Opuntia phaeacantha var. **flavispina** L. Benson. Flats, washes, and hillsides in the desert, 375-1,050 m (1,250-3,500 ft). Arizona Desert and probably upper edge of Colorado Desert. Arizona in White Tank Mts., w Maricopa Co., and in Organ Pipe Cactus National Monument, Pima Co.

The long yellow-and-red spines are the special feature of this large prickly pear.

40. Opuntia lindheimeri Engelmann
Texas prickly pear

Large suberect to sprawling shrubs, 1-3(3.5) m high, 1-5+ m diam; trunk, if present, very short; larger terminal joints green (in w central and s Texas sometimes blue-green), obovate to orbiculate or rarely greatly elongate, usually 15-25(30) cm (rarely 1.2 m) long, (6.2)12-20(30) cm broad, ±2 cm thick; leaves narrowly conical, 3-9 mm long; areoles elliptic, ±4.5 mm long, ±3 mm broad, typically 2.5-4 cm apart; spines occurring usually in all but lower areoles of joint (but some plants spineless), yellow or sometimes whitish-yellow (the extreme bases sometimes black, brown, or red), 1-6(8) per areole, usually 1 spreading and others lying fairly near surface, straight, the longer (1)1.2-4(7.5) cm long, basally ±0.7 mm broad, subulate, very narrowly elliptic in section, not barbed; glochids yellow or turning brown in age, 3-6 mm long; flower 5-7.5(10.5) cm diam and 5-8 cm long; sepaloids greenish-yellow or greenish-red, obovate, 6-35 mm long, 6-15(25) mm broad, mucronate to acuminate, somewhat crisped; petaloids yellow or rarely red, cuneate-obovate, 30-40(50) mm long, 12-25(40) mm broad, mucronate, undulate; filaments 6-12 (15) mm long; anthers 2 mm long; style greenish-yellow, 12-20 mm long, 3-6 mm diam; stigmas 6 or 8, 4.5-6 mm long, slender to fairly thick; ovary

Distinctive Characters of the Varieties of **Opuntia lindheimeri**

Character	a. var. lindheimeri	b. var. tricolor	c. var. lehmannii	d. var. cuija	e. var. linguiformis
Joint growth	Determinate	Determinate	Determinate	Determinate	Apically meristematic, therefore indeterminate
Shape of larger terminal joints	Obovate to sometimes orbicular, flat	Obovate, flat	Broader than long, wavy	Obovate, flat	Elongate, lanceolate to linear-lanceolate, flat
Size of larger terminal joints	15-25(30) cm long, 12.5-20(25) cm broad	17.5-20(25) cm long, 15-17.5(20) cm broad	22.5-25 cm long, (22.5)25-30 cm broad	15-20 cm long, 6.2-7.5 cm broad	45-90(120) cm long, 10-12.5(17.5) cm broad
Spine distribution on joint	1-6 per areole, usually in all but lower areoles	1-3(6) per areole, in nearly all the areoles	Mostly 3 or 4 per areole, in all but lower areoles	3-8 per areole, on nearly all the joint	1-3 per areole, distributed irregularly or on some joints lacking
Spine color	Yellow, the bases not red	Yellow, the bases not red	Yellow, the bases not red	Pale yellow, the bases red	Yellow
Spine length	1.2-4 or 5 cm	5-7.5 cm	2-3 cm	4.4 cm	1.2-2 cm
Altitude	1.5-300 m (5-1,000 ft)	Sea level to 120 m (400 ft)	Sea level to 25 m (80 ft)	Introduced near sea level; altitude in Mexico unknown	±250 m (800 ft)
Floristic association	Great Plains Grassland; Edwards Plateau; Rio Grande Plain; rare in Chihuahuan Desert	Rio Grande Plain	Rio Grande Plain	Native area in Mexico; association undetermined	Great Plains Grassland

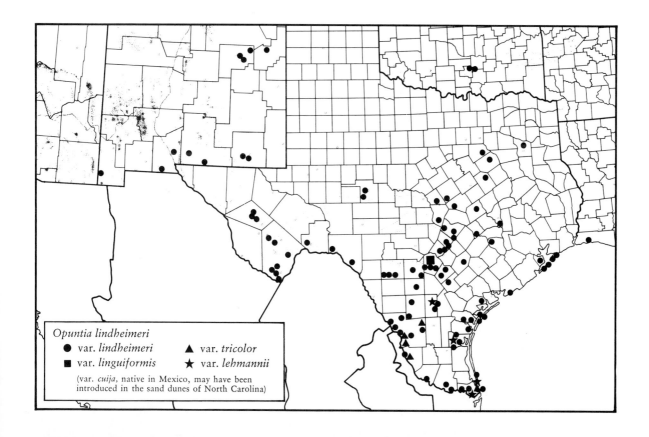

Opuntia lindheimeri

● var. *lindheimeri*   ▲ var. *tricolor*

■ var. *linguiformis*   ★ var. *lehmannii*

(var. *cuija*, native in Mexico, may have been
introduced in the sand dunes of North Carolina)

Fig. 497. Texas prickly pear, *Opuntia lindheimeri* var. *lindheimeri*, growing on the edge
of Deciduous Forest near Waco, Texas, in 1909. (D. A. Saunders)

in anthesis not spiny; fruit purple, fleshy at maturity, obovate or elongate, the areoles and glochids small, 3-7 cm long, 2.5-3(4) cm diam, the umbilicus shallow, the fruit not persistent; seeds tan, asymmetrically elliptic, 3-4 mm long, 2.5-3 mm broad, 1.5 mm thick.

40a. Opuntia lindheimeri var. lindheimeri.

Texas prickly pear. Sandy, gravelly, or relatively rich soils of hills, valleys, and plains in grasslands or brushlands at 1.5-300 m (5-1,000 ft). Great Plains Grassland, Edwards Plateau, Rio Grande Plain, and (rarely) Chihuahuan Desert. New Mexico (rare) from Guadalupe Co. to Dona Ana and Eddy Cos. and perhaps Hidalgo Co.; s central Oklahoma (rare) in Murray Co.; Texas in Jeff Davis, Brewster, and Sutton Cos. and along the Rio Grande from Big Bend National Park downstream and E to Gulf Coast, abundant in central and s Texas; sw Louisiana (rare). Mexico as far s as San Luis Potosí, Hidalgo, and Tamaulipas.

The shrubs are big plants, often as large as O. *phaeacantha* var. *discata* farther west. The yellow, instead of nearly white, spines and green, instead of bluish-green, stems give a different aspect. The plants may be solitary or in large thickets.

Fig. 498. *Opuntia lindheimeri* var. *lindheimeri*, in cultivation, with fruits. (David Griffiths)

Fig. 499. Texas prickly pear, *Opuntia lindheimeri*, ×.6, except as indicated. *1*, Joint with flower buds and a flower. *2*, Areole, showing spines and glochids, ×3. *3*, Flower in longitudinal section. *4*, Fruit. *5*, Fruit in longitudinal section. *6*, Seed, ×5.

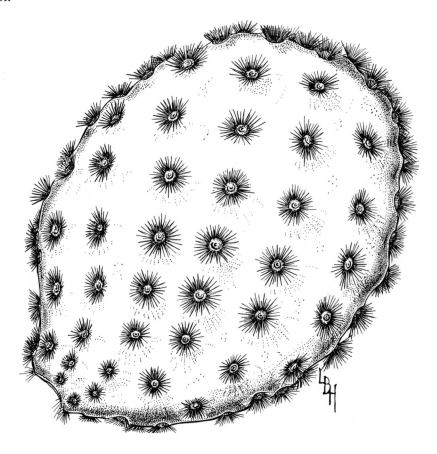

Fig. 500. *Opuntia lindheimeri* var. *lindheimeri*, spineless form with large brown glochids, collected by Griffiths and brought into cultivation as "*Opuntia aciculata*," half natural size. Spineless joints and the unusual abundance and size of the glochids occur in other plants of this species and in other species. In this case, these characters are maintained together because the plants are propagated in cultivation without sexual reproduction.

40b. Opuntia lindheimeri var. **tricolor** (Griffiths) L. Benson. Plains, to 120 m (400 ft). Rio Grande Plain. Texas in Webb, Zapata, w Duval, and Cameron Cos.

The long yellow spines give the plant a shaggy appearance. This may distinguish the variety, even from a distance.

40c. Opuntia lindheimeri var. **lehmannii** L. Benson. Sandy plains in grassland and among mesquites, to 25 m (80 ft). Rio Grande Plain. Texas in McMullen Co., on King Ranch in Kleberg Co., and s to Cameron Co.

The plants are relatively lower and more inclined to sprawl than those of var. *lindheimeri*. They are mostly 1-1.5 m (3-5 ft) high. Each joint is nearly circular but somewhat broader than long, the size of a large dinner plate, and with a wavy rather than flattened aspect. Thus, although this variety is conspicuous, it has long been overlooked because it occurs largely within the restricted area of the King Ranch. This area was visited in 1965 through the kindness of Mr. V. W. Lehmann, the wildlife manager, who wished to determine which cacti grew on the ranch.

40d. Opuntia lindheimeri var. **cuija** (Griffiths & Hare) L. Benson. Native of San Luis Potosí, Querétaro, and Hidalgo, Mexico; may be introduced in sand dunes in North Carolina.

A collection from beach sand dunes at Beaufort, North Carolina (R. L. Borney in 1930, US, 1038808), which may be this variety, was referred by Small (Man. S. E. Fl. 910. 1933) to *O. cantabrigiensis* Lynch, a cultivated plant. The specimen consists of two small joints about 10 cm long, with single small spines in some of the upper areoles; they are almost certainly immature and therefore not representative. A good photograph by Duncan Johnson, mounted on the same herbarium sheet, indicates a large plant with much larger joints. It could be either var. *cuija* or var. *lindheimeri*. Similar plants at Beaufort were mentioned by Engelmann (1857, preprint 1856) as *O. tuna* (L.) Miller of the West Indies. The plant was not found at Beaufort in 1956, but there was insufficient time for a thorough search.

Fig. 501. *Opuntia lindheimeri* var. *tricolor* in cultivation. (David Griffiths)

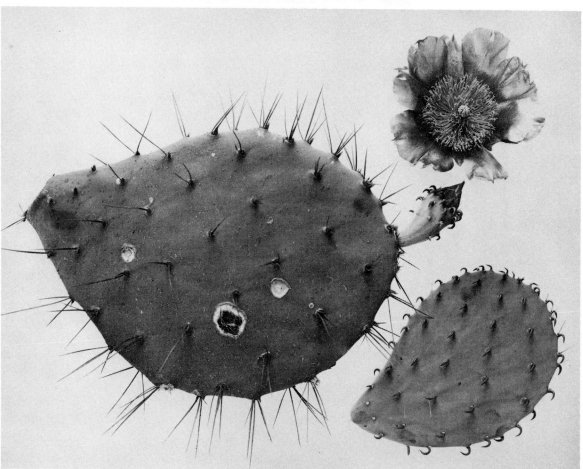

Fig. 502. *Opuntia lindheimeri* var. *tricolor*, young joint with leaves; mature joint with spines and a flower bud; a flower. The stamens have not been touched, and remain spread. (David Griffiths)

493

Fig. 503. *Opuntia lindheimeri* var. *lehmannii* in cultivation, showing the immense size of the joints. (David Griffiths)

Fig. 504. *Opuntia lindheimeri* var. *lehmannii* in cultivation. (David Griffiths; see Credits)

40e. Opuntia lindheimeri var. linguiformis

(Griffiths) L. Benson. Cow's tongue, lingua de vaca. At ±250 m (800 ft). Occasional near San Antonio, Texas. The variety was introduced into cultivation by David Griffiths about 1908, and it has escaped in various localities. During 66 years the plant has not been demonstrated to occur still as a native variety.

The elongate, lance-shaped joints that provide the name "cow's tongue" are almost as wide as those of the other varieties but up to a meter (yard) long. For this reason this tall variety is cultivated in many gardens as a curiosity.

Fig. 506. *Opuntia lindheimeri* var. *linguiformis*, young joints with leaves and an older joint; flower buds and flowers, the stamens closed together, having been touched. The terminal bud does not die or become dormant after the early weeks of the first season, as is the case with nearly all other prickly-pear joints, but continues the growth and elongation of the joint. (David Griffiths)

Fig. 505. Cow's tongue or lingua de vaca, *Opuntia lindheimeri* var. *linguiformis*, in cultivation; known only from plants descended from those collected near San Antonio, Texas, by Griffiths in 1906. (David Griffiths)

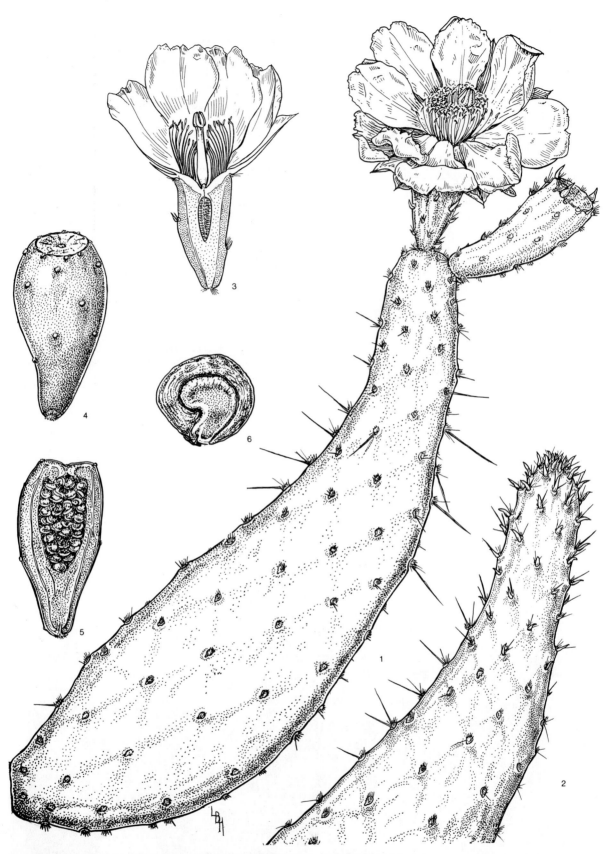

Fig. 507. Cow's tongue or lingua de vaca, *Opuntia lindheimeri* var. *linguiformis*, ×.6, except as indicated. *1*, Joint with a flower and a young fruit. *2*, Growing tip of a long joint, the upper part immature and bearing leaves, the rest of the joint lacking leaves but with mature spines. *3*, Flower in longitudinal section. *4*, Fruit. *5*, Fruit in longitudinal section. *6*, Seed, ×6.

41. **Opuntia stricta** Haworth

Sprawling or erect shrub 0.5-2 m high, 1-2.5 m diam; trunk lacking or short; larger terminal joints green, narrowly obovate or narrowly elliptic to nearly oblong, 10-25(40) cm long, usually 7.5-15(25) cm broad, 1.2-2 cm thick; leaves conical, sharp-tipped, 4.5-6 mm long; areoles ±4.5 mm diam, typically 3-5 cm apart; spines none or a few along margin or (var. *dillenii*) numerous and from all areoles, yellow (or brown in age), 0-11 per areole, spreading in all directions, straight or slightly curving, the longer 1.2-4(6) cm long, basally 1-1.5 mm broad, subulate, nearly linear in cross section, not markedly barbed; glochids yellow, relatively few, short, inconspicuous, slender or stout and to 7.5 mm long; flower ±5-6 cm diam and long; sepaloids greenish with yellow margins, broadly deltoid-obovate to narrowly obovate, 10-25 mm long, 6-12 mm broad, mucronate to short-acuminate, entire or slightly crisped; petaloids light yellow (reported to be sometimes red), obovate or cuneate-obovate, 25-30 mm long, 12-20 mm broad, apically rounded or truncate, emarginate, entire

Fig. 509. *Opuntia stricta* vars. *dillenii* (left) and *stricta* (right).

Fig. 508. Southern spineless cactus, *Opuntia stricta* vars. *stricta* and *dillenii*: *left*, var. *stricta*, from Fernandino Beach, Florida, this variety spineless; *right*, var. *dillenii*, from Coot Bay, Everglades National Park, Florida. (From *Plant Taxonomy, Methods and Principles*)

or slightly undulate; filaments yellow, 12 mm long; anthers yellow, 1.5 mm long; style yellowish or yellow, 12-20 mm long, ±4.5 mm diam; stigmas 5 or 10(?), 4.5 mm long, very thick; ovary in anthesis with a few prominent glochids; fruit purple, fleshy at maturity, smooth, spineless (areoles few and glochids small), 4-6 cm long, 2.5-3 (4) cm diam, the umbilicus of moderate depth, the fruit maturing during fall or winter and then deciduous; seeds light tan, nearly orbiculate, somewhat irregular, 4-5 mm long, 4-4.5 mm broad, 2 mm thick.

Distinctive Characters of the Varieties of **Opuntia stricta**

Character	a. var. **stricta**	b. var. **dillenii**
Shape of larger terminal joints	Narrowly elliptic, narrowly obovate, or sometimes obovate	Obovate
Size of larger terminal joints	17.5-25 cm long, 7.5-12.5 cm broad	10-30(40) cm long, 12.5-15(25) cm broad
Spines	None (sometimes a few solitary small ones in some marginal areoles)	1-11 per areole, 1.2-4(6) cm long
Altitude	Near sea level	Near sea level
Floristic association	Deciduous Forests (coastal plain types) and Caribbean Tropical Forest (uncommon)	Caribbean Tropical Forest and edges of Deciduous Forests (coastal plain types)

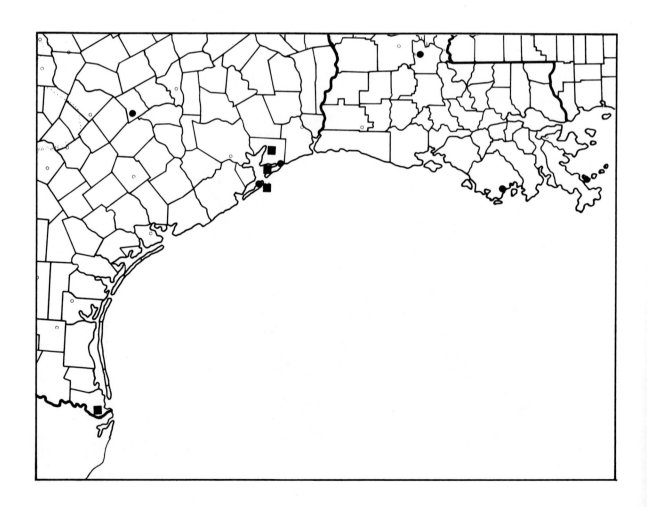

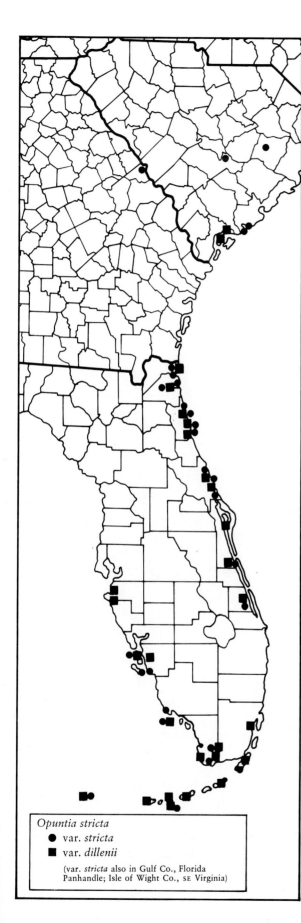

Opuntia stricta
● var. *stricta*
■ var. *dillenii*

(var. *stricta* also in Gulf Co., Florida
Panhandle; Isle of Wight Co., SE Virginia)

Fig. 510. Plant intermediate between *Opuntia stricta* vars. *stricta* and *dillenii*. In Florida, plants with all of the possible character recombinations are abundant. On the islands of the Caribbean, var. *dillenii* occurs alone; the plants there are of an extreme stout-spiny form. In this species the spines are yellow. (David Griffiths)

41a. Opuntia stricta var. stricta. Southern spineless cactus. Sandy soils of coastal woods and dunes, jungles, shell mounds, and swamp borders just above sea level. Caribbean Tropical Forest and Deciduous Forests (in various woods and pinelands along or not far from coast). Texas, rare from Nueces Co. E; rare in S Louisiana and in W South Carolina; Virginia in Isle of Wight Co.; rare in NW Florida, but common on Gulf Coast below Tampa and on E coast and Keys. Western Cuba; Bahamas (the type specimen of *O. bahamana* Britton & Rose being *O. stricta*).

The spineless joints, narrower than those of related large prickly pears, render the plants quite striking.

This variety occurs even in jungles along the Everglades, where the water table is only a few centimeters below the surface.

A plant collected on Big Pine Key, Florida Keys (*L. & R. L. Benson 15362, Pom*), during four years of culture produced only spineless joints, although the original joint from which they grew was still present and strongly spiny.

Hybridizes with *O. humifusa* var. *humifusa* in northeastern Florida.

41b. Opuntia stricta var. **dillenii** (Ker-Gawler) L. Benson. Sandy soils and shell mounds of woods, pinelands, and thickets near sea level; mostly coastal but sometimes occurring inland. Caribbean Tropical Forest and adjacent vegetation types (Deciduous Forests). Rare on Gulf Coast in Texas and on Atlantic Coast in sw South Carolina; most abundant in Florida, on Gulf Coast below Tampa, on E coast, and on Keys. On E coast of Mexico to N South America; West Indies; Bermuda.

Var. *dillenii* is impressive for its clusters of stout, yellow spines. On the islands of the Caribbean (see below) the plants are truly forbidding, and even the hybridized ones in Florida are formidable.

In Florida, intergradation between vars. *stricta* and *dillenii* is common, and few populations are clearly one or the other. Nearly any form from one extreme, var. *stricta*, to the mainland extreme of var. *dillenii* may be collected wherever these plants occur within the state. The forms of var. *dillenii* on the Caribbean islands are more strongly differentiated, and var. *stricta* does not occur there.

Hybridizing with *O. humifusa* vars. *humifusa* and *austrina* also occurs in Florida.

Fig. 511. *Opuntia stricta* var. *dillenii* in dense brush of second-growth jungle on Big Pine Key, Florida. (Randy Willich)

Fig. 514 (*above*). *Opuntia stricta* var. *dillenii*, fruits. (David Griffiths)

Fig. 512. *Opuntia stricta* var. *dillenii*, mature joint with spines typical of plants in the southern states. (David Griffiths)

Fig. 513. *Opuntia stricta* var. *dillenii*, mature joint; a young joint with leaves but not yet with spines; a flower bud and two flowers. (David Griffiths)

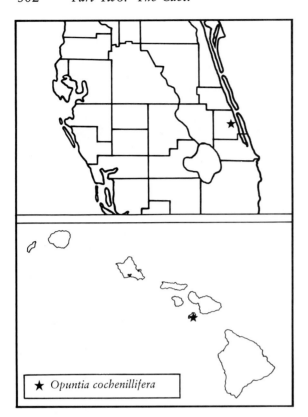

★ *Opuntia cochenillifera*

42. Opuntia cochenillifera (Linnaeus) Salm-Dyck

Shrubs or trees to ±4 m (reportedly to 9 m) high, several meters diam; trunk 15-20 cm diam; larger joints green, narrowly elliptic to sometimes narrowly obovate, 15-25 (reportedly 50) cm long, 6-7.5(15) cm broad; areoles ±2 mm diam, ±2.5 cm apart; spines none, except for reportedly) minute ones sometimes occurring on upper margins of older joints or in specimens probably representing intergrades with *O. auberi* Pfeiffer of Mexico *(US)*; spines (when present) grayish-tan, 1-3 per areole, spreading, straight, the longer ±0.9 cm long, basally 1 mm diam, acicular, nearly circular in cross section; glochids numerous, falling away early, none on mature joint; flower 1.2-1.5 cm diam, 5-6 cm long; sepaloids with midribs brilliant red, some with green along middles (scales on inferior floral cup covering the ovary green), succulent, the largest ovate-acute, to 12 mm long, to 7.5 mm broad, apically acute, entire or undulate; petaloids bright red, the largest oblong-obovate, to 20 mm long, 10 mm broad, apically rounded, entire; filaments pink, 30-40 mm long, much longer than perianth; anthers pink, 1.5 mm long; style pink, 40-45 mm long, 1-1.5 mm greatest diam, except for basal swelling, ±3 mm diam; stigmas 6 or 7, 3 mm

long, slender, ±0.5 mm diam; ovary in anthesis ±1.5 cm long; fruit red, fleshy at maturity, without surface appendages from the small areoles, ellipsoid, 2.5-3.8 cm long, 2.5-3 cm diam, the umbilicus developed but not prominent; seeds gray or tannish, smooth, thickened-discoid, ±3 mm diam, 1.5 mm thick.

Sandy soils of dunes and fields at low elevations. In openings in Caribbean Tropical Forest. Mexico; grown by Aztecs; long cultivated in the West Indies and tropical America and occasionally escaped from cultivation, as (perhaps) on Kahoolawe, Hawaii, and in Florida (near St. Lucie Sound, 6 mi s of Ft. Pierce, *L. & R. L. Benson 15374, Pom*).

The plants occur in cultivation in tropical or nearly tropical areas. Rarely, they escape. The usually spineless dark-green joints and the small but colorful flowers and bright red fruits are

Fig. 515. *Opuntia cochenillifera*, grown as a host for the cochineal scale insect, the source of the royal purple dye used by the Aztec emperor. Spineless joint with flower buds and a flower (note the very short sepaloids and petaloids and the more elongate style); young joint with leaves; flowers and fruits. See Figs. 228 and 229 (and text) and color plates 50 and 51. (David Griffiths)

attractive. The elongate stamens and style far surpass the perianth, and thus the shape of the flower is far different from that in other species of *Opuntia*.

O. *cochenillifera* (cochineal-bearer) is named for its use as host plant in the culture of the cochineal scale insect (*Dactylopius coccus*), the source of cochineal dye. The insects occur on various prickly pears, and often they are mistaken for other white woolly insects, such as the cottony-cushion scale. The reddish pigment, however, is an obvious distinguishing feature. O. *cochenillifera* and many other species (e.g., O. *littoralis* and its many hybrids with O. *ficus-indica* in southern California) are also hosts for other species of cochineal scale insects (see pp. 236-37).

43. Opuntia oricola Philbrick

Typically treelike, with short trunk (to 30 cm high), but sometimes shrubby, 1-3 m high, spreading 1-2+ m; larger joints very dark green, broadly obovate or orbicular to broadly elliptic, some usually broader than long, 15-20(25) cm long, 12.5-20 (22.5) cm broad, ±2 cm thick; areoles 4.5-6 mm diam, typically 1.2-2 cm apart; spines rather dense on joint, yellow and at first translucent (in age changing through brownish-gray to black, as do yellow spines of other cacti), (4)8-16 per areole, spreading in various directions, the lower in the areole larger and with a downward trend, the longer gently and irregularly curving or twisting, 2-2.5(3) cm long, basally 0.7-1 mm broad, subulate, very narrowly elliptic in cross section, not

Fig. 516. *Opuntia oricola* in a grassy disturbed area formerly of California Chaparral, along ocean bluffs north of Malibu, Los Angeles Co., California.

markedly barbed; glochids yellow, abundant and prominent, mostly 3-4.5 mm long, those on flower buds to 20 mm long; flower 5-5.5 cm diam and long; sepaloids with midribs green and margins purplish-red, the largest obovate, short-acuminate, to 25 mm long, to 12 mm broad, short-acuminate to mucronate, with a few irregular subapical dentations; petaloids yellow, cuneate to obovate-cuneate, 30-40 mm long, 12-20 mm broad, truncate and mucronate, entire; filaments yellow, ±9 mm long; anthers yellow, linear-oblong, 2 mm long; style purplish-red, 15-22 mm long, 3-4.5 mm greatest diam, in bulbous base to 9 mm diam; stigmas green, 10-12, 2-4.5 mm long, ±1 mm broad; ovary in anthesis ±2.5 cm long; fruit red, fleshy at maturity, with yellow glochids 3-12 mm long, subglobose, nearly as broad as long, 2.5-3 cm long, 2.5-2.8 cm diam, the umbilicus fairly deep, the fruit persisting several months; seeds gray, nearly circular, discoid, the rim enclosing the embryo narrow and smooth, 3 mm diam, 1.25 mm thick.

Older trees arise like massive sentinels high above the bushes of coastal bluffs and hillsides. Younger plants resemble piles of large, platelike dark-green disks. The plates are the more impressive for their dense clusters of short, stout yellow to brown or black spines.

Sandy soils of valleys, flats, and low hills in coastal grassy disturbed areas at 6-150 m (20-500 ft). Disturbed areas on south-facing slopes in California Chaparral (coastal sagebrush stage). California along coast and on islands from Santa Barbara Co. to San Diego Co.; inland to Fullerton and Santa Ana Canyon in Orange Co. Mexico on NW coast of Baja California.

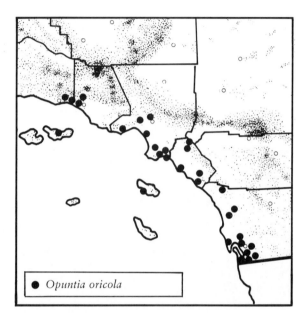

Fig. 517. *Opuntia oricola*, sprawling plant in a grassy, disturbed area along a road cut; north of Malibu.

Fig. 518. *Opuntia oricola*, plant about 3 m (10 ft) high; near the California coast. (David Griffiths)

Fig. 519. *Opuntia oricola*, joint showing the peculiar and characteristic curvature of the spines. (David Griffiths)

44. Opuntia chlorotica Engelmann & Bigelow
Pancake pear

Arborescent plant or erect shrub (0.6)1-2 m high, 1-1.2 m diam; trunk ±30 cm long, 7.5-20 cm diam; larger terminal joints blue-green, orbiculate to broadly obovate, 15-20 cm long, 12.5-17.5 cm broad, 12-20 mm thick; areoles elliptic, 4.5 mm long, 3 mm broad, typically ±2 cm apart; spines, in all but a few basal areoles of joint, light yellow to sometimes straw-colored (blackened or dirty gray in age or in old herbarium specimens), 1-6 per areole, all deflexed, straight or curving at extreme bases, the longer 2.5-4 cm long, basally (0.5)1 mm broad, subulate, tapering through entire length, narrowly elliptic to linear in cross section, not markedly barbed; glochids yellow, mostly 4.5 mm long; flower 4-6 cm diam, 5-7.5 cm long; sepaloids yellow, but reddish in middles, subulate-lanceolate to obovate-acuminate, 12-30 mm long, 3-15 mm broad, attenuate to acuminate, the margins essentially entire; petaloids light yellow, with external reddish flush, broadly obovate to cuneate-obovate, 20-30 mm long, 10-20 mm broad, truncate or rounded and mucronate, essentially entire; filaments yellow, ±12 mm long; anthers yellow, 2.25 mm long; style greenish-yellow, 20-25 mm long, to 4.5 mm diam; stigmas ±10, 4.5 mm long, thick; ovary in anthesis with many glochids and

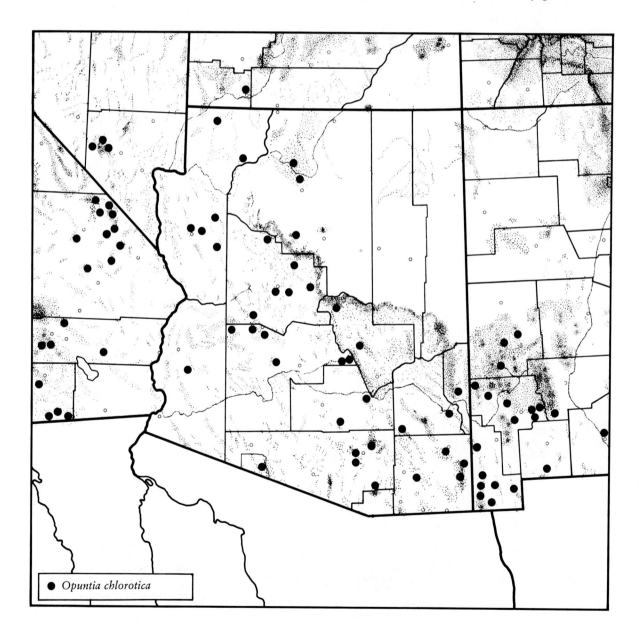

● *Opuntia chlorotica*

some slender spines; fruit grayish tinged with purple, fleshy at maturity, subglobose to ellipsoid, without spines, 4-6 cm long, 2-3.5 cm diam, the umbilicus bowl-like or sometimes shallow, the fruit maturing the summer or fall after flowering; seeds light tan, nearly elliptic but asymmetrical, smooth, 2.25-3 mm long, slightly less broad, 1.5 mm thick.

Rocky or sandy soils of ledges, steep slopes, canyons, or sometimes flats in the desert or just above it at 900-1,200 m (3,000-4,000 ft); extreme occurrences at 600 m (1,800 ft) and 2,000 m (6,000 ft). Mojavean Desert; Colorado Desert (rare); Arizona Desert; desert-edge phase of California Chaparral; Southwestern Oak Woodland; Juniper-Pinyon Woodlands; Desert Grassland. California in s and e Mojave Desert in San Bernardino Co. and on w edge of Colorado Desert (and in specialized chaparral just above it) from Riverside Co. to San Diego Co.; s Nevada in Charleston Mts., Clark Co.; Utah in Zion Canyon; Arizona from Mohave Co. to lower parts of N and s Coconino Co. and se in canyons, mountains, and hills below Mogollon Rim to Greenlee, Pima, and Cochise Cos.; sw New Mexico from Catron and Hidalgo Cos. to Socorro and Dona Ana Cos. Mexico in N Baja California and Sonora.

This species occurs on the tobosa grass (*Hilaria mutica*) flats northeast of Aguila, Arizona. Despite its more characteristic occurrence on rocky mountainsides, it here attains its greatest size, becoming 1.5 m or more in height and having hundreds of joints.

Plants intermediate between this species and *O. violacea* (possibly var. *santa-rita*) occur in the Perilla, Swisshelm, and Huachuca Mts. and on limestone hills just east of the Mule Mts. (*L. Benson 10264, Pom*) in southeastern Arizona.

Combinations of the characters of *O. chlorotica* and *O. phaeacantha* var. *discata* are shown in some plants collected in New Mexico: HIDALGO Co. Guadalupe Canyon, *Castetter 878, UNM.* LINCOLN Co. Jicarilla Mts., *P. Pierce 914, UNM.*

Fig. 521. *Opuntia chlorotica*, joints with the characteristic yellow spines; near Salome, Yuma Co., Arizona. (From *The Native Cacti of California*)

Fig. 520. Pancake pear, *Opuntia chlorotica*, miniature tree at the southeasternmost extension of the Mojavean Desert near Aguila, Arizona. (From *The Native Cacti of California*)

Fig. 522. *Opuntia chlorotica* in cultivation, the plant with young joints, flowers, and fruits.

Fig. 523. *Opuntia chlorotica*, joints with yellow spines (the shadows making the number seem larger), the upper mature joint bearing two flower buds, a flower, and a young fruit.

Fig. 524. *Opuntia chlorotica*, the joint of Fig. 523, showing the flower parts.

508

Fig. 525. Pancake pear, *Opuntia chlorotica*, ×.5, except as indicated. *1*, Joint with a flower bud and flowers. *2*, Areole with spines, glochids, and wool, ×2.2. *3*, Flower in longitudinal section. *4*, Fruit. *5*, Fruit in longitudinal section. *6*, Seed, ×4.

45. Opuntia strigil Engelmann

Ascending or sprawling plants, 0.6-1 m high, 1.3-2 m diam; larger terminal joints green, slightly glaucous, obovate, mostly 10-12.5(20) cm long, 8.8-10(15) cm broad, ±1.2 cm thick; areoles 3 mm diam, typically 0.9 cm apart; spines of moderate density, not obscuring joint, the larger reddish-brown with yellow tips, 1-8 per areole, usually 1 much larger than others, all turned downward or the principal(s) ascending from each of the uppermost areoles, straight or curving a little, the longer 1.2-4 cm long, basally 0.75 mm broad, subulate or acicular, only a little flattened basally, not markedly barbed; glochids reddish-tan, 6 mm long; flower ±5 cm diam, ±4.5 cm long, cream-colored, not available for description; fruit red, fleshy at maturity, the surface smooth, spheroidal, ±1.2-1.9 cm long and diam, the umbilicus not very prominent, the fruit persisting through most of winter; seeds light tan, nearly circular, the margin narrow, 3 mm diam, ±1.5 mm thick.

45a. Opuntia strigil var. strigil. Limestone soils of hills and plains in or near the desert at 900-1,350 m (3,000-4,500 ft). Chihuahuan Desert. Texas from Pecos Co. to Crockett and Terrell Cos., also in Nolan Co.

This medium-sized prickly pear is conspicuous for its reddish-brown and yellow spines. It spots the broad valleys and gentle slopes.

45b. Opuntia strigil var. flexospina (Griffiths) L. Benson. Hills. At about 115 m (450 ft). Lower Rio Grande Plain. Near Laredo, Webb Co., Texas, near the Rio Grande.

Distinctive Characters of the Varieties of **Opuntia strigil**

Character	a. var. **strigil**	b. var. **flexospina**
Joint size	10-12.5 cm long, 8.8-10 cm broad	17.5-20 cm long, ±15 cm broad
Spines	5-8 per areole, one much longer and much greater diam than others	1-3 per areole, one slightly larger than but otherwise similar to others
Altitude	900-1,350 m (3,000-4,500 ft)	About 115 m (450 ft)
Floristic association	Chihuahuan Desert	Rio Grande Plain

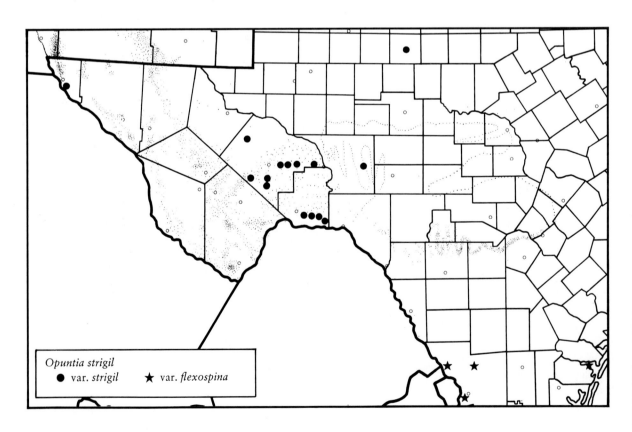

Opuntia strigil
● var. *strigil*　★ var. *flexospina*

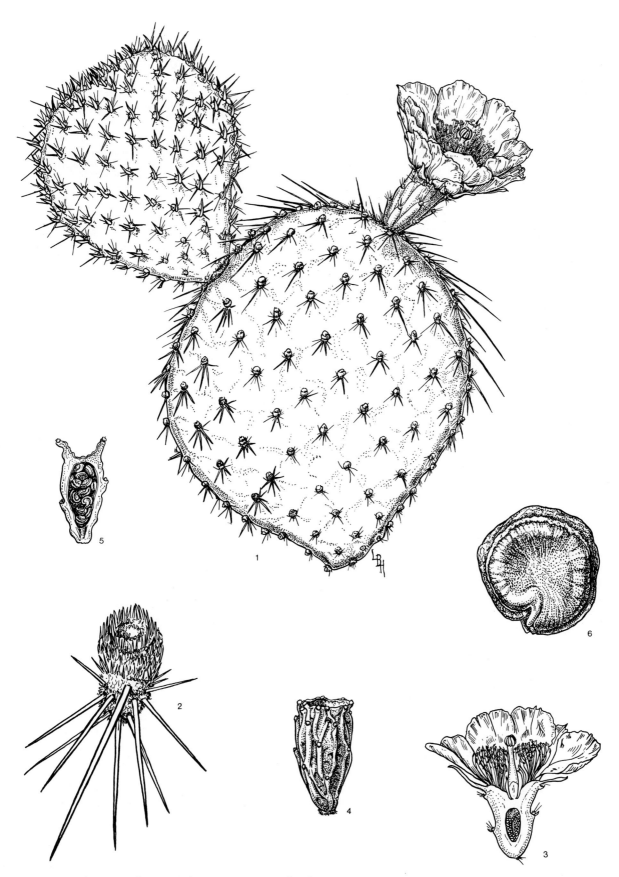

Fig. 526. *Opuntia strigil* var. *strigil*. *1*, Mature joint with a flower, young joint with leaves, ×.6. *2*, Areole with spines, large glochids, and wool, ×5. *3*, Flower in longitudinal section, ×.6. *4*, Fruit (fleshy at maturity, but this one having dried later), ×.9. *5*, Same fruit in longitudinal section, ×.9. *6*, Seed, ×7.5.

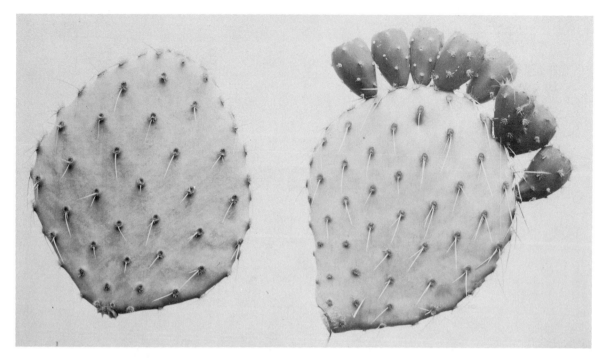

Fig. 527. *Opuntia strigil* var. *flexospina*, joints, one with fruits; from the type collection. (David Griffiths)

46. **Opuntia ficus-indica** (Linnaeus) Miller
Indian fig

Tree 3-5(7) m high and diam; trunk 60-120 cm long, 80-120 cm diam; larger terminal joints green, broadly to narrowly obovate or oblong, (22.5)30-60 cm long, 20-40 cm broad, 2-2.5 cm thick; areoles narrowly elliptic, 2-4.5 mm long, 3 mm broad, typically 2-5 cm apart; spines none, few, or abundant, white or sometimes on some joints tan or pale brown, 1-6 per areole, some spreading and some deflexed, straight, the longer ones 1.2-2.5(4) cm long, basally ±0.8 mm broad, subulate, flattened, narrowly elliptic in cross section, not barbed; glochids yellow, numerous, early deciduous; flower about 5-7 cm diam, ±6-7 cm long; sepaloids yellow with reddish or green middles, broadly cuneate to obdeltoid or ovate-acute, up to 20 mm long, 15-20 mm broad, truncate or acute, mucronate-acuminate, margins entire or denticulate; petaloids yellow or orange-yellow, externally pink-tinged, obovate or cuneate, ±25-30 mm long, 15-20 mm broad, truncate to rounded, mucronate, entire; filaments yellow, ±6 mm long; anthers yellow, ±2 mm long, slender; style greenish, 15 mm long, bulging, to ±3 mm diam; stigmas 8-10, ±2 mm long; ovary in anthesis with a few later deciduous short spines; fruit yellow, orange, red, or purplish in various strains, fleshy at maturity, edible, spineless or sometimes with spines, 5-10 cm long, 4-9 cm diam, the umbilicus low and concave, the fruit persistent for several months; seeds gray or tan, elliptic-orbiculate, the embryo-bearing margin narrow and smooth, the body 4-5 mm long, 3.5-4 mm broad, 1.5 mm thick.

Long known from most of tropical America, the spineless horticultural forms (cultivars) have been prized for their fruit since prehistoric times and consequently have probably spread widely by trading; now cultivated throughout the warm parts of the world. Escaped and naturalized in many areas, in some becoming a pest (e.g., in Australia and in the eastern part of Cape Province, South Africa). Naturalized on dry leeward southeastern sides of probably all the Hawaiian Islands; occasional as an escape and common as one of the parents of plants in the vast hybrid prickly-pear swarms of southern California; occasional as a local escape or relic around old dwellings in southern Arizona, southern New Mexico, southern Texas, and (reportedly) Florida. Collected once in southern New Mexico.

Except in Hawaii, the species is nowhere common as an escape in the United States. In southern

California, it becomes established only where there is deep soil and a little subirrigation, as along washes in valleys or at the mouths of small canyons. The pollen of the species, widely distributed by bees and beetles, has had a profound influence on the cactus populations in southern California and a minor influence in other areas in the U.S.

Probably the species is native in Mexico, where there are numerous cultivars and many hybrids with other species. Two types of plants are common in cultivation in the warm, moderately dry regions of the world, especially in Mediterranean climates: one, known as *O. ficus-indica*, is spineless and relatively less variable in other characters; the other, known as *O. megacantha*, is spiny and relatively more variable in other characters. The *megacantha* form, known originally from Mexico, has been postulated by Griffiths to be nearer the wild type, the spineless form perhaps having arisen in cultivation. The introduced forms of both types vary from country to country, probably owing to the widespread propagation of clones introduced by chance. Any form was chosen in Mexico or tropical America for propagation elsewhere if the fruit was good. For exam-

ple, the spineless form covering the south face of the Acropolis of Athens differs from that common type in eastern Cape Province and other areas of South Africa. The spiny form in South Africa differs from those in California and in Hawaii.

The introduction of *O. ficus-indica* from Mexico and its hybridization with the native varieties of *O. littoralis* have been discussed and illustrated by Benson and Walkington (1965), and an abridged account appears in Benson (1969c).

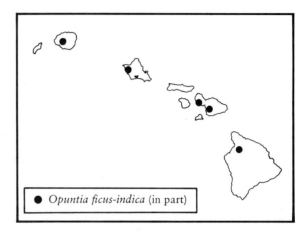

● *Opuntia ficus-indica* (in part)

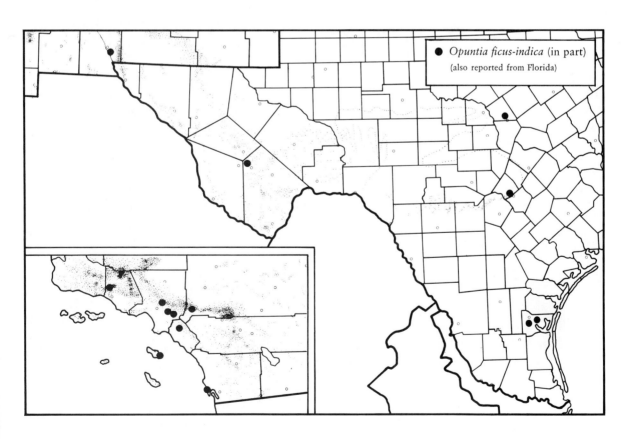

● *Opuntia ficus-indica* (in part)
(also reported from Florida)

Fig. 528. Indian fig or mission cactus (California), *Opuntia ficus-indica*, spineless type, growing in the Huntington Botanical Gardens, San Marino, California.

Fig. 529. *Opuntia ficus-indica*, spineless type, in cultivation by C. C. Molby, Browns Valley, California, September 15, 1915, from stock purchased directly from Luther Burbank; one of Burbank's "thornless" prickly pears, the plants bearing abundant fruits. (David Griffiths)

514

Fig. 530. *Opuntia ficus-indica*, spineless type, a joint with (in this case) orange-red fruits. (David Griffiths)

Fig. 531. *Opuntia ficus-indica*, spineless type, young joint with leaves; two flowers. (David Griffiths)

Fig. 532. Indian fig or mission cactus, *Opuntia ficus-indica*, spiny type known as "*Opuntia megacantha*," probably the wild type (but in this case with slight introgression of genes from varieties of *O. littoralis*). The plant is growing in disturbed California Chaparral at the type locality for *Opuntia occidentalis* Engelm. & Bigelow, near Cucamonga, San Bernardino Co., California, but the plant so named was an introduction from Mexico. (From *The Native Cacti of California*)

Fig. 534. *Opuntia ficus-indica*, spiny type, mature spiny joint bearing a young joint with leaves and a flower bud; flowers. (David Griffiths; from *The Native Cacti of California*)

Fig. 533. *Opuntia ficus-indica*, spiny type, in the Huntington Botanical Gardens, in fruit.

Hybrid population "**occidentalis**" (*Opuntia occidentalis* of authors, not of Engelmann & Bigelow; *O. rugosa* Griffiths). The southern Californian prickly pears are most abundant in the disturbed soils of washes and alluvial fans, since after floods (as noted at Claremont in 1938 by Philip A. Munz), joints from prickly pears are distributed over large areas. They soon root and grow, bringing into new situations any types to be found in the more stable populations in the foothills. Thus the production of hybrids and mixed populations is common, and the instability of characters is not surprising. Since the area has been one of occasional great floods for thousands of years, disturbed habitats have been available for some time.

Below is a description summarizing the characteristics commonly found in numerous combinations in the vast, irregular hybrid swarms resulting (as indicated by morphological data and chemical evidence; Walkington, see pp. 63-67) from the interbreeding of *O. littoralis* var. *vaseyi* (and, to a lesser extent, var. *austrocalifornica*) with mostly the spiny form of *O. ficus-indica* (known commonly as *O. megacantha*).

Suberect or sprawling shrubs, 1-1.5(2) m high, 1-4.5 m or much greater diam; trunk none or when present very short; larger terminal joints markedly to only slightly glaucous, narrowly elliptic, narrowly obovate, sometimes broadly either of these or rhombic, 17.5-37.5 cm long, 10-20 cm broad, 2-2.5 cm thick; areoles elliptic, 6 mm long, typically 25-30 mm apart; spines in all or nearly all areoles, each brown or red on at least lower half, or sometimes all white or gray, 4-7 per upper areole, fewer in lower areoles, spreading or some deflexed, straight or rarely curving, the longer 1.2-3.4(4.7) cm long, basally 1-1.25 mm broad, subulate, very narrowly elliptic in cross section, not barbed; glochids yellow or brown, 3-6+ mm long; flower 7.5-11 cm diam, 6-9 cm long; sepaloids with midribs green and margins yellow (or partly reddish in age), the largest cuneate or cuneate-obovate, 6-25+ mm long, 6-22 mm broad, truncate, mucronate, undulate, or toothed; petaloids yellow to orange-yellow, becoming reddish in age, the largest obovate, 40-55 mm long, 20-45 mm broad, mucronate, nearly entire; filaments yellow, 12-15 mm long; anthers yellow, ±2 mm long; style greenish, 12-20 mm long, 4.5-7.5 mm greatest diam; stigmas ±10, 3-4.5 mm long, thick; ovary in anthesis not spiny; fruit red to purple, fleshy at maturity, smooth, not spiny, with some glochids, obovoid, 4-7 cm long, 2.5-4.5 cm diam, the umbilicus shallow but cuplike, the fruit maturing and deciduous during early winter; seeds tan, variable, nearly orbiculate, the embryo-bearing margin from prominent and irregular to narrow and smooth, the body 3-6 mm long, slightly less broad, 1.5+ mm thick.

Sandy, gravelly, or partly clay soils of hillsides and valleys, and, to a lesser extent, of alluvial fans and washes at 150-900 m (500-3,000 ft). Disturbed or naturally open areas in California Chaparral. Coastal side of mountains of s California from near Glendora, Los Angeles Co., to San Bernardino and Riverside Cos., and s through interior foothill region to San Diego Co.

The California cochineal insect is common on these plants, as well as on other species.

In 1769, when Father Junipero Serra founded Mission San Diego, he unknowingly began the transformation not only of California's landscape, but also in some ways, of its flora and vegetation.* After the establishment of the missions, settlers from Mexico and Spain brought agriculture and livestock, including sheep. As range animals were taken from the Mediterranean region to Mexico and other parts of the world, weed seeds were carried along in their wool or hair and in mud on their hoofs. Wherever sheep walked or died, weeds sprang up. Over many centuries of hybridizing and selection, these plants had adapted to areas about the dwellings of man and his cultivated fields and pasturelands. They had evolved in Mediterranean areas of summer drought and on land disturbed by fire, overgrazing, or agriculture, and so were adjusted perfectly to the California climate and to the newly disturbed ground. Ultimately they reached a dynamic ecological equilibrium with the native species. This equilibrium shifts from year to year in correspondence with the highly erratic incidence of winter rainfall.

The founders of the California missions also brought with them fruit-bearing plants from Mexico and Spain. Besides grapes, figs, and other fruits of mild climates, they introduced the large, cultivated fruit-tree cacti of Mexico, which are now known as mission cacti in the United States. The original cactus stock was primarily of two kinds, which have been called *Opuntia ficus-indica*, a spineless type, and *O. megacantha*, a similar plant with flattened white (or on some joints brownish) spines in all the areoles. These two plants

---

* Much of the following discussion is adapted from previous publications (Benson & Walkington 1965; Benson 1969c) by permission of the Missouri Botanical Garden.

were quite similar, and the evolutionary origin of those known as O. *ficus-indica* from those called O. *megacantha* (as the wild type) was postulated by David Griffiths (*Journal of Heredity* 5: 222. 1914). Both are members of a complex of cultivated prickly pears abundant in Mexico, many of them representing horticultural forms or hybrids of O. *ficus-indica*.* The mission Fathers and others found these cacti useful not only for their fruit but also as a source of mucilaginous binding material for the adobe bricks of the mission buildings. In the course of time, the two cacti were also planted about the buildings of the great Spanish ranchos, and they appeared wherever there were Spanish, Mexican, and eventually American settlers.

In many places the large cultivated prickly pears have hybridized with the small native species (as pointed out by Baxter, 1935). Field studies, especially in Los Angeles, San Bernardino, Riverside, and Orange counties, indicate this hybridization to be vastly more extensive than had been supposed. The introduced cacti in their original form often survive in the lowlands or on the edges of hills about the sites of old dwellings, especially near the coast, where there is less frost. Here and there they have spread a short distance, but they are restricted to the better-watered, deeper soils along washes in the valleys or at the mouths of canyons. They cannot grow on the drier hills.

The genes of the cultivated mission cacti are given rapid air transportation by several species of native bees and by beetles, especially *Carpophilus pallipennis* (Say) (Nitidulidae). Sometimes the local hillside population of cacti includes plants with character combinations ranging from almost those of the mission cacti (usually of the spiny type long known as "*Opuntia megacantha*") to those of the native species, but more commonly the character combinations are restricted. In a few areas (e.g. east of Fullerton), the prevailing spiny plants are near the end of the series approaching O. *ficus-indica*, but this is rare. Com-

monly the population is composed of plants varying in characters from about those of the postulated F_1 generation to those of the native species. Most individuals in this range of phenotypes, compared to those more like mission cacti, are better-adapted physiologically to the dry, shallow soils of south-facing slopes, where cacti have the least competition. The hillside populations away from the immediate coast are dominated mostly by plants of about the middle of this half-series— i.e. "quarter-breeds." By contrast, gravelly or sandy places in the beds of dry washes, shady places with few grasses or shrubs beneath trees, or rocky mountainous areas without much brush are strongholds of varieties of the native species.

Fire has been a major factor in the evolution of prickly pears in southern California. Cacti do not grow in the chaparral or brushland because about once every five to thirty years there is a very hot fire. Cactus plants cannot survive a chaparral fire, and even a summer grass fire sweeping through a patch of prickly pears is devastating. The small plants are killed outright, and often the larger ones are killed, too. However, sometimes parts sheltered by the piling up of cactus stem-joints during the fire are not killed, and new joints may arise from any living fragment.

Among the weeds introduced into California from the Mediterranean region are many annual grasses, especially of the genus *Bromus*, and these have formed a dense cover in the lowlands and on hillsides. The plants of the modified grassy areas become like tinder during the dry summer months, and grass fires are intense and frequent. Thus in each locality for two centuries there has been a rigid trial by fire every few years, determining which prickly pears are best adapted to withstanding intense heat.

Selection by fire has favored not the introduced or the native species but the larger hybrid plants, especially sprawling ones capable of forming dense patches from which grasses are more or less excluded. These thickets of cactus joints are vulnerable to fire only around the fringes. They form vigorous resistant centers that grow rapidly outward and occupy more and more space after each grass fire. By contrast, the smaller native species is enveloped where grass is present, and on the open hillsides each fire tends to reduce its numbers. It is for this reason that the trend in the large areas of dry grass is toward the ascendancy of a vast array of hybrid types about intermediate between the postulated F_1 generation and the small native species. Both morphological and chemical characters indicate this trend (see p. 63).

---

* The identity of the entire complex of cultivated plants is subject to investigation. Several species of Mexican prickly pears occur now in cultivation in southern California. Some of these have been brought from various parts of Mexico by immigrants or by visitors to that country, and probably introductions have been made during much of two centuries. The identity of *Opuntia ficus-indica*, based originally on material cultivated in Europe, is not really certain, and research on this problem is necessary. Leía Scheinvar has identified a specimen from one of the escaped colonies of "*Opuntia megacantha*" as O. *amyclea* Tenore, a proposed species also based on unpreserved plants from cultivation in Europe.

Figs. 535–41. Effects of grass fires upon prickly pears. Fig. 535. *Opuntia ficus-indica*, spiny type, established in subirrigated ground at the mouth of a small canyon or rincon near Puddingstone Lake, between Pomona and San Dimas, Los Angeles Co., California. These large plants are surrounded by O. *littoralis* vars. *littoralis, vaseyi,* and *austrocalifornica* and a complex hybrid swarm. O. *ficus-indica* is nearly confined to the area of extra moisture, on lower ground, where it forms an extensive thicket central to the complex. However, because the thicket is more or less open, high grass grows within it, and in the summer there is danger of fire within the area, lethal to the large plants. The dense thicket of the lower-growing O. *littoralis* var. *littoralis* growing behind the largest plants is capable of excluding fire; so are many of the patches of various types of hybrids. However, the small plants of O. *littoralis* var. *vaseyi,* hidden or partly hidden in the grasses on the hillsides, were vulnerable to destruction by fire, and they *were* destroyed three years after the picture was taken.

Fig. 536. *Left,* the small native plant *Opuntia littoralis* var. *vaseyi,* almost completely enveloped (center and upper left) in weedy introduced Mediterranean grasses, principally wild oats (*Avena barbata*) and ripgut grass (*Bromus rigidus*), near Puddingstone Reservoir. (From *The Native Cacti of California.*) *Right,* O. *littoralis* var. *austrocalifornica,* nearly engulfed in introduced grasses (especially ripgut grass); Claremont, Los Angeles Co., California.

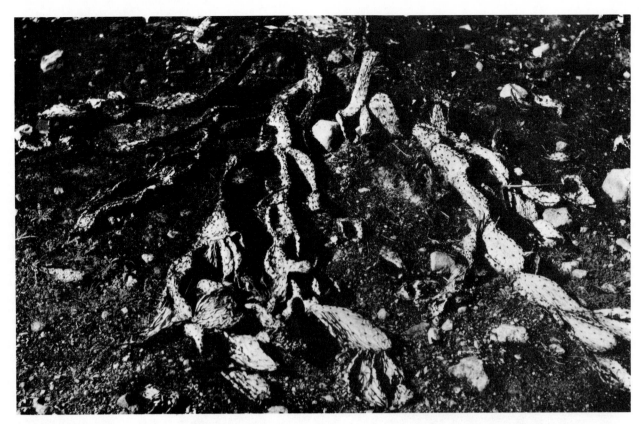

Fig. 537 (*above*). Tall, nearly erect hybrid approaching *Opuntia ficus-indica* in characters; plant killed by fire in the tall grasses beneath it even though they were only one-fourth to one-sixth its height, the heat above the fire having been intense. In the plants of all the other figures, killing by fire has been due to envelopment of the cactus by grasses; and this has been the reason for the destruction of the native species. The plant shown here was not enveloped but only underlain by grasses, yet its destruction was complete; this accounts for the elimination of *O. ficus-indica* from fields. Thus, plants of both extremes of form are likely to be killed by fire, and the only survivors ultimately are the intermediate spreading plants that form thickets. Their selection, however, requires many years and many fires.

Fig. 538. Grassy area after a fire, even the large prickly pears being almost destroyed; note regeneration of a small area of the plant in the foreground, a hybrid of *O. littoralis* var. *vaseyi* and *O. ficus-indica* (spiny type) but a plant not large enough to exclude the fire from its center. (From *The Native Cacti of California*)

Fig. 539. A surviving large thicket-forming hybrid with densely branching sprawling stems; only the joints along the edges have been killed by the intense grass fire.

Fig. 540. *Left*, a hybrid swarm of prickly pears on a hillside, the larger plant at the left with genes derived about three-fourths from *O. littoralis* var. *vaseyi*, one-fourth from the spiny type of *O. ficus-indica*. The small plants enveloped in the grass are var. *vaseyi*; the others are of mixed ancestry and intermediate. *Right*, portion of a hybrid clone covering about half an acre from which fire is almost completely excluded; often, rodents, living under a hybrid cactus thicket, forage just outside its protection and reduce the number of grass plants. Plants near the Puddingstone Reservoir. (From *The Native Cacti of California*)

Fig. 541. The results of natural selection during trial-by-fire. Nearly all the plants on the hillside are those forming large thickets that have excluded fires in the past. Near Puddingstone Reservoir.

During the last half of the nineteenth century and two-thirds of the twentieth, all botanical authors used the name *Opuntia occidentalis* for elements in the populations of hybrid cacti, which are common everywhere except along the immediate coast. However, each author had a different mental image of this "species," for each had in mind a different plant or range of plants in the vast hybrid swarm. Usually this was one or a few of the many combinations about midway between the F₁ generation and the native species. No population can be exactly reconciled with the description of *O. occidentalis* appearing in any book or paper, because no two plants are alike and the total variation is extreme. Thus, from the standpoint of classification, the common conception of "*O. occidentalis*" is a will-o'-the-wisp. In each book, it was based on one or more transitory

combinations of genes that disappeared with the individual plant(s) or clone(s) on which the description was based. Furthermore, nomenclaturally *O. occidentalis* is a metanym for *O. ficus-indica*, since the type specimen is of the spiny form of that species. It was not derived from a wild plant but from one that must have been a cultivar or a recent escape.

In 1876, Engelmann (in Brewer & Watson, Bot. Calif. 1: 248) concluded that the several early collections from coastal southern California represented varieties of "*Opuntia engelmannii*," i.e. *O. phaeacantha* var. *discata* of California to Texas and adjacent Mexico, and relationship to that variety is close. Var. *discata* occurs along the desert edges of all southern Californian mountains from San Bernardino Co. to San Diego Co., in the eastern Mojave Desert, and rarely along

Fig. 543. Hybrid population *"occidentalis,"* joints of the plant in Fig. 542, representing one of innumerable character combinations in the hybrid swarms, approximately the plant most authors have had in mind as *O. occidentalis* (the name misapplied and the presumed species nonexistent).

Fig. 542. Hybrid population *"occidentalis," Opuntia ficus-indica* × *O. littoralis* var. *vaseyi*, and sometimes var. *austrocalifornica*, a fire-resistant, thicket-forming plant surrounded by introduced Mediterranean weedy grasses in disturbed California Chaparral, at Claremont, Los Angeles Co., California. The other hybrids, unable to exclude fire, have been killed.

the coast in Orange Co. Distinction of some plants in the coastal southern Californian hybrid swarms from *O. phaeacantha* var. *discata* and from var. *major*, which occurs at higher elevations in the same parts of southern California and eastward to Kansas, Texas, and northern Mexico, is difficult.

Distinction of *O. littoralis* from the *O. phaeacantha* complex is also not wholly clear, since acicular spines grade into flattened spines. Thus, segregation must be partly arbitrary, as is all classification.

Hybrid population "**demissa**" (*Opuntia demissa* Griffiths). Joints elliptic, obovate, or rhombic, 20-27.5 cm long, 12.5-20(25) cm broad; spines yellow, 3-6 in each upper areole of joint, 2-3.5 cm long; petaloids yellow or with some reddish pigment basally; seeds discoid, ±3 mm diam.

Sandy or partly clay soils of foothills, valleys, ocean bluffs, and dunes at 3-150(300) m (10-500 or 1,000 ft). California Chaparral or more commonly in coastal grasslands. California from near Ventura, Ventura Co., s to San Diego Co., mostly through lower valleys along coast but ranging inland through valleys for 10-25 mi. in some areas, and occurring on Santa Catalina I.

Fig. 545. Hybrid population *"demissa,"* joint with flower buds. (David Griffiths; see Credits)

Fig. 544. Hybrid population *"demissa,"* *O. ficus-indica* × *O. littoralis* var. *littoralis* or *O. oricola*, large plant in an area of disturbed California Chaparral. (David Griffiths; see Credits)

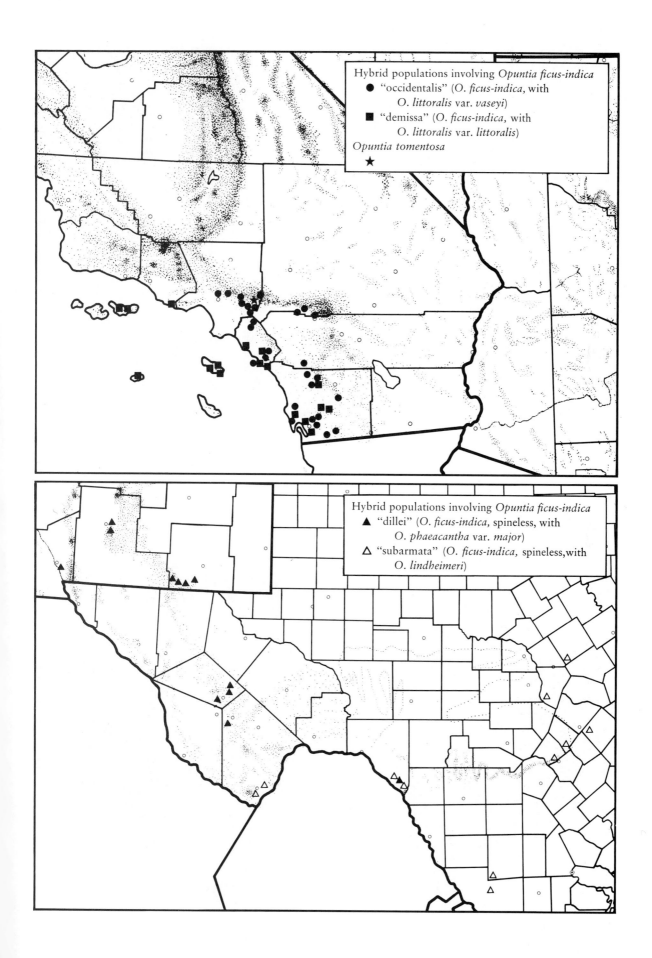

Hybrid populations involving *Opuntia ficus-indica*
- ● "occidentalis" (*O. ficus-indica*, with *O. littoralis* var. *vaseyi*)
- ■ "demissa" (*O. ficus-indica*, with *O. littoralis* var. *littoralis*)

Opuntia tomentosa
- ★

Hybrid populations involving *Opuntia ficus-indica*
- ▲ "dillei" (*O. ficus-indica*, spineless, with *O. phaeacantha* var. *major*)
- △ "subarmata" (*O. ficus-indica*, spineless, with *O. lindheimeri*)

Fig. 546. Hybrid population "*dillei*," *Opuntia ficus-indica* × *O. phaeacantha* vars. *major* and *discata*, the type plant of *Opuntia dillei* Griffiths, on a ledge in Andreas Canyon, Sacramento Mountains, Otero Co., New Mexico. (David Griffiths; see Credits)

Fig. 547. Hybrid population "*dillei*," a young joint with leaves and a mature joint, from plant in cultivation in Texas. The plant is stated to be more spiny than those in the wild, but observation in western Texas indicates great variability. (David Griffiths)

Fig. 548. Hybrid population *"subarmata," Opuntia ficus-indica* ✕ an undetermined native species, the type plant of *O. subarmata* Griffiths, at Devil's River, Val Verde Co., Texas. (David Griffiths; see Credits)

Fig. 549. Hybrid population *"subarmata,"* from the type collection, a young joint with leaves, an older joint, a flower bud, and flowers. (David Griffiths)

Fig. 550. *Opuntia tomentosa* in cultivation.

Fig. 551. *Opuntia tomentosa*, joints of a spineless plant, with flowers and fruits. Note the dense velvety covering of hairs on both joints and ovaries.

Hybrid population "**dillei**" (*Opuntia dillei* Griffiths). Joints large, orbiculate, and spineless, ±20-25 cm long.

Rock and sand of canyonsides in the desert at about 1,200 m (4,000 ft). Desert Grassland. New Mexico (rare) in Dona Ana, Otero, and Eddy Cos.; Texas in Canyon of Limpia Creek NE of Ft. Davis, Davis Mts., Jeff Davis Co.

These plants may have originated through hybridizing of the spineless forms of the mission cactus, *O. ficus-indica*, with *O. phaeacantha* var. *discata* or var. *major*. The colonies are not extensive.

Hybrid population "**subarmata**" (*Opuntia subarmata* Griffiths). Joints orbiculate or obovate, spineless, large, commonly 20-30 cm long, 15-25 cm broad.

Texas at widely scattered stations from Brewster Co. in the Big Bend of the Rio Grande to edge of plains in Bastrop and Comal Cos.

This form may have been derived from sporadic crosses of the cultivated spineless mission cactus, *O. ficus-indica*, with *O. lindheimeri*.

47. Opuntia tomentosa Salm-Dyck

Trees 3-8 m high, spreading over an area 1-5 m diam; trunk 1-1.6 m long, to 30 cm diam; larger terminal joints dark green, reflecting high and low lights from dense, white, velvety tomentum, velvety to touch, 20-30 cm long, 7.5-12.5 cm broad, 2-3 cm thick; areoles 2 mm diam, typically 2.5-3 cm apart; spines none, sometimes 1 or a few in some upper marginal areoles, sometimes in all areoles; spines when present gray or partly brown, spreading in various directions, straight, the longer to 3 cm long, basally 0.5-0.7 mm diam, acicular, nearly circular in cross section, not markedly barbed; glochids yellow, well barbed, early deciduous, 2 mm long; flower 4-5 cm diam, 5-6 cm long; sepaloids with midribs red and margins shading to yellow, the largest cuneate, to 25 mm long, 12-20 mm broad, rounded or obtuse and cuspidate, minutely denticulate; petaloids red in middles and orange on margins, the largest cuneate-obovate to obovate, 25-40 mm long, ±20 mm broad, rounded to emarginate or retuse; filaments pale green tinged with rose, ±12 mm long; anthers white, tinged with pink but pollen yellow, ±2 mm long; style dark red, ±12 mm long, 3 mm greatest diam; stigmas 5 or 6, white tinged with pink, 4.5 mm long, very thick, closely appressed; ovary in anthesis 3 cm long; fruit red, fleshy at maturity, densely tomentose, obovoid,

3-4 cm long, ±2.5 cm diam, the umbilicus shallow, the fruit persisting until spring; seed light tan, orbiculate, the rim enclosing embryo ±1 mm thick, smooth, the body 5-6 mm diam, 1-1.5 mm thick.

Deep soils with water available. Native of central Mexico; escaped occasionally, notably in Australia. California Chaparral (in U.S.). Sporadic near Thompson Creek N of Claremont, Los Angeles Co., California, at 450 m (1,500 ft) (*Louis C. Wheeler* in 1962, *Pom*).

This large tree cactus forms parts of open woodlands in Mexico. In the United States it is known as a fine horticultural plant and a rare escape.

According to Léia Schinvar, in Mexico birds eat the seeds of this species in preference to those of others.

See map for Hybrids of *O. ficus-indica* (preceding).

48. Opuntia leucotricha DeCandolle

Tree or arborescent, 1-3(4.5) m high; trunk 60-90 cm long, 15-30 cm diam; larger terminal joints green or blue-green, mostly oblong but some nearly orbiculate, 10-27.5 cm long, 7.5-15 (20) cm broad, ±12 mm thick; areoles 2.25-3 mm

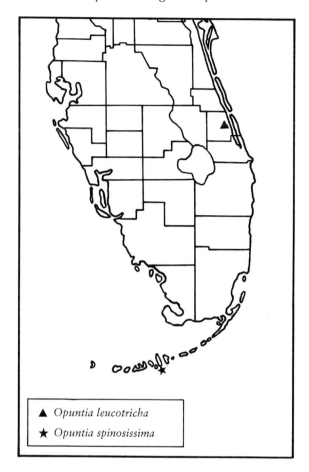

▲ *Opuntia leucotricha*
★ *Opuntia spinosissima*

Fig. 552. *Opuntia leucotricha* on a hillside in Mexico. (C. H. Thompson; see Credits)

Fig. 553. *Opuntia leucotricha* on a flat in Mexico. The basket is for gathering the edible fruits. (David Griffiths; see Credits)

Fig. 554 (*right*). A semaphore cactus, *Opuntia leucotricha*, young plant in cultivation, showing the long, flexible spines on the lower joints of the stem. (David Griffiths)

Fig. 555. *Opuntia leucotricha*, joints from the middle and upper portions of a plant. The joints are of three ages, the youngest retaining leaves, the other two showing stages of spine development. (David Griffiths)

diam, typically 2-2.5 cm apart; spines in all but very lowest areoles of joint, white or gray, 1-5(6) per areole, those on new joints ±1.2-2 cm long, straight, those on trunk and older joints 5-7.5 cm long, on new joints basally 0.5 mm broad, filiform, flexible, curving irregularly, narrowly elliptic in cross section, not barbed; glochids brownish, bristlelike, to ±9 mm long; flower 5 cm diam and long; sepaloids greenish, lanceolate, 5-20 mm long, 3-4.5(6) mm broad, acuminate to mucronate; petaloids yellow, obovate-cuneate, ±25 mm long, 12-15 mm broad, mucronate, minutely denticulate; filaments yellow, ±9 mm long; anthers yellow, 1.5 mm long; style 9 mm long, 1.5 mm diam; stigmas 10(?), 3 mm long, thick; ovary in anthesis with some distal spines; fruit red or white, fleshy at maturity, edible, with deciduous clusters of spines, 4-6 cm diam, the umbilicus developed but not prominent, the surface layers separating readily from pulp; seeds tan, discoid, smooth, ±4 mm diam, ±1.5 mm thick.

Native of central Mexico. Cultivated. Naturalized in a hammock s of Ft. Pierce, St. Lucie Co., Florida, there within the Caribbean Tropical Forest.

This tree forms open woodlands in Mexico, where it is prized also in cultivation.

49. Opuntia spinosissima (Martyn) Miller
Semaphore cactus

Miniature tree 1-3(4.5) m high; trunk 0.5-2.5 m long, 7.5 cm diam, nearly cylindroid; larger terminal joints light green, standing mostly at right angles to older joints, all somewhat flattened but relatively thick, elliptic to elongate or asymmetrical, length 2-4 times breadth, 15-27.5 cm long, 5-8.5 cm broad, 6-9 mm thick; areoles elliptic, 1.5 mm long, typically 0.75-1.5 cm apart; spines numerous, in all areoles (or some joints spineless), salmon to straw-colored, changing to brown in age, 2 or 3(4) per areole, spreading or some deflexed, straight, the longer 2.5-5(11) cm long, basally 0.25-0.5 mm diam, acicular, nearly circular in cross section, twisted, somewhat barbed; glochids tan or brown, abundant, 1-1.5 mm long; flower 1.2-2.5 cm diam, 3-7.5 cm long; sepaloids green to orange-red, ovate-deltoid, mostly 3-6 mm long and broad, acute or obtuse; petaloids orange-yellow, changing to red, broadly ovate-acute to obovate, 9-12 mm long, 4.5-9 mm broad, acute or truncate and mucronate, entire; filaments yellow, 6 mm long; anthers yellow, 0.5 mm long;

Fig. 556. A semaphore cactus, *Opuntia spinosissima*, joints with the long, slender spines. (David Griffiths)

style 6-7.5 mm long, 0.5 mm diam; stigmas 5, 1.5 mm long, thick; ovary in anthesis spiny; fruit yellow, fleshy at maturity, spiny, often flattened, 2.5-6 cm long, 2-4 cm diam, the umbilicus deep; seeds few, irregular, the edges crested, the sides hairy, 6-8 mm diam.

Bare rocks with slight covering of humus in jungle hammocks near sea level. Caribbean Tropical Forest. Big Pine Key, Florida. On s coast of Jamaica; Virgin Islands.

This tree is one of the plants known in the Caribbean region as semaphore cacti because it is upright with elongate drooping joints reminiscent of a railway semaphore.

Fig. 557. Brazilian cactus, *Opuntia brasiliensis*, branch with cylindroid main joints and flattened lateral joints. Below are a fruit in longitudinal section, a seed in two views, and the curved embryo in two views (the cotyledons incumbent). (See Credits)

Fig. 558. Brazilian cactus, *Opuntia brasiliensis*, in cultivation about 1910. (David Griffiths; see Credits)

50. **Opuntia brasiliensis** (Willdenow) Haworth
Brazilian cactus

Tapering, polelike trees, 3-6(9) m high; trunk and primary branches cylindroid, indeterminate, 5-15 cm diam, the secondary branches flattened, thin, determinate; branches spreading horizontally or declined from main trunk, 30-90 cm long; larger terminal joints bright green, obovate to oblong to nearly lanceolate, 7.5-12.5 cm long, 4-6 cm broad, thin, ±6 mm thick, the joint surface undulating in very large, flat tubercles; areoles about 1-2 mm diam, 1-3 cm apart; spines numerous, several per areole on trunk and cylindroid branches, few and only 1 per areole on flat terminal joints, white with brown tips, spreading, straight, the longer 1.2-4 cm long, basally 1-1.5 mm diam, subulate; glochids barely visible, minute and ineffective; flower 2.5-4 cm diam and long; sepaloids green and yellow, ovate, to ±12 mm long, 6-9 mm broad, truncate or rounded, entire; petaloids light lemon yellow, cuneate-obovate or obovate, 12-25 mm long, 12-15 mm broad, rounded or truncate, entire; filaments pale yellow, 6-9 mm long; anthers yellow; style pale yellow, 9-12 mm long, thick; stigmas 4 or 5, pale yellow, ovate; fruit light yellow, fleshy at maturity, with chestnut-colored glochids (these deciduous), ovoid to subglobose, 2.5-4.5 cm long, 2.5-4 cm diam, the umbilicus obsolete; seeds only 1-4, nearly spherical, enveloped in cottony fibers, 6-8 mm diam.

Subtropical and warm temperate areas of South America from central Bolivia to s Brazil and Argentina.

Reported by Britton and Rose (Cactaceae 1: 209. 1919) and by Small (1933) to be naturalized in Florida, but no specimens have been found. According to Small: "Hammocks, mostly on shell-mounds, or occasionally in waste-places, pen. Fla. and the keys."

These dark green trees become large in cultivation, and they are unusual for their cylindroid trunks bearing flattened branches.

3. Schlumbergera

Plants low, trailing. Stems branching, forking repeatedly, flat; larger joints ovate, elliptic, or oblong, 4-5(12.5) cm long, 2-2.5(3.8) cm broad, 3 mm thick; ribs none; tubercles none. Leaves not discernible in adult plant. Areoles minute. Spines none in mature plant. Flowers and fruits on new growth of current season, therefore near apex of a terminal joint of a main branch. Flower 5-10 cm diam; floral tube with a sharp bend above junction with ovary, tubular-funnelform, with the color of flower (reddish to lavender). Fruit fleshy at maturity, without surface appendages, narrowly obovoid, 1.5-2 cm long, 7.5-9 cm diam, indehiscent; floral tube deciduous. Seeds dark brown or brownish-black, shining.

A small genus, of three species: *S. truncata*, described below; *S. russelliana*, Brazil; and *S. bridgesii*, Brazil and/or Bolivia, the Christmas cactus of cultivation.

1. Schlumbergera truncata (Haworth) Moran

Stems numerous, branching widely, trailing, the clumps to several meters diam; joints green, ovate, elliptic, or oblong, 3.8-5 cm broad, 3 mm thick, marginally sharp-serrately lobed, the lobes turned or curving upward, 6 mm long; spines none on mature stems; flower bilaterally symmetrical, 5(10) cm diam, 5-6.2(10) cm long; sepaloids reddish to pink, the largest broadly

Fig. 559. *Schlumbergera truncata*, the flower buds not fully opened.

Fig. 560. *Schlumbergera truncata*, joints and (below, left to right) embryo, seed, stamen, ovary in longitudinal section at base of flower, and (smaller scale) two longitudinal sections of the flower, showing the remoteness of the sepaloids and petaloids. (See Credits)

lanceolate-acute above, ±40 mm long, 9-12 mm broad, acute, entire; petaloids reddish to lavender, largest narrow below, ovate-lanceolate in the upper spreading portions, ±20-30 mm long, ±12 mm broad, acute, entire; filaments pale, about 30 mm long; anthers yellow, 1.25 mm long; style purple, 45-50 mm long, 0.5 mm greatest diam; stigmas 5, red, 4.5 mm long, rather stout, appressed; ovary in anthesis 12 mm long; fruit purple, fleshy at maturity, without surface appendages, narrowly obovoid, 1.5-2 cm long, 7.5-9 mm diam, the umbilicus conspicuous; seeds dark brown or brownish-black, shining.

A commonly cultivated species of hanging baskets and pots. Native in the mountains of the state of Rio de Janeiro, Brazil. Escaped into the Asian-Pacific Insular Flora about Honolulu and perhaps elsewhere on Oahu, Hawaii.

The well-known Christmas cactus is *Schlumbergera bridgesii*, but often the name is applied to *Schlumbergera truncata* also.

References: McMillan, 1969; Moran, 1953; Tjaden, 1966.

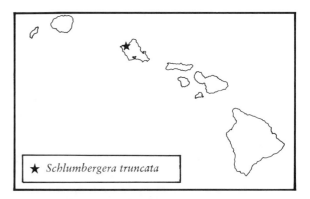

★ *Schlumbergera truncata*

Fig. 561. *Schlumbergera truncata*, branch showing the teeth on the joints; a flower and opening flower buds.

4. Rhipsalis

Plants occurring on tree branches, rocks, logs, or other objects, usually epiphytic but sometimes growing in soil. Stems freely branching, somewhat flexible, the longer ones dangling, cylindroid to broad and thin and flat or with winglike angles, jointed, sometimes with aerial roots, the year-old and 2-year-old stems usually 20+ cm long, 3-9 mm diam or 7.5 cm broad; ribs none; tubercles none. Leaves not discernible in adult plants. Areoles circular, very small. Spines none on mature plants, small, bristle-like, straight, and numerous on juvenile stems. Flowers and fruits in areoles along the sides of the stem-joints of new growth. Flower 3-25 mm diam; floral tube not continuing above junction with ovary. Fruit fleshy at maturity, without appendages, subglobose to ellipsoid, 4.5-12 mm long, indehiscent; floral tube deciduous. Seeds (of species in U.S.) black, finely reticulate, narrowly asymmetric-obovoid or -ellipsoid, longer than broad (hilum to opposite side), 1.5 mm long; hilum obviously basal; embryo nearly straight; cotyledons very large, continuing the axis of the hypocotyl.

The genus is primarily tropical, and it is composed of a large, undetermined number of species —Britton and Rose (1923) recognized 57. Inasmuch as the plants are epiphytes, many of which occur high in the trees of tropical rain forests where they are not seen readily from the ground, the problems of research are even more difficult than for most cacti. Thus, the limits of the genus and its internal organization need study; as with most plant groups growing in regions remote from the university belt of the world, investigation has been largely superficial and sporadic.

Because only one species occurs in the U.S. and the others are poorly understood, the extraterritorial species are not listed.

Perhaps as many as 50 species in the American tropics. Plants of the Old World Tropics of Africa and Ceylon may or may not be native there (see Introduction, p. 114); no other genus of the Cactaceae is possibly native to the Eastern Hemisphere.

1. Rhipsalis baccifera (J. Miller) W. T. Stearn

Growing on trees or rocks; older clumps dangling, the stems 0.3-1(10) m long; branches green, in dense clusters, cylindroid, weak, sometimes with aerial roots; joints mostly 10-20 cm long, the year-old and 2-year-old ones 3 mm and 6 mm diam respectively, year-old joints with ±8-10 ribs; areoles on ribs in spirals rising ±12 mm per turn, areoles 1 mm diam, typically with 5-9 white bristles, but these deciduous; flower ±6 mm diam and long; sepaloids scalelike, green, 2-5, deltoid, 2 mm or less long; petaloids white, ±5, largest elliptic, 2-3 mm long, 1-1.5 mm broad, acute, the tips entire; filaments 1-2 mm long; anthers yellow, broadly oblong, 0.2-0.3 mm long; style white, 2 mm long; stigmas 3, white, 1 mm long, relatively broad; fruit white or pink, fleshy, with no areoles or appendages, smooth, maturing rapidly, ellipsoid, 4.5-7.5 mm long, the umbilicus not evident; seeds black, appearing smooth but finely reticulate, narrowly asymmetric-obovoid or -ellipsoid,

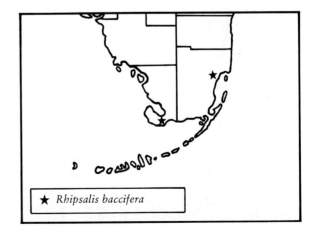

★ *Rhipsalis baccifera*

1.25 mm long, 0.5 mm broad, 0.25 mm thick; hilum obviously basal.

Rain forests in the Tropics at low elevations. Caribbean Tropical Forest. Florida in the Cape Sable region (E of Flamingo) and (introduced or native) w of Kendall, Dade Co. Central America and West Indies and southward to s Bolivia. Tropical Africa and Ceylon.

Fig. 563. *Rhipsalis baccifera*, dangling branch tips with fruits of varying ages, the dried sepaloids and petaloids persistent at the apex of each fruit.

Fig. 562. *Rhipsalis baccifera* (long known as *R. cassutha*), plant in a pot but drooping in characteristic fashion as if it were an epiphyte growing on a tree branch in a tropical jungle. (C. H. Thompson, February 1908; courtesy of Missouri Botanical Garden)

5. Cereus

Plants of various forms. Stems branching slightly to freely, the larger ones elongate, cylindroid to prismatic, length of mature stems 15-100 times diam, 0.3-16 m long, 6 mm to 75 cm diam; ribs 3-20+; tubercles coalescent through nearly their entire height and adnate with ribs. Leaves not discernible in adult plant. Areoles usually circular to elliptic. Spines smooth and gray, yellow, straw-colored, tan, brown, red, or white; central spines sometimes differentiated; spines 1 to many per areole, straight, usually 1.5-7.5 cm long, basally usually 0.1-1.5 mm diam, acicular, broadly elliptic in cross section. Flowers and fruits on old growth of preceding years, therefore below growing apex of stem or branch, in a felted area within at least the edge of the spine-bearing part of the areole or merging into it. Flower usually 2.5-15 (22.5) cm diam; floral tube above junction with ovary almost obsolete to funnelform or long and tubular. Fruit fleshy at maturity, usually pulpy, in some species edible, with or without tubercles, scales, spines, hairs, or bristles, usually orbicular to ovoid or ellipsoid, mostly 1.2-7.5 cm long, indehiscent; floral tube deciduous or persistent. Seeds usually black, smooth to reticulate or papillate, longer than broad (hilum to opposite side), usually 1-2 mm long; hilum obviously basal, sometimes oblique; embryo curved; cotyledons minute, much smaller than hypocotyl, incumbent.

A large but undetermined number of species occurring from California, Arizona, New Mexico, Texas, and Florida to South America, including the Galápagos Islands. Seventeen species native or introduced in the United States.

Reference: A. Berger, 1905.

From Latin *cereus*, a torch, since the earliest known species resembled candelabras.

Numerous "genera" segregated from *Cereus* have been proposed, either within the framework of a particular theory of classification or in amazement at the differences between the extreme forms in a somewhat heterogeneous mass. The species occurring in the United States, in fact, are extremes occurring far from the more southerly center of distribution; they represent the ends of several lines of development, but commonly each has been taken to be complete in itself.

As pointed out in the Introduction (p. 82), there is insufficient information available for an adequate reclassification of *Cereus*, and the proposed systems of division now existing are not satisfactory. Consequently, I have continued a "wait and see" policy pending the further accumulation of information. The task of reevaluating *Cereus* is enormous, and it will require extensive and intensive field and laboratory studies. Such a study cannot be based on the material in cultivation, though these plants are of help in some phases of research.

More than 1,000 species have been proposed under *Cereus*; countless others are under numerous other generic names. Britton and Rose (1923) proposed 34 additional genera for species of *Cereus* that do not occur in North America (and other genera have been proposed since the publication of these): *Monvillea, Espostoa, Browningia, Stetsonia, Escontria, Corryocactus, Pachycereus, Leptocereus, Eulychnia, Erdisia, Leocereus, Dendrocereus, Machaerocereus, Nyctocereus, Brachycereus, Heliocereus, Trichocereus, Jasminocereus, Borzicactus, Binghamia, Rathbunia, Arrojadoa, Oreocereus, Cleistocactus, Zehntnerella, Myrtillocactus, Neoraimondia, Wilmattea, Mediocactus, Deamia, Weberocereus, Werckleocereus, Aporocactus,* and *Strophocactus.*

To facilitate reference, the species occurring north of the Rio Grande are linked below with their probable relatives abroad and with the genera proposed by Britton and Rose. The extraterritorial species have not been evaluated, and those described recently are not included.

Perhaps a thorough restudy of *Cereus* would lead to the recognition of species in the United States as taxa composing such proposed genera as

Carnegiea, Harrisia, Eriocereus, Hylocereus, Selenicereus, Acanthocereus, Cephalocereus, Lemaireocereus, Lophocereus, Bergerocereus, and *Peniocereus.* However, this remains to be seen; and segregations, if any, are likely to be along new lines, into units absorbing all or some of these fragments. I have attempted working out keys to the proposed genera listed above on a segregated basis, but each time the project has bogged down because of the shortage of information and the probable artificiality of the units.

[Genus CEREUS of Britton & Rose]

    C. *hexagonus* (West Indies & N South America)
    C. *hilmannianus* (Brazil; = C. *hexagonus*?)
    C. *alacriportanus* (s Brazil & Paraguay)
    C. *validus* (N Argentina)
    C. *forbesii* (N Argentina)
    C. *jamacaru* (Brazil)
    C. *horridus* (Venezuela)
    C. *tetragonus* (Brazil)
    C. *stenogonus* (Paraguay & NE Argentina)
    C. *xanthocarpus* (Paraguay)
    C. *dayamii* (N Argentina)
    C. *argentinensis* (N Argentina)
  1. C. *peruvianus*
    C. *perlucens* (Brazil)
    C. *variabilis* (Brazil)
    C. *fernambucensis (pernambucensis)* (s Brazil & Uruguay)
    C. *obtusus* (Brazil?)
    C. *azureus* (Brazil)
    C. *chalybaeus* (N Argentina)
    C. *aethiops* (Brazil)
    C. *repandus* (West Indies)
    C. *insularis* (Brazil)

[Genus CARNEGIEA of Britton & Rose]

  2. C. *giganteus*

[Genus HARRISIA of Britton & Rose]

  3. C. *eriophorus*
    var. a. *fragrans*
        eriophorus (Cuba)
    C. *portoricensis* (Puerto Rico)
    C. *nashii* (Haiti)
    C. *brookii* (Bahamas)
  4. C. *gracilis*
    vars. a. *simpsonii*
       b. *aboriginum*
        gracilis (Jamaica)
    C. *tortuosus* (E Argentina)
    C. *pomanensis* (Argentina)

  5. C. *martinii*
    C. *adscendens* (Brazil)
    C. *bonplandii* (Brazil, Paraguay, Argentina)
    C. *guelichii* (Argentina)

[Genus ACANTHOCEREUS of Britton & Rose]

  6. C. *pentagonus*
[Britton and Rose listed six other species under this proposed genus, all described as new.]

[Genus SELENICEREUS of Britton & Rose]

  7. C. *grandiflorus*
    vars. a. *grandiflorus*
       b. *armatus*
    C. *hondurensis* (Honduras & Guatemala)
    C. *urbanianus* (Cuba & Hispaniola)
    C. *donkelaarii* (Yucatan)
  8. C. *pteranthus*
    C. *kunthianus* (Honduras?)
    C. *boeckmannii* (Mexico, Cuba, Hispaniola)
    C. *macdonaldiae* (Central America; reported from Uruguay & Argentina)
    C. *hamatus* (E & s Mexico)
    C. *vagans* (w Mexico)
  9. C. *spinulosus*
    C. *inermis* (Colombia & Venezuela)
    C. *wercklii* (Costa Rica)
    C. *setaceus* (Brazil to Argentina)

[Genus HYLOCEREUS of Britton & Rose]

    C. *ocamponis* (Mexico?)
    C. *polyrhizus* (Panama & Colombia)
  10. C. *undatus*
    C. *lemairei* (Trinidad & Tobago)
    C. *monacanthus* (Panama & Colombia)
    C. *stenopterus* (Costa Rica)
    C. *extensus* (Trinidad)
    C. *trigonus* (West Indies)
    C. *triangularis* (Jamaica)
    C. *calcaratus* (Costa Rica)
    C. *minutiflorus* (Guatemala & Honduras)

[Genus CEPHALOCEREUS of Britton & Rose]
[Britton and Rose listed 48 species, but not all are given here; the list includes a few species not listed by Britton and Rose.]

    C. *senilis* (Hidalgo & Guanajuato: the old man cactus; a favorite in cultivation because of its long spines, which even on a young plant resemble gray human hair)
    C. *hoppenstedtii* (s Mexico)
    C. *fluminensis* (Brazil)
    C. *macrocephalus* (Puebla)
    C. *pentaedrophorus* (Brazil)

C. polycephalus (E Mexico)
C. russellianus (Colombia & Venezuela)
C. gounellei (Brazil)
C. leucostele (Brazil)
11. *C. robinii*
   vars. a. *robinii*
        b. *deeringii*
C. monoclonos (Hispaniola?)
C. moritzianus (Venezuela)
C. arrabidae (Brazil)
C. urbanianus (West Indies)
C. nobilis (West Indies)
C. swartzii (Jamaica)
C. polygonus (Hispaniola)
C. chrysacanthus (Puebla & Oaxaca)
C. lanuginosus (West Indies)
C. brooksianus (Cuba)
C. royenii (West Indies)
C. cometes (San Luis Potosí)
C. leucocephalus (Sonora & Chihuahua)
C. alensis (w Mexico)
C. catingicola (Bahia, Brazil)
C. phaeacanthus (Brazil)
C. piauhyensis (Brazil)
C. colombianus (Colombia)
C. chrysotele (Brazil)
C. aybrowskii (Brazil)
C. purpureus (Brazil)
C. bapalacanthus (Brazil)
C. salvadorensis (Brazil)

[Genus LEMAIREOCEREUS of Britton & Rose]
[Britton & Rose listed 21 proposed species; not all are included here.]
C. hollianus (Puebla; the fruit is about 10 cm long)
C. hystrix (West Indies)
C. griseus (West Indies & Venezuela; common as a hedge plant)
C. pruinosus (s Mexico)
C. chichipe (Puebla & Oaxaca; a fruit tree, known as *chichipe*, the fruits as *chichituna*)

C. chende (Puebla & Oaxaca)
C. aragonii (Costa Rica; common there as a hedge plant)
C. stellatus (s Mexico; the fruit is known in the markets as *joconostle*)
C. deficiens (Venezuela; used as a hedge plant)
C. weberi (Puebla & Oaxaca; known as *cardon* or *candebobe*)
C. queretaroensis (central Mexico)
12. *C. thurberi*
C. laetus (Ecuador & N Peru)
C. dumortierii (central Mexico)
C. beneckii (central Mexico)
C. euphorbioides (N Mexico)
C. godingianus (Ecuador)
C. littoralis (s Baja California)
C. marginatus (central Mexico)
C. martinezii (w Mexico)

[Genus BERGEROCACTUS of Britton & Rose]
13. *C. emoryi*

[Genus LOPHOCEREUS of Britton & Rose]
14. *C. schottii*
C. gatesii (Baja California)

[Genus PENIOCEREUS of Britton & Rose]
15. *C. greggii*
   vars. a. *greggii*
        b. *transmontanus*
Peniocereus johnstonii (Baja California)
Peniocereus maculatus (central Mexico)
Peniocereus macdougallii (s Mexico)
Peniocereus rosei (w central Mexico)

[Genus WILCOXIA of Britton & Rose]
C. viperinus (Puebla)
16. *C. poselgeri*
17. *C. striatus*
C. papillosa (Sinaloa)
C. tamaulipensis (Tamaulipas)
C. viperina (Puebla)

KEY TO THE SPECIES OF CEREUS

1. Roots *not* forming tubers; larger stems 2-60 cm in diameter; spines or some of them nearly always 12+ mm long or longer (rarely shorter, in plants of the coasts of the Gulf of Mexico and E Florida).
2. Superior floral tube slender, 3.8+ cm long; plants *either* shrubby or sprawling and with slender, elongated stems *or* sometimes trees; tropical (except the tree, *C. giganteus*, of the deserts of Arizona and adjacent California).
3. Stems *not* bearing aerial roots.
4. Floral tube with an abscission layer near mid-level, separating crosswise at this

point and the upper part falling away when the fruit is young; ovary nearly naked, bearing only a few scales, these sometimes with a few hairs from the vestigial axillary areoles; introduced in Hawaii............1. **C. peruvianus**

4. Floral tube *not* with an abscission layer in the middle, *not* separating crosswise; ovary with scales and often spines, bristles, or hairs in the areoles, these present on the fruit at least until maturity.

    5. Ovary at flowering time completely covered by green scales, these *not* enlarging with growth of the fruit (as in *C. undatus*) but obvious on the fruit, the areoles in their axils *not* bearing discernible spines, bristles, or hairs; plant a tree with a tall trunk; stem with usually only 1-15(25) branches (but gigantic plants 8-16 m high having larger numbers), with little rebranching; stems 30-75 cm in diameter, narrower at ground level than above; fruit splitting lengthwise along 3 (rarely 4) lines, green outside and brilliant red inside; deserts of Arizona and adjacent California and of N Sonora............

    .... 2. **C. giganteus**

    5. Ovary at flowering time *not* completely covered by green scales, the fruit *not* scaly; the areoles bearing spines, bristles, or hairs; plant *not* treelike, but either clambering or shrubby; stems branching and rebranching many times at ground level and above; stems 1-5 cm in diameter, at least as large at ground level as above; fruit opening irregularly, if at all.

      6. Stems cylindroid, with (4)6-11 ribs, not sharply angled; areoles of the inferior floral tube and later of the fruit either spineless or with flexible hairlike spines; Florida and the Caribbean region.

        7. Central and radial spines *not* obviously different; fruit orange-red to yellow, not tuberculate, not regularly dehiscent, the superior floral tube deciduous just above ovary; stem ribs 8-12.

          8. Hairs of the areoles on the floral tube 10-15+ mm long, white, flexible, forming conspicuous tufts; inner petaloids entire, narrowly lanceolate or oblanceolate, *not* markedly expanded above; sepaloids *not* acuminate, very narrow; scale leaves of the lower superior floral tube ±1.5 mm broad, flat, the continuation along the tube below the point of attachment nearly flat; fruit at maturity (in the U.S.) obovoid, orange-red; E and S Florida and the Keys.......3. **C. eriophorus**

          8. Hairs of the areoles on the floral tube 6-8(10) mm long, white or tawny-brown, flexible or rather stiff, *not* forming conspicuous tufts; inner petaloids erose-denticulate above, oblanceolate, expanded above; sepaloids slightly acuminate; scale-leaves of the lower superior floral tube 1.5-3 mm broad, swollen basally and the swelling continued along the tube below the point of attachment; fruit at maturity globular or depressed-globose, yellow or orange-red; W and S Florida and the Keys....................4. **C. gracilis**

        7. Central and radial spines clearly differentiated, the single central much longer than the radials; fruit red, irregularly somewhat tuberculate, dehiscent, the superior floral tube and the dried flower parts persistent; stem ribs 4-5; introduced in Hawaii.................5. **C. martinii**

      6. Stems or most of them essentially triangular in cross section, sharply 3-angled; areoles of the inferior floral tube and later of the fruit with hairs and many stiff spines about ±1.2 cm long; coasts of Texas and Florida......

      ....6. **C. pentagonus**

3. Stems bearing aerial roots; tropical forests and the more open or disturbed places near them.

    4A. Floral tube and ovary *not* bearing large scalelike leaves, the small scales, if any, not enlarging as the fruit matures, the areoles of the floral tube spiny; stems essentially cylindroid, with 4-8 relatively broad ribs.

      5A. Spines not clearly divided into central and radial, 1-12(15) mm long; flower 12.5-20 cm in diameter, 17.5-30 cm long; sepaloids 7.5-10 cm long; petaloids 7.5-10 cm long; areoles of the floral tube bearing long, flexible, hairlike spines or hairs; filaments 38-50 mm long; anthers 1.5 mm long, rectangular; style 15-20 cm long.

        6A. Longer spines 4.5-12(15) mm long; spines 6-18 per areole, the bulbous bases inconspicuous; stem joints 1.2-2.5 cm in diameter..............

        ....7. **C. grandiflorus**

6A. Longer spines 1-3 mm long; spines 1-5 per areole, the bulbous bases more conspicuous than upper parts; stem joints 2.5-5 cm in diameter.......
....**8. C. pteranthus**
5A. Spines clearly 1 central and 6-7 radial, 1 mm long; flower 7-8.5 cm in diameter, 10-12.5 cm long; sepaloids 5-6 cm long; petaloids ±6 cm long; areoles of the floral tube *not* bearing long, flexible, hairlike spines or hairs; filaments ±30 mm long; anthers 2.5-3 mm long, elongate-rectangular; style ±8 cm long...**9. C. spinulosus**
4A. Floral tube and ovary bearing large, scalelike leaves, these enlarging greatly as the fruit matures, the areoles of the floral tube spineless; stems or most of them essentially triangular in cross section, 3-angled or the angles usually extending into ribs or wings...**10. C. undatus**
2. Superior floral tube below the attachment of the stamens relatively broad, *not more* than 1.5 cm long; shrubs or plants with suberect to erect elongate stems arising from near ground level; tropical areas or deserts or dry seacoasts.
3A. Flower 1 per areole; areoles of the stems all with similar spines; fruit with or without scales, spiny or spineless.
4B. Ovary naked or with only a few small scales, the areoles sometimes with a few short hairs; Florida and the Caribbean region................**11. C. robinii**
4B. Ovary with scales, the areoles with spines and often bristles, long flexible hairs, or wool.
5B. Spines gray, black, or brownish; petaloids pink; trees or arborescent plants 3-7 m high at maturity, the stems numerous from a low central trunk or base, 10-15(20) cm in diameter; deserts of s Arizona and of Baja California and Sonora...**12. C. thurberi**
5B. Spines yellow (turning black or dirty dark gray in age and often in herbarium specimens); petaloids yellow; stems forming dense colonies by branching from the bases, the colonies often several to many meters in diameter, the stems 3.8-5 cm in diameter; coastal and insular s California and adjacent Baja California..**13. C. emoryi**
3A. Flowers 2 to several (rarely 1) per areole; areoles of the lower part of the stem (in the U.S.) spineless or with ±8-10 stout spines ±1.2 cm long and with conspicuous bulbous bases, the areoles of the upper part of the stem with ±30 slender spines 1.2-3.8(7.5) cm long and without bulbous bases; fruit with scales but spineless (or rarely with a few basal spines); Arizona; Baja California and Sonora.......
....**14. C. schottii**
1. Root(s), either the taproot or a cluster of principal roots, forming one or more large tubers, these fleshy, reminiscent (in form) of a sweet potato and (in texture) of a raw white potato; stems slender, basally ±4.5-6 mm in diameter, or enlarging above to 6-12 mm, with as many as 8 branches above; spines (in the U.S. species) slender and weak, sometimes with bulbous bases, to 9 mm long; deserts from Arizona to Texas and N Mexico.
2A. Stems with 4-6 ribs, the ribs conspicuous and the intervening troughs deep; style and stamens *not* projecting above the perianth; tuber single, an enlarged taproot weighing 0.7-20 kg (1.5-43 lb); spines mostly parallel to stem surface, but 1 or more nearly at right angles; superior floral tube 10-15 cm long; Arizona to Texas and N Mexico...**15. C. greggii**
2A. Stems with 6-10 grooves, the ridges only ±1-1.5 mm high; style and stamens often (perhaps always) projecting beyond the perianth; tubers several, each developed from a major root; spines all parallel to stem surface; superior floral tube 0.9-2.5 cm long.
3B. Flower to 5 cm long; areoles 3-4.5 mm apart; stems 6-9 mm in diameter; superior floral tube 0.9-1.2 cm long, funnelform; spines 1 central, 12-16 radial, tan or the central brown, the central 6-9 mm long, the radials 3-4.5 mm long; s Texas along the Rio Grande; Coahuila...............................**16. C. poselgeri**
3B. Flower 7.5-15 cm long; areoles ±6-15 mm apart; stems ±6 mm in diameter; superior floral tube 2.5+ cm long, tubular-funnelform; spines in 3 groups by position in the areole, some white, some white with black tips, 1.5-3 mm long; middle southernmost Arizona; Baja California, and Sonora............**17. C. striatus**

1. Cereus peruvianus (Linnaeus) Miller

Plant to 6-7 m high; trunk 30-90 cm high, to 30+ cm diam; larger branches with powdery bluish wax covering, cylindroid, the ultimate branches 30-60 cm long, ±10-12.5 cm diam; ribs 4-9, mostly ±6, the number increasing on upper part of plant, the grooves 4-6 cm deep; areoles brown to gray, ±6 mm diam, typically 10-25 mm apart; spines not obscuring stem, gray, brown, or black, mostly 6-8 per areole, longer ones spreading, some others reflexed, straight or basally bent, the longer 1.2-3.8(10.6) cm long, basally 0.75 mm diam, acicular, nearly circular in cross section; flower nocturnal, ±7.5-10 cm diam, to 15 cm long; sepaloids dorsally green and pink, uppermost margins of longer ones white, the largest narrowly oblong or narrowly lanceolate or somewhat spathulate, 5 cm long, to 12 cm broad, the lower apically rounded, the upper sharply acute, entire, thick; petaloids white, largest oblanceolate-spathulate, 4.4-7.5 cm long, 1-2 cm broad, acute, mucronulate, entire; filaments greenish to often greenish-white, 25-45 mm long, very slender; anthers dull tan, oblong, 1.5-2 mm long; style pale green, 7.5-10 cm long, 1.5-2.5 mm greatest diam; stigmas pale green, ±12-15, 9-11+ mm long, very slender; ovary in anthesis ±12 mm long; fruit red or rose, changing to amber, fleshy at maturity but usually splitting along 1 side, the pulp white, juicy, sweet, the surface nearly smooth and almost lacking scales, 5-7.5 cm long, 4.4-5 cm diam, the umbilicus inconspicuous; seeds black, nearly smooth but papillate on periphery, irregularly obovoid, 2 mm long, 1.5 mm broad, 1 mm thick.

Escaped on rich volcanic soils of pastures and hills at low elevations. Native of South America. On s Kauai, Hawaii; according to report, introduced by the Moir family. The plant has become common, and it sometimes is a pest in pastures.

This is the standard large cactus of outdoor cultivation throughout the warm parts of the world. Left alone, it is an arborescent plant or compact fruit tree with a short trunk and many thick branches; but commonly it is pruned into symmetry to emphasize either the tree form or a group of several branches erect from spreading bases. The fruit is a delicacy valued for its light, perfumed flesh peppered with small black seeds.

Fig. 564. *Cereus peruvianus* in cultivation at Claremont, Los Angeles Co., California, the tree form due partly to pruning.

Fig. 565. *Cereus peruvianus* in cultivation at Claremont; the stem joints with relatively young areoles. The nocturnal flowers were photographed soon after sunrise.

Fig. 567. *Cereus peruvianus*, with young fruits and a dehiscent red mature fruit, revealing the edible, delicately aromatic, white pulp and embedded black seeds; the styles (and stigmas) still persistent.

Fig. 566 (*left*). *Cereus peruvianus*, flower.

545

2. Cereus giganteus Engelmann
Saguaro, giant cactus

Tree 3-16 m high (Peebles, 1936, stated 53 ft); trunk 30-75 cm diam, for many years unbranched, but in time with 1-5 or ultimately up to 25(50) branches, these bending or curving abruptly upward, far above stem base, with little rebranching, green; ribs ±12-30, prominent, mostly ±2.5-3.8 cm high; areoles broadly elliptic, ±12 mm diam, typically ±12 mm apart; spines relatively dense on the stem, gray or with pink tinge, 15-30 per areole, spreading in all directions, on younger stems (and lower portions of older trunks) the longer ones deflexed, straight, ±3.5 cm long, but on upper parts of old stems spreading and 2.5-3.8 cm long, basally to 1.3 mm diam, acicular or on young stems flattened or angular; flower nocturnal but remaining open next day, 5-6 cm diam, 8.7-12.5 cm long; sepaloids with middles green and margins paler to whitish, largest obovate or spatulate-obovate, 2-2.5 cm long, to 9 mm broad, rounded, undulate; petaloids white, largest more or less obovate, to ±2.5 cm long, ±15 mm broad, rounded, undulate; stamens to 3,482 per flower (counted by Bessey; see Cutak, 1946); filaments ±6 mm long; anthers ±1.3-1.5

mm long; style ±5 cm long, to almost 3 mm greatest diam; stigmas ±12 mm long, slender; ovary in anthesis ovoid-cylindroid, ±40 mm long, with green scales, these with axillary tufts of short wool; fruit green tinged with red, fleshy at maturity, with scales (those covering the floral tube at flowering time) *not* growing as the fruit develops; fruit scaly but otherwise smooth, obovoid to ellipsoid, 5-7.5 cm long, ±2.5-4.4 cm diam, the umbilicus not prominent, the fruit maturing in late June and July, dehiscent along 3(4) regular vertical lines and exposing the conspicuous red lining; seeds black, irregularly obovoid, 2 mm long, 1.3 mm broad, 1 mm thick; hilum oblique.

Rocky or gravelly well-drained soils of foothills, canyons, and benches and along washes in sandy or gravelly plains in the desert at 180-1,080 (1,350) m (600-3,600 or 4,500 ft). Arizona Desert and upper edge of Colorado Desert. California near Colorado R., a few individuals occurring from Whipple Mts. to Laguna Dam; Arizona from s Mohave Co. to Graham (Aravaipa), Yuma, and Pima Cos.

The saguaro is the prime feature of the Arizona Desert, and, regardless of all else present, it dominates the landscape. The young plants stand like

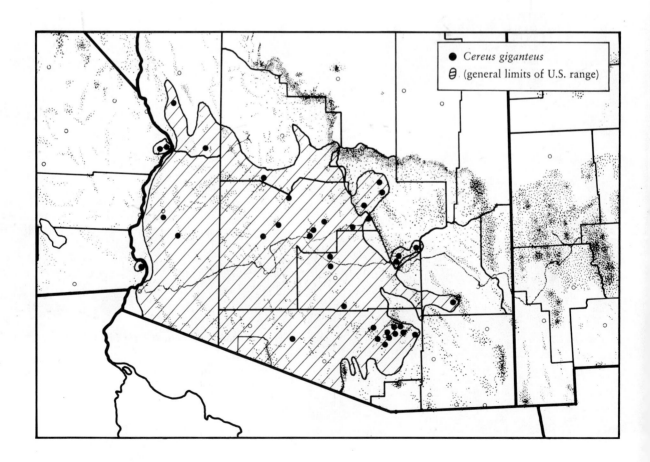

Fig. 568. The opening illustration of the saguaro, *Cereus giganteus*, and the Arizona Desert in George Engelmann, "Cactaceae in the Boundary," in William H. Emory, *Rept. U.S. & Mex. Bound. Surv.* 1859. The title is "View along the Gila, Cereus giganteus." This was the first view that a waiting world had of the cactus desert of Arizona. Recent visits suggest that the scene was sketched by J. M. Stanly near the site of the present Coolidge Dam, where the saguaro was discovered by Emory in 1846 (the artist, Paulus Roetter, evidently worked from Stanly's sketch). The plants at the lower right suggest a prickly pear and a creosote bush, but the rest of the vegetation is omitted. (Paulus Roetter in Engelmann/Emory, *pl. facing p. 78*)

Fig. 570. *Cereus giganteus*, a cluster of plants in the Rincon Mts., the holes in the upper stems made by nesting flickers and other woodpeckers (see Fig. 577).

Fig. 569. Saguaro or giant cactus, *Cereus giganteus*, part of a grove in the Saguaro National Monument, Rincon Mts., Pima Co., Arizona. Arizona Desert: foothill palo verde, *Cercidium microphyllum*, just left of center; velvet mesquite, *Prosopis juliflora* var. *velutina*, extreme right; *Condalia warnockii* var. *kearneyana* (known as *C. spathulata*), right foreground; burro weed, *Haplopappus tenuisectus*, bushes in open area, left foreground; cane cholla, *Opuntia spinosior*, among shrubs at right. (George A. Grant, October 1935; courtesy of U.S. National Park Service)

Fig. 571. *Cereus giganteus,* an enormous plant in the Rincon Mts.; 49 branches and an estimated height of 15 m (51 feet). (Robert H. Peebles; see Credits)

pillars on the hills, and the older, branching ones are like great candelabra towering above the rocks and shrubs. The desert mountains are majestic in themselves, but much more so with saguaros.

The vernacular (Indian) name, pronounced "sa-wår-o," has been transliterated in various ways, but the best choice is saguaro. The English name giant cactus is used also in the United States, but more commonly outside of Arizona.

In May the saguaro flowers open at about 10 P.M. and remain open most of the next day. Pollination is effected by any of the numerous animal visitors—bats and probably moths at night, bees, other insects, and birds (including the white-winged dove) by day.

The "red flowers" reported during midsummer and appearing on picture postcards are the opened fruits, which have bright red pulp. This pulp is eaten by birds of many species, and the seasonal range of the white-winged dove, for example, is almost identical with the distributional area of the saguaro.

Birds, including the sparrow-sized elf owl, nest in abandoned woodpecker holes in the saguaro trunks, drilled in the first instance by the Gila woodpecker or the gilded flicker. Many other birds occupy the holes after they have been abandoned by their makers.

The Indians gather saguaro fruit for use in conserves and beverages, as well as for the seeds, which are rich in fats. The ribs of the woody carcass of the plant are used for shelters, fences, and novelty furniture and trinkets. The wood is heavy and is impregnated with mineral crystals that dull woodworking tools.

According to Shreve (1935), many older saguaros are 150-200 years old. A plant 10 cm (4 in.) tall may be 8-25 years old, and a plant 4.5 m (15 ft) tall 60-100 years of age. A large fallen saguaro at the foot of the Santa Catalina Mts. near Sabino Canyon, northeast of Tucson, was measured by Shreve in 1915. Measurements to determine the volume and weight on the basis of weighed samples indicated a total weight of 9 tons (8.2 metric tons). This gigantic saguaro is described in letters to Dr. F. V. Coville, accompanied by photographs taken by Dr. D. T. McDougal in 1903 and 1911, *US.*

In the desert landscape of Arizona and Sonora the saguaro dominates steep mountainsides or alluvial fans and occurs also in valleys. At the northern end of its distributional range in Arizona it is primarily on the warmer south and especially on the southwest slopes, which are the least affected by winter cold. A little south of the Mexican boundary saguaros are abundant on both the north-facing and south-facing slopes, but in the warmer areas at the southern end of its range in Mexico the species is restricted to the north-facing slopes. *C. giganteus* thus follows a pattern typical of many north-temperate species.

Extensive saguaro forests are common in southern Arizona. The original section of the Saguaro National Monument in the Rincon Mts. southeast of Tucson includes an old forest in which, because of earlier overgrazing, there was little reproduction for many years. Consequently, although there are many gigantic saguaros in this stand, there are few young ones. (Various species of cacti besides the saguaro are abundant, however.) Excellent younger, and reproducing, forests are

Text continued on p. 555

Fig. 572. Opening of the saguaro flower, *Cereus giganteus*: the same flower cluster photographed from the opening of the buds the evening of May 23, 1940, to the following morning. The flowers close during late afternoon, the time varying with the weather. *Upper left*, 10:05 p.m.; *upper right*, 10:54 p.m.; *lower left*, 11:55 p.m.; *lower right*, 9:50 a.m. (Robert H. Peebles; see Credits)

Fig. 574. *Cereus giganteus*, stem-apex with flower buds, flowers, and a young fruit, showing the scale-leaves on the floral tube covering the ovary and the transition from these into sepaloid, then petaloid perianth parts. Note the relatively short, but slender, spines on the upper part of the plant, these having developed during the mature stage, in contrast with those produced during the juvenile stage, which are much larger and stouter and are deflexed (see Figs. 582–84). Juvenile spines persist on the lower part of the stem. (Robert H. Peebles)

Fig. 575. *Cereus giganteus*, flower, showing the multitudinous stamens. (Robert H. Peebles)

Fig. 573. Flowers of the saguaro, *Cereus giganteus*, stem-apex with flower buds, flowers, and young fruits, each flower arising from a feltlike cushion within the upper portion of the spine-bearing areole (see also development of buds, Fig. 574), but the spines mostly on the lower side of the areole. (Robert H. Peebles; see Credits)

551

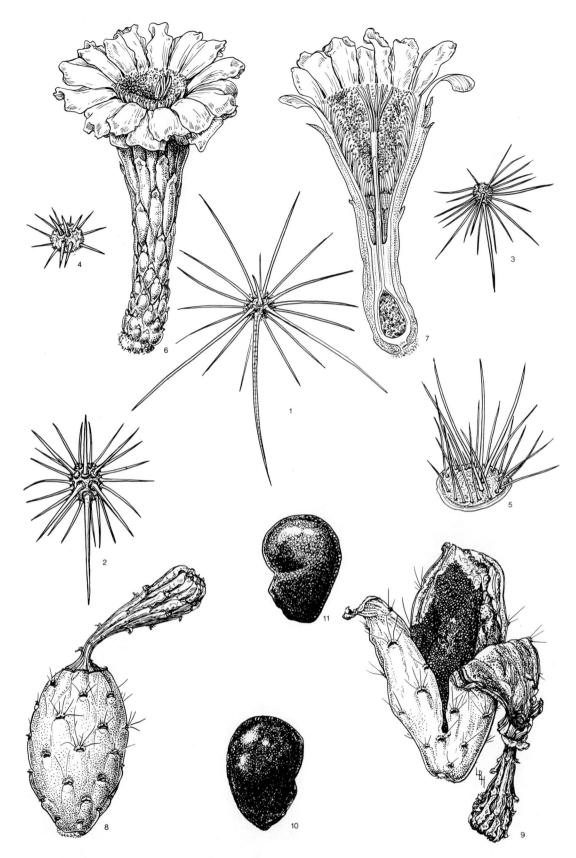

Fig. 576. Saguaro or giant cactus, *Cereus giganteus*, ✕.8, except as indicated. *1*, Areole with spines; from a young plant, the principal spine strongly deflexed. *2*, Areole with intermediate type of spines. *3, 4, 5*, Areoles from the upper part of the plant, from areas developed after the plant was mature (*5*, from the flowering area); the spines much shorter and more slender. *6*, Flower, showing the scale-leaves on the floral cup covering the ovary. *7*, Flower in longitudinal section. *8*, Fruit, the upper portion of the flower persisting, but the scale-leaves fallen from the ovary. *9*, Dehiscence of the fruit, exposing the red lining and the numerous black seeds. *10, 11*, Seed in two views, ✕13.

Fig. 577 (*above left*). *Cereus giganteus*, with holes made by the Gila woodpecker and the gilded flicker, which use them for nests; later, many other birds, often the sparrow-sized elf owl, will become tenants of the condominium.

Fig. 578 (*above right*). *Cereus giganteus*, woody skeleton, the softer outer tissues disintegrating, leaving the ribs. The wand-like structures are branches of the ocotillo, *Fouquieria splendens*.

Fig. 579. *Cereus giganteus*, the ribs of a dead stem separating after decay of the fleshy tissues; Tucson Mts., Pima Co., Arizona. A velvet mesquite, *Prosopis juliflora* var. *velutina*, is at the right; foothill palos verdes, *Cercidium microphyllum*, are in the background.

553

Fig. 580. *Cereus giganteus*, portion of a fallen woody skeleton of a large plant. (Homer L. Shantz; see Credits)

Fig. 581. *Cereus giganteus*, hard structures formed as callus around woodpecker holes. (Homer L. Shantz; see Credits)

in the western section of the Monument in the Tucson Mountains west of the city and at the south end of Santa Rosa Valley in western Pima County.

Other ecological factors governing occurrence of the saguaro are complex, involving production and dispersal of seeds, germination of seeds and establishment of seedlings, and growth and survival of the plants, as follows:

Production and dispersal of seeds. Fruits are produced in considerable numbers, and each one may contain up to 2,000 seeds; a plant with 200 fruits, then, might produce as many as 400,000 seeds in a single season. Inasmuch as establishment of even one of these as a new plant is unlikely, the occurrence of just the right set of factors must be rare (McGregor, Alcorn, & Olin, 1962).

The fruit matures in June or early July, and the highly nutritious seeds are too valuable to desert animals to be left lying around on the ground until the rains begin in July. They are dispersed by ants, rodents, birds, and other animals, and each carrier takes its toll. Ants may remove every seed from the original location, but a few may germinate later. When larger animals eat the seeds, some may survive their digestive tracts and be deposited, along with fertilizing and water-holding material, elsewhere, perhaps in a favorable spot. Nevertheless, survival and deposition in a suitable place is the lot of only a very small number of seeds.

Germination of seeds and the establishment of seedlings. The first requirement is proper soil. The saguaro will grow in a wide range of desert soils, but it is most abundant and becomes largest at low elevations on the dry, southwest-facing slopes of alluvial fans and on the adjacent lower rocky slopes of the mountains. The plants become established more frequently in the coarse, gravelly soils at the upper ends of the fans or *bajadas* than in the finer soils at the lower ends of the fans or in the valleys below them. Dark-colored soils are less favorable, since they absorb more heat and therefore dry more rapidly (Niering, Whittaker, & Lowe, 1963).

Moisture is vital to the saguaro seed for germination, and both moisture and shade are needed for the seedling's development. However, at the latitude of Arizona, the north-facing slopes where moisture and shade are available are too cold for the saguaro. Here, at the northern end of the species range, the best situations are the warmer ones on south or southwest slopes, but only where there is extra water from concentration in slightly depressed troughs or draws or near washes or between and along the lower edges of rocks. In Yuma County, where the rainfall of less than 12.5 cm (5 in) per year will not support saguaros on the open desert, the threadlike washes below the mountains are marked by lines of them running for miles.

The germination of seeds and most of the growth of both seedlings and adults occur during the summer rainy season. This limits the occurrence of the saguaro in the United States to the Arizona Desert and excludes the species from all but the eastern margin of California.

Shade is necessary for the establishment of seedlings (Shreve, 1931a; Turner, Alcorn, Olin, & Booth, 1966), and usually it is provided by other plants or by rocks. Inasmuch as the seedling has a high ratio of surface to volume and little storage capacity, it is vulnerable to drying. In experimental plots all the unshaded seedlings died within a year, whereas about 35 percent of the shaded plants survived. Most seedlings planted during the summer rains survived that moist period whether they were in sun or shade, but all the unshaded ones died when the rains ceased.

Growth and survival of plants. The most critical factors are water (already discussed) and temperature. The most suitable temperatures occur at the upper ends of the alluvial fans and on the adjacent lower rocky slopes. Locally, cold air drains downward and concentrates in the valleys on still nights, and the temperatures there drop lower. However, greater changes of altitude, such as those occurring on the mountains above, result in overall temperature differences that tend in the opposite direction. For each increase of 300 m (1,000 ft) of altitude the average annual temperature decreases about 2.2°C (4°F). Near Tucson (elevation 730 m/2,400 ft) the saguaro is abundant and best developed up to 1,070 m (3,500 ft) elevation; but above that level it thins out and becomes smaller, and above 1,370 m (4,500 ft) it disappears (see Niering, Whittaker, & Lowe, 1963). This is caused by periodic killing frosts in which the cold continues through 24 hours or longer, as in 1962, when the saguaros along the Soldier Trail Highway into the Santa Catalina Mts. were injured severely. Temperature affects both the seedlings struggling for establishment and the older plants, but frequently the younger ones are sheltered by rocks, which may radiate heat at night, and by other plants. Consequently, the percentage of survival of younger individuals

Fig. 582 (*above left*). *Cereus giganteus*, seedling about 4 dm (16 inches) tall; all the spines stout, the principal one in each areole much longer than the others and turned downward, forming a "drip-tip" upon which the water from even a light rain accumulates into drops before falling off and soaking the soil. This feature is significant for small plants but not for larger ones with wider-spreading root systems. The spines also provide protection from rodents, their downward direction enhancing that function.

Fig. 583 (*above right*). *Cereus giganteus*, young plant about 6 dm (2 feet) high; Organ Pipe Cactus National Monument, Pima Co., Arizona. A medium-sized velvet mesquite, *Prosopis juliflora* var. *velutina*, serves as a nurse tree.

Fig. 584. *Cereus giganteus*, juvenile plant about 1.2 m (4 feet) high, showing the narrow stem base and larger upper trunk characteristic of the saguaro and of some other species of *Cereus*; Organ Pipe Cactus National Monument, Pima Co., Arizona. Arizona Desert: right foreground, a young staghorn cholla, *Opuntia acanthocarpa* var. *major*; in the tangle of desert shrubs, many other species; and in the background, older (but still mostly unbranched) saguaros and the organ pipe cactus, *Cereus thurberi*.

556

Fig. 585. *Cereus giganteus*, plant about 3 m (10 feet) tall, soon to overtop its nurse tree, a foothill palo verde, *Cercidium microphyllum*; Arizona Desert.

may be higher than that of older ones. Among older plants the advantage is with those of greater stem diameter, since the ratio of surface to volume is less and heat is retained longer (Felger & Lowe, 1967).

Anchorage may limit local occurrence of the saguaro. Strong winds commonly occur during rainy weather, when the ground is soft; and root anchorage in sandy or loamy soil sometimes is not adequate to support the heavy plant body swaying in the wind. In one cactus forest in Sonora, A. A. Nichol found that half the giant cacti had been blown over in one direction by the wind and partly buried in alluvial soil.

During the last century the range of the saguaro has been altered by the coming of European man. In the 1880's the desert was heavily overstocked with cattle, and the grasses and browse plants were depleted rapidly. As the plant cover was reduced, the desert's capacity to support livestock declined, and many cattle died of starvation. Thus, except for the spreading of cities into the desert, there has been a tendency toward stabili-

zation at a lower level of vegetation. Loss of the original vegetative cover reduced the soil capacity to retain water and retard flow, changing the Santa Cruz River at Tucson, for example, from a year-round clear stream to a sandy wash carrying only flash floods. These conditions have affected the soil, seedbeds, and shade needed by saguaro seedlings. In some of the older forests there are no young plants, and the older ones (100-200 years) are disappearing a few at a time. According to Niering, Whittaker, & Lowe (1963), the reproduction of the saguaro on the mountain slopes can be correlated with the less intensive grazing there. Probably the saguaro will continue in its dominant role in the Arizona Desert, since its chief enemy, overgrazing, reached a peak and subsided long ago. However, for the several reasons above it will still tend to grow on the alluvial fans and lower mountain slopes, which are bothered less by man and livestock.

A form of bacterial rot that affects the saguaro can be serious; but this enemy has been present for a long time, and it attacks only injured plants, which have strong abilities to seal off the infected areas. In forests that are not reproducing, the rot may finish off many older plants.

References: Alcorn, 1961, *Natural history of the saguaro*; Alcorn & May, 1962, *Attrition of a saguaro forest*; Alcorn & Kurtz, 1959, *Some factors affecting the germination of seed of the saguaro cactus (Carnegiea gigantea)*; Alcorn, McGregor, Butler, & Kurtz, 1959, *Pollination requirements of the saguaro (Carnegiea gigantea)*; Alcorn, McGregor, & Olin, 1961, *Pollination of saguaro cactus by doves, nectar-feeding bats, and honey bees*; Brum, G. D., 1973, *Ecology of the saguaro: Phenology and establishment in marginal populations*; Hastings & Alcorn, 1961, *Physical determinations of growth and age in giant cactus*; Herbert, 1969, *Papago saguaro harvest*; Hodge, 1969, *Monarch of the desert: Saguaro*; Kurtz & Alcorn, 1960, *Some germination requirements of saguaro cactus seeds*; McGregor, Alcorn, Kurtz, & Butler, 1959, *Bee visitors to saguaro flowers*; McGregor, Alcorn, & Olin, 1962, *Pollination and pollinating agents in the saguaro*; Mitich, 1972, *The saguaro: A history*; Niering, Whittaker, & Lowe, 1963, *The saguaro: A population in relation to environment*; Peebles, 1943, *Watching the saguaro bloom*, 1947, *Saguaro fruit*; Shantz, 1937, *The saguaro forest*; Shreve, 1910, *The rate of establishment of the giant cactus*, 1931a, *Physical conditions in sun and shade*, 1931b, *The cactus and its home*, 1935, *The longevity of cacti*, 1951, *Vegetation of the Sonoran Desert*; Shreve and Wiggins, 1964, *Vegetation and flora of the Sonoran Desert*; Thackery & Leding, 1929, *The giant cactus of Arizona*; Turner, Alcorn, Olin, & Booth, 1966, *The influence of shade, soil, and water on saguaro seedling establishment*; Turner, Alcorn, & Olin, 1969, *Mortality of transplanted saguaro seedlings*.

Fig. 586. *Cereus eriophorus* var. *fragrans* growing in a tangle of shrubs in an area devastated by a hurricane a few years earlier; a palm trunk at left. Caribbean Tropical Forest at Cape Sable, Everglades National Park, Florida.

3. Cereus eriophorus Pfeiffer

Canelike plant with several to many stems sprawling through surrounding vegetation, mostly 1-5 m long, 2.5-5 cm diam; trunk none; larger terminal joints green, cylindroid, greatly elongate; ribs 8-12, prominent, the grooves between ribs obvious but not deep; areoles 1.5-3 mm diam, typically ±12 mm apart; spines numerous, more or less covering joint, either brown with black tips or the older ones grayish-tan with yellow tips and the younger somewhat yellowish all over, 8-15 per areole, spreading in all directions,

straight, rigid, longest 1.2-4.4 cm long, basally to ±0.75 mm diam, acicular, nearly circular in cross section, not markedly barbed; flower nocturnal but persisting into next day, faintly scented, 7.5-10 cm diam, 15-17.5 cm long; scale-leaves of lower portion of floral tube 1.5 mm broad, thin, flat, the continuation of each leaf along the tube below the attachment thin and flat; hairs of areoles on floral tube 10-15 mm long, white, flexible; sepaloids with midribs purplish-brown and margins paler to pink or white, largest lanceolate-

Fig. 587 *(above)*. *Cereus eriophorus* var. *fragrans*, the spines longer than those in Fig. 589 (as is the case in some individuals).

Fig. 589 *(left)*. *Cereus eriophorus* var. *fragrans*, stem with a fruit, showing the characteristic wool-like spines in the areoles of the floral tube enveloping and adnate with the true fruit. The dark structure trailing down from the fruit (and out of focus) is composed of the dried floral tube and the now amorphous perianth.

Fig. 588. *Cereus eriophorus* var. *fragrans*, portion of a stem, with fruit; and a flower. (Mary E. Eaton; see Credits)

linear, to 5.5 cm long, to 4.5 cm broad, attenuate; petaloids pale pink or white, the largest narrowly oblanceolate, to 6.2(7.5) cm long, 12(15) mm broad, acuminate-attenuate, entire; filaments white or nearly so, ±50-55 mm long; anthers yellow, 2-2.5 mm long; style pale green, 12.5-15 cm long, 1 mm greatest diam; stigmas ±15, ±6 mm long, slender; ovary in anthesis ±12 mm diam, appearing woolly; fruit orange-red or (in Cuba) yellow, fleshy at maturity, smooth, with some wool-like spines, obovoid, 5-6.2 cm long, 40-45 mm diam, persistent until midwinter; seeds black, nearly oblong but slightly constricted above the middles, 3 mm long, 1.5 mm broad, 1 mm thick, finely and deeply pitted.

3a. Cereus eriophorus var. fragrans (Small) L. Benson. Plants to 3-5 m high; stems with 10-12 ribs; spines gray with yellow tips or yellowish all over when young, 2-3 cm long, 9-13 per areole; fruit orange-red.

Sandy soils of low areas in jungles and woods along the coast at 1-4 m (3-13 ft). Caribbean Tropical Forest. Florida on Atlantic Coast from Turtle Mound, Volusia Co., to St. Lucie Sound (Indian River), St. Lucie Co.; Cape Sable and Big Pine Key, Monroe Co.

This canelike or shrubby plant may be nearly lost in other vegetation growing up in disturbed areas of fields or the edges of the forest. Sometimes it stands above herbs and bushes. The largest plants in my memory occurred in an area of slowly regenerating forest land at Cape Sable, where a hurricane had struck some years earlier.

See map for *C. gracilis* (next species).

Cereus eriophorus var. eriophorus. Plants to 4 m tall; stems bearing 8 or 9 ribs; spines brown with black tips, 6-9 per areole, 2.5-4.5 cm long; fruit yellow. Caribbean Tropical Forest. Not native in the U.S. Western and central Cuba; Isle of Pines.

4. Cereus gracilis Miller

Canelike plant with several to many stems growing in suberect colonies or sprawling through jungle vegetation, 3-5(7) m high, 2.5-4 cm diam; trunk none; larger terminal joints green, cylindroid, greatly elongate; ribs 9-11, the intervening grooves pronounced but shallow; areoles ±3-4.5 mm diam, typically 12 mm apart; spines numerous, almost covering joint, grayish-tan or pale

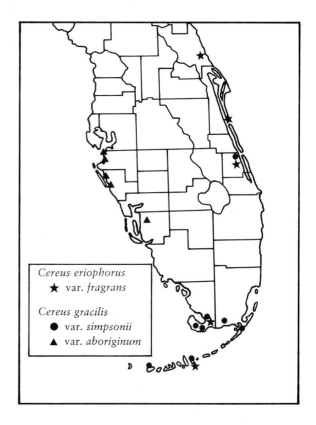

Cereus eriophorus
★ var. *fragrans*

Cereus gracilis
● var. *simpsonii*
▲ var. *aboriginum*

gray with dark tips, 7-16 per areole, spreading in all directions, straight, rigid, the longer ±2.5 cm long, basally ±0.5 mm diam, acicular, nearly circular in cross section, not markedly barbed; flower nocturnal, 10-12 cm diam, 15-20 cm long; scale-leaves on lower portion of superior floral tube 1.5-3 mm broad, swollen basally, the swelling continued on floral tube below point of attachment; hairs of areoles on tube 6-8(10) mm long, white or brown, flexible or stiff; sepaloids with purplish-brown midribs and paler to pink or white margins, the largest lanceolate-linear, to ±6 cm long, 6 mm broad, slightly acuminate, entire; petaloids white, largest oblanceolate, to 6(7.5) cm long, 15-20 mm broad, mucronate or short-acuminate, erose-dentate above the broadest area; filaments white or nearly so, ±50 mm long; anthers yellow, 3 mm long; style pale green, ±11(12.5) cm long, 1 mm greatest diam; stigmas 11+, ±9 mm long, slender; ovary in anthesis ±12 mm long; fruit orange-red or yellow, fleshy at maturity, smooth, with some persistent hairlike spines, depressed-globose, 3-4 cm long, 3-6.2 cm diam, persisting until midwinter; seeds black, the surface finely and deeply pitted, more or less oblong but slightly constricted above middle, 2 mm long, 1.5 mm broad, 1 mm thick.

Distinctive Characters of the Varieties of **Cereus gracilis**

Character	a. var. **simpsonii**	b. var. **aboriginum**	var. **gracilis** (Jamaica)
Hairs of areoles on floral tube	White, soft, mostly ± 8 mm long	Tawny brown, rather stiff, mostly ±6 mm long	White, soft, mostly ±8 mm long
Color of fruits at maturity	Orange-red	Yellow	Yellow

[All three varieties occur near sea level in dry areas on the fringes of the Caribbean Tropical Forest. They are poorly known and of doubtful status.]

4a. Cereus gracilis var. **simpsonii** (Small) L. Benson. Sandy soils of jungles and hammocks. Low elevations along the coast. Caribbean Tropical Forest. In s Florida from Cape Sable and Ft. Pierce to the Florida Keys.

4b. Cereus gracilis var. **aboriginum** (Small) L. Benson. Coastal hammocks and shell mounds at low elevations. Caribbean Tropical Forest. Gulf Coast of Florida from Tampa Bay (Manatee Co.) to Lee Co.

Cereus gracilis var. **gracilis**. Caribbean Tropical Forest. Not native in the U.S. Jamaica.

Fig. 590. *Cereus gracilis* var. *simpsonii*, in cleared land on Lower Matecumbe Key, Florida; in the background, trunkless saw-palmetto, *Serenoa repens*. (Robert K. Willich)

5. Cereus martinii Labouret

Plant clambering over vegetation or in clumps to 2 m high; stems branching freely, the larger green, cylindroid, ±2.5 cm diam; ribs 4 or 5, irregularly cordlike, the intervening grooves deep; areoles 3-4.5 mm diam, typically 15-25 mm apart; spines not dense, radials and central sharply differentiated; central spine yellowish with black tip, solitary, somewhat deflexed, straight, to 2-3.8 cm long, basally to 1.5 mm diam, acicular, nearly circular in cross section; radial spines gray or black, 1-3 per areole, spreading irregularly, straight, very short, to 3 mm long, stout, narrowly conical, acicular in cross section; flower 15-17.5 cm diam, 15-22.5 cm long; sepaloids green or pink-tinged, the largest narrowly lanceolate, 5-10 cm long, 6-9 mm broad, somewhat attenuate, entire; petaloids white to pink-tinged or rose-red, largest obovate-oblanceolate, 6-10 cm long, 25-30 mm broad, acuminate, undulate; filaments white to pale yellow, 25-30 mm long; anthers yellow, ±1.5 mm long; style green, ±5 cm long; stigmas ±8, green, ±9 mm long, rather slender; ovary in anthesis ±12 mm long; fruit red, irregularly globular, fleshy at maturity, dehiscent, with some tuberculate roughening and with small

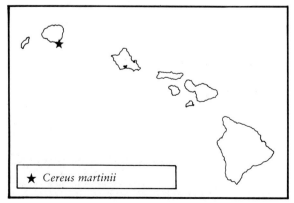

★ *Cereus martinii*

Fig. 591. *Cereus martinii*, ×.6, except as indicated. *1*, Branch (drooping downward) bearing a flower. *2*, Areole with spines and wool, ×3.3. *3*, Flower in longitudinal section. *4*, Fruit, now dehiscent, exposing the seeds embedded in pulpy material; the upper floral parts still attached. *5*, Fruit in longitudinal section. *6*, Seed, ×14.

scale-leaves, 3.8-5 cm diam, the superior floral tube and dried flower parts persistent; seeds black, conspicuous on white pulp of fruit, longer than broad, irregularly and narrowly domelike, papillate, ±2.5 mm long, nearly 2 mm broad, 1 mm thick; hilum very small.

Rich volcanic soils. Asian-Pacific Insular Forest. Native of Argentina. Introduced on Kauai, Hawaii; reported to be originally from the garden of the Moir family.

The plant is a rambling, tangled mass covering other vegetation.

6. Cereus pentagonus (Linnaeus) Haworth
Barbed-wire cactus

Suberect to sprawling plants; stems weak and commonly arching, and in jungles scrambling through other vegetation, to several meters long, 2.5-5 cm diam; larger terminal joints dark green, elongate, mostly 30-100 cm long; ribs of mature branches 3(4 or 5), strongly divergent, sharply angled; ribs of juvenile stems 4-6, low, not divergent, with slender, weak spines, the basal portions of elongating joints retaining these characters; areoles 1.5-3 mm diam, typically 25-38 mm apart; spines not obscuring surface of joint, gray,

Fig. 592. Barbed-wire cactus, *Cereus pentagonus*, originally on Lower Matecumbe Key, Florida, now growing in cultivation in Miami; the three prominent ribs of the mature stems are characteristic. (Robert K. Willich)

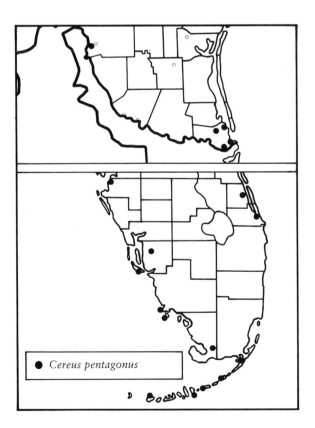

● *Cereus pentagonus*

mostly 7 or 8 per areole, 1 or 2(4) central, others radial, spreading in all directions, straight, the largest mostly 2.5-4 cm long, basally to 1.5 mm diam, acicular or somewhat flattened, elliptic in cross section; flower nocturnal, ±10 cm diam, 17.5-25 cm long; sepaloids with green midribs (or these tinged with red-purple) and lighter margins, the largest lanceolate-linear, to 9 cm long, to 10 mm broad, acuminate; petaloids white to greenish, the largest narrowly oblanceolate, ±5 cm long, to ±10 mm broad, mucronate, entire or minutely denticulate; filaments white, ±40-50 mm long; anthers yellow, ±3 mm long; style 17.5-20 cm long, 1.5 mm greatest diam; stigmas 10-15(?), ±12 mm long, slender; ovary in anthesis greenish-blue, ±25 mm long, with scale-leaves to 12 mm long; fruit bright red, shiny, fleshy at maturity, sweet, with many spines each ±12 mm long, the fruit elliptic or elongate-ellip-

Fig. 593. Barbed-wire cactus, *Cereus pentagonus*, ×.6, except as indicated. *1*, Joint with (despite the name) the characteristic three ribs. *2*, Areole with spines and wool, ×5. *3*, Flower. *4*, Flower in longitudinal section. *5*, Fruit. *6*, Fruit in longitudinal section, showing the seeds embedded in pulpy material. *7*, Seed, ×9.

Fig. 594. *Cereus pentagonus*, mature joint of the stem (left) with three ribs and large spines, universal at this stage of development; joint of juvenile plant (right) with five ribs below and three above. This transition from about five ribs to three is characteristic; the name of the species was based on the form of the juvenile plants.

tic, 3-6(10) cm long, 2.5-4(7.5) cm diam; seeds black, shiny, nearly smooth, flattened-obovoid, basally acute, 3 mm long, ±2.5 mm broad, ±1.5 mm thick; hilum not prominent.

Sandy soils of jungles and bottomlands of coastal areas at low elevations. Caribbean Tropical Forest. Texas along Rio Grande from Laredo (Webb Co.) to Gulf of Mexico; peninsular Florida from Lee and St. Lucie Cos. s and on the Keys. Thence s to N South America.

The large, three-angled stems are a striking feature, even though commonly they are obscured by the other vegetation of disturbed areas.

7. Cereus grandiflorus (Linnaeus) Miller

Plant vinelike, clambering or trailing, the stems numerous, to several m long, 1.2-2.5 cm diam; ribs 5-8; areoles ±1-2 mm diam, typically 12-20 mm apart along ribs; spines abundant or sparse, reddish-brown, tan, or sometimes yellow, slender

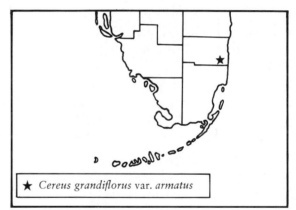

★ *Cereus grandiflorus* var. *armatus*

Distinctive Characters of the Varieties of **Cereus grandiflorus**

Character	a. var. **grandiflorus**	b. var. **armatus**
Stem ribs	Usually 7 or 8	5 or 6
Spine-bearing areoles	Each with several basal reflexed hairlike spines, those of floral tube from nearly white to tawny	Each with 1 or a few basal reflexed hairlike spines, those of floral tube white
Flowers	17.5-22.5 cm long	25-30 cm long
Floral tube above ovary	7.5-8.7 cm long	±11 cm long
Petaloids	Acute, the style longer than petaloids	Apiculate, the style much shorter than petaloids

[Both varieties occur near sea level in the Caribbean Tropical Forest region.]

but rigid, 6-18 per areole, spreading in all directions, straight, the longer 4.5-12(15) mm long, basally ±0.25 mm diam, acicular, elliptic to circular in cross section, bulbous basally; hairlike spines few, from the basal portion of the areole, reflexed; flower nocturnal, 12.5-17.5 cm diam, 17.5-22.5(30) cm long; floral tube above ovary 7.5-8.7(11) cm long, without scale-leaves, bearing many white to tawny, slender, flexible spines; sepaloids brownish to bronze, salmon, light orange, or lemon-yellow, largest linear-attenuate, 7.5-10 cm long, averaging 4.5 mm broad, attenuate, margins entire; petaloids white, largest narrowly lanceolate, 7.5-10 cm long, mostly 9-12 mm broad, acute or sometimes apiculate, entire; filaments white, 38-50 mm long; anthers yellow (?), 1.5 mm long, rectangular; style 15-20 cm long, usually longer than petaloids, 1.5 mm greatest diam; stigmas 5(?), ±7.5 mm long, slender; ovary in anthesis ±25 mm diam, covered with white or tawny, coarse, wavy, hairlike spines to 25 mm long, these transitional to shorter and slightly coarser spines; fruit chiefly white but partly pink, fleshy at maturity, with numerous brownish, flexible, slender, hairlike spines, ovoid, 5-9 cm long, 4.5-7 cm diam, the umbilicus small and inconspicuous.

Cereus grandiflorus is the source of a heart tonic.

7a. Cereus grandiflorus var. grandiflorus. Caribbean Tropical Forest. Jamaica and Cuba. Appearing in the United States only in gardens or as a probably momentary escape.

The plant is a ropelike vine, best known for its enormous night-blooming flowers. According to Rowley (Cactus & Succ. Jour. Gr. Brit. 18: 91. 1956), "During her long imprisonment in the Temple, Queen Marie Antoinette kept up her spirits by watching the daily growth of buds on a favorite night-blooming *Cereus*. When the great day arrived for the first flower to open, Redouté [the best-known illustrator of plants of the time] was summoned and painted the first flower at midnight before the assembled court and royal family.... Doubtless the plant was *Selenicereus* [*Cereus*] *grandiflorus*." Rowley refers to C. Leger, Redouté et Son Temps (Paris, 1945).

7b. Cereus grandiflorus var. armatus (K. Schumann) L. Benson. Sandy soil near the ocean at low elevations. Caribbean Tropical Forest. Introduced in Broward Co., Florida. Native on tropical E coast of Mexico.

Fig. 595. *Cereus grandiflorus* var. *grandiflorus*, pendulous branch with a flower; Huntington Botanical Gardens.

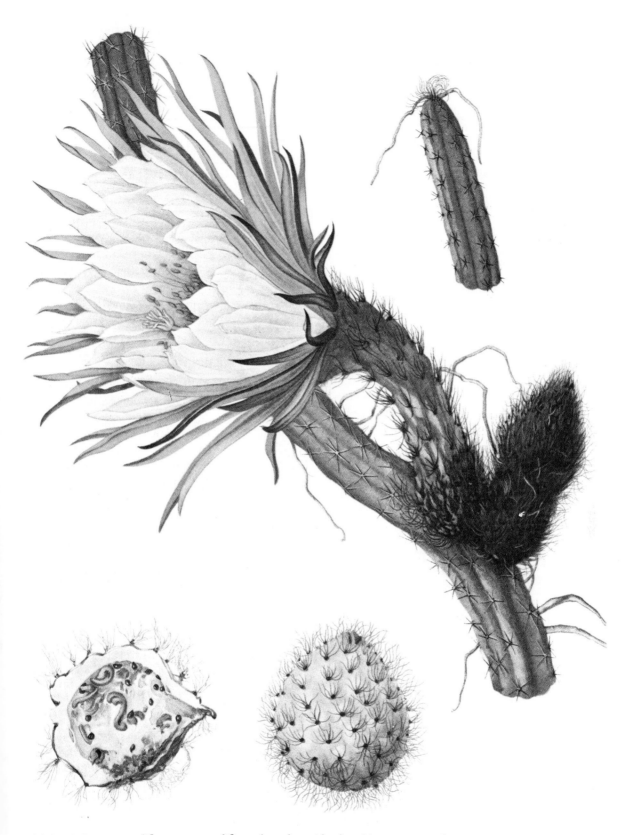

Fig. 596. *Cereus grandiflorus* var. *grandiflorus*, branches with adventitious roots, areoles bearing spines, a flower bud, and a flower; a separate fruit; a fruit in longitudinal section, the seeds germinating within the fruit, and some embryos considerably developed. (Mary E. Eaton; see Credits)

8. Cereus pteranthus Link & Otto

Plant clambering or sprawling, the stems numerous, several meters long, mostly 2.5-5 cm diam, with 4-6 angles; areoles 1.5-3 mm diam, typically 20-25 mm apart; spines short and few, inconspicuous, brownish, rigid, 1-5 per areole, spreading, straight, the largest 1-3 mm long, very short above bulbous bases, just above these ±0.25 mm diam, acicular, nearly circular in cross section; flowers nocturnal, similar to those of *C. grandiflorus*, ±20 cm diam, 25-30 cm long, fragrant; floral tube above ovary ±12.5 cm long; petaloids acuminate; style ±20 cm long, much longer than petaloids; fruit red, spheroidal, to 4.5 cm diam, covered densely with yellowish spines to 1 cm long and with darker, flexible, hairlike spines; seeds black, cuneate-obovate, rather elongate, 2.25 mm long, 1.3 mm broad, ±1 mm thick; hilum oblique.

Sand dunes and stabilized sandy areas at low elevations near the coast. Caribbean Tropical

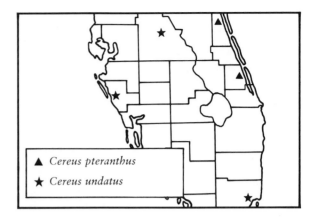

Forest. Native of Mexico known mostly from cultivation. Introduced in Florida from Brevard Co. to St. Lucie Co.

The snakelike stems sprawl through and over other vegetation or form great masses.

9. Cereus spinulosus DeCandolle

Plant vinelike, trailing or clambering, the stems numerous, to 4-5 m long, 1-2 cm diam; ribs 4-6, acute; areoles 1.5-2 mm diam, 15-25 mm apart along the ribs; spines brown, 7 or 8, 1 central and 6 or 7 radial, to 1 mm long, basally 0.25 mm diam above the swollen bases, apically attenuate-conical, circular in cross section, the bulbous bases 0.5 mm diam; hairlike spines none; flower nocturnal, 7-8.5 cm diam, 10-12.5 cm long; floral tube above ovary ±5 cm long, without scale-leaves, with 7-12 brownish spines 4-5 mm long,

Fig. 597. *Cereus pteranthus*, branches with adventitious roots, a flower, and a flower bud. (George Nicholson; see Credits)

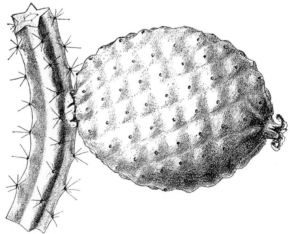

Fig. 598. *Cereus pteranthus*, branch with spines and a fruit. (T. Gürke; see Credits)

these not flexible or hairlike; long hairs none; sepaloids brownish-green, 5-6 cm long, 3-4 mm broad, attenuate, the margins entire; petaloids white, ±6 cm long, 5-7 mm broad, apically somewhat attenuate, entire; filaments white, ±30 mm long; anthers yellow, 2.5-3 mm long, 1 mm broad, elongate-rectangular; style ±8 cm long, exceeding the petaloids, 1 mm diam; stigmas 10(?), 6-7 mm long, slender; ovary in anthesis ±10 mm diam, not bearing hairs in areoles; fruits and seeds not available.

Caribbean Tropical Forest. Texas, probably near the mouth of the Rio Grande. Tropical E coast of Mexico.

The single collection from Texas (*Rose* in 1909, *NY*) bears no data except the state.

Fig. 599. *Cereus spinulosus*, branch bearing spines, an adventitious root, and a fully opened flower. (The stem with the smaller flower is of *Weberocereus panamensis*, a species not occurring in the United States.) (Mary E. Eaton; see Credits)

10. Cereus undatus Haworth
Night-blooming cereus

Creeping, sprawling, or clambering plant, the stems several meters long, the larger 4-7.5 cm overall diam, winged, the wings usually 3, ±25 mm broad, crenately lobed but the lobes directed upward, callus-margined; areoles ±2 mm diam, typically 38-50 mm apart; spines few, inconspicuous, gray-brown, 1-3 per areole, spreading in various directions, straight, the longest to ±3 cm long, basally 1 mm diam, more or less acicular, nearly circular in cross section; flower 15-25 cm diam, 25-27 cm long; sepaloids with greenish midribs and mostly white margins, the largest lanceolate-linear to linear, 10-15 cm long, 10-15 mm broad, mucronate, tending to be reflexed, entire; petaloids white, largest narrowly oblanceolate, to 15 cm long, to ±2.5 cm broad, mucronate, entire; filaments cream-colored, 50-75 mm long; anthers 4.5 mm long; style cream-colored, 17.5-20 cm long, 6 mm greatest diam; stigmas to 24, 2-2.3 mm long, slender; ovary in anthesis ±25 mm long, clothed with scale-leaves to 40 mm long; fruit red, fleshy at maturity, with scale-leaves to 25 mm long, oblong, 5-12.5 cm long, ±4-9 cm diam, the umbilicus small; seeds black, narrowly pyriform, 2 mm long, 1 mm broad, 0.8 mm thick; hilum very small.

Sandy soils of hammocks at low elevations. Caribbean Tropical Forest. Native in the American Tropics, naturally widely distributed. Introduced at numerous points, among them s Florida, including reportedly the Keys, and abundant near the Deering Estate, Miami (R. K. Willich).

This species is cultivated for its numerous nocturnal flowers. It forms the well-known hedge of the Punahou School in Honolulu, reported (Cutak, 1945) to have as many as 5,000 open flowers on a single night. The hedge, more than a century old, is about 2 m (6-7 ft) high and 0.8 km (0.5 mi.) long.

See map for *C. pteranthus* (above).

Fig. 601 (*above*). *Cereus undatus*, stems and flower buds; Huntington Botanical Gardens.

Fig. 600 (*left*). Night-blooming cereus, *Cereus undatus*, in the jungle near the Deering Estate, Miami, Florida. (Robert K. Willich)

Fig. 604. *Cereus undatus*, the deeply three-angled branches bearing a flower and a fruit. (Mary E. Eaton; see Credits)

Fig. 603. *Cereus undatus*, the world-famous hedge of night-blooming cereus at the Punahou School, Honolulu, Hawaii. (Courtesy of Punahou School)

Fig. 602. *Cereus undatus*, photographed in the early morning. (Courtesy of Punahou School)

571

11. Cereus robinii (Lemaire) L. Benson

Large, erect shrub or small tree, 3-10 m high; branches cylindroid, 5-10 cm diam; trunk none or 0.3-1 m long; ribs 9-13, 10-12 mm high; spines dense, at first yellowish, becoming gray or tinged with pink, mostly 10-20 per areole, spreading in all directions, straight, the longer 1-1.5(2.5) cm long, basally ±0.25 mm diam, acicular, nearly circular in cross section; flower 2.5-5 cm diam, 5-6 cm long, opening in afternoon, at first usually with an onion or garlic odor; sepaloids light green with green to brownish-green or brownish-purple midribs, largest cuneate, 1.2-2.5 cm long, ±7.5 mm broad, rounded, obtuse, or acute, entire or minutely denticulate, tending to be mucronate-acuminate; petaloids white, the largest spathulate or nearly oblong, 1.2-2.5 cm long, 7.5 mm broad, tending to be acuminate, entire; filaments ±6-12 mm long; anthers oblong, 1.25-1.5 mm long; style ±3 cm long, 1-1.5 mm greatest diam; stigmas ±5, 3 mm long, rather broad; ovary in anthesis ±9 mm long; fruit red, fleshy at maturity, almost naked but with a few scales, nearly globose, 2-4.5 cm long; seeds black, irregularly cuneate-obovate in outline, 2 mm long, 1.25 mm broad, ±0.7 mm thick; hilum conspicuous, appearing to be on one edge of the acute end of the seed.

11a. Cereus robinii var. robinii.

Sandy soils of brushy areas just above high-tide level. Caribbean Tropical Forest. Florida on Big Pine Key, Umbrella Key, and Key West, Florida Keys, Monroe Co. Cuba near Havana and Matanzas.

The little groves of giant, canelike stems, bearing Spanish moss, are a striking feature of the limited areas in which the plants occur. Preservation of the southeastern part of Big Pine Key has been recommended to both the State of Florida and the National Park Service. These plants, *Opuntia cubensis*, *O. triacantha*, and *O. spinosissima*, should all be protected there.

11b. Cereus robinii var. deeringii (Small) L. Benson.

Sandy soils of jungle areas just above high-tide level. Caribbean Tropical Forest. Florida on Upper and Lower Matecumbe Keys, Florida Keys, Monroe Co.

The status of the variety needs further investigation in the field. However, housing developments have exterminated many populations on the Matecumbe Keys, and there may be no plants left to study.

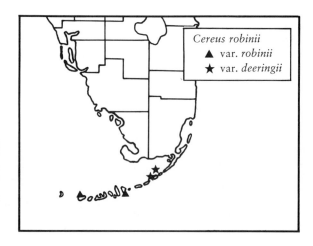

Cereus robinii
▲ var. *robinii*
★ var. *deeringii*

Distinctive Characters of the Varieties of **Cereus robinii**

Character	a. var. **robinii**	b. var. **deeringii**
Stem branching	Profuse	Limited
Stem ribs	10-13	9-10
Color of young stems	Blue-green	Gray-green
Spines per areole	10-20	±16-20
Color of sepaloids	Brownish-green	Light green
Apices of sepaloids	Angled (lower) to rounded (upper)	Rounded or nearly truncate
Style	Exserted	Included
[Both varieties occur near sea level in the Caribbean Tropical Forest region.]		

Fig. 607. *Cereus robinii* var. *robinii*, the stem with ribs and spine-bearing areoles.

Fig. 605 (*above*). *Cereus robinii* var. *robinii*, in dense second-growth jungle on Big Pine Key, Florida. (Randy Willich)

Fig. 606 (*right*). *Cereus robinii* var. *robinii*, jungle, Caribbean Tropical Forest, on Big Pine Key, Florida. Spanish moss, *Tillandsia usneoides*, is epiphytic on the lower parts of some stems. (Randy Willich)

Fig. 608. *Cereus robinii* var. *deeringii*, stem with a flower; fruit (dehiscent and showing seeds); and a seed. (Mary E. Eaton; see Credits)

12. Cereus thurberi Engelmann
Organ pipe cactus, pitahaya

Large arborescent cactus; plant as a whole commonly 3-7 m high, 2-6 m diam; branches numerous, columnar, in the plants of the U.S. arising from ground level and reminiscent of organ pipes; trunk none or (in Mexico) sometimes present and short; larger terminal joints green, cylindroid, usually (unless the plant has been killed back by frost) 3-7 m long, 10-15(20) cm diam; ribs 12-19, 9-12 mm high; areoles ±6 mm diam, typically 6-12 mm apart; spines rather dense on the stem, dirty-gray, black, or brownish, 11-19 per areole, spreading all directions, straight, the longer 1.2-2.5 cm long, basally to 0.5 mm diam, acicular, nearly circular in cross section; flower nocturnal, opening a little before dark, often remaining open through part of the next morning, ±5 cm diam, 6-7.5 cm long; floral tube imbricated with conspicuous scale-leaves; sepaloids with reddish midribs and lighter margins, largest narrowly obovate, to 2 cm long, ±6 mm broad, apically rounded to slightly angular; petaloids lavender, margins white, largest oblanceolate, 2-2.5 cm long, 9-12 mm broad, spreading, the tips recurved, acute, entire; filaments white, ±20 mm long; anthers yellowish, 1.5 mm long; style ±4 cm long, 1.2 mm greatest diam; stigmas 5-10(?), 3 mm long, yellowish; ovary in anthesis ±15 mm diam, densely covered with short scales and spines; fruit red, fleshy at maturity, edible, with dense but deciduous spine cover, spheroidal, 3-7.5 cm diam, the umbilicus not prominent, maturing during late summer or fall; seeds black, irregularly obovoid, 2-2.5 mm long, 1.5-2 mm broad, 1 mm thick; hilum somewhat on the diagonal.

Rocky or sandy soils of hills, mesas, and valleys in the desert at 300-1,050 m (1,000-3,500 ft). Arizona Desert and (in Mexico) the other Sonoran Deserts. Arizona in Pinal and Pima Cos. w from the Growler Mts. sw of Ajo to (according to Nichol) the Picacho and Roskruge Mts. Mexico in Baja California and w Sonora.

The majestic groups of columns dominate the rocky desert hillsides and in some places combine with saguaros and large chollas, forming cactus forests.

A large plant about 4.5 m high and with 22 stems was reported (Anonymous, 1938) north of Red Rock, Pinal County. The report, based on a newspaper account, was confirmed by Whitehead (1939).

Pollination under experimental conditions has been effected by honeybees and by bats, but natural nocturnal pollinators have not been studied (Alcorn, McGregor, & Olin, 1962).

The form of the plant is determined partly by local climate, and in Arizona the plants branch more than in the warmer climate of Sonora. The more severe winter frosts of Arizona seldom kill the entire plant but often freeze the tender terminal buds; new shoots may then arise from near ground level, or a lateral bud near the top of each stem may replace the terminal bud, causing an offset in the branch. Once a stem tip is killed, its elongation ceases; but the stem may continue to live for an indefinite time, and it may increase remarkably in girth (see Wiggins, 1937).

Felger and Lowe (1967) have shown the surface-to-volume ratio of the stem to be correlated with geographical distribution of the large columnar cacti. The organ pipe cacti with the thickest stems, and thus with the lowest ratio of surface to volume, occur farther northward in northern Sonora and northern Baja California and in southern Arizona. Those with more slender stems occur farther southward near the Gulf of California and along the Mexican coast, where the rainfall is somewhat higher and water loss is reduced. Thus gradients in ratio of surface to volume parallel gradients in annual (and especially summer) precipitation.

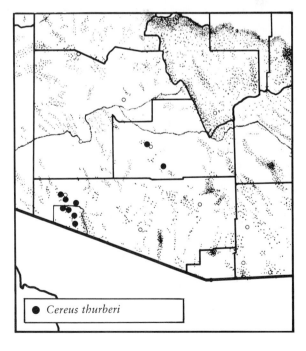

● *Cereus thurberi*

Text continued on p. 583

Fig. 609. Organ pipe cactus or pitahaya, *Cereus thurberi*, large plants in the Arizona Desert; Organ Pipe Cactus National Monument, Pima Co., Arizona. At lower left and right are staghorn chollas, *Opuntia acanthocarpa* var. *major*; the low bushes are mostly a bur sage, *Ambrosia deltoidea*; at left margin, a foothill palo verde, *Cercidium microphyllum*, and in the middle ground, ocotillos, *Fouquieria splendens*.

Fig. 610 (*below*). *Cereus thurberi*, about 7 m (22 feet) high; a fallen skeleton at the right. (Note the nearly complete, only perforated, cylinder of wood; there are no elongate ribs like those of the saguaro.) The tall shrub is a foothill palo verde, *Cercidium microphyllum*; the low shrubs in the foreground are brittle bush, *Encelia farinosa*.

Fig. 611. *Cereus thurberi*, plant about 10 or 12 m (33 to 38 feet) tall; Sonora, Mexico, where commonly the species does not sprawl basally and may even have a short trunk. (Homer L. Shantz; from *The Cacti of Arizona*, eds. 1 and 2; see also Credits)

Fig. 612. *Cereus thurberi*, with numerous flower buds just before blooming. At the left is an ocotillo, *Fouquieria splendens*. (Frank P. McWhorter)

Fig. 614. *Cereus thurberi*, young fruit, the leaves gone and the spines enlarging. (Homer L. Shantz; from *The Cacti of Arizona*, eds. 1 and 2; see also Credits)

Fig. 613. *Cereus thurberi*, stem-apex with flower buds and fruits and with the young spine-bearing areoles on the stem ribs near the growing point. (Homer L. Shantz; from *The Cacti of Arizona*, eds. 1 and 2; see also Credits)

Fig. 615. *Cereus thurberi*, stem-apex with open flowers and maturing fruits, one fruit almost mature and covered densely with spines. (Robert H. Peebles)

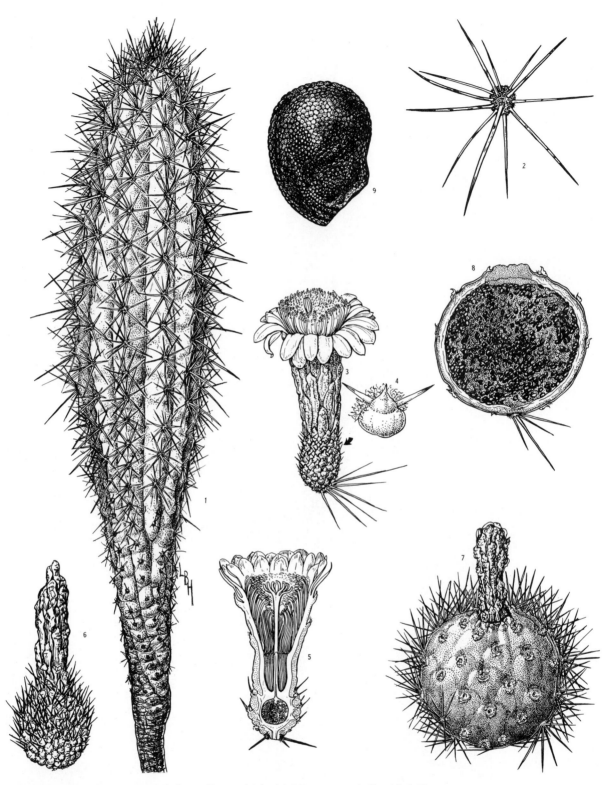

Fig. 616. Organ pipe cactus or pitahaya, *Cereus thurberi*, ×.8, except as indicated. *1*, Young plant, ×.5. *2*, Areole with spines and wool, from a young plant, ×1.1. *3*, Flower, showing the large scale-leaves on the superior floral tube and the smaller scale-leaves and spines on the inferior floral tube covering and adnate with the ovary. *4*, Young areole with a scale-leaf, spines, and wool from the point in *3* indicated by the arrow. *5*, Flower in longitudinal section. *6*, Young fruit, the spines on the floral tube covering the ovary now larger and more numerous. *7*, Mature fruit, the spine clusters falling away. *8*, Fruit in longitudinal section. *9*, Seed, ×17.

Fig. 617. Extrusion of seeds of *Cereus emoryi*: upper left, spiny fruit with the remains of the upper parts of the flower at the apex; upper right, beginning of extrusion of seeds beneath the remains of upper portion of flower; lower left, seeds extruded like toothpaste in a stream of mucilage; lower right, seeds in dried mucilage. (Reid Moran; see Credits)

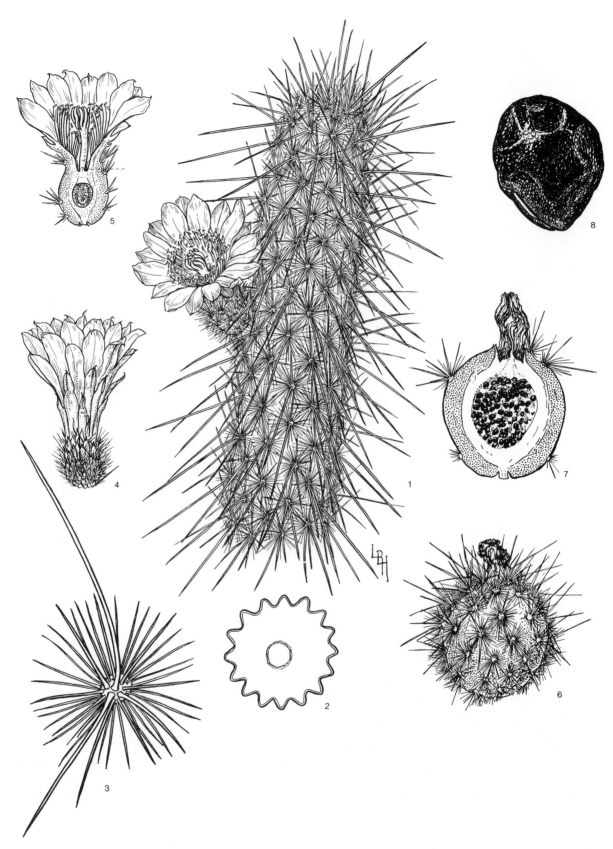

Fig. 618. *Cereus emoryi*, ×.9, except as indicated. *1*, Joint bearing a flower. *2*, Outline of cross section of a joint, showing (outside to inside) the epidermis, cortex, stele (woody part), and pith. *3*, Areole with spines. *4*, Flower; note the scale-leaves. *5*, Flower in longitudinal section; nectar gland indicated by dotted line. *6*, Fruit, the remains of the upper portion of the flower dry but remaining attached to the fruit. *7*, Fruit in longitudinal section. *8*, Seed, ×12.

13. Cereus emoryi Engelmann

Sprawling plant with ascending to erect branches, forming colonies 30-60 cm high and up to many meters diam; larger terminal joints green, cylindroid, 30-60 cm long, ±3.8-5 cm diam; ribs ±12-16, inconspicuous, ±3 mm high; areoles ±3 mm diam, typically 6-7.5 mm apart; spines very dense, obscuring joint, clear yellow, ±20-30 per areole, the centrals 1-3, the largest one tending to be deflexed, the other centrals and the radials spreading in all directions, straight or the principal central curving a little, the longer to 5 cm long, basally 0.4 mm diam, acicular, nearly circular in cross section; flower 2.8-4 cm diam, 3.8-4.4 cm long; sepaloids with greenish midribs and yellow margins, largest oblanceolate, mostly 1.2-2 cm long, to ±4.5 mm broad, acute and slightly mucronate, irregularly serrulate; petaloids yellow, largest obovate-oblanceolate, ±2-2.5 cm long, to ±7.5 mm broad, mucronulate, irregularly serrulate; filaments yellow, ±9 mm long; anthers yellow, elliptic-oblong, ±1 mm long; style yellowish, ±1.2 cm long, 1.5 mm greatest diam; stigmas 10, ±4.5 mm long, rather

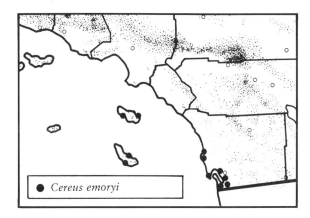

broad; ovary in anthesis nearly globose, ±12 mm diam; fruit drying at maturity, densely spiny, globose, 2.5-3 cm diam, the umbilicus not prominent, deciduous; seeds black, shiny, finely reticulate, flattened-obovoid, 3 mm long, 2 mm broad, 1.5 mm thick; hilum oblique.

Sandy soils of open hillsides along the coast at 30-60 m (100-200 ft). Baja Californian phase of California Chaparral. Southern California on Santa Catalina and San Clemente Islands and on coastal hills in San Diego Co. from San Clemente and Oceanside (Frick; plants perhaps exterminated) and from Del Mar s. In NW Baja California as far s as lat. 29° 48′ N.

The great yellow thickets of ascending densely spiny stems are conspicuous on hillsides near the ocean.

Reference: Moran, 1966.

14. Cereus schottii Engelmann
Senita

Shrub with (in Sonora) sometimes several hundred elongated ascending branches, 3-7 m high, 2-5 m diam; trunk none; larger terminal joints green, 2+ m long, ±11-13 cm diam; ribs (5)6 or 7(9), evident, ±25 mm high; areoles ±6 mm diam, on upper part of stem typically ±6 mm apart, on lower part 20-25 mm apart; spines of upper stem gray and suggesting gray human hair or with a pinkish tinge, ±30(50) per areole, tending to be deflexed, bristle-like, twisted, to 7.5 cm long, strongly flattened, striate; spines of lower stem gray, ±8-10 per areole, straight, 1 central and 7-9 radial, short and bulbous-based, the longer ±1.2 cm long, stout, ±1.5 mm diam just above bulbous bases, circular to angular in cross section; flowers 1 to several per areole, nocturnal, with an unpleasant odor, 2.5-3.8 cm diam, ±2.5-3.8 cm long; sepaloids with pinkish-green midribs

Fig. 619. *Cereus emoryi*, stems bearing the spiny fruits. (Edward F. Anderson)

and pink margins, largest more or less lanceolate, to 2.5 cm long, 4.5 mm broad, mucronate; petaloids pink, largest oblanceolate, to 2.5 cm long, 6 mm broad, mucronate, sparsely denticulate; filaments ±20 mm long; anthers yellow, 1 mm long; style ±2 cm long, 0.75 mm greatest diam; stigmas probably 10, 3 mm long, slender; ovary in anthesis ±7.5-9 mm diam, with a few short scale-leaves subtending short-woolly areoles; fruit red, fleshy at maturity, with a few scales, nearly globular to ovoid, ±2.5-3 cm long, 2-2.5 cm diam, the umbilicus not prominent, ripening in fall, bursting irregularly; seeds black, finely reticulate, nearly smooth, semicircular-obovoid, 2.5-3 mm long, 1.5 mm broad, 1 mm thick; hilum extending across the truncate base.

Heavy or sandy soils of valleys and plains in the desert at 450 m (1,500 ft) or less. Sonoran Deserts. Southern edge of Arizona mostly at extreme s margin of Organ Pipe Cactus National Monument, Pima Co. Mexico in Baja California and Sonora.

The largest plants are those in dense colonies on grassland plains in Sonora. These may develop several hundred branches. A. A. Nichol counted 134 branches on one plant in Abra Val-

ley, southeast of Ajo, Arizona; but most of the plants in the United States are relatively small, and they are struggling for survival in the unfavorable conditions at the northern limit of their range. In 1939, Nichol estimated that only 50 plants remained in the United States, and that not more than 100 had been present at the time of the Boundary Survey in the early 1850's. An old clump may include several separate plants, but most or all of these are clones developed vegetatively from a single individual.

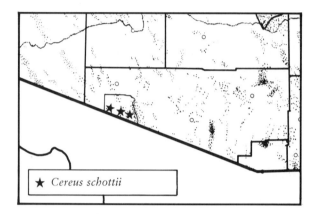

★ *Cereus schottii*

Fig. 620. Senita, *Cereus schottii*, in the Arizona Desert, the stems strongly ribbed. The lower parts of the stems bear short spines; the upper parts bear elongate spines that form a shaggy, hairlike covering. (Robert H. Peebles)

Fig. 621. *Cereus schottii*, upper portion of the stem with flowers and flower buds, the spines slender, deflexed, flattened, and twisted, the spine bases not bulbous (compare the spines produced while the stem is younger, Fig. 623: *1, 3*; these remain on its lower portions in age). (Robert H. Peebles; see Credits)

Fig. 622. *Cereus schottii*, flower buds and a flower, these developed clearly within the spine-bearing areole, several in one areole in this species. (Homer L. Shantz; from *The Cacti of Arizona*, eds. 1 and 2; see also Credits)

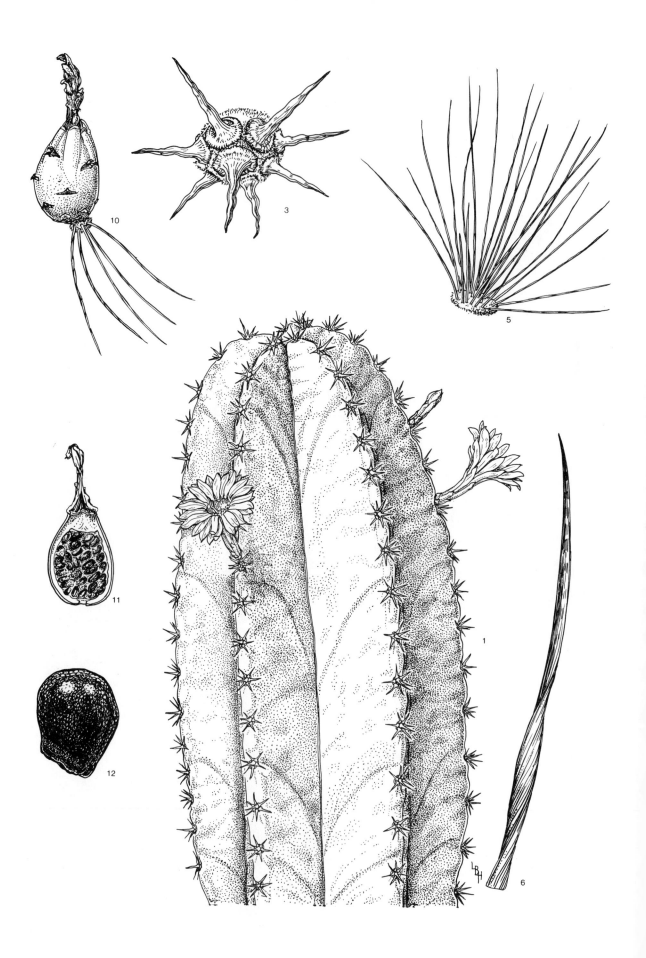

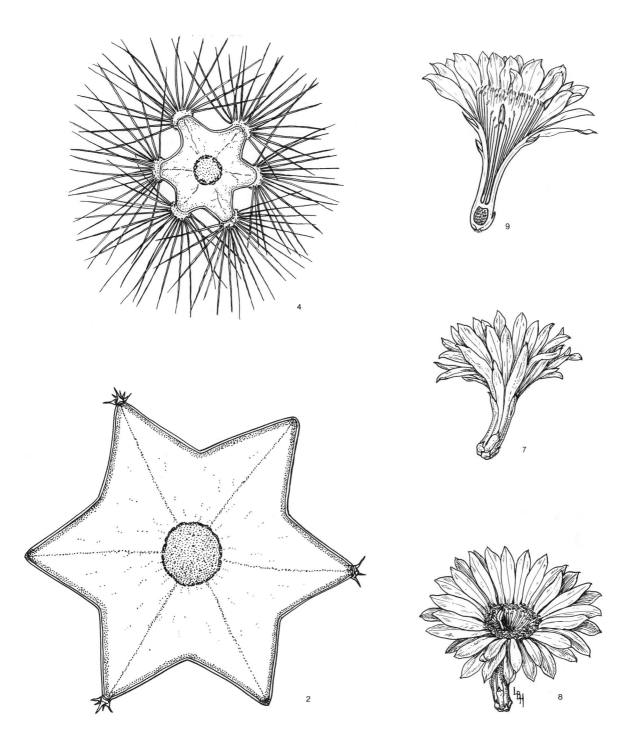

Fig. 623 (*facing page and above*). Senita, *Cereus schottii*, ×.9, except as indicated. *1*, Apex of a young stem with a flower bud and flowers. *2*, Cross section of such a stem with areoles on the ribs and with (outside to inside) epidermis, cortex, stele (thin woody part) and pith. *3*, Areole from such a stem, with short, stout, terete, bulbous-based, spreading spines and with wool, ×3.5. *4*, Upper part of an older stem in cross section (see Figs. 620 and 624), with the areoles on the ribs and with the tissues listed in 2. *5*, Areole from the upper part of an older stem, with long, slender, flattened, twisted, nonbulbous spines, these deflexed. *6*, Spine of *5*, ×4.5. *7, 8*, Flowers. *9*, Flower in longitudinal section. *10*, Fruit, in the spine-bearing areole. *11*, Fruit in longitudinal section. *12*, Seed, ×11.

Fig. 624. *Cereus schottii*, stems, the middle one with flower buds, flowers, and fruits, one fruit dehiscent. The righthand stem is in transition from earlier production of short, stout, bulbous-based spines to later formation of the longer, slender, nonbulbous spines that crown the older stems; the stem bears a few flower buds. (Robert H. Peebles)

15. Cereus greggii Engelmann
Desert night-blooming cereus

Slender, exceedingly inconspicuous plants with the appearance of dead sticks or branches of the creosote bush (*Larrea tridentata*); root very large and turniplike; stems erect or sprawling, 0.3-0.6 (2.4) m long, to 12 mm diam, the lower parts slender, only ±6 mm diam; trunk none; stems not branched or with 2-5+ branches, strongly ribbed above, minutely and densely canescent; ribs 4-6; areoles elongate-elliptic or nearly circular, 1.5-4.5 mm long, typically 4.5-6 mm apart; spines abundant but small, ±11-13 per areole, ±6-8 upper ones only 0.8 mm long, dark, ±3-5 lower ones approximately 3 mm long, 2-4 of these white, the other(s) dark, mostly parallel to stem, straight, basally bulbous, acicular, nearly circular in cross section, pubescent; flower nocturnal, 5-7.5 cm diam, 15-21 cm long; floral tube 10-15 cm long, with minute spines but no scale-leaves;

sepaloids with red but greenish-tinged midribs and whitish margins, largest lanceolate-linear, to 5 cm long, 6 mm broad, attenuate or acuminate, entire or minutely ciliolulate; petaloids white, largest narrowly oblanceolate, 25-75 cm long, 12 mm broad, mucronate, entire; filaments cream, ±25 mm long; anthers yellow, ±1.5-2.5 mm long; style white, 10-15 cm long, 3 mm greatest diam; stigmas ±10, 10-15 mm long, slender; ovary in anthesis ±25 mm long; fruit at first bright red, later relatively dull, ripening during late summer, at maturity fleshy, with areoles bearing short spines, the fruit ellipsoid, 5-7.5 cm long, 2.5-3.8 cm diam, the umbilicus not depressed; seeds black, obovoid, 3 mm long, 2.25 mm broad, 1.5 mm thick; hilum on the truncate seed-base.

The lower part of the stem is slender, brittle, and readily broken, and the surrounding woody vegetation usually provides protection from the movement of animals. Often the plants occur under creosote bushes with similarly colored stems, and one may pass by many plants without seeing them. Most stems are under a meter long, but a record length of 3.6 m (11 ft 10 in) was reached in a cultivated plant owned by Mrs. William H. Kitt (*US*, photograph).

The root of the desert night-blooming cereus is large and tuberous. A sample of 27 roots weighed in the 1930's by Nichol at the University of Arizona ranged from 0.7-20 kg (1.5-43 lbs) apiece. Both Indians and Mexicans occasionally slice the tubers and fry them in deep fat. Nichol reported the flavor to be turniplike but relatively mild. Slices bound on the chest are a supposed cure for congestions.

Flowering tends to be concentrated into one or sometimes two nights during late June (rarely, as early as late May), when nearly all the mature plants bloom. This night is a long-anticipated annual event. A few flowers may appear earlier or later, and, according to Nichol, under unusual conditions a few may bloom on nights scattered over almost a month. Opening occurs just after dark, when the petaloids and other floral structures open in a series of jerks. The odor is sweet, and a single flower can be detected from 30 m (100 ft). Unless the weather is unusually cool, flowering is over by about 7 A.M. Most plants produce only a few flowers each season, but as many as 44 on a single plant have been recorded.

Distinctive Characters of the Varieties of **Cereus greggii**

Character	a. var. **greggii**	b. var. **transmontanus**
Areoles	Elongate-elliptic, to ±4.5 mm long	± circular, ±1.5 mm diam
Flowers	5 cm diam, ±15 cm long	To 7.5 cm diam, to 21 cm long
Bristles of floral tube	In basal areoles 2-4 mm long, in upper areoles 8-12 mm long	In basal areoles ±9 mm long, in upper areoles 15-31 mm long
Petaloids	Lanceolate, to 2.5 cm long	Narrowly lanceolate, to 7.5 cm long
Altitude	1,200-1,500 m (4,000-5,000 ft)	300-1,050 m (1,000-3,450 ft)
Floristic association	Chihuahuan Desert	Arizona Desert

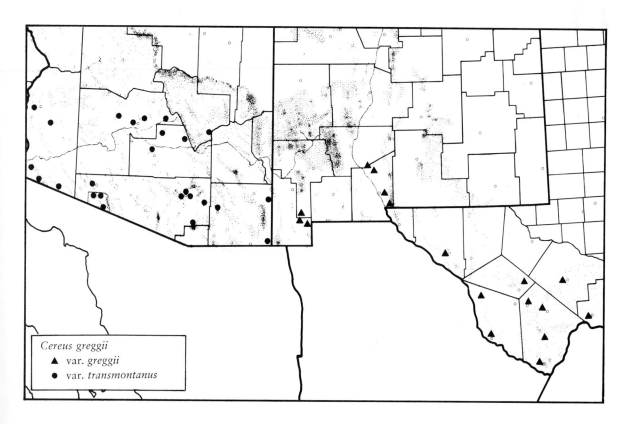

Cereus greggii
▲ var. *greggii*
● var. *transmontanus*

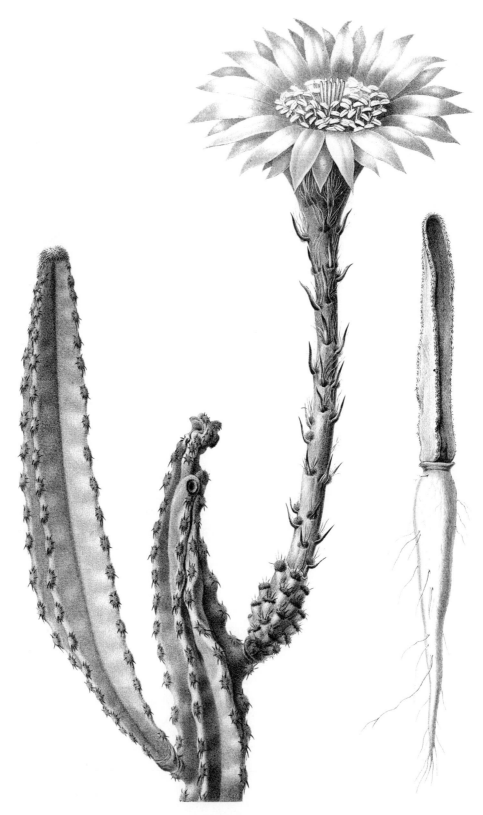

Fig. 625. Desert night-blooming cereus, *Cereus greggii* var. *greggii*, the type of New Mexico and Texas: branches and a flower; stem and tuberous root of a 3-year-old seedling. (Paulus Roetter in Engelmann/Emory, *pl. 63*)

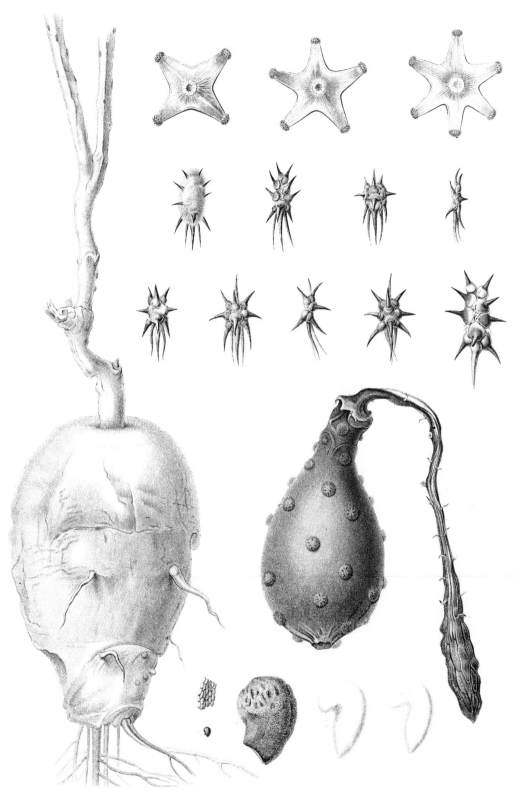

Fig. 626. *Cereus greggii* var. *greggii*: left, lower portion of the stem and the large, tuberous root, ×.5; upper row, cross sections of stems with 4–6 ribs, ×4; middle row, areoles with spines in various stages of development, the areole at the left with very young spines embedded in wool, ×4; lower row, older areoles with larger spines, ×4; fruit, with the upper floral tube and the other flower parts dried but still attached; lowest row, seeds, natural size and one much enlarged, and embryos. (Paulus Roetter in Engelmann/Emory, *pl. 64*)

15a. Cereus greggii var. **greggii.** Flats and washes in the desert at about 1,200-1,500 m (4,000-5,000 ft). Chihuahuan Desert. Arizona on E edge of Cochise Co.; s New Mexico from Hidalgo Co. to Sierra and Dona Ana Cos.; Texas from probably El Paso Co. and definitely Hudspeth Co. to Pecos, Brewster, and Terrell Cos. Mexico in Chihuahua and Zacatecas.

15b. Cereus greggii var. **transmontanus** Engelmann. Growing under trees or among the branches of bushes or shrubs in the desert mostly in flats and washes at 300-1,050 m (1,000-3,450 ft). Arizona Desert. Arizona below the Mogollon Rim from Yuma Co. E to s Gila and w Cochise Cos. Mexico in adjacent Sonora.

Fig. 628. *Cereus greggii* var. *transmontanus*, flower from above. (Homer L. Shantz; from *The Cacti of Arizona*, eds. 1 and 2; see also Credits)

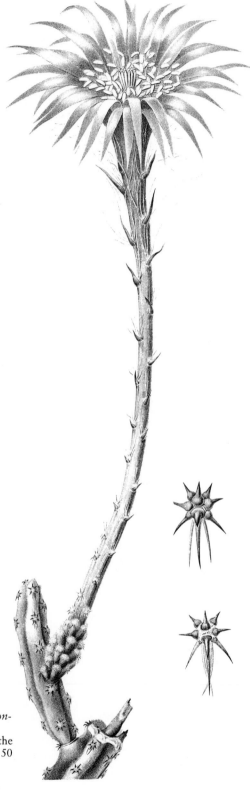

Fig. 627. Desert night-blooming cereus, *Cereus greggii* var. *transmontanus*, flower for comparison with that of var. *greggii*, Fig. 626; the spines of two areoles. The scale is not given for the illustrations of the flowers of vars. *greggii* and *transmontanus*, but the latter are about 50 percent longer and their petaloids are up to three times as long. (Paulus Roetter in Engelmann/Emory, *pl. 65*)

Fig. 630. Desert night-blooming cereus, *Cereus greggii* var. *transmontanus*, in flower (deserts of Arizona and Sonora). In a given area, nearly all flowers open early in the evening during a single night, usually in the month of June. (Homer L. Shantz; from *The Cacti of Arizona*, eds. 1 and 2; see also Credits)

Fig. 629. *Cereus greggii* var. *transmontanus*. (Homer L. Shantz; from *The Cacti of Arizona*, eds. 1 and 2; see also Credits)

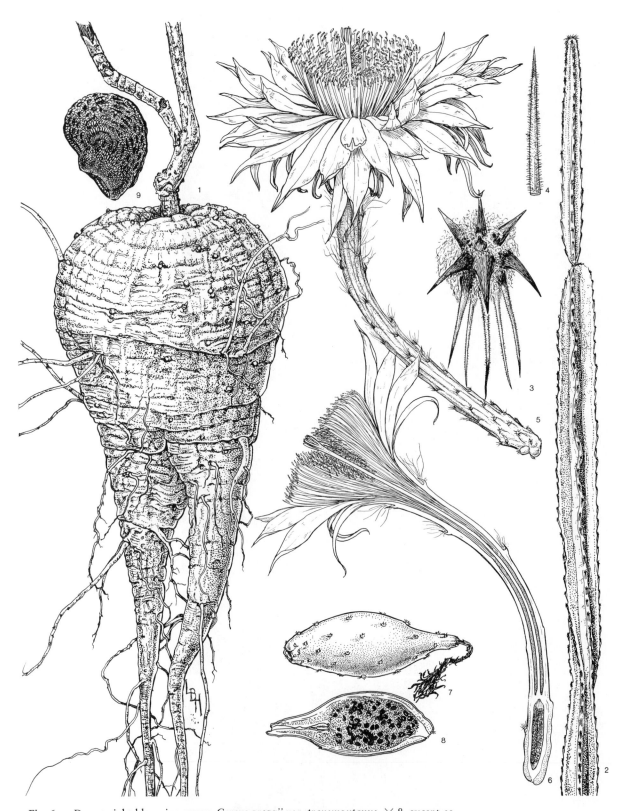

Fig. 631. Desert night-blooming cereus, *Cereus greggii* var. *transmontanus*, ×.8, except as indicated. *1*, The tuberous root and the slender cylindroid base of the stem, natural size. *2*, Strongly ribbed upper portion of the stem, ×.6. *3*, Areole with spines and wool, ×11. *4*, Tip of a spine from lower side of areole, the spine pubescent, ×22. *5*, Flower. *6*, Flower in longitudinal section. *7*, Fruit (red). *8*, Fruit in longitudinal section. *9*, Seed, ×10.

16. Cereus poselgeri Lemaire
Sacasil

Erect or suberect plant with cluster of tuberous roots, each 50-75 mm long and ±25 mm diam (also, at least sometimes propagating by filiform rhizomes); stems 30-60 cm high, 6-9 mm diam, diam gradually increasing above slender bases, with 5-8 branches above; larger terminal joints green, slender and cylindroid, 15+ cm long, 6-9 mm diam; ribs 8-10, low, conspicuous only because of the rows of areoles; areoles 1-1.5 mm diam, typically 3-4.5 mm apart; spines densely covering joint, tan or the centrals brown, appressed; central spines turned upward, straight, ±6-9 mm long, 0.2-0.3 mm diam; radial spines 12-16 per areole, appressed, 3-4.5 mm long, basally ±0.1 mm diam, subulate, elliptic in cross section; flower diurnal, opening more than 1 day, 3.8-4.5 cm diam, 4.5-5 cm long; floral tube above ovary only 9-12 mm long, the lower part without stamens, 3-6 mm long, its areoles bearing bristle-like spines and dense white wool; sepaloids pink or purple, largest lanceolate, to ±25 mm long, 6 mm broad, mucronate, entire or slightly denticulate; petaloids pink to purple, largest broadly oblanceolate, 25 mm long, to ±12 mm broad, mucronate, slightly denticulate; filaments pale green, 6-9 mm long; anthers yellow,

Fig. 632. Sacasil, *Cereus poselgeri,* branches with a flower bud and a fruit. (Photograph May 1899, perhaps by C. H. Thompson; courtesy of Missouri Botanical Garden)

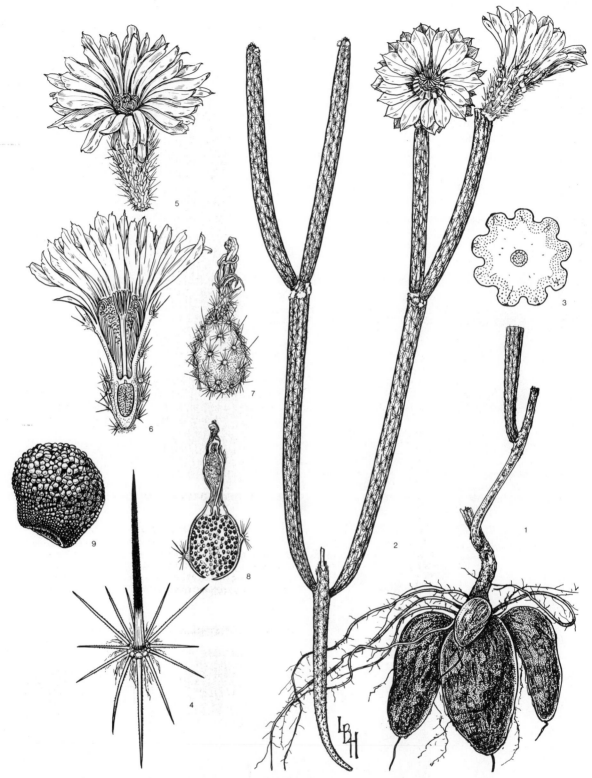

Fig. 633. Sacasil, *Cereus poselgeri*, ×.9, except as indicated. *1*, The cluster of tuberous roots and the base of the stem (the base more slender than the part above, as is true in many species of *Cereus*), ×.6. *2*, Stem with flowers, ×.6. *3*, Stem in cross section, showing the ribs and grooves, the cortex, the small stele (woody part), and the enclosed pith, ×4.5. *4*, Areole with spines and long woolly hairs. *5*, Flower. *6*, Flower in longitudinal section. *7*, Fruit. *8*, Fruit in longitudinal section. *9*, Seed, ×27.

596

61 (*left*). *Rhipsalis baccifera*, native habitat at Cape Sable, Florida; the forest here was destroyed by a hurricane, and this plant, growing on a fallen log, was the only known *Rhipsalis* survivor in 1965.

62 (*above*). Standing skeleton of a saguaro, *Cereus giganteus*.

63 (*left*). Saguaro or giant cactus, *C. giganteus*, Arizona Desert, in the Santa Catalina Mts., Pima Co., Arizona; the larger shrubs are creosote bushes, *Larrea tridentata*; the smaller, bur sage, *Ambrosia [Franseria] deltoidea*; at the right are a jumping cholla, *Opuntia fulgida*, and a teddy bear cholla, *O. bigelovii* var. *bigelovii*; the white flowers at the left are prickly poppy, *Argemone*.

64 (*below*). *C. giganteus*, flower buds and flowers. (E. H. Hamilton)

65 & 66. *Cereus giganteus*. 65 (*left*): stem apex with fruit.
66 (*above*): dehiscent fruits; the red, fleshy interiors, when seen
from the ground, are often mistaken for the petals of flowers.

67 (*below*). *C. eriophorus* var. *fragrans*, Cape Sable, Florida.

68. Barbed-wire cactus, *C. pentagonus*.

70 (*above*). *C. robinii* var. *robinii*, Big Pine Key, Florida, the spines becoming gray with age.

69 (*above*). *Cereus robinii* var. *robinii*, Big Pine Key, Florida; the woolly, gray-green epiphytes are Spanish moss, *Tillandsia usneoides*.

71 & 72. Organ pipe cactus or pitahaya, *C. thurberi*.
71 (*middle right*): stem apex with flower buds and flower.
72 (*below right*): in Arizona Desert, in the Organ Pipe Cactus National Monument; the low shrubs in the foreground are bur sage, *Ambrosia [Franseria] deltoidea*; the yellow-flowered shrubs are brittlebush, *Encelia farinosa*.
(71, J. W. Thompson; 72, R. A. Darrow)

73. Colony of *Cereus emoryi*, southwestern San Diego Co., California; at the lower left is a barrel cactus, *Ferocactus viridescens*; the patch of red protuberances in the left foreground is introduced *Mesembryanthemum*. (E. F. Anderson)

74 & 75. *C. emoryi.* 74 (*middle left*): in flower. 75 (*below left*): the exceedingly spiny fruits. (74, R. Moran; from *The Native Cacti of California*)

76. Senita, *C. schottii*, Arizona Desert.

77. Desert night-blooming cereus, *Cereus greggii* var. *transmontanus*, with 31 open flowers. (R. A. Darrow; from *The Cacti of Arizona*)

78. Sacasil, *C. poselgeri*. (S. Farwig)

79. *C. schottii*, in flower. (R. Moran)

80. *C. schottii*, in fruit. (R. Moran)

83 & 84 (*above*). *E. triglochidiatus* var. *melanacanthus*; the fruits are red at maturity, and the spines are deciduous (*lower picture*), leaving a ripe, edible fruit. (C. R. Trapp)

81 & 82 (*left*). Red-flowered hedgehog cactus, *Echinocereus triglochidiatus* var. *melanacanthus*. 81 (*top left*): Chisos Mts., Big Bend National Park, Brewster Co., Texas. 82 (*middle left*): the flower pigments are not betacyanins and are insoluble in water; in pressed flowers the color remains with little change. (81, from *The Cacti of Arizona*)

85. *E. triglochidiatus* var. *mojavensis*, Ivanpah Mts., San Bernardino Co., California; the curving spines are distinctive. (J. A. Noble)

86 (*above*). *Echinocereus triglochidiatus* var. *gurneyi*; the flower bud (center) has just burst through the epidermis. (R. H. Wauer)

88 (*below*). A hedgehog cactus, *E. pentalophus*, the petaloids markedly bicolored. (J. A. Noble)

87 (*above*). *E. triglochidiatus* var. *arizonicus*; the emergence of buds through the epidermis just above spine-bearing areoles, as shown here and in Fig. 86, is characteristic of the genus. (From *The Cacti of Arizona*)

89 (*below*). *E. pentalophus*, western Texas. (R. A. Darrow)

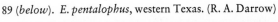

91 (*above*). *E. fasciculatus* var. *boyce-thompsonii*, the spines long and flexuous. (J. A. Noble)

93 (*below*). *E. fasciculatus* var. *fasciculatus*.

90 (*above*). *Echinocereus fendleri* var. *rectispinus*, in cultivation in the Colorado Desert, California; the white flowers in the foreground are *Chaenactis fremontii*. (J. A. Noble)

92 (*below*). *E. fasciculatus* var. *fasciculatus*.

94 & 95 (*below & right*). *Echinocereus fasciculatus* var. *bonkerae*. (94, from *The Cacti of Arizona*; 95, J. A. Noble)

96 & 97 (*left and below*). A hedgehog cactus, *E. ledingii*. 96: in flower. 97: in the Graham (Pinaleno) Mts., Graham Co., Arizona, in Southwestern Oak Woodland; two species of oak in the background, Mexican blue oak (*Quercus oblongifolia*) and bellota (*Q. emoryi*).

99 (*above*). *E. engelmannii* var. *engelmannii*. (J. A. Noble)

98 (*above*). A hedgehog cactus, *Echinocereus engel-mannii* var. *acicularis*, Yuma Co., Arizona; in the back-ground, a creosote bush, *Larrea tridentata*. (J. A. Noble)

101 (*right*). *E. engelmannii* var. *chrysocentrus*, Ivanpah Mts., Mojave Desert, San Bernardino Co., California, in the shade of a mojave yucca, *Yucca schidigera*. (J. A. Noble)

100 (*below*). *E. engelmannii* var. *armatus*. (From *The Native Cacti of California*)

102. *Echinocereus engelmannii* var. *nicholii*, at the type locality, Silverbell Mts., Pima Co., Arizona.

103 (*below*). A hedgehog cactus, *Echinocereus engelmannii* var. *nicholii*. (J. A. Noble)

104 (*below*). *E. enneacanthus* var. *stramineus*, Big Bend National Park, Brewster Co., Texas. (R. Wauer)

105. *E. enneacanthus* var. *enneacanthus*, Big Bend National Park, Brewster Co., Texas; the leaves of two seasons of honey mesquite, *Prosopis juliflora* var. *glandulosa*, are at the right. (R. Wauer)

106 (*above*). A rainbow cactus, *Echinocereus pectinatus* var. *wenigeri*, Big Bend National Park, Brewster Co., Texas, showing the distinctive spine coloration. (R. Wauer)

107 (*right*). Arizona rainbow cactus, *E. pectinatus* var. *rigidissimus*. (J. A. Noble)

108 & 109 (*below left & right*). *E. pectinatus* var. *neomexicanus*. (109, R. Wauer)

110 & 111 (*above left & right*). *Echinocereus reichenbachii* var. *reichenbachii*. (110, S. Farwig)

112 (*right*). *E. reichenbachii* var. *perbellus*.

114 (*below*). *Echinocereus reichenbachii* var. *albertii*; the type plant, near Alice, Texas.

113. *E. reichenbachii* var. *chisosensis*.

115. Peyote, *Lophophora williamsii*, near the Rio Grande in Starr Co., Texas.

116. *Lophophora williamsii*. (D. & M. Zimmerman)

117 (*left*). A barrel cactus, *Ferocactus acanthodes* var. *lecontei*, Maricopa Co., Arizona; a tall and characteristically slender plant, among young chollas growing from fallen branches of the teddy bear cholla, *Opuntia bigelovii* var. *bigelovii*; the tall shrub is a foothill palo verde, *Cercidium microphyllum*. (From *The Native Cacti of California*)

118. *Ferocactus acanthodes* var. *acanthodes*. (J. A. Noble)

119. A barrel cactus, *Ferocactus acanthodes* var. *eastwoodiae*, on a cliff in the mountains southwest of Globe, Gila Co., Arizona; at the upper right is an ocotillo, *Fouquieria splendens* (the wandlike branches); the shrubs are foothill palo verde, *Cercidium microphyllum*. (From *The Cacti of Arizona*)

120. *F. acanthodes* var. *lecontei*, showing the red central spines and the less conspicuous, flexuous radial spines. (From *The Native Cacti of California*)

121. *F. acanthodes* var. *eastwoodiae*, showing the characteristic yellow spines, the radials stouter than in other varieties and nearly straight.

122 (*above*). *Ferocactus wislizenii*, showing the large, hooked, principal central spine and the slender, whitish, irregularly curving radial spines. (J. A. Noble)

124 (*middle right*). *F. hamatacanthus*. (R. Wauer)

123 (*below left*). *F. covillei*, Ajo, Pima Co., Arizona, showing the single downward-curving central spine and the six to eight equally stout radial spines.

125 (*below right*). *F. setispinus*.

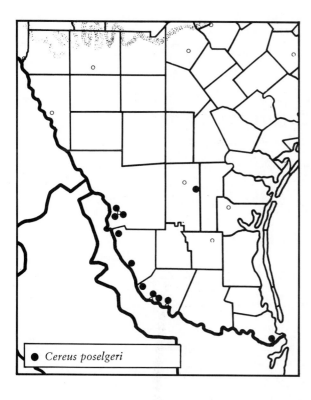

● *Cereus poselgeri*

elongate and slender; ribs 6-9, relatively broad, the intervening grooves narrow; areoles ±1 mm diam, typically 6-15 mm apart; spines appressed, numerous but very small, in each areole 5-10 white ones 1.5 mm long, a few white ones with black tips, 1.5-2 mm long and spreading radially, 2 white ones 3 mm long and pointing downward, all spines straight, basally perhaps 0.1 mm diam, acicular, elliptic in cross section; flower nocturnal or diurnal, 5.5-7.5 cm diam, ±7.5-15 cm long; superior floral tube 2.5+ cm long; sepaloids with greenish-purple midribs and pink to purple margins, the larger narowly lanceolate, to 2.5 cm long, ±2-3 mm broad; petaloids white to pink or purple, largest oblanceolate to lanceolate, to 4.5 cm long, ±8 mm broad, mucronate; filaments white to pink or purple, to 75 mm long; anthers light yellow, ±1.5 mm long; style yellowish-white, ±6 cm long, 1 mm greatest diam; stigmas ±9, 3 mm long, pale yellow; ovary in anthesis about 12 mm long, broadly ellipsoid; fruit maturing during August, scarlet at maturity, fleshy, the pulp red, the surface somewhat spiny,

ovoid, 0.5 mm long; style pale green, 1.2-2.5 cm long, less than 1 mm greatest diam; stigmas 7 or 8, green, 3-4.5 mm long, slender; ovary in anthesis ±20 mm long, densely covered with areoles bearing slender brown spines to 12-20 mm long and with white wool; fruit maturing during summer, fleshy at maturity, still covered with wool and spines, ellipsoid, ±2 cm long, ±1 cm diam, the umbilicus not prominent; seeds black, between obovoid and square, 1 mm long, slightly less broad, ±0.75 mm thick; hilum extending across the truncate seed-base.

Sandy soils of valleys and hills in semidesert brushlands at low elevations. Rio Grande Plain. Texas mostly near Rio Grande from Webb Co. to Duval and Cameron Cos. Mexico in Coahuila, N Nuevo León, and N Tamaulipas.

The plant is difficult to find among the shrubs, except when its large, starlike, pink to purple flowers are blooming. The stems alone blend with those of the neighboring bushes.

17. Cereus striatus Brandegee

Inconspicuous suberect plant; roots in clusters, each terminating in a tuber reportedly sometimes 30-40 cm long, with slender erect or suberect stems 30-70 cm high; stems ±6 mm diam, gradually enlarged upward from very slender bases, branching above; larger terminal joints green,

Fig. 634. *Cereus striatus*, older plant with the characteristic cluster of tuberous roots reminiscent of sweet potatoes. (Robert H. Peebles)

Fig. 636. *Cereus striatu*s entwined in a creosote bush, *Larrea tridentata*, at the right, from which it was disentangled during photography, then returned to its original position. In its usual habit, the plant is barely discernible among the branches of the creosote bush or another shrub.

Fig. 635. *Cereus striatus*, branches of the plant in Fig. 636.

598

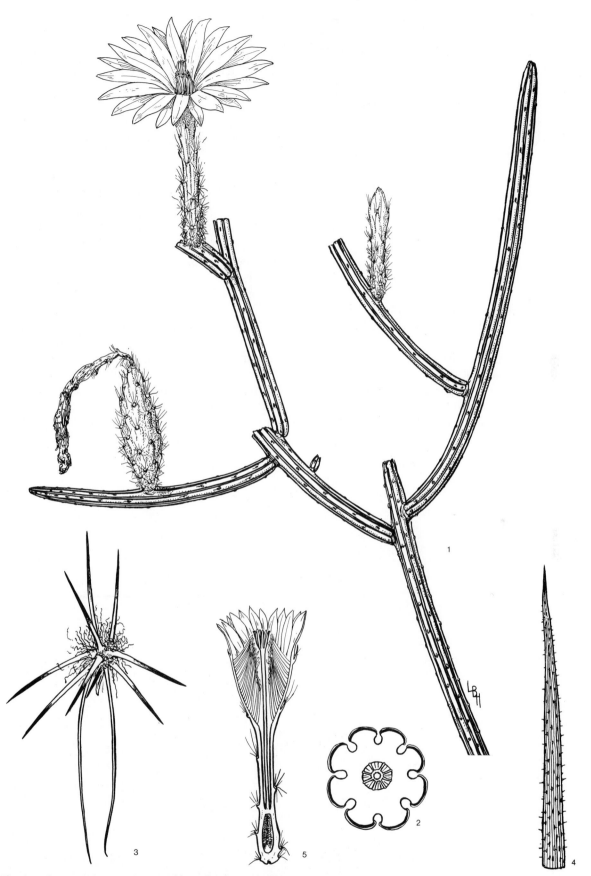

Fig. 637. *Cereus striatus. 1*, Stem and branches bearing a flower and a fruit, ×.9. *2*, Stem in cross section, showing the brown ridges and green grooves, the cortex, the stele (woody center), and the enclosed pith, ×.6. *3*, Areole with spines and long, woolly hairs, ×7. *4*, Spine tip, ×30. *5*, Flower in longitudinal section, ×.9.

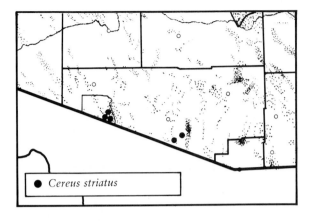

● *Cereus striatus*

the spines deciduous, pyriform, the fruit ±4 cm long, 2.5 cm diam, the umbilicus not prominent, the floral tube persistent; seeds black, shiny, tuberculate, 1 mm long, 0.8 mm broad, 0.5 mm thick.

Beneath trees and shrubs in bottoms and on hills at 60-450 m (200-1,500 ft) elevation. Border zone between the Arizona Desert and the Colorado Desert. Arizona in Yuma and Pima Cos. near the Mexican boundary from the Tule Desert (according to Nichol) to Quijotoa Valley, mostly on the Papago Indian Reservation. The vegetative plant is inconspicuous, and it may occur through a much greater area in Arizona than the few collections indicate. It is distributed widely in Baja California and Sonora, Mexico.

The plant is slender and vinelike, and it depends upon shrubs like the creosote bush for support. It is even more inconspicuous than *C. greggii*, the desert night-blooming cereus.

The yamlike, tuberous roots are light tan. There may be as many as two or three dozen of these roots, but they rarely appear in herbarium specimens because they are overlooked when the plant is collected.

Commonly the seeds are described as "shining," but a recent collection (*Annetta Carter, 4905, UC*) indicates that this feature varies, at least in herbarium specimens, according to the amount of fruit juice dried upon the seed coat.

As with *C. greggii*, nearly all the seeds are eaten by birds. Similarly, the distribution of the species is determined partly by the roosting places of the birds in shrubs or in small trees like the mesquites.

6. Echinocereus

Stems 1-500, branching profusely near ground, the larger usually cylindroid, 5-60 cm long, 2.5-7.5 (10) cm diam; ribs 5-13; tubercles coalescent with the ribs beneath them, contributing half to usually nearly all the height of projection from the stem. Leaves not discernible in mature plant. Areoles circular to linear, diam various. Spines smooth and white, gray, tan, brown, yellow, pink, red, or black; central spines straight or curving, 1-100 mm long, basally 0.25-1.5 mm diam, acicular or subulate, narrowly to broadly elliptic in cross section; radial spines 3-32, straight or curving, 3-30 mm long, basally 0.25-1 mm diam, acicular. Flower buds, flowers, and fruits on old growth of preceding years and therefore mostly well below apex of stem or branch, the bud bursting through the epidermis just above the spine-bearing areole, the area of emergence forming a persistent, irregular scar. Flower 2-12.5 cm diam; floral tube above ovary funnelform to obconic, green or tinged with the perianth color. Fruit fleshy at maturity, bearing spines, the areoles ultimately deciduous, the fruit globular to ellipsoid, 6-50 mm long, 6-40 mm diam, with the floral tube persistent, not regularly dehiscent. Seeds black, obovoid or domelike, reticulate or papillate, usually longer than broad (hilum to opposite side), mostly 1-1.5 mm long; hilum obviously basal, large; embryo nearly straight; cotyledons minute, incumbent, not foliaceous.

About 20-30 species occurring from California to South Dakota (Black Hills) and Oklahoma and southward to the vicinity of Mexico City; 13 species in the U.S.

The extraterritorial species of *Echinocereus* have not been evaluated carefully in the list that follows; the relationships of some are not clear, and the genus is in need of further study.

1. *E. triglochidiatus*
   vars. a. *melanacanthus*
       b. *mojavensis*

   c. *neomexicanus*
   d. *gurneyi*
   e. *paucispinus*
   f. *arizonicus*
   g. *gonacanthus*
   h. *triglochidiatus*
       pacificus (Baja California)
   E. acifer (Durango & Coahuila; status uncertain)
   E. leeanus (area and status undetermined)
   E. salmianus (Chihuahua & Durango)
   E. scheeri (Chihuahua)
   E. huitcholensis (Jalisco)
   E. gentryi (Sonora)
   E. delaetii (Coahuila)
   E. pensilis (Baja California)
2. *E. berlandieri*
   vars. a. *berlandieri*
       b. *papillosus*
       c. *angusticeps*
3. *E. pentalophus*
   var. *ehrenbergii* (central Mexico; not evaluated)
   E. brandegeei (Baja California)
   E. chlorophthalmus (Hidalgo)
   E. subinermis (w Mexico)
   E. knippelianus (Mexico, but locality unknown)
   E. pulchellus
   vars. *pulchellus* (Hidalgo)
       amoenus (San Luis Potosí)
   E. weinbergii (Mexico?; status unknown)
   E. ferreirianus (Baja California)
   E. maritimus (Baja California)
   E. merkerii (Coahuila to Durango & San Luis Potosí)
   E. sarissophorus (Coahuila)
   E. barthelowanus (Baja California)
   E. longisetus (Coahuila)
4. *E. fendleri*
   vars. a. *fendleri*
       b. *rectispinus*
       c. *kuenzleri*

5. *E. fasciculatus*
   vars. a. *fasciculatus*
       b. *boyce-thompsonii*
       c. *bonkerae*
6. *E. ledingii*
7. *E. engelmannii*
   vars. a. *engelmannii*
       b. *acicularis*
       c. *armatus*
       d. *munzii*
       e. *chrysocentrus*
       f. *variegatus*
       g. *purpureus*
       h. *nicholii*
       i. *howei*
8. *E. enneacanthus*
   vars. a. *enneacanthus*
       b. *brevispinus*
       c. *stramineus*
       d. *dubius*
           conglomeratus (Nuevo León)
   E. cinerascens (central Mexico)
9. *E. lloydii*
10. *E. pectinatus*
   vars. a. *rigidissimus*
       b. *pectinatus*
       c. *wenigeri*

       d. *minor*
       e. *neomexicanus*
E. grandis (islands in Gulf of California;
   status uncertain, but near *E. pectinatus*)
E. sciurus (Baja California, status uncertain,
   but near *E. pectinatus*)
E. websterianus (Baja California; status
   uncertain, but near *E. pectinatus*)
E. stoloniferus (Sonora; status uncertain)
E. adustus (Chihuahua)
E. palmeri (Chihuahua; status uncertain)
11. *E. reichenbachii*
   vars. a. *reichenbachii*
       b. *perbellus*
       c. *albertii*
       d. *fitchii*
       e. *chisosensis*
       f. *albispinus*
12. *E. viridiflorus*
   vars. a. *viridiflorus*
       b. *davisii*
       c. *correllii*
       d. *cylindricus*
13. *E. chloranthus*
   vars. a. *chloranthus*
       b. *neocapillus*
E. tayopensis (Sonora)

KEY TO THE SPECIES OF ECHINOCEREUS

1. Petaloids red or red-and-yellow (with no admixture of blue; probably with plastid pigments, these not water-soluble); areoles of the mature parts of stems bearing white felt or cobwebby hairs; flower *not* closing at night, remaining open 2-3 days until the end of flowering...**1. E. triglochidiatus**
1. Petaloids *either* lavender to purple (probably pigmented with betacyanins, these in solution in the cell sap) *or* yellow (but at least the sepaloids yellow with a lavender tinge), green, brownish, or reddish (but then with an admixture of blue); areoles of the mature *vegetative* parts of stems *not* bearing white felt or cobwebby hairs, the felt of young areoles persistent 1(2) years; flower closing at night, reopening the next morning (in hot weather sometimes withering at the end of a single day).
   2. Flower 4-12.5 cm in diameter and length.
       3. Stem ribs 4-6 (rarely 8 and bearing prominent tubercles on the ribs); stem joints creeping but the terminal ones ascending, slender and elongate, 2-3 cm in diameter, the spines not obscuring the joints, gray to brown or nearly black.
           4. Petaloids narrowly oblong to linear-lanceolate, apically acute and mucronate, usually (6)9-12 mm broad; stem joints 5-15(17.5) cm long, 2-2.5(3) cm in diameter, with 5-6 ribs; central spine usually 20-25 mm long, slender, basally 0.5 mm in diameter; radial spines shorter than central, 6-12 mm long, very slender, 0.25 mm in diameter; papillae on the seed coat large..............
           ....**2. E. berlandieri**
           4. Petaloids broadly oblanceolate to cuneate, apically rounded or truncate, the distal margins often erose, 9-15 mm broad; stem joints 5-10 cm long, 1.2-1.6 cm in diameter, with 4-5 ribs; longer central spines (if any) ±10(20) mm long, basally 0.75 mm in diameter, absent from many to nearly all areoles; radial spines about as long as most centrals, relatively stout, 0.5 mm in diameter; papillae on the seed coat small.......................**3. E. pentalophus**

3. Stem ribs 9-22 (rarely 7-8 in varieties of *E. enneacanthus*); stem joints, *if* at maturity less than 5 cm in diameter, *then* either (1) with joint length only 1-3 times diameter *or* (2) not decumbent *or* (3) with at least some straw-colored spines *or* (4) with the spines tending to obscure the joints.

  4A. Areoles practically circular; spacing and density of spines variable; branching variable.

    5. Central spine(s) usually dissimilar and the lower one dominant (the rare exceptions occurring w of the Continental Divide; in these cases *either* (1) very rarely central spines none *or* (2) 1-4 and the principal or only one much longer than the radials *or* (3) 2-4 and the principal one flattened *or* (4) 1-3 or sometimes 4 and about as long as the longer radials [E central Arizona]); areoles 12-20 mm apart; spines *usually not* obscuring the stem; stems (except in young plants) often branching from the bases; Utah to Colorado, Arizona, and Texas.

      6. Principal central spine *not* flattened, basally nearly circular to broadly elliptic in cross section, solitary or with 1(2-3) short upper accessory centrals (rarely, in E central Arizona, only 6-7.5 cm long and thus about equal to the other centrals and to the longer radials; very rarely, in s central New Mexico, central spines none), turned downward or curving either up or down.

        7. Spines *not* yellow or straw-colored; principal central spine straight or curving gently *upward*, tapering very gradually from base to apex, the base 0.25-0.5 mm in diameter; stems ovoid to cylindroid, 7.5-30(47.5) cm long.

          8. Central spine 1, *either* gray and brown-tipped or black-tipped *or* at first very dark brown or nearly black, becoming gray in age, *either* curving slightly upward *or* straight; radial spines 5-9 per areole, relatively short, 9-12 mm long, the lowest one longest, 0.75-1 mm in diameter; stem solitary or with 1-5 branches, flabby, usually ovoid to cylindroid-ovoid, 7.5-17(25) cm long; SE Utah to s Colorado, E Arizona, and westernmost Texas.................**4. E. fendleri**

          8. Central spines nearly always 2-4, of various colors, the principal one and the 1-2(3) short accessory centrals above it straight; radial spines 11-13 per areole, slender, the longest 12-20 mm long, slender, to 0.5 mm in diameter; stem at maturity with (3)5-20 branches, firm, cylindroid, elongate, 16-30(45) cm long; E Arizona s of Mogollon Rim. ....**5. E. fasciculatus**

        7. Spines yellow or straw-colored; principal central spine curved strongly *downward* at the broad base, tapering rapidly from base to apex, the base ±1.25 mm in diameter; stems elongate-cylindroid, 25-50 cm long. ....**6. E. ledingii**

      6. Principal central spine basally flattened, narrowly elliptic in cross section, deflexed, the 4 central spines all well developed but not equal.

        7A. Radial spines mostly ±0.8-1.2 cm long; flower usually 5-7.5 cm in diameter and length; petaloids acuminate; spines *either* (1) strongly differentiated into centrals and radials and the centrals of more than 1 type *or* (2) (rarely, in California mountains) mostly curved and twisted; w of Continental Divide from California to Utah, Arizona, and Sonora ....**7. E. engelmannii**

        7A. Radial spines (at least longer ones) 20-30 mm long; flower (5)7.5-12.5 cm in diameter and length; petaloids apically rounded; spines not strongly differentiated into centrals and radials, straight; E of Rio Grande in s New Mexico and Texas; Mexico E of Continental Divide (Sierra Madre Occidentál)....................**8. E. enneacanthus**

    5. Central spines all similar and no one dominant, 2-5, acicular, the longest central shorter than the longest radial; areoles ±6-10 mm apart; spines obscuring the stem; stems usually unbranched; Pecos R. Valley in SE New Mexico and adjacent Texas....................................**9. E. lloydii**

  4A. Areoles vertically elongate, elliptic to linear, close-set, 2-6 mm apart; spines often obscuring the ribs of the stem; stems usually unbranched or with few branches.

    5A. Spines of the entire floral tube stout and rigid, the hairs of the areoles short; flower 6.2-12.5 cm in diameter; petaloids apically rounded; stigmas ±3 mm long, stout; fruit 2-6 cm long; seeds 1.2-1.3 mm long......**10. E. pectinatus**

5A. Spines of the entire floral tube slender and somewhat flexible, the hairs of the areoles long and cobwebby; flower 5-7.5 cm in diameter; petaloids acuminate; stigmas ±6 mm long, broad; fruit ±1.5 cm long; seeds 1.5 mm long...**11. E. reichenbachii**
2. Flower 2-2.5 cm in diameter and length.
   3A. Areole vertically elongate or elliptic, with 1-2 series of spines; central spines none or 1(2-4) per areole, 0.5-0.7 mm in basal diameter; petaloids 3-4 mm broad....
   ....**12. E. viridiflorus**
   3A. Areole circular, with 3 series of spines (arbitrarily, the innermost series central and the 2 outer series radial); central spines 5-6, 0.3-0.4 mm in basal diameter; petaloids 2-3 mm broad................................**13. E. chloranthus**

1. Echinocereus triglochidiatus Engelmann
Red-flowered hedgehog cactus

Plants of most varieties branching several to many times from base, frequently forming dense mounds to 30 cm high and 30-120 cm diam; larger terminal joints green or bluish-green, cylindroid to ovoid-cylindroid, 5-30(40) cm long, 2.5-15 cm diam; ribs 5-10(12), slightly tuberculate; areoles nearly circular, 3-4.5 mm diam, typically 6-12 mm apart; spines from sparse to dense on joint, usually gray but sometimes pinkish, straw-colored, pale gray, or black, (2 or 3) 8-12(16) per areole, variable among varieties; flower 2.5-5(6.4) cm diam, (2.5)3-7 cm long; sepaloids with greenish midribs and red margins, largest narrowly elliptic, 1.5-2.5 cm long, 6-9 mm broad, rounded apically, mucronulate, margins entire; petaloids red (with no admixture of blue), largest broadly cuneate or cuneate-obovate, 2-2.5 cm long, 6-12 mm broad, apically rounded but outer

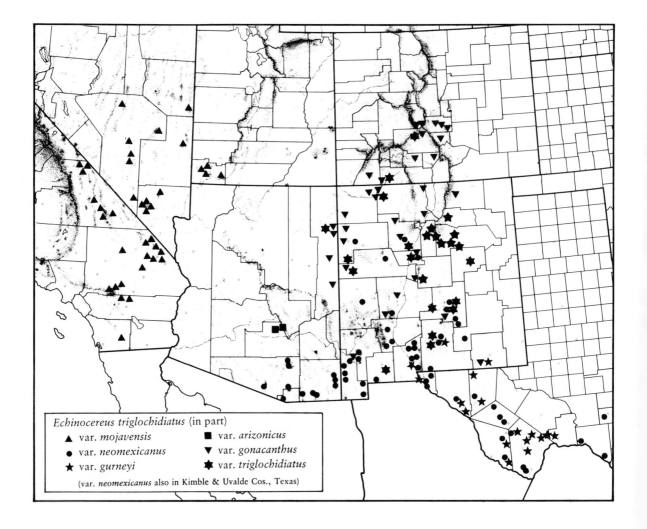

Echinocereus triglochidiatus (in part)
▲ var. *mojavensis*   ■ var. *arizonicus*
● var. *neomexicanus*   ▼ var. *gonacanthus*
★ var. *gurneyi*   ✶ var. *triglochidiatus*
(var. *neomexicanus* also in Kimble & Uvalde Cos., Texas)

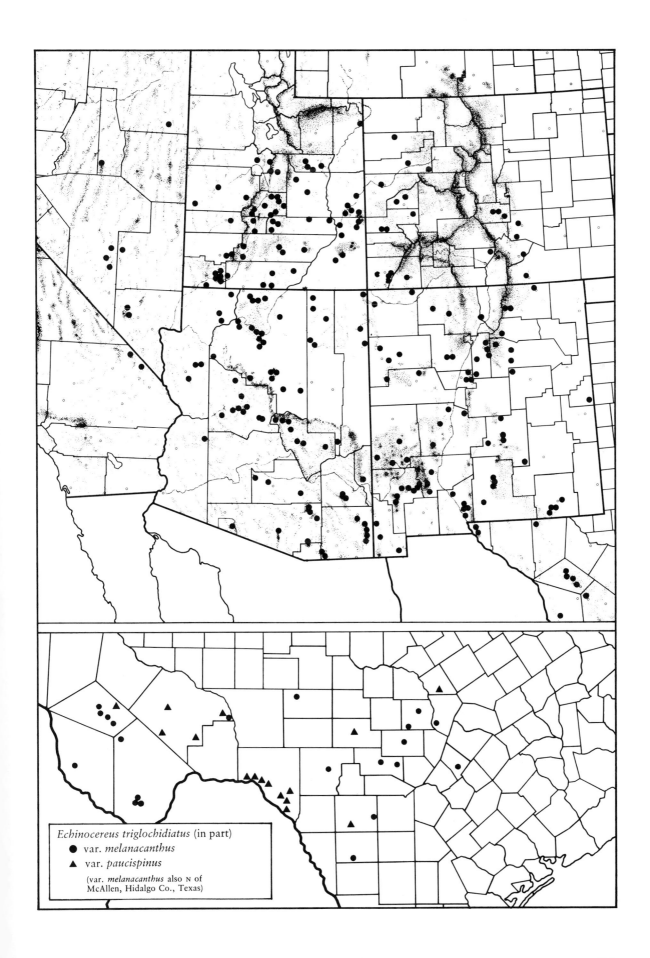

Echinocereus triglochidiatus (in part)

● var. *melanacanthus*
▲ var. *paucispinus*

(var. *melanacanthus* also N of
McAllen, Hidalgo Co., Texas)

ones slightly mucronulate, entire; filaments white or pale green, 9-12 mm long; anthers pale yellow, about 0.5-0.75 mm long, 1-1.5 mm greatest diam; style greenish, 12-20 mm long, 1-2 mm diam; stigmas ±10, 3-4.5 mm long, rather slender; ovary in anthesis 9-12 mm diam, the areoles with spines and white hairs; fruit red, with a deciduous mass of spines, obovoid to cylindroid, 12-25 mm long, 10-15 mm diam; seeds strongly papillate, 1.5-2 mm long, 1.2-1.5 mm broad, 0.8-1 mm thick.

The status of *E. triglochidiatus* has been both misunderstood and hotly debated. The species is composed of a complex group of local populations, and the appearance of the extreme types differs remarkably. The most strikingly variable

characters are stem size and the number, size, and smoothness or angularity of the spines. Differing combinations of these readily visible characters produce extreme types that are seemingly distinct, and as a result many new "species" have been segregated. These determinations have resulted not from the study of natural populations in the field but from observation of a few plants in cultivation. Most reports either have given no data relating the plants to their places in nature or have shown knowledge of only a local flora involving one or a few forms of the species.

The number of herbarium specimens available for this species is small, but the existing collections indicate both the instability of many char-

Distinctive Characters of the Varieties of **Echinocereus triglochidiatus**

Character	a. var. **melanacanthus**	b. var. **mojavensis**	c. var. **neomexicanus**	d. var. **gurneyi**
Stems	Up to 500, 3.8-7.5 (15) cm long, 2.5-5 (6.2) cm diam	Up to 500, 3.8-7.5 (15) cm long, 2.5-5 (6.2) cm diam	Mostly 5-45, 20-30 cm long, 7.5-10 cm diam	Few, 20-30 cm long, 10-15 cm diam
Stem ribs	Mostly 9 or 10, tuberculate	Mostly 9 or 10, tuberculate	8-12 (mostly 10), not markedly tuberculate	10-12, not markedly tuberculate
Spines (in general)	Gray, black, pink, or basally tan, or sometimes straw-colored, to 2.5-6.2 cm long, straight, smooth, rarely angled	Gray, pink, or at first straw-colored, to 4.4-7 cm long, curving and twisting, smooth or angled	Tan or pink, becoming light gray, to 3.8 cm long, nearly straight, not angled	Pinkish-tan, to 1.9 cm long, nearly straight, not angled
Central spines	1-3, light or dark in color, spreading or the longest deflexed, smooth, to 0.7 mm basal diam	1-2, light in color, usually twisting, often striate, to 0.7 mm basal diam	2-4, gray, spreading, smooth, to 0.5-1+ mm basal diam	1(2), tan, gray, or pinkish, spreading, smooth, to 0.5 mm basal diam
Radial spines	5-11, half to sometimes nearly as long as central(s), straight	5-8, half to sometimes nearly as long as central(s), straight	9-12, ± half as long as centrals, straight	7-9, ± equal to central(s), straight
Flower	Slender, 2.5-3.8 cm diam, 3-5(6.2) cm long	Slender, ±3.8-5 cm diam, 3-5(6.2) cm long	Slender, ±3.8 cm diam, 5-7 cm long	Slender, ±3.8 cm diam, 5-7 cm long
Style	1 mm diam; equal to or longer than perianth	1 mm diam; equal to or longer than perianth	1 mm diam; ± equal to or longer than perianth	1.5 mm diam; shorter than perianth
Altitude	1,050-2,400(2,900) m (3,500-8,000 or 9,600 ft)	1,050-2,400(3,000) m (3,500-8,000 or 10,000 ft)	1,350-2,100 m (4,500-7,000 ft)	1,200-1,500 m (4,000-5,000 ft)
Floristic association	Rocky Mountain Montane Forest; Southwestern Oak Woodland; Sagebrush Desert; Navajoan Desert; edges of Desert Grassland and Great Plains Grassland	Northern Juniper-Pinyon Woodland; desert-edge California Chaparral; upper Mojavean Desert; lower Rocky Mountain Montane Forest	Southwestern Oak Woodland and oak woodlands of Texas and NW Mexico; Southern Juniper-Pinyon Woodland; Desert Grassland	Chihuahuan Desert; Desert Grassland

acters and the extensive intergradation of the populations of proposed new species with common types known to be *E. triglochidiatus*. Only extensive, intensive, and long-continued study of natural populations in the field can reveal the nature of the problems underlying the classification of the group. Thirty-six years of such study have not been sufficient, but lines of combination and segregation are emerging.

Even though the natural populations are composed chiefly of individual plants with character combinations falling within a definable range of variability, each population includes a broad range of genetic combinations. In every case studied some individuals do not fall clearly within the variety represented by the general population in which they occur; they have some characters more common in other varieties. In any direction from any given center there is a gradual reduction of the frequency of occurrence of some characters and a weakening of character combinations. Concurrently there is an irregular trend toward combinations most common in other geographical (or otherwise segregated) varieties. A parallel case is the shifting of hereditary character combinations in human populations from region to region, as from the Orient to Europe or Africa, or from Europe to Africa.

The most abundant and wide-ranging member of the *E. triglochidiatus* complex is var. *melana-*

Distinctive Characters of the Varieties of **Echinocereus triglochidiatus** (cont.)

Character	e. var. **paucispinus**	f. var. **arizonicus**	g. var. **gonacanthus**	h. var. **triglochidiatus**
Stems	Few, 15-20 cm long, 6.2-10 cm diam	Few, 22.5-40 cm long, 7.5-10 cm diam	Few or sometimes to 200, 7.5-12.5 cm long, 5-7.5 cm diam	Few, 15-30 cm long, ±7.5 cm diam
Stem ribs	5-7, not strongly tuberculate	±10, tuberculate	±8, tuberculate	5-8, tuberculate
Spines (in general)	Gray, to 3-3.8 cm long, nearly straight, smooth, acicular or rarely somewhat angled or flattened	Dark gray (but radials pinkish-tan), to 2.5-3.8 cm long, nearly straight, not angled	Gray or tan, to 2.5-4.4 cm long, nearly straight, (3)6-angled	Gray, to 1.9-2.5 cm long, nearly straight, 3-angled
Central spines	None	1-3, gray or pinkish, the largest deflexed, with minute striations, to 1.5 mm basal diam	(0)1(2), gray, spreading, angled, to 1.25 mm thick basally (6-7-angled)	None (or rarely 1 and then like the radials; see below)
Radial spines	4-6 (no centrals), straight	5-11, shorter than central(s), often slightly curved	5-8 (centrals too variable for comparison), to 1 mm diam	3-6, as long as central (when it is present), spreading or recurving, to 1.5 mm diam
Flower	Slender, ±3.8 cm diam, 2.5-3.8 cm long	Broad, ±5 cm diam, ±7 cm long	Broad, ±6.4 cm diam, ±6.2 cm long	Broad, ±5 cm diam, 5-6.2 cm long
Style	1.5 mm diam; equal to perianth	2 mm diam; equal to perianth	No data	No data
Altitude	150-300 m (500-1,000 ft)	1,050-1,410 m (3,500-4,700 ft)	1,680-2,370 m (5,600-7,900 ft)	1,300-2,070 m (4,350-6,900 ft)
Floristic association	Chihuahuan Desert	Southwestern Oak Woodland; Southwestern Chaparral	Southern Juniper-Pinyon Woodland	Southern Juniper-Pinyon Woodland

canthus. Through the entire central range of the species and at many points on the periphery the character combinations of this variety can be observed in at least some individuals of other varieties. From California to Colorado and Texas and south in Mexico to Durango, at one point or another var. *melanacanthus* is in contact with each of the other varieties, and it intergrades with all of them (though with var. *arizonicus* indirectly through var. *neomexicanus*). Thus there is a central main population with peripheral extremes. In the outlying localities small breeding populations are shielded from the general population, and evolution has proceeded rapidly. Local differences have tended to become partly stabilized; and in such cases first geographical races, then varieties, and ultimately species develop. In *E. triglochidiatus* only the varietal level has been reached.

1a. Echinocereus triglochidiatus var. melanacanthus (Engelmann) L. Benson. Rocky or grassy hillsides, ledges, and canyons; mostly on igneous rocks at 1,050-2,400(2,900) m (3,500-8,000 or 9,600 ft). Rocky Mountain Montane Forest; Juniper-Pinyon Woodlands; Southwestern Oak Woodland; Sagebrush Desert; Navajoan Desert; edges of Desert Grassland and Great Plains Grassland. California on Clark Mt. and in New York

Mts., Mojave Desert region in San Bernardino Co.; Nevada in Antelope Mts., Eureka Co., and in SE Nye Co. and adjacent Lincoln Co.; Utah from Juab, Carbon, and Uintah Cos. S; Colorado from the Colorado R. drainage to Pueblo Co. and S; Arizona, except in lower deserts of Yuma, Maricopa, W Pinal, and W Pima Cos.; New Mexico in all higher areas, but not on Great Plains or in deserts; Texas in trans-Pecos region and in granitic areas of the Edwards Plateau and its escarpment as far E as Granite Mt., Burnet Co., and Hays Co. Mexico, especially in the region of the Sierra Madre Occidental, as far S as Durango and San Luis Potosí.

This variety is the central one of the species, and it intergrades with all the others. Intermediate plants are common along the zones of geographical contact.

In the Mojave Desert of California and in adjacent Clark Co., Nevada, the variety is represented partly by individuals in the populations of var. *mojavensis* displaying some or all the characters of var. *melanacanthus*, the segregation of var. *mojavensis* rarely being complete.

Variations in characters of the spines are especially common. Long- and short-spined plants grow in the same natural populations, and various intergrading forms occur with them (e.g., above Spire Rock, Canyon de Chelly, Arizona,

Fig. 638. Red-flowered hedgehog cactus, *Echinocereus triglochidiatus* var. *melanacanthus*, plant with 125–200 stems growing in rocky ground in northern Arizona. A young century plant, *Agave palmeri*, is at the right. (A. A. Nichol)

L. & R. L. Benson 14658, Pom, 14658a, Pom). In some individual plants occurring intermittently the basal portions of the longest spines are marked by striations or angles. The spines are of various colors, but the occurrence of yellow or black spines is restricted. Some populations in west-central Utah have long, yellow spines (cf. MILLARD CO. Skull Rock Pass west of Sevier Lake, *L. & R. L. Benson 15700, Pom*; Fremont Road south of Emery-Sevier county line, *B. Harrison 7346, Mo, BrY.* GARFIELD CO. About 15 miles north of Panguitch, *L. Benson 16036, Pom).* Black spines (responsible for the epithet *melanacanthus*) are rare, but they occur, for example, in New Mexico in some plants growing near the type locality (15 miles southeast of Santa Fe, *L. & R. L. Benson 14694, Pom).*

Var. *melanacanthus* grows in clumps, and old plants form cushions or mounds at first half a meter in diameter but enlarging to a meter or more. Ultimately, the stems run into the hundreds, and the mounds become knee-high. In the pine belt at the upper limit of distribution the plants may remain smaller or with only a few stems, reflecting slow growth, short life, or both. At all levels the flowers form bright red masses relatively early in the spring, and the plant is a favorite with color photographers.

Fig. 640. *Echinocereus triglochidiatus* var. *melanacanthus,* stem of a plant in flower. (Paul C. Standley; courtesy of Missouri Botanical Garden)

Fig. 639. *Echinocereus triglochidiatus* var. *melanacanthus* forming clumps of hundreds of stems; northern Arizona, 1929. (Homer L. Shantz)

Fig. 641. *Echinocereus triglochidiatus* var. *melanacanthus*, stems from above, showing the felted young areoles at the apex of the stem. (Homer L. Shantz)

Fig. 643. *Echinocereus triglochidiatus* var. *melanacanthus*, flower. (Paul C. Standley; courtesy of Missouri Botanical Garden)

Fig. 642. *Echinocereus triglochidiatus* var. *melanacanthus*, closer view of the stems, showing ribs and spines. (Robert H. Peebles)

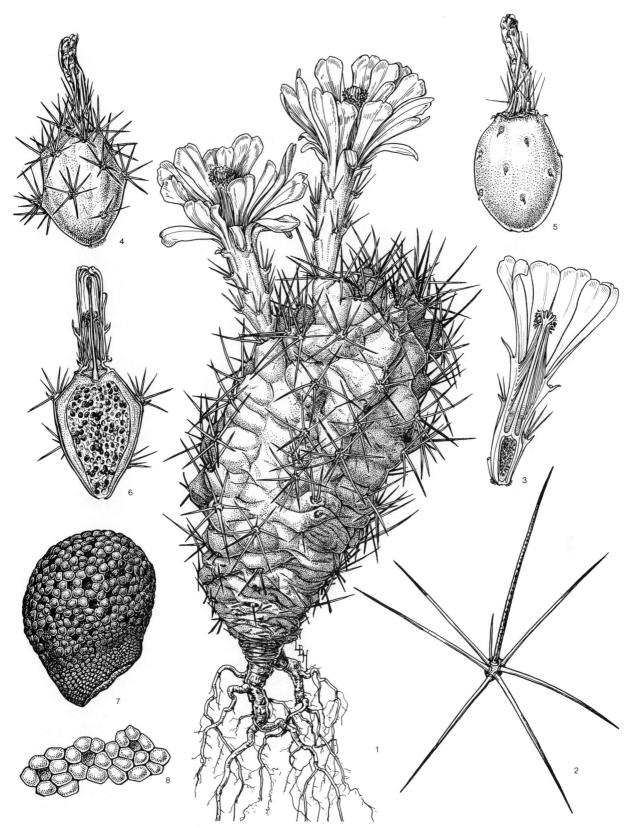

Fig. 644. Red-flowered hedgehog cactus, *Echinocereus triglochidiatus* var. *melanacanthus*, ×.9, except as indicated. *1*, Young, unbranched plant with flowers. *2*, Areole with spines and wool, ×1.8. *3*, Flower in longitudinal section. *4*, Fruit. *5*, Fruit (red and edible) after shedding of the spines. *6*, Fruit in longitudinal section. *7*, Seed, ×45. *8*, Papillate surface of the seed, ×90.

Fig. 645. A red-flowered hedgehog cactus, *Echinocereus triglochidiatus* var. *mojavensis*, in the Rancho Santa Ana Botanic Garden; plant with many stems, showing the characteristic curving spines. The spines of this variety, like those of the others, are variable.

1b. Echinocereus triglochidiatus var. **mojavensis** (Engelmann & Bigelow) L. Benson. Rocky hillsides and canyons in woodland above and in the deserts at 1,050-2,400(3,000) m (3,500-8,000 or 10,000 ft). Northern Juniper-Pinyon Woodland and California Chaparral (desert-edge phase), upper Mojavean Desert, and lower Rocky Mountain Montane Forest. California at Kane's Springs Wash, San Diego Co., and from Inyo Co. s to desert side of San Bernardino Mts. and to Little San Bernardino and San Jacinto Mts. (Riverside Co.) and E; s central and s Nevada from Nye and Clark Cos. E; Utah in Washington Co.; Arizona in w Mohave Co. (according to map prepared by A. A. Nichol in Benson et al., 1940, 1950, but this not so far confirmed by specimens).

Var. *mojavensis* forms dense mounds of long stems, and Parish reported more than 400 stems in one individual. At flowering time, during April or May, the mass of many red flowers is a major attraction of the Mojave Desert. The plants are similar to those of var. *melanacanthus*, but the stems are a little larger, and the nearly white masses of curving and twisting spines are conspicuous.

All populations of this variety are composed of plants ranging from the extreme Californian form to those having at least some characters of var. *melanacanthus*. At the extreme eastern end of the range in which characters of var. *mojavensis* occur, along the zone of contact with var. *melanacanthus* in southeastern Washington Co., Utah, only an occasional plant actually suggests var. *mojavensis* (Springdale, *L. Benson 13703, Pom*). In the Charleston Mts. of southern Nevada features of var. *mojavensis* are dominant, but those of var. *melanacanthus* are proportionately more frequent in occurrence than they are in the California populations.

Fig. 647. *Echinocereus triglochidiatus* var. *mojavensis*, a clump with elongate, curving, but somewhat sparse spines; Joshua Tree National Monument, California.

Fig. 646. *Echinocereus triglochidiatus* var. *mojavensis*; plant in the population of Fig. 647, Joshua Tree National Monument, having straight spines and mostly matching the characters of var. *melanacanthus*. Segregation of the populations is incomplete, even far from the occurrence of var. *melanacanthus* in Utah and Arizona. In this plant the spines are unusually numerous and dense.

613

Fig. 648. *Echinocereus triglochidiatus* var. *mojavensis*, clumps of plants in the Rancho Santa Ana Botanic Garden, the near one with sparse, short, but curving spines.

Fig. 649. Red-flowered hedgehog cactus, *Echinocereus triglochidiatus* var. *neomexicanus*, apex of the robust stem, with its long, straight spines. (Robert H. Peebles)

1c. Echinocereus triglochidiatus var. **neomexicanus** (Standley) Standley *ex* W. T. Marshall. Soils of igneous origin in woodlands and grasslands at 1,350-2,100 m (4,500-7,000 ft). Southwestern Oak Woodland and oak woodlands of w Texas and NW Mexico; Southern Juniper-Pinyon Woodland; Desert Grassland. Arizona from Pima and Santa Cruz Cos. to Cochise Co.; New Mexico from McKinley Co. to Bernalillo, Hidalgo, Chaves, and Eddy Cos.; Texas w of Pecos R. from El Paso Co. to Culberson, Sutton, and Brewster Cos. Mexico from Chihuahua to Durango.

Var. *neomexicanus* mostly forms clumps of several stems, though sometimes large mounds. All parts of the plants are larger than those of var. *melanacanthus*, and the flowers are even more conspicuous.

Intergrades with vars. *melanacanthus, gurneyi, paucispinus, arizonicus, gonacanthus,* and *triglochidiatus*.

1d. Echinocereus triglochidiatus var. **gurneyi** L. Benson. Rocky hillsides in either granitic or limestone soils in the desert at 1,200-1,500 m (4,000-5,000 ft). Chihuahuan Desert and Desert Grassland. New Mexico from s Dona Ana Co. (uncommon) to near Carlsbad in Eddy Co.; Texas w of Pecos R. from El Paso Co. to Presidio and Terrell Cos. Mexico in n Chihuahua.

Var. *gurneyi* forms small clumps of very thick stems with only short spines.

This variety intergrades with vars. *melanacanthus*, *neomexicanus*, and *paucispinus*.

Fig. 651. *Echinocereus triglochidiatus* var. *gurneyi*, stem showing the young apical areoles and spines and the inside of the flower.

Fig. 650. Red-flowered hedgehog cactus, *Echinocereus triglochidiatus* var. *gurneyi*, showing areoles and spines of various ages, and flowers.

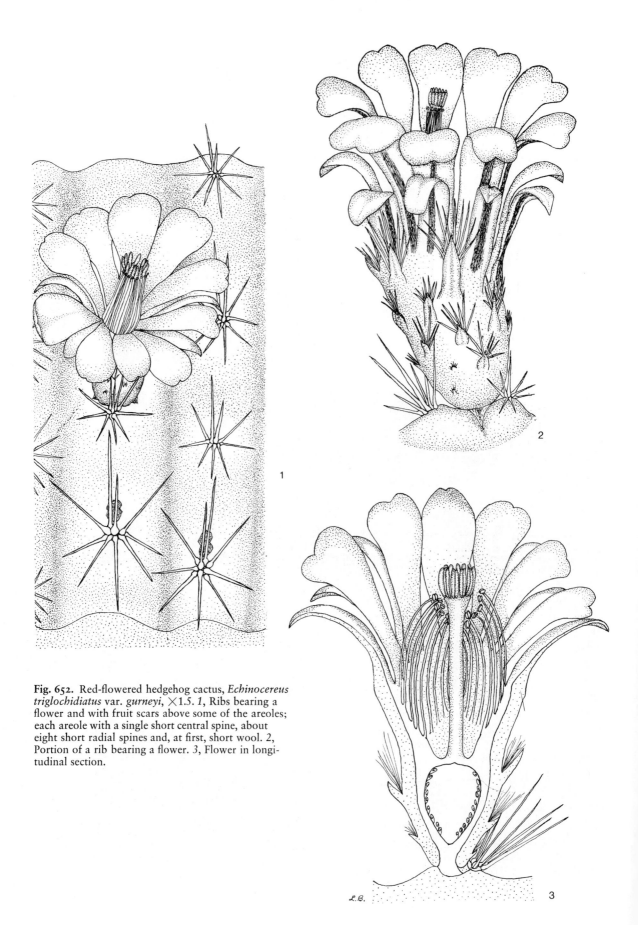

Fig. 652. Red-flowered hedgehog cactus, *Echinocereus triglochidiatus* var. *gurneyi*, ×1.5. *1*, Ribs bearing a flower and with fruit scars above some of the areoles; each areole with a single short central spine, about eight short radial spines and, at first, short wool. *2*, Portion of a rib bearing a flower. *3*, Flower in longitudinal section.

Fig. 653. Red-flowered hedgehog cactus, *Echinocereus triglochidiatus* var. *paucispinus*, showing the relatively stout spines; the flowers of very deep hue. (A. R. Leding, U.S. Acclimatization Station, Las Cruces, New Mexico)

1e. Echinocereus triglochidiatus var. **paucispinus** (Engelmann) Engelmann *ex* W. T. Marshall. Rocky igneous or limestone soils in the desert or in grassland at about 150-300 m (500-1,000 ft). Chihuahuan Desert. Texas near Rio Grande from Davis Mts. to Val Verde and Kimble Cos.

The greenness and stoutness of the stems are the feature first noticed in the field. This variety possesses large stems and few spines, as does var. *triglochidiatus*, and acicular or slightly angular spines, as does var. *melanacanthus*. There is no central spine.

Intergrades with vars. *melanacanthus, neomexicanus,* and *gurneyi*.

1f. Echinocereus triglochidiatus var. **arizonicus** (Rose) L. Benson. Woodland in the mountains at about 1,050-1,410 m (3,500-4,700 ft). Southwestern Oak Woodland; Southwestern Chaparral. Arizona in the mountainous area near the line between Gila and Pinal Cos.

This is the most robust of all the varieties. Its usually few large branches grow in clumps that are often hidden away among granite boulders.

Intergrades with var. *neomexicanus.*

Fig. 654. Red-flowered hedgehog cactus, *Echinocereus triglochidiatus* var. *arizonicus*, plant in cultivation at Sacaton, Pinal Co., Arizona. (Robert H. Peebles)

Fig. 655. *Echinocereus triglochidiatus* var. *arizonicus*, showing the ribs, spines, and flowers. (Robert H. Peebles)

1g. Echinocereus triglochidiatus var. **gonacanthus** (Engelmann & Bigelow) Boissevain. Rocky hillsides mostly in or near woodlands at 1,680-2,370 m (5,600-7,900 ft). Southern Juniper-Pinyon Woodland. Colorado from Chaffee and Fremont Cos. to La Plata, Archuleta, and Rio Grande Cos.; Arizona in easternmost Apache Co.; W New Mexico sparingly from San Juan and Rio Arriba Cos. to Grant and Socorro Cos. and in forms transitional to vars. *melanacanthus* and *neomexicanus* E to Colfax and Eddy Cos.

This variety occupies a range northwest and north of var. *triglochidiatus*, with which it also intergrades. It also shades into var. *melanacanthus*.

Var. *gonacanthus* is both robust and mound-forming. Its large, cushionlike clumps are in evidence along steep slopes, cliffs, and ledges in the mountains.

1h. Echinocereus triglochidiatus var. **triglochidiatus**. Rocky or gravelly soils of ridges, hills, and canyons in woodland areas at 1,300-2,070 m (4,350-6,900 ft). Southern Juniper-Pinyon Woodland. Southern Colorado in Saguache Co. and near Arboles, Archuleta Co. (there in a population transitional to var. *gonacanthus*); Arizona near Ft. Defiance, Apache Co. (the population probably transitional to var. *gonacanthus*; see discussion under that variety); New Mexico from McKinley Co. to Rio Arriba, Mora, San Miguel, Luna, and Otero Cos.

Var. *triglochidiatus* forms clumps of a few large, robust, angular, bare-looking stems. These bear striking clusters of mostly three or four short, stout spines that tend to grow in a bird's-foot pattern.

Intergrades with vars. *melanacanthus*, *neomexicanus*, and *gonacanthus*.

2. Echinocereus berlandieri
(Engelmann) Engelmann *ex* Rümpler

Plant spreading, the stems procumbent, arising from a short slender rhizome, forming clumps mostly 10-15 cm high and to 1 m or more diam; larger terminal joints green or tinged with purple, prismatic or cylindroid, 3.8-15(17.5) cm long, 2-

Fig. 656. Red-flowered hedgehog cactus, *Echinocereus triglochidiatus* var. *gonacanthus*, on a cliff near the Royal Gorge, Fremont Co., Colorado; a clump of many stems, showing the relatively sparse, stout spines.

Fig. 657. *Echinocereus triglochidiatus* var. *gonacanthus*, individual stems, the spines variable, few per areole, and stout.

Fig. 658. Red-flowered hedge-hog cactus, *Echinocereus triglochidiatus* var. *triglochidiatus*, plant with a single stem (in this variety, the stems are solitary or few) growing on a rocky ledge south of Las Vegas, San Miguel Co., New Mexico. This variety, alone, has as few as three spines per areole, the basis for the Latin epithet *triglochidiatus*.

Fig. 659. *Echinocereus triglochidiatus* var. *triglochidiatus*, the ribs almost tuberculate, a condition due partly to drought. The spines, 2–4 per areole, are usually very stout and short, as in the second plant from right; occasionally they are more slender, as in the three other plants by chance selected for the photograph.

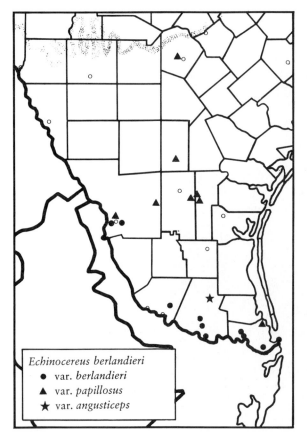

Echinocereus berlandieri
• var. *berlandieri*
▲ var. *papillosus*
★ var. *angusticeps*

2.5(3) cm diam; ribs 5 or 6, prominent to faint, somewhat to strongly tuberculate, the tubercles projecting 3-9 mm; areoles circular, 2.25 mm diam, typically 9-12 mm apart; spines not obscuring joint, gray, straight; central spines usually 1 per areole, brown, gray, or nearly black, 6-12(25) mm long, basally 0.5 mm diam, acicular, circular in cross section; radial spines 6-8 per areole, whitish to gray, very slender and rather weak, the longest usually 6-12 mm long, usually basally 0.25 mm diam; flower 6.2-7.5 cm diam, 6.2-8 cm long; sepaloids with greenish midribs and usually purple margins, largest mostly cuneate-oblanceolate, 2.5-4 cm long, ±3-7.5 mm broad, rounded and weakly cuspidate, irregularly denticulate or entire; petaloids *either* rose-purple or lighter *or* yellow with red bases, largest oblanceolate, 2.5-5 mm long, (6)9-12 mm broad, cuspidate, irregularly denticulate; filaments rose-purple, ±10 mm long; anthers yellow, 1.2-1.5 mm long; style green and purplish, 25-30 mm long, 1.5 mm greatest diam; stigmas 7-13, 6-9 mm long, slender, green; ovary in anthesis obovoid, spiny, to ±20 mm long, 12 mm diam; fruit reddish, fleshy at maturity, with numerous reddish-brown or mottled deciduous spines, obovoid, 20-25 mm long, 12-20

Distinctive Characters of the Varieties of **Echinocereus berlandieri**

Character	a. var. **berlandieri**	b. var. **papillosus**	c. var. **angusticeps**
Stems	Mostly 25-50, not forming dense mats	1-10, forming a small mat (to ±30 cm diam)	5-95, forming a mat to ±30 cm diam (as large in var. *papillosus* but with only 1-10 stems)
Joints	Mostly 5-15 cm long, 2-2.5 cm diam	10-17.5 cm long, 3-5 cm diam	3.8-7.5 cm long, ±2.5 cm diam
Central spine	0.6-1.2 cm long	0.6-1.2 cm long	0.8 cm long
Petaloids	Apically rounded, weakly cuspidate, irregularly denticulate, rose-purple or lighter, 3.8-5 cm long, 0.9-1.2 cm broad	Acuminate, pale yellow with red bases, ±2.5 cm long, 0.9 cm broad	Slightly apiculate or rounded, pale yellow with drab purplish bases, ±2.5 cm long, 1 cm broad

[All three varieties grow at low elevations on the Rio Grande Plain.]

mm diam, not persistent, the umbilicus not prominent; seeds black, basally truncate, coarsely papillate, 1 mm long, 0.8 mm broad, ±0.5 mm thick; hilum broad, across truncate end of seed.

2a. Echinocereus berlandieri var. **berlandieri.** Deep, fine soils of plains, washes, and low hills, in thickets of mesquite and in grassland areas at low elevations. Rio Grande Plain. In s Texas from Webb Co. to Nueces and Cameron Cos. Northeastern Mexico.

Except during dry seasons, the loose mats of stems are inconspicuous among grasses or under bushes. When the grasses and other herbs are dry, each mat becomes a contrasting patch of dark green with nearly white to gray slender spines like ornaments on the protruding stem tips.

2b. Echinocereus berlandieri var. **papillosus** (Linke) L. Benson. Light sandy loam or red gravel or limestone in grass and mesquite lands at low elevations. Rio Grande Plain. In s Texas from vicinity of San Antonio, Bexar Co., to the Rio Grande in Webb, Starr, and Cameron Cos.

The mats are like those of var. *berlandieri*, but the joints have irregular tuberculate ribs, and they are stouter.

2c. Echinocereus berlandieri var. **angusticeps** (Clover) L. Benson. Open mesquite woods. Rio Grande Plain. Near Linn, N of Edinburg, Hidalgo Co., Texas.

The mats are about as large as those of the other varieties but dense and with shorter stem joints.

Fig. 660. *Echinocereus berlandieri* var. *berlandieri*, fruits and seeds: left, fruit after the spines have fallen, ×1.3; center, fruit in longitudinal section, ×1.3; right, seed, ×50.

Fig. 661. A hedgehog cactus, *Echinocereus berlandieri* var. *berlandieri*. *1*, Plant with a flower bud and a flower. *2–4*, Spine clusters, showing the elongate central spine in each areole. *5*, Fruit, with separate illustrations of the seed. *6*, Seeds: *a*, natural size; *b*, ×9; *c*, the papillae of the seed coat, ×36. (Paulus Roetter in Engelmann/Emory, *pl. 58*)

3. Echinocereus pentalophus
    (DeCandolle) Rümpler
Alicoche

Spreading, procumbent, forming clumps or mats to ±10 cm high and ±1 m diam; larger terminal joints green, prismatic, to ±10 cm long, 1.2-1.6 cm diam; ribs 4 or 5; tubercles ±6 mm high; areoles nearly circular, 1.5-3 mm diam, typically about 10 mm apart; spines numerous but not obscuring joint; central spine 0 or 1, only slightly longer than radials, 0.75 mm diam; radial spines gray or brown to black, 4-6 per areole, spreading, straight, longer 10-20 mm long, basally ±0.5 mm broad, more or less subulate, elliptic in cross section; flower 7.5-10 cm diam, ±7.5 cm long; sepaloids with greenish midribs and reddish-violet margins, the largest cuneate-linear, 2.5-3.8 cm long, ±6 mm broad, apically rounded and irregularly dentate, mucronate; petaloids reddish-violet with yellow bases (flower having a yellow center), largest broadly oblanceolate to cuneate, truncate, 3.8-4.5 cm long, 9-15 mm broad, obtuse to rounded, somewhat mucronulate, nearly entire to irregularly dentate; filaments white tinged with green, ±12 mm long; anthers yellow, oblong, 1 mm long; style white tinged with violet, ±25 mm long, 0.75 mm greatest diam; stigmas dark green, ±10, ±6(7.5) mm long, rather slender; ovary in anthesis ellipsoid, ±12 mm long, spiny; seeds black, somewhat enlarged upward, strongly papillate, 1 mm long, ±0.8 mm broad, 0.5 mm thick; hilum broad, across truncate base of seed.

Fine soils of flats and plains in the mesquite and grass country at low elevations. Rio Grande Plain. In s Texas near Rio Grande from Webb Co.

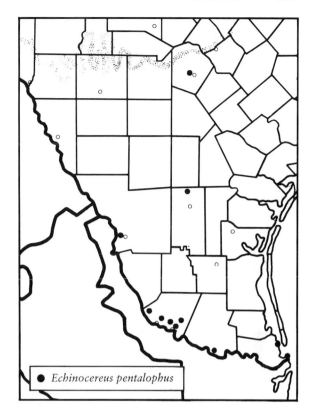

● *Echinocereus pentalophus*

to Cameron Co. and to northward (sparingly) on the coastal plain (Bexar and Duval Cos.). Southward to San Luis Potosí, Mexico.

Echinocereus pentalophus forms much larger, deeper mats or clumps than *E. berlandieri*, and the stems appear less spiny. The spines are shorter and stouter and of greater rigidity. The very large flowers are of two contrasting colors—reddish violet with a yellow center—and they are much sought by photographers.

Fig. 662. *Echinocereus pentalophus*, stems showing the four or five ribs and the short spines.

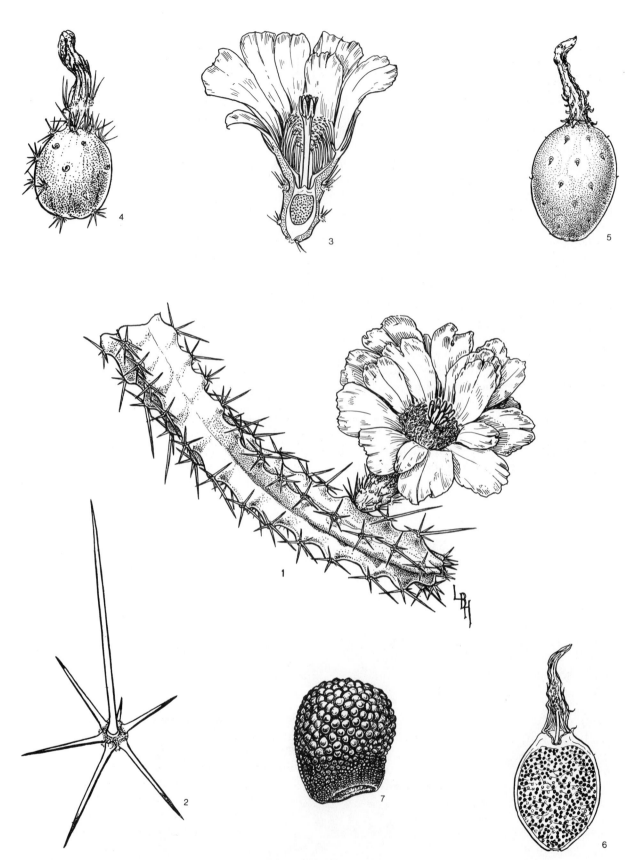

Fig. 663. A hedgehog cactus or alicoche, *Echinocereus pentalophus*. *1*, Stem with a flower. *2*, Areole with spines and wool, ×6. *3*, Flower in longitudinal section. *4*, Fruit, the spines becoming deciduous. *5*, Fruit after fall of spines. *6*, Fruit in section. *7*, Seed, ×30.

Fig. 664. A hedgehog cactus or alicoche, *Echinocereus pentalophus*, in the Huntington Botanical Gardens, showing the sprawling habit.

4. Echinocereus fendleri Engelmann

Mature stems usually 1 but up to 5, flabby, the clumps not dense; larger stems green, ovoid to ovoid-cylindroid or cylindroid, 7.5-17 (25) cm long, 3.8-6.2 cm diam; ribs (8)9 or 10, not markedly tuberculate; areoles circular, 4.5 mm diam, not bearing white felt at maturity, typically 20-25 mm apart; spines not obliterating stem surface; central spine at first very dark but in age changing to gray or pale gray tipped with brown or black, solitary in the areole or (var. *kuenzleri*) none, curving slightly upward through entire length or straight, rigid, (12)25-38 mm long, basally 0.5-0.75 mm diam, acicular, circular in cross section, tapering gradually; radial spines usually white or pale gray, sometimes yellow or like the central spine, 5-7(9) per areole, spreading at low angles, straight or rarely (var. *kuenzleri*) 1, curving, short, the lowest longer than others, the longer 9-12 mm long, basally 0.5-1 mm diam (but in var. *kuenzleri* stout, 1.5 mm diam, and the lowest one curving), acicular; flower 5-6.2 cm diam and long; sepaloids with greenish to brownish midribs and magenta margins, largest lanceolate, to 3(3.8) cm long, 6-9 mm broad, acute, mucronate, entire; petaloids magenta, largest elliptic-cuneate, 3-3.8 cm long, ±12 mm broad, acute, mucronulate, entire; filaments pinkish, ±9 mm long; anthers yellow, oblong, 1-1.5 mm long; style green and pink, 20-25 mm long, 2-2.5 mm greatest diam; stigmas ±10, ±4-5 mm long, green; ovary in anthesis ±12 mm long; fruit green, turning reddish, 20-30 mm long, 12-25 mm diam; seeds reticulate-punctate, 1.5 mm long, 1.2-1.3 mm broad, 0.8 mm thick.

4a. Echinocereus fendleri var. fendleri. Sandy or gravelly soils of grasslands and woodlands at mostly 1,800-2,400 m (6,000-8,000 ft). Great Plains Grassland, Southern Juniper-Pinyon Woodland, and lower edge of Rocky Mountain Montane Forest. Colorado in Fremont (Canyon City), Montezuma, and La Plata Cos.; Arizona from Coconino Co. E and s above the Mogollon Rim and sparingly s at higher levels to Santa Cruz and Cochise Cos.; New Mexico from San Juan Co. E to Taos Co. and s to Hidalgo and Chaves Cos.; Texas in El Paso Co. and w Hudspeth Co. Mexico

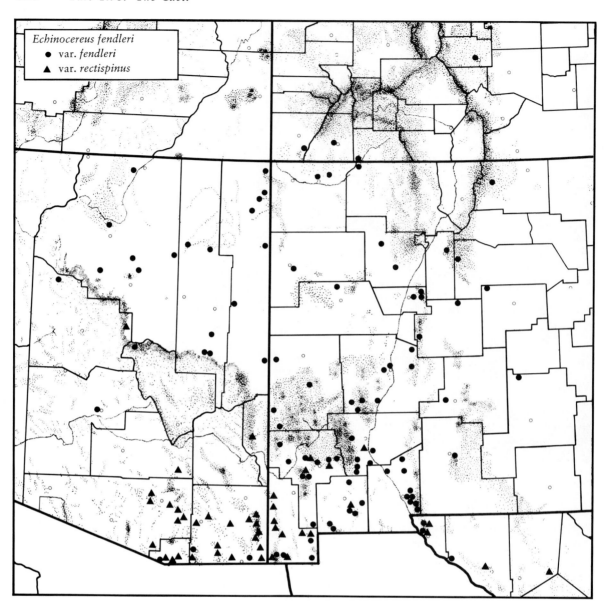

Echinocereus fendleri
- ● var. *fendleri*
- ▲ var. *rectispinus*

in Chihuahua (Candelario, *E. Stearns 322*, May 15, 1912, *US*).

The solitary or few stems are usually inconspicuous among clumps of grasses on the rolling hills and plains. The brown to gray spines blend with the dry grass stems and leaves, but during a few days of each year the lavender to purplish flowers make large spots of color.

4b. Echinocereus fendleri var. **rectispinus** (Peebles) L. Benson. On sandy or gravelly soils of grassland at mostly 900-1,650(2,040) m (3,000-5,500 or 6,800 ft). Desert Grassland and edges of Arizona Desert and Chihuahuan Desert. Arizona from near Oracle, Pinal Co., and E Pima Co. to near Clifton, Greenlee Co., and s to Santa Cruz and Cochise Cos.; sw New Mexico from Grant Co. to Hidalgo and Sierra Cos.; Texas from El Paso Co. to Culberson Co.

The plant is larger than var. *fendleri*, and the spines standing at right angles to the stem catch the eye more quickly than the upward-curving spines of the other variety, which blend into the outline of the stem, especially at its apex.

Intergrades with *E. fasciculatus* var. *fasciculatus*.

Distinctive Characters of the Varieties of **Echinocereus fendleri**

Character	a. var. **fendleri**	b. var. **rectispinus**	c. var. **kuenzleri**
Stems	Ovoid to ovoid-cylindroid (in age some cylindroid), 7.5-15(25) cm long	Cylindroid, 10-17.5(25) cm long	Cylindroid, to 25 cm long
Central spine	At first nearly black to dark brown, in age gray or pale gray tipped with brown, curving upward entire length, 2.5-3.8 cm long	Pale gray, tipped with black or brown, projecting perpendicularly to stem, 1.2-3.8 cm long	None or rare
Radial spines	Straight, 0.9-1.2 cm long, 0.25-0.5 mm diam	Straight, 0.9-1.2 cm long, 0.25-0.5 mm diam	Lower longest and curved, upper dagger-like and sometimes longer than lateral, 1.2-1.9 cm long, to 1.5 mm diam
Altitude	1,800-2,400 m (6,000-8,000 ft)	900-1,650(2,040)m (3,000-5,500 or 6,800 ft)	±1,500 m (5,000 ft)
Floristic association	Great Plains Grassland; Southern Juniper-Pinyon Woodland; lower edge of Rocky Mountain Montane Forest	Desert Grassland; edges of Arizona Desert and Chihuahuan Desert	Unknown: Juniper-Pinyon Woodland or Great Plains Grassland

Fig. 665. A hedgehog cactus, *Echinocereus fendleri* var. *fendleri*, showing the upward-curving central spine in each areole and a spiny young fruit. (Robert H. Peebles; from *Cacti of Arizona*, eds. 1–3)

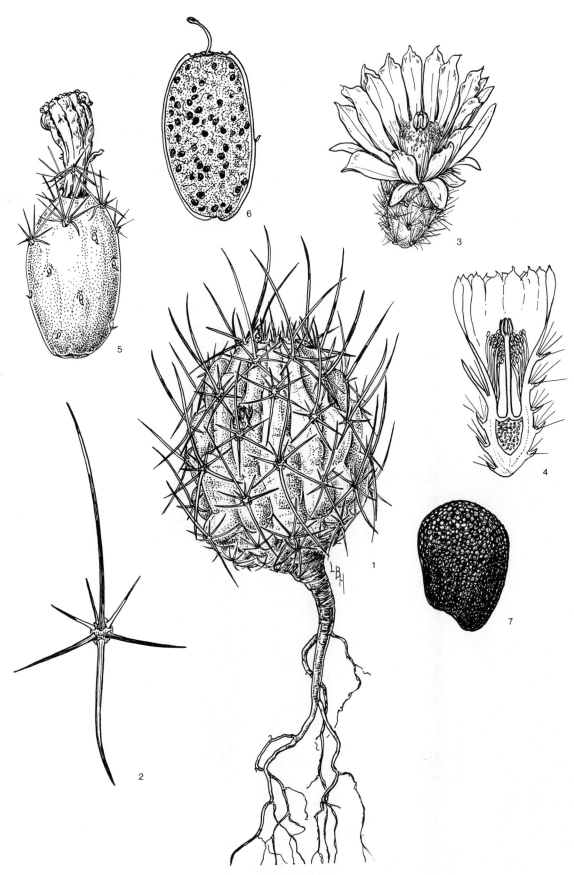

Fig. 666. A hedgehog cactus, *Echinocereus fendleri* var. *fendleri*, natural size, except as indicated. *1*, Plant from near the Grand Canyon, Arizona, showing the upward-curving spines. *2*, Areole with spines and wool, ×2. *3*, Flower. *4*, Flower in longitudinal section. *5*, Fruit at maturity after fall of some of the spine clusters. *6*, Fruit in longitudinal section. *7*, Seed, ×6.

Fig. 667. A hedgehog cactus, *Echinocereus fendleri* var. *rectispinus*, in a patch of Desert Grassland; Colossal Cave, Rincon Mts., Pima Co., Arizona. This and the other photographs show variations of spine types; all plants have a single straight central spine protruding at right angles to the stem and a single cycle of shorter radial spines.

Fig. 668. *Echinocereus fendleri* var. *rectispinus*, with long spines; Desert Grassland near Willcox, Cochise Co., Arizona.

Fig. 670. *Echinocereus fendleri* var. *rectispinus*, plant transplanted from nature into a garden; with short central spines and with flower buds and flowers. (Robert H. Peebles)

Fig. 669. *Echinocereus fendleri* var. *rectispinus*, showing the tuberculate ribs and spines of intermediate length; a young fruit at the left, covered with clusters of small white spines.

4c. Echinocereus fendleri var. **kuenzleri** (Castetter, Pierce & Schwerin) L. Benson, *comb. nov.* (for nomenclature, see Documentation). Woodland and grassland at about 1,500 m (5,000 ft). Southern Juniper-Pinyon Woodland or Great Plains Grassland. New Mexico in Otero or Lincoln Co. in NE Sacramento Mt. foothills; reported to occur at higher elevations than var. *fendleri*. Mexico in Chihuahua.

The stems are more conspicuous than the spines, but the small clusters of thick spines are curiosities in themselves.

5. Echinocereus fasciculatus
(Engelmann) L. Benson

Stems of mature plants (3)5-20, tissues firm, not flabby, clumps not dense; larger stems green, cylindroid, elongate, 16-30(45) cm long, 4-6(7.5) cm diam; ribs 8-18, not markedly tuberculate; areoles circular, 4.5 mm diam, not bearing white felt at maturity, typically 20-25 mm apart; spines not obliterating stem surface; central spines *either* pale gray with brown or black tips *or* straw-colored, white, light brown, tan, or reddish-brown, the principal central prominent, spreading or deflexed, straight, accompanied by 1 or 2(3) short accessory centrals, 2.5-7.5 cm long (in var. *bonke-*

rae only 6-7.5 mm), basally 0.5-0.75(1) mm diam, acicular, circular in section, tapering gradually; radial spines usually white or pale gray, sometimes yellow or like the central spine, 11-13 per areole, spreading at low angles, straight, longest 12-20 mm long, basally to 0.5 mm diam, acicular; flower 5-6.2 cm diam and long; sepaloids with greenish to brownish midribs and magenta to reddish-purple margins, largest lanceolate, to 3 (3.8) cm long, 6-9 mm broad, acute, mucronate, entire; petaloids magenta to reddish-purple, largest elliptic-cuneate, 3-3.8 cm long, ±12 mm broad, acute, mucronulate, entire; filaments pinkish, ±9 mm long; anthers yellow, oblong, 1-1.5 mm long; style green and pink, 20-25 mm long, 2-2.5 mm greatest diam; stigmas ±10, ±4.5 mm long, green; ovary in anthesis ±12 mm long; fruit green, turning reddish, 20-30 mm long, 12-25 mm diam; seeds reticulate-punctate, 1.5 mm long, 1.2-1.3 mm broad, 0.8 mm thick.

This species has larger and more numerous stems than *E. fendleri*, and it grows principally in the desert, where usually it is not concealed by grasses. Consequently, the clumps can be seen from a considerable distance. For a brief period during the spring, masses of the large magenta to reddish-purple flowers of this or the other varieties make gorgeous spots on the desert.

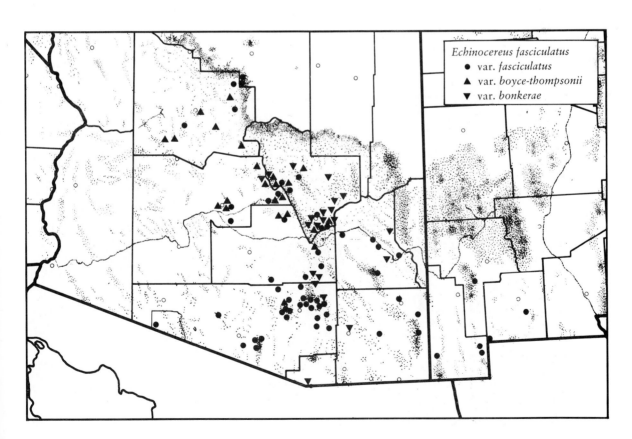

5a. Echinocereus fasciculatus var. **fasciculatus.** Sand, gravel, and rocks of hillsides and washes in the desert at 750-1,050(1,500) m (2,500-3,500 or 5,000 ft). Arizona Desert and edge of Desert Grassland. Arizona from Yavapai Co. and s Coconino Co. (Oak Creek Canyon) s through desert mountains and higher desert near the Mogollon Rim to Gila Co. and thence to Pima and Cochise Cos.; New Mexico (rare) to Hidalgo and Grant Cos.

Intergrades with *E. engelmannii* var. *acicularis* and *E. fendleri* var. *rectispinus.*

Distinctive Characters of the Varieties of Echinocereus fasciculatus

Character	a. var. **fasciculatus**	b. var. **boyce-thompsonii**	c. var. **bonkerae**
Stems	5-20, 17.5-45 cm long	3-12, 10-25 cm long	Usually 5-15 (sometimes more), 12.5-20 cm long
Ribs	8-10	(12)14-18+	(11)13-16
Principal central spine	Perpendicular to stem or deflexed, somewhat flexible, 2.5-7.5 cm long	Deflexed, flexible and very slender, 3.8-5(10) cm long	Perpendicular to stem, rigid, stout, only 0.6-0.75 cm long
Principal central spine color	Pale gray but at least tipped with brown or black	Light-colored, yellow or either straw-colored, reddish-tan, or white tipped with light brown	White or pale gray tipped with brown
Altitude	750-1,050(1,500) m (2,500-3,500 or 5,000 ft)	(300)600-900 m (1,000 or 2,000-3,000 ft)	900-1,500(1,800) m (3,000-5,000 or 6,000 ft)
Floristic association	Arizona Desert; edge of Desert Grassland	Arizona Desert	Desert Grassland

Fig. 671. A hedgehog cactus, *Echinocereus fasciculatus* var. *fasciculatus*, growing on the Papago Indian Reservation, Pima Co., Arizona. (A. A. Nichol)

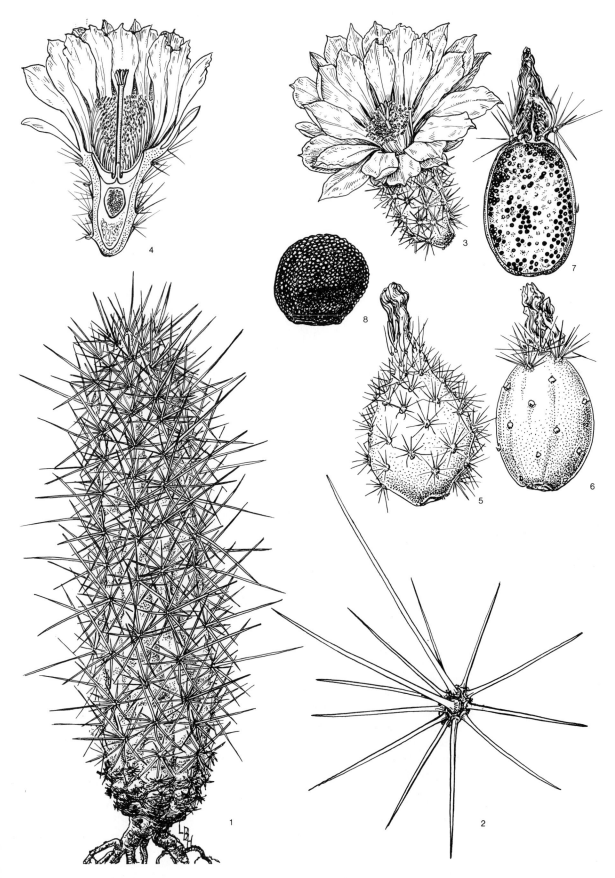

Fig. 672. A hedgehog cactus, *Echinocereus fasciculatus* var. *fasciculatus*, ×1.2, except as indicated. *1*, Stem taken from a cluster of six. *2*, Areole with spines and wool, ×1.5. *3*, Flower. *4*, Flower in longitudinal section. *5*, Fruit. *6*, Fruit after fall of the spines. *7*, Fruit in longitudinal section. *8*, Seed, ×16.

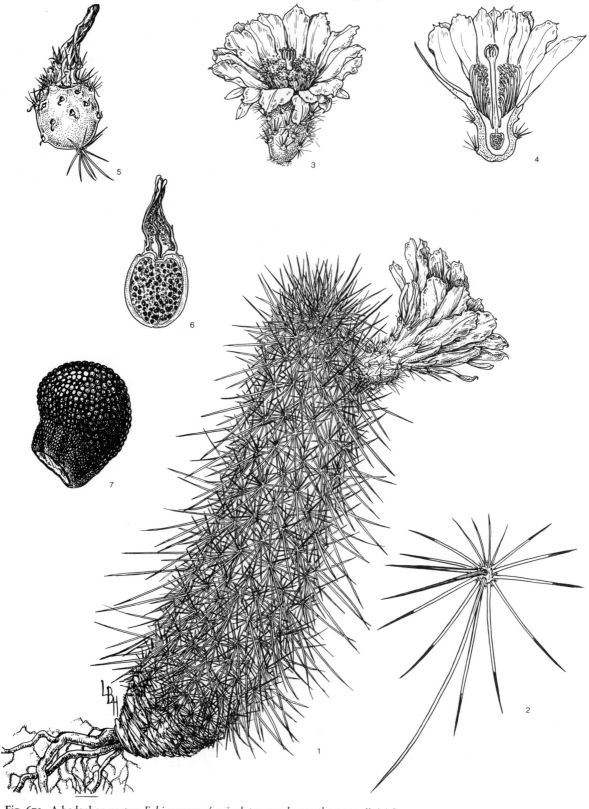

Fig. 673. A hedgehog cactus, *Echinocereus fasciculatus* var. *boyce-thompsonii*, ×.8, except as indicated. *1*, Young, unbranched plant with a flower. *2*, Areole with spines and wool, ×1.6. *3*, Flower. *4*, Flower in longitudinal section. *5*, Fruit (red) at maturity, most of the spines already deciduous. *6*, Fruit in longitudinal section. *7*, Seed, ×22.

5b. Echinocereus fasciculatus var. boyce-thompsonii (Orcutt) L. Benson. Rocky or gravelly slopes in the desert at (300)600-900 m (1,000 or 2,000-3,000 ft). Arizona Desert. Arizona below the Mogollon Rim from Yavapai Co. to E Maricopa Co. and to Gila and NE Pinal Cos.

This variety forms stem clumps similar to those of var. *fasciculatus*, but it is commonly distinguished by yellow to golden spines. Each plant of var. *boyce-thompsonii* forms a golden mass on the desert hillside.

Intergrades with *E. engelmannii* var. *acicularis*.

5c. Echinocereus fasciculatus var. bonkerae (Thornber & Bonker) L. Benson. Sandy or gravelly soils of plains, hilltops, and canyonsides in grassland at 900-1,500(1,800) m (3,000-5,000 or 6,000 ft). Desert Grassland. Arizona, common in Gila Co. and rare in Pinal, Graham, and NW Cochise Cos. and near Nogales, Santa Cruz Co.

Coulter (Contr. U.S. Nat. Herb. 3: 384. 1896) described a plant of this variety and considered it to be *Cereus ctenoides*. Probably the specimen was from Oracle, Arizona, but it was labeled "Tucson" (*W. H. Evans* in 1891, *US*, carton; vege-

Fig. 674. A hedgehog cactus, *Echinocereus fasciculatus* var. *boyce-thompsonii*, showing the dense cover of spines, the longer ones directed mostly downward (less markedly so than usual), and a mature fruit in the process of losing spine clusters. (Robert H. Peebles; from *The Cacti of Arizona*, eds. 1–3)

Fig. 675. A hedgehog cactus, *Echinocereus fasciculatus* var. *bonkerae*, large plant at the Arizona-Sonora Desert Museum, Tucson, Arizona, showing the characteristic stem clump and the short spines.

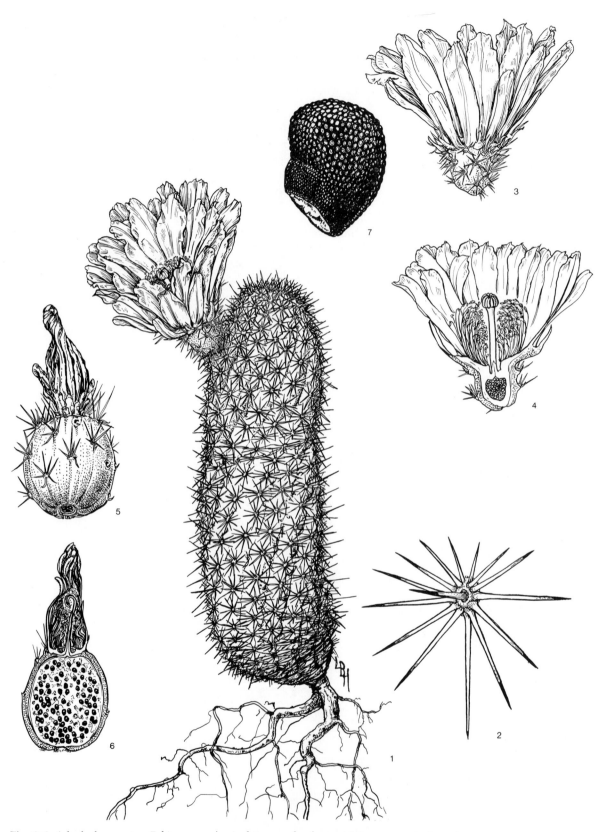

Fig. 676. A hedgehog cactus, *Echinocereus fasciculatus* var. *bonkerae*, ×.9, except as indicated. *1*, Relatively young plant in flower. *2*, Areole with spines and wool, ×5. *3*, Flower. *4*, Flower in longitudinal section. *5*, Fruit. *6*, Fruit in longitudinal section, the floral tube and the ovary deep pink, the pulp white. *7*, Seed, ×22.

Fig. 677. *Echinocereus fasciculatus* var. *bonkerae*, in flower and with a very young fruit; Arizona Desert in east-central Arizona. A banana yucca, *Yucca baccata*, is in the background at right. (Homer L. Shantz)

tative material). Britton and Rose (*Cactaceae* 3: 37, *f. 45.* 1922) published a photograph of this plant as *Echinocereus fendleri.*

Except during the brief period of flowering, when the plant becomes a mass of reddish-purple, many-pointed stars, this variety looks wholly different from the others. Each stem in the clump seems a smooth mass of short spines, as if it had been mowed carefully with electric clippers. There is none of the shaggy effect of the long, uneven spines characteristic of the other varieties.

6. Echinocereus ledingii Peebles

Stems of mature plants usually 4-10, the clumps not dense; larger stems green, with firm tissues, ovoid to cylindroid, often elongate, 2.5-5 cm long, commonly 6-7.5 cm diam; ribs usually 12-14 (16), not markedly tuberculate; areoles circular, 4.5 mm diam, not bearing white felt at maturity, typically 20-25 mm apart; spines tending to obliterate stem surface, yellow or straw-colored (as with other yellow spines, turning black in age or sometimes in pressed specimens); central spine accompanied by 1-4 short accessory centrals, principal central strongly curved downward near base, stout and rigid, 20-25 mm long, basally very thick and 1.25 mm diam, acicular, circular in cross section, tapering very rapidly from the broad base, other centrals (if any) small; radial spines ±9-11 per areole, spreading at a low angle, the longer 12-15 mm long, basally ±0.5 mm diam, acicular; flower 5-6 cm diam and long; sepaloids with greenish to brownish midribs and magenta to rose-purple margins, largest lanceolate, to 30(38) mm long, 6-9 mm broad, acute, mucronate, entire; petaloids magenta to rose-purple, largest elliptic-cuneate, 30-38 mm long, ±12 mm broad, acute, mucronulate, entire; filaments pinkish, 9 mm long; anthers yellow, oblong, 1-1.5 mm long; style green and pink, 20-25 mm long, 2-2.5 mm greatest diam; stigmas ±10, green, ±4.5 mm long; ovary in anthesis ±12 mm long; fruit green, turning reddish, 20-30 mm long, 12-25

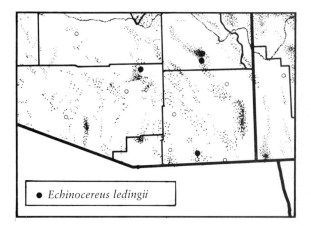

● *Echinocereus ledingii*

mm diam; seeds reticulate-punctate, 1.5 mm long, 1.2-1.3 mm broad, 0.8 mm thick.

Rocky, gravelly, or sandy mountain slopes in grassland, woodland, and chaparral at 1,200-2,000 m (4,000-6,500 ft). Southwestern Oak Woodland and Southwestern Chaparral; edge of Desert Grassland. Arizona, known from specimens from Santa Catalina Mts. in Pima Co., Graham or Pinaleno Mts. in Graham Co., and Mule Mts. in Cochise Co.; reported by A. A. Nichol to occur also in Quinlan, Santa Rita, Huachuca, and Chiricahua Mts. (cf. map in L. Benson, *Cacti Ariz.*, ed. 2.89. *f. 23, upper left.* 1950).

Fig. 678. A hedgehog cactus, *Echinocereus ledingii*, growing at lower edge of the Southwestern Oak Woodland in the Graham (Pinaleno) Mts., Graham Co., Arizona. (Dale A. & Marian A. Zimmerman)

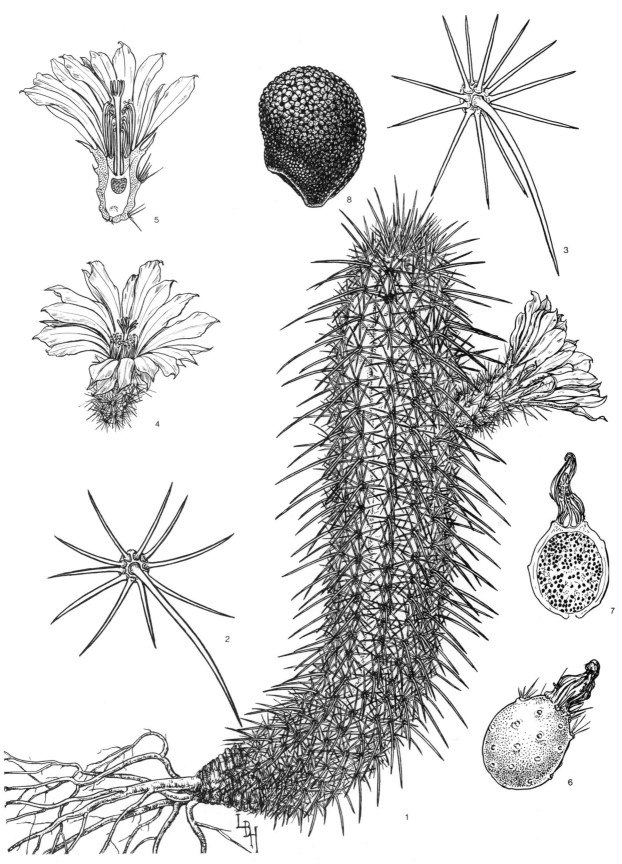

Fig. 679. A hedgehog cactus, *Echinocereus ledingii*, ×1.2, except as indicated. *1*, Plant with a flower (note here and in *2* the large, recurving central spine), ×.6. *2*, *3*, Areoles with spines and wool, ×1.8. *4*, Flower. *5*, Flower in longitudinal section. *6*, Fruit, the spines having fallen with most of the areoles. *7*, Fruit in longitudinal section. *8*, Seed, ×24.

Distinctive Characters of the Varieties of **Echinocereus engelmannii**

Character	a. var. **engelmannii**	b. var. **acicularis**	c. var. **armatus**
Stems	5-15, not forming dense masses, erect	5-15 or rarely aggregated in clumps of 50 or more, commonly erect	5-25, not densely aggregated, suberect or erect
Joint size	15-20(25) cm long, 5 cm diam	15-20 cm long, 3.8-5 cm diam	15-20(30) cm long, ±5 cm diam
Spine color	Yellow, pink, or gray; lower central slightly lighter	Pink to yellow; lower central same as others	Pink to yellow; lower central same as others
Lower (deflexed and flattened) central spine	Stout, rigid, almost straight, 3-4.4 cm long, basally ±1.2 mm broad	Relatively weak and flexible, straight, 2.5-3.8 cm long, basally 1 mm broad	Stout, rigid, curving and to some extent twisting, 3.8-4.4 cm long, basally 1.5 mm broad
Other central spines	Straight, strong, some almost equalling lower central, basally ±1 mm diam	Straight, flexible and weak, some to ±2.5 cm long, basally ±0.5 mm diam	Curving and twisting, but very strong, the longer equal to lower central, basally 1.5 mm diam
Flower diameter	5-6.2 cm	±6.2 cm	6.2-7.5 cm
Petaloid color	Magenta, medium intensity	Purplish to magenta, medium intensity	Reddish-purple, medium intensity
Altitude	600-1,500 m (2,000-5,000 ft)	300-900 m (1,000-3,000 ft)	±900 m (1,000 ft)
Floristic association	Colorado Desert; lower Mojavean Desert	Arizona Desert; edges of Mojavean and Colorado deserts	Mojavean Desert

Character	d. var. **munzii**	e. var. **chrysocentrus**	f. var. **variegatus**
Stems	5-60, becoming aggregated in mounds or clumps, suberect or erect	3-10, not densely aggregated, erect	3-6, not densely aggregated, erect
Joint size	10-20 cm long, ±5 cm diam	12.5-20(32.5) cm long, 5-6.2 cm diam	7.5-15 cm long, 3.8-5 cm diam
Spine color	Pink changing to pale gray or tan; lower central often paler	Red to yellow or reddish-brown, varying from dark to light; lower central white or pale gray	Dark red to almost black (radials nearly white); lower central white or pale gray
Lower (deflexed and flattened) central spine	Somewhat flexible, curving and twisting, 2.5-5 cm long, basally 1-1.3 mm broad	Rigid, swordlike, straight or slightly curving or twisting, 3.8-5.6 cm long, basally 1.2-1.5 mm broad	Rigid, nearly straight, 3.8 cm long, basally to 1 mm broad
Other central spines	Curving and twisting, but strong, resembling lower central, but half as long, basally 0.5-0.8 mm diam	Straight, strong, shorter than lower central, dark-colored or sometimes yellow, basally ±1 mm diam	Straight, strong, shorter than lower central, at first dark-colored, basally ±0.5 mm diam
Flower diameter	±6.2 cm	6.2-7.5 cm	±5 cm
Petaloid color	Magenta, medium intensity	Purplish to magenta, medium to dark	Purplish to magenta, rather dark
Altitude	1,950-2,400 m (6,500-8,000 ft)	900-1,500(2,160) m (3,000-5,000 or 7,200 ft)	1,150-1,710 m (3,800-5,700 ft)
Floristic association	Pacific Montane Forest; higher desert border California Chaparral	Mojavean Desert	Great Plains Grassland; Southern Juniper-Pinyon Woodland; Navajoan Desert

Distinctive Characters of the Varieties of **Echinocereus engelmannii** (cont.)

Character	g. var. **purpureus**	h. var. **nicholii**	i. var. **howei**
Stems	4-10, not densely aggregated, erect	Mostly 20-30, not densely aggregated, erect	Several, not densely aggregated, suberect
Joint size	5-20 cm long, ± 5 cm diam	30-60 cm long, 5-7.5 cm diam	±45 cm long, ±8.7 cm diam
Spine color	Dark purplish-red; lower central same as others	Clear yellow to straw or nearly white, turning black or gray; lower central same	Straw-yellow, all spines same color
Lower (deflexed and flattened) central spine	Rigid, slightly curving, 2.5(3) cm long, basally 1 mm broad	Rigid, straight, 5-6.2 cm long, basally 1.2-1.5 mm broad	Rigid, straight, ±5 cm long, basally 2 mm broad, differing little from other centrals
Other central spines	Straight to slightly curving, slender, shorter than lower central, basally 0.7-0.8 mm diam	Straight, stout, shorter than lower central, basally ±1 mm diam	Straight, very stout, almost equal to lower central, 6 forming a ring with it around a single porrect central (radials small, in 1 series)
Flower diameter	5-6.2 cm	5-6.2 cm	±7.5 cm
Petaloid color	Purple, very dark	Lavender, pale	Purplish lavender, medium intensity
Altitude	±860 m (2,900 ft)	300-900 m (1,000-3,000 ft)	±430 m (1,400 ft)
Floristic association	Mojavean Desert	Arizona Desert and upper edge of Colorado Desert	Mojavean Desert

7. Echinocereus engelmannii (Parry) Lemaire

Stems 3-60, forming open or dense clumps, masses, or mounds, to 30-60 cm high and 60-90 cm diam; larger stems green, cylindroid, usually elongate, 15-60 cm long, 3.8-8.7 cm diam; ribs commonly 10-13; tubercles not prominent; areoles circular, ±6 mm diam, typically 20-30 mm apart, not bearing white felt after first year; spines numerous but not obliterating stem surface; central spines varying among varieties, 2-6 per areole, the lower one declined and flattened, others variable, straight, curved, or twisted, the longer 2.5-7.5 cm long, basally 1-1.5 mm broad, flattened, narrowly elliptic in cross section; radial spines variable among varieties, 6-12 per areole, spreading close to stem, straight, the longer mostly 8-12 mm long, basally averaging ±0.5 mm broad, acicular, elliptic in section; flower 5-7.5 cm diam and long; sepaloids with magenta to purple or lavender midribs and lighter or green margins, the largest lanceolate-oblong, to 3.8-4.5 cm long, 3-7.5 mm broad, acute or obtuse, mucronate, entire; petaloids purple to magenta or lavender, the largest cuneate-oblanceolate, 3.8-5 cm long, 20-25 mm broad, rounded, mucronulate; filaments purplish, ±12 mm long; anthers yellow, 1.2-1.3 mm long; style pinkish, 20-30 mm long, 1.5 mm greatest diam; stigmas 8-10, 3-4.5 mm long, rather stout; ovary in anthesis 12-20 mm long; fruit green, turning to red at maturity, with spine clusters deciduous, 20-30 mm long, ±12-25 mm diam; seeds deeply reticulate-pitted, 1.5 mm long, 1.2 mm broad, 1 mm thick.

The plentiful red fruits are edible, and they are eaten by birds and rodents. The ovary is rich in sugar and the seeds in fats. The Pima Indians consider the fruits a delicacy.

Echinocereus engelmannii is larger and more formidable than its relatives E. *fendleri* and E. *fasciculatus*. The stem clumps are larger and composed of larger joints, and the spines are stouter. The presence of four major central spines produces an impressive array of protruding points.

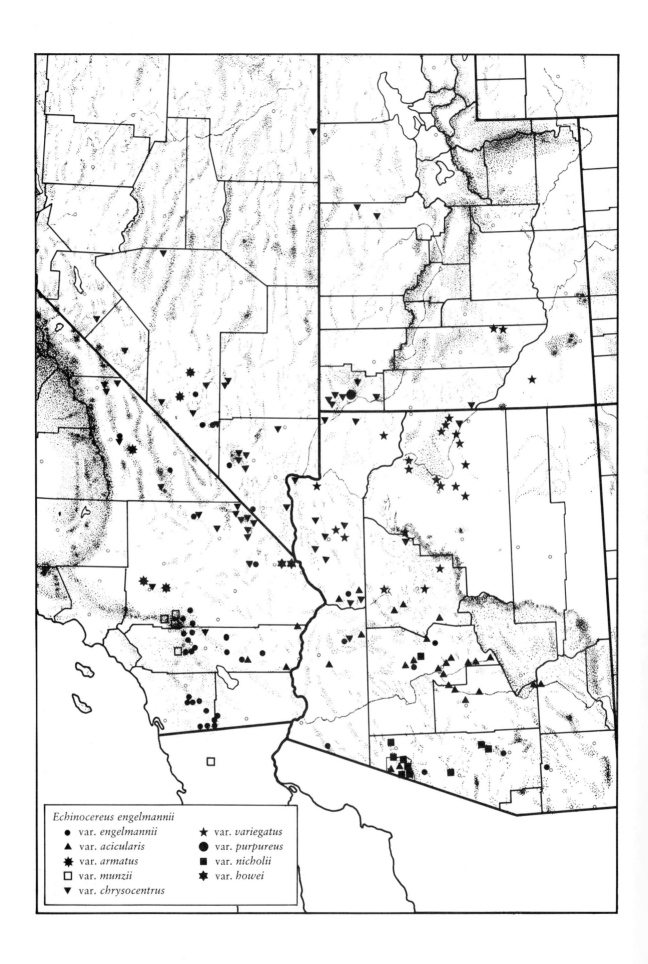

Echinocereus engelmannii
- ● var. *engelmannii*
- ▲ var. *acicularis*
- ✳ var. *armatus*
- □ var. *munzii*
- ▼ var. *chrysocentrus*
- ★ var. *variegatus*
- ⬤ var. *purpureus*
- ■ var. *nicholii*
- ✶ var. *howei*

Fig. 680. A hedgehog cactus, *Echinocereus engelmannii* var. *engelmannii*, typical stem cluster, the spines rather stout, Colorado Desert near Palm Springs, Riverside Co., California. Brittle bush or incienso, *Encelia farinosa*, in the background.

7a. Echinocereus engelmannii var. engelmannii. Gravelly, sandy, or rocky soils of hillsides, washes, and canyons in the desert at 600-1,500 m (2,000-5,000 ft). Mojavean and Arizona deserts but principally Colorado Desert. California in lower elevations of Mojave Desert and in mountains of N and w Colorado Desert from Inyo and San Bernardino Cos. to San Diego Co. and w edge of Imperial Co.; Nevada in s Nye and N Clark Cos.; Arizona (rare) in s Mohave Co. and Yuma Co. and from NE Maricopa Co. to Pima Co. and Benson, Cochise Co. Mexico in N Baja California and NW Sonora.

The prominent spine mass of var. *engelmannii* attracts attention even when the plant is not flowering, and the clumps are magnificent when flowers are present.

7b. Echinocereus engelmannii var. acicularis L. Benson. Rocky, sandy, or gravelly hillsides, washes, and plains in the desert at 300-900 m (1,000-3,000 ft). Arizona Desert and adjacent edges of Mojavean and Colorado Deserts. California in E Riverside Co.; Arizona from s Mohave Co. near Bill Williams R. to s Yavapai Co. and to Yuma, Maricopa, w Graham, Pinal, and w Pima Cos. Mexico in adjacent Baja California and in Sonora.

The variety was the basis for the illustration in Emory, Rept. U.S. & Mex. Bound. Surv. 2: Cactaceae, *pl. 57.* 1859.

Var. *acicularis* is smaller than most other varieties of the species, but it is conspicuous on the desert floor and hillsides because of its golden masses of slender, needlelike spines.

Intergrades with *E. fasciculatus* vars. *boyce-thompsonii* and *fasciculatus*.

In Palm Canyon in the Kofa Mts., Yuma Co., Arizona, there is a slender, creeping form of this variety. Colonies with 50 or more stems up to 60 cm long and only ±5 cm diam occurred among rocks and on the flat tops of boulders and ledges

Fig. 681. A hedgehog cactus, *Echinocereus engelmannii* var. *acicularis*, in flower; Arizona Desert in central Arizona. (Homer L. Shantz)

Fig. 682. *Echinocereus engelmannii* var. *acicularis* in flower, showing the slender, somewhat flexible spines.

644

(*Benson & Darrow 10870, Pom, Ariz*). Specimens of the form were collected in 1941, but when the area was visited about 15 years later many plants had been killed by drought. During subsequent visits few plants have been found.

A collection of var. *acicularis* from the Apache Trail near Fish Creek, Maricopa Co., Arizona, has principal central spines as much as 10 cm long (*McKelvey 735, US 1532949, GH*). The two accessory centrals are as much as 3 cm long. Keil and Lehto found a similar plant (but with the spines broad, as in var. *engelmannii*) near Lake Pleasant, Maricopa Co., north of Phoenix (*ASU, Pom, Keil & Lehto 10401, ASU*). Later study in the field near New River opposite the Black Canyon Refuge (*L. Benson 16617, Pom*) revealed a highly heterozygous population in which long spines occurred in a few of many character com-binations. Parental types of the population appeared to include *Echinocereus engelmannii* vars. *engelmannii* and *acicularis* and *E. fasciculatus* vars. *fasciculatus* and *boyce-thompsonii*.

7c. Echinocereus engelmannii var. **armatus** L. Benson. Among granite boulders of hillsides in the desert at about 900 m (3,000 ft). Mojavean Desert. California in Argus Mts., Inyo Co., and in granite dells and on hillsides E of Victorville, San Bernardino Co.; Nevada at Nevada Test Site, Nye Co. (s of Ribbon Cliffs and NW of Pahute Mesa).

The clumps of stems are conspicuous because of their numerous and very stout golden spines. The remarkably numerous spines protect the plants well from desert animals seeking the stored water.

Fig. 683. A hedgehog cactus, *Echinocereus engelmannii* var. *armatus*, the spines very dense and stout, but elongate and somewhat curving; near Twenty-nine Palms, San Bernardino Co., California. In the background is a mojave yucca, *Yucca schidigera*.

7d. Echinocereus engelmannii var. **munzii** (Parish) Pierce & Fosberg. Rocky, gravelly, or sandy soil of mountainsides and canyons in pine woods and chaparral (some of which resembles superficially a Juniper-Pinyon Woodland) at 1,950-2,400 m (6,500-8,000 ft). Pacific Montane Forest and California Chaparral. Southern California in the San Bernardino, San Jacinto, and (reportedly) Laguna Mts. Mexico in adjacent Baja California.

This variety resembles its geographical neighbor *Echinocereus triglochidiatus* var. *mojavensis* in form and in its masses of curving and twisting light gray spines. It is distinguished readily, however, by the betacyanin pigmentation of its flowers (magenta, i.e. red and blue coloring); the flowers of *E. triglochidiatus* var. *mojavensis* are a pure red with some yellow tinges. In the vegetative state the plants are recognized easily by the four central spines (except in an occasional areole). These contrast with the single centrals found in *E. triglochidiatus* var. *mojavensis*.

7e. Echinocereus engelmannii var. **chrysocentrus** (Engelmann & Bigelow) Engelmann *ex* Rümpler. Sandy hills, low mountains, and washes in the desert at 900-1,500(2,160) m (3,000-5,000 or 7,200 ft). Mojavean Desert. California from White Mts., Inyo Co., to higher desert mountains of Riverside Co.; SE Nevada from Esmeralda Co. to Clark Co. and sparingly NE to Nye and Elko Cos.; Utah in Great Salt Lake Desert (rare) and in Washington Co. and s Kane Co.; Arizona in Mohave Co., in N Yuma Co., at Lee's Ferry on the Colorado R. in Coconino Co., and in N Yavapai Co. Rarely in the Sagebrush Desert, as near the Great Salt Lake.

The long, white, and deflexed lower central spine, which has the appearance of a sword, is in the field the most conspicuous feature of this variety. Engelmann, who provided the name for the variety, knew the spine to be white, and the epithet *chrysocentrus* is unexplained.

Fig. 684. A hedgehog cactus, *Echinocereus engelmannii* var. *munzii*, showing the long, twisting spines; desert-edge California Chaparral at 2,025 m (7,000 feet) elevation in the San Bernardino Mts., California.

Fig. 685. A hedgehog cactus, *Echinocereus engelmannii* var. *chrysocentrus*, typical clump of stems on limestone desert pavement in the upper Mojavean Desert, Beaverdam Mts., Washington Co., Utah. Each central spine is white and daggerlike, each slants downward.

Fig. 686. *Echinocereus engelmannii* var. *chrysocentrus*, plant growing in a crevice of limestone rocks; upper Mojavean Desert, Beaverdam Mts., Washington Co., Utah.

647

7f. Echinocereus engelmannii var. **variegatus**
(Engelmann & Bigelow) Engelmann *ex* Rümpler.
Rocky or gravelly soils of hillsides in grasslands,
woodlands, and deserts at 1,150-1,710 m (3,800-
5,700 ft). Great Plains Grassland, Southern Juniper-Pinyon Woodland, and Navajoan Desert.
Utah in Henry Mts., Garfield Co.; Arizona in N
Mohave Co. and E to N Coconino Co. and rare
in Gila Co.

This small variety has only a few stems. These
are covered by dark spines, partly brown and
partly purplish.

7g. Echinocereus engelmannii var. **purpureus**
L. Benson. Sandy and gravelly soils derived from
the red sandstones of the Navajo country in the
desert at 860 m (2,900 ft). Mojavean Desert. SW
Utah in the vicinity of St. George, Washington
Co.

This small local variety has only a few stems.
It is striking because of its purplish spines, which
are conspicuous against the brownish or tannish-
red sand and rock of its habitat.

7h. Echinocereus engelmannii var. **nicholii** L.
Benson. Gravelly or sandy flats and hillsides in
the desert at 300-900 m (1,000-3,000 ft). Arizona
Desert and upper edge of Colorado Desert. Arizona in White Tank Mts., Maricopa Co., and in
Pima Co. from Organ Pipe Cactus National Monument to Silver Bell Mts.; reported by A. A.
Nichol from Mohawk Mts., Yuma Co. Mexico in
adjacent Sonora.

Var. *nicholii* is a giant among the varieties, and
its golden-yellow spine masses are visible from
far away. They make the numerous tall, slender
stems of the clumps conspicuous. The patina-cov-
ered "black" limestone of the background rocks

Fig. 687. A hedgehog cactus, *Echinocereus engelmannii* var. *variegatus*, with the typical small clumps of stems and the typical scattered occurrence on limestone desert pavement; Navajoan Desert, Navajo Reservation, south of the Marble Canyon of the Colorado River, Coconino Co., Arizona.

in most habitats is in strong contrast to the plants. The flowers are pale and much less obvious than those of the other varieties.

7i. Echinocereus engelmannii var. **howei** L. Benson. Desert hills at about 430 m (1,400 ft). Mojavean Desert. California, San Bernardino Co. opposite extreme tip of s Nevada.

This rare plant is the largest of all the varieties of the species, and its yellow spines are among the stoutest.

8. Echinocereus enneacanthus Engelmann

Stems up to 120-350 or more (counted by Clark Champie for var. *stramineus*), forming extensive clumps sometimes to 30+ cm high and 0.6(2) m diam; larger stems light or dark green, cylindroid, 15-30 cm long, 3.8-7(10) cm diam; ribs 7-13; areoles 3-4.5 mm diam, typically 12-45 mm apart; spines dense to sparse in different varieties; central spines straw-colored or gray at maturity, at first tan to brown or reddish-brown, 1-4 per areole, tending to be solitary in young plants (and therefore also solitary on lower parts of older stems) but often 3 or 4 centrals on later growth of older plants, spreading, straight, longer 1.2-8.7 cm long, basally ±1 mm broad, somewhat flattened, elliptic in cross section; radial spines straw-colored or gray, 6-14(15) per areole, parallel to stem surface, straight, longer 1.2-3 cm long, basally 0.75-1.5 mm diam, acicular; flower (5)7.5-12.5 cm diam and long; sepaloids with reddish-purple midribs and magenta to purple margins, largest cuneate, 2.5-4 cm long, 12-20 mm broad, apically rounded to nearly truncate, mucronate; petaloids magenta to purplish, largest obovate-cuneate, 5-6.2 cm long, 25-30 mm broad, rounded and mucronate, somewhat toothed; filaments lavender to red or purple or rarely green, 12 mm long; anthers yellow, narrowly oblong, 1.2 mm long; style tinged with magenta, 40-45 mm long, 3 mm greatest diam; stigmas 8-10, flat, ±9 mm long, ±1.5 mm broad; ovary in anthesis ±25 mm long; fruit red, with ultimately deciduous spines, 38-50 mm long, 30-38 mm diam; seeds (according to the variety) strongly tuberculate to pitted, 1-1.4 mm long, ±1 mm broad, ±0.7 mm thick.

Distinctive Characters of the Varieties of **Echinocereus enneacanthus**

Character	a. var. **enneacanthus**	b. var. **brevispinus**	c. var. **stramineus**	d. var. **dubius**[a]
Stems	Mostly clustered, becoming numerous, decumbent	Clustered, several or sometimes numerous, decumbent	Mound-forming, up to 350 or more, mostly erect or suberect	Clustered, usually several to 100, decumbent
Stem diameter	3.8-5 cm	3.8-4.5 cm	5-7.5 cm	5-7(10) cm
Ribs	(7)8-10	7-8	Mostly 10-12	7-9(10)
Radial spines	Not markedly obscuring stem, gray to straw-colored, 7-12, mostly 8 per areole	Not obscuring stem, gray or straw-colored, 10-13 per areole	Obscuring stem, forming a conspicuous straw-colored mass, 9-14 per areole	Sparse, not obscuring stem, gray to straw-colored, 6-12, mostly few per areole
Central spines	Usually 1, 2-3.8(5) cm long, ±1 mm basal diam	Usually 1, 1.2-2.2 cm long, ±0.75 mm basal diam	2-4, in upper areoles (only 1 in lower, on juvenile part of stem), 5-8.7 cm long, 1 mm basal diam	1 (sometimes more in upper areoles), 5-7 cm long, stout, to 1.5 mm basal diam
Flower diameter	5-8.7 cm	5-5.6 cm	10-12.5 cm	7.5-10 cm
Altitude	To 900 m (3,000 ft)	Low altitudes near sea level	1,200-1,600 m (4,000-5,300 ft)	840-1,200 m (2,800-4,000 ft)
Floristic association	Chihuahuan Desert; Edwards Plateau; Rio Grande Plain	Rio Grande Plain	Chihuahuan Desert	Chihuahuan Desert

[a] Var. *dubius* also differs from the three other varieties as follows: areoles 1.9-4.5 cm apart (others 1-2 cm); petaloids 10-15 cm long (others 15+); surface reticulum of the seed obscurely tuberculate, the pits more conspicuous than the tubercles (others tuberculate, the tubercles obscuring the intervening pits).

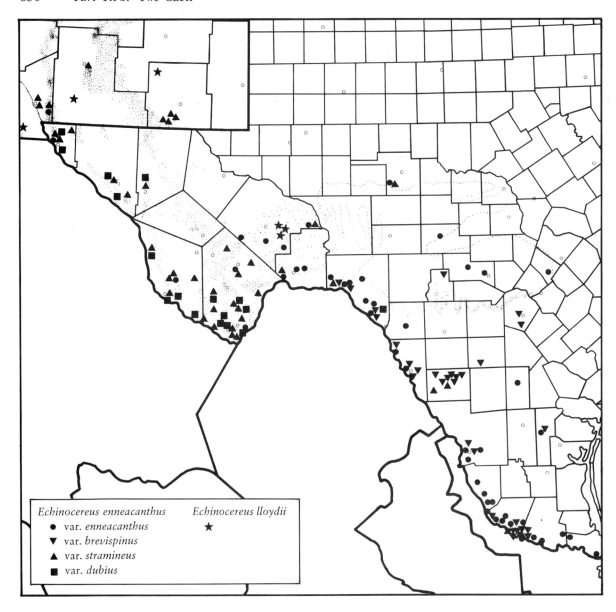

Echinocereus enneacanthus   Echinocereus lloydii
● var. *enneacanthus*   ★
▼ var. *brevispinus*
▲ var. *stramineus*
■ var. *dubius*

The characters of the three varieties *enneacanthus*, *stramineus*, and *dubius* may be found in various combinations in areas of intermediate altitude (e.g. TEXAS. 60 mi. s of Alpine, Brewster Co., 3,700 ft, *L. & R. L. Benson 15492, Pom, 15493, Pom*).

8a. Echinocereus enneacanthus var. enneacanthus. Mostly limestone soils but sometimes clay-loam soils of rocky or gravelly hills and washes or plains in the desert, brushlands, or grasslands at mostly 900 m (3,000 ft) or less. Chihuahuan Desert and adjacent grasslands or brushlands of Edwards Plateau and Rio Grande Plain. New

Mexico in Ash Canyon, Dona Ana Co.; Texas in mixed populations with the other varieties along the Rio Grande near and below El Paso and occasional (and better segregated) from valley of lower Pecos R. E across Edwards Plateau to Hays and Jim Wells Cos. but mostly SE near the Rio Grande to Cameron Co. Mexico in Chihuahua, Coahuila, and Nuevo León.

The numerous, closely packed but erect stems are primarily green, the surfaces being little obscured by spines. The greenness of the clump makes it inconspicuous in or between thickets of other vegetation except when the numerous and large magenta to purple flowers appear.

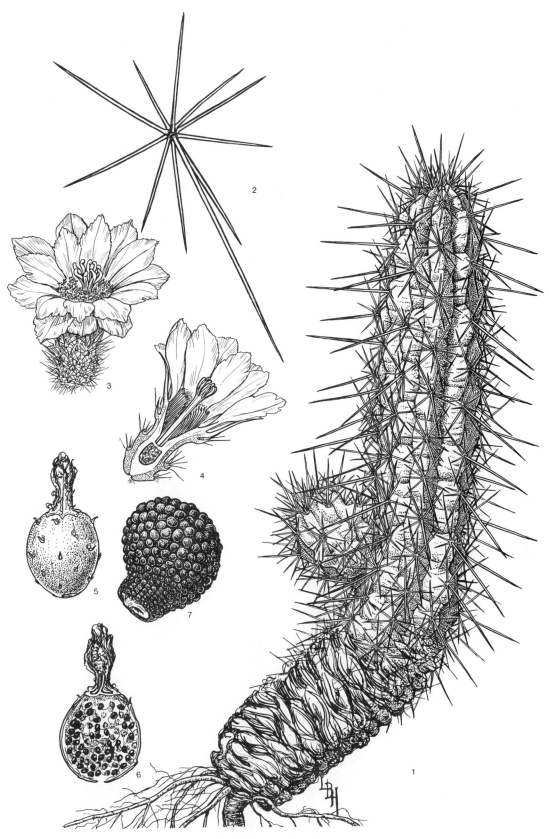

Fig. 688. A hedgehog cactus, *Echinocereus enneacanthus* var. *enneacanthus*, ×.9, except as indicated. *1*, A developed stem and a young branch, ×.6. *2*, Areole with spines and a little wool, ×1.8. *3*, Flower. *4*, Flower in longitudinal section. *5*, Fruit, after fall of the spines. *6*, Fruit in longitudinal section. *7*, Seed, ×26.

Fig. 689. A hedgehog cactus, *Echinocereus enneacanthus* var. *enneacanthus*, showing the close spacing of the areoles along the ribs; Roma, Starr Co., Texas. Flower buds are developing.

Fig. 690. A hedgehog cactus, *Echinocereus enneacanthus* var. *stramineus*, mound of more than 100 stems, each densely covered with a mass of straw-colored spines; Big Bend National Park, Brewster Co., Texas.

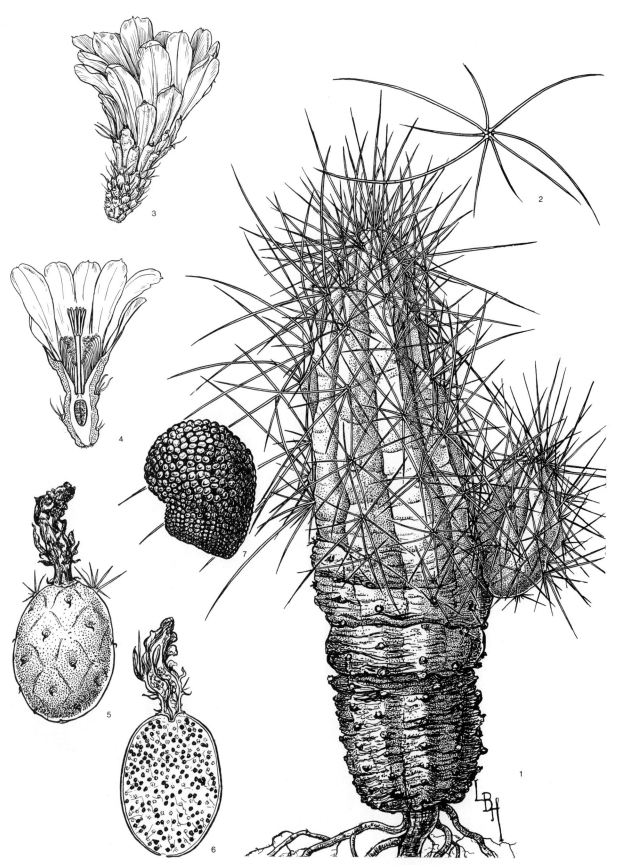

Fig. 691. A hedgehog cactus, *Echinocereus enneacanthus* var. *stramineus*, ×.6, except as indicated. *1*, Stem with a younger joint developing from the lower part. *2*, Areole, showing the spines. *3*, Flower. *4*, Flower in longitudinal section. *5*, Fruit, after fall of most of the spines. *6*, Fruit in longitudinal section. *7*, Seed, ×24.

8b. Echinocereus enneacanthus var. **brevispinus** (W. O. Moore) L. Benson. Gravelly soils and loam in grasslands and on edge of desert at low elevations. Rio Grande Plain. Texas along lower Rio Grande from Langtry, Val Verde Co., to Hidalgo Co. and E to Real, Bexar, and Jim Wells Cos. Probably common on Mexican side of Rio Grande, but known definitely from only Monclova, Coahuila, and Nuevo Laredo, Tamaulipas.

Similar in appearance to var. *enneacanthus*, but smaller.

8c. Echinocereus enneacanthus var. **stramineus** (Engelmann) L. Benson. Mostly limestone soils of hills and washes in the desert at 1,200-1,600 m (4,000-5,300 ft). Chihuahuan Desert. New Mexico in Dona Ana, Otero, and Eddy Cos.; Texas w of Pecos R. from El Paso Co. to s Pecos and w

Val Verde Cos. Mexico from N Chihuahua to San Luis Potosí.

The large, rounded clumps of stems resemble mounds of straw, except that the "straws" (spines) protrude from radiating internal cylinders. At some time during April these apparent straw-stacks turn to masses of lavender and purple flowers.

8d. Echinocereus enneacanthus var. **dubius** (Engelmann) L. Benson. On limestone soils of valleys and washes in the desert at 840-1,200 m (2,800-4,000 ft). Chihuahuan Desert. Texas near El Paso (rare) and near Rio Grande w of Pecos R. from Hudspeth Co. to Presidio and Brewster Cos. and near Del Rio. Doubtless on Mexican side of river in N Chihuahua.

The stems are more in evidence than the sparse spines, and the clumps are green or lead-green.

Fig. 692. A hedgehog cactus, *Echinocereus enneacanthus* var. *dubius*, in cultivation at Tucson, Arizona. Though the spines are long, the areoles are widely spaced, and the stem ribs are conspicuous.

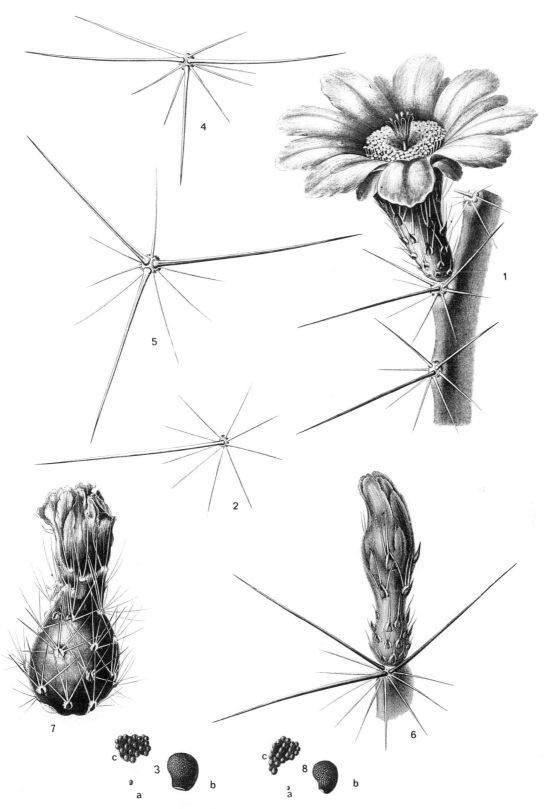

Fig. 693. A hedgehog cactus, *Echinocereus enneacanthus* var. *dubius*. *1*, Portion of a rib of the stem, with a flower. *2, 4, 5*, Areoles with spines and wool; note the small number of spines per areole in this variety. *3, 8*, Seeds: *a*, natural size; *b*, ×8; *c*, enlargement, showing the tubercles of the surface of the seed coat. *6*, Areole with a flower bud. *7*, Fruit, with the spine clusters still present. (Paulus Roetter in Engelmann/Emory, *pl. 50*)

9. Echinocereus lloydii Britton & Rose

Plant with a single stem or with several in a clump 15-20 cm high and 30+ cm diam; larger stems green, cylindroid, 15-20 cm long, ±7.5-10 cm diam; ribs 12; tubercles distinguishable along ribs; areoles circular, ±4.5 mm diam, typically 6-9 mm apart on rib; spines rather dense but only partly obscuring stem; central spines red with some gray surface coating, 2-5 per areole, spreading, straight, shorter than longest radial spine in same areole, longer to 12 mm long, basally to 0.8 mm diam, acicular, nearly circular in cross section; radial spines colored like centrals, 8 or 9 per areole, spreading irregularly but nearly parallel to stem, straight, longer to 15 mm long, basally 0.8 mm diam, acicular; flower ±5 cm diam, ±6 cm long; sepaloids with purplish midribs and lavender margins, the largest narrowly elliptic-oblong, 3 cm long, 6 mm broad, obtuse, mucronulate, undulate; petaloids lavender or magenta, the largest cuneate-oblanceolate, ±4 cm long, 12 mm broad, rounded, mucronulate, entire; filaments 6-9 mm long; anthers yellow, narrowly oblong, 1 mm long; style 25 mm long, 3 mm greatest diam; stigmas green, numerous (±20), 9 mm long, slender; ovary in anthesis ±25 mm long; fruit green tinged with pink, with white spines about 15 mm long, the fruit 25-30 mm long, 12-20 mm diam; seeds black, strongly papillate, domelike, broader than long, 1 mm long, ±1.5 mm broad and thick; hilum large.

Sandy or gravelly soils of flats in the desert at ±900 m (3,000 ft). Chihuahuan Desert. New Mexico from s Dona Ana Co. to Eddy Co.; Texas in Pecos Co.

These rare and beautiful plants are difficult to find, and the first reaction of the finder is usually amazement and triumph. The color pattern produced by the spines of the usually solitary stem is intricate and attractive.

See map for *E. enneacanthus* (preceding species).

10. Echinocereus pectinatus
(Scheidweiler) Engelmann

Stem solitary or with 2 or 3 basal branches; larger stems green, cylindroid, 10-30 cm long, 6-10 cm diam; ribs 15-22; areoles elliptic to narrowly so, 4.5-6 mm long, typically ±6 mm apart; spines dense, obscuring stem, pink to pale gray, straw-colored, brown, or white; central spines 0-9 per areole, in 1-3 vertical series, perpendicular to stem, straight, the longer 1-12 mm long, basally 0.35-0.5 mm diam, acicular, circular in cross section; radial spines 7-22 per areole, strongly pectinate to spreading rather irregularly, straight or curving downward in a low arc, longer 6-19 mm long, basally 0.25-0.5 mm diam, acicular, nearly circular in cross section; flower 5-12.5 cm diam and long; areoles of floral tube with short hairs and rather stout spines; sepaloids with brown or green midribs and yellow or pink to lavender margins, largest oblanceolate, 3.8-5 cm long, to 10-15 mm broad, acute, nearly entire; petaloids magenta to light purple or lavender or yellow, sometimes magenta and yellow, largest oblanceolate but with rounded apices, 4.5-6 cm long, to 12-15 mm broad, apically rounded to acute, mucronate, dentate; filaments pink or yellow, 9-12 mm long; anthers yellow, 1.5 mm long, oblong; style white, lavender, or yellowish, 25-40 mm long, 1.5-3 mm greatest diam; stigmas 13-18, ±3 mm long, stout; ovary in anthesis 12-15 mm long; fruit green or greenish-purple, with clusters of deciduous spines, subglobose or ellipsoid, 20-62 mm long, 15-45 mm diam; seeds papillate, 1.2-1.3 mm long, ±1 mm broad, ±0.7 mm thick.

In some works the varieties of *Echinocereus pectinatus* have been segregated arbitrarily into species, or even groups of species, merely on the basis of flower color. Transitional coloring involving both yellow plastid pigments and betacyanins (pink to light purple) in the petaloids appears occasionally (see Documentation). Even the plant used here in black and white to illustrate *E. pectinatus* var. *neomexicanus* (normally yellow-flowered; long ago described as a separate species, *E. dasyacanthus*) had pink to purple flowers. The plants described as *Cereus ctenoides* Engelmann combined the spine characters of var. *pectinatus* with the yellow flowers of var. *neomexicanus*.

Aside from flower color, the most striking difference between var. *neomexicanus* and vars. *pectinatus* and *wenigeri* is the greater number and size of central spines and the more disorderly placement of radials. This produces a superficially different plant. In var. *neomexicanus* the central spines are crowded into two or three irregularly segregated rows; in keeping with their small number, in vars. *pectinatus* and *wenigeri* they are usually in a single row. Sometimes in var. *pectinatus* the number of central spines is greater than usual, and through crowding they are forced into two irregular rows. The radial spines of vars. *pecti-*

Distinctive Characters of the Varieties of **Echinocereus pectinatus**

Character	a. var. rigidissimus	b. var. pectinatus	c. var. wenigeri	d. var. minor	e. var. neomexicanus
Central spines	None	3-5, in 1 or sometimes 2 vertical series, 1-3 mm long	1-3, in 1 vertical series, 2-3 mm long	2-5, in 2 vertical series or irregular, 8-12 mm long	(3)7-9, irregularly arranged, 3-7.5 mm long
Radial spine arrangement	18-22 per areole, obviously pectinate	12-16 per areole, spreading ± irregularly	14-16 per areole, spreading rather regularly	7-15, spreading ± irregularly	18-22, spreading ± irregularly
Radial spine size	7.5-9 mm long, 0.5 mm diam, stout	6-7.5 mm long, 0.25-0.35 mm diam, rigid	±6 mm long, 0.35 mm diam, slender but rigid	4.5-19 mm long, 0.25 mm diam, slender and ± flexible	9-12 mm long, 0.25-0.35 mm diam, of moderate thickness but rigid
Flower color	Purplish-lavender	Pinkish-lavender	Magenta	Magenta	Yellow
Flower diam	6.2-8.7 cm	6.2-8.7 cm	5-7.5 cm	6.2-7.5 cm	7.5-12.5 cm
Altitude	1,200-1,550 m (4,000-5,200 ft)	1,150-1,350 m (3,500-4,500 ft)	800-1,200 m (2,700-4,000 ft)	1,200 m (4,000 ft)	1,200-1,500 m (4,000-5,000 ft)
Floristic association	Desert Grassland; lower edge of Southwestern Oak Woodland	Chihuahuan Desert; Desert Grassland	Chihuahuan Desert	Chihuahuan Desert	Chihuahuan Desert; Desert Grassland

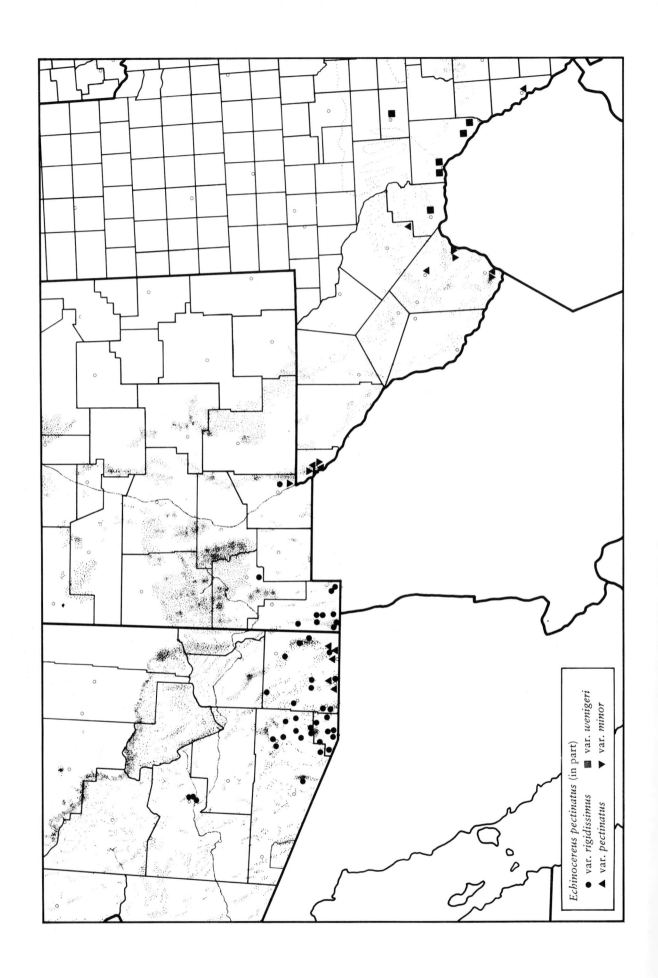

Echinocereus pectinatus (in part)

● var. rigidissimus ■ var. wenigeri

▲ var. pectinatus ▼ var. minor

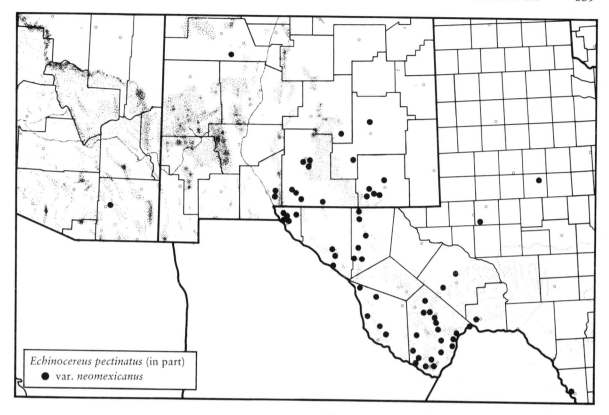

Echinocereus pectinatus (in part)
● var. *neomexicanus*

natus and *wenigeri* are intermediate in regularity in direction of spreading between the disarray of var. *neomexicanus* and the primly pectinate arrangement of var. *rigidissimus*, which has no central spines. These variations in spine types are paralleled in the more delicate spines of the varieties of *E. reichenbachii*.

Reference: Benson, 1968.

10a. Echinocereus pectinatus var. **rigidissimus** (Engelmann) Engelmann *ex* Rümpler. Limestone outcrops of hills primarily in grasslands at 1,200-1,550 m (4,000-5,200 ft). Desert Grassland and lower edge of Southwestern Oak Woodland. Southern Arizona at least formerly near Phoenix and Tempe in Maricopa Co., in Graham Co. (Galiuro Mts.), and in Pima, Santa Cruz, and Cochise Cos.; New Mexico in Hidalgo Co. and s Grant Co. Mexico in N Sonora.

The solitary, red-and-white banded stems are attractive among the grass clumps and rocks of the grassland hillsides. The opening of the large purplish-lavender flowers is an extravaganza.

10b. Echinocereus pectinatus var. **pectinatus.** Limestone hills and flats in the desert and in grasslands at 1,150-1,350 m (3,500-4,500 ft). Chihuahuan Desert and Desert Grassland. Southeast cor-

Fig. 694. *Echinocereus pectinatus* var. *rigidissimus*, showing the red and white horizontal bands of spines that give this and some other varieties of the species the name rainbow cactus; rocky outcrop in Desert Grassland near Willcox, Cochise Co., Arizona.

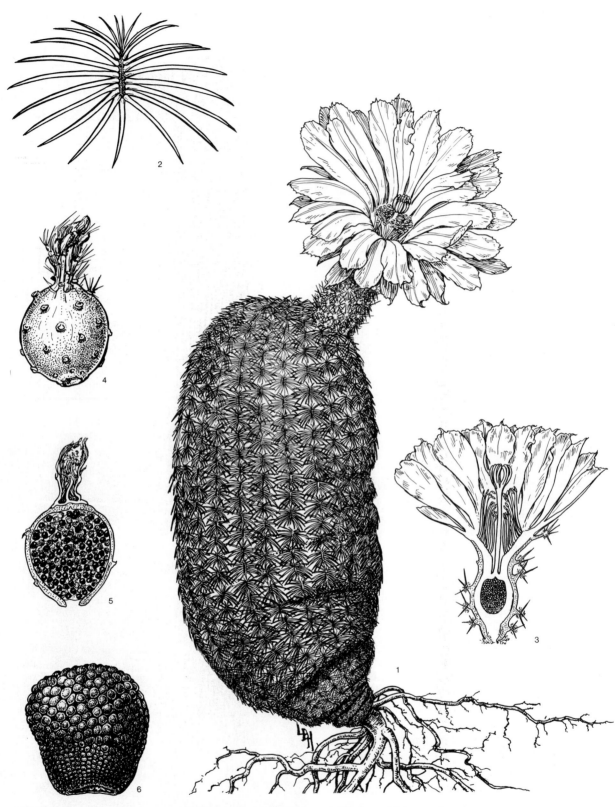

Fig. 695. Arizona rainbow cactus, *Echinocereus pectinatus* var. *rigidissimus*, ×.5, except as indicated. *1*, Plant in flower. *2*, Areole, with only radial spines, these like the teeth of a comb on each side, ×3.25. *3*, Flower in longitudinal section. *4*, Fruit after fall of the spines. *5*, Fruit in longitudinal section. *6*, Seed, ×22. (See Credits)

Fig. 696. Arizona rainbow cactus, *Echinocereus pectinatus* var. *rigidissimus*, showing the spine-bearing areoles along the ribs and an emerging flower bud (white object at left); rocky places in Desert Grassland near Willcox, Cochise Co., Arizona.

ner of Arizona (sw Cochise Co. from Mule Mts. E); Texas, rare near Rio Grande from El Paso Co. to Maverick Co. From adjacent Mexico s to San Luis Potosí and E to Victoria, Tamaulipas.

The stems have a smooth appearance because the radial spines are relatively short and the centrals minute. The pinkish-lavender flowers are especially attractive.

10c. Echinocereus pectinatus var. wenigeri L. Benson. Limestone hills in the desert at about 800-1,200 m (2,700-4,000 ft). Chihuahuan Desert. Texas in Rio Grande region from Sutton Co. to Brewster, Terrell, and Val Verde Cos. Mexico in adjacent Coahuila.

The color of the spines and the banding pattern make this an attractive plant for cultivation.

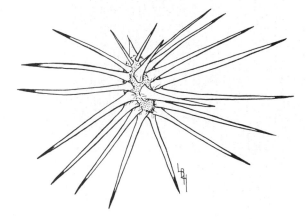

Fig. 697. A rainbow cactus, *Echinocereus pectinatus* var. *wenigeri*, an areole, ×6. The central spines are in a single row and few (in this case only two), and the radial spines are more or less like the teeth of a comb along each side. The areole of var. *pectinatus* is similar. (See Credits)

10d. Echinocereus pectinatus var. **minor** (Engelmann) L. Benson. Rocky hills and alluvial fans at about 1,200 m (4,000 ft). Chihuahuan Desert. New Mexico near Rio Grande just N of El Paso; Texas near El Paso and in Big Bend region, Brewster Co. Mexico from Sonora and NW corner of Sinaloa to Coahuila (rarely collected).

Because of its longer, more slender spines, this variety is softer in appearance than the other varieties.

Fig. 699 *(right)*. *Echinocereus pectinatus* var. *minor*, three areoles from the same plant, showing the variable number and disposition of the central spines, which tend to be in more than one row; ×5.5. The elongate, slender radial spines are characteristic of the variety. (See Credits)

Fig. 698 *(below)*. *Echinocereus pectinatus* var. *minor*, in Chihuahuan Desert at Lower Tornillo Creek, Big Bend National Park, Brewster Co., Texas. The radial spines, completely covering the stem, are longer, more slender, and more interlaced than those of vars. *pectinatus* and *wenigeri*.

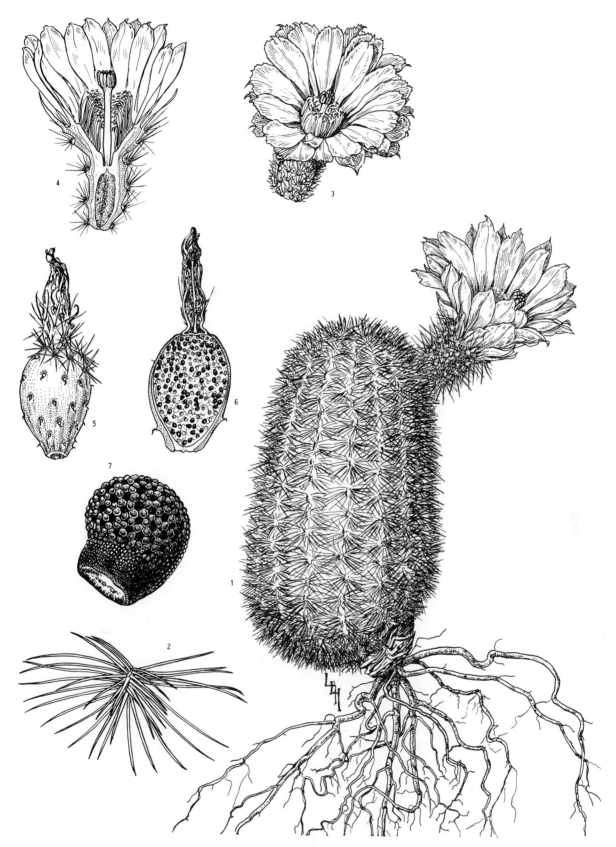

Fig. 700. A rainbow cactus, *Echinocereus pectinatus* var. *minor*, ×.6, except as indicated. *1*, Plant in flower, showing the numerous slender spines. *2*, Areole with a number of central spines and with relatively long, slender radial spines (see Fig. 699), ×2. *3*, Flower. *4*, Flower in longitudinal section. *5*, Fruit after fall of most of the spines, ×.9. *6*, Fruit in longitudinal section, ×.9. *7*, Seed, ×25.

10e. Echinocereus pectinatus var. **neomexicanus** (Coulter) L. Benson. On limestone hills and on flats in the desert and in grassland at mostly 1,200-1,500 m (4,000-5,000 ft). Chihuahuan Desert and Desert Grassland. Arizona near Benson, Cochise Co.; SE New Mexico from Valencia Co. to Chaves Co. and S; Texas from El Paso Co. to Mitchell and Terrell Cos. Mexico in N Chihuahua and perhaps NW Coahuila.

The large yellow flowers have made this variety a long-time garden favorite (under the name "*E. dasyacanthus*"). In the field the irregularity of both central and radial spines gives the stems a roughened, slightly shaggy appearance.

The distribution in Arizona is reported to be greater than the actual documentation by specimens indicates. The variety also occurs, according to J. J. Thornber, in the southern part of the Baboquivari Mts., Pima Co., and, according to A. A. Nichol, in the Perilla and Guadalupe Mts., Cochise Co., as well as perhaps in modified form in the Oro Blanco Mts. west of Nogales, Santa Cruz Co., and at Altar and Pitiquito in adjacent Sonora.

Fig. 701. Yellow-flowered rainbow cactus, *Echinocereus pectinatus* var. *neomexicanus*, in flower on a steep hillside in desert pavement in an "island" of the Chihuahuan Desert near Marathon, Brewster Co., Texas.

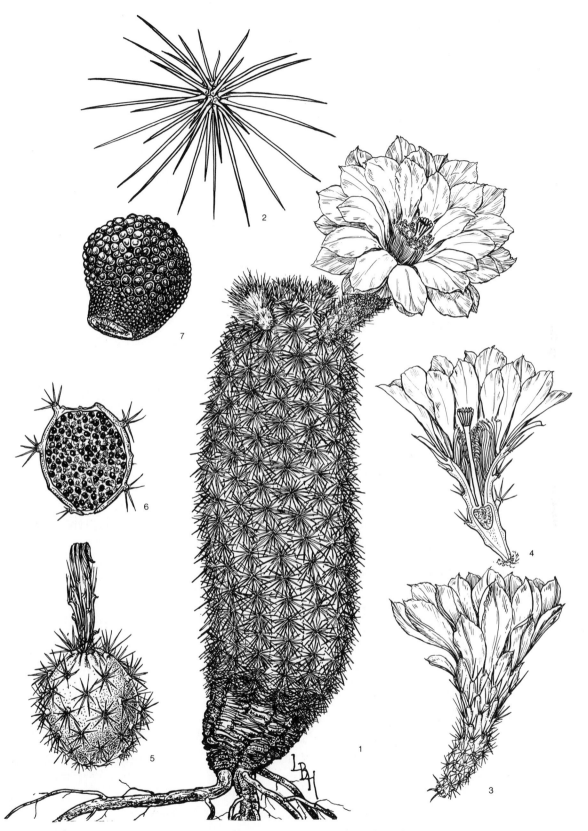

Fig. 702. *Echinocereus pectinatus* var. *neomexicanus*, ×.6, except as indicated. *1*, Plant in flower. *2*, Areole with spines, ×3.75. *3*, Flower (yellow). *4*, Flower in longitudinal section. *5*, Fruit with the spines still persistent, ×.9. *6*, Fruit in longitudinal section, ×.9. *7*, Seed, ×27.

11. Echinocereus reichenbachii
(Terscheck) Haage, *f.*, *ex* Britton & Rose

Stems solitary or sometimes to 5-12, the larger green, cylindroid, 7.5-15(22.5, or in var. *perbellus* 40) cm long, 2.5-5 cm diam; ribs about 12-18; areoles narrowly elliptic to linear, 1.5-3 mm long vertically, typically 2-4.5 mm apart; spines dense, obscuring the stem; central spines none or 1-7 per areole, much smaller than the radials but otherwise similar to them, straight, the longer 1-12 mm long; radial spines basally straw-colored, pale gray, or pink and distally pink to red, 12-32 per areole, curving downward in a low arc or straight and spreading irregularly, the longer 3-12(25) mm long, 0.2-0.35 mm diam, acicular, circular in cross section; flower 5-7.5 cm diam, 2-6 cm long; areoles of floral tube with conspicuous fine wool and weak spines; sepaloids with green midribs and pink margins, largest oblanceolate, 2.5-3 cm long, 3-7.5 mm broad, short-acuminate, entire; petaloids pink to light purple, largest oblanceolate, 2.5-3.5 cm long, ±9 mm broad, short-acuminate, entire; filaments pale yellow or pink, ±9 mm long; anthers yellow, 1.5 mm long, oblong; style pink, 20-30 mm long, 1-2 mm greatest diam; stigmas 16-20, green, ±6 mm long, broad; ovary in anthesis ±9 mm long; fruit green (with pink tinge?), with short spines and soft, conspicuous, deciduous, long wool in areoles, ±15 mm long, 9 mm diam; seeds strongly tuberculate, asymmetrical, 1.5 mm long, 1 mm broad, 0.7 mm thick.

Distinctive Characters of the Varieties of Echinocereus reichenbachii

Character	a. var. **reichenbachii**	b. var. **perbellus**	c. var. **albertii**
Areoles	Very narrow, 3 mm long	Elliptic, 2 mm long	Elliptic, 1.5 mm long
Central spines	None	None or 1 and minute, 1 mm long	None or 1, 2-3 mm long (very dark purple)
Radial spines	22-32, each curving in a low arc, 4.5-6 mm long	12-16(20), spreading ± irregularly at low angles, 4.5-6 mm long	14-16, closely pectinate, 3-4(6) mm long
Radial spine color	Basally straw-colored to pale gray, distally pink	Straw-colored to pink	White, with very dark purple tips
Altitude	Sea level to 450 m (1,500 ft)	600-1,200 m (2,000-4,000 ft)	Near sea level
Floristic association	Great Plains Grassland; Edwards Plateau	Great Plains Grassland	Rio Grande Plain

Character	d. var. **fitchii**	e. var. **chisosensis**	f. var. **albispinus**[a]
Areoles	Elliptic, 2 mm long	Elliptic, 2 mm long	Narrowly elliptic, 2 mm long
Central spines	4-7, 2-6 mm long	1-4 (not in a row), 6-12 mm long	1-3, the longest ± 3 mm long
Radial spines	18-22, spreading but ± irregular, curving slightly downward, 6-7.5 mm long	12-14, spreading ± irregularly, 6-12 mm long	12-14, spreading at various low angles, to 12(25) mm long
Radial spine color	White or straw-colored, distally tan or brownish	White or ashy	Dark, basally pink, distally red (some forms white, yellow, or brownish)
Altitude	90-300 m (300-1,000 ft)	600-900 m (2,000-3,000 ft)	400-600 m (1,300-2,000 ft)
Floristic association	Rio Grande Plain	Chihuahuan Desert	Great Plains Grassland

[a] In var. *albispinus* two characters are in need of further study (as they are in the other varieties): the petaloids are spathulate, acute, and serrate, and the fruit is nearly dry and is dehiscent; the occurrence of these characters in the complex intergrading populations in Oklahoma is not well understood.

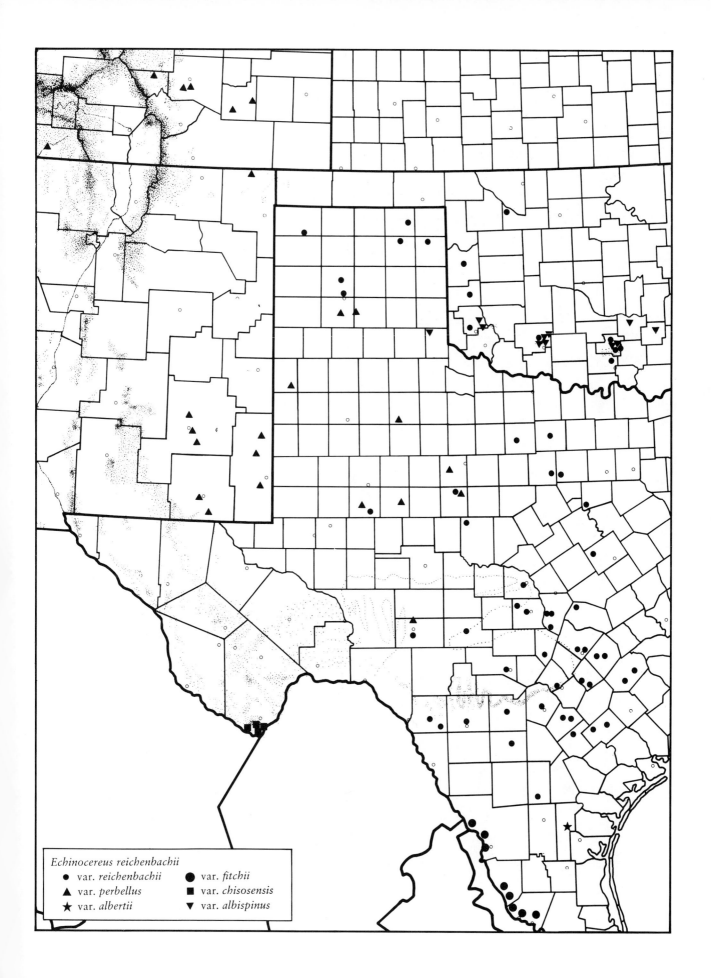

Echinocereus reichenbachii
- var. reichenbachii
- ▲ var. perbellus
- ★ var. albertii
- ● var. fitchii
- ■ var. chisosensis
- ▼ var. albispinus

667

11a. **Echinocereus reichenbachii** var. **reichenbachii.** Gravelly, rocky, or sandy soils of various origins, including especially limestone but reportedly also granitic rocks, in grasslands from near sea level to about 450 m (1,500 ft). Great Plains Grassland; Edwards Plateau. Reported from Kansas; Oklahoma in Major, Roger Mills, Beckham, Greer, Comanche, and Murray Cos.; Texas on the Canadian R. drainage in N Panhandle in Dallam, Ochiltree, Roberta, Hemphill, and Potter Cos. and in the central portion, especially on E declivity of Edwards Plateau, from Taylor, Jacks, and Johnson Cos. S to Sutton, Kinney, Frio, McMullen, DeWitt, and Austin Cos., with W outliers in Howard Co. Mexico S to San Luis Potosí.

The stem is cylindroid, but it ends in a dome. The short, appressed spine mass covers the stem but adheres strictly to its outline, forming a shining, satiny covering. Both the form of the stem and the proportionately enormous pink flowers have made the species a garden favorite for more than a century.

Fig. 703. *Echinocereus reichenbachii* var. *reichenbachii*, in rock crevices and fissures on the eastern edge of the Edwards Plateau, central Texas. The flower buds bear conspicuous fine, white wool in the areoles, as the fruits will later.

Fig. 704. *Echinocereus reichenbachii* var. *reichenbachii*, showing the vertically elongate areoles and the arrangement of the radial spines like the teeth of a comb along each edge; plants from north of Amarillo, Potter Co., Texas.

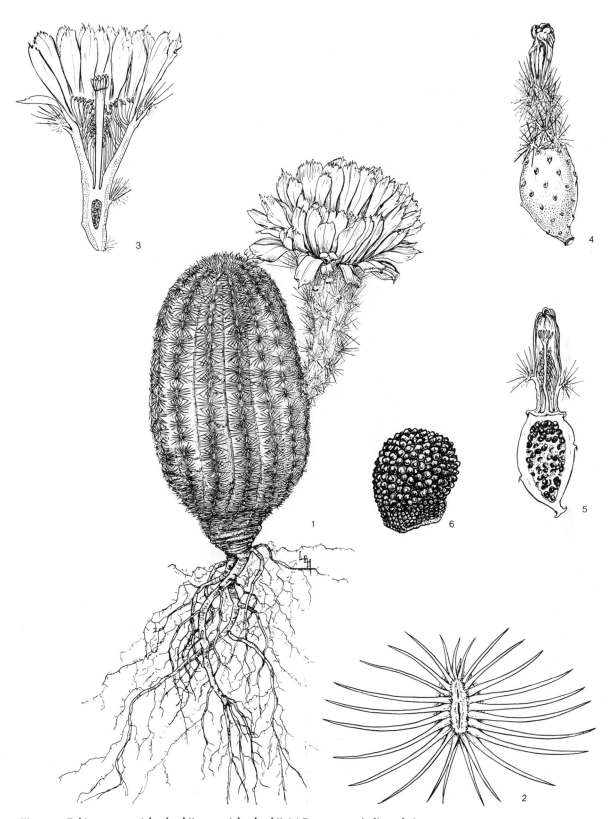

Fig. 705. *Echinocereus reichenbachii* var. *reichenbachii*, ×.7, except as indicated. *1*, Plant in flower. *2*, Areole, with radial spines and wool but without central spines, ×3.5. *3*, Flower in longitudinal section; note the long wool in the areoles of the ovary. *4*, Fruit, after fall of the spines and wool of the areoles. *5*, Fruit in longitudinal section. *6*, Seed, ×18.

Fig. 706. *Echinocereus reichenbachii* var. *perbellus*, distinguished from var. *reichenbachii* (Figs. 704 and 705) by its elliptic areoles and fewer spines; Spur, Dickens Co., Texas. Note the white wool in the areoles of the ovaries, characteristic of the species.

11b. Echinocereus reichenbachii var. perbellus (Britton & Rose) L. Benson. Sandy or rocky soil on limestone formations in the desert and in grasslands at 600-1,200 m (2,000-4,000 ft). Great Plains Grassland. Colorado in Custer, Pueblo, Archuleta, and Otero Cos.; E New Mexico in Union, Quay, Chaves, Eddy, and Lea Cos.; Texas Panhandle from Palo Duro Canyon in Randall and Armstrong Cos. s to Taylor and Sutton Cos.

This is an attractive variety usually found in out-of-the-way places. Sometimes it is abundant on rocky hills in the grasslands.

11c. Echinocereus reichenbachii var. albertii L. Benson. Fine soils near mesquite thickets in plains near sea level. Rio Grande Plain. Texas in Jim Wells Co. near Alice.

This rare variety is inconspicuous in the disturbed areas of brushland. The dark spines and purplish-lavender flowers make it unusual and attractive.

11d. Echinocereus reichenbachii var. fitchii (Britton & Rose) L. Benson. Gravelly, usually limestone soils of semidesert brushlands at 90-300 m (300-1,000 ft). Rio Grande Plain. Texas near Rio Grande from Webb Co. to Starr Co.

The plants are little gems partly hidden in underbrush and commonly overlooked.

11e. Echinocereus reichenbachii var. chisosensis (W. T. Marshall) L. Benson. Limestone soils of plains and hills in the desert at about 600-900 m (2,000-3,000 ft). Chihuahuan Desert. Texas in Big Bend National Park, Brewster Co., near Big Bend of Rio Grande.

The elongate-cylindroid stems are most conspicuous for their tendency toward whiteness of the spine mass. The white wool and slender spines of the floral tubes catch the eye at once.

11f. Echinocereus reichenbachii var. albispinus (Lahman) L. Benson. Granitic outcrops of

Fig. 707. *Echinocereus reichenbachii* var. *albertii* among mesquite leaflets in its natural habitat under a mesquite, *Prosopis juliflora* var. *glandulosa*, near Alice, Jim Wells Co., Texas; the flower larger than the stem.

hills and plains in grassland at about 400-600 m (1,300-2,000 ft). Great Plains Grassland. Southern Oklahoma from Greer Co. to Pontotoc and Johnston Cos.; Texas in Childress Co. at SE extremity of the Panhandle.

The fruit is nearly dry, and it is dehiscent; the petaloids are spathulate, acute, and serrate.

In varietal rank, use of the epithet *albispinus* is mandatory but unfortunate. It was applied to a transitory form.

In Oklahoma this variety and var. *reichenbachii* interbreed, producing perplexing hybrid swarms, individuals of which have been taken to be new species. The only collection from Texas is from a hybrid swarm derived partly from var. *perbellus* (10 mi. E of Memphis, *L. & R. L. Benson 15653, Pom*).

12. Echinocereus viridiflorus Engelmann

Stems usually solitary but sometimes a few in a clump, the larger green, ovoid to cylindroid or barrel-shaped, 2.5-20(25) cm long, (0.9)2.5-7.5 cm diam; ribs mostly 10-14, sometimes 6-9; tu-

bercles more or less prominent; areoles 2-3 mm long, elliptic or elongate, 3-6 mm apart; spines dense, obscuring stem, occurring in horizontal light and dark bands, this associated with time of development; central spines, when present, red, reddish-brown, white, pale gray, or greenish-yellow, 0-4 (usually 1) per areole, number varying at different levels on the same stem, the solitary or principal central deflexed except in areoles near the growing point, longer 12-20(30) mm long, basally 0.5-0.7 mm diam, acicular or subulate, elliptic or flattened in cross section; radial spines usually same colors as central, but lighter, the upper and sometimes lower in areole small and pale, 8(11) per areole, pectinate, almost parallel to stem, straight, the longer usually 3-9 mm long, basally 0.15-0.2 mm diam, acicular; flower (2)2.5 cm diam and long; sepaloids with magenta midribs and green or magenta margins, largest narrowly oblong to linear-lanceolate, to 1.2 cm long, to 3 mm broad, apically acute, rounded and mucronate, entire; petaloids green to magenta or reddish, largest narrowly lanceolate to oblanceolate, to 2 cm long, to 3-4 mm broad, acute, en-

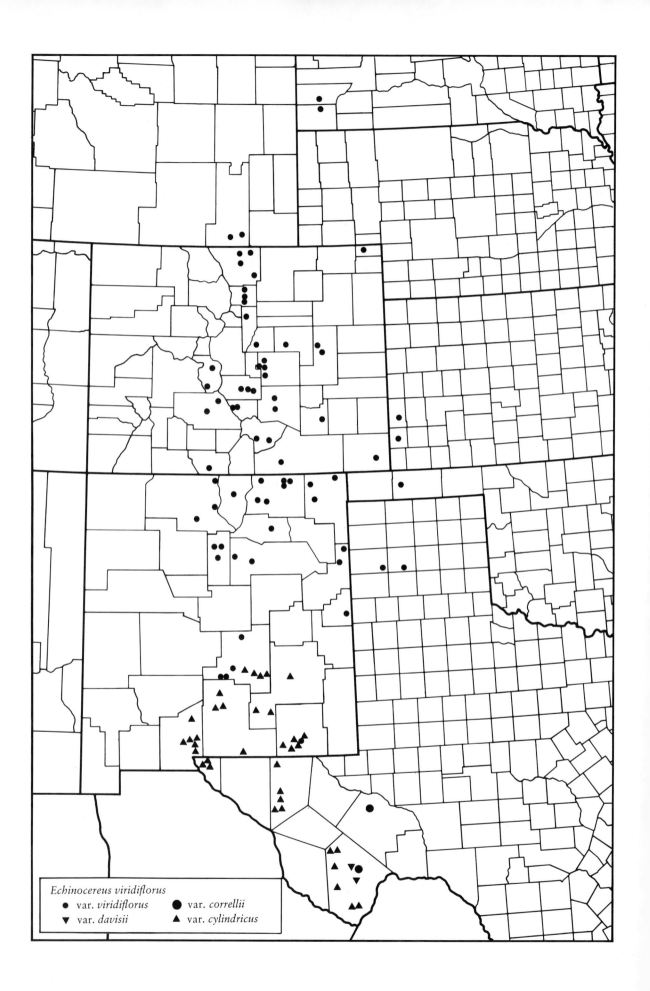

Echinocereus viridiflorus

- • var. *viridiflorus*   ● var. *correllii*
- ▼ var. *davisii*   ▲ var. *cylindricus*

tire or minutely sparsely serrulate; filaments pale green to pale pink, 6 mm long; anthers yellow, oblong, 0.7-1.3 mm long; style pale green to pink, 12-20 mm long, ±1 mm greatest diam; stigmas 5-8, ±3 mm long, relatively broad; ovary in anthesis 3-6 mm long; fruit green (or turning to red?), ±6-12 mm diam and long; seeds black, tuberculate on the reticulate pattern, in one variety the depressions in the reticulum obscure and in another obvious, 1-1.5 mm long, ±1 mm broad, 0.7 mm thick.

12a. Echinocereus viridiflorus var. viridiflorus. Gravelly soils of foothills, plains, and washes in grassland or along edges of woodlands at 1,500-2,100(2,700) m (5,000-7,000 or 9,000 ft). Rocky Mountain Parkland; Great Plains Grassland; edge of Southern Juniper-Pinyon Woodland. Higher w parts of Great Plains; foothills and outliers of adjacent Rocky Mountains and the "parks" among the eastern ranges. Wyoming near Colorado border; Colorado between E ranges of Rocky Mountains, in foothills of Front Range, and in hilly areas of mostly w portions of Great Plains; New Mexico in similar areas southward as far as N Otero, Curry, and Eddy Cos. (in the southernmost localities at about 2,400-2,700 m in the mountains); South Dakota near Wind Cave and Hot Springs, Black Hills; sw Kansas in Hamilton and Stanton Cos.; Oklahoma Panhandle in Texas

Distinctive Characters of the Varieties of **Echinocereus viridiflorus**

Character	a. var. **viridiflorus**	b. var. **davisii**	c. var. **correllii**	d. var. **cylindricus**
Stems	Small, ovoid or elongate-ovoid	Dwarf, turbinate or turbinate-ovoid	Medium, elongate-ovoid or cylindroid	Large, cylindroid or sometimes barrel-shaped
Stem size	2.5-5(12.5) cm long, 2.5-3.8 cm diam	1.2-2(2.5) cm long, 0.9-1.2(2) cm diam	7.5-12.5 cm long, 3.8-5 cm diam	10-20(25) cm long, 5-7.5 cm diam
Stem ribs	10-14	6-9	10-14	10-14
Spine color	Red, reddish-brown, white, or pale gray	Gray tipped with red or wholly gray or white	Greenish-yellow and ashy white in horizontal bands	Red, reddish-brown, white, or pale gray
Radial spines	Relatively slender, acicular, 3-4.5 mm long, 0.4 mm diam, nearly alike in all mature areoles, the lateral in areole larger	Slender to stout, variable, acicular, pectinate, 6-15 mm long, 0.2-0.5 mm diam, differing markedly on parts of plant[a]	Broad, subulate, the larger laterals ±9 mm long, 0.5 mm diam, nearly alike in all mature areoles, the lateral in areole larger	Stout, acicular, ± 9 mm long, 0.5-0.75 mm diam, nearly alike in all areoles, the upper in areole smaller
Petaloid color	Green	Yellow-green	Yellow-green	Magenta to nearly red
Anthers	Ovoid, 0.7 mm long	Ovoid, 0.75 mm long	Narrow, lanceolate, 1 mm long	Long, narrow, 1.3 mm long
Fruit length	6-9 mm	±6 mm	Unknown	12 mm
Seed coat	Tubercles of surface obscuring pits	Unknown	Unknown	Tubercles of surface not obscuring pits
Altitude	1,500-2,100(2,700) m (5,000-7,000 or 9,000 ft)	1,200-1,350 m (4,000-4,500 ft)	900-1,350 m (3,000-4,500 ft)	1,200-1,620 m (4,000-5,400 ft)
Floristic association	Rocky Mountain Parkland; Great Plains Grassland; edge of Southern Juniper-Pinyon Woodland	Desert Grassland	Desert Grassland	Great Plains Grassland; Chihuahuan Desert; Desert Grassland

[a] Radial spines of var. *davisii*: spines of first-formed areoles (low on stem) pale gray or white, slender, ±7 on each side of areole, ±6 mm long, 0.2 mm diam; spines of later-formed areoles (at stem apex) differentiated, the upper rudimentary, the lateral ±4 on each side, basally gray, tipped with red, for a plant 1.2-2 cm high very large and stout, to 15 mm long, ±0.5 mm basal diam.

Fig. 709. *Echinocereus viridi-*
florus var. *viridiflorus*, detail of
ribs and areoles, the plant at
the left with central spines and
fruits, that at the right without
central spines; Black Hills,
South Dakota.

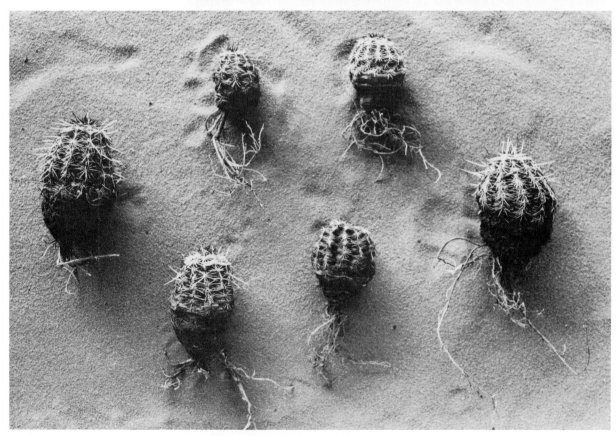

Fig. 708. *Echinocereus viridiflorus* var. *viridiflorus*, with stems of various shapes and sizes, some
with central spines and some without; west of Pueblo, Pueblo Co., Colorado.

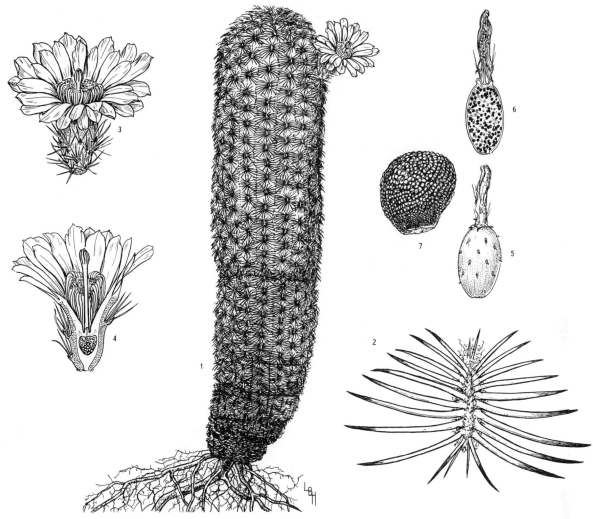

Fig. 710. *Echinocereus viridiflorus* var. *viridiflorus*, ×1.75, except as indicated. *1*, Plant from cultivation, grown proportionately much taller than those common in nature, ×1.2. *2*, The elongate or elliptic areole with pectinately arranged radial spines (often like the teeth of a comb), in this case with no central spine(s), ×6. *3*, Flower. *4*, Flower in longitudinal section. *5*, Fruit after fall of the spines. *6*, Fruit in longitudinal section. *7*, Seed, ×16.

Co.; Texas Panhandle in Oldham and Potter Cos.

Except for two smaller varieties of the same species, this is the smallest and least conspicuous hedgehog cactus in the United States. The stem is a pink-and-white, cylindroid-based dome with or without conspicuous protruding central spines.

12b. Echinocereus viridiflorus var. **davisii** (A. D. Houghton) W. T. Marshall. Rock crevices, the small stems mostly subterranean and often covered by other low-growing plants, such as a diminutive *Selaginella* (little club moss). Hills at about 1,200-1,350 m (4,000-4,500 ft). Desert Grassland. Texas s of Marathon, Brewster Co.

This is the pygmy of *Echinocereus*, and only a few protruding spines may be visible, except when the flowers are present. These are much larger than the hidden stems, which by themselves would be passed by.

12c. Echinocereus viridiflorus var. **correllii** L. Benson. Rock crevices on hills in grassland at 900-1,350 m (3,000-4,500 ft). Desert Grassland. Texas from vicinity of Ft. Stockton, Pecos Co., to the area about Marathon, Brewster Co.

The variety is small and often hidden among grasses. The greenish-yellow-tan color combination of stems and spines is distinctive.

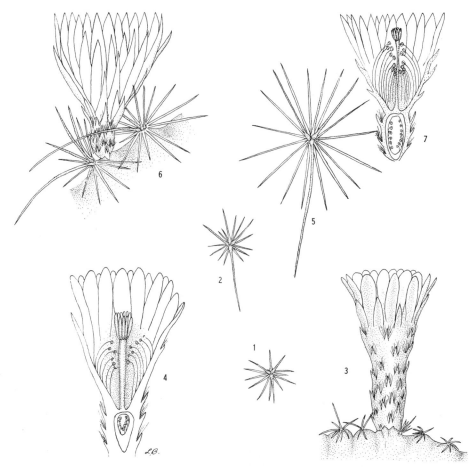

Fig. 712. *Echinocereus viridiflorus* vars. *viridiflorus* and *cylindricus*. Var. *viridiflorus*: 1, Areole with central and radial spines. 2, Areole with a long central spine. 3, Flower and adjacent rib of the stem, showing the area where the flower bud burst through the epidermis. 4, Flower in longitudinal section; note the small anthers. Var. *cylindricus*: 5, Areole with the much larger and longer central and radial spines. 6, Flower and the adjacent rib of the stem, the epidermis similarly ruptured. 7, Flower in longitudinal section; note the large anthers.

Fig. 711. *Echinocereus viridiflorus* var. *cylindricus*, cultivated plant with flowers, these small for an *Echinocereus* of this size. (A. R. Leding, U.S. Acclimatization Station, Las Cruces, New Mexico)

12d. Echinocereus viridiflorus var. cylindricus (Engelmann) Engelmann *ex* Rümpler. Rocky hillsides, especially limestone, in the desert at 1,200-1,620 m (4,000-5,400 ft). Great Plains Grassland, Chihuahuan Desert, and edges of Desert Grassland. New Mexico from Dona Ana Co. to Lincoln, Chaves, and Eddy Cos.; Texas w of Pecos R. from El Paso Co. to Culberson, Jeff Davis, and Brewster Cos. Chihuahua, Mexico, near the Rio Grande.

This is the largest variety of the species, and its elongate, cylindroid stems are detectable from as far as 30 m (100 ft).

13. Echinocereus chloranthus Engelmann

Stems solitary or few, the larger green, cylindroid, 7.5-17.5(25) cm long, ±7.5 cm diam; ribs mostly 11-17; tubercles more or less evident; areoles circular, ±3 mm diam, ±3 mm apart; spines very dense, obscuring stem; central spines red or red-and-white or brown, 5-6(10) per areole, straight, the longer 5-55 mm long, slender, but basally 0.3-0.4 mm diam, acicular, nearly circular in section; radial spines in 2 series, the inner series partly colored like the centrals and partly white, the outer white, 15-20(40) per areole, spreading at various angles, straight, the longer ±12 mm long, basally 2-4 mm diam, acicular; flower ±2.5 cm diam and long; areoles of the floral cup covering the ovary sometimes very spiny; sepaloids with reddish midribs and pale or green margins, the largest oblanceolate-linear, ±12 mm long, 2 mm broad, apically rounded; petaloids green to red, the largest narrowly oblanceolate to linear, 12-15 mm long, 2-3 mm broad, apically

rounded and mucronate, entire; filaments greenish or pinkish, 6 mm long; anthers yellow, 1 mm long, oblong; style ±12 mm long, 1 mm greatest diam; stigmas ±10, 3 mm long, rather broad; ovary in anthesis ±3 mm long; fruit 9-12 mm long and diam; seeds black, tuberculate, the tubercles coalescent and outlining the intervening pits in the reticulum, 1-1.2 mm long, nearly 1 mm broad, ±0.7 mm thick.

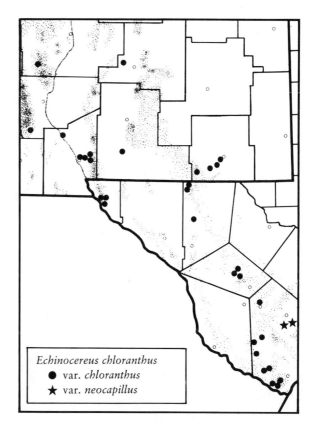

Echinocereus chloranthus
● var. *chloranthus*
★ var. *neocapillus*

Distinctive Characters of the Varieties of **Echinocereus chloranthus**

Character	a. var. **chloranthus**	b. var. **neocapillus**
Juvenile areoles (low on stem)	Spiniferous, not producing dense, fine, elongate, flexible hairs	Not spiniferous, producing dense, fine, elongate, flexible hairs, these persisting on bases of old stems
Central spines	Usually 5-6 per areole, red, red-and-white, or brown	5-10 per areole, clear translucent yellow or chalky white
Radial spines	15-20	30-40
Altitude	900-1,350 m (3,000-4,500 ft)	±1,350 m (4,500 ft)
Floristic association	Chihuahuan Desert and adjacent oak woodland and Desert Grassland	Desert Grassland

13a. Echinocereus chloranthus var. **chloranthus.** Limestone hills and slopes in the desert at about 900-1,350 m (3,000-4,500 ft). Chihuahuan Desert and adjacent oak woodland. Southern New Mexico from Socorro and Luna Cos. E to Lincoln and Eddy Cos.; Texas w of Pecos R. from El Paso Co. to Culberson, Jeff Davis, and Brewster Cos.

13b. Echinocereus chloranthus var. **neocapillus** Weniger. Hills in grassland at about 1,350 m (4,500 ft). Grassland. Texas s of Marathon, Brewster Co.

Fig. 714. *Echinocereus chloranthus* var. *chloranthus,* cultivated plant with flower buds, flowers, and young fruits. (A. R. Leding, U.S. Acclimatization Station, Las Cruces, New Mexico)

Fig. 713 (*below*). *Echinocereus chloranthus* var. *chloranthus* in flower on a rocky hillside in the Basin, Chisos Mts., Big Bend National Park, Brewster Co., Texas.

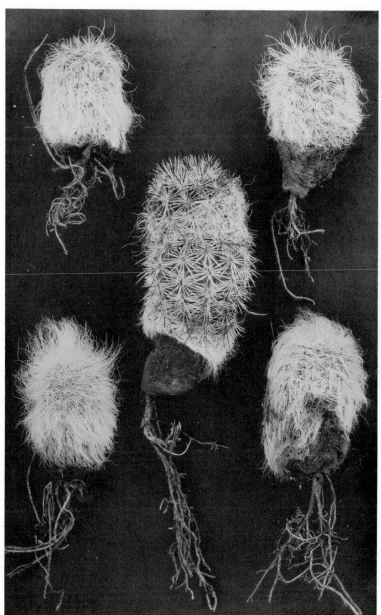

Fig. 715. *Echinocereus chloranthus* var. *neocapillus*, a variety with long, woolly spines during the juvenile period of growth, the older plant at the right with juvenile spines on the lower part of the stem and adult spines on the (later-formed) upper part. The central individual of the group at the left produced adult spines for a time, then temporarily reverted to forming the juvenile type. (A. R. Leding, discoverer of this variety; see Credits)

7. Lophophora

Stems solitary to numerous (numerous especially after injury to terminal bud), the larger short-cylindroid or hemispheroidal, mostly 2.5-7.5 cm long, 5-10 cm diam; ribs commonly ±8, the tubercles adnate with ribs and protruding far above them. Leaves none (or microscopic during early development). Areoles nearly circular, bearing compact tufts of long, persistent hairs. Spines none in mature plants; areoles of seedlings bearing a few bristle-like spines. Flowers and fruits on new growth of current season near apex of stem, each at apex of the low tubercle in a felted area adjoining spine-bearing part of areole and partly merging with it, after fall of fruit this area persistent as a circular scar. Flower 1.2-2.5 cm diam;

floral tube above ovary funnelform, pink. Fruit red, fleshy but at maturity with wall thin, transparent, and bare, elongate, clavate or nearly cylindroid, 1.2-2 cm long, ±3-4.5 mm diam. Seeds black, resembling those of *Cereus*, enlarged upward from hilum, papillate, longer than broad, 1.3 mm long; hilum obviously basal; cotyledons accumbent, not foliaceous.

One species, *L. williamsii*, in Texas and Mexico. One extraterritorial species, *L. diffusa*, in Querétaro, Mexico. See pp. 238-41.

The name means "crest-bearer," referring to the tufts of hairs in the areoles. The name "mescal," properly the name of an *Agave*, often is applied erroneously to peyote.

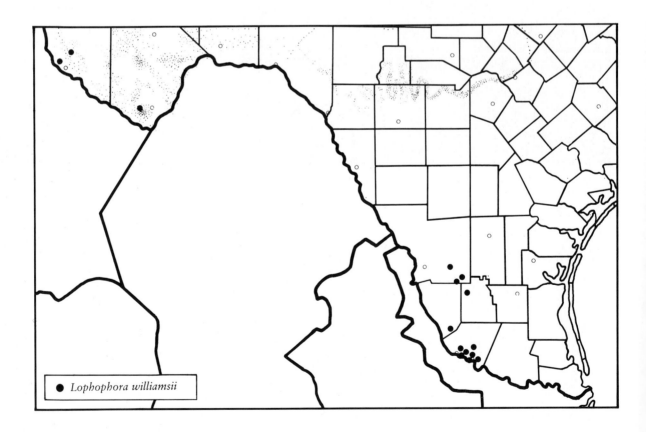

● *Lophophora williamsii*

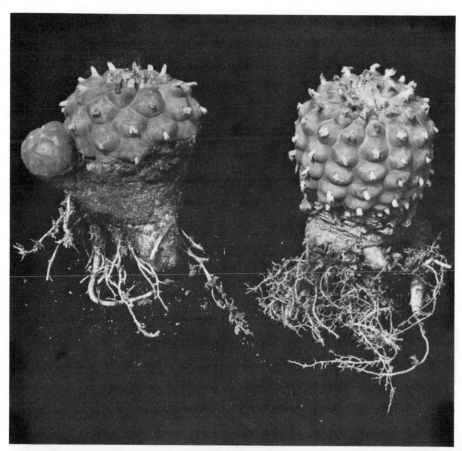

Fig. 716. Peyote, *Lophophora williamsii*, one of the plants showing the growth of a new branch with low, rounded tubercles (the basis for some described "species"); each mature areole bearing a tuft of white, more or less silky hairs.

Fig. 717. *Lophophora williamsii* in flower. (F. E. Lloyd; courtesy of Missouri Botanical Garden)

1. Lophophora williamsii (Lemaire) Coulter
Peyote

Stems solitary to numerous, glaucous-green, depressed-globose to depressed-cylindroid, moundlike, mostly 2.5-7.5 cm long, mostly 5-10 cm diam; ribs mostly ±8-12; younger tubercles at stem-apex bulging, to 5 mm high, the older flattening out as stem enlarges, irregularly hexagonal, to 25 mm diam; areoles 2-4 mm diam, typically 12-25 mm apart; spines none on mature plant, the seedlings with a few weak, bristlelike spines in areoles; during first year of growth the mature areole bearing a dense tuft of white and more-or-less silky hairs to 7-10 mm long, these later in a compact cylindroid tuft and with the ends often broken off; flower 12-25 mm diam, 12-30 mm long; sepaloids with greenish middles

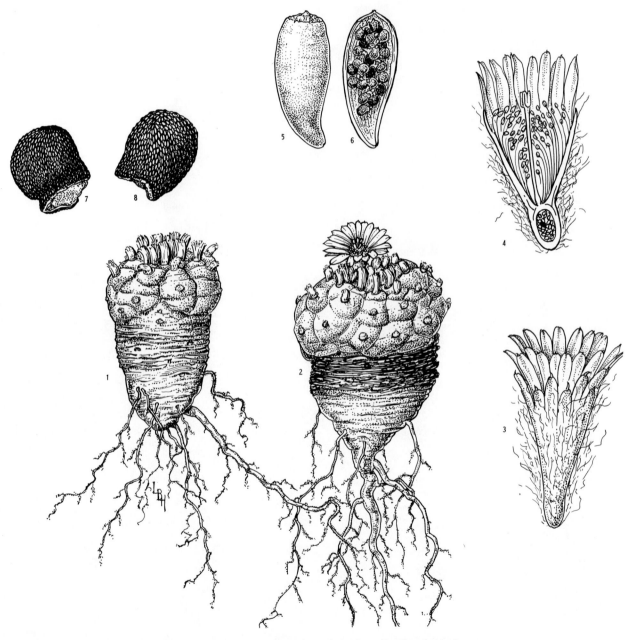

Fig. 718. Peyote, *Lophophora williamsii*, ×1.8, except as indicated. *1*, Plant showing the underground part of the stem (roughly half) and the tubercles and areoles above ground, the areoles with tufts of hairs but without spines, ×.6. *2*, Plant in flower. *3*, Flower. *4*, Flower in longitudinal section. *5*, Fruit. *6*, Fruit in longitudinal section. *7, 8*, Two views of a seed, ×15.

and pink margins, largest narrowly oblanceolate, 9-15 mm long, to 3 mm broad, acute and strongly cuspidate, the margin entire; petaloids pink in middles, pale to nearly white at margins, largest oblanceolate, 12-15 mm long, to 4 mm broad, acute and cuspidate, entire; filaments pale, ±2 mm long; anthers yellow, 1-1.4 mm long; style white, tinged with pink(?), to 9 mm long, ±1-1.5 mm greatest diam; stigmas 5, 2 mm long, 1+ mm broad, thin and flattened; ovary in anthesis turbinate, 3-4.5 mm long, smooth, not scaly, surrounded by hairs to 12 mm long; fruit red, the wall thin and transparent, fleshy at maturity, without tubercles, scales, spines, hairs, or glochids, elongate, clavate, or nearly cylindroid and enlarged gradually upward, 12-20 mm long, ±3-5 mm diam; seeds densely papillate, 1.25 mm long, 1+ mm broad, 0.8 mm thick.

Limestone or partly limestone soils of hills, alluvial fans, and flats in the desert at 150-1,200 m (500-4,000 ft). Chihuahuan Desert and Rio Grande Plain. Texas near Rio Grande from Presidio Co. to Starr Co. and E to Jim Hogg Co. Mexico s to San Luis Potosí and Querétaro.

8. Ferocactus

Plant columnar or rarely with divergent basal stems. Stems unbranched or branched (branched especially after injury to terminal bud), the larger cylindroid to ovoid or depressed-globose, 15 cm to 3 m long, 5-60 cm diam; ribs 13-30; tubercles coalescent and adnate with stem ribs. Leaves not distinguishable on mature tubercles. Areoles nearly circular to elliptic. Spines annulate or smooth, red, pink, white, tan, brown, or yellow, often with surface layer of ashy gray or becoming gray in age; central spines 4 (rarely 1 or 8), straight, curved, or hooked, to 16 cm long, basally 0.5-4 mm diam, acicular to subulate, broadly to narrowly elliptic in cross section; radial spines either colored like the central or more often lighter or white, 6-20 per areole, straight or curved, 1-7.5 cm long, basally 0.25-1(3) mm diam or width, acicular or subulate. Flowers and fruits on new growth of current season, near apex of stem or branch, developed at apex of tubercle in a felted area adjacent to spine-bearing part of areole and merging with it, this area persistent and forming semicircular to circular scar. Flower 4-7.5 cm diam; color of sepaloids and petaloids various; floral tube above ovary obconical to barely funnelform, green or tinted like perianth. Fruit fleshy at maturity, with numerous or sometimes only 10-15 broad scales, these with scarious margins, fimbriate or denticulate, short-cylindroid, ovoid, or globular, 0.8-4.5 cm long, 0.8-3.5 cm diam; floral tube persistent, opening by a short crosswise or lengthwise slit between base and middle. Seeds black, finely reticulate, reticulate-pitted, or papillate, narrowly compressed-obovoid to semicircular or obovoid with base flaring around the micropyle, longer than broad, 1-3 mm long; hilum obviously basal or "sub-basal"; cotyledons accumbent, not foliaceous.

About 20-30 species occurring from California to Texas, western Mexico, and Mexican Plateau. Six species in U.S.

The name of the genus means "wild" or "fierce" cactus.

In the list that follows, the classificational and nomenclatural status of the extraterritorial species (the unnumbered species not treated herein) has not been evaluated fully.

F. fordii
vars. fordii (Baja California)
    grandiflorus (Baja California)
F. townsendianus
vars. townsendianus (Baja California)
    santa-maria (Baja California)
F. peninsulae
vars. peninsulae (Baja California)
    viscainensis (Baja California)
F. rectispinus (Baja California)
F. chrysacanthus (I. Cedros, Baja California)
F. gracilis
vars. gracilis (Baja California)
    coloratus (Baja California)
F. gatesii (Baja California)
1. F. acanthodes
vars. a. acanthodes
    b. lecontei
        tortulospinus (Baja California)
    c. eastwoodiae
2. F. wislizenii
vars. wislizenii (in U.S. but not treated
        separately in text)
    tiburonensis (I. Tiburon, Baja California)
F. johnstonianus (I. Angel de la Guarda, Baja California)
F. diguetii
vars. diguetii (islands of Baja California)
    carmenensis (I. Carmen, Baja California)
3. F. covillei
F. robustus (Puebla)
F. echidne
vars. echidne (San Luis Potosí to Hidalgo)
    victoriensis (Tamaulipas)

F. alamosanus
vars. *alamosanus* (Sonora)
   platygonus (Sonora)
F. glaucescens (E central Mexico)
F. flavovirens (Puebla)
F. melocactiformis (E Mexico)
F. Histrix (Durango to Jalisco & Puebla; the
   flesh is used to make candy, and the fruits
   are sold in the markets)
F. macrodiscus (San Luis Potosí & southward)
4. *F. viridescens*

F. nobilis (E Mexico)
F. robustus (Baja California; status uncertain)
F. recurvus (E Mexico)
F. pilosus (N central Mexico; the acid fruits
   are sold as substitutes for lemons)
F. latispinus (Mexico)
5. *F. hamatacanthus*
vars. a. *hamatacanthus*
   b. *sinuatus*
6. *F. setispinus*
F. herrerae (W Mexico)

KEY TO THE SPECIES OF FEROCACTUS

1. Spines, or some of them, strongly and conspicuously cross-ribbed, some over 2 mm broad or in diameter; stem commonly 0.5-3 m tall, 30-60 cm in diameter; rind of the fruit yellow at maturity, thick, the pulp not very juicy.
   2. Outer radial spines *either* (1) bristlelike, flexible, white, and *not* straight but irregular *or* (2) (in a rare variety of s Arizona) rather slender but stiff, yellow, and curving.
      3. The 4 central spines surrounded by a series of radial spines of similar texture, only the outer spines slender, flexible, and curving irregularly (except in var. *eastwoodiae*, in which the radial spines are all similar to the centrals and *yellow*); plant flowering profusely during May or June after the winter rains and sporadically after the summer rains; principal central spine red to pink with a yellow tip or rarely straw-colored, *not* hooked or recurved at the apex (at least not so in most areoles of the plant; sometimes curved as much as 90°, but not recurved), the largest 5-16 cm long, 2-3(4) mm broad; stigmas terete, ±0.5 mm in diameter; seeds with the hilum clearly basal, deeply reticulate-punctate...**1. F. acanthodes**
      3. The 4 central spines surrounded by few or no spines of similar texture, all or nearly all the radial spines slender, flexible, and irregularly curving, the mature spines *not* yellow; plant flowering profusely during late summer and sometimes sporadically during spring; principal central spine red with a surface layer of ashy gray, hooked or recurved at the apex, 3.8-5 cm long, 1.5-3 mm broad; stigmas flattened, 1.2 mm broad; seeds with the hilum appearing "sub-basal," shallowly reticulate...**2. F. wislizenii**
   2. Outer radial spines *neither* (1) bristlelike *nor* (2) yellow and rigid.
      3A. Principal (and only) central spine spreading away from the stem, *not* strongly deflexed, usually apically curved or hooked; stem elongate-ovoid, 0.6-1.5(2.5) m long, 30-60 cm in diameter; sc and s Arizona and Sonora.........**3. F. covillei**
      3A. Principal central spine very stout, rigid, pointing downward through its entire length, this evident in the older areoles on the side of the plant; stem short and turgid, but length usually greater than diameter, 15-30(45) cm long, 20-35 cm in diameter; coastal s California (near San Diego) to Baja California............ ....**4. F. viridescens**
1. Spines *not* cross-ribbed, or inconspicuously so, slender, 1.25 mm or less broad or in diameter; stem at maturity 0.1-0.2 m (rarely to 0.3 m; reported to 0.6 m) tall, usually 4-15 cm in diameter; rind of the fruit green or red, thin, the pulp juicy.
   2A. Fruit green, broadly ellipsoid, ±3 cm long, with usually ±30-40 scales; seeds minutely pitted; stems 15-30 (reportedly to 60) cm high, 7.5-15 cm in diameter; central spines 4(8), to (4)6-10 cm long, to ±1.2 mm broad; anther length twice breadth.. ....**5. F. hamatacanthus**
   2A. Fruit red, spheroid, ±9-12 mm diam, with ±10-15 scales; seeds minutely papillate; stems 3.8-10(20) cm long, 3.8-5 cm in diameter; central spine 1 (sometimes with 2-3 accessory centrals), 1.2-3.8 cm long, 0.5-0.7 mm in diameter or broad; anther length 3 times breadth.....................................**6. F. setispinus**

1. Ferocactus acanthodes
(Lemaire) Britton & Rose

Plant columnar or sometimes barrel-shaped; larger stems nearly always solitary (actually un-branched), cylindroid, and usually elongate, the younger ones sometimes ovoid-cylindroid, usually 1-3 m long, averaging ±30 cm diam; ribs mostly 18-27; tubercles nearly indistinguishable; areoles elliptic, 12 mm diam, typically ±12 mm apart; spines dense, partly obscuring stem; central spines at first yellowish or red-and-yellow, usually turning red except apically, later often becoming gray (however, in var. *eastwoodiae* all spines yellow or straw-yellow), usually 4 per areole, these in a cross, the upper and lower broader, longer, and thicker, the lower usually apically curving a little, sometimes to 90°, but never hooked, the longer to 5-14 cm long, basally 2-3 (4.5) mm broad, the larger narrowly elliptic in section; radial spines colored like centrals, 6-8(14) inner ones 3.8-6.2 cm long, basally 0.5-1.5 mm diam, nearly elliptic in section, the 6-12 outer ones white, as long as inner ones but ±0.5 mm diam, flexible, curving irregularly in and out (outer radials lacking in var. *eastwoodiae*), all but the slender outer radials strongly cross-ribbed; flower 3.8-6 cm diam; 3-6 cm long; sepaloids with greenish and pink to red middles and yellowish margins, largest oblanceolate or narrowly oblong, 15-30 mm long, 4.5-9 mm broad, acute or obtuse, fimbriate (the shorter outer ones more strongly so); petaloids yellow with some red, especially along basal portions of veins, largest oblanceolate, 20-45 mm long, 4.5-6 mm broad, acute to mucronate-acuminate, somewhat serrulate-dentate; filaments yellow, 9-12 mm long; anthers yellow, narrowly oblong, 1 mm long; style yellow, 12-20 mm long, 1.5-2 mm greatest diam; stigmas ±6, ±7.5 mm long, terete and very slender, ±0.5 mm diam; ovary in anthesis 9-12 mm long; fruit yellow, fleshy at maturity, with numerous rounded, scarious-margined scales, the wall thick, usually 3-3.8 cm long, ±1.5-2 cm diam; seeds minutely reticulate-pitted, compressed-obovoid, 2-3 mm long, 1.5-2 mm broad, 1-1.5 mm thick; hilum clearly basal.

Flowering almost wholly during late spring or early summer following the winter rains; sometimes flowering sporadically after summer rains where these occur.

For recent name changes, see Documentation.

Distinctive Characters of the Varieties of Ferocactus acanthodes

Character	a. var. **acanthodes**	b. var. **lecontei**	c. var. **eastwoodiae**
Principal (lower) central spine:			
Length	7.5-14 cm	5-7 cm	7.5-8.1 cm
Basal width	2-3 mm	±2(3, or rarely 4.5) mm	±2.5 mm
Apical curvature	To about 90°, but not recurved	Curving slightly	Curving slightly
Color at maturity	Red or becoming gray	Red or becoming gray	Conspicuously yellow or straw-yellow
Inner radial spines (similar to centrals)	6-8, 1-1.5 mm diam	6-8, 1-1.5 mm diam	12-14, 0.5 cm diam
Outer radial spines (unlike centrals)	Nearly white, flexible, curving irregularly in and out, 3.8-6.2 cm long, 0.5 mm diam	Nearly white, flexible, curving irregularly in and out, 3.8-5 cm long, 0.5 mm diam	Outer form lacking; all radials similar to centrals (nearly straight, rigid)
Altitude	60-450(600) m (200-1,500 or 2,000 ft)	750-1,500 m (2,500-5,000 ft); in central and sw Arizona at 300-900 m (1,000-3,000 ft)	390-1,140 m (1,300-3,800 ft)
Floristic association	Colorado Desert	Mojavean Desert; Arizona Desert; upper edge of Colorado Desert	Arizona Desert

1a. Ferocactus acanthodes var. **acanthodes.**
Gravelly or rocky hillsides, canyon walls, alluvial
fans, and wash margins in the desert at 60-450
(600) m (200-1,500 or 2,000 ft). Colorado Desert.
California in San Bernardino (Barstow and the
New York and Whipple Mts.), Riverside, San
Diego, and Imperial Cos.; Arizona in s Yuma Co.
Mexico in adjacent Baja California.

The tall, slender, columnar plants stand alone
like sentinels or cluster in small groups on the
rocky desert hillsides. The mass of elongate, twisting, stout red to gray spines is conspicuous along
the ribs. Because of the irregular length and form,
the spine mass has a ragged appearance.

1b. Ferocactus acanthodes var. **lecontei** (Engelmann) Lindsay. Gravelly or rocky hillsides,
canyon walls, alluvial fans, and wash margins
or sometimes sandy flats in the desert at mostly
750-1,500 m (2,500-5,000 ft) or, in central and sw
Arizona, 300-900 m (1,000-3,000 ft). Mojavean
and Arizona Deserts and upper edge of Colorado
Desert. California in mountains of E and s Mojave Desert and s to upper edge of w Colorado
Desert in Riverside and San Diego Cos. and rare
in E Imperial Co.; Nevada in Clark Co.; Utah in
Washington Co. s and w of St. George; Arizona
from Mohave Co. to Coconino (Grand Canyon
and lower Little Colorado R. to about 1,350 m,

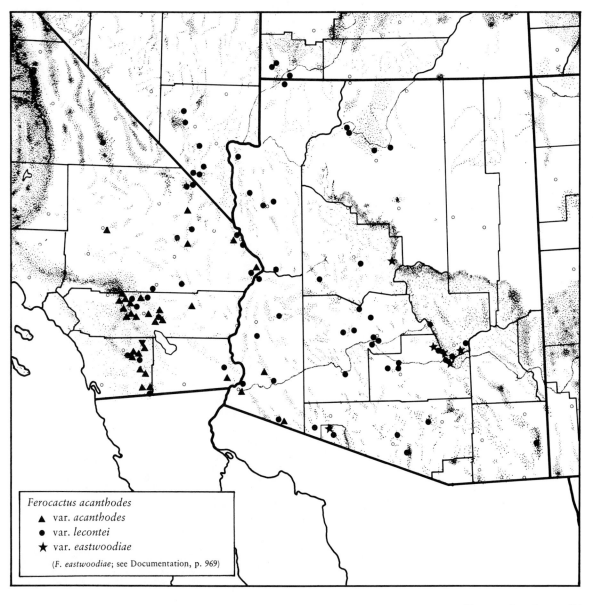

Ferocactus acanthodes
▲ var. *acanthodes*
● var. *lecontei*
★ var. *eastwoodiae*
　(*F. eastwoodiae*; see Documentation, p. 969)

Text continued on p. 692

Fig. 719. A barrel cactus, *Ferocactus acanthodes* var. *acanthodes*, over 2 m (more than 6 feet) tall and about 0.5 m (1.6 feet) in diameter; Colorado Desert near Whitewater, Riverside Co., California. The darker shrubs are creosote bush, *Larrea tridentata*; the lighter ones, brittle bush, *Encelia farinosa*.

Fig. 720. *Ferocactus acanthodes* var. *acanthodes*, medium-sized plant showing the spines; Colorado Desert, Mason Valley, San Diego Co., California.

688

Fig. 721. *Ferocactus acanthodes* var. *acanthodes*, relatively young plant showing the curving and twisting of the spines common in this species. (Robert H. Peebles)

Fig. 722. *Ferocactus acanthodes* var. *acanthodes*, top of a plant, the flowers in a typical apical circle. (Homer L. Shantz)

Fig. 723. A barrel cactus, *Ferocactus acanthodes* var. *lecontei*, about 2 m high (more than 6 feet) and 0.5 m (1.6 feet) in diameter; near the Santa Maria River in the Mojavean Desert in Yavapai Co., Arizona. Green ephedra or Mormon tea, *Ephedra viridis* var. *viridis*, right foreground; a cholla, *Opuntia echinocarpa* var. *echinocarpa*, middle right; foothill palo verde, *Cercidium microphyllum*, left background on the skyline.

Fig. 724. *Ferocactus acanthodes* var. *lecontei*, showing the broad, curving but not twisting central spines, and the narrow, flexible, undulating radial spines.

690

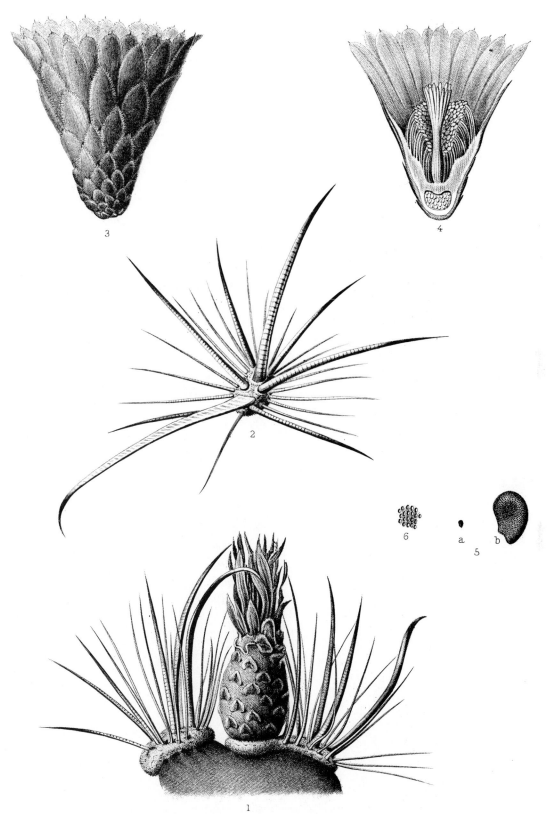

Fig. 725. A barrel cactus, *Ferocactus acanthodes* var. *lecontei. 1*, A spine-bearing areole (left) and (at right) an areole with a young fruit in the reproductive (flower-bearing) area. *2*, Areole with spines and felt, the largest (the principal central) spine turning downward at the tip. *3*, Flower. *4*, Flower in longitudinal section. *5*, Seed: *a*, natural size; *b*, ×12. *6*, Papillae of the surface of the seed coat, enlarged. (Paulus Roetter in Engelmann/Emory, *pl. 27*)

or 4,500 ft), Gila, w Graham, Yuma, and Pima Cos. (rare in E Pima Co.). Mexico in adjacent Sonora and probably N Baja California.

The columnar stems resemble those of var. *acanthodes*, but the spines are shorter and merely curved. Consequently, the plants appear relatively smooth. The red of the spines tends somewhat to mask the green stem.

1c. Ferocactus acanthodes var. **eastwoodiae** L. Benson. Mostly on rocky (often inaccessible) ledges in the desert at 390-1,140 m (1,300-3,800 ft). Arizona Desert. Arizona in w Pima Co. near Organ Pipe Cactus National Monument and in the Dripping Springs and Mescal Mts. in Pinal and Gila Cos.

Var. *eastwoodiae* is a cliffhanger—one species in little danger of extinction, since the huge, yellow-spined stems are mostly perched on ledges far out of reach of man and other large mammals. The plants are attractive and are to be recommended for cultivation from seeds.

Fig. 726. A barrel cactus, *Ferocactus eastwoodiae* (see new combination, Supplement to Documentation; treated as *Ferocactus acanthodes* var. *eastwoodiae* in the text), large plant growing at the Arizona-Sonora Desert Museum, in Tucson, Arizona, in an essentially natural setting of the Arizona Desert. Other plants are the teddy-bear cholla, *Opuntia bigelovii* var. *bigelovii* (two young plants); the jumping cholla, *Opuntia fulgida* var. *fulgida* (trunk at upper right, chains of fruits at upper left); the ocotillo, *Fouquieria splendens* (upper left center); and a bur sage, *Ambrosia deltoidea* (low shrub through much of picture).

Fig. 727. *Ferocactus eastwood-iae* (see Fig. 726), stem ribs bearing the stout yellow spines, the radials of this variety stiff and similar to the centrals but smaller. (Robert H. Peebles)

2. Ferocactus wislizenii
(Engelmann) Britton & Rose

Barrel-shaped or sometimes columnar plant, with rarely more than 1 stem (sometimes branching following injury); larger stems massive, becoming especially so after damage to terminal bud, cylindroid or (especially in younger plants) ovoid, 0.6-1.6(3) m long, 45-83 cm diam; ribs ±20-28; tubercles not conspicuous; spines somewhat obscuring stem; central spines red with ashy gray surface layer, 4 per areole, forming a cross but *not* flattened against stem, strongly cross-ribbed, at least some lower ones hooked, largest 3.8-5 cm long, basally 1.5-3 mm broad, narrowly elliptic in cross section; radial spines ashy gray, mostly 12-20 per areole, spreading, curving irregularly back and forth, not cross-ribbed, the longer to 4.5 cm long, basally mostly 0.25-0.5 mm diam, nearly acicular, elliptic in cros section; flower 4.5-6 cm diam, 5-7.5 cm long; sepaloids with greenish to reddish midribs and orange-yellow margins, the largest narrowly ovate-oblong to narrowly elliptic, 25-35 mm long, 5-10 mm broad, apically rounded, marginally scarious and fimbriate-toothed; petaloids orange-yellow, largest narrowly lanceolate, 25-38 mm long, ±4.5 mm broad, apically sharply acute and mucronate, irregularly serrulate; filaments orange-yellow, ±12 mm long; anthers yellow, oblong, 1 mm long; style 12-20 mm long, 2-3 mm greatest diam; stigmas ±20, 7.5-9 mm long, flat and relatively broad, ±1.2 mm broad; ovary in anthesis 6-9 mm long; fruit yellow, barrel-shaped, fleshy at maturity, with numerous nearly circular, shallowly fimbriate scales, 3-4 cm long, 2.5-3.4 cm diam; seeds minutely and shallowly reticulate, commonly semicircular, 2-2.5 mm greatest dimension, ±1.5 mm at right angles to this, 1 mm thick; hilum appearing "sub-basal."

Rocky, gravelly, or sandy soils of hills, flats, canyons, wash margins, and alluvial fans in deserts or grasslands at (300)600-1,600 m (1,000 or 2,000 to 5,600 ft). Eastern edge of Arizona Desert; Desert Grassland; Chihuahuan Desert. Southeastern Arizona mostly from vicinity of Phoenix to Pima Co. and E; s New Mexico from Hidalgo Co.

to sw Lincoln Co.; Texas in El Paso Co. Mexico s to Sinaloa and NW Chihuahua.

Occurring only in areas with summer rainfall. Flowering profusely during summer, sporadically during late spring.

The plants of *Ferocactus wislizenii* are great hulks on the open desert or in thickets along washes. They are the largest barrel cacti in the United States, being as tall as *F. acanthodes* but of greater diameter. A mature plant 2.4-3 m (8-10 ft) or more high, ±0.6 m (2 ft) in diameter, and covered with stout, hooked spines is a memorable discovery.

Fig. 728. A barrel cactus, *Ferocactus wislizenii*, giant plant 2.5 m (8 feet) high, about 1 m (3 feet) in diameter; Arizona Desert in the Organ Pipe Cactus National Monument, Pima Co., Arizona. (Robert H. Peebles)

Fig. 729. *Ferocactus wislizenii,* gigantic plant showing the hooked principal central spines; Organ Pipe Cactus National Monument. The tree is a blue palo verde, *Cercidium floridum.*

Fig. 730. *Ferocactus wislizenii,* giant plant growing in the Arizona Desert in the Tucson Mts., Pima Co., Arizona, among creosote bushes, *Larrea tridentata.*

695

Fig. 732. *Ferocactus wislizenii,* young plant in flower, the flowers in an apical circle, the characteristic spines as in Fig. 731. (Homer L. Shantz)

Fig. 731. *Ferocactus wislizenii,* stem, ribs, tubercles, and spines. The central spines are stout and rigid, the principal one hooked; the radial spines are lighter-colored, flexible, very slender, and undulating.

696

Fig. 734. *Ferocactus wislizenii,* stem-apex showing the spine-bearing areole near the growing end of each rib and a fruit-attachment scar just above it. The flower bud, then the flower, then the fruit are produced in a special area just at the upper edge of the spine-bearing areole, and after fall of the fruit this area is left as a scar; the spots on the scars are the broken vascular bundles that entered the fruits.

Fig. 733. *Ferocactus wislizenii,* apex of the stem ringed by fruits, each in the axil of a spine-bearing areole.

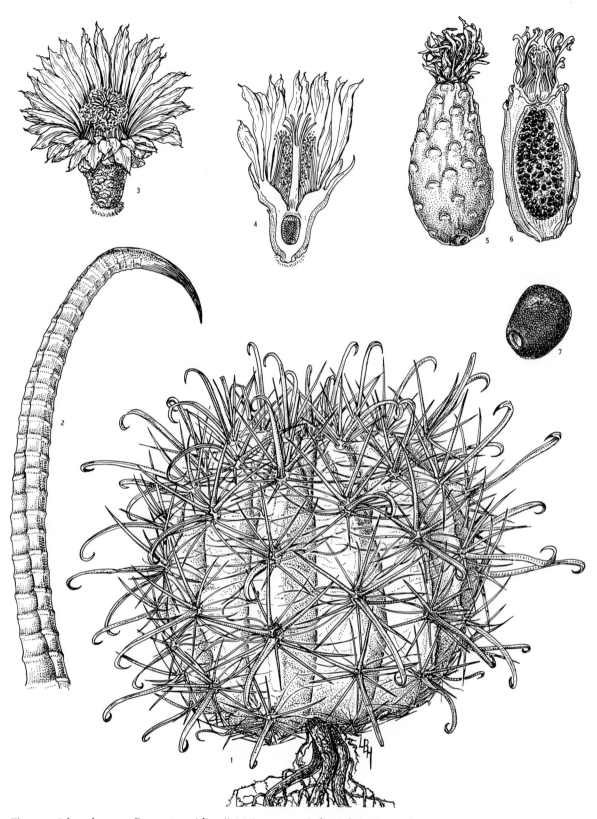

Fig. 735. A barrel cactus, *Ferocactus wislizenii*, ×.6, except as indicated. *1*, Young plant, natural size; four central spines in each areole, the principal (lower) one turning downward and hooked, all or most of the radial spines slender and curving irregularly. *2*, Enlarged principal central spine, showing the cross-ribs, the surface finely hairy. *3*, Flower. *4*, Flower in longitudinal section. *5*, Fruit, showing the scaly surface and the persistent dried upper parts of the flower. *6*, Fruit in longitudinal section. *7*, Seed, the hilum small and obviously basal, ×7.

698

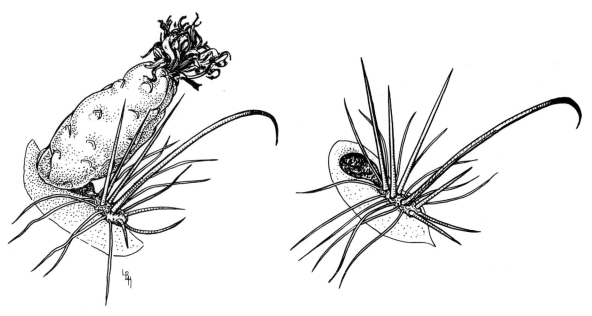

Fig. 736. *Ferocactus wislizenii*, relationship of the fruit and the spine-bearing areole. *Left*, Fruit in the special reproductive area adjacent to the upper side of the spine-bearing areole. *Right*, Scar left after fall of the fruit.

3. Ferocactus covillei Britton & Rose

Plant barrel-shaped to ovoid or sometimes columnar, stem unbranched except after injury to terminal bud, green, 0.6-1.5(2.5) m long, 30-60 (100) cm diam; ribs usually 20-30; tubercles projecting only slightly; areoles elliptic, 12-15 mm long, typically ±25 mm apart; spines only partly obscuring stem; central spine red but in age developing surface layer of ashy gray, solitary, standing at right angles to stem, curving a little through entire length, commonly (in Arizona) hooked or strongly curved at apex, strongly cross-ribbed, 7.5-10 cm long, basally to ±4-5 mm broad, flat above, rounded below, semicircular in cross section; radial spines all same texture and color as central, mostly 7-9 per areole, spreading, straight or slightly curving, the longer 5-7.5 cm long, basally 2-3 mm broad, somewhat flattened, elliptic in cross section; flower about 7.5 cm diam and long; sepaloids purplish-red, largest oblanceolate or spathulate-oblanceolate, to ±25 mm long, ±6 mm broad, apically acute, minutely ciliate; petaloids purplish-red, the largest narrowly lanceolate, ±38 mm long, ±4.5-6 mm broad, apically short-acuminate, fimbriate-serrulate; filaments 7.5-15 mm long; anthers yellow, ±1.5 mm long; style ±13 mm long, 3 mm diam; stigmas ±18, very slender, ±15 mm long;

ovary in anthesis broadly obovoid, 15 mm long; fruit yellow at maturity, with relatively few to 25-30(40) semicircular, scarious-margined, fimbriate or crenulate scales, 2.5-4.5 cm long, 2.5-3 cm diam; seeds reticulate, narrowly obovoid, 2.5 mm greatest dimension, 1.5 mm at right angles to this, 1 mm thick; hilum obviously basal but diagonal.

Gravelly, rocky, or sandy soils of hillsides, wash margins, alluvial fans, grassy mesas, or flats in the desert at 450-750(900) m (1,500-2,500 or 3,000 ft). Arizona Desert and upper edge of Colorado Desert (in U.S.). Arizona from the Sierra Estrella, Maricopa Co. (according to A. A. Nichol), to Organ Pipe Cactus National Monument and Papago Indian Reservation, Pima Co. Adjacent Sonora, Mexico.

Often this barrel cactus is set off by the strong contrast of the red spines with a background of black rock, usually limestone with a black patina or sometimes black lava or basalt. The plant is massive, but too elongated to be really reminiscent of a barrel.

The young plant is enclosed in a sphere of bright red, interlacing, recurved spines, which protect it from deer and rodents. An uprooted specimen may bounce like a tennis ball as it rolls down a hillside.

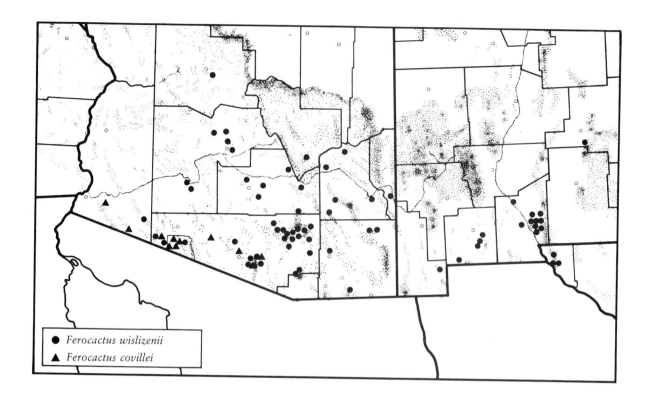

● *Ferocactus wislizenii*
▲ *Ferocactus covillei*

Fig. 737. A barrel cactus, *Fero-cactus covillei*, showing the hooked central spine of each areole and the several nearly equal but straight radial spines; Arizona Desert in the Organ Pipe Cactus National Monument, Arizona.

Fig. 738. *Ferocactus covillei*, large plant about 2.5 m (8 feet) high and 1 m (3 feet) in diameter; Papago Indian Reservation, Pima Co., Arizona. (A. A. Nichol)

Fig. 739. *Ferocactus covillei*, with flowers and young fruits at the apex of the stem, the ribs with areoles each bearing a single slightly curving central spine and several nearly equal radial spines. The scar of a fruit is above each areole. (Robert H. Peebles)

701

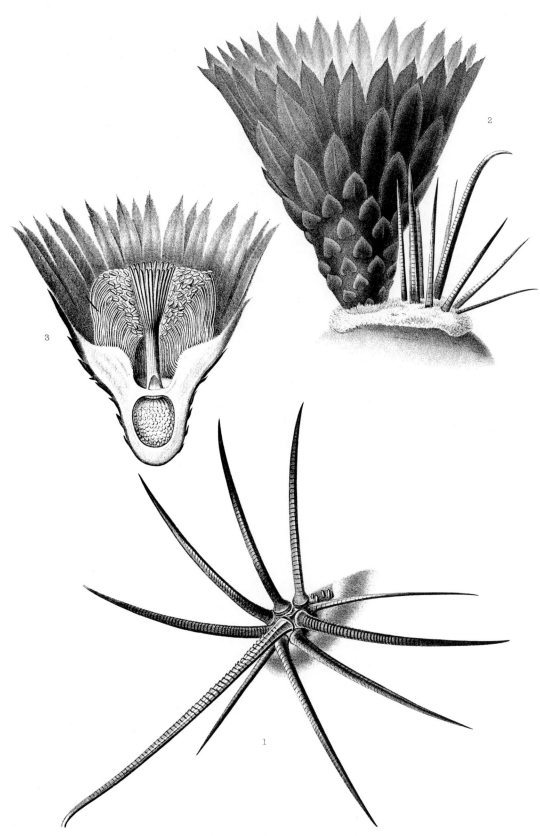

Fig. 740. A barrel cactus, *Ferocactus covillei*. *1*, Areole with spines and felt; the single central spine hooked or strongly curved and also turned downward, the 7–9 radial spines stout and cross-ribbed like the central spine. *2*, Flower at the edge of a developing spine-bearing areole; as in other members of the genus, the flower-bearing area felted and merging with the spine-bearing portion. *3*, Flower in longitudinal section. (Paulus Roetter in Engelmann/Emory, *pl. 28*)

Fig. 741. *Ferocactus covillei,* relatively young plant, showing the spines as in Fig. 739, each upper areole subtending the attachment scar of a fallen fruit. (Frank P. McWhorter)

4. Ferocactus viridescens
(Nuttall) Britton & Rose

Stems depressed-globose or hemispheroidal to (in older plants) ovoid or cylindroid, often of greater diameter than length, 15-30(45) cm long, 20-35 cm diam; ribs usually 15-20; tubercles barely protruding; areoles elliptic, 9-12 mm long; spines more or less obscuring the stem; central spines red, in age becoming grayish or yellowish, 4 per areole, forming a cross, spreading from stem at about 45° angles, the lower (principal) one slightly curving, strongly cross-ribbed, 3-4.5 cm long, basally ±2 mm broad, very narrowly elliptic in cross section; radial spines similar to central but smaller, of various sizes, 10-20 per areole, spreading irregularly, stiff, straight, the longer 1.2-2 cm long, basally 1 mm broad, subulate, elliptic (mostly narrowly so) in cross section; flower 3-4.5 cm diam, 2.5-3 cm long; sepaloids with green and red midribs and greenish-yellow margins, the largest spathulate-oblanceolate, ±12 mm long, ±6 mm broad, apically rounded, fimbriolate to denticulate; petaloids pink, green, and yellow, largest broadly oblanceolate, 12-15 mm long,

±6 mm broad, apically rounded to acute, irregularly denticulate; filaments greenish-yellow, 3-6 mm long; anthers yellow, oblong, 0.8 mm long; style yellowish, ±6-9 mm long, ±1.5 mm greatest diam; stigmas 13-15, 7.5-10 mm long, very slender; ovary in anthesis ±6 mm long; fruit red, fleshy at maturity, with ±30 fimbriolate-denticulate semicircular scales, barrel-like, 1.5-2 cm long and diam; seeds strongly but minutely reticulate, elongate-obovoid, 1.7 mm in greatest dimension,

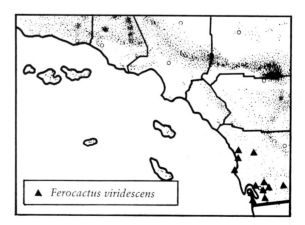

▲ *Ferocactus viridescens*

1.2 mm at right angles to this, 0.7-0.8 mm thick; hilum obviously basal but oblique.

Sandy or gravelly soils of hillsides in the chaparral at 10-150 m (30-500 ft). California Chaparral (San Diego Co. phase). California near coast from Del Mar s and inland nearly as far as Otay. Mexico in NW Baja California.

This species must be sought among bushes or grass clumps. It is relatively inconspicuous for its size, and its depressed form and low stature make it hard to find. The stem is dark green, and the older spines are dull and not in strong contrast. Nevertheless, a barrel cactus growing in chaparral areas near the coast is an unusual sight.

Fig. 742. A barrel cactus, *Ferocactus viridescens*, in Rancho Santa Ana Botanic Garden under conditions similar to those in nature; a species of southernmost coastal California and northwestern Baja California.

Fig. 743. *Ferocactus viridescens*, closer view of the ribs and spines, the plant a neotype of the species.

Fig. 744. *Ferocactus viridescens*, large plant with an open flower and a series of flower buds about to open.

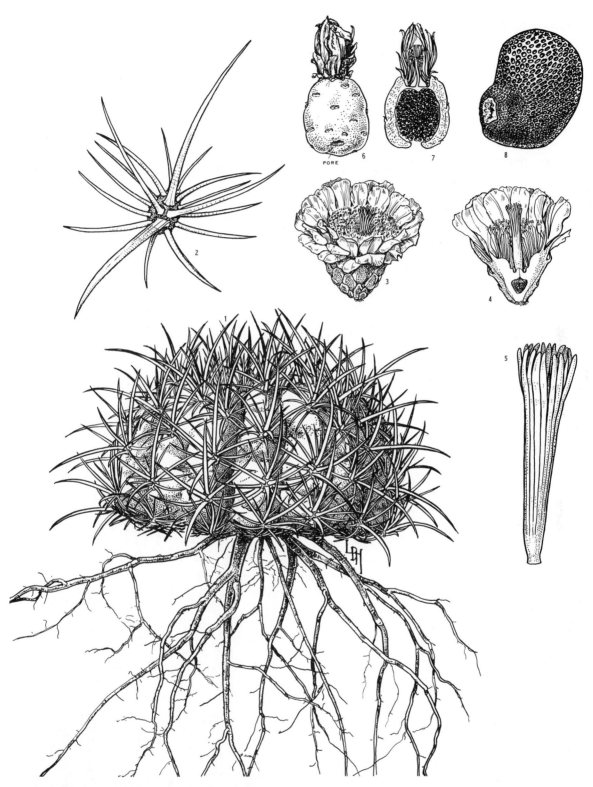

Fig. 745. A barrel cactus, *Ferocactus viridescens*, ×.8, except as indicated. *1*, Plant with the characteristic short, broad form of the species. *2*, Areole with spines and felt, the principal central spine curving downward in a gentle arc, the other three turned more or less upward, the radial spines rigid and resembling the centrals but smaller, ×1.2. *3*, Flower. *4*, Flower in longitudinal section. *5*, Stigmas, ×4.5. *6*, Fruit, showing basal pore through which the seeds are released gradually (a characteristic of several preceding species as well). *7*, Fruit in longitudinal section. *8*, Seed, somewhat asymmetrical, the hilum obviously basal, ×20.

5. Ferocactus hamatacanthus
(Mühlenpfordt) Britton & Rose

Larger stems of mature plants (see below for characters of juvenile plants) ovoid or ovoid-cylindroid, 15-30 (reportedly 60) cm long, mostly 7.5-15 cm diam; ribs ±12-17, relatively thin; spines fairly dense but not obscuring stem; central spines straw-colored to brown, 4(8) per areole, the lower (largest) perpendicular to stem, cross-ridged, hooked, nearly straight to flexuous, the others straight or usually so, the longer (4)6-10 cm long, basally (0.5)1-1.2 mm diam or breadth, acicular or subulate, elliptic to very narrowly elliptic in cross section; radial spines usually brown or some straw-colored, 8-20 per areole (at top and bottom of areole), spreading, straight, the longer 15-40 mm long, basally ±5-7 mm diam, acicular, nearly circular in cross section; flower usually 6.5-7.5 cm diam, usually 6-7 cm long; sepaloids with green and red midribs and middles and yellow margins, largest oblanceolate-cuneate, to 25-30 mm long, 7-10 mm broad, apically rounded to right-angled, fimbriolate or largest entire; petaloids yellow except for red bases, largest oblanceolate, 30-40 mm long, ±10 mm broad, acute and mucronulate, marginally entire; filaments yellow, ±12 mm long, filiform; anthers yellow, 0.7 mm long, oblong, length ±twice breadth; style yellow, ±25 mm long, ±2 mm greatest diam; stigmas ±12, 4.5-6 mm long, slender; ovary in anthesis usually cylindroid, 12 mm long, 6 mm diam; fruit green, fleshy and juicy at maturity, with usually ±30-40 scales, these fimbriolate-scarious at margins, broadly ellipsoid, ±2.5-3 cm long, ±20 cm diam; seeds finely pitted, asymmetrically obovoid, ±1.5 mm long, 1 mm broad, 0.7 mm thick; hilum large, obviously basal.

Juvenile plants known as *Echinocactus longihamatus* Galeotti var. *brevispinus* Engelm. (in Emory, Rept. U.S. & Mex. Bound. Surv. 2: Cactaceae 22. 1859) are, according to Engelmann, perhaps ". . . the young plant, as these plants often flower when quite young, and before the character of the plant is yet fully developed. This in a very marked degree in *E. uncinatus* [*Ancistrocactus uncinatus*] . . . which begins to bloom while the central spine is yet quite short and terete." Juvenile plants have central spines 30-50 mm long and only 8-11 radial spines 12-30 mm long; all spines are relatively slender. This is shown by young and old plants in the same collection of var. *hamatacanthus*, including young branches from an older plant (Santa

Elena Canyon, Big Bend National Park, Texas, *L. & R. L. Benson 15507, Pom*).

5a. Ferocactus hamatacanthus var. **hamatacanthus.** In soil from igneous rocks and on old river gravels in the desert and grasslands at about 10-1,500 m (30-5,000 ft). Chihuahuan Desert and Desert Grassland; Rio Grande Plain. New Mexico in Cornudas Mts., Otero Co. (Castetter, personal communication, July 13, 1966); Texas mostly near Rio Grande or Pecos R. from El Paso Co. to Cameron Co. s to San Luis Potosí, Mexico.

This small barrel cactus is not a major feature of the landscape, as are its massive relatives to the westward. Its spines are large for the size of the plant, elongate, and strongly hooked. They are in strong contrast to the relatively small and thick stem.

5b. Ferocactus hamatacanthus var. **sinuatus** (Dietrich) L. Benson. Modified grassland near sea level. Rio Grande Plain. Texas on the Gulf Coast in San Patricio Co. Northeastern Mexico.

The relatively broad and somewhat papery spines are the most noticeable feature of this variety.

Fig. 746. A barrel cactus, *Ferocactus hamatacanthus* var. *hamatacanthus*, in the Huntington Botanical Gardens.

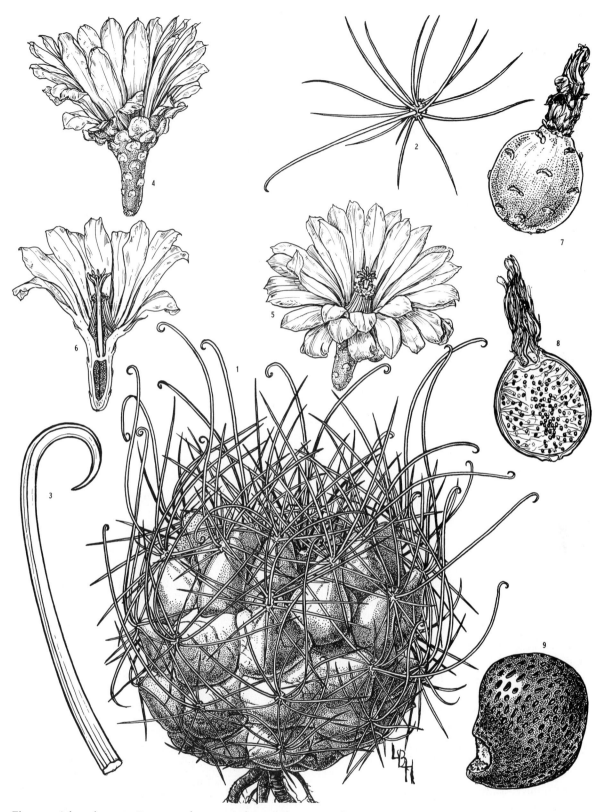

Fig. 747. A barrel cactus, *Ferocactus hamatacanthus* var. *hamatacanthus*. *1*, Plant, ×.9. *2*, Areole with spines and felt, showing the hooked principal central spine surrounded by other, unhooked spines, ×.9. *3*, Upper portion of the principal central spine, ×4.5. *4, 5*, Flower, ×.6. *6*, Flower in longitudinal section, ×.6. *7*, Fruit, showing the scales on the surface, ×1.2. *8*, Fruit in longitudinal section, ×1.2. *9*, Seed, showing the hilum with an almost "lateral" appearance (or "basal," according to interpretation; actually *per se* basal), ×23. (See Credits)

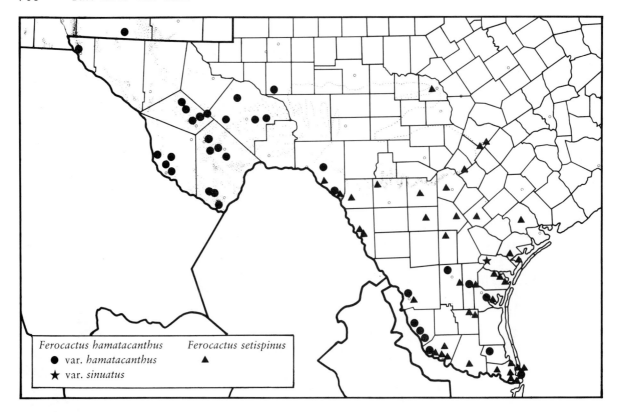

Distinctive Characters of the Varieties of **Ferocactus hamatacanthus**

Character	a. var. **hamatacanthus**	b. var. **sinuatus**
Ribs	Not much compressed	Strongly compressed
Central spine form	Angled or flattened, twisting but not flexuous	Principal (lower) strongly flattened, markedly flexuous
Central spine size	6-10 cm long, 1-1.2 mm diam	4-9.5 cm long, 1 mm broad
Flower diameter	6.5-7.5 cm	5.5-6.5 cm
Fruit length	±30 cm	±25 cm
Altitude	10-1,500 m (30-5,000 ft)	Near sea level
Floristic association	Chihuahuan Desert; Desert Grassland; Rio Grande Plain	Rio Grande Plain

6. Ferocactus setispinus (Engelmann) L. Benson

Larger stems green, solitary to sometimes several or numerous, ovoid or cylindroid, 3.8-10(20) cm long, 3.8 cm diam; ribs ±13, narrow, areoles 1.5 mm diam, typically 9-12 mm apart; spines rather dense but not obscuring stem; principal central spine straw-colored to reddish-brown with lighter tip, strongly hooked (sometimes with 2 or 3 additional smaller straight upper centrals per areole), perpendicular to stem, finely scaberulous-canescent, 1-3.8 cm long, basally 0.5(0.7) mm diam or breadth, usually acicular but rarely flattened, nearly circular to sometimes narrowly elliptic in cross section; radial spines straw-colored or white to brown, varying within the areole, 12-15 per areole, spreading, nearly straight, the longer mostly to 12 mm long, the upper radials sometimes much longer, basally 0.25 mm diam,

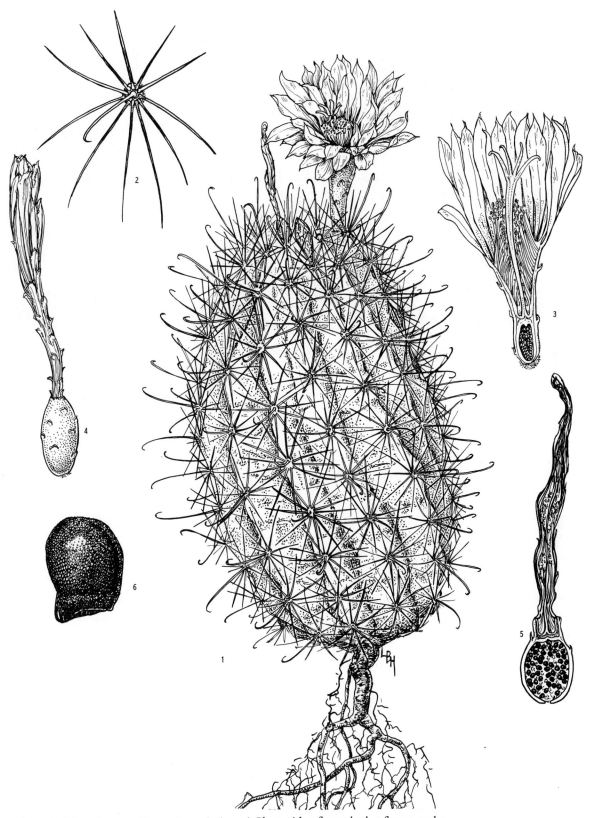

Fig. 748. A barrel cactus, *Ferocactus setispinus*. *1*, Plant with a flower bud, a flower, and a young fruit, ×.9. *2*, Areole, showing the hooked central spine and the radials, ×2.5. *3*, Flower in longitudinal section, ×1.25. *4*, Fruit, showing the scales on the bright red surface, the other flower parts dry and persistent, ×1.9. *5*, Fruit in longitudinal section, ×1.9. *6*, Seed, the hilum broad and obviously basal, ×19.

Fig. 749. A small barrel cactus, *Ferocactus setispinus*, vegetative plant showing the ribs and areoles.

acicular, nearly circular in section; flower 4-5.5 cm diam, 3.8-5 cm long; sepaloids with the midribs and broad adjacent areas green, margins red, the largest cuneate-oblanceolate, to 20 mm long, to 6(9) mm broad, the lower obtuse, uppermost acute and fimbriolate; petaloids clear yellow with red bases, largest oblanceolate, 20-25 mm long, 6-9 mm broad, acute, cuspidulate, the margins entire; filaments pale yellow to white, ±6 mm long, very slender; anthers yellow, narrowly oblong, length ±3 times breadth, 0.7 mm long; style greenish-yellow, 15-20 mm long, 1 mm greatest diam; stigmas 5-8, 3-4.5 mm long, slender; ovary in anthesis ±4.5 mm long and diam or more elongate; fruit red, fleshy at maturity, with ±10-15 scales (these with fimbriolate-scarious margins), globular, ±9-12 mm long and diam; seed minutely papillate, obovoid, but base flaring around micropyle, usually 1-1.4 mm long, 0.8-1 mm broad, ±0.5-0.6 mm thick; hilum obviously basal.

Black or clay soils and leaf mold on hills and flats in grasslands, usually in mesquite thickets at or below 300 m (1,000 ft). Rio Grande Plain and Edwards Plateau. Texas from Val Verde and San Saba Cos. E and s to Rio Grande and E to Travis, Refugio, and Cameron Cos. Mexico near lower Rio Grande.

The plant is a miniature barrel cactus, and its slender hooked spines and its tendency to branch are not reminiscent of its gigantic western relatives.

The chief basis for the proposed genus *Hamatacanthus* Britton & Rose was the form of the superior floral tube, commonly referred to as "narrow, funnelform." However, in sectional view it is not markedly of that form. In essential characters the tube is like those of the other species of *Ferocactus*. The often slender ovary gives the false impression of a narrow tube.

See map for *F. hamatacanthus*.

9. Echinocactus

Plant columnar or with divergent basal branches; stems branching or unbranched, the larger 50-60 cm long, 5-30 cm diam; ribs 8-27, the coalescent tubercles barely projecting, or in some species only slits occurring between tubercles. Leaves not discernible in adult plant. Areoles nearly circular to elliptic; size and spacing various. Spines, when present, annulate; central spines red, sometimes covered partly by ashy gray, (0)1-4 per areole, straight or curving, 2.5-7.5 cm long, basally 1.5-10 mm broad, nearly acicular to subulate, narrowly elliptic in cross section; radial spines like central but smaller, 5-11 per areole, 2 cm long, basally 1-3 mm broad, nearly acicular to subulate. Flowers and fruits produced on new growth of current season and therefore near apex of stem or branch, developed at apex of tubercle in a felted area adjacent to spine-bearing part of areole and merging with it, this area forming a long-persistent circular or semicircular scar. Flower 3.8-7 cm diam; floral tube above ovary obconical to slightly funnelform, green or tinted like perianth. *Sepaloids aristate or spinose-tipped.* Fruit becoming dry or fleshy at maturity, with scales (and in some species the hairs axillary to them) obscuring fruit, 15-20 mm long, 10-20 mm diam. Seed black or brown, reticulate, irregularly obovoid or ovoid or irregularly pyramidal and then with a large collar around the hilum enclosing a chamber around the funiculus, usually broader than long or rarely the reverse, 2-4 mm greatest dimension; hilum usually appearing "lateral" or oblique; cotyledons accumbent, *not* foliaceous.

Twelve (possibly more) species occurring from California to Texas and into Mexico as far as Querétaro; four species in the U.S.

From Gr. *echinos* (hedgehog).

In the list that follows, the status of the extraterritorial species has not been evaluated fully.

E. *grusonii* (San Luis Potosí to Hidalgo; widely cultivated as "golden ball")
E. *ingens* (Mexico; status uncertain)
E. *platyacanthus*
  vars. *platyacanthus* (E Mexico; commonly cultivated; stem dark green with purplish stripes)
    visnaga (San Luis Potosí)
E. *grandis* (Puebla)
E. *palmeri* (Coahuila to Zacatecas)
1. E. *polycephalus*
  vars. a. *polycephalus*
    b. *xeranthemoides*
E. *parryi* (Chihuahua)
2. E. *horizonthalonius*
  vars. a. *horizonthalonius*
    b. *nicholii*
3. E. *texensis*
4. E. *asterias*
  E. *myriostigma* (N central Mexico to San Luis Potosí; spineless)
  E. *capricornis* (N Mexico; spiny)
  E. *ornatus* (Hidalgo & Querétaro; spiny)

KEY TO THE SPECIES OF ECHINOCACTUS

1. Stem of the adult plant bearing spines, the surface *not* bearing minute scales with long hairs on the margins; seed black, the hilum depressed but *not* in an elaborate chamber; stem ribs 7-27, not as broad as the intervening grooves.
2. Fruit remaining densely woolly after drying at maturity, dehiscent by an apical pore.
3. Radial spines from all sides of the areole; central spines (3)4, spreading or curving in various directions, at maturity red or yellow or partly obscured by a pale gray layer; flowers yellow; fruit ovoid; stem ribs 13-21, nearly vertical, usually not markedly spiny; stems several to many, forming dense clumps, elongate-ovoid ....1. E. polycephalus

3. Radial spines lacking on the extreme lower side of the areole; principal central spine strongly deflexed, at maturity dark or dirty gray; flowers pink; fruit narrowly cylindroid; stem ribs 7-13, commonly 8, markedly spiral, spiny; stem solitary, spheroid to sometimes elongate-ovoid..........2. **E. horizonthalonius**
    2. Fruit ultimately becoming naked, scarlet, at first pulpy and juicy, but soon drying and bursting irregularly..3. **E. texensis**
1. Stem of the adult plant *not* bearing spines, the surface bearing minute scales with long woolly hairs on the margins; seed brown, the hilum enclosed in the greatly elaborated margin of the seed coat, the funiculus entering the chamber around the hilum through the porelike apex; stem ribs 8, many times broader than the intervening grooves..4. **E. asterias**

1. Echinocactus polycephalus
Engelmann & Bigelow

Stems branching, (1-4 or) in clumps of 5-30, these to 0.6 m high and 1.2 m diam; larger stems gray-green, spheroidal to cylindroid, 30-60 cm long, to 10-20 cm diam; ribs 13-21; tubercles almost completely coalescent; areole elliptic, the spine-bearing portion ±1.2 mm diam, areoles typically 12 mm apart; spines dense, obscuring stem; central spines red or yellow with ashy surface layer, in the common variety with a dense, felty canescence, which may peel off in sheets as spine ages, 4 per areole, spreading irregularly, lowest (principal) one curving slightly downward, others nearly straight, strongly cross-ribbed, the longer 6-7.5 cm long, basally 2.5-3 mm broad,

subulate, flattened, narrowly elliptic in cross section; radial spines similar to centrals but smaller, 6-8 per areole, spreading irregularly or slightly curving in low arcs, the longer 3-4.5 cm long, basally 1-1.5 mm broad, somewhat flattened, elliptic in cross section; flower ±5 cm diam and long; sepaloids with pink midribs and yellowish margins, largest subulate, each forming a spine ±20-25 mm long, basally ±1 mm broad; petaloids yellow or midribs tinged with pink, largest oblanceolate, ±20 mm long, ±3 mm broad, acute to mucronate or aristulate, sparsely minutely toothed; filaments yellow, ±10 mm long; anthers yellow, oblong, 1 mm long; style yellow, ±20 mm long, 2 mm greatest diam; stigmas ±10, 3 mm long, relatively broad and flat; ovary in anthesis ±3 mm long; fruit dry at maturity, densely encased in matted

Distinctive Characters of the Varieties of Echinocactus polycephalus

Character	a. var. **polycephalus**	b. var. **xeranthemoides**
Stems	In clumps of 10-20(30), the longest in middle	In clumps or solitary, (1)5-12, the longest (according to A. A. Nichol) on margin
Spines	Densely canescent, the felt peeling away in sheets, the spine surface under the felt red or pink, the apex straight or somewhat curving	Glabrous or glabrate with the hairs falling away separately, the spine surface red or sometimes varying to pink, the apex straight or curving slightly
Seed form	Irregularly obovoid-oblong, markedly papillate-reticulate, not shiny	Obovoid, papillate-reticulate but the pattern not prominent, shiny
Seed size	2-2.5 mm long, 2.5-3.5 mm broad, 1.5 mm thick	±2 mm long, ±2.5 mm broad, 1-1.25 mm thick
Altitude	30-750 m (100-2,500 ft)	1,080-1,500 m (3,800-5,000 ft)
Floristic association	Mojavean Desert	Navajoan Desert; edge of Northern Juniper-Pinyon Woodland

woolly white hairs 12-20 mm long, the ovary 20-25 mm long, 9-12 mm diam; seeds black, reticulate-papillate, irregularly obovoid but sharply irregularly angled from compression, 2-2.5 mm long, 2-3.5 mm broad, 1-1.5 mm thick; hilum appearing "lateral."

The clumps of medium-sized stems are reddish masses on the rocky desert hills, and they resemble gigantic easter eggs carefully placed on end or in groups and diverging from a common basal support.

1a. Echinocactus polycephalus var. **polycephalus.** Rocky or gravelly soils of dry, hot slopes of low mountains and sometimes clay soils of the valleys in deserts at 30-750 m (100-2,500 ft). Mojavean Desert. California in Mojave Desert region from Kern and Inyo Cos. to Little San Bernardino Mts., Riverside Co., and to NE Imperial Co.; also E of Clark Dry Lake, San Diego Co.; Nevada in westernmost Nye Co. and Clark Co.; Arizona in Mohave and Yuma Cos. Mexico in NW Sonora.

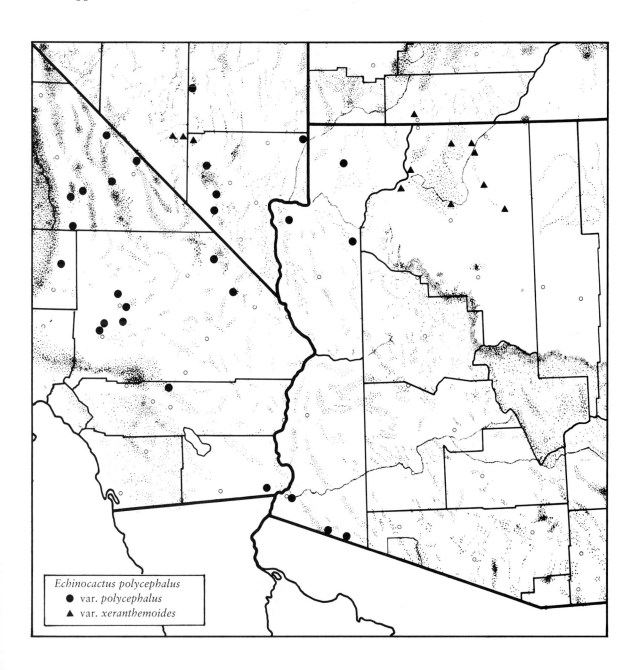

Echinocactus polycephalus
● var. *polycephalus*
▲ var. *xeranthemoides*

Fig. 751. *Echinocactus poly-cephalus* var. *polycephalus*, typical cluster of six stems. The cottonlike material at the top of the stem is the wool of the fruits, which are dry at maturity. (Frank P. McWhorter)

Fig. 750. *Echinocactus poly-cephalus* var. *polycephalus*, stem tops showing the spines and a circle of white-woolly, dry fruits.

714

Fig. 752. A barrel cactus, *Echinocactus polycephalus* var. *polycephalus*, on an alluvial fan of the Inyo Mts., northeast of Lone Pine, Inyo Co., California, in an area transitional between the Sagebrush Desert and the Mojavean Desert. (Frank P. McWhorter)

1b. Echinocactus polycephalus var. **xeranthemoides** Coulter. On rocky, mostly south-facing ledges of canyons or on rocky hillsides in desert or on edge of woodland above it at 1,080-1,500 m (3,800-5,000 ft) or more. Navajoan Desert and edge of Northern Juniper-Pinyon Woodland. Nevada in s Nye Co. and NW Clark Co.; Utah about Kanab, Kane Co.; Arizona in N Coconino Co. near Colorado R. and tributaries, such as Kanab Creek and Little Colorado R.

2. Echinocactus horizonthalonius Lemaire
Turk's head

Stems solitary, depressed-globose to ovoid or sometimes columnar, the longer blue-green, 10-15(50) cm long, 10-15 cm diam; ribs 7-13, com-monly 8; tubercles coalescent, with only slits between upper portions; areoles circular, ±10 mm diam, typically 9-12 mm apart; spines dense, more or less obscuring stem, glabrous; central spines pale gray or sometimes black, this covering underlayers of red or red-and-yellow, 3-5 per areole, 1 usually curving downward in low arc, 2.5-3 cm long, basally 2-3 mm broad, somewhat flattened, elliptic in cross section, the 2 more slender upper centrals curving upward or straight; radial spines gray, this covering underlayers of red or yellow, 5-7 per areole, curving slightly outward in low arcs, the longer 2-2.5 cm long, basally ±1-1.5 mm diam, essentially acicular but a little flattened, elliptic in cross section; flower 5-6.5 cm diam, 5-6.2 cm long; sepaloids with red midribs and pink margins, largest narrowly lan-

Fig. 753. A barrel cactus, *Echinocactus polycephalus* var. *xeranthemoides*, near the Colorado River in the Navajoan Desert of northern Arizona. (Homer L. Shantz)

Fig. 754. *Echinocactus polycephalus* var. *xeranthemoides*, apex of the stem with dry, woolly fruits. (Homer L. Shantz)

716

Distinctive Characters of the Varieties of **Echinocactus horizonthalonius**

Character	a. var. **horizonthalonius**	b. var. **nicholii**
Stem form	Depressed-globose to broadly ovoid	Depressed-globose to broadly ovoid, in age becoming columnar
Stem size	Usually 10-15 cm long and diam	Ultimately to 40-50 cm high, 12.5-15(20) cm diam
Spines	Gray, usually pale gray covering red or red-and-yellow	Some nearly black or dark gray, with some underlayers of red
Central spines	3(5), the lower 1 curving downward or nearly straight, similar to but larger than others, the upper 2 usually short and straight	3, 1 black and curving strongly downward and much shorter than others, 2 red or basally pale gray and curving upward
Radial spines	Usually 6(7) per areole	5 per areole
Seeds	Broader than long, 2 mm long, 3 mm broad	Longer than broad, 3-3.5 mm long, 2 mm broad
Hilum	Appearing "lateral" to basal, 0.5 mm diam	"Sub-basal," ±1 mm diam
Altitude	900-1,650 m (3,000-5,500 ft)	900-1,050 m (3,000-3,500 ft)
Floristic association	Chihuahuan Desert	Arizona Desert

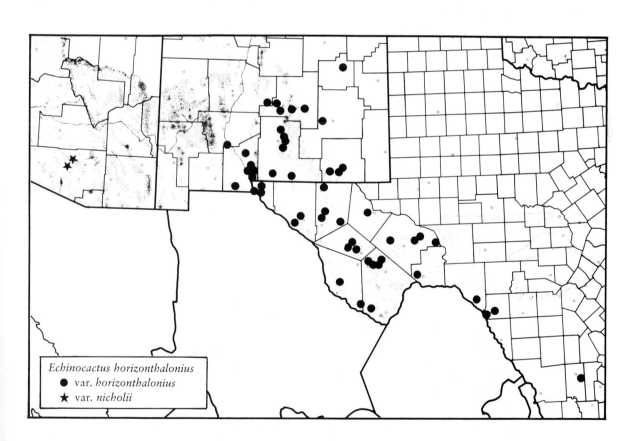

Echinocactus horizonthalonius
- ● var. *horizonthalonius*
- ★ var. *nicholii*

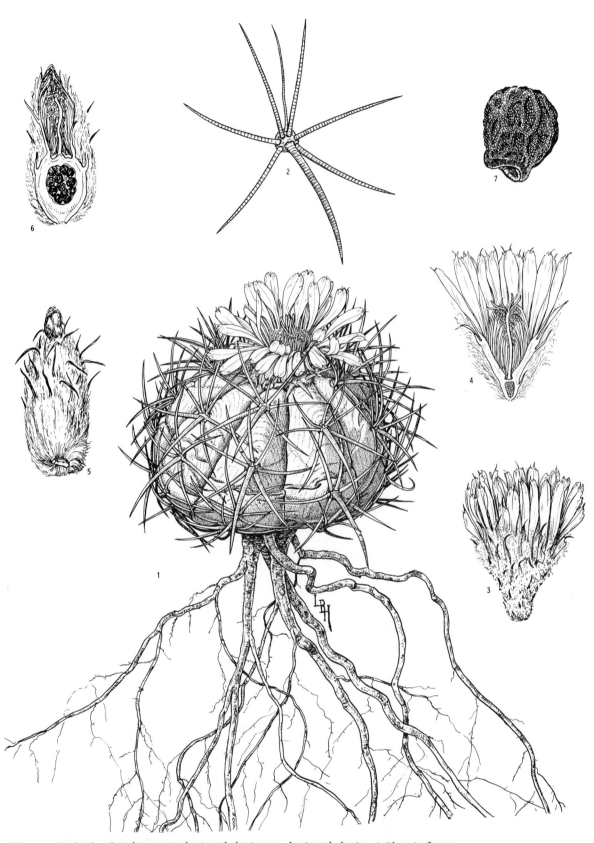

Fig. 755. Turk's head, *Echinocactus horizonthalonius* var. *horizonthalonius*. *1*, Plant in flower, ×.6. *2*, Areole with spines and wool, showing the downward-curving lower central spine and the relatively stout radials, ×1.2; all spines cross-ribbed. *3*, Flower, showing the sharply spinose scale-leaves of the ovary and of the spine-tipped sepaloid perianth parts, these characteristic of the genus, ×.6. *4*, Flower in longitudinal section, ×.6. *5*, Fruit, dry at maturity and covered with long, woolly hairs, ×1.2, still bearing the spinose scale-leaves. *6*, Fruit in longitudinal section, ×1.2. *7*, Seed, the hilum in this case obviously basal, ×12.

718

ceolate, attenuate into long aristate tips ±3 mm long, sepaloids 20-25 mm long, basally ±3-5 mm broad; petaloids pink, largest obovate-spathulate, long-stalked, 25-30 mm long, 6(12) mm broad, apically rounded to acute, mucronate, and irregularly toothed, marginally undulate (crisped) and entire; filaments pinkish, ±12 mm long; anthers yellow, narrowly oblong, 1-2 mm long; style pink, 19-22 mm long, 1.5-2 mm greatest diam; stigmas pink, 7 or 8, 3-4.5 mm long, slender; ovary in anthesis ±3 mm long; fruit at first juicy, but at maturity soon dry, covered densely with white, soft, woolly hairs, ±25 mm long, 12 mm diam; seeds black, papillate and reticulate, irregularly ovoid, 2-2.5 mm long, 2-3 mm broad, 1.5 mm thick; hilum appearing "lateral," "sub-basal," or obviously basal.

2a. Echinocactus horizonthalonius var. horizonthalonius. Limestone soils of rocky hills in the desert at 900-1,650 m (3,000-5,500 ft). Chihuahuan Desert. New Mexico from Sierra and Hidalgo Cos. to De Baca and Eddy Cos.; Texas w of Pecos R. and near Rio Grande in Val Verde Co. Mexico s at least to San Luis Potosí.

The stems are spiny, grayish, domelike low mounds. The flowers are large and delicately colored, with a memorable shade of pink.

Fig. 757. The Turk's head of Arizona, *Echinocactus horizonthalonius* var. *nicholii*, tall plant of the original collection in the cactus garden of the University of Arizona, Tucson (early 1930's); the remains placed in the University Herbarium by the writer. (Homer L. Shantz; from *The Cacti of Arizona*, ed. 1; see also Credits)

Fig. 756. The Turk's head of Arizona, *Echinocactus horizonthalonius* var. *nicholii*, at the Arizona-Sonora Desert Museum, Tucson, Arizona, in conditions similar to those of its natural habitat.

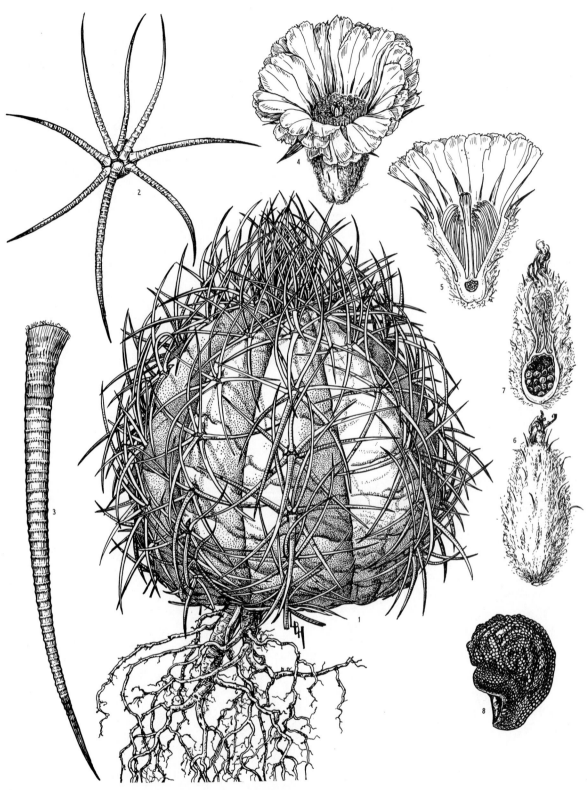

Fig. 758. The Turk's head of Arizona, *Echinocactus horizonthalonius* var. *nicholii*. *1*, Plant, ×.6. *2*, Areole with spines and felty wool, showing the three central spines, the principal (lower) one black and curving downward, and the few radial spines, ×.8; all spines cross-ribbed. *3*, Principal central spine, ×2.8. *4*, Flower, ×.6. *5*, Flower in longitudinal section, ×.6. *6*, Fruit, dry and woolly at maturity, ×1.2. *7*, Fruit in longitudinal section, ×1.2. *8*, Seed, the large hilum appearing "sub-basal," ×9.

2b. Echinocactus horizonthalonius var. nicholii
L. Benson. Black limestone (with desert varnish)
in desert mountains at about 900-1,050 m (3,000-
3,500 ft). Arizona Desert. Occasional in Arizona
in sw Pinal Co. and N central Pima Co.

Much of the information concerning this variety may be attributed to A. A. Nichol, formerly
of the University of Arizona and the Arizona State
Game and Fish Department. During the 1930's,
Mr. Nichol located the plants in a number of
areas, and he thought the Arizona plants to be
different from those occurring in Texas. The
areas of occurrence are remote from habitations.

The plants are taller and darker than those of
var. *horizonthalonius*, and they tend to form dark
gray cylinders.

3. Echinocactus texensis Hoppfer
Horse crippler, devil's head

Larger stems green, hemispheroidal, 12-20 cm
long, to 30 cm diam; ribs 13-27; areoles 10-15 mm
diam, typically ±25 mm apart; spines dense but
not obscuring joint, red but basally whitened,
strongly cross-ribbed, stout and rigid; central
spine 1 per areole, turned and curving rigidly
downward and exceeding radials, the longer 3-7.5
cm long, basally 3-9 mm broad, subulate, flattened but angular, tapering; radial spines usually
(5)6(7) per areole, each spreading at a low angle
or in a low arc, the longer 2.5-5 cm long, basally
1.5-3 mm broad, subulate, tapering, flattened;
flower 5-6 cm diam and long; sepaloids numer-

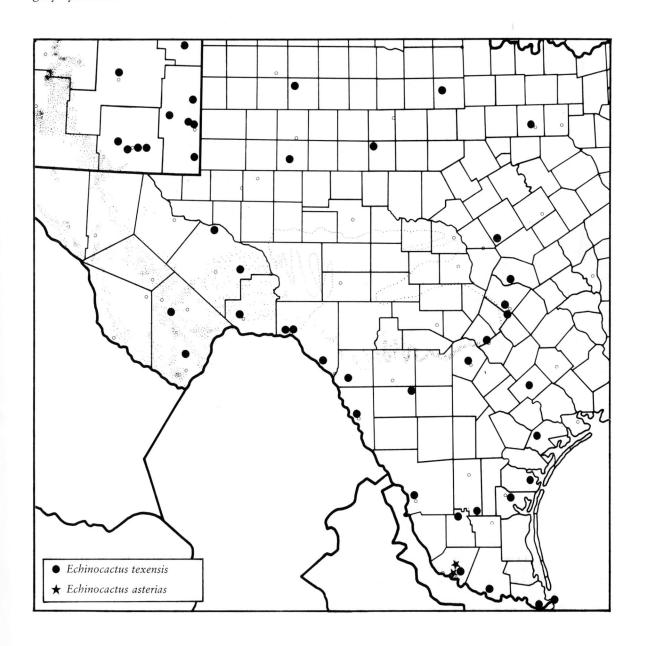

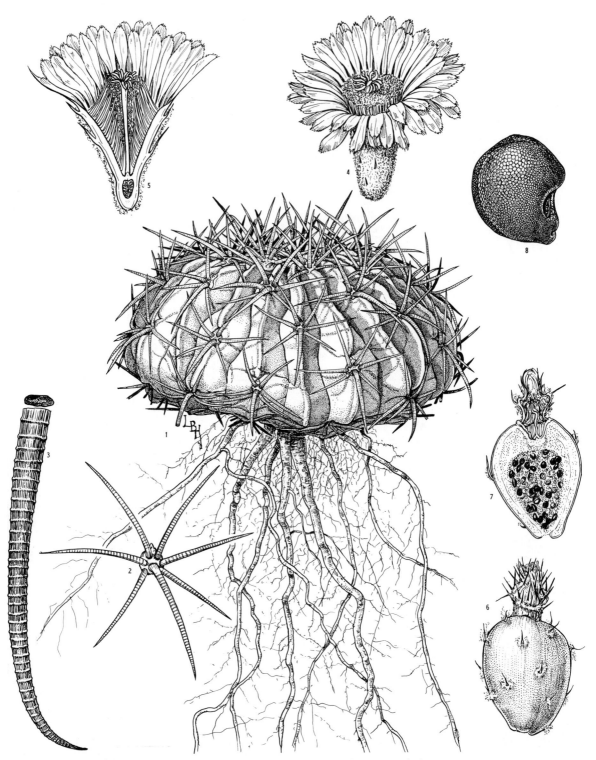

Fig. 759. Horse crippler or devil's head, *Echinocactus texensis*. *1*, Plant, the stem with the characteristic ratio of length to breadth, ×.5; note the downward-curving stout lower central spine, responsible for the common name. *2*, Areole with spines and felty wool, showing the single central spine and the few radials, ×1.1. *3*, Central spine, enlarged, with a diagrammatic cross section, ×4.5. *4*, Flower, showing the sharply spinose scale-leaves on the ovary and on the similar sepaloid perianth parts, these characteristic of the genus, ×.8. *5*, Flower in longitudinal section, ×.8. *6*, Fruit, retaining the scale-leaves and fleshy and red at maturity, ×.8. *7*, Fruit in longitudinal section, ×.8. *8*, Seed, the hilum appearing more or less "lateral," ×14.

722

ous, with pink midribs, the lower margins covered by long wool, the upper lacerate-fimbriate, feathery, largest oblanceolate, 25 mm long, to 4.5 mm broad, each acute but attenuate into a long spine; petaloids numerous, with pale purple to violet midribs, basally scarlet, then orange, and distally pale pink to white, largest oblanceolate, ±25 mm long, to 7.5 mm broad, rounded, not spinose, lacerate-fimbriate; filaments red, 10 mm long; anthers yellow, oblong, length 3 times breadth, ±1 mm long; style pink, ±25 mm long, 1.5 mm greatest diam; stigmas ±10-17, irregular, ±3 mm long, pink; ovary in anthesis obovoid, ±6 mm long, embedded in wool; fruit red, fleshy at maturity but soon drying and splitting irregularly, with the scales more or less deciduous, ±50 mm long, ±25-38 mm diam; seeds black, finely reticulate, irregularly obovoid, 2 mm long,

2.5 mm broad, 1.5 mm thick; hilum oblique, deeply incurved.

Loam, limestone, or sandy soils of plains, valleys, and hills in grasslands from sea level to 1,000 m (3,300 ft). Great Plains Grassland, Edwards Plateau, Rio Grande Plain. Southeastern New Mexico from Chaves and Roosevelt Cos. to E Otero, Eddy, and Lea Cos.; Texas from Pecos R. Valley and N Brewster Co. NE to Garza, Young, and Tarrant Cos. and S and E to Travis, Refugio, and Cameron Cos. Adjacent Mexico in Coahuila, Nuevo León, and Tamaulipas.

The horse crippler stem is a hemispheroidal mound often half hidden among the plains grasses, and its sharp, stout, downward-curving spines are a menace to animals, including man. Its varicolored flowers are striking, but the ring of bright red fruits the size of small walnuts is even more so.

Fig. 760. Star cactus, *Echinocactus asterias*, southernmost Texas near the Rio Grande. (Archie D. Wood)

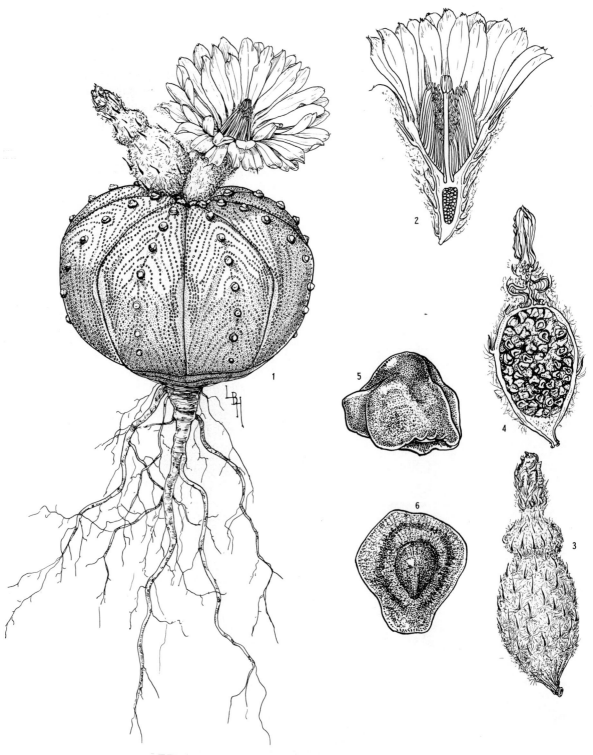

Fig. 761. Star cactus, *Echinocactus asterias*, ×1.1, except as indicated. *1*, Plant with a flower and a fruit, showing the spineless areoles and the irregular rows of small scales on the stem-ribs. *2*, Flower in longitudinal section. *3*, Fruit, green and fleshy at maturity, the surface covered with spinose scale-leaves and woolly hairs. *4*, Fruit in longitudinal section. *5*, Seed in side view, the lower half a broad collar surrounding a large cavity around the small hilum, ×14. *6*, Seed in top view, showing the flaring basal collar, ×14.

4. Echinocactus asterias Zuccarini
Star cactus

Larger stems green, with covering of white or yellowish, more-or-less circular scales, some of which may be fringed, ±2.5-7.5 cm long, 7.5 (reportedly to 23.7) cm diam; ribs usually 8, separated by narrow grooves; areoles ±3 mm diam, typically 6-9 mm apart, bearing many hairs; spines in adult plant none; flower 3.8-5 cm diam, 4.5-5.3 cm long; sepaloids with dense, long wool on midribs and margins, the largest lanceolate-attenuate, to nearly 25 mm long, basally 3-4.5 mm broad, attenuate to aristate; petaloids pale straw-yellow, bases red, largest lanceolate-acuminate, ±25 mm long, 6-9 mm broad, mucronate to aristate, marginally entire; filaments yellowish, ±12 mm long; anthers yellow, linear, 1.5 mm long; style 15-20 mm long, 1-1.5 mm greatest diam; stigmas ±10, 4 mm long, rather broad; ovary in anthesis ±6 mm long; fruit green or pink, fleshy at maturity, obscured by white, woolly hairs from areoles, the scale-leaves of ovary specialized as setose spines 2-3 mm long, the fruit 15-20 mm long, ±12 mm diam; seed brown, shiny, finely reticulate on a larger and more conspicuous scale below than apically, irregularly pyramidal but the edges rounded off, the basal part a remarkable collar surrounding the hilum, the rim of the collar turned inward and forming a membranous covering around the threadlike funiculus, this entering the chamber about the hilum as through a hole in the roof, the seed basally broader than long (hilum to opposite point, the seed proper occupying only the apex of the visible structure), 2 mm long, 3 mm broad, the base being nearly an equilateral triangle; hilum small, at center of floor of cavity.

Gentle slopes and flats of grasslands and brushlands at low elevations. Rio Grande Plain. Texas in Starr Co. near the Rio Grande. Mexico in Nuevo León and Tamaulipas (Clover, 1933).

The star cactus is a little gem partly hidden among bushes. Its circular form is overshadowed by the beauty of its symmetrical markings, and the lack of spines permits these to predominate.

Reference: Rowley, 1958.

10. Sclerocactus

Stems solitary or sometimes with a few branches (perhaps due to injury of terminal bud), largest cylindroid, ovoid, globose, or depressed-globose, 5-20(40) cm long, 4-10(15) cm diam; ribs ±12-17, the tubercles coalescent, the protruding portions usually of less height than ribs; tubercles mostly 6-12 mm long vertically, 6-9 mm broad, protruding 3-6 mm. Leaves none on mature stem, each represented in early development of tubercle by small hump of tissue below developing areole. Areoles circular to elliptic. Spines smooth, *not* with crosswise ridges; central spines gray, white, yellow, red, or brown, (0)1-6(11) per areole, usually of 2 or 3 distinct types and usually 1 or more hooked, the longer 1.2-9 cm long, acicular or subulate or commonly some of each type; radial spines white or gray or sometimes some pink or brown, 6-11(15) per areole, straight, the longer shorter than centrals, acicular or subulate. Flowers and fruits on new growth of current season and therefore near apex of stem or branch, developed on upper side of tubercle in felted area adjacent to and merging with new spiniferous areole, this area forming a persistent circular to irregular or uncommonly oblong scar. Flower 2.5-6 cm diam; floral tube above ovary short, funnelform; petaloids white, yellow, or pink to reddish-purple. Fruit green, thin-walled, turning reddish and becoming dry at maturity, naked or with a few broad, thin scales, the body 10-25 mm long, 9-13.5 mm diam, the umbilicus obscured by persistent superior floral tube and attached perianth and other flower parts, *either* opening along a circular, nearly horizontal, regular or somewhat irregular line above base to below or a little above middle *or* (in 2 species) along 2 or 3(4) short vertical lines. Seeds black, papillate-reticulate, asymmetrical, angled on 1 side of hilum, rounded on other, broader than long, 1.5-2.5 mm long (hilum to point opposite), (2.5)3-4 mm broad, 1-1.5 mm thick; hilum appearing "lateral" or "diagonal"; cotyledons accumbent, *not* foliaceous.

From Gr. *scleros* (hard).

Eight species occurring from Mojave Desert, California, to Great Salt Lake Desert, Utah, and the Colorado Plateau and east to western Colorado and northwestern New Mexico.

The genus was proposed to classify two highly specialized species occurring in western North America. The other six described here include three unknown then and three known only from inadequate herbarium material and misinterpreted. In addition, a new variety has come to light. Several of these taxa are relatively less specialized in obvious spine structure than the original two.

Dorothea Woodruff has supplied new information, acknowledged for some species, for the descriptions of *Sclerocactus wrightiae, pubispinus, spinosior, whipplei,* and *parviflorus.*

1. *S. glaucus*
2. *S. mesae-verdae*
3. *S. wrightiae*
4. *S. pubispinus*
5. *S. spinosior*
6. *S. whipplei*
7. *S. parviflorus*
   vars. a. *parviflorus*
        b. *intermedius*
8. *S. polyancistrus*

KEY TO THE SPECIES OF SCLEROCACTUS

1. Central spines 1-4, *none hooked*; perianth pink to lavender or reddish-purple; seeds ±2.5 mm broad (greatest dimension); scale-leaves of the fruit none or 1 or 2; stem tubercles merging only basally with the ribs, the free portion of the tubercle as high as the rib beneath it; E Utah and w Colorado.....................**1. S. glaucus**

1. Central spines 0-11 *the lower (principal) one (when present) hooked* (except sometimes in the areoles of juvenile stems, which later in mature stems persist as the lower areoles); perianth color various; seeds 3-4 mm broad; scale-leaves of the fruit none or a few; stem-tubercles various.
   2. Fruit *not* bearing scale-leaves; stem-ribs not prominent, the free portions of the tubercles nearly as conspicuous as the rib; lower central spine (if present) not more than 1.5 cm long.
      3. Central spines *usually* none but sometimes the lower (principal) one present, this dark, terete, and hooked; stem-tubercles of older plants not as high as the rib beneath them; perianth yellow; sw Colorado and NW New Mexico . . . .**2. S. mesae-verdae**
      3. Central spines 4, the lower (principal) one hooked, dark brown or black, terete, the two lateral upper centrals dark, terete, not hooked, the uppermost (median) one white, basally broad and flattened; stem-tubercles of older plants as high as the rib beneath them; perianth pink to white; sw Utah . . . .**3. S. wrightiae**
   2. Fruit bearing a few scale-leaves, these separated widely from the sepaloids; stem-ribs evident, only the tops of the tubercles separate; lower (principal) central spine hooked, 1.5-9 cm long.
      3A. Hooked central spine(s) of mature stems 1 (rarely 2) per areole, to 2.5-5 cm long; hairs on ovary usually shorter than or slightly exceeding and protruding beyond the scales; upper, flattened, white central spine 1, median, ±2.5-5 cm long; style glabrous or pubescent; scales on the ovary not fimbriate, not membranous-bordered or only slightly so.
         4. Fruit opening along 2 or 3 short vertical slits; spines of juvenile stems (often still discernible at the bases of older stems) conspicuously and densely white-pubescent; *not only* the upper median central spine of each areole of the mature stem flattened and white *but also* often 1 or 2 lateral upper centrals basally flattened, broad, and white; style glabrous; scales on the ovary not scarious-membranous-bordered, not fimbriate; E edge of Nevada, w Utah, and middle northernmost Arizona.
            5. Lower central spine (in mature plants) red to almost black, all other spines white or the 2 lateral centrals pink to pale brown, the lower central hooked; flower cream to yellow or pinkish; petaloids cream with pale yellow to greenish or pink middles and yellow to pale pink margins; sepaloids with pink to yellowish-brown middles and cream to yellow or pink margins, apically rounded, usually not mucronate; E edge of Nevada and w Utah from Box Elder Co. to Beaver Co. . . . .**4. S. pubispinus**
            5. Lower 3 central spines usually brown, the principal one and sometimes the 1 or 2 laterals hooked; flower reddish-violet to lavender or reddish-purple or rarely brownish; petaloids with reddish-violet to reddish-purple or lavender or brownish middles and lighter margins; sepaloids with greenish or reddish-brown middles and pink to purple margins, mucronate; w edge of Utah and middle northernmost Arizona. . . . .**5. S. spinosior**
         4. Fruit opening horizontally near base; spines of juvenile stems *not* densely white-pubescent, sometimes finely canescent; *only* the upper median central spine of each areole of the mature stem flattened and white or pale, the lateral upper centrals not flattened or very rarely so; style finely pubescent with hooked hairs; scales on the ovary remarkably scarious-membranous-bordered, tending to be fimbriate; Colorado Plateau in E Utah, w Colorado, N Arizona, and NW New Mexico.
            5A. Flower buds brownish, their length less than diameter, opening completely only in bright sunshine, the petaloids increasing rapidly in size within a few hours, usually yellow; upper central spine flat, ribbonlike, white, conspicuous, basally 1.5-3 mm broad, subulate; lower (hooked) central spine to 2.5-3.8 cm long, purplish-pink; stems depressed-globose to short-ovoid, to 7.5 cm long (rarely longer), to 9 cm in diameter; N Arizona on Little Colorado drainage in Navajo and Apache Cos. . . . .**6. S. whipplei**
            5A. Flower buds greenish, their length greater than diameter, opening with or without bright light, even without light, the petaloids with no striking increase in size after the opening of the bud, purple, pink, or white; upper central spine flat to somewhat flattened or angled, not necessarily ribbonlike, pale pink or white, much less conspicuous to inconspicuous, basally 1-1.5 mm broad, linear to narrowly subulate; lower (hooked) central spine 3.8-4.5(5) cm long, reddish; stems elongate, cylindroid, 7.5-15(20) cm long,

5-6(10) cm in diameter; E Utah to w edge of Colorado and middle north-ernmost Arizona.....................................7. **S. parviflorus**
3A. Hooked central spines of the mature stems 6-8 per areole, to 7.5-9 cm long; hairs on the ovary about twice as long as the scales, protruding far beyond them; upper white, broad, flattened central spines usually 3, the single median one 7.5-9 cm long; style glabrous; scales on the ovary *not* fimbriate, slightly membranous-bordered; California in Mojavean Desert and Nevada in Esmeralda Co. ....8. **S. polyancistrus**

1. Sclerocactus glaucus (K. Schumann) L. Benson

Stems solitary or sometimes 2 or 3, green but somewhat glaucous, ovoid or nearly globular, 4-6 cm long, 4-5 cm diam; ribs ±12; tubercles ±9 mm long, 6-9 mm broad, each protruding 6-9 mm above the rib; areoles ±3 mm diam, typically ±9 mm apart; spines dense, obscuring stem; central spines 1-3, the upper 1 or 2 (when present) white but only partly flattened, narrowly elliptic in cross section, resembling and not wholly distinguish-able from radials, to 2.5 cm long, ±0.7 mm broad; lower central spine light to dark brown, *not hooked* but sometimes curving, somewhat flattened, to 2.5 cm long, basally 1 mm broad, subulate, very narrowly elliptic in cross section; radial spines white or some brown, straight or nearly so, 6-8 per areole, spreading in a circle or those above missing, the longer to 2 cm long, bas-ally ±0.5 mm diam, acicular, nearly circular in cross section; flower 4-5 cm diam, 3-3.8 cm long; sepaloids with lavender midribs and pink mar-gins, the larger very narrowly elliptic, to 25 mm long, to 6 mm broad, apically narrowly rounded, marginally entire and slightly scarious; petaloids pink, largest nearly lanceolate, to 30 mm long, to 6 mm broad, apically acute, the margins entire; filaments greenish-white or green, to 12 mm long; anthers yellow, oblong, 1 mm long; style to 20 mm long, 1.5 mm greatest diam; stigmas ±12, 3.5 mm long, rather slender; ovary in anthesis ±6 mm long; fruit with a few broad membranous scales especially at apex, ±9-12 mm long, 9 mm

Fig. 762. *Sclerocactus glaucus,* near Delta, Delta Co., Colorado.

Fig. 764. *Sclerocactus glaucus*, apex of the stem with fruits, the dried floral tube and perianth of each persistent. Note the few dry scales on each fruit. (Dorothea Woodruff)

Fig. 763. *Sclerocactus glaucus*, plants from the population of Fig. 762, showing individual variation and differences due to age. The stem is tuberculate.

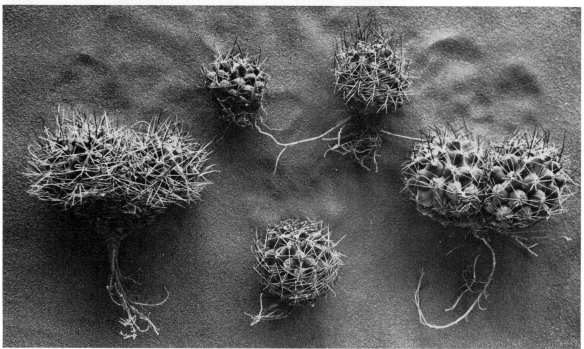

diam, umbilicus covered by persistent perianth, barrel-shaped; seeds 1.5+ mm long, 2.5 mm broad, 1 mm thick.

Gravelly soils of hills and mesas in or near desert at 1,200-1,500(1,800) m (4,000-5,000 or 6,000 ft). Navajoan Desert. Utah near Green R.; Colo-rado from near Colorado R. in Mesa Co. to Grand Mesa and Delta, Delta Co.

The gray-green plants blend with the river-worn gravels or the rocks of the soil on which the cactus grows, and the plants can be found only after much searching.

2. Sclerocactus mesae-verdae
(Boissevain *ex* Hill & Salisbury) L. Benson

Stems pale green or gray-green, broadly ovoid or depressed-globose, mostly 4-6(18) cm long, 4-6(7.5) cm diam; ribs 13-17; tubercles of older plants inconspicuous; areoles 3-4.5 mm diam, typically ±12 mm apart, with dense, short wool; spines dense on ribs, but stem with obvious space between ribs; central spines none (rarely 1 or possibly 2-4), some upper spines suggesting white upper centrals of other species, gray with dark tips, hooked, ±10-12 mm long; radial spines pale tannish or straw-colored, 8-10 per areole, spreading irregularly, straight or slightly curving, the longer to 12 mm long, basally to 1 mm diam, acicular, elliptic to circular in cross section, the bases slightly bulbous; flower (1.5)2.5-3 cm diam, 2-2.5 cm long; sepaloids with greenish-purple midribs and yellow to greenish-yellow margins, the larger oblanceolate-obovate, to 20 mm long, to 6 mm broad, obtuse to rounded, some tending toward mucronulate, entire or minutely and sparsely denticulate or undulate; petaloids yellow to greenish-yellow, the largest oblanceolate, to 20 mm long, to 4 mm broad, mucronate to cuspidate, entire or nearly so; filaments pale yellow, ±1.5 mm long; anthers yellow, narrowly elliptic, 1.5 mm long; style pale green, 15 mm long, 1-1.5 mm greatest diam; stigmas 6-8, ±2 mm long, rather narrow; ovary in anthesis ±3 mm long, surrounded by wool; fruit green, becoming tan when dry at maturity, bare or essentially so, but floral tube bearing scales above ovary, becoming wrinkled lengthwise and papery, irregularly short-cylindroid, to ±4.5-5 mm long, to ±8 mm diam, dehiscent irregularly transversely above middle; seeds 2 mm long, 3 mm broad, 1.5+ mm thick; hilum very small.

Low hills and mesas in desert at about 1,200-1,500 m (4,000-5,000 ft). Navajoan Desert. Southwestern corner of Colorado near Mesa Verde and adjacent NW corner of New Mexico s to vicinity of the Ship Rock and town of Shiprock.

The pale gray spines blend with the peculiar fine soil on which the plants grow. They have almost no competition, and they occur in places where presumably no cactus could live.

This species resembles *Pediocactus knowltonii* and especially *P. bradyi* in its spines, and *P. bradyi* in its flowers; but the fruit follows the irregular pattern of opening circularly at, below, or above the middle common in *Sclerocactus*.

Sclerocactus mesae-verdae is distinguished, also, from *Pediocactus*, to which it is probably related, by the following characters:

1. Tubercles of stems *of larger plants* coalescent into ribs.

2. Fruit not clearly both with top coming off like a lid and with a dorsal slit, but opening by an irregular, circular, and horizontal slit above the middle.

The species is distinguished further from the probably related *Pediocactus bradyi* by the following characters:

1. Fruit not constricted basally, not stalked.

2. Seeds papillate but not with larger mounds, ±3 mm broad (as opposed to 2 mm).

3. Radial spines not pectinate, 8-10 (instead of 14-15) per areole, mostly 7.5-12 mm long (instead of 3-6 mm); stems mostly 5-6(10) cm long (instead of 4-5(6) cm).

Lack of central spines was the chief feature of the proposed genus *Coloradoa*. However, Boissevain and Davidson (1940, 55) described the rare occurrence of central spines in this species (as *Coloradoa mesae-verdae*) as follows: "Central spine usually wanting but when present 1, 1 cm. long,

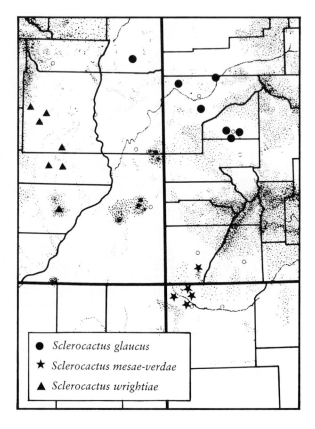

● *Sclerocactus glaucus*
★ *Sclerocactus mesae-verdae*
▲ *Sclerocactus wrightiae*

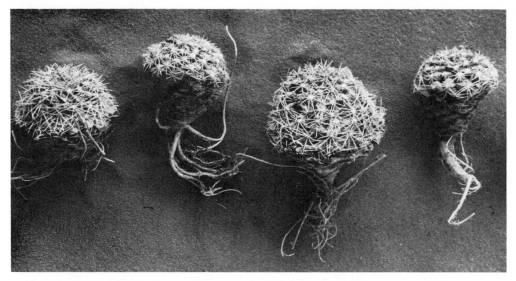

Fig. 765. *Sclerocactus mesae-verdae*, plants from a population in the vicinity of Mesa Verde, Montezuma Co., Colorado.

Fig. 766. *Sclerocactus mesae-verdae*, upper part of the stem, showing the irregular separation of the upper and lower portions of the fruits. (Dorothea Woodruff)

731

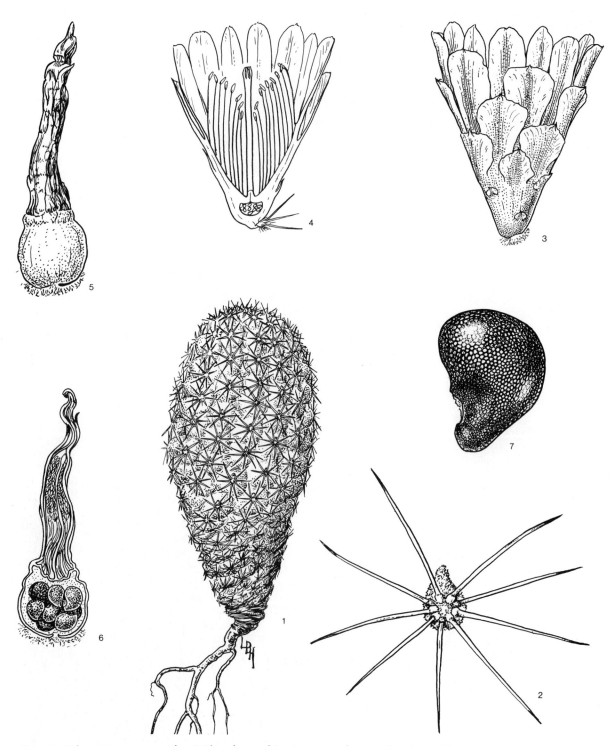

Fig. 767. *Sclerocactus mesae-verdae. 1*, Plant from cultivation, more elongate than is usual in nature, ×1.25. *2*, Areole with spines and wool, ×3.75; central spine none (rarely present). *3*, Flower, showing the transition from scale-leaves to sepaloid, then petaloid, perianth parts, ×1.8. *4*, Flower in longitudinal section, ×1.8. *5*, Fruit, ×3.75. *6*, Fruit in longitudinal section, ×3.75. *7*, Seed, in the hilum appearing "lateral," ×19.

Fig. 768. *Sclerocactus mesae-verdae*, plant with a hooked central spine similar to those of *S. wrightiae*, a connecting link to the other species of *Sclerocactus*. (See Credits)

subulate, gray with dark tip, porrect or ascending, straight or sometimes hooked." Central spines have occurred in only one of some hundreds of plants examined in the field in sw Colorado (*L., E. L., & R. L. Benson 14756, Pom, 16155, Pom*) and NW New Mexico (*L., E. L., & R. L. Benson 16158, Pom*) and in herbarium specimens. A collection of one plant from w of the Ship Rock, New Mexico, has solitary, hooked, dark-tipped centrals (*L., E. L., & R. L. Benson 16159, Pom*). Similar spines are in a collection by Marilyn Colyer (s of Jackson Butte, Montezuma Co., Colorado, March 1963, *Pom*). These spines are reminiscent of those of *Sclerocactus whipplei* and related species. Other plants have upper spines suggesting the white upper central spines of the other species of *Sclerocactus*.

The discovery in 1961 and the securing in 1965 of good material of *Sclerocactus wrightiae* have indicated the close relationship of this species to *S. mesae-verdae*, and this affinity is a bridge to the rest of the genus.

3. Sclerocactus wrightiae L. Benson

Stems unbranched, globose (depressed-globose to obovoid), 5-5.5(9) cm long, 5-7.5 cm diam; ribs ±13; tubercles more prominent and on even the older stems about as high as the rib beneath them, 12 mm long, 9 mm broad, protruding 6-9 mm; areoles 3-4 mm diam, typically ±9 mm apart, the scar of the fruiting area ventral to areole vertically elongate (length 2-4 times breadth); spines not obscuring stem; central spines 4, the

principal (lower) one hooked, pale on upper side, dark brown on lower, often stout, ±12(15) mm long, somewhat curved as well as hooked, in older plants ±0.5-1 mm broad, elliptic in cross section, the 2 lateral upper central spines slightly curving, dark to light brown, to 12 mm long, the uppermost (median) central pale straw or ashy, the longer centrals 1.2-2 cm long, basally 0.8-1.5 mm broad, somewhat flattened, thus relatively broad; radial spines white, 8-10 per areole, spreading almost perpendicularly to tubercle, nearly straight, the longer 6-12 mm long, basally 0.25-0.4 mm broad, subulate; flower 2-2.5(4) cm diam and long, fragrant; sepaloids with light reddish-brown, reddish-green, or lavender middles and pale pink to white margins, the larger obovate-oblanceolate, 5-12 mm long, 3-8(12) mm broad, rounded, entire to undulate or with irregular minute teeth; petaloids nearly white to pink, midribs brownish, largest lanceolate to oblanceolate, 12-20 mm long, (3)4.5-6(10) mm broad, acute to rounded, often mucronulate, entire to undulate or irregularly minutely toothed; filaments pink, 6-12 mm long, slender; anthers yellow, narrowly elliptic-oblong, 0.7-1 mm long; style green, 12 mm long, 1 mm diam; stigmas 5-8, 1.5-2 mm long, slender to broad; ovary in anthesis ±10 mm long, 5-6 mm diam; fruit with 1 or 2 scales or none, 9-12 mm long and diam, barrel-shaped; seeds 2 mm long, 3.5 mm broad, 1.5 mm thick.

Hills in desert at about 1,350-1,860 m (4,500-

Fig. 769. *Sclerocactus wrightiae* in flower, showing the tubercles, spine clusters in the areoles, and scars of fallen fruits, one scar above each areole. (Irving G. Reimann)

Fig. 770. *Sclerocactus wrightiae*, flowers from above. (Irving G. Reimann)

5,800 ft). Navajoan Desert. Utah through a known area about 80 km (50 miles) in diameter on upper drainage of Dirty Devil R.

This rare plant is an obscure, fat green barrel occurring in out-of-the-way places.

This species is related to both *Sclerocactus mesae-verdae* and *S. whipplei*, and it is a connecting link between them. It provided further evidence for amalgamation of the proposed genera *Sclerocactus* and *Coloradoa* (the evidence having been already sufficient). There is also a relationship to *S. spinosior* and *S. parviflorus*.

4. Sclerocactus pubispinus
(Engelmann) L. Benson

Mature stems solitary, domelike, to ±6 cm high, to 9 cm diam; ribs ±13; tubercles protruding prominently above ribs, ±10 mm long, (5)10 (17) mm broad, protruding 4-6 mm, about as high as the ribs beneath; areoles circular to elliptic, 3-4.5 mm diam, typically 12-15 mm apart; spines not obscuring stem, those of juvenile plants densely white-pubescent, hygroscopic, all but lower central usually white or pale; central spines (0-3) 4(5), the single lower central red to nearly black, not flattened, elliptic or sometimes rhombic in cross section, hooked, 1.5-3 cm long, 0.5-1.5 mm diam, the middle (0-1)2 centrals tending to resemble the lower, though smaller, red or reddish-brown, slender, 1-2 cm long, ±0.5 mm diam, the upper 1 central white or tip dark, flattened,

nearly straight, (7)15-25(35) mm long, basally ±0.7 mm broad; radial spines white or with dark tips, (6)9-11(16), straight or slightly curving, acicular, spreading, mostly 5-12 mm long and 0.3-0.4 mm diam; flower 2-4 cm diam, 2.5-3.5 cm long; sepaloids with pink to yellowish-brown midribs and cream to yellow or pink margins, the larger variable but mostly oblanceolate, 10-20 mm long, 4-8 mm broad, apically rounded, marginally entire or sometimes undulate, obtuse to acute, finely irregularly apically toothed and sometimes mucronulate; petaloids cream with pale yellow to greenish or pink middles and pale cream to yellow or pale-pink margins, largest very narrowly elliptic-oblanceolate, 15-20 mm long, (4)4.5-6 mm broad, acute and sometimes mucronulate, marginally entire or slightly undulate or apically minutely toothed; filaments cream or yellow or greenish, 6-12 mm long; anthers yellow, ±1 mm long; style greenish to yellowish, 12-25 mm long, 1-2 mm greatest diam; stigmas (6)8 or 9(10), 1.5-2 mm long, greenish to yellow, densely pubescent, tending to be broad; ovary in anthesis 6-7 mm long, 6-10 mm diam; fruit green and pink but becoming dry at maturity, barrel-shaped, with 1-4 scales, these only slightly scarious on margins, and the hairs (if any) in axils short, the fruit ±10 mm long and diam, splitting along 2 or 3 vertical lines.

Rocky hillsides of woodland and upper desert mountains at about 1,800-2,100 m (6,000-7,000 ft). Northern Juniper-Pinyon Woodland and up-

Fig. 771. *Sclerocactus pubispinus*, plants in flower. (Dorothea Woodruff)

per Sagebrush Desert. Nevada along E edges of Elko and White Pine Cos.; NW Utah from Box Elder Co. to Beaver Co.

The white balls or domes are seldom seen, and they blend into the light-colored soils of hills and flats in the deserts and woodlands.

This species was named from juvenile specimens with pubescent spines. The young plants are indistinguishable from those of *Sclerocactus spinosior*, and the writer once thought the name combination *Echinocactus pubispinus*, based on juvenile plants, to have been applied to young individuals of the plant named simultaneously by Engelmann as *S. whipplei* var. *spinosior*. However, two collections (*Wiegand* in 1954, *Pom*; *D. Wright* [*Woodruff*] in 1961, *Pom*) were anomalous and thought possibly from a different taxon: one specimen (*Wiegand* in 1954, *Pom*) appeared to be derived from a juvenile plant; the other specimen consisted of a single living plant in Salt Lake City and a photograph of it at Pomona College. In 1970 Mrs. Woodruff obtained excellent specimens of mature plants from the type locality of *E. pubispinus*, and these proved to be similar to the plant from Elko Co., Nevada, cultivated at Salt Lake City. Mrs. Woodruff established the existence of two species, one (*S. pubispinus*) occurring westward at higher elevations, the other (*S. spinosior*) eastward at lower levels and on different underlying rock formations.

Fig. 773. *Sclerocactus pubi-spinus*, adult plant in flower, showing the dark hooked principal lower central spines; the other spines usually white. (Dorothea Woodruff)

Fig. 772. *Sclerocactus pubi-spinus*, young plants showing the markedly pubescent spines of juvenile individuals. (Dorothea Woodruff)

736

Fig. 774. *Sclerocactus pubispinus*, upper part of the stem, showing the younger areoles and spines; one developing areole with a longitudinally dehiscent fruit (one or two slits now showing). (Dorothea Woodruff)

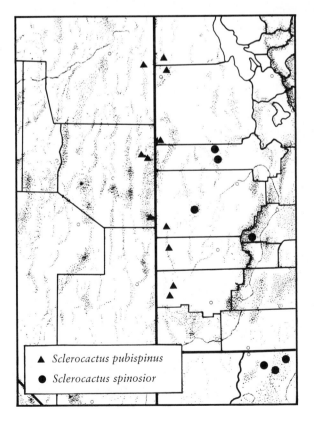

▲ *Sclerocactus pubispinus*
● *Sclerocactus spinosior*

5. Sclerocactus spinosior
(Engelmann) Woodruff & Benson

Mature stem depressed-globose to ovoid, solitary, 4-7.5(14) cm long, 4.5-6(9) cm diam; ribs 13(14), tuberculate but not deeply so; tubercles one-fourth to one-half as high as rib beneath, 6-11(17) mm long, 6-15 mm broad, protruding ±3-4 mm; areoles circular to elliptic, 3-6 mm broad, typically 6-12 mm apart; spines rather dense but not wholly obscuring stem, those of juvenile plants densely white-pubescent, somewhat hygroscopic, those produced later glabrous; central spines white on juvenile stems and therefore on older (lower) parts of mature stems, the lower centrals of upper areoles 3, tan to brown, reddish, or almost black except sometimes basally, usually rhombic in section, the upper centrals white, ±6 per areole, the principal lower one and sometimes 1 or 2 others hooked, otherwise nearly straight, the principal lower usually 2-3 cm long, basally 1-1.2 mm broad, more or less acicular but elliptic in section, the lateral (usually 2) centrals similar to but lighter-colored than the lower, the upper median central white, flat, 2-5(6) cm long,

Fig. 775. *Sclerocactus spinosior*, growing at the type locality, the stem about the size of a tennis ball, showing the dark hooked lower central spines, the lower three usually brown, at least one hooked.

Fig. 776. *Sclerocactus spinosior*, stem with the characteristic covering of spines, but in this still rather young individual the white spines predominating; a flower bud emerging apically. (Dorothea Woodruff)

Fig. 777. *Sclerocactus spinosior*, apex of the stem with flowers, showing both dark lower central spines and broad, white, flat upper central spines.

Fig. 778. *Sclerocactus spinosior*, upper areoles with dark, hooked middle lower central spines, dark hooked lateral or nearly straight lower centrals, and flat, thin, white lateral and flattened, straight or curving upper centrals. The fruit at the upper left is dehiscent along a vertical line (one visible, one or two not seen from this side). (Dorothea Woodruff)

Fig. 779. *Sclerocactus spinosior,* apex of the stem with young areoles and two dehiscent fruits, showing the ribbonlike character of the white upper central spines and the absence or lesser degree of flattening in the dark lower central spines. (Dorothea Woodruff)

to 1.6 mm broad, the 1 or 2 adjacent (probably also central) spines similar but smaller; radial spines white, to ±8 per areole, spreading, flexible, not quite straight, slender, the longer mostly 1-2.5 (3.5) cm long, basally 2.5-5 mm broad, acicular to subulate, elliptic or narrowly so in cross section; flower 2-4 cm diam and long; sepaloids with greenish-brown or reddish-brown midribs and pink to reddish-purple margins, the larger usually oblanceolate, mostly 10-20 mm long, mostly 4.5-7 mm broad, mucronate, nearly entire or with a few irregular apical minute teeth, acute to narrowly rounded; petaloids with reddish-purple to red-violet or lavender or brownish middles and lighter margins, largest narrowly oblanceolate, ±25 mm long, 6-7.5 mm broad, mucronate, nearly entire; filaments red-violet to pink, pale green, or yellow, 6-12 mm long; anthers yellow, elliptic to oblong, 1-1.5 mm long; style usually pink to reddish-violet, glabrous, 15-20 mm long, 1-1.7 mm greatest diam; stigmas usually yellow, 5 or 6(10), 1.5-3 mm long, 0.5 mm broad, usually long and narrow; ovary in anthesis ±6 mm long and diam; fruit green, at first somewhat fleshy but becoming reddish and dry at maturity, with (0)1 or 2 somewhat scarious-margined scales and with no or short hairs from the areoles beneath them, barrel-shaped, 9-12 mm long and diam, opening along 2-4 vertical slits; seeds 2-2.5 mm long, 3-4 mm broad, 1.5-2 mm thick.

Rocky soils of hills in desert at 1,500-1,800 m (5,000-6,000 ft) and perhaps higher. Sagebrush Desert and Navajoan Desert. Utah from sw Tooele Co. to Iron and Sevier Cos. and perhaps in region near Kanab, Kane Co.; Arizona in N Coconino Co. about Houserock Valley.

The domes or balls are a mixture of the red or reddish-brown of the hooked central spines and the white of the usually three flattened upper centrals. In younger plants the white spines predominate, but in mature plants the darker spines develop and the color of the mass changes.

6. Sclerocactus whipplei
(Engelmann & Bigelow) Britton & Rose

Stems solitary or sometimes 2 or 3, green, ovoid to depressed-globose, mature ones to 7.5 cm long (rarely longer), to 9 cm diam; ribs ±13-15, well developed but upper portions of tubercles standing above ribs, 6-12 mm long and broad and protruding 6-10 mm; areoles 4.5-6 mm diam, typically 9-12 mm apart; central spines mostly 4, the lower one purplish-pink, terete or somewhat angled, hooked, porrect, 2.5-3.8 cm long, ±1 mm diam, turned or curving somewhat downward, the 2 laterals similar to lower but a bit shorter and not hooked, the upper white, straight or nearly so, flat, ribbonlike, conspicuous, narrowly elliptic in cross section, 2.5-5 cm long, 1.5-3 mm broad, erect; radial spines mostly 7-11, all but 2 of lower spreading ones white, these like lateral centrals, with which they form a cross, the longer mostly ±2.5 cm long, basally 1-1.5 mm broad, acicular, elliptic or rhombic in section; flower ±2.5-3.5 cm diam, 1.5-2.5 cm long; sepaloids with greenish midribs and yellow margins, the larger narrowly oblanceolate, ±20 mm long, 4.5-5 mm broad, mucronate, marginally membranous and crisped and irregularly minutely hooked; petaloids usually yellow, largest narrowly oblanceolate, ±25 mm long, ±6 mm broad, mucronate, apically slightly irregularly toothed; filaments yellow, 6-12 mm long; anthers yellow, 1-3 mm long; style green or tinged with yellow, 15-25 mm long, 1-1.5 mm greatest diam, covered with *minute* hooked hairs; stigmas 5 or 6, 1.5 mm long, 0.5-1 mm broad; ovary in anthesis ±6 mm long; fruit green or tan or tinged with pink, dry at maturity, with a few scarious-margined, minutely toothed, membranous-fringed scales, 1.2-2(2.5) cm long, 6-10 mm diam, separating irregularly along a horizontal cleft at or just above or below middle; seeds 2 mm long, 3 mm broad; hilum not deeply indented.

Low gravelly hills and canyons in desert at about 1,500-1,800 m (5,000-6,000 ft). Lower parts of Navajoan Desert. Arizona on Little Colorado R. drainage in Navajo and Apache Cos.

The inconspicuous, domelike stems are reminiscent of tiny, old-fashioned beehives, each with many upraised swords—the flat upper-central spines of the areoles.

See map for *S. parviflorus* (next species).

7. Sclerocactus parviflorus Clover & Jotter

Stems solitary or sometimes 2 or 3, green, elongate and cylindroid or the younger ovoid, the mature ones 7.5-15(20) cm long, 5-6(10) cm diam, one huge plant (according to Donald G. Davis) weighing 17 pounds; ribs ±13-15, well developed but upper portions of tubercles standing above ribs 6-12 mm long and broad and protruding 6-10 mm; areoles 4.5-6 mm diam, typically 9-12 mm apart; central spines mostly 4, the lower reddish, terete or somewhat angled, hooked, porrect, 3.8-4.5(5) cm long, ±1 mm diam, turned or curving somewhat downward, the 2 laterals similar to the lower but shorter and not hooked, the upper central pink or white, straight or nearly so, angled or somewhat flattened to flat and narrowly ribbonlike, rather inconspicuous, elliptic to rhombic in cross section, 2.5-5 cm long, 1-1.5 mm broad, erect; radial spines 7-11, all but 2 of lower spreading ones white, these like lateral centrals, with which they tend to form a cross, the longer mostly ±2.5 cm long, basally ±1 mm diam, acicular, elliptic or rhombic in cross section; flower 2-5.5(7)

Fig. 780. *Sclerocactus whipplei* in flower, showing the very broad, flat, ribbonlike, white upper central spines. (Dorothea Woodruff; see Credits)

cm diam, 3.5-5 cm long; sepaloids with greenish midribs and rose to purple, pink, or white margins, the larger oblanceolate, 25-45 mm long, 6-10 mm broad, mucronate, marginally membranous and crisped or irregularly minutely toothed; petaloids rose to purple, pink, or rarely white, largest oblanceolate, 15-50 mm long, 6-12 mm broad, mucronate, apically slightly irregularly toothed; filaments yellow, 6-12 mm long; anthers yellow, 1-3 mm long; style green or tinged pink or purple, 15-25 mm long, 1-1.5 mm greatest diam, covered with *minute* hooked hairs; stigmas 5 or 6, 1.5 mm broad; ovary in anthesis ±6 mm long; fruit green or tan or tinged with pink, dry at maturity, with a few scarious-margined, minutely toothed, membranous-fringed scales, 12-20(25) mm long, 6-10 mm diam, separating irregularly along a horizontal cleft at or just above or below middle; seeds 2 mm long, 3 mm broad; hilum not deeply indented.

Segregation of *Sclerocactus parviflorus* as a species is based on recent studies of the flowers of this species and *S. whipplei* by Dorothea Woodruff. As indicated in the key, the flower buds of *S. parviflorus* are greenish and of greater length than diameter, and they do not require bright light, or even any light, for opening; the petaloids do not increase markedly in size at the beginning of anthesis. In *S. whipplei* the buds are brownish and of less length than diameter, and they open only in bright sunshine; the petaloids increase rapidly in size within a few hours. According to Woodruff, development of the flower buds of *S. polyancistrus* parallels that of *S. parviflorus*; that of the other species is similar to that of *S. whipplei*. These differences, added to the several other, less sharply defined characters (Benson, 1969c, 176) indicate the validity of specific rank for *S. parviflorus*.

Fig. 781. *Sclerocactus parviflorus* var. *parviflorus*, stem showing the dense mass of spines, the principal central of each areole hooked and not flattened, the uppermost central somewhat flattened and light-colored, but not markedly ribbonlike.

Distinctive Characters of the Varieties of **Sclerocactus parviflorus**

Character	a. var. **parviflorus**	b. var. **intermedius**
Upper central spine	Pale pink, somewhat flattened or angled, elliptic or rhombic in cross section, not subulate, ±1 mm broad	White, flat, very narrowly elliptic in cross section, narrowly subulate, ribbonlike, basally 1-1.5 mm broad
Flower diameter[a]	2-7 (average 4-4.5) cm	2-4.5 (average ±3) cm
Altitude	1,050-1,500(2,000) m (3,500-5,000 or 6,700 ft), but mostly at lower levels	1,050-1,500(2,100) m (3,500-5,000 or 7,000 ft), but mostly at higher levels
Floristic association	Lower parts of Navajoan Desert, near major rivers	Northern Juniper-Pinyon Woodland; higher Navajoan Desert

[a] Flower length is about the same in both varieties, 3-5.5 cm (average 4 cm).

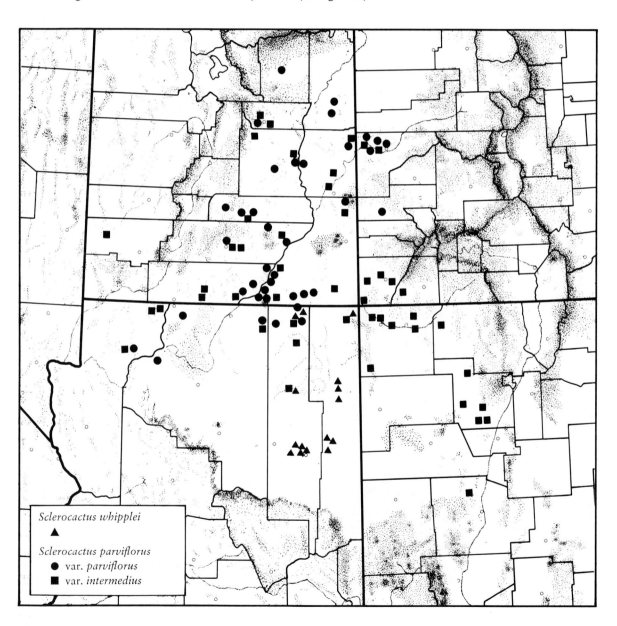

Sclerocactus whipplei
▲

Sclerocactus parviflorus
● var. *parviflorus*
■ var. *intermedius*

Fig. 782. *Sclerocactus parviflorus* var. *parviflorus*, stem showing the tuberculate ribs and in each areole the dark hooked lower central spine and the only somewhat flattened erect, white upper one. (Perhaps C. H. Thompson, 1899; courtesy of Missouri Botanical Garden)

Fig. 783. *Sclerocactus parviflorus* var. *parviflorus* in flower. (Homer L. Shantz)

7a. Sclerocactus parviflorus var. **parviflorus**. Red sand from red sandstones of the Navajo country and other sandy or gravelly soils in desert at 1,050-1,500(2,000) m (3,500-5,000 or 6,700 ft). Lower parts of Navajoan Desert. Almost restricted by altitude to areas near major watercourses, i.e., the Fremont, Colorado, Green, and San Juan Rivers in SE Utah and adjacent W Colorado and N Arizona; occurring mostly from vicinity of Capitol Reef, Moab, and Mexican Hat downstream to Havasupai Canyon and SE to Kayenta.

The solitary, cylindroid, uniformly blond or pink stems are conspicuous shaggy little figures standing on the sandy hillsides of the Navajo country.

7b. Sclerocactus parviflorus var. **intermedius** (Peebles) Woodruff & Benson. Gravelly or sandy (especially red sandstone) soils in desert or more frequently woodland at 1,050-1,500(2,100) m (3,500-5,000 or 7,000 ft). Northern Juniper-Pinyon Woodland and higher parts of Navajoan Desert. Colorado R. drainage from S and E Utah to W edge of Colorado, northernmost Arizona, and New Mexico (SE to San Ysidro and N Socorro Co.).

The common variety, long supposed by authors to be *S. spinosior*.

The solitary cylindroid stems are mottled with some gray, red, or brown spines and some white spines. The erect upper white central spines contrast with the others.

There may be a basis for recognizing distinct varieties. Plants collected in the adjacent parts of Utah, Colorado, Arizona, and New Mexico indicate the need for further intensive field study, but they may or may not represent unnamed taxa.

Some collections from the gravel-hill region along the San Juan River in San Juan Co., northwestern New Mexico, have very broad uppermost median central spines. These are ribbonlike below, but daggerlike in their overall shape, and they are reminiscent of those of *S. whipplei*. Otherwise the plants are more like var. *intermedius*. (The collections are by Robert Reeves, UNM, bearing E. F. Castetter's garden numbers *2508-2611, 2904-2906, 2950,* and *2954*. Number *2952* is a large plant; the others are relatively small.)

Plants of a few collections from the Colorado Plateau have yellow spines, and occasionally there is a report or photograph of a plant with curving but not hooked central spines. Authentic speci-

Fig. 785. *Sclerocactus parviflorus* var. *intermedius*, plant from the type collection, in cultivation; the upper central spine of each areole somewhat though not strongly flattened. (Robert H. Peebles)

Fig. 784. *Sclerocactus parviflorus* var. *intermedius* growing near Pipe Spring, Mohave Co., Arizona.

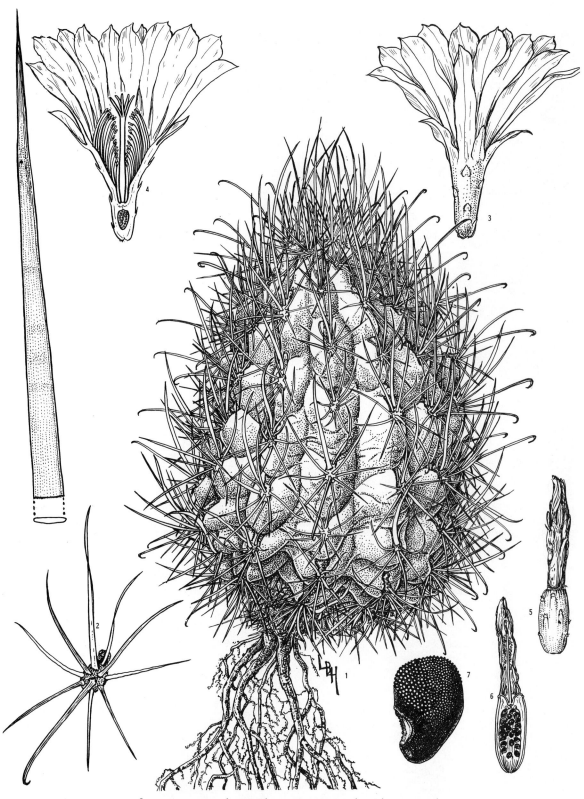

Fig. 786. *Sclerocactus parviflorus* var. *intermedius. 1*, Plant, ×1.1. *2*, Areole with spines and felty wool, showing the lower (principal) hooked central spine and the white, ribbonlike upper central spine as well as two laterals and the few radial spines, ×1.75. *3*, Flower, ×1.1. *4*, Flower in longitudinal section, ×1.1. *5*, Fruit, ×.6. *6*, Fruit in longitudinal section, ×.6. *7*, Seed, the hilum appearing "lateral," ×14.

Fig. 787. *Sclerocactus polyancistrus,* showing the exceedingly dense mass of spines, the six to eight lower and lateral central spines relatively thick, reddish, hooked, the upper three flat, thin, white, not hooked. (Perhaps C. H. Thompson, about 1900; courtesy of Missouri Botanical Garden)

mens with records of localities of collection are lacking. However, in 1965 a very large living plant with only curving spines was seen.

8. Sclerocactus polyancistrus
(Engelmann & Bigelow) Britton & Rose

Stem solitary, green, cylindroid, usually 10-15 cm long, 5-6(7.5) cm diam; ribs clearly developed, ±13-17; tubercles adnate basally with ribs, ±12 mm long vertically, 10 mm broad, protruding 6 mm; areoles elliptic, ±6-7.5 mm long, typically ±9 mm apart; spines very dense, almost obscuring stem; central spines 9-11, the usually 6-8 lower and lateral central spines red or reddish-brown, the longer as long as the median upper central, basally to 0.7 mm diam, acicular, nearly circular in cross section, all but 1 or 2 hooked, the (usually) 3 upper centrals white, flat, conspicuous, erect (parallel to stem), the median 1 usually 7.5-9 cm long, the lateral pair one-third to two-thirds as long, to 3+ mm broad; radial spines white, 10-15 per areole, spreading in a circle, straight, the longer mostly ±2 cm long, basally 0.5 mm broad, somewhat flattened, elliptic in cross section; flower ±5 cm diam, 5-6 cm long; sepaloids with greenish-purple midribs and rose-purple or magenta margins, the larger cuneate-spathulate, ±25 mm long, 6-9 mm broad, angled, entire or finely toothed; petaloids rose-purple to magenta, largest broadly ovate-lanceolate, ±25-40 mm long, 9-12 mm broad, apically angled or mucro-

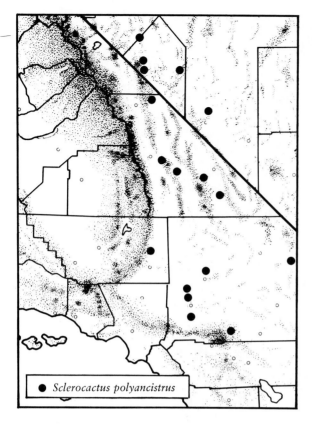

● *Sclerocactus polyancistrus*

nate, entire or margins slightly irregular; filaments greenish-yellow, ±6-12 mm long; anthers creamy yellow, nearly 2 mm long, 1 mm broad, narrowly oblong; style green to cream, ±25 mm long, 1.5 mm greatest diam; stigmas pink, 10, 3 mm long, slender; ovary in anthesis ±10 mm long, with a few toothed scale-leaves; ovary at maturity with a few white scales, these irregularly somewhat serrate, the hairs from the areoles white and twice as long as the subtending scales; fruit green to tan, dry at maturity, barrel-shaped, ±25 mm long, 15-20 mm diam; seeds black, markedly reticulate-papillate, 3 mm long, 2.3 mm broad, ±1.5 mm thick.

Limestone and other gravelly or rocky soils of hills and canyons in desert at 750-1,500(2,100) m (2,500-5,000 or 7,000 ft). Mojavean Desert. California in Mojave Desert; Nevada in Esmeralda and Nye Cos. Reported from Antelope Valley, Los Angeles Co., California (anonymous, Desert [Pl. Life] 2: 5. 1930).

This is the giant of the genus, and the cylindroid stems may be picked out from 15 or 20 paces away. The red spines and white spines contrast sharply, and their unusual length and density produce a shaggy effect.

11. Pediocactus

Stems solitary or sometimes clustered, rarely more than 2-5, 1-7.5(15) cm long, 1-7.5(15) cm diam, green or glaucous, cylindroid to globose or depressed-globose; ribs none; tubercles more or less pyramidal, conical, truncate-conical, cylindroid, or mammillate, prominent, not coalescent. Leaves none or microscopic. Areoles 1-6 mm diam, typically 1-6(12) mm apart. Spines more or less obscuring surface of joint, variable in color, number per areole, direction, texture, and flattening, the longer (1)6-12(30) mm long, basally (0.1)0.3-1 mm diam or broad, acicular or in 1 species subulate, circular or narrowly elliptic in cross section. Flowers and fruits on new growth of current season and therefore near apex of stem or branch. Flower 1-2.5 cm diam, 1-2.5(4) cm long; sepaloids with pink, green, brown, or maroon midribs and white, pink, or yellow margins, largest 6-18 mm long, (1)3-9 mm broad, obtuse, rounded, truncate, fimbriate, denticulate, or entire but undulate; petaloids white or with pink or yellow on at least the midribs, largest oblanceolate, obovate-oblanceolate, or narrowly oblong-cuneate, (4) 12-20(25) mm long, (1.5)4.5-6 mm broad, acute to rounded, entire or mucronate or shallowly indented, marginally entire or minutely denticulate; anthers yellow or perhaps sometimes white, 0.75-1.25 mm long; style more or less green or yellow, 6-20 mm long, 0.5-1.5 mm greatest diam; stigmas 5-8 or perhaps more, 0.75-1.5 mm long. Fruit green, often changing toward tan or yellow, dry at maturity, naked or with a few scale-leaves, otherwise smooth except for veins, more or less obovoid, subglobose, or cylindroid but tending to be enlarged upward and narrow basally, 4-15 mm long, 4.5-7.5 mm largest diam, the umbilicus shallow, both circumscissile on the broad apical margin and dehiscent along a dorsal slit produced by another abscission layer. Seeds black or gray, papillate-tessellate, irregularly or obliquely obovoid in outline or broadly so and somewhat flattened, actually broader than long, 1-3 mm long, 1.5-4.5 mm broad, 0.7-1.5 mm thick; hilum obovate or elliptic, appearing to be on edge of seed, i.e., "lateral"; cotyledons accumbent, not foliaceous.

Seven species occurring in mountainous areas; Columbia R. Basin, Great Basin, Rocky Mountain system, and Colorado Plateau. Six species and their varieties are restricted endemics of the Colorado Plateau. Related species occur in Mexico, but whether they warrant assignment to the genus *Pediocactus* remains to be determined (see *Pediocactus* list).

The genus *Pediocactus* was proposed by Britton and Rose (in Britton & Brown, 1913) to encompass a single species, *Echinocactus simpsonii* Engelm., thought to occur in the range of Britton and Brown's *Illustrated Flora*. This territory in eastern North America included few cacti, and the globular to ovoid one supposedly occurring on the Great Plains was given a name of Greek derivation denoting a habitat on a plain. Actually, this species is characteristic of mountainous areas and of the Sagebrush Desert farther west. It was reported once from Kansas, but only one collection from a Great Plains state has been seen, and this is from a higher elevation in the Black Hills in Custer County, South Dakota.

Aside from remarkable variations in the spines, the seven species occurring in the western United States form a coherent unit, and the gaps between spine types are becoming less marked as new species and varieties come to light.

Of the seven species listed here, only three were known in the time of Engelmann. *Pediocactus papyracanthus* was described (under *Mammillaria*) in 1848; and *P. simpsonii* (composed of three varieties) and *P. sileri* were discovered during Engelmann's later years (1863-83). Only the same three species were known to Britton and Rose (Cactaceae, 1919-1923). Nearly 60 years after Engelmann's publications and over 40 years ago, the discovery of *P. peeblesianus* near

Holbrook, Arizona, and in 1940 of the related *Sclerocactus mesae-verdae* near Cortez, Colorado, reawakened interest in searching for the small localized cacti of this group. Four new taxa—*P. paradinei, P. knowltonii, P. peeblesianus* var. *fickeiseniae,* and *P. bradyi*—have been found only recently. Conservatively interpreted new species and varieties rarely compose such a high percentage of the taxa in a genus of plants occurring in a well-studied area like the United States.

Most species of *Pediocactus* are found in the field only infrequently or rarely. All species but one are small, of narrow geographical ranges, and limited to areas difficult to reach until recently and still not much visited. At maturity some species are of no greater diameter than a medium-sized coin, and they may stand no higher above ground level than the thickness of the coin. Even when their approximate location is known, days of searching may be consumed in finding the plants. Most species grow hidden in particular kinds of gravel or rocks, and during the dry season they retract into the substrate (see *P. bradyi,* below); thus the season during which plants may be found is limited. *Pediocactus papyracanthus* often occurs in fairy rings in blue grama grass (*Bouteloua gracilis*), and it is hidden among the seasonally dry leaves of the grass. These look almost exactly like the spines of the cactus.

Probably the living species of *Pediocactus* are relics of a more variable group of plants that once occupied suitable intervening sites between the present areas of distribution. A subsequent long evolutionary period in isolation is indicated by (1) the structural differentiation of the species; (2) extremely disjunct distribution, together with the lack of any special means of seed dispersal; and (3) the physiological limitation of each species to a specific underlying rock type or an unusual desert pavement or a special soil type. Only *Pediocactus simpsonii* is both widespread and variable, occupying a range (mostly north of those of the other species) in the Columbia River Basin, the Great Basin, and the middle portions of the Rocky Mountain system. The other species are restricted to small areas of specialized habitats in the Navajoan Desert on the Colorado Plateau in northern Arizona and northwestern New Mexico. The distribution of this group of species is one fragment of evidence supporting the floristic coherence and validity of the Navajoan Desert as a floristic association. Lacking a fossil record, the time of conditions more favorable to the genus is a matter of mere speculation. Possibly, they oc-

curred during the warmer (hypsothermal) period of 2,500-9,000 years ago, following the last Pleistocene glaciation.

In this reclassification of the cactus genera of the United States, *Pediocactus* is the keystone of the arch. In relationships, it and a few other small genera are intermediate between *Echinocactus, sensu latu,* on the one hand and *Coryphantha* and *Mammillaria* on the other; therefore, classification of this group of anomalous species is of first importance in the realignment of the Cactaceae. The genus is characterized most obviously and readily by: (1) the similarities of the tuberculate (rather than ribbed) stems; (2) the position of the flower (in a circular floriferous area just ventral to the spiniferous area at the apex of a newly forming tubercle); (3) the opening of the fruit (dry at maturity and dehiscent both along a dorsal slit and along a ring around the circumscissile apex); (4) the strong similarity of the flowers (of the barrel-cactus type); and (5) the position of the hilum (just above what appears to be the base of the seed).

The relationship of *Pediocactus* to the other proposed genera is still under study. The genus is related to certain groups of species occurring in Mexico.

The proposed genus *Strombocactus* Britton & Rose (*Turbinicarpus* [Backeberg] Buxbaum & Backeberg; included in *Toumeya,* as genus, by W. T. Marshall) is in need of study. It may or may not form a part of *Pediocactus.* Several species of *Strombocactus* have been described, these occurring from Tamaulipas to San Luis Potosí.

References: Benson, 1961-1962; Frank, 1963, 1965; Kladiwa, 1963.

Section 1. PEDIOCACTUS
1. *P. simpsonii*
   vars. a. *simpsonii*
      b. *minor*
      c. *robustior*
2. *P. bradyi*
3. *P. knowltonii*
4. *P. paradinei*
5. *P. sileri*

Section 2. NAVAJOA
6. *P. peeblesianus*
   vars. a. *fickeiseniae*
      b. *peeblesianus*

Section 3. TOUMEYA
7. *P. papyracanthus*

KEY TO THE SPECIES OF PEDIOCACTUS

1. Spines not strongly flattened, acicular, circular to elliptic in cross section; stems globular, depressed-globular, obovoid, or short-cyindroid, the length little greater than the diameter or rarely about twice as great.
  2. Surface of the spine smooth, often more or less polished, rarely finely canescent; sepaloids and scales of the floral tube above the ovary entire to fimbriate (Section 1. PEDIOCACTUS).
    3. Sepaloids and the few (if any) scales of the floral tube above the ovary either minutely toothed or short-fimbriate or entire and often undulate; seeds black, 1-2.3 mm broad; petaloids pink-and-white, white, magenta, or yellow; areole not more than 3 mm in diameter; larger spines slender, 0.1-0.3(0.7) mm in diameter.
      4. Central spines none or, when present, rigid, gradually curving or straight, in fully mature plants wholly or at least distally reddish-brown or reddish, 7.5-12(27) mm long, (0.3)0.5-0.7 mm in diameter; petaloids marginally *either* pink, magenta, or white with pink midribs or middles *or* wholly yellow.
        5. Central spines present, except in juvenile plants or in the lower (juvenile) areoles persisting in adult plants, straight, 5-8(11) (in younger plants 0-3) per areole; radial spines nearly straight, spreading irregularly from the circular areole, 6-10(19) mm long; stems 2.5-12.5(30) cm long, 2.5-10(12.5) cm in diameter, standing well above ground level; ovary with a few scales; scales of the perianth tube toothed or often short-fimbriate; seeds to ±1.5 mm long...1. P. simpsonii
        5. Central spines none or rarely present; radial spines slightly recurved, pectinate along the elliptic or elongate areole, 1-6 mm long; stems at maturity only 2.5-6 cm long, 1.2-6 cm in diameter, often barely protruding above ground level; ovary practically lacking scales; scales of the perianth tube minutely toothed; seed ±1.5 *or* 2 mm long.
          6. Radial spines glabrous, pale yellowish-tan or sometimes white, straight or nearly so, 3-6 mm long, 14-15 per areole; areole elliptic; stems mostly 3.8-5(6.2) cm long, 2.5-5 cm in diameter; flower pale straw-yellow, 1.5-3 cm in diameter; fruit ±7.5 mm in diameter, basally constricted into a very short stalk; seeds 2 mm long, papillate and with larger mounds on the surfaces....................................2. P. bradyi
          6. Radial spines finely canescent, white, gradually recurving, 1-1.4 mm long, mostly 18-23 per areole; areole elongate, narrow; stems to 3.8 cm long, ±1.2-2.5 cm in diameter; flower pink, ±2 cm in diameter; fruit ±3 mm in diameter, not stalked; seeds ±1.5 mm long, papillate but *not* with larger mounds on the surfaces......................3. P. knowltonii
      4. Central spines flexible and hairlike, bending and curving irregularly or straight, uniformly colored, white or ashy gray, turning to straw- or cream-colored in age, 2.5-3+ cm long, ±0.3 mm in diameter; petaloids white or with pink midribs...4. P. paradinei
    3. Sepaloids and scales of the floral tube and ovary long-fimbriate; seeds gray, ±4.5 mm broad; petaloids yellow or yellow with maroon veins; areole ±6 mm in diameter; larger spines rather stout, 0.7-1 mm in diameter..........5. P. sileri
  2. Surface of the spine and the tissues beneath it spongy-fibrous; sepaloids and the scales (if any) of the ovary and of the lower floral tube scarious-margined, never fimbriate (Section 2. NAVAJOA).............................6. P. peeblesianus
1. Spines strongly flattened, subulate, several times broader than thick, puberulent; stems elongate, the length at least twice the diameter (Section 3. TOUMEYA).............
....7. P. papyracanthus

1. Pediocactus simpsonii
(Engelmann) Britton & Rose

Stems solitary or sometimes clustered and the clumps to 30 cm diam; larger stems or branches globular to depressed-ovoid or sometimes elongate-ovoid, 2.5-12.5(30) cm long, 2.5-10(12.5) cm diam; tubercles more or less pyramidal, mostly 6-9 mm long, basally ±4.5-7.5 mm broad; areoles to 3 mm diam; central spines reddish-brown or sometimes red or on basal halves pale yellow to cream, 5-8(11) (in young plants 0-3), spreading widely, straight, the longer 7.5-12(27) mm long, basally ±0.3(0.7) mm diam, acicular, elliptic to circular in section; radial spines whitish to cream or sometimes pale reddish-brown, 12-30 per areole, spreading at right angles to the tubercle, nearly straight, 6-10(19) mm long; flower 1.2-2.5(5) cm diam, 1.2-2.5(4) cm long; sepaloids either with greenish and purple midribs and pink margins or yellow with slight median and marginal pink tinges, the larger narrowly oblanceolate-oblong, 9-12(25) mm long, 3-9 mm broad, rounded, each with ±0.5 mm of the margin petal-like and (in the smaller sepaloids) often shallowly fimbriate; petaloids pink to nearly white or sometimes magenta or yellow, largest narrowly oblong-cuneate, 12-20(25) mm long, 4.5-6(9) mm broad, mucronate or cuspidulate, apically irregularly and shallowly indented; filaments yellow or greenish-yellow, 6(9) mm long; anthers yellow, 0.7 mm long; style greenish, to 12-20 mm long, usually 1 mm greatest diam; stigmas 5-9 (5, 6, or 9 on the same plant), 0.7 mm long, acute; fruit greenish, tinged with red, smooth, with a few fimbriate scales on upper portion, fundamentally short-cylindroid but bulging irregularly and widened upward, 6-9 mm long, 4.5-7.5 mm diam, the umbilicus depressed and having a thin border; seeds gray or nearly black, tessellate-tuberculate, obovoid or obliquely so in outline but the oblique hilum forming a long straight line along 1 side, ±1.5 mm long, to 2 mm broad, 1.2-1.3 mm thick; hilum obovate, 1 mm long, with sharply raised border.

According to Arp (1972b), *P. simpsonii* is limited in occurrence on mountainsides because some slopes are unstable and the soil slides gradually down the mountains. *P. simpsonii* is not adapted to this.

Reference (use of the computer in correlation of data concerning the varieties of *Pediocactus simpsonii*): Arp & Rogers, 1970.

1a. Pediocactus simpsonii var. simpsonii. Fine powdery soils of valleys, flats, and hillsides in dry areas at mostly 1,800-2,850 m (6,000-9,500 ft). Northern Juniper-Pinyon Woodland and Sagebrush Desert; Rocky Mountain Montane Forest. Eastern Oregon (rare); s Idaho to s half of Wyoming and to N central and NE Nevada, N Arizona (Grand Canyon), N New Mexico, w South Dakota, and reportedly (though probably not) Montana and w Kansas.

Distinctive Characters of the Varieties of **Pediocactus simpsonii**

Character	a. var. **simpsonii**	b. var. **minor**	c. var. **robustior**
Stem branching and shape	Usually unbranched, globular to broadly obovoid	Unbranched or rarely branching, globular	Usually branching, usually elongate
Stem size	5-12.5(20) cm long, 7.5-10 (12.5) cm diam	2.5(7.5) cm long, 2.5-5.5 cm diam	5-10(30) cm long, 5-6.2(7.5) cm diam
Spine habit	Spreading widely	Spreading widely	Suberect
Central spines	Reddish-brown (or red) or pale and yellowish or cream on the lower half, 5-8(11), 9-12(19) mm long, 0.3 mm diam	Dark reddish-brown, 5-8, 7.5-10.5(13.5) mm long, 0.3 mm diam	Dark reddish-brown, 6-11, 15-27 mm long, 0.7 mm diam
Radial spines	Whitish or cream, 15-30, slender, 6-9 mm long	Whitish or cream, 20-28, slender, 6 mm long	Pale reddish-brown, 12-25, stout, 12-19 mm long
Flower diameter	1.9-2.5 cm	1.2-1.9 cm	3.1-5 cm
Sepaloid shape	Narrowly oblanceolate-oblong, sometimes narrowly obovate	Narrowly oblanceolate-oblong	Obovate to spathulate-obovate or nearly lanceolate
Petaloid color	Pink to magenta, white, yellow, or salmon	Pink to magenta or nearly white	Magenta
Altitude	1,800-2,850 m (6,000-9,500 ft)	2,500-3,300 m (8,800-11,000 ft)	450-900(1,500 or reportedly 3,000) m (1,500-3,000 to 5,000 or 10,000 ft)
Floristic association	Northern Juniper-Pinyon Woodland; Sagebrush Desert; Rocky Mountain Montane Forest	Rocky Mountain Montane Forest; Rocky Mountain Parkland; Juniper-Pinyon Woodlands	Sagebrush Desert

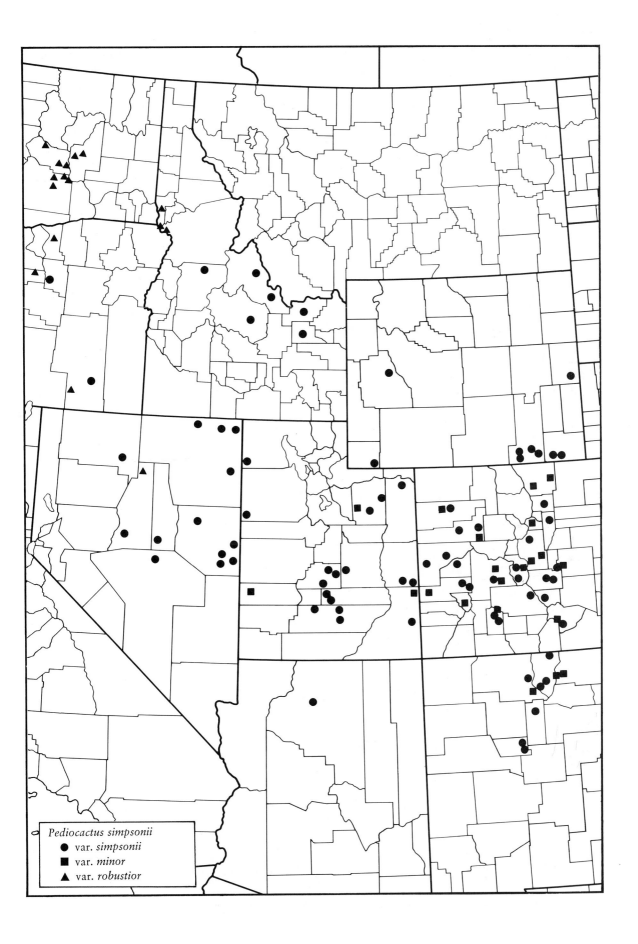

Pediocactus simpsonii
● var. simpsonii
■ var. minor
▲ var. robustior

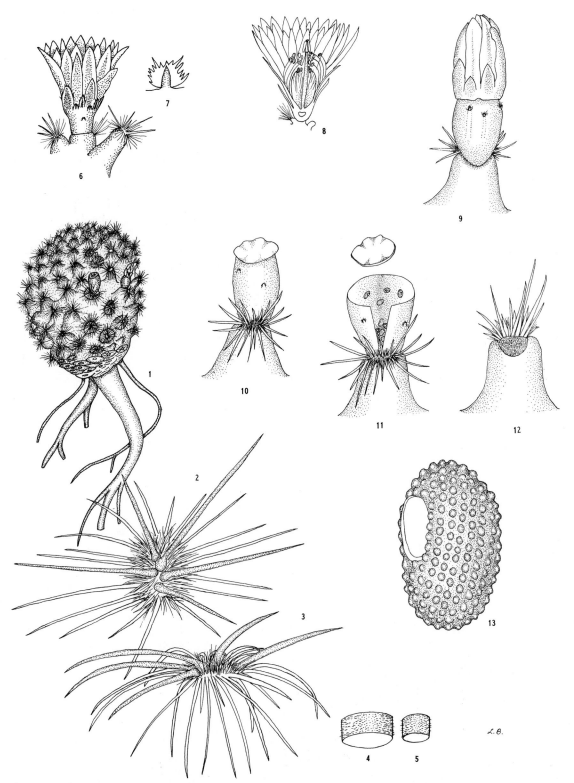

Fig. 788. *Pediocactus simpsonii* var. *simpsonii*, ×1.25, except as indicated. *1*, Relatively young plant, ×.9. *2*, Areole of a mature plant from above, showing several central spines, the more numerous radial spines, and the woolly hairs, ×6. *3*, Side view of the areole, the central spines brown, the radials white, ×6. *4*, *5*, Sectional views of central and radial spines, ×18. *6*, Flower on a developing tubercle; two somewhat older tubercles adjacent to the flower. *7*, Scale-leaf from the floral tube covering and adnate with the ovary, ×12. *8*, Flower in longitudinal section. *9*, Young fruit, the remains of the upper parts of the flower shriveling. *10*, Mature fruit with the tubercle and the spine-bearing area that merges with the spine-bearing areole. *11*, Dehiscence of the fruit along one line, and the circumscissile separation of the upper part of the floral tube like a lid. *12*, Scar left after the fall of the fruit. *13*, Seed, the hilum appearing "lateral," ×17.

The plants are gray-white balls under bushes and, for their size—about that of a cantaloupe—difficult to find. They blend with the gray-green of the bushes.

Especially in most of Nevada, some plants may have pale yellow-gray spines and yellow flowers (e.g., Silver Zone Pass region, Nevada, just w of Great Salt Lake, *D. Wright [Woodruff] & L., E. L., & R. L. Benson 16153, Pom*).

1b. Pediocactus simpsonii var. minor (Engelmann) Cockerell. Rocky soils of high valleys and mountainsides in grasslands and at edges of forests near timberline at 2,500-3,300 m (8,800-11,000 ft). Rocky Mountain Montane Forest, Rocky Mountain Parkland, and Juniper-Pinyon Woodlands. Dry areas of Rocky Mountain system. Utah in Duchesne Co. and La Sal Mts.; Colorado from Garfield Co. to Larimer, Mineral, and Huerfano Cos.; New Mexico from e Rio Arriba and Taos Cos. to Bernalillo Co.

The plants are baseball-sized masses of dark brown to almost black spines.

Further field study of var. *minor* is needed to determine its limits of occurrence and degree of distinction from var. *simpsonii*. Small plants from southern Utah, southern Colorado, and northern New Mexico are referred to this variety, but some have relatively light-colored spines.

Fig. 790. *Pediocactus simpsonii* var. *minor*, stem about the size of a baseball, with two branches. (Perhaps C. H. Thompson, about 1900; courtesy of Missouri Botanical Garden)

Fig. 789. *Pediocactus simpsonii* var. *simpsonii* in flower; in cultivation in Salt Lake City, Utah. (Dorothea Woodruff)

1c. Pediocactus simpsonii var. robustior (Coulter) L. Benson. Gravelly soils of mostly lava or basalt hillsides in the desert at mostly 450-900 (1,500 or reportedly 3,000) m (1,500-3,000 to 5,000 or 10,000 ft). Sagebrush Desert. Disjunct in occurrence: E Washington (between Ellensburg and Columbia R. and in Yakima and Grant Cos.); Oregon (Jefferson and Harney Cos.); Idaho (Snake R. Canyon near confluence with Salmon R.); and Nevada (Humboldt and Havallah Mts. and N of Battle Mountain).

The stems are ball-like and usually clustered. Each is a dark spiny mass up to half the diameter of a soccer ball. The spines are longer than those of the other varieties, and the appearance is ragged. Against the black lava the dark brown to nearly black spines are inconspicuous. This was my first cactus, collected May 5, 1929. The flowers were visible 100 m up the side of a hill in eastern Washington.

Occurrence (but not identification) of this variety in Washington was noted first by Geyer (London Jour. Bot. 5: 25. 1846), and later by Piper (Fl. Wash., Contr. U.S. Nat. Herb. 11: 397. 1906).

2. Pediocactus bradyi L. Benson

Stem solitary (rarely 2), green but obscured by the white or yellowish-tan spines, subglobose to obovoid, 3.8-6.2 cm long, 2.5-5 cm diam; tubercles cylindroid-ovoid or elongate-ovoid, apically nearly truncate, ±3-4.5 mm long and diam; areoles elliptic, 1.5-3 mm long, 0.7-1.5 mm broad, typically ±3 mm apart, densely white-villous or yellow-villous; spines dense on joint, obscuring tubercles; central spines 0 or (in 2 collections) 1 or 2 per areole, these straight, darker than radials, ±4 mm long; radial spines white or yellowish-tan,

Fig. 791. *Pediocactus bradyi*, showing the vertically elongate areoles; plant collected originally by L. G. Brady and grown at the Desert Botanical Garden, Papago Park, Phoenix, Arizona. (W. Hubert Earle; see also Credits)

glabrous, smooth, appearing more or less cartilaginous, ±14 or 15 per areole, spreading, nearly pectinate, nearly straight but the tips curving slightly downward, about equal, 3-6 mm long, at bases of main shafts ±0.2 mm diam, acicular, tapering gradually from bulbous bases, nearly circular in cross section; flower 1.5-3 cm diam, 1.5-2 cm long; lower sepaloids with green and (especially at tips) purplish-red midribs, the upper with green midribs and pale straw-yellow margins, larger obovate-oblanceolate, to 12(15) mm long, to 3-4.5 mm broad, acute or blunt and minutely and irregularly denticulate, marginally entire; petaloids pale straw-yellow, largest oblanceolate, to 12-15 mm long, 3-4.5 mm broad, acute and apically minutely denticulate, marginally entire; filaments yellow, 3-4.5 mm long; anthers golden-yellow, 1 mm long; style pale straw-yellow, 6-9 mm long, 1 mm greatest diam; stigmas

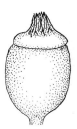  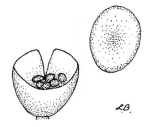

Fig. 792. *Pediocactus bradyi*, fruit. Left, fruit at maturity before dehiscence. Center, circumscissile dehiscence, the top of the ovary and the remains of the other flower parts coming off like a lid. Right, fruit after both circumscissile and longitudinal dehiscence, ×4; both modes of dehiscence occurring throughout *Pediocactus*.

Fig. 793. *Pediocactus bradyi*, plants of the type collection in fruit.

Fig. 794. *Pediocactus bradyi*, the plants of Fig. 793, side view.

about 8, ±1.5 mm long; fruit green, tardily turning brownish at maturity, smooth except for irregularity around the areoles, without surface appendages, broadly turbinate, 6 mm long, 7.5 mm diam at maturity, basally constricted into short stalk, the umbilicus slightly convex, thin and membranous; seeds black, with minute beadlike papillae, but these on larger irregular projections, acutely obovoid, 2 mm long, 2.3 mm broad, 1.5 mm thick; hilum appearing "lateral."

Colorado Plateau at about 1,200 m (4,000 ft). Navajoan Desert. Arizona in Coconino Co. near Marble Canyon of Colorado River. The species occurs at least sparsely over an area about 25 km (15 miles) long.

Even when the plants are distended with water, finding them may require days of searching. They are inconspicuous, and they blend into the rock fragments around them.

This and other species of small desert cacti may retract into the ground during the dry season. W. Hubert Earle and John H. Weber of the Desert Botanical Garden at Papago Park, Tempe, Arizona, marked the locations of plants later restudied in May during the drought period. By that time some of them had shrunk into the ground, and they were obscured completely by as much as 12 mm of wind-blown sand and soil.

The collection of plants with central spines is by *Donald G. Davis*, Nov. 6, 1963, *Pom*. Similar plants are reported by Stanley J. Farwig and Victor Girard, 1971.

References: Benson, 1961-1962; Earle, 1962.
See map for *P. peeblesianus* (species 6).

3. Pediocactus knowltonii L. Benson

Very small plants with the stems solitary or a few in a cluster; stem to 3.8 cm high and to ±2.5 cm diam, barely protruding above ground level, remarkably inconspicuous; tubercles cylindroid, conical, or pyramidal, 1.5-2.5 mm long, 1.5-2 mm diam; areoles ±1 mm greatest diam, typically 1-3 mm apart; spines dense but not obscuring tubercles, white or sometimes turning reddish-tan or pink or tipped with pink, finely canescent with white hairs, spines ±18-23 per areole, all radial, spreading pectinately from the elongate areole and moderately recurving, the longer 1-1.4+ mm long, basally 0.1 mm broad, subulate, tapering gradually to apices, flattened, elliptic in cross section; flower ±2 cm diam when spread open, ±10 mm long; perianth spreading rotately; sepaloids mostly ±10 mm long, to 3 mm broad, pink

with pale margins, apically rounded or obtuse, largest oblanceolate; petaloids pink, to 10 mm long, 3 mm broad, apically sharply acute, essentially entire; filaments ±4-5 mm long, yellow; anthers yellow, ±0.6-0.7 mm long; style ±8-10 mm long, 1.5 mm greatest diam; stigmas 4 or 5, yellow or rose, ±1 mm long; fruit green to tannish, without scales, obovoid-turbinate, ±4 mm long, about 3 mm diam; seeds black, irregularly obovoid, 1.5 mm long, 1-1.2 mm broad, ±0.6-0.7 mm thick.

Gravelly soils of hills in dry areas at about 1,800 m (6,000 ft). Southern Juniper-Pinyon Woodland. Northernmost New Mexico near Los Pinos R. Probably also in Colorado near state line.

This beautiful miniature cactus is long to be sought in the field and seldom to be found. Mature plants range from the size of a quarter to that of a fifty-cent piece, and they blend into the rock mosaic around them or into the debris under shrubs. The stem is studded with tiny bumps, each bump crowned with a parasol of white spines.

Although the distinctive spines differ from those of juvenile plants of *Pediocactus simpsonii* vars. *simpsonii* and *minor*, publication of this species was considered to be unwise until evidence of maturity of the Knowlton plants of the original collection (in 1958, *Pom*) could be obtained. Field study in southern Utah in June, 1960 (south side of La Sal Mountains, *L. & R. L. Benson 16054, Pom*), confirmed the differences in the type of spine occurring in the juvenile plants of the smaller forms of *P. simpsonii*. In August, 1960, Prince Pierce and a group of others from Albuquerque, New Mexico, visited the general area in which Mr. Knowlton found the small *Pediocactus* and collected specimens. Where Mr. Pierce found the plants, "The ground . . . was not disturbed at all. . . ." This was an area of ". . . untouched wilderness." The largest plants, undoubtedly mature, were of the same size as the plants collected by Knowlton. This point was confirmed by field study in the same area, April 12 and August 25, 1962 (*L., E. L., & R. L. Benson 16160, Pom*). The plants were in undisturbed soil, and there is no question of their maturity. The largest stems were 2.5 cm in diameter, but most of the mature ones were only 1.2-2 cm. The examination of hundreds of plants of reproductive age in various habitats in the field has revealed no developmental change during later stages.

Plants collected near the Colorado National Monument, Mesa County, Colorado (*W. A. Weber 12110*, May 25, 1964, *Colo*) appeared similar

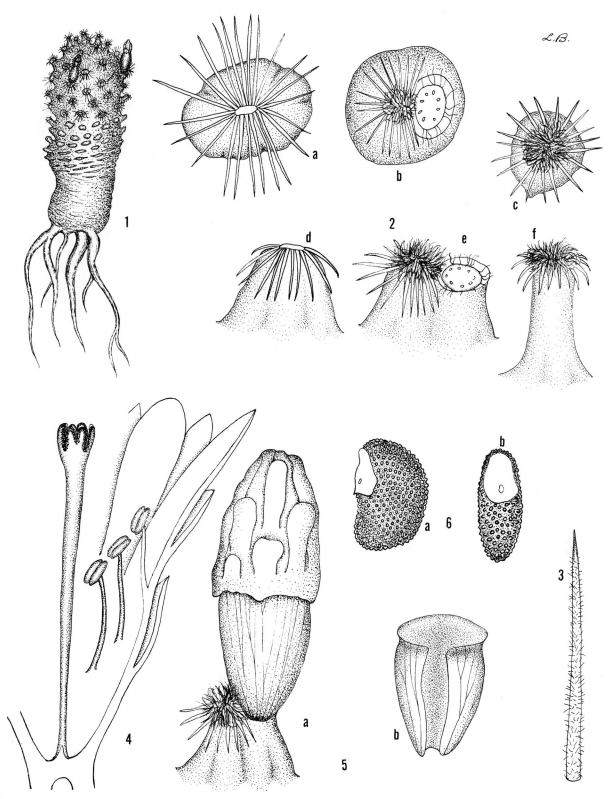

L.B.

Fig. 795. *Pediocactus knowltonii*. Drawn from the type specimen, collected south of La Boca, Colorado, perhaps in adjacent New Mexico. *1*, Full-grown plant with fruits; only 4 cm (1.6 inches) high, including the part below ground. *2*, Tubercles: *a–c*, from above, showing the radial spines, there being no centrals, and in *b* the attachment scar of a fruit; *d–f*, from the side; *c, f*, young tubercles; *a, d*, old tubercles; *b, c*, tubercles after fall of the fruit, the areas of flowers and fruits exposed. *3*, Tip of a spine enlarged, showing the fine covering of hairs characteristic of the species. *4*, Portion of a longitudinal section of a flower. *5*, Fruits: *a*, young fruit attached to the tubercle on the ventral side of the spine-bearing area of the young areole, the drying remains of the upper portion of the flower still attached above; *b*, old fruit after dehiscence along the back and (circumscissile) disarticulation of the upper part of the floral tube, which formed a lid. *6*, Seeds: *a*, in side view; *b*, in ventral view (toward the axis of the stem).

759

Fig. 796. *Pediocactus knowltonii*, plant about the diameter of a 25-cent piece, emerging from underground after the dry season, each spine-bearing tubercle about the size of a match head; the dark objects at the apex of the stem are flower buds. (Robert L. Benson)

to *Pediocactus knowltonii*, but differed as follows: spines 19 per areole, 3-4 mm long; stem 2.8-4.5 cm diam. In *P. knowltonii*, the corresponding vegetative characters are as follows: spines ±22 per areole, 1-2 mm long; stem 1.2-2.5 cm diam. The spines of the Colorado plant were pubescent, as in *P. knowltonii* and sometimes in juvenile plants of *P. simpsonii*. A series of specimens collected later in the same place (*L. & E. L. Benson 16590*, June 13, 1965, *Pom*) shows that the Colorado National Monument plants soon develop dark central spines as growth continues and are thus juvenile forms of *P. simpsonii*. This was observed in numerous plants, several of them now pressed and in the specimen cited above.

See map for *P. peeblesianus* (species 6).

4. Pediocactus paradinei B. W. Benson

Depressed plant, the stem solitary, 2.5-5 cm high, 2.5-5(8) cm diam; tubercles truncate-conical, ±3 mm diam, to 4.5 mm high; areoles circular, 3 mm diam, typically 3 mm apart; central spines hairlike, usually dense but sparse in some young plants, white to pale gray, becoming straw- or cream-colored in age, the apical portions sometimes darker, 4-6 per areole, the centrals and the

approximately 20 radials not clearly distinguished, all spines flexible, straight or curving irregularly, the longer mostly 2.5-3+ cm long, basally ±0.2-0.3 mm diam, acicular, elliptic to nearly circular in cross section; flower 2-2.5 cm diam, to 2 cm long; sepaloids reddish-green with white margins, the larger obovate, to 20 mm long, 6 mm broad, rounded or blunt, undulate and minutely irregularly denticulate; petaloids white with pink midribs, largest oblanceolate-obovate, to 20 mm long, to 6 mm broad, rounded and mucronulate, minutely denticulate; filaments yellowish, to 6 mm long; anthers yellow, oblong, ±0.6-0.7 mm long; style greenish, 10-12 mm long, 1.5 mm greatest diam; stigmas 5 or 6(?), 1.5 mm long, relatively broad; ovary in anthesis 3 mm long, smooth; fruit greenish-yellow or becoming tan, smooth except for veins and bare except sometimes for minute subapical scales, nearly cylindroid but enlarged upward, 7.5-10.5 mm long, 4.5-6 mm diam; seeds nearly black, tessellate-tuberculate, obliquely obovoid, 1.5 mm long, about 2 mm broad, 1 mm thick; hilum elliptic.

Gravelly soils of alluvial fans and flats in desert or grassland at 1,500-1,800 m (5,000-6,000 ft). Transitional areas of Sagebrush Desert, Navajoan Desert, and Great Plains Grassland. Northern

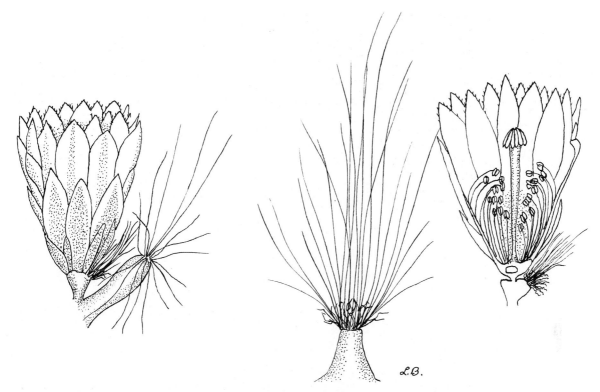

Fig. 797. *Pediocactus paradinei.* Center, tubercle with an areole bearing wool and the characteristic long, threadlike spines, the upper, longer ones centrals, the lower, shorter ones radials. Left, young tubercle with a flower (2–5 cm long), the spine-bearing immature areole at the side; and an older tubercle. Right, flower and young tubercle in longitudinal section.

Arizona from NE Mohave Co. to vicinity of Houserock Valley, Coconino Co.

The plants appear as little masses of coarse gray hairs protruding from a flat or moundlike body. They are well hidden under shrubs or grasses, and even an extended search may not be successful.

Living material has been collected by Leonard Heaton in northeastern Mohave County, Arizona, and probably the plant occurs intermittently along the northern front of the Kaibab Plateau and in the outlying hills. Thus the known range of this ecologically restricted species is 50 airline miles.

See map for *P. peeblesianus* (species 6).

5. Pediocactus sileri (Engelmann) L. Benson

Stems solitary, depressed-ovoid or sometimes ovoid, 5-10(13) cm long, 5-7.5(10) cm diam; tubercles truncate-conical, 6-10.5 mm diam, protruding 9-12 mm; areoles ±6 mm diam, typically ±12 mm apart; spines densely covering stem; central spines wholly or partly brownish-black, becoming pale gray or nearly white in age, 3-7 per areole, nearly porrect, straight or slightly curving at tips, the longer 2-2.8 cm long, basally 0.7-1 mm diam, acicular, nearly circular in section, tapering evenly from base to apex; radial spines smaller, white, 10-15 per areole, rigid, acicular; flower ±2.5 cm diam, ±2 cm long; sepaloids with maroon midribs and yellowish margins, the larger obovate-oblanceolate, to 15 mm long, ±3-4.5 mm broad, rounded, marginally scarious and long-fimbriate; petaloids yellowish or straw-colored with maroon veins, largest obovate-oblanceolate, 15-20 mm long, 4.5-6 mm broad, apically rounded, minutely denticulate; filaments yellowish, 3 mm long; anthers yellow, 1.2 mm long; style yellowish, 12 mm long, 1 mm greatest diam; stigmas ±5 or 6, ±2 mm long; fruit greenish-yellow, with several long-fimbriate scales above, nearly cylindroid but enlarged upward, 12-15 mm long, 6-9 mm diam; seeds gray, finely tessellate-tuberculate, obliquely obovate, 3 mm long, 4.5 mm broad, 1.5 mm thick; hilum incurved in side view.

Hills in desert at 1,400-1,500 m (4,700-5,000 ft). Transitional areas between Navajoan Desert, Sagebrush Desert, and Mojavean Desert. Northern Arizona in Mohave Co. from Hurricane Cliffs to vicinity of Pipe Spring and Fredonia; reported from adjacent Utah; collected in 1975 in Utah

Fig. 798. *Pediocactus sileri* growing near Pipe Spring, Mohave Co., Arizona.

Fig. 799. *Pediocactus sileri*, fruit after dehiscence along a vertical slit, the upper part of the floral cup still attached (just beginning to separate). (Robert H. Peebles)

Fig. 800. *Pediocactus sileri*, flower and sectioned flower and tubercle, showing the flower structure and the complete areole, with both spine- and flower-bearing portions. (Robert H. Peebles)

about 65 km (40 mi) w of Pipe Spring (*Stanley L. Welsh, BrY*).

The plants are relatively large, as large as those of *P. simpsonii*, but they are not conspicuous. The mixture of nearly white and dark spines blends into the light gray and white soil background. Although the species is abundant over limited areas, it seldom is seen.

This plant has been known as "*Utahia*," and the type collection (*A. L. Siler*, May, 1883, Mo) may have been made in Kane Co., Utah, near Kanab, because it is labeled, "Southern Utah." In 1883 the state boundary may not have been clear, and probably the plant was collected barely within northern Arizona near Pipe Spring. Few localities in adjacent Utah are suited to this ecologically

Fig. 801. *Pediocactus sileri*, showing the tubercles, areoles, and spines, and a flower. (Robert H. Peebles; from *The Cacti of Arizona*, eds. 1–3; see also Credits)

highly specialized species. So far, only one that appears favorable has been found, but the cactus was not present there. Another collection (two flowers) was made in 1882 and labeled "Southern Utah," *Ph*. Probably these collections were attributed to Utah because Siler lived at Kanab.

References: anonymous, 1931; Buchanan, 1931; Lindsay, 1941; Marshall, 1948, 1953b; Wright, 1932.

See map for *P. peeblesianus* (next species).

6. Pediocactus peeblesianus (Croizat) L. Benson

Obscure plant; stem(s) solitary or rarely clustered, somewhat glaucous, obovoid, globose, ovoid-cylindroid, or depressed-globose, often only the summit protruding above ground level, largely retracted into soil during dry weather, to 1.5-3.8(6.2) cm long, to 1.5-3.8 cm diam; tubercles mammillate to truncate-pyramidal, 3-6(9) mm broad, 3-4.5(6) mm high; areoles 1-3 mm diam, typically 3-6 mm apart; spines usually nearly covering but not obscuring surface of upper portion of stem; central spines none or 1 per areole, ashy white to pale gray, rather flexible, turned upward, curving slightly upward, remarkably variable in size from plant to plant, longer 0.6-2(3.4) cm long, 0.5-1 mm basal diam, acicular, circular to elliptic in cross section, the surface layers of spine remark-ably spongy-fibrous; radial spines 3-7 per areole, similar to central but usually smaller in 1 variety (see table); flower ±1.5-2.5 cm diam, 12 mm long; sepaloids with brownish-purple midribs and pale green or maroon margins, the larger oblanceolate or broadly oblong, 6-9 mm long, to 4.5 mm broad, acute to somewhat rounded, entire or sparsely and minutely serrulate; petaloids yellow to yellowish-green, sometimes pale or reportedly white, usually with median band of green or pale pink, largest lanceolate, ±6-9 mm long, ±3 mm broad, acute to subacute, mucronulate to apiculate, minutely serrulate; filaments whitish or pale green, 6 mm long; anthers yellow, 0.5 mm long; style cream-colored, 9 mm long, 1 mm greatest diam; stigmas 6-8; ovary in anthesis 3 mm long; fruit greenish, changing to tan during drying at maturity, without surface appendages or with 1 or a few scales on upper portion, subcylindroid but broader above, 6-9 mm long, 4.5-7.5 mm diam; seeds black to dark grayish-brown or dark gray, asymmetrically (obliquely) obovoid, 1.5-2 mm long, 2.5 mm broad, ±1 mm thick; hilum slightly curved.

6a. Pediocactus peeblesianus var. fickeiseniae
L. Benson. Confined to exposed layers of rock on the margins of canyons or hills in desert at about 1,200-1,500 m (4,000-5,000 ft). Navajoan Desert

Distinctive Characters of the Varieties of **Pediocactus peeblesianus**

Character	a. var. **fickeiseniae**	b. var. **peeblesianus**
Plant size	Larger	Smaller
Stem	Occasionally with 2-4 branches, to 2.5-3.8(6.2) cm long, 2.5-3.8 cm diam	Unbranched, to 2.5 cm long, 1,530-1,560 m (5,100-5,200 ft)
Central spines	Solitary, erect and prominent (small or lacking in young plants), clearly differentiated from radials, highly variable	None, but upper radial spine frequently longer than others, to 6(7.5) mm long
Radial spines	Usually 6 (sometimes 7), straight, spreading irregularly, variable in size, 3-6 mm long, 0.25-0.5 mm diam	Usually 4 but in some areoles sometimes 3 or 5, recurving, with the appearance of a cross, the lower usually 3-4.5(6) mm long, 0.3-1 mm diam
Altitude	1,200-1,500 m (4,000-5,000 ft)	1,530-1,560 m (5,000-5,100 ft)
Floristic association	Navajoan Desert and areas transitional to Great Plains Grassland	Navajoan Desert

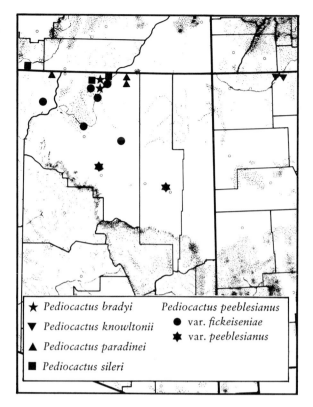

and areas transitional to Great Plains Grassland. Northern Arizona from hills in NE Mohave Co. to vicinity of Colorado and Little Colorado rivers in region of Grand Canyon and SE in Coconino Co. The known range is about 200 km (125 miles).

The white spines arise from the plant like tiny horns pointing in a variety of directions. In contrast to the prim, precise arrangement of spines in var. *peeblesianus*, the disposition of spines in this variety yields a ragged appearance.

Distinction of the populations of the Grand Canyon region and near Cameron from those of var. *peeblesianus* is difficult because of the paucity of collections and knowledge of both populations. The (so far) consistent points of difference are the presence of a central spine and the presence of six or seven radial spines instead of four (rarely three or five). There are differences in size, but no clear gaps between sizes of parts. The specimens in Figs. 802–3 (*L. & R. L. Benson 15745, Pom, L. & E. L. Benson 16086, Pom*) illustrate the extreme variability of the spine and other quantitative characters from individual to individual in the populations occurring near Cameron, and thus the possibility of further variation in other populations. Some of the plants from Mohave County, so far as these are available, are uniform, having a long, basally stout, gradually tapering central spine and closely spreading, slender radial spines. The same type occurs, along with a host of others, among the plants growing near Cameron. Thus, pending additional data, there is no justification for the segregation of the plants occurring northwest of the Grand Canyon from those of the Cameron region.

Fig. 802 (*above*). *Pediocactus peeblesianus* var. *fickeiseniae*, the type collection, showing the extreme variation in spines to be found in a single population of this variety.

Fig. 803. *Pediocactus peeblesianus* var. *fickeiseniae*, the plants of Fig. 802 in side view.

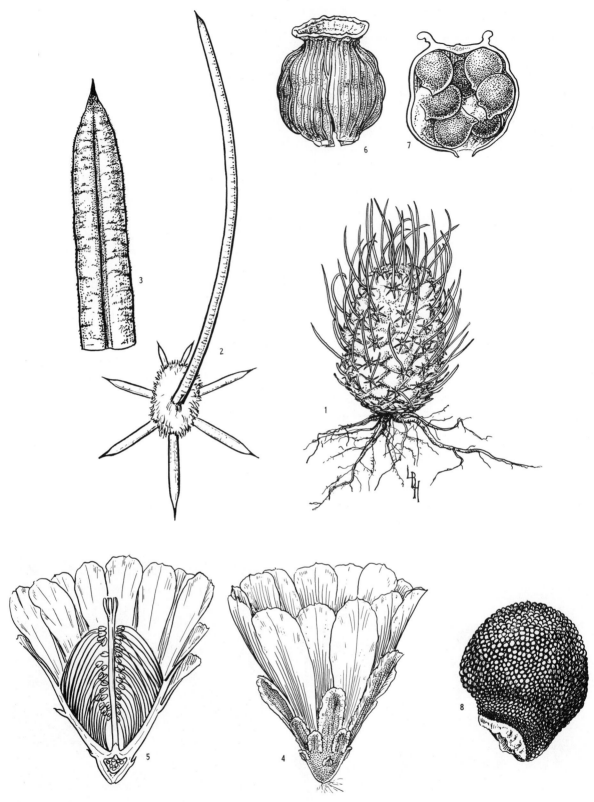

Fig. 804. *Pediocactus peeblesianus* var. *fickeiseniae*. *1*, Plant, ×1.3. *2*, Areole with the characteristic single long central spine, the half dozen radial spines, and wool, ×4; all the spines having remarkably spongy surfaces and interiors; the spine highly variable (see Fig. 802). *3*, Spine-tip, the spongy-fibrous areas, ×18. *4*, Flower, ×2.6. *5*, Flower in longitudinal section, ×2.6. *6*, Fruit, both circumscissile at top and splitting along dorsal side, ×4. *7*, Fruit in longitudinal section, ×4. *8*, Seed, the hilum more obviously basal than in the rest of the genus, ×26.

Fig. 806. *Pediocactus peeblesianus* var. *peeblesianus*, grafted plant (on another cactus) in flower; type collection. (Robert H. Peebles)

Fig. 805. *Pediocactus peeblesianus* var. *peeblesianus*, in one phase of its natural habitat; near Holbrook, Navajo Co., Arizona. *Left*, older plant about the diameter of a quarter (American 25-cent piece) and three match-head-sized young plants, emphasizing the typical cruciform spine clusters in the areoles of this variety. *Right*, plant the size of an American penny (1-cent piece), emphasizing the proportionately large tubercles, with three shorter spines and one longer in the areole, as occasionally occurs in this variety, but indicating a slight tendency toward the characters common in var. *fickeiseniae*. Plants with the characters of var. *fickeiseniae* are rare in the populations of the region. (*Left*, Steven L. Timbrook; *right*, Stanley J. Farwig)

767

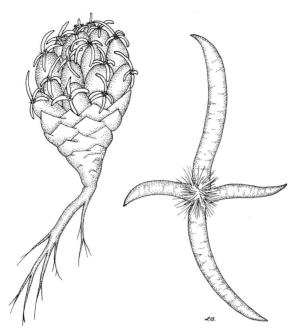

Fig. 807. *Pediocactus peeblesianus* var. *peeblesianus.* Left, mature plant, ×1.1. Right, a single areole with the peculiar "cross" of four radial spines, and with hairs, ×4.

6b. Pediocactus peeblesianus var. peeblesianus. Sandy soils of hills in desert at about 1,530-1,560 m (5,000-5,100 ft). Navajoan Desert. Northern Arizona in Navajo Co. from near Joseph City to Marcou Mesa region NW of Holbrook.

The plants are minute, and their precise arrangement of little white crosses of spines is both curious and attractive. If they were of stone, they could be sold in art stores. More man-days of searching have been devoted to this cactus than to any other in the United States, except perhaps the grama grass cactus (*Pediocactus papyracanthus*).

References: Cowper, 1955, 1956; Marshall, 1955; Benson, 1961-1962.

7. Pediocactus papyracanthus
(Engelmann) L. Benson
Grama grass cactus

Stems solitary, elongate, cylindroid or obconical-cylindroid, 2.5-7.5 cm long, 1.2-2 cm diam; tubercles more or less elongate-mammillate to elongate-conical, 3-4.5 mm long and broad, ±1.5 mm high; areoles 1-1.5 mm diam, typically ±3 mm apart; spines dense, obscuring surface of stem; central spines whitish or pale brown, changing to gray, flexible, 1 per areole (or 2-4 and up-

per ones smaller), curving upward, the mass of centrals overarching apex of stem, the longer usually 2-3 cm long, basally to ±1.2-1.3 mm broad, subulate, strongly flattened, involute and midrib evident on ventral side, it and margins puberulent, cross section very narrow; radial spines ashy white or pale gray, flexible, 6-8 per areole, spreading parallel to stem surface, straight, the longer ±3 mm long, 0.5 mm broad, flat, very thin; flower 2-2.5 cm diam, ±2.5 cm long; sepaloids with purplish- to reddish-brown midribs and nearly white margins, the larger spathulate, to 20 mm

Fig. 808. *Pediocactus papyracanthus,* grafted plant (on another cactus) in flower, the upper areoles with the long, papery central spines, the lower with only the short radial spines. (Robert H. Peebles)

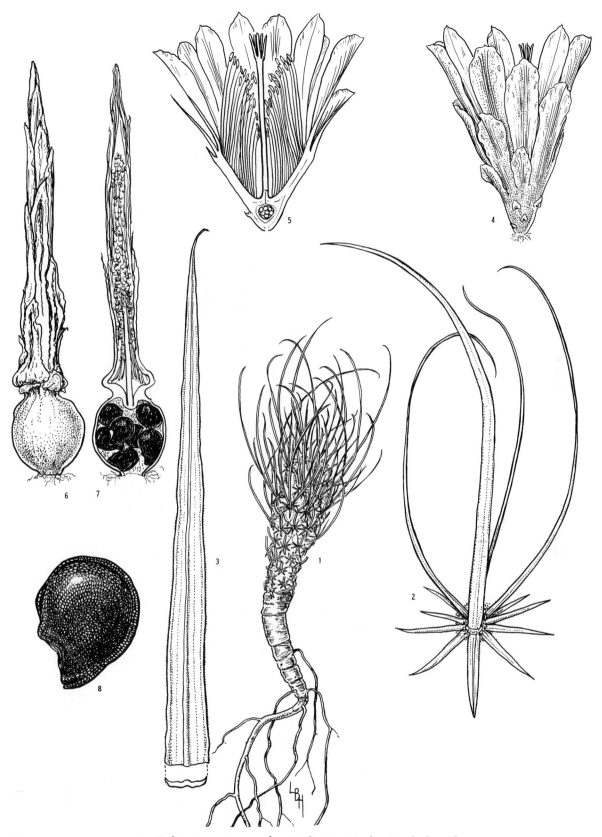

Fig. 809. Grama grass cactus, *Pediocactus papyracanthus*. *1*, Plant, ✕2.5, showing the long, flat spines, resembling grass blades (especially of blue grama grass, *Bouteloua gracilis*) in clumps of which the species grows. *2*, Areole with the elongate central spines and the shorter, spreading radials, and with wool, ✕5. *3*, Tip of a central spine, showing the median groove, and a cross section, ✕12. *4*, Flower, ✕2.5. *5*, Flower in longitudinal section, ✕2.5. *6*, Fruit, with the upper flower parts persistent, ✕4.25. *7*, Fruit in longitudinal section, ✕4.25. *8*, Seed, in hilum appearing more or less basal, more so than usually in this genus, ✕12.

769

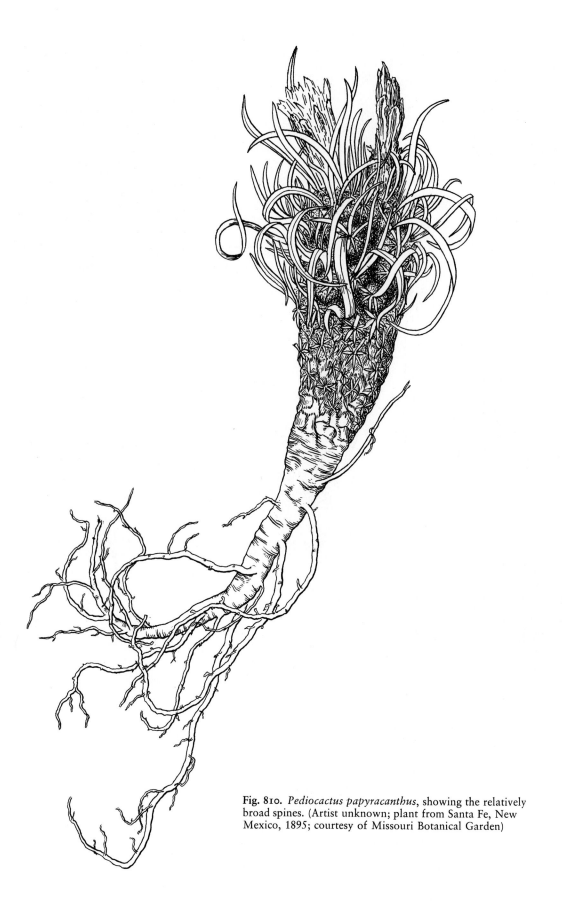

Fig. 810. *Pediocactus papyracanthus*, showing the relatively broad spines. (Artist unknown; plant from Santa Fe, New Mexico, 1895; courtesy of Missouri Botanical Garden)

long, ±3 mm broad, apically obtuse, scarious, with a few irregular teeth; petaloids white with brownish midribs, largest oblanceolate, ±20 mm long, 4.5 mm broad, apically sharply acute, mucronate, marginally entire; filaments whitish, 6-9 mm long; anthers pale yellow (?) or whitish, 1 mm long, relatively broad; style greenish, ±20 mm long, 0.5 mm greatest diam; stigmas 5, 1.5 mm long; ovary in anthesis with or without a few toothed scales; fruit green, changing to tan, with a few or no persistent scales, subglobose, ±4.5-6 mm long, to 4.5 mm diam; seeds black, finely papillate-tessellate, broadly obovoid but irregular,

Fig. 811. Grama grass cactus, *Pediocactus papyracanthus*, showing the flat, papery central spines and the rosette of short radials. (Perhaps C. H. Thompson, 1910; courtesy of Missouri Botanical Garden)

somewhat flattened, ±2.5 mm long, 3 mm broad, 1 mm thick; hilum relatively small.

Red sandy soils of open flats in grasslands and woodlands at 1,500-2,200 m (5,000-7,200 ft). Southern Juniper-Pinyon Woodland and Great Plains Grassland. Arizona in s Navajo Co.; New Mexico from SE Rio Arriba Co. and McKinley Co. to Grant and Dona Ana Cos. Inconspicuous and probably irregular in occurrence; consequently commonly overlooked.

The plants grow in or near fairy rings of blue grama grass (*Bouteloua gracilis*), and usually they are not noticed because the spines resemble the dried leaves of the grass. Finding the first one required many days of searching bent over or on hands and knees.

Boke (1961) has shown this species to be similar in microscopic development to the genus *Coryphantha*.

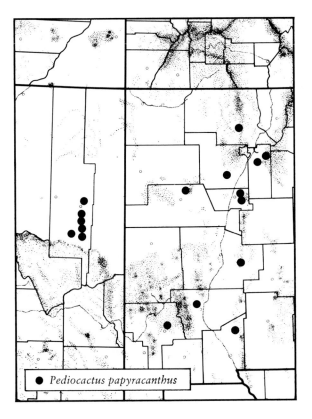

● *Pediocactus papyracanthus*

12. Epithelantha

Stems unbranched or branching and in clumps, the larger irregularly ovoid-cylindroid to cylindroid, 2.5-6 cm long and diam; ribs none; tubercles separate. Leaves not discernible on mature tubercles, each a microscopic hump of tissue on a young tubercle. Areoles nearly circular. Spines smooth, white or ashy gray, those in upper portion of areole longer than others, making a tuft in the depression at stem apex, but ultimately breaking at the middles, the terminal tuft thereby giving way as stem grows to an area of seemingly shorter spines on sides of stem, 20-100 per areole, in 2-5 series, straight, 3-6 mm long, basally ±0.1 mm diam, acicular, broadly elliptic in cross section. Flowers and fruits on new growth of current season near apex of stem or branch, each developed at apex of a tubercle in felted area adjacent to the spine-bearing part of areole and merging with it, this area forming a persistent circular to semicircular scar. Flower 3-12 mm diam; floral tube above ovary funnelform, like perianth in color but paler. Fruits red and with 6-11 seeds or some small, colorless, and with only 1-5 seeds, fleshy at maturity, without surface appendages, with floral tube deciduous, clavate, 3-12 mm diam, indehiscent. Seeds black, impressed-reticulate and sometimes also papillate, more or less obovoid-acute, broader than long, 1-1.5 mm broad; hilum appearing "lateral"; cotyledons accumbent, not foliaceous.

Probably only two species, occurring from Arizona to Texas and northern Mexico.

The name of the genus is derived from the Greek words for "on," "nipple," and "flower."

The species of *Epithelantha* are similar in appearance to *Mammillaria lasiacantha*. However, the flowers of *Epithelantha* are developed at the growing point at the top of the stem, each at the apex of a young tubercle and adjacent to the spine-bearing portion of the areole, rather than away from the stem apex and between the bases of older tubercles. This point may be difficult to determine in dried specimens, and the following may be easier: in *Epithelantha* the spines about the stem apex are much longer than those on the sides of the stem because, after a season or so, they disarticulate near the middles and the upper portion of each one falls away; this does not occur in *Mammillaria lasiacantha*.

No list of species is necessary: *E. micromeris* and *E. bokei* are described below; *E. micromeris* var. *greggii*, the other taxon, is a Mexican plant not evaluated in the preparation of this study. The status of some proposed species has not been investigated.

KEY TO THE SPECIES OF EPITHELANTHA

1. Spines of each areole in 2 or sometimes 3 series, 20-30; flowers usually obscured by the longer spines of the stem, small, ±3-4.5 mm long, ±6 mm in diameter; petaloids from more or less semicircular to deltoid, ±1 mm long and broad; stamens 10-15; stems usually irregularly short-cylindroid to ovoid, the spine-bases giving the stem a relatively rough, irregular appearance.........................1. E. micromeris
1. Spines of each areole in 4 or 5 series of ±25-28 (outer series) to ±10 (inner series); flowers relatively conspicuous, protruding well beyond the spines of the stem, relatively large, 10-12 mm long and in diameter; petaloids bluntly oblanceolate, ±9 mm long, ±3 mm broad; stamens 35-40; stems cylindroid, the spine-bases giving the stem a shining, smooth appearance....................................2. E. bokei

1. **Epithelantha micromeris** (Engelmann) Weber

Stems solitary or sometimes in small clumps to 6 cm high and 15 cm diam; stem green but obscured by the white or pale gray spines, usually irregularly ovoid-cylindroid with a slight apical depression, 4-6 cm long, 2.5-6 cm diam (in a Mexican type to 12.5 and 7.5 cm); tubercles conic-cylindroid, in 20-35 rows, ±1.5 mm long, ±1.5 mm broad, protruding ±3 mm; areoles ±1 mm diam, typically ±2 mm apart; spines numerous and very dense, obscuring stem, arranged in 2(3) series, 20-30 per areole, accompanied by white woolly hairs, 6 mm long, basally ±0.1 mm diam, acicular, with numerous forward-directed minute barbs; spines of upper areoles (before disarticulating) ±twice as long as in lower areoles; flower small, usually obscured by the long spines near apex of stem, ±3-4.5 mm diam, ±6 mm long; sepaloids 3-5, with pink midribs and pale pink margins, the larger elongate-semicircular, 1 mm long and broad, apically rounded, irregularly denticulate; petaloids pale pink, largest approaching obdeltoid but with upper sides somewhat curving, 1 mm long and broad, acute, entire; stamens ±10-15; filaments tinged with red, ±0.5-0.7 mm long;

anthers white or pale yellow, 0.25 mm long and broad; style yellowish, ±4.5 mm long, 0.25 mm greatest diam; stigmas 3, 0.5 mm long and broad; ovary in anthesis ±1 mm long; fruit red (or some small, colorless, and with only 1-3 seeds, the seeds usually 4-11), fleshy at maturity, clavate, the lower portion not producing seeds, 3-12 mm long, 1.5-6 mm diam, the umbilicus inconspicuous; seeds minutely reticulate-impressed, asymmetrically obovoid-acute, 1+ mm long, 1.5 mm broad, ±0.8 mm thick; hilum oblique, elongate.

Limestone or sometimes igneous soils of rocky hills and ridges in desert and grasslands at 1,020-1,500 m (3,400-5,000 ft). Chihuahuan Desert and Desert Grassland. Arizona, rare in Santa Cruz and Cochise Cos.; New Mexico in Sandoval and Hidalgo Cos. and from Sierra Co. to Chaves and Eddy Cos.; w Texas from El Paso Co. to Pecos and Val Verde Cos. and in Bandera Co. South into N Mexico.

The stems are fuzzy white balls or bullets, the green obliterated by the furlike cover of spines. The flowers are inconspicuous, but the crown of bright red fruits is beautiful and striking against the white background.

Fig. 812. A button cactus, *Epithelantha micromeris*, plant in cultivation. The tuft of spines at the top is characteristic; the lower spines appear shorter because the upper portion of each has fallen off. (Norman H. Boke)

Fig. 813. *Epithelantha micromeris*, much-enlarged emerging spines at the apex of a young stem. (Norman H. Boke)

Text continued on p. 779

Fig. 814. *Epithelantha micromeris*, apex of the stem, with flowers at the center; a little farther from the apex, a fruit from a previously developed turn of the spiral of tubercles. (Norman H. Boke)

Fig. 815. *Epithelantha micromeris*, areoles, each with 20–30 white spines in two or three spirals, and with woolly white hairs. (Norman H. Boke)

Fig. 816. *Epithelantha micromeris*, two areoles enlarged. (Norman H. Boke)

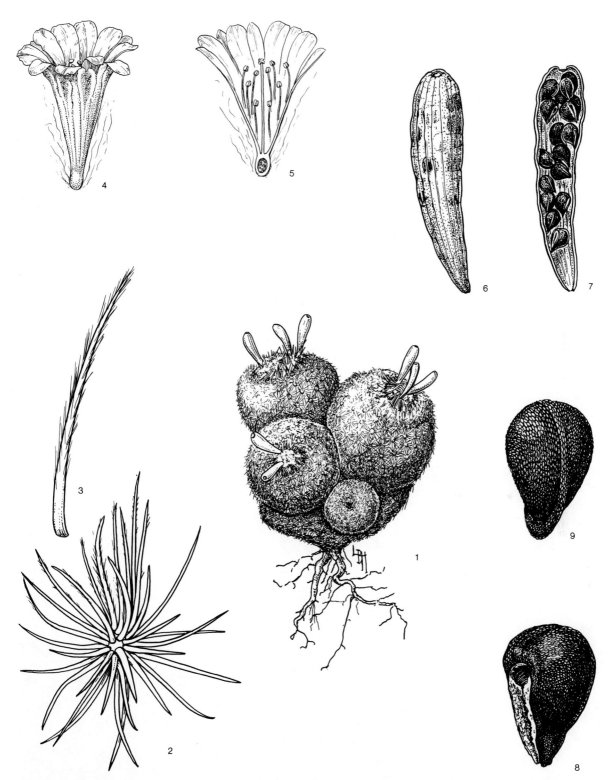

Fig. 817. A button cactus, *Epithelantha micromeris*. *1*, Plant in fruit, showing the full-length spines at the top of the stem, natural size; lower on the stem the remaining lower portions of the spines after disarticulation of the upper portions following the first year of growth. *2*, Areole with about three series of spines, ×8. *3*, Tip of a spine, showing the forward-directed barbs or hairs, ×16. *4*, Flower, ×10. *5*, Flower in longitudinal section, ×10. *6*, Fruit, ×3.25. *7*, Fruit in longitudinal section, ×3.25. *8*, *9*, Two views of the seed, ×40.

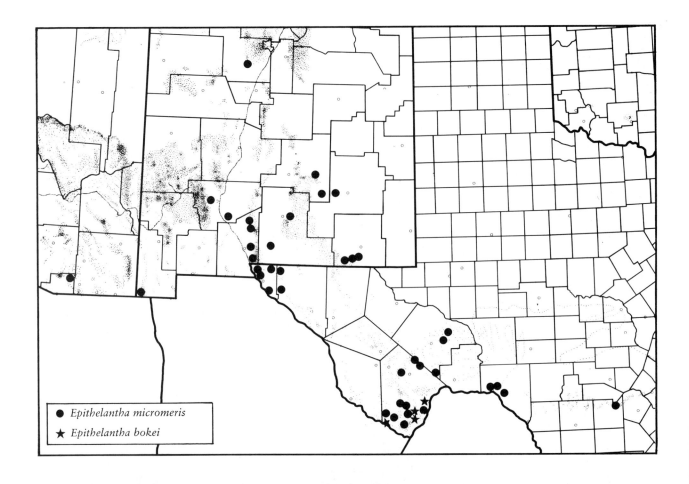

Fig. 818. A button cactus, *Epithelantha bokei*, branches, emphasizing the extreme smoothness of the spiny covering of all but the apex of the stem after the upper portion of each spine has fallen; only the apical spines are of full length. (Norman H. Boke)

Fig. 819. *Epithelantha bokei*, with an apical tuft of flowers. (Norman H. Boke)

Fig. 820. *Epithelantha bokei*, with an apical tuft of fruits, these elongating rapidly at maturity and now red. (Norman H. Boke)

Fig. 821. *Epithelantha bokei*, apex of a young stem, the young areoles with emerging spines. (Norman H. Boke)

Fig. 822. *Epithelantha bokei*, areoles with mature spines in four or five series, about 25–28 spines in the outer series and about 10 in the inner. (Norman H. Boke)

Fig. 823. *Epithelantha bokei*, two areoles enlarged. (Norman H. Boke)

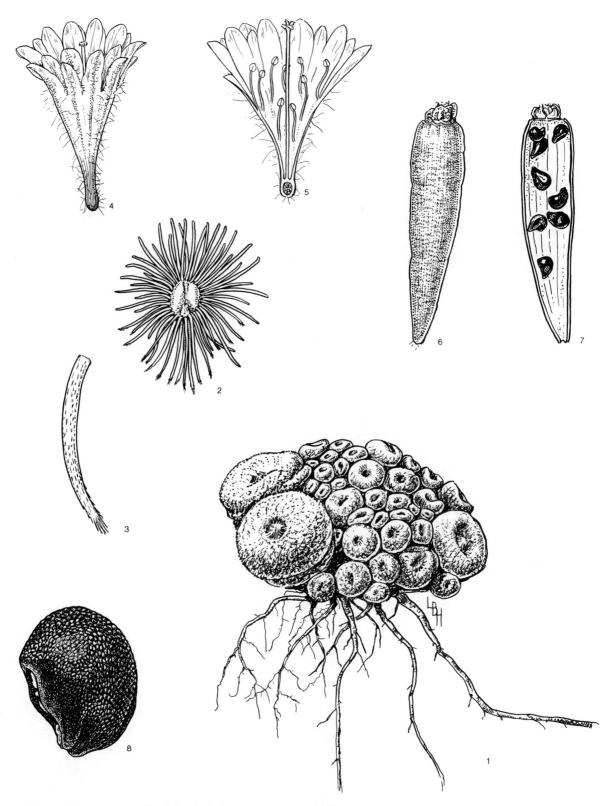

Fig. 824. A button cactus, *Epithelantha bokei*, ×3.5, except as indicated. *1*, Plant forming a large cluster of stems, most of these still young, ×.9. *2*, Areole from beneath, ×4.75. *3*, Tip of a spine, showing barblike apical hairs, ×28. *4*, Flower. *5*, Flower in longitudinal section. *6*, Fruit. *7*, Fruit in longitudinal section. *8*, Seed, ×48.

2. Epithelantha bokei L. Benson

Stems solitary or few, mostly green, cylindroid, mostly 2.5-5 cm long and diam; tubercles conic-cylindroid, ±1.5 mm long, 1.5 mm broad, protruding 3 mm; areoles 1 mm diam, typically ±2 mm apart; spines very dense, obscuring stem, white, in each areole in 4 or 5 series of ±25-28 (outer) to ±10 (inner), spreading parallel to stem, the longer on upper sides of young areoles, ±3-4.5 mm long, ±0.1 mm diam, acicular, those of inner series shorter; flower 10-12 mm diam and long; sepaloids with pink midribs and pale pink margins, the largest narrowly oblong, 3 mm long, 0.7 mm broad, blunt, laciniate; petaloids pink, largest bluntly oblanceolate, ±9 mm long, ±3 mm broad, truncate, retuse, entire; stamens 35-40; filaments pale yellow, 1 mm long; anthers pale yellow, 0.5 mm long; style pale yellowish, ±10 mm long, ±0.25 mm greatest diam; stigmas 3, 0.5 mm long, stout; ovary in anthesis ±2 mm long; fruit red and with 5-10 seeds or some fruits gray and small and with 1-5 seeds, 3-9 mm long, 1.5-2.25 mm diam, the umbilicus obscure; seeds impressed-reticulate and papillate, obovoid-acute, 0.7 mm long, 1 mm broad, 0.5 mm thick; hilum elongate.

Limestone soils of rocky hilltops and ridges in desert at 750-1,200 m (2,500-4,000 ft). Chihuahuan Desert. Texas near the Rio Grande in Big Bend region in w Brewster Co. Adjacent Mexico.

The plants are dense clusters of balls, domes, or short cylinders. Each stem is covered by a dense cloak of white, close-set spines. Because the spine tips disarticulate evenly, the surface of the spine mass has the appearance of satin.

13. Thelocactus

Stems solitary or several, the larger hemispheroidal to ovoid or long-ovoid, 7.5-10(12.5) cm long, 5-10 (12.5) cm diam; ribs 8-12, the tubercles coalescent through much of their height or sometimes (in Mexican plants) nearly separate. Leaves not discernible on mature tubercles. Areoles nearly circular. Spines smooth, straw-colored or tinged with pink; central spines 1-4 per areole, straight or curved, 2-4.5 cm long, basally less than 1 mm diam, subulate, narrowly elliptic in cross section; radial spines 3-17 per areole, straight or curved, 1.2-3 cm long, the upper basally 0.5-1.5 mm broad, subulate. Flowers and fruits produced on new growth of current season and thus located near apex of stem or branch, developed on upper side of tubercle in a felted area adjoining spine-bearing part of areole, the flower buds emerging next to the spines, but flower-bearing area *not* connected with spine-bearing area by an isthmus, the scar persistent, elongate, and narrow or slit-like, extending ±half length of tubercle. Flower 2.5-6 cm diam; floral tube above ovary obconic to funnelform, green tinged with perianth color, i.e., with pale yellow to red or purple. Fruit dry at maturity, with 5-20 scales, subcylindroid, ±12 mm long, 6-12 mm diam, opening diagonally at base, floral tube persistent, the seeds black, so far as known finely reticulate-papillate, obovoid but basally truncate, longer than broad, ±1.75 mm greatest dimension; hilum obviously basal; cotyledons accumbent, not foliaceous.

A number of species occurring in Texas and Mexico, these little known and less understood. One species represented in Texas, along the Rio Grande.

From Greek, "nipple" cactus.

The extraterritorial species in the list that follows have not been evaluated, and they are in need of study.

T. *hexaedrophorus* (central Mexico to San Luis Potosí)
T. *rinconensis* (Nuevo León)

T. *lophothele* (Chihuahua)
T. *conothelos* (NE Mexico)
T. *phymatothele* (Mexico)
T. *buekii* (Mexico)
T. *leucanthus* (Hidalgo)
T. *nidulans* (Mexico)
T. *fossulatus* (San Luis Potosí)
T. *tulensis* (Tamaulipas)
T. *lloydii* (Zacatecas)
1. T. *bicolor*
   vars. a. *schottii*
      b. *flavidispinus*
         bicolor (central Mexico s as far as San Luis Potosí)
         pottsii (Chihuahua & Coahuila)
T. *gielsdorfianus* (NE Mexico)
T. *hastifer* (Mexico)
T. *knuthianus* (central Mexico)
T. *saveri* (NE Mexico)
T. *wagnerianus* (E Mexico)

1. Thelocactus bicolor (Galeotti) Britton & Rose

Stems solitary, green, ovoid or long-ovoid, 7.5-10(13) cm long, 5-7.5(12) cm diam; ribs ±8, low; tubercles adnate basally with ribs, crowded tightly against each other and separated by only slit-like spaces, 9-12 mm long, ±12-20 mm broad, protruding 9-12 mm; areoles circular, ±3 mm diam, typically 4-9 mm apart; spines usually densely covering the rows of tubercles, the centrals and most radials either straw-colored or tinged with pink; central spines 4, the upper 3 spreading with radials, lower 1 porrect, straight, 2.5-3 cm long, 1 mm broad, basally flattened; radial spines 10-17 per areole, radiating nearly parallel to stem surface, all but upper ones 1-2.5(3) cm long, basally to ±0.7-0.8 mm diam, acicular, broadly elliptic in cross section, upper 1-3 radials white or straw-colored, to 7.5 cm long, ±1.5 mm broad, flat, thin, ribbonlike; flower 5-6 cm diam and long; sepaloids with green midribs tinged with rose and pale rose margins, the larger oblanceo-

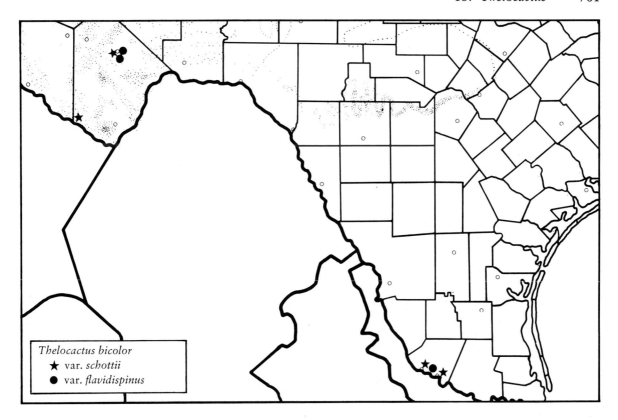

Thelocactus bicolor
★ var. *schottii*
● var. *flavidispinus*

Distinctive Characters of the Varieties of **Thelocactus bicolor**

Character	a. var. **schottii**	b. var. **flavidispinus**	var. **bicolor** (Mexico)
Stems	Ovoid or long-ovoid, 7.5-10(13) cm long, 5-7.5(12) cm diam	Ovoid or long-ovoid, 7.5-9 cm long, 5-6 cm diam	Nearly globose, to 11-14 cm long, 10-13 cm diam
Central spines	Tinged with pink, relatively long, the longest (upper) one to 4.5 cm long and with a keel	Straw-colored or with a slight tinge of pink, relatively short, the longest (upper) one ±2 cm long and not keeled	Tinged with pink, relatively short, the longest (upper) one 2-3 cm long and not keeled
Radial spines	15-17, most tinged with pink, the upper flattened 1-3 spines straw-colored or white and 5-10 cm long, ±1.5 mm broad	±12-14, straw-colored or with a slight tinge of pink, the upper flattened 1-2 spines yellowish and 2.5-3.8 cm long, to 0.5 mm broad	8-10(11), most tinged with pink, the upper flattened 1-3 spines straw-colored or white and ±3 cm long, ±1 mm broad
Altitude	90-1,200 m (300-4,000 ft) in the U.S.; no data on Mexican occurrence	90-1,200 m (300-4,000 ft) in the U.S.; no data on Mexican occurrence	No data, but in areas mostly above 1,200 m (4,000 ft) in Mexico
Floristic association	Desert Grassland; Rio Grande Plain; Chihuahuan Desert	Desert Grassland and Rio Grande Plain	Chihuahuan Desert and adjacent grasslands

late, to 40 mm long, to 7.5 mm broad, rounded to acute, minutely very shallowly fimbriate; petaloids rose but basally red, largest oblanceolate, to 45 mm long, to 12 mm broad, acute or mucronate, entire to minutely and irregularly apically denticulate; filaments nearly white, ±10 mm long; anthers yellow, 1.5 mm long; style nearly white, 20-30 mm long, 1.5 mm average diam; stigmas ±10 or 11, ±4.5 mm long, red with orange cast; ovary in anthesis broadly cylindroid, ±6 mm long, with short-fimbriate scales; fruit green, dry at maturity, with 15-20 fimbriate scales, ±12 mm long, 9-12 mm diam; seeds finely reticulate-papillate, obovoid but basally truncate, 2-2.5 mm long, 1.75 mm broad, 1.25 mm thick.

1a. Thelocactus bicolor var. **schottii** (Engelmann) Krainz. Gravelly soils of hills and alluvial fans in desert or grassland at 90-1,200 m (300-4,000 ft). Chihuahuan Desert, Desert Grassland, and Rio Grande Plain. Texas near Rio Grande in Big Bend region in Brewster and Starr Cos. Mexico in adjacent Tamaulipas.

The long red-and-white spines are the obvious feature of the plant, except when the gorgeous large flowers are present.

1b. Thelocactus bicolor var. **flavidispinus** Backeberg. Gravelly hills in desert or grassland at 90-1,200 m (300-4,000 ft). Desert Grassland and Rio Grande Plain. Texas in vicinity of Rio Grande in NE Brewster Co. and Starr Co.

The dirty yellow spines make the plant much less attractive and less conspicuous than var. *schottii*.

Thelocactus bicolor var. **bicolor.** Central Mexico in an undetermined range as far south as San Luis Potosí; not occurring in the U.S. This variety is included for comparison because it is widely distributed and because it occurs in cultivation.

Fig. 825. *Thelocactus bicolor* var. *schottii*, growing under shrubs, in this case *Opuntia leptocaulis*; Roma, Starr Co., Texas. The conspicuous central spine in each areole is the long, flattened, pink-tinged upper one.

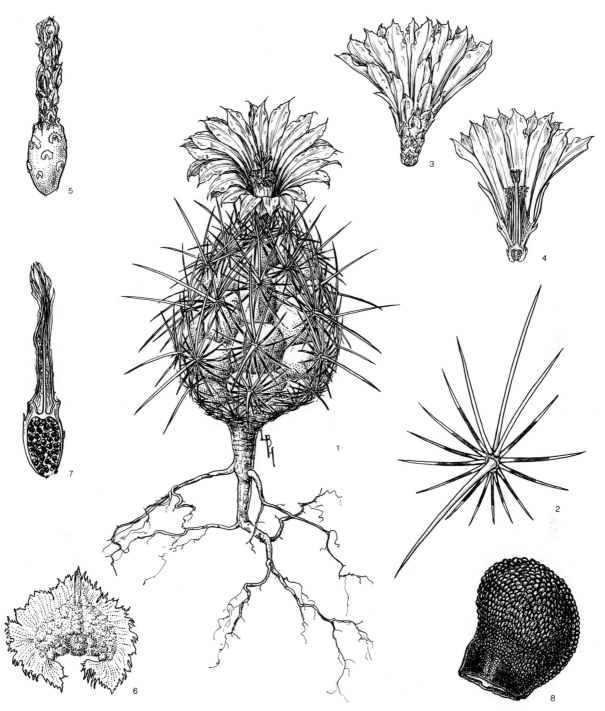

Fig. 826. *Thelocactus bicolor* var. *schottii*, ×1.2, except as indicated. *1*, Plant in flower. *2*, Areole with the 4 central spines and with 13 (in this variety usually 15–17) radial spines, the lower central spine pink, the upper three white or nearly so, ×2.5. *3*, Flower. *4*, Flower in longitudinal section. *5*, Fruit. *6*, Scale from the ovary, ×7.5. *7*, Fruit in longitudinal section. *8*, Seed, ×25. (See Credits)

Stems branched or unbranched, the larger ovoid or cylindroid, 5-15(40) cm long, 2.5-7.5(12.5) cm diam, tuberculate or slightly to clearly ribbed. Leaves not discernible on mature tubercles. Areoles nearly circular to elliptic. Spines smooth, black to dark brown or tan, chalky blue, straw-colored, purplish, or pink, sometimes dark-tipped, in age becoming gray or black; central spines 1-8 per areole, straight or rarely (in Mexico) curved or almost hooked, 1.2-4.5 cm long, basally 0.4-1.5 mm diam, acicular or subulate, broadly or very narrowly elliptic in cross section; radial spines white or similar to centrals but usually smaller and lighter colored, 3-32 per areole, straight, 0.6-3 cm long, basally 0.2-1.5 mm diam, acicular. Flowers and fruits on new growth of current season and therefore near apex of stem or branch, each on upper side of a tubercle in a felted area distant from spine-bearing part of areole and connected by an isthmus running length of tubercle, this area persisting and forming an elongate, narrow scar. Flower 2.5-7.5 cm diam; floral tube above ovary funnelform to obconical, green and pink to purple. Fruit dry at maturity, with a few or to 20 broad, membranous scales, ellipsoid to short-cylindroid, 6-12 mm long, ±6-9 mm diam, dehiscent basally or along 1-3 longitudinal slits. Seeds black, reticulate, reticulate-papillate, or only papillate, broader than long or the reverse, often crescentic-ellipsoid, 1.5-2.5 mm greatest dimension; hilum either obviously basal or appearing "lateral"; cotyledons accumbent, *not* foliaceous.

About 12-15 species occurring from California to Texas and south to northern Sonora and San Luis Potosí, Mexico. Seven species in California, Arizona, New Mexico, and Texas.

The name is for Professor Francis E. Lloyd, 1868-1947.

Not all the extraterritorial species proposed by recent authors have been evaluated. *Echinomastus macdowellii* is a *Neolloydia*, but the status of the taxon has not been worked out.

1. N. conoidea
    N. ceratites (Mexico) (status uncertain)
2. N. warnockii
3. N. gautii
4. N. mariposensis
    N. unguispinus (Chihuahua to Zacatecas)
    Echinomastus macdowellii (N Mexico)
    N. durangensis (Durango & Zacatecas)
5. N. intertexta
    vars. a. intertexta
          b. dasyacantha
6. N. erectocentra
    vars. a. erectocentra
          b. acunensis
7. N. johnsonii

KEY TO THE SPECIES OF NEOLLOYDIA

1. Fruit dehiscent basally along a diagonal line of abscission; central spines basally 0.4-0.6 (0.75) mm in diameter; radial spines 0.2-0.5 mm in diameter; Texas and NE Mexico (N. intertexta), also in SE Arizona and S New Mexico.
    2. Lower central spine longer than the others, the central spines black or dark brown; stems branching, forming clumps, green; seeds longer than broad, the hilum obviously basal ....1. N. conoidea
    2. Lower central spine shorter than the others, the central spines *either* dull tan tipped with chalky blue *or* blue-brown *or* pinkish *or* grayish-straw-colored; stems, so far as known, unbranched (except perhaps after injury to the terminal bud); seeds broader than long, the hilum appearing "lateral" or perhaps transitional between "lateral" and basal.
        3. Central spines dull tan tipped with chalky blue or blue-brown; stem with a bluish powdered wax over the surface.

4. Radial spines chalky blue, ±12-14 per areole, in a single series but not pectinate, spreading irregularly at low angles, blurring but not obscuring the stem; central spines similar to the radials, 4 (or possibly 6, with 2 additional ones above), the upper 3 about 20-25 percent longer than the lower (porrect) one; seed ±2 mm broad (greatest dimension)...................**2. N. warnockii**
4. Radial spines ashy white, (16)26-32 per areole, pectinate, spreading at a low angle against the stem, obscuring the stem; central spines various, as in leads 5, below; seeds ±1.5 mm broad, as far as is known.
5. Lower central spine much longer than the upper 1-2, all centrals straight and turned upward, ±2 cm long; radial spines 16-20 per areole, ±9-12 mm long, 0.4 mm in diameter................................**3. N. gautii**
5. Lower central spine turned and curving downward, 50-70 percent the length of the upper 1-3, which point upward, 0.6-1.5 cm long; radial spines 26-32 per areole, ±0.6 cm long, 0.2 mm in diameter.........**4. N. mariposensis**
3. Central spines usually grayish or straw-colored with the upper parts pink or red or sometimes the whole spine red; stem green................**5. N. intertexta**
1. Fruit dehiscent along 1-3 vertical slits; central spines basally 1-1.25(1.5) mm in diameter; radial spines 0.5-0.75 mm in diameter; California to sw Utah, Arizona, and N Sonora.
2A. Flowers pink or pale pink; central spines 1-4, *either* (1) solitary *or* (2) dissimilar in length, bending, or curvature, the 1-3 upper spreading more or less like the radials, the principal one either nearly porrect or turned upward and much longer than the radials ....**6. N. erectocentra**
2A. Flowers magenta to yellow; central spines 4-9, all similar, spreading in all directions ....**7. N. johnsonii**

1. Neolloydia conoidea
(DeCandolle) Britton & Rose

Stems solitary to many, clumps to 10 cm high, 20-30+ cm diam; larger stems green, ovoid to cylindroid, to 7.5-10 cm long, 2.5-6 cm diam; ribs, if any, faintly developed, probably none; tubercles 9-12 mm long, 9-18 mm broad, protruding 6-12 mm; areoles ±2-3 mm diam, typically ±9-12 mm apart; spines dense, obscuring stem; central spines black or dark brown, mostly 4 per areole, the lower (principal and longest) central turned slightly downward, upper 1-3 turned upward, straight or (Saltillo, Coahuila, Mexico, *Palmer 500*, April 9, 1905, *GH*) rarely hooked or nearly so, the longer to 2-3 cm long, basally ±0.5 mm diam, acicular, tending toward circular in cross section; radial spines white, (13)15-28 per areole, spreading parallel to stem, straight, longer to 1 cm long, basally ±0.25 mm diam, acicular, nearly circular in cross section; flower to 4-6 cm diam, ±2 cm long; perianth rotate; sepaloids magenta to purplish, larger broadly oblanceolate, to 25 mm long, to 10 mm broad, mucronate, entire; petaloids magenta to purplish, the largest broadly oblanceolate, to 25 mm long, 6 mm broad, mucronate, entire; filaments orange-yel-

Fig. 827. *Neolloydia conoidea*, stem showing the tubercles, the areoles, and a flower.

low, slender, 6 mm long; anthers orange, ±1 mm long; style yellow, 10 mm long, less than 1 mm greatest diam; stigmas 6 or 7, ±3 mm long, slender; ovary in anthesis ±3 mm long and diam; fruit not available; seeds gun-metal gray and black, strongly papillate, longer than broad, the hilum obviously basal, 1.5 mm long, 1.25 mm broad, 1 mm thick.

Limestone hills in desert at 690-1,200 m (2,300-4,000 ft). Chihuahuan Desert. Texas from El Paso Co. to Brewster and Terrell Cos. and in Edwards Co. Northern Mexico.

The stems form dark-green clumps, and their color is more prominent than the gray of the relatively short spines and the areoles. The tubercles are clearly visible.

2. Neolloydia warnockii L. Benson

Stems solitary, blue-green, ovoid to long-ovoid, 7-11 cm long, 5-7.5 cm diam; ribs or tubercle rows 13-21; tubercles ±10 mm long, 6 mm broad, protruding 10 mm; areoles elliptic, 3 mm long, typically ±10 mm apart; spines dense, obscuring

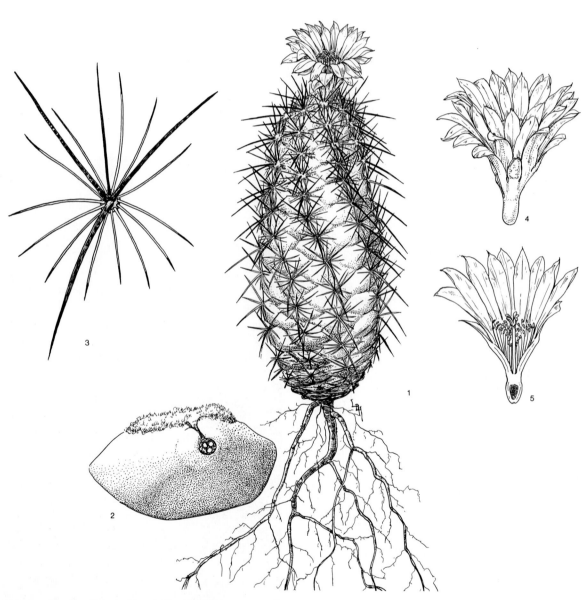

Fig. 828. *Neolloydia conoidea. 1*, Plant in flower, ×.6. *2*, Tubercle, the areole with the spines cut off, showing the groove between the spine-bearing area and the felted to woolly flower- and fruit-bearing area, ×2.25. *3*, Areole, showing the four central spines and the radial spines, ×2.25. *4*, Flower, ×1.1. *5*, Flower in longitudinal section, ×2.25. (See Credits)

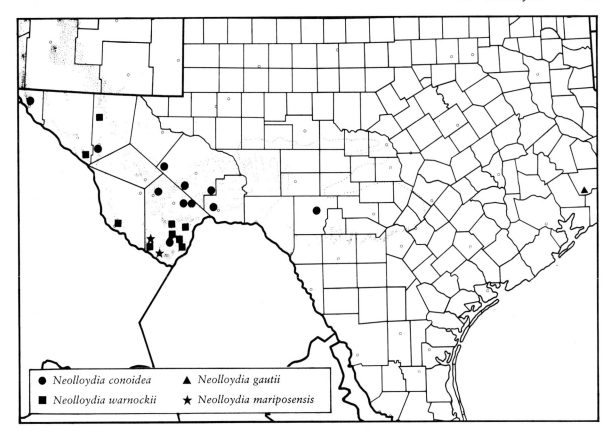

● *Neolloydia conoidea* ▲ *Neolloydia gautii*
■ *Neolloydia warnockii* ★ *Neolloydia mariposensis*

stem; central spines dull tan but tips chalky blue or partly brown, 4 per areole or perhaps with 2+ additional above upper median one, straight, the lower porrect, others pointing upward, similar to lower but 20-25 percent longer, the longer 1.2-2.5 cm long, basally ±0.4 mm diam, acicular, nearly circular in section; radial spines like centrals but dark tips shorter and diam a little less, 12-14 per areole, spreading rather irregularly at low angles; flower ±2.5 cm diam and long; sepaloids with green midribs and white-scarious to pink margins, larger lanceolate, 9-12 mm long, to 4.5 mm broad, acute, marginally undulate; petaloids pink, largest oblanceolate, ±12 mm long, 4.5-6 mm broad, acute, marginally scarious and undulate; filaments pale yellowish, 3 mm long; anthers yellow, oblong, 0.7 mm long; style green, ±10 mm long, slender, 0.7 mm greatest diam; stigmas ±5, 1 mm long, relatively broad; ovary in anthesis ±6 mm long; fruit green, becoming brownish at maturity, with a few very broad membranous scales, spheroidal, ±6 mm diam, the umbilicus covered by persistent floral tube and perianth; seeds black, papillate in a reticulate pattern, flattened-obovoid except for incurved hilum, 1.5 mm long, 2 mm broad, 1 mm thick; hilum appearing "lateral."

Limestone of hills in desert at 560-900(1,200) m (1,900-3,000 or 4,000 ft); sometimes on gypsum flats at 1,350 m (4,500 ft). Chihuahuan Desert. Texas mostly near Rio Grande from E Hudspeth Co. to Culberson and Brewster Cos.

This small, cylindroid plant is detected readily among the low desert shrubs because of its conspicuous bluish-gray spines and stem.

3. Neolloydia gautii L. Benson

Stem solitary, 7.5 cm high, 5.6 cm diam; mature spines chalky blue, darker at tips; central spines 2 or 3, all pointing upward, lower (principal) one exactly central in areole, ±2 cm long, 0.75 mm basal diam, straight or slightly curving upward, other central spines straight and much smaller, tapering, basally elliptic in cross section; radial spines ±16-20, spreading regularly in single series and lying flat against stem, 9-12 mm long, basally to 0.4 mm diam; flowers and fruits unknown.

Sour Lake, Hardin Co., Texas; Gulf Coastal Plain, far from other cacti of this group or any other but prickly pears. Known from only the type specimen, which differs markedly from related species.

4. Neolloydia mariposensis (Hester) L. Benson

Stem blue-green, ovoid- or obovoid-cylindroid, 6-10 cm long, 4-6 cm diam; ribs none, the usual position shown by tubercles; tubercles 6 mm long vertically, 6 mm broad, protruding 3 mm; areoles elliptic, 3 mm diam, typically 6 mm apart; spines very dense, radials obscuring stem; central spines dull tan with chalky blue or partly brown tips, 2-4 per areole, lower central turned and curving downward, mostly 0.5-0.7 times as long as but similar to upper 1-3, these straight, turned upward, the longer 1.5-2 cm long, basally 0.6 mm diam, acicular, nearly circular in cross section; radial spines white (ashy), 26-32 per areole, spreading evenly and parallel to stem, straight, pectinate, the longer ±6 mm long, basally 0.2 mm diam, acicular; flower to 4 cm diam, ±2.5 cm long; sepaloids with green and reddish-purple midribs and pink margins, largest elliptic-lanceolate, to 12 mm long, 3 mm broad, rounded, marginally scarious and undulate; petaloids pink, largest oblanceolate, to 20 mm long, 3 mm broad, acute to rounded, entire; filaments ±7.5 mm long; anthers ±1 mm long; style 10 mm long, 1 mm greatest diam; stigmas ±5, 2 mm long, green, rather broad; ovary in anthesis 3 mm broad; fruit not available; seed black, papillate in a reticulate pattern, in side view forming a parallelogram, 1.3 mm long, 1.5 mm broad, 1 mm thick; hilum "lateral" but transitional to obviously basal type.

Limestone of hills in desert at about 750-900 m (2,500-3,000 ft). Chihuahuan Desert. Texas near Rio Grande in sw Brewster Co. Central Coahuila, Mexico.

Small cylindroid plants bearing light bluish spines and stems, which may either contrast or blend with the surroundings. Usually found in obscure places among small desert shrubs.

5. Neolloydia intertexta (Engelmann) L. Benson

Stem solitary, almost globular to cylindroid, 5-15 cm long, 4-7.5 cm diam; ribs ±6-9 mm high beneath the tubercles; tubercles 6-9 mm long, ±3 mm broad, protruding ±3 mm; areoles ±2.2 mm diam, typically ±6 mm apart; spines covering and obscuring stem; central spines pinkish or mostly (all but tips) grayish to straw-colored, usually 4 per areole, the 3 upper pointing more or less upward and appearing to be radials, 1.2-2(4) cm long, basally to 0.6 mm diam, acicular, elliptic in cross section, the lower (obviously central) spine similar to the upper or at right angles to stem, 1-3 mm or 1.5-2(4) cm long, elongate-conical; radial spines similar to upper centrals, 13-20 (reportedly 25) per areole, spreading, slightly curving, the longer 9-15(20) mm long, basally ±0.5 mm diam, acicular, elliptic in cross section; flower 2.5-3 cm diam, 2-3 cm long; sepaloids with purplish-brown midribs and pale pink to white margins, the larger spathulate-oblanceolate, 12-20 mm long, to 4.5 mm broad, slightly obtuse to acute or mucronate, marginally membranous and usually minutely denticulate; petaloids pink or pale pinkish-white on margins, each with broad pink median section, largest lanceolate, to 20 mm long, to 3 mm broad, acute to sharply acute or cuspidate, entire or essentially so; filaments pale yel-

Distinctive Characters of the Varieties of Neolloydia intertexta

Character	a. var. intertexta	b. var. dasyacantha
Stems	At first globular, becoming ovoid or obovoid to cylindroid, 5-7.5(15) cm long	Soon elongate-ovoid to cylindroid, 7.5-15 cm long
Upper central and radial spines	Appressed against stem, each forming a low arc, mostly to 1.2-1.5 cm long, the larger basally 0.5-0.6 mm diam	*Not* markedly appressed against stem, tending to spread in various directions, commonly some to 1.5-2(4) cm long, the larger basally 0.4-0.5 mm diam
Lower central spine (center of areole)	Usually 1-3 mm long, elongate-conical, much shorter than other centrals	1.5-2(4) cm long, acicular, a little shorter than but similar to the upper centrals
Altitude	±1,200-1,500 m (4,000-5,000 ft)	900-1,500 m (3,000-5,000 ft)
Floristic association	Desert Grassland (mostly); edge of Chihuahuan Desert	Chihuahuan Desert (mostly); Desert Grassland

126. A barrel cactus, *Echinocactus polycephalus* var. *polycephalus*, near Victorville, San Bernardino Co., California, showing the characteristic curving central spines. (From *The Native Cacti of California*)

127. A barrel cactus, *Echinocactus polycephalus* var. *polycephalus*, the flower in a mass of stout spines. (R. Wauer)

128. Turk's head, *Echinocactus horizonthalonius* var. *horizonthalonius*, Big Bend National Park, Brewster Co., Texas. (R. Wauer)

130 (*below*). Horse crippler, *Echinocactus texensis*, in fruit.

129. Turk's head, *Echinocactus horizonthalonius* var. *horizonthalonius*, collected in Texas. (S. Farwig)

132. *Sclerocactus spinosior*. (D. W. Woodruff)

131. *Sclerocactus mesae-verdae*, southwestern Colorado. (R. L. Benson)

133. *Sclerocactus whipplei*, near Holbrook, Arizona. (S. Farwig)

134 (*below left*). *Sclerocactus whipplei*, in cultivation. (S. Farwig)

135 (*below right*). *Sclerocactus parviflorus* var. *parviflorus*.

137 (*above*). *Pediocactus simpsonii* var. *simpsonii*, Belmont, Nevada, a yellow-flowered form common there. (S. Farwig)

136. *Sclerocactus polyancistrus*. (S. Farwig)

139 (*below*). *Pediocactus simpsonii* var. *minor*.

138 (*left*). *Pediocactus simpsonii* var. *simpsonii*, Burnt Fork, Wyoming. (D. W. Woodruff)

140. *Pediocactus knowltonii*, San Juan Co.,
New Mexico, in bud.

141. *Pediocactus knowltonii*, northern edge of
New Mexico. (P. Pierce)

142. *Pediocactus paradinei*, Coconino
Co., Arizona. (D. & M. Zimmerman)

143. *Pediocactus sileri*, Mohave Co.,
Arizona. (S. Farwig)

144. *Pediocactus peeblesianus* var.
peeblesianus. (S. Farwig)

145. *Pediocactus peeblesianus* var. *fickeiseniae*, near Little
Colorado River, Coconino Co., Arizona.

146. *Pediocactus papyracanthus*,
Sandoval Co., New Mexico. (D. & M.
Zimmerman)

147 (*right*). Button cactus,
Epithelantha micromeris, in
fruit.

148 (*below*). Button cactus,
Epithelantha bokei.
(S. Farwig)

150. *Thelocactus bicolor* var. *flavidispinus*, near Marathon, Brewster Co., Texas. (D. & M. Zimmerman)

149. *Thelocactus bicolor* var. *schottii*. (R. Wauer)

151. *Neolloydia conoidea*.

152 & 153 (*below left & right*). *Neolloydia mariposensis*. (Both R. Wauer)

154 (*above left*). *Neolloydia intertexta* var. *intertexta*. (R. Wauer)
155 (*above right*). *Neolloydia intertexta* var. *dasyacantha*, collected in Texas. (S. Farwig)

157. *Neolloydia johnsonii*, Utah. (D. W. Woodruff)

156 (*above*). *Neolloydia erectrocentra* var. *erectrocentra*. in cultivation. (J. A. Noble)

158. *Neolloydia johnsonii*, Utah. (D. W. Woodruff)

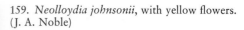

159. *Neolloydia johnsonii*, with yellow flowers. (J. A. Noble)

160 (*above*). *Neolloydia johnsonii*, from White Hills, Arizona, with the more common magenta flowers (betacyanin pigments). (S. Farwig)

161. *Neolloydia johnsonii*, southeast of Death Valley, Inyo Co., California, showing another color form. (S. Farwig; from *The Native Cacti of California*)

162. *Ancistrocactus uncinatus* var. *wrightii*. (S. Farwig)

163. *Coryphantha macromeris* var. *runyonii* .(S. Farwig)

164. *Coryphantha macromeris* var. *macromeris.*

165. *Coryphantha macromeris* var. *macromeris*, Doña
Ana Co., New Mexico. (D. & M. Zimmerman)

166. *Coryphantha minima*, near Marathon, Brewster
Co., Texas. (D. & M. Zimmerman)

167. *Coryphantha vivipara* var. *bisbeeana*. (W. P. Martin)

169 (*below*). *Coryphantha vivipara* var. *desertii*. (J. A. Noble)

168. *Coryphantha vivipara* var. *arizonica*. (S. Farwig)

170. *Coryphantha vivipara* var. *alversonii*. (J. A. Noble)

171 & 172 (*above left & right*). *Coryphantha vivipara* var. *rosea*. 171: from Hunt's Canyon, Nevada. (Both S. Farwig; 172 from *The Native Cacti of California*)

173 (*left*). *Coryphantha hesteri*. (S. Farwig)

174. *Coryphantha ramillosa*. (R. Wauer)

176. *Coryphantha dasyacantha* var. *dasyacantha*. (R. Wauer)

175. *Coryphantha cornifera* var. *echinus*, from Texas. (S. Farwig)

177 (*below*). *Coryphantha recurvata*, near Nogales, Santa Cruz Co., Arizona. (D. & M. Zimmerman)

178. *Coryphantha duncanii*, Big Bend National Park, Brewster Co., Texas. (D. & M. Zimmerman)

179. *Coryphantha missouriensis* var. *marstonii*, in flower and fruit. (S. Farwig)

180. *Coryphantha missouriensis* var. *marstonii*, in fruit.

181. Living rock, *Ariocarpus fissuratus*. (S. Farwig)

182. *Mammillaria heyderi* var. *macdougalii*, Arizona. (J. A. Noble)

184 (*below*). *Mammillaria heyderi* var. *meiacantha*, with few but stout spines in each areole, the tubercles somewhat pyramidal, and the fruits purplish. (R. Wauer)

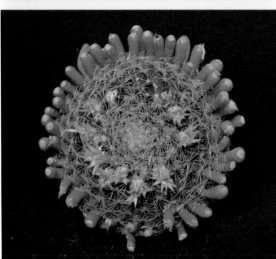

183 (*above*). *Mammillaria heyderi* var. *heyderi*.

185. *Mammillaria heyderi* var. *heyderi*. (R. Wauer)

186 (*above left*). *Mammillaria lasiacantha.*
(R. Wauer)

187 (*above right*). *Mammillaria pottsii.*
(S. Farwig)

188 (*right*). *Mammillaria dioica.* (J. A. Noble)

189 (*below left*). *Mammillaria microcarpa*, near
Superior, Pinal Co., Arizona. (From *The Cacti
of Arizona*)

190 (*below right*). A fish-hook cactus,
Mammillaria thornberi. (W. P. Martin)

191. A fish-hook cactus, *Mammillaria viridiflora*, near Tyrone, Grant Co., New Mexico. (D. & M. Zimmerman)

192. A fish-hook cactus, *Mammillaria grahamii* var. *grahamii*, near Colossal Cave, Pima Co., Arizona.

193 (*above*). A fish-hook cactus, *Mammillaria wrightii*, at 1,950 m (6,000 ft), Grant Co., New Mexico. (D. & M. Zimmerman)

194 (*left*). A fish-hook cactus, *Mammillaria wrightii*. (W. P. Martin)

lowish, 4.5-6 mm long; anthers pale yellow, elliptic, to 1 mm long; style pale yellowish-green, ±12
mm long, 0.5 mm greatest diam; stigmas red, ±8-
10, 1 mm long, of moderate width; ovary in anthesis ±3 mm long, with a few scales; fruit green,
drying to tan or brown, with a few short, broad,
membranous scales, ellipsoid-cylindroid, ±12
mm long, ±6 mm diam, the umbilicus covered
by persistent superior floral tube; seed black,
minutely and regularly papillate-reticulate except
near hilum, crescentic-ellipsoidal, 1.5 mm long,
2 mm broad, 1 mm thick; hilum incurving in
middle of the crescent.

5a. Neolloydia intertexta var. intertexta. Lime-
stone hills in grasslands at ±1,200-1,500 m
(4,000-5,000 ft). Desert Grassland and edge of
Chihuahuan Desert. Arizona from SE Pima Co. to
Santa Cruz and Cochise Cos.; New Mexico from
Bernalillo Co. to Luna and Dona Ana Cos.; Texas
from El Paso Co. to Jeff Davis and Brewster Cos.
Mexico in N Sonora and Chihuahua.

Globular or egg-shaped plants about the size of
baseballs, but in age becoming more elongate and
covered with grayish to straw-colored spines.
Often found among the grasses of hillsides, but
obscure.

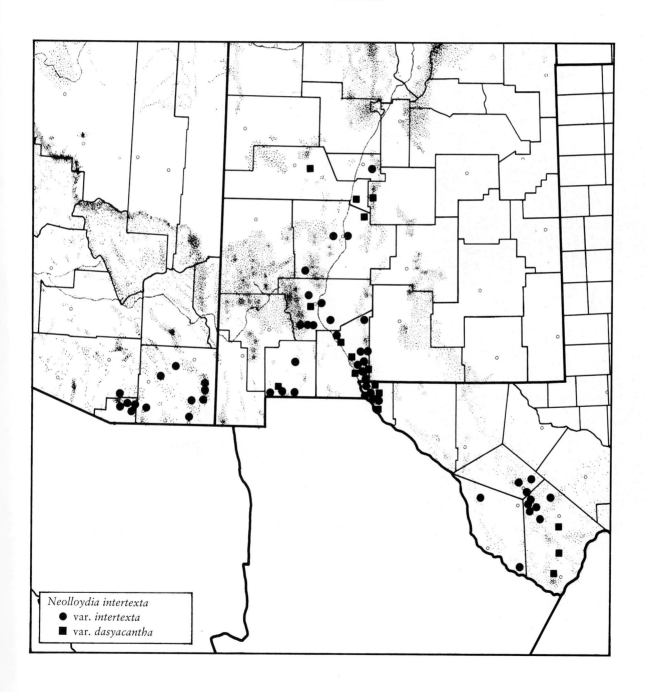

Neolloydia intertexta
● var. *intertexta*
■ var. *dasyacantha*

Fig. 829. *Neolloydia intertexta* var. *intertexta*. *1*, Plant in flower, natural size. *2–8*, Areoles of various ages. *9*, Fruit. *10*, Seed: *a*, natural size; *b*, ×10; *c*, papillate surface; *d*, contents; *e*, embryo. (Paulus Roetter in Engelmann/Emory, *pl. 34*)

5b. Neolloydia intertexta var. **dasyacantha** (Engelmann) L. Benson. On limestone hills and mountains in desert at 900-1,500 m (3,000-5,000 ft). Mostly Chihuahuan Desert; Desert Grassland. New Mexico from Luna and Valencia Cos. to Bernalillo and Dona Ana Cos.; Texas in El Paso and Brewster Cos.

The cylindroid plants are majestic for their size, and they are conspicuous when one is near by. The coat of tannish or brownish to straw-colored spines is shaggy.

Fig. 830. *Neolloydia intertexta* var. *intertexta* in flower, showing the spines in the areoles on the tubercles along the ribs of the stem. (Perhaps C. H. Thompson; courtesy of Missouri Botanical Garden)

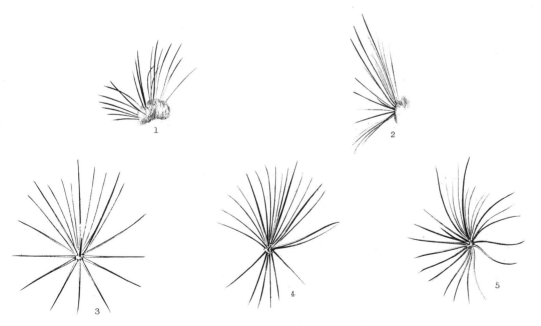

Fig. 831. *Neolloydia intertexta* var. *dasyacantha*, areoles with spines. (Paulus Roetter in Engelmann/Emory, *pl. 35*)

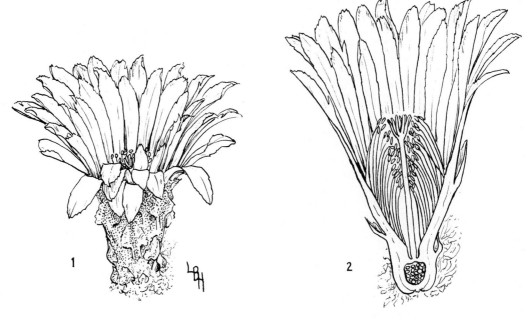

Fig. 832. *Neolloydia intertexta* var. *dasyacantha*, ×2. *1*, Flower. *2*, Flower in longitudinal section.

6. Neolloydia erectocentra (Coulter) L. Benson

Stem solitary, ovoid or somewhat cylindroid, 10-22.5(37) cm long, 7.5-10(12) cm diam; ribs ±15-21, the indentations between tubercles sharp and narrow; tubercles mammillate, ±6-12 mm long, 6 mm broad, protruding 6 mm; areoles 3-4.5 mm long, narrow, typically ±6 mm apart; spines dense, obscuring surface of stem; central spines dark-tipped, reddish, pink, or purplish, or sometimes the lower halves straw-colored, 1-4 per areole, the upper turned upward, the lower (principal) central spreading or turned upward, straight or slightly curving, the longer 1.2-3.5 cm long, basally ±1 mm diam, acicular, circular in cross section; radial spines either similar to the central or straw-colored and half the diam, 11-15 per areole, appressed, the lateral often pectinate, straight, the longer 1.2-2.5 cm long, basally 0.5-0.8 mm diam, acicular, nearly circular in cross section; flower 3.8-5 cm diam, ±4-5 cm long; sepaloids

Distinctive Characters of the Varieties of **Neolloydia erectocentra**

Character	a. var. **erectocentra**	b. var. **acunensis**
Stems	1-15(37) cm long, to 7.5-12 cm diam	To 22.5 cm long, to 10 cm diam
Tubercles	6 mm long vertically	12 mm long vertically
Central spines	1 or 2, the longer to 1.2-2.2 cm long, basally 1 mm diam	3 or 4, the longer to 2.5-3.5 mm long
Radial spines	To 1.2-1.5 cm long, basally to 0.5+ mm diam	To 2.5 cm long, to ±0.7-0.8 mm diam
Flower	To 3.8-4.4 cm diam and long, the petaloids pink	To 5 cm diam and long, the petaloids coral or orange-pink
Altitude	900-1,300 m (3,000-4,300 ft)	400-600 m (1,300-2,000 ft)
Floristic association	Upper Arizona Desert; mostly Desert Grassland	Colorado Desert; Arizona Desert

with purplish-green midribs and pale pink to coral or orange-pink margins, the larger oblanceolate, to 25-30 mm long, to 6-7.5 mm broad, angular or cuspidate, entire; petaloids pink or rarely white, the largest spathulate-oblanceolate, to 30-40 mm long, to 10 mm broad, each with a small cusp, entire; filaments very slender, ±6 mm long; anthers yellow, ellipsoidal, to ±1 mm long; style 12-15 mm long, 1.5 mm greatest diam; stigmas probably 10, 1.5+ mm long, stout; ovary in anthesis broadly obconical; fruit green, drying to tannish, with several membranous, minutely and sharply denticulate scales, subcylindroid, ±10 mm long, ±7.5 mm diam, opening by a dorsal slit or along 2 lines, these sometimes irregular; seeds minutely and regularly papillate except near hilum, crescentic-ellipsoidal, broader than long, 1.5 mm long, 2 mm broad, 1 mm thick; hilum incurving in middle of crescent.

6a. Neolloydia erectocentra var. erectocentra. Limestone of alluvial fans and hills in upper desert and in grassland at about 900-1,300 m (3,000-4,300 ft). Upper part of Arizona Desert and Desert

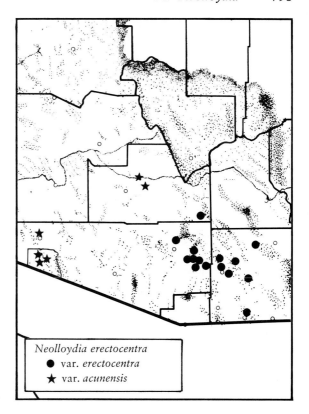

Neolloydia erectocentra
● var. *erectocentra*
★ var. *acunensis*

Fig. 833. *Neolloydia erectocentra* var. *erectocentra* on limestone in southeastern Pima Co., Arizona.

Grassland. Southeastern Arizona from se Pinal Co. and e Pima Co. to w Cochise Co.

The reddish-spined cylindroid stems are hidden among grasses during the summer rainy season, but they are more conspicuous at other times of the year.

6b. Neolloydia erectocentra var. **acunensis** (W. T. Marshall) L. Benson. Limestone hills and flats in desert at 400-600 m (1,300-2,000 ft). Colorado and Arizona Deserts. Arizona in Organ Pipe Cactus National Monument, w Pima Co., and e to Sand Tank Mts., Maricopa Co., and to Pinal Co. Mexico in adjacent Sonora.

The egg-shaped to cylindroid plants are inconspicuous among the large rock fragments or gravel of desert hillsides.

Fig. 834. *Neolloydia erectocentra* var. *erectocentra*, stem, showing the erect central spine in each areole. (C. H. Thompson, 1910; courtesy of Missouri Botanical Garden)

Fig. 835. *Neolloydia erectocentra* var. *erectocentra* in flower. (Homer L. Shantz)

Fig. 836. *Neolloydia erectocentra* var. *acunensis* on limestone at the type locality in Acuña Valley, Organ Pipe Cactus National Monument, Pima Co., Arizona.

Fig. 837. *Neolloydia erectocentra* var. *acunensis*, showing the tubercles and spines, including the erect principal central spine.

Fig. 838. *Neolloydia erectocentra* var. *acunensis* in flower.

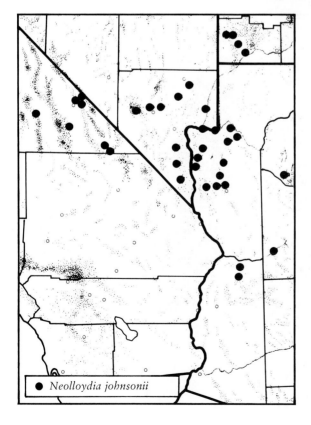

● *Neolloydia johnsonii*

7. Neolloydia johnsonii (Parry) L. Benson

Stem solitary or rarely branching (perhaps following injury to terminal bud), ovoid-cylindroid to ellipsoid-cylindroid, mostly 10-15(25) cm long, 5-10 cm diam; ribs 17-21, clearly developed but strongly indented just above each tubercle and gradually rising to the next; tubercles ±12 mm long, ±6 mm broad, protruding ±6 mm; areoles elliptic, 4.5 mm long, 3 mm broad, typically ±12 mm apart; spines dense, obscuring stem; central spines pink to reddish, in age blackened, 4-9 per areole, divaricately spreading, straight or slightly curving, the longer 3-4 cm long, basally 1-1.25 (1.5) mm diam, acicular, nearly circular in cross section; radial spines similar but smaller and sometimes lighter in color, ±9 or 10 per areole, longer 1.2-2(2.5) cm long, basally ±0.5-0.75 mm diam, acicular, circular to elliptic in cross section; flower 5-7.5 cm diam, 5-6 cm long; sepaloids with purplish or purplish-brown midribs and magenta to pink margins or yellow or greenish-yellow, larger oblanceolate or broadly so, 25-30 mm long, 6-10 mm broad, mucronulate, entire but middle scales scarious-margined and lower fimbriate; petaloids magenta to pink or greenish and turning to yellow, largest broadly oblanceolate, ±30 mm long, ±10 mm broad, acute to mucronulate, entire; filaments pink, 6-9 mm long; anthers slender, ±1.5 mm long; style probably pink, ±25 mm long, ±1.5 mm greatest diam; stigmas ±10, 1.5-3 mm long, rather thick; ovary in anthesis ±9-12 mm long, the scales fimbriate; fruit green, drying to tan, with several scarious-margined fimbriate scales, ellipsoid-cylindroid, ±12 mm long, 10 mm diam, splitting open along dorsal side; seeds minutely papillate except near hi-lum, 2 mm long, 2.5 mm broad, 1.5 mm thick; hilum deeply depressed.

Granitic soils of hills and alluvial fans in desert at 500-1,200 m (1,700-4,000 ft). Mojavean Desert and edge of Colorado Desert. California in Death Valley region, Inyo Co.; Nevada in Clark Co.; Utah in Washington Co.; Arizona in Mohave, w Yavapai, and n Yuma Cos.

These small barrels, known to some as keg cacti, have a dense covering of usually brown to red spines. They are visible for as much as 15-30 m (50-100 ft).

Fig. 839. *Neolloydia johnsonii* on granitic soil in the Mojavean Desert near the Santa Maria River, Yavapai Co., Arizona.

15. Ancistrocactus

Stems strongly succulent, solitary or rarely (probably after injury to terminal bud) with a few branches, dark green, nearly globose in young plants, varying to obovoid, ellipsoid, obovoid-cylindroid, obconical, turbinate, or globose in older plants; ribs of stem clearly present or in younger stems ribs none and tubercles separate. Leaves not visibly developed on mature tubercles. Central spines on juvenile stems 1 per areole, on mature stems 3 or 4, lowest hooked, others straight and turned upward; radial spines 6-22, straight or some of lower ones hooked. Flowers and fruits from new tubercles on growth of current season, on rib segments near stem apex; flower-bearing portion of areole of young stem nearly circular to elliptic and adjacent to spine-bearing portion of areole at apex of tubercle; flowers of later seasons produced lower and lower on the new tubercles and ultimately from their bases, the felted connecting groove becoming longer and longer and finally extending full length of the tubercle, these grooves persisting for many years. Flower ±2.5-3 cm diam and long; floral tube obconic to funnelform; sepaloids various; petaloids green to cream-colored, pale yellow, red, or rose-purple; anthers yellow or golden-yellow; style greenish or reddish; stigmas 6-10; ovary not obscured by hairs. Fruit at maturity green or red or with a rosy flush, fleshy, indehiscent, bearing (1)2-13 (or numerous) membranous scales. Seed dark brown or black, finely papillate, domelike, broader than long or the reverse, ±1.5-2 mm greatest dimension; hilum obviously basal or appearing "lateral"; cotyledons accumbent, *not* foliaceous.

Three species occurring in southern Texas and adjacent Mexico in the Rio Grande region, a fourth occurring farther south.

The name means "fishhook cactus."

The closest relationship of this species group is to *Coryphantha* and *Neolloydia,* all the proposed genera being in the vast and complex group of plants standing more or less intermediate between *Mammillaria* and *Echinocactus, sensu latu,* as interpreted by Engelmann. Although not all the genera proposed in this group are valid, some are, and the writer is attempting to unscramble the complex mosaic of relationships. Here, *Ancistrocactus* is accepted tentatively as valid. Clarification of some of its component species has been undertaken by the writer (Benson, Cactaceas y Suculentas Méxicanas 11: 3-8, 25-26. 1966).

As currently understood, the genus comprises four species, one of them extraterritorial.

1. *A. tobuschii*
2. *A. scheeri*
3. *A. uncinatus*
   vars. a. *wrightii*
              uncinatus (Mexico)
   A. crassihamatus (Querétaro)

KEY TO THE SPECIES OF ANCISTROCACTUS

1. Radial spines not hooked; principal central spine (lower hooked one) 1.2-4.5 cm long; petaloids green or cream to yellow; ovary and fruit bearing (1)2-13 scale-leaves, green or red-tinged at maturity, thin-walled, not juicy; seed broader than long, the hilum therefore appearing "lateral."
   2. Spines finely hairy (scaberulous-canescent); radial spines 7-9 per areole, spreading rather irregularly; stem almost flat-topped, turbinate or obconical, arising only slightly above ground level. . . . . .1. **A. tobuschii**
   2. Spines glabrous; radial spines 12-20 per areole, spreading rather uniformly; stem at maturity obovoid-cylindroid, elongate (beginning to flower while still juvenile and obovoid), rising conspicuously above ground level. . . . . .2. **A. scheeri**

1. Radial spines (some longer ones) hooked; principal central spine (lower hooked one) 5-7.5(11.2) cm long; petaloids red; ovary and fruit bearing numerous scale-leaves, red at maturity, fleshy, thick-walled, juicy; seed longer than broad, the hilum therefore obviously basal . . . . .3. **A. uncinatus**

1. Ancistrocactus tobuschii
W. T. Marshall *ex* Backeberg

Roots fibrous; stems normally solitary, rarely branching and then probably because of injury to terminal bud; larger stems obconical or turnip-shaped, 4-5 cm long, 4-5 cm diam; ribs unknown; tubercles 6-9 mm long, 6 mm broad, protruding ±9-12 mm; areoles ±4.5 mm diam, typically ±9-12 mm apart; spines rather dense and somewhat obscuring tubercles, finely scaberulous-canescent; central spines at first light yellow with red tips, changing to gray, 3 per areole, upper 2 straight and turned upward, the lower one hooked and spreading, perpendicular to stem, the upper ones longer than lower, to 2.2 cm long, basally to ±0.4 mm broad, subulate, somewhat flattened, narrowly elliptic in cross section; radial spines like centrals but smaller, 7-9 per areole, spreading somewhat irregularly, straight, the longer to 12 mm long, basally ±0.2 mm diam, acicular, broadly elliptic in section; flower to 3-4 cm diam and long; sepaloids with brownish-red midribs and pale yellow margins, the larger elliptic-oblong, 12-15 mm long, ±6 mm broad, apically rounded, entire; petaloids light yellow or cream-colored, largest nearly oblanceolate but somewhat rounded apically, ±15 mm long, ±4.5 mm broad, irregularly indented; filaments cream-colored, 6 mm long; anthers golden-yellow, ±0.7 mm long; style green, ±17 mm long, 1 mm diam; stigmas 6 or 7, ±1 mm long, rather broad; ovary in anthesis ±4 mm long, 6 mm diam; fruit green at maturity (reportedly with a "rosy flush" when fully ripe), with apparently only 1-3 scales, these broad, membranous, and irregularly lobed, the fruit 2.5-3 cm long, ±9-15 mm diam; seeds black, finely papillate, 1.5 mm long, 1.5+ mm broad, 1 mm thick.

Limestone of hills and flats; among junipers, oaks, and grasses at about 420 m (1,400 ft). Edwards Plateau. Texas in Bandera Co. near Vanderpool.

The rounded biscuitlike plants are obscure and rare, and they have been collected only three or four times.

2. Ancistrocactus scheeri
(Salm-Dyck) Britton & Rose

Roots fibrous or tuberous; stem solitary, ellipsoid to nearly globose or obovoid or elongate-obovoid, 2.5-10(15) cm long, 2.5-5(10) cm diam; ribs present, adnate with tubercles; tubercles ±6-12 mm long, 6-9 mm broad, protruding 6-12 mm; areoles ±1.5-3 mm diam, typically 6-9 mm apart; spines dense, in older plants obscuring stem; principal central spines ventrally pale grayish or whitish and tending dorsally to be black on the lower portions and on the curve of the hook, porrect, strongly hooked; spines variable from plant to plant and commonly but not always differing according to maturity of stem, as follows: (1) *juvenile plants* and some mature ones (known commonly as *A. scheeri*) and lower (first-formed) portions of older stems:—longer principal central spines 0.9-1.2 cm long to curve of hook, basally to 0.8 mm diam, acicular, nearly circular in cross section, the upper centrals 0-2(3), pale gray, flattened, the middle central (if present) usually short and weak, the 2 laterals to 0.9-1.2 cm long; radial spines gray or tannish, 15-22 per areole, radiating precisely parallel to stem, straight, the longer ±6 mm long, basally ±0.2 mm diam, acicular, nearly circular in cross section; (2) *mature plants* (known commonly as "*A. brevihamatus*"):—longer principal central spines ±2.5-4.5 cm long to curve of hook, basally 1 mm diam, acicular, nearly circular in cross section, the upper centrals whitish, usually 3, flattened, the middle upper central 0.9-1.5 cm long, weak, the 2 lateral centrals to 3 cm long, stouter; radial spines nearly white (pale gray), 12 (to ±20) per areole, spreading, but usually not as precisely as in juvenile plants, longer ±9 mm long, basally ±0.3 mm diam, acicular, nearly circular in cross section; flower funnelform, ±2.5-3 cm long; sepaloids dorsally with greenish to purplish midribs and greenish-white margins, ventrally purple-tinged, larger narrowly lanceolate, 10-15(20) mm long, 2-4 mm broad, marginally scarious and denticulate; petaloids greenish with a median purplish tinge, largest lanceolate, 20-30 mm long, 2-3 mm broad, acute and short-acuminate, entire; stamens numerous; filaments reddish, 7-10 mm long; anthers yellow, oblong, 0.5 mm long; style greenish-white, 12-15 mm long, 1.2 mm greatest diam; stigmas ±10, red, 2 mm long, 0.5 mm broad, slender; ovary in anthesis 6-8 mm long, bearing a few scales; fruit green, somewhat fleshy but thin-walled and finally dry at maturity, with 8-13 membranous scales, 1.2-2.5 cm long, 6-9 mm diam; seeds brown, finely papillate, 1.5 mm long, 2 mm broad, 1 mm thick.

Grassy plains and open hills or brushy areas in grasslands at low elevations. Rio Grande Plain. Texas on plains and hills mostly near Rio Grande from Val Verde Co. to Jim Wells and Hidalgo Cos. Northern Mexico in Nuevo León and Tamaulipas.

The green cylinders have a thin to dense and shaggy coat of spines, which forms a pepper-and-salt mixture of gray, brown, and black like the fur of a jackrabbit. Younger plants and some genetically different older ones do not have a real coat of spines, and the green shows more prominently, though it is punctuated by short, hooklike central spines. These cacti grow among bushes and in the openings between them. For their size, they are relatively inconspicuous.

The first-described species was *Echinocactus scheeri* Salm-Dyck in 1850. There was no type specimen, and the interpretation of Engelmann was accepted and validated (L. Benson, *Cactaceas y Suculentas Méxicanas* 11: 8. 1966) by naming as a neotype the specimen Engelmann had in mind. His illustration and description are of a juvenile plant, and the epithet *scheeri* has been applied in various books to juvenile plants thought to be adults. In the herbaria the juvenile plants

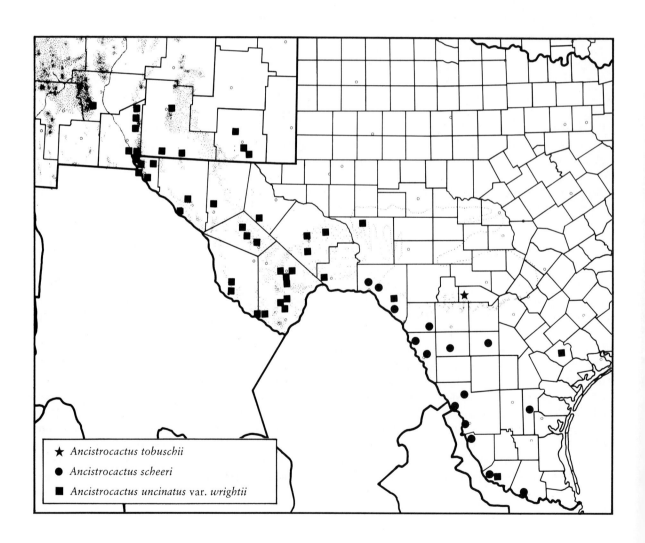

★ *Ancistrocactus tobuschii*

● *Ancistrocactus scheeri*

■ *Ancistrocactus uncinatus* var. *wrightii*

Fig. 840. *Ancistrocactus scheeri,* five plants illustrating the great variation from individual to individual: central plant the type known commonly as *A. scheeri;* lower two plants the type long called *Sclerocactus* or *Echinocactus brevihamatus;* upper two intermediate; all plants from the same population.

and the adults (described as *Ancistrocactus brevihamatus*) are shown to have the same geographical range, and in the field they occur together, both or neither showing the tuberous roots of the proposed *A. megarhizus* (Rose) Britton & Rose. Often the lower (juvenile) part of a stem may show the spine characters of *A. scheeri,* whereas the upper (mature) part of the same stem (above a transition zone) has those of *A. brevihamatus.* Parallel to this is a transition of flower development and position: *low on the stem,* there is a nearly circular to elliptic flower-bearing portion of the areole at the apex of each tubercle; *midway up the stem,* an elongate flower-bearing segment of the areole reaches to about midlevel of the ventral side (toward the growing point at the stem apex) of the tubercle; and *on the upper part of*

the stem, a greatly elongate, slitlike flower-bearing segment extends the full length of the tubercle. Thus the key characters of the two proposed species may be those of stages in development of the same individual—though there are some similar variations among adult plants (cf. *L. Benson 16526, 16534, 16535, 16542, 16543, 16546,* all *Pom*). Flower color, the other "key character," has not been known well enough for correlation. Originally it was given by Engelmann as green for *A. scheeri* and rose-purple for *A. brevihamatus.* In 1973, Archie D. Wood of Roma, Texas, made many collections of both types of plants and intermediates (*Pom*). These all had green flowers. The description given here is based on mature plants that flowered in December 1973.

According to Wood (letter of September 9,

Fig. 842. *Ancistrocactus scheeri*, plant of the "*brevi-hamatus*" type, shaggy with dense, long spines; in fruit.

1971), *Ancistrocactus scheeri* flowers over a long period at the coldest time of year along the lower Rio Grande; and since few botanists collect at this time of year, there have been no intact flowers or fruits in herbarium specimens. The flowering, as with many cacti of the Mexican Plateau, "seems to be triggered by a photoperiod comparable [to that of] the shortest day of the year" at about the 30th parallel of latitude. Wood reports that he did not see "these plants in flower until . . . after the monte got a good soaking in the hurricane of September, 1967." The flowers open toward noon in bright sunshine, and each flower opens on two, three, or more days. The flowering period during the winter of 1967-68 began about November 30 and ended in early March. On April 7 the plants bore green and maturing fruits. On March 2, 1969, all plants had finished flowering, and on March 9 fruits were maturing. On May 10, 1970, plants that had flowered during the preceding winter bore "heavy crowns of mature fruit[s]." The plants do not respond to rains during the late spring or the summer.

Fig. 841. *Ancistrocactus scheeri*, plant of the "*scheeri*" type with few and short spines, the fruits green at maturity.

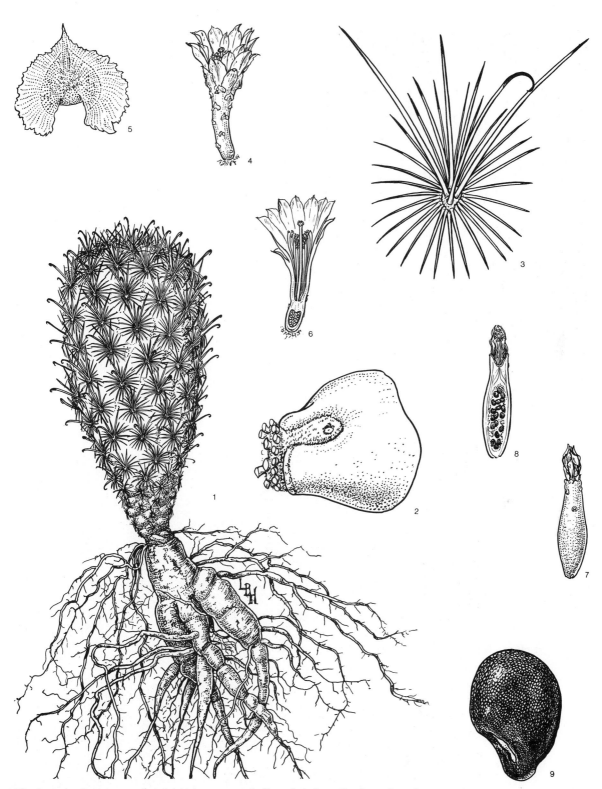

Fig. 843. *Ancistrocactus scheeri*, ×1.1, except as indicated. *1*, Juvenile plant, the only type long recognized as belonging to this species, the spines small, ×.9. *2*, Tubercle with the spines cut off, ×3; the flower-bearing area (of the areole of a juvenile plant) almost merging with the spine-bearing area, the connecting groove short or none. *3*, Areole with four central spines, the lower one hooked, and with a circle of radial spines, ×2.25. *4*, Flower. *5*, Scale-leaf from the floral cup covering and adnate with the ovary, ×5.5. *6*, Flower in longitudinal section. *7*, Fruit, the scale-leaves of the surface few. *8*, Fruit in longitudinal section. *9*, Seed, the hilum seemingly "oblique," ×23. (See Credits)

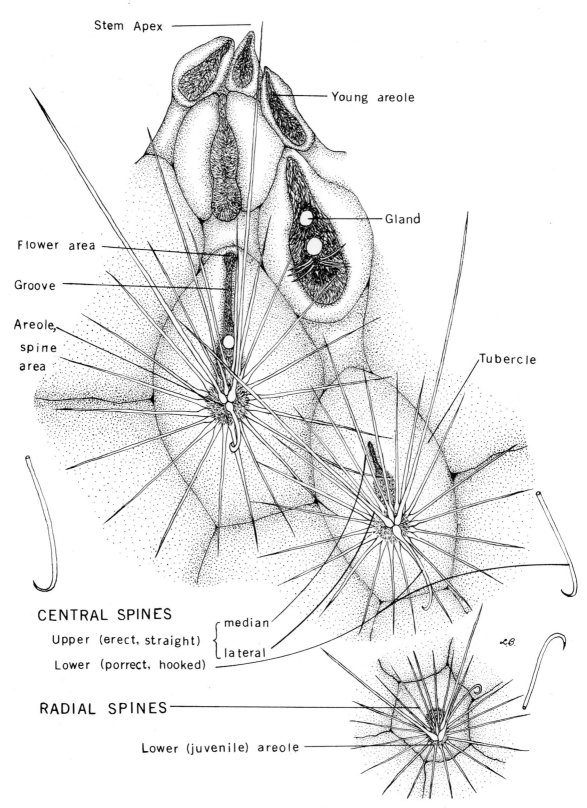

Stem Apex

Young areole

Gland

Flower area

Groove

Areole,
spine
area

Tubercle

CENTRAL SPINES
Upper (erect, straight) { median
Lower (porrect, hooked) lateral

RADIAL SPINES

Lower (juvenile) areole

Fig. 844. *Ancistrocactus scheeri*, enlargement of a few tubercles of various ages showing the developmental stages of the areoles they bear, several tubercles from the upper part of the plant and one from the lower part produced when the plant was in the juvenile stage. In the upper areoles the felted groove between the spine- and flower-bearing portions of the areole becomes longer and longer. (See Credits)

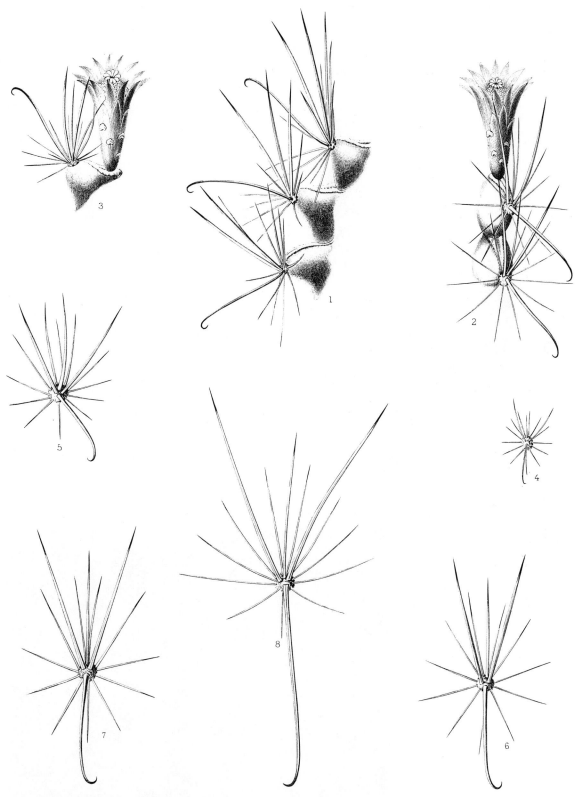

Fig. 845. *Ancistrocactus scheeri*, areoles and flowers. *1–3*, Tubercles with the spine-bearing and flower-bearing areas connected by a long groove, this extending from the base to the apex of each tubercle, illustrating the relationship of spines and flowers in mature plants. *4–8*, Spine clusters. (Paulus Roetter in Engelmann/Emory, *pl. 19*)

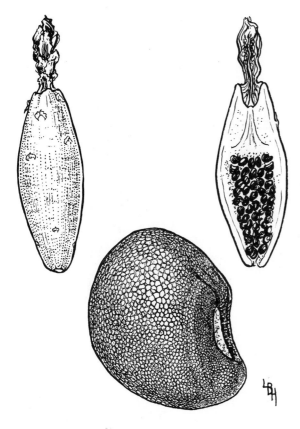

Fig. 846. *Ancistrocactus scheeri,* fruit and a seed. *Left,* mature fruit, ×2. *Right,* fruit in longitudinal section, ×2. *Center,* seed, ×26.

3. **Ancistrocactus uncinatus** (Galeotti) L. Benson

Stems unbranched, green, cylindroid-ovoid to ovoid, 7.5-15 cm long, 5-7.5(10) cm diam; ribs present, but constrictions between tubercles basally slitlike; tubercles elongate, 20-25 mm long, 6-9 mm broad, protruding 9-15 mm; areoles ±4.5 mm diam, typically 10-25 mm apart; spines abundant and conspicuous on joint; central spines light-colored (i.e. tannish-white) to straw-colored or pinkish, in mature stems 1-4 per areole, principal central turned upward, conspicuously and effectively hooked, 5-7.5(11.2) cm long, basally ±1(1.3) mm broad, somewhat flattened, elliptic in cross section; lower radial spines reddish or reddish-tan, some hooked, only slightly flattened, the upper radials pale, tan or straw-colored, not hooked, flattened, middle upper radial markedly so, 8-10 per areole, perpendicular to axis of tubercle, the longer 2.5-5 cm long, basally mostly ±1 mm broad or diam, the lower radials acicular, the upper subulate, elliptic to linear in section, the most flattened and uppermost radial (which may be interpreted as a central) basally to 1.5 mm broad; flower 2.5-3 cm diam, 2-4 cm long; sepaloids with brownish midribs, adjacent areas red, the margins white-scarious, the larger broadly oblanceolate, 12-20 mm long, to 6 mm broad, acute, fimbriolate-denticulate; petaloids brick red

Fig. 847. *Ancistrocactus uncinatus* var. *wrightii,* relatively young plant in cultivation, just beginning to produce the long, strongly hooked, upward-turned principal central spines. (Perhaps C. H. Thompson, about 1905; courtesy of Missouri Botanical Garden)

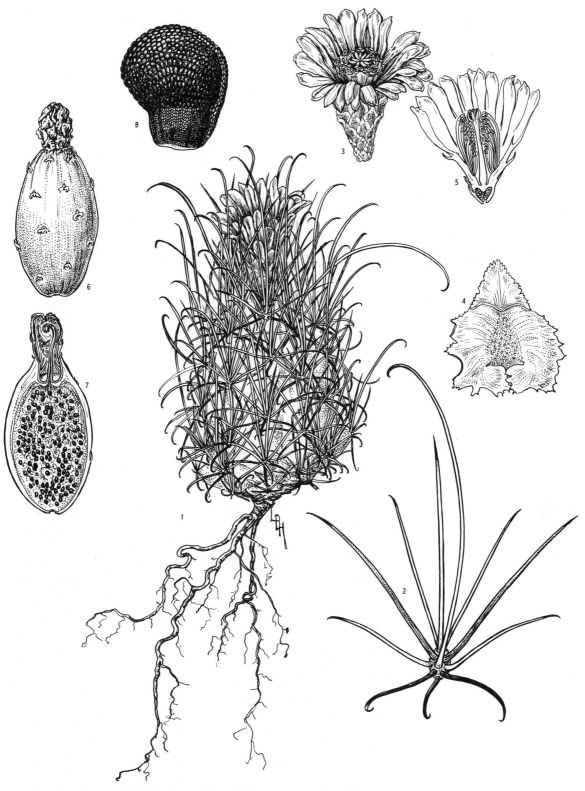

Fig. 848. *Ancistrocactus uncinatus* var. *wrightii*, ×1.1, except as indicated. *1*, Young plant in flower, ×.6. *2*, Areole with four central spines; the lower or principal central hooked and pale tan, the two lateral ones light red, and the upper (also interpreted by some as a radial spine) light-colored; and with several radial spines, the lower ones dark red and hooked. *3*, Flower. *4*, Scale-leaf from the floral tube covering and adnate with the ovary of the flower, the center maroon and the edges white, ×12. *5*, Flower in longitudinal section, ×12. *6*, Fruit. *7*, Fruit in longitudinal section. *8*, Seed, ×23.

or with some purple, largest oblanceolate, ±12 mm long, 4.5 mm broad, acute, sparsely minutely denticulate; filaments yellow, 6 mm long; anthers yellow, narrowly oblong, 1 mm long; style reddish, to 12 mm long, ±1.5 mm greatest diam; stigmas ±10, to 3 mm long, slender; ovary in anthesis covered with fimbriolate-dentate scales, broadly obconical, 6 mm long; fruit red, fleshy at maturity, with numerous conspicuous auriculate, deltoid scales ±4.5 mm long, the fruit 2-2.5 cm long, 12-15 mm diam, indehiscent, the perianth persistent; seed with the upper two-thirds minutely papillate and basal portion smooth, irregularly oblong-obovoid, 1.5 mm long, 1 mm broad, 0.8 mm thick; hilum obviously basal, surrounded by a broad border.

3a. Ancistrocactus uncinatus var. **wrightii** (Engelmann) L. Benson. Radial spines 8-10; upper sepaloids obtuse; petaloids obtuse to acute; seed

curving somewhat, the rim around hilum conspicuous, ±1-1.2 mm across. Limestone soils of hills and alluvial fans in desert at 900-1,200 m (3,000-4,000 ft). Chihuahuan Desert. New Mexico from Sierra to s Chaves and Eddy Cos.; Texas from El Paso Co. to Crockett and Val Verde Cos. and rare in Starr and Victoria Cos. Mexico in Chihuahua.

This cactus forms a conspicuous light-colored spot against the darker background of soil and desert plants. The plant is forbidding, covered everywhere with long, protruding, light tan fishhooks that divert attention from other characters.

Ancistrocactus uncinatus var. **uncinatus.** Radial spines 7 or 8; upper sepaloids aristate; petaloids acuminate and aristate; seeds markedly curving, the rim around the hilum small, ±0.8 mm across. Mexico from Chihuahua and Coahuila to San Luis Potosí; not in the U.S.

16. Coryphantha

Stems solitary or branching, sometimes forming mounds of 200+ stems, the larger subglobose to cylindroid, 2.5-10(12.5) cm long, 2.5-7.5 cm diam; ribs none; tubercles separate. Leaves not discernible on mature tubercles. Areoles circular to elliptic. Spines smooth, white to gray, pink, yellow, brown, or black; central spines 1-10+ per areole, grading into radials, straight, curved, hooked, or somewhat twisted, 3-25(50) mm long, basally 0.2-1 mm diam or width, acicular or sometimes subulate, narrowly to broadly elliptic in cross section; radial spines usually same color as or lighter than centrals, 5-40 per areole, usually straight, 3-25 mm long, basally 0.1-0.5 mm diam, acicular. Flowers and fruits on new growth of current season at apex of stem or branch, developed in special area at base of upper side of tubercle distant from spine-bearing part of areole and connected with it by a narrow isthmus persisting for many years as an elongate felted groove on tubercle. (On immature stems, and on all stems of *Coryphantha macromeris*, the flower-bearing area is nearly circular and at or above midlevel on the tubercle; see Boke (1952) for development in *Coryphantha vivipara*.) Flower 1.2-5 cm diam; floral tube above ovary funnelform, green or tinged with perianth color, i.e. with pink, magenta, reddish-purple, yellow-green, or yellow. Fruit fleshy, green or red at maturity, thin-walled, without surface appendages, usually ellipsoid, clavate, or cylindroid, 30-55 mm long, 2-20 mm diam; floral tube deciduous, indehiscent. Seeds tan, brown, or black, smooth and shining or punctate or reticulate, *usually* broader than long, 1-2 mm greatest dimension; hilum usually appearing "lateral" but sometimes obviously basal or "oblique"; cotyledons accumbent, not foliaceous.

Some 30-40 species occurring from southern Alberta to central Mexico; 15 in Canada and the U.S.

The generic name, which means "top flower," derives from the position of the flowers at the apex of the stem.

A large genus, with about two-thirds of its described species reported from south of the Rio Grande. The extraterritorial species have not been studied fully.

1. C. *minima*
2. C. *macromeris*
   vars. a. *macromeris*
       b. *runyonii*
   C. *ottonis* (central Mexico)
   C. *poselgeriana* (Coahuila to Nuevo León & Zacatecas)
   C. *difficilis* (Mexico)
3. C. *scheeri*
   vars. a. *scheeri*
       b. *valida*
       c. *uncinata*
       d. *robustispina*
   C. *echinoidea* (Durango)
   C. *clava* (Hidalgo; near C. *octacantha*)
   C. *octacantha* (central Mexico)
   C. *exsudans* (Hidalgo)
   C. *asterias* (Mexico)
   C. *erecta* (Hidalgo)
   C. *elephantidens* (central Mexico)
   C. *bumamma* (Mexico; near C. *elephantidens*)
   C. *andreae* (Vera Cruz; near C. *elephantidens*)
   C. *pseudoechinus* (Coahuila)
   C. *schwartziana* (central Mexico)
   C. *unicornis* (Coahuila)
   C. *werdermannii* (N Mexico)
4. C. *vivipara*
   vars. a. *vivipara*
       b. *radiosa*
       c. *bisbeeana*
       d. *arizonica*
       e. *desertii*
       f. *alversonii*
       g. *rosea*
5. C. *hesteri*
6. C. *ramillosa*

7. *C. sulcata*
   vars. a. *sulcata*
       b. *nickelsiae*
   C. connivens (Valley of Mexico)
   C. sulcolanata (Hidalgo?)
   C. retusa (Oaxaca)
   C. palmeri (Durango to San Luis Potosí)
   C. compacta (Chihuahua)
8. *C. cornifera*
   vars. a. *echinus*
           cornifera (Mexico)
   C. gladiispina (Coahuila)
   C. clavata (San Luis Potosí)
   C. salm-dyckiana (Chihuahua)
   C. pallida (Puebla)
   C. pycnantha (Oaxaca)
   C. durangensis (N Mexico)
9. *C. recurvata*
10. *C. strobiliformis*
    vars. a. *strobiliformis*
        b. *durispina*

   c. *orcuttii*
   C. chihuahuensis (Chihuahua)
   C. chaffeyi (Zacatecas)
   C. lloydii (Zacatecas)
   C. muehlenbaueriana (N Mexico)
   C. roseana (N Mexico)
11. *C. sneedii*
    vars. a. *sneedii*
        b. *leei*
12. *C. dasyacantha*
    vars. a. *dasyacantha*
        b. *varicolor*
13. *C. robertii*
14. *C. duncanii*
15. *C. missouriensis*
    vars. a. *missouriensis*
        b. *marstonii*
        c. *caespitosa*
        d. *robustior*
   C. asperispina (N Mexico; status unknown)

KEY TO THE SPECIES OF CORYPHANTHA

1. Spines cylindroid with abruptly acute apices, the largest (the upper 3 of the innermost series) strongly bulbous-based, to 4.5 mm long, the spines about 20 in 2 or 3 series, gradually diminishing outward in size, especially in the upper part of the outer series (third series or vestige of a fourth); plants ovoid, about 1.2-2(2.5) cm long; near Marathon, Brewster Co., Texas . . . . .1. **C. minima**
1. Spines *not* cylindroid and *not* with abruptly acute apices, of various numbers of series and of centrals and radials; plants of various shapes and sizes.
   2. Fruit (as far as is known) green at maturity, commonly cylindroid, clavate, or ellipsoid; seeds usually brown, rarely black, usually, though not always, broader than long, the hilum usually appearing "lateral" but sometimes obviously basal; central spines usually present and differentiated from the radials.
      3. Flowers at the apex of the stem from a single series of new developing tubercles (some fruits of plants that bloom more than once a year relatively lower on the stem); central spines various.
         4. Ovary in flower and fruit bearing a few scales; flower and fruit developed at midlevel on the tubercle, the groove even in mature plants only half as long as the tubercle . . . . .2. **C. macromeris**
         4. Ovary in flower and fruit bearing no scales; flower and fruit, except on juvenile stems (or fruit scars on lower tubercles), developed at the base of the ventral (upper) side of the tubercle, and the groove as long as the tubercle (in immature stems, the groove at first much shorter than the tubercle, but becoming longer on each new crop of tubercles).
            5. Tubercles protruding 2.5-4 cm, conspicuous; central spines to 3.8 cm long, 1-1.5 mm in diameter, straw-yellow with dark red tips . . . . . . .3. **C. scheeri**
            5. Tubercles protruding no more than 1.2(2) cm; central spines no more than 1.7 cm long (if the bases are as much as 1-1.5 mm in diameter).
               6. Lower (porrect) central spine *either* shorter than the upward-directed upper ones *or* lacking; sepaloids fringed with hairs; seeds reticulate (but unknown in *C. hesteri*).
                  7. Longest spines 12-19(25) mm long; radial spines 9-25 mm long; flower 2.5-5 cm in diameter; petaloids apically mucronate to acuminate or attenuate; stigmas 1.5-3 mm long . . . . .4. **C. vivipara**

7. Longest spines 9-11 mm long; radial spines 3-9 mm long; flower 1.5-2 cm in diameter; petaloids apically acute; stigmas ±1-2 mm long..... .... **5. C. hesteri**
6. Lower (porrect) central spine longer than the upward-directed upper ones; sepaloids *not* fringed with hairs (this point not determined for *C. ramillosa*); seeds smooth and shining, *not* reticulate, sometimes minutely punctate (but unknown in *C. ramillosa*).
7A. Central spines at first dark chocolate brown, the lower porrect (principal) one remaining so; petaloids pale pink to rose-purple, not yellow; Texas near the Rio Grande in Brewster and Terrell Cos. .... **6. C. ramillosa**
7A. Central spines at first pink, yellow, or gray, the lower porrect (principal) one changing, like the others, to white or light gray; petaloids at least partly yellow; distribution as in leads 8, below.
8. Flower opening each day for 2-3 days; each petaloid yellow apically but pink basally, *not* with a bristle-like terminal lobe; seeds smooth, not punctate; s central Texas.....................**7. C. sulcata**
8. Flower opening only once, then for 1-2 hours; each petaloid yellow, with apical teeth and an elongate, bristle-like terminal lobe; seeds smooth but minutely punctate; w Texas.........**8. C. cornifera**
3. Flowers produced at the same time on several turns of a spiral near the apex of the stem, therefore some from tubercles more or less at the side of the stem; principal central spine (commonly the only one, but occasionally 1 of 2) curving downward in a low arc; s central Arizona and adjacent Sonora......... .... **9. C. recurvata**
2. Fruit red at maturity (except in some plants with persistent woody basal tubercles after fall of the spines or on mat-forming plants), of various shapes; seeds various, as in leads 3A and 4A; central spines not necessarily differentiated from the radials.
3A. Fruit elongate, either cylindroid, clavate, or ellipsoid; central spines (1-4)5-11 per areole *or* (in *C. duncanii*) the numerous spines not differentiated into centrals and radials; flowers pink or white; seeds various.
4A. Seed broader than long, the hilum appearing "lateral," the seed coat brown; stems usually branching (in 1 species profusely so).
5A. Radial spines on the upper side of the areole *not* markedly longer than those on the lower side; fruit usually bright red (rarely green) at maturity; mature stems 2.5-5 cm in diameter, 5-12.5(20) cm long, solitary or forming clumps of several branches.....................**10. C. strobiliformis**
5A. Radial spines on the upper side of the areole much longer than those on the lower side; fruit green at maturity; mature stems 1.2-2.5 cm in diameter, 2.5-7.5 cm long, branching profusely and forming extensive mats........ .... **11. C. sneedii**
4A. Seed longer than broad, the hilum obviously basal, the seed coat brown to black; stems solitary or several.
5B. Spines clearly differentiated into 1 series of larger centrals and 1 of smaller radials, 17-38 per areole altogether; seeds dark brown to black; stems solitary to numerous.
6A. Stems (so far as is known) solitary; mature stems cylindroid, 5-7.5 cm in diameter, 7.5-17.5 cm long; anthers oblong, twice as long as broad.... .... **12. C. dasyacantha**
6A. Stems branching, often profusely so; mature stems obovoid, 2-2.5 cm in diameter, (3.8)5-12 cm long; anthers ovoid, 1.5 times as long as broad .... **13. C. robertii**
5B. Spines in several series, *not* clearly differentiated into centrals and radials, but the inner series gradually somewhat larger, 30-75 per areole; seeds black; stems solitary or rarely 2-3.....................**14. C. duncanii**
3A. Fruit globular; central spines lacking or solitary or rarely 2, except in position little differentiated from the radials, straight; flowers yellow or rarely red; seeds black, slightly longer than broad, the hilum obviously basal................ .... **15. C. missouriensis**

Fig. 849. *Coryphantha minima*, in flower, showing the spines, these narrowed gradually upward and with abrupt acute apices.

1. Coryphantha minima Baird

Plant simple or infrequently sparingly branched, ovoid, 1.2-2(2.5) cm long, 1.2 cm diam; tubercles subcylindroid, 1.5-2.25 mm long and broad, protruding 3 mm; areoles only slightly woolly, 1 mm diam, typically 3-4.5 mm apart; spines dense, tending to obscure stem, ±20 per areole, pale

ashy gray or sometimes pinkish, in 2 or 3 vague turns of a spiral, all spreading parallel to stem surface, those of inner series longer and thicker, those of 2 outer series smaller and smaller, especially in the upper part of areole where largest spines of areole form part of inner series, the 3 largest spines ±4.5 mm long, basally bulbous (much more so than in other species), above bulb 0.5 mm diam, cylindroid with abruptly acute apex, nearly circular in cross section; flower ±2 cm diam and long; sepaloids with greenish midribs and somewhat reddish-purple margins, the larger narrowly spathulate-oblanceolate, to 12 mm long, 2-3 mm broad, ciliate-fimbriate; petaloids reddish-purple, oblanceolate, entire, apically acuminate or apiculate, largest 8-12 mm long, 2-3 mm broad; filaments pale greenish-yellow, ±4.5 mm long, very slender; anthers bright yellow, minute, ±0.5 mm long and broad; style greenish, ±7.5 mm long, ±0.5 mm diam; stigmas ±5, green, ±1 mm long, rather broad; fruit not available.

Gravelly soil of hills in grasslands at about 1,200-1,350 m (4,000-4,500 ft). Desert Grassland. Texas in vicinity of Marathon, Brewster Co.

See map for *C. macromeris* (next species).

2. Coryphantha macromeris
(Engelmann) Orcutt

Solitary or with many stems forming clumps to 15 cm high and 30-100 cm diam; larger stems green, cylindroid to elongate-ovoid, 5-15 cm long, to 5 cm diam; tubercle prominent and elongate, grooved (unlike those of the other species) on only upper half, to ±15 mm long, to 6-9 mm broad, protruding to 12-25 mm; areoles ±3 mm diam, typically ±12 mm apart; spines rather dense but not obscuring tubercles; central spines black or dark to pale gray or reddish brown, 4-6 per areole, lower (principal) one a little longer, the upper 3-5 less conspicuous, spreading irregularly, straight or somewhat curved or twisted, the longer 25-50 mm long, basally to 1 mm broad, subulate, narrowly elliptic in cross section; radial spines dark to pale gray, lighter than centrals, 9-15 per areole, spreading parallel to stem surface, straight to slightly curving, the longer mostly 20-25 mm long, basally ±0.5 mm broad, acicular or nearly so, approaching circular in cross section; flower 3-4.5 cm diam, 4.5-5 cm long; sepaloids with greenish midribs and reddish-purple margins, the larger narrowly oblanceolate, to 25 mm long, to 6 mm

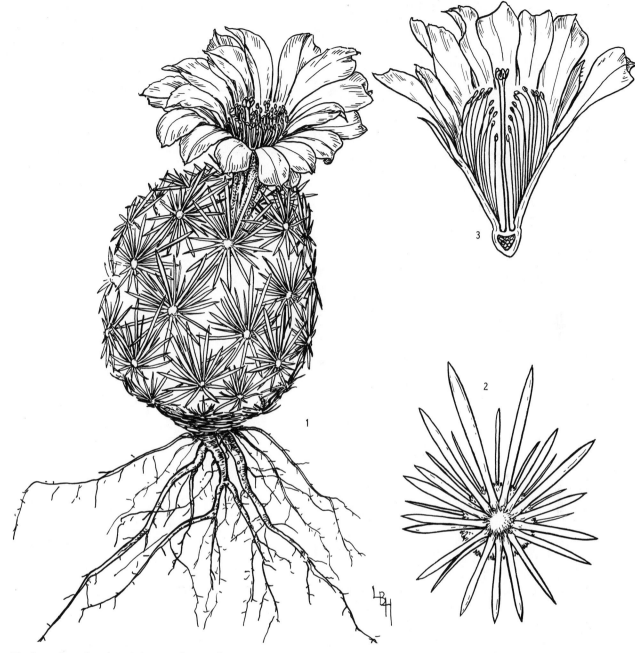

Fig. 850. *Coryphantha minima*. *1*, Plant in flower, ×5. *2*, Areole, showing the spines and hairs, the spines narrowed abruptly at the apices, ×14. *3*, Flower in longitudinal section, ×7.

broad, apically fimbriate-ciliate; petaloids reddish-purple to rose, the largest narrowly oblanceolate, to 30 mm long, ±6-9 mm broad, minutely fimbriate; filaments reddish-purple to rose, to 12 mm long; anthers yellow, oblong, ±1 mm long; style yellow, ±20 mm long, 1.5 mm greatest diam; stigmas 7 or 8, ±4.5 mm long, slender; ovary in anthesis ±7.5 mm long, 4.5 mm diam, with a few fimbriate scales; fruit green at maturity, the fimbriate scales with woolly axils, 16-25 mm long, 6-9 mm diam; seeds golden brown, reticulate, broader than long, ±1.25 mm long, 2 mm broad, ±1 mm thick; hilum appearing "lateral."

Reference: Hodgkins, Brown, & Massingill, 1967. (Alkaloids found in this species.)

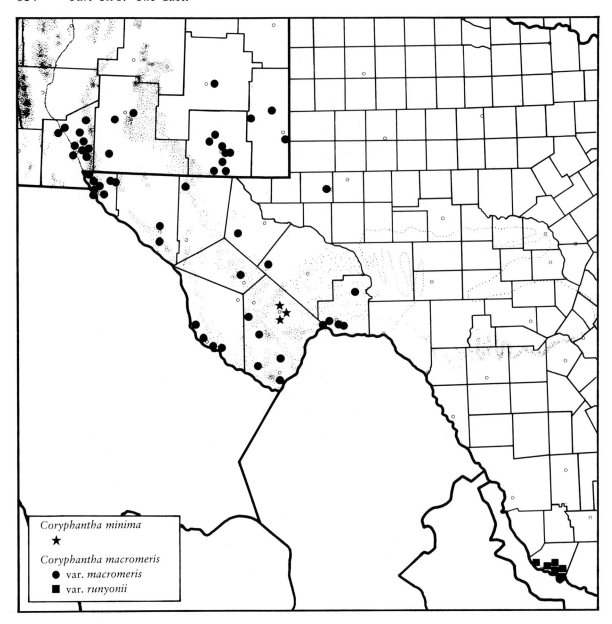

Coryphantha minima
★

Coryphantha macromeris
● var. macromeris
■ var. runyonii

Distinctive Characters of the Varieties of **Coryphantha macromeris**

Character	a. var. **macromeris**	b. var. **runyonii**
Stems	Green, to 10-15 cm long, to 5 cm diam, in clumps to 0.3 m diam	Gray-green, to ±5-7.5 cm long, 2.5-3.8 cm diam, in clumps to 1 m diam
Tubercles	To 15 mm long, ±6-9 mm broad, protruding 1.5-2.5 cm	Mostly to 7.5 mm long, ±4.5 mm broad, protruding ±1.2 cm
Altitude	750-1,350 m (2,500-4,500 ft)	Near sea level
Floristic association	Chihuahuan Desert	Rio Grande Plain

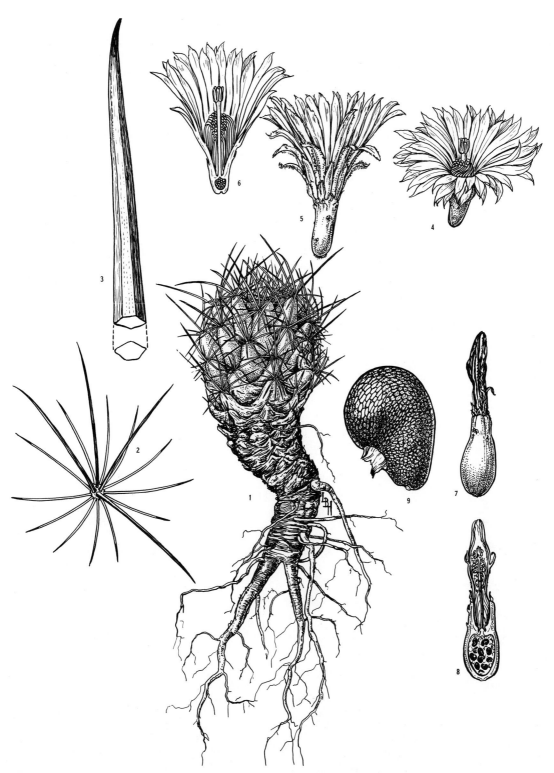

Fig. 851. *Coryphantha macromeris* var. *macromeris*, ×1.1, except as indicated. *1*, Relatively young plant, ×.6; note the young branch developing from a tubercle on the right side of the stem. *2*, Areole with four reddish-brown (to black) central spines and with white radial spines. *3*, Tip of a radial spine, ×12. *4, 5*, Flower. *6*, Flower in longitudinal section. *7*, Fruit, with a few scales on the floral tube covering and adnate with the ovary (these lacking in the other species of the genus). *8*, Fruit in longitudinal section. *9*, Seed, the hilum appearing "lateral," ×16.

2a. Coryphantha macromeris var. **macromeris.**
Yellow clay and gravelly soils of low hills in desert at mostly 750-1,350 m (2,500-4,500 ft). Chihuahuan Desert. New Mexico from Dona Ana Co. to Chaves and Lea Cos.; Texas w of Pecos R. and in Ector Co. South in Mexico through Chihuahua to Zacatecas.

The stems are either solitary or in low, irregular aggregations. The tubercles are the most conspicuous structure of the stem.

2b. Coryphantha macromeris var. **runyonii** (Britton & Rose) L. Benson. Gravelly and white silt soils of low hills and flats in desert at low elevations. Rio Grande Plain. Texas near Rio Grande from Starr Co. to (reportedly) vicinity of Brownsville, Cameron Co.

The plants are smaller, and they tend to be less conspicuous and more matlike than those of var. *macromeris.*

Reference: Keller & McLaughlin, 1972.

3. Coryphantha scheeri Lemaire

Stems usually solitary or sometimes in clusters, the larger green, ellipsoid, 10-17 cm long, 7.5-10 cm diam; tubercles elongate, prismatic-cylindroid, 12-20 mm long, 12-25 mm broad, protruding 25-40 mm; areoles 6 mm diam, typically ±10 mm apart; spines dense, tending to obscure upper tubercles; central spines straw-colored with dark-red tips or pink, 1-4(5) per areole, at first inclined upward, later spreading at right angles to stem, straight or curving or hooked, longer to 38 mm long, basally to 1-1.5 mm diam, acicular, nearly circular in cross section; radial spines colored like centrals, 6-16 per areole, spreading irregularly, straight, longer to 30 mm long, basally ±0.75 mm diam, acicular, elliptic in cross section; flower ±5-7.5 cm diam, ±5-6 cm long; sepaloids with yellow or red midribs and yellow margins, the larger commonly 2-3 cm long, usually 3-4.5 mm broad, rounded, mucronate, denticulate; petaloids yellow or with red streaks, largest narrowly

Fig. 852. *Coryphantha macromeris* var. *macromeris,* in flower near Presidio, Presidio Co., Texas. (Perhaps C. H. Thompson, 1900; courtesy of Missouri Botanical Garden)

Fig. 853. *Coryphantha macromeris* var. *runyonii* growing in a wash near Roma, Starr Co., Texas. The plants are much smaller than those of var. *macromeris* occurring farther west, and they tend to form mats.

oblanceolate, ±30 mm long, to 9 mm broad, slightly acuminate to acute, entire or with a few sharp teeth; filaments 9-12 mm long; anthers 1 mm long, oblong; style 30-35 mm long, 1.5 mm greatest diam; stigmas ±10, 3 mm long, rather stout; ovary in anthesis ±6 mm long; fruit green, ellipsoid, ±30-55 mm long, 12-20 mm diam; seeds brown or perhaps becoming black, very finely reticulate, ovate-acute, 2 mm long, 3 mm broad, 1 mm thick; hilum in a slight curve.

The clusters of stems are conspicuous for the dark green tubercles, which are much more conspicuous than the spines. However, in the varieties the central spine stands like a pole or a hook on the end of each tubercle.

3a. Coryphantha scheeri var. **scheeri.** Sandy flats in desert; sometimes in areas occasionally flooded for short periods; at ±1,200 m (4,000 ft). Chihuahuan Desert. New Mexico near Pecos R.

in Eddy Co.; Texas in Pecos R. region in Reeves Co. and in Big Bend region s of Alpine, Brewster Co. Mexico, reportedly from Chihuahua to Zacatecas.

3b. Coryphantha scheeri var. **valida** (Engelmann) L. Benson. Deep, more or less sandy soils of flats and bottomlands in grasslands and deserts at ±1,200 m (4,000 ft). Desert Grassland and other Texan and Mexican grasslands; Chihuahuan Desert. Southeastern Arizona in s Pima Co., near Nogales in Santa Cruz Co., and in San Simon Valley in Cochise Co.; s New Mexico as far E as Dona Ana Co.; Texas from El Paso Co. to Davis Mts. in Jeff Davis Co. and vicinity of Alpine, Brewster Co. Mexico in N Chihuahua.

The cylindroid stems, about 15 cm high, are either conspicuous in the open or hidden under bushes. The tubercles are the most obvious feature of the stem.

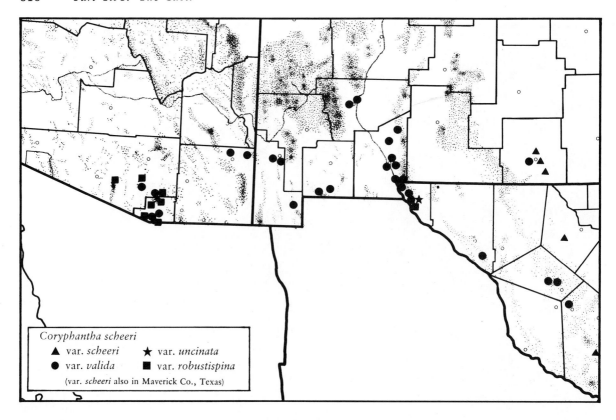

Coryphantha scheeri
▲ var. *scheeri*   ★ var. *uncinata*
● var. *valida*   ■ var. *robustispina*
(var. *scheeri* also in Maverick Co., Texas)

Distinctive Characters of the Varieties of **Coryphantha scheeri**

Character	a. var. **scheeri**	b. var. **valida**	c. var. **uncinata**	d. var. **robustispina**
Stem	Solitary	Solitary	Branching unknown	Branching and forming clumps
Young areoles	Not covered with wool	Covered densely with wool	Covered densely with deciduous wool	Covered densely with deciduous wool
Central spine(s)	1, to 3.8 cm long, to 1 mm diam, not strongly curved or hooked	1-4(5), the primary one to 3.8 cm long, to 1 mm diam, not strongly curved and *not* hooked	1-3 in young plants, 3 and equal in mature plants, 2.5 cm long, 1 mm diam, all strongly arcuate and apically hooked	1 to 2.8 cm long, to 1.5 mm diam, curved and hooked, tapering abruptly at apex
Radial spines	6-10(11), to 2 cm long	(9)12-16, to 3 cm long	About 16, ±2.5 cm long	(±6, young plants) or 10-15, 1.9-2.2 cm long
Sepaloids	With glabrous margins	Ciliate	(Flowers unknown)	Ciliate on lower margins
Petaloids	Yellow with red streaks	Yellow	———	Yellow, salmon, or rarely white
Floral tube	Relatively broad	Relatively broad	———	Relatively narrow
Altitude	±1,200 m (4,000 ft)	±1,200 m (4,000 ft)	±1,200 m (4,000 ft)	700-1,500 m (2,300-5,000 ft)
Floristic association	Chihuahuan Desert	Desert Grassland; Texan and Mexican grasslands; Chihuahuan Desert	Chihuahuan Desert	Arizona Desert (upper edge); Desert Grassland; lower edge of Southwestern Oak Woodland

Fig. 855. *Coryphantha scheeri* var. *valida* in flower, in gravelly sand at Anthony, El Paso Co., Texas; central spines nearly straight.

Fig. 854. *Coryphantha scheeri* var. *valida* growing in sand at Anthony, El Paso Co., Texas.

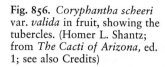

Fig. 856. *Coryphantha scheeri* var. *valida* in fruit, showing the tubercles. (Homer L. Shantz; from *The Cacti of Arizona,* ed. 1; see also Credits)

3c. Coryphantha scheeri var. **uncinata** L. Benson. Rocky hillsides in desert at about ±1,200 m (4,000 ft). Chihuahuan Desert. Vicinity of El Paso, Texas.

The plant is like a mass of short, blunt hooks.

3d. Coryphantha scheeri var. **robustispina** (Schott) L. Benson. Alluvial valleys, mesas, and hillsides in desert, grassland, or woodland at 700-1,500 m (2,300-5,000 ft). Arizona Desert (upper edge); Desert Grassland; Southwestern Oak Woodland (lower edge). Arizona from Baboquivari Mts. and Sierrita (s of Tucson) to Santa Cruz Co. Mexico in N Sonora.

The relatively large cylindroid stem has both conspicuous tubercles and very stout hooked spines.

Fig. 857. *Coryphantha scheeri* var. *robustispina* in cultivation; central spines curved to hooked in the young plant, hooked as plant grows older. (Robert H. Peebles)

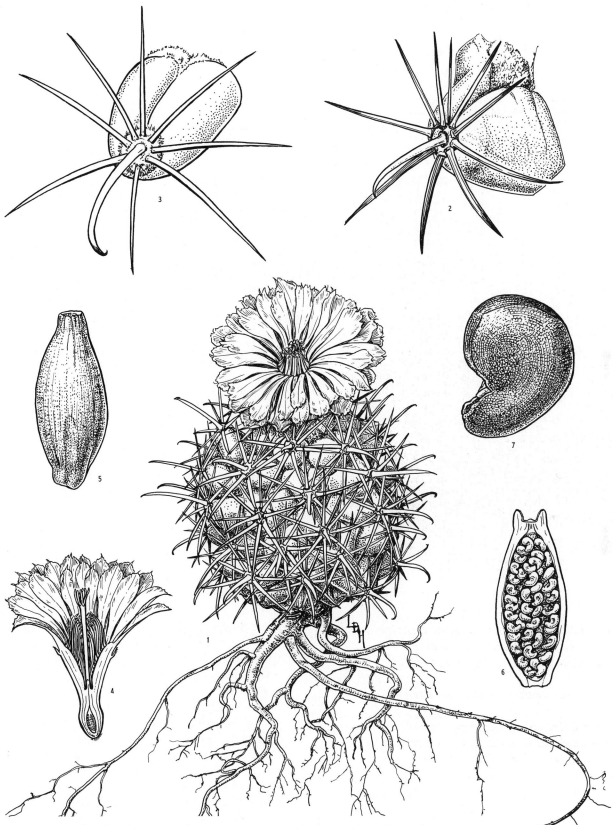

Fig. 858. *Coryphantha scheeri* var. *robustispina*, ×1.1, except as indicated. *1*, Plant in flower, ×.6. *2, 3*, Tubercles with areoles, showing the single hooked central spine. *4*, Flower in longitudinal section. *5*, Fruit. *6*, Fruit in longitudinal section. *7*, Seed, ×12.

Distinctive Characters of the Varieties of **Coryphantha vivipara**

Character	a. var. **vivipara**	b. var. **radiosa**	c. var. **bisbeeana**
Stems	Solitary or numerous and forming mounds to 30-60 cm diam, depressed-globose to ovoid, 2-5 cm long and diam	Solitary or branching, sometimes forming mounds, ovoid to cylindroid, 5-7.5 cm long, 2-5.6 cm diam	Solitary or branching, often forming mounds to 60+ cm diam, ovoid, 5-7.5 cm long, 5-6.2(6.9) cm diam
Central spines	4, the lower one turned downward, red and relatively dark-colored or basally white, 1.2-1.9 cm long, rather prominent among the radials	3 or 4, the lower one turned downward, pink to red, ±1.5-2.2 cm long, relatively less prominent among the radials than in var. *vivipara*	5 or 6, brown or gray with pink or brown tips, 1.2-1.5 cm long, seeming to mingle with the mass of radials
Radial spines	12-20, white, mostly 0.9-1.2 cm long, slender, ±0.2 mm diam	20-40, white to pink, mostly 1.2-1.9 cm long, very slender, 0.2 mm diam	20-30, white to brown, mostly 0.9-1.2 cm long, 0.1-0.2 mm diam (variable within the areole)
Flower diameter	±3.8 cm	±3.8 cm	±3.8-5 cm
Petaloids	Dark purplish pink, narrowly lanceolate-subulate, 1.5-2 cm long, 2 mm broad	Dark purplish pink, narrowly lanceolate-subulate, attenuate, 1.5-2.2 cm long, ±3 mm broad	Pink, narrowly lanceolate, the tips acuminate, 2.5-3 cm long, ±4.5 mm broad
Fruit length	1.2-2 cm	1.9-2.5 cm	±2 cm
Seed breadth	1.5-1.8 mm	2 mm	2 mm
Altitude	300-2,400 m (1,000-8,000 ft)	180-1,800(2,400) m (600-6,000 or 8,000 ft)	900-1,600 m (3,000-5,200 ft)
Floristic association	Great Plains Grassland; also Juniper-Pinyon Woodlands	Great Plains Grassland; lower Southern Juniper-Pinyon Woodland; Edwards Plateau; Chihuahuan Desert	Desert Grassland

4. Coryphantha vivipara
(Nuttall) Britton & Rose

Stems depressed-globose to ovoid or cylindroid, in some varieties forming clumps of 200 or more stems, the clumps to 30 cm high, 60+ cm diam; larger stems green, 2-15 cm long, 2-10(15) cm diam; tubercles 6-9 mm long and broad, protruding 6-20 mm; areoles 1.5-3 mm diam, typically ±6 mm apart; spines dense, obscuring stem in various degrees according to variety; central spines usually white basally but tipped for various distances with pink, red, or black, 3-12 per areole, spreading at various angles, straight, the longer 12-25 mm long, basally 0.3-0.6(1) mm diam, acicular, nearly circular in cross section; radial spines white, 12-40 per areole, spreading, straight, the longer 9-25 mm long, basally mostly 0.2-0.5 mm diam, acicular, nearly circular in cross section;

flowers in some varieties open only 1-2 hours on 1 day in the year, but in others often several series of flowers produced at different times in a single year; flower 2.5-5 cm diam and long; sepaloids with greenish midribs and pink, red, lavender, yellow-green, or straw-yellow margins, the longer linear-lanceolate to lanceolate, 12-25 mm long, 3-4.5 mm broad, mucronate to attenuate, ciliate-fimbriate; petaloids pink, red, lavender, or yellow-green, the largest lanceolate-linear to narrowly lanceolate-attenuate, 1.2-3(5) cm long, 2-7.5 mm broad, mucronate to acuminate or attenuate, entire; filaments ±6 mm long; anthers yellow, 1 mm long, oblong, length ±twice breadth; style 12-25 mm long, ±1 mm greatest diam; stigmas 5-10, 1.5-3 mm long; ovary in anthesis ±6 mm long; fruit green, rarely with a few scales, ellipsoid, 12-25 mm long, 9-15 mm diam; seed brown, retic-

Distinctive Characters of the Varieties of **Coryphantha vivipara** (cont.)

d. var. arizonica	e. var. desertii	f. var. alversonii	g. var. rosea
Solitary or forming mounds to 60+ cm diam, ovoid, 5-10 cm long, 5-6.2 diam	Solitary or few, cylindroid to ovoid, 7.5-15 cm long, 7.5-8.7 cm diam	Appearing unbranched but sometimes with branching rhizomes under the sand, cylindroid, 10-15 cm long, ±6.2-7.5 cm diam	Solitary or branching, ovoid-globose, 7.5-12.5 (17.5) cm long, 7.5-10 (15) cm diam
5-7, red, but white basally, 1.5-1.9 cm long, except for color seeming to mingle with the mass of radials	4-6, white, tipped with pink or red, 1.2-1.9 cm long, seeming to mingle with the radials, relatively stout	8-10, white, tipped with dark red or black, 1.2-1.5 cm long, forming a remarkably dense mass with the radials, stout	10-12, white with red tips, 1.9-2.5 cm long, robust, 1 mm diam, individually prominent
20-30, white, 1.2-1.5 cm long, ±0.2 mm diam	12-20, white, 0.9-1.2 cm long, 0.2 mm diam	±12-18, white, 1.2-1.5 (1.9) cm long, ±0.3 mm diam	±12-18, white, 1.5-2 (2.5) cm long, ±0.5 mm diam
±3.8-5 cm	To 2.5-3 cm	±3 cm	3-5 cm
Deep pink, narrowly lanceolate, acute and mucronate, to 2.5-3 cm long, ±4.5 mm broad	Straw-yellow, yellow-green, or pink, narrowly lanceolate, mucronate, ±1.2-2.5 cm long, ±3 mm broad	Magenta to pink, lanceolate-linear, ±2 cm long, ±2 mm broad	Magenta to purplish, narrowly lanceolate, 2-3 cm long, 3-7.5 mm broad
±2 cm	±2.5 cm	±2.2 cm	(Fruits not known)
2 mm	1.5 mm	1.3 mm	2 mm
1,400-2,160 m (4,700-7,200 ft)	300-1,620(2,400) m (1,000-5,400 or 8,000 ft)	75-600(1,200) m (250-2,000 or 4,000 ft)	1,500-2,700 m (5,000-9,000 ft)
Juniper-Pinyon Woodlands; Rocky Mountain Montane Forest	Mojavean Desert; Northern Juniper-Pinyon Woodland or Sagebrush Desert	Border zone of Colorado Desert and Mojavean Desert	Northern Juniper-Pinyon Woodland; upper Mojavean Desert

ulate, nearly semicircular but a little broader on one side, 1.1-1.2 mm long, 1.5-2 mm broad, ±0.7 mm thick; hilum appearing "lateral," near narrow side of seed.

Fischer (1972, unpublished) has prepared a study of the *Coryphantha vivipara* complex based on herbarium and field studies; investigations of morphology, anatomy, and ecology; and some experimental work. He considers *C. vivipara* var. *alversonii* to be a distinct species, describes a new varietal taxon under *C. vivipara* (northern Arizona), and considers var. *neomexicana* to be a taxon occurring in western and southern New Mexico (see note under var. *radiosa*).

4a. Coryphantha vivipara var. vivipara. Various soil types but mostly on limestone in grassland and woodland at 300-2,400 m (1,000-8,000 ft), according to latitude and local climate. Typically of Great Plains Grassland but occurring in Juniper-Pinyon Woodlands. Alberta to sw Manitoba, Canada; Steen Mts. in E Oregon to E Montana, Minnesota, Kansas, NE Utah, NE New Mexico, Texas panhandle and Archer Co., and w Oklahoma.

The individual plants, or even mounds of them, may be nearly obliterated by plains grasses or they may occur in the open or under shrubs or bushes. They are conspicuous only at flowering time.

The flowering of this variety is photoperiodic, being governed by the length of day. Plants collected at several places in South Dakota, Wyoming, and Colorado all flowered each spring on the same day in Claremont, California. Flowering lasts for only an hour or two.

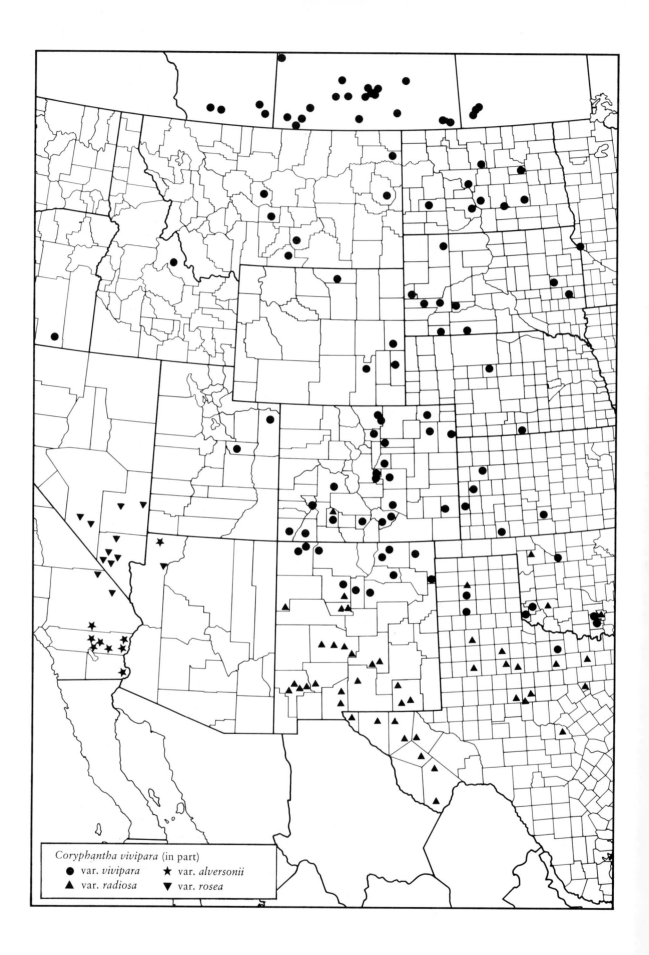

Coryphantha vivipara (in part)

● var. vivipara   ★ var. alversonii
▲ var. radiosa   ▼ var. rosea

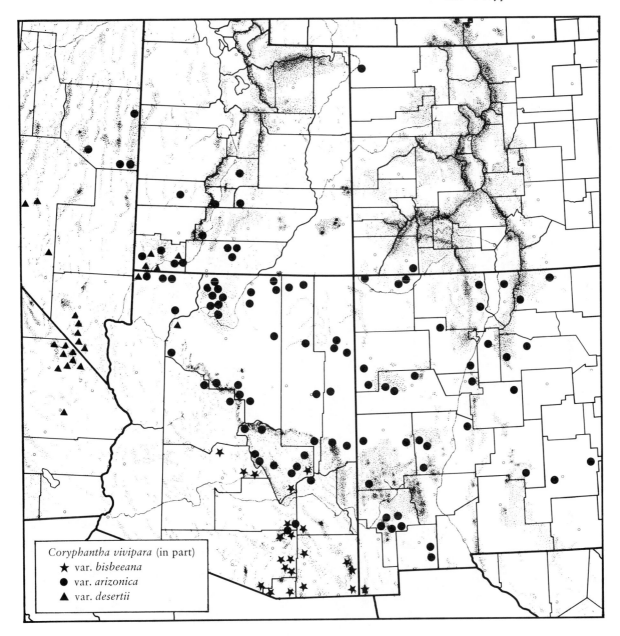

Coryphantha vivipara (in part)
★ var. *bisbeeana*
● var. *arizonica*
▲ var. *desertii*

According to Thomas Nuttall (Gen. N. Amer. Pl. 295–296. 1818), "In spite of its armature the wild antelope of the plains finds means to render it subservient to its wants by cutting it up with its hooves."

4b. Coryphantha vivipara var. radiosa (Engelmann) Backeberg. Mostly on limestone soils in grassland and woodland and along edge of desert at 180–1,800(2,400) m (600–6,000 or 8,000 ft). Great Plains Grassland, lower parts of Southern Juniper-Pinyon Woodland, Edwards Plateau, and Chihuahuan Desert. Mostly on Great Plains and adjacent regions. New Mexico from Valencia,

Sandoval, Grant, and Hidalgo Cos. E to w Oklahoma and Arbuckle Mts. in s Oklahoma and to w Texas and sparingly to Wise and Hood Cos. and Edwards Plateau in central Texas.

Fischer (1972) recognizes *Coryphantha vivipara* var. *neomexicana* (Engelm.) Backeberg, applying the epithet to plants occurring in western and southern New Mexico and westernmost Texas. Although these plants are included here in var. *radiosa*, they are considered transitional to vars. *arizonica*, *vivipara*, and perhaps *bisbeeana*. Fischer's additions to knowledge sharpen the problem, but whether the suggested taxon is capable of clear delimitation as a consistent unit is a com-

Fig. 859. *Coryphantha vivipara* var. *vivipara*, plant in flower in the Great Plains Grassland. (Perhaps C. H. Thompson, about 1900; courtesy of Missouri Botanical Garden)

plex question. The area of occurrence is a meeting ground for several varieties, and each apparently contributes some genes to a highly variable pool. The case for detachment of these plants from var. *radiosa* may be stronger than that for consideration of them as a variety in their own right, and they are regarded as an irregular swarm of intermediate individuals. The writer has no strong opinion on this point, and further study is needed.

4c. **Coryphantha vivipara** var. **bisbeeana** (Orcutt) L. Benson. Various soils, including especially limestone, of plains and hillsides in grassland at 900-1,600 m (3,000-5,200 ft). Desert Grassland. Arizona in E Maricopa, Pinal, Gila, sw Graham, Pima, Santa Cruz, and Cochise Cos.; New Mexico in Hidalgo Co. Adjacent Sonora.

The plants form clusters of blond, relatively smooth, spiny balls.

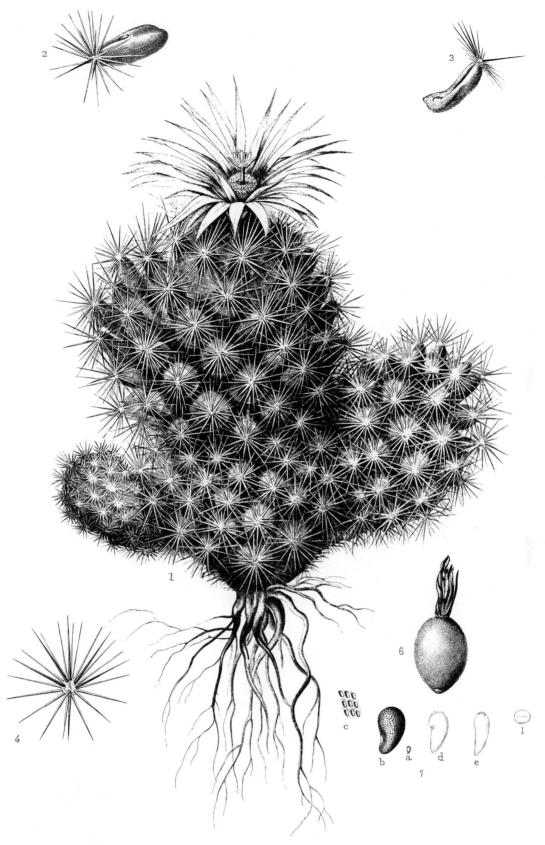

Fig. 860. *Coryphantha vivipara* var. *radiosa*. *1*, Plant in flower. *2*, Tubercle of a juvenile plant, the spine- and flower-bearing areas separated by half the length of the tubercle and connected by an isthmus. *3*, Tubercle of a mature plant, the spine- and flower-bearing areas separated by the full length of the tubercle. *4*, Mature areole with central and radial spines. (*5*, Number not used.) *6*, Fruit. *7*, Seed: *a*, natural size; *b*, ×9; *c*, reticulate surface; *d*, contents; *e*, embryo with minute cotyledons, in side view; *f* (appearing as *l*), top view of the embryo showing the minute cotyledons. (Paulus Roetter in Engelmann/Emory, *pl. 13*)

Fig. 861. *Coryphantha vivipara* var. *bisbeeana*, plant with a cluster of stems; Papago Indian Reservation, Pima Co., Arizona. (A. A. Nichol)

Fig. 862. *Coryphantha vivipara* var. *bisbeeana* in Desert Grassland, southeastern Arizona. (Homer L. Shantz)

Fig. 863. *Coryphantha vivipara* var. *bisbeeana* in flower, showing the central and radial spines. (A. R. Leding, U.S. Acclimatization Station, College Station, New Mexico)

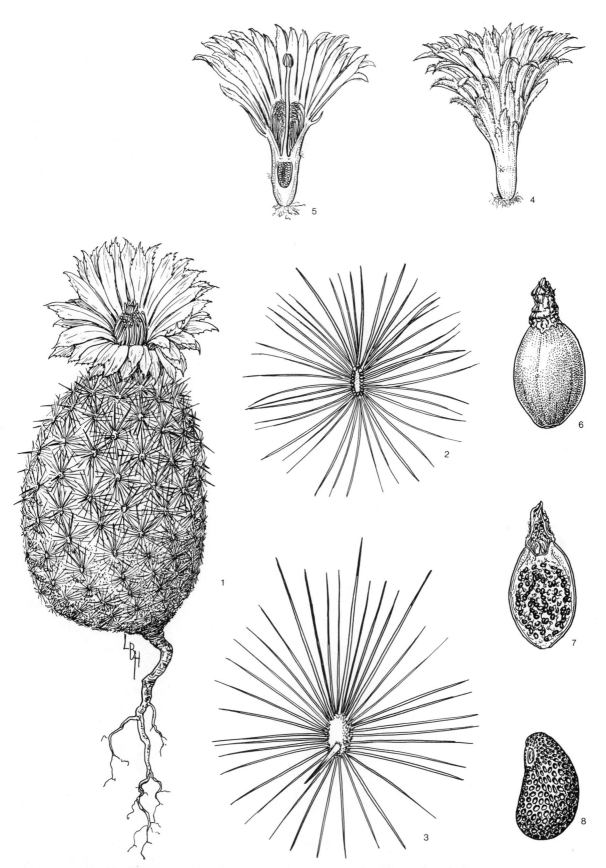

Fig. 864. *Coryphantha vivipara* var. *bisbeeana*, natural size, except is indicated. *1*, Unbranched plant in flower. *2*, Juvenile spine cluster, the areoles with no lower central spine, ×3.25. *3*, Mature spine cluster, the lower central spine present, ×3.25. *4*, Flower. *5*, Flower in longitudinal section. *6*, Fruit (green at maturity). *7*, Fruit in longitudinal section. *8*, Seed, ×16.

Fig. 865. *Coryphantha vivipara* var. *arizonica*, forming a mound; near south rim of the Grand Canyon, Coconino Co., Arizona.

Fig. 866. *Coryphantha vivipara* var. *arizonica* in flower, showing the more numerous spines in the areoles of older plants. (Robert H. Peebles)

Fig. 867. *Coryphantha vivipara* var. *arizonica* in flower, though the plant is juvenile; the spines fewer than in older plants and the central spines developed only in the upper areoles. (Robert H. Peebles)

4d. Coryphantha vivipara var. **arizonica** (Engelmann) W. T. Marshall. Sandy and rocky soils in mountains and on high plains in juniper and yellow pine belts at 1,400-2,160 m (4,700-7,200 ft). Juniper-Pinyon Woodlands and Rocky Mountain Montane Forest. Eastern Nevada in White Pine Co.; s Utah; Colorado in Moffat and s La Plata Cos.; N and E Arizona; New Mexico except on the plains.

The reddish-brown central spines make the solitary, clumped, or mounded stems much darker than those of the other varieties occurring from the mountains of w New Mexico westward.

4e. Coryphantha vivipara var. **desertii** (Engelmann) W. T. Marshall. Limestone areas of hills and flats in desert at 300-1,620(2,400) m (1,000-5,400 or 8,000 ft). Mojavean Desert; Northern Juniper-Pinyon Woodland; Sagebrush Desert. California in E San Bernardino Co.; Nevada in Nye and Clark Cos.; Utah in Washington Co.; Arizona in N Mohave and w Coconino Cos.

Usually the stems are few and blond.

Fig. 868. *Coryphantha vivipara* var. *desertii*, showing the central and radial spines, the latter light-colored.

Fig. 869. *Coryphantha vivipara* var. *desertii* on limestone in the Beaverdam Mts., Washington Co., Utah.

4f. Coryphantha vivipara var. **alversonii** (Coulter) L. Benson. Sandy areas in desert at 75-600 (1,200) m (250-2,000 or 4,000 ft). California along border zone between Mojavean and Colorado deserts in s edge of San Bernardino Co., in Riverside Co., and near Bard, Imperial Co.; Arizona at Pagumpa, Mohave Co. (probably an old mine or a ghost town).

This is the giant among varieties of this species, and its gray, spiny stems remind one of the fur of a gray fox.

4g. Coryphantha vivipara var. **rosea** (Clokey) L. Benson. Limestone slopes and gravelly areas in woodland or desert mountains at 1,500-2,700 m (5,000-9,000 ft). Northern Juniper-Pinyon Woodland and upper edge of Mojavean Desert. California in E San Bernardino Co.; s Nevada from s Nye Co. to w Clark Co. and E Lincoln Co.; Arizona N of Peach Springs, Mohave Co.

The plant is usually a solitary, light-colored, spiny ball.

Fig. 870. *Coryphantha vivipara* var. *alversonii* in granitic sand, gravel, and rock in middle southern San Bernardino Co., California. The dense spines are the source of the name foxtail cactus.

Fig. 871. *Coryphantha vivipara* var. *rosea* in desert pavement, Charleston Mts., Clark Co., Nevada. The small cholla is *Opuntia whipplei* var. *multigeniculata*, a very rare variety.

5. Coryphantha hesteri Y. Wright

Stems producing branches from lower tubercles, sometimes forming clumps 10-15 cm diam; stems green, broadly obovoid to turbinate or subglobose, 2.5-4(5) cm long, 2-3(4.5) cm diam; tubercles broad and prominent, 3-4.5 mm long, 6-9 mm broad, protruding 6-9 mm; areoles 1.5 mm diam, typically 6-7.5 mm apart; spines not obscuring stem; central spines white or sometimes red-tipped, 1-3(4) per areole, all in upper portion and turned upward, the longer 9-11 mm long, tapering, at extreme bases 0.5 mm diam, acicular; radial spines white, 12-14 per areole, spreading uniformly, straight, the longer 3-9 mm long (uppers longest), basally 0.2 mm diam, acicular; flower 1.5-2 cm diam and long; sepaloids with greenish-brown midribs and lavender or pale pink margins, the larger oblanceolate, 7.5-10 mm long, to 3 mm broad, markedly fimbriate, the solid portions acute; petaloids lavender, oblanceolate or broadly so, 12-15 mm long, 3-4.5 mm broad, acute, entire to sharply denticulate at apices; filaments pale yellow, nearly white, ±1.5-3 mm long; style green, lavender above, 9-12 mm long, ±0.5 mm greatest diam; stigmas 4-6, ±1-2 mm long, narrow, flat, the margins stigmatic; ovary in anthesis ±1.5-2 mm long; fruit obscured by spines, dry and green or yellowish at maturity, with the wall thin and transparent, nearly spheroidal, 6-7 mm long, 3-6 mm diam; seeds brown, the surfaces pitted, 0.7-1 mm long, ±1 mm broad, ±0.6-0.7 mm thick.

Limestone and other soils of hills and alluvial fans in desert and grassland at 1,200-1,500 m (4,000-5,000 ft). Desert Grassland. Texas in N Brewster Co.

The plants are relatively small and often difficult to locate among grasses and other herbs.

Fig. 872. *Coryphantha hesteri*, showing the tubercles, spines, and a flower.

4 mm broad in the upper third, not ciliate; ... [sepaloids] lighter colored, broader, and with a light green stripe through the middle; scales on flower tube light green, gradually assuming a light purplish tint as they merge into the outer perianth segments; filaments short, white, attached to the tube, the topmost reaching only the bases of the stigma lobes, approximately 7.8 mm long; pollen golden yellow to orange; style slender, white, about 18 mm long; stigma lobes 6-7, from 4 to 7 mm long; ovary whitish, approximately 15 mm long; fruit not seen."

Limestone soils of hills in desert at 750-1,050 m (2,500-3,500 ft). Chihuahuan Desert. Texas near Rio Grande in Brewster and s Terrell Cos. Mexico in NW Coahuila.

The Santa Rosa collection by *Bigelow*, Jan. 1853, *Mo* (on two sheets) was the *Mammillaria scolymoides* of Engelmann, in Emory, Rept. U.S. & Mex. Bound. Surv. 2: Cactaceae 14. 1859. However, this was not Santa Rosa, New Mexico, but Santa Rosa, Chihuahua, across the Rio Grande from Big Bend National Park, Texas. Bigelow was not at Santa Rosa, New Mexico, until September 1853. Hence, reports of occurrence of this species in New Mexico are incorrect.

6. Coryphantha ramillosa Cutak

Stems dark green, solitary, nearly globular or broadly obovoid, 6-7.5 cm long, ±6 cm diam; tubercles broad and prominent, 6 mm long, 12-15 mm broad, protruding 12-15 mm; areoles ±3 mm diam, typically ±12 mm apart; spines abundant but not obscuring stem; central spines 4 with 1-3 accessory ones above them, straight or somewhat curved, the lower one dark brown, porrect, 25-40 mm long, the upper 3+ nearly white with some brown, turned upward, more slender, the longer 20-25 mm long, the principal centrals basally 0.75 mm diam, acicular; radial spines white, 9-20 per areole, spreading rather irregularly, nearly straight, the longer 12-20 mm long, basally ±0.3 mm diam, acicular; (because complete flowers are not available, the remainder of the description is quoted from the original publication, Cutak, Cactus & Succ. Jour. 14: 164. 1942) "flowers large, showy, very variable, pale pink to deep rose purple, about 65 mm long and 50 mm broad when fully opened; ... [petaloids] white, the upper half to third pink to purple or deep rose to crimson, 25 mm long, only 2 mm broad in the lower half and

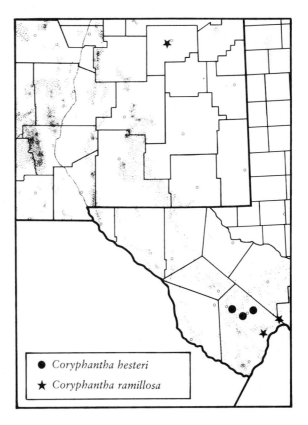

● *Coryphantha hesteri*
★ *Coryphantha ramillosa*

Fig. 873. *Coryphantha ramillosa*, showing the large tubercles, projecting central spines, and spreading radial spines.

7. Coryphantha sulcata
(Engelmann) Britton & Rose

Stems branching, forming clumps to 30 cm diam; larger stems green, subglobose or obovoid, 4-13 cm long and diam; tubercles 10 mm long and broad, protruding 12 mm; areoles 3 mm diam, typically 12 mm apart; spines not obscuring stem, at first either pink or yellow and pink, later either gray or with overlying gray or white; central spines (1)2 or 3 per areole, spreading, slightly curving, longer 9-12 mm long, basally 0.3-0.5 mm diam, acicular, nearly circular in cross

section; radial spines 6-8 per areole, similar to centrals but shorter, ±3 mm long; flower 3.8-6 cm diam and long; sepaloids with green midribs and yellow margins, largest oblong-linear, to 25 mm long, ±3 mm broad, acute, margins entire, glabrous; petaloids red basally, yellow distally, largest oblanceolate, apiculate and apically ciliate-erose, 25-30 mm long, to 6 mm broad; filaments

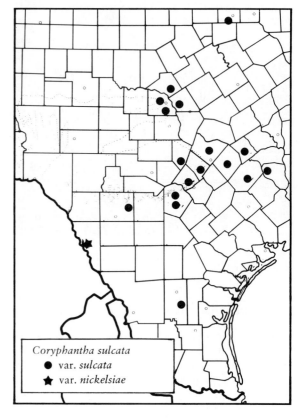

Coryphantha sulcata
● var. *sulcata*
★ var. *nickelsiae*

Distinctive Characters of the Varieties of **Coryphantha sulcata**

Character	a. var. **sulcata**	b. var. **nickelsiae**
Stems	Subglobose, 7.5-13 cm long and diam	Obovoid, ±5 cm long, ±4-5 cm diam
Spines	At first yellow-and-pink or pink, later this overlain by gray or white, stouter, (0.3)0.4-0.5 mm diam	Pink overlain by gray or white from outset, slender, 0.3-0.4 mm diam
Flower diam	To 5-6 cm	±3.8 cm
Altitude	Low elevations, under 150 m (500 ft)	Low elevations, ±100 m (300 ft)
Floristic association	Rio Grande Plain and southern edge of Edwards Plateau escarpment	Rio Grande Plain

yellowish, 3-6 mm long; anthers yellow, narrowly oblong, 1 mm long; style ±25 mm long, 1.5 mm greatest diam; stigmas 7-10; ovary in anthesis 6-9 mm long; fruit green, fleshy at maturity, ellipsoid, ±30 mm long, 20 mm diam; seeds brown, smooth and shining, semicircular, 1 mm long, 2 mm broad, ±0.7 mm thick.

7a. Coryphantha sulcata var. **sulcata.** Sandy or gravelly soil of plains in grasslands, at low elevations. Rio Grande Plain. Texas in lower hill country below E and S edge of escarpment of Edwards Plateau from Tarrant Co. to Uvalde, Austin, and Duval Cos.

The stems are large green balls with obvious tubercles and spines. They may be in bare places or partly hidden among grasses and small herbs or bushes.

7b. Coryphantha sulcata var. **nickelsiae** (K. Brandegee) L. Benson. Valley soils in grasslands and thickets at low elevations. Rio Grande Plain. Texas perhaps at Laredo, Webb Co. Mexico in Nuevo León near Mt. La Mitra.

Fig. 874. *Coryphantha sulcata* var. *sulcata,* in natural habitat near San Diego, Duval Co., Texas.

Fig. 875. *Coryphantha sulcata* var. *sulcata*, showing the tubercles, strongly curving central spines, and spreading radial spines.

Fig. 876. *Coryphantha sulcata* var. *sulcata*, cultivated plant in flower, showing the tubercles; the central spines, in this case, only slightly curved. (Robert Runyon, about 1920; courtesy of Missouri Botanical Garden and Robert Runyon)

8. Coryphantha cornifera
(DeCandolle) Lemaire

Stems solitary or sometimes several, the larger cylindroid, the younger globose, 7.5-10 cm long, 4.5-6 cm diam; tubercles ±6 mm long and broad, protruding 9-12 mm; areoles ±1.5 mm diam, typically ±10 mm apart; spines white to pale gray, very dense, obscuring stem; central spines gray or sometimes reddish, 1-4 per areole (0 in juvenile, 1 in intermediate plants), the lower (principal) one perpendicular to stem, straight or curving, others turned upward and resembling radials, the longer 9-17 mm long, basally 1-1.5 mm diam, acicular, nearly circular in cross section; radial spines 16-26 per areole, spreading parallel to stem, straight, largest 12-28 mm long, basally 0.5-1 mm diam, acicular, nearly circular in cross section; flowering each season restricted to a single circle of areoles; flower opening for only 1-2 hours on a single afternoon, ±5 cm diam and long; sepaloids with greenish midribs and yellow margins, the larger narrowly lanceolate, 20-25 mm long, 3-4.5 mm broad, sharply acute and acuminate; petaloids yellow, largest narrowly oblanceolate, 25-30 mm long, ±6 mm broad; filaments partly red, 6 mm long; anthers yellow, ±1 mm long, oblong, length ±3 times breadth; style yel-low, 20-25 mm long, 1-1.5 mm greatest diam; stigmas 10-12, ±4.5 mm long, slender; ovary in anthesis ±6 mm long, ±4.5-6 mm diam; fruit green, fleshy at maturity, ±25 mm long, ±10 mm diam; seeds brown, smooth and shining, minutely punctate, approaching semicircular but broader at one end, ±1.2 mm long, 2 mm broad, ±0.7 mm thick.

8a. Coryphantha cornifera var. echinus (Engelmann) L. Benson. Central spines 3 or 4, the lower one somewhat larger than others, straight or curving, 12-17 mm long, relatively slender, tapering gradually, basally 1-1.5 mm diam; radial spines 16-26, to 28 mm long on upper side of areole, to ±12 mm long on lower, slender, basally 0.5-0.7 mm diam. Limestone soils of hills in desert at 660-900(1,440) m (2,200-3,000 or 4,800 ft). Chihuahuan Desert and Desert Grassland; Edwards Plateau. Texas from El Paso Co. to Howard, Val Verde, and Webb Cos. and in Cooke Co. Mexico probably in adjacent Chihuahua and Coahuila.

The solitary or clustered stems are hidden beneath desert shrubs or bushes and among grasses. The brown, usually downward-curved spines are the most noticeable feature.

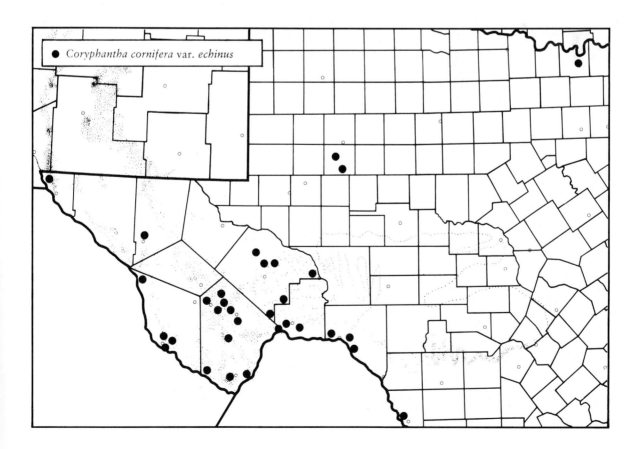

Coryphantha cornifera var. echinus

Fig. 877. *Coryphantha cornifera* var. *echinus* in fruit. *1*, Unbranched but mature plant with fruits. *2, 3*, Tubercles, each showing the groove or isthmus connecting the spine- and flower-bearing areas; the groove extends the entire length of the tubercle in *2*, where it was formed on a mature (upper) portion of the stem; the tubercle in *3* was formed on what is now the lower portion of the stem developed when the plant was younger. *4–9*, Areoles, each with stouter central spines and slender radials, the principal (lower) central projecting at right angles to the stem (porrect) and straight or curving. *10*, Fruit. *11*, Seed: *a*, natural size; *b*, ×10. (Paulus Roetter in Engelmann/Emory, *pl. 10*)

Fig. 878. *Coryphantha cornifera* var. *echinus* in flower (as a juvenile plant). *1*, Unbranched young plant, showing the tubercles without central spines; new joints of this type are found at the bases of older plants with central spines. *2–3*, *8–9*, Tubercles: *2* and *3*, from a juvenile plant; *8* and *9* from an adult plant, showing the groove between the apical spine-bearing area and the basal flower-bearing area. *4–7*, Areoles. *10*, Seed: *a*, natural size; *b*, ×10. (Paulus Roetter in Engelmann/Emory, *pl. 11*)

Coryphantha cornifera var. **cornifera**. Central spine 1, curving slightly downward to almost hooked, ±6-15 mm long, narrowly conical, basally ±1-1.5 mm diam; radial spines 16-20, gray, nearly equal on all sides of areole, 6-12 mm long. Plains, valleys, and low hills in grasslands to about 450 m (1,500 ft). Mexico; not in the U.S. Specimens have been given a wide variety of specific epithets.

9. Coryphantha recurvata
(Engelmann) Britton & Rose

Stems forming clumps of to 50, these to ±30 cm high and 30-100 cm diam; larger stems green, cylindroid, 10-25 cm long, 7.5-15 cm diam; tubercles cylindroid, ±6-10 mm long, 6 mm broad, protruding 10 mm; areoles 4.5 mm diam, typically 10 mm apart; spines dense, obscuring stem; central spine(s) at first yellow, later gray, tips red, 1(2) per areole, curving downward in a low arc, the longer 15-20 mm long, ±1 mm diam, acicular, nearly circular in cross section; radial spines colored like central, (12)15-20 per areole, spreading parallel to stem, but each curving slightly in a low arc, the longer 12-15 mm long, basally ±0.5 mm diam, acicular, nearly circular in cross section; flower 2.5-4 cm diam and long; sepaloids with greenish midribs and yellowish margins, the larger broadly oblanceolate or lanceolate, to 12 mm long, ±3 mm broad, acute and mucronate, denticulate; petaloids greenish-yellow or reportedly lemon-yellow, largest oblanceolate, ±12-15 mm long, ±3-4.5 mm broad, markedly mucronate, denticulate-serrulate; fruit green, fleshy at maturity, spheroidal, ±7.5 mm diam; other data not available.

Alluvial soils of valleys, mesas, and foothills in grassland and oak belts at 1,200-1,800 m (4,000-6,000 ft). Desert Grassland and Southwestern Oak Woodland. Arizona in w Santa Cruz Co. (from Nogales and Tumacacori Mts. w). Mexico in adjacent Sonora.

The plants are moundlike clusters of several tannish and grayish domes capping cylindroid bases. They occur in grassy and sometimes rocky places either in the open or among trees.

See map for *C. strobiliformis* (next species).

Fig. 881. *Coryphantha recurvata*, a plant in cultivation, showing the spreading radial spines, as well as the central spines. (Robert H. Peebles)

Fig. 880. *Coryphantha recurvata* in the Arizona-Sonora Desert Museum, Tucson, Arizona, showing the downward-curving, usually solitary, central spines.

843

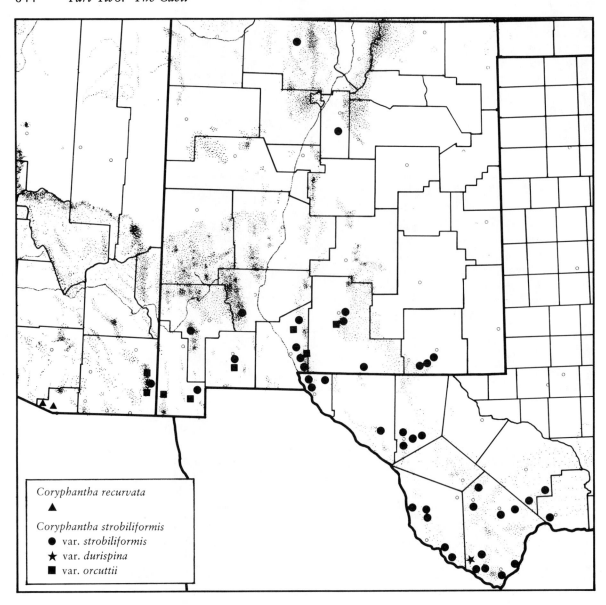

Distinctive Characters of the Varieties of **Coryphantha strobiliformis**

Character	a. var. **strobiliformis**	b. var. **durispina**	c. var. **orcuttii**
Stems	5-12.5 cm long, 2.5-5 cm diam	15-20 cm long, ±5 cm diam	5-12.5 cm long, 2.5-5 cm diam
Central spines	Central 1 longest, surrounded by 5-7 smaller centrals	Central 1 or 2 surrounded by 4-6 centrals, some longer, some shorter	Central 2-4 shorter than the surrounding 4-6 centrals
Spine size	Principal one to 1.2-1.5 cm long, to 0.3 mm diam	Some to 1.5-2 cm long, some ±0.6 mm diam	Several to 1-1.2 cm long, 0.25 mm diam
Altitude	750-1,500 m (2,500-5,000 ft)	±600 m (2,000 ft)	±1,200 m (4,000 ft)
Floristic association	Chihuahuan Desert; Desert Grassland	Chihuahuan Desert	Desert Grassland

10. Coryphantha strobiliformis (Poselger) Moran

Stems solitary or clumps of to 8-12, these 20-30 cm diam, the larger glaucous-green, cylindroid, 5-12(20) cm long, 2.5-5 cm diam; tubercles cylindroid, ±3 mm long and broad, protruding 10 mm, becoming spineless, hard, and persistent on lower part of stem; areoles 1.5 mm diam, typically 3-4.5 mm apart; spines dense, tending to obscure stem; central spines straw-yellow, *usually* tipped with pink or pale red, principal 1(2-4) central(s) surrounded by 4-7 smaller, straight, the longer ±10-20 mm long, basally 0.25-0.6 mm diam, acicular, nearly circular in cross section; radial spines pale straw-colored, white, or pale gray, 20-30 per areole, spreading, straight, the longer 12 mm long, basally 0.2 mm diam, acicular, nearly circular in cross section; flower 2-3 cm diam and long; sepaloids with green to red midribs and pink margins, the longer lanceolate, 12-20 mm long, 3 mm broad, acute, marginally scarious and fimbriate; petaloids pink, the longer lanceolate, 15-20 mm long, 3-4.5 mm broad, sharply acute, entire; filaments pale yellow, 4.5-6 mm long; anthers yellow, 0.5 mm long, ovate; style pale pink, 9-12 mm long, 1 mm greatest diam; stigmas 6 or 7, 3 mm long, rather broad; ovary in anthesis 6 mm long, ±3 mm diam; fruit red or sometimes some of them green, narrowly ellipsoid-cylindroid, 12-20 mm long, 6-7.5 mm diam; seeds brown, punctate, broader than long, 0.8 mm long, 1 mm broad, 0.6 mm thick; hilum very small, appearing "sublateral."

The plants are conspicuous little white cylinders, single or in clumps among rocks or under bushes.

This species is known to intergrade with *C. sneedii* var. *sneedii* (sp. 11a).

10a. Coryphantha strobiliformis var. **strobiliformis.** Limestone soils of hills, canyons, and alluvial fans in deserts and grasslands at 750-1,500 m (2,500-5,000 ft). Chihuahuan Desert and Desert Grassland. Arizona in Chiricahua Mts., Cochise Co.; s New Mexico from Hidalgo and Luna Cos. to Eddy Co. and in Rio Arriba and Santa Fe Cos.; Texas from El Paso Co. to Presidio and Terrell Cos. Mexico in Chihuahua.

Fig. 882. *Coryphantha strobiliformis* var. *strobiliformis*, plant in the Huntington Botanical Gardens, with flower buds and a closed flower; showing the persistent old lower tubercles after the fall of the spines (see Fig. 884).

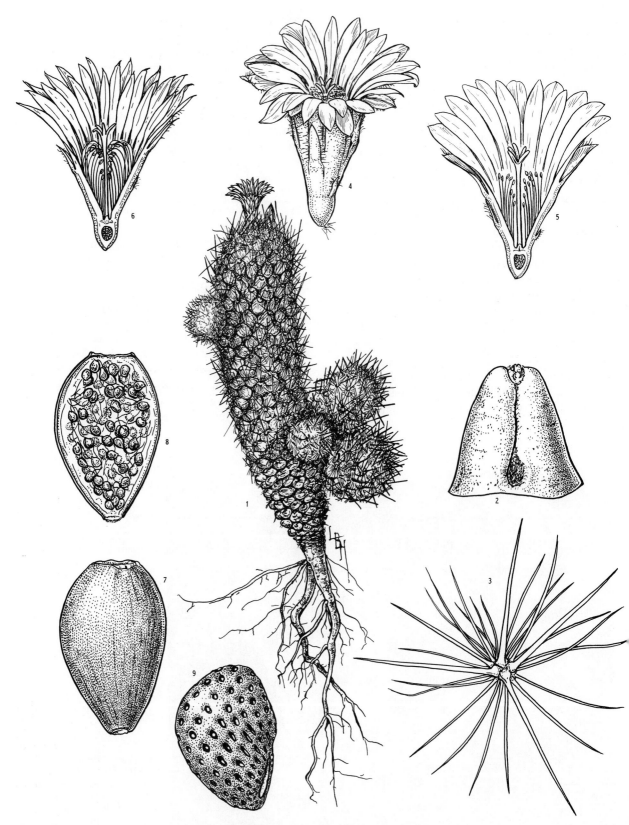

Fig. 883. *Coryphantha strobiliformis* var. *strobiliformis*. *1*, Plant in flower, showing the lower woody tubercles that remain after the areoles have fallen away, ×.5. *2*, Tubercle with the spines cut away from the top, showing the groove or isthmus connecting the spine- and flower-bearing areas, ×4.25. *3*, Areole, showing the central and radial spines, ×2. *4*, Flower, ×1.5. *5, 6*, Flowers in longitudinal section, 6 with the sensitive stamens closed inward, ×1.5. *7*, Fruit, ×3.25. *8*, Fruit in longitudinal section, ×3.25. *9*, Seed, the hilum appearing "lateral," but the seed merely broader than long, ×32.

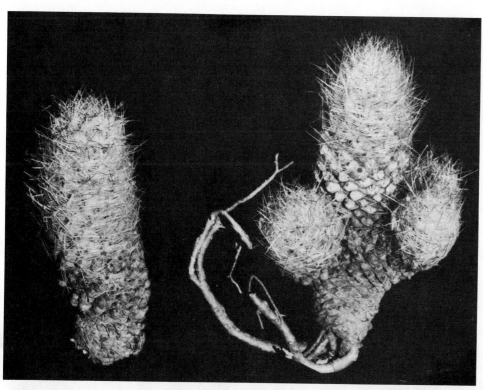

Fig. 884. *Coryphantha strobiliformis* var. *strobiliformis*, stems, the upper tubercles covered densely with spines, the old lower bare tubercles conspicuous after fall of the spines.

Fig. 885 (*below*). *Coryphantha strobiliformis* var. *orcuttii*, plant with a cluster of stems, these tending to be more rounded than in var. *strobiliformis* and to be in larger aggregations; Florida Mts., Luna Co., New Mexico. (Dale A. & M. A. Zimmerman)

Fig. 886. *Coryphantha organensis,* proposed species from the Organ Mts., Dona Ana Co., New Mexico, named by Allan D. and Dale A. Zimmerman; published while this book was in proof and not yet studied in detail by the author (see Documentation section). (Dale A. Zimmerman)

10b. Coryphantha strobiliformis var. durispina (Quehl) L. Benson. Rocky hills at ±600 m (2,000 ft). Chihuahuan Desert. Near Rio Grande in Presidio-Brewster Co. region of Texas. Northern Mexico.

10c. Coryphantha strobiliformis var. orcuttii (Bödeker) L. Benson. Limestone hills in grassland at about 1,200 m (4,000 ft). Desert Grassland. Arizona in E Cochise Co.; New Mexico from Hidalgo Co. to Otero Co. See discussion in Documentation section concerning particularly the recent studies of Allan D. Zimmerman and Dale A. Zimmerman.

See Documentation section for the proposed species *Coryphantha organensis.*

11. Coryphantha sneedii (Britton & Rose) Berger

Stems much branched, forming clumps 30+ cm diam; larger stems green, cylindroid, 2.5-7.5 cm long, 1.2-2.5 cm diam; tubercles 2 mm long and broad, protruding 3 mm, persistent and hard after fall of spines; areoles 1.5 mm diam, typically 3 mm apart; spines very dense, obliterating stem; central spines white, tipped with pink or lavender, about 6-9 per areole, the strictly central one short, straight, larger 4.5-9 mm long, basally to 0.3 mm diam, acicular, nearly circular in cross section; radial spines white, 25-35 per areole, spreading, straight, those on upper side of areole 4.5-6 mm long, those on lower ±3 mm long, basally 0.1 mm diam, acicular; flower 1.2-2 cm diam and long;

sepaloids with tan or brown to green median sections and white or pink margins, the larger lanceolate, ±5 mm long, 1 mm broad, each often with a short awn; petaloids white or at least the midribs pink, rose, magenta, or partly brownish, largest lanceolate-acuminate, ±6 mm long, 1 mm broad; filaments pale, ±3 mm long; anthers yellow, nearly square, 0.5 mm long; style cream-colored, ±4 mm long, ±0.5 mm diam; stigmas 3-5, cream-colored, ±1 mm long, relatively broad; fruit green or tinged with brown or red, clavate, to 15 mm long, to 6 mm diam, sometimes with up to several pilose scale-leaves; seeds reddish-brown, strongly reticulate, broader than long, 0.75-1 mm long, 1.25-1.5 mm broad, ±0.75 mm or less thick; hilum appearing "sub-basal."

The plants are masses of numerous and very small white-spined balls. The effect may be that of a gray-white shag rug with a coarse pattern. Sometimes a few larger stems protrude above the rest.

11a. Coryphantha sneedii var. sneedii. Limestone ledges of high hills in desert and in grassland at (1,300)1,500-1,650 m (4,200 or 5,000-5,500 ft). Chihuahuan Desert and Desert Grassland. New Mexico in Florida Mts., Luna Co., and Franklin Mts., Dona Ana Co.; Texas in Franklin Mts., El Paso Co.

In the Franklin Mts. *C. sneedii* var. *sneedii* intergrades with *C. strobiliformis* (New Mexico above Anthony Pass, *C. Champie & L. Benson 16453 to 16457, Pom*). Plants described by Dale A. Zimmerman (Cactus & Succ. Jour. 44: 114. *f. 1-4. 1972*) as *C. organensis* appear to be similar, but their status has not been evaluated. The proposed species is based upon specimens collected in the adjacent southern part of the Organ Mts. at 2,150-2,450 m (7,000-8,000 ft) elevation. See Documentation section.

Coryphantha sneedii var. *sneedii* and *C. strobiliformis* differ in the characters shown in the key and in the following additional characters:

C. sneedii var. *sneedii*. Central spines 4.5-6 mm long; radial spines on upper side of areole as long

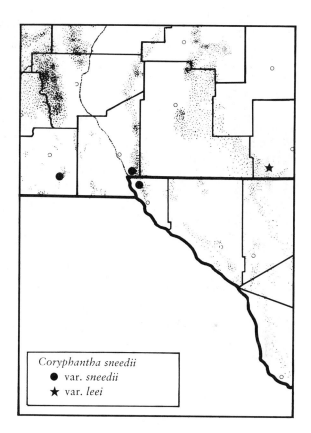

Coryphantha sneedii
● var. *sneedii*
★ var. *leei*

Distinctive Characters of the Varieties of Coryphantha sneedii

Character	a. var. **sneedii**	b. var. *leei*
Spines	All spreading parallel to stem surface, *not* deflexed	On medium and small stems deflexed and drooping toward stem from top of tubercle
Flower color	Pale or medium rose to magenta	Dull, medium brownish-pink
Seed size	0.75 mm long, 1.25 mm broad	1 mm long, 1.5 mm broad
Altitude	(1,300)1,500-1,650 m (4,200 or 5,000-5,500 ft)	1,200-1,500 m (4,000-5,000 ft)
Floristic association	Chihuahuan Desert; Desert Grassland	Chihuahuan Desert

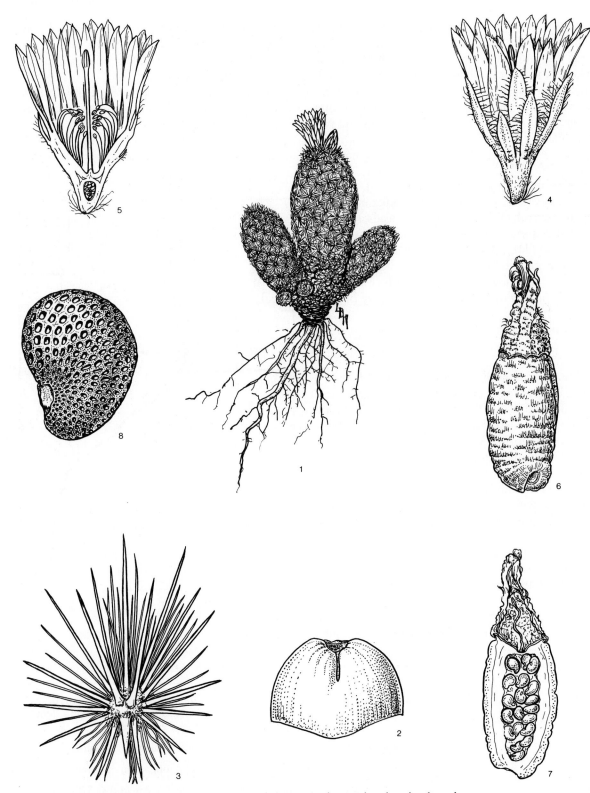

Fig. 887. *Coryphantha sneedii* var. *sneedii*. *1*, Relatively young plant with only a few branches, in flower, ×.9. *2*, Apex of a tubercle with the spines removed, ×17; the scar of flower attachment very short, as in young plants still in the stage of juvenile development. *3*, Areole with stouter central spines and more slender radial spines, the latter in several series, ×4.5. *4*, Flower, ×3.5. *5*, Flower in longitudinal section, ×3.5. *6*, Fruit, ×4.5. *7*, Fruit in longitudinal section, ×4.5. *8*, Seed, the hilum appearing "lateral," but the seed merely broader than long, ×28.

Fig. 888. *Coryphantha sneedii* var. *sneedii*, typical mat-forming plant with many small branches of various ages; specimen from Clark Champie; Franklin Mts., El Paso Co., Texas.

as centrals, those on lower side only ±3 mm long; fruit red or green, ±9 mm long, 4.5 mm diam.

C. strobiliformis. Central spines 12-15 mm long; radial spines nearly equal around the areole, largest about 12 mm long; fruit red (sometimes green), 12-15 mm long, 6-7.3 mm diam.

11b. Coryphantha sneedii var. **leei** (Rose *ex* Bödeker) L. Benson. Limestone ledges in desert at 1,200-1,500 m (4,000-5,000 ft). Chihuahuan Desert. Guadalupe Mts., Eddy Co., New Mexico.

12. Coryphantha dasyacantha
(Engelmann) Orcutt

Stems solitary (so far as known), the larger green, those of young plants globose but if older elongate-cylindroid or reportedly expanding upward, when mature 7.5-17.5 cm long, 5-7.5 cm diam; tubercles persisting on lower part of stem after fall of spines and becoming hard, 3-4.5 mm long, 3-6 mm apart; spines either dense and obscuring stem or sparse; central spines varying up-

ward from light-colored bases through pink, then red, to black, ±1-4(5) per areole, one usually porrect to directed downward, others tending upward, straight, longer 9-12 mm long, basally 0.25 (0.5) mm diam, acicular, nearly circular in cross section; radial spines white or straw-colored, 16-28 per areole, spreading, straight, the longer 6-10 mm long, basally 0.1 mm diam, acicular; flower 2-2.5 cm diam and long; sepaloids with purple to magenta midribs and pink margins, the larger lanceolate-subulate, 9-12 mm long, 2 mm broad, acute, ciliate-fimbriate; petaloids pink, largest narrowly lanceolate, ±12 mm long, 3 mm broad, acute, entire; filaments pale, 4.5 mm long; anthers yellow, 0.7 mm long, oblong, twice as long as broad; style pale yellow, 9-12 mm long, 2 mm greatest diam; stigmas 5 or 6, 2 mm long, rather broad; ovary in anthesis ±4.5 mm long, 2 mm diam; fruit red, fleshy at maturity, cylindroid to narrowly ellipsoid, 12-20 mm long, 4.5-6 mm diam; seeds dark brown to "almost black," obovoid, 1 mm long, 0.7 mm broad, 0.5 mm thick; hilum large, obliquely basal.

12a. Coryphantha dasyacantha var. **dasyacantha**. Soil from igneous rocks and probably limestone in oak woodland and grassland and to some extent in desert at 800-1,700 m (2,700-5,800 ft). Chihuahan Desert, Desert Grassland, and a Texan version of oak woodland. Texas from El Paso to Big Bend region. Reported from Chihuahua, Mexico.

The variety is relatively uncommon, reportedly because many plants have been collected for sale.

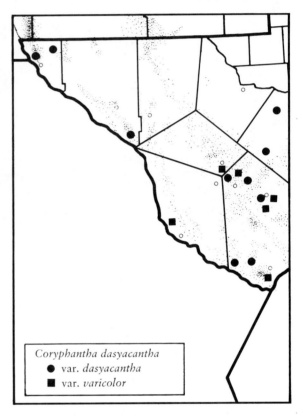

Coryphantha dasyacantha
● var. *dasyacantha*
■ var. *varicolor*

Fig. 889. *Coryphantha dasyacantha* var. *dasyacantha* in cultivation. (A. R. Leding, U.S. Acclimatization Station, College Station, New Mexico)

Distinctive Characters of the Varieties of **Coryphantha dasyacantha**

Character	a. var. **dasyacantha**	b. var. **varicolor**
Spines	Relatively dense, obscuring stem, their light color predominating	Not dense, the green of the stem predominating
Radial spines	White, ±24-28 per areole, the longer ±7.5-10 mm long	Straw-colored or some smaller ones white, 16-18 per areole, ±6 mm long
Tubercles	Relatively stout	Relatively slender
Altitude	800-1,700 m (2,700-5,800 ft)	1,080-1,440 m (3,600-4,800 ft)
Floristic association	Chihuahuan Desert; Desert Grassland and oak woodland	Desert Grassland

The stems are white cylinders of dense spines occurring among rocks, under bushes, or among grasses. The plants are not quickly distinguishable from *C. strobiliformis* unless the seeds are examined; these are not at all alike.

12b. Coryphantha dasyacantha var. varicolor (Tiegel) L. Benson. Hills of igneous rocks, limestone, or novaculite in grasslands at 1,080-1,440 m (3,600-4,800 ft). Desert Grassland. Texas in Presidio, s Jeff Davis, and N Brewster Cos.

The green cylinders are recognizable from several meters away.

Fig. 891. Comparison of seeds: *Coryphantha strobiliformis* and *C. dasyacantha* var. *dasyacantha*. Left, *C. strobiliformis*, the hilum appearing "lateral," the seed being actually merely broader than long and the hilum being *per se* basal. Right, *C. dasyacantha*, the hilum being obviously basal, because the seed is longer than broad. (Paulus Roetter in Engelmann/Emory, *pl. 12, f. 15b, 21*)

Fig. 892. *Coryphantha dasyacantha* var. *varicolor*, stem showing the relatively light covering of spines, as opposed to the dense covering in var. *dasyacantha*.

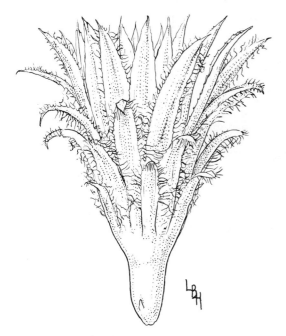 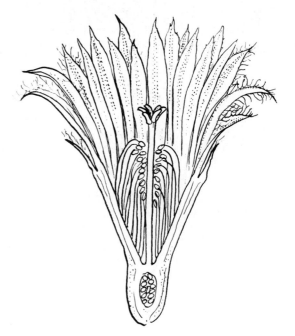

Fig. 890. *Coryphantha dasyacantha* var. *dasyacantha*, flowers. *1*, Flower, ×3. *2*, Flower in longitudinal section, ×3.

13. Coryphantha robertii Berger

Stems branching or individuals growing together and forming clumps ±10 cm high and 60-100 cm diam; larger stems green, at first cylindroid to ovoid-cylindroid and ultimately cylindroid, (3.8)5-12 cm long, 2-2.5 cm diam; tubercles 6 mm long vertically, 6 mm broad, protruding 6-9 mm, not hard or persistent; areoles 1.5 mm diam, typically 3 mm apart; spines very dense, obscuring stem; central spines pale yellow with dark red, brown, or black tips, 5-8 per areole, mostly turning upward, straight, larger to 12 mm long, basally ±0.2-0.25 mm diam, acicular, nearly

circular in cross section; radial spines white, numerous, mostly 20-30 per areole, spreading irregularly, straight, the larger to 10 mm long, basally ±0.1 mm diam, acicular; flower bronze-pink, 2-2.5 cm diam and long; sepaloids with greenish-purple midribs and magenta or pink margins, the larger lanceolate, to 15 mm long, 3 mm broad, acute, fimbriate; petaloids lavender to pale purple, largest lanceolate, 9-11 mm long, 3 mm broad, short-acuminate, marginally entire; filaments yellow, 3 mm long; anthers yellow, 1 mm long, oblong, 1.5 times as long as broad; style green and pink, 12-15 mm long, 1 mm max diam; stigmas 6 or 7, green, 2 mm long, rather broad; ovary in an-

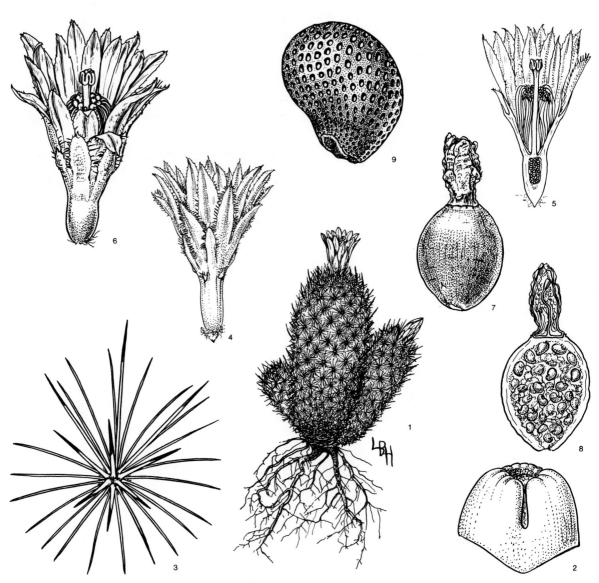

Fig. 893. *Coryphantha robertii*, ×3.3, except as indicated. *1*, Relatively young, unbranched plant bearing a flower bud and a flower, ×1.1. *2*, Apex of a tubercle with the spines cut off, ×5.5, showing the short groove leading to the flower-bearing area from the spine-bearing area, the groove in juvenile plants not running the full length of the tubercle. *3*, Areole with central and radial spines. *4*, Flower, ×1.6. *5*, Flower in longitudinal section, ×1.6. *6*, Another view of a flower. *7*, Fruit. *8*, Fruit in longitudinal section. *9*, Seed, showing the obviously basal hilum, ×33.

thesis ±3 mm long, ±2 mm diam; fruit red, fleshy at maturity, globose to ellipsoid, 6-9 mm diam; seeds black or brown, punctate, hemispheroidal to hemispheroidal-obovoid, 1-1.25 mm long, 1 mm broad, 0.75 mm thick; hilum clearly basal.

Limestone of hillsides in desert or grassland to about 300 m (1,000 ft). Chihuahuan Desert and Rio Grande Plain. Texas near Rio Grande from Devil's R., Val Verde Co., to Duval and Hidalgo Cos. Adjacent Mexico from Coahuila to Tamaulipas.

The whitish-brown masses or clumps are like clusters of eggs or short cylinders beneath bushes or between them.

In addition to the characters shown in the Key, the following distinguish *C. robertii* from *C. strobiliformis*:

C. robertii. Anthers 1 mm long, oblong, length twice breadth; style ±12-15 mm long, ±6-7 times as long as stigmas, these 2 mm long.

C. strobiliformis. Anthers 0.5 mm long, ovoid, length 1.5 times breadth; style 9-12 mm long, ±3-4 times as long as stigmas, these 3 mm long.

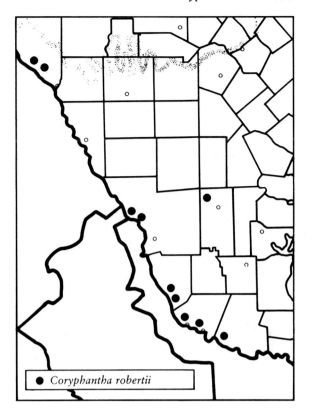

● *Coryphantha robertii*

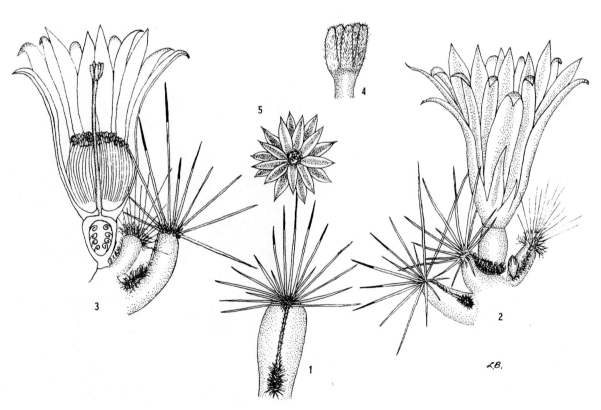

Fig. 894. *Coryphantha robertii. 1,* Tubercle with an areole, ×4.5, showing the isthmus between the spine- and flower-bearing areas; from a mature portion of the stem where the isthmus runs the full length of the tubercle. *2,* Flower, showing the position of the flower and of a fruit scar on the adjacent tubercle, ×2.3. *3,* Flower in longitudinal section, ×2.3. *4,* Stigmas, ×7. *5,* Top view of the flower, ×.4.

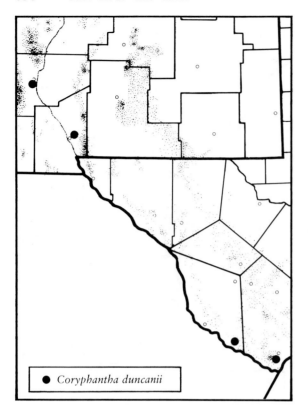

● *Coryphantha duncanii*

pitted, obovoid, 1-1.25 mm long, 0.8 mm broad, 0.7 mm thick; hilum obviously basal.

Limestone hills in desert at 1,030-1,650 m (3,400-5,400 ft). Chihuahuan Desert and Desert Grassland. Near Rio Grande; New Mexico in Sierra and Dona Ana Cos.; Texas in SE Presidio and S Brewster Cos., including Big Bend National Park.

15. Coryphantha missouriensis (Sweet) Britton & Rose

Stems solitary or branching and forming clumps 5-10 cm high, 15-30 cm diam, the larger dark green, hemispheroidal to depressed-globose, 2.5-5 cm long, 3.8-5(10) cm diam; tubercles elongate, 6-9 mm long and broad, protruding to 12-15 mm; areoles 1.5-2 mm diam, typically ±6 mm apart, white-woolly when young; spines rather dense, partly obscuring stem, at first yellowish but becoming dark gray, *pubescent*; central spines none (sometimes 1, rarely 2 or perhaps 4 per areole), not conspicuously differentiated; radial spines 10-20 per areole, spreading, straight, slender, longer 10-20 mm long, basally to 0.3 mm

14. Coryphantha duncanii (Hester) L. Benson

Stems solitary or rarely with 2 or 3 branches, green, broadly turbinate or subglobose to obconical, 2.5-6 cm long and diam; tubercles cylindroid, 2-3 mm long and broad, protruding 4.5-6 mm, *not* hard and persistent; areoles 1 mm diam, typically 3-4.5 mm apart; spines exceedingly dense, completely obscuring stem, in several series, the innermost larger, but distinction of central and radial spines not clear, white or with short dark-brown tips, 30-75 per areole, straight, bent, curved, or twisted through crowding against spines of adjacent areoles, slender, fragile, those on lower part of stem breaking off, longer 9-12 (22) mm long, basally 0.1-0.2 mm diam, acicular; flower 10-12 mm diam and long; sepaloids with greenish midribs and pink margins, largest oblong-lanceolate, 4 mm long, 1.5-2 mm broad, acute, scarious-margined and at least basally fimbriate-ciliate; petaloids pink, largest lanceolate, ±6 mm long, 1.5 mm broad, acute, cuspidate, marginally undulate; filaments pale, 3 mm long, ovate; anthers yellow, oblong, 0.5 mm long; style 6-7.5 mm long, 0.5 mm greatest diam; stigmas 4 or 5, 0.5 mm long, relatively broad; ovary in anthesis 2 mm long; fruit red, clavate, 10 mm long, ±3-4 mm diam; seeds black, shiny, with surface

Fig. 895. *Coryphantha duncanii* in flower, showing the fimbriolate-ciliate sepaloids; on limestone in the Big Bend National Park, Brewster Co., Texas. (Roland H. Wauer)

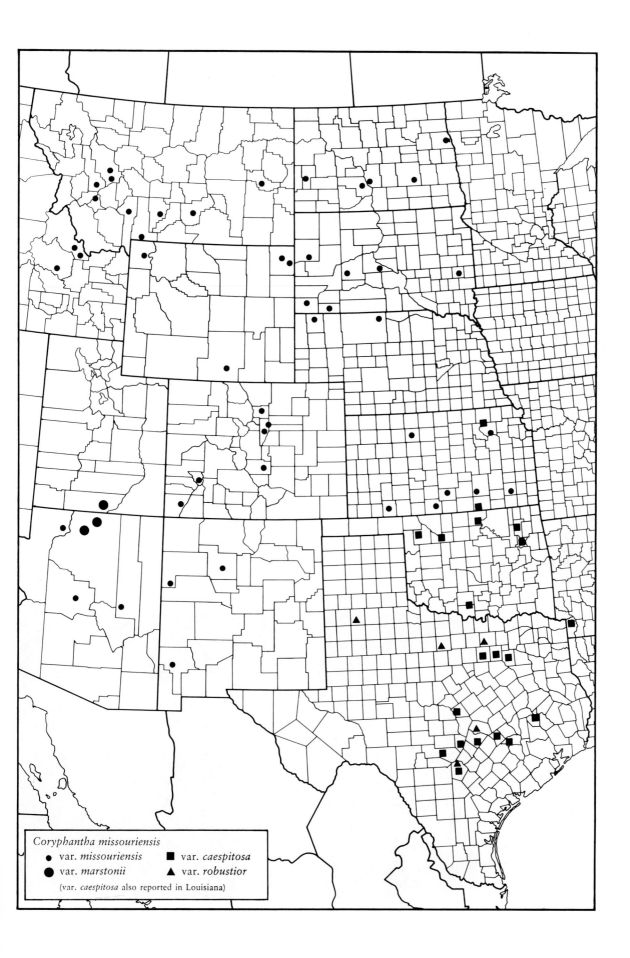

Coryphantha missouriensis
- • var. *missouriensis*   ■ var. *caespitosa*
- ● var. *marstonii*   ▲ var. *robustior*

(var. *caespitosa* also reported in Louisiana)

857

diam, acicular, nearly circular in cross section; flower 2.5-6.2 cm diam and long; sepaloids with green midribs and yellow to nearly white margins, larger linear-lanceolate, 12-40 mm long, 12 mm broad, sharply acute, fimbriate or entire; petaloids yellow or sometimes pink, red, or yellow tinged with red, the largest linear-lanceolate, 12-40 mm long, 1.5-4.5 mm broad, sharply acute, acuminate, or attenuate, entire; filaments yellow or green, 3-6 mm long; anthers yellow, ±1 mm long; style green, 12-25 mm long, to 1 mm greatest diam; stigmas 3-6, 1.5-4.5 mm long, rather broad; ovary in anthesis to 3 mm long; fruit red, 10-20 mm long and diam; seeds black, obviously punctate, helmetlike, 1-2.5 mm long, 1.5-2 mm broad, 0.5-1 mm thick; hilum clearly basal, slightly oblique.

The plants are inconspicuous and difficult to find, except during the flowering season, when the yellow, starlike flowers attract attention. At this time the stems are swollen with water and stand above ground level; but during the dry seasons they may retract nearly to the soil surface.

Distinctive Characters of the Varieties of Coryphantha missouriensis

Character	a. var. missouriensis	b. var. marstonii	c. var. caespitosa	d. var. robustior
Radial spines	Usually 13-20	10-13(19)	Usually 12-15	Usually 12-15
Flower size	2.5 cm diam and long	3.8-5 cm diam and long	±5-6.2 cm diam and long	±4.4-5 cm diam and long
Sepaloids	Fimbriate	Fimbriate	Fimbriate	*Not* fimbriate
Petaloids	Acute	Attenuate	Acuminate-attenuate	Abruptly long-acuminate
Fruits	Nearly globular, ±1 cm diam	Unknown	Globular to ellipsoid, 1.5-2 cm long	Globose, ±1 cm diam
Seed length	1 mm	2-2.5 mm	2-2.5 mm	Seeds not available
Altitude	600-1,800(2,700) m (2,000-6,000 or 9,000 ft)	1,500-2,100 m (5,000-7,000 ft)	Low elevations	300-600 m (1,000-2,000 ft)
Floristic association	Great Plains Grassland; Juniper-Pinyon Woodlands	Rocky Mountain Montane Forest; Southern Juniper-Pinyon Woodland	Great Plains Grassland	Great Plains Grassland; Edwards Plateau

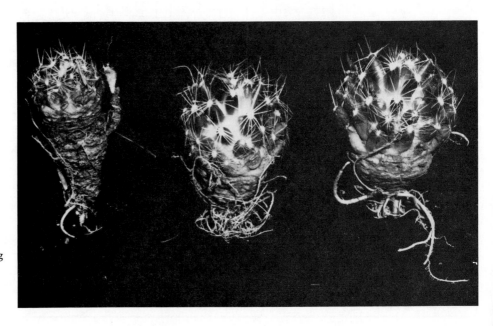

Fig. 896. *Coryphantha missouriensis* var. *missouriensis*, plants sent from North Dakota by Larry W. Mitich, showing the solitary erect central spine and the spreading radial spines in each areole.

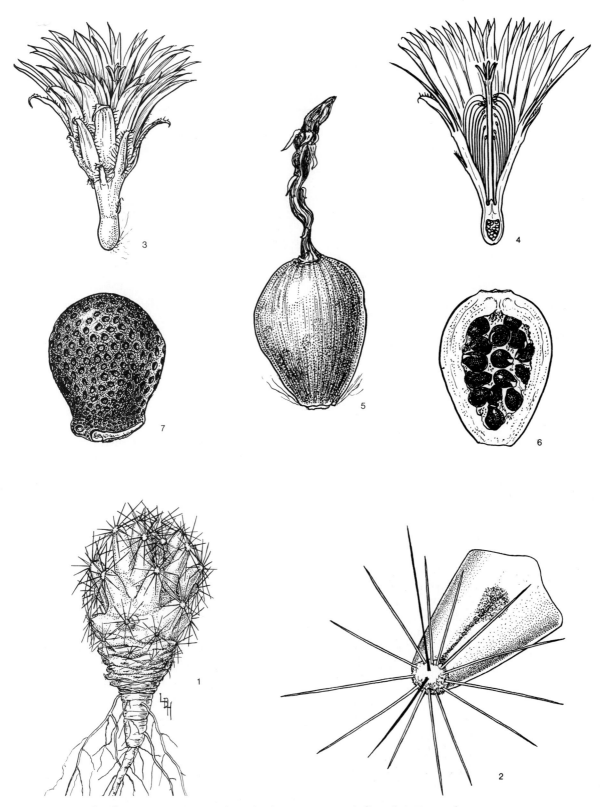

Fig. 897. *Coryphantha missouriensis* var. *missouriensis*, ×3, except as indicated. *1*, Young plant, ×1.25. *2*, Tubercle, showing the central spines, the radial spines, and the groove or isthmus between the spine- and flower-bearing areas, this from a juvenile stem and therefore not extending the length of the tubercle. *3*, Flower. *4*, Flower in longitudinal section. *5*, Fruit. *6*, Fruit in longitudinal section. *7*, Seed, the hilum obviously basal, ×28.

Fig. 898. *Coryphantha missouriensis* var. *caespitosa*, plant with a withered flower and a young fruit; collected in the Indian Territory (Oklahoma) in 1895. (Artist unknown; courtesy of Missouri Botanical Garden)

15a. Coryphantha missouriensis var. **missouriensis.** Plains and hills; desert edge and especially grasslands and among junipers on lower mountains at 600-1,800(2,700) m (2,000-6,000 or 9,000 ft). Great Plains Grassland; Juniper-Pinyon Woodlands. Central Idaho to North Dakota, Kansas, N Arizona, and w New Mexico.

15b. Coryphantha missouriensis var. **marstonii** (Clover) L. Benson. Mountainsides in forest or woodland at 1,500-2,100 m (5,000-7,000 ft). Rocky Mountain Montane Forest and Southern Juniper-Pinyon Woodland. Utah from s side of Aquarius Plateau to s Kane Co.; Arizona on Kaibab Plateau (known, also, as Buckskin Mts.).

15c. Coryphantha missouriensis var. **caespitosa** (Engelmann) L. Benson. Plains in grassland at low elevations. Great Plains Grassland. From SE Kansas (Cowley and Riley Cos.) to E Oklahoma and central Texas mostly in hills E of Edwards Plateau and s as far as Kerr, Bexar, Walker, and Austin Cos. and Nueces R.; Arkansas on Red R.; Louisiana (in "prairies"; presumably in the present state rather than elsewhere in old Louisiana Territory).

15d. Coryphantha missouriensis var. **robustior** (Engelmann) L. Benson. Prairies and grassy woodlands at about 300-600 m (1,000-2,000 ft). Great Plains Grassland and Edwards Plateau. Texas from Canadian R. (in Panhandle) to Hale, Denton, Travis, and Bexar Cos.

17. Ariocarpus

Stems usually unbranched, turbinate, the portion above ground flattened or depressed-globose, usually 6-12.5 cm diam; ribs none; tubercles separate, often flattened and imbricated like petals of a cultivated rose, in the local species sculptured, cartilaginous, tending to be triangular or prismatic; tissues with extensive mucilage canal systems. Roots large and fusiform. Leaves not distinguishable in mature plant. Areoles none or vestigial in adult, either an apical or a subapical point on upper side of tubercle or at base of median woolly groove, spine-bearing portion either a minor vestige or missing. Spines present only in very young plants. Flowers and fruits on new tubercles on growth of current season near apex of stem, at the base of the obscure hair-covered upper side of the tubercle in an area distant from the vestige (if any) of the spine-bearing part of areole and (in species occurring in U.S.) connected with it by an isthmus, this area persisting as an elongate, narrow groove on upper side of tubercle, or in some Mexican species groove absent. Flower 2-5 cm diam, between saucer-shaped and bell-shaped; floral tube above ovary obconical, white or magenta. Fruit greenish to red or reddish-purple, ultimately turning brown, fleshy at maturity, the surface bare, globose to oblong, 6-50 mm long, 2-12 mm diam, persistent in wool at apex of stem. Seeds black, shiny, globose, slightly longer than broad, 0.75-1 mm long; hilum obviously basal; cotyledons accumbent, not foliaceous.

Six species occurring in the Chihuahuan Desert from near the Rio Grande in the southern Big Bend region and south on the Mexican Plateau to Querétaro. Only one species occurs in the U.S.

The name derives from *Aria* (a plant genus) and Gr. *karpos* (fruit)—i.e., with fruit similar to that of *Aria*.

Reference: Anderson, 1960-64.

As monographed by Anderson, the genus comprises six species in two subgenera; one species occurs north of the Rio Grande.

Subgenus 1. ARIOCARPUS (Mexico)
    A. retusus (Coahuila to Tamaulipas & San Luis Potosí)
    A. agavoides (Tamaulipas)
    A. trigonus (Tamaulipas)
    A. scapharostrus (Nuevo León)

Subgenus 2. ROSEOCACTUS (U.S. & Mexico)
    A. kotschoubeyanus (Nuevo León & Tamaulipas to Querétaro)
1. *A. fissuratus*
    vars. a. *fissuratus*
           lloydii (Coahuila to San Luis Potosí)

1. Ariocarpus fissuratus
(Engelmann) K. Schumann
Living rock

Stem usually solitary, gray-green, very inconspicuous, more or less turnip-shaped, only the flattened or somewhat convex top protruding above ground level, usually 4-5 cm long, to 10 cm diam; ribs none; tubercles flattened or somewhat angular on top, exposed portion deltoid, deeply fissured-tuberculate above, exposed portion usually 12-25 mm long, 20-25 mm broad; areoles to 12 mm long and 3-6 mm broad, densely woolly; spines none on mature plant; flower on morphologically upper side of tubercle at end of groove connecting with potential spine-bearing area, to 3.5(4) cm diam and long; sepaloids with magenta midribs and pale magenta to whitish margins, the larger oblanceolate, to 20-25 mm long, to 4.5(6) mm broad, mucronulate, entire or slightly undulate; petaloids pale magenta, largest cuneate, to 30 mm long, to 15 mm broad, apically rounded, entire or finely and irregularly toothed; filaments pale, ±6 mm long; anthers yellow, 0.7 mm long, plump; style pale, 15-19 mm long, ±1 mm greatest diam; stigmas 5-10, mostly 3-4.5 mm long, slender; ovary in anthesis 3-4.5 mm long; fruit white to greenish, at first fleshy but drying at ma-

Fig. 899. Living rock, *Ariocarpus fissuratus*, almost hidden among limestone desert-pavement rock fragments in the Chihuahuan Desert. The plants rise only barely above the pavement. (Edward F. Anderson)

Fig. 900. *Ariocarpus fissuratus*, showing the deeply fissured, reticulate, wedgelike tubercles of two plants crowded against each other, these flat against the soil surface and overtopped by the surrounding limestone fragments. (Edward F. Anderson)

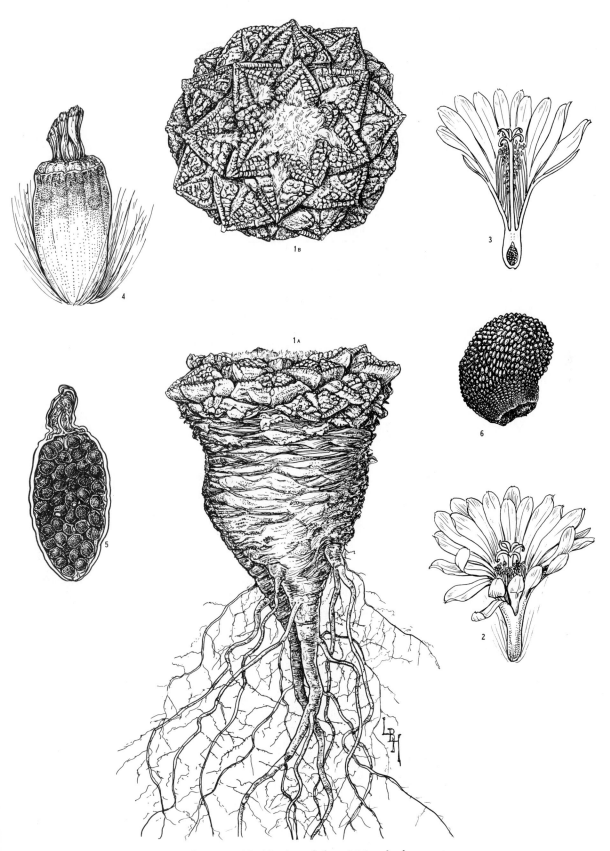

Fig. 901. Living rock, *Ariocarpus fissuratus. 1A*, side view of plant, ×.6, only the upper-most portion of which was above ground. *1B*, Top view, ×.6, showing the deeply fissured tubercles and the woolly hairs at the apex of the stem, the flowers emerging from the mass of hairs. 2, Flower, ×1.2. 3, Flower in longitudinal section, ×1.2. 4, Fruit, ×2.4. 5, Fruit in longitudinal section, ×2.4. 6, Seed, ×30.

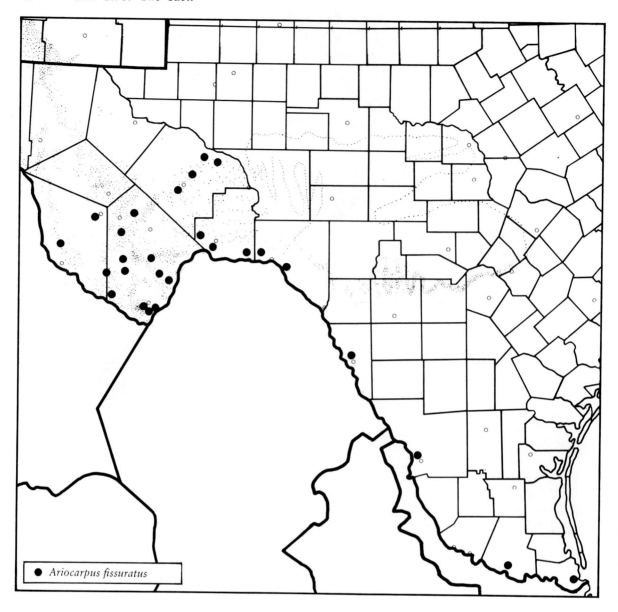

● *Ariocarpus fissuratus*

turity and ultimately becoming brown, without tubercles, scales, spines, hairs, or bristles, globose to oblong, 6-15 mm long, 3-6 mm diam, remaining embedded in wool, finally disintegrating; seeds irregularly obovoid, 0.8 mm long, 0.6 mm broad, 0.5 mm thick.

Limestone soils often with rock fragments. Hills or ridges in desert at 500-1,170 m (1,650-3,900 ft). Chihuahuan Desert. Texas from Presidio Co. SE

along Rio Grande and near lower Pecos R. Mexico near Rio Grande in adjacent Chihuahua and Coahuila.

These spineless cacti are like irregular stars forming decorations in desert pavements of flat limestone flakes. They are seen only from almost straight above; ordinarily they cannot be detected from a distance.

18. Mammillaria

Stems simple or branching, the larger ovoid to cylindroid, globose, or turbinate, 2.5-10(30) cm long, mostly 2.5-7.5(20) cm diam; tubercles separate, each corresponding with an enlarged leaf base (Boke, 1953, 1958). Leaves not discernible on mature tubercles. Areoles usually circular or nearly so. Spines smooth, with a wide range of colors; central spines none to several or sometimes central and radial spines not differentiated, straight, curved, or hooked, mostly 6-20(25) mm long, slender, basally usually 0.1-0.3 mm diam, acicular, broadly elliptic in cross section; radial spines usually smaller and of lighter color, 10-80 per areole, not hooked, acicular. Flowers and fruits on old growth of preceding seasons below apex of stem or branch, developed between tubercles and not obviously connected with them or with the areoles upon them, sometimes appearing in minor spine-bearing areoles (or the areole with rudimentary structures corresponding with spines; Boke, 1953, 1958) between tubercles. Flower usually 6-25(50) mm diam; floral tube above ovary funnelform or obconic, green tinged with the color of the perianth. Fruit fleshy at maturity, without surface appendages, globular to elongate, usually 6-25 mm long, 6-20 mm diam; floral tube deciduous, indehiscent. Seeds black to brown, rugose-reticulate, reticulate-pitted, or smooth and shiny, the surface more prominent than the pits, or tuberculate, longer than broad, usually 1-2 mm greatest dimension; hilum usually obviously basal but sometimes appearing oblique, crater-like; cotyledons accumbent, *not* foliaceous.

Perhaps 100 species (many more having received names), occurring from California to southern Nevada, southwestern Utah, New Mexico, western Oklahoma, and Texas, south to Mexico and Central America, with outliers in the Caribbean and Venezuela. Thirteen species in the U.S.

Some species of the genus are known as fish-hook cacti.

Britton and Rose (1923) listed 150 species as *Neomammillaria* (superfluous equivalent of *Mammillaria*, now conserved) and five more under *Phellosperma*, *Dolichothele*, and *Solisia*. These are in need of thorough study and evaluation. The extraterritorial species are too numerous and too uncertain to be included in the following list.

1. *M. longimamma*
   vars. a. *sphaerica*
      longimamma (Mexico)
2. *M. heyderi*
   vars. a. *heyderi*
      b. *hemisphaerica*
      c. *meiacantha*
      d. *macdougalii*
         gummifera (Chihuahua)
3. *M. prolifera*
   vars. a. *texana*
      prolifera (Caribbean)
4. *M. lasiacantha*
5. *M. pottsii*
6. *M. dioica*
7. *M. mainiae*
8. *M. microcarpa*
9. *M. thornberi*
10. *M. viridiflora*
11. *M. grahamii*
    vars. a. *grahamii*
       b. *oliviae*
12. *M. wrightii*
    vars. a. *wrightii*
       b. *wilcoxii*
13. *M. tetrancistra*

David R. Hunt (1971) has published a provisional arrangement of the species of *Mammillaria* according to infrageneric taxa; this appears to be a good, though not final, treatment of the subgenera, sections, and series within the genus. However, since relatively few species are included in the present study, a complete evaluation of his allocations cannot be made. According to Hunt, the species appearing in this book are members of the following infrageneric taxa:

Subgenus DOLICHOTHELE

Section DOLICHOTHELE

Series DOLICHOTHELE
1. *M. longimamma*

Subgenus MAMMILLARIA

Section MAMMILLARIA

Series MACROTHELE
2. *M. heyderi*

Section HYDROCHYLUS

Series STYLOTHELE
3. *M. prolifera*

Series LASIACANTHAE
4. *M. lasiacantha*

Series LEPTOCLADODAE
5. *M. pottsii*

Series ANCISTROCANTHAE
6-13. [All other U.S. & Canadian species]

KEY TO THE SPECIES OF MAMMILLARIA

1. Fruit green; petaloids stalked, yellow; superior floral tube elongate; tubercles soft, protruding 1.5-2.5 cm; flowers 2.5-5 cm in diameter; spines straight; Texas and Mexico ....**1. M. longimamma**
1. Fruit red; petaloids not stalked, pink, purple, magenta, yellow, salmon, or white; superior floral tube cuplike; tubercles usually firm, protruding 0.3-0.5(2.4) cm; flowers less than 2.5 cm in diameter or, if larger, not yellow; spines straight, curved, or hooked.
   2. Juice of the stems milky; stem broadly turbinate or depressed-globose, the apex flattened or shallowly convex, often barely protruding above ground level; tubercles conical or pyramidal, conspicuous, not obscured by spines; spines straight or slightly curving, none recurved, like fishhooks; SE Arizona and s New Mexico to Texas and Mexico......................................**2. M. heyderi**
   2. Juice of the stems *not* milky; stem cylindroid to ovoid, the apex *not* markedly flattened or shallowly convex, standing well above ground level (except in *M. mainiae*, which has hooked, yellow central spines); tubercles conical to cylindroid, obscured by spines; spines various.
      3. Spines not hooked; SE Arizona and s New Mexico to Texas and Mexico.
         4. Radial spines flexible, hairlike, turning irregularly; central spines 8-10 per areole, red, puberulent; Texas and Mexico...............**3. M. prolifera**
         4. Radial spines *not* flexible or hairlike; central spines various (cf. leads 5 and 6), *not both* red and puberulent.
            5. Spines (40)50-80 per areole, white, in several undifferentiated series; stems globose, rarely more than 3.8 cm in diameter; flowers saucer-shaped, 9-12 mm in diameter; petaloids white with red midstripes; New Mexico, Texas, and Mexico ....**4. M. lasiacantha**
            5. Spines 23-48 per areole, clearly and sharply differentiated into central and radial series; stems cylindroid or globose, if globose then 5-10 cm in diameter at maturity; flowers campanulate or funnelform, 6-30 mm in diameter; petaloids pink or reddish-purple.
               6. Central spines 7-11, in 2 series, the principal one purplish-brown on the upper half, the others light tan; radial spines much more slender than the centrals and readily overlooked; stems cylindroid, 7.5-10+ cm long, 2-2.5(4.5) cm in diameter; flowers campanulate, 6 mm in diameter; petaloids reddish-purple; Texas and Mexico.................**5. M. pottsii**
               6. Central spines 3, in 1 series, white or reddish-brown-tipped, the most nearly central one shorter than the 2 upper (those toward the edge of the areole); radial spines more slender than the centrals but conspicuous; stems ovoid to spheroidal, 4.5-6(11) cm in diameter; flowers funnelform, 20-30(40) mm in diameter; petaloids pink; Arizona and Sonora................. ....**11b. M. grahamii** var. **oliviae**
      3. Spines (1 or more of the central spines but not the radials) hooked; largely w of the Continental Divide.
         4A. Base of the seed not enlarged, i.e., the aril, if present, *not* markedly thickened or corky; hooked central spine(s) 1 (to 3-5, in *M. wrightii* and rarely in *M. viridiflora*); straight centrals 0-2(3); radial spines 10-35.

5A. Stem with vestigial areoles between the tubercles, these each bearing hairs and a cluster of a few relatively weak, undifferentiated spines and ultimately the flowers and fruits; some plants with only sterile male flowers, the pollen viable but not released from the anthers; (stems of older plants usually branching; areoles numerous, closely packed); coastal s California near San Diego and the w edge of the Colorado Desert in California and Baja California.......................................**6. M. dioica**

5A. Stem with *no* visible spine-bearing areoles between the tubercles, but the flowers between tubercles; plants bisexual, the stamens and pistils similar in the flowers of all plants; Arizona and some species E to the w edge of Texas; adjacent Mexico.

  6A. Central spines yellow except at the apices, 0.5-0.7 mm in diameter, the hooks nearly all turned counterclockwise; stigmas red; sepaloids bearing very short hairs on the margins, the hairs much less than 0.3 mm long .... **7. M. mainiae**

  6A. Central spines *not* even partly yellow, 0.2-0.4 mm in diameter, the hooks not turned consistently in any direction; stigmas of various colors; sepaloid margins various.

    7. Apical hook of the central spine 2-3 mm across from the tip to the opposite side of the curve, this spine usually solitary but accompanied by a single, straight, smaller and paler accessory central; stem at maturity typically branching basally, it or each branch basally truncate; (flower 20-28 mm in diameter; petaloids reddish-purple, ±10, 3-4.5 mm broad; stigmas green, ±3 mm long)..........**8. M. microcarpa**

    7. Apical hook of the central spine 1.5 mm across; stem commonly unbranched, but in some species a few plants branching, the stem clusters (if any) usually of separate individuals or (in *M. thornberi*) connected at first by slender ephemeral rhizomes.

      8. Petaloids *not* brilliant magenta, ±10, acute, 2-8 mm broad; hooked central spine 1 per areole (rarely 2 hooked central spines in a few areoles or, in *M. viridiflora*, rarely 2-4 in old plants); fruits 4.5-13 mm in diameter; flowers 15-30 mm in diameter, 12-40 mm long, the diameter not greater than the length.

        9. Central spine 1, hooked (but sometimes in a few areoles accompanied by 1 shorter, paler, straight accessory upper central; old plants of *M. viridiflora* sometimes with 2-4 hooked centrals); radial spines basally bulbous, 14-24, tan or straw-colored basally and reddish-brown apically; areoles circular; flower 15-20 mm in diameter; petaloids lavender or green or tinged with pink, to 9-12 mm long.

          10. Stem slender-cylindroid but expanding gradually into the base, 5-10(26) cm long, 1.2-2.5 (in very long stems 5) cm in diameter, the stems connected by slender, ephemeral rhizomes; stigmas bright red, 7, 3-5 mm long; petaloids lavender; anthers rectangular, 0.6-0.7 mm long; radial spines straw-colored but brown-tipped, 15-20 per areole; sepaloids finely ciliate; flowers of 1 turn of the spiral opening a few at a time on different days, well down the stem........................**9. M. thornberi**

          10. Stem ovoid, basally truncate, 7.5-10 cm long, 5-7.5 cm in diameter, *not* with rhizomes; stigmas green, 3-8, 1 mm long and relatively broad; petaloids green or green tinged with pink; anthers nearly square, 0.3 mm long; radial spines white, 14-24 per areole; sepaloids strongly fimbriate; flowers of 1 turn of the spiral all opening the same day, only 1 or 2 tubercles away from the stem apex ....**10. M. viridiflora**

        9. Central spines 3, the principal one hooked and longer than the 2-3 pale, straight, accessory upper marginal centrals; radial spines not basally bulbous, 20-35, white; areoles elliptic; flower 20-30(45) mm in diameter; petaloids reddish-purple to pink or the margins sometimes pink or pale pink, 12-25 mm long, white to pale pink or lavender; (radial spines white or pale tan; stigmas 7-10, pale green or tannish-green, (2)3-8 mm long; flowers of 1 turn of the spiral opening a few at a time on different days, well down the stem).....................**11. M. grahamii** var. **grahamii**

8. Petaloids brilliant magenta, 15-40, attenuate, 2-3 mm broad; hooked central spines 3 (2 or 4 or 5; in juvenile plants 1, later 2) per areole; fruits 13-25 mm in diameter; flowers 33-75 mm in diameter, 35-50 mm long, the diameter greater than the length; (flowers of 1 turn of the spiral all opening the same day, only 1 or 2 tubercles away from the stem apex)..........................**12. M. wrightii**

4A. Base of the seed corky, the aril being a conspicuous enlarged outgrowth at least half as large as the seed body; hooked central spines (1)2-4, straight centrals several or sometimes none; radial spines 30-46(60); deserts near the Colorado River in California, Nevada, Utah, Arizona, and adjacent Mexico..........
....**13. M. tetrancistra**

1. Mammillaria longimamma DeCandolle

Stems numerous, forming dense mounds or clumps to ±5 cm high and 30+ cm diam; larger stems green, cylindroid, ±5 cm long, 2.5-6 cm diam; tubercles soft and turgid, mammiform-cylindroid, 12-25(50) mm long, 6-9 mm broad, protruding 12-25 mm; areoles 1.5 mm diam, typically 6 mm apart; spines not dense, not obscuring stem; central spines reddish-tan, 1-4 per areole, spreading perpendicular to stem, straight, minute, 1-3 mm long, basally 0.25 mm diam, acicular, long-conical; radial spines gray, 12-14 per areole, spreading and paralleling the stem, straight, slender, longer 6-10 mm long, basally 0.1 mm di-

am, acicular; flower ±25-50 mm diam and long, funnelform; floral tube constricted above ovary; sepaloids with greenish to reddish-green midribs and yellow margins, larger narrowly elliptic-lanceolate, 12-25 mm long, 3-4.5 mm broad, acute, entire; petaloids yellow, largest oblanceolate, 20-30 mm long, 4.5-6 mm broad, acute or slightly acuminate, entire; filaments yellowish, 6-12 mm long; anthers yellow, 0.4-0.7 mm long; style yellowish, 12-25 mm long, 1 mm greatest diam; stigmas 5-8, 6-7.5 mm long, very slender; ovary in anthesis 3-6 mm long; fruit not available.

The relationship of this species to *Coryphantha*, with which it is a connecting link, was pointed out by Engelmann (in Emory, 1859). Boke (1961), on the basis primarily of minute structures, considered the relationship with *Coryphantha vivipara* to be evident.

1a. Mammillaria longimamma var. **sphaerica** (Dietrich) K. Brandegee. Tubercles 1.2-2.5 cm long; spines glabrous; central spines 1-4; radial spines 12-14, 6-9 mm long. Grasslands and thickets near sea level. Rio Grande Plain. Texas along lower Rio Grande from Maverick Co. to Cameron Co. and E to Gulf Coast in San Patricio and Nueces Cos. Adjacent N Mexico.

The plants are small, inconspicuous, irregular mats among bushes or in gravelly spots among grasses.

Mammillaria longimamma var. **longimamma.** Tubercles ±2.5-5 cm long; spines puberulent; central spines 1-3; radial spines 6-12, (5)10-20 mm long. Central Mexico; not occurring in the U.S.

2. Mammillaria heyderi Mühlenpfordt

Low-growing plant with usually solitary, rarely clustered stems, longer turbinate to subglobose, the part above ground flat or depressed or shal-

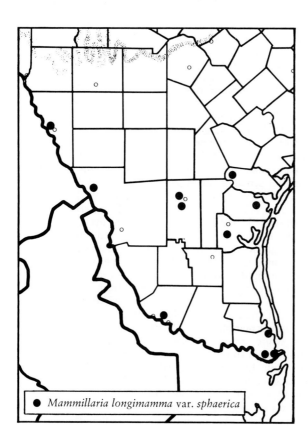

● *Mammillaria longimamma* var. *sphaerica*

Fig. 902. *Mammillaria longimamma* var. *sphaerica*, showing the elongate tubercles and the central and radial spines.

lowly convex, 7.5-10(15) cm diam; tubercles sub-conical to subpyramidal, 9-11 mm long, 6-7.5 mm broad, protruding 9-12 mm; areoles circular, 1.5-2.2 mm diam, typically 6-12 mm apart; spines rather dense but not obscuring stem; central spines brown, reddish-brown, or tan, 0-2(4) per areole, at right angles to stem, straight, the longer 3-9 mm long, basally 0.2-0.5 mm diam, acicular, nearly circular in cross section; radial spines tan to brown or nearly white, 6-22 per areole, spreading parallel to stem, straight, longer 6-16 mm long, basally 0.2-0.5 mm diam, acicular, nearly circular in cross section; flower 25-30 mm diam and long; sepaloids with green or pink midribs and pink or white margins, larger linear-lanceolate, 10-20 mm long, 3 mm broad, apically acute to acuminate or mucronate, entire to denticulate or fimbriate; petaloids pink, white, or cream or mixtures of these colors, largest linear-lanceolate, 10-20 mm long, 1.5-3(4.5) mm broad, acute to acuminate or mucronate, entire to denticulate; filaments white to pink or cream, 3 mm long; an-

thers yellow, rectangular, longer than broad, 0.7 mm long; style pink or cream, 9-22 mm long, 1 mm greatest diam; stigmas ±10, 3-4.5 mm long, slender; ovary in anthesis ±4.5 mm long; fruit red, fleshy at maturity, narrowly obovoid, mark-edly enlarged upward, 12-40 mm long, 6-9 mm diam; seeds brown, rugose-reticulate, obovoid, 1 mm long, 0.8 mm broad, 0.6 mm thick.

The plants are spiny pincushions protruding from the soil. Pricking the tubercles yields a milky juice, which oozes quickly to the surface.

2a. Mammillaria heyderi var. heyderi. Gravel-ly limestone soils in deserts and grasslands from near sea level to about 1,350 m (4,500 ft). Chi-huahuan Desert and Desert Grassland. South-easternmost corner of Arizona in Cochise Co.; New Mexico from Grant and Hidalgo Cos. to Guadalupe and Eddy Cos.; Oklahoma in Greer Co.; Texas from El Paso Co. to San Saba and San Patricio Cos. and s to Edwards Plateau and Rio Grande Plain. Mexico (area undetermined).

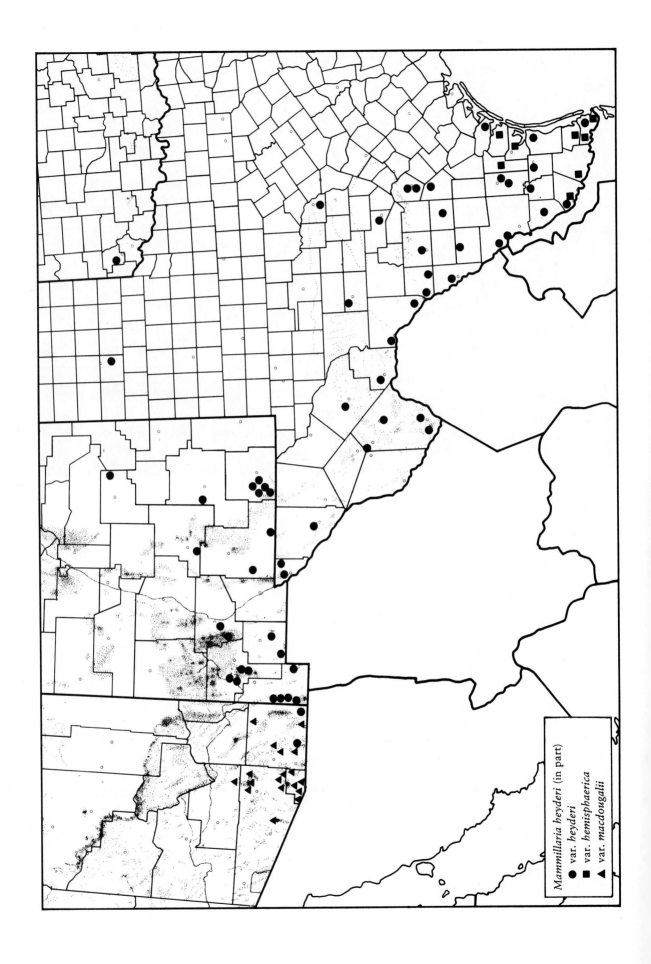

Mammillaria heyderi (in part)

● var. *heyderi*
■ var. *hemisphaerica*
▲ var. *macdougalii*

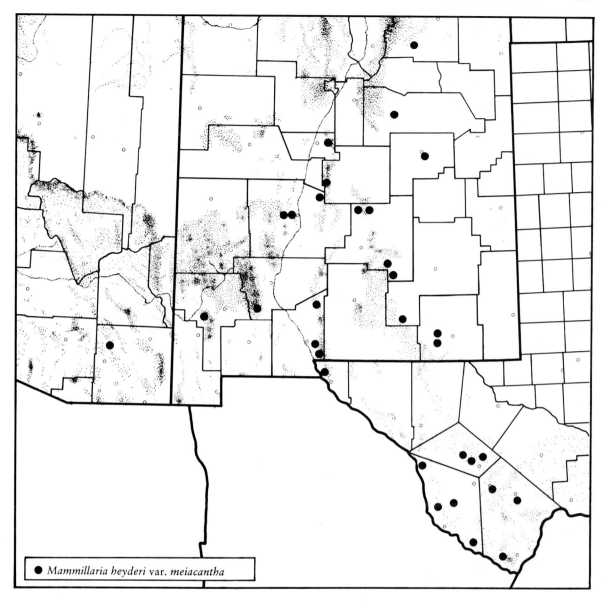

● *Mammillaria heyderi* var. *meiacantha*

2b. Mammillaria heyderi var. **hemisphaerica** (Engelmann) L. Benson. In deeper soils of valleys and plains; grasslands and thickets near sea level. Rio Grande Plain. Texas near mouth of Rio Grande and on plains from Jim Hogg and Starr Cos. to Nueces and Cameron Cos. Mexico in adjacent Tamaulipas and Nuevo León.

2c. Mammillaria heyderi var. **meiacantha** (Engelmann) L. Benson. Gravelly and rocky soils, usually of limestone origin, in desert and grasslands at 1,200-1,600 m (4,000-5,300 ft). Chihuahuan Desert, Great Plains Grassland, and Desert Grassland (in U.S.). Arizona in Texas Canyon, Dragoon Mts., Cochise Co.; New Mexico from Colfax Co. to Grant and Eddy Cos.; Texas from El Paso Co. to Jeff Davis and Brewster Cos. Mexico s to Zacatecas.

2d. Mammillaria heyderi var. **macdougalii** (Rose) L. Benson. Hillsides and valleys in mountains and on plains in grassland at 1,080-1,500 m (3,600-5,000 ft). Desert Grassland. Arizona on s edge of Pinal Co. and from Pima Co. to Santa Cruz and Cochise Cos. Mexico in adjacent Sonora.

Mammillaria heyderi var. **gummifera** (Engelmann) L. Benson. Collected at only the type locality, Cosihuiriachi, Chihuahua, Mexico; not known in the U.S.

Distinctive Characters of the Varieties of **Mammillaria heyderi**

Character	a. var. heyderi	b. var. hemisphaerica	c. var. meiacantha	d. var. macdougalii	var. gummifera (Mexico)
Stem apex	Flattened to concave	Hemispheroidal (with a smooth appearance)	Hemispheroidal	Flattened or concave to hemispheroidal	Flattened or concave to hemispheroidal
Tubercles	Subconical	Conical	Subpyramidal	Subconical	Subpyramidal
Central spine(s)	1, 6-7.5 mm long	1, 3-4.5 mm long	0 or 1, 3-6 mm long	1 or 2, 7.5-9 mm long	1, 2, or 4, 3-4 mm long
Radial spines	(10)14-22, 7.5-9 mm long, 0.2 mm diam	7-12(14), to 16 mm long, 0.3 mm diam	6-9, 7.5-10.5 mm long, 0.5 mm diam	10-12, 7.5-13.5 mm long, 0.2 mm diam, those on lower side of areole elongate	9-12, the upper 6 or 7 much longer, to 1.5 cm long, to 0.5 mm diam, those on upper side of areole elongate
Flower	Pink to nearly white or cream, to 2 cm diam	Cream to pinkish, to 2.5 cm diam	Pink or pink-and-white, to 2.5-3 cm diam	Cream, to 3 cm diam	Pink or red-and-white, to 2.5-3 cm diam
Sepaloid margins	Entire	Entire	Entire or minutely denticulate	More or less fimbriate	Fimbriate
Fruit color	Red	Red	Purplish	Red	Unknown
Altitude	Sea level to 1,350 m (4,500 ft)	Near sea level	1,200-1,600 m (4,000-5,300 ft)	1,080-1,500 m (3,600-5,000 ft)	Unknown; perhaps 1,500 m (5,000 ft)
Floristic association	Chihuahuan Desert and Desert Grassland; Edwards Plateau; Rio Grande Plain	Rio Grande Plain	Great Plains Grassland to Desert Grassland (in U.S.)	Desert Grassland	Unknown

Fig. 903. *Mammillaria heyderi* var. *heyderi*, growing in the shadow of a creosote bush on Lower Tornillo Creek in the Chihuahuan Desert, Big Bend National Park, Brewster Co., Texas. The plant is both obscure and well hidden.

Fig. 904. *Mammillaria heyderi* var. *heyderi*. 1, Plant from above, showing the tubercles and spines, ×.7. 2, Fruit, ×2. 3, Fruit in longitudinal section, ×2. 4, Seed, ×30.

873

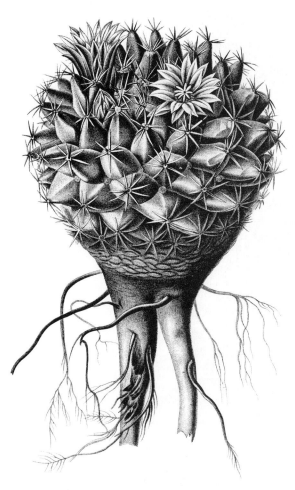

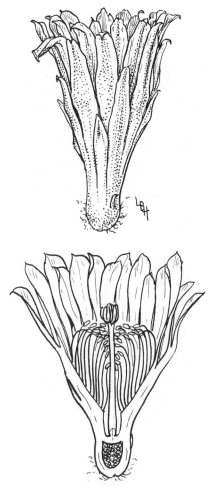

Fig. 905. *Mammillaria heyderi* var. *meiacantha*, plant in flower, showing the more or less prismatic tubercles. (Paulus Roetter in Engelmann/Emory, *pl. 9, f. 1*)

Fig. 906. *Mammillaria heyderi* var. *meiacantha*, ×2½. Above, flower. Below, flower in longitudinal section.

Fig. 907. *Mammillaria heyderi* var. *macdougalii*, showing the sparse central and radial spines. Each tubercle of the uppermost (apical) one or two turns of the spiral subtends a flower; these are mature tubercles and therefore not at the stem apex.

874

Fig. 908. *Mammillaria heyderi* var. *macdougalii* in the lower edge of the Desert Grassland. The two desert shrubs are ocotillo, *Fouquieria splendens* (upper left), and the brittle bush, *Encelia farinosa* (upper right).

Fig. 909. *Mammillaria heyderi* var. *macdougalii* among limestone boulders near Colossal Cave, Rincon Mts., Pima Co., Arizona; lower edge of the Desert Grassland.

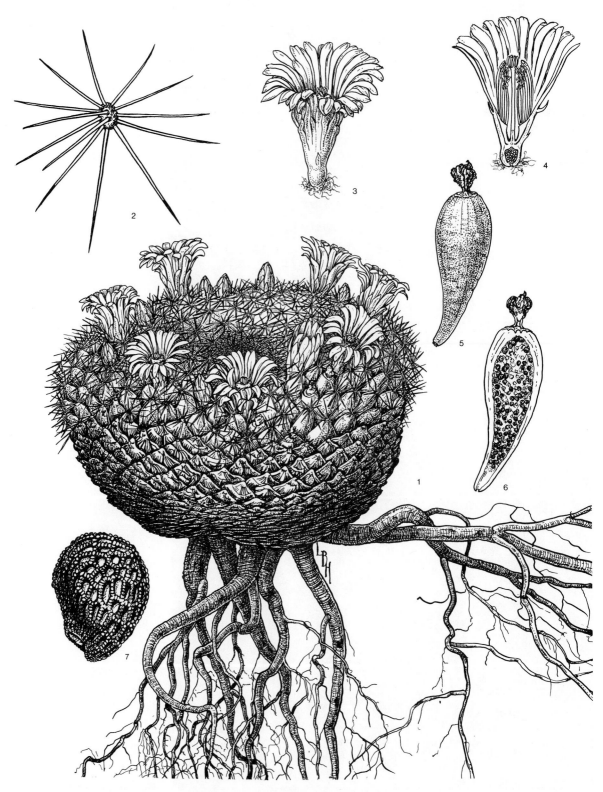

Fig. 910. *Mammillaria heyderi* var. *macdougalii*, ×1.1, except as indicated. *1*, Plant, ×.6, bearing flower buds in a turn of a spiral well back from the stem-apex (which is in the central depression) and bearing fruits outside of these (fruits shown a little right of center); only the spiny part of the stem above ground level. *2*, Areole with central and radial spines and wool, ×3. *3*, Flower. *4*, Flower in longitudinal section. *5*, Fruit. *6*, Fruit in longitudinal section. *7*, Seed, ×28.

3. **Mammillaria prolifera** (Miller) Haworth

Plant with dense stem clusters forming mounds or clumps 2.5-7.5 cm high and to 30+ cm diam; larger stems green, cylindroid to short-ovoid, 2-5 (7.5) cm long, 1.2-2.5(6) cm diam; tubercles mammiform, 3 mm diam, protruding 4.5-6 mm; areoles 1-1.5 mm diam, typically 3 mm apart; spines densely covering and obscuring the stem, with intermingling hairs nearly as long; central spines red, puberulent, 8-10 per areole, straight, longer 6-9 mm long, basally 0.1 mm diam, acicular; radial spines white, 30-60 per areole, spreading irregularly, hairlike, mostly winding and twisting, longer as long as centrals but of much less diam; flower closed-campanulate, 12 mm diam when spread out, of greater length; sepaloids with reddish midribs but yellowish tips, larger narrowly oblong, blunt, 4.5 mm long, 1.5 mm broad; petaloids dirty-yellow to whitish-yellow, reddish, or pink-and-yellow, the largest narrowly oblong, 10 mm long, 2-3 mm broad, apically acute and moderately serrulate, marginally entire; filaments 4.5 mm long; anthers yellow, nearly square, 0.4 mm long; style ±9 mm long, 0.5 mm greatest diam; stigmas ±4, 1.5 mm long, narrow; ovary in anthesis ±2 mm long; fruit red, the wall very thin but fleshy at maturity, without surface appendages, nearly cylindroid but enlarged upward, 20 mm long, 4.5 mm diam; seeds black, reticulate-pitted, asymmetrically obovoid, 1 mm long, 0.7-0.8 mm broad, 0.6 mm thick.

3a. Mammillaria prolifera var. **texana** (Engelmann) Borg. Plant 1.2-2.5 cm diam; central spines 8-10, with dark-brown tips; flowers nearly white to salmon-yellow or partly reddish or pink-and-yellow; fruit 9-12 mm long. Grasslands at low elevations. Rio Grande Plain. South Texas from Val Verde Co. to Bexar and Hidalgo Cos. Adjacent N Mexico.

The little mounds of furry, egglike stems are hidden away among grasses or under bushes, where their white color contrasts with the soil and vegetation.

Mammillaria prolifera var. **prolifera**. Plant 2.5-6 cm diam; central spines 5-12, with yellow tips; flowers yellowish-white; fruit 1.5-2 cm long. Cuba and Hispaniola and SE on Caribbean Islands to Trinidad; not native in the U.S.

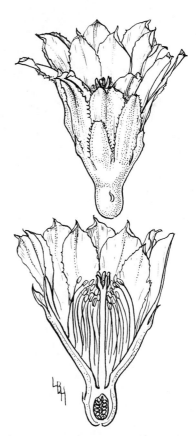

Fig. 911. *Mammillaria prolifera* var. *texana*, ×4. Above, flower. Below, flower in longitudinal section.

● *Mammillaria prolifera* var. *texana*

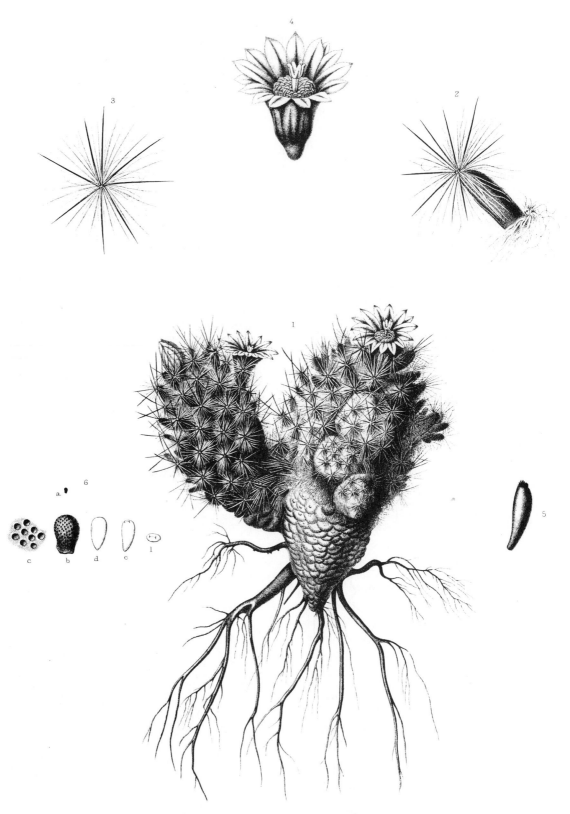

Fig. 912. *Mammillaria prolifera* var. *texana*. *1*, Plant in flower. *2*, Tubercle bearing an areole, showing the central spines and very fine hairlike radial spines. *3*, Areole, top view. *4*, Flower. *5*, Fruit. *6*, Seed: *a*, natural size; *b*, ×10; *c*, surface; *d*, contents; *e*, embryo, showing the minute apical cotyledons; "*l*," the embryo from above. (Paulus Roetter in Engelmann/Emory, *pl. 5*)

4. **Mammillaria lasiacantha** Engelmann

Small plant nearly hidden in soil, the stem (sometimes 2 or 3 stems) projecting only slightly above surface; larger stems turbinate or turnip-shaped, 2-3.8(10) cm long and diam; tubercles basally 1.5-2 mm long and broad, protruding 3 mm; areoles ±1 mm diam, typically 3 mm apart; spines very dense, obscuring stem, white, ±40-80 per areole, in several series, the number per series decreasing upward, straight, the longer ±3 mm long, basally ±0.1 mm diam, acicular, nearly circular in section, white-pubescent or glabrous; flower rotate, when fully expanded 9-12 mm diam and long; sepaloids with red midribs and white margins, the larger obovate-oblanceolate, ±6 mm long, 1.5 mm broad, nearly acute or mucronate, entire; petaloids white with red midstripes, largest very narrowly elliptic, usually ±10 mm long, 2 mm broad, apically rounded, entire; filaments yellowish, 2 mm long; anthers yellow, oblong-ovate, 0.5 mm long; style greenish-white, 7.5-10 mm long, ±0.7 mm greatest diam; stigmas 4 or 5, 1 mm long, 0.7 mm broad; ovary in anthesis 1.5-3 mm long; fruit red, fleshy but thin-walled, at maturity drying, shrivelling, and turning gray, persistent between tubercles, at first cylindroid to clavate, 12-20 mm long, 30-45 mm diam; seeds brown with some dark gray or black surface covering, clearly reticulate-pitted, obovoid but with an abrupt basal reduction of diam, 1+ mm long, 0.8 mm broad, 0.7 mm thick.

Limestone of hills and tablelands in desert at 900-1,300 m (3,000-4,300 ft). Chihuahuan Desert; Desert Grassland and possibly other grasslands. Arizona; SE New Mexico from Lincoln to Otero and Eddy Cos.; Texas near Rio Grande from El Paso Co. to Pecos and Brewster Cos. and in w Val Verde Co. The species has been reported by Alan Blackburn (Saguaroland Bull. 6: 32. 1952; 7: 54. *f.* 1953) to occur near Sonoita, Santa Cruz Co., Arizona. The photograph indicates this species, but no specimen has been seen.

The small white dome protrudes only a little above ground level.

Mammillaria lasiacantha is confused readily with the species of *Epithelantha*, and especially with *E. micromeris* (*Epithelantha* sp. 1), the two often growing together.

A distinction has been made between *Mammillaria lasiacantha* with pubescent spines and the proposed *M. denudata* with glabrous spines. In the field either type may be found growing alone;

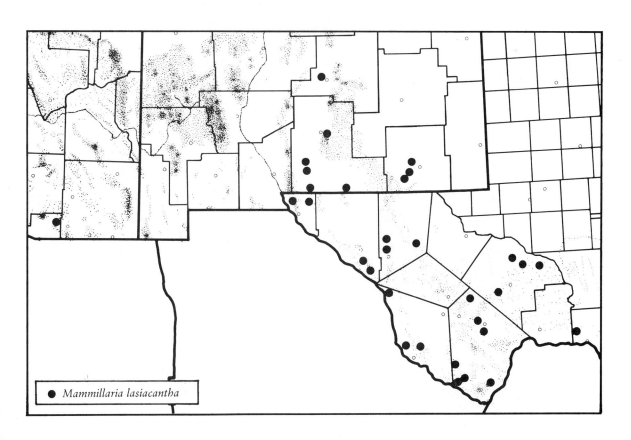

● *Mammillaria lasiacantha*

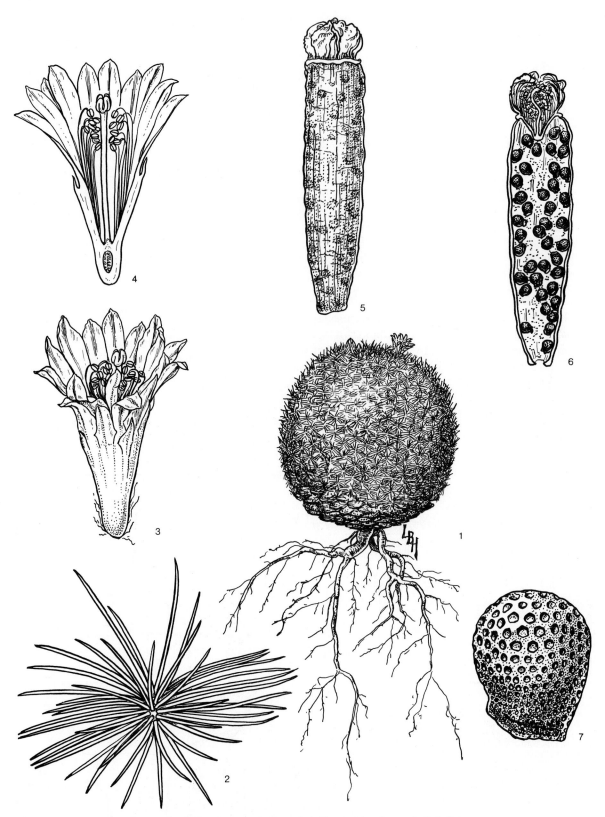

Fig. 913. *Mammillaria lasiacantha*, ✕5.5, except as indicated. *1*, Plant with a flower, ✕2. *2*, Spine cluster, showing the numerous series of spines, ✕7. *3*, Flower. *4*, Flower in longitudinal section. *5*, Fruit. *6*, Fruit in longitudinal section. *7*, Seed, ✕38.

but usually the two are together, and, so far as determined, the single character is not correlated with any other. For example, a collection from about 50 miles south of Alpine, Texas (*L. & R. L. Benson 15490, Pom*), includes nine plants with pubescent spines, eight with glabrous spines, and two with slightly pubescent spines. Similar mixtures occur in Texas at distant points (e.g., midway between Terlingua and Lajitas, *Boke* in 1955, *Pom*; Franklin Mts. near El Paso, *Gurney* in 1955, *Pom*). Thus, there is no indication of an extensive population either with or without spine pubescence or of the occurrence of either in a consistent combination with other characters. Even the type material of the two proposed taxa came from a single collection later sorted out according to pubescence or lack of it.

5. Mammillaria pottsii Engelmann

Stems usually in clusters of several or perhaps many, apparently rather widely branching below ground level, the larger cylindroid or somewhat clavate or sometimes ovoid, 7.5-10+ cm long, 2-2.5(4.5) cm diam; tubercles ±3 mm long and broad, protruding 3 mm; areoles 1.5 mm diam, typically 3-4.5 mm apart; spines dense, obscuring stem; central spines mostly pale tan, 7-11 per areole, in 1 or 2 series, the upper series of 1 or 2 inner centrals (or the uppermost spine of a single series) much longer and apically purplish and curving gently upward, the centrals, except the principal one, straight and spreading at 30°-45° from stem surface, the principal central 9-12 mm long, basally 0.3 mm diam, acicular, nearly cir-

Fig. 914. *Mammillaria pottsii* in the Huntington Botanical Gardens.

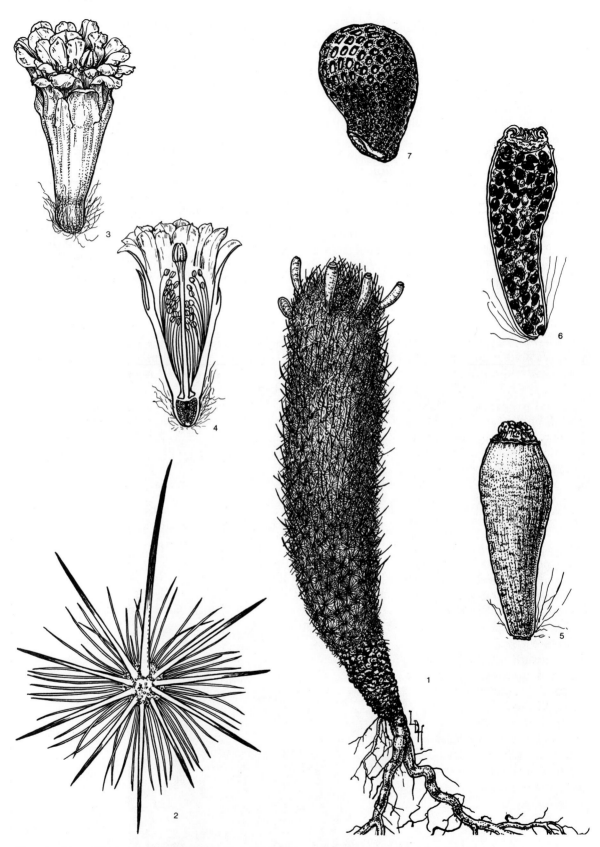

Fig. 915. *Mammillaria pottsii*, ×3.5, except as noted. 1, Plant with fruits, ×.9. 2, Areole, with central and radial spines and wool, ×4.5. 3, Flower. 4, Flower in longitudinal section. 5, Fruit. 6, Fruit in longitudinal section. 7, Seed, ×35.

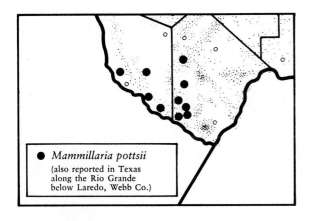

● *Mammillaria pottsii*
(also reported in Texas
along the Rio Grande
below Laredo, Webb Co.)

droid but gradually enlarging upward, larger 10-15(30) cm long, mostly 4-5(6) cm diam; tubercles unusually numerous, cylindroid, 6 mm long and broad, protruding 10 mm; areoles 1.5-3 mm diam, typically ±6 mm apart; flowers between tubercles in vestigial areoles with hairs and weak spines; spines rather dense, more or less obscuring stem; central spines 1-4 per areole, the principal (most nearly central) spine hooked, dark red, accompanied by 1-3 shorter, basally white and apically red, straight accessory centrals, in coastal form the longer centrals 9-12(15) mm long, in desert form 10-15(20) mm long, basally 0.25-0.5 mm diam, acicular, nearly circular in cross section; radial spines light tan to red, mostly 12-18 per areole, spreading parallel to stem, straight, longer 5-9(10) mm long, basally ±0.2 mm diam, acicular; flowers 20-25(40) mm diam and long, those of some plants with sterile anthers but large, functional stigmas; sepaloids with green-and-purple midribs and light yellow to pale cream or nearly white margins, larger lanceolate, ±12 mm long, 3-4.5 mm broad, apically acute to rounded, entire, the lower sometimes fimbriate; petaloids sometimes with purplish midribs, the rest light yellow to pale cream or white, largest oblanceolate, 15-22 mm long, ±4.5 mm broad, acute, mucronulate, entire; filaments yellow, 2-3 mm long; anthers

cular in cross section, the remaining centrals light tan, 3-4.5 mm long, ±0.2 mm diam; radial spines pale tan, much more slender than centrals, very inconspicuous, 27-37 per areole, spreading somewhat away from stem, a little shorter than outer centrals, about 3 mm long, basally 0.1 mm diam, acicular; flower campanulate, 6 mm diam and long; sepaloids with broad reddish-purple midstripes and white margins, the largest cordate, 2-3 mm long, ±1.5 mm broad, apically acute, entire or sparsely and minutely denticulate; petaloids reddish-purple, obovate-elliptic, 3-4 mm long, ±2 mm broad, apically acute, entire or sparsely and minutely denticulate or irregular; filaments pale, 1.5 mm long; anthers yellow, nearly square, 0.25 mm long; style reddish-purple, 4.5-6 mm long, 0.2-0.5 mm greatest diam; stigmas 4 or 5, ±1 mm long, relatively broad, reddish-purple; ovary in anthesis ±1 mm long; fruit red, fleshy but very thin-walled at maturity, transparent when pressed, 9-15 mm long, 2-4.5 mm diam; seeds very dark brown, essentially black, deeply reticulate-pitted, irregularly obovoid, 1 mm long, 0.8 mm broad, 0.7 mm thick.

Gravelly areas of hills and washes in desert at 750-900 m (2,500-3,000 ft). Chihuahuan Desert. Texas near Rio Grande in Presidio and Brewster Cos. and reportedly along river below Laredo in Webb Co. Chihuahua to Nuevo León and Zacatecas, Mexico.

The clusters of slender stems are striking for their pale tan background of radial spines with protruding purplish centrals. Sometimes there are small, bell-shaped, reddish-purple flowers. The plant is a beautiful one for cultivation.

6. Mammillaria dioica K. Brandegee

Stems of older plants usually branching, often forming small clumps, green, more or less cylin-

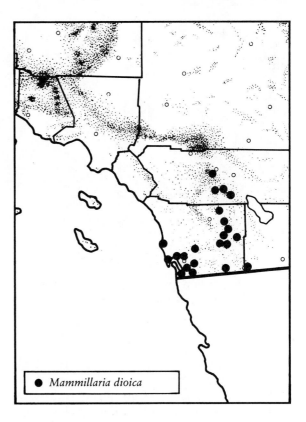

● *Mammillaria dioica*

Fig. 916. *Mammillaria dioica* in the Colorado Desert in Mason Valley, San Diego Co., California; under a cholla, *Opuntia bigelovii* var. *hoffmannii*.

yellow, 1-1.25 mm long, in flowers of sterile male plants the stamens 0.5 mm long, narrow, and with the pollen tightly enclosed and not released; style pale cream, 9-12 mm long, ±0.5 mm greatest diam; stigmas 3-5, green, 1.5-3 mm long, slender; ovary in anthesis 3-4.5 mm long; fruit red, fleshy at maturity, ellipsoid or gradually enlarged upward, 12-25 mm long, 3-6 mm diam; seeds black, with shiny surface and pits about equal in prom-

inence, the reticulate nature of pattern evident, 1-1.25 mm long, 0.9 mm broad, 0.7 mm thick.

Rocky or gravelly or coarse sandy soils of hillsides and washes in chaparral or desert at 15-150 m (50-500 ft) near the coast and 300-1,500 m (1,000-5,000 ft) in desert in the immediate rainshadow on E side of coastal mountains. Baja Californian phase of the California Chaparral; Colorado Desert. California near ocean from vicinity of Del Mar, San Diego Co., s and on w side of Colorado Desert from San Jacinto Mts. Mexico, in much of Baja California.

The coastal form is like a cluster of cante-loupes, and often of about the same grayish white. Frequently the desert form is somewhat more elongate, and the spines may form tannish masses.

The California coastal and desert forms might be considered to be two varieties. However, the segregation is weak, and both extend southward into Baja California, where the distinction seems not to be clear.

According to Bemis, Berry, and Deutschman (1972), *Mammillaria dioica* is not dioecious; it has sterile male individuals, i.e., plants with normally developed pollen but with thickened anther walls, which do not open and release the pollen.

Fig. 918. *Mammillaria dioica* in flower among granite boulders.

Fig. 917. *Mammillaria dioica*, showing the dark hooked central spines and the light-colored radial spines (see Fig. 916).

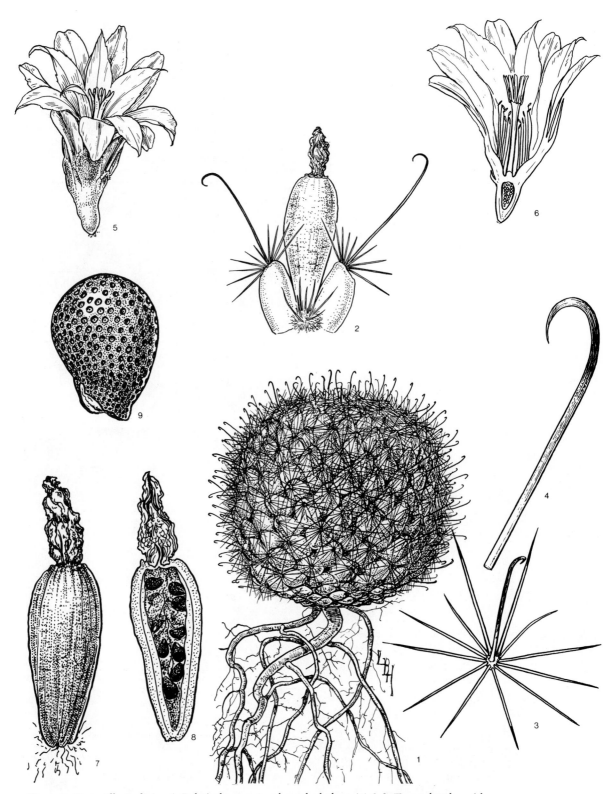

Fig. 919. *Mammillaria dioica.* 1, Relatively young, unbranched plant, ×.6. 2, Two tubercles with a minor spine-bearing areole and a fruit between them, ×1.8; the small spiniferous areoles occurring between tubercles are characteristic of this and some other species of *Mammillaria*, but in most species there are no spines between tubercles. 3, Areole, with a single hooked lower or principal central spine, two upper straight centrals, and radial spines, ×3.5. 4, Tip of the hooked central spine, ×11. 5, Flower, ×2.5. 6, Flower in longitudinal section, ×2.5. 7, Fruit, ×3.5. 8, Fruit in longitudinal section, ×3.5. 9, Seed, ×32.

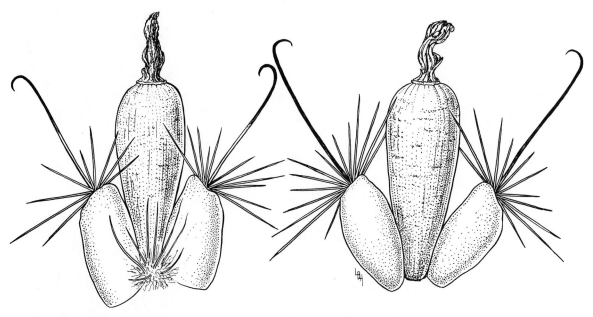

Fig. 920. *Mammillaria dioica* and M. *microcarpa*, comparison of tubercles and areoles. In M. *dioica* (left), the flowers and fruits are produced each in a small spiny areole between tubercles; in M. *microcarpa* (right), they develop in the same position, but there is no visible association with development there of a spine-bearing areole.

7. **Mammillaria mainiae** K. Brandegee

Stem gray-green or blue-green, often solitary, rarely branching, hemispheroidal or ovoid to sub-globose, 6-12.5 cm long, 5-7.5 cm diam; tubercles mammiform-cylindroid, ±9 mm long and broad, protruding 12-15 mm; areoles 1.5 mm diam, typically 10 mm apart; spines rather dense, partly obscuring stem; central spine yellow with brown tip, usually 1 per areole (reportedly sometimes 2 additional straight centrals present), hooked, the hook 1.5 mm across, 12-20 mm long, basally 0.5-0.7 mm diam, acicular, nearly circular in cross section, the hooked centrals turned counterclock-wise in the areoles around the stem; radial spines yellow with brown tips, 10-15 per areole, spreading parallel to stem, straight, longer 6-9 mm long, basally 0.2 mm diam, acicular; flower 12-20 mm diam, ±2 cm long; sepaloids with greenish-pink thickened middles and pale pink and very thin margins, narrowly oblong, to 6-9 mm long, 2 mm broad, apically rounded, marginally white, densely ciliate-fimbriate; petaloids with dark pink mid-dles and conspicuous contrasting white or pale pink thin margins, lanceolate, ±12 mm long, 3 mm broad, apically acuminate-cuspidate, sparsely ciliate; filaments pink, ±3 mm long; anthers pur-plish-tinged, oblong, ±1 mm long; style pink, ±10 mm long, 0.5 mm diam; stigmas 5, pinkish-purple, ±4.5 mm long, slender, 0.2-0.4 mm diam;

fruit red, fleshy at maturity, obovoid, 6-12 mm long, 3-6 mm diam; seeds black, *not* shiny, with surface strongly reticulate-pitted, 1 mm long, 0.8 mm broad, 0.7 mm thick.

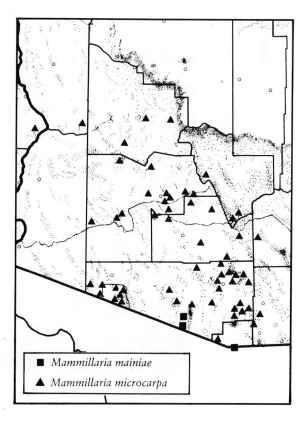

■ *Mammillaria mainiae*
▲ *Mammillaria microcarpa*

Fig. 921. *Mammillaria mainiae* with several stems, developed perhaps because of injury to the terminal bud; Baboquivari Mts., Pima Co., Arizona.

Fig. 922. *Mammillaria mainiae*, showing the long curved central spines and short radial spines, and two fruits far from the apex of the stem.

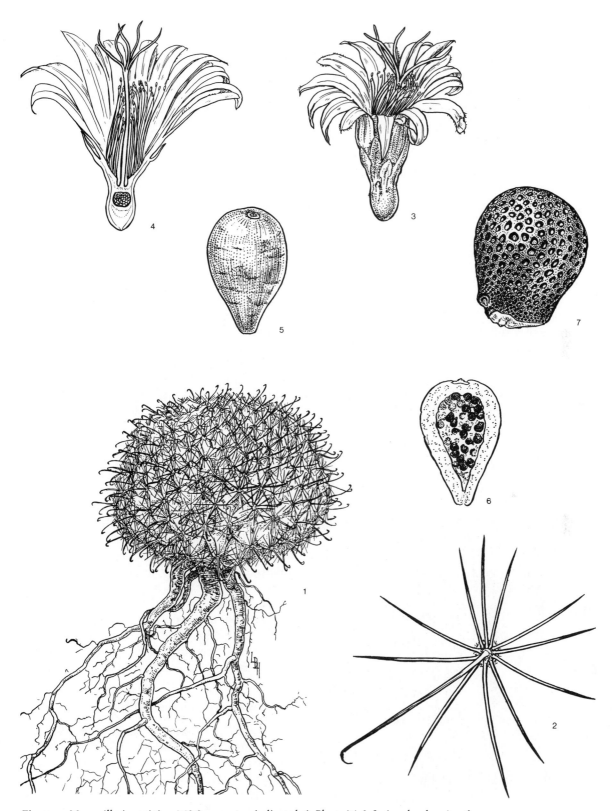

Fig. 923. *Mammillaria mainiae*, ✕2.3, except as indicated. *1*, Plant, ✕.6. *2*, Areole, showing the single hooked central spine, the radials, and the woolly hairs. *3*, Flower. *4*, Flower in longitudinal section. *5*, Fruit. *6*, Fruit in longitudinal section. *7*, Seed, ✕35.

Gravelly or coarse sandy soils of hills, washes, and alluvial fans in desert or grassland at 600-1,200 m (2,000-4,000 ft). Arizona Desert; Desert Grassland; Southwestern Oak Woodland. Arizona near Mexican boundary; on Papago Indian Reservation in Pima Co. and near Nogales, Santa Cruz Co. Mexico in Sonora and Sinaloa.

The yellow, ball-like spine masses are dominated by the large, hooked central spines, which form a counterclockwise whorl.

8. Mammillaria microcarpa Engelmann

Stems green, solitary at first but tending to branch as the plant becomes older, cylindroid, the bases truncate at maturity (rather than tapering as in *M. thornberi*), 7.5-12.5(15) cm long, 4-5 cm diam; tubercles mammiform-cylindroid, ±10 mm long and broad, protruding 12-15 mm; spine-bearing areoles only at tops of tubercles, *not* also between tubercles as in *M. dioica*, 1.5 mm diam,

Fig. 924. *Mammillaria microcarpa* in the Arizona Desert, showing the solitary hooked, dark-colored central spine in each areole and the light-colored radial spines. (Robert H. Peebles)

typically ±10 mm apart; spines rather dense, partly obscuring stem; principal central spine dark red or sometimes black-purple, hooked (sometimes also 1 accessory central per areole shorter, lighter-colored, straight), nearly perpendicular to stem, gently curving or essentially straight except for hook, this 2-3 mm across, longer centrals usually 12-15 mm long, basally 0.3 mm diam, acicular, nearly circular in cross section; radial spines light tan to red, 18-28 per areole, spreading parallel to stem, straight, longer mostly 6-12 mm long, basally 0.2-0.25 mm diam, acicular; flower 20-30 mm diam, ±20 mm long; sepaloids with green midribs and lavender margins, the larger broadly lanceolate, ±10, 9-12 mm long, 3-4.5 mm broad, acute, entire; petaloids lavender to reddish-purple, largest oblanceolate, 12-15 mm long, 3-4.5 mm broad, short-acuminate, entire; filaments yellowish, 3 mm long; anthers yellow, oblong, 0.8 mm long; style pink, 9-12 mm long, 0.5 mm greatest diam; stigmas 5, but some branching, averaging ±3 mm long, slender, green; ovary in anthesis ±2 mm long; fruit red, fleshy at maturity, cylindroid to tapering gradually upward, usually 12-28 mm long, to 4.5 mm diam; seeds black, with the shiny surface more prominent than pits in reticulum, asymmetrically obovoid, 0.8-1 mm long, 0.7 mm broad, 0.6 mm thick.

Sandy or gravelly soils of canyons, washes, alluvial fans, and plains in desert at 300-900 m (1,000-3,000 ft). Arizona Desert and (rare) Colorado Desert. Whipple Mts., San Bernardino Co., California (according to I. Craig, Cactus & Succ. Jour. 10: 8. 1938); Arizona from SE corner of Mohave Co. to Graham and Pima Cos.

The single or somewhat clustered cylindroid stems are visible for 15 m (50 ft) or more. They form grayish to tannish or reddish masses of spines from which the large, dark red to black-purple, hooked central spines protrude. The flowers are attractive and large for the genus.

9. Mammillaria thornberi Orcutt

Low-growing plant with single stem, but individual stems closely associated in clumps of to 100, having arisen from slender, ephemeral connecting rhizomes; stem elongate, cylindroid or narrowly so, 5-10(26) cm long, 1.2-2.5 (very long stems to 5) cm diam, *tapering* gradually into root; tubercles mammiform, 6-9 mm long and broad, protruding 9-12 mm; areoles 2 mm diam, typ-

Fig. 925. *Mammillaria microcarpa* in flower, the flowers in a circle above old tubercles on the side of the stem. (Robert H. Peebles)

ically 6-9 mm apart; spines of moderate density, somewhat obscuring stem; central spine solitary, reddish-brown, darkened gradually apically, perpendicular to stem, apically hooked, with the hook 1.5 mm across, the longer centrals 9-12 mm long, basally 0.4 mm diam, nearly circular in cross section; radial spines basally straw-colored, tips reddish-brown, 15-20 per areole, spreading parallel to stem, longer 6-9 mm long, basally ±0.2 mm diam; flower 15-20 mm diam, 12-15 mm long; sepaloids with green midribs and lavender margins, larger narrowly ovate-acute, 4.5-6 mm long, 1.5-2 mm broad, acute, finely ciliate; petaloids ±10, lavender to reddish-purple, largest lanceolate, 9-12 mm long, 3-4.5 mm broad, acute, entire; filaments pale greenish, 6 mm long; anthers yellow, rectangular, 0.6-0.7 mm long; style pink, 10 mm long, 0.5 mm greatest diam; stigmas 7, red, 3-5 mm long, slender, 0.3-0.4 mm broad; ovary in anthesis 4.5-6 mm long; fruit red, fleshy at maturity, 9-12(15) mm long, 4.5-7.5 mm diam; seeds black, with the shiny surface more prominent than the pits in reticulum, irregularly obovoid but base narrow, 1 mm long, 0.7-0.8 mm broad, 0.6-0.7 mm thick.

Sandy or fine soils under shrubs of flats and washes (particularly tolerant to alkaline conditions) in desert at 240-720 m (800-2,400 ft). Arizona Desert. Arizona in Pinal and (mostly) w Pima Cos.; largely on Papago Indian Reservation. Mexico in N Sonora.

The slender, elongate stems form obscure masses under bushes in remote parts of the desert.

Many stems grow together, but these are separate but crowded individuals of a clone. Initially the stems are connected by slender ephemeral rhizomes (Stockwell, 1932). The few herbarium specimens and study in the field do not indicate stem branching. This point appears to have been unknown to Britton and Rose (1923).

Apparently Britton and Rose were unaware of the geographical and ecological significance of the great distance intervening between the area of *Mammillaria thornberi* on the lower Gila River and that of the plants of the middle Gila, which they considered *M. fasciculata*. In 1923 few appreciated the environmental differences of the regions. See the discussion under *Echinocereus fasciculatus* (*Echinocereus* sp. 5), the species upon which the name *M. fasciculata* was based.

Fig. 926. *Mammillaria thornberi* on the Papago Indian Reservation, Pima Co., Arizona; stem clusters composed of individuals at first developed from very slender, ephemeral rhizomes. (A. A. Nichol)

Fig. 927. *Mammillaria thornberi* in flower, the long, hooked central spines in contrast with the short radials. (Robert H. Peebles)

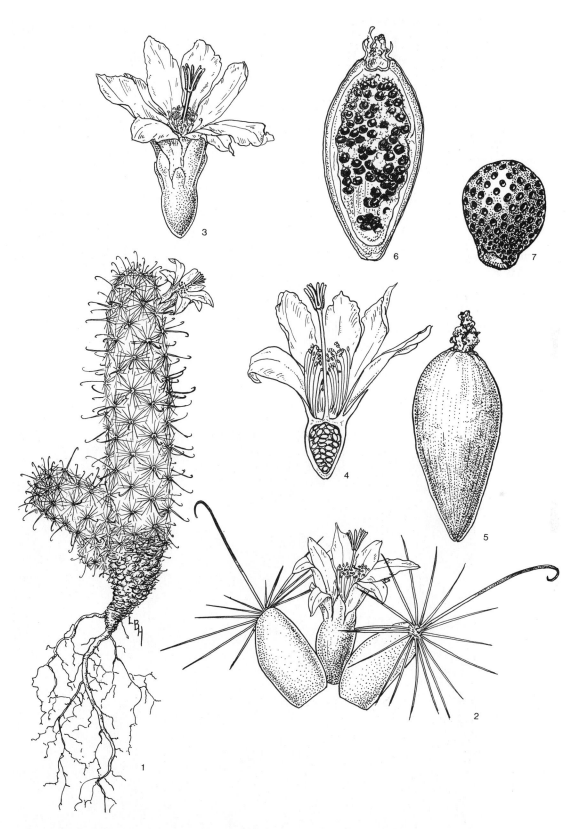

Fig. 928. *Mammillaria thornberi.* *1,* Plant in flower, ✕.65; basal branching uncommon or absent, except through short, slender, ephemeral rhizomes. *2,* Flower between two tubercles and not associated with a minor discernible areole, ✕2.6; areoles with the single hooked central spine and the radials. *3,* Flower, the stigmas red (green in the related species), ✕2.6. *4,* Flower in longitudinal section, ✕2.6. *5,* Fruit, ✕4. *6,* Fruit in longitudinal section, ✕4. *7,* Seed, ✕24.

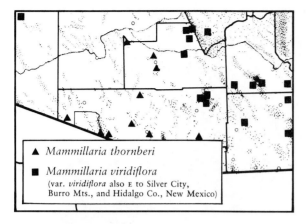

▲ *Mammillaria thornberi*

■ *Mammillaria viridiflora*
   (var. *viridiflora* also E to Silver City,
   Burro Mts., and Hidalgo Co., New Mexico)

10. Mammillaria viridiflora
(Britton & Rose) Bödeker

Stems solitary or some branching, orbicular to ovoid, the larger 7.5-10 cm long, 5-7.5 cm diam; tubercles mammiform-cylindroid, ±4.5 mm long and broad, protruding 6-12 mm; areoles circular, 1.5 mm diam, 5-8 mm apart, in 8 and 13 spirals; spines dense, more or less obscuring stem; central spines 1(2-4), reddish-brown, glabrous or pubescent, projecting and somewhat curving, 9-31 mm long, 0.25 mm diam, with the apical hook 1.5 mm across; radial spines pale tan, 14-24 per areole, arranged in a circle and spreading parallel to stem, straight, the longer 8-10.5 mm long, with tan to brown basal bulbs, these 0.2 mm diam; flower 15-34 mm diam, 20-38 mm long; sepaloids with greenish midribs and lighter margins, the larger lanceolate, 6-9 mm long, 2 mm broad, acute, strongly fimbriate; petaloids green or tinged with pink or from greenish-white or yellowish-white to numerous shades of pink or flesh-pink and to wine-red or carmine, the margins always markedly paler, 10-25, the largest lanceolate, to 10 mm long, 2 mm broad, acute, entire or faintly toothed, spreading near tips but forming a bowl below; filaments pale, 2-10 mm long; anthers yellow, nearly square, 0.3 mm long; style green, 10 mm long, 0.5 mm greatest diam; stigmas 3-8, green, 1 mm long, relatively broad; ovary in anthesis 3 mm long; fruit green to dull red, juicy at maturity, subglobose or ellipsoid, 10-22 mm long, ±4.5-13 mm

Fig. 929. *Mammillaria viridiflora*, apex of a stem with flowers. (Dale A. Zimmerman)

Fig. 931. *Mammillaria viridiflora* in flower, an individual with many stems (usually solitary); south of Tyrone, Grant Co., New Mexico. (Dale A. & M. A. Zimmerman)

Fig. 930. *Mammillaria viridiflora* in flower, the stem solitary (as is usual), showing the circle of flowers only one or two tubercles back from the growing apex of the stem; central spine hooked and usually solitary (sometimes two to four), the radial spines relatively long. (Dale A. & M. A. Zimmerman)

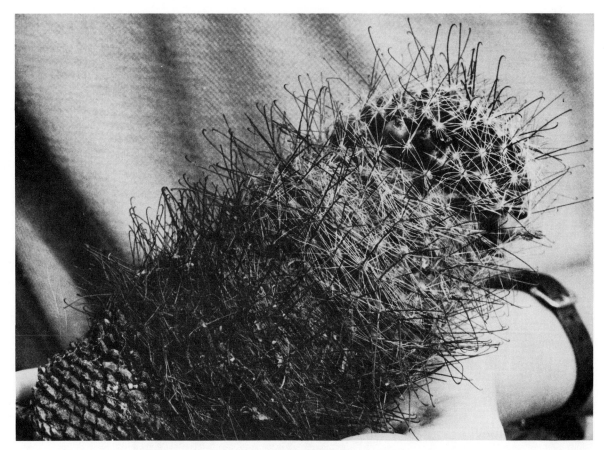

Fig. 932. *Mammillaria viridiflora*, tall plant grown in shade, bearing the small mature fruits (see fruits of *M. wrightii*, Fig. 940). (Dale A. & M. A. Zimmerman)

diam; seeds black or dark brown, the surface smooth and shiny and more prominent than the pits, 1-1.5 mm long, 0.7-1 mm broad, 0.5-0.7 mm thick.

Sandy granitic soils of high hills and mountainsides in oak woodland and at edge of forest at 1,500-2-100 m (5,000-7,000 ft). Southwestern Oak Woodland and Southwestern Chaparral; Northern and Southern Juniper-Pinyon Woodlands; lower edge of Rocky Mountain Montane Forest. Arizona on Hualpai Mountain, Mohave Co., and from E tip of Maricopa Co. to NE Pima, S Graham, C Greenlee, and N Cochise Cos.; New Mexico in NW Grant Co.

These rare plants are obscure little balls growing under grasses or bushes.

Flowering occurs mostly in the spring, a season rarely free for study in New Mexico. New information concerning especially the flowers and fruits and an interpretation of the New Mexican plants have been furnished by Allan D. and Dale A. Zimmerman.

Most collections from New Mexico are of plants with only a single pubescent hooked cen-tral spine per areole. A large plant of *L. & E. L. Benson 16641* had two or three central spines per areole. The natural populations of *M. wrightii* and *M. viridiflora* have long needed the thorough study given them recently by the Zimmermans (1975, 1977).

11. Mammillaria grahamii Engelmann

Stems solitary or little branched, green, ovoid to spheroidal, 5-7.5(10) cm long, 4.5-6(11) cm diam; tubercles mammiform-cylindroid, ±4.5 mm long and broad, protruding 6-12 mm; areoles elliptic, 1.5 mm long, typically ±6 mm apart; spines fairly dense and partly obscuring stem; central spines dark reddish-brown or red to nearly black, (1 or 2)3 per areole, spreading, acicular, nearly circular in cross section, basally 0.1-0.2 mm diam, *either* with principal central apically recurved and curving somewhat below, 12-25 mm long, basally 0.2 mm diam, with the hook ±1.5(2) mm broad straight across from point, and the up-per marginal centrals much shorter, less deeply colored, and straight, *or* with all or nearly all centrals white, *not* hooked and only 4-8 mm long; radial spines white or pale tan, 20-35 per areole, spreading at right angles to stem, straight, to 6-8 mm long, basally 0.1-0.2 mm diam; flower 20-30 (45) mm diam and long; sepaloids with brownish-greenish-purple or purple midribs and reddish-purple or pink or sometimes pale pink margins, the larger lanceolate to oblanceolate, 9-14 mm long, 1.5-5 mm broad, blunt, minutely ciliate; petaloids ±10, rose-purple to pink or sometimes the margins pale pink, lanceolate or oblanceolate, 12-25 mm long, ±4-8 mm broad, blunt, entire; filaments red, 3-6 mm long; anthers yellow, nearly square to oblong, 0.5-0.7(1) mm long; style pale, to 10 mm long, 0.5 mm greatest diam; stigmas green or creamy-green, ±7-10, (2)3-8 mm long, slender; ovary in anthesis ±3 mm long; fruit red, fleshy at maturity, subglobose or barrel-shaped, 12-25 mm long, to 6 mm diam; seeds black, smooth and shining, with the pits occupying less space than the shiny surface of reticulum between pits, the seeds asymmetrically short-obovoid, almost as broad as long, 1 mm long, 0.8 mm broad, ±0.6 mm thick; hilum very broad, as is base of seed.

Distinctive Characters of the Varieties of **Mammillaria grahamii**

Character	a. var. **grahamii**	b. var. **oliviae**
Central spines	Dark reddish-brown or red to nearly black, (1 or 2)3, one hooked and curving a little, 12-25 mm long, much longer than the 1 or 2 upper ones (if any)	White or the lower one sometimes dark-tipped, 3, straight and usually none hooked or curved, 4-8 mm long, the lower one shorter than the upper 2
Altitude	900-1,500 m (3,000-5000 ft)	About 900 m (3,000 ft)
Floristic association	Desert Grassland; upper edges of Chihuahuan Desert and Arizona Desert	Arizona Desert; Desert Grassland

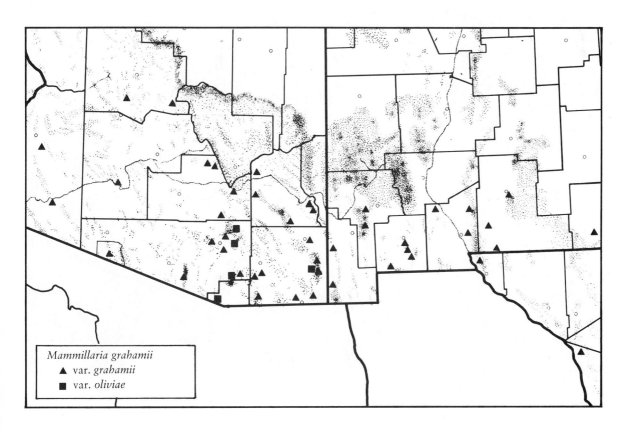

Mammillaria grahamii
▲ var. *grahamii*
■ var. *oliviae*

11a. Mammillaria grahamii var. grahamii. Hills and washes in grassland at 900-1,500 m (3,000-5,000 ft). Desert Grassland and upper edges of Arizona and Chihuahuan deserts. Arizona in E Pinal, Graham, and E Pima Cos., in Santa Cruz and Cochise Cos., and at scattered localities in W mountains mostly just above desert in Yuma, Yavapai, Maricopa, and W Pima Cos.; New Mexico as far E as Otero Co.; Texas in Franklin Mts. near El Paso and Sierra Tierra Vieja (Sierra Vieja), Presidio Co.

The stems are green, fat cylinders occurring under bushes or grasses.

11b. Mammillaria grahamii var. oliviae (Orcutt) L. Benson. Rocky or gravelly soils along upper edge of desert and lower edge of grassland at about 900 m (3,000 ft). Arizona Desert and Desert Grassland. Arizona in E Pima Co. and (rare) in Santa Cruz and Cochise Cos. Mexico in N Sonora.

The plant also has been classified as a variety of *M. microcarpa* because the specimens of some collections have a few hooked central spines. However, these hooked centrals are the same as those of *M. grahamii*, and both the lectotype and the duplicate cited in the Documentation section (see var. *oliviae*) include stems with a few central spines like those of var. *grahamii*. A specimen specially collected from near the type locality (Colossal Cave, *Fosberg 8640, Pom, DS*) is made up of comparative material of both varieties. Recent observation there confirms the intergradation. The flowers of the two varieties are similar.

The white of the radial spines dominates the cylindroid stems.

Fig. 933. *Mammillaria grahamii* var. *grahamii*, showing the hooked, dark, long central spines; among limestone rocks near Colossal Cave, Rincon Mts., Pima Co., Arizona.

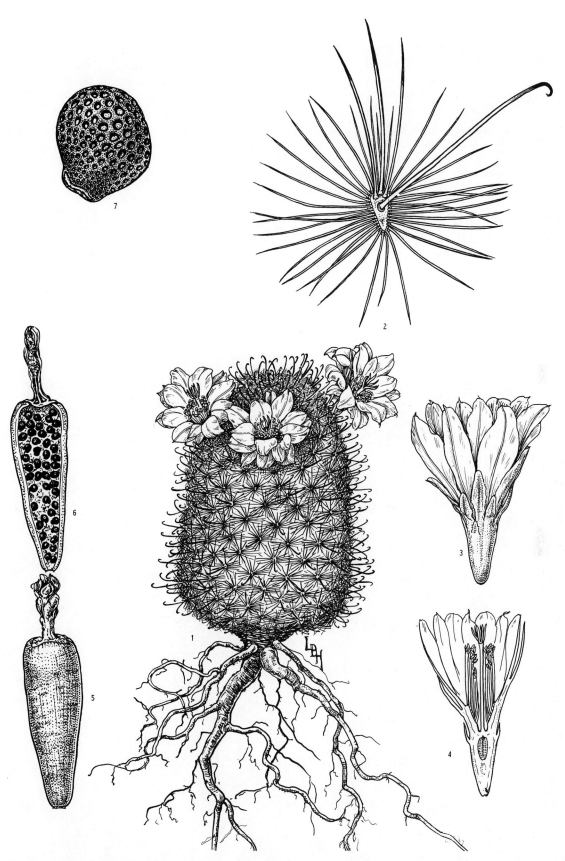

Fig. 934. *Mammillaria grahamii* var. *grahamii*. *1*, Plant in flower, ×.9. *2*, Areole, ×2.3, showing the principal (lower, hooked) central spine, the two lateral dark-colored and one upper light-colored accessory straight central spines, and the radial spines, as well as wool; the principal central spine measuring about 1.5 mm (1/16 inch) across the hook. *3*, Flower, ×1.8. *4*, Flower in longitudinal section, ×1.8. *5*, Fruit, ×2.3. *6*, Fruit in longitudinal section, ×2.3. *7*, Seed, ×30.

Fig. 935. *Mammillaria grahamii*, three mature stems and a young one from different plants: left, with the central spines of var. *grahamii*; right, with the obscure, straight, light-colored central spines of var. *oliviae* (one or two upper ones longer and darker); middle, above, intermediate plant with some central spines of each type.

Fig. 936. *Mammillaria grahamii* var. *oliviae* among limestone rocks near Colossal Cave, Pima Co., Arizona (in a special area removed from var. *grahamii*). The short, straight, light-colored central spines are hidden among the radials.

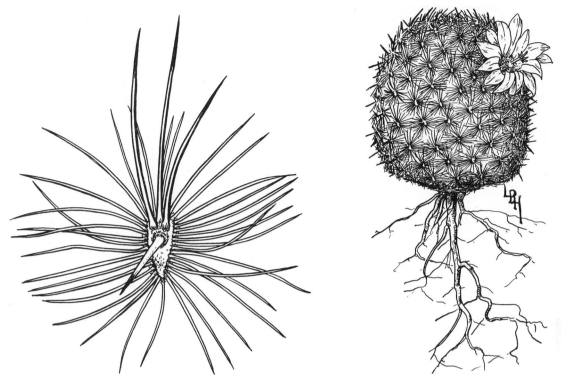

Fig. 938. *Mammillaria grahamii* var. *oliviae*. Right, plant in flower. Left, areole, ×4, showing the short, straight, lower or principal central spine, the two straight lateral spines, and the single upper one, as well as the radial spines and the wool.

Fig. 937. *Mammillaria grahamii* var. *oliviae*, the radial spines prominent, the centrals difficult to distinguish. (Robert H. Peebles)

12. Mammillaria wrightii Engelmann

Stem green, usually solitary, globose, depressed-globose, or turbinate, 4-10 cm long, 4-7.5 cm diam; tubercles mammiform or somewhat cylindroid, 3-4.5 mm long and broad, protruding 3-24 mm; areoles elliptic, ±1.5 mm diam, 6-9 mm apart; in 5 and 8 spirals; spines dense, partly obscuring the stem; the color effect gray-tan; central spines dark reddish-brown, in adult plants 3 (also 2 or 4 or 7; in juvenile plants 1, later 2) per areole, spreading, all somewhat curved and apically hooked, equal, ±25 mm long, basally 0.2-0.3 mm diam, the hook small, ±1.5 mm across from the tip, acicular, nearly circular in cross section; radial spines white or reddish-tan, later becoming gray, ±8-30 per areole, arranged in an ellipse, parallel to surface of stem, straight, the longer to 13.5 mm long, basally 0.3 mm diam, acicular; flower 22-75 mm diam, 19-52 mm long; sepaloids with greenish midribs and pale pink-and-tan or pink or green margins, the larger linear-lanceolate, 15-25 mm long, 2-3 mm broad, attenuate, somewhat ciliate-fimbriate; petaloids 15-40, brilliant magenta, the margins sometimes pale rose, the largest lanceolate-linear, 25-30 mm long, the innermost 2-3 mm broad, spreading widely and thus forming a shallow bowl; fila-

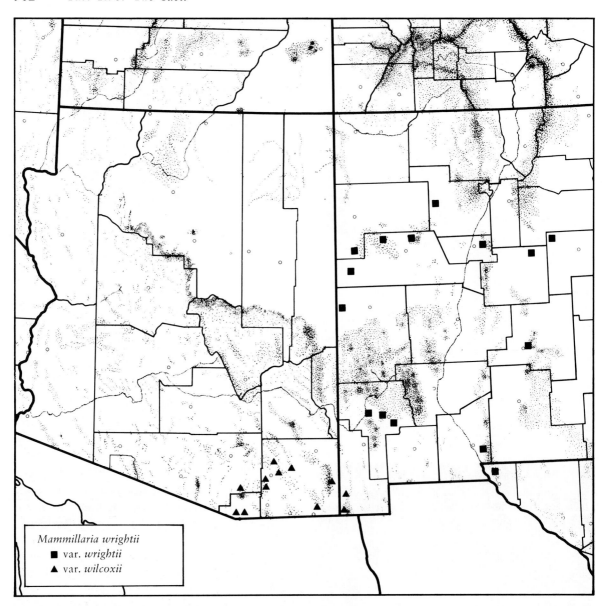

Distinctive Characters of the Varieties of **Mammillaria wrightii**

Character	a. var. **wrightii**	b. var. **wilcoxii**
Hooked central spines	1-5(7), average 2.3, per areole	1-5, average 1.6, per areole
Radial spines	8-20 per areole, average 13	12-30 per areole, average 20
Flowers	27-75 mm diam, average 45 mm; 25-52 mm long, average 35 mm	22-48 mm diam, average 35 mm; 19-38 mm long, average 29 mm
Fruits	14-28 mm long, average 19 mm; 11-26 mm diam, average 15 mm	9-20 mm long, average 15 mm; 6-15 mm diam, average 11 mm
Altitude	1,500-2,400 m (5,000-8,000 ft)	1,050-1,500 m (3,500-5,000 ft)
Floristic association	Great Plains Grassland; Southwestern Oak Woodland; Southern Juniper-Pinyon Woodland; edge of Desert Grassland	Desert Grassland and its borders

NOTE: Characters as given by D. A. and A. D. Zimmerman.

ments magenta, mostly ±10 mm long; anthers yellow, narrowly oblong, 1.3 mm long; style reddish-purple to green, 12-22 mm long, 1 mm diam; stigmas green to orange, 8-10, 2-5 mm long, flat, 0.5-1 mm broad; ovary in anthesis 4.5 mm long; fruit green to purplish, ovoid or nearly orbicular, to 9-28 mm long, 6-26 mm diam; seeds brownish black, with surfaces of reticulum occupying less space than pits, the seeds irregularly obovoid, 1.5 mm long, 1-1.2 mm broad, 0.8-0.9 mm thick; hilum oblique.

Flowering occurs mostly after the summer rains. For this and other information concerning especially the flowers and fruits, the writer is grateful to Allan and Dale A. Zimmerman.

Juvenile plants of *Mammillaria wrightii* may be mistaken for *M. viridiflora*, since the vegetative characters are similar. On the young stem at first there is only one central spine per areole, and the areole is nearly circular. This changes gradually in the new areoles as the stem grows. As with many other cacti, reproduction begins while the plant is still juvenile in vegetative characters.

12a. Mammillaria wrightii var. **wrightii.** Among grasses; clay soils of low hills in grassland and woodland at 1,500-2,400 m (5,000-8,000 ft). Great Plains Grassland; Desert Grassland;

Fig. 939. *Mammillaria wrightii* var. *wrightii* in flower; near the type locality at Silver City, Grant Co., New Mexico. (Dale A. Zimmerman)

Southwestern Oak Woodland; Southern Juniper-Pinyon Woodland. Arizona (according to report) near Springerville, Apache Co., and collected just across state line in New Mexico (*L. & R. L. Benson 15580, Pom*); New Mexico from Zuni in McKinley Co. to Sandoval, Guadalupe, Grant, and Dona Ana Cos.; Texas in Franklin Mts. in El Paso Co. and at Samuels (probably in El Paso Co.).

The ball- or domelike mature stems appear as masses of reddish-tan, slender, hooked central spines.

12b. Mammillaria wrightii var. wilcoxii

(Toumey ex K. Schumann) W. T. Marshall. Commonly among grasses on low hills mostly in grasslands or along the edges of woodlands. Primarily Desert Grassland. Arizona in Santa Cruz and Cochise Cos.; New Mexico in s Hidalgo Co.

The appearance of the plant is similar to that of var. *wrightii*.

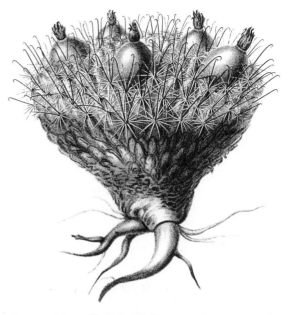

Fig. 940. *Mammillaria wrightii* var. *wrightii*, mature plant in fruit, with three hooked central spines per areole. (Paulus Roetter in Engelmann/Emory, *pl. 8, f. 1*)

Fig. 941. *Mammillaria wrightii* var. *wilcoxii*, showing the proportionately enormous, ellipsoid, almost globular, or obovoid fruits; central spines one in each lower areole but two to four above. (Dale A. Zimmerman)

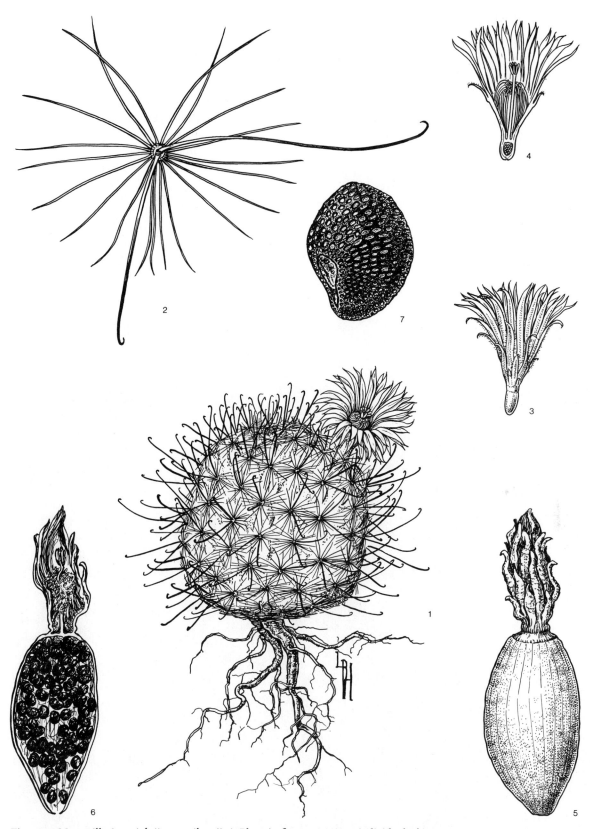

Fig. 942. *Mammillaria wrightii* var. *wilcoxii*. *1*, Plant in flower, ×.6; an individual of intermediate age, still with only two hooked central spines per areole. *2*, Areole with three hooked central spines, radial spines, and felty wool, ×2.5. *3*, Flower, ×1.2. *4*, Flower in longitudinal section, ×1.2. *5*, Fruit, ×3.7. *6*, Fruit in longitudinal section, ×3.7. *7*, Seed, ×25, turned to show the hilum and therefore appearing broader than long (actually the reverse).

13. Mammillaria tetrancistra Engelmann

Stem solitary, the larger plants ovoid-cylindroid to cylindroid, 7.5-15 cm long, 4-6 cm diam; tubercles elongate, mammiform-cylindroid, 10 mm long and broad, protruding 12-15 mm; areoles 1.5 mm diam, typically 6-9 mm apart; spines very dense, obscuring stem; central spines spreading at various angles, longer (hooked) ones 12-25 mm long, basally 0.3-0.4 mm diam; principal (hooked) central spines 1-4 per areole, shading from red to nearly black above, white near bases; accessory central spines none to several, straight, ranging from color of principal centrals to white; radial spines white or sometimes the longer tipped with red or red-and-black, intergrading with outer centrals, 30-46 (reportedly 60) per areole, in 2(3?) series, straight, longer 9-12(25) mm long, basally usually 0.2 mm diam; flower 25-30 mm diam and long; sepaloids with green midribs and pink to purple margins, larger lanceolate, 10-15 mm long, 1.5-2 mm broad, acute or mucronate, the lower sparsely to densely long-ciliate; petaloids rose-pink to purple, the largest oblanceolate, 15-20 mm long, 2-3 mm broad, acute to short-acuminate-aristate, entire; filaments pale, 3-4.5 mm long; anthers yellow, oblong, 0.8 mm long; style green, 15-20 mm long, ±1 mm greatest diam; stigmas 5, green, 1.5 mm long, rather broad; fruit red, cylindroid to clavate, 20-30 mm long, 9-10.5 mm diam; seeds black, dull, tuberculate, spheroidal with hilum invested by nearly white corky tissue of aril almost as large as seed, seed proper 2 mm long (one-third covered and obscured by aril), 1.5

Fig. 943. *Mammillaria tetrancistra*, showing the two to four dark, hooked central spines; Colorado Desert near Dome Rock, Yuma Co., Arizona.

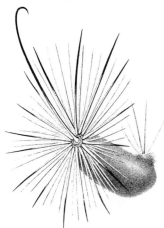

Fig. 946. *Mammillaria tetrancistra*. Seed in two views, showing the extreme size of the aril (lower part) around the hilum before drying; at right, two views of the embryo, showing the minute cotyledons. (Paulus Roetter in Engelmann/Emory, *pl. 7, f. 9*)

Fig. 945. *Mammillaria tetrancistra*, tubercle with spine-bearing areole (juvenile with only one hooked central spine); and a small areole, of the type produced between the tubercles in this species and in *M. dioica*. (Paulus Roetter in Engelmann/Emory, *pl. 7, f. 3*)

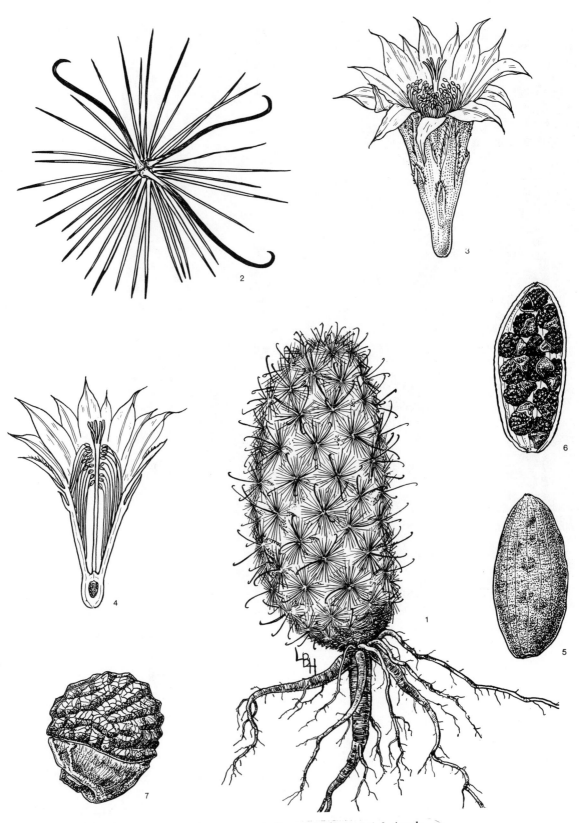

Fig. 947. *Mammillaria tetrancistra*, ×1.6, except as indicated. *1*, Plant, ×.6. *2*, Areole, with three hooked central spines and numerous radial spines, ×2.25. *3*, Flower. *4*, Flower in longitudinal section. *5*, Fruit. *6*, Fruit in longitudinal section. *7*, Seed, ×17, showing (lower part) the conspicuous aril, which, even when the seed is dry (as here), is almost as large as the body of the seed (compare Fig. 945).

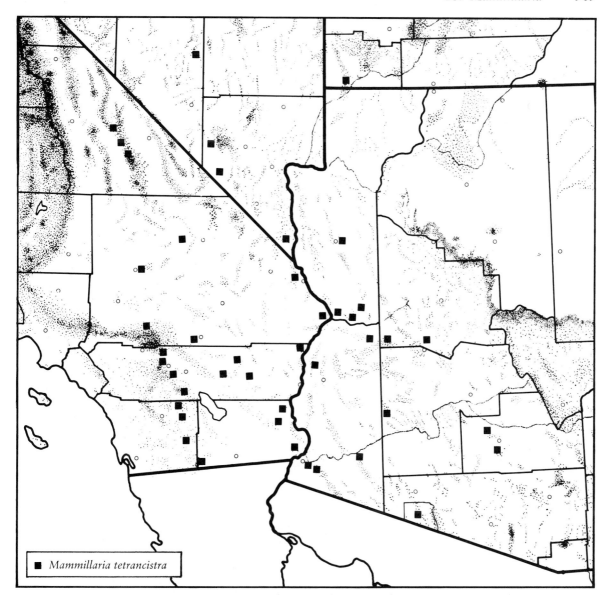

■ *Mammillaria tetrancistra*

mm broad, 1.5 mm thick, the aril ±1-1.5 mm long in dried specimens, according to Engelmann (in Emory, 1859, 7. *pl.* 7), "1.2-1.5 line long," i.e., 2.4-3 mm (1 line = 2 mm), this probably based on size in living material before shriveling during drying at maturity, the undried aril with 3 symmetrical inflated areas, as in Engelmann's illustration.

Sandy soils of hills, valleys, and plains in desert at 135-720 m (450-2,400 ft) or in Nevada and Arizona to even 1,500 m (5,000 ft). Colorado Desert and lower levels of Mojavean and Arizona deserts. California from Inyo Co. (Panamint Mts.) to San Diego and Imperial Cos.; Nevada in s Nye Co. and in foothills of Charleston Mts. and w of Davis Dam in Clark Co.; Utah near St. George; Arizona in Mohave, Yuma, w Yavapai, w Maricopa, w Pinal, and w Pima Cos.

The relatively large cylindroid stems are masses of gray, white, and tan, and the hooked central spines are the most conspicuous feature.

The distinctive aril of M. *tetrancistra* was the only basis for the "genus" *Phellosperma* proposed by Britton and Rose. However, there is no correlation between occurrence of this character and others differing from those in the usual combinations in *Mammillaria*. Shurly (1956) reports large arils in the seeds of M. *calleana*, M. *pennispinosa*, M. *sanluisensis*, and M. *tetrancistra*. "Two have hooked centrals, two have straight centrals," there being little correlation of seed features with other characters.

Documentation

(See also Supplement to Documentation, end of this section)

This section documents the research underlying classification, the use of reference materials for the solution of problems of nomenclature, and the basis for statements of geographical distribution of the cacti.

In the pages that follow, an entry is included for each taxon occurring in the United States or Canada. The material is furnished in the sequence of the main text and keyed to the text by species number (and variety letter) and by the running heads at the tops of the pages.

Documentation for the names of sections (in Opuntia and Pediocactus) and series (in Opuntia), given in the text only in the species lists and the keys, appears below under the documentation of the generic names, but the names applicable to the subordinate taxa are listed separately.

Research underlying classification. To facilitate both the rechecking of earlier research and the undertaking of new studies, the results of investigation must be documented. Pressed and dried plant specimens are the basic form for storage of taxonomic data; they may be supplemented, but not replaced, by photographs or by material preserved in fluid in glass containers. Specimens serve both as a record of the data studied and as a precise reference to the plants classified as species or other taxa; they also provide correlative materials for investigation of new specimens representing new research.

The research on classification is documented here by listing the most significant herbarium specimens recording data upon which conclusions are based. These include specimens from many natural populations studied in the field. However, the specimens that can be listed here are only a few of those examined and recorded. For some rare taxa they are all that is known; for more common ones they provide a solid reference to the plants discussed or described or they document the nature of plants occurring on the periphery of distribution of the taxon, where commonly there is most variation. Herbarium specimens often show the intergradation of taxa or other facts supporting or undermining their taxonomic status. Many unusual features noted in the text are documented here by reference to the specimens in which they were observed. Unfortunately, space limitations prevent citing the thousands of other specimens examined and thus providing a full documentation of the nature of each taxon and of its local and ecological ramifications. The new specimens from this study are all included in the Herbarium of Pomona College, indicated by the symbol Pom.

Problems of nomenclature. Nomenclatural research is documented here by listing the names applied to each taxon, a full reference to the place of publication, information needed for determining the type specimen, and the herbarium in which it or its substitute has been found. The location of the type is indicated by an herbarium symbol, as are its duplicates (isotypes). In many instances there is no type, and a substitute is designated: if material studied by the original author exists, the substitute is drawn from it and is termed a lectotype; if no such material exists, the substitute is chosen from other collections or collected especially for the purpose, and is called a neotype.

Statements of geographical distribution. Available space limits citation of specimens documenting distribution to cases subject to debate or of special interest--for their rarity, perhaps, or their occurrence as outposts.

Herbaria Studied

Relevant specimens in the herbaria listed below have been studied, and in all but a few instances all the specimens have been examined. The references to specimens in the herbaria are cited in the text according to the standard symbols, cf. J. Lanjouw and F. A. Stafleu, Index Herbariorum, ed. 5, part 1 (Regnum Vegetabile 31). 1964.* These are as follows:

A	Arnold Arboretum, Harvard University, Cambridge, Massachusetts
Ariz	University of Arizona, Tucson
ASC	Northern Arizona University, Flagstaff
ASU	Arizona State University, Tempe
BH	Bailey Hortorium, Cornell University, Ithaca, New York
BM	British Museum, Natural History, London
Bish	Bernice P. Bishop Museum, Honolulu, Hawaii
BrY	Brigham Young University, Provo, Utah
___	Boyce Thompson Southwestern Arboretum, University of Arizona, Superior
Can	National Herbarium, Natural History Branch, National Museum of Canada, Ottawa
CAS	California Academy of Sciences, San Francisco, California
CM	Carnegie Museum, Carnegie Institute, Pittsburgh, Pennsylvania
Colo	University of Colorado Herbarium, Museum, Boulder
CU	Cornell University Herbarium, Ithaca, New York
DAO	Plant Research Institute, Research Branch, Department of Agriculture, Ottawa, Canada
Des	Desert Botanical Garden of Arizona in Papago Park, Phoenix
DS	Dudley Herbarium, Stanford University, California
F	Field Museum of Natural History, Chicago, Illinois
G	Conservatoire et Jardin Botanique, Geneva, Switzerland
Ga	University of Georgia, Athens
GH	Gray Herbarium, Harvard University, Cambridge, Massachusetts
ISC	C. C. Parry collection, Iowa State University, Ames
Ill	University of Illinois, Urbana, Illinois
Jeps	Jepson Herbarium, University of California, Berkeley
K	Royal Botanic Gardens, Kew, Surrey, England
LA	University of California, Los Angeles
Linn	Linnean Society of London, England
LL	Lundell Herbarium, Texas Research Foundation, Renner, Texas
Mich	University of Michigan, Ann Arbor
MNA	Museum of Northern Arizona, Flagstaff
MtMG	MacDonald College, McGill University, Quebec, Canada
NDA	North Dakota State University, Fargo (only duplicates of certain specimens)
NMC	Wooton and Standley Herbarium, New Mexico State University, Las Cruces
NY	New York Botanical Garden, New York City
Obi	California Polytechnic State University, San Luis Obispo
Ore	University of Oregon, Eugene
___	Organ Pipe Cactus National Monument, Ajo, Arizona
OSC	Oregon State University, Corvallis
Oxf	Oxford University, England
P	Muséum d'Histoire Naturelle, Laboratoire de Phanérogamie, Paris, France
Penn	University of Pennsylvania, Philadelphia
Ph	Academy of Natural Sciences, Philadelphia, Pennsylvania
Pom	Pomona College, Claremont, California
QUK	Queens University, Kingston, Ontario, Canada
RSA	Rancho Santa Ana Botanic Garden, Claremont, California
S	Botanical Department, Naturhistoriska Riksmuseum, Stockholm, Sweden
SBBG	Santa Barbara Botanic Garden, Santa Barbara, California
SD	San Diego Natural History Museum, San Diego, California
SMU	Southern Methodist University, Dallas, Texas
SRSC	Sul Ross State College, Alpine, Texas
TAES	Texas Agricultural & Mechanical University, College Station
Tex	University of Texas, Austin
Trin	University of the West Indies, St. Augustine, Trinidad
TSH	Test Site Herbarium, University of California at Los Angeles, Laboratory of Nuclear Medicine and Radiation Biology, Los Angeles, and at Mercury, Nevada

* Symbols formed from initials are written in capital letters (ASU, Arizona State University); those formed as abbreviations are written in capital and small letters (Ariz, University of Arizona); those from combinations may be written in other ways, e.g., BrY, Brigham Young University. In Regnum Vegetabile all letters are capitals. The slight change here is intended to make initials and abbreviations more readily recognizable. For example, Des is derived from Desert Botanical Garden, not from the initial letters of three separate words.

UC   University of California, Berkeley
UNM   University of New Mexico, Albuquerque
US   United States National Herbarium, Smithsonian Institution, United States National Museum, Washington, D.C.
USFS   United States Forest Service Herbarium, Department of Agriculture, Washington, D.C.
USNA   United States National Arboretum, Department of Agriculture, Washington, D.C.
Ven   Instituto Botienico, Ministry of Agriculture (and Central University of Venezuela), Caracas, Venezuela
Vt   Pringle Herbarium, University of Vermont, Burlington
WillU   Peck Herbarium, Willamette University, Salem, Oregon
WS   Washington State University, Pullman, Washington
WTU   University of Washington, Seattle, Washington
YU   Herbarium of Yale University, New Haven, Connecticut

Order of Citation of Specimens

The order of statement of geographical distribution of species and varieties and of citation of specimens, so far as this is possible, parallels the progression on a printed page. Thus, on the map, it proceeds from west to east and north to south. Within each state an approximation of a similar order is maintained.

HAWAII

ALASKA

CANADA

Yukon, Mackenzie, British Columbia, Alberta, Saskatchewan, Manitoba, Ontario, Quebec, Labrador, Newfoundland, Prince Edward Island, New Brunswick, Nova Scotia

UNITED STATES (except Hawaii and Alaska, above)

Western
   (Coastal) Washington, Oregon, California
   (N interior) Nevada, Idaho, Montana, Wyoming
   (S interior) Utah, Colorado, Arizona, New Mexico

Great Plains
   North Dakota, South Dakota, Nebraska, Kansas, Oklahoma, Texas

Middle West
   (N) Minnesota, Wisconsin, Michigan
   (S) Iowa, Missouri, Illinois, Indiana, Ohio

Middle Atlantic
   New York, Pennsylvania, West Virginia, New Jersey

New England
   (N) Vermont, New Hampshire, Maine
   (S) Massachusetts, Connecticut, Rhode Island

Southern and Border
   (W) Missouri, Arkansas
   (C) Kentucky, Tennessee
   (Gulf) Louisiana, Mississippi, Alabama
   (Atlantic Coastal) Maryland, Delaware, District of Columbia, Virginia, North Carolina, South Carolina, Georgia
   (Peninsular) Florida

1. Pereskia

Pereskia, as genus [Plumier ex L.] Miller, Gard. Dict. Abr. ed. 4. 1754. Type species: *Cactus pereskia* L. (lectotype, Britton & Rose, Cactaceae 1: 9. 1919). For spelling of generic name, cf. Croizat, Des. Pl. Life 15: 76. 1943.

1. Pereskia aculeata Miller

Cactus pereskia L. Sp. Pl. 1: 469, 1753. *Pereskia pereskia* Karsten, Deutsche Fl. ed. 1. 888. 1882. tautonym. "Habitat in America Calidiore, Jamaica, Margaretha." Linnean specimen: Specimen No. 8 (number of Savage), Linn. photograph, F 1374149. Leaf narrowly elliptic in outline, attenuate at both ends. 3.5 cm long; 13.5 mm broad; petiole slender. 4-5 mm long. See Suppl.

Pereskia aculeata Miller, Gard. Dict. ed. 8. (under P, pages numbered). 1768. "Plum. Nov. Gen. 37. tab. 26. Cactus Lin. Gen. Pl. 539." "Spanish West Indies."

FLORIDA. MANATEE CO. Oneco, Reasoner Bros. in 1910, US. HIGHLANDS CO. Avon Park, J. B. McFarlin 6346, Mich. ST. LUCIE CO. Hammock 6 mi. S of Ft. Pierce, Small 8458, Dec. 20, 1917, Mo, NY, GH, US, Mich, 8751, NY. PALM BEACH CO. West Palm Beach, Small, Britton, & De Winkler 9220, NY.

2. Pereskia grandifolia Haworth

Pereskia grandifolia Haw. Suppl. Pl. Succ. 85. 1819. *Cactus grandifolius* Linke, Enum. Pl. Hort. Berol. 2: 25. 1822. *Rhodocactus grandifolius* Knuth in Backeberg & Knuth, Kaktus-ABC 97. 1935. "HABITAT in Brasilia...in horto Kewense A.D. 1818."

FLORIDA. HIGHLANDS CO. Avon Park, J. B. McFarlin 6344, Mich.

2. Opuntia

Synonymy appears under the subgenera and sections below.

Subgenus 1. Cylindropuntia

Section 1. CYLINDRACEAE

Cylindraceae, as section, DC. Prodr. 3: 471. mid-March, 1828. Lectotype species designation, Moran and Benson: *Opuntia rosea* DC., loc. cit. and Mem. Hist. Nat. Paris 17: pl. 15. July 18, 1828.

Cylindricae, as section, Engelm. Proc. Amer. Acad. 3: 305. 1857 (preprint 1856). Lectotype species designation: *Opuntia arborescens* Engelm. (= *O. imbricata* Haw.).

Cactodendron, indefinitely as genus, Bigelow, U. S. Senate Rept. Expl. & Surv. R. R. Pacific Ocean 3: 102; 4: 7, 11, notes and corrections iii. 1857, illegitimate name, Art. 34 (1), Note 2, Example 1. The two species mentioned are described as of "shrubby form" and "arborescent," but they appear only as *Opuntia arborescens* (a synonym of *O. imbricata*) and *O. whipplei*, further described and illustrated in the same volume. The name *Cactodendron* is indicated to represent a new genus, but the species mentioned are retained formally under *Opuntia*. Cf. also Britton & Rose, Cactaceae 1: 43. 1919, who, working under the American Code of Botanical Nomenclature, superseded in 1934, stated that publication of *Cactodendron* by Bigelow "...was apparently not intended to be a formal publication, but as a definite species is indicated, the name is published." This is not acceptable under the present Code.

Cylindropuntia, as subgenus, Engelm. Proc. Amer. Acad. 3: 302. 1857 (preprint, 1856); as genus, Knuth in Backeberg & Knuth, Kaktus-ABC 117, 410. 1935; as section, Moran ex H. E. Moore, Baileya 19: 166. 1975. Type species: *Opuntia arborescens* Engelm. (= *O. imbricata* Haw.)

Section 2. CLAVATAE

Clavatae, as section, Engelm. Proc. Amer. Acad. 3: 302. 1857 (preprint 1856); as series, K. Schum. Gesamtb, Kakt. 657, 658, 660. 1898. Type species: *Opuntia clavata* Engelm.

Corynopuntia, as genus, Knuth in Backeberg & Knuth, Kaktus-ABC 114, 410. 1935; as subgenus, W. T. Marshall, Saguaroland Bull. 11: 105. 1957, nom. nud., without reference to the basionym or a Latin diagnosis; only *Opuntia stanlyi* mentioned; as subgenus, Bravo, Cact. y Suc. Mex. 17: 118. 1972; as section, L. Benson, Cacti Ariz. ed. 3. 63. 1969. Type species: *O. clavata* Engelm.

Micropuntia, as genus, Daston, Amer. Midl. Nat. 36: 661. 1947. Type species: *M. brachyrhopalica* (lectotype, Byles, Nat. Cact. & Succ. Jour. 10: 82. 1955; Dict. Gen. & Sub-Gen. Cactaceae 21. 1955) (= *Opuntia pulchella* Engelm.).

Subgenus 2. Opuntia

Section 1. OPUNTIA

Opuntia, as genus, [Tourn.] Miller, Gard. Dict. abridged ed. no. 4. 1754. Type species: *Cactus opuntia* L. (lectotype, Britton & Rose, Smithsonian Misc. Coll. 50: 503. 1908) (= *O. compressa* [Salisb.] Macbr.).

Nopalaea, as genus, Salm-Dyck, Cact. Hort. Dyck 1849: 63. 1850. Type species: *Opuntia cochenillifera* Miller (lectotype, Britton & Rose, Cactaceae 1: 33. 1919).

Platopuntia, as subgenus, Engelm. Proc. Amer. Acad. 3: 290. 1857 (preprint, 1856); as section, Weber in Bois. Dict. Hort. 893. 1893-1899. Lectotype species designation: *Cactus tuna* L. (= *Opuntia tuna* Miller). *Platopuntia* or *Platyopuntia* is invalid as either a subgenus or a section, because the type subgenus or section is named automatically by repetition of the name of the genus (Art. 22).

Ficindica, as genus, St. Lager, Ann. Soc. Bot. Lyon 7: 70. 1880. Type species: *Cactus ficus-indica* L. (= *Opuntia ficus-indica* [L.] Miller).

Tunas, as genus, Dodonaeus ex Nieuwland & Lundell, Amer. Midl. Nat. 4: 479. 1916. Lectotype species designation: *Tunas polyacantha* (Haw.) Nieuwland & Lundell (= *Opuntia polyacantha* Haw.).

Section 2. CONSOLEA

Consolea, as genus, Lemaire, Rev. Hort. 1862: 174. 1862; as subgenus, Berger, Kakteen 64. 1929; as section, L. Benson,

Cactus & Succ. Jour. 46: 80. 1974. Type species: <u>Opuntia</u> <u>rubescens</u> Salm-Dyck (lectotype, Britton & Rose, Cactaceae 1: 43. 1919).

<u>Brasiliopuntia</u>, as subgenus, K. Schum. Gesamtb. Kakteen 655. 1898; as genus, Berger, Entwicklungslinien Kakteen 94. 1926. Type species: <u>Cactus brasiliensis</u> Willd. (= <u>Opuntia brasiliensis</u> [Willd.] Haw.).

1. Opuntia parryi Engelmann

1a. Opuntia parryi var. parryi

<u>Opuntia parryi</u> Engelm. Amer. Jour. Sci. II. 14: 339. 1852. <u>Cactus parryi</u> Lemaire, Cactées 88. 1868. <u>Cylindropuntia parryi</u> Knuth in Backeberg & Knuth, Kaktus-ABC 124. 1935. "Eastern slope of the California Mountains near San Felipe [San Diego County]." TYPE: not found, <u>cf</u>. also Coulter, Contr. U. S. Nat. Herb. 3: 441. 1896. NEOTYPE designation: San Felipe Valley, San Felipe Ranch 1/2 mile from the canyon of Banner Grade, San Diego Co., California, <u>Lyman Benson 16384</u>, July 14, 1963, <u>Pom 305014</u>. In Engelmann's later publications (<u>cf</u>. Engelm. & Bigelow, U. S. Senate Rept. Expl. & Surv. R. R. Route Pacific Ocean. Botany 4: 48-49. <u>f</u>. <u>4-7</u>. 1897) this plant was considered doubtfully to be that later named O. parishii Orcutt, West. Amer. Sci. 10 (Whole No. 81): 1. 1896 (= <u>O. stanlyi</u> var. <u>parishii</u>). Var. <u>parishii</u> is not known to occur in or near the area about San Felipe.

<u>Opuntia bernardina</u> Engelm. ex Parish, Bull. Torrey Club. 19: 92. 1892. "...Coast Range to San Bernardino Mts., in the San Jacinto and San Bernardino Valleys." LECTOTYPE designation: "Arid plains about San Bernardino and along the mountain bases," <u>George Engelmann</u>, November 9, 1880, <u>Mo</u>. DUPLICATE: <u>Pom 317796</u>.

<u>Opuntia parkeri</u> Engelm. in Coulter, Contr. U. S. Nat. Herb. 3: 446. 1896, pro. syn. <u>O. echinocarpa</u> Engelm. & Bigelow var. <u>parkeri</u> Coulter, loc. cit. "Type, C. F. Parker of 1879 in Herb. Mo. Bot. Gard...San Diego County, California, east side of mountains facing desert." Coulter omitted the key word, "Campo," a town on the coastal rather than the desert watershed, and var. <u>parryi</u> occurs there, <u>Lindsay & Benson 16368</u>, <u>Pom</u>. TYPE: <u>J. C. Parker</u> [not C. F. Parker] in 1879, <u>Mo 39396</u>, <u>39397</u>.

<u>Opuntia bernardina</u> Engelm. var. <u>cristata</u> K. Schum. Monatsschr. Kakteenk. 12: 20. 1902, <u>nom. nud</u>. <u>O. bernardina</u> Engelm. f. <u>cristata</u> Schelle, Handb. Kakteenkultur 40. 1907, <u>nom. nud</u>. Horticultural.

CALIFORNIA. SAN LUIS OBISPO CO. Cuyama Valley, <u>Schreiber 1106</u>, <u>UC</u>; E of Big Rocks, Los Padres National Forest, <u>T. M. Hendrix</u>, May 25, 1939, <u>UC</u> (box). SANTA BARBARA CO. 9 mi. W of New Cuyama, <u>L. Benson 16085</u>, <u>Pom</u>; 3 mi. below Green Canyon (road to Wasioja), Cuyama Valley, <u>C. B. Wolf 9478</u>, <u>RSA</u>, <u>DS</u>. VENTURA CO. Santa Susana Quadrangle, <u>P. L. Johannsen</u>, Feb. 26, 1934, <u>RSA</u>. SAN BERNARDINO CO. Santa Ana River, 3 mi. above Seven Oaks, San Bernardino Mts., 6,000 ft., <u>C. B. Wolf 2484</u>, <u>RSA</u>, <u>Pom</u>, <u>US</u> (box), <u>DS</u> (box); E of Barton Flats, S fork of Santa Ana River, San Bernardino Mts., 6,200 ft., <u>L. Benson, P. Baker, & J. Adams 16645</u>, <u>Pom</u>.

<u>Opuntia parryi</u> vars. <u>parryi</u> and <u>serpentina</u> intergrade, as pointed out by George Lindsay: CALIFORNIA. SAN DIEGO CO. Barrett, NW of Tecate Mt., <u>L. Benson 16362-16365</u>, <u>Pom</u>.

1b. Opuntia parryi var. serpentina (Engelmann) L. Benson

<u>Opuntia serpentina</u> Engelm. Amer. Jour. Sci. 14: 338. 1852. <u>O</u>. <u>parryi</u> Engelm. var. <u>serpentina</u> L. Benson, Cactus & Succ. Jour. 41: 33. 1969. "...Dry hillsides, San Diego," California, <u>C. C. Parry</u> in 1849 or 1850. TYPE: not found (<u>cf</u>. also Coulter, Contr. U. S. Nat. Herb. 3: 447. 1896). A collection (<u>Mo</u>) from the Parry Herbarium may have been added after Engelmann's death. NEOTYPE (Benson, <u>loc</u>. <u>cit</u>.): "Hills of Tia Juana, U. S. side of line," San Diego Co., Calif., <u>LeRoy Abrams 3474</u>, May 14, 1903, <u>Pom 156430</u>. DUPLICATES: <u>NY</u>, <u>DS 30544</u>.

<u>Cereus californicus</u> Torrey & Gray, Fl. N. Amer. 1: 555. 1840. <u>Opuntia californica</u> Cov. Proc. Biol. Soc. Wash. 13: 114. 1899, not Engelm. in Emory, Notes Mil. Reconn. Ft. Leavenworth to San Diego. App. 2. 158. <u>f</u>. <u>11</u>. 1848. <u>Cylindropuntia californica</u> Knuth in Backeberg & Knuth, Kaktus-ABC 125. 1935. "...Near San Diego, California, uncommon. <u>Nutt</u>." TYPE: not found, <u>BM</u>, <u>NY</u>, <u>GH</u>, <u>Ph</u>. NEOTYPE designation: <u>Abrams 3474</u>, as in the paragraph above.

CALIFORNIA. SAN DIEGO CO. San Diego, <u>Schott</u>, in 1854, <u>Mo</u>, <u>Parry</u>, Nov., 1880, <u>ISC</u>, <u>Engelmann</u>, in 1880, <u>Mo</u>, <u>Vasey 217</u>, in 1880, <u>NY</u>, <u>Parry</u>, in 1882, <u>ISC</u>, <u>Orcutt</u>, in 1884, <u>Mo</u>, <u>G. Sykes</u>, in 1905, <u>NY</u>, <u>Toumey</u>, July 20, 1896, <u>US</u>, <u>Parish</u>, in 1916, <u>US</u>, <u>Orcutt</u>, in 1922, <u>US</u>, <u>Gander</u>, Wolf's No. 9740, <u>RSA</u>, <u>CAS</u>; La Mesa, <u>Griffiths 7993</u>, <u>US</u>; Florida Canyon, San Diego, <u>G. Lindsay 2959</u>, <u>Pom</u>; Bailey St., E San Diego, <u>C. B. Wolf 9471</u>, <u>RSA</u>, <u>Tex</u>, <u>DS</u> (box), <u>9472</u>, <u>RSA</u>, <u>DS</u> (box); San Ysidro, 1 mi. N of Mexican boundary, <u>L. Benson 16356</u>, <u>Pom</u>, <u>16357</u>, <u>Pom</u>; San Diego Co., opposite Tijuana, <u>Abrams 3474</u>, <u>Pom</u>, <u>NY</u>, <u>DS</u>.

2. Opuntia wigginsii L. Benson

<u>Opuntia wigginsii</u> L. Benson, Cacti Ariz. ed. 3. 19, 32. 1969. <u>Cylindropuntia wigginsii</u> H. Robinson, Phytologia 26: 175. 1973. TYPE: "South of Quartzsite, Yuma County, Arizona. 900 feet elevation, <u>Lyman & Evelyn L. Benson 16465</u>, March 30, 1965." <u>Pom 296264</u>.

CALIFORNIA. SAN DIEGO CO. Cane Brake Canyon, S of Agua Caliente Springs on Road to Carrizo, <u>C. B. Wolf 9393</u>, <u>RSA</u>, <u>DS</u>, (box). IMPERIAL CO. S of Palo Verde, <u>Wiggins 8571</u>, <u>DS 272044</u> (box), <u>RSA</u>.

ARIZONA. YUMA CO. S of Quartzsite, <u>Wiggins 6635</u>, <u>US</u>, <u>DS</u> (box), <u>Wiggins 8574</u>, <u>DS</u> (box), <u>L. & E. L. Benson 16465</u>, <u>Pom</u>, <u>L. Benson 16711</u>, <u>Pom</u>; NW of Tyson, along old road to Kofa and Quartzsite, <u>Wiggins 8628</u>, <u>DS</u> (box). MARICOPA CO. Aguas Calientes (Agua Caliente), <u>G. Hockderffer</u> in 1906, <u>US</u>.

3. Opuntia echinocarpa Engelmann & Bigelow

3a. Opuntia echinocarpa var. echinocarpa

<u>Opuntia echinocarpa</u> Engelm. & Bigelow, Proc. Amer. Acad. 3: 305. 1857 (preprint, 1856); U. S. Senate Rept. Expl. & Surv. R. R. Route Pacific Ocean. Botany 4: 49. <u>pl</u>. <u>18</u>, <u>f</u>. <u>5-10</u>. 1857. <u>Cactus echinocarpus</u> Lemaire, Cactées 88. 1868. <u>Cylindropuntia echinocarpa</u> Knuth in Backeberg & Knuth, Kaktus-ABC 124. 1935. "In the Colorado Valley, near the mouth of Williams' River." TYPE: not found (<u>cf</u>. also Coulter, Contr. U. S. Nat. Herb. 3: 446. 1896). NEOTYPE designation: 23 miles west of Needles, San Bernardino Co., California; 1,200 feet elevation, [in fruit], <u>Lyman Benson 10374</u>, <u>Pom 274071</u>. Typical for flowers: "Needles, California," <u>Marcus E. Jones</u>, May 7, 1884, <u>Pom 83456</u>.

<u>Opuntia deserta</u> Griffiths, Monatss. Kakteenk. 23: 132. photograph. 1913. "Die Beschreibung und Photographie wurden bei Searchlight in Nevada am 28 April 1912 in Gelände aufgenommen....Das Original trägt meine [Griffiths] Nummer 10535...." TYPE: US 2607619 (box "A"). ISOTYPE: <u>Pom 294989</u>.

3b. Opuntia echinocarpa var. wolfii L. Benson

<u>Opuntia echinocarpa</u> Engelm. & Bigelow var. <u>wolfii</u> L. Benson, Cactus & Succ. Jour. 41: 33. 1969. TYPE: "Base of Mountain Springs Grade, Imperial County, western edge of the Colorado Desert on U. S. 80 west of El Centro, <u>Carl B. Wolf 9429</u>, June 12, 1938, <u>RSA 20700</u> and material from propagation, <u>RSA 96387</u> (the two sheets together the holotype)." Cf photograph, Rancho Santa Ana Bot. Gard. Occ. Papers I. (2): 76. <u>f</u>. <u>21</u>. 1938. ISOTYPES: <u>US</u> (box), <u>UC 1043499</u> (Balls from living plant at <u>RSA</u>), <u>592967</u> (box), <u>CAS</u>, <u>DS</u> (box).

CALIFORNIA. RIVERSIDE CO. Palms-to-Pines Highway, <u>L. Benson 16717</u>, <u>Pom</u>. SAN DIEGO CO. Headquarters, Borrego State Park, <u>C. B. Wolf 8472</u>, <u>DS</u> (box), <u>Balls 19055</u>, <u>RSA</u>; Sentenac Canyon, San Felipe Creek, <u>Peirson 7853</u>, <u>RSA</u>; Boulder Park, 3,000 feet, U. S. 80, Laguna Mts., <u>H. Rush 119</u>, <u>Pom</u>; plateau above Mt. Springs, <u>E. A. McGregor 887</u>, June 10, 1919, <u>DS</u>; between Jacumba and Mt. Springs, <u>R. S. Ferris 7058</u>, <u>DS</u>. IMPERIAL CO. Mt. Springs, <u>Mearns 2981</u>, <u>US</u>, <u>3046</u>, <u>US</u>, <u>3151</u>, <u>US</u>, <u>L. Benson 16371</u>, <u>Pom</u>, <u>16372</u>, <u>Pom</u>, <u>16373</u>, <u>Pom</u>; base of Mt. Springs Grade, <u>C. B. Wolf 9429</u>, <u>RSA</u>, <u>US</u> (box), <u>CAS</u>, <u>UC</u> (& box), <u>DS</u> (box).

4. Opuntia acanthocarpa Engelmann & Bigelow

4a. Opuntia acanthocarpa var. coloradensis L. Benson

<u>Opuntia acanthocarpa</u> Engelm. & Bigelow var. <u>coloradensis</u> L. Benson, Cacti Ariz. ed. 3. 20, 34. 1969. TYPE: "West of South Pass, U. S. Highway 66, 23 miles west of Needles, San Bernardino County, California; Mojave Desert; 2,200 feet elevation, <u>Lyman Benson 10375</u>, July 14, 1940," <u>Pom 244022</u>. ISOTYPE: <u>Ariz 137142</u>.

CALIFORNIA. KERN CO. Freeman Quadrangle, 3 mi. E of Inyokern, <u>E. Armstrong 1192</u>, <u>UC</u> (spines few).

NEVADA. CLARK CO. Charleston Mts., <u>Coville & Funston 384</u>, March 7, 1891, <u>US</u>; Wilson's Ranch, <u>Clokey 8024</u>, <u>UC</u> (& box), <u>DS</u>, <u>USNA</u>, <u>Ph</u>, <u>NY</u> (fls.), <u>WillU</u>, <u>OSC</u>, <u>BH</u>, <u>Mich</u>, <u>F</u>, <u>WTU</u>, <u>8433</u>, <u>UC</u>, <u>Pom</u>, <u>RSA</u>, <u>Mo</u>, <u>NY</u>, <u>UPa</u>, <u>WillU</u>, <u>OSC</u>, <u>UO</u>, <u>GH</u>, <u>Ill</u>, <u>CU</u>, <u>BH</u>, <u>Mich</u>, <u>F</u>, <u>Tex</u>, <u>TAES</u>, <u>SMU</u>, <u>US</u> (& box), <u>BrY</u>, <u>USFS</u>, <u>USNA</u>, <u>Ariz</u>, <u>DS</u>; 40 mi. NE of Las Vegas, <u>J. P. Hester</u>, June, 1950, <u>US</u> (box), <u>Pom</u>; 13.4 mi. W of Davis Dam, <u>Dress 2970</u>, <u>BH</u>.

UTAH. WASHINGTON CO. Beaverdam Mts., <u>L. Benson 13715</u>, <u>Pom</u>; NW of Santa Clara, <u>L. Benson 13713</u>, <u>Pom</u>; 10 mi. NW of St. George, <u>E. L. Benson 315</u>, <u>Pom</u>.

ARIZONA. MARICOPA CO. Near Harquahala, <u>F. A. Greeley</u>, June, 1921, <u>US</u>; 18 mi. N of Hassayampa, <u>L. Benson 10001</u>, <u>Pom</u>, <u>CAS</u>, <u>Ariz</u>; S side of Black Canyon Refuge, <u>L. Benson 16615</u>, <u>Pom</u>. GILA CO. 10 mi. SW of Globe, <u>L. Benson 16621</u>, <u>Pom</u>; 3 mi. SE of Cutler on old road to Coolidge Dam, <u>L. Benson 16627</u>, <u>Pom</u>.

4b. Opuntia acanthocarpa var. major
(Engelmann & Bigelow) L. Benson

Opuntia echinocarpa Engelm. & Bigelow var. major Engelm. & Bigelow, Proc. Amer. Acad. 3: 305. 1857 (preprint, 1856); in Emory, Rept. U. S. & Mex. Bound. Surv. 2: Cactaceae 56. 1859, not O. phaeacantha Engelm. var. major Engelm. in 1856. O. echinocarpa var. robustior Coulter, Contr. U. S. Nat. Herb. 3: 446. 1896, nom. nov. O. acanthocarpa Engelm. & Bigelow var. major L. Benson, Cacti Ariz. ed. 3. 20, 35. 1969. "β in Sonora," cf. U. S. Senate Rept. Expl. & Surv. R. R. Route Pacific Ocean. Botany 4: 49. 1857. TYPE: "In deserts on both sides of the Colorado River, and in Sonora, Schott." Not found. NEOTYPE (Benson, loc. cit.): Headquarters, Organ Pipe Cactus National Monument, Arizona, W. F. Steenbergh 5-2662-1, May 26, 1962, Pom 306088. DUPLICATE: Herbarium of the Organ Pipe Cactus National Monument.

Opuntia acanthocarpa Engelm. & Bigelow var. ramosa Peebles, Cactus & Succ. Jour. 9: 37. f. on p. 38 (mislabelled as "Opuntia thornberi," not f. on p. 36, which is O. acanthocarpa var. thornberi). 1937. Cylindropuntia acanthocarpa (Engelm. & Bigelow) Knuth var. ramosa Backeberg, Cactaceae 1: 181. 1958. TYPE: Sacaton, Pinal Co., Arizona, 1920, A. R. Leding SF 2, US 1699996. ISOTYPE: Ariz. 94443.

CALIFORNIA. SAN BERNARDINO CO. 20 mi. N of Vidal Jct., 1,200 ft., F. H. Tschirley 83, March 19, 1962, Ariz.

ARIZONA. YUMA CO. Yuma, Wilson in 1907, US (box). GRAHAM CO. 5 mi. E of Coolidge Dam, F. H. Tschirley 36, June 2, 1961, Ariz; Geronimo, Toumey, Dec., 1896, US.

4c. Opuntia acanthocarpa var. ganderi (C. B. Wolf) L. Benson

Opuntia acanthocarpa Engelm. & Bigelow subsp. ganderi C. B. Wolf, Rancho Santa Ana Botanic Garden Occ. Papers I (2): 75. f. 20. 1938. Opuntia acanthocarpa Engelm. & Bigelow var. ganderi L. Benson, Cactus & Succ. Jour. 41: 33. 1969. TYPE: 3 mi. below the old Vallecito Stage Station, San Diego County, California, C. B. Wolf 9424, June 12, 1938, RSA 18631. ISOTYPES: US (box), UC 592964 (box), DS 271973 (box).

CALIFORNIA. RIVERSIDE CO. Palms-to-Pines Highway, 4,000 ft., L. &. R. L. Benson 14838, Pom, 15627, Pom; 4 mi. NE of Aguanga, L. Benson 16141, Pom. SAN DIEGO CO. San Felipe Valley NW of Las Arenas Ranch, C. B. Wolf 9891, RSA; 1 1/2 mi. N of Scissors Crossing, L. Benson 16146, Pom (tending toward Opuntia parryi); middle of Sentenac Canyon, L. Benson 15778, Pom; Wagon Wash near Sentenac Canyon, Jepson 12501, UC-Jeps; Sentenac Valley near jct. of Grapevine and San Felipe Creeks, Jepson 8874, UC-Jeps; Headquarters of Borrego State Park, C. B. Wolf 8472, RSA, CAS; upper end of Mason Valley, L. Benson 15781, Pom; below Vallecito stage station, C. B. Wolf 9424, RSA, UC (box), DS; Agua Caliente Springs, E base Laguna Mts., C. B. Wolf 9396, RSA; Cane Brake Canyon, C. B. Wolf 9395, RSA. IMPERIAL CO. 6.9 mi. NW of Ocotillo, Balls & Everett 22768, RSA, UC.

4d. Opuntia acanthocarpa var. acanthocarpa

Opuntia acanthocarpa Engelm. & Bigelow, Proc. Amer. Acad. 3: 308. 1857 (preprint, 1856); U. S. Senate Rept. Expl. & Surv. R. R. Route Pacific Ocean. Botany 4: 51. pl. 18, f. 1-3. 1857. Cylindropuntia acanthocarpa Knuth in Backeberg & Knuth, Kaktus-ABC 124. 1935. "On the mountains of Cactus Pass, about 500 miles west of Santa Fe." Yavapai Co., Arizona, J. M. Bigelow in 1854. Coulter, Contr. U. S. Nat. Herb. 3: 454. 1896, cites "Type, Bigelow in 1854 in Herb. Mo. Bot. Gard." Specimen not found. NEOTYPE designation: McCloud Mountains, 3 1/2 miles west of Hillside, Yavapai Co., Arizona [about 62 miles southeast of Cactus Pass]; 3,800 feet; Lyman Benson & Robert Darrow 10874, April 18, 1941, Pom 274024. DUPLICATES: CAS 500838, Ariz (not found).

UTAH. WASHINGTON CO. N of Virgin, L. Benson 16021, Pom.

ARIZONA. MOHAVE CO. Peach Springs, Rusby 622, July, 1883, NY, Ph, Mo (box), US, Mich, NY, DS (some plants at NY and US approaching var. thornberi); Kingman, Eastwood 18068, CAS; Pocum Canyon, C. W. McCormick, June 22, 1961, MNA; Hualpai Mt., L. Benson 16201, Pom (this specimen approaching var. coloradensis), 16713, Pom; Big Sandy Wash, 25 mi. SE of Kingman, L. Benson 15852, Pom; summit between Burro Creek and Big Sandy Wash, L. Benson 16712, Pom. YAVAPAI CO. Summit of McCloud Mts., W of Hillside, L. Benson & R. A. Darrow 10874, Pom, CAS, Ariz (not found).

4e. Opuntia acanthocarpa var. thornberi (Thornber & Bonker) L. Benson

Opuntia thornberi Thornber & Bonker, Fantastic Clan 133, 148. f. on p. 135. 1932. O. acanthocarpa Engelm. & Bigelow var. thornberi L. Benson, Proc. Calif. Acad. Sci. IV. 25: 247. 1944. Cylindropuntia acanthocarpa (Engelm. & Bigelow) Knuth var. thornberi Backeberg, Cactaceae 1: 184. 1958. "Southern Arizona." NEOTYPE designation: Bumblebee, Yavapai Co., Arizona; 2,700 feet elevation, Lyman Benson 9671, June 16, 1939, Pom 274018. DUPLICATE: Ariz 158257.

ARIZONA. MOHAVE CO. Peach Springs, Rusby 622, July, 1883, UPa, NY (see note on mixed collection under var. acanthocarpa).

MARICOPA CO. Mormon Flats, A. R. Leding SF 92, March 7, 1926, Ariz. PINAL CO. Hills below Superior, Peebles SF 437, March 10, 1932, Ariz; 9 mi. W of Superior, L. Benson 14620, Pom. GRAHAM CO. Aravaipa Valley, C. Hope SF 514, April 16, 1932, Ariz. (More common in Yavapai and Gila counties.)

5. Opuntia tunicata (Lehmann) Link & Otto

5a. Opuntia tunicata var. tunicata

Cactus tunicatus Lehmann, Ind. Sem. in Hort. Hamburg. 6: 16. 1827 (nom. nud.?); Pugillus Pl. Bot. Hamburg. Hort. in Nova Acta Acad. Caes. Leop. Carol. (Nat. Cur.) 16 (1): 319. 1832 (1828). Opuntia tunicata Link & Otto in Pfeiffer, Enum. Cact. 170. 1837. Cereus tunicatus Link & Otto, loc. cit., pro. syn., based upon Lehmann's parenthetical use of Cereus. Cylindropuntia tunicata Knuth in Backeberg & Knuth, Kaktus-ABC 126. 1935. Pfeiffer gives, loc. cit. 1, only one reference to Lehmann's works, as follows: "LEHMANN pugillus plantarum in botan. Hamburgensium horto occurrentium 1828 in: Nova acta physico-medica academ. caesar. mat. cur. XVI. P. I. 1832" p. 319. According to Pfeiffer, loc. cit. 170, "Pa: Mexico (sec. LEHM. Brasilia merid.)." According to Lehmann (second reference): "Habitat in Brasilia meridionali."

TEXAS. PECOS CO. Gap Tank, Glass Mts., Warnock 47-455, April 15, 1947, SRSC; outlier of Glass Mts., Anthony 649, US, 650, Mich, US, 676, Mich, US; Split Gap, Glass Mts., Warnock & Benson 16496, Pom. BREWSTER CO. Split Tank, Glass Mts., Anthony 4, SRSC; Glass Mts., 15-20 mi. NE of Marathon, J. P. Hester, March 28, 1940, DS.

5b. Opuntia tunicata var. davisii
(Engelmann & Bigelow) L. Benson

Opuntia davisii Engelm. & Bigelow, Proc. Amer. Acad. 3: 305. 1857 (preprint, 1856); U.S. Senate Rept. Expl. & Surv. R. R. Route Pacific Ocean. Botany 4: 49. pl. 16, f. 1-4. 1857. Cylindropuntia davisii Knuth in Backeberg & Knuth, Kaktus-ABC 124. 1935. O. tunicata (Lehmann) Link & Otto var. davisii L. Benson, Cactus & Succ. Jour. 41: 124. 1969. TYPE: "...common on the Upper Canadian, eastward and westward of Tucumcari hills [New Mexico in Quay County], near the Llano Estacado." Specimen not found. NEOTYPE (Benson, loc. cit.): New Mexico State University Northeastern Agricultural Station just NE of Tucumcari, Quay County, New Mexico, E. F. Castetter 1051, A, B, C, D, & E, UNM 45293.

NEW MEXICO. SANTA FE CO. Ft. Marcy, P. Pierce 2138, UNM, QUAY CO. New Mexico State Univ., Agric. Exp. Sta., NE of Tucumcari, Castetter 1051 A-E, UNM.

OKLAHOMA. GREER CO. M. S. Lahman, July 5, 1932, US. HARMON CO. Dry hills near Red River, Goodman & Barkley 2052a, US.

TEXAS. Widespread but scattered and not common, the following being outliers: HANSFORD CO. C. Polaski in 1968, Pom. POTTER CO. Bushland, Weniger 295, Oct. 7, 1963, UNM. PARMER CO. Friona, Weniger 304, Oct. 7, 1963. CHILDRESS CO. 10 1/2 mi. N of Childress, Cory 50-149, SMU. PRESIDIO CO. Marfa, Orcutt 54, in 1924, US; S of Paisano Pass, Anthony 1147, Mich; San Esteban Canyon, Warnock & MacBryde 15420, SRSC, Warnock 17350, SRSC. TOM GREEN CO. San Angelo, Parks & Cory 6730, TAES, Cory 6731, Pom.

6. Opuntia whipplei Engelmann & Bigelow

6a. Opuntia whipplei var. whipplei

Opuntia whipplei Engelm. & Bigelow, Proc. Amer. Acad. 3: 307. 1857 (preprint, 1856); U.S. Senate Rept. Expl. & Surv. R. R. Route Pacific Ocean. Botany 4: 50. pl. 17, f. 1-4. 1857. Cylindropuntia whipplei Knuth in Backeberg & Knuth, Kaktus-ABC 124. 1935. Var. laevior, loc. cit., was intended as the typical variety; var. spinosior is the basis for the later-published O. spinosior, cf. below. "From the elevated country about Zuñi to the head of Williams's River..." LECTOTYPE designation: Zuni, J. M. Bigelow, Nov. 22, 1853, Mo (obviously the specimen from which the plate was drawn). DUPLICATE: Pom 317795.

Opuntia whipplei Engelm. & Bigelow var. enodis Peebles, Jour. Wash. Acad. Sci. 30: 473. 1940; Des. Pl. Life 13: 32. f. 1941. Cylindropuntia whipplei (Engelm. & Bigelow) Knuth var. enodis Backeberg, Cactaceae 1: 180. 1958. TYPE: "North end of Hualpai Mountain, Mohave County, Ariz., altitude 4,200 feet, Peebles SF 883, April 19, 1935," US 1786533 & photograph. ISOTYPE: Ariz 95988. Observation in the field at the type locality shows (L. Benson 15581, Pom) the characters of the fruits to be due to reaction to larvae of parasitic insects.

Opuntia hualpaensis Hester, Cact. & Succ. Jour. 15: 191. f. 94, upper right. 1943. Cylindropuntia hualpaensis Backeberg, Cactaceae 1: 178. 1958. TYPE: "...Dudley Herbarium, Stanford University, No. 285575, [box] ...Highway 66, 11 or 12 miles east of Peach Springs and 2 or 3 miles west of Hyde Park, Arizona, by J. Pinckney Hester, July, 1942." Possible ISOTYPES: Mo (labelled only Hualapai Indian Reservation), GH (sent by Hester, Aug. 30, 1942, with no locality).

UTAH. BEAVER CO. Summit W of Milford, L. & R. Benson 15191, Pom. IRON CO. Paragoonah [Paragonah], Palmer in 1877, Mo. WASHINGTON CO. Upper Santa Clara Crossing, _____, May 16, 1891, Mo (photograph); St. George, Palmer in 1877, Mo; Crater Hill, Zion Nat. Park, G. & C. Trapp 67-70, 67-81 to 67-85, Pom.

ARIZONA. GILA CO. Roosevelt Dam, Eastwood in 1928, CAS; road to Winkelman, Eastwood 17477, CAS. PINAL CO. Between Tucson and Oracle, McKelvey 1123, NY; Oracle, _____, May 30, 1912, NY.

NEW MEXICO. RIO ARRIBA CO. El Rito, Rusby, Aug. 1, 1880, US; Espanola, V. Bailey, Oct. 19, 1904, US. SANTA FE CO. Santa Fe, P. Pierce 2138, UNM. SOCORRO CO. Puertocito Mts., Wooton 3008, NMC. GRANT CO. Ft. Bayard, Blumer 155, US (box).

6b. Opuntia whipplei var. multigeniculata (Clokey) L. Benson

Opuntia multigeniculata Clokey, Madroño 7: 69. pl. 4, f. A. 1943. Cylindropuntia multigeniculata Backeberg, Cactaceae 1: 186. 1958. O. whipplei Engelm. & Bigelow var. multigeniculata L. Benson, Cacti Ariz. ed. 3. 20, 38. 1969. TYPE: "...east of Wilson's Ranch, Charleston [Spring] Mountains, Clark County, Nevada, ... Blue Diamond mill to the mine, ...1400 meters; Clokey 8430...." Not found. LECTOTYPE (Benson, loc. cit.): Same place, Clokey 8630, UC 872689 (box). DUPLICATES: Pom 265219, 275347, Mo 1244341, BM, NY, WillU 30290, 30292, OSC, GH, US 1828523, Ill, BH, DS 270338 (box & photographs), Ariz 21473, UO, Tex, Mich, SMU, F, Ph 815140, K, WTU 74000, USNA 289540, UFS 94508.

Opuntia abyssi Hester, Cact. & Succ. Jour. 15: 193. f. 94, upper left and below. 1943. Cylindropuntia abyssi Backeberg, Cactaceae 1: 184. 1958. TYPE: "...Peach Springs Canyon,...Hualpai Indian Reservation, northwestern Arizona, by J. Pinckney Hester in 1939...." DS 285624 (box & fluid, excluding one stem of "Opuntia hualpaensis [= Opuntia whipplei]"). ISOTYPES: Mo (box), UC 901702, US (not yet numbered).

NEVADA. NYE CO. Between Mercury and the Ranger Mts., Beatley, Aug. 27, 1967, TSH 5307. CLARK CO. Below Lee Canyon, Charleston Mts., L. Benson 16728, Pom; E of Wilson's Ranch, Clokey 8427, UC, 8630 (lectotype, see list of duplicates), 8639, UC (box), DS (box), NY, Ariz, 8760, UC (box), NY, WillU, Ill, WTU, DS, USNA. "Just one area in southern Nevada," J. P. Hester, April 25, 1942, UC 901707 (possibly a large Opuntia echinocarpa or O. acanthocarpa var. acanthocarpa; no fruits).

ARIZONA. MOHAVE CO. Peach Springs Canyon, J. P. Hester in 1939, DS, UC, US, Mo.

6c. Opuntia whipplei var. viridiflora (Britton & Rose) L. Benson

Opuntia viridiflora Britton & Rose, Cactaceae 1: 55. 1919. Cylindropuntia viridiflora Knuth in Backeberg & Knuth, Kaktus–ABC 124. 1935. O. imbricata Engelm. var. viridiflora Weniger, Cacti S. W. 231. 1970, nom. nud. (Art. 33). O. whipplei Engelm. & Bigelow var. viridiflora L. Benson, Cactus & Succ. Jour. 46. 79. 1974. TYPE: "...Vicinity of Santa Fe, New Mexico,...about 2,224 meters, by Paul C. Standley, July 6, 1911 (No. 6493, type)...," US 685515.

NEW MEXICO. SANTA FE CO. N of Santa Fe off road to Hyde Park, Castetter 2171, Oct. 10, 1963, UNM; Santa Fe, Standley 6493, US, Rose & Fitch 17776, NY, K, Cockerell in 1912, NY; Ft. Marcy, Santa Fe, A. R. Leding, in 1932, UNM. HARDING CO. Ute Creek, Canadian River drainage, junction of routes 39 & 65, 10 mi. E of Mosquero, Castetter 1930, UNM. Other collections cited by authors as Opuntia viridiflora, US, are O. imbricata.

7. Opuntia spinosior (Engelmann) Toumey

Opuntia whipplei Engelm. & Bigelow var. spinosior Engelm. Proc. Amer. Acad. 3: 307. 1857 (preprint, 1856); U.S. Senate Rept. Expl. & Surv. R. R. Route Pacific Ocean. Botany 4: 51. pl. 17, f. 5-6; pl. 18, f. 4 (all labelled inadvertently as O. arborescens [imbricata]). 1857. O. spinosior (Engelm. & Bigelow) Toumey, Bot. Gaz. 25: 119. 1898. O. whipplei Engelm. & Bigelow f. spinosior Schelle, Handb. Kakteenkultur 39. 1907. Cylindropuntia spinosior Knuth in Backeberg & Knuth, Kaktus–ABC 126. 1935. "Var.β...Schott south of the Gila River,...he also discovered the flower of this plant...." Specimen not found. LECTOTYPE designation: "Santa Cruz river valley and further East." A. Schott, no. 5, VI, 1855, Mo. DUPLICATE: Pom 317797.

Opuntia spinosior (Engelm.) Toumey var. neomexicana Toumey, Bot. Gaz. 25: 119. 1898. "...Southern Arizona..." According to Britton & Rose, Cactaceae 1: 68. 1919, "Mr. Toumey writes...original material...from the low foothills north of the Rillito River near Tucson [near Sabino Canyon, Santa Catalina Mts.]." LECTOTYPE designation: specimen bearing this name and labelled "Tucson," Toumey, Feb. 5 and Apr. 20, 1896, Pom 83393. Probable DUPLICATES: Mo (with the same dates but for 1895), NY, BH, UC (2).

ARIZONA. MARICOPA CO. Paradise Valley N of Scottsdale, E. R. Blakley 1871, Des; 12 mi. N of Scottsdale, Blakley & Speck 214, Des. PINAL CO. Sacaton, M. F. Gilman in 1913, NY, US; Casa Grande, Leding SF 14, in 1921, Ariz. GILA CO. S of Sierra Ancha, E. F. Wiegand 116 in 1950, Pom; South Rim of Salt River Canyon,

L. & R. L. Benson 15735, Pom. GRAHAM CO. Klondyke to Safford, R. B. Ross, July 1, 1922, US; Safford, SCS [Soil Conservation Service] 782, Ariz; 26 mi. S of Safford, F. H. Tschirley 34, Ariz; 3 mi. NE of Clifton Jct., L. Benson 9473, Pom. PIMA CO. (W). Near Gunsight, W. F. Steenbergh, Jan. 31, 1962, Pom; NW corner Organ Pipe Cactus Nat. Mon., W. F. Steenbergh, Jan. 10, 1962, Pom; W boundary (of same) W. F. Steenbergh, Jan. 10, 1962, Pom. (Common in Arizona S & E.)

NEW MEXICO. VALENCIA CO. S end of Zuni Mts., S of Grants, P. Pierce 1201, UNM. SOCORRO CO. Socorro, Vasey, May, 1881, NY. SIERRA CO. (NW). Fairview, Goldman 1782, US. LINCOLN CO. S of Corona, Castetter 2203, UNM. DONA ANA CO. Mt. Riley, C. Champie in 1961, UNM

8. Opuntia imbricata Haworth

8a. Opuntia imbricata var. imbricata

Cereus imbricatus Haw. Rev. Pl. Succ. 70. 1821. Opuntia imbricata DC. Prodr. 3: 471. 1828. Cylindropuntia imbricata Knuth in Backeberg & Knuth, Kaktus–ABC 125. 1935. According to DeCandolle, "Patria...ign." According to Britton & Rose, Cactaceae 1: 64. 1919, "Type locality: unknown; introduced into England by Loddiges in 1820."

Cactus cylindricus James, Trans. Amer. Philos. Soc. 2: 182. 1825, not Lam. Encyl. 1: 539. 1783. Opuntia cylindrica DC. Prodr. 3: 471. 1828. "...Journey to and from the Rocky Mountains, during the Summer of 1820...head waters of the Arkansaw and Canadian...." Long Expedition. No specimen found.

Opuntia arborescens Engelm. in Wisliz. Mem. Tour. No. Mex. 90. 1848. O. imbricata (Haw.) DC var. arborescens Weniger, Cacti S. W. 229. 1970, nom. nud. (Art. 33). "Mountains of New Mexico to Chihuahua, Parras, and Saltillo; Santa Fé (Fendler)... on Waggon-mound..." LECTOTYPE designation: Santa Fe, New Mexico, Fendler 277 in 1847, Mo (flowers and fruits, but no branches). SYNTYPE: Wislizenus, July 27, 1846, Mo (flowers but no branches or fruits). Typical specimen (for other parts): hills 3 miles NW of Santa Fe, Lyman & Robert L. Benson 14686, October 25, 1950, Pom 278909.

Opuntia vexans Griffiths, Rept. Mo. Bot. Gard. 22: 28. pl. 6 and (in part 7; 2 right-hand rows). 1912. O. imbricata Haw. var. vexans Weniger, Cacti S. W. 231. 1970, nom. nud. (Art. 33). TYPE: Griffiths "...9174, prepared at San Antonio, Texas, May 2, 1910, from plants cultivated from cuttings collected under the same number in Webb County, Texas, March 13, 1908." Only a photograph and the following found. LECTOTYPE designation: "Flowered in cultivation at the Asylum, San Antonio, Texas, 10-12-'05," David Griffiths 8174, US 2437234.

Opuntia imbricata fl. rosea Frič, Českoslov. Zehradnických Listů [Kakt. Sukk.] 1924: 122. 1924, nom. nud., not a bi- or trinomial. "Texas, USA."

COLORADO. LA PLATA CO. Durango, Diehl in 1899, Pom. EL PASO CO. Colorado Springs, Mathias 481, Mo; Fountain, Mrs. G. W. Vanderbilt, June 29, 1896, US.

ARIZONA. GILA CO. N of San Carlos, A. A. Nichol, March, 1940, Ariz. PIMA CO. Old road near San Pedro River, near Redington; plants in P. G. Nichols' garden, Tucson. COCHISE CO. Cascabel, W. W. Jones, June 14, 1947, SD.

KANSAS. MORTON CO. Richfield, Rose & Fitch 17104, US.

OKLAHOMA. (W edge of Panhandle). CIMARRON CO. Kenton, G. W. Stevens 494, May 15, 1913, GH, Ill (fr.), Mo (fr.), US (fr.), DS (fr.).

TEXAS. BURNET CO. Granite Mt., Griffiths 9386, US, Pom. BEXAR CO. San Antonio, Griffiths 8174, US, Pom. VICTORIA CO. Victoria, Lewton in 1904, US (box).

8b. Opuntia imbricata var. argentea Anthony

Opuntia imbricata Haw. var. argentea Anthony, Amer. Midl. Nat. 55: 236. f. 7. 1956. Cylindropuntia imbricata Knuth var. argentea Backeberg, Cactaceae 1: 195. 1958. "Specimen typicum ex monte dicto 'Mariscal Mountain, Big Bend National Park, [Brewster County] Texas'...[Anthony]...280." TYPE: Mich, Bot. Gard. no. 18830.

TEXAS. BREWSTER CO. Mariscal Mt., Big Bend Nat. Park, Anthony 12, SRSC, 280, Mich; Solis Ranch, Big Bend Nat. Park, Anthony 276, Mich.

9. Opuntia versicolor Engelmann

Opuntia versicolor Engelm. ex Coulter, Contr. U.S. Nat. Herb. 3: 452. 1896. O. arborescens Engelm. var. versicolor E. Dams, Monatschr. Kakteenk. 14: 3. 1894. Cylindropuntia versicolor Knuth in Backeberg & Knuth, Kaktus–ABC 125. 1935. O. thurberi Engelm. subsp. versicolor Felger & Lowe, Jour. Ariz. Acad. Sci. 6: 82. 1970. TYPE: "Specimens of Parry, Pringle, G. Engelmann, and Miller, in Herb. Mo. Bot. Gard." LECTOTYPE designation: "Mesas and foothills [probably near Tucson], C. G. Pringle, May 18, 1881, Mo. DUPLICATES: K, F, Pom 313597, NY, UPa 8558, GH, Vt, US 41045, F 98068, 404515, ISC.

ARIZONA. PINAL CO. Sacaton, H. F. Loomis SF 113, May 8, 1926, Ariz; Casa Grande, Leding SF 170, June 15, 1927, Ariz; Road to Winkelman, Pinal Mts., McKelvey 1119, GH. COCHISE CO. Benson, [Parry], Jan. 21, 1881, ISC, Rose, Standley, & Russell 12309, GH.

10. Opuntia kelvinensis V. & K. Grant

Opuntia kelvinensis V. & K. Grant, Evolution 25: 156. 1971. "Type. V. Grant, collection no. 70-29, just southeast of Kelvin, Pinal County, Arizona, June 15, 1970. Herbarium, University of Texas, Austin."

11. Opuntia prolifera Engelmann

Opuntia prolifera Engelm. Amer. Jour. Sci. II. 14: 338. 1852. Cylindropuntia prolifera Knuth in Backeberg & Knuth, Kaktus-ABC 126. 1935. "San Diego..." California, C. C. Parry in 1848-49. TYPE: not found. NEOTYPE designation: Mission Hills, San Diego, San Diego Co., California, LeRoy Abrams 3394, Mo. DUPLICATES: Pom 155594, NY, GH, UC, DS.

CALIFORNIA. SANTA BARBARA CO. Santa Barbara Islands, Abrams & Wiggins 306, DS (box); Laguna Canyon, S Shore Santa Cruz I., Balls & Blakley 23752, RSA, UC; Santa Cruz I., Balls 23751, RSA. VENTURA CO. N of Ventura, C. B. Wolf 8276, RSA, US (box), DS (box), H. M. Pollard, Sept. 24, 1945, CAS; Conejo Grade, Fosberg 8611, Pom. LOS ANGELES CO. San Nicolas I., Trask, April, 1901, NY, GH, Mo, US.

12. Opuntia fulgida Engelmann

12a. Opuntia fulgida var. fulgida

Opuntia fulgida Engelm. Proc. Amer. Acad. 3: 306. 1857 (preprint, 1856); in Emory, Rept. U.S. & Mex. Bound. Surv. 2: Cactaceae 57. pl. 75, f. 18 (seeds). 1859. O. fulgida Engelm. f. nana Weber ex Schelle, Handb. Kakteenkultur 40. 1907, nom. nud. Cylindropuntia fulgida Knuth in Backeberg & Knuth, Kaktus-ABC 126. 1935. "Mountains of Western Sonora: fl. July and August." LECTOTYPE designation: "All through the Sierras of Western Sonora." "Vela Coyote of the Sonorians [mentioned with the description]," Schott No. 8, Mo. See Suppl.

NEW MEXICO. HIDALGO CO. Between Red Rock and U.S. Highway 180, G. Wiens, June 22, 1966, UNM.

12b. Opuntia fulgida var. mamillata (Schott) Coulter

Opuntia mamillata Schott in Engelm. Proc. Amer. Acad. 3: 308. 1857 (preprint, 1856); in Emory, Rept. U.S. & Mex. Bound. Surv. 2: Cactaceae 58. pl. 75, f. 19 (seeds). 1859. O. fulgida Engelm. var. mamillata Coulter, Contr. U.S. Nat. Herb. 3: 449. 1896. Cylindropuntia fulgida (Engelm.) Knuth var. mamillata Backeberg, Cactaceae 1: 204. 1958. "South range of the Sierra Babuquibari [Baboquivari], in Sonora, and southeastward..., Schott fl. July and August." TYPE: (Coulter, loc. cit.); "Schott 6 in Herb. Mo. Bot. Gard." Not found, Mo, or F (Schott Collection). Most of the Baboquivari range is in Pima County, Arizona, where it extends N into the Quinlan Range. NEOTYPE designation: N end of the Quinlan Mountains, Papago Indian Reservation, 3,800 feet, Pima County, Arizona, Lyman and Robert L. Benson 14867, April 10, 1952, Pom 285605.

13. Opuntia munzii C. B. Wolf

Opuntia munzii C. B. Wolf, Rancho Santa Ana Botanic Garden Occ. Papers I. (2): 79. f. 23. 1938. Cylindropuntia x munzii Backeberg, Kakteen Lexikon 11. 1966. TYPE: "11 mi. east of Niland on road to Beal's Well, Chocolate Mts., Colorado Desert, Imperial Co., California,...C. B. Wolf 1875, March 12, 1931,..." RSA 5142.

CALIFORNIA. RIVERSIDE CO. Chuckawalla Well, Chuckawalla Mts., C. H. & A. Bonner, Dec. 25, 1960, Pom. IMPERIAL CO. Above Beal's Well, C. B. Wolf 9389, RSA, DS (box); Chocolate Mts., E of Niland, C. B. Wolf 1875, RSA, 9388, RSA, DS (box); Niland to Beal's Well, Balls & Everett 22760, RSA.

14. Opuntia bigelovii Engelmann

14a. Opuntia bigelovii var. hoffmannii Fosberg

Opuntia bigelovii Engelm. var. hoffmannii Fosberg, Bull. So. Calif. Acad. Sci. 32: 122. 1933, not O. hoffmannii Bravo in 1930. O. fosbergii C. B. Wolf, Rancho Santa Ana Botanic Garden Occ. Papers I. (2): 79. f. 22. 1938, nom. nov. TYPE: "...Fosberg No. 8602 from the mouth of Can Brakes [Cane Brake] Canyon...." Pom 220078.

CALIFORNIA. SAN DIEGO CO. Mason Valley, L. Benson 15780, Pom; Cane Brake Canyon, Fosberg 8602, Pom, C. B. Wolf 9392, RSA, US (box), UC (box), DS (box), Balls & Everett 22770, RSA.

14b. Opuntia bigelovii var. bigelovii

Opuntia bigelovii Engelm., Proc. Amer. Acad. 3: 307. 1857 (preprint, 1856); U.S. Senate Rept. Expl. & Surv. R. R. Route Pacific Ocean. Botany 4: 50. pl. 19, f. 1-7. 1857. Cylindropuntia bigelovii Knuth in Backeberg & Knuth, Kaktus-ABC 125. 1935. "On Williams's River, a branch of the Colorado." Mohave Co., Arizona. TYPE (Coulter, Contr. U.S. Nat. Herb. 3: 450. 1896): "Bigelow of 1854, in Herb. Mo. Bot. Gard." Not found. NEOTYPE designation: 8 miles east of Papago Well, Camino del Diablo; granite hill, Agua Dulce Mountains; 1,200 feet elevation; Lyman Benson & Robert A. Darrow 10766, April 14, 1941, Pom 274052. DUPLICATES: Ariz, CAS 500834.

Species Reported from Arizona

Opuntia ciribe Engelm. in Coulter, Contr. U.S. Nat. Herb. 3: 445. 1896. Cylindropuntia ciribe Backeberg & Knuth, Kaktus-ABC. 125. 1935. Opuntia bigelovii Engelm. var. ciribe W. T. Marshall, Arizona's Cactuses ed. 2. 23. 1953. Marshall reported a plant presumed by him to be Opuntia ciribe contrasted with Opuntia bigelovii as follows: "Spines fewer...; tubercles of fruit all alike, while...the upper tubercles are longer." "We have had our attention called to a colony of plants from Lower California near Quitobaquito in the western part of Organ Pipe Cactus National Monument by Wm. Supernaugh. The location is on the old Camino del Diablo once travelled by pack trains from Lower California...." According to a personal communication from Warren F. Steenbergh, later with the National Park Service at the Organ Pipe Cactus National Monument and a careful collector of the cacti of the area, the plant is not known to the present members of the Park Service. The reference may have been to a colony (clone) of plants of Opuntia bigelovii with an unusual character combination. However, Marshall's interpretation may have been correct.

15. Opuntia leptocaulis DeCandolle

Opuntia leptocaulis DC. Mem. Mus. Hist. Nat. 17: 118. 1828. Cylindropuntia leptocaulis Knuth in Backeberg & Knuth, Kaktus-ABC 122. 1935. "...In Mexico. Coulter, no. 22."

Opuntia frutescens Engelm. var. longispina Engelm. Proc. Amer. Acad. 3: 309. 1857 (preprint, 1856); U.S. Senate Rept. Expl. & Surv. R. R. Route Pacific Ocean. Botany 4: 53. pl. 20, f. 2-3; 24, f. 16. 1857. O. leptocaulis DC var. stipata Coulter, Contr. U.S. Nat. Herb. 3: 456. 1896, nom. superfl., as nom. nov. because of O. longispina Haw. in 1830. O. leptocaulis var. longispina Engelm. ex Berger in Engler, Bot. Jahrb. 36: 450. 1905, erroneously ascribed to Engelmann. O. vaginata DC. f. longispina Schelle, Handb. Kakteenkultur 41. 1907. Cylindropuntia leptocaulis (DC.) Knuth var. longispina Knuth in Backeberg & Knuth Kaktus-ABC 122. 1935. "...Laguna Colorado, 60 miles east of the Pecos, to Williams' River, a branch of the Great Colorado...." "The forms collected on the [Whipple] expedition belong to var. ⌐ longispina." LECTOTYPE designation: "Laguna Colorado — East of the Pecos," J. M. Bigelow, Sept. 22, 1853, Mo. The upper right-hand branch on the sheet is the one illustrated for pl. 20, f. 2. A few small branches and the fruits have dropped off.

Opuntia vaginata Engelm. in Wisliz. Mem. Tour. No. Mex. 100. 1848. O. leptocaulis DC. var. vaginata S. Wats. Bibl. Ind. N. Amer. Bot. 1: 407. 1878. O. leptocaulis DC. f. vaginata Schelle, Kakteen 54. 1926. Cylindropuntia leptocaulis (DC.) Knuth var. vaginata Knuth in Backeberg & Knuth, Kaktus-ABC. 122. 1935. "On the mountains near El Paso; in August in flower and fruit." LECTOTYPE designation: "Mountains near El Paso. Dr. A. Wislizenus leg. August 14th., 1846," Mo (flowers and fruits). The rejected possible alternative choice, labelled Opuntia vaginata Engelm. Hab. between Albuquerque and El Paso. Dr. A. Wislizenus leg. August, 1846," has no flowers or fruits.

Opuntia fragilis Nutt. var. frutescens Engelm. Pl. Lindh. I, Boston Jour. Nat. Hist. 5: 245. 1845. O. frutescens Engelm. Pl. Lindh. II, Boston Jour. Nat. Hist. 5: 245. 1845, pro syn.; Engelm. loc. cit. 6: 208. 1850. "Near the Muskit [mesquite] thickets, (vide No. 233,) on the Colorado...." Texas. LECTOTYPE designation: "Colorado bottom prairie," Texas, F. Lindheimer, August, 1844, Mo. DUPLICATES: Pom 317785, K, GH, Ph, US 1870971. 244 is the serial number of the species in Plantae Lindheimerianae.

The plants described as var. frutescens and var. brevispina have very short spines. However, short-spined plants occur with long-spined almost throughout the range of the species. Detailed study of populations may reveal lines of segregation of varieties within Opuntia leptocaulis, but present information is meager.

Opuntia frutescens Engelm. var. brevispina Engelm. Proc. Amer. Acad. 3: 309. 1857 (preprint, 1856); U.S. Senate Rept. Expl. & Surv. R. R. Route Pacific Ocean. Botany 4: 53. pl. 20, f. 4-5; 24, f. 19. 1857. O. leptocaulis DC. var. brevispina S. Wats. Bibl. Ind. No. Amer. Bot. 1: 407. 1878. O. leptocaulis (DC.) f. brevispina Schelle, Kakteen 54. 1926. Cylindropuntia leptocaulis (DC.) Knuth var. brevispina Knuth in Backeberg & Knuth Kaktus-ABC 122. 1935. "...Texas and northeastern Mexico." LECTOTYPE designation: "Texas," F. Lindheimer, May, 1846, Mo (part drawn for pl. 20, f. 4).

Cylindropuntia leptocaulis (DC.) Knuth var. glauca Backeberg, Cactaceae 6: 3583. f. 3258, left. 1962, nom. nud. "Typus

RIVIERE -- Nr. 8022 (abb. 3258 links)." Probably no type specimen. Backeberg stated that he would never make an herbarium specimen, and presumably this was a living plant in a garden.

ARIZONA. MOHAVE CO. Kingman, Braem, Sept. 12, 1927, DS; Big Sandy windmill, Mrs. F. Stevens in 1902, UC. YUMA CO. La Poza Plain, 16 miles S of Quartzsite, Wiggins 6229, Mich, DS (box); 7 miles E of Aztec, Wiggins 8661, DS (box).

OKLAHOMA. MURRAY CO. Turner Falls, Arbuckle Mountains, E. J. Palmer 42055, GH, Mo, NY, Dowell in 1950, RSA.

Yellow-fruited plants collected by Mr. and Mrs. Bone include the following: TEXAS. ZAPATA CO. South of Zapata near Falcon Lake, Bone & Bone, December 1971, Pom. Brooks Co. 14.5 miles southwest of Falfurrias, Bone & Bone, December, 1971, Pom.

16. Opuntia arbuscula Engelmann

Opuntia arbuscula Engelm. Proc. Amer. Acad. 3: 309. 1857 (preprint, 1856); in Emory, Rept. U.S. & Mex. Bound. Surv. 2: Cactaceae 60. 1859. Cylindropuntia arbuscula Knuth in Backeberg & Knuth, Kaktus-ABC 123. 1935. "On desert heights, near Maricopa village, on the Gila, Schott: fl. in June." Arizona. LECTOTYPE designation: "Gila...flower in June," Mo, with Engelmann's handwritten description with "Op. arbusculum" crossed out and "Schottii" [tentative designation] substituted.

Opuntia vivipara Rose, Smithsonian Misc. Coll. 52: 153. pl. 12. 1908. Cylindropuntia vivipara Knuth in Backeberg & Knuth, Kaktus-ABC. 124. 1935. "...near Tucson, Arizona,...J. N. Rose, April 21, 1908 (No. 11836)...." "While going from Tucson, Arizona, to the Pictured Rock, some 12 miles to the southwest [in the Tucson Mountains to the northwest]...." TYPE: US 454531 and box. ISOTYPES: NY, Pom 306400.

Opuntia neoarbuscula Griffiths, Rept. Mo. Bot. Gard. 19: 260. pl. 23 (upper). 1908 (preprint issued Nov. 6, 1908). Cylindropuntia neoarbuscula Knuth in Backeberg & Knuth, Kaktus-ABC 120. 1935; Index Kew. Suppl. 9: 82. 1935. TYPE: "...from the cultivated plant and [re-]numbered 9219 D. G. [David Griffiths], April 22, 1908; ...originally...foothills...Santa Rita Mountains, Arizona...." Field number 7771, April 16, 1905, US 2572031A. ISOTYPE: Pom 287140.

17. Opuntia kleiniae DeCandolle

17a. Opuntia kleiniae var. kleiniae

Opuntia kleiniae DC. Mem. Mus. Hist. Nat. 17: 118. 1828. Cylindropuntia kleiniae Knuth in Backeberg & Knuth, Kaktus-ABC 123. 1935. "...in Mexico. Coulter, no. 21."

Opuntia wrightii Engelm. Proc. Amer. Acad. 3: 308. 1857 (preprint, 1856); in Emory, Rept. U.S. & Mex. Bound. Surv. 2: Cactaceae 59. 1859. "...On the Limpia, Wright,...Rio Grande from Presidio del Norte to the Pecos, Parry, Bigelow;...in Mexico, Gregg: fl. June and July." LECTOTYPE designation: "...Presidio del Norte towards the Pecos." C. Wright in 1851-2, Mo.

17b. Opuntia kleiniae var. tetracantha (Toumey) W. T. Marshall

Opuntia californica Engelm. in Emory, Notes Mil. Reconn. Ft. Leavenworth to San Diego, App. 2. 158. f. 11. May-July, 1848. TYPE: "Nov. 2, 1846." No specimen preserved. The illustration matches most nearly O. kleiniae var. tetracantha. On Nov. 2 the expedition was in Arizona [not California] near the Gila River in the mountains between the Coolidge Dam and Christmas, S Gila Co. LECTOTYPE designation: "Ex Hb. Torrey, Emory," (excluding one label, "arbuscula, Emory, Nov. 13, 1846," which belongs with a collection of that species from the lower Gila), Mo 1797128. The specimen from the Torrey Herbarium matches the illustration of No. 11 of Emory's Notes (cf. above).

Opuntia tetracantha Toumey, Garden & Forest 9: 432. 1896. Cylindropuntia tetracantha Knuth in Backeberg & Knuth, Kaktus-ABC 124. 1935. O. kleiniae DC. var. tetracantha W. T. Marshall, Arizona's Cactuses 17. f. 7. 1950. "...About five miles east of Tucson...." LECTOTYPE designation: Tucson, Arizona, Toumey, Jan. 25 and April 20, 1895, Pom 83403. DUPLICATES: Mo, NY (2), US 535545, BM, UC 108230.

Opuntia congesta Griffiths, Rept. Mo. Bot. Gard. 20: 88. pl. 2, f. 4, 7; 8; 13, f. 5. 1909. Cylindropuntia arbuscula (Engelm.) Knuth var. congesta Backeberg, Cactaceae 174. 1958. O. arbuscula Engelm. var. congesta Rowley, Nat. Cactus & Succ. Jour. 13: 25. 1958. TYPE: "...9658, D. G. [David Griffiths] collected at Hillside [SW Yavapai Co.], Arizona, September 10, 1908." Griffiths 9658 is O. phaeacantha, not the plant described, and 9657 is O. phaeacantha var. major. LECTOTYPE designation: Griffiths 9567, US, from the same place, US 2437252.

ARIZONA. NAVAJO CO. Showlow-Holbrook (nearer Showlow), P. Fischer, June, 1959, Ariz. YAVAPAI CO. Hillside, Griffiths 9567, US. GILA CO. 5 miles NE of Globe, P. Fischer 803, March 3, 1961, Ariz, Pom.

18. Opuntia ramosissima Engelmann

Opuntia ramósissima Engelm. Amer. Jour. Sci. II. 14: 339. 1852. O. tessellata Engelm. Proc. Amer. Acad. 3: 309. 1857 (preprint, 1856); U.S. Senate Rept. Expl. & Surv. R. R. Route Pacific Ocean. Botany 4: 52. pl. 21, f. 1-7. 1857, nom. superfl., nom. nov. (O. ramosissima having been considered inappropriate because all species branch profusely). Cylindropuntia ramosissima Knuth in Backeberg & Knuth, Kaktus-ABC 122. 1935. "Gravelly soil near the Colorado, and in the desert." California, C. C. Parry in 1849-50. TYPE: not found, Mo or ISC. Engelmann in renaming the species as O. tessellata cited observations or collections by Parry, Bigelow, and Schott. NEOTYPE designation: "Sierra Pala, N Western Sonora, IX [September]. 1855. Schott," Mo. Engelmann's notes and discussion are with the Bigelow collection, but it lacks mature fruits.

Opuntia tessellata Engelm. var. cristata K. Schum. Monatsschr. Kakteenk. 8: 70. photograph. 1898. "...Von Herrn ALVERSON in Kalifornien...." Garden plant.

Opuntia ramosissima Engelm. f. cristata Schelle, Handb. Kakteenkultur 41. 1907, nom. nud.

CALIFORNIA. INYO CO. Head of Ryan Wash, Death Valley, M. F. Gilman 2026, June 19, 1935, US; Furnace Creek on Shoshone Road, Coville & Gilman 450, April 25, 1932, US.

NEVADA. NYE CO. W of Mercury, Beatley, Aug. 27, 1967, TSH; Ranger Mts., R. Rasp, Aug. 31, 1967, TSH; Reveal & Beatley 1158, June 6, 1968, TSH, Beatley, July 1, 1969, TSH; Spotted Range, Beatley, April 13, 1969, TSH, April 20, 1969, TSH; Mara Wash, S of Mt. Salyer, Beatley, June 3, 1971, TSH, Pom.

ARIZONA. PIMA CO. W boundary of Organ Pipe Cactus Nat. Mon., W. F. Steenbergh, Jan. 1, 1962, Pom, Organ Pipe Cactus Nat. Mon. Herb.

19. Opuntia stanlyi Engelmann

19a. Opuntia stanlyi var. stanlyi

Opuntia stanlyi Engelm. in Emory, Notes Mil. Reconn. Ft. Leavenworth to San Diego. App. 2. 158. f. 9. May-July, 1848. Corynopuntia stanlyi Knuth in Backeberg & Knuth, Kaktus-ABC 114. 1935. Grusonia stanlyi H. Robinson, Phytologia 26: 176. 1973. "Oct. 22, 1846. Abundant on the Gila." Camp of October 22, 1846 (p. 63), Lat. 23° 38' 18" N; Long. 109° 07' 30" W; Arizona-New Mexico boundary, "...in view of a rock, which we named, from its general appearance, Steeple rock." TYPE: not preserved, but only one taxon of this group occurs in the area, and it corresponds with Stanly's (in this instance relatively good) figure 9 and with the description. NEOTYPE designation: Gravelly and sandy valley land along the Gila River, 3 miles SE of Virden, Hidalgo Co., New Mexico, almost directly S of Steeple Rock, 3,500 feet, Lyman Benson 16638, April 23, 1966; flowers and fruits from the same plant, July 2, 1966, Pom 317489. See Suppl.

Plant of Uncertain Identity (perhaps Opuntia stanlyi)

Opuntia emoryi Engelm. Proc. Amer. Acad. 3: 303. 1857 (preprint, 1856); Emory, Rept. U.S. & Mex. Bound. Surv. 2: Cactaceae: 53. pl. 70-71. 1859. Cactus emoryi Lemaire, Cactées 88. 1868. "Arid soil south and west of El Paso, especially between the Sandhills and Lake Santa Maria (Wright, Bigelow), in Sonora (Wright), and on the lower Gila and in the Colorado Desert (Schott). Flowers in August and September." Two seed specimens, Mo; without locality, Bigelow in 1852, Mo; a packet of seeds (some dissected) and one of embryos, Mo (used for preparation of Engelmann's illustration). LECTOTYPE designation: the seeds mentioned above, Mo. Engelmann indicated some doubt concerning inclusion of the Schott collections from the Gila and westward, as follows (p. 54), "The specimens from the lower Gila and the Colorado [rivers] must, I have little doubt, also be referred here." However, in view of their size, probably they were O. stanlyi var. kunzei. The area "between the sand-hills and Lake Santa Maria," Chihuahua, is about 70-75 miles southwest of El Paso. This, rather than the areas in the United States farther west, should be considered the type locality. Full specimens from this area are needed to determine the nature of O. emoryi and to provide a neotype. No other material has been seen, and the plates may match the Chihuahuan plant, but they may include elements from O. stanlyi var. kunzei, the Gila collection from the U.S.

19b. Opuntia stanlyi var. peeblesiana L. Benson

Opuntia stanlyi Engelm. var. peeblesiana L. Benson, Cacti Ariz. ed. 3. 20, 64. 1969. TYPE: "5 miles southeast of Alamo (old [former] settlement at the crossing of the Bill Williams River), Yuma County, Arizona, 1,500 feet elevation; base of the Harcuvar Mountains; Colorado Desert; sandy flat, Lyman Benson 10064, March 27, 1940," Pom 274040.

ARIZONA. YUMA CO. 5 mi. SE of Alamo, 1,500 ft., L. Benson 10064, Pom; La Posa Plain, 12 mi. S of Quartzsite, L. Benson 16100, Pom; Pass on State Route 95 between Middle Mts. and Castle Dome Mts., L. Benson 16099, Pom. PINAL CO. 3.5 mi. S of Casa Grande, L. Benson 15733, Pom; 5 mi. S of Casa Grande, H. F. Loomis SF 179,

June 3, 1936, Ariz, Peebles SF 14541, Ariz; 5-20 mi. S of Casa
Grande, Peebles SF 658, Oct. 15, 1932, Ariz. PIMA CO. Grass Canyon, NE corner of Organ Pipe Cactus Nat. Mon., W. F. Steenbergh,
Feb. 17, 1962, Pom; Quitovaquita, Nichol, Apr. 26, 1939, Organ
Pipe Cactus Nat. Mon. Herb., L. Benson 9937, Pom; 10 mi. E of Gunsight, H. Rush 192, in 1951, Pom; 13 mi. E of Gunsight, Wiggins
8723, DS (box), US (box); S of Quijotoa Mts., D. T. MacDougal in
1913, NY, US; Brownell, C. Lumholz in 1909, US; Sells, collector
unknown SF 72, Pom.

19c. Opuntia stanlyi var. kunzei (Rose) L. Benson

Opuntia kunzei Rose, Smithsonian Misc. Coll. 50: 505. 1908.
O. stanlyi Engelm. var. kunzei L. Benson, Proc. Calif. Acad. Sci.
IV. 25: 248. 1944. Corynopuntia stanlyi (Engelm.) Knuth var.
kunzei Backeberg, Cactaceae 1: 360. 1958. TYPE: "...U.S. National
Herbarium, no. 535,063, collected by Dr. R. E. Kunze in Pima
County, Arizona, 1904...about forty miles south of the Ajo copper
mines,...about 25 to 35 miles north of the Mexican boundary." The
mileage figures do not check, and they may be overestimated; Ajo
is only 40 airline miles north of the International Boundary. The
Gunsight Mining Area, mentioned in Kunze's discourse quoted by
Rose, is about 20 to 25 miles southeast of Ajo. Cf. Britton & Rose,
Cactaceae 1: 80. pl. 14, f. 3, 4. 1919. LECTOTYPE designation:
"Twenty-six miles south of the Copper mine," R. E. Kunze 603, US
535063 (only a fruit on the right side of the sheet, the left side
bearing another collection) and carton. Specimens from the type
plant grown at Phoenix, Griffiths 10436, US, Pom 288233.

Opuntia wrightiana Baxter, Cactus & Succ. Jour. 4: 283. 1932
(description meager but valid); Peebles, Des. Plant Life. 9: 43.
1937. Grusonia wrightiana Baxter, Calif. Cactus. 58. 1935. O.
stanlyi Engelm. var. wrightiana L. Benson, Proc. Calif. Acad. Sci.
IV. 25: 248. 1944. Corynopuntia stanlyi (Engelm.) Knuth var.
wrightiana Backeberg Cactaceae 1: 360. 1958. "...From southwestern Arizona." TYPE: "Petrified Forest near the Colorado River,
four miles west of Quartzsite-Yuma road, 33 miles north of Yuma,
Arizona," Allan B. Clayton, April 15, 1934, DS (box).

ARIZONA. YUMA CO. 45 mi. W of Wickenburg, Peebles SF 523,
Apr. 20, 1932, Ariz; 3 mi. E of Salome, Wiggins 8449, DS (box); 10
mi. S of Quartzsite, Wiggins 8576, US (box), DS (box); 18 mi. S of
Quartzsite, Loomis & Peebles SF 248, Mar. 31, 1930, Ariz; 9.5 mi.
E of Martinez Landing, Lindsay 3189, Pom; Petrified Forest, 4 mi.
W of Yuma-Quartzsite Road, Allan B. Clayton, Apr. 15, 1934, DS
(box); Tinajas Altas, Harbison, Mar. 9, 1937. PIMA CO. 7 mi. W
of Papago Well, Wiggins 6555, DS; Papago Well, A. A. Nichol,
March, 1939, Ariz; "26 mi. s of the Copper Mine" [Ajo], R. E.
Kunze in 1904, US (box); Gunsight Mining Area, D. Griffiths 10436,
Pom (2 & photograph); Wall's Well, Organ Pipe Cactus Nat. Mon.,
A. A. Nichol, May 2, 1939, Organ Pipe Cactus Nat. Mon. Herb.;
Quitovaquita, Mearns 2735, US, DS (box), Peebles SF 14561, Ariz.

19d. Opuntia stanlyi var. parishii (Orcutt) L. Benson

Opuntia parishii Orcutt, West. Amer. Sci. 10 (whole No. 81):
1. 1896. Corynopuntia parishii Knuth in Backeberg & Knuth, Kaktus-ABC 115. 1935. O. stanlyi Engelm. var. parishii L. Benson,
Cacti Ariz. ed. 2. 39. 1950. C. stanlyi (Engelm.) Knuth var.
parishii Backeberg, Cactaceae 1: 361. 1958. "...Mohave desert
region, hitherto called O. Parryi, and under which it has been
well described." The Orcutt reference is to Engelm. Proc. Amer.
Acad. 3: 303. 1857 (preprint, 1856), and, more fully, U.S.
Senate Rept. Expl. & Surv. R. R. Route Pacific Ocean. Botany 48.
pl. 22, f. 4-7. 1857. "...Plant brought by the expedition
[Whipple Expedition; collector, J. M. Bigelow] from the Mojave
river." TYPE: not found. NEOTYPE designation: Near Piñon Wells,
dry open desert, southern edge of the Mojave Desert, 4,000 feet,
P. A. Munz 4483, May 1, 1921, Pom 9957. DUPLICATE: US.

NEVADA. NYE CO. Johnnie's Water Road below central Belted
Range, Rhoads & Beatley, July 13, 1967, TSH.

ARIZONA. MOHAVE CO. Music Mountain, E. A. Goldman 2353, US.

20. Opuntia schottii Engelmann

20a. Opuntia schottii var. schottii

Opuntia schottii Engelm. Proc. Amer. Acad. 3: 304. 1857 (preprint, 1856); in Emory, Rept. U.S. & Mex. Bound. Surv. 2: Cactaceae
54. pl. 73, f. 1-3. 1859. Corynopuntia schottii Knuth in Backeberg & Knuth, Kaktus-ABC 114. 1935. Grusonia schottii H. Robinson, Phytologia 26: 176. 1973. "Abundant on the arid hills near
the Rio Grande, between the San Pedro [of Texas] and Pecos rivers,
Wright, Schott...in July and September...in fruit." LECTOTYPE
designation: "Dry arid hills. Rio Bravo near the Mouth of the
Pecos and San Pedro, Schott, Sept., 1853." Mo. Probable DUPLI-
CATE: "Rio Bravo del Norte [Rio Grande], Schott, Nr. 80," F 42690
(Schott Herbarium).

Opuntia schottii Engelm. var. greggii Engelm. in Emory, Rept.
U.S. & Mex. Bound. Surv. 2: Cactaceae pl. 73, f. 4. 1859, nom.
nud.; ex K. Schum. Gesamtb. Kakteen 665. 1898. O. greggii
Engelm. ex K. Schum., loc. cit. 829 (index reference to var.
greggii on p. 665), incorrectly ascribed to Engelmann.

TEXAS. SCHLEICHER CO. 20 mi. W of El Dorado, Cory 31-841,
May 9, 1939, TAES. BROWN CO. Brownwood, E. J. Palmer 11121, DS.

20b. Opuntia schottii var. grahamii (Engelmann) L. Benson

Opuntia grahamii Engelm. Proc. Amer. Acad. 3: 304. 1857
(preprint, 1856); in Emory, Rept. U.S. & Mex. Bound. Surv. 2:
Cactaceae 55. pl. 72. 1859. Corynopuntia grahamii Knuth in
Backeberg & Knuth, Kaktus-ABC. 116. 1935. O. schottii Engelm.
var. grahamii L. Benson, Cactus & Succ. Jour. 41: 124. 1969.
Grusonia grahamii H. Robinson, Phytologia 26: 176. 1973. "Sandy
soil in the bottom of the Rio Grande, near El Paso, and...about
100 miles along the river, Wright, Bigelow; fl. June." LECTOTYPE
designation (Benson, loc. cit.): the only syntype, "Opuntia No.
10," Wright in 1851, Mo (one shrivelled flower) and plate 72.

NEW MEXICO. DONA ANA CO. Bishop's Cap, Organ Mts., Castet-
ter 158A, B, June 6, 1954, UNM, C. Champie, Castetter's Garden
No. 2151, UNM, J. Green, UNM. OTERO CO. Orange [near Oro Grande],
Pillsbry, Oct. 25-30, 1922, Ph.

Name of Uncertain Application (perhaps to var. grahamii)

Corynopuntia planibulpispina Backeberg, Cactaceae 6: 3603.
f. 3273. 1962, nom. nud. "Heimat nicht genau bekannt, wohl süd-
liches USA. Typus: Sammlung RIVIERE, Nr. 7951, von der höllandi-
schen Züchter JANSEN als Corynop. moelleri erhalten. (Abb. 3273)."
Backeberg was opposed to use of herbarium specimens, and presumably the reference was to a numbered plant in a living collection
and the nomenclatural combination, thus, a nomen nudum. According
to the original publication, the plant was similar to var. grahamii.

21. Opuntia clavata Engelmann

Opuntia clavata Engelm. in Wisliz. Mem. Tour No. Mex. 95.
1848. Cactus clavatus Lemaire, Cactées 88. 1868. Corynopuntia
clavata Knuth in Backeberg & Knuth, Kaktus-ABC 115. 1935. Grusonia clavata H. Robinson, Phytologia 26: 176. 1973. "About
Albuquerque (W. [Wislizenus]), about Santa Fé, on the high plains,
never on the mountains (Fendler)." TYPE: not found. LECTOTYPE
designation: Santa Fe, Fendler, Nov. 6, 1846, Mo (only flowers).
Typical specimen for vegetative parts and fruits: sandy wash, 7
miles north of Santa Fe, 6,700 feet, Lyman and Robert L. Benson
14675, October 24, 1950, Pom 285511.

22. Opuntia pulchella Engelmann

Opuntia pulchella Engelm. Trans. St. Louis Acad. Sci. 2: 201.
pl. 3. 1863. Corynopuntia pulchella Knuth in Backeberg & Knuth,
Kaktus-ABC 115. 1935. Grusonia pulchella H. Robinson, Phytologia 26: 176. 1973. "Sandy deserts on Walker River, Nevada.
Flowers in June." Page 197: "In the same year (1858) and the
following one...Henry Engelmann...." LECTOTYPE designation:
"Sandy deserts on Walker River, Nevada," Henry Engelmann, June 7,
1859, Mo.

Micropuntia brachyrhopalica Daston, Amer. Midl. Nat. 36: 661.
f. 1. 1946; cf. photographs, Cactus & Succ. Jour. 28: 194-195.
f. 157-159. 1956. Opuntia brachyrhopalica Rowley, Nat. Cact. &
Succ. Jour. 13: 5. 1958. "...Collected by Gordon Marsh in Nov-
ember of 1945 and January of 1946 near the U.S. Desert Experimental
Range in southwestern Utah...type specimens...Chicago [Field] Natural History Museum. Isotypes...University of Texas, Austin...."
Specimens not found, F, Tex, U.S. Forest Service herbaria at
Desert Experimental Range and Ogden, USFS (partly reported earlier,
Benson, Cactus & Succ Jour. 29: 19-21. 1957). Perhaps suitable
specimens cannot be collected and designated as neotypes, because
Paul C. Hutchison reports that at the type locality there is much
abnormal growth of plants injured by grazing of sheep. Possibly
this and the next two described species represent plants of this
character. However, similar features appear in growth phases of
adults in cultivation and in juvenile plants, including those of
a series of individuals of O. pulchella sent from the type locality by Ralph Holmgren. LECTOTYPE designation: Daston's photograph, F. DUPLICATE: US. Cf, also, illustrations as published.
The figures of the three described species appear to represent
run-of-the-mill juvenile plants.

Micropuntia barkleyana Daston, loc. cit. 662. f. 2. Opuntia
barkleyana Rowley, loc. cit. (Cf. discussion above.) LECTOTYPE
designation: Daston's photograph, F. DUPLICATE: US. Cf., also
illustrations as published.

Micropuntia spectatissima Daston, loc. cit. 662. f. 3.
Opuntia spectatissima Rowley, loc. cit. (Cf. discussion above.)
LECTOTYPE designation: Daston's photograph, F. DUPLICATE: US.
Cf., also, illustrations as published.

Micropuntia tuberculosirhopalica Wiegand & Backeberg in Backeberg, Descriptiones Cactacearum Novarum 9. 1956. Opuntia tuberculosirhopalica Rowley, loc. cit. "USA (Utah, Arizona)." No
precise locality or specimen cited.

Micropuntia pygmaea Wiegand & Backeberg, loc. cit. Opuntia
pygmaea Rowley, loc. cit. "USA (Idaho australis, Nevada)." No
precise locality or specimen cited. Occurrence in Idaho is not
documented.

Micropuntia gracilicylindrica Wiegand & Backeberg, loc. cit. Opuntia gracilicylindrica Rowley, loc. cit. "USA (Nevada)." No precise locality or specimen cited.

Micropuntia wiegandii Backeberg, Descriptiones Cactacearum Novarum 9. 1956. M. gigantea Wiegand ex Backeberg, Cactaceae 1: 370. 1958, pro syn. Opuntia wiegandii Rowley, loc. cit. "USA (Nevada, California)." No precise locality or specimen cited. Occurrence in California is not documented.

UTAH. TOOELE CO. Willow Spring [as Arizona, but shown by his diary to have been this Willow Spring], M. E. Jones, June 5, 1891, Pom; Willow Spring Pass, M. E. Jones, June 5, 1891, Pom. MILLARD CO. E of State Line, E of Lehman Caves, R. H. Kirkpatrick in 1971, Pom; Confusion Range, R. H. Kirkpatrick in 1971, Pom; Desert Experimental Range W of Milford, photographs deposited by Daston, F, dried flowers, USFS; "Desert Range Experimental Farm," E. F. Wiegand, Pom; Pine Valley, Desert Exp. Range, R. C. Holmgren, May 26, 1970, Pom.

ARIZONA. Without locality, Wheeler Expedition, Mo (flower). MOHAVE CO. Round Valley, E of Kingman, A. A. Nichol in 1940, Pom (presumably this species, but material inadequate).

23. Opuntia polyacantha Haworth

23a. Opuntia polyacantha var. polyacantha

Cactus ferox Nutt. Gen. N. Amer. Pl. 1: 296. 1818, not Willd. Enum. Pl. Hort. Berol. Suppl. 35. 1813. Opuntia polyacantha Haw. Suppl. Succ. 82. 1819, nom. nov. O. missouriensis DC. Prodr. 3: 472. 1828, nom. nov. Tunas polyacantha Nieuwl. & Lunell, Amer. Midl. Nat. 4: 479. 1916. "HAB. In arid situations on the plains of the Missouri, common." According to Nuttall in Fraser's Cat. New & Interesting Pl. Coll. Upper Louisiana, 1813, "Both these [Cactus ferox and C. fragilis] grow with the above [Cactus, i.e. Coryphantha, viviparus]," which was "collected near the Mandan Towns on the Missourie: lat. near 49°." TYPE: not found, BM, NY, GH, or Ph. Photograph, NY, of a drawing made at the Royal Botanic Gardens, Kew, by George Bond and Thomas Duncanson, 1822-1835, under direction of W. T. Aiton. Many such drawings were made from plants described by Haworth. NEOTYPE (Mitich & Benson, Cactus & Succ. Jour. 49: 7. 1977): Ft. Manuel Lisa, later Ft. Vanderburgh (on the Missouri River), Mercer Co., North Dakota, Larry W. Mitich, June, 1970 (specially collected neotype), Pom 317945, NDA. In 1811 Nuttall stayed near by at Ft. Manuel Lisa. Cactus ferox Nutt. appeared earlier in Fraser's Catalog, No. 28, 1813, but it was a nomen nudum.

Opuntia media Haw. Suppl. Pl. Succ. 82. 1819. O. missouriensis DC. var. elongata Salm-Dyck, Cact. Hort. Dyck. 1849: 67. 1850, based upon O. media Haw. "HABITAT cum praecedente [...prope flumen Missouri, in America Boreali, in aridis locis], ad longe minor spinis minoribus. CULT. in hort. Chels. A. D. 1814." According to Britton & Rose, Cactaceae 1: 200. 1919, probably based upon a less spiny plant from Nuttall's collections, growing near or within the populations of Cactus ferox Nutt., cf. above. NEOTYPE (Mitich & Benson, Cactus & Succ. Jour. 49: 7. 1977, 12 miles east of Ft. Mandan, McLean County, North Dakota, east side of the Missouri River, Larry W. Mitich, June, 1970, (specially collected neotype), Pom 317946. DUPLICATE: NDA.

Opuntia splendens Hort. Angl. ex Pfeiffer, Enum. Cact. 159. 1837. "O. missouriensis similis, sed nondum satis cognita. ... (Ill. Pr. Salm-Dyck in litt.)." Source unknown. According to David Griffiths' notes, description from a young specimen in the Salm-Dyck [living] collection.

Opuntia missouriensis DC. var. platycarpa Engelm. Proc. Amer. Acad. 3: 300. 1857 (preprint, 1856); U.S. Senate Rept. Expl. & Surv. R. R. Route Pacific Ocean. Botany. 4: 45. pl. 14, f. 4. 1857. O. polyacantha Haw. var. platycarpa Coulter, Contr. U.S. Nat. Herb. 3: 436. 1896. "Sent from the Yellowstone by Dr. Hayden." LECTOTYPE designation: Yellowstone River, F. V. Hayden in 1854, Mo. Some fruits are short and broad as in the figure; others are of normal elongation.

Opuntia missouriensis DC. var. microsperma Engelm. Proc. Amer. Acad. 3: 300. 1857 (preprint, 1856); U.S. Senate Rept. Expl. & Surv. R. R. Route Pacific Ocean. Botany. 4: 46. pl. 14, f. 5-7. 1857, not O. rafinesquei Engelm. var. microsperma Engelm., locs. cit., 295 and 41. 1856 and 1857; not O. compressa (Salisb.) Macbr. var. microsperma (Engelm.) L. Benson, Proc. Calif. Acad. IV. 25: 250. 1944. O. polyacantha Haw. var. borealis Coulter, Contr. U.S. Nat. Herb. 3: 436. 1896, nom. nov. "On the Missouri, about Fort Pierre [South Dakota]; brought down 10 years ago by the fur traders...." LECTOTYPE designation: "Specimens obtained from Fort Pierre, Upper Missouri in 1847, fl. St. Louis. May 1854" (one sheet with only joints, another with seeds and Engelmann's notes and drawings), Mo.

Opuntia missouriensis DC. var. subinermis Engelm. Proc. Amer. Acad. 3: 300. 1857 (preprint, 1856); U.S. Senate Rept. Expl. & Surv. R. R. Route Pacific Ocean. Botany. 4: 46. 1857. O. missouriensis Haw. var. subinermis J. A. Purpus, Mitt. Deutsch. Dendrol. Gesellsch. 1925: 62. 1925. "...The Upper Missouri by Dr. Hayden...." LECTOTYPE designation: "Opuntia missouriensis fr. rarum

spinulosa elongato, Ft. Pierre [South Dakota on the Upper Missouri]," F. V. Hayden in 1853, Mo.

Opuntia missouriensis DC. var. albispina Engelm. & Bigelow, Proc. Amer. Acad. 3: 300. 1857 (preprint, 1856); U.S. Senate Rept. Expl. & Surv. R. R. Route Pacific Ocean. Botany. 4: 46. pl. 14, f. 8-10. 1857. O. polyacantha Haw. var. albispina Coulter, Contr. U.S. Nat. Herb. 3: 437. 1896. O. missouriensis DC. f. albispina Schelle, Handb. Kakteenkultur 54. 1907. "Sandy bottoms and dry beds of streamlets on the Upper Canadian, 250 miles east of the Pecos...." LECTOTYPE designation: "Sandy bottoms and arroyos, Canadian [River]," J. M. Bigelow, Sept. 11, 1853, Mo.

Opuntia polyacantha Haw. var. watsonii Coulter, Contr. U.S. Nat. Herb. 3: 437. 1896. "Type, specimens cited below in Herb. Mo. Bot. Gard." Five are cited. LECTOTYPE designation: "On the divide over the Wahsatch Mountains, where the Pacific R. R. route crosses them, 7000' high [Utah]," Sereno Watson in 1869, Mo. DUPLICATES: NY, US, YU, GH (Wasatch Mts., 7,000 ft.).

Opuntia missouriensis DC. f. salmonea Schelle, Handb. Kakteenkultur 55. 1907, nom. nud. O. polyacantha Haw. var. salmonea Spᾰth ex J. A. Purpus, Mitt. Deutsch. Dendrol. Gesellsch. 1925: 63. 1925. "C. A. Purpus: Grand Mesa Kolorado 1892-93." No specimen preserved.

Opuntia missouriensis DC. f. leucospina Schelle, Handb. Kakteenkultur 55. 1907, nom. nud.

Opuntia polyacantha Haw. var. spirocentra J. A. Purpus, Mitt. Deutsch. Dendrol. Gesellsch. 1925: 63. 1925. Based upon O. missouriensis DC. var. spirocentra Hort. No specimen or locality.

BRITISH COLUMBIA. 11 mi. NNW of Cache Creek on road to Clinton, Calder & Saville 12297, DAO; 6 mi. N of Cache Creek, J. Grant 22, July 4, 1966, DAO. The following specimens are intermediate between Opuntia polyacantha and O. fragilis: Between Spence's Bridge and Cache Creek, Thompson River, Scoggan 15579, Can, QUK; 10 mi. W of Kamloops, L. Benson 14158, Pom; between Kelowna and Penticton, Okanogan Valley, Scoggan 15030, Can, QUK; 9 mi. N of Keremeos, Calder & Saville 10728, DAO.

ALBERTA. Rosedale, M. E. Moodie, July 20, 1914, US, 1040, June 26, 1915, MtMG, NY, US, F; Oldman River Valley, N of Pincher, E. H. Moss 862, Can, US; Belly River, G. M. Dawson, Geol. Surv. Can. 44472, Can; Ft. McLeod district, 20 mi. N of Lethbridge, Scoggan 16574, Can; Lethbridge, collector unknown, David Griffiths collection, P. I. G. 13024, US, Pom, H. Groh, Oct. 16, 1929, DAO; Suffield, A. W. A. Brown, June 30, 1943, QUK; Medicine Hat, Dr. & Mrs. C. D. Walcott in 1922, NY, US, F. Fyles, July 28, 1914, DAO, Dore 11970, DAO; Manyberries, Dore, July 25, 1950, DAO.

SASKATCHEWAN. 10 mi. E of Unity, Boivin & Dunbar 10430, DAO; Saskatoon, Griffiths, summer, 1916, US, Pom; Crystal Beach, Rosetown-Biggar District, Boivin & Dunbar 10396, DAO; Rosetown, Rivière de las Montagne d'Aigle, Boivin 10404, DAO; Fort Walsh, Cypress Hills, Breitung 5348, DAO, Mo; Cypress Hills, Eastend, Breitung 5400, Can, Colo; South of Shaunavon, Boivin & Perron 12120, DAO; Frenchman River Valley, R. C. Russell 5025, DAO; Bethune, Arm River, Boivin & Dore 7541, DAO; Wood Mountain Dist., Big Muddy Valley, Hudson Coulee, Brown & Gillett 8676, DAO; Radville, Boivin & Dore 7885, DAO; Fort Qu'Appelle, de Vries 742, June 26, 1950, DAO; Agassiz Coulee, Fort Qu'Appelle, Boivin & Dore 7530, DAO, 7570A, DAO; Midale, Boivin & Dore 7938, DAO; Souris Valley, Boivin & Dore 7901, DAO; Estevan, Boivin & Dore 7962, DAO.

OREGON. "Dry, sandy soil," Cusick 1389, July, 1886, UC.

IDAHO (northern). BONNER CO. Sandpoint, Christ 5826, NY. NEZ PERCE CO. Clearwater River near Lewiston, Ferris & Duthie 1291, DS, Christ 690, NY, 7320, NY.

NEVADA. ELKO CO. W of Pequop Summit, Pequop Mts., McVaugh 6420, USNA.

NEW MEXICO. GUADALUPE CO. Between Anton Chico and mouth of Gallinas River, Rose & Fitch 17634, NY. QUAY CO. Canadian River, Bigelow, Sept. 11, 1853, Mo. CHAVES CO. Bottomless Lake State Park, D. Weniger 541, May, 1964, UNM.

OKLAHOMA. CIMARRON CO. Mineral, G. W. Stevens 431 in 1913, Mo, NY, US.

TEXAS. POTTER CO. Amarillo, C. R. Ball 1676, US.

MISSOURI. WEBB CO. E. J. Palmer, Oct. 1, 1909, US.

23b. Opuntia polyacantha var. rufispina
(Engelmann & Bigelow) L. Benson

Opuntia rutila Nutt. in Torrey & Gray, Fl. N. Amer. 1: 555. 1840. "Arid clay hills in the Rocky Mountain range, near the Colorado of the West about lat. 42°. Nuttall." According to Engelmann in King, Rept. Geol. Expl. 40th. Par. 5: 119. 1871, "...near the Green River in southern Wyoming." TYPE: not found, BM, NY, GH, Ph. Griffiths visited Green River to determine the basis for

O. rutila. NEOTYPE designation: Griffiths 10762, US 2437081.
DUPLICATE: Pom 288269. The name has been misinterpreted and misapplied to plants occurring along the Colorado River farther
south. A photograph, Berger, Monatschr. Kakteenk. 14: 105. 1904,
was of var. rufispina; plants illustrated by Boissevain in Boissevain & Davidson, Colorado Cacti 34 and especially 35. 1940, were
hybrids of O. fragilis with a larger species.

Opuntia missouriensis DC. var. rufispina Engelm. & Bigelow,
Proc. Amer. Acad. 3: 300. 1857 (preprint, 1856); U.S. Senate
Rept. Expl. & Surv. R. R. Route Pacific Ocean. Botany 4: 45. pl.
14, f. 1-3. 1857. O. polyacantha Haw. var. rufispina L. Benson,
Cacti Ariz. ed. 3. 20, 70. 1969. "...Rocky places on the Pecos
[Bigelow]; Dr. Hayden...Yellowstone...." LECTOTYPE (Benson, loc.
cit.): "'Rocky places, Pecos,' J. M. Bigelow, Sept. 24, 1853,"
Mo. Near the head of the Pecos River, New Mexico. The spines are
reddish-brown and much darker than in all but a few plants of this
variety -- hence the unfortunate choice of the epithet rufispina.

23c. Opuntia polyacantha var. juniperina (Engelmann & Bigelow) L. Benson

Opuntia sphaerocarpa Engelm. & Bigelow, Proc. Amer. Acad. 3:
300. 1857 (preprint, 1856); U.S. Senate Rept. Expl. & Surv. R. R.
Route Pacific Ocean, Botany. 4: 47. pl. 13, f. 6-7. 1857. "...
Eastern declivity of the Sandia Mountains, near Albuquerque."
LECTOTYPE designation: "Sandia Mountains near Albuquerque," J. M.
Bigelow, Oct. 10, 1853, Mo; photographs NY, US.

Opuntia juniperina Britton & Rose, Cactaceae 1: 197. f. 243-
244. 1919. O. erinacea Engelm. & Bigelow var. juniperina W. T.
Marshall, Arizona's Cactuses ed. 2. 36. 1953. O. polyacantha
Haw. var. juniperina L. Benson, Cacti Ariz. ed. 3. 20, 69. 1969.
TYPE: "...Vicinity of Cedar Hill, San Juan County, New Mexico,
altitude about 1,900 meters, August 17 [7], 1911, Paul C. Standley
(No. 8051)," US 686991. ISOTYPE: NY (marked "co-type").

WYOMING. SWEETWATER CO. Green River, Griffiths 10762, US,
Pom, M. Cary 699, Sept. 19, 1911, US.

UTAH. SALT LAKE CO. S of Brighton, A. E. Nalch, Dec., 1922,
NY. UINTAH CO. Uinta River along Lapoint-Neola road, E. H.
Graham 9312, Mo. Mich; Colorado line E of Vernal, L. Benson 4747,
Pom; 20 mi. S of Vernal, E. H. Graham 6172, Mo. GRAND CO. 12 mi.
N of Moab, L., E. L., & R. L. Benson 16042. SAN JUAN CO. S of
Moab, Clover & Jotter 1990, Mich; La Sal Mts., Griffiths 10739,
US, Pom; Natural Bridge, between Moab and Monticello, Clover &
Jotter 2016, Mich.

COLORADO. CLEAR CREEK CO. Clear Creek Canyon, G. H. French,
June 30, 1874, F. CHAFFEE CO. 10-15 mi. W of Salida, E. B. Karr,
June 19, 1963, UNM; Poncha Pass, E. F. Wiegand 64, 65, 149, 152,
153, 154, all in 1950, all Pom. EL PASO CO. Garden of the Gods,
Manitou Springs, Ehlers 7591.5, Mich. LAS ANIMAS CO. 3 mi. N of
Raton Pass, L. & R. L. Benson 14719A, Pom.

ARIZONA. COCONINO CO. W edge of Kaibab Plateau, L. Benson
14255, Pom. APACHE CO. N end of Carrizo Mts., Standley 7375, US.

23d. Opuntia polyacantha var. trichophora (Engelmann & Bigelow) Coulter

Opuntia missouriensis DC. var. trichophora Engelm. & Bigelow,
Proc. Amer. Acad. 3: 300. 1857 (preprint, 1856); U.S. Senate
Rept. Expl. & Surv. R. R. Route Pacific Ocean. Botany. 4: 46.
pl. 15, f. 1-4. 1857. O. polyacantha Haw. var. trichophora
Coulter, Contr. U.S. Nat. Herb. 3: 437. 1896. O. missouriensis
DC. f. trichophora Schelle, Handb. Kakteenkultur 54. 1907. O.
trichophora Britton & Rose, Smithsonian Misc. Coll. 50: 535.
1908. "Only on the volcanic rocks about Santa Fe, and on the
Sandia mountains [near Albuquerque]." LECTOTYPE designation: Santa
Fe Creek, J. M. Bigelow, Oct. 3, 1853, Mo. DUPLICATE: Pom 317787.

UTAH. SAN JUAN CO. Road to White Rim, 3 mi. S of Potash
Point, Welsh 7047, BrY; Glen Canyon, old Mormon road across river
from Hole-in-the-Wall, L. Benson 16305, Pom; 6 mi. N of Mexican
Hat, L., E. L., & R. L. Benson 16059, Pom; Desha Canyon, A. J.
Lindsey, May 13, 1960, MNA.

OKLAHOMA. CIMARRON CO. Black Mesa, G. J. Goodman 4347, Tex;
Kenton, G. W. Stevens 495, May 15, 1913, Mo, NY, Ill, US, DS;
Mineral, G. W. Stevens 431, May 30, 1930, US

24. Opuntia fragilis (Nuttall) Haworth

24a. Opuntia fragilis var. fragilis

Cactus fragilis Nutt. Gen. N. Amer. Pl. 1: 296. 1818.
Opuntia fragilis Haw. Suppl. Pl. Succ. 82. 1819. Tunas fragilis
Nieuwl. & Lunell, Amer. Midl. Nat. 4: 479. 1916. "HAB. From the
Mandans to the mountains...." According to Nuttall in Fraser's
Cat. New & Interesting Pl. Coll. Upper Louisiana. 1813, "Both
these [Cactus ferox and Cactus fragilis] grow with the above [Cac-
tus, i.e. Coryphantha, viviparus]," which was "...collected near
the Mandan Towns on the Missourie: lat. near 49°." TYPE: not
found, BM, NY, GH, Ph. According to Haworth, loc. cit., "CULT.

in Hort. Chels. A. D. 1814." NEOTYPE (Mitich & Benson, Cactus &
Succ. Jour. 49: 8. 1977): Richardson, Stark Co., North
Dakota, Larry W. Mitich, June, 1970, Pom 317947. DUPLICATE: NDA.
This is near Ft. Mandan and Ft. Manuel Lisa (Ft. Vanderburgh) where
Nuttall collected plants in 1811. Cactus fragilis Nutt. appeared
earlier in Fraser's Catalog, No. 24. 1813, but as a nomen nudum.

Opuntia sabinii Pfeiffer, Enum. Cact. 147. 1837, pro syn.
for Cactus fragilis Nutt.

Opuntia schweriniana K. Schum. Monatsschr. Kakteenk. 9:
148. photograph. 1899. O. polyacantha Haw. var. schweriniana
Backeberg, Cactaceae. 1: 607. 1958. "Staat Colorado, bei Sapinero: PURPUS n. XIII." Cultivated plants. Short spines like
those in the photograph often appear in cultivated plants of O.
fragilis, and several individuals in pots at the time of writing
show this phenomenon on newer mature joints, even though the
originally planted joints retain their longer spines. So far no
suitable specimen is available for a neotype.

Opuntia fragilis (Nutt.) Haw. f. caespitosa Späth ex Schelle,
Handb. Kakteenkultur 52. 1907, nom. nud. O. fragilis (Nutt.)
Haw. var. caespitosa Hort.; L. H. Bailey, Stand. Cyclop. Hort. 4:
2363. 1916. "Colo."

Opuntia fragilis (Nutt.) Haw. var. tuberiformis Hort. ex
L. H. Bailey, Stand. Cyclop. Hort. 4: 2363. 1916. "Colo."

Opuntia fragilis (Nutt.) Haw. var. parvinconspicua Backeberg,
Descriptiones Cactacearum Novarum 10. 1956. "Hab. ?" Spineless
form; cf. Backeberg, Cactaceae 1: 595. f. 577. 1958.

Opuntia fragilis (Nutt.) Haw. var. denudata Wiegand & Backeberg in Backeberg, Descriptiones Cactacearum Novarum 10. 1956.
"USA (Utah australis)." Nearly spineless form; cf. Backeberg,
Cactaceae 1: 595-6. f. 578. 1958. "USA (Utah, in Utah-Bassin
westlich von Steptoe Valley)." Steptoe Valley is in Nevada.

BRITISH COLUMBIA. Beatton River, 5 mi. ENE of Ft. St. John,
Peace River (the northernmost cactus collection), Calder & Gillett
24615, DAO; dry bluff, N bank of Peace River at Taylor Flat, 58°
8' N, 1,600 feet, Raup & Abbe 3586, GH, Can; 4 mi. W of Taylor, N
side of Peace River, Calder & Gillett 24599, WTU, DAO, Calder &
Kukkonen 26788, DAO.

ALBERTA. Dunvegan, Peace River, E. H. Moss 7445, DAO, Boivin
& Dunbar 10568, DAO; Peace River Valley, E. H. Moss 7548, DAO;
Smoky River Mission, Peace River, Macoun, Geol. Surv. Can. 59868,
Can, NY; Watino, Smoky River, E. H. Moss 7690, DAO; Kleskun Hill
N of Grande Prairie, Wapiti River, E. H. Moss 8120, DAO.

SASKATCHEWAN & MANITOBA. Now known from numerous specimens,
mostly in the Canadian herbaria.

ONTARIO. Just off Lake-of-the-Woods Provincial Park, McCros-
son Township, G. E. Gorton 9213, DAO; small island, extreme E
end of Sturgeon Lake, S of Atikokan, W. McInnis, July 26, 1896,
Can; S of Kaladar, Dore & Senn 671, DAO, M. I. Moore 2765, DAO,
Dore 22811, DAO, Zavitz, Garwood, Vanderkleet, et al, 2379, QUK,
Mellon Creek near Highway 41, Besdrel & Bartman 15887, QUK,
15888, QUK, Can, 15889, QUK.

CALIFORNIA. SISKIYOU CO. 20 mi. NE of Weed, C. B. Wolf
11074, RSA, NY, UC, DS, 11477, RSA; Shasta Valley, B. Wise, May
26, 1931, Jeps.

NEVADA. ELKO CO. Contact, L. S. Rose 32383, CAS.

NEW MEXICO. SANDOVAL CO. W of Cuba, R. Reeves, Sept. 15,
1963, UNM. CURRY CO. Pleasant Hill, P. Pierce 2192, UNM.

KANSAS. LANE CO. "Plains," A. S. Hitchcock 187, Aug. 14,
1895, NY, GH, US. ELLSWORTH CO. Ellsworth, Fisher, June, 1893,
US. SALINE CO. Salina, C. D. Marsh in 1922, US. PRATT CO.
Pratt, Rose & Fitch 17161, NY, US.

OKLAHOMA. CIMARRON CO. Mineral, G. W. Stevens 432, May 13,
1913, NY, GH.

TEXAS. HUTCHINSON CO. "Panhandle" [he collected at Plemons
that day], Griffiths 10662, US, Pom. POTTER CO. Amarillo, Ball &
Townsend 1660, US.

MINNESOTA. REDWOOD CO. Redwood Falls, Redwood River, P.
Jones, July 27, 1930, GH. PIPESTONE CO. Pipestone, M. Menzel
1011, June, 1895, YU (2), July, 1895, Ill, YU (2). MOWER CO. 15
mi. SW of Adams, A. M. Fuller, Aug. 21, 1955, SMU. ROCK CO.
Luvane, J. B. Patten, June 16, 1895, GH.

WISCONSIN. WAUPACA CO. New London, Fassett 13679, Mo, GH.
JUNEAU CO. NE of Lyndon, G. C. Shaw, May 3, 1942, WS; Quincy, A.
M. Fuller 1274, Aug. 21, 1925, UPa. SAUK CO. Baraboo, T. J. Hale
in 1861, Mo, GH.

MICHIGAN. MARQUETTE CO. Huron Mt., A. Russell, Sept. 1,
1916, Mich, V. Bailey, Aug. 26, 1926, US, G. E. Nichols, June,
1936, YU.

IOWA. LYON CO. Gitchie Manitou State Park, <u>Shimek</u>, June 11, 1925, <u>Mo</u>, <u>GH</u>.

ILLINOIS. JO DAVIESS CO. Hanover, <u>F. C. Gates 2622</u>, <u>Mich</u>, <u>H. A. Gleason</u>, Aug. 18, 1908, <u>GH</u>. CARROLL or WHITESIDE CO. <u>G. S. Winterringer</u>, April, 1951, <u>Ill</u>.

24b. Opuntia fragilis var. brachyarthra
(Engelmann & Bigelow) Coulter

Opuntia brachyarthra Engelm. & Bigelow, Proc. Amer. Acad. 3: 302. 1857 (preprint, 1856); U.S. Senate Rept. Expl. & Surv. R. R. Route Pacific Ocean. Botany 4: 47. pl. 12, f. 9. 1857. O. frag-ilis (Nutt.) Haw. var. brachyarthra Coulter, Contr. U.S. Nat. Herb. 3: 440. 1896; Boissevain in Boissevain and Davidson, Colo-rado Cacti 31. 1940. O. fragilis (Nutt.) Haw. f. brachyarthra Schelle, Handb. Kakteenkultur 56. 1907. "At the foot of the Inscription Rock near Zuñi under pine-trees...." TYPE: Inscrip-tion Rock near Zuni, New Mexico, <u>J. M. Bigelow</u>, Nov. 19, 1853, <u>Mo</u>. ISOTYPE: <u>Pom 317798</u>.

25. Opuntia arenaria Engelmann

Opuntia arenaria Engelm. Proc. Amer. Acad. 3: 301. 1857 (preprint, 1856); in Emory, Rept. U.S. & Mex. Bound. Surv. 2: Cactaceae 52. pl. 75, f. 15 (seed). 1859. "Sandy bottoms of the Rio Grande near El Paso, <u>Wright</u>: fl. May." LECTOTYPE designation: "Sandy ridges at Frontera [on the Rio Grande then in New Mexico, now in NW El Paso, Texas]," <u>Charles Wright 311</u>, May 15, 1852, <u>Mo</u>. DUPLICATE: <u>Pom 287038</u>.

NEW MEXICO. <u>Wright</u> in 1851-52, <u>Ph</u>. DONA ANA CO. Valley of the Rio Grande, below Donana, <u>Wright 2</u> in 1851-52, <u>NY</u>; Mesquite Lake, Mesilla Park, <u>Standley</u>, June 30, 1910, <u>NMC</u>, <u>Griffiths 12087</u>, <u>US</u>, <u>Pom</u>, <u>Tex</u>, <u>Rose</u>, <u>Standley</u>, & <u>Russell 12246</u>, <u>US</u>, <u>NY</u>; Agricul-tural College, <u>Rose</u>, <u>Standley</u>, & <u>Russell 15203</u>, <u>NY</u>; Vado, Rio Grande, 3,850 ft., <u>Castetter 440</u>, <u>UNM</u>; Anthony, <u>C. Champie C2117</u>, Aug. 5, 1963, <u>UNM</u>, <u>Castetter 2118</u>, <u>2121</u>, <u>UNM</u>, <u>L. Benson 16461</u>, <u>Pom</u>, <u>16462</u>, <u>Pom</u>; N of Frontera, <u>C. Champie</u>, July, 1961, <u>Pom</u>; vicinity of El Paso, Texas, in New Mexico just W of Rio Grande, <u>Rose & Fitch 17866</u>, <u>US</u>; Rio Grande, <u>Parry</u> in 1867, <u>Mo</u>, <u>Rose 13866</u>, <u>NY</u>.

TEXAS. EL PASO CO. Anthony, 4,000 ft., <u>L. Benson 16459</u>, <u>Pom</u>; Canutillo, <u>A. R. Leding SF 407</u>, Aug. 1930, <u>Ariz</u>; Rio Grande Valley above El Paso, <u>Griffiths 12087</u>, <u>US</u>, <u>Pom</u>; Frontera, <u>Wright</u>, May 15, 1852, <u>Mo</u>, <u>Pom</u>, July, 1852, <u>Mo</u>; El Paso, <u>Wright</u> in 1854, <u>Mo</u>, July 12, 1854, <u>Mo</u>, <u>Rose & Fitch 17866</u>, <u>NY</u>; E of El Paso, <u>C. Champie</u>, July 10, 1955, <u>UNM</u>. HUDSPETH CO. 30 mi. below San Elizario, Bound. Surv., June 14, 1852, <u>US</u>.

26. Opuntia erinacea Engelmann & Bigelow

26a. Opuntia erinacea var. erinacea

Opuntia erinacea Engelm. & Bigelow, Proc. Amer. Acad. 3: 301. 1857 (preprint, 1856); U.S. Senate Rept. Expl. & Surv. R. R. Route Pacific Ocean. Botany 4: 47. pl. 13, f. 8-11. 1857. O. hystri-cina Engelm. & Bigelow var. bensonii Backeberg, Cactaceae 1: 609. 1958, nom. nov. for O. erinacea, but an illegitimate epithet (Art. 57). O. erinacea and O. hystricina were published simultan-eously, but the writer had reduced O. hystricina to varietal status under O. erinacea in 1944, and the reverse combination was illegi-timate. "West of the great Colorado near the Mojave Creek...." TYPE: Mojave Creek [River], <u>J. M. Bigelow</u>, March 4, 1854, <u>Mo</u>.

NEVADA. MINERAL CO. Candelaria, <u>W. H. Shockley 274</u>, June, 1882, <u>Jeps</u>. ESMERALDA CO. Chiatovitch Creek, White Mts., <u>Duran 2773</u>, <u>US</u>, <u>Mich</u>, <u>CAS</u>, <u>UC</u>, <u>Ariz</u>, <u>WTU</u>; N slope of Boundary Peak, <u>Train 3968</u>, <u>RSA</u>. WHITE PINE CO. Egan Canyon, <u>Griffiths 10769</u>, <u>US</u>, <u>Pom</u>, <u>10771</u>, <u>US</u>, <u>Pom</u>, <u>M. E. Jones</u> in 1923, <u>US</u>.

COLORADO. MONTROSE CO. Montrose, <u>Griffiths 10698</u>, <u>US</u>, <u>Pom</u>.

NEW MEXICO. CATRON CO. 12 mi. W of Datil, <u>R. S. Ferris 1215</u>, <u>CAS</u>, <u>DS</u>.

The following are examples of specimens of thick-jointed hybrid plants probably derived through crossing of Opuntia fragi-lis, source of the thickened joints, with a larger species, such as O. polyacantha or O. erinacea:

UTAH. CARBON CO. E of Wellington, <u>Mr. and Mrs. S. A. Hatton</u>, ca. 1947, <u>Pom</u>. UTAH CO. Colton, <u>Griffiths 10746</u>, <u>US</u>, <u>Pom</u>. SEVIER CO. Salina Canyon, <u>M. E. Jones 5416</u>, June 14, 1894, <u>US</u>. GARFIELD CO. Panguitch, <u>Eggleston 8128</u>, <u>USNA</u>. SAN JUAN CO. La Sal, <u>L.</u>, <u>E.</u>, & <u>R. L. Benson 16051</u>, <u>16053</u>, <u>Pom</u>.

COLORADO. GARFIELD CO. Near Rifle, <u>P. Pierce</u> in 1956, <u>UNM</u>, June 6, 1963, <u>UNM</u>; near Carbondale, <u>L. & R. L. Benson 16223-16227</u>, <u>Pom</u>. MONTROSE CO. Near Montrose, <u>E. Wiegand 66</u>, <u>Pom</u>, <u>E. Karr</u> in 1963, <u>Pom</u>. GUNNISON CO. Sapinero, <u>Griffiths 10688</u>, <u>US</u>, <u>Pom</u>.

Names of Uncertain Application (perhaps to var. erinacea)

Opuntia xerocarpa Griffiths, Proc. Biol. Soc. Wash. 29: 15. 1916. "...About 15 miles southeast of Kingman, Arizona, in May, 1912,...[Griffiths] 10,579...in cultivation since that time...

[and] previously." TYPE: <u>US 317779</u>, <u>2576146A</u>. ISOTYPE: <u>Pom</u>. The fruit is described as dry and with 1-3 short, white spines per areole, each 5-7 mm long. However, the type specimen, which bears only flower buds and no flowers or fruits, gives no indication that this will be so. The theoretical type, above, is not the plant described, but is O. phaeacantha var. superbospina. The plant described seems to be some form of O. erinacea or its varie-ties or hybrids.

Opuntia barbata K. Brandegee ex C. A. Purpus, Monatschr. Kak-teenk. 10: 97. 1900; J. A. Purpus, Mitt. Deutsch. Dendrol. Gesell-sch. 1925: 58. 1925. "Gegen Nässe ist sie weniger empfindlich wie O. ursina." "Wurde von C. A. Purpus in Jahre 1900 im west-lichen Utah bei Moah [Moab] gefunden wo sie an Sandsteinfelsen wächst." No type specimen; cf. under O. erinacea var. utahensis.

Opuntia barbata K. Brandegee var. gracillima K. Brandegee ex C. A. Purpus, Montaschr. Kakteenk. 10: 97. 1900; J. A. Purpus, Mitt. Deutsch. Dendrol. Gesellsch. 1925: 58. 1925. "C. A. Purpus fand diese Varietät in höheren Regionen der La Sal Mts. in Utah." No type specimen, cf. under O. erinacea var. utahensis.

26b. Opuntia erinacea var. columbiana (Griffiths) L. Benson

Opuntia columbiana Griffiths, Bull. Torrey Club 43: 523. 1916. O. erinacea Engelm. & Bigelow var. columbiana L. Benson, Cactus & Succ. Jour. 41: 124. 1969. "...Sandy lands along the Columbia and Snake River valleys,...No. 10041, from Pasco, Wash-ington...." TYPE: "Pasco, Washington, <u>Griffiths 10,041</u>," <u>US 2572081A</u>. ISOTYPE: <u>Pom 288191</u>.

OREGON. WHEELER CO. Mitchell, <u>W. E. Lawrence 1033</u>, <u>OSC</u>. GRANT CO. W of Dale Vale, <u>Lawrence & Powell 2705</u>, <u>OSC</u>, <u>DS</u>. GIL-LIAM CO. Arlington, <u>Henderson</u>, May 11, 1899, <u>UO</u>, <u>GH</u>.

IDAHO. OWYHEE CO. Oreana, <u>J. P. Hester</u>, June, 1950, <u>US</u>.

The following collections represent probable hybridization of Opuntia erinacea var. erinacea and O. phaeacantha var. major, markedly differing dry- and juicy-fruited species (cf. Text):

UTAH. WASHINGTON CO. Springdale, <u>L. Benson 13696-13700</u>, <u>Pom</u>. <u>13705-13708</u>, <u>Pom</u>. KANE CO. Paria River above Paria, Buckskin Mts., <u>L. & R. L. Benson 15200-15201</u> (<u>15201</u> approaching closely O. nicholii), Pom.

Collections of single specimens representing apparent hybrids include the following (cf. discussion under Opuntia nicholii):

UTAH. MILLARD CO. Delta, <u>Becraft 2696</u>, <u>Pom</u>. WASHINGTON CO. 10 mi. E of St. George, <u>E. W. Nelson 155 (09.355)</u>, Oct. 3, 1909, <u>K</u>. Numerous intergradations between this species and O. phaeacantha var. major were observed in Bridge Canyon and along Glen Canyon in 1963 before much of the area was flooded (e.g. Bridge Canyon, <u>L. Benson 16318</u>, <u>Pom</u>, <u>16319</u>, <u>Pom</u>).

ARIZONA. COCONINO CO. Vermilion Cliffs N of Navajo Bridge, <u>E. Benson 317</u>, <u>Pom</u>.

In Coconino Co., Arizona, there is a similar series involving O. erinacea var. erinacea and O. littoralis var. martiniana (<u>L. & R. L. Benson 15748-15753</u>, <u>Pom</u>).

Flattening of at least the basal portions of the larger spines is a basis (not wholly clear-cut in some areas) for segregation of Opuntia erinacea and O. polyacantha. An example of specimens col-lected in an intergrading population between O. erinacea var. erinacea and O. polyacantha var. rufispina is as follows: four herbarium sheets from a population in Kyle Canyon, Charleston Mts., Clark Co., Nevada, <u>L. Benson 15054</u>, <u>Pom</u>. A series of plants ap-pearing to involve the genes of var. erinacea, var. utahensis, and O. polyacantha var. rufispina is represented also on four herbarium sheets collected near Cardinal Lodge W of Bishop, Inyo Co., Cali-fornia (<u>E. Wiegand 78</u>, <u>79</u>, <u>109</u>, and <u>111</u> in 1951, <u>Pom</u>). Other cases are discussed under the other varieties of O. erinacea.

26c. Opuntia erinacea var. ursina (Weber) Parish

Opuntia rubrifolia Engelm. ex Coulter, Contr. U.S. Nat Herb. 3: 424. 1896. TYPE: "Palmer 3 [May, 1877] in Herb. Mo. Bot. Gard. St. George, Utah," <u>Mo</u>.

Opuntia ursina Weber in Bois, Dict. Hort. 896. 1897, metanym. O. erinacea Engelm. & Bigelow var. ursina Parish in Jepson, Fl. Calif. 2: 542. 1936. O. hystricina Engelm. var. ursina Backeberg, Cactaceae 1: 610. 1958. "Desert de Californie." According to Weber, Bull. Soc. Nat. d'Acclimatation 49: 14-15. 1902, "...sous le 36° degré de latitude, et a 1.700 mètres d'altitude." Accord-ing to Parish, loc. cit., Ord Mountains, south of Barstow, Mojave Desert, in San Bernardino Co., California. NEOTYPE designation: "Ord Mountain near Aztec Spring, <u>C. B. Wolf 8575</u>, May 5, 1937," <u>Pom 244286</u>. DUPLICATES: <u>RSA 21341</u>, <u>US</u>, <u>UC</u>, <u>DS</u>.

Opuntiae Ursus horribilis Walton, Cactus Jour. 2: 121. 1899, illegitimate name. "...A lone mountain in the Mojave desert; the elevation may be 2,000 or 3,000 feet...," A. H. Alverson. TYPE: "...Near the Ord Mountains...," <u>A. H. Alverson</u> in 1894 (cf. Cactus

& Succ. Jour. 5: 520. *f.* 1934). This collection, probably not preserved, formed the basis for both this name and var. *ursina* above. The following specimen may or may not be a duplicate: "Mojave Desert. A. H. Alverson," US (box).

NEVADA. MINERAL CO. Candelaria, W. H. Shockley 274, June, 1882, GH, DS; Montgomery Pass, C. H. Bonner 21, Pom. EUREKA CO. N end of Antelope Range, Kobeh Valley, L. Benson 16610, Pom, 16611, Pom.

UTAH. WASHINGTON CO. 10 mi. NW of St. George, E. L. Benson 314, Pom; St. George, Griffiths 10753, US, Pom, 10755, US, Pom.

ARIZONA. COCONINO CO. Vermilion Cliffs, Blakley & Earle 238, June 21, 1951, Des. NAVAJO CO. Above Kayenta, J. Fishback, TAES.

26d. Opuntia erinacea var. utahensis (Engelmann) L. Benson

Opuntia sphaerocarpa Engelm. & Bigelow var. utahensis Engelm. Trans. St. Louis Acad. Sci. 11: 199. 1863, not O. utahensis J. A. Purpus, Monatschr. Kakteenk. 19: 133. 1909. O. erinacea Engelm. & Bigelow var. utahensis L. Benson, Cacti Ariz. ed. 3. 20, 78. 1969. "...Pass west of Steptoe Valley [Nevada], in the Utah basin. In flower and fruit...July." "In the same year (1858) and the following one...Henry Engelmann...." Simpson Expedition. TYPE: "'Pass west of Steptoe Valley, Utah [site of Ely, Nevada],' Henry Engelmann, July 19, 1859," Mo. The only spine is flattened.

Opuntia rhodantha K. Schum. Monatschr. Kakteenk. 6: 111. July, 1896; Gesamtb. Kakteen. 735. 1898. O. erinacea Engelm. & Bigelow var. rhodantha L. Benson, Proc. Calif. Acad. IV. 25: 249. 1944. "...Staate Colorado...in dem SPÄTH'schen Baumschule in Rixford...." "Colorado; bei 2000-2300 m. Höhe: [C. A.] PURPUS; blühte bei SPÄTH in Juni...." No specimen found. The collections of C. A. Purpus, at Darmstadt, Germany, where his brother, J. A. Purpus, was Inspektor des Botanischen Gartens, were destroyed during the Second World War. No suitable material for a neotype found. The July, 1896, publication is barely valid, the description being minimal.

Opuntia xanthostemma K. Schum. Monats. Kakteenk. 6: 111. 1896; Gesamtb. Kakteen. 735. 1898. O. rhodantha K. Schum. var. xanthostemma Rehder, Jour. Arn. Arb. 7: 149. 1926. O. rhodantha K. Schum. f. xanthostemma Rehder, Bibl. & Cult. Trees & Shrubs 478. 1949. O. erinacea Engelm. & Bigelow var. xanthostemma L. Benson, Leafl. West. Bot. 4: 209. 1945. "Colorado Mesa Grande bei 2000 m. Höhe: [C. A.] PURPUS; blühte im Juni bei SPÄTH...." The statements above for O. rhodantha, published simultaneously, apply also to publication and typification of O. xanthostemma.

Opuntia rhodantha K. Schum. formae schumanniana, brevispina, pisciformis, & flavispina Späth ex Schelle, Handb. Kakteenkultur 55. 1907, nom. nud. Mesa Grande, Colorado, C. A. Purpus. No specimens.

Opuntia xanthostemma K. Schum. formae elegans, fulgens, gracilis, orbicularis, & rosea Späth ex Schelle, Handb. Kakteenkultur 55. 1907, nom. nud. No specimens.

Opuntia rhodantha K. Schum. var. spinosior Boissevain in Boissevain & Davidson, Colorado Cacti 29. 1940, nom. nud. (without Latin diagnosis); Cactus & Succ. Jour. 15: 138. 1943. "Southwestern Colorado [state] Desert, Cortez." No specimen found. NEOTYPE designation: 3 mi. W of U.S. 666 in McElmo Canyon, W of Cortez, Montezuma County, Colorado, Lyman and Robert L. Benson 14748, October 31, 1950, Pom 278862. No. 14750 from the same place has only 1-4 spines per areole as opposed to the 4 or more described for var. spinosior and occurring in 14748. Probably no consistent pattern of genes is involved.

NEW MEXICO. SOCORRO CO. Chupadera Mesa, NE of Bingham, Castetter 314, UNM. COLFAX CO. Baton, P. Pierce 2081, UNM, 2082A & B, UNM. UNION CO. Seneca, NE of Clayton, P. Pierce 791, UNM.

26e. Opuntia erinacea var. hystricina (Engelmann & Bigelow) L. Benson

Opuntia hystricina Engelm. & Bigelow, Proc. Amer. Acad. 3: 299. 1857 (preprint, 1856); U.S. Senate Rept. Expl. & Surv. R. R. Route Pacific Ocean. Botany 4: 44. pl. 15, f. 5-7. 1857. O. erinacea Engelm. & Bigelow var. hystricina L. Benson, Proc. Calif. Acad. IV. 25: 249. 1944. "...Colorado Chiquito and on the San Francisco mountains." LECTOTYPE designation: "Colorado Chiquito [Little Colorado River in Arizona]," J. M. Bigelow, Dec. 8, 1853, Mo. DUPLICATE: Pom 317790 (spines).

ARIZONA. COUNTY uncertain. Colorado Chiquito, Bigelow, Dec. 8, 1853, Mo, Pom. COCONINO CO. Bright Angel Trail, Grand Canyon, Goldman 2044, NY; San Francisco Mt., Bigelow, Dec. 27, 1853, Mo; 20 mi. N of Flagstaff, C. J. King SF 588 & photograph, June, 1932, Ariz. NAVAJO CO. Marsh Pass, Kayenta to Red Lake, Peebles & Smith SF 1062, Ariz; W of Holbrook, L. & R. L. Benson 14641, Pom. APACHE CO. SE of Chambers, L. & R. L. Benson 14644, Pom.

NEW MEXICO. SAN JUAN CO. N of Aztec, P. Pierce 337A, Aug. 19, 1960, UNM.

27. Opuntia nicholii L. Benson

Opuntia nicholii L. Benson, Cacti Ariz. ed. 2. 48. 1950. O. hystricina Engelm. & Bigelow var. nicholii Backeberg, Cactaceae 1: 610. 1958. TYPE: "Hills at 5,000 feet elevation along the highway 5 miles south of Navajo Bridge [Colorado River], Navajo Indian Reservation in Coconino County, Arizona, October 16, 1949, L. Benson 14,247," Pom 277226.

UTAH. SAN JUAN CO. Glen Canyon, Colorado River: Lower Ticaboo, E bank, opposite Ticaboo Canyon, L. Benson 16271, Pom, 16279, Pom; Bridge Canyon, 1 mi. below Rainbow Bridge, L. Benson 16318, Pom; 1 mi. NE of Forbidding (Aztec) Canyon but in Glen Canyon, Colorado River, L. Benson 16324, Pom.

ARIZONA. COCONINO CO. Soap Creek, 7 mi. W of Navajo Bridge, L. & E. L. Benson 16088, Pom (fls.); Navajo Bridge, Peebles SF 993, US, Ariz, Peebles & Parker SF 14651, Ariz, L. & R. L. Benson 13517, Pom, L. Benson 14249, Pom, 14250, Pom, E. Benson 318, Pom (3), 319, Pom (2), J. P. Hester, June, 1950, US (box), E. R. Blakley & W. H. Earle, June 23, 1951, Des; 2 mi. SE of Navajo Bridge, L. & R. L. Benson 15754, Pom, 4 mi. S[E] of Navajo Bridge, A. A. Nichol, Jan. 15, 1940, Pom; 5 mi. S[E] of Navajo Bridge, Peebles & Parker SF 14651, Ariz, L. Benson 14247, Pom; 10 mi. S of Navajo Bridge, E. R. Blakley B-1745, Des; Lee's Ferry, E. W. Nelson, Aug. 26, 1909, NY, US.

28. Opuntia basilaris Engelmann & Bigelow

28a. Opuntia basilaris var. basilaris

Opuntia basilaris Engelm. & Bigelow, Proc. Amer. Acad. 3: 298. 1857 (preprint, 1856); U.S. Senate Rept. Expl. & Surv. R. R. Route Pacific Ocean. Botany 4: 43. pl. 13, f. 1-5. 1857. "On William's River, the Colorado, and the Mojave, and down to the Gila: flowers April and May." LECTOTYPE designation: "Cactus Pass, Bill Williams fork, etc.," J. M. Bigelow, Feb. 1, 1854, Mo. DUPLICATE: Pom 317791.

Opuntia basilaris Engelm. & Bigelow var. ramosa Parish, Bull. Torrey Club 19: 92. 1892. O. basilaris Engelm. & Bigelow f. ramosa Parish ex Schelle, Handb. Kakteenkultur 47. 1907. LECTOTYPE (Benson, Amer. Jour. Bot. 28: 361. 1941): "Borders of the Colorado Desert, Whitewater, San Diego [Riverside] Co." S. B. & W. F. Parish 169, April, 1882, DS 109124. DUPLICATES: Mo, Ph, US, F, YU.

Opuntia basilaris Engelm. & Bigelow var. cordata F. Fobe, Monatschr. Kakteenk. 16: 46. 1906. O. basilaris Engelm. & Bigelow f. cordata Schelle, Handb. Kakteenkultur 47. 1907. No specimen.

Opuntia basilaris Engelm. & Bigelow f. nana Haage, f., ex Schelle, Handb. Kakteenkultur 47. 1907, nom. nud.

Opuntia basilaris Engelm. & Bigelow f. cristata Schelle, Handb. Kakteenkultur 47. 1907, nom. nud.

Opuntia humistrata Griffiths, Bull. Torrey Club 43: 83. 1916. O. basilaris Engelm. & Bigelow var. humistrata Griffiths ex W. T. Marshall in Marshall & Bock, Cactaceae 65. 1941, incorrectly ascribed to Griffiths. O. brachyclada Griffiths subsp. humistrata Wiggins & Wolf in Abrams, Illustr. Fl. Pac. States 3: 148. 1951. TYPE: Griffiths 10787, "...collected in the mountain cañons above San Bernardino, California, September 17, 1912...description... from cultivated plants, grown at Chico, California, July 28, 1914." TYPE: not found, US, Pom.

Opuntia whitneyana Baxter, Calif. Cactus 37. photograph 1935. O. basilaris Engelm. & Bigelow var. whitneyana Baxter ex W. T. Marshall in Marshall & Bock, Cactaceae 65. 1941, incorrectly ascribed to Baxter. O. basilaris Engelm. & Bigelow subsp. whitneyana Munz, Aliso 4: 94. 1958. TYPE: "...F. W. Leuders... Alabama Hills," Inyo County, Calif. Specimen labelled: "Alabama Hills, near Lone Pine, 6000-8000 ft." F. W. Leuders, DS (in fluid; no number). In this area O. basilaris intergrades at higher altitudes with O. polyacantha var. rufispina and with O. erinacea var. utahensis, and the peculiarities of Baxter's plants likely are derived from crosses, (cf., Lake Sabrina road, Inyo Co., L. Benson 6009, Pom; 1/2 mile south of Tom's Place, U.S. 395, Mono Co., Glade, July, 1963, Pom).

Opuntia whitneyana Baxter var. albiflora Baxter, Calif. Cactus 39. photograph. 1935, not O. albiflora K. Schum. Gesamtb. Kakteen. Nachtr. 152. 1903, not O. basilaris var. albiflorus Walton, Cactus Journal 2: 163. f. 1899. TYPE: "...Dudley Herbarium of Stanford University...garden of Mrs. Wm. Otte, Santa Barbara, California...[From] rounded mountain top 'flats'...eastern Sierra Nevada...near Mount Whitney." Not found, DS.

CALIFORNIA. TULARE CO. Near Rancheria, A. W. Sampson 461, May 3, 1909, NY, US, Pom (photograph), USFS. VENTURA CO. Moorpark, D. T. MacDougal, May 24, 1921, US, NY. LOS ANGELES CO. Los Angeles, J. C. Nevin in 1882, GH. SAN DIEGO CO. Extreme NW corner of county, Gander 3266, SD; Oak Grove, Gander, Oct. 24, 1935, SD.

28b. Opuntia basilaris var. brachyclada (Griffiths) Munz

Opuntia brachyclada Griffiths, Proc. Biol. Soc. Wash. 27: 25. 1914. O. basilaris Engelm. & Bigelow var. brachyclada Munz, Man. So. Calif. Bot. 325, 599. 1935. TYPE: "...No. 10,768...mountain valleys above San Bernardino, California," US 2576145A, ISOTYPE: Pom 288598.

CALIFORNIA. LOS ANGELES CO. Valyermo, Wiegand 184, Pom; Mescal Creek, San Gabriel Mts., Ewan 9917a, GH, Mo, J. & N. Ewan 9967, GH; Rock Creek, N slope San Gabriel Mts., F. W. Pierson 3546, RSA; E side of San Gabriel Mts., 6 mi. [N] from Big Pine Camp, Wiggins 8775, DS (2 & box); L. A. County road N4, near Wrightwood-Pear Blossom road, L. Benson 16705, Pom. SAN BERNARDINO CO. Mountain valleys above San Bernardino, Griffiths 10768, US, Pom; Wrightwood, E. Wiegand 202, Pom; Lone Pine Canyon, H. M. Hall, June, 1899, UC, DS, June 1-3, 1900, UC, C. B. Wolf 2630, RSA; N of Cajon Pass, Stark in 1927, RSA, L. Benson 12242, Pom; Cajon Pass, Parish, June 15, 1916, DS, E. Wiegand 22, in 1950, Pom; Bear Valley, San Bernardino Mts., Parish 1054, July 21, 1898, UC; Bonanza King Mine, E slope of Providence Mts., Munz, Johnston, & Harwood 4296, Pom, UC. SAN DIEGO CO. Vulcan Mt., H. M. Hall, May, 1899, UC.

28c. Opuntia basilaris var. longiareolata
(Clover & Jotter) L. Benson

Opuntia longiareolata Clover & Jotter, Bull. Torrey Club 68: 418. f. 6. 1941. O. basilaris Engelm. & Bigelow var. longiareolata L. Benson, Cacti Ariz. ed. 2. 43. 1950. TYPE: (Clover and Jotter 2302) growing at base of steep talus, near water's edge, Granite Rapids (Gard. 16852), Grand Canyon, Coconino Co., Arizona," Mich.

28d. Opuntia basilaris var. aurea (Baxter) W. T. Marshall

Opuntia aurea Baxter, Calif. Cactus 27, 28. 1933. O. basilaris Engelm. & Bigelow var. aurea W. T. Marshall in Marshall & Bock, Cactaceae 65. 1941, without reference to the basionym; Arizona's Cactuses ed. 2. 28. 1950. O. lubrica Griffiths var. aurea Backeberg, Cactaceae 1: 585. 1958. TYPE: "1/2 mile north of Pipe Springs...Arizona...1930 by Percy and Helen McCabe...," DS 213750 (box). Peebles in Kearney & Peebles, Flowering Plants and Ferns of Arizona, U.S.D.A. Misc. Publ. 423: 610. 1942, reported, "An amazing variety of forms was observed at the type locality." He cited character combinations and postulated natural crossing. Cf. Peebles & Parker SF 14694, Ariz, 14697-14699, Ariz. Cf., also, Peebles in Kearney & Peebles, Arizona Flora 581. 1951, 1960. Collections were made at the type locality on August 8, 1953, and in a postulated hybrid swarm from interbreeding of var. aurea (L. & R. L. Benson 15210, Pom, 15214, Pom) with O. erinacea var. utahensis (L. & R. L. Benson 15211, Pom, approaching this variety). L. & R. L. Benson 15212, Pom, 15213, Pom, illustrate intermediate types.

UTAH. WASHINGTON CO. 11 mi. NW of Short Creek, J. P. Hester, June, 1950, US (box), Pom; road over mts. W of Zion, D. Woodruff, Garden at Salt Lake City; Springdale, M. E. Jones 5261n in 1894, Pom; Zion Nat. Park, W side of Checkerboard Mesa, W. S. Boyle Z227, June 27, 1938, UC; Zion Canyon, Plateau between Sentinel and North Fork of Virgin River, G. & C. Trapp 67-35, June 14, 1967, Pom; Zion Canyon, Mt. of the Sun, G. & C. Trapp 67-37, June 14, 1967, Pom; Observation Point Road, Zion Nat. Park, G. & C. Trapp 67-46, June 18, 1967, Pom. KANE CO. E of Zion Nat. Park Boundary, L. Benson 13692, Pom; red sand dunes, 9 mi. NW of Kanab, L. & R. L. Benson 15760, Pom; same, 8 mi. NW, L. Benson 13471, Pom; Kanab, Wiegand 73-77, in 1948, Pom; Chalk Hill about 20 mi. E of Kanab, L. & R. L. Benson 15206, Pom; grade to Paria E of Buckskin Mt., L. Benson 15203, Pom, 15204, Pom.

ARIZONA. MOHAVE CO. 0.9 mi. N of Pipe Spring, L. & R. L. Benson, 15210, Pom, 15214, Pom; 1/2 mi. N of Pipe Spring, P. & H. McCabe in 1930, DS; Pipe Spring, G. Lindsay, Aug., 1939, Ariz, Peebles & Parker SF 14694 & 14697-14699, Ariz (hybrid swarm); 5 mi. SW of Pipe Spring, Peebles & Parker SF 14701, Ariz.

28e. Opuntia basilaris var. treleasei (Coulter) Coulter

Opuntia treleasii [treleasei] Coulter, Contr. U.S. Nat. Herb. 3: 434. 1896. O. basilaris Engelm. & Bigelow var. treleasei Coulter ex Toumey in Bailey, Stand. Cyclop. Hort. 3: 1147. 1901, incorrectly ascribed to Coulter. "At Caliente, in the Tehachapi Mountains, California. Type, growing in Mo. Bot. Gard. 1893,... Trelease in 1892." Not found, Mo. NEOTYPE designation: sand ridge at the lower end of the W side of Caliente Wash, E of the Edison Oil Field, 14 miles E and a little S of Bakersfield; 600 feet, Lyman Benson 15782, Feb. 14, 1958, Pom 288546, 288956.

Opuntia treleasei Coulter var. kernii Griffiths & Hare, New Mex. Agric. Exp. Sta. Bull. 60: 81. 1906. TYPE: "...No. 8321 D. G. [David Griffiths], collected near Kern [East Bakersfield], May 27, 1906," US 2607622. Griffiths refers to gradations from spineless to spiny forms of "Opuntia treleasei" (cf. Caliente Wash, L. Benson 4377, Pom, 8698, Pom, sand ridge west of Caliente Wash, L. Benson 15783-15784, Pom), and continuation of this sequence [beginning with var. basilaris] to the proposed var. kernii, the type of which has stout brown spines up to 3 cm long, far exceeding those observed in the field populations. The plants in

the region vary not only in degree of spininess but also in joint size (cf. Kern Canyon Road, L. Benson 15708-15710, Pom). Cf. L. Benson, Amer. Jour. Bot. 28: 361. 1941.

CALIFORNIA. SAN BERNARDINO CO. Near Big Pine Recreation Area, San Gabriel Mts., E. F. Wiegand 134 in 1950, Pom; Turtle Mts., Colorado River region, C. H. & A. Bonner, May, 1959, Pom.

ARIZONA. MOHAVE CO. NW Arizona near the Colorado River, J. Whitehead, April-May, UC 822527 (seeds and photographs), UC 901710.

29. Opuntia rufida Engelmann

Opuntia rufida Engelm. Proc. Amer. Acad. 3: 298. 1857 (preprint, 1856): in Emory, Rept. U.S. & Mex. Bound. Surv. 2: Cactaceae 51. 1859. O. microdasys (Lehmann) Pfeiffer var. rufida K. Schum. Gesamtb. Kakteen 706. 1898. "...Presidio del Norte,... Rio Grande,...Bigelow;...lower valley of the Nazas, southeastern Chihuahua Gregg: fl. May." LECTOTYPE designation: "Mountain rocks at Presidio del Norte,...J. M. Bigelow, Aug., 1952," Mo.

Opuntia rufida Engelm. var. tortiflora Anthony, Amer. Midl. Nat. 55: 240. f. 15. 1956. TYPE: "BREWSTER CO [Texas]...limestone slopes n.w. of Hot Springs, 2,000 ft., April 18, 1947, [Anthony] No. 39c..." Mich.

30. Opuntia cubensis Britton & Rose

Opuntia cubensis Britton & Rose, Torreya 12: 14. 1912. TYPE: "...U.S. Naval Station, Guantanamo Bay, March [17-30], 1909, N. L. Britton 2064," NY. ISOTYPE: US 538823.

Opuntia antillana Britton & Rose, Brooklyn Bot. Gard. Mem. 1: 73. 1918. TYPE: "...St. Kitts, (Rose, Fitch, and Russell 3230)." According to Britton & Rose, Cactaceae 1: 115. 1919, "Near Basse Terre, St. Christopher, Rose, Fitch, & Russell, No. 3230, February 2, 1913." According to the label "BASSE TERRE, ST. KITTS," US 639383.

Opuntia ochrocentra Small in Britton & Rose, Cactaceae 4: 262. 1923. "...Southeastern end of Big Pine Key, Florida. Type...December 1921, by J. K. Small, in the herbarium of the New York Botanical Garden." TYPE: not found. LECTOTYPE designation: "Hammock, southern end of Big Pine Key, John K. Small, George K. Small, & Paul Matthews, December 11, 1921," US 1111245 (some spines yellowish).

FLORIDA. MONROE CO. Big Pine Key, J. K. & G. K. Small & P. Matthews, Dec. 11, 1921, US, Small, May 17, 1922, US, Killip 31423, US, 42026, F, L. & R. L. Benson 15368A, Pom, L. Benson, T. Alexander, & C. Dodson 16576, Pom.

31. Opuntia triacantha (Willdenow) Sweet

Cactus triacanthos Willd. Enum. Pl. Suppl. 34. 1813. Opuntia triacantha Sweet, Hort. Brit. 172. 1826. No specimen or locality. Representative specimen: FLORIDA. MONROE CO. Southeastern corner of Big Pine Key, Lyman & Robert L. Benson 15367, Pom 285314 (on 2 sheets), 317654.

Opuntia militaris Britton & Rose, Cactaceae 1: 104. 1919. TYPE: "Collected by Dr. N. L. Britton, March 17 to 30, 1909, at the Naval Station, Guantanamo Bay, Oriente, Cuba (No. 1957)," US 535814.

Opuntia abjecta Small in Britton & Rose, Cactaceae 4: 257. 1923. "On edge of hammock, southern end of Big Pine Key, Florida. Type collected in May 1921 by J. K. Small,...New York Botanical Garden." TYPE: not found. LECTOTYPE designation: "Hammock, southern tip of Big Pine Key, J. K. Small and Paul Matthews, April 12, 1921," NY.

FLORIDA. MONROE CO. Big Pine Key, J. K. Small & P. Matthews, Apr. 12, 1921, NY, May 17, 1922, NY, US, G. S. Miller 1710, Feb. 22, 1935, US, Killip 31712, US, L. & R. L. Benson 15363, Pom, 15367, Pom, T. Alexander, Mar. 14, 1964, Pom, L. Benson, T. Alexander, & C. Dodson 16577, Pom.

32. Opuntia pusilla (Haworth) Nuttall

Cactus pusillus Haw. Misc. Nat. 188. 1803. O. pusilla Haw. Syn. Pl. Succ. 195. 1812, not Salm-Dyck, Obs. Bot. 10. 1822; in Pfeiffer, Enum. Cact. 145. 1840. "HABITAT in America meridionali?" Cf. below under C. foliosus.

Cactus foliosus Willd. Enum. Pl. Suppl. 35. 1813. Opuntia foliosa Salm-Dyck in DC. Prodr. 3: 471. 1828. No locality or specimen. O. pusilla Haw. is given in synonymy, and one species is taken to be based upon the other. According to Salm-Dyck in DC., "...in America calidiore, O. pusilla Haw. syn 195. non Salm. Cactus foliosus Willd." This species was illustrated by Pfeiffer & Otto, Abb. & Beschr. Blühende Kakteen 1: pl. 18. 1840, and the illustration was copied by Britton & Rose, as stated, Cactaceae 1: 106. f. 129. 1919. According to Pfeiffer & Otto, "Sie [O. foliosa] war von Haworth zuerst unter dem Namen Opuntia pusilla beschrieben worden, welcher Name aber auf ein ganz andere Art übertragen, und der Name O. foliosa für diese Art allgemein allgenommen wurde." Earlier publication of the combination than that by Haworth has not come to light, and Pfeiffer & Otto may have had in mind horticultural use of the combination rather than its publication. NEOTYPE designation: The illustration by Pfeiffer & Otto, loc. cit., for both C. pusillus Haw. or O. pusilla (Haw.) Haw. and C. folious Willd. or O. foliosa (Willd.) Salm-Dyck.

Opuntia drummondii Graham in Maund, Botanist 5: pl. 246. 1846. "Plants of the species now described were received both at the Botanic Garden, Edinburgh, and by Dr. Neill, Canonmills, from Mr. Drummond, in 1835. They were gathered by him in Apalachicola, and flowered with Dr. Neill (and with him, and at the Caledonian Horticultural Society's Garden, only, as far as I know), in July, 1838 and 1839." The following is quoted from a letter of February 23, 1970, from D. M. Henderson, Regius Keeper, Royal Botanic Garden, Edinburgh: "We have had a search for the specimen of Opuntia drummondii Graham but I regret very much that we have been unable to find it. There are only a few Graham specimens in Edinburgh. For the rest, all we have ever been able to find out, is a note in Hooker's London Journal of Botany for 1846, referring to the impending sale of Graham's herbarium." Later collections from Apalachicola consist only of fragments. NEOTYPE designation: FLORIDA. ST. JOHN'S CO. Dunes 5 miles south of Ponte Verde, Lyman & Robert L. Benson 15388, Sept. 2, 1954, Pom 283363 (on two sheets).

Opuntia Pes-Corvi Le Conte in Engelm. Proc. Amer. Acad. 3: 346. 1857 (preprint, 1856). "Sandy coast of Georgia, Major Le Conte, and Florida, Dr. Chapman." No specimen collected clearly prior to 1856 found. NEOTYPE designation: Materials from plants collected by Chapman at Apalachicola, Florida, pressed by Engelmann in April, July, and November 1860, Mo. DUPLICATE: F 99199. Either these were from the original material grown at St. Louis or from plants received later from Chapman and placed in cultivation.

Opuntia frustulenta Gibbes, Proc. Elliott Soc. Nat. Hist. 1: 273. 1859. "...obtained within a few miles of Charleston...." The following is quoted from a letter from Albert E. Sanders, Curator of Natural Sciences, Charleston Museum, March 2, 1970: "I am sorry to say that our herbarium does not contain any botanical specimens collected by Gibbes. It is quite probable that the specimens in which you are interested were at one time in the Museum herbarium but likely did not survive the closing days of the Civil War. During the seige of Charleston, many of the more fragile items were taken into the country for safekeeping. However, some of this material was burned by Sherman's raiders, and it is possible that the Gibbes herbarium specimens were among those items that went up in smoke. Fortunately, the Elliott herbarium survived and is in the Museum today." NEOTYPE designation: SOUTH CAROLINA. CHARLESTON COUNTY. Folly Island, near Charleston, John K. Small, February 15, 1916, US (unnumbered).

Opuntia tracyi Britton, Torreya 11: 152. 1911. TYPE: "... Coast, Biloxi, Mississippi, S. M. Tracy, May [11], 1911; flowered at New York Botanical Garden May 12-13, 1911 (33786, type)," NY.

Opuntia macateei Britton & Rose, Cactaceae 1: 113, 221. f. 292-293. 1919. TYPE: "...W. L. McAtee at Rockport, Texas, December 28, 1910 (No. 1992)," US 1812772. ISOTYPE: NY (sheet bearing No. 1992 but the date, "1911").

TEXAS. ARANSAS CO. Rockport, W. L. McAtee 1992 in 1910, US. CHAMBERS CO. Anahuac, Griffiths, US.

MISSISSIPPI. FORREST CO. Hattiesburg, W. Cliburn, June 27, 1961, Pom. HARRISON CO. Biloxi, C. L. Pollard, Aug. 1, 1896, NY, US, S. M. Tracy, March, 1910, NY, US (2), Pom, May 12, 1911, NY, Feb. 1, 1912, NY.

ALABAMA. BALDWIN CO. Navy Cove, C. Mohr, July 27, 1888, US.

NORTH CAROLINA (northernmost). HYDE CO. Cape Hatteras National Seashore, Ocracoke, C. J. Bosworth 235, April 14, 1965, BrY.

33. Opuntia vulgaris Miller

Opuntia vulgaris Miller, Gard. Dict. ed. 9. No. 1. 1768. "J. B. 1. 154." According to Britton & Rose, Cactaceae 1: 156. 1919, "O. vulgaris was based on Bauhin's figure (Hist. Pl. 1: 154. 1650), which was taken from Lobelius (Icones 2: 24. 1591)...."

Cactus monacanthos Willd. Enum. Pl. Suppl. 33. 1813. Opuntia monacantha Haw. Suppl. Pl. Succ. 81. 1819. No locality or specimen.

HAWAII. OAHU. Honolulu: Punchbowl St. near Prospect and Pele Sts., Westgate & St. John, July 30, 1932, Bish (part on a second sheet, mixed with Opuntia ficus-indica); Punchbowl, Pemberton, Sept. 26, 1944, Bish; Kamehameha Heights, Kamehameha Girls School, Judd, Nov. 12, 1930, Bish, Judd, Bryan, & Neal, June 6, 1932, Bish.

FLORIDA. POLK CO. Crooked Lake, McFarlin 3235 (hybrid with Opuntia compressa var. ammophila) 3375a, F, DS, 5609, Mich, 5610,

Mich, 6061, UC, 6589, Mich, 6590, Tex, 6591, Mich, 6594, Mich; Lake Alfred, McFarlin 3962, Mich (hybrid with Opuntia compressa var. ammophila).

34. Opuntia humifusa (Rafinesque) Rafinesque

34a. Opuntia humifusa var. humifusa

Cactus opuntia L. Sp. Pl. 468. 1753. C. compressus Salisb. Prodr. 348. 1796, superfl. nom. nov. for C. opuntia L. Opuntia opuntia Karsten, Deutsche Fl. ed. 1. 882. 1882; Coulter, Contr. U.S. Nat. Herb. 3: 432. 1896, tautonyms. O. compressa Macbr. Contr. Gray Herb. (65): 41. 1922; Backeberg, Cactaceae, Jahrb. Deutsche Kakteen Gesellschaft 7. 1944. "Habitat in America calidiore." "Cactus compressus articulatus ramosissimus, articulatis ovatis; spinis setaceis. Hort. Cliff. 183. Hort. ups. 120. Gron. virg. 54. Roy, lugdb. 280...Habitat in America Peru, Virginia...." Gronovius, Fl. Virginica 54. 1739, cites L. Hort. Cliff. and refers to "Clayt. n. 43." LECTOTYPE designation: Linnaean Herb. S, "Cactus articulata prolifer, orbiculatis ovatis: spinis setaceis. Linn. Spec. plant. 468, 16." "Fl. U. 1. 120. 8." "Hort."

Cactus opuntia L. var. nana DC. in Redouté & DC. Pl. Succ. Hist. (Pl. Grasses) 2: pl. opposite 138 (pages unnumbered). 1804; as Opuntia nana on the next page, but definitely intended as a variety of C. opuntia, as shown in later pages. O. nana Visiani, Fl. Dalmatica 3: 143. 1852. O. vulgaris Miller var. nana K. Schum. Gesamtb. Kakteen 715. 1898. O. vulgaris Miller f. nana Schelle, Handb. Kakteenkultur 50. 1907. "Hort. Paris." No locality or specimen. LECTOTYPE designation: plate by Redouté (opposite 138).

Cactus humifusus Raf. Annals Natur. 15. 1820. Opuntia humifusa Raf. Med. Fl. U.S. 2: 247. 1830. O. compressa (Salisb.) Macbr. var. humifusa Weniger, Cacti S. W. 202. 1970, nom. nud. (Art. 33). "...the common Cactus of the United States·[as then defined],...mistaken for C. Opuntia by all our botanists...New York to Kentucky and Missouri...."

Opuntia mesacantha Raf. in Seringue, Bull. Bot. 216. 1830. Page 215: "Trois se trouvent dans le Kautucky [Kentucky]: l'une est son O. humifusa, décrit en 1820..; le deux autres sont inédites; en voici les caractères:...."

Opuntia cespitosa Raf. in Seringue, Bull. Bot. 216. 1830. Page 215: Same statement as for O. mesacantha, above.

Opuntia intermedia Salm-Dyck, Hort. Dyck. 1834: 364. 1834. "An O. italica Tenor?"

Opuntia prostrata Monville & Lemaire ex Förster, Handb. Cact. 478. 1846, pro syn., nom. nud. O. intermedia Salm-Dyck var. prostrata Salm-Dyck, Cact. Hort. Dyck. 1849. 69. 1850, with only the reference above.

Opuntia rafinesquei Engelm. Proc. Amer. Acad. 3: 295. 1857 (preprint, 1856); U.S. Senate Rept. Expl. & Surv. R. R. Route Pacific Ocean. Botany. 4: 41. pl. 11, f. 1-3. 1857, nom. superfl. O. vulgaris Miller var. rafinesquei A. Gray, Man. Bot. ed. 2. 136. 1856. No specimen cited. "Rafinesque had already observed it in Kentucky, and, in his usual careless manner, had indicated 3 species.... As it seems impossible from his incomplete descriptions to make out what he meant by three different names, and as we know only one species in those states of the Mississippi valley, I take the liberty of discarding those names and of substituting the name of the author of the western species." Illegitimate name; superfluous when published. LECTOTYPE designation: "St. Louis, May 1856," young joints on one sheet and flowers on another, June, 1856, Mo. No specimens labelled by Engelmann as O. rafinesquei include mature joints.

Opuntia rafinesquei Engelm. & Bigelow var. microsperma Engelm. & Bigelow, Proc. Amer. Acad. 3: 295. 1857 (preprint, 1856); U.S. Senate Rept. Expl. & Surv. R. R. Route Pacific Ocean. Botany. 4: 41. 1857. O. mesacantha Raf. var. microsperma Coulter, Contr. U.S. Nat. Herb. 3: 429. 1896. O. humifusa Raf. var. microsperma Heller, Cat. N. Amer. Pl. ed. 2. 8. 1900. O. compressa (Salisb.) Macbr. var. microsperma L. Benson, Proc. Calif. Acad. 25: 250. 1944. "Opuntia compressa var. microsperma (Eng.) non Benson," Weniger, Cacti S. W. 206. 1970, nom. nud. (Art. 33) and nom. dubium. No locality or specimen. LECTOTYPE (Coulter, loc. cit.): "Type cult. in Mo. Bot. Gard. 1854 [1855] and preserved in Herb. Mo. Bot. Gard.," probably the following specimen. "Cult. in ------'s garden, St. Louis. April, 1854 [1855], Mo (fruits and seeds).

Opuntia fuscoatra Engelm. Proc. Amer. Acad. 3: 297. 1857 (preprint, 1856); U.S. Senate Rept. Expl. & Surv. R. R. Route Pacific Ocean. Botany 4: 55. pl. 11, f. 4. 1857. O. compressa (Salisb.) Macbr. var. fuscoatra Weniger, Cacti S. W. 207. 1970, nom. nud. (Art. 33). "Sterile places in prairies, west of Houston, Texas: fl. May." LECTOTYPE designation: Same data, F. Lindheimer 33, May, 1842, Mo.

Opuntia rafinesquei Engelm. var. minor Engelm. U.S. Senate Rept. Expl. & Surv. R. R. Route Pacific Ocean. Botany. 4: 55. pl. 11, f. 1. 1857. O. mesacantha Raf. var. parva Coulter, Contr. U.S. Nat. Herb. 3: 429. 1896, nom. nov. O. humifusa Raf. var. parva Heller, Cat. N. Amer. Pl. ed. 2. 8. 1900. O. rafinesquei Engelm. var. parva Haage & Schmidt, Verzeichnis Blumenzwiebeln 1915: 29. 1915. No type indicated. LECTOTYPE (Coulter, loc. cit.): "...Engelmann of 1845 in Herb. Mo. Bot. Gard. Sandstone rock in southern Missouri." The following is the only specimen, the lectotype: "Naked sandstone ledges at Mine la Motte...." G. Engelmann, Nov. 1845, Mo.

Opuntia rafinesquei Engelm. var. arkansana Engelm. ex Rümpler, in Förster, Handb. Cacteenk. ed. 2. 922. 1885, incorrectly ascribed to Engelmann. O. rafinesquei Engelm. f. arkansana Schelle, Handb. Kakteenkultur 50. 1907. O. arkansana Engelm. ex Hirscht, Monatschr. Kakteenk. 8: 115. 1898, nom. nud., incorrectly ascribed to Engelmann; Britton & Rose, Cactaceae 1: 128. 1919. Rümpler referred to Engelmann's works only by the abbreviation, but probably U.S. Senate Rept. Expl. & Surv. R. R. Route Pacific Ocean. Botany 4: 42. 1857. "...near Fort Smith,... Arkansas." LECTOTYPE designation: "Fort Smith," J. M. Bigelow, June, 1853, Mo. Probably this also was the basis for O. arkansana Hort. ex J. A. Purpus, Mitt. Deutsch. Dendr. Gesellsch. 1925: 59. 1925; O. rafinesquei arkansana L. Späth ex J. A. Purpus, loc. cit.

Opuntia allairei Griffiths, Rept. Mo. Bot. Gard. 20: 83. pl. 2, f. 2; 5; 12, upper; 13, f. 9. 1909. O. compressa (Salisb.) Macbr. var. allairei Weniger, Cactus & Succ. S. W., nom. nud. (Art. 33). TYPE: "...No. 322, San Antonio garden [Texas]...Allaire near the mouth of Trinity River, Texas, in April, 1908," US 2576159A (fls.)

Opuntia xanthoglochia Griffiths, Rept. Mo. Bot. Gard. 21: 166. f. 20, lower. 1910. TYPE: "...July 11, 1908...collected on that date near Milano, Texas...type specimen is No. 9,355 D. G. [David Griffiths]...." US 2576293A. ISOTYPE: Pom 288116.

Opuntia nemoralis Griffiths, Monatschr. Kakteenk. 23: 133. 1913. TYPE: "Das Original trägt meine Seriennummer 10480 und ist bei Longview in Texas im Oktober 1911 gesammelt," US 2576133A. ISOTYPE: Pom 288237, 294981. In cultivation some joints were elongate and up to 1.5 dm long.

Opuntia youngii C. Z. Nelson, Galesburg Republican Register, Galesburg, Illinois, July 20, 1915; Trans. Ill. Acad. Sci. 12: 119. 1919. "Type loc: nine miles north of Tampa, Fla." Nelson corresponded with F. G. Young of Haines City, Florida.

Opuntia calcicola Wherry, Jour. Wash. Acad. Sci. 16: 12. f. 1. 1926. TYPE: "...North of Bolivar, Jefferson County, West Virginia ...Type specimens...June 9, 1925...in the U.S. National Herbarium (no. 1,242,156, type) and the New York Botanical Garden." Not found. NEOTYPE designation: "Limestone ledges northwest of Bolivar, E. T. Wherry, June 10, 1932," UPa.

ONTARIO. Pointe Pelée, Lake Erie, T. J. W. Burgess, June 30, 1882, BM, MtMG, Aug. 17, 1886, DAO, BM, MtMG, A. Saunders, July 1, 1882, DAO, Macoun, Sept. 18, 1884, GH, A. A. Wood, July 9, 1934, DAO, E. W. Hart 1067, DAO, A. E. Porsild 16549, Can, Victorin, Germain, & Dominque 46060, BM, DAO, J. H. Soper 2480a, GH, DAO, P. F. Maycock & O. B. Mzrynizk 5519, MtMG; Pelée Island, E. W. Hart 1131A, DAO, R. D. Usshen, July 14, 1968, DAO; Caledon (?), crevices of granitic rock, W. T. MacClement, May, 1934, GH.

MONTANA. CASCADE CO. Great Falls [introduced?], Griffiths 10740, US, Pom.

UTAH. UTAH CO. R. R. right of way [introduced?], La Mar Mason 6570, July 29, 1935, US.

NEW MEXICO. GUADALUPE CO. Anton Chico [introduced?], Griffiths 10326, US, Pom.

KANSAS. SHAWNEE CO. Topeka, Rose & Fitch 17003, NY. CROWLEY CO. Arkansas City, E. J. Palmer, Sept. 26, 1922, NY.

OKLAHOMA. TULSA CO. M. S. Lahman, April 27, 1933, US. MARSHALL CO. 6 mi. N of Madill, D. Weniger 559, June, 1964, UNM. BRYAN CO. 4 mi. E of U.S. 70 bridge across Lake Texoma, J. & C. Taylor 2079, Pom.

WISCONSIN. MONROE CO. Cataract, Michel, April 10, 1942, Mo. NY. SAUK CO. Baraboo Bluffs, Hale in 1861, Mo (2); Sauk City, H. F. Luders, July 7, 1883, UC. DANE CO. Bluffs of Wisconsin River, E. H. Walker, May 19, 1928, USNA.

MICHIGAN. OCEANO CO. 9 mi. SW of Hesperia, Voss 7192, Mich. NEWAYGO CO. 1 mi. W of Croton Dam, D. S. Bullock, Nov. 3, 1930, Mich; Brooks Twp. ca. 5.5 mi. ESW of Newaygo, Voss 7207, Mich. MUSKEGON CO. SE of Whitehall, Voss 2861, Mich. ALLEGAN CO. Yuncker 732, Aug. 16, 1917, Ill; 4 mi. W of Allegan, Voss 7223, Mich; 3 mi. W of Allegan, McVaugh 11260, Mich.

NEW YORK. (common around lower Hudson River). COURTLAND CO. Courtland Park, E. P. Bicknell, Ph.

MASSACHUSETTS. BARNSTABLE CO. (numerous collections). HAMPDEN CO. Southwick, E. Gillett (Rose, Standley, & Russell's No. 15057), US.

34b. Opuntia humifusa var. ammophila (Small) L. Benson

Opuntia ammophila Small, Jour. N. Y. Bot. Gard. 20: 29. 1919. O. compressa (Salisb.) Macbr. var. ammophila L. Benson, Cactus & Succ. Jour. 41: 124. 1969. O. humifusa (Raf.) Raf. var. ammophila L. Benson, Cactus & Succ. Jour. 48: 59. 1976. "...South of Ft. Pierce, collected in December, 1917, by J. K. Small." TYPE: "Hammock on sanddune, St. Lucie Sound, 6 miles south [of] Ft. Pierce, J. K. Small, December 20, 1917," NY (on 2 sheets, 1 with the field number 8456). The habit of the plant is shown by the following topotype: "Ancient dunes, near Fort Pierce, Small, Small, & DeWinkler, Sept. 6, 1922," NY.

Opuntia lata Small, Jour. N. Y. Bot Gard. 20: 26. 1919. TYPE: "Pine woods, 12 miles west of Gainesville," Florida, J. K. Small, Dec. 13, 1917, NY (flowers on a second sheet).

Opuntia impedata Small in Britton & Rose, Cactaceae 4: 257. f. 235. 1923. "...Dunes at Atlantic Beach, Florida, in April 1921, by J. K. Small." TYPE: "Atlantic Beach, east Jacksonville," NY. ISOTYPE: US 1111253. Nearest to var. ammophila.

Opuntia turgida Small in Britton & Rose, Cactaceae 4: 265. 1923. "...About 5 miles south of Daytona, in December [November 30] 1919, by J. K. Small, [N. L. Britton, & J. B. DeWinkler]...." TYPE: NY (on 2 sheets.)

Name Applied to a Hybrid.

Opuntia pisciformis Small in Britton & Rose, Cactaceae 4: 258. f. 236. 1923. "Sand dunes, estuary of the Saint Johns River, Florida...Dunes at Atlantic Beach, Florida, in April 1921, by J. K. Small." TYPE: Specimen marked, "type," labelled, "Dunes, Pilot Island, John K. Small, April 26, 1921." NY. This is var. ammophila X O. stricta, but nearer var. ammophila. The joints are similar to those of O. stricta, 17.5–22.5 cm long, 5–7.5 cm broad. The spines are as in O. compressa var. austrina, but a little more slender, 2–5 per areole and the larger ones 2.5–4.4 cm long.

34c. Opuntia humifusa var. austrina (Small) Dress

Opuntia austrina Small, Fl. S.E. U.S. 816, 1335. 1903. O. compressa (Salisb.) Macbr. var. austrina L. Benson, Cactus & Succ. Jour. 41: 125. 1969. O. humifusa var. austrina Dress, Baileya 19: 165. 1975. "Type, Miami, Fla., Small & Nash, no. 198, in Herb. N. Y. B. G." TYPE: Not found, NY. Notation on sheet bearing label: "Drawing out for use in monograph. May, 1916." LECTOTYPE (or a NEOTYPE, if collection date was later than publication) (Benson, loc. cit.): "...J. K. Small & J. J. Carter, Oct. 28 – Nov. 28, 1903. In pinelands Miami, Florida," US 1739032. DUPLICATES: GH, Ph (unnumbered), Ph 570992.

Opuntia pollardii Britton & Rose, Smithsonian Misc. Coll. 50: 523. 1908. "Biloxi, Harrison County, Mississippi, August 1, 1896, C. L. Pollard (no. 1138)." TYPE: NY. ISOTYPES: Mo, GH, US 271679, 1812771 (fr.), F 171235, CU.

Opuntia polycarpa Small, Man. S. E. Fl. 906. 1506. 1933. "Caxambas Island [Cape Romano Region], Fla., Small, May 11, 1922, in herb. N. Y. B. G." TYPE: "Sand-dunes," NY (on three sheets, including on one sheet plants with spines to 7.5 cm long and on a second no spines; on a third no spines). ISOTYPE: US 1111246 (spines to 4.4 cm long).

Opuntia cumulicola Small, Man. S. E. Fl. 907. 1506. 1933. "Beach, opp. Lemon City, Fla., Small, Small, & Carter No. 970, in herb. N. Y. B. G." TYPE: "Beach. Bull Key, opposite Lemon City, J. K. Small & J. J. Carter, 970, Nov. 6, 1903," NY. ISOTYPE: US (but 1 joint 26 cm long).

Name Applied to a Hybrid.

Opuntia eburnispina Small in Britton & Rose, Cactaceae: 24: 260. f. 237. 1923. "Coastal sands, Cape Romano, Florida...May 1922, by J. K. Small." TYPE: "Sanddunes, Cape Romano, J. K. Small May 10, 1922," NY. An arrow on a map on the label points to the tip of Cape Romano. Notes: Joints of the O. humifusa type, obovate to nearly orbiculate, 3.8–12.5 cm long, 3.8–7.5 cm broad; spines 2–5 per areole, of the O. humifusa type, but the longer ones about 1.2 cm long, clustered as in O. stricta var. dillenii. However, the 2 larger joints at the top of the type sheet have only 2 spines per areole. Because of the spine clusters, the plant gives the impression of a minute var. dillenii, but otherwise it resembles O. humifusa.

35. Opuntia macrorhiza Engelmann

35a. Opuntia macrorhiza var. macrorhiza

Opuntia macrorhiza Engelm. Bost. Jour. Nat. Hist. 6: 206. Jan. 13 (cf. p. 205 and p. 213), 1850. O. mesacantha Raf. var. macrorhiza Coulter, Contr. U.S. Nat. Herb. 3: 430. 1896. O. compressa (Salisb.) Macbr. var. macrorhiza L. Benson, Proc. Calif. Acad. IV. 25: 251. pl. 25, f. A, 1, 2. 1944. "...On the Upper Guadaloupe. Flowers (in St. Louis) in June." LECTOTYPE designation: "Between the Piccardinalis [Pierdenales or Perdenales River] & [the] Guadaloupe...." and including two packets labelled "Western Texas, 1847," F. Lindheimer 1251 in 1847, Mo (only flowers from cultivated material, St. Louis, June 30, 1849, and fruits). Typical specimen (for joints): Comanche Spring, New Braunfels, etc., F. Lindheimer 827, May, 1851, Mo. DUPLICATES: BM, F, Ph, NY, GH, F, UC 143909, NMC 19022, Tex, Ariz, US.

Opuntia tortispina Engelm & Bigelow, Proc. Amer. Acad. 3: 293. 1857 (preprint, 1856); U.S. Senate Rept. Expl. & Surv. R. R. Route Pacific Ocean. Botany 4: 41. pl. 5, f. 2-3. 1857. "On the Camanche plains, near the Canadian River, east of the plateau of the Llano Estacado." LECTOTYPE designation: Camanche Plains, J. M. Bigelow, Sept. 12, 1853 (1 sheet, "Septr., 1853"), Mo. DUPLICATE: Pom 317789. This form is transitional to O. phaeacantha.

Opuntia cymochila Engelm. & Bigelow, Proc. Amer. Acad. 3: 295. 1857 (preprint, 1856); and as "sub-species," but in the form for a species, U.S. Senate Rept. Expl. & Surv. R. R. Route Pacific Ocean. Botany 4: 42. pl. 12, f. 1 3. 1857. O. mesacantha Raf. var. cymochila Coulter, Contr. U.S. Nat. Herb. 3: 430. 1896. O. rafinesquei Engelm. f. cymochila Schelle, Handb. Kakteenkultur 50. 1907. O. tortispina Engelm. & Bigelow var. cymochila Backeberg, Cactaceae 1: 483. 1958. "On the Camanche plains east of the Llano Estacado, near the 100th. degree of longitude, and from there to Tucumcari hill, 80 miles east of the Pecos." New Mexico. LECTOTYPE designation: "Plaza Laya Tucumcari hills near Llano Estacado, J. M. Bigelow, Sept. 21, 1853," Mo.

Opuntia cymochila Engelm. & Bigelow var. montana Engelm. & Bigelow, Proc. Amer. Acad. 3: 296. 1857 (preprint, 1856); U.S. Senate Rept. Expl. & Surv. R. R. Route Pacific Ocean. Botany 4: 42. 1857. "...Sandia mountains, near Albuquerque...." LECTO-TYPE designation: Sandia Mountains, J. M. Bigelow, Oct. 10, 1853, Mo. Another collection of this variety bearing the same date has no spines, and it is not included in the lectotype.

Opuntia stenochila Engelm. & Bigelow, Proc. Amer. Acad. 3: 296. 1857 (preprint, 1856); (as "sub-species," see above) U.S. Senate Rept. Expl. & Surv. R. R. Route Pacific Ocean. Botany 4: 43. pl. 12, f. 4-6. 1857. O. mesacantha Raf. var. stenochila Coulter, Contr. U.S. Nat. Herb. 3: 430. 1896. O. compressa (Salisb.) Macbr. var. stenochila Weniger, Cacti S. W. 211. 1970, nom. nud. (Art. 33). At the cañon of Zuñi...in November...." LECTOTYPE designation: "Cañon de Zuñi. Mt. valleys," J. M. Bigelow, Nov. 17, 1853, Mo.

Opuntia fusiformis Engelm. & Bigelow, Proc. Amer. Acad. 3: 297. 1857 (preprint, 1856); (as "sub-species," see above) U.S. Senate Rept. Expl. & Surv. R. R. Route Pacific Ocean. Botany 4: 43. pl. 12, f. 7-8. 1857. "Cross-timbers [present town is in Hickory County, Missouri] longitude 97°-99° [Bigelow]...Also...Dr. Wislizenus in the same longitude, but farther north, on Cow creek and the Little Arkansas, [on the road from Independence to Santa Fe], and by Dr. Hayden, of the United States army, on the Missouri, below the Big Bend. Fl. in May...description of the flower is from the specimen collected by Dr. Wislizenus." LECTOTYPE designation: "Opuntia bulbosa. Deer Creek, denuded prairies. With large tuberous roots. J. M. Bigelow, August 26, 1853," Mo.

Opuntia mesacantha Raf. var. greenei Coulter, Contr. U.S. Nat. Herb. 3: 431. 1896. O. greenei Engelm. ex Coulter, loc. cit., pro syn. O. greenei Britton & Rose, Smithsonian Misc. Coll. 50: 523. 1908. TYPE: "Greene of 1870, in Herb. Mo. Bot. Gard... COLORADO (E. L. Greene of [October] 1870, Golden City...)," Mo.

Opuntia mesacantha Raf. var. oplocarpa Coulter, Contr. U.S. Nat. Herb. 3: 431. 1896. O. oplocarpa Engelm. ex Coulter, loc. cit., pro syn. The combination O. mesacantha var. sphaerocarpa Coulter ex Wooton & Standley, Contr. U.S. Nat. Herb. 19: 446. 1915, pro syn., was an inadvertance, the epithet oplocarpa having been intended. O. rafinesquei Engelm. f. oplocarpa Schelle, Handb. Kakteenkultur 50. 1907. TYPE: "Greene of 1870 in Herb. Mo. Bot. Gard....COLORADO (E. L. Greene of [October] 1870. Golden City)...." Mo.

Opuntia plumbea Rose, Smithsonian Misc. Coll. 50: 524. 1908. TYPE: "...F. V. Coville in the San Carlos Indian Reservation, Arizona, altitude 1,500 meters, June [28], 1904...." US 399804, photographs, US, NY. ISOTYPE: Pom 306405.

Opuntia utahensis J. A. Purpus, Monatsschr. Kakteenk. 19: 133. 1909, not O. sphaerocarpa Engelm. var. utahensis Engelm. in 1863, not O. erinacea Engelm. var. utahensis L. Benson in 1969. "Utah, Piñonvalley Mountains bei 2300 m. C. A. Purpus 1900." J. A. Purpus was Inspektor des Botanischen Gartens in Darmstadt. A specimen of "Opuntia utahensis J. A. Purpus," US, from plants grown in the Botanical Garden at Darmstadt in 1909, was identified by J. N. Rose as O. rhodantha (O. erinacea var. utahensis). However, the plants were O. macrorhiza Engelm. NEOTYPE designation: Rose 17206, collected Bot. Gard., Darmstadt, grown, then pressed June 22, 1902, US 638961; photographs, NY, US.

Opuntia roseana Mackensen, Bull. Torrey Club 38: 142. April 7, 1911. "...Kerrville, Texas, in May, 1910...." TYPE: US 618290. ISOTYPES: Pom 313584, NY, BH (probably this plant). Cuttings from the type plant, US 2436902; Pom 288235.

Opuntia leptocarpa Mackensen, Bull. Torrey Club 38: 141. April 7, 1911. TYPE: US 618292. ISOTYPES: "San Antonio, B. Mackensen in 1910," NY (3), Pom 314635. Habitat photo by Mackensen, US. "From seed from Mackensen." "Collected at Sinclair Farm, San Antonio, Texas," Griffiths 9024 (P.I.G. 10540), Pom 287277; P.I.G. 14072, US 2576292A, Pom 288236.

Opuntia mackensenii Rose, Contr. U.S. Nat. Herb. 13: 310. pl. 67. April 11, 1911. "...Bernard Mackensen, near Kerrville, Texas, August, 1909." TYPE: US 617434. ISOTYPES: NY (2), Pom 313578. Plants intermediate between O. macrorhiza and O. phaeacantha var. major.

Opuntia sanguinocula Griffiths, Proc. Biol. Soc. Wash. 27: 26. 1914. Griffiths "...9359...near Taylor, Texas, in July, 1908...description from cultivated plants at Chico, California, July, 1913." TYPE: US 2571051A. ISOTYPE: Pom 288117.

Opuntia seguina C. Z. Nelson, Galesburg Republican Register. July 20, 1915; Trans. Ill. Acad. Sci. 12: 120. 1919. "Type loc: Seguin, Texas." LECTOTYPE designation: Cultivated, Galesburg, C. Z. Nelson in 1916, US.
Opuntia loomisii Peebles, Cactus & Succ. Jour. 9: 109. photographs. 1938. TYPE: "H. F. Loomis No. SF 298, Prescott, Arizona, Aug. 10, 1930, US 1699995; photographs of type plant, US. ISOTYPE: Ariz 94345.

CALIFORNIA. SAN BERNARDINO CO. N side of Clark Mt., C. H. Bonner, Dec., 1961, Pom.

IDAHO. MINIDOKA CO. Minidoka, Nelson & Macbride 1990, GH. BANNOCK CO. Pocatello, Blankinship, June 27, 1902, NMC.

WYOMING. LARAMIE CO. "Shyenn--," Hayden, July 13(?), 1859, Mo.

UTAH. WASHINGTON CO. Stratton Ranch, SE of Central, F. W. Gould 1534, UC. SALT LAKE CO. Salt Lake City, A. O. Garrett 2143, Nov., 1909, US, Pom, US (photo). GARFIELD CO. Hell's Backbone road from Boulder, L. Benson 16603, Pom. KANE CO. Johnson, M. E. Jones 5289, May 23, 1894, US. SAN JUAN CO. Pinyon Valley, La Sal Mts., from Darmstadt Bot. Gard. ex C. A. Purpus, Rose 17206, June 22, 1912, US 638961 (photo), NY, Griffiths 10743, US, Pom; Cumings Mesa, A. J. Lindsey, April 22, 1960, MNA.

MINNESOTA. YELLOW MEDICINE CO. Granite Falls, L. R. Moyer 362, July 20, 1913, NY. NICOLLET CO. Upper St. Peters, Parry in 1848, ISC.

WISCONSIN. MARQUETTE CO. Budsin Corners, D. Ugent, Aug. 9, 1960, Pom. GREEN LAKE CO. Marquette, McAtee, Nov. 5, 1908, US, Fassett, Uhler, Warren, & McLaughlin 9203, CU, F, Shinners 3424, Sept. 10, 1940, UPa. SAUK CO. Baraboo, T. J. Hale in 1861, US, Ph, GH, YU; "Cactus Bluff" along Wisconsin River, D. Ugent 60-10h, July 17, 1960, Pom; Top of Lodi Mills Bluff, D. Ugent, July 13, 1960, Pom (2). DANE CO. Between Mazomanie and Sauk City, Univ. of Wisc. Botany 162 class, Sept. 28, 1935, GH; Mazomanie, D. Ugent 60-7b, July 17, 1960, Pom, 60-7f, July 17, 1960, Pom; Pine Bluff, D. Ugent, July 17, 1960, Pom; Sandstone ledge, Ugent & Clarke, July 21, 1960, Pom, Fassett 3100, NY, GH.

MICHIGAN. MUSKEGON CO. Whitehall Twp., Voss 2861, SMU

IOWA. ALLAMAKEE CO. Elon, A. Haydon 4085 in 1937, Ph. POLK CO. Sandy prairie at Polk City, T. Van Bruggen 3127, UC.

ILLINOIS. LA SALLE CO. Ottawa, H. L. Bottwood, June 1, 19--, YU. HENDERSON CO. N of Oquawka, H. N. Patterson, June 29, 1892, F; Oquawka, H. N. Patterson, F.

OHIO. HAMILTON CO. E of Cincinnati, R. R. Cut [introduced], Wherry, Sept. 10, 1922, NY, US.

LOUISIANA. CAMERON PARISH. Cameron, McAtee 1953, Dec. 3, 1910, NY, 1955, Dec. 3, 1910, NY. PARISH UNCERTAIN. Sparta, Thieret in 1968, Pom.

Epithet Applied to Hybrid Plants

Opuntia grandiflora Engelm. Proc. Amer. Acad. 3: 295. 1857 (preprint, 1856). O. rafinesquei Engelm. var. grandiflora Engelm. U.S. Senate Rept. Expl. & Surv. R. R. Route Pacific Ocean. Botany 4: 55. pl. 11, f. 2-3. 1857. O. mesacantha Raf. var. grandiflora Coulter, Contr. U.S. Nat. Herb. 3: 429. 1896. O. grandiflora Small, Fl. S.E. U.S. 816, 1335. 1903. O. compressa (Salisb.) Macbr. var. grandiflora Weniger, Cacti S. W. 210. 1970, nom. nud. (Art. 33). "On the Brazos, Texas." LECTOTYPE designation: "Industry, Texas, sent by Lindheimer, cult. St. Louis, June 1847," Mo (fl.), and Engelmann's figure (cited above), which shows a joint of the plant. This is a large-flowered Texan Gulf Coast plant with spineless joints. It is intermediate (except for the large flowers) between O. macrorhiza and O. stricta. Hybrids of these species with O. lindheimeri, probable source of the large flowers, are not uncommon.

35b. Opuntia macrorhiza var. pottsii (Salm-Dyck) L. Benson
Opuntia pottsii Salm-Dyck, Cact. Hort. Dyck. 1849: 236. 1850. O. macrorhiza Engelm. var. pottsii L. Benson, Cacti Ariz.

ed. 3. 20, 89. 1969. "Recenter cura Dom. Potts e Chihuahua...." No specimen preserved. NEOTYPE (Benson, loc. cit.): "'Vicinity of Chihuahua; altitude 1,300 meters,' Edward Palmer 124, April 8-27, 1908, Mo 1797126." DUPLICATE: US.

Opuntia setispina Engelm. in Salm-Dyck, Cact. Hort. Dyck. 1849. 239. 1850. No locality or specimen. According to Engelmann, Proc. Amer. Acad. 3: 294. 1857 (preprint, 1856), "Pine woods in the mountains west of Chihuahua [Mexico], Dr. Wislizenus." LECTOTYPE designation: "Mountains of Cosihuiriachi," Wislizenus, Nov., 1846, Mo.

The date of publication of Opuntia pottsii Salm-Dyck and of O. setispina Engelm. in Salm-Dyck is 1850 (title page). The signature of the "Lectore benevolo" introducing Salm-Dyck's work is dated "...ultimo die Decembris 1849." If this date (December 31, 1849) represents completion of the manuscript, publication probably did not occur as early as January 13, 1850, and O. macrorhiza Engelm. (cf. above), published then, is taken to have priority.

Opuntia tenuispina Engelm. & Bigelow, Proc. Amer. Acad. 3: 294. 1857 (preprint, 1856); in Emory, Rept. U.S. & Mex. Bound. Surv. 2: Cactaceae 50. pl. 75, f. 14 (seed). 1859. O. phaeacantha Engelm. var. tenuispina Weniger, Cacti S. W. 197. 1970, nom. nud. (Art. 33). "Sand-hills on the Rio Grande near El Paso, from Doña Ana to San Elizario, Wright; fl. May." LECTOTYPE designation: "Sandy hillocks below El Paso," Charles Wright 332, May 19, 1852, Mo, photograph, US. DUPLICATE: Pom 317702.

Opuntia filipendula Engelm. Proc. Amer. Acad. 3: 294. 1857 (preprint, 1856); in Emory, Rept. U.S. & Mex. Bound. Surv. 2: Cactaceae 51. pl. 68. 1859. "...Near Doña Ana, about El Paso, and at San Elizario, below it...between El Paso and the Limpia, Wright, fl. May and June." LECTOTYPE designation: "Rio Grande bottom near San Elisario," Charles Wright 337, May 29, 1852," Mo; photograph Pom 317793. DUPLICATE: GH.

Opuntia ballii Rose, Contr. U.S. Nat. Herb. 13: 309. pl. 64. April 11, 1911. "...C. R. Ball at Pecos, Texas, August 1909 (no. 1506)." TYPE: US 615499. ISOTYPES: NY, Pom 306407.

Opuntia delicata Rose, Contr. U.S. Nat. Herb. 13: 310. April 11, 1911. TYPE: "...J. N. Rose at Calabas[s]. April 30, 1908 (no. 11951)," Santa Cruz County, Arizona, US 454622.

36. Opuntia littoralis Engelmann

36a. Opuntia littoralis var. littoralis

Opuntia engelmannii Salm-Dyck var. littoralis Engelm. in Brewer & Watson, Bot. Calif. 1: 248. 1876. O. lindheimeri Engelm. var. littoralis Coulter, Contr. U.S. Nat. Herb. 3: 422. 1896. O. littoralis Cockerell, Bull. So. Calif. Acad. Sci. 4: 15. 1905. O. engelmannii Salm-Dyck f. littoralis Schelle, Handb. Kakteenkultur 52. 1907. O. occidentalis Engelm. var. littoralis Parish in Jepson, Man. Fl. Pl. Calif. 657. 1925. "...Coast from Santa Barbara and the islands in its Gulf (O. Tittman) to San Diego, and southward, G. N. Hitchcock." Tittmann's collection from the islands is of fruit alone; his mainland collection produced a much better specimen. Collection by Hitchcock not found, Mo, UC (State Geological Survey collection upon which the Botany of California was based), or YU (Brewer Collection). LECTOTYPE (Benson & Walkington, Ann. Mo. Bot. Gard. 52: 268. 1965): "Santa Barbara, California, Otto Tittmann, Jan., 1874, Mo." DUPLICATE: Pom 317794. The statement of Coulter, loc. cit., is difficult to understand, "Type, Tittum [Tittmann ?] and Mallinckrodt of 1874 in Herb. Mo. Bot. Gard." No collection found.

Opuntia semispinosa Griffiths, Bull. Torrey Club 43: 89. 1916. Griffiths "...10353...San Pedro, California, September 22, 1911." TYPE: US 2437085. ISOTYPE: Pom 290309. Status doubtful.

36b. Opuntia littoralis var. vaseyi (Coulter) Benson & Walkington

Opuntia mesacantha Raf. var. vaseyi Coulter, Contr. U.S. Nat. Herb. 3: 431. 1896. O. rafinesquei Engelm. var. vaseyi K. Schum. Gesamtb. Kakteen 717. 1898. O. humifusa Raf. var. vaseyi Heller, Cat. N. Amer. Pl. ed. 2. 8. 1900. O. vaseyi Britton & Rose, Smithsonian Misc. Coll. 50: 532. Feb. 28, 1908. O. covillei Britton & Rose var. vaseyi Engelm. ex Anon., Des. Pl. Life 18: 12. 1946, erroneously ascribed to Engelmann. O. occidentalis Engelm. & Bigelow var. vaseyi Munz, Aliso 4: 94. 1958. O. littoralis (Engelm.) Cockerell var. vaseyi Benson & Walkington, Ann. Mo. Bot. Gard. 52: 268. 1965. "Type in Nat. Herb. Western Arizona. Specimens examined: Arizona (G. R. Vasey of 1881, Yuma; H. H. Rusby of 1883, Ft. Verde)." LECTOTYPE (Benson & Walkington, Ann. Mo. Bot. Gard. 52: 269. 1965): "Yuma, Arizona, G. R. Vasey in 1881, US 62,105, photographs Pom 175,019, NY, US...." DUPLICATE: Ph. Various authors have followed Britton & Rose, Cactaceae 1: 146. 1919, in discounting the Arizonan locality as erroneous and in attributing the epithet to this variety because the Vasey collection is clearly of this taxon.

Opuntia covillei Britton & Rose, Smithsonian Misc. Coll. 50: 532. Feb. 28, 1908. O. occidentalis Engelm. & Bigelow var. covillei Parish in Jepson, Man. Fl. Pl. Calif. 657. 1925. O. phaeacantha Engelm. var. covillei Fosberg, Bull. So. Calif. Acad.

Sci. 33: 102. 1934. "...San Bernardino, California, by G. R. Vasey in 1891...." TYPE: US 40809; photograph, Pom 175019.

Opuntia magenta Griffiths, Rept. Mo. Bot. Gard. 19: 268. Nov. 9, 1908. O. vaseyi (Coulter) Britton & Rose var. magenta Parish in Jepson, Man. Fl. Pl. Calif. 657. 1925. "...No. 7876 D. Griffiths...Redlands, California, May, 1905." TYPE: US 2572045A. These plants combine characters of var. vaseyi and var. austrocalifornica, but the combinations are much nearer those of the former.

Opuntia intricata Griffiths, Proc. Biol. Soc. Wash. 29: 10. 1916. Griffiths "...10,372 from near San Bernardino, California, May, 1912." TYPE: US 2571223A. ISOTYPE: Pom 288599. Tending toward var. austrocalifornica, but not that variety.

Opuntia rubiflora Davidson, Bull. So. Calif. Acad. Sci. 15: 33. July, 1916, not O. rubiflora Griffiths, Bull. Torrey Club 43: 529. Nov. 7, 1916. "Type station Hollywood reservoir." Type not found in any southern Californian herbarium. According to Bonnie C. Templeton, Los Angeles Co. Museum, letter of April 1, 1970: "The type of Opuntia rubiflora Davidson does not appear to be in the Type Collection...A number of types [or taxa described by]... Davidson are not [here]. Some had been deposited in other institutions and others were held by the original collectors. During the early part of the [Second World] war years, when it became necessary to store all type material and rare objects in a depository in Colorado, I made a record of all types in the Museum's collection...; the type you are interested in does not appear in these records either." According to Louis C. Wheeler, letter of June 5, 1970, neither this specimen nor probably any other of Davidson's is in the Herbarium of the University of Southern California. LECTOTYPE designation: photograph, original publication.

36c. Opuntia littoralis var. austrocalifornica Benson & Walkington

Opuntia littoralis (Engelm.) Cockerell var. austrocalifornica Benson & Walkington, Ann. Mo. Bot. Gard. 52: 269. 1965. "Sand and gravel, coastal sagebrush (a successional, disturbed) phase of the California Chaparral, just SE of Indian Hill, Claremont, Los Angeles County, California, Lyman Benson 15,132, June 3, 1953. Type: Pom 285,263."

CALIFORNIA. LOS ANGELES CO. SE of Indian Hill, Claremont, L. Benson 15132, Pom. SAN BERNARDINO CO. 5 mi. above San Bernardino on Cajon Pass Road, Wiggins 8771, DS; near San Bernardino, Parish 10491, in 1916, NY; San Bernardino Valley, Parish 10975, May, 1916, DS; San Bernardino, Griffiths 10598, US, E. Wiegand 165, Pom. RIVERSIDE CO. 3 mi. SE of Redlands, Crystal Springs, L. Benson 15617, Pom; Santa Rosa Mts., 3 1/2 mi. E of Anza on road to Palms-to-Pines Hwy., C. B. Wolf 9421, RSA, US (box), DS (box).

36d. Opuntia littoralis var. piercei (Fosberg) Benson & Walkington

Opuntia phaeacantha Engelm. var. piercei Fosberg, Bull. So. Calif. Acad. Sci. 33: 102. 1934. O. covillei Britton & Rose var. piercei Munz, Man. So. Calif. Bot. 327. 1935. O. occidentalis Engelm. & Bigelow var. piercei Munz, Aliso 4: 94. 1958. O. littoralis Cockerell var. piercei Benson & Walkington, Ann. Mo. Bot. Gard. 52: 270. 1965. "...Fosberg No. 8637 from Gold Mountain, San Bernardino Mountains, San Bernardino County, Calif., above Baldwin Lake, altitude 2,100 m. approximately." TYPE: Pom 220076.

CALIFORNIA. SAN BERNARDINO CO. San Bernardino Mts. Whiskey Spring, Bear Valley, Parish 2951, June 19, 1894, DS (near var. vaseyi); Gold Mt. above Baldwin Lake, Fosberg 8637, Pom; N side of Baldwin Lake, L. & R. L. Benson 14764, Pom; Baldwin Lake, Parish 10805, June 17, 1916, US, 10969, June 16, 1916, UC; Doble Mine (Lucky Baldwin Mine), L. Benson, P. C. Baker, & J. Adams 16650, Pom; Doble [Mine?], Stark, Sept. 5, 1931, RSA; Doble to Arrastre Flat, Peirson 9013, RSA; desert side of Johnson Grade 3.1 mi. below summit, C. B. Wolf 9912, RSA; 1/2 mi. N of Cactus Flats, desert slope San Bernardino Mts., Stark, May 28, 1933, RSA, DS; S Fork Santa Ana River E of Barton Flats, L. Benson 15400, Pom (2), 15608, Pom, 15609, Pom (3), 15610, Pom.

36e. Opuntia littoralis var. martiniana (L. Benson) L. Benson

Opuntia charlestonensis Clokey, Madroño 7: 71. pl. 4. f. C. 1943. O. phaeacantha Engelm. var. charlestonensis Backeberg, Cactaceae 1: 508. 1958. "...Griffith's mine [Charleston Mountains, Clark County, Nevada]...about 2450 meters, Clokey 7203, 7592, 8029 (type), 8688, 8770. Flower, July to August; fruit September to October." TYPE: UC 905408. ISOTYPES: UC 872654, Pom 265222, 275346, Mo 1244224, BM (2 sheets), WillU 30243, OSC, UO, GH, US 1828521, Ph 815139, Ill, BH, F 1120167, Mich (2), NY, WTU 74008, USNA 289548, 289570, USFS 94507, SMU, Ariz, Tex. The type colony (L. Benson 15075, Pom, 15076, Pom, 15077, Pom) shows, as do some other populations of var. martiniana, a tendency toward inclusion of some characters of O. phaeacantha var. major, which occurs at lower elevations. The holotype has some flattened spines in each areole; particularly the single (moderate-sized) deflexed spine is flattened and rather slender. The upper spines are pale gray or whitish and flattened, the lower are yellow or red and acicular.

Opuntia macrocentra Engelm. var. martiniana L. Benson, Cacti Ariz. ed. 2. 64. 1950. O. littoralis (Engelm.) Cockerell var.

martiniana L. Benson, Ann. Mo. Bot. Gard. 52: 270. 1965. "King-
man Road on the north side of Hualpai Mountain, Mohave County,
Arizona, L. Benson 10169, March 30, 1940." TYPE: Pom 274107.
ISOTYPE: Ariz (not found in 1965).

CALIFORNIA. SAN BERNARDINO CO. S of Cima, Stark, June 28,
1931, RSA; Barnwell, C. B. Wolf 3296, RSA.

37. Opuntia atrispina Griffiths

Opuntia atrispina Griffiths, Rept. Mo. Bot. Gard. 21: 172.
pl. 26, lower. 1910. "...9411 D. G. [David Griffiths]...near
Devil's River [Val Verde Co.], Texas, July 20, 1908." TYPE: US
2576305A, 2576306A. ISOTYPE: Pom 288123.

Opuntia macrocentra Engelm. var. minor Anthony, Amer. Midl.
Nat. 55: 244. f. 21. 1956. "PRESIDIO CO.: ...2700 ft., 1.4 mi.
from Ruidosa along road to Presidio, Aug. 26, 1948, [Anthony] No.
1081." TYPE: Mich. ISOTYPE: US 2346133. The character combination is with some tendency toward those of O. violacea var. macrocentra. Another collection (Santa Elena Canyon, Big Bend National
Park, Brewster County, Anthony 1211, Mich) suggests O. violacea
var. castetteri.

TEXAS. TAYLOR CO. Camp Barkley, Abilene, Tolstead 7685, SMU
(2). MITCHELL CO. Colorado City, Pohl 5145, SMU. NOLAN CO. 8
mi. S of Sweetwater, C. H. Muller 8669, LL. BEE CO. Blanconis,
E. Martin, spring, 1915, YU. UVALDE CO. Near local road 1022, D.
Weniger 196, June 21, 1963, UNM, SW corner of county, D. Weniger
197A & B, June 21, 1963, UNM.

38. Opuntia violacea Engelmann

38a. Opuntia violacea var. violacea

Opuntia violacea Engelm. in Emory, Notes Mil. Reconn. Ft.
Leavenworth to San Diego. App. 2. 157. f. 8. May-July, 1848.
"October 28th, 1846, common on the Gila." On October 26-27, the
expedition camped on the Gila River opposite the mouth of Bonita
Creek about 6 miles east and a little north of Solomon, Graham
Co., Arizona. October 28: "One or two miles ride, and we were
clear of the Black mountains, and again in the valley of the Gila,
which widened out gradually to the base of Mount Graham, abreast
of which we encamped. Almost for the whole distance, twenty
miles...." NEOTYPE (L. Benson, Cacti Ariz. ed. 3. 21. 1969):
"Four miles east and a little north of Solomon: steeply slanting
embankment above the bottomlands of the south side of the Gila
River two or three miles above the mouth of Bonita Creek; 3,100
feet elevation, Lyman Benson 16,632, April 22, 1966," Pom 311337
(from the first point at which large, conspicuously violet, specimens were encountered as described by Emory).

TEXAS. HUDSPETH CO. Sierra Blanca, Neally or Evans in 1891,
US, Rose, Standley, & Russell 12230, US.

38b. Opuntia violacea var. gosseliniana (Weber) L. Benson

Opuntia gosseliniana Weber, Bull. Soc. Acclim. France 49: 83.
1902. O. violacea Engelm. var. gosseliniana L. Benson, Cacti
Ariz. ed. 3. 21, 92. 1969. "...Du littoral de la Sonora et s'est
trouvée parmi les Cactées qui y ont été recueillies en 1897
par...M. Leon Diguet." LECTOTYPE designation: Roland-Gosselin.
f. 309 in 1904, P (two flowers). Cited (Benson loc. cit.) as the
type.

ARIZONA. PIMA CO. Quijotoa Mts., E. R. Blakley 189, March
6, 1951, Des; Twin Buttes, S of Tucson Mts., L. Benson 8868, Pom;
Florida Canyon, Santa Rita Mts., L. Benson 9748, Pom.

38c. Opuntia violacea var. santa-rita (Griffiths) L. Benson

Opuntia chlorotica Engelm. var. santa-rita Griffiths & Hare,
N. Mex. Agric. Exp. Sta. Bull. 60: 64. 1906. O. santa-rita Rose,
Smithsonian Misc. Coll. 52: 195. 1908. O. gosseliniana Weber
var. santa-rita L. Benson, Cacti Ariz. ed. 2. 65. 1950. O. vio-
lacea Engelm. var. santa-rita L. Benson, Cacti Ariz. ed. 3. 21,
92. 1969. "...No. 8157 D. G. [David Griffiths]...Celero [Santa
Rita] mountains, Arizona, October 8, 1905." Pima Co. TYPE:
US 2607623. ISOTYPE: Pom 287241.

Opuntia shreveana C. Z. Nelson, Galesburg Republican Register, July 20, 1915; Trans. Ill. Acad. Sci. 12: 121. 1919. "Type
loc: Tucson, Arizona." Nelson corresponded with Forrest Shreve,
Desert Laboratory, Tucson.

38d. Opuntia violacea var. macrocentra (Engelmann) L. Benson

Opuntia macrocentra Engelm. Proc. Amer. Acad. 3: 292. 1857
(preprint, 1856); in Emory, Rept. U.S. & Mex. Bound. Surv. 2:
Cactaceae 49. pl. 75, f. 8. (seeds). 1859. O. violacea Engelm.
var. macrocentra L. Benson, Cacti Ariz. ed. 3. 21, 92. 1969.
"...Rio Grande near El Paso, also on the Limpia, Wright. fl. in
May." LECTOTYPE designation: "Sandhills in the Rio Grande Bottom, near El Paso, Charles Wright" in 1852, Mo (on 2 sheets, "May,
1852," on 1).

ARIZONA. PIMA CO. N end of Coyote Mts., Wiggins 8680, US,
DS. COCHISE CO. Benson, Rose 11961, US, Rose, Standley, & Russ-
ell 12231, US; E of Benson, Toumey, Sept. 20, 1898, US; Bowie,
Toumey, Aug. 2, ____, US; Bisbee, Toumey, Sept. 20, 1898, US.
Some other collections are intermediate between vars. violacea and
macrocentra.

TEXAS. TERRELL CO. W of Sanderson, Anthony 739, Mich, 742,
US. WEBB CO. Laredo, Griffiths 8638, US. LA SALLE CO. Encinal,
Griffiths 6365, US.

38e. Opuntia violacea var. castetteri L. Benson

Opuntia violacea Engelm. var. castetteri L. Benson Cactus &
Succ. Jour. 41: 125. 1969. "Hueco Mountains south of U.S. 62
and 180 (combined), 4,300 feet elevation, limestone, Lyman & Robert
L. Benson 15,433, July 11, 1955." TYPE: Pom 284747 (on 2 sheets).

ARIZONA. COCHISE CO. San Pedro Valley, Toumey, July 28,
1894, US, Aug. 2, ____, US.

NEW MEXICO. OTERO.CO. Hueco Mts., N of Hueco Tanks, Castet-
ter 545, UNM, Pom, 546 & 547A-C, UNM, P. Pierce, Nov., 1961, Pom;
Alamo Mt., J. Findley (C920), UNM; Orange [near Oro Grande],
Pillsbry, Oct. 26-30, 1922, Ph. The following collections approach
var. castetteri: SIERRA CO. 5 mi. N of Truth or Consequences,
Castetter 455, June 12, 1954, UNM. HIDALGO CO. Granite Pass,
Little Hatchet Mts., Castetter 2174, Oct., 1956, UNM.

. TEXAS. EL PASO CO. U.S. 62 and 180, Hueco Mts., L. & R. L.
Benson 15433, Pom (2). PRESIDIO CO. Marfa, C. Champie, in 1965,
Pom. BREWSTER CO. About 40 mi. S of Alpine, L. & R. L. Benson
15481, July 15, 1955, Pom (transitional to vars. gosseliniana &
macrocentra). REEVES CO. Pecos, Rose & Fitch 17902, US. CRANE
CO. W of Crane, Warnock & Mullins 14388, SRSC.

39. Opuntia phaeacantha Engelmann

39a. Opuntia phaeacantha var. phaeacantha

Opuntia phaeacantha Engelm. Pl. Fendl., Mem. Amer. Acad. 4:
52. 1849. "...About Santa Fé, and on the Rio Grande...flowering
in May and June." Engelmann described two plants, the first later
forming the basis for his var. nigricans (Proc. Amer. Acad. 3: 293.
1857 [preprint, 1856]), this being var. α and, according to his
custom, the typical variety. The second, a larger plant with fewer
spines, was the basis for his var. major (loc. cit.), described
below. The flowers described for O. phaeacantha are from some member of the Polyacanthae, and Engelmann later excluded them (in
Emory, Rept. U.S. & Mex. Bound. Surv. 2: Cactaceae 50. 1859 and
in Ives, Rept. Colo. River 14. 1861). LECTOTYPE designation:
"Santa Fe, near the Rio del Norte [Rio Grande], A. Fendler, Nov.,
1846," Mo; photograph, US. The plant has long spines over the
upper two-thirds of the joint.

Opuntia dulcis Engelm. Proc. Amer. Acad. 3: 291. 1857 (preprint, 1856); in Emory, Rept. U.S. & Mex. Bound. Surv. 2: Cactaceae 48. pl. 75, f. 5-7 (seeds). 1859. O. lindheimeri Engelm.
var. dulcis Coulter, Contr. U.S. Nat. Herb. 3: 421. 1896. O.
engelmannii Salm-Dyck var. dulcis Engelm. ex K. Schum. Gesamtb.
Kakteen 3: 421. 1896, incorrectly ascribed to Engelmann. "...Rio
Grande, near Presidio del Norte, &c....very sweet fruit." LECTO-
TYPE designation: "El Paso ??" "West Texas ? Sweet!" Wright in
1852, Mo.

Opuntia zuniensis Griffiths, Bull. Torrey Club 43: 86. 1916.
"...Near Zuni, New Mexico, August 31, 1911...[Griffiths] 10345."
TYPE: US 2436949. ISOTYPE: Pom 288211.

UTAH. SAN JUAN CO. La Sal Mts., Griffiths 10743, US, Pom.

TEXAS. "El Paso? West Texas? Probably Presidio del Norte
[more likely not]" (lectotype of Opuntia dulcis Engelm.), Wright
in 1852, Mo. JEFF DAVIS CO. SE of Ft. Davis, D. Weniger 373,
Oct., 1963, UNM. BREWSTER CO. Victor Pierce Ranch, Glass Mts.,
Anthony 1161, Mich; Allison Ranch, Glass Mts., Anthony 695, Mich.
TERRELL CO. 5 mi. E of Dryden, D. Weniger 84, Apr. 16, 1963, UNM.

39b. Opuntia phaeacantha var. camanchica
(Engelmann & Bigelow) L. Benson

Opuntia camanchica Engelm. & Bigelow, Proc. Amer. Acad. 3:
293. 1857 (preprint, 1856); U.S. Senate Rept. Expl. & Surv. R. R.
Route Pacific Ocean. Botany 4: 40. pl. 9, f. 1-5. 1857. O.
phaeacantha Engelm. subsp. camanchica Borg, Cacti ed. 2. 96.
1951. O. phaeacantha Engelm. var. camanchica L. Benson, Cactus &
Succ. Jour. 41: 125. 1969. O. phaeacantha Engelm. var. camanchica
Weniger, Cacti S. W. 196. 1970, nom. nud. (Art. 33). "...Llano
Estacado...to the Tucumcari hills, near...the Canadian River."
LECTOTYPE (Benson, 1969): "'Plains,' J. M. Bigelow, Sept. 23,
1853," Mo. The expedition was at Tucumcari Peak on Sept. 21, 1853.

Opuntia camanchica Engelm. & Bigelow vars. albispina, longispina, major, gigantea, minor, pallida, rubra, and salmonea Hort
ex Borg, Cacti ed. 2. 96-97. 1951, nomina nud. (without Latin
diagnoses). No localities or specimens. All these and f. orbic-

ularis appeared earlier as formae, Schelle, Handb. Kakteenkultur 53. 1907, nom. nud., but Borg gave no reference.

NEW MEXICO. LINCOLN CO. 5 mi. SW of Ancho, Wooton 3025, NMC. SAN MIGUEL CO. Plains [Bigelow was at Tucumcari on Sept. 16 & 21, 1853, headed westward], Bigelow, Sept. 23, 1853, Mo. GUADALUPE CO. Anton Chico, Griffiths 10329, US, Pom. QUAY CO. Tucumcari, Griffiths 10664, US, Pom (2 + photos), Tex (2); Tucumcari Peak, L. Benson 14706, Pom (2). CURRY CO. Clovis, P. Pierce 2209A-B, Oct. 18, 1963, UNM. CHAVES CO. 3 mi. S of Hagerman, Castetter 103, Pom. EDDY CO. N of Loving, D. Weniger 330, Oct. 14, 1963, UNM. The following collections represent plants intermediate between var. camanchica and var. major: QUAY CO. Llano Estacado, Bigelow, Sept. 21, 1853, Mo, US (photograph), Sept. 16, 1853, Mo; Tucumcari hills, Bigelow, Sept. 16, 1853, Mo.

OKLAHOMA. CIMARRON CO. West Carrizo Creek, N of Black Mesa, W of Kenton, Waterfall 8665, Aug. 23, 1948, Ph. ELLIS CO. Pack Saddle Bridge, Canadian River Valley, Goodman 2581, Mo. MAJOR CO. W of Orienta, D. Weniger 584, June, 1964, UNM. GREER CO. 3 mi. SW of Mangum, L. & R. L. Benson 15654, Pom; 1/2 mi. W of Mangum, D. Weniger 6, UNM, 112, UNM, 613, UNM. MURRAY CO. Arbuckle Mts., W. H. Emig, Aug. 20, 1917, Mo (box). MARSHALL CO. 5 mi. NE of Madill, D. Weniger 557, June, 1964, UNM. JOHNSTON CO. Top of Devil's Canyon [Devil's Den?], Little 3958, Sept. 26, 1936, GH.

TEXAS. HUTCHINSON CO. SW of Plemons, Griffiths 10658, US, Pom, Tex, 10659, US, Pom. RANDALL CO. Canyon City, Griffiths 9326, US, Pom. BRISCOE CO. Between Silverton and Memphis, L. & R. L. Benson 15651, Pom. FLOYD CO. Floydada, D. Weniger 286, 287, Sept. 1, 1963, UNM. LAMPASAS CO. Lampasas, Griffiths 9348, US, Pom. GREGG CO. Longview, Griffiths 10552, US, Pom.

MISSOURI. JASPER CO. Webb City, E. J. Palmer, Oct. 12, 1909, NY, US (photograph).

39c. Opuntia phaeacantha var. spinosibacca (Anthony) L. Benson

Opuntia spinosibacca Anthony, Amer. Midl. Nat. 55: 246. f. 22-23. 1956. O. phaeacantha Engelm. var. spinosibacca L. Benson, Cactus & Succ. Jour. 41: 125. 1969. "...Limestone hill just west of ranger's quarters, Boquillas, Big Bend National Park, Brewster County, Texas." TYPE: Mich (unmounted in 1964). ISOTYPE: US 2346076.

TEXAS. PRESIDIO CO. Ruidosa, Anthony 1073, Mich. BREWSTER CO. Glass Mts., Anthony 1154, US; Nine-point Mesa, Anthony 1270, Mich; 7 mi. S of Terlingua, Anthony 1219, Mich, US, 1186, US; Santa Elena Canyon, Anthony 1209, Mich; N of Painted Desert Jct., L. & R. L. Benson 15508, Pom; Chisos Mts., C. H. Muller 8103, F; 5 mi. SE of Panther Jct., D. Weniger 420, Nov., 1963, UNM; near Hot Springs, Big Bend Nat. Park, D. Weniger 274, Sept. 11, 1963, UNM; Hot Springs to Boquillas, Anthony 235, US, Mich; Boquillas Canyon, Anthony 3, SRSC (3), 7, SRSC; Boquillas, Anthony 36, Mich, 236, Mich (unmounted), 241, Mich, 243, US, Mich, 127, UNM, L. Benson 16507, Pom; mouth of Reagan Canyon, wax factory at Las Vegas de Ladrones, Rio Grande, Warnock & McVaugh 47-412, SRSC (3).

39d. Opuntia phaeacantha var. laevis (Coulter) L. Benson

Opuntia laevis Coulter, Contr. U.S. Nat. Herb. 3: 419. 1896. O. phaeacantha var. laevis L. Benson, Cacti Ariz. ed. 3. 21, 98. 1969. "Pringle of [May 17] 1881 (distributed as O. angustata) in Herb. Coulter. Arizona." TYPE: F 98070. ISOTYPES: Mo, K, Vt, GH, US 795860.

39e. Opuntia phaeacantha var. major Engelmann

Opuntia phaeacantha Engelm. var. major Engelm. Proc. Amer. Acad. 3: 293. 1857 (preprint, 1856). "...near Santa Fé." LECTOTYPE designation: "4 miles east of Santa Fé on the south side of a rocky hill," A. Fendler, Dec. 22, 1846, Mo.

Opuntia engelmannii Salm-Dyck var. cyclodes Engelm. & Bigelow, Proc. Amer. Acad. 3: 291. 1857 (preprint, 1856); U.S. Senate Rept. Expl. & Surv. R. R. Route Pacific Ocean. Botany 4: 37. pl. 8, f. 1. 1857. O. lindheimeri Engelm. var. cyclodes Coulter, Contr. U.S. Nat. Herb. 3: 422. 1896. O. cyclodes Rose, Contr. U.S. Nat. Herb. 13: 309. 1911. "On the upper Pecos, in New Mexico." LECTOTYPE designation: "Hunah [Hanah ?] Creek near the Pecos," J. M. Bigelow, Sept. 25, 1853, Mo.

Opuntia angustata Engelm. & Bigelow, Proc. Amer. Acad. 3: 292. 1857 (preprint, 1856); U.S. Senate Rept. Expl. & Surv. R. R. Route Pacific Ocean. Botany 4: 39. pl. 7, f. 3-4. 1857. O. phaeacantha Engelm. var. angustata Engelm. ex W. T. Marshall, Arizona's Cactuses 39. 1950, incorrectly ascribed to Engelmann. "From the foot of Inscription Rock, near Zuñi [New Mexico], to Williams River, and westward as far as the Cajon Pass of the California mountains." The collection from Inscription Rock, Bigelow, Nov. 18, 1853, Mo, is O. phaeacantha; that from Cajon Pass, Bigelow, March 16, 1854, Mo, is O. littoralis var. vaseyi (fig. 4, adorned with a fruit of O. imbricata or O. whipplei). Britton & Rose, Cactaceae 1: 142. 1919, eliminated these leaving the Bill Williams River collection (fig. 3, showing a fruit not to be found with the specimen) as the basis for O. angustata. LECTOTYPE designation: Bill Williams fork, bottoms, suberect,

J. M. Bigelow, Feb. 4, 1854, Mo; photograph, US. The specimen is an elongate joint, 25 cm long, 10 cm broad. Spines slender, to 2.8 cm. long. The elongation of the joints is the principal feature in common among the three discordant elements included originally in O. angustata.

Opuntia phaeacantha Engelm. var. brunnea Engelm. Proc. Amer. Acad. 3: 293. 1857 (preprint, 1856); in Emory, Rept. U.S. & Mex. Bound. Surv. 2: Cactaceae 50. 1859. O. phaeacantha Engelm. f. brunnea Schelle, Kakteen 72. 1926. "Common about El Paso...[near] river, Wright." LECTOTYPE designation: "Sandhills in the Rio Grande bottoms, El Paso," Charles Wright in 1852, Mo; photograph, US.

Opuntia toumeyi Rose, Contr. U.S. Nat. Herb. 12: 402. May 10, 1909. "...J. N. Rose near Desert Laboratory, Tucson, Arizona, April, 1908 (no. 11750)." TYPE: US 454445.

Opuntia blakeana Rose, Contr. U.S. Nat. Herb. 12: 402. pl. 45. May 10, 1909. "...J. N. Rose near Desert Laboratory, Tucson, Arizona, April, 1908 (no. 11753)." TYPE: US 454451. ISOTYPES: US 2572044A, Pom 313567. Cuttings from type plant, Griffiths 10443, US 2576139A, Pom 288612.

Opuntia gregoriana Griffiths, Rept. Mo. Bot. Gard. 22: 26. 1912. "...Near El Paso, Texas, July 29, 1905...[Griffiths] 8020." TYPE: US 2570047A to 2570049A. ISOTYPE: Pom 287158.

Opuntia confusa Griffiths, Proc. Biol. Soc. Wash. 27: 28. 1914. "...Tumamoc Hill [Griffiths] 10,441...." Tucson, Arizona. TYPE: US 2576135A, 2576136A, 2576137A. ISOTYPE: Pom 291200, 313370.

Opuntia expansa Griffiths, Proc. Biol. Soc. Wash. 29: 14. 1916. Griffiths "...10,324 near Anton Chico, New Mexico, August 1911." TYPE: US 2571227A to 2571231A. ISOTYPE: Pom 288203.

Opuntia recurvospina Griffiths, Proc. Biol. Soc. Wash. 29: 12. 1916. "Near Pantano, Arizona, [Griffiths] 10456." TYPE: US 317781, 2576140A to 2576143A. ISOTYPE: Pom 317781. The number 10456 is duplicated in a collection of O. macrorhiza.

Opuntia caesia Griffiths, Proc. Biol. Soc. Wash. 29: 13. 1916. "...Between Crozier and Hackberry, Arizona, the first of May, 1912,...[Griffiths] 10555." TYPE: US 2576149A. ISOTYPE: Pom 317784.

Opuntia magnarenensis Griffiths, Proc. Biol. Soc. Wash. 29: 9. 1916. "...On the Big Sandy, 30-50 miles south [SE] of Kingman, Arizona...[Griffiths] 10,560,...near Owens Post Office, Arizona, May 3, 1912." LECTOTYPE designation: US 2576148A. DUPLICATE: Pom 317815.

Opuntia flavescens Peebles, Cactus & Succ. Jour. 9: 67. 1937. O. engelmannii Salm-Dyck var. flavescens L. Benson, Cacti Ariz. ed. 2. 58. 1950. "...A. R. Leding No. SF 66, near Sells, Pima County, Arizona, Oct. 30, 1925," TYPE: US 1699997. ISOTYPES: Ariz 94390, 94391, 94393. With some characters of var. discata.

Opuntia woodsii Backeberg, Descriptiones Cactacearum Novarum 10. 1956. "USA (Nevada)." Backeberg, Cactaceae 1: 497, 511. 1958, refers to R. S. Woods, Cact. & Succ. Jour. 8: 94. f. 1936. Described from the literature. No type specimen, but the name, applied before 1958, is valid. Woods' plant was from Zion National Park, Utah [not Nevada]. O. phaeacantha var. discata occurs there, and so does a bewildering array of hybrids derived from it and vars. discata and major and O. erinacea var. utahensis. Doubtless the plant from Zion was one of these, and Mr. Woods' photograph indicates one similar to var. major. The "red" or purplish or lavender flower color probably was contributed by O. erinacea var. utahensis. For a plant with some of the characters taken by Backeberg from Woods' description, cf. flats of Virgin River, Zion Lodge, L. Benson 16020, Pom. This plant was essentially O. phaeacantha var. major with reddish flowers.

CALIFORNIA. SAN LUIS OBISPO CO. San Luis Obispo SW of Cuesta Pass, D. T. MacDougal, Oct. 28, 1920, US, NY; 4 mi. SW of Pozo, T. M. Hendrix 197, May 21, 1937, UC; NW of Stanley, Mt. Nipomo Quadrangle, H. C. Lee 667, June 13, 1936, UC (2); Nipomo, W. H. Brewer 413, Apr. 10, 1861, US; N edge of Santa Maria Valley, Nipomo-Guadalupe Road, R. F. Hoover 1731b, Obi; between Suey Creek and Cuyama River, R. F. Hoover 6479, Obi; 5 mi. E of U.S. 101, Cuyama Valley 32 mi. E on the Santa Maria-Maricopa road, L. Benson 16084, Pom; Cuyama Valley 50 mi. W of Maricopa, L. Benson 5797, Pom. KERN CO. W of La Rosa, Mojave Quadrangle, E. Armstrong 1181A, UC (2). LOS ANGELES CO. Hills W of Palmdale, T. W. Minthorn, June, 1958, RSA; Meadow Wash Canyon, W. H. Earle in 1968, Pom.

NEVADA. LINCOLN CO. Karshaw, Meadow Valley Wash, Goodding 970, CU. CLARK CO. Willow Creek, Spring Mts., Beatley & Reveal 10842, Pom.

UTAH. SAN JUAN CO. Square Flat, Canyonlands Nat. Park, Welsh 7031, BrY; mi. 74 above Lee's Ferry, Glen Canyon, L. Benson 16315, Pom.

COLORADO. MONTROSE CO. Naturita, Payson 3858, US. MONTEZUMA CO. Chapin Mesa, Mesa Verde Nat. Park, J. A. Erdman, S. L. Welsh, & G. Moore 2181, BrY. BOULDER CO. Junction of Colorado Highways 7 & 66 N of Boulder, L. & R. L. Benson 16214, Pom, 16212, Pom; 7 mi. N of Boulder, Weber 3920, Ariz; Boulder, D. M. Andrews in 1900, Mo (photograph). FREMONT CO. Penrose, C. H. Boissevain, Sept., 1941, UC. LAS ANIMAS CO. Trinidad, Biltmore Herb. 1-942, Aug. 26, 1896, US, Rose & Fitch 17519, US. OTERO CO. La Junta, Rose & Fitch 17051, US.

SOUTH DAKOTA. FALL RIVER CO. [Probably Smithwick], Claude A. Barr, June 25 [probably 1939], Mich.

KANSAS. ELLIS CO. Ft. Hayes, T. L. Timmons, June, 1941, Tex. KEARNEY CO. Lakin, Arkansas River, C. R. Ball 1578, US (photograph and fruit).

Names Applied to Hybrids of vars. major, discata, etc.

Opuntia arizonica Griffiths, Rept. Mo. Bot. Gard. 29: 93. pl. 2, f. 8; 10; 13, f. 8, March 22, 1909. "...9559 D. G. [David Griffiths]...near Kirkland, Arizona, September 8, 1908." TYPE: US 2572032A. ISOTYPE: Pom 288135. Intermediate between vars. major and discata.

Opuntia cañada Griffiths, Rept. Mo. Bot. Gard. 20: 90. 1909. O. laevis Coulter var. cañada Peebles, Cactus & Succ. Jour. 9: 68. 1937. "...9593 D. G. [David Griffiths]...Santa Rita Mountains [Pima Co.], Arizona, September 17, 1908." According to Thornber, at the dam just above the Forest Service experiment station in Florida (Stone Cabin) Canyon. TYPE: US 2572071A. ISOTYPES: Pom 288140, Mo. Specimens from the Florida Canyon dam include typical var. laevis (L. Benson 9883, Pom, Ariz) and the O. cañada type (L. Benson 9884, Pom, Ariz, Darrow in 1939 Ariz, Pom. Vars. laevis, major, and discata intergrade freely, forming a variable population at the type locality (Griffiths 7774, US, Pom, 7787, US, Pom, 8159, US, Pom, in April, 1906, US, 8208, US, 8209, Pom, 8219, Pom, 8596, US, 9592, US, Pom, 9596, US, Pom, L. Benson 9845, Pom, 9884, Ariz, Pom, Darrow, Dec. 1, 1939, Ariz, Pom). The plants described as O. cañada are intermediate between those of O. phaeacantha vars. laevis, major, and discata. Plants of about this type occur in the Santa Rita, Santa Catalina, and Baboquivari Mts. The fruits are obovoid, like those of var. laevis, and the spines are similar to those of var. major but distributed over the entire joint. The joints are green, as in var. laevis. The type specimen approaches var. discata.

Opuntia gilvescens Griffiths, Rept. Mo. Bot. Gard. 20: 87. pl. 2, f. 5; 7; 13, f. 6. 1909. "...9619 D. G. [David Griffiths] ...Santa Rita Mountains, Arizona, September 23, 1908." TYPE: US 2572070A. Joints obovate, spiny over half or two-thirds of the surface; base of the fruit not markedly constricted. This plant is almost identical with O. cañada Griffiths, first collected in the same vicinity. The lack of spines on the basal portion of the joint is the only difference worthy of note, and this is variable in the hybrid swarm population in Florida Canyon. One sheet of L. Benson 9884 (cf. above, under Opuntia cañada) is of this type of plant.

39f. **Opuntia phaeacantha** var. **discata** (Griffiths) Benson & Walkington

Opuntia procumbens Engelm. & Bigelow, Proc. Amer. Acad. 3: 292. 1857 (preprint, 1856); U.S. Senate Rept. Expl. & Surv. R. R. Route Pacific Ocean. Botany 4: 39. pl. 6, f. 4-5. 1857. "From the San Francisco mountains [westward] to Cactus Pass, at the head of [Bill] Williams' River, in rocky localities," Arizona. Both the Bigelow collections from the two localities specifically mentioned consist of only 1 or 2 areoles. They are different species. The spine cluster in fig. 5 appears to be from the Cactus Pass collection, a rather long-spined plant of var. discata or probably var. superbospina. The more elaborate fig. 4 probably was reconstructed on the basis of a fragment of a joint forming a collection from Aztec Pass, this showing several areoles, the spine clusters of some matching those in the figure, which are typical of var. discata. The third collection, not figured, from the San Francisco Mts. [Peaks] is O. littoralis var. martiniana. LECTOTYPE designation: "Aztec Pass," J. M. Bigelow, Jan. 22, 1853, Mo. This is not from Aztec, Yuma Co., but a pass in western Yavapai Co. between San Francisco Peaks near Flagstaff, visited (earlier, westward bound) by Bigelow on December 27, 1853. Cactus Pass in Mohave County was visited January 29, 1854. Photograph, US.

Opuntia discata Griffiths, Rept. Mo. Bot. Gard. 19: 265. pl. 27, upper. 1908. O. engelmannii Salm-Dyck var. discata C. Z. Nelson, Galesburg Republican Register, July 20, 1915; Trans. Ill. Acad. Sci. 12: 124. 1919. O. phaeacantha Engelm. var. discata Benson & Walkington, Ann. Mo. Bot. Gard. 52: 265. 1965. "...7790 D. G. [David Griffiths]...foothills of the Santa Rita Mountains [Pima Co.], Arizona, April, 1905." TYPE: US 2572028A, 2572029A, 2572032A. ISOTYPE: Pom 287144.

Opuntia megacarpa Griffiths, Rept. Mo. Bot. Gard. 20: 91. 1909. O. engelmannii Salm-Dyck var. megacarpa Fosberg, Bull. So. Calif. Acad. 33: 100. 1934. O. occidentalis Engelm. & Bigelow var. megacarpa Munz, Aliso 4: 94. 1958. "...9501 D. G. [David Griffiths],...near Banning, California, August 25, 1908." TYPE: US 2572034A, 2572035A. ISOTYPE: Pom 288132 and a plant grown from a seed of the type material, Pom 288145. In this form or possible variety the maximum spine length is 5-7.5 cm. The plant is reminiscent of O. phaeacantha var. superbospina. The epithet has been applied in Californian references to all material of var. discata, rather than to the specialized local plant collected by Griffiths. For this only fairly good matching material has been collected recently, Benson & Walkington 16349, 16350, Pom, near Cabazon and 16345, Pom, near Redlands. In each case the individual plants were associated with others with numerous differing character combinations. The following older collections approach the type of O. megacarpa: SAN BERNARDINO CO. San Bernardino, Vasey in 1881, US 40809. RIVERSIDE CO. Near Riverside, Toumey, Sept. 25, 1896, US, Pom; Banning, Griffiths 8292, US, Pom, Tex, 9501, US, Pom, 9675, US, Pom. SAN DIEGO CO. E of Jacumba, 2,000 feet, MacDougal, May 23, 1913, US. The long spines may have been acquired through interbreeding with O. phaeacantha var. major which occurs nearby.

Opuntia valida Griffiths, Proc. Biol. Soc. Wash. 27: 24. 1914. Griffiths "...9194, vicinity of San Antonio, New Mexico, in 1908." TYPE: US 2572057A. ISOTYPE: Pom 287288.

Opuntia eocarpa Griffiths, Proc. Biol. Soc. Wash. 29: 11. 1916. "...Near Pantano, Arizona, in September, 1911, [Griffiths] 10452." TYPE: US 2576138A.

CALIFORNIA. ORANGE CO. Hills N of Newport Beach, L. Benson 16614, Pom. SAN DIEGO CO. 6 mi. S of Julian, L. Benson 16376, Pom; San Felipe Valley near Banner, L. Benson 15775, Pom, 16378, Pom. INYO CO. Panamint Mts., Coville & Funston 544, April 3, 1891, NY.

UTAH. WASHINGTON CO. Above Springdale, L. Benson 13709, Pom; probably the same place, J. P. Hester 529, US, Pom.

Names of Uncertain Application (perhaps to var. discata)

Opuntia microcarpa Engelm. in Emory, Notes Mil. Reconn. Ft. Leavenworth to San Diego. App. 2. 157. f. 7. May-July, 1848. nom. dub. "'Very abundant on the Del Norte and Gila.' No date or statement whether the figure represents the natural size or smaller." The status of O. phaeacantha, with 10 varieties, depends upon application of the epithet microcarpa, because, unfortunately, this epithet (1848) has priority over phaeacantha (1849). Thus, care in interpretation is of first importance. The fruit measurements in the description require interpretation. Engelmann had only Emory's notes and Stanly's drawing. In view of his statement, "If the figure represents the natural size, this species ought to bear the name O. microcarpa," the fruit length given in the description must represent a misprint or an inadvertence. He could not have intended to say, "...berries...only 3 or 4 inches long." Interpretation of fruit size depends upon the proportions in figure 7, as published. Judging by Engelmann's assessment of the joint-measurements, the original drawing (not found, Mo) must have been about four or five times the size of the reduction. This would allow in the drawing for joints 1 1/2 to 2 1/2 inches long, as assumed doubtfully by Engelmann and, for fruits about 1/4 to 5/8 inch long. No fleshy-fruited prickly pear in the region, not even O. macrorhiza, is commonly of this small size, and the length and distribution of spines do not suggest those of O. macrorhiza. Thus, probably the representation of length in the figure is a considerable reduction from the original plant. The light-colored spines appearing over the whole joint could indicate only O. phaeacantha var. discata, the most striking prickly pear along most of the route of the expedition on the Rio Grande (Del Norte) in New Mexico and much of the Gila River in New Mexico and Arizona. The joints of this plant are 9 to 12 inches long, five times the length of those in the original drawing. This would allow for a fruit length of 1 1/4 to 3 inches. In the varieties of O. phaeacantha normal fruit length is 1 1/4 to 2 1/4 or rarely 3 inches. This is in harmony with the characters shown in the following collection representative of var. discata as it occurs near the upper Gila River: 12 miles W and somewhat N of Duncan, Greenlee Co., Arizona, Lyman Benson 7395, August 26, 1935, Pom. Although this interpretation would allow the possibility of applying the epithet to var. discata, the basis requires too much interpretation, and the application would be forever in doubt. In this instance the Stanly illustration cannot be associated with the travel of a single day or with a campsite, and there are no distinctive features which pin the illustration down to a special plant occurring in a limited area. Consequently, O. microcarpa is considered a nomen dubium.

Opuntia riparia Griffiths, Proc. Biol. Soc. Wash. 27: 26. 1914. "...Santa Rita Mountains, Arizona...April, 1908...." No specimen indicated. There may be one in the Griffiths collection, US, Pom, but many specimens cannot be placed for lack of the original data. The description indicates var. discata, and probably the plant was this variety or an intermediate between it and var. major.

39g. **Opuntia phaeacantha** var. **wootonii** (Griffiths) L. Benson

Opuntia wootonii Griffiths, Rept. Mo. Bot. Gard. 21: 171. pl. 26, upper; 27. 1910. O. engelmannii Salm-Dyck var. wootonii Fosberg, Bull. So. Calif. Acad. Sci. 30: 71. 1931; Anthony, Amer. Midl. Nat. 55: 249. f. 28. 1956. O. phaeacantha Engelm.

var. <u>wootonii</u> L. Benson, Cactus & Succ. Jour. 41: 125. 1969.
"...Wooton...Organ Mountains, New Mexico. ⌈Griffiths⌉ 9171...
May 4, 1910, from a cultivated plant the cutting for which was
secured April, 1908, from...Wooton's collection...no 3030." TYPE:
<u>US 736498</u>, <u>2572052A</u>, <u>2572053A</u>, <u>2576297A</u>, <u>2576298A</u>. ISOTYPES: <u>Pom
288300</u>, <u>NMC 18999</u>.

39h. Opuntia phaeacantha var. superbospina (Griffiths) L. Benson

Opuntia superbospina Griffiths, Proc. Biol. Soc. Wash. 29:
13. 1916. <u>O. phaeacantha</u> Engelm. var. <u>superbospina</u> L. Benson,
Cactus & Succ. Jour. 46: 79. 1974. Griffiths "...10574, about
15 miles southeast of Kingman, Arizona...." TYPE: <u>US 2576147A</u>.

   <u>ARIZONA</u>. MOHAVE CO. Hualpai Mountain (N side), <u>L. Benson
16714</u>, <u>Pom</u>; about 15 miles SE of Kingman, <u>Griffiths 10574</u>, <u>US</u>,
<u>10579</u>, <u>US</u>, <u>Pom 317779</u>, the theoretical type of <u>Opuntia xerocarpa</u>
Griffiths but not the plant described; near Owens Post Office,
Arizona, <u>Griffiths 10564</u>, <u>US</u>, <u>Pom</u>, <u>Tex</u>.

39i. Opuntia phaeacantha var. mojavensis (Engelmann) Fosberg

Opuntia mojavensis Engelm. Proc. Amer. Acad. 3: 293. 1857
(preprint, 1856); U.S. Senate Rept. Expl. & Surv. R. R. Route
Pacific Ocean. Botany 4: 40. <u>pl. 9</u>, <u>f. 6–8</u>. 1857. <u>O. phaeacan-
tha</u> Engelm. f. <u>mojavensis</u> Schelle, Kakteen 72. 1926. <u>O. phae-
acantha</u> Engelm. var. <u>mojavensis</u> Fosberg, Bull. So. Calif. Acad.
33: 103, 1934. "On the Mojave Creek....Only a few fragments were
brought home, together with sterile fruit." LECTOTYPE designation: "Mojave Creek ⌈River⌉, March 15, 1854." <u>J. M. Bigelow</u>, <u>Mo</u>
(spines).

   Opuntia curvospina Griffiths, Bull. Torrey Club 43: 88. <u>pl.
2</u>. 1916. "...Between Nipton, California, and Searchlight, Nevada,
in April 1912,...⌈Griffiths⌉ 10530." LECTOTYPE designation: <u>US
2576150A</u>, <u>2576151A</u>, <u>2576152A</u>, <u>2576153A</u>. DUPLICATE: <u>Pom 313376</u>.
This plant indicates also the characters of <u>O. mojavensis</u> Engelm.
the type of which consists of only a few spine clusters.

   <u>CALIFORNIA</u>. SAN BERNARDINO CO. Mojave Creek ⌈River⌉, <u>J. M.
Bigelow</u>, March 15, 1853; Bonanza King Mine, Providence Mts., <u>Munz,
Johnston, & Harwood 4303</u>, <u>Pom</u> (spines pale gray); N of Windmill
Station, Ivanpah Range, <u>H. Rush 120 & 121</u>, May 2, 1950, <u>Pom</u>
(spines pale gray); between Nipton and Searchlight ⌈Nevada⌉,
<u>Griffiths 10530</u>, <u>US</u>, <u>Pom</u>.

39j. Opuntia phaeacantha var. flavispina L. Benson

Opuntia phaeacantha Engelm. var. <u>flavispina</u> L. Benson, Cactus
& Succ. Jour. 46: 79. 1974. TYPE: Alamo Canyon, Ajo Mountains,
Organ Pipe Cactus National Monument, 2,300 feet elevation, <u>A. A.
Nichol</u>, April 27, 1939, <u>Pom 306987</u>. ISOTYPES: <u>Ariz 64930</u>, <u>83680</u>,
Organ Pipe Cactus National Monument Herbarium, <u>U.S. National Park
Service Herbarium</u> at Santa Fe.

   <u>ARIZONA</u>. MARICOPA CO. White Tank Mts., 1,250 ft., <u>Pinkava &
Lehto 4217</u>, <u>ASU</u>, 1,600 ft., <u>D. Keil 6064</u>, <u>ASU</u>, <u>Pom</u>; (with shorter
spines) E base of White Tank Mts., <u>J. P. Hester</u>, June, 1950, <u>US</u>
(box), <u>Pom</u>. PIMA CO. Organ Pipe Cactus National Monument: Alamo
Canyon, Ajo Mts., 2,300 ft., <u>A. A. Nichol</u>, April 27, 1939, <u>Pom</u>,
<u>Ariz</u>, Organ Pipe Cactus Nat. Mon. Herb., <u>U.S. Nat. Park Service
Herbarium</u> at Santa Fe; Boulder Canyon, <u>W. F. Steenburgh</u>, May 24,
1962, <u>Pom</u>, Organ Pipe Cactus Nat. Mon. Herb. The following
specimens are essentially of this variety but with the longest
spines only 4 cm long: flat 10 miles E of Organ Pipe Cactus Nat.
Mon. Headquarters on road to Ajo Mts., <u>L. Benson 15615</u>, <u>Pom</u> (3);
W side of Ajo Mts., <u>A. A. Nichol</u>, March 1939, <u>Pom</u>, <u>Ariz</u>, <u>U.S. Nat.
Park Service</u> at Santa Fe, <u>Hoy</u>, April 30, 1963, <u>Pom</u> (1 sheet var.
<u>major</u> or approaching it). The following specimens from the Papago
Indian Reservation approach this variety, but they include charac-
ters of var. <u>major</u>: 10 miles W of Sells on Ajo Road, <u>Wiggins 8719</u>,
<u>DS</u>; 36 miles W of Tucson on road to Ajo, <u>Wiggins 8676</u>, <u>DS</u>, <u>US</u>.

40. Opuntia lindheimeri Engelmann

40a. Opuntia lindheimeri var. lindheimeri

Opuntia lindheimeri Engelm. Pl. Lindh. II, Bost. Jour. Nat.
Hist. 6: 207. 1850. "About New Braunfels." <u>Lindheimer</u>. LECTO-
TYPE designation: "Texas, New Braunfels," <u>F. Lindheimer</u> in 1845,
<u>Mo</u> (fruit and seeds). Typical specimen for parts not shown by the
lectotype: 8 miles W of New Braunfels, <u>L. & R. L. Benson 15314</u>,
<u>Pom 284778</u>; also New Braunfels, <u>L. & R. L. Benson 15317</u>, <u>Pom</u>.

   Opuntia winteriana Berger in Engler, Bot. Jahrb. 36: 455.
1905. "Heimat und Herkunft unbekannt." Drawings are in the Alwin
Berger Succulent Herbarium, NY.

   Opuntia haematocarpa Berger in Engler, Bot. Jahrb. 36: 456.
1905. No locality. Specimen in the Alwin Berger Succulent Herbarium, <u>NY</u> (fls. and Berger's description).

   Opuntia cacanapa Griffiths & Hare, N. Mex. Agr. Exp. Sta.
Bull. 60: 47. 1906. <u>O. engelmannii</u> Salm-Dyck var. <u>cacanapa</u> Weniger, Cacti S. W. 177. 1970, <u>nom. nud.</u> (Art. 33). Griffiths
"...8393...Encinal, La Salle County, Texas, August 12, 1906." <u>No.
8393</u> not found, but one sheet with no number labelled as follows:

"Opuntia cacanapa. Cult. S.A.G. Coll 4/29 '09. Original cuttings from Encinal, Tex." LECTOTYPE designation: <u>US 2572059A</u> (the
specimen cited above).

   Opuntia ferruginispina Griffiths, Rept. Mo. Bot. Gard. 19:
267. 1908. "...9207 D. G. ⌈David Griffiths⌉, collected near San
Antonio, Texas, April 21, 1908." TYPE: <u>US 2572037A</u>, <u>2572136</u>.

   Opuntia texana Griffiths, Rept. Mo. Bot. Gard. 20: 92. <u>pl. 9</u>;
<u>13</u>, <u>f. 1</u>. 1909. <u>O. engelmannii</u> Salm-Dyck var. <u>texana</u> Weniger,
Cacti S. W. 174. 1970, <u>nom. nud.</u> (Art. 33). "...9640 D. G.
⌈David Griffiths⌉, collected at San Antonio, Texas, October 1,
1908." TYPE: <u>US 2572068A</u>, <u>2572069A</u>. ISOTYPE: <u>Pom 288144</u>.

   Opuntia alta Griffiths, Rept. Mo. Bot. Gard. 21: 165. <u>pl. 19</u>;
<u>20</u>, <u>upper</u>. 1910. <u>O. engelmannii</u> Salm-Dyck var. <u>alta</u> Weniger,
Cacti S. W. 175. 1970, <u>nom. nud.</u> (Art. 33). "...9914 D. G. ⌈David
Griffiths⌉, collected March 13, 1910, near Brownsville, Texas...
flowers...from the same plant April 20, 1910." TYPE: <u>US 2571234A</u>,
<u>2571235A</u>. ISOTYPE: <u>Pom 288222</u>.

   Opuntia sinclairii Griffiths, Rept. Mo. Bot. Gard. 21: 173.
<u>pl. 28</u>. 1910. "...9003 D. G. ⌈David Griffiths⌉...near San Anton-
io, Texas." TYPE: <u>US 2572065A</u> to <u>2572067A</u>. ISOTYPE: <u>Pom 287274</u>.

   Opuntia tardospina Griffiths, Rept. Mo. Bot. Gard. 22: 34.
<u>pl. 11</u>, <u>above</u>; <u>15</u>. 1912. "...9338 D. G. ⌈David Griffiths⌉...
Lampasas, Texas, July 3, 1908...." TYPE: <u>US 2572042A</u>, <u>2572294A</u>.
ISOTYPE: <u>Pom 288111</u>.

   Opuntia convexa Mackensen, Bull. Torrey Club 39: 290. 1912.
"...About San Antonio ⌈in 1911⌉." TYPE: <u>US 619756</u>; type material
from cultivation by David Griffiths, <u>10474</u>, <u>US</u>, <u>Pom 317782</u>,
<u>317798</u>. ISOTYPES: <u>NY</u>, <u>F 324715</u>.

   Opuntia griffithsiana Mackensen, Bull. Torrey Club 39: 291.
1912. TYPE: "...619758 in the U.S. National Herbarium." San Antonio, Texas, <u>Mackensen</u>. Specimens grown "from seeds of Mackensen's type." <u>Griffiths 10470</u>, <u>US 2576134A</u>, <u>Pom 288234</u>.

   Opuntia reflexa Mackensen, Bull. Torrey Club 39: 292. 1912.
"...619754 in the U.S. National Herbarium. SAN ANTONIO," Texas,
<u>Mackensen</u> in 1911. TYPE: <u>US 619754</u> (additional material on <u>US
619755</u>). ISOTYPE (from Griffiths' cutting): <u>Pom 288693</u>. Possible isotype: San Antonio, B. Mackensen in 1911, <u>NY</u>. From seeds
of type: <u>US</u>, <u>Pom 288234</u>.

   Opuntia deltica Griffiths, Bull. Torrey Club 43: 84. 1916.
"...Vicinity of Brownsville, Texas, in 1908...," <u>Griffiths 10501</u>.
TYPE: <u>US 2576154A</u>.

   Opuntia aciculata Griffiths, Proc. Biol. Soc. Wash. 29: 10.
1916. <u>O. engelmannii</u> Salm-Dyck var. <u>aciculata</u> Weniger, Cacti S. W.
178. 1970, <u>nom. nud.</u> (Art. 33). <u>O. lindheimeri</u> Engelm. var.
<u>aciculata</u> Bravo, Cact. y Suc. Mex. 19: 47. 1974. Griffiths "...
10300...near Laredo, Texas, June 26, 1911....Description from cultivated plants...Chico, California, May 26, 1914." No. <u>10300</u> has
not been found in the Griffiths collection, and on specimen sheet
no. <u>10360</u> mixing of numbers is mentioned. LECTOTYPE designation:
<u>Griffiths 10360</u>, <u>US 2571266A</u>. DUPLICATE: <u>Pom 288217</u>. Note: The
large glochids and the absence of spines were the basis for the
proposed species. A specimen collected in the vicinity of Laredo,
Webb County, Texas, <u>Rose 18031</u>, <u>US</u>, includes spineless joint sections, and one joint with glochids of the <u>aciculata</u> type bears
slender yellow spines up to 5 cm long. In Griffiths' original
description only an occasional spine in a few of many areoles was
noted. The plants described as <u>O. aciculata</u> Griffiths from Laredo
and <u>O. tardospina</u> Griffiths from Lampasas both have spineless
joints and abundant large brown glochids. However, both appear to
represent sporadic gene combinations rather than segregated natural
populations.

   Opuntia longiclada Griffiths, Bull. Torrey Club 43: 525.
1916. "...S. T. G. ⌈South Texas Garden, Brownsville⌉ 2838...
grown...in Texas besides ⌈at⌉ Chico, California... Its natural
habitat is unknown." TYPE: "Original at Lalule, east of Brownsville, Texas." <u>S. T. G. 2838</u>, <u>US</u>. ISOTYPE: <u>Pom 291213</u>.

   Opuntia pyrocarpa Griffiths, Bull. Torrey Club 43: 90. 1916.
"...Near Marble Falls, Texas, July, 1908...⌈Griffiths⌉ 9392...."
TYPE: <u>US 2576302A</u> to <u>2576304A</u>. ISOTYPE: <u>Pom 288120</u>.

   Opuntia lindheimeri Engelm. var. <u>chisosensis</u> Anthony, Amer.
Midl. Nat. 55: 252. <u>f. 26</u>. 1956. "Basin of Chisos Mountains,
Big Bend National Park, Brewster County, Texas." TYPE: <u>Mich</u>.
Similar plants occur in a hybrid swarm of <u>O. lindheimeri</u> and <u>O.
phaeacantha</u> vars. <u>major</u> and <u>discata</u> in The Basin one-half mile S
of Panther Pass, Chisos Mts., Brewster Co., Texas, <u>L. & R. L.
Benson 15512–15514</u>, <u>Pom</u>.

   <u>NEW MEXICO</u>. HIDALGO CO. Skeleton Canyon, SE of Apache,
Ariz., W slope of Peloncillo Mts., <u>Castetter 1823</u>, Apr. 23–24,
1963, <u>UNM</u>. DONA ANA CO. E Potrillo Mts., <u>Castetter & P. Pierce
1718A</u>, <u>B</u>, <u>UNM</u>; Hill, close to Dona Ana, <u>P. Pierce 2037A</u>, <u>B</u>, <u>UNM</u>.
OTERO CO. Jarilla Mts. NW of Orogrande, <u>P. Pierce 1026</u>, <u>UNM</u>;
Cornudas Mt., <u>Castetter 2522</u>, <u>UNM</u>. GUADALUPE CO. 1 mi. E of
Santa Rosa, <u>L. & R. L. Benson 14700</u>, <u>Pom</u>, <u>Castetter 1054</u>, <u>UNM</u>;

5.7 mi. S of U.S. 66 jct. with U.S. 84, E of Santa Rosa, P. Pierce 521, UNM; 6 mi. E of Newkirk, P. Pierce 2590, UNM. QUAY CO. Northernmost foothill of Tucumcari Peak, L. & R. L. Benson 14704, Pom (2). EDDY CO. Foothills of Guadalupe Mts., P. Pierce 1025A, B, UNM; Adm. Bldg., Carlsbad Nat. Park, Castetter 2215, UNM.

OKLAHOMA. MURRAY CO. Sulphur, G. M. Merrill 560, GH, 1324, GH, 1653, GH; Platt Nat. Park, G. M. Merrill & W. A. Hagan 1653, F, June 3, 1935, F (fls).

LOUISIANA. CAMERON PARISH. Cameron, W. L. McAtee 1956, NY (2), US.

Plant of Uncertain Identity (probably var. lindheimeri)

Opuntia aciculata Griffiths var. orbiculata Backeberg, Descr. Cact. Nov. 10, 1956. "Hab?" No type specimen, but valid because of publication before 1958.

40b. Opuntia lindheimeri var. tricolor (Griffiths) L. Benson

Opuntia tricolor Griffiths, Rept. Mo. Bot. Gard. 20: 85. pl. 4, upper. 1909. O. lindheimeri Engelm. var. tricolor L. Benson, Cactus & Succ. Jour. 41: 125. 1969. "...8651 D. G. [David Griffiths], prepared October 2, 1908, from cultivated specimens collected March 29, 1907, near Laredo, Texas, under the same collection number." TYPE: US 2571219A to 2571221A. ISOTYPE: Pom 287271.

40c. Opuntia lindheimeri var. lehmannii L. Benson

The Griffiths type specimens of the references below are determined now to have been applied in specific rank to var. lehmannii, with which the writer became acquainted in the field in 1965. Earlier the Griffiths plants were considered to represent large forms of O. stricta var. dillenii, and they have been reinterpreted only recently.

Opuntia gomei Griffiths, Rept. Mo. Bot. Gard. 21: 167. pl. 21; 22, lower. 1910. "...9913 D. G. [David Griffiths], collected near Brownsville, Texas, March 13, 1910." TYPE: US 2571237A, 2571238A. ISOTYPE: Pom 288221.

Opuntia cyanella Griffiths, Rept. Mo. Bot. Gard. 22: 30. pl. 9, below; 10. 1912. "The type specimen consists of four sheets, bearing my collection number 9702, two prepared in the type locality, Loma Alta, Texas, May 13, 1909, and...two from a cultivated specimen...May 18, 1911." TYPE: US 2571241A, 2607632 to 2607634. ISOTYPE: Pom 288148 (on 2 sheets). Griffiths' plants had purplish flowers, but otherwise they have characters of var. lehmannii.

Opuntia lindheimeri Engelm. var. lehmannii L. Benson, Cactus & Succ. Jour. 41: 125. 1969. "King Ranch in Kleberg County, Texas, 10 miles south of the Ranch Headquarters at Kingsville, V. W. Lehmann & Lyman Benson 16,557, April 19, 1965." TYPE: Pom 317076 (on 4 sheets).

TEXAS. McMULLEN CO. 5 mi. E of Tilden, J. D. Dodd 64-6, April 28, 1964, TAES, Pom. KLEBERG CO. King Ranch, 10 mi. S of Kingsville, V. W. Lehmann & L. Benson 16557, Pom. CAMERON CO. Near Brownsville, Griffiths 9913, US, Pom; Loma Alta, Griffiths 9702, US, Pom.

40d. Opuntia lindheimeri var. cuija (Griffiths & Hare) L. Benson

Opuntia engelmannii Salm-Dyck var. cuija Griffiths & Hare, N. Mex. Agr. Exp. Sta. Bull. 60: 44. pl. 2. 1906. O. cuija Britton & Rose, Smithsonian Misc. Coll. 50: 529. 1908. O. lindheimeri Engelm. var. cuija L. Benson, Cactus & Succ. Jour. 41: 125. 1969. "Number 7636, San Luie [Luis] Potosi, Mexico, is the botanical type." The plants of this collection pressed after cultivation were given the number 7596. Griffiths often renumbered specimens when they were cultivated, but usually he referred to the field number, in this case, 7636. TYPE: US 2576155A, 2576156A. ISOTYPE: Pom 287125.

Name of Undetermined Application (perhaps to var. cuija)

Opuntia cantabrigiensis Lynch, Gard. Chron. III. 33: 98. 1903. "...A feature of the Cambridge Botanical Garden." A specimen sent by R. I. Lynch in 1912, US, has small, probably young joints with a few small spines. The plant may have been Opuntia lindheimeri var. cuija, but there is little evidence of its identity.

40e. Opuntia lindheimeri var. linguiformis (Griffiths) L. Benson

Opuntia linguiformis Griffiths, Rept. Mo. Bot. Gard. 19: 270. pl. 27, lower. 1908. O. lindheimeri Engelm. var. linguiformis L. Benson, Cactus & Succ. Jour. 41: 125. 1969. O. engelmannii Salm-Dyck var. linguiformis Weniger, Cacti S. W. 181. 1970. nom. nud. (Art. 33). "...Evidently a native of southern Texas... The type is no. 8377 D. G. [David Griffiths], collected near San Antonio, Texas, August, 1906." TYPE: US 2571222. ISOTYPE: Pom 317780. The collection, found in 1970, includes only joints. Neotype designated before the type was rediscovered, a better specimen showing

characters missing in the type (Benson, loc. cit.): "Roadside planting at Cisco, Eastland County, Texas, L. Benson 11,079, Jan. 1, 1942, Pom 287,034 (on two sheets)."

Opuntia lindheimeri Engelm. var. brava Schulz & Runyon, Texas Cacti, Proc. Tex. Acad. Sci. 14: 57. f. on p. 55. 1930, illegitimate name. "This form...for ease of record was designated as O. lindheimeri var. brava...The form named [thus]...was named O. linguiformis by Dr. Griffiths, but as there is little doubt that it is a lethal mutation and cannot perpetuate itself, it is doubtful if it should receive specific standing." The above dubious discussion was under a centered heading "OPUNTIA LINGUIFORMIS -- Cow-Tongue Cactus." The discussion of another species appears between this and O. lindheimeri, which follows rather than precedes it. Thus, the variety was not accepted by its author (Art. 34).

41. Opuntia stricta (Haworth) Haworth

41a. Opuntia stricta var. stricta

Cactus strictus Haw. Misc. Nat. 188. 1803. Opuntia stricta Haw. Syn. Pl. Succ. 191. 1812. According to the second reference, "Cult. ante 1796" [no locality or specimen mentioned] "Cactus strictus. Nobis in misc. nat. p. 168 [188].--Cactus Opuntia inermis. Plant. grass. [Redouté & DC. Pl. Hist. Succ. (Pl. Grass.) 138. 1804] cum icone." LECTOTYPE designation: illustration by Redouté. The dates of publication of parts of Redouté and DeCandolle's book are uncertain, and apparently the illustration had been seen by Haworth prior to 1804.

Cactus opuntia L. var. inermis DC. in Redouté & DC. Pl. Hist. Succ. (Pl. Grass.) 2: 138. f. 1804. Opuntia inermis DC. Prodr. 3: 473. 1828. No locality or specimen. LECTOTYPE designation: the illustration by Redouté.

Opuntia bartramii Raf. Atl. Jour. 146. 1832. "See my Flora Medica, vol. ii. page 247, and Bartram's travels." First reference no information; description in second indicates O. stricta. New Smyrna region of Florida.

Opuntia macrarthra Gibbes, Proc. Elliott Soc. Nat. Hist. 1: 273. 1859. "...Within a few miles of Charleston....A prostrate species, joints from ten to fifteen inches long and three inches wide, one-third of an inch thick; no spines, fruit two and a half inches long, slender, clavate." The Gibbes collection disappeared from the Charleston Museum during the American Civil War. Cf. under O. pusilla.

Opuntia parva Berger, Hort. Mortol. 411. 1912. No type given. "In habit it almost resembles the figure given in DeCandolle's Plantes Grasses [Pl. Hist. Succ. 138. 1804] as Cactus Opuntia nana, but it is not procumbent." It is also "...about 1/2 m. high...." and therefore not the same as C. opuntia L. var. nana DC., which is O. compressa.

Opuntia bentonii Griffiths, Rept. Mo. Bot. Gard. 22: 25. pl. 1-2. 1912. "...Prepared April 24, 1910, from a cultivated specimen, numbered 8374 D. G. [David Griffiths], and collected originally by Harmon Benton at McClenny, Florida, April 26, 1906." Some specimens in the Griffiths Collection were pressed April 28, 1909, and in October, 1911. TYPE: US 2607635 to 2607638. DUPLICATES: Pom 287290, 288045 (on two sheets). The type collection includes joints with a few marginal spines, indicating a population tending toward var. dillenii.

Opuntia keyensis Britton & Small, Jour. N. Y. Bot. Gard. 20: 31. 1919. "...Boot Key, April, 1909, by N. L. Britton...." TYPE: "537, April 7-12, 1909," NY. ISOTYPE: US 535811.

Opuntia magnifica Small, Man. S. E. Fl. 910. 1933. "...Amelia Island, Fla." LECTOTYPE designation: "Sand-dunes, Southern part of Amelia Island" [NE corner of Florida], J. K. Small, John W. Small, & John B. DeWinkler, August 21, 1922, US 1111234, DUPLICATE: NY. Note: The joint is as large as those of O. ficus-indica, 32.5 cm long and 22.5 cm broad, but it is not glaucous, and the plant is almost surely nearest O. stricta. In the upper areoles there are one or two spines under 2.5 cm long. These are dark, but probably they were yellow when the joint was alive, having followed the usual pattern of discoloration. The plant may have resulted from a cross with O. ficus-indica, followed by selection and back-crossing to O. stricta.

41b. Opuntia stricta var. dillenii (Ker-Gawler) L. Benson

Cactus dillenii Ker-Gawler, Edwards Bot. Reg. 3: pl. 255. 1818. Opuntia dillenii Haw. Suppl. Pl. Succ. 79. 1819. O. stricta Haw. var. dillenii L. Benson, Cactus & Succ. Jour. 41: 126. 1969. "Tuna major, spinis validis flavicantibus flore sulphureo. Dillen. elth. 398. 296. f. 382." "It flowered...at Eltham before 1732, and was represented by Dillenius, in his Hortus Elthamensis, but the figure has not been applied by Linnaeus to any species." LECTOTYPE (Benson, loc. cit.): "Plate 255 (ibid.)."

Cactus humilis Haw. Misc. Nat. 187. 1803. Opuntia humilis Haw. Syn. Pl. Succ. 189. 1812. O. horrida Salm-Dyck in DC. Prodr. 3: 472. 1818, nom. nov. No specimen or locality. "...in Americâ calid.?"

Opuntia maritima Raf. Atl. Jour. 146. 1832. "On the sea shore from Florida to Carolina."

Opuntia dillenii (Ker-Gawler) Haw. var. minor Salm-Dyck, Hort. Dyck. 185. 1834, nom. nud. No locality or specimen.

Opuntia dillenii (Ker-Gawler) Haw. var. orbiculata Salm-Dyck, Cact. Hort. Dyck. 1849. 67. 1850, nom. nud. No locality or specimen.

Opuntia tunoidea Gibbes, Proc. Elliott Soc. Nat. Hist. 1: 272. 1859. "...Obtained within a few miles of Charleston." "...Erect, or sub-erect, with large ovate joints, armed with yellowish spines, tipped with brown, about three-quarters of an inch long. The flowers and fruit we have not yet procured." The Gibbes collection disappeared from the Charleston Museum during the American Civil War. Cf. under O. pusilla. NEOTYPE designation: SOUTH CAROLINA. Rockville, S. C. Small, February 6, 1919, NY.

Opuntia gilvoalba Griffiths, Rept. Mo. Bot. Gard. 22: 35. pl. 9, above; 16; 17. 1912. "La Tule, Texas, March 5, 1908... [Griffiths] 9046, put up May 4, 1910, at San Antonio, Texas, from a cultivated plant grown from a cutting of the original collection...." TYPE: US 2572043A; photograph, Mo. ISOTYPE: Pom 287279.

Opuntia laxiflora Griffiths, Bull. Torrey Club 43: 85. 1916. "...9915 D. G. [David Griffiths], collected at Loma Alta, near Brownsville, Texas, August 18, 1912." TYPE: US 2572072A, 2572076A. ISOTYPES: Pom 289518, 291205, 299918.

Opuntia anahuacensis Griffiths, Bull. Torrey Club 43: 92. 1916. "...C. B. Allaire near Anahuac, Texas, at the mouth of the Trinity River...[Griffiths] 9217...." TYPE: US 2436973. ISOTYPE: Pom 288106.

Opuntia zebrina Small, Jour. N. Y. Bot. Gard. 20: 35. pl. 226. 1919. "...Middle Cape Sable, December, 1917, by J. K. Small...." Not found, NY. LECTOTYPE designation: plant labelled, "type, Sand-Dunes, Cape Sable (East Cape), MONROE COUNTY. Cruise of the 'Barbee', November, 1916, November 28, 1916," NY.

Opuntia atrocapensis Small, Man. S. E. Fl. 905, 1506. 1933. "Type, dunes, Cape Sable (E. Cape), Small, November 25, 1916, in herb. N. Y. B. G." Not found.

Opuntia nitens Small, Man. S. E. Fl. 906. 1933. "...Hammock, 5 m. S of Daytona, Fla., Small, Small, & DeWinkler, Aug. 23, 1922, in herb. N.Y.B.G." Type: as above with "Green mound" on the label, NY. DUPLICATE: US.

TEXAS. CHAMBERS CO. Anahuac, C. B. Allaire, Griffiths No. 9215, US, Pom, Tex, Griffiths 9217, US, Pom. GALVESTON CO. Galveston, G. L. Fisher 33201, US (in part). CAMERON CO. Loma Alta near Brownsville, Griffiths 9702, US, Pom, 9913, US, Pom, 9985, US, Pom.

SOUTH CAROLINA. CARTERET CO. Beaufort, Tourney in 1896, GH. COUNTY UNDETERMINED. Rockville, Small, Feb. 6, 1919, NY, US, Aug., 1922, US.

42. Opuntia cochenillifera (Linnaeus) Miller

Cactus cochenillifer L. Sp. Pl. 468. 1753. Opuntia cochenillifera Miller, Gard. Dict. ed. 8. No. 6. 1768. Nopalea cochenillifera, Salm-Dyck, Cact. Hort. Dyck. 1849. 64. 1850. O. cochenillifer Karsten, Deutsche Fl. ed. 1. 888. 1882. "Habitat in Jamaica & America calidiore." Ref. to L. Hort. Ups. 121. 1748, "Habitat in Jamaica." Introduced there. NEOTYPE designation: 6 miles south of Ft. Pierce, St. Lucie County, Florida, Lyman & Robert L. Benson 15374, Pom 285307, 288540. (Introduced.)

HAWAII. KAHOOLAWE. Kuheia, "cult. near houses," [also escaped ?], E. H. Bryan, Jr., 1408, Jan. 7, 1939, Bish.

FLORIDA. ST. LUCIE CO. 6 mi. S of Ft. Pierce, L. & R. L. Benson 15374, Pom.

43. Opuntia oricola Philbrick

Opuntia oricola Philbrick, Cactus & Succ. Jour. 36: 163. 3 f. 1964. TYPE: "San Ysidro Canyon, one mile northeast of Montecito, Santa Barbara County, California, U. S. A., 4 July 1964, R. N. Philbrick 0443...." SBBG. ISOTYPES: BH, Pom 306803.

44. Opuntia chlorotica Engelmann & Bigelow

Opuntia chlorotica Engelm. & Bigelow, Proc. Amer. Acad. 3: 291. 1857 (preprint, 1856); U.S. Senate Rept. Expl. & Survey R. R. Route Pacific Ocean. Botany 4: 38. pl. 6, f. 1-3. 1857. O. tidballii Bigelow, loc. cit. 11, an inadvertence. "On both sides of the Colorado, from the San Francisco mountains to the headwaters of [Bill] Williams' River...and to the Mojave Creek [River]." LECTOTYPE designation: "Bill Williams Mt., [Arizona], Jan. 2nd., 1853, Bigelow," Mo.

Opuntia palmeri Engelm. ex Coulter, Contr. U.S. Nat. Herb. 3: 323. 1896. "Type, Palmer of [June] 1877, in Herb. Mo. Bot. Gard." Not found. However, the description indicates O. chlorotica.

NEVADA. NYE CO. Crystal Spring Canyon, Spring Mts., Beatley & Reveal 10507, Pom. CLARK CO. Lower Clark Canyon, Spring Mts., Beatley & Reveal 10727, Pom; Buck Spring Canyon, Spring Mts., Beatley & Reveal 11231, Pom; Charleston Mts., Coville & Funston 313, Feb. 14, 1891, US.

UTAH. WASHINGTON CO. Zion Canyon, G. & C. Trapp 67-78, Sept. 4, 1967, Pom.

45. Opuntia strigil Engelmann

45a. Opuntia strigil var. strigil

Opuntia strigil Engelm. Proc. Amer. Acad. 3: 290. 1857 (preprint, 1856); in Emory Rept. U.S. & Mex. Bound. Surv. 2: Cactaceae 47. pl. 67. 1859. "Western Texas, west of the Pecos, in crevices of flat limestone rocks; Wright, Bigelow." LECTOTYPE designation: 6 miles W of the Pecos, Wright in 1851, Mo. DUPLICATE: Pom 217786.

TEXAS. "Below El Paso," Wright in 1852, Mo. NOLAN CO. "Desert plains," F. A. Barkley, Aug. 4, 1934, Mo. CROCKETT CO. Ozona, D. Weniger 654, 655, 656, Nov., 1964, UNM. PECOS AND TERRELL COS. Common.

45b. Opuntia strigil var. flexospina (Griffiths) L. Benson

Opuntia flexospina Griffiths, Bull. Torrey Club 43: 87. 1916. O. engelmannii Salm-Dyck var. flexispina [flexispina] Weniger, Cacti S. W. 178. 1970, nom. nud. (Art. 33). O. strigil Engelm. var. flexospina L. Benson, Cactus & Succ. Jour. 46: 79. 1974. "...Vicinity of Laredo, Texas...June, 1911,...[Griffiths] 10301." TYPE: US 2571224A, 2571225A. ISOTYPES: Pom 299916, 290308.

46. Opuntia ficus-indica (Linnaeus) Miller

Cactus ficus-indica L. Sp. Pl. 468. 1753. Opuntia ficus-indica Miller, Gard. Dict. ed. 8. No. 2. 1768. "Habitat in America calidiore." Not found, Linn or L. Choice of a lectotype or a neotype will require further study.

Opuntia megacantha Salm-Dyck, Hort. Dyck 1834: 363. 1834. "Habitat in Mexico." Not preserved.

Opuntia engelmannii Salm-Dyck, Cact. Hort. Dyck. 1849. 67. 1850, pro syn., nom. nud., in Engelm. Pl. Lindh. II, Boston Jour. Nat. Hist. 6: 208. 1850. "From El Paso to Chihuahua, indigenous and cultivated, Dr. Wislizenus. No doubt also on the Texas side of the Rio del Norte [Rio Grande]." LECTOTYPE (Benson & Walkington, Ann. Mo. Bot. Gard. 52: 273. 1965): "North of Chihuahua, common as high up as El Paso, A. Wislizenus, Aug., 1846," Mo, photographs, Pom, NY. This name has been applied erroneously to the large, conspicuous prickly pear occurring from the deserts of California to those of Texas, but the type is from a cultivated individual of the spiny "Opuntia megacantha" type. The plants described commonly as "Opuntia engelmannii" are O. pheacantha var. discata.

Opuntia occidentalis Engelm. & Bigelow, Proc. Amer. Acad. 3: 219. 1857 (preprint, 1856) (publication in specific rank in the correct form but clouded by the statement: "The following may be considered as a sub-species;"); U.S. Senate Rept. Expl. & Surv. R. R. Route Pacific Ocean. Botany 4: 38. pl. 7, f. 1-2. 1857. O. engelmannii Salm-Dyck var. occidentalis Engelm. in Brewer & Watson, Bot. Calif. 1: 248. 1876. O. engelmannii Salm-Dyck f. occidentalis Schelle, Handb. Kakteenkultur 52. 1907. LECTOTYPE (Benson & Walkington, Ann. Mo. Bot. Gard. 52: 264-265, 273. 1965): "Near Los Angeles, Cal.," actually, from near Cucamonga, 43 miles east of Los Angeles in San Bernardino Co., J. M. Bigelow, March 19, 1852, Mo; photographs US, Pom.

The species escapes here and there, but its occurrence is little documented.

HAWAII. KAUAI. Road to Waimea Canyon and Kokee (spiny type), L. Benson 15841, Pom. Observed on the dry leeward sides of the other islands, notably at various points on Oahu, Maui, and Hawaii.

CALIFORNIA. VENTURA CO. Ojai Valley near Matilija Canyon (spineless, the other specimens listed below being spiny), H. M. Pollard, Aug. 19, 1949, CAS. LOS ANGELES CO. "Mt. Wilson," D. T. MacDougal in 1906, NY (3); about a winter spring, canyon mouth N of Carrion House, E of Puddingstone Reservoir, Pomona, L. Benson 16345, Pom, Walkington 194, Pom. SAN BERNARDINO CO. Alluvial fan above Cucamonga, L. Benson 16242, Pom. SAN DIEGO CO. Pt. Loma, San Diego, A. J. Stover 195, Feb. 21, 1939, SD.

NEW MEXICO. DONA ANA CO. Mesilla, Wooton 3032, NMC (perhaps with introgression of genes of Opuntia phaeacantha var. major and with a few small spines).

TEXAS. (Spineless type): BREWSTER CO. 7 mi. W of Alpine, Warnock 47-450, SRSC (2). VAL VERDE CO. Del Rio, Griffiths 9410, US. LAMPASAS CO. Lampasas, Griffiths 9339, US, 9342, US, Pom (other sheets of this no. are O. lindheimeri). COMAL CO. New Braunfels, Griffiths 9402, US, Pom, 9404, US. KLEBERG CO. King Ranch, V. W. Lehmann in 1955, Pom (also spiny type, Pom).

Hybrid population "occidentalis"

For the epithet occidentalis, see Opuntia ficus-indica.

Opuntia rugosa Griffiths, Proc. Biol. Soc. Wash. 27: 27. 1914. Griffiths "...10364, and...near Pomona, California." According to a letter from David Griffiths to S. B. Parish, Feb. 16, 1916, Parish Botany Library of Pomona College (583.471 C 113 V.1), "Opuntia rugosa I secured on a circuitous trip which I took from Pomona to Claremont." TYPE: US 2576077A. ISOTYPES: Pom 285257, 288613, 291217.

Hybrid population "demissa"

Opuntia demissa Griffiths, Rept. Mo. Bot. Gard. 22: 29. pl. 9. 1912. "...East of San Diego, California, April 2, 1909...[Griffiths] 9647." TYPE: US 2571236A. Except that the joints are somewhat larger, the following match the type well: San Diego, Griffiths 7864, Pom, 7998, US, Pom.

Hybrid population "dillei"

Opuntia dillei Griffiths, Rept. Mo. Bot. Gard. 20: 82. pl. 2, f. 10; 4, lower; 13, f. 7. 1909. "...9460 D. G. [David Griffiths], collected in San Andreas canyon of the Sacramento Mountains of New Mexico, about 15 miles south of Alamogordo, August 3, 1908." TYPE: US 2576308A, 2576309A. ISOTYPE: Pom 288128. The specimen is intermediate between O. ficus-indica and O. phaeacantha var. major.

Hybrid population "subarmata"

Opuntia subarmata Griffiths, Rept. Mo. Bot. Gard. 20: 94. pl. 2, f. 1; 11; 13, f. 4. 1909. O. engelmannii Salm-Dyck var. subarmata Weniger, Cacti S. W. 180. 1970, nom. nud. (Art. 33). "...9422 D. G. [David Griffiths], collected near Devils River [Val Verde Co,], Texas, July 22, 1908." TYPE: US 2572063A, 2572064A. ISOTYPE: Pom 288607, 288608.

Opuntia ellisiana Griffiths, Rept. Mo. Bot. Gard. 21: 170. pl. 25. 1910. "...No. 8626 D. G. [David Griffiths], cultivated plant...Mexican gardens at Corpus Christi, Texas, in 1907." TYPE: US 2571232A, 2571233A. ISOTYPE: Pom 287269.

47. Opuntia tomentosa Salm-Dyck

Opuntia tomentosa Salm-Dyck, Observ. Bot. 3: 8. 1822. Cactus tomentosus Link, Enum. Hort. Berol. 2: 24. 1822. "Omnes species in America calidiore habitant." No specimen or locality; native in central Mexico. Salm's plants not preserved.

48. Opuntia leucotricha DeCandolle

Opuntia leucotricha DC. Mém. Mus. Hist. Nat. Paris 17: 119. 1828. "...In Mexico. Coulter, N⁰ 2." No specimen in Coulter collection, Herbarium of Trinity College, Dublin.

FLORIDA. ST. LUCIE CO. Hammock 6 mi. S of Ft. Pierce, "naturalized during the Seminole wars," Small, Dec. 16, 1918, NY.

49. Opuntia spinosissima Miller

Opuntia spinosissima Miller, Gard. Dict. ed. 8. No. 8. 1768. Cactus spinosissimus Martyn, Cat. Hort. Cantebrig. 88. 1771. Consolea spinosissima Lemaire, Rev. Horticol. 1862. 174. 1862. Jamaica.

Consolea corallicola Small, Addisonia 15: S.25. pl. 493. 1930. Opuntia corrallicola Werdermann in Backeberg, Neue Kakteen 66. 1931; in Fedde, Repert. Sp. Nov. 30: 59. 1932. "...Spring of 1919...Big Pine Key," Florida, May, 1919. J. K. Small, NY. ISOTYPE: US.

FLORIDA. MONROE CO. Hammock, SE end of Big Pine Key, Small, May 19, 1919, NY, US, Small, Small, & DeWinkler, Dec. 12, 1921, NY, US.

50. Opuntia brasiliensis (Willdenow) Haworth

Cactus brasiliensis Willd. Enum. Suppl. 33. 1813. Opuntia brasiliensis Haw. Suppl. Pl. Succ. 79. 1819. No locality or specimen mentioned in the original publication. Near Rio de Janeiro, Brazil.

3. Schlumbergera

Schlumbergera, as genus, Lemaire, Rev. Hort. IV. 7: 253. 1858, not E. Morr. in 1878 (Bromeliaceae). Type species: Epi-phyllum russellianum Gardner ex Hooker (= Schlumbergera russelliana [Gardner] Britton & Rose).

Zygocactus, as genus, K. Schum. in Martius, Fl. Bras. 4(2): 223. 1890; as subgenus of Epiphyllum, Berger, Kakteen 98. 1929; as subgenus of Schlumbergera, Moran, Gent. Herb. 8: 329. 1953. Type species: Epiphyllum truncatum Haw. (lectotype, Britton & Rose, Cactaceae 4: 177. 1923) (= Schlumbergera truncata [Haw.] Moran).

1. Schlumbergera truncata (Haworth) Moran

Epiphyllum truncatum Haw. Suppl. Pl. Succ. 85. 1819. Cactus truncatus Link, Enum. Pl. Hort. Berol. 2: 24. 1822. Cereus truncatus Sweet, Hort. Brit. 172. 1827. Zygocactus truncatus K. Schum. in Martius, Fl. Bras. 4(2): 224. 1890. Schlumbergera truncata Moran Gentes Herb. 8: 329. 1953. "HABITAT in Brasilia... in horto Kewense A.D. 1818."

HAWAII. OAHU. Malu.Lane, Honolulu, Anna Coker, Bish, cf. Gent. Herb. 8: 329. 1953.

4. Rhipsalis

Hariota, as genus, Adans. Fam. 2: 243. 1763, nom. rejic. Based on Cactus parasiticus inermis, aphyllus, ramosus Plum. Pl. Amer. 1: 190. pl. 197. f. 2. 1755.

Rhipsalis, as genus, Gaertner, Fruct. Sem. 1: 137. pl. 28. 1788, nomen conservandum. Type species: Rhipsalis cassutha Gaertner (lectotype, Britton & Rose, Cactaceae 4: 219. 1923) (= Rhipsalis baccifera [J. Miller] W. T. Stearn).

Cassyta Miller, Illustr. Sex. Syst. Linn. 1771-1777. pl. 29. 1800, not Cassytha L. Sp. Pl. 35. 1753 (Lauraceae). Type species: Cassyta baccifera Miller (= Rhipsalis baccifera [Miller] W. T. Stearn).

1. Rhipsalis baccifera (J. Miller) W. T. Stearn

Cassyt[h]a baccifera J. Miller, Illustr. Sex. Syst. Linn. Class. IX. Ord. I. 1771. Rhipsalis baccifera W. T. Stearn, Cactus & Succ. Jour. Gt. Brit. 7: 107. 1939. According to Stearn, loc. cit. "Johann Sebastian Miller (1715-c.1790), a German draughtsman and engraver, who came to London from Nürnberg in 1744 and anglicised his name to John Miller, should not be confused with his contemporary, Philip Miller (1691-1771) of the Chelsea Physic Garden, whose works he helped to illustrate. His figure and description of Cassyta baccifera are obviously done from the living plant, almost certainly one cultivated at Chelsea or Kew, and as Gaertner later based his Rhipsalis Cassutha on a specimen sent from Kew by Sir Joseph Banks, the two names may actually have had the same type....[The species], according to Aiton, was introduced into cultivation from the West Indies by Philip Miller in 1758." LECTOTYPE designation: the original published illustration.

Rhipsalis cassutha Gaertner, Fruct. Sem. 1: 137. pl. 28. 1788. Hariota cassutha Lemaire, Cact. Gen. Nov. Sp. 75. 1839. A specimen sent to the Royal Botanic Gardens, Kew, by Sir Joseph Banks (not found), "Ad Cacti genus referri posse censet Ill. BANKS, in litt. sed Cacti femines albumen farinosum, & embryo subspiralis est." LECTOTYPE designation: original illustration of Cassytha baccifera J. Miller (see above) is designated as the lectotype, also, of Rhipsalis cassutha Gaertner.

FLORIDA. DADE CO. Wallerstein's Hammock, west of Kendall, C. A. Mosier, Aug. 5, 1923, NY, US; E of Flamingo, observed in 1965 but not collected because of its rarity and of the few plants in the single known surviving clump, L. Benson 16578, Pom, photographs, supplemented from an earlier collection of living material from the same place growing at the University of Miami (courtesy of Taylor R. Alexander).

5. Cereus

Cereus, as genus, Miller, Gard. Dict. abridged ed. 4 (genera alphabetical). 1754. Type species: Cactus hexagonus L. (lectotype, Britton & Rose, Cactaceae 2: 3. 1920).

Cephalocereus, as genus, Pfeiffer, Allg. Gartenz. 6: 142. 1838; as subgenus, Berger, Ann. Rept. Mo. Bot. Gard. 16: 61. 1905. Type species: Cereus senilis Haw. (lectotype, Britton & Rose, Contr. U.S. Nat. Herb. 12: 415. 1909).

Cephalophorus, as genus, Lemaire, Cact. Aliq. Nov. XII. 1838, not Cephalophora Cav. in 1801. Type species: Cereus senilis Haw. (lectotype designated here).

Pilocereus, as genus, Lemaire, Cact. Gen. Sp. Nov. 6. 1839, not K. Schum. in 1894, not Backeberg in 1941; as subgenus, Engelm. Proc. Amer. Acad. 3: 287. 1857 (preprint, 1856). Type species:

Cereus senilis Haw. (lectotype, Britton & Rose, Contr. U.S. Nat. Herb. 12: 415. 1909).

Lepidocereus, as subgenus, Engelm. Proc. Amer. Acad. 3: 287. 1857 (preprint, 1856); as subgenus, Berger, Rept. Mo. Bot. Gard. 16: 65. 1905. Type species designation: Cereus giganteus Engelm. (cf. Berger, loc. cit.).

Lophocereus, as subgenus, Berger, Ann. Rept. Mo. Bot. Gard. 16: 62. 1905; as genus, Britton & Rose, Contr. U.S. Nat. Herb. 12: 42. 1909. Type species: Cereus schottii Engelm. (lectotype, Britton & Rose, loc. cit.).

Eriocereus, as subgenus, Berger, Ann. Rept. Mo. Bot. Gard. 16: 74. 1905; as genus, Riccobono, Boll. R. Ort. Bot. Palermo 8: 238. 1909. Type species: Cereus platygonus Otto (lectotype, Byles, Nat. Cactus & Succ. Jour. 11: 36. 1956; Dict. Gen. & Sub-Gen. Cact. 32. 1956). The earlier choice of Cereus gracilis Miller (R. S. Byles, Nat. Cact. & Succ. Jour. 10: 33. 1955; Dict. Subg. Cactaceae 13. 1955) is invalid, because this species was not mentioned by Berger under the proposed subgenus Eriocereus.

Hylocereus, as subgenus, Berger, Ann. Rept. Mo. Bot. Gard. 16: 72. 1905; as genus, Britton & Rose, Contr. U.S. Nat. Herb. 12: 428. 1909. Type species: Cactus triangularis L. (lectotype, Britton & Rose, loc. cit.) (= Cereus triangularis [L.] Haw.).

Selenicereus, as subsection, Berger, Ann. Rept. Mo. Bot. Gard. 16: 76. 1905; as genus, Britton & Rose, Contr. U.S. Nat. Herb. 12: 429. 1909; as subgenus, Berger, Kakteen 110. 1929. Type species: Cactus grandiflorus L. (lectotype, Britton & Rose, loc. cit.) (= Cereus grandiflorus [L.] Haw.)

Acanthocereus, as subsection, Berger, Ann. Rept. Mo. Bot. Gard.16: 77. 1905; as genus, Britton & Rose, Contr. U.S. Nat. Herb. 12: 432. 1909; as subgenus, Berger, Kakteen 124. 1929. Type species: Cactus pentagonus L. (lectotype, Britton & Rose, loc. cit.) (= Cereus pentagonus [L] Haw.).

Peniocereus, as subsection, Berger, Ann. Rept. Mo. Bot. Gard. 16: 77. 1905; as genus, Britton & Rose, Contr. U.S. Nat. Herb. 12: 428. 1909; as subgenus, Berger, Kakteen 126. 1929. Type species: Cereus greggii Engelm. (lectotype, Britton & Rose, loc. cit.).

Harrisia, as genus, Britton, Bull. Torrey Club 35: 561. 1908 (1909); as subgenus, Berger, Kakteen 127. 1929. Type species: Cereus gracilis Miller.

Carnegiea, as genus, Britton & Rose, Jour. N.Y. Bot. Gard. 9: 188. Nov., 1908. Type species: Cereus giganteus Engelm. The earlier subgeneric name Lepidocereus Engelm., based upon the same type, was brushed aside by Britton and Rose with the vague statement that it was "...neither necessary nor desirable to maintain..." this name.

Lemaireocereus, as genus, Britton & Rose, Contr. U.S. Nat. Herb. 12: 424. July 21, 1909; as subgenus of Cereus, Berger, Kakteen 161. 1929; as subgenus of Pachycereus, Bravo, Cact. Suc. Méx. 17: 119. 1972. Type species: Cereus hollianus Weber.

Wilcoxia Britton & Rose, Contr. U.S. Nat. Herb. 12: 434. 1909. Type species: Cereus poselgeri (Lemaire) Coulter.

Bergerocactus, as genus, Britton & Rose, Contr. U.S. Nat. Herb. 12: 435. 1909; as subgenus, Berger, Kakteen 133. 1929. Bergerocereus, Britton & Rose, loc. cit., nom. nud. Type species: Cereus emoryi Engelm.

Piptanthocereus, as subgenus, Berger, Rept. Mo. Bot. Gard. 16: 70. 1905; as genus, Riccobono, Boll. R. Ort. Bot. Palermo 8: 225. 1909. Type species: Cereus peruvianus Miller (lectotype, by inference, cf. Britton & Rose, Contr. U.S. Nat. Herb. 12: 414. 1909).

Stenocereus, as genus, Riccobono, Boll. R. Ort. Bot. Palermo 8: 253. 1909. Type species: Cereus stellatus Pfeiffer.

Neoevansia, W. T. Marshall in Marshall & Bock, Cactaceae 84: 1941. Type species: Cereus diguetii Weber. (= Cereus striatus Brandegee).

Marshallocereus, as genus, Backeberg, Cactus & Succ. Jour. 22: 154. 1950. Type species: Cereus aragonii Weber.

Pilosocereus, as genus, Byles & Rowley, Cactus & Succ. Jour. Gt. Brit. 19: 66. 1957. Type species: Pilocereus leucocephalus Poselger.

1. Cereus peruvianus (Linnaeus) Miller

Cactus peruvianus L. Sp. Pl. 467. 1753. Cereus peruvianus Miller, Gard. Dict. ed. 8. No. 4. 1768. Piptanthocereus peruvianus Riccobono, Boll. R. Ort. Bot. Palermo 8: 232. 1909. "Habitat in Jamaica, Peru apricis aridis maritimus."

HAWAII. KAUAI. Koloa, S. Au, Jan. 12-14, 1959, Bish.

2. Cereus giganteus Engelmann

Cereus gigantens [giganteus] Engel. in Emory, Notes. Mil. Reconn. Ft. Leavenworth to San Diego, App. 2. 158. 1848. Pilocereus engelmannii Lemaire, Illus. Hort. 9: misc. 97. 1862, nom. nov. for C. giganteus. P. giganteus Rümpler in Förster, Handb. Cacteenk. ed. 2. 662. 1885. Carnegiea gigantea Britton & Rose, Jour. N.Y. Bot. Gard. 9: 188. 1908. "In your [Emory's] letter you figure and describe a cactus plant, of which you have set before me the seeds..." Emory's notes and seeds not found, Mo. Later additions by Engelmann to the description of the species were from verbal reports by C. C. Parry and from collections by George Thurber, Mo, GH (flowers and seeds). According to the itinerary of the Military Reconnaissance, on November 1, 1846, the Emory expedition was at the site of the Coolidge Dam in southern Gila County, Arizona. According to Emory, loc. cit., "At the point where we left the Gila [to travel through mountains above its deep canyon in which the dam is located now], there stands a cereus six feet in circumference, and so high, I could not reach half way to the top of it with the point of my sabre by many feet; and a short distance up the ravine is a grove of these plants, much larger than the one I measured and with large branches." The grove is still there. This is the first point at which a traveller paralleling Emory's route down the Gila encounters the species. NEOTYPE designation: original site, L. Benson 16630, April 22, 1966, Pom 317572. TOPOTYPE: L. Benson 7401, August 26, 1935, Pom.

Carnegiea gigantea cristata, Anonymous, Cactus & Succ. Jour. 8: 113. f. 1937, nom. nud., label for photograph; G. Turner, Cactus Jour. 8: 31, 33. 1939, nom. nud.; Hester, Des. Pl. Life 12: 84. fs. 1940, nom. nud.

CALIFORNIA. SAN BERNARDINO CO. Whipple Mts., Jepson 5231, UC-Jeps; Copper Basin, Whipple Mts., C. B. Wolf 3159, RSA, Pom, Mo, NY, GH, UC, US, DS. IMPERIAL CO. 5 mi. above Laguna Dam, C. B. Wolf 1883, RSA, Munz 12834, Pom.

3. Cereus eriophorus Pfeiffer & Otto

3a. Cereus eriophorus var. fragrans (Small) L. Benson

Harrisia fragrans Small in Britton & Rose, Cactaceae 2: 149. 1920 (cf. Addisonia 17: 29-30. pl. 559. 1932). Cereus eriophorus Pfeiffer var. fragrans L. Benson, Cactus & Succ. Jour. 41: 126. 1969. TYPE: "Coastal sand-dunes, Brevard and St. Lucie Counties, Florida...sand-dunes 6 miles south of Fort Pierce, December [20], 1917," John K. Small, NY (on 2 sheets). ISOTYPES: US 1738304, GH. Specially-collected TOPOTYPE: L. & R. L. Benson 15375, Pom.

FLORIDA. VOLUSIA CO. Turtle Mound, E. Norman 101, Pom. BREVARD CO. Islands E of Malabar, P. H. Rolfs, Nov. 3, 1903, NY, Small in 1903, NY. ST. LUCIE CO. Hammock S of Ft. Pierce, Small 8457, NY (2 & in preservative), GH, US, L. & R. L. Benson 15375, Pom. MONROE CO. E of Flamingo, Everglades Nat. Park, L. Benson 16578, Pom; Big Pine Key, L. Benson, T. Alexander, & C. Dodson 16575, Pom.

Cereus eriophorus var. *eriophorus* (not in U.S.)

Cereus eriophorus Pfeiffer & Otto, Enum. Cact. 94. 1837. C. subrepandus Hort. ex Pfeiffer, loc. cit., pro syn., not Haw. Suppl. Pl. Succ. 78. 1819. Harrisia eriophora Britton, Bull. Torrey Club 35: 562. 1908. "Pa: Insula Cuba." "H. BEROL." NEOTYPE designation: illustration, Pfeiffer & Otto, Abbild. Beschr. Cact. 1: pl. 22. 1842.

4. Cereus gracilis Miller

4a. Cereus gracilis var. simpsonii (Small) L. Benson

Harrisia simpsonii Small in Britton & Rose, Cactaceae 2: 152. 1920 (cf. Addisonia 17: 59-60. pl. 574. 1932). Cereus gracilis Miller var. simpsonii L. Benson, Cactus & Succ. Jour. 41: 126. 1969. TYPE: "...Between Cape Sable and Flamingo [southern Florida], John K. Small, November 29, 1916." Not found, NY. LECTOTYPE (Benson, loc. cit.): "Hammock near Flamingo, J. K. Small, May, 1919," NY (a flower, divided lengthwise). Typical specimen for other characters (Benson, loc. cit.): "Old road to Bear Lake, Everglades 3 miles west of Coot Bay, Everglades National Monument, 3–4 miles north of Flamingo, Lyman and Robert L. Benson 15,345, August 29, 1954, Pom 284,785 (on 3 sheets)."

FLORIDA. MANATEE CO. "On old shell mounds," J. T. Rothrock, spring, 1887, F; Terra Ceia Island, W. T. Swingle in 1917, US, Small, Cuthbert, & DeWinkler, April 29, 1919, NY (& in preservative), US. SARASOTA CO. Sarasota Key, Coville, Feb. 18, 1924, US; Osprey, J. G. Webb, July 8, 1911, NY (fl.), US (fl.). LEE CO. Ft. Myers, A. S. Hitchcock, July-Aug., 1900, F.

4b. Cereus gracilis var. aboriginum (Small) L.Benson

Harrisia aboriginum Small in Britton & Rose, Cactaceae 2: 154. 1920. Cereus aboriginus Little, Amer. Midl. Nat. 33: 445. 1945. C. gracilis Miller var. aboriginum L. Benson, Cactus & Succ. Jour. 41: 126. 1969. "Ten Thousand Islands... Type collected by J. K. Small on Terra Ceia Island, April 1919." Not found. LECTOTYPE (Benson, loc. cit.): "Hammock, western shore of Terra Ceia Island,

John K. Small, Alfred Cuthbert, & John B. DeWinkler, April 29, 1919," NY. DUPLICATE: US 989391.

Cereus gracilis var. *gracilis* (not in U.S.)

Cereus gracilis Miller, Gard. Dict. ed. 8. no. 8. 1768. Cactus gracilis Weston, Bot. Univers. 1: 33. 1770. Harrisia gracilis Britton, Bull. Torrey Club 35: 563. 1908.

5. Cereus martinii Labouret

Cereus martinii Labouret, Ann. Soc. Hort. Haute Garonne 1854. Eriocereus martinii Riccobono, Boll. R. Ort. Bot. Palermo 8: 241. 1909. Harrisia martinii Britton, Addisonia 2: 55. pl. 68. 1917; Britton & Rose, Cactaceae 2: 155. 1920. No locality given.

HAWAII. KAUAI. Poipu, S. Uhara, Oct. 15, 1959, Bish.

6. Cereus pentagonus Linnaeus

Cactus pentagonus L. Sp. Pl. 1: 467. 1753. Cereus pentagonus Haw. Syn. Pl. Succ. 180. 1812. Acanthocereus pentagonus Britton & Rose, Contr. U.S. Nat. Herb. 12: 432. 1909. "Habitat in America." No specimen, Linn.

Acanthocereus floridanus Small in Britton & Rose, Cactaceae 4: 276. 1923. "...J. K. Small, on Key Largo, December 1917 and 1918...." LECTOTYPE designation: "Hammock, Key Largo, J. K. Small Dec." and "Plants from Key Largo, Dec. 1917 [grown at Buena Vista]," NY (2 sheets and material preserved in fluid). DUPLICATE: US 1814254.

7. Cereus grandiflorus (Linnaeus) Miller

7a. Cereus grandiflorus var. grandiflorus

Cactus grandiflorus L. Sp. Pl. 1: 476. 1753. Cereus grandiflorus Miller, Gard. Dict. ed. 8. sp. no. 11. 1768. Selenicereus grandiflorus Britton & Rose, Contr. U.S. Nat. Herb. 12: 430. 1909. "Habitat in Jamaica, Vera Cruce." TYPE: Linn; photograph, F 1373996.

7b. Cereus grandiflorus var. armatus (K. Schumann) L. Benson

Cereus nycticallis Link. var. armatus K. Schum. Gesamtb. Kakteen. ed. 1. 147. 1898. C. grandiflorus (L.) Miller var. armatus L. Benson, Cactus & Succ. Jour. 41: 126. 1969. "...In den Garten...." No specimen or locality.

Cereus coniflorus Weingart, Monatsschr. Kakteenk. 14: 118. 1904. Selenicereus coniflorus Britton & Rose, Contr. U.S. Nat. Herb. 12: 430. 1909. "Meine Pflanze erhielt ich am 6. März 1896 von ROTHER, Gross-Rosenburg, als Steckling.... Die Triebe stimmen in Form und Stacheln mit einem 1903 von Herrn HARTMANN in Hamburg erhaltenen Original aus Haiti gut überein."

FLORIDA. BROWARD CO. 4 mi. W of Hallendale, Small, April, 1919, NY.

8. Cereus pteranthus Link & Otto

Cereus pteranthus Link & Otto, Allg. Gartenz. 2: 209. 1834. Selenicereus pteranthus Britton & Rose, Contr. U.S. Nat. Herb. 12: 431. 1909. "Habitat in Mexico." "Der botanische Garten erhielt diesen Cactus durch Herrn Deppe aus Mexico im Jahre 1829... Unter dem Namen Cereus Antoini wurde dieser Cactus aus dem botanischen Garten in Wien gefandt."

Cereus nycticallus Link in A. Dietr. Verh. Ver. Beförd. Gartenb. 10: 372. 1834. nom. nov. (Refs. to C. pteranthus Link and C. brevispinus Salm-Dyck). "Habitat in Mexico."

Cereus brevispinulus Salm-Dyck, Hort. Dyck. 1834: 339. 1834. "Habitat in Mexico."

FLORIDA. BREVARD CO. J. M. Hollister, Feb. 12, 1946, US (color transparency photograph). ST. LUCIE CO. Hammock on sand dune, 6 mi. S of Ft. Pierce, St. Lucie Sound [Indian River], Small 8455, Dec. 20, 1917, NY, GH, US.

9. Cereus spinulosus DeCandolle

Cereus spinulosus DC. Mém. Mus. Hist. Nat. Paris 17: 117. 1828. "...in Mexico. Coulter, n° 27." Selenicereus spinulosus Britton & Rose, Contr. U. S. Nat. Herb. 12: 431. 1909.

10. Cereus undatus Haworth

Cereus undatus Haw. Syn. Pl. Succ. Phil. Mag. 7: 110. 1830. Harrisia undata Britton, Bull. Torrey Club 35: 564. 1909. Hylocereus undatus Britton & Rose in Britton, Fl. Bermuda 256. 1918. "Habitat in Sinâ. Exindè Hort. Soc. Londini nuper introduxit...."

FLORIDA. POLK CO. Winter Haven, J. B. McFarlin, Sept., 1931, Mich. MANATEE CO. Osprey, J. G. Webb, May 18, 1906, NY, US (2). DADE CO. Hammocks, Miami, Small & Carter 1010, Oct. 28-Nov. 28, 1903, NY, US.

11. Cereus robinii (Lemaire) L. Benson

11a. Cereus robinii var. robinii

Pilocereus robinii Lemaire, Illustr. Hort. II. 1: Misc. 74. 1864. Cephalocereus robinii Britton & Rose, Cactaceae 2: 39. 1920. Pilocereus robinii Byles & Rowley, Cactus & Succ. Jour. Gt. Brit. 19: 67. 1957. Cereus robinii L. Benson, Cactus & Succ. Jour. 41: 126. 1969. "...Par M. Robin, qui dit l'espece commune dans le lagunes, sur le bord de l'Ocean, non loin de la Havane." Cephalocereus keyensis Britton & Rose, Contr. U.S. Nat. Herb. 12: 416. 1909. Cereus keyensis Vaupel, Monatsschr. Kakteenk, 23: 23, 26. 1913. Pilocereus keyensis Knuth in Backeberg & Knuth, Kaktus-ABC 331. 1935. Pilosocereus keyensis Byles & Rowley, Cactus & Succ. Jour. Gt. Brit. 19: 67. 1957. Cereus robinii var. keyensis L. Benson ex Long & Lakela, FL. Trop. Fla. 631. 1971, an inadvertance. "Hammock, Key West, Florida, N. L. Britton, April 7, 1909, no. 518, type...." TYPE: NY (including fluid-preserved material); photograph, US 535808.

FLORIDA. MONROE CO. Big Pine Key, Small, May, 1919, NY (& in preservative), Killip 31426, US, 31714, US, UC, 32405, US, 41951, F, G. S. Miller, Jr., 1714, Feb. 22, 1935, US, Robert F. Martin 1307, USNA, L. Benson, T. Alexander, & C. Dodson 16574, Pom, R. K. Willich in 1970, Pom; Umbrella Key, Hitchcock, Mar. 28-30, 1906, F, J. K. & E. W. Small 4880, NY, Rose, May 20, 1915, NY, Small, May 2-3, 1917, NY, US.

11b. Cereus robinii var. deeringii (Small) L. Benson

Cephalocereus deeringii Small, Jour. N. Y. Bot. Gard. 18: 201: pl. 532. 1917. Pilocereus deeringii Knuth in Backeberg & Knuth, Kaktus-ABC 330. 1935. Pilosocereus deeringii Byles & Rowley, Cactus & Succ. Jour. Gt. Brit. 19: 67. 1957. Cereus robinii (Lemaire) L. Benson var. deeringii L. Benson, Cactus & Succ. Jour. 41: 126. 1969. "Rocky hammocks, Lower Matecumbe Key, Florida, J. K. Small 7790...." April 8, 1916. TYPE: NY (including fluid-preserved material). ISOTYPE: US 1814252.

FLORIDA. MONROE CO. Hammock, Upper Matecumbe Key, Small & Britton 9321, Dec. 12, 1919, NY; hammock, Lower Matecumbe Key, Small 7790, April 8, 1916, NY, US.

12. Cereus thurberi Engelmann

Cereus thurberi Engelm. Amer. Jour. Sci. II. 17: 234. 1854. Pilocereus thurberi Rümpler in Förster, Handb. Cacteenk. ed. 2. 689. 1885. Lemaireocereus thurberi Britton & Rose, Contr. U.S. Nat. Herb. 12: 426. 1909. Neolemaireocereus thurberi Backeberg, Cactaceae, Jahrb. Deutschen Kakteen-Gesellsch. 1943-1944: 57. 1944, nom. nud. Marshallocereus thurberi Backeberg, Cactus & Succ. Jour. 23: 121. 1951. Stenocereus thurberi F. Buxbaum, Bot. Studien 12: 101. 1961. Pachycereus thurberi Bravo, Cact. Suc. Méx. 17: 119. 1972. "Collected in 1851, in a rocky cañon near the mountain pass of Bacuachi, a small town on the road to Arispe, Sonora...." George Thurber. TYPE: Mo (flower and a very young fruit). Typical specimen for other characters: "Hills and mesas near Altar, Sonora," Mexico, Pringle, Aug. 25, 1884, US 41026 & 795791.

13. Cereus schottii Engelmann

Cereus schottii Engelm. Proc. Amer. Acad. 3: 288. 1857 (preprint, 1856); in Emory, Rept. U.S. & Mex. Bound. Surv. Cactaceae 44. 1859. Pilocereus schottii Lemaire, Rev. Hort. 1862: 428. 1862. Lophocereus schottii Britton & Rose, Contr. U.S. Nat. Herb. 12: 427. 1909. "Sierra de Sonoyita, and southeast towards Santa Magdalena...Schott..." TYPE: Mo (spines and seeds). Typical specimen for other characters: University of Arizona Cactus Garden, Tucson, plant brought from the Organ Pipe Cactus National Monument in Arizona 2-3 miles N of Sonoita, Sonora, by A. A. Nichol in the 1930's, Lyman Benson 10342, May 29, 1940, Pom 274004.

Lophocereus schottii (Engelm.) Britton & Rose f. monstrosus Hort. ex Y. Ito, Cacti 1952: 147. 1952, nom. nud. (no Latin diagnosis).

ARIZONA. "Arizona," Schott in 1856, Mo; monument 174, Mexican boundary line, Mearns 2788, US. PIMA CO. 1 mi. E of Quitovoquita, E. R. Blakley, June 2, 1951, Des (fls.); Puerto Blanco Mts., Peebles & Parker 14800, Ariz; Desert Star Mine Road, Organ Pipe Cactus Nat. Mon., L. Benson 14880, Pom; Gray's Well, A. A. Nichol, May 4, 1939, Organ Pipe Cactus Nat. Mon. Herb.

14. Cereus emoryi Engelmann

Cereus emoryi Engelm. Amer. Jour. Sci. 14: 338. 1852; in Emory, Rept. U.S. & Mex. Bound. Surv. 2: 40. pl. 60, f. 1-4. 1859. Echinocereus emoryi Rümpler in Förster, Handb. Cacteenk. ed. 2. 80. 1885. Doubtless Rümpler was describing C. emoryi, and his reference to Echinocactus emoryi Engelm., almost certainly was due to momentary confusion of names. Bergerocactus emoryi Britton & Rose, Contr. U.S. Nat. Herb. 12: 435, 474. 1909. Bergerocereus emoryi Britton & Rose, Cactaceae 2: 227. 1920, nom. nud. (in index but not text; omitted from reprints), an inadvertance. "In thick patches, on dry hills near the sea-shore, about the boundary line. ...California...San Diego...patches 10 to 20 feet square, Dr. Parry...." 1850. TYPE: Mo (fruit). Typical specimen for other characters: <u>CALIFORNIA</u>. SAN DIEGO CO. "1/2 mile from the ocean, 1/2 mile from Mexico, elevation 50 feet." <u>Lyman Benson 14337</u>, April 29, 1950, <u>Pom 285764</u>.

15. Cereus greggii Engelmann

15a. Cereus greggii var. greggii

Cereus greggii Engelm. in Wisliz. Mem. Tour. No. Mex. 102. 1848. <u>C. greggii</u> Engelm. var. <u>cismontanus</u> Engelm. Proc. Amer. Acad. 3: 287. 1857 (preprint, 1856); in Emory, Rept. U.S. & Mex. Bound. Surv. Cactaceae 41, <u>pl. 63–64</u>. 1859, intended as the typical variety. <u>Peniocereus greggii</u> Britton & Rose, Contr. U.S. Nat. Herb. 12: 428. 1909. LECTOTYPE designation: "...Dr. Gregg ...near Cadena, south of Chihuahua, in flower, from which I completed the description," May 9, 1847, <u>Mo</u>.

15b. Cereus greggii var. transmontanus Engelmann

<u>Cereus greggii</u> Engelm. var. <u>transmontanus</u> Engelm. Proc. Amer. Acad. 3: 287. 1857 (preprint, 1856); in Emory, Rept. U.S. & Mex. Bound. Surv. Cactaceae 2: 42. <u>pl. 65</u>. 1859. <u>Peniocereus greggii</u> (Engelm.) Britton & Rose var. <u>transmontanus</u> (Engelm.) Backeberg, Cactaceae 4: 1945. 1960. "...To the Gila, <u>Emory</u>; and Sonora, <u>Thurber</u>, <u>Schott</u>...." LECTOTYPE designation: "Table lands of the Gila and San Bernardino," <u>George Thurber</u>, July and August, 1852, <u>F</u>.

<u>Cereus greggii</u> Engelm. var. <u>roseiflorus</u> R. Kuntze, Monatss. Kakteenk. 20: 172. 1910. Arizona. No specimen. See Suppl.

16. Cereus poselgeri (Lemaire) Coulter

<u>Cereus tuberosus</u> Poselger, Allg. Gartenz. 21: 135. 1853, not Pfeiffer in 1837. <u>Echinocereus poselgeri</u> Lemaire, Cactées 57. 1868, nom. nov. E. tuberosus Rümpler in Förster, Handb. Cacteenk., ed. 2. 783. 1885. C. <u>poselgeri</u> Coulter, Contr. U.S. Nat. Herb. 3: 398. 1896. <u>Wilcoxia poselgeri</u> Britton & Rose, Contr. U.S. Nat. Herb. 12: 434. 1909. "Habitat in Texas." LECTOTYPE designation: "Rio Grande [near Laredo] above Belleville" and "Dr. Poselger coll 1850" (fruit) and "On the Rio Grande. 1850" (fruit) and "From an original seedling of Dr. Poselger cult. in Goebel's Garden, St. Louis. George Engelmann...April & May 1859," (flowers) <u>Mo</u> (on 3 sheets). Typical specimen (for other parts) Laredo, Texas. <u>Marcus E. Jones 29587</u>, March 24, 1932, <u>Pom 215607</u>. DUPLICATE: <u>Mo 1021792</u>.

17. Cereus striatus Brandegee

<u>Cereus striatus</u> Brandegee, Zöe 2: 19. 1891. <u>Wilcoxia striata</u> Britton & Rose, Contr. U.S. Nat. Herb. 12: 434. 1909. <u>Neoevansia striata</u> Sanchez-Mejorada, Cact. y Suc. Méx. 18: 22. 1973. TYPE: San Jose Del Cabo, <u>T. S. Brandegee 243</u>, Sept. 30. 1890, <u>UC 108249</u>, photograph, <u>US</u>. ISOTYPES: <u>GH</u>, Ph.

<u>Cereus diguetii</u> Weber, Bull. Mus. Hist. Nat. Paris 1 (1895): 319. 1895. <u>Wilcoxia diguetii</u> Diguet & Guillaumin, Arch. Hist. Nat. Soc. Nat. d'Acclim. 4: 222. 1928. Neoevansia diguetii W. T. Marshall in Marshall & Bock, Cactaceae 84. 1941. <u>W. diguetii</u> Peebles, Leafl. West. Bot. 5: 192. 1949; Cactus & Succ. Jour. 22: 13. 1950, later homonym. <u>Peniocereus diguetii</u> Backeberg, Cactus & Succ. Jour. 23: 119. 1951. "Le Cactées de la Basse-Californie," "Le plupart de ces documents ont été recueillis aux environs de 27° latitude Nord." TYPE: <u>P</u> (5 sheets of stems and tubers, no flowers or fruits). ISOTYPE: <u>UC 168560</u> (piece of a stem).

<u>ARIZONA</u>. PIMA CO. Gray's Well, Organ Pipe Cactus Nat. Mon., <u>A. A. Nichol</u>, May 4, 1939, <u>Organ Pipe Cactus Nat. Mon. Herb.</u>, <u>L. Benson 16707</u>, <u>Pom</u>; 8 mi. NE of Sonoyta, <u>A. A. Nichol</u>, April 20, 1939, <u>Ariz</u>; near San Miguel, Papago Reservation, <u>Lindsay</u>, Jan. 25, 1942, <u>Ariz</u>; near Rusty Shovel, W. of San Miguel, <u>Lindsay</u>, Jan. 25, 1942, <u>DS</u> (box); W of Baboquivari Mts., <u>Mr. and Mrs. Ed Gay</u> in 1969, <u>Pom</u>.

6. Echinocereus

<u>Echinocereus</u>, as genus, Engelm. in Wisliz. Mem. Tour. No. Mexico 91. 1848; as subgenus, Engelm. Proc. Amer. Acad. 3: 278. 1857 (preprint, 1856). Type species, Echinocereus viridiflorus Engelm. (lectotype, Britton & Rose, Cactaceae 3: 3. 1922).

<u>Triglochidiata</u>, as section, Bravo, Cact. y Suc. Méx. 18: 108. 1973. Type species: Echinocereus triglochidiatus Engelm.

1. Echinocereus triglochidiatus Engelmann

<u>Echinocereus triglochidiatus</u> received its first contingent of names as a species during 1848 -- 5 or, according to some authors, 6 under four genera. The names applied that year, each to a variety of the species, are listed below.

<u>Cereus roemeri</u> Mühlenpfordt, Jan. 15 (var. <u>melanacanthus</u>) <u>Echinopsis octacantha</u> Mühlenpfordt, Jan. 15 (of uncertain application; misapplied to var. <u>melanacanthus</u>)

<u>Echinocereus triglochidiatus</u> Engelm., <u>ca</u>. Apr. 2 (var. <u>triglochidiatus</u>) <u>Echinocereus coccineus</u> Engelm., <u>ca</u>. Apr. 2 (var. <u>melanacanthus</u>) <u>Echinocereus polyacanthus</u> Engelm., <u>ca</u>. Apr. 2 (var. <u>neomexicanus</u>)

<u>Mammillaria aggregata</u> Engelm., May 18–July 19 (var. <u>melanacanthus</u>)

The names by Mühlenpfordt appeared in the Allgemeine Gartenzeitung for January 15, 1848.

The first 3 names by Engelmann were published in Wislizenus, <u>Memoir of a Tour to Northern Mexico</u> [which included New Mexico and Texas] in 1846 and 1847, published for the United States Senate, Miscellaneous No. 26. The year date, 1848, appears on the title page, along with "January 13, 1848.-- Ordered that 5,000 copies be printed for the use of the Senate, and 200 additional for Dr. Wislizenus." According to the Senate Journal, First Session, Thirtieth Congress, p. 85, on Jan. 3, 1848, an earlier resolution (30th Cong., 1st sess. Senate, Misc. Document no. 22) was read authorizing the printing of Dr. Wislizenus' <u>Memoir</u>, a small publication of 115 pages. The following appears on the verso of the title page "IN THE SENATE OF THE UNITED STATES, January 13, 1848. The Committee on Printing, to whom were referred the resolutions submitted by Mr. Benton, viz: 'Resolved, that there be printed...[quotation of the resolution of Jan. 3, 1848]' report [Senate Journal, pp. 108–109], that there be printed for the use of the Senate 5,000 copies of the tour, and that there be lithographed a like number of maps accompanying the same; also 200 copies for the use of Dr. Wislizenus. Attest: ASBURY DICKINS, Secretary." Thus the publication date appeared to be January 13, 1848. The booklet, according to the last page, was completed in December, 1847, approved January 3, 1848, and published January 13, 1848. (Cf. L. Benson, Cactus & Succ. Jour. 46: 74. 1974.)

However, there was a delay in publication of the booklet by Wislizenus. According to the Senate Journal, page 225, on March 21, 1848, the following resolution was passed: "...That the Secretary of the Senate be directed to inquire into the execution of the Senate's order, of January 13, directing the report of Dr. Wislizenus to be printed, and report the progress, if any, made into the execution of said order." On March 23, Senate Journal, page 230, "The Vice President laid before the Senate a report of the Secretary of the Senate, made in pursuance of the resolution of the Senate in relation to the causes of delay in printing the report of Dr. Wislizenus: which was read." However, there was no indication of what was read. This problem, called to attention by Terry L. Corbett, stimulated a further search (cf. L. Benson, Cactus & Succ. Jour. 47: 40–43. 1975.

Fortunately, a record exists in the National Archives, as follows (Sen. 30D-A1 and Letter Book, 24th.-32nd. Cong.). The letter of March 23, 1848, from the Secretary of the Senate to the Vice President, included the following: "...respecting the printing of the Report of Dr. Wislizenus, ...[the Secretary of the Senate] is informed by the printers, Mssrs Ritchie & Heiss for Mssrs Tippin & Streeper, that considerable progress has been made in the work, and that it will probably be completed in about 10 days or perhaps less." Thus, according to the existing data, the publication date was almost certainly between March 23 and April 2, 1848, most likely about April 2.

Thus, the publication of the species by Mühlenpfordt, <u>Beiträge zur Cacteenkunde</u>, Allgemeine Gartenzeitung 16: 17–20. January 15, 1848, has priority over that of Engelmann in Wislizenus' <u>Memoir</u>. However, the status of each of the names applied by Mühlenpfordt is as follows:

<u>Cereus roemeri</u>, not <u>C. roemeri</u> Engelm. in 1849 (see under <u>Echinocereus triglochidiatus</u> var. <u>melanacanthus</u>). <u>C. roemeri</u> Mühlenpfordt cannot be transferred to <u>Echinocereus</u> because the combination, <u>Echinocereus roemeri</u> Rümpler, based upon <u>C. roemeri</u> Engelm. was published in 1885.

<u>Echinopsis octacantha</u> is a <u>nomen dubium</u>, not applied to <u>Echinocereus triglochidiatus</u>, as assumed by Coulter and other authors (<u>cf</u>. discussion, Documentation section, following var. <u>melanacanthus</u>).

The names published in Wislizenus' <u>Memoir</u>, <u>circa</u> April 2, 1848, have the following stati:

<u>Echinocereus triglochidiatus</u>, valid and available (cf. under var. <u>triglochidiatus</u>, Documentation section).

<u>Echinocereus coccineus</u>, valid but not available to replace E. triglochidiatus (<u>cf</u>. under var. <u>melanacanthus</u>, Documentation section), under Article 57, "the rule of the first reviser." In 1941, W. T. Marshall treated the two proposed species of Engelmann as varieties of a single species, E. triglochidiatus, and he published the subordinate combination, E. triglochidiatus var. <u>coccineus</u>.

<u>Echinocereus polyacanthus</u>, valid but not available to replace E. triglochidiatus (cf. var. <u>neomexicanus</u>, Documentation section), under Article 57. E. polyacanthus was reduced to varietal status

under E. triglochidiatus, as var. polyacanthus, L. Benson, Proc. Calif. Acad. Sci. IV. 25: 253. 1944.

Thus, the two names published by Engelmann simultaneously with Echinocereus triglochidiatus no longer compete with it, but another name was published by Engelmann in 1848, as follows:

Mammillaria aggregata Engelm. in Emory, Notes of a Military Reconnaissance from Fort Leavenworth in Missouri [now in Kansas] to San Diego in California, App. 2. 157. f. 1. 1848 (cf. under var. melanacanthus, Documentation section). According to the date of authorization by the Senate on the title page, February 17, 1848, this publication could have appeared before Wislizenus' Memoir, circa April 2. If so, the epithet aggregata(-us) would have priority over triglochidiatus.

The Senate Journal, First Session, 1847-48, includes various orders of the Senate for publication of Emory's Report (December 9, 16, and 21, 1847; February 9 and 17, 1848). The order of February 17 appears on the title page, and commonly it has been considered the date of publication. The Journal includes later entries (1848) (March 4, 17, 18; May 29; June 30; July 19) concerning printing of additional copies but no indication of the time when the first copies were released. The entry of June 30 seems significant: "Ordered, That ten thousand additional copies of the report of the Secretary of War of the 15th. December, 1847, and the report of Lieutenant Emory, communicated therewith, be printed for the use of the Senate; and that said copies, as well as those already printed, be bound in muslin." Thus, copies had been printed before or by June 30, 1848, but whether any unbound copies had been released, thus effecting botanical publication, is uncertain. The following information has been supplied by the National Archives and Record Service: According to the letter (Letter Book, p. 259) of the Secretary of the Senate to G. & W. Endicott, dated...May 18, 1848, "The printing of Emory's Report has been finished and a large number of sets of the drawings lithographed by Weber & Co. have been received. But the complete copies of the work cannot be delivered for want of the drawings lithographed by you." On (ibid.) p. 263, "As the Report is urgently called for, I trust your engravings will be sent without delay." Therefore, publication could have occurred no earlier than May 18 and perhaps after June 30, and the later publication date excludes the epithet aggregatus from consideration for priority over triglochidiatus.

1a. Echinocereus triglochidiatus var. melanacanthus (Engelmann) L. Benson

Cereus roemeri Mühlenpfordt, Allg. Gartenz. 16: 19. Jan. 15, 1848, not Engelm. in 1849. Echinocereus roemeri Rydb. Bull. Torrey Club 33: 146. 1906, later homonym, not Engelm. ex Rümpler 1885. "...Durch Herrn Dr. Roemer in Hildsheim aus dem nördl. Texas mitgebracht." The following is quoted from Engelmann, U.S. Senate Rept. Expl. & Surv. R. R. Route Pacific Ocean 4: Botany 35. 1857, "Cer. roemeri Mühlenpf., not Engelm., from the San Saba, in Texas...." The San Saba River flows within 30 miles of the Llano River, the type locality for Cereus roemeri Engelm., published one year later than C. roemeri Mühlenpfordt. Probably the collections reaching Mühlenpfordt were by Dr. F. Roemer, geologist of the University of Bonn, because likely Roemer sent plants to both authors while Lindheimer also sent some to Engelmann. The plants of the Roemer collections were not necessarily identical but both were drawn from the only taxon of this type occurring in the area. NEOTYPE designation: Balanced Rock; granitic outcrop 4 miles due north of Fredericksburg, Gillespie Co., Texas, L. Benson 16563, April 23, 1965, Pom 317376. About 53 airline miles from San Saba River.

Echinocereus coccineus Engelm. in Wisliz. Mem. Tour No. Mex. 93. ca. Apr. 2, 1848. (For publication date cf. discussion under E. triglochidiatus and L. Benson, Cactus & Succ. Jour. 48: 40-43. 1975.) Cereus coccineus Engelm. in A. Gray, Pl. Fendl., Mem. Amer. Acad. 4: 51. 1849, not Salm-Dyck in 1828. C. phoeniceus Engelm. Proc. Amer. Acad. 3: 284. 1857 (preprint, 1856), nom. nov. for E. coccineus Engelm. (this being necessary under Cereus but not Echinocereus). E. phoen[i]ceus Engelm. ex Rümpler in Förster, Handb. Cacteenk. ed. 2. 788. 1885, incorrectly ascribed to Engelmann, nom. superfl. (E. coccineus, based upon the same type specimen available and legitimate under Echinocereus). E. polyacanthus Engelm. var. X phoeniceus Frič, Českoslov. Zahradnichých Listů [Kakt. Sukk.] 1924: 121. 1924, nom. nud. E. triglochidiatus Engelm. var. coccineus Engelm. ex W. T. Marshall in Marshall & Bock, Cactaceae 117. 1941, erroneously attributed to Engelmann. "With the foregoing [E. triglochidiatus], also about Santa Fé." "On Wolf Creek, in pine woods...." New Mexico, east of Santa Fe, "...June 24, 1846...." LECTOTYPE designation: Wolf Creek, Wislizenus, June 24, 1846, Mo (on 2 sheets).

Mammillaria aggregata Engelm. in Emory, Notes Mil. Reconn. Ft. Leavenworth to San Diego App. 2. 157. f. 1, May-July, 1848. Cereus aggregatus Coulter, Contr. U.S. Nat. Herb. 3: 396. 1896. Echinocereus aggregata Rydb. Bull. Torrey Club 33: 146. 1906. Coryphantha aggregata Britton & Rose, Cactaceae 4: 47. 1923. M. vivipara (Nutt.) Haw. var. aggregata L. Benson, Proc. Calif. Acad. Sci. IV. 25: 262. 1944. Escobaria aggregata F. Buxbaum, Österr. Bot. Zeitschr. 98: 78. 1951. Coryphantha vivipara (Nutt.) Britton & Rose var. aggregata W. T. Marshall, Arizona's Cactuses ed. 1. 93. 1950. "Oct. 18, 1846. Head waters of the Gila, 6,000 feet above the sea."

Whether the plant figured and described was a Coryphantha or an Echinocereus affects the status of names under both genera. The combinations under Cereus and Echinocereus in publications prior to Britton & Rose, Cactaceae 3: 47-48. pl. 4. & f. 47. 1922. were based upon formation of large clusters of stems like those in the original illustration and in E. triglochidiatus var. melanacanthus. Stem mounds occur also in some varieties of Coryphantha vivipara, including both var. bisbeeana (to which Britton & Rose referred Mammillaria aggregata Engelm. under the new combination Coryphantha aggregata) and var. arizonica. This departed from Engelmann's reinterpretation (in Ives, Rept. Colo. R. West Part 4. Botany 13. 1861) of the proposed species as Echinocereus, which he then placed under Cereus. It differed also from the then recent interpretations of other authors, e.g., Coulter, Contr. U.S. Nat. Herb. 3: 396. 1896. Four years after Britton & Rose's work appeared, Engelmann's interpretation was reinstated by Orcutt (Cactography 3. 1926), and Orcutt proposed Coryphantha bisbeeana as a nomen novum for the plant (Coryphantha vivipara var. bisbeeana) described as Coryphantha aggregata by Britton & Rose.

Either Echinocereus triglochidiatus var. melanacanthus or Coryphantha vivipara var. arizonica could be found in the area in Grant Co., New Mexico, in which the sketch was made on October 18, 1846. This was on rocky hills between the Mimbres River and Santa Rita. However, var. bisbeeana, to which Mammillaria aggregata was referred by Britton & Rose, is known only from Arizona and Sonora. Furthermore, occurrence at 6,000 feet elevation indicates that the plant was either var. melanacanthus or var. arizonica, which grow at higher levels than var. bisbeeana.

The original drawing (in Emory, Notes Mil. Reconn. Ft. Leavenworth to San Diego App. 2. 157. f. 1. Feb. 17, 1848) shows the form and habit of the plant well, but structural features are vague. The stems are of the shape of those of Echinocereus triglochidiatus var. melanacanthus, rather than those of Coryphantha vivipara var. bisbeeana or arizonica (cf., for example, Britton & Rose, pl. 4), which would have the appearance of a pile of balls, rather than of a cluster of more elongate structures. E. triglochidiatus var. melanacanthus often forms dense clusters on rocky ledges; var. arizonica does not. The vague crossed lines may indicate tubercles rather than ribs, supporting the Coryphantha theory. However, the significance of these lines is doubtful, and most likely they are only shading. The description could apply to either plant, except that the stem dimensions and proportions are those shown in the figure, and these could apply only to var. melanacanthus. For a matching photograph, cf. L. Benson, Cacti of Arizona ed. 3. 123. f. 3.1. 1969 (Echinocereus triglochidiatus var. melanacanthus).

There is no reason to disallow Engelmann's own reinterpretation of the species he described. In Ives' Report he refers Mammillaria aggregata to Cereus phoeniceus, a synonym for Echinocereus triglochidiatus var. melanacanthus, as follows: "This is Mammillaria aggregata, Emory's Report, 1848, and the 'Aggregated Cactus' of the explorers of the western parts of New Mexico [which then included Arizona] and the Gila regions.... It was found from Camp 64 to Camp 78 (Yampai Valley to Partridge Creek). In flower in April." However, Yampai is in Western Coconino Co., Arizona, far from Santa Rita, New Mexico, and, although the Newberry collection ("Camp 64-78, Newberry, Ives Expedition, April, 1858," Mo) is the specimen Engelmann had in mind, the material preserved is not adequate to become a neotype because it consists of only a flower.

On October 17, 1846, the military reconnaissance expedition under Lieutenant W. H. Emory made camp in the mountains just west of the Mimbres River, en route from approximately the site of the present town of San Lorenzo to the then quiescent "Copper Mines" of Santa Rita. "Mammillaria aggregata" was drawn sometime on October 18 in a "rocky succession of hills and valleys covered with cedar [juniper], live oak and some long-leafed pine [Pinus ponderosa]." NEOTYPE designation: Near the campsite from which the party started on October 18, 1846; canyon between Santa Rita and the Mimbres River, 2.5 miles above San Lorenzo, 6,000 feet, Lyman Benson 16660, July 2, 1966, Pom 317382.

Cereus coccineus (Engelm.) Engelm. var. melanacanthus Engelm. in A. Gray, Pl. Fendler., Mem. Amer. Acad. 4: 51. 1849. Echinocereus triglochidiatus Engelm. var. melanacanthus L. Benson, Proc. Calif. Acad. IV. 25: 254. 1944. E. melanacanthus Engelm. ex W. H. Earle, Cacti Southw. 61. 1963, incorrectly ascribed to Engelmann, nom. superfl., antedated by E. coccineus (1848) which appears in synonymy. "...Fendler...Santa Fe...." LECTOTYPE designation: "Santa Fe," A. Fendler, Nov. 26, 1846, Mo. In varietal rank the epithet melanacanthus (1849) has almost a century of priority over coccineus (1941), and several other epithets also have priority in varietal rank over coccineus.

The epithet melanacanthus (black-spined) is disturbing to some, because usually the spines are gray to pink, tan, or straw-colored. From plant to plant the color varies within each population. Near the type locality, Santa Fe, there are plants with black spines, but the character is uncommon and not correlated with any other (15 miles SE of Santa Fe, 7,400 ft., L. Benson 14694, Pom, 14694a, Pom). "However, the purpose of giving a name to a taxon is not to indicate its characters or history, but to supply a means of referring to it, and a legitimate name or epithet must not be rejected merely because it is inappropriate or disagreeable, or because another is preferable or better known, or because it has lost its original meaning" (Art. 62). If the epithet has been applied to a type specimen derived from any plant of a taxon, it must apply to the whole taxon. The degree of predominance or prevalence of this element makes no difference in nomenclature.

Cereus coccineus (Engelm.) Engelm. var. cylindricus Engelm. in A. Gray, Pl. Fendl., Mem. Amer. Acad. 4: 51. 1849, not Cereus viridiflorus (Engelm.) Engelm. var. cylindricus Engelm. in 1856. "...Fendler...Santa Fé...." LECTOTYPE designation: Fendler 17/9/46 [Sept. 17, 1846], Mo.

Cereus roemeri Engelm. in A. Gray, Pl. Fendl., Mem. Amer. Acad. 4: 51. 1849; Pl. Lindh., Boston Jour. Nat. Hist. 6: 204. 1850, later homonym, not Mühlenpfordt in 1848. Echinocereus roemeri Engelm. ex Rümpler in Förster, Handb. Cacteenk. ed. 2. 792. 1885, incorrectly ascribed to Engelmann; epithet considered newly published in 1885. "Western [central] Texas." "Granitic region about Liano; flowers (in St. Louis) in May...Dr. F. Roemer ...Sent also in numerous specimens by Lindheimer." No collections by Roemer found. LECTOTYPE designation: "Liano [Llano] River, Lindheimer in 1887," Mo (on 2 sheets).

Cereus hexaedrus Engelm. Proc. Amer. Acad. 3: 285. 1857 (preprint, 1856); U.S. Senate Rept. Expl. & Surv. R. R. Route Pacific Ocean 4: Botany 34. pl. 5, f. 1. 1857. Echinocereus hexaedrus Engelm. ex Rümpler in Förster, Handb. Cacteenk. ed. 2. 807. 1885, incorrectly ascribed to Engelmann. E. paucispinus (Engelm.) Engelm. ex Rümpler var. hexaedra [hexaedrus] K. Schum. Gesammtb. Kakteen 281. 1898. E. paucispinus (Engelm.) Engelm. ex Rümpler f. hexaedrus Schelle, Handb. Kakteenkultur 137. 1907. E. triglochidiatus Engelm. var. hexaedrus Boissevain & Davidson, Colo. Cacti 36. 1940. "Near [15 miles W of] Zuñi, in Western New Mexico." LECTOTYPE designation: "Near Zuñi. Cedar woods. Sandy soil." J. M. Bigelow, Nov. 28, 1853, Mo. In 1856 Arizona was part of the New Mexico Territory. The present boundary is 10 miles by airline, 12 by road, west of Zuñi, New Mexico. Probably the specimen was collected barely in Apache Co., Arizona. This plant has been confused with var. triglochidiatus or var. gonacanthus because of the "angular spines." However, the spines are very slender and are angular only on close inspection, as sometimes in var. melanacanthus. Spines of this type are found in some of the innumerable character assemblages among hybrids in the transitory populations abundant where two or more of the varieties occur.

Cereus conoideus Engelm. & Bigelow, Proc. Amer. Acad. 3: 284. 1857 (preprint, 1856); U.S. Senate Rept. Expl. & Surv. R. R. Route Pacific Ocean 4: Botany 35. pl. 4, f. 4-5. 1857, as to type specimen but not classification. C. phoeniceus Engelm. subsp. conoideus Engelm. U.S. Senate Rept. Expl. & Surv. R. R. Route Pacific Ocean 4: Botany 35. pl. 4. f. 4-5. 1857. Echinocereus phoeniceus Rümpler [illegitimate name] var. conoideus K. Schum. Gesambt. Kakteen 283. 1898. E. phoeniceus "Lem." f. conoideus Engelm. ex Schelle, Handb. Kakteenkultur 138. 1907, incorrectly ascribed to Engelmann. E. coccineus Engelm. var. conoideus Engelm. ex Weniger Cacti S.W. 42. 1970, nom. nud. (Art. 33), erroneously ascribed to Engelmann. "Rocky places on the Upper Pecos [River], and perhaps San Francisco Mountain." "On rocky and mountainous localities on the Pecos." LECTOTYPE designation: Anton Chico, upper Pecos River, New Mexico, J. M. Bigelow, Sept. 24, 1853, Mo.

Cereus mojavensis Engelm. & Bigelow var. zuniensis Engelm. & Bigelow, Proc. Amer. Acad. 3: 28. 1857 (preprint, 1856); U.S. Senate Rept. Expl. & Surv. R. R. Route Pacific Ocean 4: Botany 33. pl. 4, f. 9. 1857. C. bigelovii Engelm. var. zuniensis Engelm. in Engelm. & Bigelow, loc. cit., pl. 4, f. 9., bigelovii being doubtless an epithet discarded before publication and replaced by mojavensis in the text but not changed on the plate. Echinocereus mojavensis Engelm. & Bigelow var. zuniensis (Engelm. & Bigelow) Engelm. ex Rümpler in Förster, Handb. Cacteenk. ed. 2. 803. 1885, incorrectly ascribed to Engelmann. "...Near Cañon Diablo, on the Colorado Chiquito, about 120 miles west of Zuñi [New Mexico]." "...December 18, 1852 [1853]...." By highway Canyon Diablo is 34 miles east of Flagstaff. The date given above is corrected, because in December, 1852, the expedition was still on the Great Plains. The type of Echinocactus whipplei (ibid. 28) was collected December 3-4, 1853, on the Colorado Chiquito about "90 miles" west of Zuni; a specimen identified as Cereus phoeniceus (ibid. 34) was collected farther west on the San Francisco Mountains, Dec. 18, 1853. LECTOTYPE designation: "Colorado Chiquito," J. M. Bigelow, Dec. 14, 1853, Mo. DUPLICATE: Pom 317803. The spines are slightly angled as in forms of var. melanacanthus similarly transitional to var. gonacanthus.

Echinocereus krausei De Smet in Förster, Handb. Cacteenk. ed. 2. 789. 1885. "Vaterland unbekannt."

Echinocereus phoen[i]ceus (Engelm.) Engelm. ex Rümpler [an illegitimate combination] vars. albispinus, longispinus, and rufispinus Rümpler in Förster, Handb. Cacteenk. ed. 2. 789. 1885, nom. nud. Horticultural names. Spines answering similar color or form descriptions can be found in most species or varieties.

Echinocereus phoeniceus (Engelm.) Engelm. ex Rümpler [an illegitimate combination] var. inermis K. Schum. Monatsschr. Kakteenk. 6: 150. 1896. E. coccineus Engelm. var. inermis J. A.

Purpus, Mitt. Deutsch. Dendrol. Gesellsch. 1925: 49. 1925. E. phoeniceus "Lem." f. inermis Schelle, Handb. Kakteenkultur 138. 1907. E. triglochidiatus Engelm. var. inermis Rowley, Repert. Pl. Succ. 22: 9. 1973; Arp, Cactus & Succ. Jour. 44: 132. 1973. "Herr C. A. Purpus aus Colorado an die hiesige berühmte Gärtneri von SPÄTH schickte...." According to J. A. Purpus, loc. cit., "Die typische Form fand C. A. Purpus auch in der Hügelregion der Bookcliffs in Utah...best an denen Plateaus der Mesas bei 1600-2200 m und in den La Sal Mts. in Utah bei 1900 m." Book Cliffs are in E Grand Co., Utah, and adjacent Mesa Co., Colorado. No specimens seen. The Purpus collection at Darmstadt was destroyed during the Second World War. NEOTYPE designation: "Road along Brumley Ridge, in pinyon-juniper woods, on Morrison formation, La Sal Mts., San Juan County, Utah, June 5, 1970, N. D. Atwood & S. L. Welsh 9,933," Pom 317984. DUPLICATE: BrY.

Echinocereus phoeniceus (Engelm.) Engelm. ex Rümpler [an illegitimate combination] f. brevispinus Engelm. ex Schelle, Handb. Kakteenkultur 138. 1907, nom. nud., incorrectly ascribed to Engelmann. Two other nomina nuda, formae densus and utahensis, are ascribed by Schelle, loc. cit., to horticulture.

Echinocereus canyonensis Clover & Jotter, Bull. Torrey Club 68: 417. f. 1 (4). 1941. "TYPE (Clover and Jotter 2317) collected in a sandy pocket on a steep limestone outcrop 100 yards from the [Colorado] river, Bass Cable below Hermit Creek Rapids, Grand Canyon, Coconino County, Arizona. Locally abundant." TYPE: "Near Hermit Creek Rapids, Grand Canyon," Elzada U. Clover & Lois Jotter 2317, July 23, 1938, Mich (not numbered). ISOTYPE: same field number, but labelled, "2 miles above Bass Cable, right bank of the Colorado River," US 2346041.

This variety is collected more frequently than most cacti, and there are numerous specimens from Utah, Colorado, Arizona, and New Mexico and fewer from western and central Texas. Collections from Mexico are few. Relatively few significant specimens, mostly those outlining the periphery of the range of the variety, are cited below:

CALIFORNIA. SAN BERNARDINO CO. Pacific Fluoride Co. Mine, N side of Clark Mt., 5,000 feet, C. H. & A. Bonner, Dec., 1961, Pom; Copper Queen Mine, New York Mts., (approaching var. mojavensis) Everett & Balls 23155, RSA, UC, SD. Var. melanacanthus is missing from most books and papers on the flora of California. The collections cited above may represent occurrence of the character combinations of var. melanacanthus in populations prevailingly of var. mojavensis. However, although this phenomenon has been observed in various populations, for the Bonner collection there is no evidence of intergradation. Thus, at least this specimen must be placed under var. melanacanthus. Field populations of var. mojavensis occurring from California to SW Utah (Washington Co.) and NW Arizona (W Mohave Co.) include individuals not, or barely, distinguishable from var. melanacanthus. Other plants, clearly var. mojavensis, are more abundant in the populations. These differ strikingly in superficial ways, and Californian authors, unaware of the nature of the broader classification problem, have not thought of the possibility of inclusion of var. mojavensis in the complex of varieties growing farther eastward. Examples of Californian plants matching var. melanacanthus but occurring in the variable local populations primarily of var. mojavensis are shown by the following specimen series: Cushenberry Canyon, San Bernardino Mts., Parish 11717, UC, Parish 11718, UC, L. & R. L. Benson 15663A-E, Pom. Similar intergradation occurs, for example, near Hidden Valley, Joshua Tree National Monument. In Nevada, the percentage of melanacanthus-like plants occurring in the Charleston Mountains is higher (e.g., between Lee Canyon and Deer Creek, L. & R. L. Benson 15067-15069, Pom).

NEVADA. EUREKA CO. N end of Antelope Mts., 7,000 feet, L. Benson 16609, Pom. NYE CO. North Belted Range, J. Beatley, June 1, 1969, TSH; Johnnie's Water road, Central Belted Range, J. Beatley, July 12, 1967, TSH; Stone Mountain Canyon below Oak Spring Butte, J. Beatley, June 16, 1968, TSH; Timpahute Range, J. Beatley, June 15, 1969, TSH; below Mt. Stirling, E side Spring Mts., J. Beatley & J. L. Reveal 10871, Pom, TSH. Plants approximating this variety occur in the Charleston Mts., Clark Co. as extremes in the local populations of var. mojavensis.

UTAH. northernmost distribution: JUAB CO. Mts. E of Nephi, J. W. Moore 2625, Ph. MILLARD CO. Canyon just W of Sevier Lake, 7,000 feet, L. & R. L. Benson 15700, Pom; 7 mi. S of Kanosh, Barkley & Blondeau 4047, Pom, USNA; Halfway Hills, Desert Experimental Range, M. G. Barlow 187, June 1, 1964, BrY. CARBON CO. Helper, Trelease & Saunders 4429, Mo; Price, E. Stearns, Sept. 8, 1905, US (box), J. Hopkins, May 9, 1924, US; Wellington, 5,500 feet, L. & R. L. Benson 15698, Pom; Sunnyside, M. E. Jones, Sept. 5, 1907, US (box). UINTAH CO. Split Mountain Canyon above Island Park, Green River, E. H. Graham 9146, US; Rainbow, Asphalt Canyon Drainage, N. H. Holmgren, J. L. Reveal, & C. La France 1835, BrY, WTU.

COLORADO, extreme NW collections. MOFFAT CO. Split Mountain Canyon, Dinosaur Nat. Mon., J. Tannenholz, (sent) Oct., 1968, Pom. RIO BLANCO CO. Below Piceance Creek, on White River, E. H. Graham 9107, Mo, Pom. GARFIELD CO. Silt, Weber 3361, Colo, Pom, Ph, WS, RSA, UC, CAS, Tex, DS; Carbondale, L. & R. L. Benson 14728, Pom. MESA CO. Grand Junction, Eastwood, US (box); 10 mi. NW of

Delta, L. Benson 16251, Pom; 15 mi. W of Delta, Rollins 2153, GH, US, 2452, GH.

TEXAS. E and S escarpment of Edwards Plateau: KERR CO. "Guadalupe," Gregg 662, Dec. [?]. 1848, Mo (box); Guadalupe River 2 mi. S of Hunt, D. Weniger 229, Sept. 1, 1963, UNM; Kerrville, Heller 1747, Mo, F, GH, CU, Mackenson, Aug. 10, 1909, US, April 14, 1912, NY, US, Turtle Creek, W. L. Bray 232, US. GILLESPIE CO. Balanced Rock, Fredericksburg, L. Benson 16563, Pom. LLANO CO. Llano River, Lindheimer in 1847, Mo; Enchanted Rock, C. M. Rogers & G. L. Webster 6718, March 20, 1949, Tex. BURNET CO. Granite Mountain, A. M. Ferguson, Apr. 30, 1901, Tex, C. M. Rowell 7025, Tex. HAYS CO. R. E. Kunze, US (box). Southern Texas: UVALDE CO. Sabinal, R. Runyon, March, 1922, US (photo), D. Weniger 841, March, 1962, UNM.

Name of Uncertain Application (misapplied to var. melanacanthus)

Echinopsis octacantha Mühlenpfordt, Allg. Gartenz. 16: 19. Jan. 15, 1848. Cereus octacanthus Coulter, Contr. U.S. Nat. Herb. 3: 395. 1896. Echinocereus octacanthus Britton & Rose, Cactaceae 3: 13. 1922. E. coccineus Engelm. var. octacanthus Boissevain & Davidson, Colo. Cacti. 39. 1940. E. triglochidiatus Engelm. var. octacanthus Mühlenpfordt ex W. T. Marshall in Marshall & Bock, Cactaceae 118. 1941, incorrectly ascribed to Mühlenpfordt. "... Durch Herrn Dr. Roemer in Hildsheim aus dem nördl. [central] Texas mitgebracht.

If this name could be shown to have been applied to any element of Echinocereus triglochidiatus, the epithet octacanthus would have priority of publication, cf. L. Benson, Cactus & Succ. Jour. 46: 74. 1974; 47: 40-43. 1975.

Classification by Coulter under Cereus (Echinocereus) was based upon application of Echinopsis octacantha to a group of four collections thought to include some special characters in common. The type was stated to be unknown, and the specimens cited were as follows: "TEXAS (Evans of 1891, about El Paso); NEW MEXICO (Fendler 272, of 1846, in part); UTAH (Mrs. Thompson); also cultivated in Mo. Bot. Gard. from Herb. Torr." None was from central Texas. This represents an improbable distributional pattern for a taxon proposed to be segregated from the wide-ranging Echinocereus triglochidiatus var. melanacanthus, and the expected explanation is the occurrence of some one or two characters in these specimens and their lack in the few other collections Coulter had available. The extant specimens themselves are unintelligible fragments not representing even corresponding parts of individuals, as follows: (1) Evans, US, a remnant of a plant which died in the garden; (2) Fendler 272, Mo, flowers; (3) Mrs. Thompson, not found; (4) Torrey Herbarium cultivated at St. Louis in 1896, not found. Thus Coulter's application of the epithet octacanthus is based upon practically nothing.

Britton & Rose, attempting (Cactaceae 3: 13. 1922) to follow Coulter, reported vaguely, "Type locality: Northern Texas" and known "definitely only from northwestern Texas," but continued as follows: "M. Cary in 1907 collected at Dolores, Colorado, a plant which comes nearer to this species than anything which we have seen, except a plant from Marathon, Texas, which has the armament and flowers called for by the original description." There are collections of var. melanacanthus from Dolores, dated 1892 (NY, labelled "Herb. St. Agr. Coll.," but without a collector's name), and other specimens and photographs by Cary in 1907, US. Any of four varieties occurs near Marathon, which is in neither "northern" nor "northwestern" nor central Texas.

Thus, both Coulter and Britton and Rose, as well as Backeberg and others following them, applied the epithet to miscellaneous collections from the enormous area from Utah to Colorado and Texas. No type collection was indicated, and there is no evidence that the existing specimens taken alone represent a natural population rather than individual plants with an occasionally recurring character or of a pair of characters, "green stems" and "light-colored spines," to be found anywhere in the widespread and variable populations of var. melanacanthus. More recent authors have sought to apply the epithet to local plants or to horticultural specimens, each merely adopting the interpretation of Coulter.

The plants described by Coulter and the other authors do not match Mühlenpfordt's description. According to Mühlenpfordt, the plants were with many stems ("polycephala"), the aggregation of stems 6 1/2 inches ("Zoll," 2.54 cm, as with the English inch) and 3 inches high. The largest single stems were described as 2 inches high and 2 wide. The stem-ribs were 7 or 8. The 1 central and the 7 radial spines were described as all rigid and robust ("kräftig"), except for sometimes one radial. All were basally naillike ("nagelartig") and thickened ("verdickt"). Nails during the Nineteenth Century were unlike the machine-produced cylindroid "wire nails" of the Twentieth Century. In 1848, during winter days "square" nails were handmade at a small forge in the chimney corner. These nails, seen now in museums or in the timbers of old buildings, were flattened (rectangular, rather than square) in cross section. Stout spines of this sort, one-half to three-quarters of an inch long, could have been found in central Texas only in some sort of barrel cactus, perhaps a juvenile. However, the only barrel cactus native as far north as central Texas is the horse crippler, Echinocactus texensis, which has unbranched stems. Inasmuch as European gardeners kept no records of the original

localities of most of the plants they cultivated, Echinopsis octacantha could have come from cultivation, perhaps having been brought by the geologist, Dr. Roemer, from a garden in Texas. The description does not match mature or juvenile plants of any of the native species of central Texas, and certainly it does not apply to Echinocereus triglochidiatus var. melanacanthus.

The wisdom expressed by K. Schumann, Gesamtb. Kakt. 285. 1898, has been overlooked: "Ich bin der Meinung, dass nur eine solche unsichere Bemerkung hin die gut begründeten und heute noch bekannten ENGELMANN'schen Arten [Echinocereus roemeri Engelm., not Mühlenpfordt] nicht zu Gunsten der ganz unbekannten MÜHLENPFORDT'schen fallen gelassen werden dürfen." Echinopsis octacantha Mühlenpfordt is still wholly unknown, as it was even in Germany in Schumann's time. In the absence of a type specimen, it is merely a name. Whatever plant may have received this name combination probably persisted in cultivation for a time then disappeared.

Names of Uncertain Application (perhaps to var. melanacanthus)

Echinocereus kunzei Gürke, Monatsschr. Kakteenk. 17: 103. 1907. E. coccineus Engelm. var. kunzei Backeberg, Cactaceae 4: 2070. 1960. "Die Pflanze findet sich selten in der Gegebung von Phoenix in Arizona." "Herr Dr. KUNTZE sandte an den Kgl. botan. Garten zu Dahlem ein Examplar, das zur blute kam, und nach welchen die verstehende Beschreibung entwerfen ist." The herbarium at Berlin (Dahlem) was destroyed during the Second World War. No locality mentioned. The flower color is described as, "floribus scarlatinie-kermesinie," and as follows: "...an ersten Tage ist sie an der inneren Seite der Blütenhüllblätter feuerrot, bald scharlachrot werdend,...und dritten Tage prächtig lacherot." Thus the plant described would seem to have been one of the varieties of E. triglochidiatus, but the spines are much shorter than in the other varieties (to only 10-12 mm long). According to Britton & Rose, Cactaceae 3: 31. 1922, "Echinocereus kunzei...is usually stated to be from Arizona. It was doubtless sent out from Phoenix, Arizona, where Dr. Kunze lived, but we have a specimen in the U.S. National Herbarium labeled 'southern New Mexico' in Dr. Kunze's handwriting." Another specimen, US (box), is E. lloydii Britton & Rose; it does not match the description, and it is not the type specimen. It could have come from south[east]ern New Mexico.

Echinocereus monacanthus Heese, Gartenflora 53: 215. f. 32, except the legend (which is interchanged with f. 33). 1904). "Vaterland: An der Grenze zwischen Mexiko und Texas." Plants similar to that in the photograph have been seen, and those observed are a form of E. triglochidiatus var. melanacanthus having only one spine per areole.

Echinocereus conoideus Engelm. & Bigelow var. cristata Houghton, Cactus & Succ. Jour. 2: 490. 1931, nom. nud.

Proposed Taxon of Uncertain Status (perhaps var. melanacanthus)

Echinocereus decumbens Clover & Jotter, Bull. Torrey Club 68: 417. f. 7. 1941. E. engelmannii (Parry) Lemaire var. decumbens L. Benson, Proc. Calif. Acad. IV. 25: 258. 1944 (interpretation based primarily upon plants similar vegetatively). "...Limestone ledge...rocky talus at Mile 16 1/2 Marble Canyon, Coconino Co. Arizona (Clover & Jotter 2212)." TYPE: Mich. ISOTYPE: Pom 275345 (spines). The specimens cannot be classified satisfactorily at present. They may represent a variety of E. triglochidiatus similar to var. melanacanthus, but this is not certain. Field work is needed to determine the nature of the local populations in the Grand Canyon. Stems to 42 cm long and only about 2.5 cm diam; spines brown, 9-10 per areole, 1.2-2.5 cm long, very slender, 0.2-0.3 mm diam. A collection similar to the type specimen is as follows: Coconino Co., Arizona, "Rock ledge below Mooney Falls," Clover 7028, Sept. 4, 1943, Mich, Ariz, SMU.

1b. Echinocereus triglochidiatus var. mojavensis
(Engelmann & Bigelow) L. Benson

Cereus mojavensis Engelm. & Bigelow, Proc. Amer. Acad. 3: 281. 1857 (preprint, 1856); U.S. Senate Rept. Expl. & Surv. R. R. Route Pacific Ocean 4: Botany 33. pl. 4, f. 8. 1857. C. bigelovii Engelm. in Engelm. & Bigelow, loc. cit., pl. 4, f. 8 (on the plate), probably a discarded name intended to have been replaced by C. mojavensis. Echinocereus mojavensis Engelm. ex Rümpler in Förster, Handb. Cacteenk. ed. 2. 803. 1885, erroneously ascribed to Engelmann. E. triglochidiatus Engelm. var. mojavensis L. Benson, Proc. Calif. Acad. IV. 25: 255. 1944. "Found between the Rio Colorado and Mojave creek [River]...March 4, 1854." TYPE: "Mojave Creek," J. M. Bigelow, March 4, 1854, Mo. ISOTYPE: Pom 317804.

Echinocereus sandersii Orcutt, Cactography 5. 1926. "Orcutt 1926: 8. Black canon, Providence mountains, 30 miles north of Fenner, Cal., at an altitude of 5,000 feet. Collected by F. Gibson and M. Sanders in 1925...." No specimen found.

Common in California in Inyo and San Bernardino Cos. and more restricted along W edge of desert in Riverside and San Diego Cos.; occasional in S Nevada. Geographically significant specimens:

CALIFORNIA. RIVERSIDE CO. S side of San Jacinto Mts., 5,000 ft., S. B. & W. F. Parish in 1882, Mo, US. SAN DIEGO CO. Kane Springs Wash, Jepson 15541, Jeps.

NEVADA. NYE CO. (northern). Dobbin Basin, 48 miles SE of Austin, G. W. Gullion, June 29, 1958, Pom; Last Chance Creek, 7,000 feet, J. M. & M. Lindsdale 753, May 23, 1932, CAS; Cherry Creek, Quinn Range, Maguire & Holmgren 25330, NY, GH, US, UC. LINCOLN CO. Pioche, 5,800 feet, Train 1787, UC, USNA (tending toward var. melanacanthus).

UTAH. WASHINGTON CO. Copper Mine, 4,000 feet, M. E. Jones 5004b, May 3, 1894, Pom; Beaverdam Mts. W of St. George, Tidestrom 9334, US; Santa Clara Creek, Goodding 900, US; 15 miles W of St. George, M. E. Jones 5004b, April 3, 1894, US; 20 miles N of St. George, C. N. Ainslie, Oct., 1910, US; Springdale, L. Benson 13703, Pom, a single plant in a hybrid population tending strongly toward var. melanacanthus (cf. L. Benson 13702, Pom, 13704, Pom).

1c. Echinocereus triglochidiatus var. neomexicanus (Standley) L. Benson

Echinocereus polyacanthus Engelm. in Wisliz., Mem. Tour. No. Mex. 104. ca. Apr. 2, 1848, cf. discussion of date under E. triglochidiatus. Cereus polyacanthus Engelm. in A. Gray, Pl. Fendler., Mem. Amer. Acad. 4: 51. 1849. E. triglochidiatus Engelm. var. polyacanthus L. Benson, Proc. Calif. Acad. IV. 25: 253. 1944. "Cosihuiriachi," Chihuahua, Mexico. LECTOTYPE (Benson loc. cit.): "Cosihuiriachi," Wislizenus in 1847, Mo. (sheet and carton). DUPLICATE: Pom 317823, 317830 (spines).

Echinocereus neo-mexicanus Standley, Bull. Torrey Club 35: 87. 1908. Cereus neomexicanus Tidestrom in Tidestrom & Kittell, Fl. Ariz. & N. Mex. 298. 1941. E. triglochidiatus Engelm. var. neomexicanus Standley ex W. T. Marshall in Marshall & Bock, Cactaceae 118. 1941, incorrectly ascribed to Standley. E. polyacanthus Engelm. var. neomexicanus Weniger, Cacti S. W. 44. 1970, nom. nud. (Art. 33). Mesa west of Organ Mts., Dona Ana Co., New Mexico, Paul C. Standley 383. TYPE: Mo. ISOTYPE: US 1821069; photographs, NY.

Echinocereus rosei Wooton & Standley, Contr. U.S. Nat. Herb. 19: 457. 1914. E. triglochidiatus Engelm. var. rosei W. T. Marshall, Arizona's Cactuses. ed. 1. 63. 1950. E. polyacanthus Engelm. var. rosei Weniger, Cacti. S. W. 43. 1970, nom. nud. (Art. 33). "TYPE LOCALITY: Agricultural College, New Mexico... Paul C. Standley in 1907 (no. 1235)." TYPE: US 535093. ISOTYPE: Mo, GH, UNM (but this specimen being near var. gurneyi, with which this plant has been confused by all authors). Cf. illustration of var. gurneyi Britton & Rose, Cactaceae 3: 15. f. 13. 1922, as E. rosei.

Echinocereus polycephalus vars. albispina, brevi-nigrispina, nigrispina, spinosissima, and X phoeniceus Frič, Ceskoslov. Zahradnickych Listě [Kakt. Sukk.] 1924: 121. 1924, nom. nud. Var. X phoeniceus, Frič, loc. cit. Plants reported to have come from New Mexico.

Echinocereus polyacanthus Engelm. formae galtieri (E. galtieri, pro syn.), bergeanus, rufispinus, nigrispinus, albispinus, and longispinus, Hort. ex Schelle, Kakteen 179. 1926. No indication of origin or of specimens. Presumably but not certainly var. neomexicanus.

Echinocereus polyacanthus Engelm. var. galtieri (Rebut) Borg, Cacti. ed. 2. 228. 1951, nom. nud. E. galtieri Rebut ex Borg, loc. cit., pro syn., nom. nud.

Echinocereus polyacanthus Engelm. vars. nigrispinus and longispinus Hort ex Borg, Cacti ed. 2. 228. 1951, nom. nud. (no Latin diagnoses). No statements of origin or references to specimens.

ARIZONA, westernmost collections. PIMA CO. Baboquivari Canyon, Baboquivari Mts., D. D. Porter SF 109, Apr. 8, 1926, Ariz. SANTA CRUZ CO. Sycamore Canyon, Oro Blanco Mts., L. Benson 10984, Pom, Ariz.

NEW MEXICO, northernmost collection. McKINLEY CO. Ft. Wingate, Palmer 73, in 1869, US.

TEXAS, except El Paso Co. HUDSPETH CO. Sierra Blanca, 5,000 feet, Rose in 1910, NY, M. B. Gurney, July, 1957, Pom. CULBERSON CO. 10 mi. N of Van Horn, W. O. Moore 343, Mich, 344, Mich. JEFF DAVIS CO. 12 mi. S of Kent, Davis Mts., L. & R. L. Benson 15471, Pom; "porphyritic cliffs," E. J. Palmer 3Q618, GH, 30782, GH; Ft. Davis, E. J. Palmer 33420, GH; Limpia Canyon 2 mi. below Ft. Davis, L. & R. L. Benson 15473, Pom. PRESIDIO CO. Canyon below Lake Esteban, L. C. Hinckley 1487, US, L. Benson 16501, Pom; Fresno Canyon, 80 mi. S of Marfa, L. C. Hinckley 2434, USNA. BREWSTER CO. W of Alpine, 2,600 feet, Warnock 11036, SRSC, 11081, SRSC, 11083, SRSC; Lost Mine Mt., Chisos Mts., O. E. Sperry 1903, Ariz; Glenn Spring, Chisos Mts., O. E. Sperry 1905, Ariz. SUTTON CO. Highway 189 near Devil's River, 30 mi. SW of Sonora, D. Weniger, Feb. 4, 1963, UNM. UVALDE CO. Uvalde, A. P. Dodd, April, 1925, US.

1d. Echinocereus triglochidiatus var. gurneyi L. Benson

Echinocereus triglochidiatus Engelm. var. gurneyi L. Benson, Cactus & Succ. Jour. 41: 126. 1969. "Igneous rocks south of Marathon, Brewster County, Texas, 4,100 feet elevation, Donovan S.

& Helen S. Correll & Lyman & Evelyn L. Benson 16,488, April 4, 1965." TYPE: Pom 317078.

NEW MEXICO. DONA ANA CO. Mesa W of Organ Mts., Standley 494, UNM, 1235, UNM (type number of Echinocereus rosei Standley, but this "duplicate" approaching var. gurneyi), Wooton & Standley, July, 1906, US; N end of Franklin Mts., L. Benson 16458, Pom. OTERO CO. San Andreas Canyon Road, SE of Alamogordo, P. Pierce, Oct. 3, 1961, UNM; Alamo Canyon, E of Alamogordo, G. Wiens, Feb. 16, 1964, UNM. EDDY CO. NE of White City, S. L. Glowenke 10674, UPa.

TEXAS. EL PASO CO. Frontera, Wright 41 in 1851, Mo; El Paso (doubtless Franklin Mts.), Wright in 1851, Mo, in 1852, Mo, Toumey, May 20, 1896, Pom, US (transitional to var. melanacanthus), Eggert, May 12, 1907, Mo, E. Stearns 136, in 1911, US. HUDSPETH CO. Vicinity of Sierra Blanca Pass, Rose, Standley, & Russell 12219, US, NY, Pom, M. B. Gurney (2 localities), March 30, 1956, Pom, Sept., 1957, Pom, L. & R. L. Benson 15466, Pom; Indian Hot Springs, B. L. Turner 351, March 20, 1949, SRSC. CULBERSON CO. Near Nickle, W. O. Moore 346, Mich; Sierra Diablo, Warnock, March 30, 1947, SRSC; near Van Horn, R. O. Albert 21, April 13, 1959, Pom. PRESIDIO CO. Elephant Mt., T. J. Allen 363, March 28, 1959, SRSC; Robber's Roost Canyon, L. C. Hinckley, April 19, 1946, US. BREWSTER CO. Near Alpine, C. R. Orcutt, June, 1926, SD; Marathon, Rose 176, May 15, 1901, US; S of Marathon, R. M. King 2582, Pom, Tex, C. Hanson & D. S. Correll 4681, LL, D. S. & H. S. Correll and L. & E. L. Benson 16488, Pom. PECOS CO. NW of Longfellow, McVaugh & Warnock 5107, SRSC, Warnock, March 30, 1947, SRSC. TERRELL CO. Near Sanderson, April 16, 1960, Pom, Tex, D. Weniger, April 16, 1963, UNM (approaching var. paucispinus).

1e. Echinocereus triglochidiatus var. paucispinus (Engelmann) Engelmann ex W. T. Marshall

Cereus paucispinus Engelm. Proc. Amer. Acad. 3: 285. 1857 (preprint, 1856); in Emory, Rept. U.S. & Mex. Bound. Surv. 2: Cactaceae 37. pl. 56. 1859. E. paucispinus Engelm. ex Rümpler in Förster, Handb. Cacteenk ed. 2. 794. 1885, incorrectly ascribed to Engelmann. E. triglochidiatus Engelm. var. paucispinus Engelm. ex W. T. Marshall in Marshall & Bock, Cactaceae 118. 1941, incorrectly ascribed to Engelmann. "From the San Pedro [Texas] to the mouth of the Pecos...Wright, Bigelow." LECTOTYPE designation: Cultivated "...from the original seeds," Mo.

Echinocereus paucispinus (Engelm.) Engelm. ex Rümpler f. flavispinus Schelle, Handb. Kakteenkultur 137. 1907.

TEXAS. JEFF DAVIS CO. Star Mt., near [the] Limpia, M. S. Young, April 11, 1914, Tex. BREWSTER CO. S of Marathon, 4,100 feet, D. S. & H. S. Correll & L. & E. L. Benson 16488. PECOS CO. Tunas Springs E of Ft. Stockton, D. S. & H. S. Correll & L. & E. L. Benson 16492, Pom; Sheffield, M. E. Jones 26304, April 13, 1930, Pom, DS, No; 24 mi. N of Sanderson, R. O. Albert 28, April 19, 1959, Pom. TERRELL CO. Near Sanderson, C. Hanson & D. S. Correll 472, LL. VAL VERDE CO. Near Langtry, Rose 11604, US, R. M. King 2561, Tex, Pom; road to Amstad Dam, D. S. & H. S. Correll 27143, LL; W of Pecos River, R. M. King 2561, Tex, Pom; Devil's River near Del Rio, Rose in 1913, NY, E. J. Palmer 11356, GH, US, H. C. Hanson, March 11, 1919, Ill, R. M. King 2557, Tex, Pom, L. Benson 16523, Pom; N of Del Rio, D. Weniger, March, 1964, UNM. KIMBLE CO. W of Junction, L. N. & G. B. Upton & J. C. Van Deman, March 23, 1930, CU.

1f. Echinocereus triglochidiatus var. arizonicus (Rose) L. Benson

Echinocereus arizonicus Rose ex Orcutt, Cactography 3. 1926. E. triglochidiatus Engelm. var. arizonicus L. Benson, Cacti Ariz. ed. 3. 21, 129. 1969. "On the Superior-Miami highway, near boundary monument between Pinal and Gila Counties, Ariz., at 4,700 feet elevation,...July, 1922." Charles Russell Orcutt. LECTOTYPE (Benson, loc. cit.): NY (photographs, US, Pom 313363). DUPLICATE: US 73376.

ARIZONA. PINAL-GILA CO. line. Orcutt in 1926, NY (photos US, Pom), US, H. F. Loomis SF 173, Sept. 10, 1927, Ariz, Pom, L. Benson 16625, Pom, 16657, Pom.

1g. Echinocereus triglochidiatus var. gonacanthus (Engelmann & Bigelow) L. Benson

Cereus gonacanthus Engelm. & Bigelow, Proc. Amer. Acad. 3: 285. 1857 (preprint, 1856); U.S. Senate Rept. Expl. & Surv. R. R. Route Pacific Ocean. Botany 4: 283. 1857. Echinocereus gonacanthus Engelm. ex Rümpler in Förster, Handb. Cacteenk. ed. 2. 806. 1885. E. paucispinus (Engelm.) Engelm. ex Rümpler [illegitimate combination] var. gonacanthus K. Schum. Gesamtb. Kakteen 281. 1898, incorrectly ascribed to Engelmann. E. paucispinus (Engelm.) Engelm. ex Rümpler f. gonacanthus Schelle, Handb. Kakteenkultur 137. 1907. E. triglochidiatus Engelm. var. gonacanthus Boissevain in Boissevain & Davidson, Colo. Cacti 36. 1940; Engelm. & Bigelow ex W. T. Marshall in Marshall & Bock, Cactaceae 117. 1941, incorrectly ascribed to Engelmann & Bigelow. "...Near the natural well, about 40 miles west of Zuñi, near the 109th. degree...." New Mexico Territory in 1856; now in Apache Co., Ariz. Zuni, New Mexico, is 10-12 miles from the Arizona boundary; the 109th. Meridian is about 3 mi. E of the state line. The "natural well" may be Witch Well, 26 mi. SW of Zuni. LECTOTYPE designation: "Cedar woods 35 miles [3 days march] west of Zuñi, J. M. Bigelow, Nov. 29, 1853," Mo. DUPLICATE: Pom 317801.

COLORADO. CHAFFEE CO. E approach to Monarch Pass, L. & R. L. Benson 14737, Pom, 14739-14741, Pom. FREMONT CO. Arkansas Canyon, Greene, June 23, 1873, Mo, June 3, 1874, Mo, in 1874, Mo (box), UC; near Cañon City, Brandegee 641 in 1873, YU, Engelmann, Sept. 26, 1874, Mo, Biltmore Herbarium 1-940, Aug. 28, 1896, US, L. & R. L. Benson 14735, Pom; Florence, F. Tweedy 131, US, Osterhout 2542, NY. RIO GRANDE CO. Del Norte, V. Bailey in 1904, US (box). LA PLATA CO. Durango, Eastwood 5316, CAS. ARCHULETA CO. Arboles (now submerged in a reservoir), C. F. Baker 474, June 10, 13, & 15, 1899, Pom, Mo, NY, US, GH, F, NMC, Tex, Weber & Livingston 6252, WS, NY, RSA, SMU, WTU. Some plants of the Arboles collections tend toward var. triglochidiatus, as does, also, the following collection: CHAFFEE CO. Salida, A. S. Plimpton in 1913, US.

ARIZONA. APACHE CO. Ft. Defiance, Palmer 136, June 16, 1869, Mo, US, Pom, Cutler 2134, June 12, 1938, GH, MNA, (the plants of the 2 preceding sheets variable but nearest var. gonacanthus), CAS, GH (the plants of the 2 preceding sheets at least approaching var. melanacanthus); 35 miles west of Zuni, Bigelow, Nov. 29, 1853, Mo, Pom.

NEW MEXICO. SAN JUAN CO. Tunitcha Mts., Navajo Indian Reservation, Standley 7734, US; south of La Boca [Colorado], P. Pierce 2059, UNM. McKINLEY CO. Gallup, Toumey & Ashman, Oct. 20, 1896, US. RIO ARRIBA CO. San Antonio Peak, P. Pierce, June 26, 1962, UNM. SANDOVAL CO. N of Cuba, Castetter 335, UNM. GRANT CO. Little Burro Mts., G. Wiens, April 10, 1965, UNM. SOCORRO CO. Springtime Canyon, San Mateo Mts., P. Pierce, July 22, 1963, UNM.

Var. gonacanthus is intermediate in a trend between the wide-ranging var. melanacanthus and the extreme and relatively local var. triglochidiatus (mostly from McKinley Co. to Rio Arriba, San Miguel, Luna, and Eddy Cos., New Mexico). Var. gonacanthus occurs from SC and SW Colorado to the E edge of N Arizona, and NW and N New Mexico. As indicated above, presumed duplicate specimens collected at the former town of Arboles include recombinations of characters of vars. triglochidiatus and gonacanthus, and a collection from Salida, Chaffee Co., Colorado, varies similarly, as does one from near Ft. Defiance, E edge of N Arizona, Cutler 2132, GH, 2134, GH, MNA. The Cutler collection includes also plants referrable to var. melanacanthus (e.g., CAS 27121). Through especially S Colorado (e.g., 10 mi. W of Salida, Chaffee Co., L. & R. L. Benson 14737-14741, Pom), var. gonacanthus grades almost imperceptibly and irregularly into var. melanacanthus. Thus, var. gonacanthus as a whole is composed essentially of a series of populations transitional from var. triglochidiatus to var. melanacanthus. Even collections of var. melanacanthus from far westward in Utah are suggestive of intergradation with var. gonacanthus (Wellington, Carbon Co., L. & R. L. Benson 15698, Pom; canyon W of Sevier Lake, Millard Co., L. & R. L. Benson 15700, Pom). Similar reflections of the characters of var. gonacanthus occur in NC Arizona (e.g., N of The Gap, L. Benson 14240, Pom). The extreme western var. mojavensis is intermediate in some spine characters between vars. gonacanthus and melanacanthus.

Elsewhere, var. gonacanthus intergrades with other varieties. Vars. neomexicanus and paucispinus are in some respects in positions of intermediacy between it and var. melanacanthus. Intergradation of var. gonacanthus with var. neomexicanus is common in New Mexico.

1h. Echinocereus triglochidiatus var. triglochidiatus

Echinocereus triglochidiatus Engelm. in Wisliz. Mem. Tour. No. Mex. 93. ca. Apr. 2, 1848. Cereus triglochidiatus Engelm. in A. Gray, Pl. Fendl., Mem. Amer. Acad. II. 4. 50. 1849. E. paucispinus (Engelm.) Engelm. ex Rümpler var. triglochidiatus K. Schum., Gesamtb. Kakteen 281. 1898, invalid because in specific rank triglochidiatus was published 8 years earlier than paucispinus. E. paucispinus (Engelm.) Engelm. ex Rümpler f. triglochidiatus Schelle, Handb. Kakteenkultur 136. 1907. "On Wolf Creek, in pine woods, flowers in June; Santa Fé. (Fendler)." LECTOTYPE (L. Benson, Proc. Calif. Acad. Sci. IV. 25: 253. 1944): "On Wolf Creek," Wislizenus in 1846, Mo (2 sheets & box). DUPLICATE: Pom 317800.

COLORADO. SAGUACHE CO. Cochetopa [now Rio Grande] Nat. For., road to Bonanza, 8,400 ft., C. E. Taylor 449, June 15, 1922, USFS. ARCHULETA CO. Arboles (cf. discussion of collections indicating intergradation with var. gonacanthus).

ARIZONA. APACHE CO. Ft. Defiance, Graham Heid, Pom (photograph) and intergrading plants discussed under var. gonacanthus.

NEW MEXICO, periphery of distribution. RIO ARRIBA CO. E of Bloomfield, Navajo Reservation near Navajo Dam, P. Pierce, Oct. 31, 1962, UNM; Stone Lake, Castetter 342, 343, UNM. McKINLEY CO. 25 mi. N of Gallup, Wooton, Aug. 4, 1904, US, Pom; S of Zuni P. Pierce 1110, UNM. VALENCIA CO. South of Zuni Reservation, Wooton, July 27, 1904, US. SANDOVAL CO. Sandoval (Corrales), J. Findley, April 21, 1962, UNM. LUNA CO. Florida Mts., P. Pierce, Nov. 28, 1961, UNM. SAN MIGUEL CO. Starvation Peak, near Rowe, P. Pierce

1182, UNM; Starvation Rock, near Bernal, P. Pierce 746, 747, UNM; Las Vegas, G. C. Brondhend, Aug., 1880, Mo; "Pecos" [River], Bigelow, Oct. 14, 1853, Mo; S of Las Vegas on U.S. 84, L. & R. L. Benson 14699, Pom; between Las Vegas and Anton Chico, Rose & Fitch 17770, NY, US. GUADALUPE CO. E of Santa Rosa, Castetter 114, UNM. EDDY CO. Tributary of Rattlesnake Canyon, Carlsbad National Park, Castetter 1346, UNM.

2. Echinocereus berlandieri (Engelmann) Engelmann *ex* Rümpler

2a. Echinocereus berlandieri var. berlandieri|

Cereus berlandieri Engel. Proc. Amer. Acad. 3: 286. 1857 (preprint, 1856); in Emory, Rept. U.S. & Mex. Bound. Surv. 2: Cactaceae 38. pl. 58. 1859. Echinocereus berlandieri Engelm. ex Rümpler in Förster, Handb. Cacteenk. 777. 1885. E. blanckii (Poselger) Rümpler var. berlandieri Backeberg, Cactacea 4: 1999. 1960. "On the Nueces, in Southern Texas: fl. May and June." "On the Nueces, Berlandier." LECTOTYPE designation: plate 58 (above) and "...flumen...las Nueces, Abrilo, 1834," Berlandier 2433, Mo (flowers).

Names misapplied to Echinocereus berlandieri

Cereus blanckii Poselger, Allg. Gartenz. 21: 134. 1853. Echinocereus blanckii Poselger ex Rümpler in Förster, Handb. Cacteenk, ed. 2. 779. 1885, incorrectly ascribed to Poselger. E. berlandieri Engelm. var. blanckii P. Fournier, Cactées & Pl. Grasses 21. 1935 [Encycl. Prat. Nat. 28], illegitimate combination. "Prope Camargo." Tamaulipas. "Meinem Freunde Herrn Apotheker P. A. Blanck in Berlin zu Ehren."

Echinocereus blankii Hort. ex F. Palmer, Rev. Hort. 36: 92. color pl. 1865, pro syn., nom. nud., and not accepted by its author; Lemaire, Cactees 56. 1868, nom. nud. Probably based on Cereus blanckii Poselger, but with no reference, direct or indirect, to that species and to be treated as a different name with a different epithet. Horticultural plants.

There is no evidence that "Blankii" was based upon "Blanckii," and it is considered to be a different epithet; therefore this name combination is not an obstacle to use of the combination E. blanckii (Poselger) Poselger ex Rümpler for the Mexican plants to which it was applied. Palmer merely discussed and halfway adopted the horticultural designation E. blankii but rejected it as follows: De plus, la description, ainsi que la figure du Berlandieri que donne Engelman[n] (United States and Mexican boundary survey, Saint-Louis, 1858 [1859]), se rapportent si bien à notre plante, que je suis porté à croire que le deux plantes n'en font qu'une; [Furthermore, the description, as well as the figure, of Berlandieri given by Engelmann...agrees so well with our plant that I must believe that the two are only one]." Probably the epithet blankii brought in from horticulture arose from corruption of Cereus blanckii Poselger, but there is no evidence of this, and Poselger's epithet (honoring P. A. Blanck) and Palmer's with an unknown basis (possibly a personal name, Blank) cannot be proved to be the same. They are applied in different genera.

Terry L. Corbett has called attention to discrepancies in the original description of Echinocereus blanckii Poselger with the plants known under that name. In particular, the ribs of the stem are stated to be 8-10, not 5-6 as in Texas plants. For this reason the first-published epithet applied clearly to the Texan species is taken up, instead of E. blanckii. According to Dale Morrical, plants matching the original description of E. blanckii occur near Monterrey in Mexico.

Echinocereus procumbens Engelm. var. longispinus Hirscht, Monatsschr. Kakteenk. 12: 135. 1902. No locality or specimen.

2b. Echinocereus berlandieri var. papillosus (Linke) L. Benson

Echinocereus papillosus Linke ex Rümpler in Förster, Handb. Cacteenk. ed. 2. 783. 1885. Cereus papillosus Berger, Rept. Mo. Bot. Gard. 16: 80. 1905. E. blanckii (Poselger) Poselger ex Rümpler var. papillosus L. Benson, Cactus & Succ. Jour. 41: 126. 1969. E. berlandieri Engelm. var. papillosus L. Benson, Cactus & Succ. Jour. 48: 1976 (in press). "Vaterland unbekannt." NEOTYPE (Benson, loc. cit., 1975): Schumann & Gürke, Blühende Kakteen 2: pl. 115. 1910.

Echinocereus texensis Rünge ex Matthson, Monatsschr. Kakteenk. 4: 61. 1894, not Jacobi in 1856. E. rungei K. Schumann, Monatsschr. Kakteenk. 5: 124. 1895, nom. nov. "...Von Herrn C. Rünge in S. Antonio, Texas...." "Der ganze Vorrat, soweit er nach Europe kommt, gelangt in die Mände des Herrn ERNST BERGE in Leipzig...."

TEXAS. WEBB CO. Laredo, R. L. Crockett 6486, US; N of Bruno, D. Weniger 213, Aug. 14, 1963, UNM. BEXAR CO. San Antonio, Toumey & Ashmun, Mar. 20, 1897, US, Pom. DUVAL CO. San Diego, M. B. Croft in 1886, NY, US. McMULLEN CO. 26 mi. N of Freer, D. Weniger 57, Mar. 20, 1963, UNM. JIM WELLS CO. NW of Alice, R. O. Albert & L. Benson 16549, Pom; SE of San Diego, F. B. Jones 1117, Apr. 20, 1965, SMU. HIDALGO CO. N of La Joya, Clover 1869, Mich, CAS, Tex, Ariz. CAMERON CO. Laguna Atascosa Wildlife Refuge, R. G. Fleetwood 3, Apr. 29, 1970, Pom.

2c. Echinocereus berlandieri var. angusticeps (Clover) L. Benson

Echinocereus angusticeps Clover, Rhodora 37: 79. pl. 327. 1935; reprinted, Cactus & Succ. Jour. 7: 173-174. pl. 327, f. 1, 1936. E. papillosus Linke var. angusticeps W. T. Marshall in Marshall & Bock, Cactaceae 119. 1941. E. blanckii (Poselger) Poselger ex Rümpler var. angusticeps L. Benson in Lundell, Fl. Tex. 2: 260. 1970. E. berlandieri Engelm. var. angusticeps L. Benson, Cactus & Succ. Jour. 48: 1976 (in press). "15261... Linn, Hidalgo County, Texas...." TYPE: Mich (sheet not numbered). Note on specimen, "Type number cited is 15261, but Dr. Clover states (verbally, 1950) that this serial no. was assigned at Hort. Bot. Univ. Mich. to same plant (living) from which her no. 1870 was derived." ISOTYPES: Mich, Tex, Ariz (no number), DS 247841.

3. Echinocereus pentalophus (DeCandolle) Rümpler

Cereus pentalophus DC. Mém. Mus. Hist. Nat. Paris 17: 117. 1828. Echinocereus pentalophus Rümpler in Förster, Handb. Cacteenk. ed 2. 774. 1885; W. T. Marshall in Kelsey & Dayton, Stand. Pl. Names. ed. 2. 71. 1942. Mexico, Coulter. TYPE: not found, G; not at Trinity College, Dublin (Coulter collection). NEOTYPE designation: 12 miles NE of Roma, Starr Co., Texas, 200 feet, Lyman Benson 16545, April 16, 1965, Pom 317936 & 317937 (on 3 sheets).

Cereus pentalophus DC. vars. simplex, subarticulatis, and radicans DC. Mém. Mus. Hist. Nat. Paris 17: 117. 1828. "...in Mexico. Cl. --Coulter hic conjungit tres varietas in posterum forsan separandas, nempe."

Cereus propinquus DC. in Salm-Dyck ex Otto in Otto & Dietr., Allg. Gartenz. 1: 366. 1833. "C. propinquus Salm-Dyck (C. pentalophus ∝ simplex De Cand. Rev. des Cactées p. 117)."

Cereus procumbens Engelm. Pl. Fendl., Mem. Amer. Acad. II. 4. 50. 1849; Pl. Lindh. II , Bost. Jour. Nat. Hist. 6: 203. 1850. Echinocereus procumbens Rümpler in Förster, Handb. Cacteenk. ed. 2. 781. 1885. E. pentalophus (DC.) Rümpler var. procumbens P. Fournier, Cactees & Pl. Grasses 25. 1935. "...Rio Grande, below Matamoras...St. Louis Volunteers in 1846." LECTOTYPE designation: "...Burita near the mouth of the Rio Grande below Matamoras by the Missouri Volunteers, 1846, and cultivated at St. Louis. fl. May 1848," Mo.

"C[ereus] leptacanthus DC.," ex Pfeiffer, Enum. Diagn. Cact. 101. 1837, pro syn. C. pentalophus DC. var. leptacanthus Salm-Dyck, Cact. Hort. Dyck. 1849: 42. 1850. Echinocereus leptacanthus K. Schum. Gesamtb. Kakteen 260. 1898. Based upon Salm-Dyck's reference. "Bot. Mag. t. 3651." Curtis' Bot. Mag. 65: pl. 3651. 1839.

Echinocereus runyonii Orcutt, Cactography 5. 1926. "Orcutt 1924: 1048. Near the mouth of the Rio Grande, Texas." No specimen found.

4. Echinocereus fendleri (Engelmann) Engelmann ex Rümpler

4a. Echinocereus fendleri var. fendleri

Cereus fendleri Engelm. in A. Gray, Pl. Fendl., Mem. Amer. Acad. 4: 51. 1849. Echinocereus fendleri Engelm. ex Rümpler in Förster, Handb. Cacteenk. ed. 2. 801. 1885, incorrectly ascribed to Engelmann. C. cinerascens DC. var. fendleri Bois, Pl. Aliment. 2: 371. 1928. "Santa Fe, on elevated sandy plains...." TYPE: Santa Fe, A. Fendler 3, in 1846, Mo. ISOTYPE: Pom 317806.

Cereus fendleri Engelm. var. pauperculus Engelm. in A. Gray, Pl. Fendl., Mem. Amer. Acad. 4: 51. 1849. Same statement as above. TYPE: Santa Fe, A. Fendler, Nov. 4, 1846, Mo.

COLORADO. MONTEZUMA CO. Mancos River S of Mesa Verde, Weber 5459, Colo. LA PLATA CO. Durango, Eastwood, June, 1890, Colo; La Boca, L. & R. L. Benson 16238, Pom. FREMONT CO. Canyon City, T. S. Brandegee 2450 or 642 in 1873, Mo, NY, UC, YU.

TEXAS. EL PASO CO. Tin mine area, Franklin Mts., M. B. Gurney, Mar. 21, 1960, Pom; El Paso, Wright in 1851, Mo (2), in 1852, Mo (fr.), W. H. Evans in 1891, US (box), R. E. Kunze, US (box); Ft. Fillmore, San Elizario, Bigelow, Apr., 1852, Mo, Wright, June 15, 1852, Mo. HUDSPETH CO. Rio Grande, 40 mi. below El Paso, Bigelow, June, 1852, Mo (box).

Name of Uncertain Application (probably to E. fendleri)

Echinocereus fendleri Engelm. f. major Hildmann ex Schelle, Handb. Kakteenkultur 134. 1907, nom. nud.

Echinocereus fendleri (Engelm.) Engelm. ex Rümpler var. robustus Fobe, Monatsschr. Kakteenk. 21: 55. 1911. No specimen or locality.

4b. Echinocereus fendleri var. rectispinus (Peebles) L. Benson

Echinocereus rectispinus Peebles, Amer. Jour. Bot. 25: 675. f. 1, 3d. 1938. E. fendleri Engelm. var. rectispinus L. Benson, Proc. Calif. Acad. Sci. IV. 25: 259. 1944. TYPE: "Peebles No.

SF 905 (fig. 1), hills near Nogales, Arizona, elevation 3,900 feet, May 5, 1935...." US 1729266. ISOTYPE: Ariz 97499.

TEXAS. EL PASO CO. El Paso, Rose 11788, US (box). HUDSPETH CO. Sierra Blanco Pass area, L. Benson 16478, Pom. CULBERSON CO. Kent, A. R. Leding [probably] SF 717, Nov., 1932, Ariz.

4c. Echinocereus fendleri var. kuenzleri (Castetter, Pierce & Schwerin) L. Benson, comb. nov. (see text)

Echinocereus kuenzleri Castetter, Pierce, & Schwerin, Cactus & Succ. Jour. 48: 77. f. 1-2. 1976. "Holotype: Elk, New Mexico, Horst Kuenzler 3585, May 5, 1968, UNM 55571. Isotype: UNM 36,650." "...Sacramento Mountains in Otero County, New Mexico, where it occurs in Piñon Juniper Woodland between 6,000 and 7,000 feet (1,830 to 2,130 m.) elevation." The original area of collection was destroyed by highway construction, but other colonies have been found.

NEW MEXICO. OTERO CO. NE foothills of Sacramento Mts., H. Kuenzler in 1965, UNM, Pom.

Plants of var. fendleri somewhat resembling "E. hempelii" but with a long straight central spine are as follows: "N. Mex.," C. Ellis, US (box). TEXAS. EL PASO CO. El Paso, Rose 11788, US (box).

5. Echinocereus fasciculatus (Engelmann) L. Benson

5a. Echinocereus fasciculatus var. fasciculatus

Mammillaria fasciculata Engelm. in Emory, Notes Mil. Reconn. Ft. Leavenworth to San Diego. App. 2. 156. f. 2. May-July, 1848. Cactus fasciculatus Kunze, Rev. Gen. Pl. 1: 259. 1891. Neomammillaria fasciculata Britton & Rose, Cactaceae 4: 162. 1923. Ebnerella fasciculata F. Buxbaum, Österr. Bot. Zeitschr. 98: 89. f. 2. 1951. Chilita fasciculata F. Buxbaum, Sukkulentenk. 5: 15. 1954. Echinocereus fasciculatus L. Benson, Cacti Ariz. ed. 3. 21, 132. 1969. "2. Mammilaria, October 26, 1846. Rare." That day the Emory military reconnaissance expedition passed over mountains just S of the Gila River in Greenlee and Graham Cos., Arizona, crossing steep, rocky slopes in the vicinity of the mouths of San Francisco River (called by the party, Rio Prieto) and of Eagle Creek (called Rio Azul) and Bonita Creek (called Rio San Carlos). Camp was made on the Gila opposite the mouth of Bonita Creek, about 6-7 miles E of Solomon. The only Mammillaria found by the writer in this area was M. grahamii, the stem of which is short and simple or sometimes with a few branches. At the mouth of Bonita Creek (L. Benson 16635, Pom) and on a sharp rocky peak about 4 miles S (L. Benson 16636, Pom) only one plant with branching stems was found. This species could not be interpreted as the basis for the illustration or the description of M. fasciculata Engelm., because the stems are not only unbranched but also spheroidal to short-ovoid and not in harmony with the branching, elongate ones in the original illustration by Stanly or with the characters in the description by Emory. Throughout the area, a common cactus on flats, slopes, and rocky hillsides is a small form of the plant later named Echinocereus robustus Peebles and recombined as E. fendleri Engelm. var. robustus (Peebles) L. Benson. A collection of this plant from the embankment above the Gila River Valley near the mouth of Bonita Creek (L. Benson 16633, Pom) almost exactly fits the description and the figure. The only point of difference is the crossed lines on the stem, shown in the figure, which prompted Engelmann doubtfully to describe both this plant and No. 1 of the Stanly cactus illustrations as representing Mammillaria instead of Echinocereus. Later Engelmann shifted the status of the other plant to the equivalent of Echinocereus triglochidiatus var. melanacanthus (cf. discussion). With the original description of No. 2, Mammillaria fasciculata, he wrote as follows: "Apparently a mamilaria, though the habit of the plant is more that of an echinocereus, but all echinocerei have bunches of spines disposed in vertical ridges, which is not the case in the figure in question." The significance of the cross-hatching on the drawings 1 to 3 is doubtful, because the detail of the plants in most of the cactus drawings was passed over lightly and inaccurately. The drawings are those of an artist attempting to give quickly a general impression, in this case a silhouette, and not those of a botanical illustrator. For numbers 1 and 3 even the presence of spines barely can be detected; for number 2 they are not shown at all; for most of the other twelve drawings only half-way observation is indicated, and other succulents are thrown in with the cacti. The significance of numbers and types of spines per areole was lost upon the artist, who obviously was not a botanist. Furthermore, making a quick sketch of a plant on a rock and using crossed lines and shading and not showing any detail of the surface is understandable for a day like October 26, 1846, when the party was away from water, was crossing miles of steep slopes with loose rock fragments, and was losing twelve or fifteen precious mules, some to precipices and some to exhaustion. This was the heart of the Apache country, and an artist could neither wander alone nor linger behind the party, which was pushing rapidly westward. NEOTYPE (Benson, loc. cit.): "...Gila River two or three miles below the mouth of Bonita Creek; 3,100 feet elevation, L. Benson 16633, April 22, 1966," Pom 311339.

Echinocereus rectispinus Peebles var. <u>robustus</u> Peebles, Amer.
Jour. Bot. 25: 675. <u>f. 3c</u>. 1938. <u>E. robustus</u> Peebles, Jour.
Wash. Acad. 30: 219. 1940. <u>E. fendleri</u> Engelm. var. <u>robustus</u>
L. Benson, Proc. Calif. Acad. Sci. IV. 25: 259. 1944, not Fobe in
1911. TYPE: "Peebles No. SF 896, Tucson to Sabino Canyon, Pima
County, Arizona, August 27, 1935...." <u>US</u> 1729267. ISOTYPE: <u>Ariz</u>
97485.

5b. Echinocereus fasciculatus var. boyce-thompsonii
(Orcutt) L. Benson

Echinocereus boyce-thompsonii Orcutt, Cactography 4. 1926.
<u>E. fendleri</u> (Engelm.) Lemaire var. <u>boyce-thompsonii</u> L. Benson,
Proc. Calif. Acad. Sci. IV. 25: 260. 1944. <u>E. fasciculatus</u>
(Engelm.) L. Benson var. <u>boyce-thompsonii</u> L. Benson, Cacti Ariz.
ed. 3. 21, 133. 1969. "Grounds of the Boyce-Thompson Southwest-
ern Arboretum near Superior, Arizona, at an elevation of about
2,300 feet." TYPE: (Benson, <u>loc. cit.</u>):
Hill just north of U.S. 60-70. "...about 5 miles west of the
Boyce-Thompson [Southwestern] Arboretum. 2,400 feet elevation,
<u>Lyman Benson 14,621</u>, October 17, 1950," <u>Pom</u> 278845.

5c. Echinocereus fasciculatus var. bonkerae
(Thornber & Bonker) L. Benson

Echinocereus bonkerae Thornber & Bonker, Fantastic Clan 71-
73, 85. <u>pl. opposite 28, 72</u>. 1932. <u>E. fendleri</u> Engelm. var.
<u>bonkerae</u> L. Benson, Proc. Calif. Acad. Sci. IV. 25: 260. 1944.
<u>E. boyce-thompsonii</u> Orcutt var. <u>bonkerae</u> Peebles, Leafl. West.
Bot. 5: 192. 1949. <u>E. fasciculatus</u> (Engelm.) L. Benson var. <u>bon-
kerae</u> L. Benson, Cacti Ariz. ed. 3. 22, 136. 1969. "...Pinal
Mountains in southeastern Arizona...." According to A. A. Nichol,
the plant described by Professor Thornber was from near Oracle at
the north base of the Santa Catalina Mountains, this being in Pinal
County. Mr. Nichol planted the specimens in the University of
Arizona Cactus Garden, and in 1939 [1940] the writer [Lyman Benson]
placed the remains of the last individual in the University Herbarium. They are the closest approach to a type specimen [Benson,
<u>loc. cit.</u>, 1944]." LECTOTYPE (Benson, second ref.): this specimen,
<u>Ariz</u> 156240 (box). Flowers are shown by <u>Thornber and Bonker</u> (San
Carlos, Gila Co., Arizona), also <u>Ariz</u> 156240 (but a different collection).

6. Echinocereus ledingii Peebles

Echinocereus ledingii Peebles, Cactus & Succ. Jour. 8: 35.
1936. TYPE: "...4,500 feet elevation on slopes of Mt. Graham,
Pinaleno [Graham] Mountains, Graham Co., Arizona, <u>Louis Wankum</u>,
July 11, 1935," <u>US</u> 1634004. ISOTYPES: <u>Ariz</u> 97470, 97471.

ARIZONA. GRAHAM CO. Graham Mts., <u>L. Wankum</u>, July 11, 1935,
<u>US</u>, <u>Ariz</u>, <u>Peebles SF 982</u>, <u>Ariz</u>, <u>W. H. Earle</u>, July 25, 1953, <u>L.
Benson 16659</u>, <u>Pom</u>. PIMA CO. "Summit of the Santa Catalina Mts.,"
<u>G. R. Vasey</u>, March, 1881, <u>Ph</u>. COCHISE CO. Mule Mts., near Bisbee,
<u>W. W. Jones</u>, <u>Ariz</u> (box).

7. Echinocereus engelmannii Parry

7a. Echinocereus engelmannii var. engelmannii

Cereus engelmannii Parry ex Engelm. Amer. Jour. Sci. II. 14:
328. 1852. Echinocereus engelmannii Lemaire, Cactées 56. 1868;
Parry ex Rümpler in Förster, Handb. Cacteenk. ed. 2. 805. 1885,
incorrectly ascribed to Parry. "Mountains about San Felipe, on
the eastern declivity of the Cordilleras." Colorado Desert in San
Diego Co., California. No collection by Parry in 1849 or 1850
found, <u>Mo</u> or <u>ISC</u> (Parry Collection). NEOTYPE designation: Hill 1
mile W of Scissors Crossing, San Felipe Valley, below the Laguna
Mts., San Diego Co., California, 2,400 feet, granitic soil, <u>Lyman
Benson 16386</u>, <u>Pom</u> 311501, 311502.

NEVADA. NYE CO. NW Pahute Mesa, <u>W. Rhodes & J. Beatley</u>,
July 27, 1967, <u>TSH</u>; canyon below Mercury Ridge, NE of Mercury, <u>J.
Beatley</u>, Aug. 27, 1967, <u>TSH</u>; Spector Range, <u>J. Beatley & J. L.
Reveal</u>, <u>TSH</u>, <u>1076</u>, <u>Pom</u>.

ARIZONA. YUMA CO. Between Salome and Vicksburg, <u>Peebles SF
526</u>, <u>Ariz</u>; Tinajas Altas Mts., <u>R. J. Blackwell & A. B. Akens</u>,
April 15, 1932, <u>Ariz</u>. MARICOPA CO. Crossing of New River, Care-
free Highway, <u>L. Benson 16617</u>, <u>Pom</u>; same general area, <u>E. Lehto</u>,
<u>Pom</u>; White Tanks Mts., <u>Pinkava & Lehto 4219a</u>, <u>ASU</u>; Phoenix, <u>G. S.
Miller</u> in 1921, <u>US</u>. PIMA CO. Mesquite Mountain, 100 mi. W of
Tucson, collector unknown, April, 1913, <u>US</u>; Tucson, Rose, April
22, 1908, <u>US</u> (box). COCHISE CO. Benson, <u>Rose 11988</u>, <u>US</u> (box).

Invalid Names of Uncertain Application (perhaps to var. <u>engelmannii</u>)

Echinocereus engelmannii (Parry) Lemaire var. <u>robustior</u> Hildmann, Monatsschr. Kakteenk. 4: 194. 1894, nom. nud. <u>E. fendleri</u>
Engelm. f. <u>robustior</u> Schelle, Handb. Kakteenkultur 135. 1907.

Echinocereus engelmannii (Parry) Lemaire var. <u>versicolor</u>
Hildmann, Monatsschr. Kakteenk. 4: 194. 1894, nom. nud.

Echinocereus engelmannii (Parry) Lemaire vars. <u>albispinus</u>,
<u>fulvispinus</u>, and <u>pfersdorffii</u> Cels ex K. Schum. Gesamtb. Kakteen
276. 1898, nom. nud., pro syn.

7b. Echinocereus engelmannii var. acicularis L. Benson

Echinocereus engelmannii Parry var. <u>acicularis</u> L. Benson,
Cacti Ariz. ed. 3. 22, 138. 1969. TYPE: "Crossing of New River,
south side of Black Canyon Refuge, Maricopa County, Arizona;
1,300 feet elevation, <u>Lyman Benson 16,616</u>, April 20, 1966," <u>Pom</u>
311313.

CALIFORNIA. RIVERSIDE CO. 35 mi. N of Blythe, U.S. 95, <u>H.
Rush 184</u> in 1951, <u>Pom</u>; Corn Springs, Chuckawalla Mts., <u>Munz &
Keck 5013</u>, <u>Pom</u>; lower Palo Verde Valley, <u>Jepson 5277</u>, <u>Jeps</u>.

ARIZONA. MOHAVE CO. 13 mi. NW of Alamo, <u>L. Benson 10085</u>,
<u>Pom</u>, <u>Ariz</u>, <u>CAS</u>. YUMA CO. Palm Canyon, Kofa Mts., <u>L. Benson
10870</u>, <u>Pom</u>, <u>CAS</u>, <u>Ariz</u>; Cottonwood Canyon, Tank Pass & Cobrita
Mine, <u>J. C. Blumer 5722</u>, <u>Ariz</u>. GRAHAM CO. 5 mi. E of Coolidge
Dam, <u>Peebles SF 984</u>, <u>Ariz</u>.

SONORA, MEXICO (not previously reported). San Pedro Bay,
<u>I. M. Johnston 4374</u>, <u>US</u>; 2.6 mi. N of Tajitas [Tajito?], <u>Wiggins
8291</u>, <u>DS</u>, <u>US</u>; La Cienega, <u>Goodding 1378</u>, <u>US</u>.

7c. Echinocereus engelmannii var. armatus L. Benson

Echinocereus engelmannii Parry var. <u>armatus</u> L. Benson, Cactus
& Succ. Jour. 41: 33. 1969. TYPE: "Mojave Desert at Dead Man
Point, east of Victorville, San Bernardino County, California;
3,000 feet elevation; granitic soil; south-facing slope, <u>Lyman &
Robert L. Benson 14,767</u>, April 1, 1951," <u>Pom</u> 284927 (on 2 sheets).

7d. Echinocereus engelmannii var. munzii (Parish) Pierce & Fosberg

Cereus munzii Parish, Bull. So. Calif. Acad. Sci. 25: 48.
1926. Echinocereus engelmannii (Parry) Lemaire var. munzii Pierce
& Fosberg, Bull. So. Calif. Acad. Sci. 32: 123. 1933. <u>E. munzii</u>
L. Benson, Amer. Jour. Bot. 28: 361. 1941. TYPE: "...2 miles
below Kenworthy, Thomas Valley, Riverside County, alt. 1,400 meters,
May 21, 1922, Munz & Johnston 5570...." <u>UC</u>. ISOTYPES: <u>Pom 12619</u>,
<u>12845</u>, <u>NY</u> (2), <u>UC</u> (box), <u>CAS 50260</u>, <u>US</u> 1814253.

CALIFORNIA. SAN BERNARDINO CO. San Bernardino Mts., above
Holcomb Lake, <u>F. W. Peirson 3146</u>, <u>RSA</u>; Johnson Grade, <u>C. B. Wolf
9914</u>, <u>RSA</u>, <u>L. Benson</u>, <u>P. C. Baker</u>, & <u>J. Adams 16652</u>, <u>Pom</u>; summit
between Johnson Grade and Baldwin Lake, <u>Stark</u>, May 28, 1933, <u>RSA</u>;
Gold Mt. above Baldwin Lake, <u>Fosberg 8552</u>, <u>Pom</u>; mts. by Baldwin
Lake, <u>Munz 5759</u>, <u>Pom</u>, <u>NY</u> (2), <u>US</u> (2), <u>M. E. Jones</u>, May 30, 1934, <u>C. B.
Wolf 9911</u>, <u>RSA</u>, <u>L. Benson 14765</u>, <u>Pom</u> (2), <u>15634</u>, <u>Pom</u>. RIVERSIDE
CO. NW of Kenworthy, <u>Munz & Johnston 5570</u>, <u>Pom</u>, <u>NY</u> (2), <u>US</u>, <u>UC</u>
(box), <u>CAS</u>.

BAJA CALIFORNIA. 47 mi. SE of Tecate, <u>Munz 9612</u>, <u>Pom</u>.

7e. Echinocereus engelmannii var. chrysocentrus
(Engelmann & Bigelow) Engelmann ex Rümpler

Cereus engelmannii Parry var. <u>chrysocentrus</u> Engelm. & Bigelow,
Proc. Amer. Acad. 3: 283. 1857 (preprint, 1856); U.S. Senate Rept.
Expl. & Surv. R. R. Route Pacific Ocean Botany 4: 35. <u>pl. 5</u>, <u>f. 8-
10</u>. 1857. Echinocereus engelmannii (Parry) Lemaire var. <u>chryso-
centrus</u> Engelm. ex Rümpler in Förster, Handb. Cacteenk. ed. 2. 806.
1885, incorrectly ascribed to Engelmann. <u>E. engelmannii</u> (Parry)
Lemaire var. <u>chrysocentrus</u> Schelle, Handb. Kakteenkultur 135. 1907.
<u>E. chrysocentrus</u> Orcutt, Cactography 4. 1926; <u>E. chrysocentrus</u>
Thornber & Bonker, Fantastic Clan 65-66, 77-78. 1932. "It was
found where <u>C</u>. [<u>E. engelmannii</u> var.] <u>variegatus</u> disappears on the
lower part of William's River, and was seen from there to the Mo-
jave Creek, up that stream to the Sierra Nevada [San Bernardino
Mts.,]." LECTOTYPE designation: "Bill Williams [River]," <u>J. M.
Bigelow</u>, Feb. 13, 1854, <u>Mo</u>. The lower deflexed central spine is
white, as stated by Engelmann in a hand-written note accompanying
the specimen. The other central spines are dirty gray or blackened, as commonly with old once-yellow spines on the lower parts
of living cactus plants or in herbarium specimens. The epithet has
been misapplied by several authors to <u>E. engelmannii</u> var. <u>nicholii</u>
because of the yellow spines, the assumption being that var. <u>chrys-
ocentrus</u> must have yellow central spines because of the name. <u>Cf</u>.
discussion of this point under <u>Echinocereus triglochidiatus</u> var.
<u>melanacanthus</u>.

7f. Echinocereus engelmannii var. variegatus
(Engelmann & Bigelow) Engelmann ex Rümpler

Cereus engelmannii Parry var. <u>variegatus</u> Engelm. & Bigelow,
Proc. Amer. Acad. 3: 283. 1857 (preprint, 1856); U.S. Senate Rept.
Expl. & Surv. R. R. Route Pacific Ocean. Botany 4: 35. <u>pl. 5</u>,
<u>f. 4-7</u>. 1857. Echinocereus engelmannii (Parry) Lemaire var. <u>vari-
egatus</u> Engelm. ex Rümpler in Förster, Handb. Cacteenk. ed. 2. 806.
1885, incorrectly ascribed to Engelmann. <u>E. engelmannii</u> (Parry)
Lemaire f. <u>variegatus</u> Schelle, Handb. Kakteenkultur 135. 1907.
"On the Cactus mountains at the head of Williams's river, degrees
113 1/2 longitude." LECTOTYPE designation: "Head of Bill Williams
Fork," <u>J. M. Bigelow</u>, Feb. 1, 1854, <u>Mo</u>.

UTAH. WAYNE CO. 1/2 mi. S of Bert Avery's Corral, NW side
of Mt. Ellen, <u>I. G. Reimann</u> in 1964, <u>Pom</u>, Aug., 1965, <u>Pom</u>; south

of Fairview Ranch, I. G. Reimann in 1964, Pom. KANE CO. N end of Brigham Plains W of Cottonwood Wash, N. D. Atwood & R. Allen 02707, Pom, BrY, ca. 36 mi. E of Glen Canyon City, N. D. Atwood, S. L. Welsh, J. Murdock, & R. Allen 2707, Pom, BrY.

7g. Echinocereus engelmannii var. purpureus L. Benson

Echinocereus engelmannii Parry var. purpureus L. Benson, Cactus & Succ. Jour. 41: 126. 1969. TYPE: "Mojavean Desert north of St. George, Washington County, Utah; 2,900 feet elevation; Lyman Benson 13,637, May 5, 1949," Pom 285578 (on 2 sheets).

7h. Echinocereus engelmannii var. nicholii L. Benson

Echinocereus engelmannii (Parry) Lemaire var. nicholii L. Benson, Proc. Calif. Acad. Sci. IV. 25: 258. pl. 25, f. B. 1944. TYPE: "Silver Bell Mountains, Pima County, Arizona, L. Benson 10,720, March 28, 1941." Ariz 34989. ISOTYPES: Pom 275437, (on 3 sheets); CAS 418803.

7i. Echinocereus engelmannii var. howei L. Benson

Echinocereus engelmannii (Parry) Lemaire var. howei L. Benson, Cactus & Succ. Jour. 46: 80. 1974. TYPE: "east of Goffs, San Bernardino County, California, D. F. Howe 4,570, Pom 317,886."

CALIFORNIA. SAN BERNARDINO CO. E of Goff's, Howe 4570, Pom; same area, farther E, L. Benson 16732, Pom.

8. Echinocereus enneacanthus Engelmann

8a. Echinocereus enneacanthus var. enneacanthus

Echinocereus enneacanthus Engelm. in Wisliz. Mem. Tour. No. Mex. 112. 1848. Cereus enneacanthus Engelm. in A. Gray, Pl. Fendl., Mem. Amer. Acad. 4: 49. 1849. "Near San Pablo, south of Chihuahua; flowers in April." TYPE: Same statement, Wislizenus, April 8, 1847, Mo 83707 (only flowers); photograph, US. A paratype is representative for other characters: Parras, Coahuila, Wislizenus, Mo 83708, 83709. Duplicate: Pom 317805.

Echinocereus enneacanthus Engelm. f. intermedius W. O. Moore, Brittonia 19: 93. 1967. TYPE: "TEXAS: Starr Co.: off La Grulla Rd...Moore 431...coll. [E. U.] Clover, 23 Mar 1953," Mich.

Names of Uncertain Application (probably to var. enneacanthus)

Echinocereus carnosus Rümpler in Förster, Handb. Cacteenk. ed. 2. 796. 1885. E. enneacanthus Engelm. var. carnosus Quehl, Monatsschr. Kakteenk. 18: 114. 1898. E. enneacanthus Engelm. f. carnosus K. Schum. ex Schelle, Handb. Kakteenkultur 126. 1907. E. enneacanthus Engelm. var. carnosus K. Schum. ex Weniger, Cacti S. W. 46. 1970, nom. nud. (Art. 33), erroneously ascribed to Schumann. "Vaterland, Texas." "Haage & Schmidt in Erfurt als Species aus Texas geführt." According to Britton & Rose, Cactaceae 3: 36. 1922, this is E. enneacanthus.

Echinocereus cereiformis De Laet, Cat. Gen. 9. 1908, nom. nud.

Echinocereus enneacanthus Engelm. f. major, Schelle, Handb. Kakteenkultur 127. 1907, nom. nud. E. enneacanthus Engelm. var. major Hort. ex Borg, Cacti 223. 1951, nom. nud. (no Latin diagnosis). No specimen or locality.

Echinocereus albiflora[us] Lowry, Des. Pl. Life 8: 20. 1936, nom. subnud. "...Webb, Duval and Zapata counties [Texas]...with a white flower." No further description; no specimen; no Latin diagnosis.

Echinocereus lowryi Lowry, Des. Pl. Life 8: 20. 1936, nom. subnud. "...Found only near Laredo,...a large jointed plant close to E. enneacanthus." No further description; no specimen; no Latin diagnosis.

8b. Echinocereus enneacanthus var. brevispinus (W. O. Moore) L. Benson

Echinocereus enneacanthus Engelm. f. brevispinus W. O. Moore, Brittonia 18: 93. 1967. E. enneacanthus Engelm. var. brevispinus L. Benson, Cactus & Succ. Jour. 41: 127. 1969. TYPE: "TEXAS: Starr Co.: 8 mi e. of Rio Grande City...Moore 508, [from a] coll. [by E. U.] Clover 31 Dec 1953," Mich.

8c. Echinocereus enneacanthus var. stramineus (Engelmann) L. Benson

Cereus stramineus Engelm. Proc. Amer. Acad. 3: 282. 1856; in Emory, Rept. U.S. & Mex. Bound. Surv. 2: Cactaceae 35. pl. 46–47; 48, f. 1. 1859. Echinocereus stramineus Engelm. ex Rümpler in Förster, Handb. Cacteenk. ed. 2. 797. 1885, incorrectly ascribed to Engelmann. E. enneacanthus Engelm. var. stramineus L. Benson, Cactus & Succ. Jour. 41: 127. 1969. "...About El Paso, extending east to the Pecos and west to the Gila (Wright, Bigelow, Parry)." LECTOTYPE (Coulter, Contr. U.S. Natl. Herb. 3: 390. 1896): "Wright of 1851 in Herb. Mo. Bot. Gard," Mo; according to W. O. Moore, Brittonia 18: 90. 1966, "Charles Wright, 1851, marked

'Cereus no. 8'...(MO)." A better specimen is the following: On high gravelly tableland & Mt. slopes. El Paso-Pecos & Gila. Fl. June, fr. July & Aug. On hills, Bigelow," together with material in a carton, labelled, "Near El Paso, gravelly, rocky soil near the Rio Grande, Bigelow, 1851," Mo (sheet and boxes). However, the collection by Wright must be considered as the lectotype.

Names of Uncertain Application (perhaps to var. stramineus)

Echinocereus bolansis Rünge, Monatsschr. Kakteenk. 5: 123. 1895, nom. nud., pro syn.

Echinocereus stramineus mayor (aureispina) Fric, Ceskoslov. Zahradnickych Listu [Kakt. Sukk.] 1924: 121. 1924. "TEXAS, USA." Also, E. stramineus mayor spina rosa Fric, loc. cit. "New Mexico, USA." Both combinations are nomina nuda, and neither is a bi- or trinomial.

Echinocereus stramineus (Engelm.) Engelm. ex Rümpler f. major Schelle, Handb. Kakteenkultur 136. 1907, nom. nud. E. stramineus (Engelm.) ex Rümpler var. major Hort. ex Borg, Cacti 222. 1951. No locality or specimen.

8d. Echinocereus enneacanthus var. dubius (Engelmann) L. Benson

Cereus dubius Engelm. Proc. Amer. Acad. 3: 282. 1857 (preprint, 1856); in Emory, Rept. U.S. & Mex. Bound. Surv. 2: Cactaceae 36. pl. 50. 1859. Echinocereus dubius Engelm. ex Rümpler, Handb. Cacteenk. ed. 2. 787. 1885, incorrectly ascribed to Engelmann. E. enneacanthus Engelm. var. dubius L. Benson, Cactus & Succ. Jour. 41: 127. 1969. "Sandy bottoms of the Rio Grande, and [N. B. !] from El Paso (Wright, Bigelow) to below Presidio (Parry...). Flowers June and July." LECTOTYPE (Coulter, Contr. U.S. Natl. Herb. 3: 390. 1896): "Sandhills of the Rio Grande," "Sandy bottoms of the Rio Grande," "El Paso to below Presidio," Charles Wright, June 19, 1852, Mo, (1 herbarium sheet, the labels bearing the statements above). On June 19, 1852, Wright was in the "Rio Grande bottom" travelling eastward; on June 21 he was at Eagle Spring. Thus, the type collection was made near the Rio Grande in Hudspeth Co., Texas, not at El Paso.

9. Echinocereus lloydii Britton & Rose

Echinocereus lloydii Britton & Rose, Cactaceae 3: 37. f. 46; pl. 3, f. 4. 1922. E. roetteri (Engelm.) Engelm. ex Rümpler var. lloydii Backeberg, Cactaceae 4: 2027. 1960. "...Near Tuna Springs, Texas, in 1909, by F. E. Lloyd...." LECTOTYPE designation: "Near Tuna Springs, F. E. Lloyd, Feb. 26–28, 1909," US 691964.

NEW MEXICO. "Southern New Mexico," R. E. Kunze, US (box). DONA ANA CO. East Potrillo Mts., P. Pierce 1725A, April 7, 1963, UNM. OTERO CO. Hills W of Oro Grande, P. Pierce 1200B, in 1958, UNM. EDDY CO. 30 mi. W of Artesia, H. Kuenzler, May, 1965, UNM.

TEXAS. Without locality, J. H. Ferriss 522, US. PECOS CO. Tunas Springs, Escondido Creek, F. E. Lloyd, NY (photograph), Feb. 26–28, 1909, US, Feb. 9, 1910, US (fls.), May 11, 1916, NY, D. Weniger 183, May 17, 1963, UNM, D. S. & H. S. Correll & L. & E. L. Benson 16493, Pom.

Invalid Name of Uncertain Application (perhaps to Echinocereus lloydii)

Echinocereus viridiflorus Engelm. var. intermedius Backeberg, Cactaceae 4: 2015. f. 1919. 1960, nom. nud. (no type specimen). "Herkunft meines Wissens auch aus Texas (abb. 1919)."

10. Echinocereus pectinatus (Scheidweiler) Engelmann

10a. Echinocereus pectinatus var. rigidissimus (Engelmann) Engelmann ex Rümpler

Cereus pectinatus (Scheidw.) Engelm. var. rigidissimus Engelm. Proc. Amer. Acad. 3: 279. 1857 (preprint, 1856); in Emory Rept. U.S. & Mex. Bound. Surv. 2: Cactaceae 31. 1859. Echinocereus pectinatus (Scheidw.) Engelm. var. rigidissimus Engelm. ex Rümpler in Förster, Handb. Cacteenk. ed. 2. 818. 1885, incorrectly ascribed to Engelmann. E. pectinatus Engelm. f. rigidissimus Engelm. ex Schelle, Handb. Kakteenkultur 131. 1907, nom. nud., incorrectly ascribed to Engelmann. E. dasyacanthus Engelm. var. rigidissimus W. T. Marshall in Marshall & Bock, Cactaceae 119. 1941. "...Sierras of Pimeria Alta in Sonora, and farther west (A. Schott). Flowers in June and July." LECTOTYPE (L. Benson Proc. Calif. Acad. Sci. IV. 25: 256. 1944; Cactus & Succ. Jour. 40: 124. 1968): "'Sierra del Pajarito and farther west in similar localities,' Schott in 1855," Mo. DUPLICATE: Pom 317807.

ARIZONA. MARICOPA CO. Tempe Butte, S. C. Mason 1042, US (box); Tempe Bluffs, S. C. Mason, Nov. 1907, US (box). Phoenix, V. Bailey, Oct., 1889, US (box). GRAHAM CO. Galiuro Mts., Toumey, Sept. 20, 1898, US. PIMA CO. (W). Baboquivari Mts., Wiggins 8706, DS (box). PIMA, SANTA CRUZ, and COCHISE COS. Numerous collections.

NEW MEXICO. HIDALGO CO. Common in S half of co. GRANT CO. White Water (labelled as Chihuahua and perhaps from that state), Mearns 273, US.

Specimens from Eddy Co., New Mexico, and from near Alpine, Brewster Co., Texas, approach this variety in their character combinations. Cf.: NEW MEXICO. EDDY CO. Rattlesnake Canyon, Guadalupe Mts., Castetter 1368, UNM; Guadalupe Ridge, J. French, Oct. 5, 1964, UNM. TEXAS. BREWSTER CO. Near Alpine, J. H. Ferriss 532c in 1925, US.

Names of Uncertain Application (perhaps to var. rigidissimus)

Echinocereus rigidissimus Engelm. ex Hirscht-Zehlendorf, Monatsschr. Kakteenk. 7: 95. 1897, nom. nud., incorrectly ascribed to Engelmann.

Echinocereus pectinatus (Scheidw.) Engelm. var. robustior Hort. ex Hirscht-Zehlendorf, Monatsschr. Kakteenk. 7: 95. 1897, nom. nud.

10b. Echinocereus pectinatus var. pectinatus

Echinocereus pectinatus Scheidw. Bull. Acad. Sci. Brux. 5: 492. 1838. Echinopsis pectinata Fennel, Allg. Gartenz. 11: 282. 1843. Echinocereus pectinatus Engelm. in Wisliz. Mem. Tour. No. Mex. 110. 1848. Cereus pectinatus Engelm. in A. Gray, Pl. Fendl., Mem. Amer. Acad. 4: 50. 1849. "Habitat prope l'ida del Pennasco in locis temperatis." According to Britton & Rose, Cactaceae 3: 29-30. 1922: "...Collected by Galeotti who sent a collection to Belgium from the states of San Luis Potosí and Guanajuato, Mexico... Villa del Pennasco...not located...Figured by Lemaire (Icon. Cact. pl. 14 or 15) and Pfeiffer (Abbild. Beschr. Cact. 2: pl. 10), very likely from the type collection." According to Lemaire, "Elle croît au Mexique (lieu non designe), d'ou l'a apportee en Europe (en 1838) M. Galeotti...."

In 1845 the plant again was described and illustrated, Curtis' Bot. Mag., pl. 4190, from a specimen sent by Staines from San Luis Potosí, presumed to be the region of Galeotti's plant.

Engelmann (in Wisliz. Mem. Tour. No. Mex. 109-110. 1848) indicated a different origin of the first-described material of Echinocereus pectinatus from that suggested by Britton & Rose: "South of Chihuahua...Echinocereus pectinatus (Echinocactus pectinatus, Scheidw., E. pectiniferus, Lem., Echinopsis pectinata, Salm, in part)...The description of the plant (which died without producing flowers) found in several works, as well as in the latest publication on Cactaceae, before me, of Foerster, Leipzig, 1846, was made, as Prince Salm[-Dyck] informed me, from specimens sent from Chihuahua by Mr. Potts. It entirely agrees with my specimen from the same region.... Dr. Wislizenus has sent me a living specimen and dried flowers of E. pectinatus. Unfortunately, the plant met with a similar fate to those sent to England by Mr. Potts, and there is none now in cultivation, if I am correctly informed; but I preserve the dried specimen in my herbarium, and have been enabled to draw up from it the description." Salm-Dyck was in a much better position to know the source of the specimens described in the part of Europe near his home than were later authors. None of Galeotti's material has been found. NEOTYPE designation: "Bachimpa, south of Chihuahua," Wislizenus, "April 27, 1846-7," Mo. DUPLICATE: Pom 317808.

Echinocactus pectiniferus Lemaire, Cact. Gen. Sp. Nov. 25. 1839. Cereus pectiniferus Labouret, Monogr. Cact. 320. 1853. "...Patriam...ignoro." According to Labouret, "Près Chihuahua." NEOTYPE designation: The Wislizenus collection cited above for Echinocactus pectinatus Scheidw.

Echinocereus pectiniferus Lemaire var. laevior Lemaire, Cact. Gen. Sp. Nov. 26. 1839. Cereus pectinatus (Scheidw.) Engelm. var. laevior Salm-Dyck, Cact. Hort. Dyck 1849: 43. 1850, nom. nud. No locality or specimen.

Cereus ctenoides Engelm. Proc. Amer. Acad. 3: 279. 1857 (preprint, 1856); Rept. U.S. & Mex. Bound. Surv. 2: Cactaceae 31. pl. 42. 1859. Echinocereus ctenoides Engelm. ex Rümpler in Förster, Handb. Cacteenk. ed. 2. 819. 1885, incorrectly ascribed to Engelmann. E. dasyacanthus Engelm. var. ctenoides Backeberg, Cactaceae 4: 2021. 1960; Wagner, Cacti S. W. 25. 1970, nom. nud. (Art. 33). "From Eagle Pass to Santa Rosa [Coahuila opposite Big Bend National Park] (Bigelow); on the Pecos (Wright). Flowers June and July (St. Louis)." LECTOTYPE (L. Benson, Cactus & Succ. Jour. 40: 124. 1968): "...Dr. Bigelow at Santa Rosa — Jan. 1853," Mo (on 2 sheets)." Bigelow did not reach the area of Santa Rosa, New Mexico, until September, 1853.

These plants could be classified, according to flower color, as var. neomexicanus because the petaloids are yellow, but the other characters are of var. pectinatus. Transitional coloring of the petaloids involving both yellow (insoluble plastid) pigments and pink to light purple coloring (water-soluble betacyanins) appears occasionally as follows: TEXAS. BREWSTER CO. 51 miles south of Alpine, Brewster Co., E. F. Anderson 1034, Pom; Texas, 10 miles north of Lajitas, Fields, McBryde, & King 2574, Tex, Pom; near Lajitas Junction, west of Big Bend National Park, E. F. Anderson 1044, Pom; near Tornillo Creek, Big Bend National Park, field observation of plants with others of varieties of Echinocereus pectinatus, associated with the collection L. Benson 16504, Pom.

Echinocereus steereae Clover, Bull. Torrey Club 6: 565. f. 4. 1938. E. dasyacanthus Engelm. var. steereae W. T. Marshall, Cactus & Succ. Jour. 17: 115. 1945, not combined formally as a variety. TYPE: "...Mrs. Lois Steere in the Chisos Mts., Western Texas, March, 1937," Mich (not numbered; only flowers). The photograph (f. 4) indicates this variety.

ARIZONA. COCHISE CO. Bisbee, Orcutt 188, March 31, 1924, US, Pom; Mule Mts., E of Bisbee, J. P. Hester 596, F (photograph); Silver Creek, Douglas, W. W. Jones, Aug. 26, 1947, SD; Perilla Mts., H. V. Harlan, May 1, 1939, Ariz, E. R. Blakley & W. T. Marshall, May 26, 1952, Des; NE of Douglas, L. Benson 11113, Pom, Ariz.

TEXAS. BREWSTER CO. Near Marathon, D. S. & H. S. Correll & L. & E. L. Benson 16479, Pom; road to Boquillas Canyon, Big Bend National Park, field observation of plants growing with L. Benson 16504, Pom, but not collected. PECOS CO. "Pecos," probably in Pecos Co. near the river, not the present town, Wright in 1851, Mo; SE corner of the co., L. Vortman, Oct. 10, 1964, UNM. MAVERICK CO. Eagle Pass, Bigelow, Jan., 1853, Mo (fls.).

Names of Uncertain Application (probably to var. pectinatus.)

Echinocereus pectinatus (Scheidw.) Engelm. f. texensis Hooker ex Schelle, f. candicans Schelle, f. rufispinus K. Schum. ex Schelle, & f. cristatus Schelle, Handb. Kakteenkultur 133. 1907, nomina nuda.

10c. Echinocereus pectinatus var. wenigeri L. Benson

Echinocereus pectinatus (Scheidw.) Engelm. var. wenigeri L. Benson, Cactus & Succ. Jour. (Haworthiana, installment 3) 40: 124. f. 3. 1968, "Texas in Val Verde County near Langtry, Lyman & Evelyn L. Benson 16,521, April 13, 1965." TYPE: Pom 311338.

TEXAS. SUTTON CO. E of Ranch Experiment Station, Cory, May 5, 1947, DS. TERRELL CO. Sanderson, D. Weniger, April 16, 1963, UNM, L. Benson 16518, Pom. VAL VERDE CO. Langtry, Fields, McBryde, & King 2565, Tex, Pom, 2566, Tex, Pom, L. & E. L. Benson 16521, Pom; near Devil's River, Fields, McBryde, & King 2560, Tex, Pom; Del Rio, R. M. King 2555, Tex, Pom. MEXICO. COAHUILA. Sierra de Huacha, D. Weniger 519 in 1964, UNM; Babia, D. Weniger 518, UNM.

10d. Echinocereus pectinatus var. minor (Engelmann) L. Benson

Cereus dasyacanthus Engelm. var. minor Engelm. Proc. Amer. Acad. 3: 279. 1857 (preprint, 1856). C. roetteri Engelm. Proc. Amer. Acad. 3: 345. 1857 (preprint, 1856), nom. nov. Echinocereus roetteri Rümpler in Förster, Handb. Cacteenk. ed. 2. 829. 1885, incorrectly ascribed to Engelmann. E. pectinatus (Scheidw.) Engelm. var. minor L. Benson, Cactus & Succ. Jour. (Haworthiana, installment 3) 40: 125. f. 4. 1968, "El Paso, southward to the Sandhills...." Cf. Engelm. in Emory, Rept. U.S. & Mex. Bound. Surv. 2: Cactaceae 33. pl. 41, f. 3-5. 1859, "Sandhills south of El Paso (Bigelow); near El Paso or Frontera, (Wright). Flowers April." LECTOTYPE (Benson, loc. cit.): "Stony hillsides at Frontera," then in New Mexico, now in NW El Paso, Texas, Wright in 1851, Mo (on 2 sheets). DUPLICATE: Pom 317825.

NEW MEXICO. DONA ANA CO. Collections of Wright (in 1851-52, Mo, Tex, A in 1852, Tex, K) are labelled, "N. Mex.," and Charles Wright travelled extensively in SW New Mexico. These specimens may have come from Dona Ana Co. or from near Frontera (now in El Paso, Texas), then in New Mexico (cf. above). Living plants from Dona Ana Co. have been seen in the garden of E. F. Castetter of the University of New Mexico, Albuquerque.

TEXAS. EL PASO CO. Frontera, Wright, in 1851, Mo; El Paso, Vasey, April, 1891, DS. BREWSTER CO. Tornillo Creek, Big Bend National Park, L. Benson 16504, Pom, R. Wauer in 1969, Pom; Reagan Canyon, Warnock, April 4, 1947, SRSC.

Echinocereus pectinatus var. minor (cf. Benson, loc. cit.) occurs through a large area in northern Mexico. Because only the margin of its range is in the U.S., the variety has been little known or understood. Few collections have been made, and each has tended to be interpreted as a new species.

10e. Echinocereus pectinatus var. neomexicanus (Coulter) L. Benson

Echinocereus dasyacanthus Engelm. in Wisliz. Mem. Tour. No. Mex. 100. 1848. Cereus dasyacanthus Engelm. in A. Gray, Pl. Fendl., Mem. Amer. Acad. 4: 50. 1849. E. pectinatus (Scheidw.) Engelm. var. dasyacanthus L. Benson ex W. H. Earle, Saguaroland Bull. 25: 80. 1971, nom. nud. (Art. 33), erroneously ascribed to the writer. "El Paso del Norte," Wislizenus. Specimen not found, Mo. NEOTYPE designation: "...Chs. Wright between San Antonio and El Paso, October, 1849," ["July 1850," probably the time of pressing the specimen], Mo. DUPLICATE: Pom 317824 (spine clusters).

Cereus dasyacanthus Engelm. var. neomexicanus Coulter, Contr. U.S. Nat. Herb. 3: 384. 1896. Echinocereus pectinatus (Scheidw.) Engelm. var. neomexicanus L. Benson, Proc. Calif. Acad. Sci. IV. 23: 256. 1944, not E. neomexicanus Standley Bull. Torrey Club 35: 87. 1908. TYPE: "Wright 366 in Herb. Mo. Bot. Gard. Southeastern New Mexico." Not found, Mo. LECTOTYPE (L. Benson, Cactus & Succ. Jour. 40: 127. 1968): "N. Mex., Wright 366 in 1851," GH.

Echinocereus spinosissimus Walton, Cact. Jour. 2: 162. 1899.
"El Paso...I collected a number...." No specimen mentioned. The
large yellow flowers of the description indicate the plant to have
been var. neomexicanus.

ARIZONA. COCHISE CO. E of Benson, R. T. Craig, Dec. 24,
1951, Pom.

NEW MEXICO. VALENCIA CO. Mesa del Oro, Castetter in 1964,
UNM. LINCOLN CO. W of Sunset, Hondo Valley, Castetter & Pierce
623, UNM; Border Hill, U.S. Highway 380, P. Pierce, Mar. 21, 1962,
UNM. CHAVES CO. 38 mi. W of Artesia, L. Benson 15538, Pom; Hacho
Draw, N of Roswell, Castetter 2253, UNM. DONA ANA, OTERO, and
EDDY COS. Several collections from each co.

TEXAS. EL PASO, HUDSPETH, PRESIDIO, and BREWSTER COS. Common. PECOS CO. 25 mi. SE of Ft. Stockton, D. S. & H. S. Correll
& L. & E. L. Benson 16491, Pom. MITCHELL CO. Colorado, Evans, in
1891, US (box). UPTON CO. E of McCamey, D. S. & H. S. Correll
30893, LL. TERRELL CO. Sanderson, Rose, Standley, & Russell
12273, NY.

Names of Uncertain Application (perhaps to var. neomexicanus)

Cereus dasyacanthus Engelm. var. spurius Labouret, Monogr.
Fam. Cact. 321. 1858, nom. dub. Cereus deflexispinus Monville
var. spurius Monville ex Labouret, loc. cit., pro syn. No specimen or locality. The description indicates a plant with a more
precise arrangement of the spines in two rows than in those in
cultivation as Cereus dasyacanthus. This may have been var. pectinatus (if the flowers, not mentioned, were not yellow) or (if
they were yellow) an intermediate form between vars. neomexicanus
and pectinatus.

Echinocereus hildmannii Arendt, Monatsschr. Kakteenk. 1: 146.
pl. 11. 1892. E. dasyacanthus Engelm. var. hildman[n]ii Arendt
ex Weniger Cacti S. W. 33. 1970, nom. nud. (Art. 33), erroneously
attributed to Arendt. "...Kultivateur H. Hildmann." No locality
or specimen.

Echinocereus rubescens Dams, Montasschr. Kakteenk. 15: 92.
f. on p. 89. 1905. E. papillosus Linke var. rubescens [Dams?],
loc. cit., pro syn. Cultivated material; no specimen or origin
given.

Echinocereus degandii Rebut ex. K. Schum. Monatsschr. Kakteenk. 5: 123. 1895, nom. nud. Var. neomexicanus, according to
Britton & Rose, Cactaceae 3: 19. 1922. Texas.

11. Echinocereus reichenbachii
(Tenscheck) Haage, f., ex Britton & Rose

11a. Echinocereus reichenbachii var. reichenbachii

Echinocactus reichenbachii Terscheck, Suppl. Cacti 2 [not
found]; in Walpers, Repert. Bot. 2: 320. ["Ante Calendas Novembr.
MD CCCXLIII."] 1843. Echinocereus caespitosus Engelm. var.
reichenbachii Terscheck ex Borg, Cacti 174. 1937, illegitimate
combination, incorrectly ascribed to Terscheck. Echinocereus
reichenbachii Haage, f., ex Britton & Rose, Cactaceae 3: 25.
1922. Echinocereus pectinatus (Scheidw.) Engelm. var. reichenbachii Werdermann in Fedde, Repert. Sp. Nov. Sonderbeiheft C.,
Lief. 2. Tafel 5. 1930. "Habitat in Mexico." NEOTYPE designation: "Vicinity of Saltillo, Coahuila," Mexico, Edward F. Palmer
511, April 10, 1905, US 570013.

Echinocactus reichenbachianus Terscheck, Preis-Verz. 3. [not
found]; Terscheck ex Fennel, Allg. Gartenz. 11: 282. Sept. 9,
1843, nom. nud., pro syn. Echinopsis pectinata (Scheidw.) Fennel
var. reichenbachiana Salm-Dyck, Cact. Hort. Dyck 1844. 26. 1845.
Cereus reichem[n]bachianus Labouret, Monogr. Cact. 318. 1853.
Echinocereus reichenbachianus Linke, Wochenschr. Gärtn. Pflanzenk.
1: 183. 1857, nom. nud.; Engelm. ex Haage, f., Index Kewensis
813. 1885 (citing Terscheck, Preis-Verz. Cact. 213 [not found]),
incorrectly ascribed to Engelmann, Preisverzeichnis Cacteen 23.
1893. Probably reichenbachianus is only a variant of the epithet
reichenbachii.

Cereus caespitosus Engelm. Pl. Lindh. I. 39, Bost. Jour. Nat.
Hist. 5: 247. 1845. Echinocereus caespitosus Engelm. in Wisliz.
Mem. Tour No. Mex. 110. 1848. Mammillaria caespitosa A. Gray,
First Lessons in Bot. & Veg. Physiol. 96. 1857; Struct. Bot. ed.
5. 421. f. 838. 1858, cf. Britton & Rose, Cactaceae 3: 26. 1922.
E. pectinatus (Scheidw.) Engelm. var. caespitosus K. Schum. Gesamtb.
Kakteen 272. 1898. E. pectinatus "Engelm." f. caespitosus Schelle,
Handb. Kakteenkultur 131. 1907. "Gravelly soil, near Cat-Spring
Austin County, west of San Felipe [Waller Co.]," Texas, Lindheimer.
LECTOTYPE designation: "...Industry, Austin County, about 15 miles
from Cat Spring" and cultivated at St. Louis, [without doubt]
F. Lindheimer, June, 1845, Mo.

Cereus caespitosus Engelm. var. castaneus Engelm. Pl. Lindh.
II, Bost. Jour. Nat. Hist. 6: 202. 1850. C. reichenbachianus
(Terscheck) Labouret var. castaneus Labouret. Monogr. Cact. 319.
1853. Echinocereus caespitosus (Engelm.) Engelm. var. castaneus
Engelm. ex Rümpler in Förster, Handb. Cacteenk. ed. 2. 811. 1885,
incorrectly ascribed to Engelmann. E. pectinatus (Scheidw.)

Engelm. var. castaneus Mathsson, Monatsschr. Kakteenk. 144. 1891.
E. castaneus Orcutt, Cactography 4. 1926, not K. Schum. in 1903.
E. caespitosus (Engelm.) Engelm. var. adustus Engelm. ex Borg f.
castaneus Borg, Cacti 184. 1937. "Mr. Lindheimer...granitic
region of the Liano...." LECTOTYPE designation: "Liano [Llano],
Texas," Lindheimer in 1847, Mo. DUPLICATE: Pom 317810.

Cereus caespitosus Engelm. var. minor Engelm. Proc. Amer.
Acad. 3: 280. 1857 (preprint, 1856). LECTOTYPE designation:
"St. Louis cultis. Sent from Industry, Texas," F. Lindheimer,
June, 1845, Mo. Engelmann intended this as the typical variety,
and the lectotype is the same as for Cereus caespitosus, cf. above.

Cereus caespitosus Engelm. var. major Engelm. Proc. Amer.
Acad. 3: 280. 1857 (preprint, 1856). Echinocereus caespitosus
Engelm. var. major Engelm. ex Rümpler in Förster, Handb. Cacteenk.
ed. 2. 811. 1885, incorrectly ascribed to Engelmann. LECTOTYPE
designation: Texas, F. Lindheimer in 1851 ("New Braunfels," in
one packet), Mo (on 3 sheets).

Echinocereus purpureus Lahman, Cactus & Succ. Jour. 6: 141.
f. 1935. E. caespitosus Engelm. var. purpureus Weniger, Cacti
S. W. 23. 1970, nom. nud. (Art. 33). "TYPE LOCALITY near Medi-
cine Park, Okla." "Flower and photograph in the Herbarium of the
Missouri Botanical Garden, St. Louis, Mo." LECTOTYPE designation:
Mo (photograph and flowers), photograph US.

Invalid Names of Uncertain Application (probably to var. reichenbachii)

Echinocereus reichenbachii (Terscheck) Britton & Rose, vars.
albiflorus and aureiflorus Seela, Cactus & Succ. Jour. 12: 92.
1940, nom. nud. (no Latin diagnoses). Horticultural material from
the Arbuckle Mountains, Oklahoma; none preserved.

Echinocereus rotatus Linke, Wochenschr. Gärtn. Pflanz. 1: 85.
1858.

11b. Echinocereus reichenbachii var. perbellus
(Britton & Rose) L. Benson

Echinocereus perbellus Britton & Rose, Cactaceae 3: 24. f. 24.
1922. E. reichenbachii (Terscheck) Britton & Rose var. perbellus
L. Benson, Cactus & Succ. Jour. 41: 127. 1969. E. caespitosus
Engelm. var. perbellus Weniger, Cacti S. W. 23. 1970, nom. nud.
(Art. 33). "...Rose and Standley and Russell] at Big Springs,
Texas, February 23, 1910 (No. 12215)." TYPE: US 635015, 635016,
including photograph of flowers. ISOTYPES: NY (on 3 sheets), US
unnumbered (flowers and photographs), Pom 306419, 314659.

11c. Echinocereus reichenbachii var. albertii L. Benson

Echinocereus reichenbachii (Terscheck) Britton & Rose var.
albertii L. Benson, Cactus & Succ. Jour. 41: 127. 1969. TYPE:
TEXAS. JIM WELLS CO. "Near Alice, Richard O. Albert and Lyman
Benson 16,550, May 25, 1965," Pom 317080.

Invalid Name of Uncertain Application (Perhaps to var. albertii)

Echinocereus melanocentrus Lowry, Desert Plant Life 2: 20.
1936, nom. nud. (no Latin diagnosis); Backeberg, Cactaceae 4:
2030. 1960, nom. nud. (no type specimen). "...In a very limited
area...Kleberg...." Co., Texas.

11d. Echinocereus reichenbachii var. fitchii
(Britton & Rose) L. Benson

Echinocereus fitchii Britton & Rose, Cactaceae 3: 30. pl. 3,
f. 2. 1922. E. reichenbachii (Terscheck) Britton & Rose var.
fitchii L. Benson, Cactus & Succ. Jour. 41: 127. 1969. "...Rose
near Laredo, Texas, in 1913 (No. 18037)...." TYPE: US 1821071.
Probable ISOTYPE: NY.

TEXAS. WEBB CO. 36-38 mi. NW of Laredo, D. Weniger 475 &
480, Feb. 10, 1964, UNM; 21 mi. NW of Laredo, D. Weniger 470,
Feb. 10, 1964, UNM; Laredo, Rose in 1913, NY, April 2, 1914, NY,
18037, US. ZAPATA CO. Zapata, D. Weniger 44 & 45, Feb. 12,
1963, UNM; between Roma and Zapata, K. M. & M. C. Wiegand 1518,
CU. STARR CO. 3 mi. E of Falcon Dam, D. Weniger 205, July 26,
1963, UNM; Roma, A. D. Wood 607, March 11, 1964, Pom, L. Benson
16536, Pom; 8 mi. N of Rio Grande City, Clover 1871, Tex, Ariz,
DS.

11e. Echinocereus reichenbachii var. chisosensis
(W. T. Marshall) L. Benson

Echinocereus chisosensis W. T. Marshall, Cactus & Succ. Jour.
12: 15. cover illus., p. 1. Jan., 1940. E. reichenbachii (Terscheck) Britton & Rose var. chisosensis L. Benson, Cactus & Succ.
Jour. 41: 127. 1969. "Chisos Mountains of Texas...F. Radley on
April 10, 1939...." TYPE: DS 263216 (ref. to material in fluid).

Echinocereus fobeanus Oehme, Beitr. Sukkulent. & -Pflege
1940. 49. f. 1940. "Heimat vermutlich Arizona." No specimen
mentioned; probably from Texas. Since the combination was published in "Lfg. 3," the third and probably the last number of the

year, the date is assumed to be later than January, when the epithet chisosensis was published. In the Library of the University
of California at Los Angeles the parts of the publication were
received as follows: Lfg. 1, May 11, 1940; Lfg. 2 (not stamped);
Lfg. 3, May 19, 1941. Distribution doubtless was erratic because
of the Second World War, but issuance of Lfg. 3 in January, 1940,
is unlikely. Probably E. chisosensis has priority in specific as
well as varietal rank.

TEXAS. BREWSTER CO. Chisos Mts., J. P. Hester, June, 1950,
US (box); San Vicente to Glenn Springs, O. E. Sperry 1907, Apr.
13, 1941, Ariz; road to Boquillas, Warnock, Pom, P. H. Wauer in
1969, Pom; 15 mi. NW of Boquillas Canyon, D. Weniger 125A & 126,
May 6, 1963, UNM; N of Hot Springs, E. R. Blakley 1423, Des;
above lower Tornillo Creek, L. Benson 16505, Pom.

11f. Echinocereus reichenbachii var. albispinus (Lahman) L. Benson

Echinocereus baileyi Rose, Contr. U.S. Nat. Herb. 12: pl
56, 57. 1909. "...V. Bailey, Wichita Mountains [Oklahoma],
August, 1906...." TYPE: US 53167 and box. ISOTYPE: Pom 306412.

Echinocereus oklahomensis Lahman, Cactus & Succ. Jour. 6:
141. f. 1935, nom. nud. (no Latin diagnosis). "...Wichita National Forest Reserve, Okla." TYPE: Mo. ISOTYPE: US (box).

Echinocereus albispinus Lahman, Cactus & Succ. Jour. 6: 143.
f. 1935. E. baileyi Rose var. albispinus Backeberg, Kakteenkunde (Deutsch. Kakteen-Gesellschaft) 4. 1941. E. reichenbachii
(Terscheck) Britton & Rose var. albispinus L. Benson, Cactus &
Succ. Jour. 41: 127. 1969. "TYPE LOCALITY near Medicine Park...
Wichita National Forest Reserve, Okla." Mo (only a photograph
found). Illustration, Lahman, Nature Magazine 27: 20. 1936; same
photograph, F 904708, US. LECTOTYPE (an isotype, Benson, loc.
cit.): US 1769021.

Echinocereus longispinus Lahman, Cactus & Succ. Jour. 7: 135.
1936, nom. nud. (no Latin diagnosis). "...Mt. Scott near Medicine
Park, Oklahoma." "Type plants in the Missouri Botanical Garden,
New York Botanical Garden and the National Museum." LECTOTYPE
designation: Mo. DUPLICATE: US; not found, NY.

Echinocereus baileyi Rose vars. brunispinus, flavispinus, and
roseispinus Backeberg, Kakteenkunde 1941: 4. 1941, nom. nud. (no
Latin diagnoses).

Echinocereus baileyi Rose var. caespiticus Backeberg, Cactaceae 4: 2011. f. 1915. 1960, nom. nud. (no type specimen.) "USA
(Oklahoma, Wichita-Mountains)."

Invalid Name of Uncertain Application (perhaps to var. albispinus)

Echinocereus mariae Backeberg, Nat. Cact. & Succ. Jour. 20:
19. f. 1965, nom. nud. (no type specimen). "Habitat: United
States of America: Oklahoma, Wichita Mountains, the extreme western
part of the Headquarters Mountains, situated about 3 miles west of
Granite." The stems are described as slender, 15 cm long, 1.5-2
cm diam. This may be one of the forms in the hybrid swarms common
in Oklahoma.

12. Echinocereus viridiflorus Engelmann

12a. Echinocereus viridiflorus var. viridiflorus

Echinocereus viridiflorus Engelm. in Wisliz. Mem. Tour No.
Mex. 91. 1848. Cereus viridiflorus Engelm. in A. Gray, Pl.
Fendl., Mem. Amer. Acad. 4: 49. 1849. C. viridiflorus (Engelm.)
Engelm. var. minor Engelm. Proc. Amer. Acad. 3: 278. 1857 (preprint, 1856), the species being composed of two varieties, this
one [the type according to Engelmann's custom] including the
plants obtained at the type locality for the species. Echinocactus
viridiflorus Pritzel, Icon. Bot. Index 2: 113. 1866. "In prairies
on Wolf Creek, at an elevation of between 6,000 and 7,000 feet...."
LECTOTYPE designation: "Near Wolf Creek on Santa Fé Road," Wislizenus, June 24, 1846, Mo (on 2 sheets) and the illustration in
Emory, Rept. U.S. & Mex. Bound. Surv. 2: Cactaceae 29. pl. 36,
f. 4-15. 1859, f. 8-10 having been drawn from the lectotype.

Echinocereus labouretianus Lemaire, Cactées 57. 1868 (referred here by Britton & Rose, Cactaceae 3: 17. 1922).

Echinocereus labouretti Förster ex Rümpler in Förster, Handb.
Cacteenk. ed. 2. 811. 1885, pro syn., under Echinocereus viridiflorus.

Echinocereus standleyi Britton & Rose, Cactaceae 3: 24. f.
23. 1922. E. viridiflorus Engelm. var. standleyi Orcutt ex Weniger, Cacti S. W. 15. 1970, nom. nud. (Art. 33, no precise reference to a publication by Orcutt). No publication by Orcutt
appears in the Gray Herbarium Card Index, and apparently the
combination by Weniger was new). "...Mrs. S. L. Pattison in the
Sacramento Mountains, New Mexico, and obtained from her by Paul C.
Standley in 1906. LECTOTYPE designation: "100 miles north of El
Paso," Sadie L. Patterson [Pattison], US (carton and photograph).
The area about Cloudcroft commonly reached by visitors to the
Sacramento Mountains is about 100 miles north and somewhat east of
El Paso, Texas.

WYOMING. ALBANY CO. Foothills E of Islay, M. Carey 311,
June 25, 1909, US; base of Laramie Mts., Hayden in 1856, Mo.

SOUTH DAKOTA. FALL RIVER CO. Hot Springs, Black Hills,
Rydberg 715, NY (in part), US.

KANSAS. HAMILTON CO. Syracuse, Rose & Fitch 17048, NY, US.
STANTON CO. Plains, A. S. Hitchcock 184, Aug. 5, 1895, Mo (box),
NY. US.

OKLAHOMA. TEXAS CO. "Camp," G. W. Stevens 347 in 1913, Mo,
NY, GH.

TEXAS. OLDHAM CO. 10 mi. E of Vega, L. Benson 14711, Pom.
POTTER CO. Amarillo, C. R. Ball, Oct. 14, 1907, US (box), 1613,
US (box).

Names of Uncertain Application (perhaps to var. viridiflorus)

Echinocereus strausianus Haage, f., in Quehl, Monatsschr.
Kakteenk. 10: 70. 1900. "Von der Firma FRIEDRICH ADOLF HAAGE,
Jr., in Erfurt aus Texas eingeführt...." Horticultural material;
no specimen.

Echinocereus viridiflorus Engelm. var. gracilispinus Hort.
ex Rümpler in Förster, Handb. Cacteenk. ed. 2. 814. 1885. No
locality or specimen.

Echinocereus viridiflorus Engelm. var. major Förster,
Monatsschr. Kakteenk. 16: 142. 1906. No specimen or locality.

12b. Echinocereus viridiflorus var. davisii (A. D. Houghton) W. T. Marshall

Echinocereus davisii A. D. Houghton, Cactus & Succ. Jour. 2:
466. 1931. E. viridiflorus Engelm. var. davisii W. T. Marshall
in Marshall & Bock, Cactaceae 119. 1941, nom. nud. (no reference
to basionym and no Latin description); validated by Backeberg,
Cactaceae 4: 2017. 1960, through reference to Houghton, loc. cit.
"...Marathon..., Texas," A. R. Davis (Houghton 700). TYPE: US
1565585. ISOTYPES: UC 450442, GH. The type is a single stem
only 12 mm long. The plants flower when they are very small, and
a collection at the exact type station revealed hundreds of individuals but none with stems more than 2.5 cm long and 2 cm in diameter even though they bore as many as eight flowers each about
as large as the stem. Typical specimen including the parts not
shown by the type or isotypes: topotype, B. H. Warnock & L. Benson
16499, Pom 317432.

12c. Echinocereus viridiflorus var. correllii L. Benson

Echinocereus viridiflorus Engelm. var. correllii L. Benson,
Cactus & Succ. Jour. 41: 128. 1969. "South of Marathon, Brewster
County, Texas; hills at about 4,100 feet (1,200 m.) elevation,
Donovan S. Correll, Helen S. Correll, Lyman Benson, & Evelyn L.
Benson 16485, April 4, 1965." TYPE: Pom 317079.

TEXAS. PECOS CO. N of Ft. Stockton, Warnock 11031, SRSC.
BREWSTER CO. S of Marathon, C. A. Hanson & D. S. Correll 468e,
June 25, 1944, LL, D. S. & H. S. Correll & L. &. E. L. Benson
16485, Pom.

12d. Echinocereus viridiflorus var. cylindricus (Engelmann) Engelmann ex Rümpler

Cereus viridiflorus (Engelm.) Engelm. var. cylindricus Engelm.
Proc. Amer. Acad. 3: 278. 1857 (preprint, 1856). Echinocereus
viridiflorus Engelm. var. cylindricus Engelm. ex Rümpler in Förster, Handb. Cacteenk. ed. 2. 812. 1885, incorrectly ascribed to
Engelmann; Backeberg, Cactaceae 4: 2015. 1960. C. viridiflorus
var. tubulosus Coulter, Contr. U.S. Nat. Herb. 3: 383. 1896,
nom. nov. for var. cylindricus. E. viridiflorus (Engelm.) Engelm.
ex Rümpler var. tubulosus Heller, Cat. N. Amer. Fl. ed. 2. 8.
1900. "East of El Paso. Flowers May and June." Later Engelmann
(in Emory, Rept. U.S. & Mex. Bound. Surv. 2: Cactaceae 29, pl. 36,
f. 1-3, 16. 1859) added the following: "On the Limpia, and thence
toward El Paso; Wright. Flowers in May." No precise type found.
LECTOTYPE designation: "Valley of the Limpia"; "Valleys among the
mountains, head of the Limpio [Limpia, a creek]," Davis Mountains,
Jeff Davis Co., Texas, Charles Wright, June 11, 1851, and the
illustrations listed above drawn from the specimens. Some plants
are with, some without, central spines.

Cereus concolor Schott, U.S. Senate Rept. Expl. & Surv. R. R.
Route Pacific Ocean. Botany 4: Errata & Notes ii. 1857. Escondido Springs near the Pecos River, Texas. "In C. caespitosus
[Echinocereus reichenbachii] the flower-buds are clothed with a
dense grayish wool and bear beautiful flowers 2 inches in diameter
and 2 inches in length. In Cereus concolor the flower-buds are
perfectly naked, small, campanulate blossoms with yellowish sanguineus petals perfectly like the spines in color, 0.5 inches in
diameter and 0.8 inches in length." Probably this indicates var.
cylindricus.

Invalid Names of Uncertain Application (perhaps to var. cylindricus)

Echinocereus viridiflorus Engelm. vars. rubra and ruberissima
Frič, Českoslov. Zahradnickych Listu Kakt. Sukk. 1924: 121.
1924, nom. nud.

Echinocereus viridiflorus Engelm. formae chrysacanthus, longispinus, & gracilispinus Schelle, Kakteen 172. 1926, nom. nud. E. viridiflorus Engelm. f. faciliflorus Hildmann ex Schelle, loc. cit., nom. nud. E. viridiflorus Engelm. f. sanguineus Regel ex Schelle loc. cit., nom. nud.

Intergradation of Echinocereus viridiflorus var. cylindricus and E. chloranthus

Echinocereus viridiflorus Engelm. var. intermedius Backeberg, Cactaceae 4: 2015. f. 1919. 1960, nom. nud. (no type specimen designated). "Herkunft meines Wissens auch aus Texas (Abb. 1919)." The photograph indicates a plant perhaps nearest in relationship to var. cylindricus and perhaps collected in one of the intergrading populations between this variety and E. chloranthus. These are occasional, especially in New Mexico. NEW MEXICO. DONA ANA CO. E slope of San Andreas Mts., G. Sandborg, June 26, 1962, UNM. OTERO CO. Jarilla Mts. near Oro Grande, P. Pierce, May 2, 1962, UNM, Castetter & Pierce 1703, April 6, 1963, UNM. EDDY CO. Carlsbad, J. Blea, Aug., 1962, UNM, Castetter 2848-2850, Oct. 27, 1963, UNM. A similar collection shows a mixed population: TEXAS. BREWSTER CO. Near Panther Pass Junction, Big Bend National Park, L. & R. L. Benson 15502, Pom.

13. Echinocereus chloranthus Engelmann

13a. Echinocereus chloranthus var. chloranthus

Cereus chloranthus Engelm. Proc. Amer. Acad. 3: 278. 1857 (preprint, 1856); in Emory, Rept. U.S. & Mex. Bound. Surv. 2: Cactaceae 29. pl. 37-38. 1859. Echinocereus chloranthus Engelm. ex Rümpler in Förster, Handb. Cacteenk. ed. 2. 824. 1885, incorrectly ascribed to Engelmann. E. viridiflorus Engelm. var. chloranthus Backeberg, Cactaceae 4: 2015. 1960. "Common on stony hills and mountain sides near El Paso; Wright, Bigelow. Flowers April." LECTOTYPE designation: "El Paso" and "Stony Hills near the Rio Grande at Frontera," Charles Wright, April 2, 1852, Mo (3 sheets and carton). DUPLICATE: Pom 317832 (box). Frontera, formerly in New Mexico, now part of NW El Paso, Texas.

Echinocereus russanthus Weniger, Cactus & Succ. Jour. 41: 41. 1969. "Weniger #712 in Univ. New Mexico Herbarium." A specimen, Weniger 712, in 1968, UNM, is labelled: "A small area in SW Brewster Co., including the N part of the Chisos Mts. and the country NE of these to just past Study Butte...." Occurrence of forms of E. chloranthus in the Big Bend region and just north of it in Texas is more widespread than has been realized. There are 14 collections from Culberson, Jeff Davis, and Brewster Cos. Many do not have flowers, but some do, and the reddish coloring of those described as E. russanthus appears in some collections (e.g., E of Castolon. Cutler 667, Mo. TAES; Chisos Mountains, L. Benson 16513, Pom. In living plants flowering simultaneously at Claremont the flower color of the russanthus type (Chisos Mts. 16513) was duplicated in a collection of E. chloranthus from Tortugas Mountain, New Mexico State University, Las Cruces (L. Benson 16475, Pom). In Texas there is a wide variety of flower colors in combination with various spine characters (including color, size, form, and the tendency to turn downward), grading from those of var. chloranthus to those of the plant described as E. russanthus.

NEW MEXICO. LUNA CO. Cook's Peak, W. Hess 2503, Pom; Florida Mts., G. Wiens, Apr., 1963, UNM.

Invalid Names of Uncertain Application (perhaps to var. chloranthus)

Echinocereus chloranthus Engelm. vars. albispina and senilis Frič, Českoslov. Zahradnických Listů, Kakt. Sukk. 1924: 121. 1924, nom. nud.

Echinocereus chloranthus Engelm. var. flavispinus Y. Ito, Cacti 1952: 133. 1952, nom. nud. (no Latin diagnosis).

13b. Echinocereus chloranthus var. neocapillus Weniger

Echinocereus chloranthus Engelm. var. neocapillus Weniger, Cactus & Succ. Jour. 41: 39. f. 4. 1969. "RANGE: a very small area including only two ranches 5 to 10 miles south of Marathon, Texas. TYPE: Weniger #711, in the Univ. New Mexico Herbarium." A sheet numbered 711 is not the plant described by Weniger, but E. viridiflorus Engelm. var. correllii L. Benson, which does not correspond with the description. LECTOTYPE designation: "In a very restricted range encompassing some hills about 5 mi. to 10 mi. south of Marathon, Texas," Del Weniger 711 (originally 712), 1968, UNM 43582. The plant was described and illustrated by A. R. Leding, Jour. Hered. 327-328. f. 12. 1934; reprinted, Cactus & Succ. Jour. 14: 149-151. f. 91. 1942.

TEXAS. BREWSTER CO. 5-10 mi. S of Marathon, D. Weniger 711 (712), in 1968, UNM; W of Simpson Spring, P. Pierce 4258, UNM.

7. Lophophora

Lophophora, as a genus, Coulter, Contr. U.S. Nat. Herb. 3: 131. 1894. Lophophora, as subgenus, K. Schum, Gesamtb. Kakteen (= Lophophora williamsii [Lemaire] Coulter).

1. Lophophora williamsii (Lemaire) Coulter

Echinocactus williamsii Lemaire ex Salm-Dyck, Allg. Gartenz. 13: 385. 1845. Anhalonium williamsii Lemaire in Förster, Handb. Cacteenk, ed 2. 233. 1885. Mammillaria williamsii Coulter, Contr. U.S. Nat. Herb. 2: 129. 1891. Ariocarpus williamsii K. Schum. ex Siebert & Voss, Vilmorin's Blumengärtnerei ed. 3. 368. 1894. Lophophora williamsii Coulter, Contr. U.S. Nat. Herb. 3: 131. June 10, 1894. According to Edward F. Anderson (cf. below), in 1845 the original name appeared without description in Cel's Catalog. Salm-Dyck provided a Latin description but not the origin of the plant. Probably the first illustration was a color plate, Curtis's Bot. Mag. pl. 1296, 1847. No specimen preserved. NEOTYPE (Anderson, Brittonia 21: 304. 1969 [March, 1970]): "MEXICO: San Luis Potosí: on the flat lands n.e. of the junction of Mex. Hwys. 57 and 80 near El Huizache, Edward F. Anderson 1079, 3 Jul. 1958." Pom 298103.

Anhalonium lewinii Hennings, Gartenflora 37: 410. Abb. 92, 93. 1888. Lophophora williamsii (Lemaire) Coulter var. lewinii Coulter, Contr. U.S. Nat. Herb. 3: 131. June 10, 1894. Echinocactus lewinii K. Schum. in Engler & Prantl, Nat. Pflanzenf. 3. Abt. 6a: 173. 1894; Monatsschr. Kakteenk. 5: 94. 1895. L. lewinii Rusby, Bull. Pharm. 8: 306. 1894. Mammillaria lewinii Karsten, Deutsche Fl. ed. 2. 2: 457. 1895. L. lewinii C. H. Thompson, Rept. Mo. Bot. Gard. 9: 133. 1898. "Mexiko." "Diese neue Kakteen erhielt Herr Dr. L. LEWIN bei seinem vorjährigen Aufenthalt in Nordamerika von der Firma PARKE, DAVIS & CO. in Detroit unter der Beziehung 'Muscale Buttons.'" According to Edward F. Anderson Brittonia 21: 307. 1969 [March, 1970]: "It is not possible to find single populations that correspond to the characters attributed to Henning's Anhalonium lewinii and that are clearly distinct from L[ophophora] williamsii." NEOTYPE (E. F. Anderson, A Taxonomic Revision of Ariocarpus, Lophophora, Pelecyphora and Obregonia [Family Cactaceae], thesis deposited in the Honnold Library for the Claremont Colleges, Claremont, California. 127. 1961, ined.): "'On a low limestone hill rising to the west of the road...north of Cadereyta des Montes, Querétaro,' Edward F. Anderson, no. 1656, September 16, 1960." Pom 298101.

Lophophora williamsii (Lemaire) Coulter var. texana Frič ex Kreuzinger, Verzeichnis 9. 1935. L. texana Frič ex Roeder, Kakteenkunde 1937: 190. 1937, nom. nud. L. lutea (Rouh.) Backeberg var. texana Backeberg, Cactaceae 5: 2903. 1961. Texas.

Lophophora echinata Croizat, Des. Pl. Life 16: 43. 1944. L. williamsii (Lemaire) Coulter var. echinata Bravo, Cact. Succ. Mex. 12: 12. 1967; Weniger, Cacti S.W. 98. 1970, nom. superfl., nom. nud. (Art. 33). Based upon a figure, Schultes, Cactus & Succ. Jour. 12: 180. f. 3. 1940.

Lophophora caespitosa Frič ex Roeder, Kakteenkunde 1937: 190. 1937, nom. nud. L. williamsii (Lemaire) Coulter var. caespitosa Y. Ito, Cacti 1952: 96. 1952, nom. nud. (no Latin diagnosis).

8. Ferocactus

Ferocactus, as genus, Britton & Rose, Cactaceae 3: 123. 1922. Type species: Echinocactus wislizenii Engelm. (= Ferocactus wislizenii [Engelm.] Britton & Rose).

Hamatocactus Britton & Rose, Cactaceae 3: 104. 1922. Type species: Echinocactus setispinus Engelm.

Bisnaga, as genus, Orcutt, Cactography 1. 1926. Type species: Echinocactus cornigerus DC.

Brittonia, as genus, Houghton ex Hort. Cactus & Succ. Jour. 2: 407. f. 1930, nom. nud.; ex C. A. Armstrong, Cactus Jour. 2: 64. f. 1934. Type species: Brittonia davisii Houghton ex C. A. Armstrong (= Ferocactus hamatacanthus [Mühlenpfordt] Britton & Rose).

1. Ferocactus acanthodes (Lemaire) Britton & Rose

1a. Ferocactus acanthodes var. acanthodes

Echinocactus acanthodes Lemaire, Cact. Gen. Sp. Nov. 106. 1839. Ferocactus acanthodes Britton & Rose, Cactaceae 3: 129 1922. "Patria ei est in California." According to Schumann, Gesamt. Beschr. Kakt. Nachträge 98. 1902, "...aus der Halbinsel Kalifornien eingeführt...." I.e., from Baja California. According to Weber, Bull. Mus. Hist. Nat. Paris 4: 104. 1898, "Elle a fleuri a Monville en 1846. J'ai eu l'occasion d'en étudier un examplaire mort, conservé chez Cels. Cette espèce est absolutement identique à celle qu' Engelmann a décrite en 1852 sous le nom d' Ech. cylindraceus...." Cf. Weber in Bois, Dict. Hort. 468. 1896.

Echinocactus viridescens Nutt. var. cylindraceus Engelm. Amer. Jour Sci. II. 14: 338. 1852. E. cylindraceus Engelm. Proc. Amer. Acad. 3: 275. 1857 (preprint, 1856). Ferocactus cylindraceus Orcutt, Cactography 5. 1926. "Found near San Felipe. On the eastern slope of the California Mountains [San Diego Co.]." C. C. Parry in 1849 or 1950. Mo; photograph, DS.

Echinocactus cylindraceus Engelm. f. latispinus Schelle, Handb. Kakteenkultur 166. 1907, nom. nud.

Ferocactus rostii Britton & Rose, Cactaceae 3: 146. f. 153b. 1922. Echinocactus rostii Berger, Kakteen 238. 1929. E. acanthodes Lemaire var. rostii Munz, Man. So. Calif. Bot. 328. 1935. F. acanthodes (Lemaire) Britton & Rose var. rostii W. T. Marshall in Marshall & Bock, Cactaceae 148. 1941. TYPE: "...Lower California, 40 miles south of the...Boundary Line (Rost, No. 327)." US 2296912 (5 areoles, two abortive fruits, and the photograph appearing in the original publication [f. 153b]). Another photograph (at the right) is of Sclerocactus polyancistrus. Cf., also, Desert 2: 41. 1930.

CALIFORNIA. SAN BERNARDINO CO. Barstow, Rose 12052, US (box); Needles, Rose 12064, US (incl. box); Cedar Canyon, New York Mts., Munz & Everett 17454, RSA.

ARIZONA. YUMA CO. 14 mi. NW of Tyson, Wiggins 8629, DS (2 boxes); Yuma, G. A. Wilcox, Oct., 1907, US (box).

1b. Ferocactus acanthodes var. lecontei (Engelmann) Lindsay

Echinocactus lecontei Engelm. Proc. Amer. Acad. 3: 274. 1857 (preprint, 1856); U.S. Senate Rept. Expl. & Surv. R. R. Route Pacific Ocean. Botany 4: 29. pl. 2, f. 3-5. 1857. E. wislizenii Engelm. var. lecontei Engelm. in Rothrock in Wheeler, Rept. U.S. Geogr. Surv. W. 100th Merid. 6: Botany. 128. 1878. E. wislizenii Engelm. f. lecontei Schelle, Handb. Kakteenkultur 168. 1907. Ferocactus lecontei Britton & Rose, Cactaceae 3: 120. 1922. E. lecontei "Benson et al, 1940" ex W. H. Earle, Cacti Southw. 73. 1940, pro syn., incorrectly ascribed to the writer. F. acanthodes (Lemaire)Britton & Rose var. lecontei Lindsay, Cactus & Succ. Jour. 27: 169. 1955. "...First noticed by Dr. John L. LeConte, on the lower Gila, and also Dr. C. Parry saw it....Subsequently Dr. Bigelow met with...[it at] Cactus Pass, at the headwaters of Williams's River [Arizona], down this stream to the Colorado, and west...." LECTOTYPE designation: "Bill Williams Fork," Bigelow in 1854, Mo.

Echinocactus hert[r]ichii Weinberg, Desert 1: 40. f. 1929. Thelocactus hertrichii Borg, Cacti ed. 2. 347. 1951. "Type--- Weinberg [growing] in Huntington's Botanic Garden, San Marino, Calif....from Tortilla and Gila mountains, Arizona." Probably var. lecontei. No specimen preserved and plant not in garden.

UTAH. WASHINGTON CO. Beaverdam Mts. at Terry's Ranch, L. C. Higgins 650, May 26, 1966, BrY.
ARIZONA. PIMA CO. (E). Mesas near Tucson, Pringle, June 17, 1881, Vt; Tucson Mts., Toumey, May 2, 1895, US. The variety is rare in this area, though common northwestward.

1c. Ferocactus acanthodes var. eastwoodiae L. Benson

Ferocactus acanthodes Lemaire var. eastwoodiae L. Benson Cacti Ariz. ed. 3. 23, 166. 1969. TYPE: "Arizona in Pinal County...[on mountains above] Queen Creek; rocky canyonside at 3,200 feet, L. Benson 16,618, April 20, 1966...." Pom 311312.

ARIZONA. PIMA CO. Growler Mts. near Bates Well, L. Benson 9895, Pom, Ariz, CAS. PINAL CO. Queen Creek Canyon above Superior, L. Benson 16618, Pom. GILA CO. Near Winkelman, Eastwood 17479, CAS; about 10 mi. SW of Globe, L. Benson, photographs in 1965. For range extension and change of rank, see Suppl.

1+. Ferocactus eastwoodiae (L. Benson) L. Benson, comb. nov.
(see Supplement)

2. Ferocactus wislizenii Engelmann

Echinocactus wislizenii Engelm. in Wisliz. Mem. Tour. No. Mex. 96. January 13, 1848. Ferocactus wislizenii Britton & Rose, Cactaceae 3: 127. 1922. "Near Doñana [Rio Grande in Dona Ana Co., southern New Mexico]...." LECTOTYPE designation: Wislizenus, Mo (1 sheet with flowers and seeds, 1 with seeds and notes, and 1 ["5/X/46"] with rib-segments); photograph (first sheet), DS.

Echinocactus emoryi Engelm. in Emory, Notes. Mil. Reconn. Ft. Leavenworth to San Diego. App. 2. 157. f. 5. May-July, 1848. Echinocereus emoryi Rümpler in Förster, Handb. Cacteenk. ed. 2. 804. 1885. Ferocactus emoryi Orcutt, Cactography 5. 1926; Y. Ito, Cacti 1952: 104. 1952; F. emoryi Backeberg, Cactaceae 5: 2717. 1961. "October 25th, 1846...." That day the military reconnaissance expedition was along the Gila River in Greenlee Co., Arizona, and camp was made about 4 miles east and a little south of the mouth of San Francisco River (recorded as Rio Prieto), just west of Guthrie. Emory reports, "I found what was to us a very great vegetable curiosity, a cactus, 18 inches high, and 18 inches in its greatest diameter, containing 20 vertical volutes [ribs], armed with strong spines. When a traveller is parched with thirst, one of these split open, will give sufficient liquid to afford relief. Several of these cacti were torn from the earth, and lying in the dry bed of a stream."
In two later publications, Engelmann assumed Echinocactus emoryi to be the same as Ferocactus covillei, later collected farther west in Pima Co. S of the lower Gila River and in adjacent Sonora, a region far removed from Emory's camp, at lower altitude, and with considerable difference in its flora. F. covillei is the basis for the later descriptions and illustrations, Engelm. Proc.

Amer. Acad. 3: 275. pl. 3, f. 3. 1857 (preprint, 1856); in Emory, Rept. U.S. & Mex. Bound. Surv. 2: Cactaceae 23. pl. 28. 1859.

Britton and Rose, Cactaceae 3: 132. 1922, assumed Echinocactus emoryi Engelm. to have been collected in New Mexico, well beyond the possible range of the species they named Ferocactus covillei. "The species...has heretofore passed as Echinocactus emoryi; the type of that species, however, came from southwestern New Mexico [actually E Arizona] and has been referred by us as a synonym of Ferocactus wislizenii." However, reference of E. emoryi to E. wislizenii Engelm. [F. wislizenii Britton & Rose] is not clear from the original figure or from the information available to Britton & Rose.

Two barrel cacti are figured in Emory's Report. The first encountered (fig. 5), Echinocactus emoryi, could represent a short, broad individual of nearly any species of barrel cactus. The feature catching the interest of the artist, J. M. Stanly, was the shape of the stem. The next day, October 26, 1846, taller plants growing in the rocky hills between Guthrie and Solomon were drawn, and Engelmann identified these as E. wislizenii [Ferocactus wislizenii], which he had just described elsewhere from the collections of Wislizenus. In this instance (fig. 4) 2 enlarged ribs were illustrated, and some detail of the spines was shown. The large, protruding, strongly curved to usually hooked central spine was distinguished from the characteristic short and very slender radials, but the 3 straight upper spreading centrals were overlooked. Aside from the form of the stem and its ribs, fig. 5 (E. emoryi) shows little except that there were spines and that the apex of the stem bore a large crown of fruits. The description adds little, except the length of the fruits, and, in contrast to all else, detail, both external and internal, of the seeds, which reached Engelmann (though not found, Mo).

Ferocactus acanthodes var. lecontei occurs in Arizona along the Gila River as far upstream as the Coolidge Dam, and Emory must have encountered it several days later at this point, 100 miles downstream from Guthrie. Since two barrel cacti are illustrated, this variety was thought possibly to have been one of them. However, along the Gila it has not been found beyond the rocky outcrops about Coolidge Dam, and, so far as observed, it is absent from the river-deposited gravels in Graham County and from the rocky hills between Solomon and Guthrie, where Stanly drew fig. 4, representing F. wislizenii.

The river-gravel hills along the Gila near Guthrie and from there to York, in the area of travel on October 25, 1846, are singularly poor in cacti. However, in 1966, two plants were found along the wash leading down from the east to Guthrie, and both are Ferocactus wislizenii. One is of exactly the shape described and figured as Echinocactus emoryi, and it grew exactly as described by Emory. NEOTYPE designation: Guthrie, L. Benson 16637, April 23, 1966, Pom 311316.

Echinocactus wislizenii Engelm. var. decipiens Engelm. in Rothrock in Wheeler, Rept. U.S. Geogr. Surv. 100th Merid. 6: Botany. 128. 1878. "Dr. Rothrock collected, at Camp Bowie, Arizona, a peculiar form (492)...." TYPE: Mo.

Echinocactus thurberi Toumey, Garden & Forest 8: 154. 1885, nom. nud. "Some miles east of Phoenix...to the headwaters of the Salt and Gila Rivers in New Mexico." No specimen found.

Echinocactus wislizenii Engelm. f. latispinus Schelle, Handb. Kakteenkultur 168. 1907. No specimen.

Echinocactus wislizenii Engelm. var. albispina Toumey, Garden & Forest 8: 154. f. 24. 1895. E. wislizenii Engelm. f. albispinus Schelle, Kakteen 208. 1926. Ferocactus wislizenii (Engelm.) Britton & Rose var. albispinus Y. Ito, Cacti 1952. "...North of Tucson, on the foothills of the Santa Catalina Mountains." No specimen found.

Echinocactus arizonicus Kunze, Monatsschr. Kakteenk. 19: 149. f. 1909. Ferocactus arizonicus Orcutt, Circular to Cactus Fanciers 1922; Cactography 6. 1926. "...Pinal County in Arizona, ungefähr 75 bis 100 englische Meilen östlich von Phoenix...." "Kleine Exemplare von 9 bis 12 cm. in Durchmesser sandte ich an das U.S. Nation. Mus. in Washington und das Königl. Botanische Museum zu Berlin....Später sandte ich zwei Exemplare, das eine an HARRY FRANK in Frankfurt a. M., das andere an C. R. ORCUTT in San Diego in Kalifornien. Das grösste Exemplar behielt ich selbst zurück...." No specimen found.

Echinocactus wislizenii Engelm. var. phoeniceus Kunze, Torreya 13: 75. 1913. Ferocactus phoeniceus Orcutt, Cactography 6. 1926. E. wislizenii Engelm. f. phoeniceus Schelle, Kakteen 208. 1926. F. wislizenii var. phoeniceus Y. Ito, Cacti 1952: 105. 1952. "...Rio Gila, Rio Salada [Salt River] and Agua Fria...." Purple-flowered plant. No specimen found.

ARIZONA. YAVAPAI CO. S of Whipple, Coues, Feb., 1876, Mo. GILA CO. Globe, Toumey & Ashmun, Dec. 5, 1896, US. YUMA CO. 3 mi. E of Mohawk Mts., Wiggins 8642, DS (box). GREENLEE CO. Guthrie, L. Benson 16637, Pom.

NEW MEXICO. HIDALGO CO. Big Hatchet Mts., Castetter 424,

UNM. LINCOLN CO. W of White Mts., Wooton & Standley, June, 1906, US.

3. Ferocactus covillei Britton & Rose

Ferocactus covillei Britton & Rose, Cactaceae 3: 122. f. 138-139. 1923. Echinocactus covillei Berger, Kakteen 238. 1929. "Collected on hills and mesas near Altar, Sonora, Mexico, by C. G. Pringle, August 11, 1884 (type)...." LECTOTYPE designation: US 795801; photograph, DS. DUPLICATES: Vt, NY, Ph, UPa, F, K.

4. Ferocactus viridescens (Nuttall) Britton & Rose

Ferocactus viridescens Nutt. ex Torrey & Gray, Fl. N. Amer. 1: 554. 1840. Melocactus viridescens Nutt. in Teschemacher, Boston Jour. Nat. Hist. 5: 293. 1845. Ferocactus viridescens Britton & Rose, Cactaceae 3: 140. 1922. "Arid hills &c. near St. Diego, California...." Nuttall. TYPE: BM (flowers, these not pressed, poorly dried). Typical specimen for other characters: "Coons Ranch; hill 3/8 mile east of the ocean and 3/4 mile north of Mexico, Lyman Benson 14336, April 29, 1950," Pom 278127 (on two sheets).

Echinocactus limitus Engelm. in Coulter, Contr. U.S. Nat. Herb. 3: 374. 1896. TYPE: "Hitchcock of 1876...'boundary line south of San Diego....'" LECTOTYPE designation: "Near the initial monument of the U.S. & Mex. Boundary line, south of San Diego. Sent by Messrs. Parker & Hitchcock...May, 1876," Mo (on 2 sheets).

Name of Uncertain Application (perhaps to F. viridescens)

Echinocactus californicus Monville, Cat. 1846; in Labouret, Monogr. Cact. 199. 1853. Ferocactus californicus Borg, Cacti 235. 1937; Y. Ito, Cacti 103. 1952. "Patrie. La Californie." According to Britton & Rose, Cactaceae 3: 141. 1922, "...first grown from seed supposed to have come from California, but without definite locality...." The plant has been referred to F. viridescens and to F. orcuttii. A spine cluster labelled as "Echinocactus californicus, Hort. Dyck, Jan., 1857," Mo, includes only central spines. These may be from F. viridescens.

5. Ferocactus hamatacanthus (Mühlenpfordt) Britton & Rose

5a. Ferocactus hamatacanthus var. hamatacanthus

Echinocactus hamatacanthus Mühlenpfordt, Allg. Gartenz. 14: 371. 1846. Original spelling, hamatocanthus, changed by Britton & Rose, Cactaceae 3: 144. 1922, as an orthographic variant. Cf. Recommendation 73(b), "Before a vowel the final vowel of the stem, if any, is normally elided." E. longihamatus Galeotti var. gracilispinus Engelm. Proc. Amer. Acad. 3: 273. 1857 (preprint, 1856); Rept. U.S. & Mex. Bound. Surv. 2: Cactaceae 22. 1859, based upon E. hamatacanthus Mühlenpfordt. Ferocactus hamatacanthus Britton & Rose, Cactaceae 3: 144. 1922. Bisnaga hamatacanthus Orcutt, Cactography 1. 1926. Hamatocactus hamatacanthus (Mühlenpfordt) Backeberg & Knuth var. gracilispina [-us] Engelm. ex Borg, Cacti 219. 1937, erroneously ascribed to Engelmann. "Aus Mexiko. Das Original befindet sich in der Sammlung des Herrn Fennel im Cassel."

Echinocactus longihamatus Galeotti in Pfeiffer & Otto, Abbild. Beschr. Cact. 2: pl. 16. 1848. E. setispinus Engelm. var. longihamatus Poselger, Allg. Gartenz. 21: 119. 1853. E. hamatacanthus Mühlenpfordt var. longihamatus Coulter, Contr. U.S. Nat. Herb. 3: 365. 1896. "...Par Mr. Galeotti, qui recueillie au Mexique."

Echinocactus treculianus Labouret, Monogr. Cact. 202. 1853. E. texensis Hopffer var. treculianus Rümpler in Förster, Handb. Cacteenk. ed. 2. 504. 1885, pro syn. "Patrie. Texas. Introduit au Jardin des Plantes de Paris par M. Trecul."

Echinocactus longihamatus Galeotti var. brevispinus Engelm. Proc. Amer. Acad. 3: 273. 1857 (preprint, 1856); in Emory Rept. U.S. & Mex. Bound. Surv. 2: Cactaceae 22. 1859. E. hamatacanthus Mühlenpfordt var. brevispinus Coulter, Contr. U.S. Nat. Herb. 3: 366. 1896. E. longihamatus Galeotti f. brevispinus Schelle, Handb. Kakteenkultur 160. 1907. Hamatocactus hamatacanthus (Mühlenpfordt) Backeberg & Knuth var. brevispina [-us] Engelm. ex Borg, Cacti 219. 1937, erroneously attributed to Engelmann. "East of El Paso, near the Pecos and San Pedro Rivers [Texas], and along the middle course of the Rio Grande." LECTOTYPE designation: "Rocky mountains of the Limpia [Creek], Bigelow, July 18, 1852," Mo. This is the juvenile form of the species, cf. note in the text.

TEXAS. UPTON CO. 5 mi. E of McCamey, D. S. & H. S. Correll 30894, LL. EL PASO CO. El Paso, W. H. Evans, US (box).

Name of Uncertain Application (perhaps to F. hamatacanthus)

Brittonia davisii Frick, Cactus & Succ. Jour. 2: 407. 1931. nom. nud.; Houghton ex C. A. Armstrong, Cactus Jour. Gt. Brit. 2: 64. 1934; Houghton ex W. T. Marshall in Marshall & Bock, Cactaceae 145. 1941, nom. nud., pro syn. (without Latin diagnosis). Hamatocactus hamatacanthus (Mühlenpfordt) Backeberg & Knuth var. davisii W. T. Marshall, loc. cit., f. 98, nom. nud. (without Latin diagnosis). Hamatocactus davisii Y. Ito, Cacti 100. 1952, nom. nud.

"...Native to western Texas, extending into old Mexico...." No specimens cited; no type named; identity uncertain. Marshall, Cactus & Succ. Jour. 16: 80. 1944, placed var. davisii as a synonym for Echinocactus longihamatus Galeotti var. crassispinus Engelm. (Proc. Amer. Acad. 3: 273. 1857, preprint, 1856), classified as Hamatocactus hamatacanthus (Mühlenpfordt) "Berg." var. crassispina [-us] Borg (= Ferocactus hamatacanthus [Mühlenpfordt] Britton & Rose var. crassispinus [Engelm.] L. Benson, Cactus & Succ. Jour. 46: 80. 1974), Cacti 219. 1937, incorrectly ascribed to Engelmann. Backeberg, Cactaceae 5: 2748. f. 2067. 1961; 6: 3871. f. 3515. 1962, illustrates a plant from "USA (Texas)" perhaps identical with the common form of the lower Rio Grande and describes it under the nomen nudum of Marshall, Hamatocactus hamatacanthus var. davisii. Marshall's plant may have been the same. Backeberg's photograph indicates a juvenile form of var. hamatacanthus or of var. sinuatus. This plant was designated also as "Ferocactus Brittonia Davisii" by an anonymous author, Cactus & Succ. Jour. 2: 272. 1930. "...Discovered by Mr. A. R. Davis of Marathon, Texas."

5b. Ferocactus hamatacanthus var. sinuatus (A. Dietrich) L. Benson

Echinocactus sinuatus A. Dietr. Allg. Gartenz. 19: 345. 1851. E. setispinus Engelm. var. sinuatus Poselger, Allg. Gartenz. 21: 119. 1853. E. longihamatus Galeotti var. sinuatus Weber in K. Schum. Gesamtb. Kakteen 342. 1898. E. longihamatus Galeotti f. sinuatus Schelle, Handb. Kakteenkultur 160. 1907. Hamatocactus sinuatus Orcutt Cactography 6. 1926. Hamatocactus hamatacanthus (Mühlenpfordt) Backeberg & Knuth var. sinuatus Weber ex Borg, Cacti 219. 1937, incorrectly ascribed to Weber. Ferocactus hamatacanthus (Mühlenpfordt) Britton & Rose var. sinuatus L. Benson, Cactus & Succ. Jour. 41: 128. 1969. "...Werde vom Herrn Poselger aus Texas eingefandt." In the living collections of Hafeloff and of Linke. NEOTYPE (Benson, loc. cit.): "Western Texas, probably on the Pecos or San Pedro," Charles Wright in 1852, Mo (box and sheet with a flower and seeds); labelled by Engelmann as Echinocactus sinuatus. DUPLICATE: Pom 317819 (spine clusters).

TEXAS. "Western Texas, probably on the Pecos or San Pedro," Wright in 1852, Mo (box). "Locality not recollected," Wright in 1849, Mo. SAN PATRICIO CO. Mathis, R. O. Albert 51, Oct. 1, 1959, Pom.

6. Ferocactus setispinus (Engelmann) L. Benson

Echinocactus setispinus Engelm. Pl. Lindh. I, Bost. Jour. Nat. Hist. 5: 246. 1845. E. setispinus Engelm. var. setaceus Engelm. Pl. Lindh. II, Bost. Jour. Nat. Hist. 6: 201. 1850. Hamatocactus setispinus Britton & Rose, Cactaceae 3: 104. 1922. Ferocactus setispinus L. Benson, Cactus & Succ. Jour. 41: 128. 1969. "Texas, from the Colorado to the Rio Grande." "Muskitthickets [Mesquite thickets], on the Colorado River." The varietal epithet setaceus was intended for the plants named originally by Engelmann as Echinocactus setispinus, which in 1850 Engelmann considered to be composed of two varieties, setaceus (the equivalent of the typical var. setispinus in current usage) and hamatus. LECTOTYPE (Benson, loc. cit.): "Colorado River, Lindheimer in 1844," Mo. DUPLICATE: Pom 817319.

Echinocactus muehlenpfordtii Fennel, Allg. Gartenz. 15: 65. 1847, not Poselger in 1853. E. setispinus Engelm. var. muehlenpfordtii Coulter, Contr. U.S. Nat. Herb. 3: 370. 1896. "Das original-Pflanze ist aus Mexiko...."

Echinocactus hamatus Mühlenpfordt, Allg. Gartenz. 16: 18. Jan. 15, 1848, not Forbes in 1837. E. setispinus Engelm. var. hamatus Engelm. Pl. Lindh. II, Bost. Jour. Nat. Hist. 6: 201. 1850. E. setispinus Engelm. f. hamatus Schelle, Handb. Kakteenkultur 159. 1907. "...Durch Herrn Dr. Roemer in Hildsheim aus dem nördl. Texas mitgebracht."

Echinocactus setispinus Engelm. var. tenuis Poselger, Allg. Gartenz. 21: 118. 1853. "Texas prope Laredo."

9. Echinocactus

Echinocactus, as genus, Link & Otto, Verh. Ver. Beförd. Gartenb. 3: 420. 1827. Type species: E. platyacanthus Link & Otto (lectotype, Britton & Rose, Cactaceae 3: 167. 1922).

Astrophytum, as genus, Lemaire, Cact. Gen. Sp. Nov. 3. 1839; as subgenus, K. Schum. Gesamtb. Kakteen 292, 320. 1898. Type species: A. myriostigma Lemaire (= Echinocactus myriostigma [Lemaire] Salm-Dyck).

Homalocephala, as genus, Britton & Rose, Cactaceae 3: 181. 1922. Type species: Echinocactus texensis Hopffer.

1. Echinocactus polycephalus Engelmann & Bigelow

1a. Echinocactus polycephalus var. polycephalus

Echinocactus polycephalus Engelm. & Bigelow, Proc. Amer. Acad. 3: 276. 1857 (preprint, 1856); U.S. Senate Rept. Expl. &

Surv. R. R. Route Pacific Ocean. Botany 4: 31. pl. 3, f. 4-6.
1857. "...From 20 miles west of the Rio Colorado to about 150
miles westward up the Mojave...March." LECTOTYPE designation: On
one sheet, "On the Mohave River," and on another "Mojave Valley,"
Bigelow, March 8, 1854, Mo, on 3 sheets, one numbered 899106.

Echinocactus polycephalus Engelm. & Bigelow var. flavispina
[us] Haage, f. Monatsschr. Kakteenk. 9: 43. 1899. Valid, through
the following "description," "...mit wachsgelben Stacheln..." but
without reference to a specimen or locality.

CALIFORNIA. SAN DIEGO CO. 4 mi. E of Clark Dry Lake and 1/2
mi. N of Co. Road S-22, 330 m. A. Morley, Apr. 20, 1973, SD, Pom.
KERN CO. Red Rock Canyon, L. Benson 3527, Pom.

NEVADA. NYE CO. Between Beattie and Tonopah, McKelvey 1479,
NY, 1480, NY. CLARK CO. S of Indian Springs, near Charleston
Mts., Clokey 7578, UC (fr.), 8432, Pom, RSA, NY (box), Ph, UPa,
OSC, UO, GH, SD, Ill, CU, BH (box), US (2 boxes), Mich, TAES,
SMU, Ariz, DS, USFS, F, USNA, Mich; E of Wilson's Ranch, Clokey
8429, Pom; N end of Sheep Mt., Train 1784, UC; Searchlight,
Eastwood 18290, CAS.

ARIZONA. MOHAVE CO. Detrital Valley, 21 mi. S of Boulder
Dam, L. Benson 10149, Pom; 55 mi. S of St. George (Utah). Palmer,
April, 1867, Mo (fr.); Peach Springs, Rusby 619, July, 1883, NY
(3), UPa, Mich (2), F, UC, US (3), Ariz. YUMA CO. Yuma, T. E.
Wilcox, Oct., 1907, US (box); E of Gila Mts., [presumably] Mearns
336, US (box); Tule Well, Mearns 339, Feb. 11, 1894, US (box).

1b. Echinocactus polycephalus var. xeranthemoides Coulter

Echinocactus polycephalus Engelm. & Bigelow var. xeranthemoides Coulter, Contr. U.S. Nat. Herb. 3: 358. 1896. E. xeranthemoides Engelm. ex Coulter, loc. cit., pro syn.; Rydberg, Fl.
Rocky Mts. 579. 1917. TYPE: "Siler of 1881 and 1883,...Mo. Bot.
Gard. Extreme southwestern Utah and western Arizona, on the
Kanab plateau and southward in the region of the Colorado. Specimens examined: UTAH "Siler of 1883, ('Kanab Mts.,'); ARIZONA (Siler
of 1881, near the Colorado 'on the Kanab wash'...." Siler in 1883,
not found, Mo; fruits ("Kanab Mts., South Utah"), GH. LECTOTYPE
designation: "Kanab Wash near the Rio Colorado, Northern Arizona,"
H. [A.] L. Siler, Nov., 1881, Mo.

NEVADA. NYE CO. Mercury, J. Beatley, Aug. 27, 1967, TSH;
Red Mt., near Mercury, R. Rasp & J. Beatley, Sept. 11, 1967, TSH;
J. Beatley, Aug. 14, 1968, TSH; below Mercury Ridge, J. Beatley,
Aug. 27, 1967, TSH.

UTAH. "S. Utah," Palmer in 1877, GH (fr.). KANE CO. Kanab
Mts., A. L. Siler, March, 1883, GH (fr.).

ARIZONA. COCONINO CO. Kanab Wash, A. L. Siler, Nov., 1881,
Mo. (2); Jumpup Canyon, Kaibab Nat. For., Darrow 2993, Ariz; Lee's
Ferry, E. W. Nelson, Aug. 26, 1909, US (box): Navajo Bridge, Lind-
say in 1939, Ariz. (incl. box), L. & R. L. Benson 15195, Pom; Grand
Canyon, several collections; Navajo Falls, Havasupai Canyon, Clover
5222, Mich; 50 mi. S of Lee's Ferry, M. E. Jones, June 12, 1890,
Pom.

2. Echinocactus horizonthalonius Lemaire

2a. Echinocactus horizonthalonius var. horizonthalonius

Echinocactus horizonthalonius Lemaire, Cact. Gen. Sp. Nov. 19.
1839. E. horizontalis Hort. ex Förster, Handb. Cacteenk. 327.
1846, pro syn. E. laticostatus Engelm. U.S. Senate Rept. Expl. &
Surv. R. R. Route Pacific Ocean. Botany 4: 32. 1857, nom. nov.
(no reason given). E. horizonthalonius Lemaire var. laticostatus
Schmoll, Catalog 1947. Homalocephala horizonthalonius Weniger,
Cacti S. W. 69. 1970, nom. nud. (Art. 33) and illegitimate (not
accepted by its author).

Echinocactus equitans Scheidw. Bull. Acad. Sci. Brux. 6
(1): 88. 1839. E. horizonthalonius Lemaire var. equitans Schmoll,
Catalog 1947. "Descriptio nonnullarum Cactacearum quae domino
Galeotti in finibus Potosi, Guanaxato, et aliis, regni Mexicani
invenientur a M. J. Scheidweiler."

Echinocactus horizonthalonius Lemaire var. centrispinus
Engelm. Proc. Amer. Acad. 3: 276. 1857 (preprint, 1856); in Emory,
Rept. U.S. & Mex. Bound. Surv. 2: Cactaceae 26. pl. 21; 22, f. 1-5.
1859. "...The Pecos to El Paso, and north to Dona Ana; Wislizenus,
Wright, Bigelow, Parry." The Engelmann collection includes the
following: 1 sheet, without locality, Wright in 1851-52; 1 sheet
with packets, as follows: "Echinocactus No. 6., Chs. Wright.
1851"; "Stony hills near Frontera, Chs. Wright, Apr. 27, 1852";
Frontera, on stony hills, Chs. Wright, July, 1851," Mo.

NEW MEXICO. HIDALGO CO. Below Sitting Bull Falls, Guadalupe Mts., Castetter, May 17, 1954, UNM; (probably New Mexico)
Guadalupe Canyon near Boundary, Mearns 701, Aug. 16, 1892, US.

TEXAS. KINNEY CO. Ft. Clark, Louis & Mearns, Aug., 1898, US
(box). DUVAL CO. San Diego, M. B. Croft in 1896, NY.

Invalid Name of Uncertain Application (presumably to var.
horizonthalonius)

Echinocactus horizonthalonius Lemaire var. moelleri "Haage
Jr." ex Weniger, Cacti S. W. 68. 1970, nom. nud., without Latin
diagnosis, type specimen, or page reference to a previous publication (no publication by Haage, f., in the Gray Herbarium Card
Catalogue). "...Franklin and Guadalupe mountains [Texas] west
into Arizona."

2b. Echinocactus horizonthalonius var. nicholii L. Benson

Echinocactus horizonthalonius Lemaire var. nicholii L. Benson,
Cacti Ariz. ed. 3. 23, 175. 1969. "Arizona in Pima County, several miles southwest of Silver Bell, Silver Bell Mountains, 2,800
feet elevation, Arizona Desert, Lyman Benson 16663, July 3, 1966,"
Pom 311314.

ARIZONA. PINAL CO. SW Pinal County, according to Charles
Gilbert. PIMA CO. Abbey Waterman Mts., Papago Indian Reservation,
Shreve in 1918, US (photograph); Silver Bell Mts., A. A. Nichol
prior to 1938, plant about 10 inches high, long in cultivation at
University of Arizona (but not preserved, Ariz), E. R. Blakely,
April 15, 1951, Des, Mrs. Dale Bumstead, Ariz (photograph),
L. Benson 16663, Pom.

3. Echinocactus texensis Hopffer

Echinocactus texensis Hopffer, Allg. Gartenz. 10: 207. 1842.
Homalocephala texensis Britton & Rose, Cactaceae 3: 181. 1922.
"...Aus Samen gezogen, welchen der hiesige Königl. botanische
Garten 1835 von Texas erhielt...."

Echinocactus lindheimeri Engelm. Pl. Lindh. I. Bost. Jour.
Nat. Hist. 5: 246. 1845. "...near the Colorado River [Texas]."
LECTOTYPE designation: "St. Louis, Cult. from Texas, June, 1845,"
doubtless collected by F. Lindheimer, Mo.

Echinocactus platycephalus Mühlenpfordt, Allg. Gartenz. 16:
9. 1848, "Aus Mexico."

Echinocactus texensis var. gourgensii Cels in Labouret,
Monogr. Cact. 196. 1853, nom. nud. Homalocephala texensis (Hopffer) Britton & Rose var. gourgensii Y. Ito, Cacti 1952: 108. 1952,
nom. nud. (probably based upon the combination above). Garden
plants.

Echinocactus courantianus Lemaire ex Labouret, Monogr. Cact.
196. 1853, pro syn., nom. nud. "Id. Cat. Cels, anciens Catalo-
gues." Garden plants.

Echinocactus texensis Hopffer f. longispinus Schelle, Handb.
Kakteenkultur 161. 1907. "Texas." Garden material.

Echinocactus texensis cristata Pirtle, Cactus & Succ. Jour.
7: 71. f. 1935, nom. nud. Labelled photograph.

4. Echinocactus asterias Zuccarini

Echinocactus asterias Zucc. Abh. Bayer. Akad. Wiss. München
4(2): 13. 1845. Astrophytum asterias Lemaire, Cactées 50. 1868.
"Crescit in imperio mexicano.... Wir erhielten lebende Exemplare
dieser angezeichneten Art im Frühjahre 1843 aus Mexico.... Zugleich
belehrte uns Hr. Baron von Karwinski, dass auch der Pflanze auf
seiner zweiten Reise in Mexico gefunden und unter dem Namen Echin.
Asterias an den kaiserlichen Garten zu St. Petersburg geschicht
habe. Wir haben ihr dasswegen auch diesen Namen belassen zu
müssen geglaubt, da er den Habitus sehr passend bezeichnet."
"Plantarum novarum vel minus cognitarum, quae in horto botanico
herbarioque regio monacensi servantur." Cf. discussion by Rowley,
Nat. Cactus & Succ. Jour. 13: 7. 1958. The plant was collected
by Karwinsky in Tamaulipas, Mexico, in the spring of 1843, and it
was named in 1845 by Zuccarini in St. Petersburg. No type was
preserved, but K. Schumann had a photograph from Poselger, cf.
Monatsschr. Kakteenk. 6: 21-23, 52-53. 1896.

10. Sclerocactus

Sclerocactus, as genus, Britton & Rose, Cactaceae 3: 212.
1922. Type species: Echinocactus polyancistrus Engelm. & Bigelow
(lectotype, Britton & Rose, loc. cit.) (= S. polyancistrus [Engelm.
& Bigelow] Britton & Rose).

Coloradoa, as genus, Boissevain in Boissevain & Davidson,
Colorado Cacti 54. 1940. Type species: Coloradoa mesae-verdae
Boissevain ex Hill & Salisbury (= Sclerocactus mesae-verdae
[Boissevain] L. Benson).

1. Sclerocactus glaucus (J. A. Purpus) L. Benson

Echinocactus glaucus J. A. Purpus, Monatsschr. Kakteenk. 5:
106. 1895, nom. nud.; K. Schum. Gesamtb. Kakteen. 438. 1898, not
Karwinsky ex Pfeiffer, Enum. Diagn. Cact. 57. 1837, pro syn.
E. subglaucus Rydb. Fl. Rocky Mts. 580. 1917, nom. nov. (based

upon the supposition that E. glaucus was illegitimate). E. whip-
plei Engelm. & Bigelow var. glaucus J. A. Purpus, Mitt. Deutsch.
Dendr. Gesellsch. 1925: 50. 1925. Sclerocactus glaucus L. Benson,
Cactus & Succ. Jour. 38: 53. March 20, 1966 (concerning publica-
tion by Backeberg, see next paragraph). Pediocactus glaucus Arp,
Cactus & Succ. Jour. 44: 221. 1972. TYPE: "In Colorado auf der
Mesa Grande, am Dry Creek, bei 1800 m.; PURPUS n. 60a, 61, 64; bei
Gummison [Gunnison]: derselbe n. 62." Dry Creek in Delta County
enters the Gunnison River from the south just above Delta; hence
the plant was not collected on Mesa Grande, which is north of
Delta. If a collection was in the Berlin Museum (Dahlem), it was
destroyed during World War II. Also, according to a letter dated
Sept. 1, 1964, from Professor H. Ziegler, Director of the Botan-
isches Institut und Botanischer Garten der Techn. Hochschule,
Darmstadt, at which J. A. Purpus was Inspektor, all herbarium collections and other preserved materials of cacti and other plants,
including those collected by C. A. Purpus, were destroyed with
the Institute during the Second World War. LECTOTYPE (Benson,
loc. cit.): "Adobes am Dry Creek, Mesa grande, Delta Co. Höhe
über dem Meer: 5-6000'. C. A. Purpus. Juni 1892," F 357488.
Probable DUPLICATE: "Colorado," C. A. Purpus, UC 108274.

Sclerocactus glaucus Backeberg, Cactaceae 5: 2683. 1961,
invalidly published, probably pro syn.; combination at the end of
a discussion under Echinocactus glaucus beneath the general heading of species No. 6, Sclerocactus franklinii (cf. pages 2681 and
2682). The name appears in quotation marks as a provisional combination, invalid under Article 34. Backeberg did not necessarily
accept the combination, and he did not use it to displace Sclerocactus franklinii, though he indicated this possibility. His uncertainty is expressed on page 2677 (under Sclerocactus whipplei),
as follows: "Echinocactus glaucus K. SCH., den BRITTON u. ROSE
hierher stellen, war vielleicht der erste Name für S. franklinii,
wenn auch Unterschiede in der Griffelfarbe erkennbar ist, was aber
nicht entscheidend ist." On page 2681, the style (Griffel) of
Sclerocactus franklinii is described as greenish-yellow (grüngelb)
in contrast to the red (rötlich, p. 2676) of Sclerocactus whipplei.
On page 2682, Schumann is quoted as having described the style of
Echinocactus glaucus as white. Under Article 34, "A name is not
validly published (1) when it is not accepted by the author in the
original publication; (2) when it is merely proposed in anticipa-
tion of the future acceptance of the group concerned...(so-called
provisional name)...." The combination reappears in Backeberg,
Kakteenlexikon 402. March 25, 1966, still under "Sclerocactus
Franklinii EVANS (ein Synonym?)" as the major heading for the
species, and with the following statement: "Von Echinocactus glaucus K. SCH., den PURPUS auch im Gunnison Valley sammelte, m. E.
nicht unterscheidbar. Die Pflanze müsste demgemäss heissen; Sclerocactus glaucus (K. SCH.) BACKBG." There is still uncertainty of
acceptance of the combination by its author. Even if, despite the
question mark after "(ein Synonym ?)," the second publication by
Backeberg is considered legitimate, it is antedated by Sclerocactus glaucus L. Benson, Cactus & Succ. Jour. 38: 53. March 20,
1966. The text was unchanged for ed. 2. 1970. According to a
letter from Dr. Breyer, Editor in Chief, Gustav Fischer Verlag,
Jena und Berlin, the publishing company of Backeberg's book,
"Delivery to wholesaler as at the same time to retailers has been
effectuated at 25th March 1966 within the GDR. Abroad (Westgermany
included) date of delivery has been 1st April 1966."

Sclerocactus franklinii J. W. Evans, Cactus & Succ. Jour. 11:
74. photograph. 1939. TYPE: "South rim of Gunnison Valley, one
to two miles east of Delta, Delta County, Colorado,...5000 feet,
...." DS 255234 (partly in fluid preservative).

UTAH. UINTAH CO. Green River area, N of mouth of Sand Wash,
E. H. Graham 7908, Mich 9804.

COLORADO. C. A. Purpus, June, 1892, UC. MESA CO. NE of
Grand Junction, Mr. & Mrs. S. L. Heacock in 1967, Pom, Brinson 101,
102, & 103 in 1974, Pom; Book Cliffs area, Weber 11299, Colo; S of
Grand Junction, Brinson 104 in 1974, Pom. DELTA CO. Dry Creek,
Mesa Grande [actually S of Delta], C. A. Purpus, June, 1892, F;
near Delta, J. W. Evans, DS, L. & R. L. Benson 14746, Pom, L. &
E. L. Benson 16589, Pom.

2. Sclerocactus mesae-verdae (Boissevain) L. Benson

Coloradoa mesae verdae Boissevain in Boissevain & Davidson,
Colorado Cacti 55. 1940; C. mesae-verdae Boissevain ex Hill &
Salisbury, Index Kewensis Suppl. (10): 57. 1947, the date of
valid publication, Art. 68 (4). Echinocactus mesae-verdae L. Ben-
son, Leafl. West. Bot. 6: 163. 1951. Sclerocactus mesae-verdae
L. Benson, Cactus & Succ. Jour. 38: 54. 1966. Pediocactus mesae-
verdae Arp, Cactus & Succ. Jour. 44: 222. 1972. TYPE: "Cortez,
Colorado....Type specimen deposited with the Dudley Herbarium of
Stanford University, Palo Alto, California." Not found in 1965.
NEOTYPE designation: southwest of Mesa Verde, south of Cortez,
Colorado, Lyman, Evelyn L., & Robert L. Benson 16155, April 11,
1962, Pom 306837.

COLORADO. MONTEZUMA CO. Near Mesa Verde: L. & R. L. Benson
14756, Pom, L., E. L., & R. L. Benson 16155, Pom; near state line
of Colorado and New Mexico, C. Mieg in 1953, Des.

NEW MEXICO. SAN JUAN CO. W of The Shiprock, L., E. L., &
R. L. Benson 16158, Pom, 16159, Pom (with hooked central spines);

Colorado state line, D. & J. Cowper, Pom, P. Pierce 168-169, July
14, 1964, UNM; N of Shiprock, E. R. Blakley 1314 in 1953, Des; R.
Reeves, March 10, 1965, UNM, K. Heil, March 10, 1965, UNM; near
Shiprock, L. B. Hamilton, Pom, P. Pierce 495, UNM, R. Reeves, May
8, 1964, UNM; E of Shiprock, R. Reeves, Nov. 1, 1963, UNM; S of
Shiprock, K. Heil, March, 1965, UNM.

3. Sclerocactus wrightiae L. Benson

Sclerocactus wrightiae L. Benson, Cactus & Succ. Jour. 38:
55. f. 6. 1966. Pediocactus wrightiae Arp, Cactus & Succ. Jour.
44: 222. 1972. TYPE: "Near San Rafael Ridge, Emery County,
Utah, at about 5,000 feet elevation; Navajoan Desert; Lyman &
Evelyn L. Benson 16,595," Pom 311309.

UTAH. EMERY CO. Near San Rafael Ridge, D. Wright in 1961,
Pom, L. & E. L. Benson 16595, Pom. WAYNE CO. Fremont River, I.
G. Reimann in 1964, Pom, L. H. Bowker in 1969, Pom; Dry Valley
Wash, R. H. Kirkpatrick in 1970, Pom; N of Mt. Ellen, Henry Mts.,
I. G. Reimann in 1965, Pom, in 1970, Pom.

4. Sclerocactus pubispinus (Engelmann) L. Benson

Echinocactus pubispinus Engelm. Trans. Acad. Sci. St. Louis
2: 199. 1863; in Simpson, Rept. Expl. Gt. Basin Terr. Utah
Wagon-Route, Camp Floyd to Genoa, Carson Valley 439. 1876.
Sclerocactus pubispinus L. Benson, Cactus & Succ. Jour. 38: 103.
1966. Pediocactus pubispinus Arp, Cactus & Succ. Jour. 44: 222.
1927, nom. nud. "Pleasant Valley near Salt Lake Desert [Goshute
Range, White Pine County, Nevada]: found May 9 [1859] without
flower or fruit." TYPE: Mo (juvenile plant with pubescent spines).
Typical specimen for the characters not shown by the type, the
adult features of the plant: "Pleasant Valley, White Pine County,
Nevada, Kern Mountains," Dorothea Woodruff 20, May 10, 1970, Pom.
317913.

NEVADA. ELKO CO. Above W edge of Great Salt Lake, D. Wright
(Woodruff) in 1961, Pom (photograph) (living plant at Salt Lake
City). WHITE PINE CO. Pleasant Valley, H. Engelmann (geologist,
brother of George Engelmann), Simpson Expedition, 1 in 1859, Mo
(juvenile plant), D. Woodruff 20 in 1970, Pom, 21 in 1970, Pom;
Baker region, R. H. Kirkpatrick in 1971, Pom.

UTAH. TOOELE CO. Mountains, E. Wiegand, August 8, 1954,
Pom. BEAVER CO. Desert Experimental Range, R. C. Holmgren 331,
June 2, 1964, Desert Experimental Range Herb., BrY, in 1970, Pom,
May 5, 1972, Pom.

5. Sclerocactus spinosior (Engelmann) Woodruff & Benson

Echinocactus whipplei Engelm. & Bigelow var. spinosior Engelm.
Trans. Acad. Sci. St. Louis 2: 199. 1863; in Simpson, Rept. Expl.
Gt. Basin Terr. Utah Wagon-Route, Camp Floyd to Genoa, Carson Valley 439. 1876. E. spinosior Hirscht, Monatsschr. Kakteenk. 11:
89. 1901, nom. nud.; Brandegee ex Britton & Rose, Cactaceae 3:
213. 1922, nom. nud. with the incorrect reference: ex Purpus
Monatsschr. Kakteenk. 10: 119. 1900. E. whipplei Engelm. & Bigelow
f. spinosior Schelle, Handb. Kakteenkultur 158. 1907. Sclerocactus
whipplei (Engelm. & Bigelow) Britton & Rose var. spinosior Engelm.
ex Boissevain in Boissevain & Davidson, Colorado Cacti 51-52.
1940, incorrectly ascribed to Engelmann and applied incorrectly to
S. parviflorus var. intermedius. S. spinosior Woodruff & Benson,
Cactus & Succ. Jour. 48: 976 (in press). "Desert Valley, west
of Camp Floyd Utah...." Henry Engelmann. LECTOTYPE (Benson, Cactus & Succ. Jour. 38: 104-105. 1966): "H. Engelmann, July 29,
1859. On one sheet there are two labels in pencil, one pertaining to the flower remains and seeds obtained by Engelmann from
the plants. The seed packet is labelled clearly, '1859,' and this
agrees with one label. The flower packet bears no date. The
other label (pencil) is dated, 'October 24, 58,' but it does not
apply clearly to anything and it bears the same data... [Both
sheets] taken to be...of the collection of July 29, 1859," almost
certainly the only one, Mo. Topotypes: L. & E. L. Benson 16255,
Pom, 16606, Pom.

The Simpson Expedition on July 29, 1859, was low on water,
and it did not make camp but travelled all night. Consequently,
even if place names appearing on present-day maps were not
changed, the location of the expedition on July 29 would be
difficult to determine. After being guided by Indians to poor or
non-existent springs, an Indian paralyzed from the waist down and
walking with his hands guided the road exploration party of army
engineers to Good Indian Springs, named in his honor. The Indian
was given a certificate commending him to the United States Army
and guaranteeing protection and help if they should be needed. The
mules were allowed to drink but limited to 9 buckets of water
apiece, but one mule was allowed to drink his fill -- 14 buckets!
At 2 or 3 gallons per bucket, this would be 28 to 42 gallons of
water!

Sclerocactus pubispinus (Engelm.) L. Benson var. sileri
L. Benson, Cacti Ariz. ed. 3. 23, 179. 1969. TYPE: "Southern
Utah, A. L. Siler in 1888,...." Ph. ISOTYPE: US (fragments,
sheet unnumbered). The field work of Robert H. Kirkpatrick of
Barstow, California, has provided new information concerning
this type of plant. In some individuals of Pediocactus spinosior
the very young stems up to 2.5 cm or so high have one type of

spine, the intermediate ones up to 5 cm or more high have another, and the older stems have a third type, as described for the species. The plants with nearly all white spines, including the hooked centrals, collected by Siler were of intermediate age. Some collections by Mr. Kirkpatrick show a great mass of these spines lower on the stem but adult spines on the upper part. Re-examination of other specimens shows them to have the intermediate spine types, but for a shorter distance.

UTAH. TOOELE CO. Clifton near Ibapah, M. E. Jones 1817 in 1917, US 1929937 (& box); published note on this specimen as Echinocactus [Pediocactus] papyracanthus. JUAB CO. S of Great Salt Lake Desert, Henry Engelmann, July 29, 1859, Mo, (same spot, exact area withheld for conservation reasons) L. & E. L. Benson 16255, Pom; 4 miles west of the locality above, L. & E. L. Benson 16606, Pom. MILLARD CO. Mountainous area W of Sevier Lake, R. H. Kirkpatrick in 1969, Pom, in 1970, Pom. SEVIER CO. Joseph City, 5,500 feet, M. E. Jones, May 13, 1899, Pom, D. Woodruff in 1969, Pom. BEAVER CO. NW Beaver Co., M. E. Jones, May 15, 1906, Pom, R. H. Kirkpatrick in 1970, Pom, in 1971, Pom. IRON CO. Between Modena and Lund, R. H. Kirkpatrick in 1969, Pom. Local-ity unknown, probably in the area near Kanab, "Southern Utah," A. L. Siler in 1888, Ph, US.

ARIZONA. COCONINO CO. Houserock Valley, E. W. Nelson, Aug. 30, 1909, US (box), D. Wright (Woodruff) in 1963, Pom, D. Davis in 1964, Pom.

6. Sclerocactus whipplei (Engelmann) Britton & Rose

Echinocactus whipplei Engelm & Bigelow, Proc. Amer. Acad. 3: 271. 1857 (preprint, 1856); U.S. Senate Rept. Expl. & Surv. R. R. Route Pacific Ocean. Botany. 4: 28. pl. 1. 1857. Sclero-cactus whipplei Britton & Rose, Cactaceae 3: 213. 1922. Pedio-cactus whipplei Arp, Cactus & Succ. Jour. 44: 222. 1972. "... Lithodendron Creek, near the Colorado Chiquito, about ninety miles west of Zuñi...Dec. 3-4, 1853...." Petrified Forest east of Holbrook, Apache County, Arizona. Lithodendron Wash is a tribu-tary of Puerco River. The 90 miles was an estimate based upon travel on horseback and neither airline nor literal; the airline distance is about 57 miles. TYPE: "Colorado Chiquito," J. M. Bigelow, Dec. 3, 1853, Mo. ISOTYPE: Pom 317813.

Sclerocactus thompsonii W. T. Marshall, Saguaroland Bull. 2(6): pages not numbered. 1948, nom. nud. (without Latin diag-nosis). "...vicinity of Tonalea...[later] vicinity of Holbrook with dried flowers that were evidently yellow."

Sclerocactus whipplei (Engelm. & Bigelow) Britton & Rose var. pygmaeus Peebles, Leafl. West. Bot. 5: 192. 1949. "Peebles & Smith No. SF 1054, 15 miles north of Ganado, Apache County, Arizona, altitude 6,200 feet, June 10, 1937...." TYPE: CAS 351111. Juvenile plant.

ARIZONA. "Little Colorado," Newberry, May, 1858, Mo. NAVAJO CO. White Dog Canyon, Skeleton Mesa, M. A. Wetherill, May 9, 1959, MNA; Kayenta, R. Reeves, May 11, 1963, UNM; Marcou Mesa area E of Joseph City, E. R. Blakley B1856, Des, D. Wright, June, 1962, Pom, L. & R. L. Benson 15739, Pom, 16209, Pom; gravel hills, Holbrook, W. Hough, June, 1917, NY, US (photo), D. & J. Cowper 1252, Pom, L. & R. L. Benson 14643, Pom, 15585, Pom. APACHE CO. Ganado to Chinle, C. J. King, May 15, 1938, US, Ariz, Peebles SF 1054, CAS; Lithodendron Creek [Wash], Petrified Forest, J. M. Bigelow, Dec. 3, 1853, Mo, Pom; Painted Desert, Petrified Forest, Brooks in 1951, Pom; Blue Mesa, P. Van Cleave, June 20, 1962, Pom.

7. Sclerocactus parviflorus Clover & Jotter

7a. Sclerocactus parviflorus var. parviflorus

Sclerocactus parviflorus Clover & Jotter, Bull. Torrey Club 68: 419. f. 8. 1941. Echinocactus parviflorus L. Benson, Cacti Arizona ed. 2. 102. 1950. "...Mouth of Forbidding Canyon in Glen Canyon above Lee's Ferry, Canyon of the Colorado. Abundant 20 miles above Moki Creek, and fairly common at intervals along the lower San Juan River (plate 1)... Clover and Jotter 2398...Botani-cal...Gard. 16,844... (Fig. 8), Utah." TYPE: Mich. ISOTYPE: US 2346042.

Sclerocactus havasupaiensis Clover, Amer. Jour. Bot. 29: 172. f. 1-2. 1942. Echinocactus parviflorus (Clover & Jotter) L. Ben-son var. havasupaiensis (Clover) L. Benson, Cacti Arizona ed. 2. 104. 1950. TYPE: "...(fig. 1) was collected by William Belknap, Jr., April 26, 1941, on top of the Supai Formation in Havasupai Canyon, Arizona...." Clover 6404, Mich; photograph, Pom 286506. ISOTYPES: Mich (not numbered), US 2346047, 2346049, Pom, 275262, 311353.

Sclerocactus havasupaiensis Clover var. roseus Clover, Amer. Jour. Bot. 29: 173. f. 3-4. 1942. Echinocactus parviflorus (Clover & Jotter) L. Benson var. roseus (Clover) L. Benson, Cacti Arizona ed. 2. 102. 1950. Sclerocactus whipplei (Engelm.) Britton & Rose var. roseus L. Benson, Cactus & Succ. Jour. 38: 104. 1966. TYPE: "Specimen typicum legit E. Clover & William Belknap, Jr. (Clover 6403), in Havasupai Canyon, Arizona...." Mich. ISOTYPE: US 2346044, 2346045, Pom 275269.

UTAH. DUCHESNE CO. Duchesne, L. H. Bowker in 1969, Pom. UINTAH CO. Uteland Mine, Green River, 4,800 feet, E. H. Graham 8900, Mich. EMERY CO. Green River, M. E. Jones 5482e, June 22, 1894, US. GRAND CO. Colorado State Line on U.S. 50, L. Benson 16592, Pom; Valley of Green River, N of Moab, D. & J. Cowper in 1957, Pom. WAYNE CO. Torrey, L. H. Bowker in 1969, Pom; Fruita, Eastwood 5184 in 1899, CAS (part), B. Harrison 7406, Mo; Dead Horse Point, Colorado River, D. & J. Cowper in 1957, Pom. SAN JUAN CO. La Sal Mts., N. D. Atwood & S. L. Welsh 9922, Pom. Glen Canyon, Colorado River: lower Ticaboo opposite Ticaboo Can-yon, L. Benson 16292C, Pom, 16292D, Pom, 16292E, Pom; Glen Canyon, Mile 74 above Lee's Ferry, L. Benson 16316A, Pom; Forbidding (Aztec) Canyon, Clover & Jotter 2398, Mich, D. Wright 311, June 11, 1962, Pom, L. Benson 16323D, Pom; Glen Canyon, Mile 50 1/2 just above Last Chance Creek, L. Benson 16331B, Pom. San Juan River: Mile 38 (above the Colorado River), D. Wright 306, June 12, 1962, Pom; Piute Farms, D. Wright 304, June 12, 1962, Pom; 2 mi. below Mexican Hat, D. Wright 301, June 16, 1962, Pom; 6 mi. NE of Mexican Hat, L. Benson 16060, Pom. Both Glen Canyon and the San Juan River Canyon, which included some of the most beautiful scenery on Earth, are now drowned out forever by the Glen Canyon Dam.

COLORADO. Cf. Grand Co., Utah, specimen at the Colorado state line on U.S. 50, above. "Southwestern Colorado," T. S. Brandegee, July, ----, UC 108272; without locality, T. S. Bran-degee in 1875, US 1929943. MESA CO. Mack, M. E. Jones, May 1908, US (box); Stovepipe Canyon, Book Cliffs, W. A. Weber 11299, Colo; Grand Junction, M. E. Jones 5476f, June 21, 1894, US, Eastwood, May, 1891, Colo; S of Fruita, Colorado National Monu-ment, Weber 3767, Colo. MONTROSE CO. Nucla, E. G. Chamberlain in 1941, DS (box).

ARIZONA. COCONINO CO. Across from "The Gods," Havasupai Canyon, Clover & Belknap 6404, Mich, Pom, US; trail to Navajo Falls, Havasupai Canyon, Clover 5229, Mich, US; Havasupai Canyon, Clover & Belknap 6403, Mich, US; Inscription House, 6,700 feet, Peebles & Smith, SF 13916, Ariz. NAVAJO CO. Betatakin, J. T. Howell 24494, CAS, Ariz; Kayenta, Peebles SF 925, June 3, 1934, Ariz; Monument Valley, R. T. Craig, Oct., 1962, Pom.

7b. Sclerocactus parviflorus var. intermedius (Peebles) Woodruff & Benson

Sclerocactus intermedius Peebles, Leafl. West. Bot. 5: 191. 1949. S. whipplei (Engel. & Bigelow) Britton & Rose var. inter-medius L. Benson, Cactus & Succ. Jour. 38: 102. 1966. S. parvi-florus Clover var. intermedius Woodruff & Benson, Cactus & Succ. Jour. 48: 133. 1976. "Peebles & Parker No. 14712, 9 miles southwest of Pipe Springs, Mohave County, Arizona, altitude 5,000 feet, May 8, 1940...." CAS 351112; photograph in Benson, Cacti Ariz. eds. 1-3. 1940, 1950, 1969.

8. Sclerocactus polyancistrus (Engelmann & Bigelow) Britton & Rose

Echinocactus polyancistrus Engelm. & Bigelow, Proc. Amer. Acad. 3: 272. 1857 (preprint, 1856); U.S. Senate Rept. Expl. & Surv. R. R. Route Pacific Ocean. Botany. 4: 29. pl. 2, f. 1-2. 1857. Sclerocactus polyancistrus Britton & Rose, Cactaceae 3: 213. 1922. Pediocactus polyancistrus Arp, Cactus & Succ. Jour. 44: 222. 1972. "On gravelly hills and sandy plains at the head-waters of the Mojave, on the eastern slope of the California Cordilleras, one day's journey before reaching Cajon Pass... March 15, 1854...." TYPE: "Head of the Mojave," Bigelow, Mo.

11. Pediocactus

Section 1. PEDIOCACTUS

Pediocactus, as genus, Britton & Rose in Britton & Brown, Ill. Fl. No. St. & Can. ed. 2. 2: 569. 1913. Type species: Echinocactus simpsonii Engelm. (lectotype, Britton & Rose, Cac-taceae 3: 90. 1922) (= Pediocactus simpsonii [Engelm.] Britton & Rose).

Utahia, as genus, Britton & Rose, Cactaceae 3: 215. 1922. Type species: Echinocactus sileri Engelm.

Pilocanthus, as genus, B. W. Benson & Backeberg, Kakt. u. a. Sukk. 8: 187. 1957. Type species: Pediocactus paradinei B. W. Benson.

Section 2. NAVAJOA

Navajoa, as genus, Croizat, Cactus & Succ. Jour. 15: 88. 1943; as section of Pediocactus, L. Benson, Cactus & Succ. Jour. 34: 57. 1962. Type species: Navajoa peeblesiana Croizat. (= Pediocactus peeblesianus [Croizat] L. Benson).

Section 3. TOUMEYA

Toumeya, as genus, Britton & Rose, Cactaceae 3: 91. 1922; as section of Pediocactus, L. Benson, Cactus & Succ. Jour. 34:

61. 1962. Type species: <u>Mammillaria papyracantha</u> Engelm.
(= <u>Pediocactus papyracanthus</u> [Engelm.] L. Benson).

1. Pediocactus simpsonii (Engelmann) Britton & Rose

1a. Pediocactus simpsonii var. simpsonii

<u>Echinocactus simpsonii</u> Engelm. Trans. St. Louis Acad. Sci.
2: 197. 1863; Rept. Expl. Terr. Utah Wagon-Route Camp Floyd to
Carson Valley, Engineer Dept., U.S. Army 437. 1876. <u>Mammillaria
simpsonii</u> M. E. Jones, Zoë 3: 302. 1893. <u>Pediocactus simpsonii</u>
Britton & Rose in Britton & Brown, Illustr. Fl. ed. 2. 2: 570.
1913. "Butte Valley, in the Utah [Nevada] desert, and Kobe Valley,
farther west...." <u>Cf</u>. J. H. Simpson, Rept. Expl. Gt. Basin Terr.
Utah, Engineering Dept., U.S. Army 74-75. 1876. Kobe, Kobeh, or
Kobah Valley is in Nevada between the present towns of Eureka and
Austin. On May 24, 1859, the Simpson expedition travelled through
a pass on the north side of Antelope Mountain into Kobeh Valley.
The camp of the expedition on May 25, 1859, was at Lat. 39° 20
[29]' 13" N; Long. 116° 39' 12" W. LECTOTYPE (Benson, Cactus &
Succ. Jour. 33: 51. 1961): "Kobe Valley, Henry Engelmann, May 24,
1859," <u>Mo</u>. The Butte Valley, Nevada, collection, <u>Henry Engelmann</u>,
May 15, 1859, <u>Mo</u>, approaches slightly var. <u>robustior</u>.

<u>Mammillaria purpusii</u> K. Schum. Monatsschr. Kakteenk. 4: 165.
1894. C. A. Purpus "...sammelte im Jahre 1893 in der Umgebung
der Städte Delta und La Mesa, welche in einer höhe von 2900 m über
dem Meeresspiegel liegen und zum Staate Colorado in den Vereinigten
Staaten gehören." The photograph is of <u>Pediocactus simpsonii</u>.
TYPE: probably non-existent. LECTOTYPE designation: "Sonnige Ab-
hang am Surface Cr., Mesa gr [Grande], Delta Co. Höhe über dem
Meere: 6-7000'. C. A. Purpus. Juni 1892," <u>F</u> 357475.

<u>Pediocactus hermannii</u> W. T. Marshall, Saguaroland Bull. 8:
78. 5 photographs. 1954. <u>P. simpsonii</u> (Engelm.) Britton & Rose
var. <u>hermannii</u> W. T. Marshall, Saguaroland Bull. 11: 79. 1957;
Wiegand & Backeberg in Backeberg, Cactaceae 5: 2846. 1961.
"Type locality -- Garfield County, Utah, at 6,200 feet." "...
Mr. and Mrs. A. Hermann and their son August, Jr...in August
1953...." Near Hatch. TYPE: Des. ISOTYPE: BrY, not found. Size
of plant indicates var. <u>minor</u>, but color of central spines var.
<u>simpsonii</u>.

<u>Pediocactus simpsonii</u> var. <u>caespiticus</u> Backeberg, Nat. Cac-
tus & Succ. Soc. Jour. 14: 63. 2 lower figs. 1959, nom. nud.
(no Latin diagnosis or type specimen; Cactaceae 5: 2846. f.
2672, lower 2 photographs. 1961, nom. nud. (no type specimen).
"USA (Colorado: Salida, auf 2700 m.)...." This epithet was
applied to a large, much-branched individual reported to form a
mound 30 cm high.

OREGON. The following plants are intermediate between vars.
<u>simpsonii</u> and <u>robustior</u>, some approaching more nearly one, some
the other. JEFFERSON CO. Between Willowdale and Ashwood, on red
rhyolite, <u>K. Maerz</u>, Jan., 1964, <u>Pom</u>. WHEELER CO. Sutton Mountain,
Cronquist 6908, <u>WS</u>, <u>NY</u>; near Mitchell, <u>W. D. Wilkinson</u>, July, 1962,
<u>Pom</u>. HARNEY CO. W of Alberson, Steen Mts., 2,300 m., <u>Peck 14212</u>,
<u>DS</u>, <u>F 675710</u>; Whitehorse Ranch, E Harney Co., <u>Peck 25654a</u>, <u>WillU</u>.

IDAHO. Ladora, <u>H. M. Hall</u>, Aug., 1921, <u>US</u>; Jefferson, <u>C.
Birdseye</u> in 1912, <u>US</u>. LEMHI CO. Kirtley Ranch, Salmon, <u>Hender-
son 3481</u>, Aug. 25, 1895, <u>US</u>. CUSTER CO. Big Creek Bar, Pahsi-
meroi Ranger Station, Challis National Forest, 6,000 feet, <u>A. M.
Cusick</u>, May 28, 1929, <u>USFS</u>; Chilly, <u>Christ & Ward 10360</u>, <u>NY</u>.
CLARK CO. Kaufman, <u>J. H. Christ 11823</u>, <u>NY</u>.

MONTANA. Reported by Britton & Rose, Cactaceae 3: 90.
1922, but no specimens seen.

ARIZONA. COCONINO CO. Grand View, Grand Canyon, <u>J. H. Fer-
riss</u>, Sept., 1920, <u>NY</u>, <u>US</u> (photograph); "some 50 miles west of
Cameron Bridge on the Little Colorado River [probably the rim of
the Grand Canyon]," <u>W. N. Duane</u>, "several years before 1927," <u>US</u>.

NEW MEXICO. RIO ARRIBA CO. Rio Vallecito, <u>Castetter 1022
A-F</u>, <u>UNM</u>. TAOS CO. Canyon S of Pilar, <u>Castetter 172</u>, <u>UNM</u>, <u>C.
Comfort</u>, in 1954, <u>UNM</u>; Ute Creek Canyon, <u>V. Blake</u>, July 22, 1962,
<u>UNM</u>. SANTA FE CO. Above Santa Fe, <u>Toumey</u>, May 20, 1896, <u>US</u>.
BERNALILLO CO. Sandia Mts., <u>C. Ellis 368</u> in 1911, <u>US</u>, <u>P. Pierce</u>,
Sept., 1964, <u>UNM</u>.

SOUTH DAKOTA. CUSTER CO. <u>E. J. Palmer 37471</u>, <u>GH</u>.

KANSAS. Reported, "...according to B. B. Smith," by Britton
& Brown, Ill. Fl. N. Sts. & Can. 2: 462. 1897, but no specimens
seen and occurrence unlikely.

1b. Pediocactus simpsonii var. minor (Engelmann) Cockerell

<u>Echinocactus simpsonii</u> Engelm. var. <u>minor</u> Engelm. Trans. St.
Louis Acad. Sci. 2: 197. 1863. <u>E. simpsonii</u> f. <u>minor</u>
Schelle, Handb. Kakteenkultur 202. 1907. <u>Pediocactus simpsonii</u>
(Engelm.) Britton & Rose var. <u>minor</u> Cockerell, Torreya 18: 180.
1916; Boissevain in Boissevain & Davidson, Colorado Cacti 58.
1940. "...In Colorado Territory...near Mount Vernon...(Parry,
Hall, & Harbour)." LECTOTYPE (Benson, Cactus & Succ. Jour. 33:
51-52. 1961): "Mt. Vernon, presumably by Parry, Hall, and
Harbour," <u>Mo</u>.

UTAH. DUCHESNE CO. Fruitland, <u>R. L. Benson</u>, Aug. 24, 1963,

<u>Pom</u>. SAN JUAN CO. N of Slick Rock, La Sal Mts., <u>F. G. Knowlton</u>,
April 6, 1956, <u>Pom</u>; S side of La Sal Mts., <u>L., E. L., & R. L.
Benson 16504</u>, <u>Pom</u>.

NEW MEXICO. TAOS CO. Hondo Canyon, headwaters of Hondo
River between Dixon and Velande, <u>F. G. Knowlton</u>, March, 1958, <u>Pom</u>;
Cimarron Canyon Pass W of Eagle Nest Lake, <u>P. Pierce</u>, May 1, 1963,
<u>UNM</u>; Eagle Nest Lake S of U.S. 64, <u>P. Pierce</u>, Sept. 11, 1960, <u>UNM</u>;
E of Eagle Nest Lake, <u>P. Pierce</u>, Aug. 28, 1962, <u>UNM</u>.

1c. Pediocactus simpsonii var. robustior (Coulter) L. Benson

<u>Echinocactus simpsonii</u> Engelm. var. <u>robustior</u> Coulter. Contr.
U.S. Nat. Herb. 3: 377. 1896. <u>Pediocactus simpsonii</u> (Engelm.)
Britton & Rose var. <u>robustior</u> L. Benson, Cactus & Succ. Jour. 34:
19. 1962. <u>P. robustior</u> Arp, Cactus & Succ. Jour. 44: 222. 1972.
"Type, Watson of 1868 in Herb. Mo. Bot. Gard. From the Humboldt
Mountains of Nevada [Pershing Co.]...." LECTOTYPE (Benson, <u>loc.
cit.</u>): "Mountains of Nevada, 8-10,000' alt. from Rum River east-
ward to the Humboldt Mountains. No. IV. Sereno Watson, of King's
Party. 40° lat.," <u>Mo</u>.

<u>Pediocactus simpsonii</u> (Engelm.) Britton & Rose var. <u>nigri-
spina</u> W. T. Marshall in Marshall & Bock, Cactaceae 140. 1941, nom.
nud. (without Latin diagnosis). "Mentioned in 'The Cactaceae'
[Britton & Rose] Vol. III: pg. 91...Priests Rapids, Washington.
Material for observation supplied by A. S. Harmer of Dieringer,
Washington." The reference above is to the following quotation
by Britton and Rose from Charles A. Geyer, London Jour. Bot. 5:
25. 1846: "...On the Oregon [Columbia River, in Washington] plains
...I brought dry specimens to London and Mr. Scheer, at Kew...
raised several from seeds...[Also] gathered by Chief Factor Mac-
Donald at Fort Colville, but the exact habitat...forgotten; the one
specimen found was afterwards in possession of Dr. Tolmie on the
lower Columbia. From the information I could gather at Ft. Walla
Walla, the true habitat of this cactus is at Priests' Rapid..."
Plant supplied by Harmer not preserved; that by MacDonald (in the
possession of Tolmie) not found, <u>K</u>, <u>BM</u>.

WASHINGTON. Without locality, <u>Brandegee 793</u>, Aug., 1883, <u>GH</u>;
Northern Transcontinental Survey, <u>Canby</u>, <u>GH</u>. KITTITAS CO. Wenat-
chee Mts., near Brushie Creek, <u>J. S. Cotton</u>, Nov. 1, 1903, <u>US</u>;
E of Ellensburg, <u>F. G. Meyer 1426a</u>, <u>Mo</u>; between Ellensburg and
Vantage, <u>L. Benson 1324</u>, May 5, 1929, <u>Pom</u>, <u>DS</u>; 15 miles E of
Ellensburg, <u>L. Glowenke 11243</u>, May 8, 1948, <u>UPa</u>; W of Vantage, <u>G.
N. Jones 6587</u>, <u>Ill</u>, <u>L. & R. L. Benson 16587</u>, <u>Pom</u>; near Vantage,
<u>J. W. Thompson 11506</u>, <u>WTU</u>, <u>Pom</u>, <u>Mo</u>, <u>NY</u>, <u>GH</u>, <u>US</u>, <u>UC</u>, <u>DS</u>; rimrocks
near Vantage, <u>J. W. Thompson 8215</u>, <u>WTU</u>, <u>Mo</u>, <u>NY</u>, <u>GH</u>, <u>US</u>, <u>CAS</u>, <u>UC</u>,
<u>DS</u>; Gingko Petrified Forest Park, Columbia River near Vantage, <u>H.
W. Smith 399</u>, <u>WS</u>, <u>UC</u>. YAKIMA CO. Selah Creek, <u>R. F. Hoover</u>,
April 17, 1942, <u>SLO</u>; Moxee Hills, Yakima, <u>E. Nelson</u>, May 28, 1922,
<u>NY</u>, <u>US</u>; Sentinel Bluffs, Head of Priest Rapids, <u>J. S. Cotton</u>, July
14, 1903, <u>WS</u>, <u>US</u>, <u>M. A. McColl</u>, Oct., 1920, <u>NY</u>, <u>US</u>. GRANT CO.
North of Egbert (Iron) Springs, <u>St. John 4119</u>, <u>WS</u>; Quincy, <u>J. Pack-
ard 591</u>, <u>WS</u>.

OREGON (<u>cf</u>. also intermediate plants listed under var. <u>simp-
sonii</u>). Hay Creek, <u>J. E. Edwards</u>, Oct., 1907, <u>US</u>. JEFFERSON CO.
W of Ashwood, 4,000 to 5,000 feet, <u>K. Maerz</u>, Jan., 1964, <u>Pom</u>.
HARNEY CO. White Horse Ranch, <u>Peck</u>, June 3, 1941, <u>DS</u>.

IDAHO. IDAHO CO. Jct. Salmon and Snake rivers, <u>J. Packard
590</u>, May 5, 1939, <u>WS</u>, <u>F. G. Meyer 1598</u>, <u>Mo</u>, <u>J. H. Christ 14201</u>, <u>NY</u>.

NEVADA. Havallah Mts., 8,000 ft., <u>S. Watson</u>, June, 1868, <u>NY</u>.
LANDER CO. N of Battle Mountain, <u>Holmgren 1086</u>, <u>Ariz</u>. PERSHING
CO. Mts. 8-10,000 feet alt., from Rum River E to the Humboldt
Mts., 40° lat., <u>S. Watson</u> no. IV in 1868, <u>Mo</u>.

2. Pediocactus bradyi L. Benson

<u>Pediocactus bradyi</u> L. Benson, Cactus & Succ. Jour. 34: 19.
f. 13-14. 1962. <u>Toumeya bradyi</u> W. H. Earle, Cacti Southw. 97.
1963. <u>Pilocanthus (Pediocactus) bradyi</u> Glass & Foster, Cactus &
Succ. Jour. 45: 254. 1973, nom. nud., an inadvertance. TYPE:
"Near the Marble Canyon of the Colorado River, Coconino County,
northern Arizona, 4,000 feet, <u>Lyman & Evelyn L. Benson 16807</u>
[16087 as on page 18 and as corrected, ibid., page 57], April 21,
1961...." Pom 299971. ISOTYPE: Des.

ARIZONA. COCONINO CO. Marble Canyon area of the Colorado
River, <u>L. F. Brady</u>, June 16, 1958, <u>Des</u>, July, 1958, <u>MNA</u>, <u>L. & E.
L. Benson 16087</u>, <u>Pom</u>, <u>Des</u> (living material), <u>W. B. McDougall
2327</u>, in 1962, <u>MNA</u>, <u>D. G. Davis</u>, Nov. 6, 1963, <u>Pom</u> (plant with
central spines), <u>D. G. Davis</u>, Nov. 6, 1963, <u>Pom</u>, <u>UNM</u>.

2+. Pediocactus winkleri Heil (see Supplement)

3. Pediocactus knowltonii L. Benson

<u>Pediocactus knowltonii</u> L. Benson, Cactus & Succ. Jour. 32:
193. 1960; 33: 52-53. f. 24. 1961; 34: 19. 1962. <u>P. bradyi</u>
L. Benson var. <u>knowltonii</u> Backeberg, Descr. Cact. Nov. 3: 12.
1963, an illegitimate name combination (knowltonii having been
published earlier than <u>bradyi</u>) for an unholy alliance. TYPE:
"Los Piños River near La Boca, Colorado, on the Colorado-New
Mexico line...,<u>Fred G. Knowlton</u>, late May, 1958," Pom 288314.
Backeberg, Kakteen Lexikon 562-563. 1966, claimed there was no

Latin description. He overlooked the first reference above; the second required no Latin. The type locality most likely is in New Mexico, but probably the species occurs in Colorado. It was found in New Mexico within 50 yards of the state line, but not in similar habitats in Colorado, a stone's throw away. See Suppl.

NEW MEXICO. RIO ARRIBA CO. Los Piños River, F. G. Knowlton, late May, 1958, Pom, P. Pierce, August, 1960, Pom, April 26, 1962, UNM, R. Reeves 59, Apr. 30, 1961, UNM, L., E. L., & R. L. Benson 16160, Pom.

4. Pediocactus paradinei B. W. Benson

Pediocactus paradinei B. W. Benson, Cactus & Succ. Jour. 29: 136. f. 83-84. 1957; cf. also W. T. Marshall, Saguaroland Bull. 10: 89-91, 107. 4 figs. 1956. Pilocanthus paradinei B. W. Benson & Backeberg, Kakt. und and. Sukk. 8: 187-189. 1957. "Holotype deposited in the Boyce Thompson Southwestern Arboretum Herbarium. No. Bwb 8-1956-1. Isotype deposited in the Herbarium of Pomona College, No. 286120." Houserock Valley, Coconino Co., Arizona. Type not found; no cactus specimens preserved at the Boyce Thompson Southwestern Arboretum Herbarium. LECTOTYPE designation: Pom 286120 (fragmentary). Typical specimen for features not shown in the lectotype: just north of Houserock Valley, Lyman & Robert L. Benson 15755, Pom 286835.

5. Pediocactus sileri (Engelmann) L. Benson

Echinocactus sileri Engelm. ex Coulter, Contr. U.S. Nat. Herb. 3: 376. 1896. Utahia sileri Britton & Rose, Cactaceae 3: 215. 1922. Pediocactus sileri L. Benson, Cactus & Succ. Jour. 33: 53. 1961. "Type [A. L.] Siler of [May] 1883 [Mo]" "Cottonwood Springs and Pipe Springs, southern Utah [Arizona]." TYPE: Mo (2 sheets); photograph, NY.

UTAH. KANE CO. "Southern Utah," A. L. Siler, May, 1883, Mo, in 1882, Ph (flowers). There is no assurance that these collections came from Utah.

ARIZONA. MOHAVE CO. Near Hurricane Cliffs, R. H. Kirkpatrick in 1970, Pom; between Pipe Spring and Moccasin, Lindsay & Bool, July 3, 1939, DS (box); Pipe Spring, Lindsay, July 2, 1939, US, Ariz, Peebles & Parker, SF 14692, Ariz, Pom (photograph of seeds), UC, L. Benson 13530, Pom, P. Pierce, Sept. 5, 1954, UNM; E of Pipe Spring, L. & R. L. Benson 15207, Pom, 15757, Pom, 16152, Pom 16732, Pom; W of Fredonia E. R. Blakley, June 5, 1953, Des, E. R. Blakley & W. H. Earle, June 22, 1951, Des, R. H. Hevly, Oct., 1951, Ariz, Aug. 30, 1959, Ariz.

6. Pediocactus peeblesianus (Croizat) L. Benson

6a. Pediocactus peeblesianus var. fickeiseniae L. Benson

Navajoa fickeisenii Backeberg, Cactus & Succ. Jour. Gt. Brit. 22: 49. 2 unnumbered f. on p. 54. 1960, nom. nud.; Cactaceae 5: 2875. f. 2700-2702. 1961, nom. nud. Pediocactus peeblesianus (Croizat) L. Benson var. fickeisenii L. Benson, Cactus & Succ. Jour. 34: 59. 1962, nom. nud. Toumeya fickeisenii L. Benson ex W. H. Earle, Cacti S.W. 98. Feb., 1963, nom. nud., incorrectly ascribed to the writer; Kladiwa, Sukkulenkunde 7/8: 46. March, 1963, nom. nud. "U. S. A. (Arizona, 300 miles west of the type locality of N. peeblesiana [Holbrook]...area of the Grand Canyon, north of the river..." "...Mrs. Florence R. Fickeisen," quoted from the 1960 paper. An area 300 miles W of Holbrook, Arizona, would be in California about 50 miles W of Needles. Doubtless the intended direction was NW and the distance about 140 to 190 miles. Valid publication is dependent upon both references to Backeberg's writing. The first includes the Latin diagnosis, the second, which refers to it, seems to designate a type specimen. Given the existence of a type (Art. 37), priority in nomenclature is based upon the 1961 publication: "USA (Arizona, ca. 300 Meilen Luftlinie westlich vom Typstandort der N. peeblesianus, auf ca. 1500 m. auf den Hangen der Südseite niedriger Berge im Gebiet der Nordseite des Grand Canyon)." "Der Typus befindet sich in meiner Sammlung." This was presumed to be an herbarium specimen, rather than a living plant, and valid publication was accepted tentatively in this condition (L. Benson, Cactus & Succ. Jour. 34: 61. 1962). Unfortunately there is no evidence or likelihood of existence of any herbarium specimens preserved by Backeberg, who was strongly opposed to making them. For full discussion, cf. Benson, Cacti Ariz. ed. 3. 23-24. 1969. Thus, all the name combinations in the list above are nomina nuda.

Pediocactus peeblesianus (Croizat) L. Benson var. fickeiseniae L. Benson, Cacti Ariz. ed. 3. 24, 186. 1969. TYPE: "Watershed of the Little Colorado River west of Cameron, Coconino County, Arizona. From the originally designated type, the following are designated: LECTOTYPE: (fruiting) Lyman & Robert L. Benson 15,745. June 28, 1957, Pom 285,856. Paratype: (flowering) Lyman & Evelyn L. Benson 16,086, April 21, 1961, Pom 299,969. Two specimens from exactly the same place.

ARIZONA. MOHAVE CO. Antelope Valley, D. Wright, May 12, 1963, Pom; SW of Fredonia, P. Pierce, July 4, 1961, UNM, May 8, 1964, UNM, S. Farwig & V. Girard in 1971, Pom; without exact locality, F. Fickeisen, Pom (photograph by W. H. Earle; living plant at Des) (possible duplicate of plant sent to Backeberg);

"Grand Canyon National Monument," N. Paradine (a single living plant examined, so far as known, none being preserved in an herbarium). COCONINO CO. Marble Canyon, D. G. Davis in 1970, Pom (juvenile plant); near Cameron, D., J., & M. Cowper in 1956, Pom; N of Little Colorado River, W of Cameron, D. G. Davis, Oct. 19, 1965, Pom; near Cameron, Little Colorado River, L., E. L., & R. L. Benson 15745, Pom, L. & E. L. Benson 16086, Pom, W. H. Earle, May 31, 1956, Des, Aug. 11-17, 1956, Des, D. G. Davis, May 22, 1965, Pom; S of Cameron, L. & E. L. Benson 16150, Pom.

6b. Pediocactus peeblesianus var. peeblesianus

Navajoa peeblesiana Croizat, Cactus & Succ. Jour. 15: 89. f. 42. 1943. Toumeya peeblesiana W. T. Marshall, Cactus (Paris) 1: 5. 1946; Cactus & Succ. Jour. 19: 17. 1947. Echinocactus peeblesianus L. Benson, Cacti Ariz. ed. 2. 108. 1950. Pediocactus peeblesianus L. Benson, Cactus & Succ. Jour. 34: 58. 1962. Utahia peeblesiana Kladiwa in Krainz, Kakteen, Lief. 40. C VII b. 1969. "Arizona, Navajo Co., vicinity of Holbrook, 'apparently found by a Mr. Whittaker of the Arizona Highway Department' ...." Ariz 137135. ISOTYPES: GH, Des.

ARIZONA. NAVAJO CO. Gravelly hills NW of Holbrook, 5,100 feet, D. & J. Cowper in 1955, Pom; Holbrook, hill behind the plant quarantine station, J. Whitman Evans (collected by Whittaker?), Ariz. GH; "Hill back of the inspection station at Holbrook." "propagated as a graft from the type collection and given to the D. B. G. by Whitman Evans," pressed Aug. 20, 1955, Des; hills west of Holbrook, 5,200 feet, D. & J. Cowper, May 31, 1956, Des.

Plant of Uncertain Identity

Pediocactus peeblesianus (Croizat) L. Benson var. maianus L. Benson, Cacti Ariz. ed. 3. 24, 186. 1969. TYPE: "Prescott, Arizona, J. W. Toumey, April 23, 1897," Yavapai Co., Arizona. US 535244. This possible variety is not to be confused with the following epithet, which was not published validly and which was intended for a form of Pediocactus peeblesianus var. fickeiseniae (not var. maianus) from the lower Little Colorado River: Navajoa maia Cowper, Cactus & Succ. Jour. Gt. Brit. 23: 90. 1961, nom. nud.; 24: 16 (photograph). 1962, nom. nud. This name appears in journals and catalogs, and it is mentioned to avoid confusion. Var. maianus was collected in Arizona at or near Prescott, Yavapai County. (Relatively large plants for this species; stem unbranched ± 6.2 cm long, 3.8 cm diam; central spine none; radial spines 6, the 3 lower stout, the lowest strongly curving, the upper 1 as long but more slender, the 2 upper lateral much smaller, the average radial ± 1.2 cm long, 1 mm diam.) This plant is known from only the type collection, and publication in varietal status was delayed for many years because of the paucity of material for study. Recent collections of juvenile plants of Echinocereus fendleri, which in the early stages does not have stem-ribs, raise the question of whether the plants named as var. maianus may be immature individuals of that species. The appearance of the spines is similar. In E. fendleri, so far as juvenile material is immediately available, in the earliest stages there are 5 radial spines and 1 central spine. This is true in even the lowest areoles on the juvenile stems. At first, however, there are no radial spines directly above the central spine. In the next set of areoles, up the stem, there are 1 or 2 small or minute radials above the central spine. In later-formed areoles these are much larger. In the specimen of var. maianus, there is no indication of formation of a central spine, though perhaps the spine which appears to be an upper radial is really the central. It is long and slender, as is the central spine in juvenile plants of E. fendleri. The lower radial in both E. fendleri (juvenile plants) and P. peeblesianus var. maianus is stouter than the others, and it may be inclined to curve. In var. maianus it is definitely stouter (1 mm broad) and strongly curving; in E. fendleri both characters are uncertain and variable. The question of relationship is raised by collections made in 1971 by Stanley J. Farwig and Victor Girard. An intensive study in the vicinity of Prescott is needed. Currently, the writer has no opinion of the probable result.

7. Pediocactus papyracanthus (Engelmann) L. Benson

Mammillaria papyracantha Engelm. in A. Gray, Pl. Fendl., Mem. Amer. Acad. II. 4: 49. 1849. Echinocactus papyracanthus Engelm. Trans. Acad. Sci. St. Louis 2: 198. 1863. Toumeya papyracantha Britton & Rose, Cactaceae 3: 91. 1922. Pediocactus papyracanthus L. Benson, Cactus & Succ. Jour. 34: 61. 1962. "...Near Santa Fe, in loose, red, sandy, though fertile soil: found only once; flowering in May." TYPE: "In a valley between the lower hills near Santa Fe in loose sandy red soil. Aug. Fendler, May 15, 1847," Mo.

ARIZONA. NAVAJO CO. N of Holbrook, W. T. Marshall & W. H. Earle, April 20, 1951, Des; Holbrook-Snowflake Road, R. H. Hevly, Aug. 31, 1960, MNA; W of Snowflake, E. R. Blakley B-1732, Des, J. Burrell, Oct. 11, 1957, Ariz, Pom; SW of Taylor, L., E. L., & R. L. Benson 15738, Pom; vicinity of Showlow, Col. & Mrs. D. Bumstead, March, 1935, Ariz, US (photographs & fl.).

NEW MEXICO. San Felipe, Berlandier, April, 1882, Mo. RIO ARRIBA CO. N of Abiquiu, Blackburn, Fall, 1963, UNM, Castetter 2737, UNM. SANDOVAL CO. Near San Ysidro, P. Pierce, June, 1965, UNM, Pom. VALENCIA CO. Mt. Taylor, Castetter 479, April,

1960, UNM. SOCORRO CO. Near Old Bingham, D. B. Dunn 6072, SMU. SANTA FE CO. Los Alamos, J. Blea in 1959, UNM; near Santa Fe, A. Fendler, May 15, 1847, Mo, GH, L., E. L., & R. L. Benson 14682, Pom. BERNALILLO CO. Sandia Mountains near Albuquerque, Cowper, Pom, Castetter 1999, UNM; Albuquerque, Ashmun, Apr. 10, 1897, NY, UC; near Albuquerque, E. F. Anderson 1578, Pom, H. V. Halliday, Oct., 1942, Ariz, R. Reaves, June 8, 1958, UNM, May 4, 1961, UNM D. G. Davis, July, 1963, Pom. GRANT CO. Pinos Altos near Silver City, D. Eppele in 1961, UNM. SIERRA CO. Salt Site, W of Truth or Consequences, G. Sandberg, Nov., 1962, UNM. OTERO CO. Near Goat Springs, San Andreas Mts., E of Alamogordo, Castetter 2300-2301, Oct. 5, 1963, UNM.

12. Epithelantha

Epithelantha, as genus, Weber in Bois, Dict. Hort. 804. 1898, pro syn.; ex Britton & Rose, Cactaceae 2: 92. 1922. Type species: Mammillaria micromeris Engelm. (lectotype, Britton & Rose, Cactaceae 3: 92. 1922) (= Epithelantha micromeris [Engelm.] Weber).

1. Epithelantha micromeris (Engelmann) Weber

Mammillaria micromeris Engelm. Proc. Amer. Acad. 3: 260. 1857 (preprint, 1856); in Emory, Rept. U.S. & Mex. Bound. Surv. 2: Cactaceae 3. pl. 1; 2, f. 1-4. 1859. Cactus micromeris Kuntze, Rev. Gen. Pl. 1: 260. 1891. Echinocactus micromeris Weber in Bois, Dict. Hort. 804. 1898. Epithelantha micromeris loc. cit., pro syn.; Weber ex Britton & Rose, Cactaceae 3: 93. 1922. Cephalomammillaria micromeris Frič, Zivot v Přirodě 299: 9 [Kakt. Succ. 29]. 1925. "From El Paso to the San Pedro River [Texas]... C. Wright." LECTOTYPE designation: "Found from San Felipe Creek to the Pecos." "First seen at a creek 3 miles west of Toquete Creek thence on to the Pecos." Wright, Mo (box). DUPLICATE: Pom 317816.

ARIZONA. SANTA CRUZ CO. Mustang Mts., Pringle, July 13, 1884, Vt, D. Bryant, July, 1948, Ariz.

TEXAS. EL PASO CO. to PECOS and BREWSTER COS.: numerous collections. VAL VERDE CO. Langtry, Rose 11611, US, 11612, US, L. Benson 16520, Pom. BANDERA CO. Lake Medina, D. Weniger, March 20, 1963, UNM.

2. Epithelantha bokei L. Benson

Epithelantha bokei L. Benson, Cactus & Succ. Jour. 41: 185. f. 1-2, 3 (above, inversion corrected, 233). 1969. E. micromeris (Engelm.) Weber var. bokei Glass & Foster, Cactus & Succ Jour. 50: 185. 1978. TYPE: "Texas: Brewster County. Limestone hill near Boquillas Canyon, Big Bend National Park; 2,700 feet elevation... Norman H. Boke, July 12, 1955," Pom 285740 (on 2 sheets).

TEXAS. BREWSTER CO. Near Lajitas, E. F. Anderson 1043, Pom; Terlingua area, Warnock 11040, SRSC, L. Benson 16511, Pom; region of Study Butte, L. Benson 16509, Pom; N of intersection of Hot Springs and Boquillas roads, Boke & Massey 488, Pom; Boquillas, Boke in 1955, Pom; SE of the Chisos Mts., R. H. Wauer, Aug., 1968, Pom, Aug., 1969, Pom.

In horticulture this species appears as Epithelantha greggii, being confused with the plant described as Mammillaria micromeris Engelm. var. greggii Engelm. Proc. Amer. Acad. 3: 261. 1857 (preprint, 1856); in Emory, Rept. U.S. & Mex. Bound. Surv. 2: Cactaceae 4. pl. 2, f. 5-8. 1859. Cactus micromeris (Engelm.) Kuntze var. greggii Coulter, Contr. U.S. Nat. Herb. 3: 101. 1894. M. micromeris Engelm. f. greggii Schelle, Handb. Kakteenkultur 248. 1907. M. greggii Safford, Ann. Rep. Smiths. Inst. 1908: 531. pl. 4, f. 1. 1909. Cephalomammillaria [as Cephalomammillariae] micromeris greggii Frič, Českoslov. Zahradnických Listu [Kakt. Sukk.]. 1924: 120. 1924. Cephalomammillaria greggii Frič, Zivot v Přirodě 299: 9. [Kakt. Succ. 29]. 1925. E. greggii Orcutt, Cactography 5. 1926. E. micromeris (Engelm.) Weber var. greggii ex Borg, Cacti 212. 1937, incorrectly ascribed to Engelmann. LECTOTYPE (Benson, Cactus & Succ. Jour. 41: 186. 1969): "Mountain ridge between Azufrora and Penos Bravos near Saltillo, Coahuila, Mexico, Josiah Gregg 508, Sept. 22, 1848." A young plant in a type folder, GH, "Valley near Azufrora," Gregg in 1848-49, may be a duplicate.

13. Thelocactus

Thelocactus, as subgenus of Echinocactus, K. Schum. Gesamtb. Kakteen 298, 429. 1898; as genus, Britton & Rose, Bull. Torrey Club 49: 251. August, 1922. Type species: Echinocactus hexaedrophorus Lemaire (lectotype, Britton & Rose, Cactaceae 4: 6. 1923) (= Thelocactus hexaedrophorus [Lemaire] Britton & Rose).

Thelomastus, as genus, Frič in Kreuzinger, Verzeichnis 10. 1935.

1. Thelocactus bicolor Galeotti

1a. Thelocactus bicolor var. schottii (Engelmann) Krainz

Echinocactus bicolor Galeotti var. schottii Engelm., Proc. Amer. Acad. 3: 277. 1857 (preprint, 1856); in Emory, Rept. U.S. & Mex. Bound. Surv. 2: Cactaceae 27. 1859. E. schottii Small, Fl. S.E. U.S. 814. 1903. Thelocactus bicolor schottii Davis, ex Backeberg, Cactaceae 5: 2809. 1961, nom. nud. Thelocactus bicolor (Galeotti) Britton & Rose var. schottii Krainz, Kakteen, Lief. 18: C VIIIb. 1961; L. Benson in Lundell, Fl. Texas 2: 291. 1970. "On cretaceous hills...near Mier, on the lower Rio Grande; Schott." Mier is in Tamaulipas, Mexico, about ten miles west of Roma, Starr County, Texas. No specimen found. LECTOTYPE designation: "Cretaceous hills near Mier," Schott in 1853, F 42661; photographs: "Rio Bravo [Grande] on top of hi[gh] shady bluffs," Schott, Sept., 1853, NY, US.

Thelocactus bicolor Galeotti var. texensis Backeberg in Krainz, Kakteen C VIIIb. 1957, nom. nud.; Backeberg, Cactaceae 5: 2809. 1961, nom. nud. (no type specimen), 6: 3872. fig. 3517. 1962, nom. nud. (same, Art. 35). "USA (Texas)...Dies ist der mir bereits vor langen Jahren von Davis aus Texas gesandte Thelocactus...." The plant in the photograph appears to be var. schottii. Probably received from A. R. Davis, for many years a cactus dealer in Marathon, Texas.

TEXAS. BREWSTER CO. E of Marathon, D. S. Correll & D. C. Wasshausen 27797, LL; S of Marathon, C. A. Hanson & D. S. Correll 468f, LL, L. Vortman, Oct., 1964, UNM; Twin Wells, The Solitario, L. C. Hinckley 3604, US; Lajitas, Big Bend Nat. Park, Boke in 1955, Pom. STARR CO. Roma, L. Benson 16537, Pom; near Rio Grande City, Clover 1880, Mich (2), Tex (2), Ariz, DS.

Thelocactus bicolor var. *bicolor* (not in U.S.)

Echinocactus bicolor Galeotti in Pfeiffer & Otto, Abbild. Beschr. Cact. 2: pl. 25. 1848. Thelocactus bicolor Britton & Rose, Bull. Torrey Club 49: 251. 1922. Hamatocactus bicolor I. M. Johnston, Contr. Gray Herb. II. 70: 88. 1924. Thelocactus bicolor Frič in Kreuzinger, Verzeichnis 10. 1935. "...De la collection de feu Mr. Fennel, a été introduite du Mexique par Mr. Galeotti."

1b. Thelocactus bicolor var. flavidispinus Backeberg

Thelocactus bicolor (Galeotti) Britton & Rose var. flavidispinus Backeberg, Beitr. Sukkulentenkunde u. -pflege. 6. 1941. T. falvidispinus Backeberg, Cactus & Succ. Jour. 23: 150. 1951. Echinocactus flavidispinus Weniger, Cacti S.W. 87. 1970, nom. nud. (Art. 33). Backeberg preserved no specimens. NEOTYPE designation: "About 15 miles south of Marathon, Brewster County, Texas, 4,000 feet," Norman H. Boke, July 14, 1955," Pom 285741.

TEXAS. BREWSTER CO. Vicinity of Marathon, several collections. STARR CO. Rio Grande City, R. O. Albert, Pom.

14. Neolloydia

Neolloydia, as genus, Britton & Rose, Bull. Torrey Club 49: 251. August 1922; as subgenus of Coryphantha, Berger, Kakteen 266. 1929. Type species: Mammillaria conoidea DC. (= Neolloydia conoidea [DC.] Britton & Rose).

Echinomastus, as genus, Britton & Rose, Cactaceae 3: 147. Oct. 12, 1922. Type species: Echinocactus erectocentrus Coulter (= Neolloydia erectocentra [Coulter] L. Benson).

1. Neolloydia conoidea (DeCandolle) Britton & Rose

Mammillaria conoidea DC. Mém. Mus. Hist. Nat. Paris 17:112. 1828. Echinocactus conoideus Poselger, Allg. Gartenz. 21: 107. 1853. Cactus conoideus Kuntze, Rev. Gen. Pl. 1: 260. 1891. Neolloydia conoidea Britton & Rose, Bull. Torrey Club 49: 252. 1922. Coryphantha conoidea Orcutt, Circular to Cactus Fanciers 1922, presumably. "...In Mexico. Coulter no. 52."

Neolloydia texensis Britton & Rose, Cactaceae 4: 18. f. 18. 1923. N. conoidea (DC.) Britton & Rose var. texensis Kladiwa & Fittau in Krainz, Kakteen C VIIIb. 1971. "Collected MacDougal and Shreve at Sanderson, Texas, December 1920." "Figure 18 is from a photograph of plants collected by Dr. MacDougal and Dr. Shreve." LECTOTYPE designation: US 1821120, including the photograph appearing in figure 18.

Mammillaria strobiliformis Engelm. in Wisliz. Mem. Tour. No. Mex. 115. 1848. "Rinconada [near Saltillo, Coahuila, Mexico], on rocks: flowers June."

TEXAS. EL PASO CO. Near El Paso, W. H. Evans in 1891, US. CULBERSON CO. Van Horn, G. L. Fisher, Aug. 11, 1931, CAS, J. S. Daston in 1929, F. PECOS CO. SE corner of Co., L. Vortman, Oct. 10, 1964, UNM; Sierra Madera, Warnock 8701, SRSC. BREWSTER CO. NE of Alpine, Warnock 11064, SRSC; Dead Horse Mts., Warnock 11055, SRSC, 11058, SRSC; Overton Ranch Warnock 11977,

SRSC; E of Marathon, <u>Boke</u> in 1955, <u>Pom</u>; near county line, NE Brewster Co., <u>L. C. Hinckley 4822</u>, <u>US</u>, <u>SRSC</u>. TERRELL CO. W of Sanderson, <u>R. O. Albert 32</u>, April 19, 1959, <u>Pom</u>; Sanderson, MacDougal & Shreve, Dec., 1920, <u>NY</u>, L. Benson 16517, Pom. ED-WARDS CO. Rock Springs, <u>G. L. Fisher</u>, April 24, 1932, <u>SMU</u>. COUNTY unknown: Lozier, <u>Morehead 9</u>, June 1897, <u>US</u> (box).

2. Neolloydia warnockii L. Benson

Neolloydia warnockii L. Benson, Cactus & Succ. Jour. 41: 186. (exclude <u>f. 4</u>). 1969. Echinomastus warnockii Glass & Foster, Cactus & Succ. Jour. 47: 222. 1975. TYPE: "Southwest of Persimmon Gap, near the Big Bend National Park, 3,000 feet elevation, limestone hills, <u>Lyman Benson 16514</u>, April 12, 1965," Pom 315729.

TEXAS. HUDSPETH CO. E of Indian Hot Springs, <u>Warnock</u>, Turner, & Parks 417, March 27, 1949, SRSC. CULBERSON CO. Delaware Mts., <u>Warnock 16753</u>, <u>SRSC</u>. PRESIDIO CO. N of Presidio, <u>D. Weniger 404 & 405</u>, Oct., 1963, <u>UNM</u>. BREWSTER CO. Terlingua area, Warnock 11053, SRSC, 11083, SRSC, D. Weniger 154, May 6, 1963, UNM, L. Benson 16515, Pom; between Hot Springs and Hannolds, O. E. Sperry 1818, TAES, Ariz; 15 mi. NW of Boquillas, D. Weniger, May 6, 1963, UNM; Boquillas, Boke, July 13, 1955, Pom, L. Benson 16508, Pom; Black Gap Refuge, NW of Persimmon Gap, <u>Warnock</u>, April, 1963, <u>Pom</u>; SW of Persimmon Gap, <u>L. Benson 16514</u>, Pom; Dog Canyon, 4 mi. S of Persimmon Gap, <u>Warnock & Beuchner 47-012</u>, <u>SRSC</u>; Big Canyon on Rio Grande W of Reagan Canyon, <u>Warnock & McVaugh 47-409</u>, <u>SRSC</u> (2).

3. Neolloydia gautii L. Benson

Neolloydia gautii L. Benson, Cactus & Succ. Jour. 46: 80. 1974. TYPE: "Sour Lake, Hardin County, Texas, <u>J. H. Gaut</u>, April 11, 1905, <u>US</u> (box)."

4. Neolloydia mariposensis (Hester) L. Benson

Echinomastus mariposensis Hester, Desert Pl. Life 17: 59. <u>f</u>. 1945. <u>Neolloydia mariposensis</u> L. Benson, Cactus & Succ. Jour. 41: 188. 1969. Echinocactus mariposensis Weniger, Cacti S.W. 92. 1970, nom. nud. (Art. 33). "...S. E. of...Mariposa which is 10-15 miles N. W. of Terlingua, Brewster Co., Texas...about 3400 feet ....The type material, including plants, pressed flowers, seeds, and photographs, was deposited in Dudley Herbarium, Stanford University, California, and Boyce Thompson Southwest Arboretum of Superior, Arizona, accepted my plants under accession number P 236." Earlier description under the number "H-5," Cactus & Succ. Jour. 10: 180. 1939. TYPE: <u>DS 271943</u> (fls. & photograph and material preserved in fluid.) No herbarium specimens of cacti preserved at Boyce Thompson Southwestern Arboretum.

TEXAS. BREWSTER CO. Near Mariposa, <u>J. P. Hester H-5</u>, <u>DS</u>, D. Weniger 148, May 6, 1963, UNM 33480; Santa Elena Canyon road, W. T. Marshall & E. R. Blakley 1428a, June 21, 1952, Des (2); Ernst Valley, <u>R. H. Wauer</u>, June 18, 1968, <u>Pom</u>.

COAHUILA. Area of Quatrecienegas, <u>Ed & Betty Gay</u> in 1969, Pom.

5. Neolloydia intertexta (Engelmann) L. Benson

5a. Neolloydia intertexta var. intertexta

Echinocactus intertextus Engelm. Proc. Amer. Acad. 3: 277. 1857 (preprint, 1856); in Emory Rept. U.S. & Mex. Bound. Surv. 2: Cactaceae 27. <u>pl. 35</u>. 1859, not Phillipi, Linnaea 33: 81. 1864. Echinomastus intertextus Britton & Rose, Cactaceae 3: 149. 1922. <u>Thelocactus intertextus</u> W. T. Marshall ex Kelsey & Dayton, Stand. Pl. Names ed. 2. 78. 1942, with faint reference to basionym (the work on the "cactus genera" being credited to advice of Elzada U. Clover, W. Taylor Marshall, and R. W. Poindexter; but, in view of later publication by Marshall [Cactus & Succ. Jour. Gt. Brit. 9: 28. 1947] as a <u>nomen nudum</u>, this combination doubtless being attributable to Marshall). <u>Neolloydia intertexta</u> L. Benson, Cactus & Succ. Jour. 41: 233. Sept. 20, 1969; Cacti Ariz. ed. 3. 24: 191. Oct. 22, 1969. "On stony ridges from the Limpia to El Paso, <u>Wright</u>, <u>Bigelow</u>, and westward, <u>Parry</u>) also towards Chihuahua, <u>Wislizenus</u>...." LECTOTYPE: (Benson, <u>loc. cit</u>.): "The specimen from El Paso in 1852 (mounted on two sheets)....There is no indication of whether this specimen was collected by <u>Wright</u> or by <u>Bigelow</u>. Part was from cultivation in St. Louis in 1855," <u>Mo</u>.

Cereus pectinatus (Scheidw.) Engelm. var. centralis Coulter, Contr. U.S. Nat. Herb. 3: 386. 1896. Echinocereus pectinatus (Scheidw.) Engelm. var. centralis K. Schum. Gesamtb. Kakteen 271. 1899. Echinocereus pectinatus (Scheidw.) Engelm. f. centralis Schelle, Handb. Kakteenkultur 132. 1907. Echinocereus centralis Rose, Contr. U.S. Nat. Herb. 12: 293. 1909. Echinomastus centralis Y. Ito, Cacti 1952: 102. 1952. "Arizona, near Fort Huachuca... Wilcox of 1894 in Nat. Herb." TYPE: <u>US</u> (box). Photographs, <u>US</u>, <u>NY</u>.

ARIZONA. PIMA CO. Oak Tree Canyon, E of Rosemont, Santa Rita <u>Mts</u>., <u>L. Benson 10602</u>, <u>Pom</u> (fls., remainder lost), <u>16054</u>, <u>Pom</u> (balance of specimen), <u>H. G. Reynolds & H. Haskell</u>, April 7, 1946, <u>Ariz</u> (box).

NEW MEXICO. BERNALILLO CO. Soda Springs, W side of Sandia Mts., <u>L. Vortman 2282</u>, <u>UNM</u>.

5b. Neolloydia intertexta var. dasyacantha (Engelmann) L. Benson

Echinocactus intertextus Engelm. var. dasyacanthus Engelm. Proc. Amer. Acad. 3: 277. 1857 (preprint, 1856); in Emory, Rept. U.S. & Mex. Bound. Surv. 2: Cactaceae 28. <u>pl. 35</u>, <u>f. 1-5</u>. 1859. Echinocactus intertextus Engelm. f. dasyacanthus Schelle, Handb. Kakteenkultur 201. 1907. Echinomastus dasyacanthus Britton & Rose, Cactaceae 3: 150. 1922. <u>Thelocactus dasyacanthus</u> W. T. Marshall ex Kelsey & Dayton, Stand. Pl. Names ed. 2. 78. 1942, cf. note under var. <u>intertextus</u>. Echinomastus intertextus (Engelm.) Britton & Rose var. dasyacanthus Backeberg, Cactaceae 5: 2832. 1961. <u>Neolloydia intertexta</u> (Coulter) L. Benson var. dasyacantha L. Benson, Cactus & Succ. Jour. 41: 233. 1969. "...Var. β common about El Paso, <u>Wright</u> in 1852," <u>Mo</u>. (on 2 sheets). DUPLICATE: <u>Pom 317811</u>.

6. Neolloydia erectocentra (Coulter) L. Benson

6a. Neolloydia erectocentra var. erectocentra

Echinocactus erectocentrus Coulter, Contr. U.S. Nat. Herb. 3: 376. 1896. Echinocactus horripilus Lemaire var. erectocentrus Weber ex K. Schum. Gesamtb. Kakteen 443. 1898, pro syn. Echinomastus erectocentrus Britton & Rose, Cactaceae 3: 148. 1922. <u>Thelocactus erectocentrus</u> W. T. Marshall ex Kelsey & Dayton, Stnad. Pl. Names ed. 2. 78. 1942, cf. note under Neolloydia intertexta var. intertexta. Neolloydia erectocentra L. Benson, Cacti Ariz. ed. 3. 24, 376. 1969. "Type in Nat. Herb. and in Herb Coulter. Near Benson, Arizona, and also near Saltillo, Coahuila. Specimens examined: ARIZONA (<u>Evans</u> of 1891); COAHUILA (<u>Weber</u> of 1869)." "It seems so unlikely that this species would be found at such widely-separated stations as Benson, Arizona, and Saltillo, Coahuila, that there must be a suspicion of shifted labels on the part of one of these collectors. Mr. Evans's only Mexican collections are from Chihuahua, just across the Rio Grande from El Paso, and it is barely possible that this plant should bear a Chihuahua label...." Specimens not found. NEOTYPE: (Benson, <u>loc. cit</u>.): "east of the junction of U.S. 80 and the road to Sonoita, Pima County, Arizona, <u>L. Benson 10326</u>, April 17, 1940," <u>Pom 273980</u>. A fruiting specimen from the same place is <u>L. Benson 16673</u>, July 15, 1967, <u>Pom 311315</u>.

Mammillaria childsii Blanc, Illustr. Cat. Rare Cacti 14. <u>illus</u>. 1894. "This fine mammillaria was sent to us as <u>M. pectinata</u>." According to Britton & Rose, Cactaceae 3: 175. 1922, the description and figure indicate this species.

Echinocactus krausei Hildmann, Monatsschr. Kakteenk. 6: 125. 1896, <u>nom. nud</u>. and without name of publishing author; ex Hirscht, <u>ibid</u>. 6: 127. 1896, <u>nom. nud</u>.; ex Hirscht, <u>ibid</u>. 7: 95. 1897, <u>nom. nud</u>.; ex Mathsson, <u>ibid</u>. 7: 107. 1897. <u>Cf</u>., also, Hildmann ex K. Schum. Gesamtb. Kakteen 446. 1899. <u>Thelocactus krausei</u> W. T. Marshall ex Kelsey & Dayton, Stand. Pl. Names ed. 2. 78. 1942, nom. nud., based upon Echinomastus krausei, nom. nud., loc. cit. (<u>cf</u>. note under Neolloydia intertexta var. intertexta). "...1890 in Arizona, nahe der Station Dragoon Summit, auf steinigen Wiesen in grosser Menge gefunden und an GRUSON gesandt. Die pflanzen hatte sich aber in der Regenzeit gesammelt und sie hatten sich daher auch schlecht gehalten, so dass nur einige kümmerlich überwinterten. Auf meine Veranlassung sind aber später andere gesammelt und, wenn ich nicht irre, an HAAGE & SCHMIDT gekommen, von wo aus sie zuerst als 'Mammillaria pectinata' verkauft werden." "Nachdem ich mich an einen Examplar, welches sich in einer hiesigen Sammlung befindet und im vorigen Jahre als Echinocactus krausei Hildm. von FRIEDRICH ADOLPH HAAGE jun. bezogen war...." The Herbarium of the Berlin Museum was destroyed during World War II, and probably no specimens exist in Germany, <u>cf</u>. Wedermann, personal communications. LECTOTYPE designation: "Echinocactus krausei Hildm. by Mathsson, in Monats. f. Kakteenk. 7: 107...Arizona...Dragoon Summit Station... Mathsson; this specimen was presented by Mr. Alb. Grimer to [C. H.] Thompson and by him to the [Missouri Botanical] Garden Nov. 23, 1899," <u>Mo</u>. DUPLICATE: Pom 317814.

6b. Neolloydia erectocentra var. acunensis (W. T. Marshall) L. Benson

Echinomastus acunensis W. T. Marshall, Saguaroland Bull. 7: 33. photograph. 1953. Cf. also, W. T. Marshall, Arizona's Cactuses ed. 1. 89. 1950; ed. 2. 92. 1953. Neolloydia erectocentra (Coulter) L. Benson var. acunensis L. Benson, Cacti Ariz. ed. 3. 25, 192. 1969. "...Eastern Organ Pipe Cactus National Monument, Arizona. Cotypes deposited in the Herbaria of The Desert Botanical Garden and of Organ Pipe Cactus National Monument." "...Acuña Valley...and on the hills around the mine pit at Ajo...1700 to 1900 feet elevation." LECTOTYPE: (Benson, <u>loc. cit</u>.): "'Acuña Valley, Organ Pipe Cactus Natl. Mon., Pima Co., Arizona, Altitude 1300 to 1850 ft.; [open slope;] rocky hills; creosote bush cover,' <u>Wm</u>. <u>Supernaugh</u>, Jan. 2, 1951," <u>Des</u>. DUPLICATE: <u>Herbarium of the Organ Pipe Cactus National Monument</u>.

ARIZONA. MARICOPA CO. Sand Tank Mts., SE of Gila Bend, J. P. Hester, (received June, 1950), US (including box). PINAL CO. About 20 mi. E of Florence, <u>E. R. Blakley B-1928</u>, <u>Des</u>; 15 mi. SE of Florence, <u>Lindsay</u>, June 16, 1939. <u>US</u>, <u>Ariz</u>, the plants transitional to var. <u>erectocentra</u>. PIMA CO. Ajo, <u>Shreve</u>, letter of Feb. 24, 1916, and photograph, <u>US</u>; Acuña Valley, Organ Pipe Cactus Nat. Mon., <u>W. Supernaugh</u>, in 1951, Des, Organ Pipe Cactus Nat. Mon. Herb., <u>E. R. Blakley 1895</u>, Des, <u>D. Sands</u>, Dec. 29, 1961,

Pom, K. F. Parker 7983, US, UC, Ariz; L. Benson in 1971, Pom (photographs).

SONORA. Near Sonoyta, Shreve, March 17, 1936, Ariz, Wiggins 8333, DS (box), 8335A, DS (box), 8388, DS (box).

Invalid Names of Uncertain Application (perhaps to N. erectocentra)

Echinomastus pallidus Backeberg, Cactaceae 5: 2826. f. 2653, 2654. 1961, nom. prov., nom. nud. (no type specimen, no Latin description). Echinocactus erectocentrus Engelm. var. pallidus Weniger, Cacti S.W. 90. 1970, nom. nud. (Art. 33). Nomen provisorum is not a category intended to be used (Art. 33). Backeberg employed it occasionally as a method of getting a name into print while the author made up his mind concerning the status of the taxon. This procedure is not valid. Backeberg's plants, described as Echinomastus pallidus, doubtless from horticulture, were of unknown origin, but they were thought to be from Arizona and were obtained as cultivated material from Japan and from Eindhoven (ex Van der Steeg). The single central spine suggests some element of Neolloydia erectocentra.

Echinomastus kakui Backeberg, Descr. Cact. Nov. 3: 6. 1963, nom. nud.

7. Neolloydia johnsonii (Parry) L. Benson

Echinocactus johnsonii Parry ex Engelm. in S. Watson in King, U.S. Geol. Expl. 40th.Par. Botany 117. 1871. Ferocactus johnsonii Britton & Rose, Cactaceae 3: 141. 1922. Echinomastus johnsonii Baxter, Calif. Cactus 75. 1935. Thelocactus johnsonii W. T. Marshall ex Kelsey & Dayton, Stand. Pl. Names ed. 2. 78. 1942, cf. note under Neolloydia intertexta var. intertexta. Neolloydia johnsonii L. Benson, Cacti Ariz. ed. 3. 25, 192. 1969. "Discovered about St. George in Southern Utah by J. E. Johnson...." LECTOTYPE: (Benson, loc. cit.): "St. George, J. E. Johnson in 1870," Mo (1 sheet seeds, another spines and flowers).

Echinocactus johnsonii Parry var. octocentrus Coulter, Contr. U.S. Nat. Herb. 3: 374. 1896. "Type, Coville & Funston 278 [of 1891] in Nat. Herb. Rusting [Resting] Springs Mountains, Inyo County, California." Specimen not found. The Californian plants tend to have about 8 central spines, as opposed to about 4-6.

Echinocactus johnsonii Parry var. lutescens Parish, Bull. So. Calif. Acad. Sci. 25: 83. 1926. Echinomastus johnsonii (Parry) Britton & Rose var. lutescens Parrish [Parish] ex Glade, Cactus & Succ. Jour. 27: 106. f. 71. 1955, nomen nudum; based upon W. T. Marshall, Arizona's Cactuses 89. f. 51. 1950, with the following reference: "...in Arizona gardens is the green-yellow flowered variation referred to by Jepson in 'Desert Wild Flowers' as var. lutescens but without author or place of publication"; probably a reference to Edmund C. Jaeger, Desert Wild Flowers 168. 1940, where Echinomastus johnsonii Engelm. var. lutescens Parish is mentioned. Echinomastus johnsonii (Parry) Baxter var. lutescens Wiggins in Shreve & Wiggins, Veg. & Fl. Sonoran Des. 2: 1011. 1964. "Type in Herb. Univ. Calif...Marcus E. Jones...Searchlight [Nevada], Jan. 5, 1925." TYPE: not found. See Suppl.

Echinomastus arizonicus Hester, Cactus & Succ. Jour. 5: 504. 1934. "...Yuma County, Arizona...." 1,600 feet. NEOTYPE designation: "Butler Valley, J. P. Hester," June, 1950 [probably date of receipt at herbarium], US (box) and US 2179286 (without flowers, fruits, or seeds).

15. Ancistrocactus

Ancistrocactus, as subgenus, K. Schum. Gesamtb. Kakteen 292, 334. 1898; as genus, Britton and Rose, Cactaceae 4: 3-5. 1923. Type species: Echinocactus megarhizus Rose (= Ancistrocactus scheeri [Engelm.] Britton & Rose).

Glandulicactus, as genus, Backeberg, Blätter Kakteenforschung 1938-6. 1938; Beitr. z. Sukkulentenkunde u. -pflege, Deutschen Kakteen-Gesellschaft 32. 1939, nom. nud. (no Latin diagnosis). Type species: Echinocactus uncinatus Galeotti (= Ancistrocactus uncinatus [Galeotti] L. Benson).

1. Ancistrocactus tobuschii (W. T. Marshall) W. T. Marshall ex Backeberg

Mammillaria (Ancistrocactus) tobuschii W. T. Marshall, Saguaroland Bull. 6: 79. 3 photographs. 1952. Ancistrocactus tobuschii W. T. Marshall ex Backeberg, Cactaceae 5: 2926. 1961. Echinocactus tobuschii Weniger, Cacti S.W. 78. 1970, nom. nud. (Art. 33). Apparently Marshall's 1952 combination was intended to be published as the name for a species of Mammillaria, but with the following peculiar statement, "The flowers, fruit and plants indicated that this species was a Mammillaria as considered by the general botanist or an Ancistrocactus by a specialist in Cacti." Normally inclusion of Ancistrocactus in parentheses would indicate a subgenus, but the author intended the two generic names to be alternative. Thus, publication in 1952 of especially the name combination Ancistrocactus tobuschii is dubious, though pub-

lication of the specific epithet is not. Had Marshall's publication appeared on or after January 1, 1953, the entire publication would have been invalid (Article 34). "[G. W.] Henri Ranch, Vanderpool, Texas...type...Herbarium of the Desert Botanical Garden No. 606, [a joint number of Marshall & Blakley]. Isotype...herbarium of the University of Texas." TYPE: "2 mi. NE. of Vanderpool [Bandera County], Texas; south slope; limestone ledge; 1,400 ft.; oak-juniper cover type. W. T. Marshall & E. R. Blakley B1501 [Blakley's number = 606]. June 24, 1952," Des, sheet marked "type" [only stems and a color transparency]. ISOTYPES: Des (includes seeds), Tex.

TEXAS. BANDERA CO. NE of Vanderpool, Blakley B1043 & B1504, Des (fl. & seeds), Marshall & Blakley 606, the same as Blakley B1501, June 24, 1952, Des, Tex, D. Weniger, Feb. 4, 1963, UNM.

2. Ancistrocactus scheeri (Salm-Dyck) Britton & Rose

Echinocactus scheeri Salm-Dyck, Cact. Hort. Dyck. 1849: 155. 1850, not Coryphantha scheeri Lemaire, Cactées 35. 1868, based on Mammillaria scheeri Mühlenpfordt in 1845 (not in 1847). Ancistrocactus scheeri Britton & Rose, Cactaceae 4: 4. pl. 2, f. 2.; text-f. 2. 1923. No specimen or locality mentioned. The first interpretation of this named species was by Engelmann (who corresponded and visited with Salm-Dyck), Proc. Amer. Acad. 3: 271. 1857 (preprint, 1856); in Emory, Rept. U.S. & Mex. Bound. Surv. 2: Cactaceae 19. pl. 17. 1859. "About Eagle Pass, on the Rio Grande; Schott, Bigelow. Flowers in April." LECTOTYPE: Benson, Cact. Suc. Méx. 11: 8. 1966): "Eagle Pass," Bigelow, Mo 112098. Echinocactus brevihamatus Engelm., Proc. Amer. Acad. 3: 271. 1857 (preprint, 1856); in Emory, Rept. U.S. & Mex. Bound. Surv. 2: Cactaceae 19. pl. 18-19. 1859. E. scheeri Salm-Dyck var. brevihamatus Weber in K. Schum. Gesamtb. Kakteen 336. 1898. E. scheeri Abart [subspecies] brevihamatus Schelle, Handb. Kakteenkultur 157. 1907. Ancistrocactus brevihamatus Britton & Rose, Cactaceae 4: 5. 1923. "On the San Pedro [River, Texas], Wright; and...Eagle Pass, Bigelow. Flowers March and April." Specimens not found, Mo. NEOTYPE: Starr County, Texas, near Roma, 5 miles on Santa Maria Road from Highway 83, just past cattle guard and on hill to right, Archie D. Wood 699-7, Pom 319976.

Echinocactus megarhizus Rose, Contr. U.S. Nat. Herb. 12: 290. 1909. Ancistrocactus megarhizus Britton & Rose, Cactaceae 4: 4. f. 1. 1923. "...Palmer near Victoria, Mexico (no. 107, 1907)." TYPE: US 572337. Tuberous roots occur in some plants of various populations studied in the field and probably not in others; correlation with other characters is not evident. Rose's statement that this "species" "has differently colored spines, and differs in technical details" from A. scheeri and A. brevihamatus is not convincing.

3. Ancistrocactus uncinatus (Galeotti) L. Benson

3a. Ancistrocactus uncinatus var. wrightii (Engelmann) L. Benson

Echinocactus uncinatus Galeotti var. wrightii Engelm. Proc. Amer. Acad. 3: 272. 1857 (preprint, 1856); in Emory, Rept. U.S. & Mex. Bound. Surv. 2: Botany. Cactaceae 20. pl. 74, f. 10 (seed). 1859. Echinocactus wrightii Engelm. ex Rümpler in Förster, Handb. Cakteenk. ed. 2. 517. 1885, erroneously ascribed to Engelmann. Echinocactus wrightii Coulter in Bailey, Stand. Cycl. Hort. 513. 1900, later homonym. Echinocactus uncinatus Galeotti f. wrightii Schelle, Handb. Kakteenkultur 160. 1907. Hamatocactus wrightii Orcutt, Cactography 6. 1926. Echinomastus uncinatus (Engelm.) Knuth var. wrightii Engelm. ex Knuth in Backeberg & Knuth, Kaktus-ABC 358. 1935, incorrectly ascribed to Engelmann. Hamatocactus uncinatus (Galeotti) Orcutt var. wrightii Engelm. ex Borg, Cacti 219. 1937, nom. nud., later homonym, incorrectly ascribed to Engelmann. Thelocactus uncinatus wrightii W. T. Marshall (cf. Neolloydia intertexta var. intertexta) in Kelsey & Dayton, Stand. Pl. Names ed. 2. 78. 1942, nom. nud., probably intended to be based upon the nomen nudum and later homonym published by Borg (cf. above). Glandulicactus uncinatus (Engelm.) Backeberg var. wrightii Backeberg, Cactaceae 5: 2925. 1961. Ancistrocactus uncinatus (Galeotti) L. Benson var. wrightii L. Benson, Cactus & Succ. Jour. 41: 188. 1969. "Near El Paso, and on the river below, also at Eagle Springs...Wright, Bigelow: fl. in March and April." LECTOTYPE (Benson, loc. cit.): "'Stony hills near Frontera [then in New Mexico, but now in NW El Paso, Texas], fl. red. Charles Wright [88], March 31, 1852,' Mo." DUPLICATE: Pom 317831.

TEXAS. VAL VERDE CO. Del Rio to Alta Loma, Warnock 15017, SRSC. STARR CO. Rio Grande City, G. C. Nealley in 1891, US (box), F.

Ancistrocactus uncinatus var. uncinatus (not in U.S.)

Echinocactus uncinatus Galeotti in Pfeiffer & Otto, Abbild. Beschr. Cact. 2: pl. 18. 1848. Ferocactus uncinatus Britton & Rose, Cactaceae 3: 146. 1922. Hamatocactus uncinatus Orcutt, Cactography 6. 1926; Galeotti ex Borg, Cacti 219. 1937, incorrectly ascribed to Galeotti; F. Buxbaum, Kakt. u. a. Sukk. 2: 1, 6. 1951; Y. Ito, Cacti 1952: 100. 1952. Echinomastus uncinatus Knuth in Backeberg & Knuth, Kaktus-ABC 358. 1935. Thelocactus uncinatus W. T. Marshall in Marshall & Bock, Cactaceae 169. 1941. Glandulicactus uncinatus Backeberg, Blätter Kakteenf. 1938-6;

Beitr. z. Sukkulentenkunde und -pflege, Deutsche Kakteen-Gesellschaft 34. 1939; 1940; 7. 1942, without reference to basionym;
Jahrb. Deutsch. Kakt. Gesellsch. 1941 (2): 59. 1942. Ancistrocactus uncinatus L. Benson, Cactus & Succ. Jour. 41: 188. 1969.
"...Mexique par Mr. Galeotti."

16. Coryphantha

Coryphantha, as subgenus, Engelm. Proc. Amer. Acad. 3: 264.
1857 (preprint, 1856); as genus, Lemaire, Cactées 32. 1868.
Mammillaria subcolonata Lemaire was indicated by Britton & Mills-
paugh, Bahama Fl. 295. 1920, as the type species. The species
was mentioned and figured by Lemaire, but the source of the name,
Coryphantha, as employed by Lemaire, was Engelmann, and this
species was not even mentioned in any of Engelmann's writing. M.
calcarata Engelm. (= M. sulcata Engelm. upon which it was based)
is designated as the type (lectotype) species by Hunt & Benson,
Cactus & Succ. Jour. 48: 72. 1976. This species appeared
in both Engelmann's original publication of the subgenus Coryphantha and Lemaire's publication of the name in generic status.
Engelmann had proposed M. calcarata as a substitute for M. sulcata,
but this was a superfluous and illegitimate name. See Suppl.

Neobesseya, as genus, Britton & Rose, Cactaceae 4: 51. 1923.
Type species: Mammillaria missouriensis Sweet (= Coryphantha missouriensis [Sweet] Britton & Rose).

Escobaria, as genus, Britton & Rose, Cactaceae 4: 53. 1923.
Type species: Mammillaria tuberculosa Engelm. (= Coryphantha
strobiliformis [Poselger] Orcutt). See Suppl.

Escobesseya, as genus, Hester, Des. Pl. Life 17: 23. 1945.
Type species: Mammillaria dasyacantha Engelm. (= Coryphantha
dasyacantha [Engelm.] Orcutt).

Lepidocoryphantha, as genus, Backeberg, Blätter Kakteenforschung 3: 5. 1938, nom. nud., genus 29 in part 6: 10, 22.
1938; as section of Coryphantha Moran, Gentes Herb. 8: 318. 1953.
Type species: Mammillaria macromeris Engelm. (= Coryphantha macromeris [Engelm.] Britton & Rose).

Pseudocoryphantha, as genus, F. Buxbaum, Österr. Bot. Zeit.
98: 78. 1951. Type species: Escobaria chlorantha (Engelm.) F.
Buxbaum (= Coryphantha vivipara [Nutt.] Britton & Rose var. desertii [Engelm.] W. T. Marshall).

The taxa in the species of the Coryphantha strobiliformis
group proposed by Allan and Dale A. Zimmerman are noted in the
Taxonomic section, but there has been no opportunity to evaluate
them and to incorporate them into the text. Information concerning them came after the text was in proof, and the notes were
added then. The field studies by the Zimmermans have been remarkably thorough.

Four new taxa are proposed in a paper by E. F. Castetter,
Prince Pierce, and Karl Schwerin, Cactus and Succ. Jour. 47: 60-70.
f. 1-11. 1975, too late for critical study and evaluation. The
field study for this paper, entitled, A reassessment of the proposed genus Escobaria, has been intensive and long-continued. The
proposed taxa have not been seen. The table of diagnostic features
of Escobaria as opposed to Coryphantha is based on characters of
size, the dimensions often overlapping or meeting, and on these
and other features appearing consistently in one taxon but either
present or absent in the other. Further analysis is necessary.

The unevaluated proposed taxa are as follows:

Escobaria sandbergii Castetter, Pierce, & Schwerin, Cactus &
Succ. Jour. 47: 62. f. 1-5. 1975. "Type: Rope Springs, west slope
of San Andres Mountains [Dona Ana Co., New Mexico], Prince Pierce
3409, April 1, 1967 UNM 38,739."

Escobaria villardii Castetter, Pierce, & Schwerin, Cactus &
Succ. Jour. 47: 64. f. 6-7. 1975. "Type: Sacramento Mountains
east of Alamogordo [Otero Co., New Mexico], Bob Reaves, 3984 March
18, 1972, UNM 50,789."

See also under 10c, Coryphantha strobiliformis var. orcuttii.

1. Coryphantha minima Baird

Coryphantha minima Baird, Amer. Botanist 37: 150. 1931, not
Mammillaria minima Reichenbach in Terscheck, Suppl. Cact. Verz. 1;
in Salm-Dyck, Cact. Hort. Dyck. 1849: 100. 1850. "Type locality
near Marathon, Texas; first collected by A. R. Davis, March 1931."
Brewster Co. LECTOTYPE designation: "Texas, near Marathon, A. R.
Davis, March 1931," US 1530466 (small plant without reproductive
parts). Typical specimen for characters not shown by the lectotype: SE of Marathon, Brewster Co., Texas, Barton H. Warnock &
Lyman Benson 16497, April 9, 1965, Pom 315710.

Coryphant[h]a nellieae Croizat, Torreya 34: 15. 1934. Mammillaria nellieae Croizat, Cactus & Succ. Jour. 14: 34. 1942.
Escobaria nellieae Backeberg, Cactaceae 5: 2967. f. 2800-2803.

1961. "Mr. A. R. Davis of Marathon [Texas], has recently sent me
specimens...." TYPE: NY. Typical specimen for C. minima is
typical also for C. nellieae; probably all three collections from
the same spot, designated in 1965 by Mrs. Nellie Davis.

2. Coryphantha macromeris (Engelmann) Orcutt

2a. Coryphantha macromeris var. macromeris

Mammillaria macromeris Engelm. in Wisliz. Mem. Tour. No. Mex.
98. 1848. Echinocactus macromeris Poselger, Allg. Gartenz. 21:
102. 1853. Cactus macromeris Kuntze, Rev. Gen. Pl. 1: 260. 1891.
Coryphantha macromeris Orcutt, Circular to Cactus Fanciers 1922;
Britton & Rose Cactaceae. 4: 25. 1923. Lepidocoryphantha macromeris Backeberg, Blätter Kakteen. 6. 1938 (not formally recombined);
Cactaceae, Jahrb. Deutsch. Kakteen-Gesellsch. 1941 (2): 61. 1942.
Thelocactus macromeris L. Benson ex Hodgkins, Brown, & Massingil,
Tetrahedron Letters, Pergammon Press, Ltd., No. 14: 1321. 1967,
nom. nud. (a tentative recombination once considered momentarily
but discarded and not intended to be published). "Sandy soil near
Donana, in flower in August." Doña Ana Co., New Mexico, Wislizenus
in 1864. LECTOTYPE designation: "Near Donana, sandy soils, southern
extremity of the Jornada [del Muerto], Wislizenus," "5/8 46 [May 8,
1846]," Mo (on 2 sheets).

2b. Coryphantha macromeris var. runyonii (Britton & Rose) L. Benson

Coryphantha runyonii Britton & Rose, Cactaceae 4: 26. pl. 1,
f. 1. 1923. Mammillaria runyonii Cory, Rhodora 38: 407. 1936;
Weniger, Cacti S. W. 121. 1970, nom. nud. (Art. 33). Lepidocory-
phantha runyonii Backeberg, Cactaceae 5: 2975. 1961. C. macrom-
eris (Engelm.) Britton & Rose var. runyonii L. Benson, Cactus &
Succ. Jour. 41: 188. 1969. "...Rio Grande from Brownsville to
Rio Grande City...Robert Runyon...in 1921 (No. 15, type) and 1922."
LECTOTYPE designation: Rio Grande [City], Runyon, Aug. 10, 1921.
US. DUPLICATE: NY.

Name of Uncertain Application (perhaps to var. runyonii)

Coryphantha pirtlei Werdermann, Notizbl. Gart. u. Mus.
Berlin-Dahlem 12: 226. 1934. "Vereinigten Staaten von Nord-
amerika: Im Staate Texas, Starr County, 1931, von W. A. Pirtle,
Edinburg entdeckt. Lebend kultiviert im Garten von Mrs. [Ysabel]
Wright, Santa Barbara, California, und im Botanischen Garten,
Dahlem [suburb of Berlin]." Leuenberger, Willdenowia 8: 630. 1979,
states the type is preserved: "USA, 1931, Pirtle s. n. lebend ge-
sammelt, cult. Hort. Berol., konserviert 1938, Typus (ohne Blüten)."

3. Coryphantha scheeri (Mühlenpfordt) Lemaire

3a. Coryphantha scheeri var. scheeri

Mammillaria scheeri Mühlenpfordt, Allg. Gartenz. 15: 97.
March 23, 1847, not Mühlenpfordt, Allg. Gartenz. 13: 346. 1845
(= Neolloydia conoidea). Coryphantha scheeri Lemaire, Cactées
35. 1868, the basionym. Bottom of p. 35 to p. 38: "Avant d'ar-
river aux deux derniers genres de cette tribu... Nous adoptons
les sections qu'a établies le prince de Salm... Les sections 10
et 11 du prince de Salm retrent dans le genre Coryphantha." According to Salm-Dyck, Hort. Dyck. Anno 1849, 1850, p. 20, M.
"-- Scheeri Mühlenpf. (135).", p. 133, "(135.) M. SCHEERI
Mühlenpf... (Mühlenpfordt A. G. Z. [Allg. Gartenz.] 1847, p. 97.)"
Cactus scheeri Kuntze, Rev. Gen. et Sp. Pl. 1: 261. 1891 (cf. 290,
"4. Centralamerikanische nach Hemsley, Biol. Centr. Amer. I.
502-528:...." Hemsley, loc. cit., "214. Mammillaria Scheeri,
Mühlenpf. in Otto & Dietr. Allg. Gartenz. XV. p. 97. t. 2....").
Coryphantha scheeri (Kuntze) L. Benson, Cactus & Succ. Jour. 41:
234. Sept. 10, 1969; Cacti Ariz. ed. 3. 25, 195. Oct. 22, 1969,
but Lemaire's combination now found valid. "Habitat in Mexico."
"Original Examplare... in der Sammlung der Herrn Scheer zu Kew,
des Herrn Fürsten zu Salm-Dyck, und in meiner." Rümpler in Förster, Handb. Cacteenk, ed. 2. 405. 1885, "Vaterland, Mexiko, Real
del Monte." No specimen found, K, or by Salm-Dyck or Mühlenpfordt.
The following are nomina nova based on Mammillaria scheeri Mühlenpfordt in 1847:

Echinocactus muehlenpfordtii Poselger, Allg. Gartenz. 21:
102. 1853, not Mammillaria muehlenpfordtii Förster, Allg. Gartenz. 15: 49. Feb. 13, 1847, not Echinocactus muehlenpfordtii
Fennel, Allg. Gartenz. 15: 65. Feb. 27, 1847. Coryphantha
muehlenpfordtii Britton & Rose, Cactaceae 4: 28. 1923; treated
as newly published, 1923.

Mammillaria engelmannii Cory, Rhodora 38: 405. 1936, not
Coryphantha engelmannii Lemaire, Cactées 34. 1868, nom. nud.
This epithet was published because both sheeri and muehlenpfordtii
were illegitimate when published. Under Mammillaria they are preoccupied, and they cannot be used. In that genus use of the epithet engelmannii published by Cory is mandatory. The combination
"Mammillaria engelmannii [Cory] Benson" ex W. T. Marshall, Arizona's
Cactuses ed. 2. 93. 1953, was attributed erroneously to the writer
and this confusion was followed by Backeberg, Cactaceae 5: 3051-
3053, etc. f. 2874. 1961. Coryphantha engelmannii (Cory) Backeberg, loc. cit. (especially the caption for f. 2874), nom. nud.,
for lack of a reference to Cory's publication of the basionym
(Art. 33). This name combination was also superfluous when published and therefore illegitimate, because under Coryphantha the

epithet scheeri (validly published in 1868 by Lemaire through reference to Mammillaria scheeri Mühlenpfordt in 1847) based upon the same type was available for use. Backeberg sought to apply the epithet engelmannii to an "Arizona form," but this cannot be done because this epithet was merely a nomen novum for scheeri.

Coryphantha neoscheeri Backeberg, Cactaceae 4: 3051. 1961. This combination was also superfluous when published and therefore illegitimate, because under Coryphantha the epithet scheeri (validly published in 1868 by Lemaire through reference to Mammillaria scheeri Mühlenpfordt in 1847) based upon the same type was available for use.

3b. Coryphantha scheeri var. valida (Engelmann) L. Benson

Mammillaria scheeri Mühlenpfordt var. valida Engelm. Proc. Amer. Acad. 3: 265. 1857 (preprint, 1856); in Emory, Rept. U.S. & Mex. Bound. Surv. 2: Cactaceae 10. 1859, not M. valida J. A. Purpus, Monatsschr. Kakteenk. 21: 97. 1911 (which probably is var. scheeri from Mexico). Coryphantha scheeri (Kuntze) L. Benson var. valida L. Benson, Cacti Ariz. ed. 3. 25, 195. 1969. "Sandy ridges of the Rio Grande, from El Paso to the Cañon; also at Eagle Spring and on prairies at the head of the Limpia: Charles Wright. Flowers in July." LECTOTYPE (Benson, loc. cit.): "'Prairies at the head of the Limpio [Limpia Creek], Charles Wright, June 25, 1852," Mo.

3c. Coryphantha scheeri var. uncinata L. Benson

Coryphantha scheeri (Kuntze) L. Benson var. uncinata L. Benson, Cactus & Succ. Jour. 41: 190. 1969. "Vicinity of El Paso, Elmer Stearns 452, Sept., 1912," US 73416.

3d. Coryphantha scheeri var. robustipina (Schott) L. Benson

Mammillaria robustispina Schott ex Engelm. Proc. Amer. Acad. 3: 265. 1857 (preprint, 1856); in Emory, Rept. U.S. & Mex. Bound. Surv. 2: Cactaceae 11. pl. 74, f. 8. 1859. Cactus robustispinus Kuntze, Rev. Gen. Pl. 1: 261. 1891. Coryphantha robustispina Britton & Rose, Cactaceae 4: 33. 1923. C. muehlenpfordtii (Poselger) Britton & Rose var. robustispina W. T. Marshall, Saguaroland Bull. 7: 67. June–July, 1953; Arizona's Cactuses ed. 2. 94. Nov., 1953. C. scheeri (Kuntze) L. Benson var. robustispina L. Benson, Cacti Ariz. ed. 3. 25, 195. 1969. "...South side of the Babuquibari [Baboquivari] mountains, in Sonora; A. Schott." TYPE: "Llanos on the South side of Baboquivaria mountain," presumably on the Sonoran side of the boundary, Schott 4, Mo. ISOTYPE: F 42679.

Mammillaria brownii Toumey, Bot. Gaz. 22: 253. 1896. Cactus brownii Toumey, loc. cit., alternative name, the specific epithet valid because of publication prior to January 1, 1953, but the alternative combination, Cactus brownii, invalid (Art. 33). "Type growing in the cactus garden, University of Arizona...Herbert Brown...[Baboquivari] Mountains, in Southern Arizona...." LECTOTYPE designation: From type plant, J. W. Toumey in 1896, sent in 1899, Mo. DUPLICATE: US 535330 (fruit & seeds from type plant, garden, J. W. Toumey, Sept. 20, 1897).

4. Coryphantha vivipara (Nuttall) Britton & Rose

4a. Coryphantha vivipara var. vivipara

Cactus viviparus Nutt. in Fraser's Cat. No. 22. 1813; in Pursh, Fl. Amer. Sept. 2: 735. 1814; Gen. N. Amer. Pl. 1: 295. 1818. Mammillaria vivipara Haw. Suppl. Pl. Succ. 72. 1819. Echinocactus viviparus Poselger, Allg. Gartenz. 21: 107. 1853. M. vivipara (Nutt.) Haw. var. vera Engelm. Proc. Amer. Acad. 3: 269. 1857 (preprint, 1856)) (typical variety). Coryphantha vivipara Britton & Rose in Britton & Brown, Illustr. Fl. ed. 2. 2: 571. 1913. M. radiosa Engelm. f. vivipara Schelle, Handb. Kakteenkultur 236. 1907, illegitimate combination. Escobaria vivipara F. Buxbaum, Österr. Bot. Zeitschr. 98: 78. 1951. "Collected near the Mandan Towns on the Missourie, lat. near 49° [48°]." North Dakota near Mandan or Bismarck at the site of the Mandan Sioux Indian villages. TYPE: not found, BM, GH, NY, Ph. NEOTYPE Mitich & Benson, Cactus & Succ. Jour. 49: 8. 1977. 12 miles east of Ft. Mandan, McLean County, North Dakota, east of the Missouri River, Larry W. Mitich, June, 1971 (specially collected neotype), Pom 317948. Nuttall visited Ft. Mandan in 1811.

Mammillaria vivipara (Nutt.) Haw. var. radiosa Engelm. subvar. borealis Engelm. Proc. Amer. Acad. 3: 269. 1857 (preprint, 1856). M. vivipara subsp. radiosa Engelm. var. borealis Engelm. Rept. U.S. & Mex. Bound. Surv. 2: Cactaceae 16. pl. 74. f. 4. 1859. "In northern New Mexico." "M. vivipara, var. E[ngelm]. in Pl. Fendl. in mem. Amer. Acad. [4: 49. 1849]." "I have living specimens from Santa Fé and from the upper Missouri [including Santa Fé, Fendler 271, in 1847; Waggon Mound, Wislizenus, June, 1846]...." LECTOTYPE designation: Fendler 271, Mo (2 sheets).

ALBERTA. Ft. McLeod, Scoggan 16566, Can; Lethbridge, J. W. Blankinship, Aug., 1909, GH; Suffield, A. W. A. Brown, July 4, 1943, QUK; Medicine Hat, F. Fyles, July 31, 1914, DAO, Dore 11791, DAO.

SASKATCHEWAN. Numerous collections, especially at DAO.

MANITOBA. Deleau, Boivin & Dore 7764, DAO; Lauder, Scoggan 11016, Can, Boivin & Dore 8253, DAO; 12 mi. NE of Melita, Dore

11125, DAO; Blind River, T. L. Walker, June 27, 1889, QUK; Grand Clariere, Scoggan & Baldwin 7354, DAO; Montagne de Diable, Aweme, Boivin, Bird, & Mosquin 11042, DAO; Souris River E of Dalny, Boivin 13438, DAO; Routledge, Boivin, Marshall, & Laishley 13226, DAO.

OREGON. HARNEY CO. Steen Mts. above Alberson, Peck 14214, WillU 13148.

IDAHO. LEMHI CO. 27 mi. S of Salmon, L. Benson 13063, Pom.

UTAH. DUCHESNE CO. Theodore [Duchesne], benches of the Uinta Mts., 8,000 ft., M. E. Jones, May 13, 1908, Pom. CARBON CO. 10 mi. S of Price, M. E. Jones 5098s, US.

TEXAS (panhandle). POTTER CO. Amarillo, Ball & Townsend 16115, US. RANDALL CO. Amarillo [S side], D. Weniger 635, UNM; S of Canyon City, W. L. Bray 46, May 30, 1899, US.

MINNESOTA. GRANITE CO. Ortonville, L. R. Moyer, June 11, 1898, CU, NY.

Name of Uncertain Application (probably to Coryphantha vivipara)

Mammillaria ramosissima Quehl, Monatsschr. Kakteenk. 18: 127. f. 1908. Originally from C. R. Orcutt in San Diego, California, but no locality or preserved specimen. The photograph indicates a variety of Coryphantha vivipara.

4b. Coryphantha vivipara var. radiosa (Engelmann) Backeberg

Mammillaria radiosa Engelm. Pl. Lindh. II, Bost. Jour. Nat. Hist. 6: 196. 1850. Echinocactus radiosus Poselger, Allg. Gartenz. 21: 107. 1853. M. vivipara (Nutt.) Haw. var. radiosa Engelm. and subvar. texana Engelm. (intended as the typical subvariety), Proc. Amer. Acad. 3: 269. 1857 (preprint, 1856). M. vivipara (Nutt.) Haw. subsp. radiosa Engelm. in Emory, Rept. U.S. & Mex. Bound. Surv. 2: Cactaceae 15. 1859 and subsp. radiosa Engelm. var. texana Engelm. loc. cit. & pl. 75, f. 5. Cactus radiosus Coulter, Contr. U.S. Nat. Herb. 3: 120. 1894. M. radiosa Engelm. f. texensis Schelle, Handb. Kakteenkultur 236. 1907. Coryphantha radiosa Rydb. Fl. Rocky Mts. 581. 1917. Neomammillaria radiosa Britton & Rose ex Rydb. Fl. Prairies & Plains Cent. No. Amer. 562. 1932. Escobaria radiosa Frank, Kakt. u. a. Sukk. 11: 157. 1960. C. vivipara (Nutt.) Britton & Rose var. radiosa Backeberg, Cactaceae 5: 2998. 1961. "Sterile, sandy soil on the Pierdenales [Perdenales]: flower (St. Louis) about the middle of June." LECTOTYPE designation: "Pierdenales, in sterile, sandy plains in western [now central] Texas," cult. St. Louis, Lindheimer, June, 1846, Mo (on 2 sheets). See. Suppl.

Mammillaria vivipara (Nutt.) Haw. var. radiosa Engelm. subvar. neomexicana Engelm. Proc. Amer. Acad. 3: 269. 1857 (preprint, 1856). M. vivipara (Nutt.) Haw. var. neomexicana Engelm. U.S. Senate Rept. Expl. & Surv. R. R. Route Pacific Ocean. Botany 4: 28. 1857 (cf. Engelm. in Emory, Rept. U.S. & Mex. Bound. Surv. 2: Cactaceae pl. 13. 1859). Cactus radiosus Engelm.) Coulter var. neomexicanus Coulter, Contr. U.S. Nat. Herb. 3: 120. 1894. Cactus neomexicanus Small, Fl. S.E. U.S. 812. 1903. M. radiosa Engelm. f. neomexicana Schelle, Handb. Kakteenkultur 236. 1907. M. neomexicana A. Nelson in Coulter & Nelson, Man. Bot. Rocky Mts. 327. 1909. Coryphantha neomexicana Britton & Rose, Cactaceae 4: 45. 1923. Escobaria neomexicana F. Buxbaum, Österr. Bot. Zeitschr. 98: 78. 1951. Coryphantha vivipara (Nutt.) Britton & Rose var. neomexicana Backeberg, Cactaceae 5: 2999. 1961. E. vivipara (Nutt.) F. Buxbaum var. neomexicana F. Buxbaum in Krainz, Kakteen C VIIIc. 1973. "From western Texas to New Mexico and Sonora." LECTOTYPE designation: "South New Mexico," Charles Wright in 1849, Mo (box).

Coryphantha columnaris Lahman, Cactus & Succ. Jour. 6: 27. 1 photograph. 1934. "Near Altus, Jackson Co., Oklahoma..." TYPE: Mo 1064502 (sketch), 1064499 (photograph); photograph, US.

Coryphantha fragrans Hester, Des. Pl. Life 13: 152. 1941. Mammillaria fragrans Weniger, Cacti S. W. 132. 1970, nom. nud. (Art. 33). "...Railroad right-of-way and Highway 90, a few miles west of Sanderson, Texas...." DS 278622.

Coryphantha oklahomensis Lahman, Cactus & Succ. Jour. 21: 165. f. 107. 1949. Escobaria oklahomensis F. Buxbaum, Österr. Bot. Zeitschr. 98: 78. 1951. TYPE: "Type locality, Caddo Co., Oklahoma." Not found. The plant may have been this variety or var. vivipara; the characters indicate a possible hybrid origin. The spelling in the Gray Herbarium Card Index is emended to oclahomensis.

4c. Coryphantha vivipara var. bisbeeana (Orcutt) L. Benson

Coryphantha bisbeeana Orcutt, Cactography 3. 1926. Escobaria bisbeeana Borg, Cacti 305. 1937; W. T. Marshall in Marshall & Bock, Cactaceae 175. 1941, nom. nud. Mammillaria bisbeeana Orcutt ex Backeberg, Cactaceae 5: 2971. 1961, pro syn., nom. nud., incorrectly ascribed to Orcutt. C. vivipara (Nutt.) Britton & Rose var. bisbeeana L. Benson, Cacti Ariz. ed. 3. 25, 197. 1969. Orcutt's intention was to rename the plant described as Coryphantha aggregata by Britton and Rose, Cactaceae 4: 47. f. 47 & pl. 4. 1922, as Coryphantha bisbeeana. This was because he adopted Engelmann's reinterpretation of Mammillaria aggregata as the equivalent of Echinocereus triglochidiatus var. melanacanthus (in Ives, Rept. Colo. R. West part 4. Botany 13. 1861). This interpretation by Engelmann was not mentioned by Britton & Rose, loc. cit., and it seems to have been overlooked by contemporary authors. (See discussion under Echinocereus triglochidiatus var. melanacanthus.) The only collection by Rose (US staff) from Benson, Arizona, is at the National Herbarium to which the plant reported to have flowered at NY (where Britton was director) may have been returned. LECTOTYPE (Benson, loc. cit.): Benson, Arizona, Rose 11958, US, the probable basis for Britton & Rose's figure 47. Orcutt excluded Britton & Rose (pl. 4) as "not true C. arizonica" but an undescribed species, though for no reason the writer can discern, because both it and the specimen and other photographs by Ruth C. Ross represent var. bisbeeana, NY, US (photographs). See Suppl.

NEW MEXICO. HIDALGO CO. San Luis Pass, Castetter 987, UNM.

4d. Coryphantha vivipara var. arizonica (Engelmann) W. T. Marshall

Mammillaria arizonica Engelm. in S. Watson in King, U.S. Geol. Expl. 40th Par. Botany 120. 1871. Cactus radiosus (Engelm.) Coulter var. arizonicus Coulter, Contr. U.S. Nat. Herb. 3: 121. 1894. M. radiosa Engelm. var. arizonica Engelm. ex K. Schum. Gesamtb. Kakteen 481. 1898, erroneously ascribed to Engelmann. M. radiosa Engelm. f. arizonica Schelle, Handb. Kakteenkultur 235. 1907. Coryphantha arizonica Britton & Rose, Cactaceae 4: 45. 1923. M. vivipara (Nutt.) Haw. var. arizonica L. Benson, Proc. Calif. Acad. Sci. IV. 25: 263. 1944; Weniger, Cacti S. W. 131. 1970, nom. nud. (Art. 33). C. vivipara (Nutt.) Britton & Rose var. arizonica W. T. Marshall, Arizona's Cactuses ed. 1. 94. 1950. Escobaria arizonica F. Buxbaum, Österr. Bot. Zeitschr. 98: 78. 1951, not Hester in 1941, nom. nud. "On sandy and rocky soil in northern Arizona, from the Colorado eastward (Coues, Palmer, F. Bischoff), and into southern Utah (J. E. Johnson); probably in southeastern California." LECTOTYPE designation: "Arizona," Coues & Palmer, Mo (stem with spines). Typical specimen for other parts: summit about 3 miles east of Peach Springs, Mohave County, Arizona, Lyman Benson 10191, March 30, 1940, Pom 273982. See Suppl.

NEVADA. WHITE PINE CO. Head of Pleasant Valley, L. Benson 16607, Pom; 10 mi. W of Ely, L. & R. L. Benson 15241, Pom; Connors Pass, U.S. 6, E of Ely, L. & R. L. Benson 15234, Pom; Lehman Creek, N side of Mt. Wheeler, L. Benson 15240, Pom.

4e. Coryphantha vivipara var. desertii (Engelmann) W. T. Marshall

Mammillaria chlorantha Engelm. in Wheeler, Rept. U.S. Geol. Surv. West 100th. Merid. Engineer Dept., U.S. Army 6: Botany 128. 1878. Cactus radiosus (Engelm.) Coulter var. chloranthus Coulter, Contr. U.S. Nat. Herb. 3: 121. 1894. M. radiosa Engelm. var. chlorantha Engelm. ex K. Schum. Gesamtb. Kakteen 481. 1898. M. radiosa Engelm. f. chlorantha Schelle, Handb. Kakteenkultur 235. 1907. M. vivipara (Nutt.) Haw. var. chlorantha L. Benson, Cacti of Arizona ed. 2. 117. 1950. Escobaria chlorantha F. Buxbaum, Österr. Bot. Zeitschr. 98: 78. 1951. "Southern Utah, east of Saint George (Dr. Parry, I[J]. E. Johnson)." LECTOTYPE designation: "St. George," C. C. Parry, May, 1874, Mo.

Mammillaria desertii Engelm. in Brewer, Watson, & Gray, Bot. Calif. 2: 449. 1880. Cactus radiosus (Engelm.) Coulter var. desertii Coulter, Contr. U.S. Nat. Herb. 3: 121. 1894. M. radiosa Engelm. var. desertii Engelm. ex K. Schum. Gesamtb. Kakteen 481. 1898. M. radiosa Engelm. f. desertii Schelle, Handb. Kakteenkultur 236. 1907. M. arizonica Engelm. var. desertii Engelm. ex Davidson & Moxley, Fl. So. Calif. 244. 1923, incorrectly ascribed to Engelmann. Coryphantha desertii Britton & Rose, Cactaceae 4: 46. 1923. M. vivipara (Nutt.) Haw. var. desertii L. Benson, Proc. Calif. Acad. Sci. IV. 25: 263. 1944. C. vivipara (Nutt.) Britton & Rose var. desertii W. T. Marshall, Arizona's Cactuses ed. 1. 1950. Escobaria desertii F. Buxbaum, Österr. Bot. Zeitschr. 98: 78. 1951. "At Ivanpah, 30 [140] miles northeast of San Bernardino, in one of the mountain ranges stretching into the desert, S. B. Parish." LECTOTYPE designation: "Ivanpah," S. B. & W. F. Parish 455 [13993] in 1880, Mo (on 3 sheets). DUPLICATES: NY, Ph, F, DS 109117. See Suppl.

Mammillaria utahensis Hildmann ex K. Schum. Gesamtb. Kakteen 481. 1898, pro syn. Britton and Rose, Cactaceae 4: 43. 1923, suggested this combination may have been applied to "Coryphantha chlorantha."

4f. Coryphantha vivipara var. alversonii (Coulter) L. Benson

Cactus radiosus (Engelm.) Coulter var. alversonii Coulter, Contr. U.S. Nat. Herb. 3: 122. 1894. Mammillaria alversonii Coulter ex Zeissold, Monatsschr. Kakteenk. 5: 70. 1895, incorrectly ascribed to Coulter. M. radiosa Engelm. var. alversonii K. Schum. Gesamtb. Kakteen 481. 1898. M. radiosa Engelm. f. alversonii Schelle, Handb. Kakteenkultur 235. 1907. M. arizonica Engelm. var. alversonii Coulter ex Davidson & Moxley, Fl. So. Calif. 244. 1923, incorrectly ascribed to Coulter. Coryphantha alversonii Orcutt, Cactography 3. 1926. M. vivipara (Nutt.) Haw. var. alversonii L. Benson, Cacti Ariz. ed. 2. 118. 1950. C. vivipara (Nutt.) Britton & Rose var. alversonii L. Benson, Cacti Ariz. ed. 3. 26, 200. 1969. "In the desert region of extreme southeastern California. Specimens examined: SOUTHERN CALIFORNIA (A. H. Alverson of 1892); also growing in Mo. Bot.

Gard. 1893." Not found. LECTOTYPE (Benson, loc. cit., 1969): "Mojave Desert, Calif., A. H. Alverson...McHaney's Mine near 29 Palms. S. B. P. [Parish]," UC 205017. See Suppl.

4g. Coryphantha vivipara var. rosea (Clokey) L. Benson

Coryphantha rosea Clokey, Madroño 7: 75. 1943. C. vivipara (Nutt.) Britton & Rose var. rosea L. Benson, Cacti Ariz. ed. 3. 26, 200. 1969. "Between Kyle Canyon and Deer Creek, Charleston Mountains, Clark County, Nevada...." Ira W. Clokey 8038, June 24, 1938. TYPE: UC 905407. ISOTYPES: Pom 265218, 275343, Mo 1244160 (including a very large plant), NY (2), OSC, UO, GH, Ill, US 1828522 Ph 815138, BH (box), Mich, F, UC 872618, 1102655, SMU, Ariz 47693, WTU 73997, DS 270339, USFS 94999, Tex, Colo, K, USNA 289564, 289571. The holotype (UC 905407) includes a stem 12.5 cm long and 10 cm diam; most of the isotypes and other collections distributed by Clokey are from much smaller plants. See Suppl.

Coryphantha alversonii (Coulter) Orcutt var. exaltissima Wiegand & Backeberg, in Backeberg, Cactaceae 5: 3001. f. 2817, right. 1961, nom. nud. No type specimen. "USA (Kalifornien, ohne nähere Standortsangabe)." A plant doubtless from the same field collection consists of a pressed flower and 2 photographs sent by Mr. Wiegand in 1956, Pom 306798. No data concerning place of collection.

CALIFORNIA. SAN BERNARDINO CO. Kingston Mts., C. B. Wolf 6860, DS; New York Mts., C. B. Wolf 9648, RSA, Munz & Everett 17451, Pom.

NEVADA. NYE CO. Monitor Range S. Farwig & V. Girard, May 18, 1970, Pom; Rainier Mesa Road, J. Beatley, June 19, 1968, TSH, Reveal 1201, TSH; Pahute Mesa, Reveal 1577, TSH. CLARK CO. Charleston Mts., numerous collections; Hidden Forest, Sheep Mts., Alexander & Kellogg 1719, UC. LINCOLN CO. Hiko, L. H. Bowker in 1969, Pom; east of Panaca, Bailey & Funston, May 18, 1891, US (box).

ARIZONA. MOHAVE CO. Peach Springs, Rusby, July 7, 1883, Mich.

5. Coryphantha hesteri Y. Wright

Coryphantha hesteri Y. Wright, Cactus & Succ. Jour. 4: 274. f. on cover (p. 273). 1932; f. and additional descriptive data, ibid. 3: 84. 1931. Escobaria hesteri F. Buxbaum, Österr. Bot. Zeitschr. 98: 78. 1951. Mammillaria hesteri Weniger, Cacti S. W. 139. 1970, nom. nud. (Art. 33). "Brewster County, Texas, J. P. Hester 1930... Type-locality: Near Mt. Ord, about 10 miles southeast of Alpine, Brewster County, Texas." "...These will be forwarded to Mrs. John D. [Ysabel] Wright, of Santa Barbara, Cal....." No specimen found. NEOTYPE designation: Hill near U.S. 385 south of Marathon, Brewster Co., Texas; 4,200 feet, Lyman Benson and Barton H. Warnock 16500, Pom 315709.

6. Coryphantha ramillosa Cutak

Coryphantha ramillosa Cutak, Cactus & Succ. Jour. 14: 166. f. 1942. Mammillaria ramillosa Weniger, Cacti S. W. 119. 1970, nom. nud. (Art. 33). "Type locality: head of Reagan Canyon, Brewster County, Texas." TYPE: Mo 1242260.

TEXAS. BREWSTER CO. Vicinity of Reagan Canyon, A. R. Davis in 1936, Mo, H. Kuenzler, Pom, R. H. Wauer in 1969, Pom. TERRELL CO. S of Sanderson, D. Weniger 91, April 16, 1963, UNM.

CHIHUAHUA. (Cultivated by Potts), Wislizenus in 1846, Mo, Pom.

COAHUILA. Santa Rosa, Bigelow, Jan., 1853, Mo (on 2 sheets), Mammillaria scolymoides as interpreted by Engelm. Proc. Amer. Acad. 3: 314. 1857 (preprint, 1856); in Emory, Rept. U.S. & Mex. Bound. Surv. 2: Cactaceae 14. 1859. During January, 1853, Bigelow was not yet with the Whipple Expedition in New Mexico, and the plant must have been collected at Santa Rosa, Coahuila, opposite the Big Bend National Park, Texas. He was not at Santa Rosa, New Mexico, until September, 1853.

Plant of Uncertain Identity (perhaps C. ramillosa)

Mammillaria scolymoides Scheidw. Allg. Gartenz. 9: 44. 1841. Echinocactus corniferus Poselger var. scolymoides Poselger, Allg. Gartenz. 21: 102. 1853. Cactus scolymoides Kuntze, Rev. Gen. Pl. 1: 261. 1891. M. radians DC. f. scolymoides Schelle, Handb. Kakteenkultur 241. 1907. "Kommt ebenfalls aus Mexiko." The U.S. collections have been confused with this plant as to name, whatever the nature of the species.

7. Coryphantha sulcata (Engelmann) Britton & Rose

7a. Coryphantha sulcata var. sulcata

Mammillaria sulcata Engelm. Pl. Lindh. I. 38, Bost. Jour. Nat. Hist. 5: 246. 1845, not Pfeiffer ex Förster, Handb. Cacteenk. ed. 1. 255. 1846, nom. nud. (cf. Engelm. in Emory, Rept. U.S. & Mex. Bound. Surv. 2: Cactaceae pl. 74, f. 1. 1859). M. calcarata Engelm. Pl. Lindh. II. Bost. Jour. Nat. Hist. 6: 195. 1850, nom. nov. (on the supposition that Pfeiffer's use of M. sulcata antedated Engelmann's). Coryphantha calcarata Lemaire, Cactées 35.

1868. Cactus calcaratus Kuntze, Rev. Gen. Pl. 1: 259. 1891. Cactus scolymoides (Scheidw.) Kuntze var. sulcatus Coulter, Contr. U.S. Nat. Herb. 496. 1898. M. radians DC. var. sulcata Coulter ex K. Schum. Gesamtb. Kakteen 496. 1898. Cactus sulcatus Small, Fl. S.E. U.S. 812. 1903. M. radians DC. f. sulcata Schelle, Handb. Kakteenkultur 241. 1907. Coryphantha sulcata Britton & Rose, Cactaceae 4: 48. 1923. Coryphantha radians (DC.) Britton & Rose, var. sulcata Y. Ito, Cacti 1952: 115. 1952. "Sandstone rocks near Industry." LECTOTYPE (Hunt & Benson, Cactus & Succ. Jour. 48: 72. 1976. "Sandstone rocks near Industry [Austin County, Texas], Lindheimer in July, 1844, Mo (sheet and box).

Mammillaria strobuliformis Mühlenpfordt, Allg. Gartenz. 16: 19. Jan. 15, 1848, not M. strobiliformis Engelm. in Wisliz. Mem. Tour No. Mex. 114. ca Apr. 2, 1848, or Scheer in Salm-Dyck, Cact. Hort. Dyck. 1849. 104. 1850. "Das Original ist Roemer's TEXAS 435."

7b. Coryphantha sulcata var. nickelsiae (K. Brandegee) L. Benson

Mammillaria nickelsiae K. Brandegee, Zoë 5: 31. 1900. Coryphantha nickelsiae Britton & Rose, Cactaceae 4: 35. 1923. C. sulcata (Engelm.) Britton & Rose var. nickelsiae L. Benson, Cactus & Succ. Jour. 41: 188. 1969. "Southward from Laredo, Texas.., Mrs. Anna B. Nickels...." LECTOTYPE (Benson, loc. cit.): "Across from Laredo, Anna B. Nickels" in 1893, F 260723.

TEXAS. WEBB CO. Laredo, Miss A. B. Nickels in 1906, NY (2) (presumably from Texas, but perhaps from near Mt. La Mitra, Nuevo Leon); R. E. Kunze in 1911, NY (photograph made at Laredo, but the plant perhaps from across the Rio Grande in Nuevo Leon). There is no certainty of occurrence in Texas.

8. Coryphantha cornifera (DeCandolle) Lemaire

8a. Coryphantha cornifera var. echinus (Engelmann) L. Benson

Mammillaria echinus Engelm. Proc. Amer. Acad. 3: 267. 1857 (preprint, 1856); in Emory, Rept. U.S. & Mex. Bound. Surv. 2: Cactaceae 13. pl. 10. 1859. M. radians DC. var. echinus K. Schum. Gesamtb. Kakteen 496. 1898. Cactus echinus Kuntze, Rev. Gen. Pl. 1: 260. 1891. M. radians DC. f. echinus Schelle, Handb. Kakteenkultur 240. 1907. Coryphantha echinus Orcutt, Circular to Cactus Fanciers 1922; Britton & Rose, Cactaceae 4: 42. 1923. Coryphantha radians DC. var. echina [echinus] Y. Ito, Cacti 1952: 15. 1952, nom. nud. Coryphantha cornifera (DC.) Britton & Rose var. echinus L. Benson, Cactus & Succ. Jour. 41: 189. 1969. "...Pecos [River], Wright; and from Presidio del Norte to Santa Rosa, Bigelow." LECTOTYPE (Benson, loc. cit.): "Western Texas, Wright in 1849," Mo 115174 α box.

Mammillaria pectinata Engelm. Proc. Amer. Acad. 3: 266. 1857 (preprint, 1856); in Emory, Rept. U.S. & Mex. Bound. Surv. 2: Cactaceae 12. pl. 11. 1859. Cactus pectinatus Kuntze, Rev. Gen. Pl. 1: 259. 1891. Coryphantha pectinata Britton & Rose Cactaceae 4: 34. 1923. Coryphantha radians (DC.) Britton & Rose var. pectinata Borg, Cacti 294. 1937. "...Pecos [River], and at Leon Spring...Charles Wright." Texas. LECTOTYPE designation: "Found on the Pecos and abundant at Ojo de Leon Valley," Wright in 1849, Mo (2 sheets & box). DUPLICATE: Pom 284045. A collection by Richard O. Albert, July 22, 1960, near Big Springs, Texas, demonstrates the probable juvenile nature of the plants described as M. pectinata Engelm. (Coryphantha pectinata Britton & Rose). R. O. Albert 56, Pom, has central spines on the upper (adult) portions of the stem, but the areoles on the lower part are identical with those of the stems of the smaller plants of R. O. Albert 55, Pom, "Coryphantha pectinata."

TEXAS. EL PASO CO. Near El Paso, W. H. Evans in 1891, US (box), NY, F; E of El Paso, Wright in 1851, Mo (box). CULBERSON CO. Van Horn flats, Eggert, May 12, 1901, Mo. HOWARD CO. R. O. Albert 55 & 56, July 22, 1960, Pom; Big Spring, D. Weniger 162, UNM. COKE CO. W of Blackwell, D. Weniger 467, Dec., 1963, UNM. WEBB CO. Laredo, R. E. Kunze, July 11, 1911, US (box).

Coryphantha cornifera var. cornifera (not in U.S.)

Mammillaria cornifera DC. Mém. Mus. Hist. Nat. Paris 17: 112. 1828. Cactus cornifer Kuntze, Rev. Gen. Pl. 1: 260. 1891. Coryphantha cornifera Lemaire, Cactées 35. 1868. "...in Mexico. [Thomas] Coulter." No specimen, Coulter collection, Herbarium of Trinity College, Dublin, Ireland.

Mammillaria radians DC. Mém. Mus. Hist. Nat. Paris 17: 111. 1828. Cactus radians Kuntze, Rev. Gen. Pl. 1: 261. 1891. Coryphantha radians Britton & Rose, Cactaceae 4: 36. 1923. "...In Mexico. [Thomas] Coulter, n° 35." No specimen, Trinity College, Dublin. Two spine clusters [one shattered] ex Salm-Dyck, Jan., 1857, Mo. This, like "Coryphantha pectinata" [cf. var. echinus] is a juvenile form, which starts flowering at an early stage before central spines are produced in the areoles.

9. Coryphantha recurvata (Engelmann) Britton & Rose

Mammillaria recurvispina Engelm. Proc. Amer. Acad. 3: 266. 1857 (preprint, 1856); in Emory, Rept. U.S. & Mex. Bound. Surv. 2: Cactaceae 12. 1859, not De Vriese, Kleine Bijdragen 8. 1839. M.

recurvata Engelm. Trans. St. Louis Acad. Sci. 2: 202. 1863, nom. nov. Cactus recurvatus Kuntze, Rev. Gen. Pl. 1: 259. 1891. Cactus engelmannii Kuntze, loc. cit. 260, nom. superfl., nom. nov. for M. recurvispina. M. nogalensis Rünge ex Hirscht, Monatsschr. Kakteenk. 6: 189. 1896, nom. nud.; 8: 22. Jan., 1898, nom. superfl., nom. nov. for M. recurvispina; Walton's Cactus Jour. 1: 29. March, 1898. Coryphantha recurvata Britton & Rose, Cactaceae 4: 27. 1923. "Eastern parts of Pimeria Alta, Sonora, especially in the Sierra del Pajarito; A. Schott." LECTOTYPE designation: "Sierra del Pajarito. Sierra Verde," Schott in 1855, Mo. DUPLICATES: F 42678, ISC.

10. Coryphantha strobiliformis (Poselger) Moran

10a. Coryphantha strobiliformis var. strobiliformis

Mammillaria strobiliformis Scheer ex Salm-Dyck, Cact. Hort. Dyck. 1849. 104. 1850, not M. strobuliformis Mühlenpfordt, Allg. Gartenz. 16: 19. Jan. 15, 1848, orthographic variant, not Engelm. in Wisliz. Mem. Tour No. Mex. 114.--after March 23, 1848; therefore M. strobiliformis Scheer a later homonym and illegitimate when published. Echinocactus strobiliformis Poselger, Allg. Gartenz. 21: 107. 1853, treated as newly published in that year (Art. 72), therefore the basionym. Cactus strobiliformis Kuntze, Rev. Gen. Pl. 1: 261. 1891. Coryphantha strobiliformis Orcutt, Circular to Cactus Fanciers 1922 (validity uncertain, publication not found); Moran, Gentes Herb. 8: 318. 1953. Escobaria strobiliformis Scheer ex Bödeker, Mamm.-Vergl.-Schlüssel 16. 1933, incorrectly ascribed to Scheer. "...Anno 1846 sub hocce nomine ex horto regio Kewensi gratissime accepi." Original specimen in Salm-Dyck's garden, cf. Engelmann, in Emory, Rept. U.S. & Mex. Bound. Surv. 2: Cactaceae. 74. 1859. LECTOTYPE (Benson, Cactus & Succ. Jour. 41: 189. 1969): "Mam. strobiliformis Scheer (Potts original specimen) Coll. Dyck in hort. Jan. 1857," Mo (tubercle and spines). Typical specimen for other characters: 20 miles S of Alpine, Texas, Texas highway 118, 4,600 feet, Lyman and Robert L. Benson 15476, Pom 284045.

Echinocactus pottsianus Poselger, Allg. Gartenz. 21: 107. 1853, not Mammillaria pottsii Scheer in Salm-Dyck, Cact. Hort. Dyck. 1849. 104. 1850 (cf. discussion under that species). Apparently not hitherto placed in synonymy under Coryphantha strobiliformis, based upon E. strobiliformis Scheer, published simultaneously. "Auf den Bergen bei Guerrero am Rio Grande." Cf. Britton & Rose, Cactaceae 4: 137. 1923: "The plant which Poselger describes under Echinocactus pottsianus, collected at Guerrero, south of the Rio Grande, is very different from Salm-Dyck's plant [see Mammillaria pottsii]...his [plant] fragment, also...[Mo], consists of a fruit, a few brownish seeds, and a spine-cluster, one attached to the top of a grooved tubercle, and is to be referred to Escobaria tuberculosa." LECTOTYPE designation: specimen cited above, "Dr. Poselger leg. south of the Rio Grande near Guerrero," 1851, Mo.

Mammillaria tuberculosa Engelm. Proc. Amer. Acad. 3: 268. 1857 (preprint, 1856); in Emory, Rept. U.S. & Mex. Bound. Surv. 2: Cactaceae 14. pl. 12, f. 1-16. 1859. Cactus tuberculosus Kuntze, Rev. Gen. Pl. 1: 261. 1891. Coryphantha tuberculosa Orcutt, Circular to Cactus Fanciers 1922; Berger, Kakteen 280. 1929; W. T. Marshall, Arizona's Cactuses ed. 1. 97. 1950, ed. 2. 99. 1953 (there the combination attributed erroneously to Fosberg). Escobaria tuberculosa Britton & Rose, Cactaceae 4: 54. 1923; Bödeker, Mam.-Vergl.-Schlüssel 16. 1933. "From the Pecos to Leon Springs [probably Lake Leon just west of Ft. Stockton], Eagle Springs, and El Paso, on the higher mountains, Wright; especially on the rocky summits of the 'Flounce Mountains,' below El Paso, Bigelow. Flowers in May and June." LECTOTYPE designation: "Flounce Mountains, below El Paso [in Chihuahua, Mexico], below San Elisario on the Rio Grande," Bigelow, June, 1852, Mo (on 2 sheets).

Mammillaria strobiliformis Scheer var. rufispina Quehl, Monatsschr. Kakteenk. 17: 87. 1907. Escobaria tuberculosa (Engelm.) Britton & Rose var. rufispina Borg, Cacti 304. 1937. No specimen or locality.

Mammillaria strobiliformis Scheer var. pubescens Quehl, Monatsschr. Kakteenk. 17: 87. 1907. Escobaria tuberculosa (Engelm.) Britton & Rose var. pubescens Borg, Cacti 304. 1937; Y. Ito, Cacti 113. 1951, nom. nud. No specimen or locality.

Mammillaria strobiliformis Scheer var. caespititia Quehl, Monatsschr. Kakteenk. 19: 173. 1909. M. strobiliformis Scheer f. caespititia Schelle, Kakteen 285. 1926. Escobaria tuberculosa (Engelm.) Britton & Rose var. caespititia Borg, Cacti 304. 1937. "Heimat unbekannt, vermutlich Mexiko."

Escobaria arizonica Hester, Desert Pl. Life 13: 189-192 [190]. f. 1941, nom. nud. The publication consists of a photograph of seeds labelled "Escobaria arizonica Sp. Nov." Two large plants (in fluid) are labelled "Escobaria arizonica Hester," DS. "Type locality is on rough limestone mountain just north of the Portal entrance to the Chiricahua Mountains Recreation Area, 8-10 miles n.w. of Rodeo, N. M., 5,000-6,000 ft." Hester 661, USNA 162351. Probable duplicates: Ariz, Pom. All these plants are clearly of typical Coryphantha strobiliformis.

Escobaria tuberculosa (Engelm.) Britton & Rose var. gracilispina Borg, Cacti ed. 2. 365. 1951. No locality or specimen.

ARIZONA. COCHISE CO. Chiricahua Mts., J. P. Hester, April,
1940, Pom, Ariz.

Plants of Uncertain Status (probably var. strobiliformis)

Escobaria bella Britton & Rose, Cactaceae 4: 56. pl. 7, f. 4,
4a. 1923. Coryphantha bella Fosberg, Bull. So. Calif. Acad. Sci.
30: 58. 1931. Mammillaria bella Weniger, Cacti S. W. 143. 1970,
nom. nud. (Art. 33). "...J. N. Rose and Wm. R. Fitch...Devil's
River, Texas (No. 17991). Plate VII, figure 4, shows the type...;
figure 4a shows a tubercle with its gland-bearing groove." LECTO-
TYPE designation: "Hills south of Devil's River," Texas, Rose &
Fitch 17991, Oct. 16, 1913, US 1821125. DUPLICATE: NY. The specimens are not very good, but probably they represent Coryphantha
strobiliformis.

Escobessya albocolumnaria Hester, Desert Pl. Life 13: 129.
figs. 1941. Mammillaria albocolumnaria Weniger, Cacti S. W. 137.
1970, nom. nud. (Art. 33). Coryphantha albicolumnaria D. Zimmerman, Cactus & Succ. Jour. 44: 157. 1972. "Mountainous limestone
area W.N.W. of Terlingua and N.E. of Lajitas, in the southern tip
of Brewster Co., Texas...." TYPE: DS 271855 (and plant preserved
in fluid). The herbarium sheet includes flowers of 2 species. No
specimen preserved at Boyce Thompson Southwestern Arboretum; the
cited plants once were in cultivation.

Dale A. Zimmerman, Cactus & Succ. Jour. 44: 157. f. 2. 1972.
considers Coryphantha ablicolumnaria to be a species distinguished
from C. strobiliformis and C. dasyacantha by the following characters: spines numerous; perianth segments numerous; fruits green;
seeds large, reddish-brown. He considers the plant to be related
closely to C. strobiliformis var. orcuttii.

Escobaria intermedia Fric, Ceskoslav. Zahradnichých Listů.
[Kakt. Sukk.] 1924: 121. 1924, nom. nud. "Texas, USA."

10b. Coryphantha strobiliformis var. durispina (Quehl) L. Benson

Mammillaria strobiliformis Scheer var. durispina Quehl, Monatsschr. Kakteenk. 17: 87. 1907. M. strobiliformis Scheer f. durispina Schelle, Kakteen 285. 1926. Escobaria tuberculosa (Engelm.)
Britton & Rose var. durispina Borg, Cacti 304. 1937. Coryphantha
strobiliformis (Poselger) Moran var. durispina L. Benson, Cactus
& Succ. Jour. 41: 189. 1969. No specimen or locality. Mexico.
"...Received from Delaet in Contich," Belgium. Horticultural
material. NEOTYPE (Benson, loc. cit.): "in Westernmost Brewster
County," Texas, Horst Kuenzler, Pom 311333.

10c. Coryphantha strobiliformis var. orcutti (Bödeker) L. Benson

Escobaria orcuttii Rose ex Orcutt, Cactography 5. 1926, nom.
nud.; Bödeker, Mam.-Vergl.-Schlüssel 17. 1933. Neolloydia orcuttii
Frič in Möller's Deutsch. Gärtner-Zeitung 142. 1926, pro syn.,
nom. nud., and not accepted by its author. Coryphantha strobiliformis (Poselger) Moran var. orcuttii L. Benson, Cacti Ariz. ed. 3.
26, 204. 1969. C. orcuttii D. Zimmerman, Cactus & Succ. Jour. 44:
156. 1972. "NM [New Mexico]." LECTOTYPE (Benson, loc. cit.):
"Escobaria orcuttii Rose, ined. Near Granite Pass, N. M. March,
1926 (type locality) C. R. Orcutt," DS 307410 (box). According to
Zimmerman, Cactus & Succ. Jour. 44: 155. 1972, publication of the
specific epithet was validated by the writer in 1969 by indication
of the lectotype. However, designation of a type specimen was not
required until 1958. Priority in specific rank dates from Bödeker
in 1933, not from "Rose ex Orcutt." The plant has been much better
known from both herbarium and living specimens than assumed by
Zimmerman (cf. below).

Coryphantha strobiliformis var. orcuttii has been studied
intensively in the field recently by Dale A. Zimmerman, Cactus &
Succ. Jour. 44: 155-157. f. 1, 3-5. 1972. According to his data,
var. orcuttii is distinguished by the following characters (see
also characters in the table in the text): spines bright white,
remarkably brittle, not conspicuously deciduous from the stem
base; central spines 15-18 (not 4-9); radial spines 30-41 (not
20-30); flowers with more color; perianth parts 36-42 (not 20-30);
fruits yellowish-green (not scarlet [however sometimes they are
green in var. strobiliformis]). Further field study is needed.

Unevaluated Proposed Taxa

Escobaria orcuttii Bödeker var. macraxina Castetter, Pierce,
& Schwerin, Cactus & Succ. Jour. 47: 66. f. 8-9. 1975. "Type:
Big Hatchet Mountains [Hildalgo Co., New Mexico] at 7,000 feet
elevation, Ken Heil 4287, December 21, 1973, UNM 54,141."

Escobaria orcuttii Bödeker var. koenigii Castetter, Pierce,
& Schwerin, Cactus & Succ. Jour. 47: 68. f. 10-11. 1975. "Type:
Florida Mountains on Koenig Ranch [Luna Co., New Mexico], eleva-
tion 5,200 feet, E. F. Castetter 961, May 7, 1962 UNM 38,768A."

ARIZONA. COCHISE CO. (Chiricahua Mts.). Keating Canyon,

E. R. Blakley 1937, June 25, 1953, Pom; W of Portal, D. Sands 2B,
3A, & 3B, Aug., 1960, Pom.

NEW MEXICO. GRANT CO. Burro Mts., Castetter 2290, UNM.
HIDALGO CO. Peloncillo Mts., Castetter 1841, UNM; Big Hatchet
Mts., Castetter 1812, UNM. LUNA CO. Florida Mts., Castetter 971,
UNM, Pom. DONA ANA CO. San Andres Mts., Castetter & Pierce
1523-1525, UNM; near Dripping Springs, Organ Mts., K. Heil in
1964, UNM; Organ Mts., Castetter 2379, Pom (status of this plant
undetermined; cf. discussion of Coryphantha organensis D. Zimmerman
under C. sneedii var. sneedii); Van Patten's, Organ Mts., Standley,
Jan. 11, 1906, US. OTERO CO. Alamo Canyon E of Alamogordo, Castetter, Pom; Dog Canyon E of Alamogordo, Castetter, Pom.

11. Coryphantha sneedii (Britton & Rose) Berger

11a. Coryphantha sneedii var. sneedii

Escobaria sneedii Britton & Rose, Cactaceae 4: 56. f. 54.
1923. Coryphantha sneedii Berger, Kakteen 280. 1929. Mammillaria
sneedii Cory, Rhodora 38: 407. 1936; Weniger, Cacti S. W. 141.
1970, nom. nud. (Art. 33). "This curious little plant was sent
to us in February 1921 by Mrs. S. L. Pattison from southwestern
Texas; it was collected by J. R. Sneed...in 1921...from a single
station in the Franklin Mountains [north of El Paso], Texas." A
letter, US, June 27, 1923, from J. N. Rose to Mrs. Pattison re-
quests the exact locality. A note in reply (bottom of letter) includes the following: "...McKelligan Canyon, Mt. Franklin, and on
west side of limestone cliffs about 8 miles north of El Paso, and
only on one cliff." [Actually, the plant is widespread in Franklin
Mts.] One sheet is labelled, "Feb. 21, 1921." LECTOTYPE designation: US (on 2 unnumbered sheets). DUPLICATE: NY.

Coryphantha pygmaea Fric, Ceskoslov. Zahradnickýck Listů
[Kakt. Sukk.] 1924: 121. 1924, pro syn. "Texas, Mexico."

Taxon of Undetermined Status

Coryphantha organensis D. A. Zimmerman, Cactus & Succ. Jour.
44: 114. f. 1972. Escobaria organensis Castetter, Pierce, &
Schwerin, Cactus & Succ. Jour. 47: 60. 1975. TYPE: "Dale A. Zimmerman and Allan D. Zimmerman No. 1535 from the Organ Mountains,
ca. 15 miles east of Las Cruces, T 23 S, R 4 E, Dona Ana County,
New Mexico, elevation 7300 feet, January 17, 1971.... Holotype deposited in the Herbarium of Western New Mexico University, Silver
City."

No specimens of Coryphantha organensis have been seen. The
photographs are reminiscent of hybrids of C. sneedii var. sneedii
and C. strobiliformis, as stated in the text. However, according
to Zimmerman (loc. cit.), they have been found in only two rugged,
isolated canyons at above 2,100 m (7,000 ft) in the Organ Mts.,
far away from and above the desert canyons in the northern Franklin
Mts. Only vegetative plants of the hybrid swarm were seen, and
other characters are not known. According to Zimmerman, C. organensis differs from C. strobiliformis vs. strobiliformis as follows:
stems soft, the spines imparting a yellow aspect; central spines
9-12 and radial spines 33-35 (in C. strobiliformis recorded as 6-8
and 20-30), very dense, tending to persist on the base of the stem;
flowers more heavily pigmented; fruits yellowish-green [however,
sometimes green in C. strobiliformis], seeds 1-1.25 mm long (as
opposed to 0.8 mm). The species is stated to differ from C. strobiliformis var. orcuttii as follows: stems softer and more slender;
spines yellowish or straw-colored, firm instead of brittle; central
spines 9-12, the bases bulbous; flower 15-16 mm in diameter; filaments pinkish or pinkish-purple. The following description is
drawn from that published by Zimmerman:

Stems densely covered with yellowish or straw-colored spines,
typically in mounds or clusters, in older plants 10-50, to 12 cm
long, to 3 cm diam; tubercles 7-10 mm long, 3-6 mm broad; areoles
circular, ± 3 mm diam; spines obscuring the stem and persistent on
the lower part; central spines 9-12, stout, straight, basally bulbous, often with reddish-brown tips, 9-19 mm long; flowers 15-16
mm diam; sepaloids pale pink with the midline maroon or brownish,
prominently fringed; petaloids pink or pinkish and bordered with
white or pale pink, 7.5-10 mm long, 1-1.5 mm broad, entire; filaments pinkish or purplish-pink; anthers yellow; styles ± 9 mm
long; stigmas 5-6, pale yellow; fruit yellowish-green, cylindroid
to slightly ovoid, tapering basally, 6-14 mm long, 3-5 mm diam,
the perianth often persistent; seeds reddish-brown, reniform, the
surface distinctly pitted, 1-1.25 mm long.

Rocky canyons at about 2,100-2,400 m (7,000-8,000 ft).
Southern Juniper-Pinyon Woodland. New Mexico in the Organ Mountains, Dona Ana Co., on the White Sands Missile Range.

11b. Coryphantha sneedii var. leei (Rose) L. Benson

Escobaria leei Rose ex Bödeker, Mam.-Vergl.-Schlüssel 17.
1933. Coryphantha sneedii (Britton & Rose) Berger var. leei L.
Benson, Cactus & Succ. Jour. 41: 189. 1969. Mammillaria leei
Weniger, Cacti S. W. 142. 1970, nom. nud. (Art. 33). "Escobaria
leei Rose (Rose als Mammillaria 1924 Nr. 282) Böd. Aus Neu-Mexiko."
LECTOTYPE (Castetter and Pierce, Madroño 18: 137-138. 1966):

"Rattlesnake Canyon, 30 miles southwest of Carlsbad [New Mexico], altitude 5500 ft., W. T. Lee, 1924," US 72134 (including carton). DUPLICATE: Pom 313262.

NEW MEXICO. EDDY CO. Rattlesnake Canyon, Guadalupe Mts., Carlsbad Caverns Nat. Park, W. T. Lee, April, 1925, US (and box), Pom, Castetter 1380, UNM, Pom.

12. Coryphantha dasyacantha (Engelmann) Orcutt

12a. Coryphantha dasyacantha var. dasyacantha

Mammillaria dasyacantha Engelm. Proc. Amer. Acad. 3: 269. 1857 (preprint, 1856); in Emory, Rept. U.S. & Mex. Bound. Surv. 2: Cactaceae 15. pl. 12, f. 17-22. 1859. Cactus dasyacantha Kuntze, Rev. Gen. Pl. 1: 259. 1891. Coryphantha dasyacantha Orcutt, Circular to Cactus Fanciers 1922; Cactography 5. 1926; Berger, Kakteen 280. 1929. Escobaria dasyacantha Britton & Rose, Cactaceae 4: 55. 1923. Escobesseya dasyacantha Hester, Desert Pl. Life 13: 192. 1941; 17: 23. 1945. "El Paso and Eagle Springs; Wright." LECTOTYPE designation: "El Paso," Charles Wright in 1852, Mo (1 sheet and carton).

12b. Coryphantha dasyacantha var. varicolor (Tiegel) L. Benson

Coryphantha varicolor Tiegel, Monatsschr. Deutsch. Kakt. Gesellsch. 3: 278. 1932. Escobaria varicolor Tiegel, loc. cit., alternative name, therefore invalid (C. varicolor published prior to January 1, 1953, therefore valid). C. dasyacantha (Engelm.) Berger var. varicolor L. Benson, Cactus & Succ. Jour. 41: 189. 1969. Mammillaria varicolor Weniger, Cacti S. W. 138. 1970, nom. nud. (Art. 33). "Heimat; südwestliches Texas." According to Backeberg, Cactaceae 5: 2957. 1961, "Die Schreibweise KNUTHS in Kaktus-ABC, 380. 1935 lautete 'varicolor'; unter diesem nom. prov. erhielt TIEGEL seinerzeit die Pflanze von mir. Ich bekan damals eine Anzahl Exemplare von Davis, Texas." Thus the original material came from A. R. Davis, for many years a cactus dealer at Marathon, Texas, in the area in which this plant grows. The description was based upon immature plants. The stems become elongate-cylindroid and large in age. NEOTYPE (Benson, loc. cit.): "Brewster County, Texas, hills south of Marathon, 3,800 feet, Barton H. Warnock 47-467, April 3, 1947." SRSC. See Suppl.

13. Coryphantha robertii Berger

Escobaria runyonii Britton & Rose, Cactaceae 4: 55. f. 53; pl. 6, f. 1. 1923, not Coryphantha runyonii Britton & Rose, loc. cit. 26. Coryphantha robertii Berger, Kakteen 280. 1929, nom. nov. C. piercei Fosberg, Bull. So. Calif. Acad. 30: 58. 1931, nom. nov. Mammillaria escobaria Cory, Rhodora 38: 405. 1936, nom. nov. "...Robert Runyon in July 1921 and again in October of the same year near Reynosa, Mexico, about 75 [30] miles up the Rio Grande from Brownsville, Texas, and on August 10, 1921, near Rio Grande City, Starr County, Texas...Plate VI, figure 1, is from a photograph of the type plant taken by Robert Runyon." LECTOTYPE designation: Rio Grande City, Robert Runyon, Aug. 10, 1921, US (not numbered) and Britton & Rose's pl. 6, f. 1. DUPLICATES: NY, Pom 313589.

13+. Coryphantha robbinsorum (W. H. Earle)
Allan D. Zimmerman (see Supplement)

14. Coryphantha duncanii (Hester) L. Benson

Escobesseya duncanii Hester, Des. Pl. Life 13: 192. 1941; 17: 24. f. 1945. Escobaria duncanii Backeberg, Cactaceae 5: 2966. f. 2799. 1961. Coryphantha duncanii L. Benson, Cactus & Succ. Jour. 41: 189. 1969. Mammillaria duncanii Weniger, Cacti S. W. 136. 1970, nom. nud. (Art. 33). "...Edwards limestone of mountains a few miles northwest of Terlingua, Brewster Co., Texas, just south of...Mariposa, on mining claim of ex-Capt. Frank Duncan ...3400 ft." TYPE: DS 271944 (photograph & fls.) and unnumbered sheet (photograph), and material preserved in fluid (with only the name of the proposed species and some marked "H4.")

NEW MEXICO. SIERRA CO. Near Truth or Consequences. P. Pierce 2346-2358, UNM, 2359-2360, UNM, 2685-2690, UNM, Castetter & Pierce 2694-2709, UNM, Pom.

TEXAS. PRESIDIO CO. W of Terlingua, J. P. Hester, April 4, 1940, DS. BREWSTER CO. Big Bend Nat. Park, J. P. Hester, April 25, 1939, DS (preservative), R. H. Wauer in 1969, Pom.

15. Coryphantha missouriensis (Sweet) Britton & Rose

15a. Coryphantha missouriensis var. missouriensis

Mammillaria missouriensis Sweet, Hort. Brit. 171. 1826. Cactus missouriensis Kuntze, Rev. Gen. Pl. 1: 259. 1891. Coryphantha missouriensis Britton & Rose in Britton & Brown, Illustr. Fl. ed. 2. 2: 570. 1913. Neobesseya missouriensis Britton & Rose, Cactaceae 4: 53. 1923. Based upon Nuttall, Gen. N. Amer. Pl. 1: 295. 1818: "On the high hills of the Missouri probably to the mountains." This, as with Coryphantha vivipara, probably was encountered about the "Mandan Towns," the Mandan Sioux Indian villages, in North Dakota near Mandan and Bismarck. No specimen found, BM, NY, GH, Ph. NEOTYPE designation (Mitich & Benson, Cactus & Succ. Jour. 49: 8. 1977: 3 mi. W. of Baldwin turnoff, 1.3 mi. E. of Missouri River, Burleigh Co., North Dakota, Larry W. Mitich, June, 1970, Pom 317949. DUPLICATE: NDA. The area is near the Missouri

River in the region where in 1811 Nuttall stayed at Ft. Manuel Lisa, later Ft. Vanderburgh. See Suppl.

Mammillaria nuttallii Engelm. Pl. Fendl., Mem. Acad. 4: 49. 1849. (Note: Cactus mammillaris Nutt. Gen. N. Am. Pl. 1: 295. 1818, not L. in 1753, was merely an identification, not a new name, and M. nuttallii was described later as a new species, as indicated by Engelmann.) M. nuttallii Engelm. var. borealis Engelm. Proc. Amer. Acad. 3: 264. 1857 (preprint, 1856) (cf. Engelm. in Emory, Rept. U.S. & Mex. Bound. Surv. 2: Cactaceae pl. 74, f. 6. 1859), nom. nov. for the typical variety. Coryphantha nuttallii Engelm. ex Rümpler in Förster, Handb. Cacteenk. ed. 2. 407. 1885, pro syn., erroneously attributed to Engelmann. M. missouriensis Sweet f. nuttallii Schelle, Handb. Kakteenkultur 241. 1907. Neobesseya nuttallii Britton & Rose ex Borg, Cacti 303. 1937, incorrectly ascribed to Britton & Rose. "...About Fort Pierre, on the Upper Missouri; flowering in May." LECTOTYPE designation: Ft. Pierre [South Dakota], Hayden in 1847 (seeds and perhaps fruit), Mo, together with Mo 899105 (flowers) (cultivated in St. Louis, May, 1848, doubtless from the same source) and Mo 899104, collected by Hayden and probably the same collection.

Mammillaria notesteinii Britton, Bull. Torrey Club. 18: 367. 1891. Cactus notesteinii Rydberg, Mem. N. Y. Bot. Gard. 1: 272. 1900. Neobesseya notesteinii Britton & Rose, Cactaceae 4: 53. 1923. Coryphantha notesteinii Clover, Marshall, & Poindexter in Kelsey & Dayton, Stand. Pl. Names ed. 2. 69. 1942 (cf. discussion under Neolloydia intertexta var. intertexta). N. missouriensis (Sweet) Britton & Rose var. notesteinii Luchsinger, Trans. Kans. Acad. Sci. 68: 394. 1965. "Deer Lodge, Mont. Prof. F. N. Notestein, 1891." TYPE: NY. ISOTYPE: US 1821122.

IDAHO. CUSTER CO. 20 mi. NE of Sun Valley, Hitchcock & Muhlick 8784, WS, NY, WTU. LEMHI CO. Leodora, H. M. Hall, Aug., 1921, NY; near the Clark Co. line, Highway 28, R. M. Spellenberg 1718, June 21, 1967, WTU.

MONTANA (eastern). Collections from scattering localities.

WYOMING. Yellowstone Nat. Park, F. Tweedy 423, US. CROOK CO. Hulett, M. Ownbey 669, Mo, WS, NY, UC, WTU; Beulah, H. E. Hayward 1326, in 1927, F. CARBON CO. 12 mi. W of Saratoga, C. B. Dugdale in 1960, Pom.

ARIZONA. MOHAVE CO. 20-30 miles S of Pipe Spring, R. H. Kirkpatrick, May, 1971, Pom; Tuweep Road, James Doman, April, 1971, Pom. YAVAPAI CO. Near Prescott, Dorothy Humphrey [Cheryl Murphy?], Des (living plant seen in the early 1960's). NAVAJO CO. Heber, probably this variety, reported, Saguaroland Bulletin 22: 76-78. f. 1968; near Heber, S. Farwig & V. Girard, April 29, 1971, Pom.

NORTH DAKOTA. BILLINGS CO. Medora, C. R. Ball, July 25, 1923, US. MORTON CO. Mandan, H. C. Overholser, June, 1918, US. MCLEAN CO. E side of Missouri River, 12 mi. from Ft. Mandan, L. W. Mitich, June, 1971, Pom. BURLEIGH CO. 3 mi. W of Baldwin turnoff, 1.3 mi. from Missouri River, L. W. Mitich, June, 1970, Pom; Bismarck, V. Bailey, July 20, 1909, US. STUTSMAN CO. Jamestown, G. Berner, US. The Mitich collections are duplicated at North Dakota State University, Fargo.

15b. Coryphantha missouriensis var. marstonii (Clover) L. Benson

Coryphantha marstonii Clover, Bull. Torrey Club 65; 412. pl. 17, f. 6. 1938. C. missouriensis (Sweet) Britton & Rose var. marstonii L. Benson, Cacti Ariz. ed. 3. 26, 204. 1969. "Known only from the type locality, 'Hell's Backbone,' a mountain ridge near Boulder, Garfield Co., Utah ([no.] 1909)." TYPE: not preserved. NEOTYPE (Benson, loc. cit.): "Utah; Kane County; east side of Buckskin Mountains, 5,200 feet elevation, Lyman [& Robert L.] Benson 15205, August 8, 1953," Pom 285320, 296309. See Suppl.

Neobessya arizonica Hester, Des. Pl. Life. Illustr. on p. 191. 1941, nom. nud; Hester ex Girard & Farwig, Cactus & Succ. Jour. 45: 129. 1973, nom. nud. A collection by Hester is labelled as follows: "Found in 1934....west side of the Buckskin Mts., N. Arizona...." J. P. Hester in 1934, US (box). DUPLICATE: Pom 306416.

UTAH. KANE CO. Buckskin Mts., Paria River, L. & R. L. Benson 15205, Pom.

ARIZONA. COCONINO CO. "Buckskin Mts." [Kaibab Plateau], J. P. Hester, June, 1950, US; "w. side of Buckskin Mts.," J. P. Hester 975 (number probably meaningless), US, in 1934, US (box), Pom; Houserock Valley, D. G. Davis, May 8, 1964, Pom.

15c. Coryphantha missouriensis var. caespitosa (Engelmann) L. Benson

Mammillaria similis Engelm. Pl. Lindh. I. 38, Bost. Jour. Nat. Hist. 5: 246. 1845. M. similis Engelm. var. caespitosa Engelm. Pl. Lindh. II, Bost. Jour. Nat. Hist. 6: 200. 1850, name for the typical variety according to Engelmann's custom, but the varietal epithet superfluous when published and then illegitimate. Echinocactus similis Poselger, Allg. Gartenz. 21: 107. 1853. M. nuttallii Engelm. var. caespitosa Engelm. Proc. Amer. Acad. 3: 265. 1857 (preprint, 1856), based upon M. similis, which was abandoned in 1857 the epithet caespitosa considered to be newly published in 1857 (cf. also Engelm. in Emory, Rept. U.S. & Mex. Bound. Surv. 2: Cactaceae pl. 74, f. 7. 1859); S. Watson, Bibl. Index N. Amer. Bot. 1: 402. 1878. Cactus missouriensis (Sweet) Kuntze var. similis Coulter, Contr. U.S. Nat. Herb. 3: 111. 1894. M. missouriensis Sweet var. similis Engelm. ex K. Schum. Gesamtb. Kakteen 498. 1898, incorrectly ascribed to Engelmann. M. missouriensis Sweet f. similis Schelle, Handb. Kakteenkultur 241. 1907. M. missouriensis Sweet f. caespitosa Schelle, loc. cit. Cactus similis Small, Fl. S.E. U.S. 812. 1903. Coryphantha similis Britton & Rose in Britton & Brown, Illustr. Fl. ed. 2. 2: 671. 1913. Neobesseya similis Britton & Rose, Cactaceae 4: 52. 1923. Coryphantha missouriensis (Sweet) Britton & Rose var. caespitosa L. Benson,Cactus & Succ. Jour. 41: 189. 1969. "Sandstone rocks, near Industry [Austin County, Texas]." LECTOTYPE (Benson, loc. cit.): "Cult. in hort Göbel, St. Louis from Texas near Industry. Coll. by F. Lindheimer, May, 1846," and "Industry, Texas," Mo (2 sheets, only flowers and seeds). Typical specimen for vegetative characters: F. Lindheimer in 1850, Mo. See Suppl.

Neobesseya roseiflora Lahmann ex Turner, Cactus & Succ. Jour. Gt. Brit. 6: 2. 1937, nom. nud.; 6: 42. f. 1. 1938, nom. nud.; Cactus & Succ. Jour. 11: 72. 1939, nom. nud. (no Latin diagnosis). Mammillaria ros[e]iflora Weniger, Cacti S. W. 124. 1970, nom. nud. (Art. 33). "...Eight miles west of Tulsa, Oklahoma...Type plant in the New York Botanical Garden." Specimen not found. Plants from the type locality of var. caespitosa (Wiegand, Pom) have red pigmentation in the petaloid perianth parts, as in "Neobesseya notesteinii," cf. var. missouriensis.

KANSAS. RILEY CO. J. B. Norton 183, Oct. 12, 1895; Roscoe H. Pond [Pound], May 29, 1897, Pom, NY. COWLEY CO. D. Weniger 651, UNM. WILSON CO. W. H. Haller in 1896, NY.

ARKANSAS. Red River, Pitcher in 1830, NY.

LOUISIANA (presumably in the state, not the earlier much larger territory). Leavenworth, NY.

15d. Coryphantha missouriensis var. robustior (Engelmann) L. Benson

Mammillaria similis Engelm. var. robustior Engelm. Pl. Lindh. II, Bost. Jour. Nat. Hist. 6: 200. 1850. M. nuttallii Engelm. var. robustior Engelm. Proc. Amer. Acad. 3: 265. 1857 (preprint, 1856). M. missouriensis Sweet var. robustior S. Watson, Bibl. Ind. N. Amer. Bot. 1: 403. 1878. Cactus missouriensis (Sweet) Kuntze var. robustior Coulter, Contr. U.S. Nat. Herb. 3: 111. 1894. M. wissmannii Hildmann ex K. Schum. Gesamtb. Kakteen 498. 1898, nom. nov. Cactus robustior Small, Fl. S.E. U.S. 812. 1903. Neobesseya wissmannii Britton & Rose, Cactaceae 4: 52. 1923. Coryphantha wissmannii Berger, Kakteen 278. 1929. N. robustior Lahman, Cactus & Succ. Jour. 7: 4. 1935; W. T. Marshall, Cactus & Succ. Jour. 19 (3): insert. 1947. Coryphantha missouriensis (Sweet) Britton & Rose var. robustior L. Benson, Cactus & Succ. Jour. 41: 190. 1969. According to Engelmann, Proc. Amer. Acad. 3: 265. 1857 (preprint, 1856), "...from the Canadian River to the Colorado River of Texas." LECTOTYPE (Benson, loc. cit.): "Pierdenales [Perdenales River, Texas], F. Lindheimer, May, 1846," Mo (flowers); Lindheimer in 1845, Mo (seeds). See Suppl.

TEXAS. HALE CO. Near Hale Center, Shinners 18637, SMU. YOUNG CO. Ft. Belknap, S. Hayes in 1858, Mo (box). DENTON CO. Roanoke, Shinners 14912, SMU. TARRANT CO. 25 mi. NW of Ft. Worth, Parks & Cory 32121, TAES. BLANCO CO [?]. Pierdenales [Perdenales] River, Lindheimer in 1845 and 1846, Mo. TRAVIS CO. Near Austin, Coville 1800, US (box). BEXAR CO. N of San Antonio, B. Mackensen in 1908, US (including 2 boxes).

17. Ariocarpus

Ariocarpus, as genus, Scheidw. Bull. Acad. Sci. Brux. 5: 491. 1838. Type species: Ariocarpus retusus Scheidw. (lectotype, Britton & Rose, Cactaceae 3: 80. 1922).

Anhalonium, as genus, Lemaire, Cact. Gen. Sp. Nov. 1. 1839. Anhalonium, as subgenus of Mammillaria, Engelm. in Emory, Rept. U.S. & Mex. Bound. Surv. 2: Cactaceae 17. pl. 16. 1859. Type species: Anhalonium prismaticum Lemaire.

Roseocactus, as genus, Berger, Jour. Wash. Acad. Sci. 15: 45. 1925. Roseocactus, as subgenus of Ariocarpus W. T. Marshall, Cactus & Succ. Jour. 18: 55. 1946. Type species: Mammillaria fissurata Engelm. (= Ariocarpus fissuratus [Engelm.] K. Schum.).

Neogomesia, as genus, Castañeda, Cactus & Succ. Jour. 13: 98. 1941. Type species: Neogomesia agavoides Castañeda.

1. Ariocarpus fissuratus (Engelmann) K. Schumann

Mammillaria fissurata Engelm. Proc. Amer. Acad. 3: 270. 1857 (preprint, 1856); in Emory, U.S. & Mex. Bound. Surv. Cactaceae 18. pl. 16. 1859. Anhalonium fissuratum Engelm. in Emory, U.S. & Mex. Bound. Surv. Cactaceae 75. 1859. Ariocarpus fissuratus K. Schum. in Engler & Prantl, Natürl. Pflanzenf. 3, 6a: 195. 1894. Roseocactus fissuratus Berger, Jour. Wash. Acad. Sci. 5: 43.

1925. "...Fairy Springs, [near]...mouth of the Pecos, and between that river and the San Pedro [Texas], Schott, Bigelow:...cañon of the Rio Grande, Parry." LECTOTYPE (Anderson, Amer. Jour. Bot. 50: 730. 1964): "Rio Bravo del Norte [Rio Grande], near Fairy Springs," Schott in October, 1852, Mo (only flowers). DUPLICATE: F42675 (Schott herbarium) (tubercle and flower remains). Plant as a whole was illustrated well in the original publication.

Anhalonium engelmannii Lemaire, Cactées 42. 79. pl. 1868. "Trouvé par Engelmann, sur des collines calcaires, près du confluent du Pecos et Rio-Grande, etc." "Croit sur les collines sabloneuses, calcaires, compactes, près du Fairy Springs (Source des Fées), non loin de l'embouchure du Pecos, et entre ce fleuve de le San Pedro, à une altitude plus élevée, sur les rochers du Cañon du Rio Grande; là elle fleurit en septembre et octobre." As pointed out by Anderson, loc. cit., Lemaire's figure is copied with reversal and some transposition, from Engelmann's. LECTOTYPE (Anderson, loc. cit.): the lectotype of Mammillaria fissurata Engelmann, Mo. Duplicate: F42675. (As above).

TEXAS. MAVERICK CO. Eagle Pass, Wright in 1851, GH. WEBB CO. Laredo, Newberry in 1906, NY (fl.). CAMERON CO. Clover 1893, US.

18. Mammillaria

Mammillaria, as genus, Haw. Syn. Pl. Succ. 177. 1812, not Stackhouse in 1809. Mammillaria (spelled in this way) is a nomen conservandum under the International Code of Botanical Nomenclature. Type species: Mammillaria simplex Haw., based upon Cactus mammillaris L.

Neomammillaria, as genus, Britton & Rose, Cactaceae 4: 65. 1923, nom. nov., nom. superfl. (Mammillaria being conserved). Type species: Mammillaria simplex Haw., based upon Cactus mammillaris L. Cactus L. is rejected under the International Code of Botanical Nomenclature. Mammillaria is the (family) type genus.

Dolichothele, as subgenus, K. Schum. Gesamtb. Kakteen 506. 1898; as genus, Britton & Rose, Cactaceae 4: 61. 1923. Type species: Mammillaria longimamma DC.

Phellosperma, as genus, Britton & Rose, Cactaceae 4: 60. 1923; as subgenus, Fosberg. Bull. So. Calif. Acad. Sci. 30: 54, 57. 1931. Type species: Mammillaria tetrancistra Engelm.

Chilita, as genus, Orcutt, Cactography 2. 1926, nom. subnud., but valid; as subgenus, Moran, Gentes Herb. 8: 324. 1953. Type species: Mammillaria grahamii Engelm.

Ebnerella, as genus, F. Buxbaum, Österr. Bot. Zeitschr. 98: 88. 1951. Type species: Mammillaria wildii Dietr.

Leptocladia, as genus, F. Buxbaum, Österr. Bot. Zeitschr. 98: 82. 1951, later homonym. Leptocladodia, as genus, F. Buxbaum ex Byles, Nat. Cactus & Succ. Jour. 10: 58. 1954; Dict. Gen. & Sub-Gen. Cact. 1954; Österr. Bot. Zeitschr. 101. 601. 1954, nom. nov.; as subgenus, Bravo, Cact. Suc. Mex. 17: 120. 1972. Type species: Leptocladia elongata (DC.) F. Buxbaum (= Mammillaria elongata DC.).

1. Mammillaria longimamma DeCandolle

1a. Mammillaria longimamma var. sphaerica (A. Dietrich) K. Brandegee

Mammillaria sphaerica A. Dietr. in Poselger, Allg. Gartenz. 21: 94. 1853. Cactus sphaericus Kuntze, Rev. Gen. Pl. 1: 261. 1891. M. longimamma DC. var. sphaerica K. Brandegee in Bailey, Stand Cyclop. Hort. 2: 975. 1900; L. Benson, Cactus & Succ. Jour. 41: 128 (inadvertance corrected, 190). 1969. Dolichothele sphaerica Britton & Rose, Cactaceae 4: 61. 1923. Neomammillaria sphaerica Fosberg, Bull. So. Calif. Acad. Sci. 30: 58. 1931. "In der Nähe der Meers bei Corpus Christi in Texas." NEOTYPE designation: The following surviving specimen (cf. Engelm. Proc. Amer. Acad. 3: 264. 1857 (preprint, 1856); in Emory, Rept. U.S. & Mex. Bound. Surv. 2: Cactaceae 9. 1859). "Rio Bravo del Norte [Rio Grande]; Eagle Pass [Maverick Co., Texas]. Hillsides," Arthur Schott, March, 1852, Mo.

Mammillaria longimamma var. *longimamma* (not in U.S.)

Mammillaria longimamma DC. Mém Mus. Hist. Nat. Paris 17: 113. 1828. Cactus longimamma Kuntze, Rev. Gen. Pl. 1: 260. 1891. Dolichothele longimamma Britton & Rose, Cactaceae 4: 62. 1923. Neomammillaria longimamma Fosberg, Bull. So. Calif. Acad. Sci. 30: 58. 1931. "...In Mexico. Coulter, n° 30." No specimen in Herbarium of Trinity College, Dublin.

2. Mammillaria heyderi Mühlenpfordt

2a. Mammillaria heyderi var. heyderi

Mammillaria heyderi Mühlenpfordt, Allg. Gartenz. 16: 20. Jan. 15, 1848. Cactus heyderi Kuntze, Rev. Gen. Pl. 1: 260. 1891.

Neomammillaria heyderi Britton & Rose, Cactaceae 4: 75. 1923.
"...Durch Herrn Dr. Roemer in Hildsheim aus dem nördl. [central]
Texas mitgebracht." According to Roemer, "Am Llanoflusse," Texas.

Mammillaria applanata Engelm. in Wisliz. Mem. Tour No. Mex.
105. ca. Apr. 2, 1848 (for publication date cf. Echinocereus
triglochidiatus, Documentation section), nom. nud., mere incidental
mention during discussion and without description or diagnostic
characters of this proposed species alone (Art. 34, example 3);
Pl. Lindh. II, Bost. Jour. Nat. Hist. 6: 198. 1850. M. heyderi
Mühlenpfordt var. applanata Engelm, Proc. Amer. Acad. 3: 263.
1857 (preprint, 1856). M. heyderi Mühlenpfordt f. applanata
Schelle, Handb. Kakteenkultur 263. 1907. Neomammillaria applanata
Britton & Rose, Cactaceae 4: 76. 1923. M. gummifera Engelm. var.
applanata L. Benson, Cacti Ariz. ed. 3. 22, 150. 1969. "...The
Pierdenales [or Perdenales River], in Texas...." LECTOTYPE:
(Benson, loc. cit.): "On the Pierdenales, western [now central]
Texas," F. Lindheimer in 1845, Mo.

Mammillaria declivis A. Dietr. Allg. Gartenz. 18: 235. 1850.
"Habitat in Texas."

Mammillaria texensis Labouret, Monogr. Cact. 89. 1853.
Cactus texensis Kuntze, Rev. Gen. Pl. 1: 261. 1891. "Patrie.
Le Texas, introduit récemment par M. Trecul, naturaliste et
voyageur Zélé du Muséum de Paris."

ARIZONA. COCHISE CO. Bisbee, Peebles SF 922, Ariz; San
Bernardino Ranch, Guadalupe Mts., L. Benson 10272, Pom, Ariz.

Mammillaria heyderi Mühlenpfordt var. bullingtoniana Castetter, Pierce, & Schwerin, Cactus & Succ. Jour. 48: 139. 1976.
"HOLOTYPE: Cliff [Grant Co.], N. M. [New Mexico], Prince Pierce
1638, April 5, 1963, UNM 33608." TYPE: UNM 33608.

2b. Mammillaria heyderi var. hemisphaerica Engelmann

Mammillaria hemisphaerica Engelm. in Wisliz. Mem. Tour No.
Mex. 106. ca. Apr. 2, 1848 (for publication date, cf. Echinocereus triglochidiatus, Documentation section), nom. nud., mere
incidental mention during discussion and without description or
diagnostic characters of this proposed species alone (Art. 34,
example 3); Pl. Lindh. II. Bost. Jour. Nat. Hist. 6: 199. 1850.
M. heyderi Mühlenpfordt var. hemisphaerica Engelm. Proc. Amer.
Acad. 3: 263. 1857 (preprint, 1856). Cactus heyderi (Mühlenpfordt) Kuntze var. hemisphaericus Coulter, Contr. U.S. Nat. Herb.
3: 97. 1894. C. hemisphaericus Small, Fl. S.E. U.S. 811. 1903.
M. heyderi Mühlenpfordt f. hemisphaerica Schelle, Handb. Kakteenkultur 263. 1907. Neomammillaria hemisphaerica Britton & Rose,
Cactaceae 4: 75. 1923. M. gummifera Engelm. var. hemisphaerica
L. Benson, Cactus & Succ. Jour. 41: 128. 1969. "Below Matamoros,
on the Rio Grande ...St. Louis Volunteers in 1846; flowers [in
St. Louis] in May." LECTOTYPE (Benson, loc. cit.): "'Cult. in
Göbels Garden, St. Louis, from Matamoros, [St. Louis Volunteers
in 1846],' flowers and fruit in 1847," Mo. Typical specimen (for
other parts): Harlingen, Cameron Co., Texas, Richard O. Albert,
Jan. 25, 1959, Pom 297247.

TEXAS. HOWARD CO. 5 mi. E of Forgan, D. Weniger 195, May
17, 1963, UNM. JIM WELLS CO. Alice, R. O. Albert, Aug. 16, 1958,
Pom. NEUCES CO. Corpus Christi Bay, Heller 1531, US. KLEBERG CO.
SE of Kingsville, A. D. Wood 601, Pom. HIDALGO CO. Penitas, 8 mi.
W. of Mission, Clover 1885, Tex, Ariz. WILLACY CO. 10 mi. SE of
Lyford, R. O. Albert, May 11, 1958, Pom. CAMERON CO. 8 mi. W. of
Boca Chica Beach, D. Weniger 78, March 20, 1963, UNM.

2c. Mammillaria heyderi var. meiacantha (Engelmann) L. Benson

Mammillaria meiacantha Engelm. Proc. Amer. Acad. 3: 263.
1857 (preprint, 1856); U.S. Senate Rept. Expl. & Surv. R. R. Route
Pacific Ocean. Botany 4: 27. 1857; in Emory, Rept. U.S. & Mex.
Bound. Surv. 2: Cactaceae 9. pl. 9, f. 1-3. 1859. Cactus mei-
acanthus Kuntze, Rev. Gen. Pl. 1: 260. 1891. Neomammillaria
meiacantha Britton & Rose, Cactaceae 4: 84. 1923. M. melano-
centra Poselger var. meiacantha Craig, Mam. Handb. 66. 1945. M.
gummifera Engelm. var. meiacantha (Engelm.) L. Benson, Cacti
Ariz. ed. 3. 22, 151. 1969. Mammillaria heyderi Poselger var.
meiacantha L. Benson, Cactus & Succ. Jour. 47: 40. 1975. "Cedar
Plains from the Llano Estacado to the Pecos, Sept. 23-27. 1853."
LECTOTYPE (Benson, loc. cit.): "Cedar plains east of the Pecos,"
J. M. Bigelow, Sept. 27, 1853. Mo.

ARIZONA. COCHISE CO. Texas Canyon, Dragoon Mts., A. Blackburn, April, 1964, Pom (photograph).

2d. Mammillaria heyderi var. macdougalii (Rose) L. Benson

Mammillaria macdougalii Rose in Bailey, Stand. Cyclop. Hort.
4: 1982. 1916. Neomammillaria macdougalii Britton & Rose, Cactaceae 4: 74. 1923. M. heyderi Mühlenpfordt var. macdougalii
L. Benson, Proc. Calif. Acad. Sci. IV. 25: 265. 1944. M. gummifera Engelm. var. macdougalii L. Benson, Cacti Ariz. ed. 3. 22,
151. 1969. "...Mountains about Tucson, Ariz., ...D. T. MacDougal
...." LECTOTYPE (Benson, loc. cit., 1969): "Santa Catalina Mts.
[Pima Co.], Arizona," D. T. MacDougal, Nov., 1909, US 1821109
(1 small juvenile plant and material in 2 cartons). DUPLICATE:
Pom 306413.

Mammillaria heyderi var. *gummifera* (Engelmann) L. Benson (not in U.S.)

Mammillaria gummifera Engelm. in Wisliz. Mem. Tour. No. Mex.
106. ca. Apr. 2, 1848 (for publication date, cf. Echinocereus
triglochidiatus, Documentation section; the epithet gummifera together with incidental mention of applanata and hemisphaerica).
Cactus gummifer Kuntze, Rev. Gen. Pl. 260. 1891. Neomammillaria
gummifera Britton & Rose, Cactaceae 3: 74. 1923. M. heyderi
Poselger var. gummifera (Engelm.) L. Benson, Cactus & Succ. Jour.
47: 40. 1975. TYPE: "Cosiquiriachi [Cosihuiriachi," now a
ghost town], Dr. Wislizenus. Oct. 1848," Mo. ISOTYPE: Pom 317822
(loose spines). TOPOTYPE: Cosihuiriachi, Chihuahua, Rose 11667,
US (box); spines as slender as in var. applanata, reddish-tan,
curving a little, 1.5 cm long, about as in the type but not blackened (during storage).

3. Mammillaria prolifera (Miller) Haworth

3a. Mammillaria prolifera var. texana (Engelmann) Borg

Mammillaria multiceps Salm-Dyck, Cact. Hort. Dyck 1849. 81.
1850. Cactus multiceps Kuntze, Rev. Gen. Pl. 160. 1891. Neomammillaria multiceps Britton & Rose, Cactaceae 4: 125. 1923.
M. prolifera (Miller) Haw. f. multiceps Schelle, Kakteen 303.
1926. Chilita multiceps Orcutt, Cactography 2. 1926. M. prolifera (Miller) Haw. var. multiceps Borg, Cacti 316. 1937. Ebnerella multiceps F. Buxbaum, Österr. Bot. Zeitschr. 98: 90. 1951.
No locality or specimen. LECTOTYPE designation: "Hort. Dyck,
Jan., 1857," Mo 1797124, material received by Engelmann from Salm-
Dyck.

Mammillaria pusilla (DC.) Sweet var. texana Engelm. Proc.
Amer. Acad. 3: 261. 1857 (preprint, 1856); in Emory, Rept. U.S.
& Mex. Bound. Surv. 2: Cactaceae 5. pl. 5. 1859. M. texana Young,
Familiar Lessons Bot. & Pl. Texas 279. 1873. Cactus stellatus
Willd. var. texanus Coulter, Contr. U.S. Nat. Herb. 3: 108. 1894.
C. texanus Small, Fl. S.E. U.S. 812. 1903. M. pusilla (DC.)
Sweet f. texana Schelle, Handb. Kakteenkultur 249. 1907. M. mul-
ticeps Salm-Dyck var. texana Engelm. ex Knuth in Backeburg & Knuth,
Kaktus-ABC 384. 1935, incorrectly ascribed to Engelmann. M. prolifera (Miller) Haw. var. texana Borg, Cacti 316. 1937. M. prolifera (Miller) Haw. f. texana Krainz, Kakteen, Lief. 27: C VIII c.
1964. "From Eagle Pass to Santa Rosa, Dr. Bigelow; and, according
to Dr. Poselger, common on the Rio Grande below." Original material not found, Mo.

TEXAS. VAL VERDE CO. Langtry, Rose, Mar. 27, 1908, US, July
4, 1908, US, G. L. Fisher, July 18, 1922, US; Devils River bridge,
Rose in 1908, US, Rose & Fitch, Oct. 16, 1913, US, G. C. Nealley,
F, D. Weniger 39, Feb. 4, 1963, UNM. WEBB CO. Laredo. J. N. &
J. S. Rose, Aug. 6-7, 1906, US, B. Mackensen, Dec. 18, 1909, US.
REAL CO. 5 mi. N of Leakey, D. Weniger 48, Feb. 12, 1953, UNM.
BEXAR CO. San Antonio, B. Mackensen, June 3, 1910, US (2).
KINNEY CO. Anacacho Mts., D. Weniger 506, March, 1906, UNM.
BROOKS CO. 7 mi. W of Rachal, R. O. Albert, Aug. 31, 1958, Pom.
HIDALGO CO. Near Sullivan City, L. L. & A. A. Lundell 9842, Mich.

Mammillaria prolifera var. *prolifera* (not in U.S.)

Cactus proliferus Miller, Gard. Dict. ed. 8. Sp. No. 6. 1768.
C. mammillaris L. var. prolifer Aiton, Hort. Kew 2: 150. 1789.
Mammillaria prolifera Haw. Syn. Pl. Succ. 177. 1812. Neomammillaria prolifera, Britton & Rose, Cactaceae 4: 124. 1923. Chilita
prolifera Orcutt, Cactography 2. 1926. Ebnerella prolifera
F. Buxbaum, Österr. Bot. Zeitschr. 98: 90. 1951. "...Natives of
the West Indies...."

4. Mammillaria lasiacantha Engelmann

Mammillaria lasiacantha Engelm. Proc. Amer. Acad. 3: 261.
1857 (preprint, 1856); in Emory, Rept. U.S. & Mex. Bound. Surv. 2:
Cactaceae 5, pl. 3. 1859. M. lasiacantha Engelm. var. minor
Engelm., loc. cit., 1859, this being the "typical" variety. Cactus lasiacanthus Kuntze, Rev. Gen. Pl. 1: 259. 1891. Neomammillaria lasiacantha Britton & Rose, Cactaceae 4: 128. 1923. Chilita
lasiacantha Orcutt, Cactography 2. 1926. Ebnerella lasiacantha
F. Buxbaum, Österr. Bot. Zeitschr. 98: 89. 1951. "About Leon
Spring and Camanche Spring, west of the Pecos,...C. Wright. Flowers April and May." LECTOTYPE designation: Texas, Wright, Mo
(sheet and box). DUPLICATE: Pom 317821. Pubescence of the spines
is variable, as in field populations. Apparently the type material
for vars. lasiacantha and denudata (below) was selected from among
the plants in the same box.

Mammillaria lasiacantha Engelm. var. denudata Engelm. in
Emory, Rept. U.S. & Mex. Bound. Surv. 2: Cactaceae 5. pl. 4. 1859.
Cactus lasiacanthus (Engelm.) Kuntze var. denudatus Coulter,
Contr. U.S. Nat. Herb. 3: 100. 1894. Neomammillaria denudata
Britton & Rose, Cactaceae 4: 129. 1923. M. lasiacantha Engelm.
f. denudata Schelle, Handb. Kakteenkultur 248. 1907. M. lasi-
acantha denudata Quehl, Monatschr. Kakteenk. 19: 79. 1909.
Chilita denudata Orcutt, Cactography 2. 1926. M. denudata
Engelm. ex Berger, Kakteen 288. 1929, erroneously ascribed to
Engelmann. Ebnerella denudata F. Buxbaum, Österr. Bot. Zeitschr.
98: 91. 1951. "About Leon Spring and Camanche Spring, west of
the Pecos,... C. Wright. Flowers April and May." LECTOTYPE
designation: Wright in 1852, Mo. (2 sheets and box). DUPLICATE:
Pom 317820.

5. Mammillaria pottsii Scheer

Mammillaria pottsii Scheer in Salm-Dyck, Cact. Hort. Dyck. 1849. 104. 1850, not Echinocactus pottsianus Poselger, Allg. Gartenz. 21: 107. 1853, which was Coryphantha strobiliformis. Cactus pottsii Kuntze, Rev. Gen. Pl. 1: 261. 1891. Neomammillaria pottsii Britton & Rose, Cactaceae 4: 136. 1923. Coryphantha pottsii Orcutt, Circular to Cactus Fanciers 1922; Berger, Kakteen 279. 1929. Chilita pottsii Orcutt, Cactography 2. 1926. Leptocladia leona F. Buxbaum, Sukkulentenkunde 5: 4. 1954, nom. nov. (based upon Chilita pottsii Orcutt, not M. leona Poselger [loc. cit. 94]). No locality or specimen. LECTOTYPE designation: "Mammillaria Pottsii vera – original coll. Dyck," Jan., 1857, the date of receipt by Engelmann who had written (then probably in press), "I have not seen this plant,..." Proc. Amer. Acad. 3: 268. 1857 (preprint, 1856); cf. Britton & Rose, Cactaceae 4: 137. 1923, Mo (unnumbered). DUPLICATE: US. The type locality is indicated by the following statements in the literature, which appeared shortly after the name was published: Walpers, Anales Botanices Systematicae 5: 37. 1851, "Hab Tex ad fl. Rio Grande, infra Laredo usque...Chihuahua." Engelmann, loc. cit., "Texas on the Rio Grande, below Laredo, and from there to Chihuahua." Possibly the original horticultural material is represented by clusters of spines with the label, "Coll. Dyck," Jan. 1857, Mo; photographs NY, US, and 2 spine clusters, US. This may or may not represent living material studied by Scheer at Kew. Typical specimen (for other characters): side canyon of the Rio Grande between Lajitas and Redford, Presidio Co., Texas, Norman H. Boke, July 12, 1955, Pom 285729.

Later Poselger published the name combination Echinocactus pottsianus apparently because in 1853 he thought another of his collections (of Coryphantha strobiliformis) to have been Mammillaria pottsii, and he thought this not to be a Mammillaria but an Echinocactus. This plant is represented also in the Engelmann Herbarium by a specimen designated (cf. under Coryphantha strobiliformis) as a lectotype. At the same time Poselger published the name Mammillaria leona for another collection of M. pottsii (next paragraph).

Mammillaria leona Poselger, Allg. Gartenz. 21: 94. 1853. "In der Nähe von La Rinconada auf Bergen, im Staate Nueva Leon." LECTOTYPE designation: On 2 sheets, one labelled "Poselger leg.," the other "Pos," Mo 1797122, 1797123.

6. Mammillaria dioica K. Brandegee

Mammillaria dioica K. Brandegee ex Orcutt, W. Amer. Sci. 9. 1884, nom. nud.; Erythea 5: 115. 1897. Neomammillaria dioica Britton & Rose, Cactaceae 4: 158. 1923. Ebernella dioica F. Buxbaum, Österr. Bot. Zeitschr. 98: 89. 1951. Chilita dioica F. Buxbaum, Sukkulentenkunde 5: 17. 1954. "From San Diego a short distance north but southward to Cape San Lucas always so far as known near the coast...." No specimens collected prior to 1897 found in Brandegee Herbarium, UC. NEOTYPE designation: "1/2 mile east of the ocean and 1/2 mile north of Mexico; San Diego County, California; 50 feet elevation, Lyman Benson 14,338," Pom 285765.

Mammillaria incerta Parish in Jepson, Fl. Calif. 2: 549. 1936. Mammillaria dioica K. Brandegee var. incerta Munz, Aliso 4: 94. 1958. "Vallecito, Parish 450 (type)...." NEOTYPE designation: "Vallecito," S. B. & W. F. Parish 450 [or 460], DS. DUPLICATES: NY, Ph (plant on right), US. The number appears also as 460, used as well for a coastal collection. Parish's numbering of specimens was inconsistent and according to at least two systems.

7. Mammillaria mainiae K. Brandegee

Mammillaria mainiae K. Brandegee, Zöe 5: 31. 1900. Neomammillaria mainiae Britton & Rose, Cactaceae 4: 154. 1923. Chilita mainiae Orcutt, Cactography 2. 1926. Ebnerella mainiae F. Buxbaum, Österr. Bot. Zeitschr. 98: 89. 1951. "Named for the collector, Mrs. F. M. Main who found it in Sonora, south of Nogales." Twin border towns, Nogales, are in Arizona and Sonora. No collection by Mrs. Main from Mexican side found in Brandegee Collection, UC. LECTOTYPE designation: "Sonora near Nogales," Mrs. F. M. Main, US 1821084. DUPLICATE: Pom 311295.

ARIZONA. PIMA CO. Near Fresnal, Baboquivari Mts., Peebles SF 148, Mar. 30, 1927, Ariz; Papago Reservation, W of Baboquivari Mts., Mr. and Mrs. Ed Gay, in 1969, Pom; Baboquivari Mts., A. J. Deutschman, Jr., May 25, 1970, Pom. Although the type was collected near Nogales, Sonora, no specimens clearly from adjacent Nogales, Arizona, have been seen.

8. Mammillaria microcarpa Engelmann

Mammillaria microcarpa Engelm. in Emory, Notes Military Reconn. Ft. Leavenworth to San Diego. App. 2. 157. f. 3. 1848. Neomammillaria microcarpa Britton & Rose, Cactaceae 4: 155. 1923. Ebnerella microcarpa F. Buxbaum, Österr. Bot. Zeitschr. 98: 89. 1951. Chilita microcarpa F. Buxbaum, Sukkulentenkunde 5: 12. 1954. "3. Mammillaria microcarpa, November 4th, 1846, abundant." According to Britton & Rose, Cactaceae 4: 155-156. 1923, "Mammillaria microcarpa was based on a drawing made by J. M. Stanly, the artist on W. H. Emory's...expedition...sent to...Engelmann...with the following note: 'November 4, 1846, abundant.' From Emory's narrative map...on that date his camp was on the eastern side of the Gila and only one day's trip by pack train from the mouth of the San Pedro [at Winkelman, southern tip of Gila County, Arizona]...." No specimen collected. NEOTYPE designation: "On upper terrace on right bank of Gila River in s. e. corner, section 15, t. 4 s. R 16 E. (Christmas Triangle). From a grove of cactus in which we believe Emory camped, Nov. 4, 1846," Mrs. Ruth C. Ross, US. DUPLICATE: NY. TOPOTYPE: L. Benson, 16623, Pom.

Mammillaria grahamii Engelm. var. arizonica Quehl, Monatss. Kakteenk. 6: 44. 1896. Horticultural plant of unknown origin.

Neomammillaria milleri Britton & Rose, Cactaceae 4: 156. f. 184a. 1923. Chilita milleri Orcutt, Cactography 2. 1926. Mammillaria milleri Bödeker, Mam. Vergl. Schlüss. 30. 1933. M. microcarpa Engelm. var. milleri W. T. Marshall, Arizona's Cactuses 104. 1950. "...C. R. Orcutt near Phoenix (No. 559a, type ...summer of 1922...." "Figure 184a is from a photograph of the type, collected by Mr. Orcutt." TYPE: US 1821083. ISOTYPE: NY (but as Orcutt 22.179, Rose's greenhouse number, normally 22. 179, meaning number 179 of 1922).

Mammillaria microcarpa Engelm. var. auricarpa W. T. Marshall, Arizona's Cactuses 106. 1950. "...W. H. Earle near Pinnacle Peak, Maricopa County...Botanical Garden Herbarium No. 101." Specimen not found, Des.

Hybrid swarms from interbreeding of Mammillaria microcarpa (Arizona Desert) and M. grahamii (Desert Grassland) occur here and there along the border zones of these floristic types. These are represented in the following collections: ARIZONA. YAVAPAI CO. Yarnell Hill, 5 mi. above Congress Junction, 3,800 ft., E. L. Benson 324, Pom. PINAL CO. Summit, 3,300 ft., on U.S. 80, 4 or 5 mi. NW of Oracle Junction, L. & R. L. Benson 14683B, Pom. PIMA CO. Loop Drive, 3 mi. N of Headquarters, Organ Pipe Cactus Nat. Mon., 2,000 ft., (here in the Arizona Desert), L. Benson 14871, Pom.

9. Mammillaria thornberi Orcutt

Mammillaria thornberi Orcutt, West. Amer. Sci. 12: 162. 1902. Chilita thornberi Orcutt, Cactography 2. 1926. "Type, Orcutt, No. 2583; Arizona." The only known collection by Orcutt, K, consists of only 2 spines, and it is without locality or collection date, marked only as "received Aug. 24, 1903." Correspondence in the folder for this species, US, indicates, letter from C. R. Orcutt to J. N. Rose, April 3, 1922, "The type locality of Mammillaria thornberi is Casa Grande, Arizona...." NEOTYPE designation: 15 miles W of the Silver Bell Mountains, Pima Co., Arizona [about 25 miles S of Casa Grande]; 1,800 feet, Lyman Benson 10606, February 2, 1941, Pom 273934. DUPLICATE: Ariz.

For many years this species was known as Mammillaria fasciculata Engelm., a name applied actually to Echinocereus fasciculatus.

ARIZONA. PINAL CO. San Tan Mts., A. E. Robinson SF 161, March 20, 1927, Ariz; Sacaton, A. E. Robinson, March 20, 1927, US; 5 mi. S of Casa Grande, Peebles SF 14542, Ariz; "On the Gila near the Pimos [sic!] villages, 40 mile desert near White's Mill," Palmer, Sept. 9, 1867, Mo (2). PIMA CO. Quitovaquita, Harbison, Nov. 28, 1939, SD; near Lukeville, L. Benson 16708, Pom; 10 mi. E of Highway 85, Mexican Boundary, W. F. Steenbergh, Jan. 26, 1962, Organ Pipe Cactus Nat. Mon. Herb., Pom; mesa E of Quijotoa Mts., F. E. Lloyd, Aug. 3, 1906, NY; Sells, R. T. Craig 183, Pom (photograph); Bigfields, Papago Reservation, Peebles SF 14542, Ariz; 15 mi. W of Silver Bell, L. Benson 10606, Pom, Ariz; Sierrita, Shreve, Apr. 20, 1921, NY, US.

10. Mammillaria viridiflora (Britton & Rose) Bödecker

Neomammillaria viridiflora Britton & Rose, Cactaceae 4: 153. 1923. Chilita viridiflora Orcutt, Cactography 2. 1926. Mammillaria viridiflora Bödeker, Mamm.-Vergl.-Schlüssel 36. 1933. M. wilcoxii var. viridiflora W. T. Marshall in Marshall & Bock, Cactaceae 182. 1941. M. wrightii Engelm. var. viridiflora W. T. Marshall, Arizona's Cactuses 100. 1950. "...C. R. Orcutt on Superior-Miami Highway, near Boundary Monument, between Pinal and Gila counties, Arizona, 4,700 feet elevation, July, 1922 (No. 608, type)...." TYPE: US 1821085. ISOTYPE: NY.

Mammillaria orestera L. Benson, Cacti Ariz. ed. 3. 22, 155. 1969. TYPE: "Santa Catalina Mountains, Pima County, Arizona, Evelyn, Lyman, & Robert L. Benson 14,864, April 9, 1952," Pom 285759.

This species has been discussed in detail by Dale A. Zimmerman and Allan D. Zimmerman, Cactus & Succ. Jour. 47: 113-115. f. 1-5. 1975; 49: 23-34, 51-62. f. 1-18. 1977.

ARIZONA. Mohave Co. Hualpai Mt., ca. 4,800 ft., D.A. & A.D. Zimmerman, 1,990, W. N. Mex. Univ., 2,718, W. N. Mex. Univ. Gila Co. W. of Miami, 1,340 mi., D.A. & A.D. Zimmerman 2,553, W. N. Mex. Univ. Graham Co. Galiuro Mts., Toumey, June 16, 1895, US; road to Ft. Grant from Safford, w. side Graham Mts., L. Benson 16,674, Pom; road to Mt. Graham, s.w. of Swift Trail Junction, D.A. & A.D.

Zimmerman 1,909, W. N. Mex. Univ. (2); about 20 mi. w. of Duncan, 1,220 m., D.A. & A.D. Zimmerman 2,472, W. N. Mex. Univ. Pinal Co. N.w. of Riverside, N. Paradine, prior to 1973, W. N. Mex. Univ.; 27 mi. e. of Florence, D.A. & A.D. Zimmerman, 2,560, W. N. Mex. Univ.; Picketpost Mt., 2,500 ft., D.A. & A.D. Zimmerman 1,907, W. N. Mex. Univ.; north of summit between Sonora and Superior, 3,500 ft., L. Benson 16,625, Pom; Pinal Mts., Superior-Miami Highway, Orcutt 608, July, 1922, US, Peebles SFl,026, May 30, 1937, Ariz. Pima Co. Sabino Canyon, 3,800 ft., L. Benson 8,873a, Pom; Upper Bear Creek, Santa Catalina Mts., 6,000 ft., L. Benson 11,087, Pom, Ariz; Soldier Trail Road, L., E.L., & R.L. Benson 14,864, Pom, below Vail Corral, 4,500 ft., L. Benson 11,059, Pom, Ariz; Santa Catalina Mts., 1,650 m. (5,400 ft.), Mt. Lemmon road, D.A. & A.D. Zimmerman 2,471, W. N. Mex. Univ. (2). Cochise Co. Texas Canyon, Little Dragoon Mts., D.A. & A.D. Zimmerman 2,553, W. N. Mex. Univ.; Bowie, Toumey, Dec. 20, 1896, US, May 11, 1897, US, Dec. 20, 1897, US (2); Chiricahua Mts., Toumey, US, UC. Two other collections from Bowie by Toumey must be rechecked: May 1, 1897, US and May 15, 1897, US.

NEW MEXICO. Grant Co. Mangas Springs, O.B. Metcalfe 797, US; Copperas Canyon, 12 mi. n. of Pinos Altos, 5,800 ft., D.A. & A.D. Zimmerman 2,643, W. N. Mex. Univ.; Bear Mountain, near Silver City, O.B. Metcalfe 819, US, UNM; Treasure Mt., 6 mi. w. of Silver City, D.A. & A.D. Zimmerman 2,496, W. N. Mex. Univ.; Burro Mts., O.B. Metcalfe 826, US; Little Burro Mts., near Tyrone, P. Pierce in 1959, UNM, 1,119, UNM, 1,621, UNM, L. Vortman, Mar. 29, 1964, UNM, L. & E.L. Benson 16,641, Pom; s. of turnoff to Tyrone Mine, D.A. & A.D. Zimmerman 1,893, W. N. Mex. Univ., 2,823, W. N. Mex. Univ. 2,364, W. N. Mex. Univ., 2,633 W. N. Mex. Univ., s. of Tyrone, D.A. & A.D. Zimmerman 1,879, W. N. Mex. Univ. Hidalgo Co. Skeleton Canyon, Peloncillo Mts., s.e. of Apache, Arizona, Castetter 1,830, UNM, 1,831, UNM, 1,832, UNM, 1,833, UNM, 1,834, UNM, 1,835, UNM, 1,836, UNM.

Plant of Uncertain Identity

Mammillaria chavezii Cowper, Nat. Cactus & Succ. Jour. 18: f. 1963, nom. nud. (no type specimen). "...Near Tyrone, New Mexico, during February, 1962." According to Edward F. Castetter, letter of August 2, 1971, the original locality has been destroyed by copper strip mining. Probably the plant discussed immediately above.

11. Mammillaria grahamii Engelmann

11a. Mammillaria grahamii var. grahamii

Mammillaria grahamii Engelm. Proc. Amer. Acad. 3: 262. 1857 (preprint, 1856); in Emory, Rept. U.S. & Mex. Bound. Surv. 2: Cactaceae 7. pl. 6, f. 1-8. 1859. Cactus grahamii Kuntze, Rev. Gen. Pl. 1: 260. 1891. Coryphantha grahamii Rydb. Fl. Rocky Mts. 581. 1917. Chilita grahamii Orcutt, Cactography 2. 1926. "Mountainous regions from El Paso, Charles Wright; southward and westward to the Gila, Dr. Parry; and Colorado, A. Schott; and up this latter river as far as William's River and Cactus Pass, Dr. Bigelow." LECTOTYPE designation: "Eastern slope of the mountains [Franklin Mts.] about El Paso," Charles Wright in 1852, Mo (including box). DUPLICATE: Pom 317833 (box) and probably, "Mountains near El Paso," Bound. Surv. in 1852, NY. A specially-collected TOPOTYPE is as follows: Lyman & Robert L. Benson 15545, Pom.

ARIZONA. YUMA CO. 12 mi. N of Roll, Wiggins 8625B, DS; Palm Canyon, Kofa Mts., Wiggins 8579, DS. YAVAPAI CO. Yarnell Hill, 5 mi. above Congress Jct., 3,500 ft., E. L. Benson 324A, Pom. MARICOPA CO. Gillespie Dam, Keck 4254, DS. PINAL CO. Summit on U.S. 80, 4 or 5 mi. NW of Oracle Jct. 3,300 ft., L. Benson 14863A, Pom. PIMA CO. (W). Loop Road 3 mi. N of Headquarters, Organ Pipe Cactus Nat. Mon., 2,000 ft., L. Benson 14871A, Pom; NE base of Quinlan Mts., H. W. Graham, June 29, 1927, DS. E. L. Benson 324A, L. Benson 14863A, and 14871A were parts of collections made in hybrid swarms of Mammillaria grahamii and M. microcarpa (see under M. microcarpa).

TEXAS. EL PASO CO. Several collections from the Franklin Mts. N of El Paso. PRESIDIO CO. S of the "Bad Lands," lower Capote Valley, Sierra Tierra Vieja, 900 m., L. C. Hinckley 1538, May 29, 1941, SMU.

11b. Mammillaria grahamii var. oliviae (Orcutt) L. Benson

Mammillaria oliviae Orcutt, West Amer. Sci. 12: 163. 1902. Neomammillaria oliviae Britton & Rose, Cactaceae 4: 135. 1923. Chilita oliviae Orcutt, Cactography 2. 1926. Ebnerella oliviae F. Buxbaum, Österr. Bot. Zeitschr. 98: 90. 1951. M. grahamii Engelm. var. oliviae L. Benson, Cacti Ariz. ed. 3. 22, 161. 1969. "Type, Orcutt, No. 2602: ...mountains and deserts of Arizona...." No specimen of this number found. According to a letter from Charles Russell Orcutt to J. N. Rose, March 4, 1921, the type locality is west of Vail and off the railway. LECTOTYPE designation: "Near Vail, Pima County, Arizona, [received at US, June, 1905] Charles Russell Orcutt in 1921 [year incorrect]," US 1821092 and material in a carton. DUPLICATE: Pom 306414.

12. Mammillaria wrightii Engelmann

12a. Mammillaria wrightii var. wrightii

Mammillaria wrightii Engelm. Proc. Amer. Acad. 3: 262. 1857 (preprint, 1856); U.S. Senate Rept. Expl. & Surv. R. R. Route Pacific Ocean. Botany 4: 27. 1857; in Emory, Rept. U.S. & Mex. Bound. Surv. 2: Cactaceae 7. pl. 8, f. 1-8. 1859, each later publication referring to the preceding. Cactus wrightii Kuntze, Rev. Gen. Pl. 1: 261. 1891. Neomammillaria wrightii Britton & Rose, Cactaceae 4: 152. 1923. Chilita wrightii Orcutt, Cactography 2. 1926. Ebnerella wrightii F. Buxbaum, Österr. Bot. Zeitschr. 98: 90. 1951. "New Mexico, on the Pecos and near the Copper Mines [Santa Rita]." "High plains near the Gallinas. Hills and rocky places near Anton Chico, on the Pecos Sept. 25. 1853 [Wright]. Santa Rita del Cobre mountains; near lake Maria, Chihuahua." LECTOTYPE (Coulter, Contr. U.S. Nat. Herb. 3: 101. 1894): "...Wright of 1851 in Herb. Mo. Bot. Gard.," the year of the Santa Rita, New Mexico, collection. "Copper Mines [Santa Rita] S. Western N. Mexico, Chs. Wright, Aug. 1851," Mo.

TEXAS. EL PASO CO. Franklin Mts., Wooton, Aug. 24, 1909, NMC; Samuels (not located, but the plants collected there indicate the El Paso area), J. H. Gaut, March 11, 1905, NY, US.

The classification of Mammillaria viridiflora and of the two varieties of Mammillaria wrightii has been clarified by the excellent work of Allan D. and Dale A. Zimmerman, Cactus and Succ. Jour. 49: 23-34, 51-62, f. 1-18. 1977.

12b. Mammillaria wrightii var. wilcoxii (Toumey ex K. Schum.) W. T. Marshall

Mammillaria wilcoxii Toumey ex K. Schum. Gesamtb. Kakteen 545. 1898. Neomammillaria wilcoxii Britton & Rose, Cactaceae 4: 153. 1923. Chilita wilcoxii Orcutt, Cactography 2. 1926. M. wrightii Engelm. var. wilcoxii W. T. Marshall, Arizona's Cactuses 100. 1950. Ebnerella wilcoxii F. Buxbaum, Österr. Bot. Zeitschr. 98: 90. 1951. "Warscheinlich in Arizona: TOUMEY." No locality was known to K. Schumann, the publishing author who wrote the description. "Mammillaria Wilcoxii msc. bei Orcutt." "Anmerkung I: Die Beschreibung wurde nach einem nicht sehr vollkommenen Stücke entworfen, das von ORCUTT stammte." This fragment has not been found; probably it was not preserved or, if it was, it was destroyed in the bombing of the Berlin Museum during World War II. There is no known duplicate. NEOTYPE (L. Benson, Cactus & Succ. Jour. 49: 35. 1977). Several miles southwest of Benson, Cochise County, Arizona, Desert Grassland, 4,500 feet elevation, Dale A. & Allan D. Zimmerman 2788, Feb. 22, 1976; flowered in cultivation, July 6, 1976; fruits from the same plants. Pom 322896. See Suppl.

Note: According to Beat Leuenberger, Wildenowia 8: 625-635. 1979, 85 type specimens of Cactaceae in the Berlin Museum Herbarium were not destroyed during World War II. However, specimens of this species are not among the 6 of Mammillaria.

Allan D. and Dale A. Zimmerman have published a thorough redefinition of Mammillaria viridiflora and M. wrightii vars. wrightii and wilcoxii, Cactus & Succ. Jour. 49: 23-34; 51-61. 1977. The confused nomenclature of var. wilcoxii was discussed by the writer in a companion paper, prepared originally as a part of that by the Zimmermans, Cactus & Succ. Jour. 49: 34-35. 1977, and a neotype was designated, there being no specimen eligible to become a lectotype. See previous discussion under Documentation.

ARIZONA. Pima Co. Santa Rita [Mts.] "near Tucson," Wooton, July 11, 1911, US. Santa Cruz Co. Calabasas, Rose 11,955, US; Warsaw Mill, E. A. Mearns, Dec. 6, 1893, US; Nogales, F.J. Dyer A330, June, 1909, US, R.E. Kunze in 1912, NY, Ashman, Dec. 1, 1897, US. Cochise Co. San Pedro Valley, Willcox road, east of junction with Redington-Benson road, 3,500 ft., L. Benson 16,733A; several miles southwest of Benson, Dale A. and Allan D. Zimmerman 2,788, Pom, W. N. Mex. Univ.; e. of Benson, R.T. Craig, Dec. 24, 1951, Pom; e. end of Texas Canyon, Little Dragoon Mts., D.A. & A.D. Zimmerman 2,789, W. N. Mex. Univ.; Ft. Huachuca, T.E. Wilcox 124 in 1894, US; Cave Creek Canyon, Chiricahua Mts., s. of Portal, 5,400 ft., A.D. Zimmerman 2,770, W. N. Mex. Univ., A.D. Zimmerman & D. Humphrey 2,774 (fls.); Chevrolet Hill, Douglas, W.W. Jones, Feb. 25, 1940, Pom (fr.).

NEW MEXICO. Hidalgo Co. Clanton Canyon, Peloncillo Mts., 5,500 ft., D.A. & A.D. Zimmerman 2,821, W. N. Mex. Univ.; Guadalupe Canyon, 4,600 ft., D.A. & A.D. Zimmerman 1,822, W. N. Mex. Univ.

The following additional collections made from 1974-76 are reported by Allan D. and Dale A. Zimmerman, Cactus & Succ. Jour. (in press, 1976): ARIZONA. PIMA CO. Madera [White House] Canyon, Santa Rita Mts., 2818. SANTA CRUZ CO. Gardner Canyon, Santa Rita Mts., 2655; Canelo Pass region, 2787. COCHISE CO. Garden Canyon, Ft. Huachuca Mil. Res., 2820; s.w. of Benson, 2788, Pom; Texas Canyon, 2789; Cave Creek Canyon, Chiricahua Mts., 2744, 2770.

13. Mammillaria tetrancistra Engelmann

Mammillaria tetrancistra Engelm. Amer. Jour. Sci. 14: 3. 1852. M. phellosperma Engelm. Proc. Amer. Acad. 3: 262. 1857 (preprint, 1856); in Emory, Rept. U.S. & Mex. Bound. Surv. 2: Cactaceae 6. pl. 7. 1859, nom. superfl., nom. nov. for M. tetrancis-

tra (see next paragraph). Cactus phellospermus Kuntze, Rev. Gen.
Pl. 1: 261. 1891. C. tetrancistrus Coulter, Contr. U.S. Nat.
Herb. 3: 104. 1894. Phellosperma tetrancistra Britton & Rose,
Cactaceae 4: 60. 1923. Neomammillaria tetrancistra Fosberg, Bull.
So. Calif. Acad. 30: 57. 1931. "...Dr. Parry's Californian Cactaceae...." "From San Diego to the junction of the Gila with the
Colorado." Parry's collection not located, Mo, ISC. NEOTYPE
designation: 1/2 mile above mouth of Whitewater Canyon, San Bernardino Mts. at edge of Colorado Desert, Riverside Co., California,
1,900 feet, gravelly soil, Lyman Benson 15716, Pom 288535 (as described for original collection, with mostly 4 hooked central
spines per areole).

This species was named Mammillaria tetrancistra by Engelmann
in 1852 on the basis of Parry's collections, 1849-50. These plants
had 4 hooked central spines, but the collections brought later to
Engelmann did not. The plants described and figured had mostly
1-2 centrals, and Engelmann hastened to change the name to M. phellosperma because he thought tetrancistra inappropriate. Formulation in 1867 of the International Rules [Code] of Botanical
Nomenclature ruled out acceptance of such name changes, because
degree of appropriateness varies, and so does human judgment.

NEVADA. "Nevada," Death Valley Expedition, E. W. Nelson 428
in 1891, US (box). NYE CO. Belted Mts., N of Mercury Basin
drainage, T. Ascherman, Apr. 13, 1969, TSH. CLARK CO. S of Indian
Springs, Charleston Mts., Clokey 8037, UC; Good Springs, D. F.
Hewitt in 1921, US.
UTAH. WASHINGTON CO. St. George, Parry in 1874, Mo.

Supplement to Documentation

References and notes based on research since the closing of this
section and literature published since each section of the descriptive text was set up in type.

Note on the Didiereaceae

The position of Dr. Werner Rauh of the University of Heidelberg on the question of nearness of relationship of the Didiereaceae and the Cactaceae is stated as follows (Rauh, Cactus & Succ.
Jour. 50: 121. 1978): "Even though the Didiereaceae belong to the
same division as the Cactaceae, namely the centrosperms [Caryo-
phyllales], there is no relationship between the two plant families.
According to our contention the Didiereaceae are more closely related to the Portulaceae, but those are represented in Madagascar
by only a very few species."

1. Pereskia

1. Pereskia aculeata Miller

The specimen in the Linnean Herbarium, London, Linn, is not
as good as that in the Linnaean Herbarium, Stockholm, S. LECTO-
TYPE designation: "CACTUS (Pereskia) caule arboreo tereti aculeis
geminis recurvis, foliis lanceolato-ovatis Syst. Nat. ed. 13. n.
22. Habitat in America calidiore Jamaica, Margaretha... Specimen ex Upps. commis--- Garten--- Metzel" (Partly illegible).
Metzel was the gardener of Linnaeus, and after the collection of
Linnaeus was taken to London, he pressed plants from the greenhouse where he had planted them for Linnaeus. The specimens were
prepared under supervision of Solander. Thus, they are authentic
Linnaean material. Gratitude is expressed to Prof. Tyckho Nor-
lindh for this information.

2. Opuntia

12a. Opuntia fulgida var. fulgida

Cylindropuntia fulgida Engelm. forma monstrosa W. H. Earle,
Sahuaroland Bull. 30: 83. 1976, nom. nud.

19a. Opuntia stanlyi var. stanlyi

TEXAS. PRESIDIO CO. Candelaria, Donald O. Kolle, in 1976,
Pom; duplicate, SRSC (not seen). The species has been reported
from Texas, but this collection is the first solid evidence that
it occurs there. Earlier collections perhaps representing this
species were fragmentary and mostly without locality.

26c. Opuntia erinacea var. ursina (Weber) Parish

Opuntiae Ursus horribilis Walton, Cactus Jour. 2: 121. 1899,
was a verbatim reproduction from Southern Florist and Gardener 5:
10-11. 1898 (cf. Larry W. Mitich) Cactus & Succ. Jour. 48: 174.
1976.

5. Cereus

15b. Cereus greggii var. transmontanus Engelmann

Cereus greggii Engelm. var. roseiflorus R. E. Kuntze,
Monatsschr. Kakteenk. 20: 172. 1910. Peniocereus greggii (Engelm.)
Britton & Rose var. roseiflorus R. E. Kuntze ex R. G. Engard,
Sahuaroland Bull. 30: 112. 1976, nom. nud. Arizona. No specimen
mentioned.

17. Cereus striatus Brandegee

Peniocereus striatus F. Buxbaum in Krainz, Kakteen Lief. 62:
CIIa. 1975.

7. Lophophora

1. Lophophora williamsii (Lemaire) Coulter

Echinocactus rapa Fischer & Meyer, Sertum Petrop. pl. 33.
1869. "Olim in horto Petropolitano cultis." (Cf. Ganders, Fred
H., Cactus & Succ. Jour. 49: 155. 1975.)

8. Ferocactus

Hamatacanthus, as subgenus of Ferocactus, H. Bravo, Cact. y
Suc. Mex. 21: 66. 1976. Type genus: Hamatacanthus Britton & Rose.

1+. Ferocactus eastwoodiae (L. Benson) L. Benson, comb. nov.

Ferocactus acanthodes (Lemaire) Britton & Rose var. eastwoodiae
L. Benson, Cacti Ariz. ed. 3. 26, 166. 1969. See treatment as
var., descriptive text and Documentation. Additional evidence of
character stability indicates specific rank. The range is extended
northwestward to eastern Yavapai County, Arizona, through a collection from between Camp Verde and Strawberry, I. G. Reimann,
Nov. 15, 1977, Pom.

10. Sclerocactus

Unevaluated proposed taxa (near Sclerocactus parviflorus
var. intermedius)

Sclerocactus whipplei (Engelm. & Bigelow) Britton & Rose
var. heilii Castetter, Pierce, & Schwerin, Cactus & Succ. Jour.
48: 79. f. 3-4. 1976. "Type: Northern San Juan County [New
Mexico], Kenneth Heil 3903A & 3903B, 7 August 1971, UNM 49,874."

Sclerocactus whipplei (Engelm. & Bigelow) Britton & Rose
var. reevesii Castetter, Pierce, & Schwerin, Cactus & Succ. Jour.
48: 80. f. 5-7. 1976. "Type: Southern San Juan County [New
Mexico], Kenneth Heil 4081, May 5, 1971, UNM 51,072."

The following newly described species have not been evaluated:

Sclerocactus contortus Heil, Cactus & Succ Jour. 51: 25.
f. 1-2. 1979. "Canyonlands National Park [further distributional
data withheld for conservation purposes]," Utah. "HOLOTYPE: deposited in the University of New Mexico Herbarium under the number
64,284. Isotypes: UNM 64,280, 64,282, 64,288." The plants are
reported to differ from Sclerocactus parviflorus in having longer
upper central and hooked central spines and larger seeds.

Sclerocactus terrae-canyonae Heil, Cactus & Succ. Jour. 51:
26. f. 3-4. 1979. "San Juan Co., Utah [further distributional
data withheld for conservation purposes]." "HOLOTYPE: deposited
at the University of New Mexico Herbarium under number 64,283.
ISOTYPE: UNM 64,279. The plant is stated to be related closely to
Sclerocactus whipplei and S. parviflorus, the major differences
being in flower and fruit color and spine length.

11. Pediocactus

2+. Pediocactus winkleri Heil

Pediocactus winkleri Heil, Cactus & Succ. Jour. 51: 28.
f. 5-8. 1979. "TYPE LOCALITY: Wayne County, Utah [further data
withheld for conservation purposes]." "HOLOTYPE: deposited at
the University of New Mexico Herbarium under the number 64,285.
ISOTYPE: UNM 64,287." The species is related to Pediocactus bradyi,
but it differs clearly as follows: stem diameter 2-2.6 cm (as opposed to 2.5-5 cm); areoles mostly woolly but naked in some plants
(as opposed to villous); radial spines mostly 9-11, sometimes to
14 (as opposed to 14-15); petaloids peach (as opposed to pale

straw-yellow to yellow); seeds black, the papillae coalescent into ridges, the surface shiny, to 3 mm long, 2-2.5 mm diam (as opposed to brown, the papillae not coalescent, the surface dull, to 2.75 mm long, 1.75-2 mm. diam.). These characters were published by the author, and, since only 1 plant with fruit has been seen, not all of them can be evaluated. However, an additional character is apparent: the fruit is not stalked as in P. bradyi, though it is similar in other respects.

3. Pediocactus knowltonii L. Benson

Toumeya knowltonii Anon. Sahuaroland Bull. 30: 41. 1976, nom. nud.

12. Neolloydia

7. Neolloydia johnsonii (Parry) L. Benson

Neolloydia johnsonii (Parry) L. Benson var. lutescens W. T. Marshall ex R. G. Engard, Sahuaroland Bull. 31: 88. f. 1. 1977, nom. nud.

16. Coryphantha

Coryphantha section Escobaria H. E. Moore, Baileya 20: 29. 1976. (Add to paragraph in list under the genus.)

4b. Coryphantha vivipara var. radiosa (Engelmann) Backeberg

Escobaria vivipara (Nutt.) Buxbaum var. radiosa D. R. Hunt, Cactus & Succ. Jour. Gt. Brit. 40: 13. 1978.

4c. Coryphantha vivipara var. bisbeeana (Orcutt) L. Benson

Escobaria vivipara (Nutt.) Buxbaum var. bisbeeana D. R. Hunt, Cactus & Succ. Jour. Gt. Brit. 40: 13. 1978.

4d. Coryphantha vivipara var. arizonica (Engelmann) W. T. Marshall

Escobaria vivipara (Nutt.) Buxbaum var. arizonica D. R. Hunt, Cactus & Succ. Jour. Gt. Brit. 40: 13. 1978.

4e. Coryphantha vivipara var. desertii (Engelmann) W. T. Marshall

Escobaria vivipara (Nutt.) Buxbaum var. desertii D. R. Hunt, Cactus & Succ. Jour. Gt. Brit. 40: 13. 1978.

4f. Coryphantha vivipara var. alversonii (Coulter) L. Benson

Escobaria vivipara (Nutt.) Buxbaum var. alversonii D. R. Hunt. Cactus & Succ. Jour. Gt. Brit. 40: 13. 1978.

4g. Coryphantha vivipara var. rosea (Clokey) L. Benson

Escobaria vivipara (Nutt.) Buxbaum var. rosea D. R. Hunt Cactus & Succ. Jour. Gt. Brit. 40: 13. 1978.

Proposed taxon

Coryphantha vivipara (Nutt.) Britton & Rose var. kaibabensis P. C. Fischer, Cactus & Succ. Jour. 51: 287. 1979. TYPE: "HOLOTYPE. P. C. Fischer 4094, collected on 31/III/69 northwest of Jacob Lake, Coconino Co., Arizona. 1890 meters (6200 ft). ...Herbarium of the University of California (UC), Berkeley, CA."

12b. Coryphantha dasyacantha var. varicolor (Tiegel) L. Benson

Escobaria dasyacantha Britton & Rose var. varicolor D. R. Hunt, Cactus & Succ. Jour. Gt. Brit. 40: 13. 1978.

13+. Coryphantha robbinsorum (W. H. Earle) Allan D. Zimmerman

Stem solitary, simple, dark green, at maturity suborbicular, 3-5 cm long, 3-5 cm diam; tubercles narrowly pyramidal-cylindroid, 3-6 mm long vertically, 5-6 or 10 mm broad basally, projecting 5-8 mm; areoles 3-4 mm diam, typically ± 5 mm apart, woolly; spines moderately dense on the stem, 11-17 per areole, those of juvenile stems densely spreading-hirsutulous and white with reddish tips, those of older stems glabrous and off-white with reddish brown to brown tips, straight, mostly radiating in a single turn of a spiral; upper spines 8-18 mm long, basally 0.4-0.7 mm thick, sometimes crowded and placed irregularly, circular to narrowly elliptic in cross section, acicular to narrowly subulate, the usually 1-3 very slender spines at the upper edge of the areole only 3-9 mm. long; the spines at the lower edge of the areole reduced, some only 3-4 mm long; flowers appearing during March and April, 1-1.5 cm. diam, ± 2 cm long; sepaloids with the midribs and adjacent apical areas brownish and the backs and margins green or the apical edges pale olive, the largest ones

obovate-oblanceolate, sharply lacerate-denticulate, 5-10 mm long, ± 2 mm broad, acute to apiculate; petaloids pale greenish yellow (reportedly sometimes with pink), the midribs brownish, the largest petaloids broadly lanceolate, ± 1-1.2 cm long, 2.5-4 mm broad, apiculate, entire; filaments white, slender, to 5 mm long; anthers yellow, 0.7 mm long, (after dehiscence) ± 0.9 mm broad; style green, ± 1.5 cm long, ± 1.5 mm greatest diam; stigmas 3-5, green, 1-2 mm long; ovary in anthesis not available; fruit maturing from July to mid-August, orange-red, fleshy at maturity, without surface appendages, cylindroid to elliptic or spheroidal, to 1 cm long, to 4.5 mm diam, if not eaten drying and persistent through the winter before disintegrating; seeds dark brown, blackish, of the Cereus type, longer than broad, 1-1.4 mm long, 0.8-1.2 mm broad, 0.7-1 mm thick, the hilum large, the basically smooth surface with deep irregular pits.

Limestone of rocky hills at about 1,280 m (4,250 ft). Desert Grassland. An undisclosed (for conservation) locality in Cochise Co., southeastern Arizona.

This species is related to Coryphantha dasyacantha, C. robertii, and C. duncanii. These species are under lead 4A (lower) of the key, and the new species fits the characters leading to that point. As in the three related species, the seed is longer than broad, and the large hilum is obviously basal, the seed being of the Cereus type, and the seed coat is brown to black. Seeds of this type are characteristic of Mammillaria, but they occur also in Coryphantha. The spines are in a single turn of a spiral, except for a few at the upper edge of the areole, and thus they are different from those of any of the related species (see leads 5B and 6A in the key). The nearest relationship is to C. duncanii, from which the species differs in the smaller number of spines, 11-17 per areole, not 30-75, and these in essentially a single turn, not several turns; the larger areoles, 3-4 mm in diameter, not 1 mm.

Cochiseia robbinsorum W. H. Earle, Sahuaroland Bull. 30: 64-66. f. 1976. Escobaria robbinsorum D. R. Hunt, Cactus & Succ. Jour. Gt. Brit. 40: 13. 1978. Coryphantha robbinsorum A. D. Zimmerman, Cactus & Succ. Jour. 50: 1978 (in press). "Topotype herbarium sheet has been deposited at the Desert Botanical Garden Herbarium, and holotype herbarium sheet at the Arizona State University Herbarium." "...Southeast Cochise County, Arizona...." TYPE: collected by James A. Robbins, Jimmy Robbins, and John Robbins, 1976. ASU. TOPOTYPE: James A. Robbins, Jimmy Robbins, and John Robbins, July 16, 1977, Pom 325313.

15a. Coryphantha missouriensis var. missouriensis

Escobaria missouriensis D. R. Hunt, Cactus & Succ. Jour. Gt. Brit. 15: 13. 1978.

15b. Coryphantha missouriensis var. marstonii (Clover) L. Benson

Escobaria missouriensis (Sweet) D. R. Hunt var. marstonii D. R. Hunt, Cactus & Succ. Jour. Gt. Brit. 40: 13. 1978.

15c. Coryphantha missouriensis var. caespitosa (Engelmann) L. Benson

Escobaria missouriensis (Sweet) D. R. Hunt var. caespitosa D. R. Hunt, Cactus & Succ Jour Gt. Brit. 40: 13. 1978.

15d. Coryphantha missouriensis var. robustior (Engelmann) L. Benson

Escobaria missouriensis (Sweet) D. R. Hunt var. robustior D. R. Hunt, Cactus & Succ. Jour. Gt. Brit. 40: 13. 1978.

17. Ariocarpus

See Mitich, Larry W. & Jan G. Bruhn. The genus Ariocarpus -- a bibliography. Cactus & Succ. Jour. 49: 122-129. f. 1-7. 1977.

18. Mammillaria

Note on further distinction of Mammillaria viridiflora and M. grahamii: M. viridiflora -- sepals attenuate, ciliate, not markedly scarious-margined. M. grahamii -- sepals rounded apically, not ciliate, markedly scarious-margined.

12b. Mammillaria wrightii Engelmann var. wilcoxii (Toumey ex K. Schum.) W. T. Marshall

Mammillaria meridiorosei Castetter, Pierce, & Schwerin, Cactus & Succ. Jour. 50: 177. 1978. TYPE: "Holotype: Clanton Canyon, one mile east of the Arizona Border, 11 miles north of the Mexican border at 6,000 feet elevation. Steven Brack (SB 3) [Castetter's Garden No.] 4335. Nov. 30, 1974. UNM 63436."

Reference Matter

Glossary

This Glossary includes botanical terms and a number of basically nonbotanical terms that have special botanical usages. Terms appearing in contexts of Part I dealing with the geographical distribution of plants and their relationship to the environment (Chapter 9), and many other terms used only once in this book, are explained in the text. A few words used commonly in other works on the cacti but not used in the text are included in the glossary; some of these are the basis for commonly used specific and varietal epithets appearing in name combinations.

A-. Without, lacking (as prefix).

AB-. Away from, on the far side of (as prefix); also different from the normal or usual arrangement or state.

ABORTIVE. Undeveloped or developed imperfectly; sterile.

ABRUPT. Ending suddenly, without tapering.

ABSCISSION. Separation through death and disintegration of a special layer of cells, as with a leaf, petal, or fruit that falls away. See *deciduous*.

ABSCISSION LAYER. A layer of cells that die and disintegrate at maturity, separating the parts of the plant occurring along the layer.

ACCESSORY. Much smaller, as a structure, than the similar structures it accompanies; additional; extra.

ACCUMBENT. Of a pair of cotyledons, lying each with the edge turned against the main axis of the embryo. If the human body were to represent the hypocotyl, the head the epicotyl, and the upraised arms the pair of cotyledons, and if the individual were to bend forward and touch his toes, keeping his hands pressed together, he would be *accumbent*. If he were to bend sidewise and do the same thing, he would be *incumbent* (and probably for the next six weeks recumbent).

ACEROSE. Needlelike.

ACICULAR. Needlelike; cylindroid, elongate, and tapering, and uniformly circular or nearly so in cross section.

ACICULATE. Having a needlelike shape.

ACULEATE. Covered with prickles.

ACUMINATE. Abruptly narrowed into a long, pointed apex. Cf. *acute*.

ACUTE. Tapering to a point, but with the sides straight along the taper (as at the tip or base of a structure). Cf. *acuminate*.

ADHERENT. Fused to a structure of a different kind, as, for example, the filaments of the stamens, adherent by their backs to the petals; *see adnate*.

ADNATE. Joined with a structure of different origin, as, for example, the fusing of the bases of the petals with the sepals or with the stamens. Cf. *approximate, coalescent, free*.

ADNATION. The fusion of one structure with another of a different origin, as, for example, the fusion of the bases of the sepals and petals. Cf. *coalescence*.

ADVENTITIOUS. Not formed in the usual place.

ADVENTITIOUS ROOT. A root developed not from the primary root system but from a stem or (rarely) a leaf.

AERIAL. In the air; not connected with the surface of the ground.

AERIAL ROOT. A root exposed to the air. This type of root occurs in humid regions, as, for example, in tropical rain forests, where plants grow on the limbs of trees, with their roots dangling in the moist air.

ALATE. Winged.

ALPINE. Occurring in the mountains above timberline. Cf. *montane*.

ALTERNATE. Having a single leaf (and the axillary bud) at each node, or joint, of the stem. The word is applied also to other structures arranged in the same manner. Cf. *opposite*.

ALVEOLATE. With a pattern of angular depressions forming a network similar to a honeycomb.

ALVEOLUS (pl. ALVEOLI). One of the depressions within an *alveolate* pattern.

AMORPHOUS. Shapeless; lacking a definite form.

AMPHIPLOID. Having two double sets of somewhat different chromosomes, as in the hybrid derivative of radish and cabbage that has two full sets of chromosomes from each of the unlike parents. See *chromosome number*.

AMPHIPLOIDY. The presence of an *amphiploid* pattern of chromosomes.

AMPHITROPOUS. Of an ovule, bent back along its stalk (funiculus) and adnate with it, but with the micropyle bent only partway to the funiculus. Narrowly distinct from anatropous. Cf. *anatropous, campylotropous, orthotropous*.

ANATROPOUS. Of an ovule, bent back along its stalk (funiculus) and adnate with it, and the micropyle almost against the funiculus; the type of ovule occurring most frequently in the flowering plants. Cf. *amphitropous, campylotropous, orthotropous*.

ANNUAL. A plant that goes through its whole life cycle in a year or less. Cf. *perennial*.

ANNULAR. In the form of a ring.

ANNULATE. Furnished with encircling, ringlike, projecting bands.

ANTHER. The upper and larger part of a stamen, consisting principally of *pollen sacs*.

ANTHESIS. Flowering time, that is, the time when pollination takes place; specifically, the process of increasing in size and opening, followed by the giving and/or receiving of pollen.

ANTHOCYANIN. One of a group of lavender to purple pigments dissolved in the sap of living cells. As with litmus paper, these pigments are indicators of acidity or alkalinity, changing toward red in an acid solution and toward blue in an alkaline (basic) solution. See *anthoxanthin, betacyanin*.

ANTHOXANTHIN. A flavonoid pigment related to the anthocyanins but orange to yellow. See also *betacyanin, betalain*.

APEX. The uppermost point; vertex; tip.

APICAL. At the apex.

APICULATE. With an abrupt, short, flexible terminal point.

APOMICTIC. Developing by *apomixis*.

APOMIXIS. *Asexual* reproduction that simulates but bypasses sexual reproduction. For example, fruits may develop roots from the ovary wall and grow into new plants; or, without fertilization, vegetative tissues in the seed may produce false embryos, as in some species of *Citrus*. See *asexual, clone*.

APPRESSED. Lying flat against the stem or other organ and pointed upward.

APPROXIMATE. Close together but not coalescent. Cf. *adnate, coalescent, free*.

ARBOREOUS. Having the form of a tree, that is, with a single main woody trunk.

ARBORESCENT. Having characters intermediate between those of a tree and those of a shrub, that is, woody and with two to several trunks and of a size intermediate between trees (larger) and shrubs (smaller).

ARCTIC. Beyond timberline in the far north.

ARCUATE. In the form of a curve or arc.

AREOLATE. Divided into small, clearly marked spaces. See *areole, reticulate*.

AREOLE. A small area. In the cacti a small, sharply defined, specialized area in which spines and (in *Opuntia*) glochids are produced. The structures in the areole are developed at a node of the stem, where they arise from the (axillary) bud in the angle above a leaf or a rudiment representing a leaf. In mature plants the rudiment is usually indiscernible.

ARIL. A large appendage formed at the *hilum* (attachment area) from the *funiculus*, or stalk, of an ovule or a seed. Sometimes the aril tends to envelop the seed.

ARILLATE. Bearing an *aril*.

ARISTA (pl. ARISTAE). A nearly rigid bristle.

ARISTATE. With a slender terminal point drawn out into a bristle.

ARTICULATE. Jointed; with conspicuous segments.

ARTIFICIAL CLASSIFICATION. A system of classification based on a predetermined supposition concerning the relative "importance" of one or more characters. See *natural classification, lumper, splitter*.

ASCENDING. Arising on an oblique angle or on a curve through the whole length of the organ.

ASEXUAL. Reproducing without sex, as in the establishment and growing of a fragment of a plant, for example a cutting. See *apomixis, clone*.

ASSURGENT. Ascending.

ATTENUATE. Tapering gradually toward the base or the apex into a point from a narrow, more or less flattened body. Cf. *awl-shaped, subulate*.

AURICULATE. With an appendage having more or less the shape of a lobe of the human ear.

AWL-SHAPED. Linear and tapering to a point from a narrow, flat body; *subulate*. Cf. *attenuate*.

AWN. A long, stout, stiff bristle.

AWNED. Having an *awn*.

AXIL. The angle above a leaf, formed by it with the stem or branch upon which it grows.

AXILE. On the *axis*. Commonly, this term describes a placenta or placentae near or at the center of an ovary.

AXILLARY. Developed in an *axil*.

AXILLARY BUD. A bud developed in the *axil* of a leaf.

AXIS. The main or central line of development of a plant or part of a plant; the main stem.

BACCATE. Like a *berry*, that is, in the form of a fruit that is fleshy or pulpy inside.

BARBATE. Bearded.

BARBED. Having a barb like that of a fishhook. Such a barb, on for example the sharp spine of a cactus, tends to prevent the spine from being pulled out of the hair or flesh of an animal.

BARBELLATE, BARBELLULATE. Minutely *bearded*.

BASIFIXED. Attached at the base.

BEAKED. Having a firm, elongate, slender, terminal structure.

BEARDED. Having a zone of hairs in an otherwise glabrous structure, or a zone of longer hairs among shorter ones.

BERRY. A fruit that is fleshy or pulpy and that has its seeds imbedded in the pulp. Strawberry and blackberry fruits are not berries; tomatoes are.

BETACYANIN. A pigment similar in behavior to the *anthocyanins* that occurs in the Cactaceae and in most plant families of the order Caryophyllales. So far as investigated, the purple-lavender pigments occurring in the cacti are betacyanins. Cf. *anthocyanin, anthoxanthin, betalain*.

BETALAIN. A pigment, either a *betacyanin* (between red and blue) or a betaxanthin (yellow to orange). The molecules include nitrogen; those of *anthocyanins* (between red and blue) and *anthoxanthins* (yellow to reddish-orange) do not.

BI-. Twice (as prefix).

BILATERAL. With two well-differentiated sides.

BISEXUAL. With both sexes represented in the same individual or organ; for example, with stamens and pistils on the same plant or in the same flower. Cf. *dioecious, imperfect, monoecious, perfect, unisexual*.

BLADE. The broad, flat part of a leaf or other flattened structure.

BLOOM. A waxy bluish to whitish powder, usually of finely divided wax particles, covering the surface of a stem, leaf, fruit, or other organ. Cf. *cuticle*; see also *glaucous*.

BOREAL. Northern.

BOTANICAL NAME. See *scientific name*.

BRACT. A leaf subtending a reproductive structure; in the flowering plants, a leaf subtending one or more flowers.

BRANCH. A division of the stem.

BRISTLE. A nearly rigid hair; a seta. See *awn*.

BUD. The young growing structure at the tip of a stem or branch or in a leaf axil. A vegetative bud encloses immature leaves, and it may be protected by scalelike outer leaves; a flower bud encloses the parts of an immature flower.

CAESPITOSE, CESPITOSE. Having numerous stems that form a dense, low tuft or mat.

CALLOSITY. A hard, thickened structure.

CALLOUS. Having the texture of a *callus*.

CALLUS. A tough, swollen area.

CALYX. Literally, a cup; the sepals of a flower or, if sepals and petals are not clearly distinguished, the outermost series of flower parts. Each sepal is fundamentally a specialized leaf, with the same number of internal vascular traces (vascular bundles) as a leaf of the species. Cf. *corolla*.

CAMBIAL ACTIVITY. Development of new cells of xylem and phloem from the cambium between these tissues.

CAMBIUM. A layer of dividing cells between the inner woody conducting tissues, the *xylem* (wood) on one side and the *phloem* (bark) on the other side. Each growing season the cambium adds new cells to both layers.

CAMPANULATE. Bell-shaped.

CAMPYLOTROPOUS. Of an ovule, having a curving body and with the micropyle therefore near the funiculus, the body and stalk of the ovule not, however, adnate. See *amphitropous, anatropous, orthotropous*.

CANESCENCE. A dense covering of short, fine, usually white or gray hair.

CANESCENT. Covered densely with short, fine, usually white or gray hairs.

CAPILLARY. A delicate elongate hair or other threadlike structure.

CAPITATE. In a dense cluster or head, as flowers.

CAPSULE. A dry, several-to-many-seeded fruit formed from more than one carpel and splitting open.

CARINATE. Having a ridge (carina) like the keel of a boat; keeled.

CARPEL. A specialized leaf composing either all or part of a pistil. In a cactus flower 3 to 20 carpels are coalescent, forming a single pistil. The only parts not coalesced are the stigmas. See *pistil*.

CARPELLATE, CARPELED. Having, of the nature of, or pertaining to a carpel or carpels.

CARTILAGINOUS. Like cartilage, that is, somewhat flexible but tough and firm.

CARUNCLE. An elevated or protruding ridge, like the keel of a boat.

CAUDATE. Having a tail.

CAULINE. On or pertaining to the stem.

CELL. A chamber or compartment. Used most frequently for a living cell, the primary unit of any living organism.

CENTRAL SPINE. One of the spines in the central part of an areole. The distinction from the *radial spines* is usually clear and obvious but sometimes arbitrary.

CENTRIFUGAL. First developing near the center and then progressing gradually outward.

CENTRIPETAL. First developing on the outside and then progressing gradually toward the center.

CHAMBER. A cavity or room, as, for example, the cavity or one of the cavities in which seeds or pollen are borne within the ovary or the anther.

CHLOROPHYLL. The green pigment of most plants. Chlorophyll aids in making the energy of light available to *photosynthesis*, that is, the manufacture of sugars from carbon dioxide and water.

CHLOROPLAST. One of the solid green bodies, within cells, that contain *chlorophyll*.

CHLOROTIC. Without *chlorophyll* or lacking the normal or expected amount.

CHROMOSOME. A structure in the nucleus of the living cell that bears the *genes*, which determine the hereditary characteristics of the individual.

CHROMOSOME NUMBER. The number of chromosomes in a particular cell, this more or less typical of the cells of the species. Numbers occur in two states: in male or female *gametes* (sex cells), usually n; in vegetative cells, usually twice as many, 2n. In flowering plants during sexual reproduction, a male and a female gamete fuse, giving rise to a new individual with 2n chromosomes, n from each parent. However, there are deviations from the usual chromosome numbers. See *amphiploid, diploid, haploid, hexaploid, octoploid, polyploid, tetraploid*.

CILIA (sing. CILIUM). Marginal hairs placed like the eyelashes of man.

CILIATE. Having *cilia*, or marginal hairs.

CILIOLATE. Ciliate, the hairs small.

CILIOLULATE. Ciliate, the hairs minute.

CINEREOUS. Like ashes; covered with light, dull, gray hairs.

CIRCUMSCISSILE. With the upper part coming off like a lid; opening along a circular horizontal line. See *dehiscent, indehiscent*.

CLASS. A major *taxon* of the Plant Kingdom, composed of *orders*.

CLAVATE. Clublike or club-shaped; elongate, nearly circular in cross section, with the diameter becoming gradually greater upward and the structure often flaring abruptly near the top or into a terminal knob.

CLEFT. Divided about to the middle into two or more parts. See *divided, lobed, parted*.

CLIMBING. Supported by clinging, usually by means of tendrils, roots, or suction pads.

CLONAL. Pertaining to a *clone*.

CLONE. A group of individual plants propagated asexually, either naturally or by man, from a single original individual. Joints of the stems of chollas and prickly pears root readily, and each joint forms a new plant; the resulting group of plants is a clone. See *apomixis, asexual.*

COALESCENCE. The joining of parts of similar origin, as, for example, the sepals of a flower. Cf. *adnation.*

COALESCENT. Joined together, said of structures of similar origin. Sepals may be coalescent with sepals, petals with petals, etc. Cf. *adnate, approximate, free.*

CONICAL. Cone-shaped, with the point of attachment at the broad base of the cone.

CONNECTIVE. The middle part of the *anther* of a flower, which joins the *pollen sacs.*

CONSERVATIVE. A botanist who requires taxa to be natural, and divides them into relatively broad and inclusive units. See *liberal, lumper, splitter.*

CORDATE. Heart-shaped.

CORIACEOUS. Of leathery texture.

CORNEOUS. Horny.

CORNICULATE. Having a small horn or horns.

COROLLA. The petals of a flower. Cf. *calyx.*

CORRUGATED. Having small wrinkles or folds.

CORTEX. The soft tissues outside the woody cylinder of a vascular plant stem. See *pith.*

CORTICAL. Of the *cortex.*

CORYMB. A flat-topped cluster of flowers, assuming this shape because the pedicels on the lower part of the short axis are longer and those farther up progressively shorter; the flowers on the outside of the cluster bloom first, and they may be in the fruiting stage while the upper flowers are buds.

COTYLEDONS. One of the first leaves of the embryo formed in the seed. In the cacti the two cotyledons are the first pair of leaves, conspicuous in the seedling.

CREEPING. With the stem lying on the ground and producing roots where it comes in contact with the soil.

CRENATE. Having rounded marginal teeth.

CRENULATE. Crenate, the teeth small.

CRESTED. With a crestlike structure; in the cacti, having a stem with a crest of abnormal *fasciated* branches.

CRISPED. With the margin undulating but entire, the undulations up-and-down rather than in the plane of the leaf or other structure.

CRISTATE. Crested.

CRUCIFORM. In the shape of a cross.

CULTIVAR. A horticultural form or strain maintained through cultivation by man and propagated usually under human control. The names of cultivars are not similar to those given to species or varieties, but are designations derived from modern languages. The name may commemorate a person, as, for example, *Camellia japonica* Mrs. Tingley. The term "horticultural variety" is obsolete, and should be avoided.

CUNEATE. Wedge-shaped; forming an isosceles triangle and attached at the sharp angle.

CUSP. A sharp, firm point, firmer than the adjacent tissue.

CUSPIDATE. Ending in a *cusp.*

CUSPIDULATE. Ending in a small or minute *cusp.*

CUTICLE. A waxy layer of material secreted by the epidermal, or surface, cells covering a plant organ. See *bloom, epidermis, glaucous.*

CYCLE. See *whorl.*

CYCLIC. Arranged in a *whorl,* verticil, or cycle.

CYLINDRIC, CYLINDROID. In the form of a cylinder.

CYME. A cluster of flowers (often flat-topped) in which the terminal bud blooms first and the axillary pair of buds (cymes with opposite branching) or bud (cymes with alternate branching) then terminates in a flower. See *raceme, spike, corymb.*

CYTOLOGY. The study of the living cell, and especially of the chromosomes.

DECIDUOUS. Falling away at the termination of each growing season. See *abscission, persistent.*

DECLINED. Turned downward.

DECUMBENT. Lying flat on the ground, but with the tips turning upward. Cf. *prostrate.*

DECURRENT. Of a leaf, having the basal margins of the petiole forming ridges along the stem below; or in other structures, being similarly arranged.

DEFLEXED. Turned or bent downward.

DEHISCE. To split lengthwise along precise lines.

DEHISCENCE. The more or less sudden process of splitting lengthwise along precise lines.

DEHISCENT. Opening lengthwise by splitting along precise lines, thus releasing the seeds or pollen. See *circumscissile, indehiscent.*

DELIQUESCENT. Absorbing water from the atmosphere, or becoming fluid when mature, and, in petals or other plant structures, becoming exceedingly wet, dying, and becoming a wet, soggy mass.

DELTOID. Like the Greek letter delta; forming more or less an equilateral triangle and attached at the middle of one side.

DENTATE. With the margin bearing angular, perpendicularly projecting teeth.

DENTATION. Toothing.

DENTICULATE. Dentate, the teeth small.

DEPRESSED. Flattened on top and the structure appearing to have been pushed down.

DESCENDING. Sloping gradually downward.

DETERMINATE. Growing to a particular size or complexity, then stopping. In the flowering plants, said of the flower formed from the terminal bud. See *indeterminate.*

DICHOTOMOUS. Forking, the two branches at each level of forking being equal.

DICOTYLEDON. A flowering plant having two *cotyledons* in the embryo, rather than one as in the *monocotyledons.* The two major groups of flowering plants differ in this respect, and in commonly associated characters.

DICOTYLEDONOUS. Having two cotyledons.

DIFFUSE. Spreading in all directions.

DIMORPHIC. Occurring normally in two dissimilar forms; said of a plant part, such as a leaf.

DIOECIOUS. Having staminate (male) or pistillate (female) flowers, but not both, on the same individual.

Cf. *bisexual, imperfect, monoecious, perfect, unisexual.*

DIPLOID. Having **2n** chromosomes per cell, that is, two chromosomes of each type. See *chromosome number.*

DISCOID. Disklike, that is, circular and flat.

DISTAL. Away from the point of attachment. Cf. *proximal.*

DISTINCT. Separate.

DIURNAL. Occurring in the daytime. Cf. *nocturnal.*

DIVARICATE. Divergent, that is, spreading widely.

DIVERGENT. Spreading away from each other.

DIVIDED. Deeply indented, that is, almost to the base or the midrib. See *cleft, lobed, parted.*

DIVISION. One of the highest-ranking *taxa* in the Plant Kingdom, each composed of related *classes* or sometimes of only one class. Also, one segment of a divided structure, such as a leaf.

DORSAL. (1) Of an organ such as a leaf, on the side facing away from the axis of the organism (for example, away from the stem). The back or lower side of a leaf is the dorsal side, because it is away from the stem axis; usually the leaf slants upward, facing the stem. (2) Of an organism such as a liverwort or a mammal, on top, that is, on the side facing away from the ground. Cf. *ventral.*

DORSOVENTRAL. Extending from the front to the back, or vice versa. A flattened or compressed structure has its broadest faces on the front and back, rather than on the sides. Cf. *lateral.*

DRIP-TIP. A drawn-out, sharply acute point of a leaf on which water accumulates until the drops become large enough to fall off. On trees growing in tropical rain forests drip-tips are common. The downward-directed spines of some cacti behave as drip-tips, concentrating light mists into droplets that wet the soil, to be taken up by the roots.

E-. A Latin prefix meaning "from" or "out of." Commonly this appears as *ex-.*

EC-. A Greek prefix meaning "out of." Before vowels this appears as *ex-.*

ECHINATE. Bearing prickles on the surface.

EGG. A female *gamete* cell that joins with the male gamete, or sex cell, in forming an *embryo.*

ELLIPSOID. Elliptic, but in three dimensions.

ELLIPTIC, ELLIPTICAL. In the form of an ellipse, that is, like a flattened circle with the length about twice the diameter, with both ends rounded, and with the widest point at the middle.

EMARGINATE. Broadly and shallowly notched at the apex.

EMBRYO. The new plant developed from a fertilized *egg* cell. In flowering plants, the embryo is the young plant in the *seed*, consisting of the *hypocotyl* and the rudiments of a *root*, a *stem* (*epicotyl*), and one or two primary leaves (*cotyledons*). The cactus embryo has two cotyledons.

ENDEMIC. Occurring naturally only in a particular geographic area. See *exotic, indigenous.*

ENDOCARP. The inner layer of the *pericarp*, or covering, of the fruit. See also *exocarp, mesocarp.*

ENDOSPERM. A cellular layer enclosing the *embryo* in immature seeds of flowering plants and often persisting in the mature seeds and becoming a food storage area. The endosperm is unique to the flowering plants, and it is formed from a large initial cell in the ovule at the time of fertilization.

ENTIRE. With a smooth, unindented *margin.*

EPHEMERAL. Enduring for only a brief time, as for a single day.

EPI-. A Greek prefix meaning "above," "upon," or on the outside (or outside edge) of.

EPICOTYL. The stem tip of the embryo, a minute area in the *seed* just above the cotyledons.

EPIDERMAL. Of or pertaining to the *epidermis.*

EPIDERMIS. The cells forming the surface layer of a plant organ. The epidermal cells of aerial organs such as stems and leaves usually secrete a layer of waxy material (*cuticle*) that retards evaporation of water. See *hypodermis.*

EPIGYNOUS. Having a floral cup or tube enclosing and adnate with the ovary, the two organs forming an inseparable unit. The flowers of all cacti except some species of *Pereskia* are epigynous. in an apple, also epigynous, the core is the ovary, and the outer edible portion is nearly all floral cup. Cf. *hypogynous, perigynous.*

EPIPHYTE. A nonparasitic plant growing upon another plant and not in contact with the ground; for example, a species of *Rhipsalis* (a cactus) growing characteristically on the limb of a tree.

EPIPHYTIC. Growing as an *epiphyte.*

EPITHET. An adjective used as a noun, often forming part of the name of a plant; for example, *flava* (yellow), as part of the name combination *Rosa flava.*

EROSE. With an irregular *margin* that appears to have been gnawed.

ESCAPE. A species or variety *introduced* from another region into cultivation but having spread into areas where it persists or spreads without the intentional aid of man. See also *endemic, exotic, native.*

ETIOLATED. Whitish because of failure to develop chlorophyll, often because of lack of light. Stems developed in darkness or with little light tend to become elongate and spindly. This phenomenon, etiolation, is particularly common in cacti whose stems have been stored.

EX-. See *e-, ec-.*

EXOCARP. The outer layer of the pericarp, or covering, of the fruit. See also *endocarp, mesocarp.*

EXOTIC. Of foreign rather than *native* origin; said of a plant *introduced* from elsewhere. See also *endemic, indigenous.*

FALCATE. Shaped like a scythe or sickle; flat, curving, and tapering gradually to a point.

FAMILY. A *taxon* composed of a group of related *genera.* The names of plant families usually end in -aceae.

FASCIATE. In a bundle.

FASCIATED. Having the stems parallel, usually flattened, and abnormally attached together, a teratological phenomenon occasional in the Cactaceae; *crested.*

FASCIATION. The quality or state of being fasciated.

FASCICLE. A cluster or a bundle.

FASCICLED, FASCICULATE. In clusters or bundles.

FASTIGIATE. Growing erect and close together.

FAVEOLATE, FAVOSE. Appearing like a honeycomb.

FELTED. With intertwining, matted hairs.

FEMALE GAMETE. The egg cell.

FERTILIZATION. The fusion of two *gametes* of opposite sex to form a *zygote*, the two usually an antherozoid and an egg in plants, a sperm and an egg in animals.

FILAMENT. The stalk bearing the upper, expanded portion of a stamen, which consists primarily of the pollen sacs.

FILIFORM. Threadlike, very slender.

FIMBRIATE. With a marginal fringe.

FIMBRIOLATE, FIMBRILLATE. Fimbriate, the fringe very fine.

FLESHY FRUIT. A fruit with juicy, soft internal tissues, the outer tissues either firm or fleshy.

FLEXUOUS. Curving in and out.

FLOCCOSE. Bearing woolly hair in tufts.

FLOCCULOSE. Floccose, the hair fine.

FLORA. Plants; the plant species occurring naturally together in a particular region, usually through one or more epochs of geologic time. Cf. *vegetation*.

FLORAL. Pertaining to flowers.

FLORAL CUP, FLORAL TUBE (according to shape). A cuplike or tubelike extension of the margin of the receptacle (a *hypanthium*) or a coalescence and adnation of the bases of the sepals, petals, and stamens. This structure bears the petals and stamens on its margin. In *perigynous* flowers the floral cup is free from the outer surface of the ovary; in *epigynous* flowers it is adnate with the ovary. In epigynous flowers and fruits, like apples, it appears to compose the outer layer of the ovary. See *epigynous*, *inferior* and *superior ovaries*.

FOLIACEOUS. Leaflike.

FOVEOLATE. Pitted.

FREE. Not *adnate* with or *coalescent* to another organ. Cf. *approximate*.

FRUIT. The matured, usually considerably enlarged, *ovary* and the enclosed seeds. In the fruit of a cactus the floral cup or tube is wholly adnate with the ovary (except across the top), and the cup or tube forms the outer coat of the fruit.

FRUTESCENT. Shrubby.

FRUTICOSE. Shrublike.

FUNICULUS (pl. FUNICULI). The stalk supporting the ovule or later the seed. See *aril*, *hilum*.

FUNNELFORM. Shaped like a funnel.

FUSIFORM. Spindle-shaped, that is, with the greatest diameter at the middle, circular in any cross section, and tapering gradually to each of the pointed ends.

GAMETE. A male or female haploid sex cell, one of the two haploid cells that join in forming the first cells of a new individual, the fertilized *egg* (*zygote* and *endosperm*).

GENE. A unit of the genetic material localized in the chromosome; a portion of a DNA (deoxyribonucleic acid) molecule that determines one (or more) hereditary character(s) of an individual. See *chromosome*.

GENE POOL. The total genetic information in the sum total of the genes in a breeding population existing at a certain time and place. See *gene*, *introgression*.

GENERIC. Of or pertaining to a *genus*.

GENUS (pl. GENERA). A *taxon* composed of a group of related *species* or sometimes a single species.

GLABRATE, GLABRESCENT. Hairy at first but the hair falling away later.

GLABROUS. Not hairy.

GLADIATE. Like a sword.

GLAND. An organ that secretes. Commonly, glands are discernible because their secretions accumulate as masses or lumps. Many glands are produced on the tips of hairs, these being known as glandular hairs.

GLAUCESCENT. More or less *glaucous*.

GLAUCOUS. With a bluish powdered wax on the surface.

GLOBOSE, GLOBULAR. Essentially spherical; spheroidal.

GLOCHID. One of the small, barbed bristles occurring in the areoles of *Opuntia* (chollas and prickly pears). Glochids are unlike the larger spines in the *areole*, and in the prickly pears usually they are strongly barbed.

GLOCHIDIATE. Having a barb at the tip.

GLOMERATE. In dense, compact clusters.

GLOMERULATE. Glomerate, the clusters small.

GLUTINOUS. Sticky or bearing stick material.

GYNOECIUM. A pistil or a group of pistils in a single flower.

HABIT. The general shape or appearance of a plant as a whole, in nature. A particular species characteristically assumes a particular habit.

HABITAT. The locality and the local combination of environmental conditions in which a plant grows. A particular habitat is characteristic of a particular species.

HAIR. A slender projection of cells. See *trichome*.

HAMATE. Having a terminal hook.

HAPLOID. Having n chromosomes per cell, that is, only one chromosome of each type. See *chromosome number*.

HERBARIUM. An organized collection of plant specimens, the specimens usually pressed.

HETEROZYGOUS. With the genes in the pair or pairs in question unlike. For example, both genes of the pair determining flower color may tend to produce yellow, both may tend to produce blue, or one may tend to yield yellow and the other blue. If the effects of the two genes duplicate, the plant is *homozygous* with respect to this pair of genes. If they are opposed, the plant is heterozygous and the resulting color will depend upon whether either gene is dominant with respect to the other. If neither gene is dominant, the color will be intermediate, for example greenish.

HEXAPLOID. Having $6n$ chromosomes per cell, that

is, six chromosomes of each type. See *chromosome number.*

HEXAPLOIDY. The state of being hexaploid.

HILUM. A scar on the seed coat at the former position of attachment of the *funiculus,* or stalk. *The hilum is the basal point of a seed.* If the seed is broader than long, the hilum may appear to be on the side. The incorrect term "lateral" has been used to describe such cases, but, by definition, the hilum is always basal. See *aril.*

HIRSUTE. Having stiff and more or less coarse hairs.

HISPID. With rigid, stiff bristles.

HISPIDULOUS. Hispid, the bristles small.

HOARY. Having short, dense, grayish-white hairs, these obscuring the stem or leaf and making it appear white, as if covered by frost.

HOLOTYPE (TYPE SPECIMEN). The particular permanently preserved specimen upon which a taxon (for example, a species) has been based and with which its scientific name is associated permanently. The specimen is so designated when the original description is published and the name is therein applied to the plant; thereafter, that name must be applied only to the taxon that includes the holotype. The type specimen should be deposited in an herbarium. See *isotype, lectotype, neotype.*

HOMOZYGOUS. Having the genes in the pair or pairs in question alike. Cf. *heterozygous.*

HOOK. A structure (such as a spine) with a long basal portion and ending in a tip that curves backward, forming an arc.

HOOKED. With a hook.

HYALINE. Thin, translucent, and resembling glass.

HYBRID. An individual whose parents differ or differed in some hereditary characters. Often the word has been used to describe individuals resulting from crossing different genera, species, or varieties. However, these taxa cannot be limited precisely, because intergradation, *introgression,* and intergeneric, interspecific, and intervarietal hybrids are common.

HYBRIDIZATION. Mating involving parents with unlike genes, often the characteristic combinations of different varieties, species, or genera.

HYBRID SWARM. A natural or cultivated plant population with abundant hybrids between two or more taxa, often produced by complete or local breakdown of isolating barriers between two or more closely related species or other taxa. Hybrids between two taxa have bred with each other and with their parents through a few to many generations and sometimes with one or more other taxa. So long as selective factors in the environment (or selection by man) are not strong enough to favor only the individuals with the genes of the parental species or particular new combinations, the hybrid swarm continues. Hybrid swarms are abundant in nature in some taxa; often also they develop among plants in disturbed habitats or in cultivation, where the environment is kept favorable to a wide range of plants, and hybrids are perhaps as well adapted as the parental species.

HYGROSCOPIC. Sensitive to the moisture available and readily obtaining it; changing form according to the moisture available, as the series of cells on one side of a fern sporangium (spore case) that curves and straightens the sporangium, thus throwing the spores into the air.

HYPANTHIUM. A *floral cup* or *floral tube* that is an extension of the stem tissue of the *receptacle* rather than a fusion of the bases of the sepals, petals, and stamens.

HYPOCOTYL. The largest part of the main axis of the *embryo,* the portion occurring below the *cotyledons.* The hypocotyl is continuous with the developing primary root.

HYPODERMIS. A layer of cells just under the *epidermis,* specialized for some particular function, such as secretion of protective materials or supplying a structural rigidity.

HYPOGYNOUS. Having no floral cup or tube. Cf. *epigynous, perigynous.*

IMBRICATE, IMBRICATED. Overlapping like shingles.

IMPERFECT. Having either functional pistil or stamens, but not both, in the same flower. Cf. *bisexual, dioecious, monoecious, perfect, unisexual.*

IMPRESSED. Imprinted deeply (in minute trenches).

INCISED. Having the margin indented as if by sharp, irregular, deep incisions.

INCUMBENT. Of a pair of cotyledons, turned so that the back of one lies flat against the main axis of the embryo and the back of the other is turned away from it. See *accumbent.*

INDEHISCENT. Not splitting open along regular lines. See *circumscissile, dehiscent.*

INDETERMINATE. Not growing to a predetermined size or state of development and then stopping; continuing at least theoretically to grow as long as conditions are favorable. See *determinate.*

INDIGENOUS. *Native* in the region under consideration. See *endemic, introduced.*

INDURATE, INDURATED. Hardened.

INFERIOR FLORAL CUP or TUBE. The part of the floral cup or tube attached to the ovary (usually to the lower part). See *superior floral cup.*

INFERIOR OVARY. An ovary enclosed by the floral cup or tube, with which all or part of its surface is adnate. All the cacti except some species of *Pereskia* have inferior ovaries. Cf. *superior ovary.*

INFLORESCENCE. The portion of a plant consisting of a terminal stem and the flowers borne thereon.

INFRASPECIFIC. Designating a rank below that of *species,* e.g. *subspecies, variety,* subvariety, forma.

INTEGUMENT. The outer coat of an ovule, later becoming the seed coat.

INTERNODE. The part of a stem lying between two nodes or "joints."

INTRODUCED. *Native* to another area and imported (intentionally or not) into the area under consideration, often becoming established and spreading without the aid of man. See also *endemic, escape, indigenous.*

INTROGRESSION. Introgressive *hybridization,* that is, hybridization followed for several generations by breeding back the hybrid and its descendants to one of the parental taxa. Later generations are less and less like the original hybrid, but they carry some genes characteristic of each parental taxon into the other. See *gene pool.*

INVESTED. Enclosed or almost surrounded by another structure.

INVOLUTE. Rolled inward, as a leaf margin.

ISOTYPE. A duplicate of the type specimen (holotype), that is, a specimen collected by the same person at the same place and time, bearing the same field number or other identification, and so far as can be determined believed by the collector to be the same collection, from the same population. See *holotype, lectotype, neotype.*

ISTHMUS. As in geography, a narrow structure connecting two broader units, as in the areoles of some cacti.

JOINT. One separable segment of a stem made up of a series of such distinguishable segments; sometimes used (inappropriately) for *node.*

KEEL. A ridge formed along the outer edge of a fold and resembling the keel of a boat.

KEELED. Having a keel; carinate.

LACERATE. Irregularly cut, as if slashed.

LACINIATE. Lacerate into narrow segments, these usually pointed.

LACUNOSE. With depressions or perforations.

LANATE. Bearing long, soft, more or less entangled hairs.

LANCEOLATE. Having the shape of a lance, that is, 4-6 times as long as broad, acute at both ends, and broadest near the attachment end.

LATERAL. Extending to the side; on the side. A laterally flattened or compressed structure has its broadest faces on its sides, rather than on the front and back. Cf. *dorsoventral.*

LATEX. An opaque, milky, and often gummy juice.

LEAF. A usually broad, flat outgrowth from the side of the stem; the primary organ of photosynthesis. Often leaves may be either vestigial or modified in form. The leaf of a flowering plant always has a bud or a potential bud or a branch in the axil, or angle, above it.

LEAF PRIMORDIUM. A hump of tissue developing into a young leaf or sometimes remaining vestigial, as in most cacti.

LECTOTYPE. A substitute for the type specimen (holotype), that is, one designated to stand in place of the type specimen if a type specimen was not designated in the original published description. A lectotype is chosen from among specimens mentioned in the original publication of the name of the taxon or from those known to have been studied by the original author. See *holotype, isotype, neotype.*

LENTICULAR. Lens-shaped, that is, like a biconvex lens.

LIBERAL. A botanist who requires taxa to be natural, but divides them narrowly into small units. See *conservative, lumper, splitter.*

LINEAR. Narrow, with parallel sides, and with the length 8 or more times the width.

LOBE. Generally, a segment of an indented leaf or other organ, especially if rounded; specifically, a short segment less than one-fourth the length or breadth of the organ as a whole.

LOBED, LOBATE. From moderately to very deeply indented toward the base or midrib; in a restricted sense, indented by more than the mere formation of teeth, but less than halfway to the base or the midrib. In a general sense, *cleft, parted,* or *divided.*

LUMPER. A botanist who does not deal with natural units, or taxa, but instead establishes broad categories made up of elements not necessarily closely related and assembles them according to arbitrarily chosen criteria. See *conservative, liberal, splitter.*

MALE GAMETE. The pollen cell (haploid nucleus) that invades the ovary to fertilize the female gamete.

MAMMIFORM. Nipple-shaped.

MAMMILLATE. Bearing small, nipplelike projections.

MEGAGAMETOPHYTE. In the flowering plants a structure developed within the ovule and consisting of seven cells that give rise to the egg cell or female gamete. Cf. *microgametophyte.*

MEGASPORANGIUM (pl. MEGASPORANGIA). In the flowering plants, a structure (the *nucellus,* in the seed plants) consisting of several layers of cells, enclosing first the megaspore, which gives rise to the *megagametophyte,* and later, after fertilization, the developing embryo. The megasporangium is enclosed by one or two seed coats (*integuments*).

MERISTEM. A tissue composed of diploid cells with the power of division, these often producing new cells adding to or replacing surrounding tissues.

MERISTEMATIC. Having cells capable of division; having the function of dividing.

MESOCARP. The middle layer of the *pericarp,* or covering, of the fruit. See also *endocarp, exocarp.*

MICROGAMETOPHYTE. In the flowering plants, the pollen grain, which produces the male gamete cell. Cf. *megagametophyte.*

MICROPYLE. The minute opening in the *integument* of the ovule (later the seed coat) through which the pollen tube enters the ovule. This passageway may be at varying distances from the *hilum.*

MICROSPECIES. In the sense used here, minute "species" resulting from an over-fine division of taxa. Commonly used for narrow taxonomic units of apomictic or other clonal origin.

MIDRIB. The vein along the middle of a leaf or other structure.

MONOCOLPATE. Of a pollen grain, having one groove or furrow in its surface.

MONOCOTYLEDON. A flowering plant having a single *cotyledon* in the *embryo.* Cf. *dicotyledon.*

MONOECIOUS. Having staminate (male) and pistillate (female) flowers on the same individual. See *bisexual, dioecious, imperfect, perfect, unisexual.*

MONTANE. Of the mountains; commonly, of areas of middle elevations in the mountains. Cf. *alpine.*

MUCRO. A short, sharp terminal point of tissue similar in texture or consistency to that of the rest of the structure.

MUCRONATE. Bearing a *mucro*.

MUCRONULATE. Mucronate, the mucro small.

NATIVE. Occurring naturally in an area; so far as is known, not introduced into the area by man. See *endemic, indigenous, introduced*.

NATURAL CLASSIFICATION. A system of classification based on patterns of observed characters, thus on assumed genetic and evolutionary relationships. See *artificial classification, lumper, splitter*.

NECTAR. A sugary secretion commonly attracting insects.

NECTARIFEROUS. Bearing nectar.

NECTARY. A gland producing nectar.

NEOTYPE. A substitute for the nomenclatural type specimen (holotype) chosen subsequently if the *holotype* is known to have been destroyed or lost. See *holotype, isotype, lectotype*.

NERVE. A rib or vein.

NETTED. In the form of a net; meshed.

NOCTURNAL. Occurring at night. Cf. *diurnal*.

NODE. A "joint" of a stem, this bearing one or more leaves, each with a bud in the angle (*axil*) above it; the point of connection between stem segments, or joints.

NOMEN. Name.

NOMEN CONFUSUM. A name invalid because of confusion concerning its application.

NOMEN CONSERVANDUM. A conserved name of a taxon, that is, one that is conserved for use despite its lack of priority in time of publication over another name or its earlier use for another plant group. An example is the genus *Mammillaria*.

NOMEN NOVUM. A new name substituted for an older one that is invalid.

NOMEN NUDUM. A name that is invalid because published without a description, or, since January 1, 1935, because published without a Latin diagnosis or description, or, since January 1, 1958, because published without the designation of a nomenclatural type specimen.

NUCELLUS (pl. NUCELLI). The *megasporangium*. (The term nucellus is used only for the seed plants.)

OB-. Prefix indicating attachment at the end opposite the usual point of attachment, as, for example, attachment of the petiole of a leaf at the small instead of the large end. A *lanceolate* leaf is attached at the broad end; an *oblanceolate* leaf is the same shape, but the attachment is at the narrow end.

OBCONIC, OBCONICAL. Conical, but attached at the apex of the cone, rather than at the base.

OBDELTOID. Deltoid, but attached at one angle, rather than on a side.

OBLANCEOLATE. Lanceolate, but attached at the narrow end, rather than at the broad end.

OBLIQUE. Diagonal; with the sides unequal or slanting.

OBLONG. About two or three times as long as broad, with more or less parallel sides.

OBOVATE. Ovate, but attached at the narrow end.

OBOVOID. Ovoid, but attached at the narrow end.

OBSOLESCENT. Almost nonexistent; rudimentary.

OBSOLETE. Abortive or only slightly or imperfectly developed.

OBTUSE. Blunt or rounded at the apex or base.

OCTOPLOID. With **8n** chromosomes of each kind in each cell. See *chromosome number*.

OPERCULATE. Having a cap or a lid.

OPERCULUM. A cap or a lid.

OPPOSITE. With two organs, as leaves, occurring at the same level and on the opposite sides of the stem or other supporting structure. Cf. *alternate*.

ORBICULAR. Nearly spherical.

ORBICULATE. Nearly circular.

ORDER. A *taxon* composed of related *families* or sometimes of only a single family.

ORGAN. A special portion of a plant, either vegetative (as a root, stem, or leaf) or reproductive (as a flower or fruit).

ORTHOTROPOUS. Of an ovule, straight, not curved or bent. Cf. *amphitropous, anatropous, camphylotropous*.

OVAL. Broadly elliptic.

OVARY. The lower, expanded portion of a pistil, containing the *ovules* that, after fertilization, develop into seeds. The ovary of a *hypogynous* or a *perigynous* flower is superior; that of an *epigynous* flower is inferior. The ovary of a cactus flower, except that of some species of *Pereskia*, is inferior. See *pistil*.

OVATE. Having the shape of an egg, about one and one-half times as long as broad, with both ends rounded, and with the apex a little narrower than the base; applied to leaves and other essentially two-dimensional objects. See *ovoid*.

OVOID. Ovate, but three-dimensional, like a hen's egg. See *ovate*.

OVULE. The structure (one of one or more in the ovary) that ultimately becomes a seed. In the ovary at flowering time the *ovule* contains the *female gamete* (reproductive cell, or egg). After fertilization the ovule begins to develop into a *seed*. After cell divisions the fertilized egg becomes an *embryo* made up of a main axis composed of the *hypocotyl* (continuous with the root) and the stem, and of *cotyledons* and leaf primordia. In the cacti there are two cotyledons (seed leaves). See *pistil*.

PANICLE. A branching inflorescence composed of racemes, spikes, or corymbs.

PAPILLA (pl. PAPILLAE). A low, usually rounded projection.

PAPILLATE. Having *papillae*.

PAPILLOSE. *Papillate*, the papillae minute.

PARENCHYMA. A soft tissue with thin-walled cells that remain alive.

PARIETAL. Borne on the margin or the outer side. For example, a parietal placenta (or seed-bearing structure) is on the outer ovary wall and not at the center, where the partitions (if any) meet.

PARTED. Indented more than halfway or nearly all the way to the base or to the midrib. See *cleft, lobed, divided*.

PECTINATE. Having structures (e.g. spines) arranged like the teeth of a comb.

PEDICEL. The stalk of a flower, in the cacti usually small, obscure, or almost nonexistent.

PERFECT. Having both functional pistil and stamens in the same flower. Cf. *bisexual, dioecious, imperfect, monoecious, unisexual.*

PERENNIAL. Lasting year after year. Cf. *annual.*

PERIANTH. The sepals and petals or corresponding structures in a flower, or the corresponding more or less undifferentiated or intergrading parts of some flowers; in the cacti the intergrading sepaloids (sepaloid perianth parts) and petaloids (petaloid perianth parts) are of a different origin from ordinary sepals and petals. See *petaloid, petaloid perianth part, sepaloid, sepaloid perianth part.*

PERIANTH PARTS. The sepals and petals or other corresponding structures constituting the *perianth*; in the cacti, the sepaloids and petaloids.

PERIANTH TUBE. A floral tube formed by fusion of the bases of the *perianth* parts, these being joined at least basally edge-to-edge, i.e. sepal-to-petal-to-sepal, etc. This type of tube is common in the monocotyledons.

PERICARP. The wall of a fruit, often composed of outer, middle, and inner layers, the *exocarp, mesocarp,* and *endocarp.*

PERIGYNOUS. Having a *floral cup* or *tube,* but the cup or tube separate from the ovary. In the cacti, perigynous flowers occur only in some species of *Pereskia.* Cf. *epigynous, hypogynous.*

PERIPHERAL. On the margin.

PERSISTENT. Remaining attached after the usual time of falling away. Cf. *deciduous.*

PETAL. In most flowers, one of the usually highly colored inner series of flower parts attractive to insects. Usually the petals or their counterparts (*petaloids* in the cacti) are more highly colored than the sepals or their counterparts (*sepaloids* in the cacti). See *petaloid, sepal, sepaloid.*

PETALOID. Similar to a petal in appearance or position; in this work, a *petaloid perianth part* (an adjective used as a noun).

PETALOID PERIANTH PART. A flower part resembling a *petal* but of a different origin. The leaves (if any) of cacti shade into sepaloid perianth parts (*sepaloids*) that shade into petaloid perianth parts (*petaloids*), and all are of a similar nature and origin. The petals of most other flowers originate through sterilization of stamens or their forerunners.

PETIOLE. The stalk of a leaf, supporting the expanded portion or blade.

PETIOLED, PETIOLATE. Having a *petiole.*

PHENOTYPE. The detectable and usually visible characters of the individual, produced by the interaction between heredity (its genetic potential) and the environment in which it finds itself. For example, a plant may have yellow flowers or lanceolate leaves.

PHLOEM. A conducting tissue carrying manufactured food downward, usually from the leaves, to places of storage or of use. See *cambium, xylem.*

PHOTOSYNTHESIS. In green plants, the process of combining carbon dioxide and water in the presence of light and *chlorophyll,* forming basic sugars.

PHOTOSYNTHETIC. Carrying on photosynthesis, as the green parts of the stems and leaves of vascular plants.

PHYLUM. A zoological term, the approximate but not exact equivalent of *division* in the Plant Kingdom.

PILOSE. Having soft, slender hairs.

PISTIL. The ovule-bearing (and later seed-producing) female organ of a flower, made up of the *stigma*(s) (receptive to pollen), which is (are) connected by a tubular *style* to the *ovary,* in which *ovules,* then *seeds,* are developed. A pistil is composed of a single *carpel* or of two or more *coalescent* carpels, each of which is a specialized leaf.

PISTILLATE. Having *pistils* but not stamens. Cf. *staminate.*

PITH. The soft tissue at the center of a vascular plant stem. Usually the pith is surrounded by a cylinder of wood. See *cortex.*

PITTED. With small depressions in the surface.

PLACENTA (pl. PLACENTAE). The tissue to which the funiculi (stalks) of the ovules or seeds are attached. This may be either on the ovary wall where carpels are joined or, if the carpels are folded inward, at the lines of meeting of the partitions of the ovary.

PLACENTATION. Manner of arrangement of the placentae and the ovules in the ovary.

PLASTID. A body within a cell, the best-known type being a *chloroplast.* Plastids commonly bear pigments such as the chlorophylls (green) and associated pigments, or red, yellow, or other pigments that are not water-soluble. Ordinarily, plastid pigments persist with little change when a plant specimen is prepared by fast drying. Some plastids (leucoplasts) contain no pigment; food may be stored in them.

PLASTID PIGMENT. The coloring matter in a *plastid* (solid body). The pigment is insoluble in water.

PLOIDY. Having reference to the number of sets of chromosomes per cell in an individual, and their varying makeup. See *chromosome number.*

POLLEN. The spheroidal structures developed in the *anther* of a flower. The mature pollen grain is a minute male plant (*microgametophyte*).

POLLEN GRAIN. Pollen; a single microgametophyte.

POLLEN SAC, POLLEN CHAMBER. One of usually four pollen-bearing cavities in the *anther* of a stamen, the two pairs of pollen sacs joined by a *connective.*

POLLEN TUBE. A tubular outgrowth of the pollen grain. The pollen grain lands on the stigma, and the pollen tube grows down through the stigma and the tubular style into the ovary, where it may bring about fertilization through the joining of an enclosed (but finally released) male gamete nucleus with the female egg nucleus.

POLYPLOID. Having more than **2n** chromosomes per cell, that is, more than two cells of each type. See *chromosome number.*

PORRECT. Directed outward and forward, as a spine.

PRICKLE. A sharp, pointed structure, as in roses, arising from the outermost cells of the surface of a stem or leaf and not connected with the woody inner tissues. See *spine, thorn.*

PRIMORDIUM. See *leaf primordium.*

PRISMATIC. Having the shape of a prism; angular, with the sides flat.

PROCUMBENT. Lying flat on the ground but not rooting. Cf. *decumbent, prostrate, repent.*

PROLIFEROUS. Reproducing by buds or special shoots. In the cacti, the term is applied particularly to the formation of buds (e.g., flower buds) from the areoles of a fruit.

PROSTRATE. Flat on the ground. Cf. *decumbent, procumbent, repent.*

PROXIMAL. Close to the point of attachment. Cf. *distal.*

PUBERULENT. *Pubescent*, the hairs fine, minute.

PUBESCENCE. Hair or down.

PUBESCENT. Hairy, with usually fine, soft hairs, the term extended commonly to denote the presence of any kind of hair. See *puberulent.*

PUNCTATE. Covered with dots or points; for example, with glands on the surface, the masses of secretions appearing as dots.

PUNGENT. Sharp-pointed.

PYRAMIDAL. In the shape of a pyramid.

PYRIFORM. Pear-shaped.

RADIAL SPINE. One of the spines around the margin of an areole, the distinction between radial and *central spines* sometimes arbitrary.

RECEPTACLE. The tip of the stem that produces the parts of a flower, formed from the upper, very short internodes and the nodes from which the flower parts grow. Except in some species of *Pereskia*, the receptacle of the cactus flower is covered up by the adnate *floral cup* and *ovary* arising from it. The stalk of the flower terminating in the receptacle is the *pedicel*, which in the cacti usually is small, obscure, or almost nonexistent.

RECURVED. Curving downward or backward, that is, in the direction opposite the usual one. See *reflexed, retrorse.*

REDUCED. Small and presumably derived from forebears with larger or more elaborate corresponding structures.

REFLEXED. Bent or turned abruptly downward or backward. See *recurved, retrorse.*

RELIC. A plant or a population persisting in only a part of its probable previous range.

RELICT. Persisting as a *relic.*

RENIFORM. In the shape of a kidney or a bean.

REPAND. With the margin winding irregularly in and out.

REPENT. Creeping; *prostrate* and rooting at the nodes. Cf. *procumbent.*

RETICULATE. In a meshwork; netlike. Cf. *areolate.*

RETICULUM. A meshwork or network.

RETRORSE. Turned downward or backward. See *recurved, reflexed.*

RETUSE. Shallowly and broadly notched at the apex, the apex broad.

RHIZOME. An underground stem growing horizontally and usually bearing roots at the nodes and producing aerial stems.

RHOMBIC. Formed like an equilateral parallelogram; essentially diamond-shaped, with the attachment at one of the sharp angles. Cf. *rhomboid.*

RHOMBOID. *Rhombic*, but in three dimensions.

RIB. A ridge running vertically or spirally along the side of the stem. The stem ribs of cacti are composites of rib tissue and the completely or incompletely coalescent and adnate *tubercles.* The apices of the tubercles may protrude from the rib, and each tubercle on the rib bears an *areole* that usually produces spines. See *vein.*

ROOT. The usually underground part of the main axis of a plant that has no nodes, internodes, or leaves and has a solid core of xylem instead of a hollow one with internal pith as in the stems of flowering plants.

ROTATE. Spreading like a saucer.

RUDIMENT. A vestige of an organ.

RUFOUS, RUFESCENT. Reddish-brown.

RUGOSE. Wrinkled.

RUPTURING. Breaking open along an irregular line. Cf. *dehiscent.*

SAC, SACK. A baglike indentation or a pocket.

SACCATE. In the form of a sac.

SALTATION. A sudden, abrupt change of characters from one taxon to another, a jump.

SCABERULOUS. Scabrous, the projections particularly minute.

SCABROUS. Bearing minute, rough or sharp projections, and rough to the touch.

SCALE, SCALE LEAF. In the cacti, a small leaf on the floral tube, especially on the part covering the ovary and adnate with it. A scale leaf may be either thin or flattened or succulent; sometimes it is elaborate in form.

SCANDENT. Climbing.

SCARIOUS. Thin, membranous, and translucent, in the manner of parchment.

SCIENTIFIC, or BOTANICAL, NAME. A name combination formed from the name of the genus and an *epithet* for the species, as *Rosa flava* (literally, yellow rose). To this the epithet of a variety may be added, as *Rosa flava* var. *montana* (mountain yellow rose).

SECTION. A group of related species that forms a natural unit within a *genus* or a *subgenus.*

SEED. The developed and matured *ovule.* The seeds of flowering plants are enclosed in an *ovary.* The seed develops a usually hard or leathery coat, and it includes the *embryo.* See *pistil.*

SEED CHAMBER. A section of the *ovary* separated by a usually vertical radial wall. The mature cactus fruit has no walls, and there is only one seed chamber.

SEED COAT. The outer hard wall of a seed; the *integument.*

SEPAL. One of the green (or at least usually not highly colored) outer *perianth* parts of most flowers, as opposed to the usually more strikingly colored *petals* (or in the cacti the sepaloids and petaloids). See *petaloids, petaloid perianth parts, sepaloids, sepaloid perianth parts.*

SEPALOID. Having the appearance of a sepal; in this work, a *sepaloid perianth part* (an adjective used as a noun).

SEPALOID PERIANTH PART. A flower part resembling a *sepal*, but of a different origin. See *petaloids, petaloid perianth parts.*

SERRATE. With marginal teeth resembling those of a saw, that is, the teeth forward-projecting and acutely angled.

SERRULATE. *Serrate*, the teeth minute.

SESSILE. Without a stalk.

SETA (pl. SETAE). A bristle.

SETACEOUS, SETIFORM. Bristlelike.

SETIFEROUS. Bearing bristles.

SETOSE. Covered with bristles.

SETULOSE. *Setose*, the bristles minute.

SHRUB. A woody plant having several to many main stems developed from about ground level. In general, shrubs are smaller than trees.

SINUATE, SINUOUS. With the margin wavy and winding in and out. Cf. *undulate.*

SINUS. An embayment or cleft or recess.

SMOOTH. Not rough.

SPATHULATE, SPATULATE. In essentially the shape of a spatula; narrowly oblong, but with the corners rounded, the basal end tapering and elongate, the apical end broadened (often abruptly so).

SPECIES (sing. & pl.). A *taxon* composed of a group of related *varieties* or a single unit. A living natural species is a reproducing population or system of populations of genetically closely related individuals. This definition applies of course to any taxon; the difference at different levels is in the degree of closeness of relationship, less for higher ranks, greater for lower ranks. (For a discussion of the nature of species, see Lyman Benson, *Plant Taxonomy, Methods and Principles,* Chapter 9, Ronald Press Company, New York, 1962; reprinted, John Wiley & Sons, 1978.)

SPECIFIC. Particular; also, pertaining to a *species*, as, for example, the characters distinguishing a species from its relatives.

SPHEROIDAL. With approximately the shape of a sphere; with the appearance of a sphere.

SPINDLE-SHAPED. See *fusiform.*

SPINE. A hard structure with a sharp point derived from a leaf or a part of a leaf. The spines of cacti develop as specialized leaves growing from the bud in the areole or from secondary buds derived from it. See *prickle, thorn.*

SPINIFEROUS, SPINESCENT. Bearing spines.

SPINOSE. Spinelike or ending in a spine.

SPIRAL. Arranged in a spiral but often appearing to alternate on the two sides of a structure such as a stem. Cf. *alternate, opposite.*

SPLITTER. A botanist who does not attempt to deal with natural units, or taxa, but instead establishes narrow categories split at random from others according to arbitrarily chosen criteria. See *conservative, liberal, lumper.*

SPORADIC. Irregular in occurrence.

SQUAMELLATE. Bearing scales.

SQUAMULOSE. Bearing minute scales.

STAMEN. The male, or pollen-producing organ of a flower, consisting of an *anther* composed chiefly of *pollen sacs* and a slender supporting *filament* or stalk.

STAMINATE. Having *stamens* but not *pistils.* Cf. *pistillate.*

STELLATE. Star-shaped.

STEM. The part of the axis of the plant above the *cotyledon*(s); usually bearing leaves and often bearing branches; the *epicotyl.*

STIGMA. The terminal, pollen-receptive part of the *pistil* of a flower, supported by the *style*, which leads to the *ovary.* A solitary style may bear more than one stigma; in the cacti, usually 3 to 20. See *pistil.*

STIGMATIC. Of the nature of a *stigma*; the stigmatic surface is the part of the stigma receptive to pollen and secreting a sugar solution in which the pollen grain germinates.

STOMA (pl. STOMATA). A porelike opening in the epidermis of a plant; in the flowering plants, surrounded by two guard cells that regulate the size of the opening.

STORAGE ROOT. A thickened root with much reserve food.

STRIATE. Having longitudinal ridges and grooves.

STYLE. The tubular organ connecting the *stigma*(s) and the *ovary* of a pistil. See *pistil.*

SUB-. A prefix meaning "nearly" or "almost" or "under."

SUBFAMILY. A *taxon* of a rank between family and genus, but higher than *tribe.*

SUBGENUS (pl. SUBGENERA). A group of related species or sections forming part of a *genus.*

SUBSPECIES (sing. & pl.). A *taxon* with a rank between that of *species* and *variety*; a group of related varieties. This taxon is employed in its correct sense by some authors, but others substitute it for variety. The term has been applied only rarely to units of the Cactaceae. See *species, taxon, variety.*

SUBTENDING. Standing beneath, or to the outside of, as a leaf (bract) subtends a flower.

SUBULATE. Shaped like a shoemaker's awl; flattened (in cross section a narrow ellipse) and tapering into a point at the apex; awl-shaped. Cf. *attenuate.*

SUCCULENT. With much soft, watery tissue and therefore fleshy.

SUCCULENT METABOLISM. Absorption of carbon dioxide from the air at night (when evaporation of water is low), combining the CO_2 into organic acids, then using it in photosynthesis the next day (when evaporation would be rapid if the stomata were open).

SULCATE. Grooved.

SUPERIOR FLORAL CUP OR TUBE. The part of the *floral cup* or *tube* above and free from an *inferior ovary.* See *inferior floral cup.*

SUPERIOR OVARY. An ovary above, rather than adnate with, the floral cup or tube. See *inferior ovary.*

SYNONYM. A name or a name combination not to be used because it is illegitimate or because it was applied earlier to a different plant or because there is an earlier name applied to the taxon in question.

SYNONYMY. The condition of being a *synonym.* For

each species or other taxon there may be a list of discarded names; these are said to be in synonymy.

TAPROOT. A continuation of the main plant axis from the *hypocotyl* into the primary root from which branch roots arise; in some plants, descending deeply into the ground.

TAXON (pl. TAXA). A taxonomic unit, that is, a category of classification; for example, a species or one of the varieties composing it. The taxon of the first magnitude is Regnum Vegetabile, the Plant Kingdom, which is composed of taxa of the next rank, that is, *divisions*, and in turn *classes, orders, families, genera, species, subspecies,* and *varieties.*

TAXONOMIC. Pertaining to taxonomy.

TAXONOMY. The principles of classification of living organisms and the construction of a natural system of classification, that is, of classification according to (presumed) natural genetic or phylogenetic (evolutionary) relationships.

TERATOLOGY. The study of biological monstrosities. See *fasciation.*

TERETE. Elongate-cylindroid, that is, approximately circular in cross section, but of varying diameter, slender.

TESSELLATE. With a surface like a cobblestone pavement.

TETRAPLOID. Having **4n** chromosomes in each cell, that is, four chromosomes of each type. See *chromosome number.*

TETRAPLOIDY. The state of being *tetraploid.*

THORN. A sharp, pointed branch. See *prickle, spine.*

TOMENTOSE. See *woolly.*

TOMENTULOSE. *Tomentose,* the wool minute.

TOMENTUM. Wool.

TOOTH. A small marginal projection.

TRANSPIRATION. Evaporation of water from the tissues of a plant.

TRANSVERSE. Across.

TREE. A usually large woody plant with a single main trunk that may branch above.

TRIBE. A *taxon* of a rank between family and genus, but lower than *subfamily.*

TRICHOME. A *hair* of a plant. Plant hairs usually are composed each of more than one cell.

TRICOLPATE. Of a pollen grain, bearing three grooves or furrows, as the pollen grains of most dicotyledonous plants.

TRUNCATE. Ending abruptly, as if chopped off at right angles to the axis.

TUBER. A thickened underground stem, as a white potato, specialized as a storage organ. See *tuberous.*

TUBERCLE. A projection; in the cacti, a stem projection bearing an *areole.*

TUBERCULATE. Bearing tubercles.

TUBEROUS. Having the aspect of a *tuber.* Structures other than stems (for example, roots) may be tuberous, but not tubers. A sweet potato is tuberous.

TUBULAR. Forming a hollow, elongate cylinder, or essentially a cylinder.

TURBINATE. Top-shaped.

TURGID. Swollen.

TYPE. See *holotype.*

TYPE LOCALITY. The locality in which the *type specimen* of a taxon was collected.

TYPE SPECIES. The species of a genus with which the generic name is associated permanently. If all other species are transferred to other genera and this one remains, the name of the genus still must be used in the restricted definition.

TYPE SPECIMEN. See *holotype.*

UMBILICUS. A cuplike apical depression.

UNCINATE. Hooked.

UNDULATE. With the margin irregular and winding gently in and out; wavy. Cf. *sinuate.*

UNISEXUAL. With only one sex represented in the same individual or organ; for example, with either pistils or stamens, but not both, on the same plant or in the same flower. Cf. *bisexual, dioecious, imperfect, monoecious, perfect.*

VARIETAL. Pertaining to a variety.

VARIETAS. The Latin and official name for *variety,* which is the English name for an infraspecific *taxon.*

VARIETY. The lowest ranking *taxon* commonly recognized; a subdivision of a *species* or (if subspecies is used) of a *subspecies.* The technical term is *varietas;* variety is the English word.

VASCULAR BUNDLE. A fiber of xylem and phloem.

VASCULAR PLANT. A plant having xylem and phloem, which constitute the vascular tissues.

VASCULAR TISSUES. A structural portion of the plant containing both *xylem* (wood) and *phloem* (the main ingredient of bark), both of these being conducting tissues.

VASCULAR TRACE. A vascular bundle of xylem-and-phloem fibers leading into a leaf, a branch, or a reproductive part of the flower.

VEGETATION. The covering of plants in an area, whatever their floristic origin. Types of vegetation cover include forest, woodland, grassland, tundra, and desert. Cf. *flora.*

VEGETATIVE. Nonreproductive, said of a part of a plant not normally reproductive, such as a root, stem, or leaf.

VEGETATIVE REPRODUCTION. Growth of plant fragments asexually into new individuals.

VEIN. A thread of conducting tissue in a leaf or a flower part. See *rib.*

VELUTINOUS. Velvety.

VENTRAL. (1) Of an organ such as a leaf, on the side facing toward the axis of the organism (for example, the stem). (2) Of an organism such as a liverwort or a mammal, on the side facing toward the ground. The front or upper side of a leaf is the ventral side, because ordinarily it slants upward at an angle, facing the stem. Cf. *dorsal.*

VERTICIL. See *whorl.*

VERTICILLATE. Arranged in a whorl, verticil, or cycle.

VESICLE. An air cavity or bladder.

VESTIGE. A rudiment.

VESTIGIAL. Poorly developed; rudimentary.

VILLOUS. Covered with soft, long, more or less interlaced hairs. See *woolly.*

VISCID. Sticky.

WAX. See *bloom, cuticle, glaucous.*

WEED. A plant growing where it is not wanted, often but not necessarily introduced from another area (that is, not native).

WHORL. A group of three or more organs appearing at the same level, as, for example, three or more leaves at the same node of a stem; a verticil, or cycle.

WING. A thin and membranous or leathery expansion of the surface of an organ such as a stem or a fruit.

WOOLLY. Covered with long, matted, strongly interlaced hairs. See *villous.*

XERIC. Dry, arid; said of habitats. See *xerophytic.*

XEROPHYTE. A plant that lives under remarkably dry conditions, such as those in deserts or chaparral.

XEROPHYTIC. Adapted to, and preferring, a dry environment. See *xeric.*

XYLEM. Wood; the elongated, thick-walled cells that constitute wood. Xylem cells conduct water and dissolved salts from the soil upward to the higher parts of the plant; they serve also in supporting the body of the plant. See *cambium, phloem.*

ZYGOTE. The fertilized egg resulting from the joining of the male and female gamete nuclei. The other cell contents, contributed mostly by the egg, join also, but they are of relatively less-known significance in heredity.

References Cited

The books and papers listed below are pertinent to subjects discussed in the Introduction and the text. A few papers merely establishing the occurrence of a species at a particular place or documenting a minor point are cited in the text but not included here. The numerous publications cited under Documentation (p. 910) are not listed here unless they relate also to text discussion of a principle. Reference to publications in the Introduction and in the text is by the method customary in the biological sciences, that is, by author and year of publication. "Jones, 1970," or "Jones (1970)" indicates a paper in this list by Jones published during 1970. Occasionally, the title of a work is included in a text citation in order to convey to the reader the subject matter and general character of the work.

Compiling a bibliography is like painting the Golden Gate Bridge. Painting starts at one end of the bridge and continues to the other, but by the time the far end is reached, it is time to start over at the beginning; there is no completing the job. The production of botanical literature, like the research underlying it, is never finished, and the text for this work was set in type before additions to the bibliography were closed. Thus, there are some references here that are not reflected in the main parts of the text.

Abrams, LeRoy. 1923/1944/1951/1960. Illustrated flora of the Pacific States: Washington, Oregon, and California. 1-4 (4 with Roxanna S. Ferris). (Cactaceae by Ira L. Wiggins and Carl B. Wolf.) Stanford Univ. Press, Stanford, Calif.

———— 1929. Endemism and its significance in the California flora. Internat. Congress of Plant Sciences at Ithaca, N.Y. 2: 1520-24.

Adams, Charles C. 1902. Postglacial origin and migration of the life of the northeastern United States. Jour. Geography 1: 300-310, 352-57.

Adams, John. 1946. The flora of Canada. Canada Year Book, 1938, as revised in 1945. Edmond Cloutier, King's Printer, Ottawa.

Addicott, W. O. 1969. Tertiary climatic change in the marginal northeast Pacific Ocean. Science 165: 583-86.

Agurell, S., J. G. Bruhn, and K. Sheth. 1972. Structure and biosynthesis of alkaloids in *Carnegiea gigantea*. Deutsche Akad. Wiss. Abh. 275-78.

Alcorn, Stanley M. 1961. Natural history of the saguaro. Arid Lands Colloquia, 1959-60, 1960-61. Univ. Ariz. Press, Tucson.

Alcorn, Stanley M., and Edwin B. Kurtz, Jr. 1959. Some factors affecting the germination of seed of the saguaro cactus (*Carnegiea gigantea*). Amer. Jour. Bot. 46: 526-29.

Alcorn, Stanley M., and C. May. 1962. Attrition of a saguaro forest. Pl. Disease Rept. 46: 156-58.

Alcorn, Stanley M., S. E. McGregor, G. D. Butler, Jr., and Edwin B. Kurtz, Jr. 1959. Pollination requirements of the saguaro (*Carnegiea gigantea*). Cactus & Succ. Jour. 31: 39-41.

Alcorn, Stanley M., S. E. McGregor, and George Olin. 1961. Pollination of saguaro cactus by doves, nectar-feeding bats, and honey bees. Science 133: 1594-95.

———— 1962. Pollination requirements of the organ pipe cactus. Cactus & Succ. Jour. 34: 135-38. *f. 90-93*.

Alston, Ralph E., and B. L. Turner. 1963. Biochemical systematics. Prentice-Hall, Englewood Cliffs, N.J.

Anderson, Edward F. 1958. A recent field trip in search of *Ariocarpus*. Cactus & Succ. Jour. 30: 171-74. *f. 96-97*.

———— 1960-64. A revision of *Ariocarpus* (Cactaceae). Amer. Jour. Bot. 47: 582-89. *f. 1-23*. 1960; 49: 615-22. *f. 1-14*. 1962; 50: 724-32. *f. 1-10*. 1963; 51: 144-51. *f. 1-16*. 1964.

———— 1961. A study of the proposed genus *Roseocactus*. Cactus & Succ. Jour. 33: 122-27. *f. 1-23*.

———— 1965. A taxonomic revision of *Ariocarpus* (Cactaceae). Cactus & Succ. Jour. 37: 39-49. *f. 1-16*.

———— 1969. The biography, ecology, and taxonomy of *Lophophora* (Cactaceae). Brittonia 21: 299-310. *f. 1-8*.

———— 1973. Research—how the Society can help. Cactus & Succ. Jour. 45: 12-14. *f. 1-3*.

———— 1980. Peyote: the divine cactus. Univ. Ariz. Press, Tucson.

Anderson, Edward F., and Margaret S. Stone. 1974. Pollen analysis of *Lophophora* (Cactaceae). Cactus & Succ. Jour. 43: 77-82. *f. 1-9*.

Anonymous. 1930. [*Sclerocactus*] *polyancistrus* hard to find. Des. [Pl. Life] 2: 5.

Anonymous. 1931. Rare *Utahia sileri* Engelmann rediscovered by John S. Wright. Cactus & Succ. Jour. 3: 88-89.

Anonymous. 1938. (Los Angeles newspaper account of the occurrence of *Cereus thurberi*, cited by Whitehead, 1939, but without publishing data.)

Anonymous. 1940. *Toumeya papyracantha*. Cactus & Succ. Jour. 12: 101. *f*.

Anthony, Harold E. 1948. How *Rhipsalis,* an American cactus, may have reached Africa. Jour. N.Y. Bot. Gard. 49: 33-38.

Anthony, Margery S. 1956. The Opuntiae of the Big Bend region of Texas. Amer. Midl. Nat. 55: 225-56.

Arp, Gerald. 1972a. The ecology of two varieties of *Echinocereus triglochidiatus.* Cactus & Succ. Jour. 44: 62-63. *f. 1-3.*

——— 1972b. Notes on the ecology of *Pediocactus simpsonii.* Cactus & Succ. Jour. 44: 108-9. *f. 1-3.*

——— 1972c. A revision of *Pediocactus.* Cactus & Succ. Jour. 44: 218-22.

——— 1973a. *Coryphantha, Escobaria,* and *Neobesseya* [Colorado]. Cactus & Succ. Jour. 45: 30-31. *f. 1.*

——— 1973b. *Opuntia compressa* and *Opuntia macrorhiza* [Colorado]. Cactus & Succ. Jour. 45: 56-57.

——— 1973c. The spineless hedgehog [cactus]. Cactus & Succ. Jour. 45: 132-33. *f. 1-4.*

——— 1973d. An interesting hybrid *Opuntia* from southwestern Colorado. Cactus & Succ. Jour. 45: 219-21.

Arp, Gerald, and David J. Rogers. 1970. A computer-aided classification of the varieties of *Pediocactus simpsonii* (Engelm.) B. & R. Cactus & Succ. Jour. 42: 40-43.

Axelrod, Daniel I. 1939. A Miocene flora from the western border of the Mohave Desert. Carnegie Inst. Wash. Publ. 516: 1-129.

——— 1940. Late tertiary floras of the Great Basin and border areas. Bull. Torrey Bot. Club 67: 477-88.

——— 1944. The Sonoma flora. Carnegie Inst. Wash. Publ. 553: 167-206.

——— 1948. Climate and evolution in western North America during Middle Pliocene time. Evolution 2: 127-44.

——— 1950a. Classification of the Madro-Tertiary flora. Carnegie Inst. Wash. Publ. 590: 1-22.

——— 1950b. Evolution of desert vegetation in western North America. Carnegie Inst. Wash. Publ. 590: 215-306.

——— 1952. Variables affecting the probabilities of dispersal in geologic time. Bull. Amer. Mus. Nat. Hist. 99: 177-88.

——— 1956. Mio-Pliocene floras from west-central Nevada. Univ. Calif. Publ. in Geol. Sciences 33: 1-322.

——— 1957. Late Tertiary floras and the Sierra Nevadan uplift. Bull. Geol. Soc. Amer. 68: 19-45.

——— 1958. Evolution of the Madro-Tertiary Geoflora. Bot. Rev. 24: 433-509.

——— 1959. Late Cenozoic evolution of the Sierran bigtree forest. Evolution 13: 9-23.

——— 1966a. A method for determining the altitudes of Tertiary floras. Paleobotanist 14: 144-71.

——— 1966b. Origin of deciduous and evergreen habits in temperate forests. Evolution 20: 1-15.

——— 1966c. Potassium-argon ages of some western Tertiary floras. Amer. Jour. Science 264: 497-506.

——— 1966d. The Eocene Copper Basin flora of northeastern Nevada. Univ. Calif. Publ. Geol. Sci. 60: 1-83.

——— 1966e. The Pleistocene Soboba flora of southern California. Univ. Calif. Publ. Geol. Sci. 60.

——— 1967a. The evolution of the California closed-cone pine forest. Proc. Symp. on the Biology of the California Islands, 93-149. Santa Barbara Bot. Gard.

——— 1967b. Geological history of the Californian insular flora. Proc. Symp. on the Biology of the California Islands, 267-315. Santa Barbara Bot. Gard.

——— 1967c. Drought, diastrophism, and quantum evolution. Evolution 21: 201-9.

——— 1967d. Quaternary extinctions of large mammals. Univ. Calif. Publ. Geol. Sciences 74: 1-42.

——— 1968. Tertiary floras and topographic history of the Snake River Basin, Idaho. Geol. Soc. Amer. Bull. 79: 713-34.

——— 1972a. Edaphic aridity as a factor in angiosperm evolution. Amer. Naturalist 106: 311-20.

——— 1972b. Ocean-floor spreading in relation to ecosystematic problems. Univ. Arkansas Mus. Occ. Paper 4: 15-76.

——— 1973. History of the Mediterranean ecosystem in California. *In* F. Di Castri and Harold A. Mooney (eds.), Ecological Studies, Analysis and Synthesis, 225-77. Springer-Verlag, Berlin-Heidelberg-New York.

——— 1974. Revolutions in the plant world. Geophytology. Paleobotanical Soc., Lucknow, India.

——— 1975a. Evolution and biogeography of Madrean-Tethyan sclerophyll vegetation. Ann. Mo. Bot. Gard. 62: 280-334.

——— 1975b. Plate tectonics and problems of angiosperm history. Mémoires du Muséum d'Histoire Naturelle. N. S. Série A, Zoologie 88: 72-86.

——— 1976. History of the coniferous forests, California and Nevada. Univ. Calif. Publ. Botany 70: 1-62.

——— 1977. Outline history of California vegetation. *In* Michael G. Barbour and Jack Major (eds.), Terrestrial vegetation of California, 140-93. Wiley-Interscience, Somerset, N.J.

——— 1978. The origin of coastal sage vegetation, Alta and Baja California. Amer. Jour. Bot. 65: 1117-31.

——— 1979. Age and origin of Sonoran Desert vegetation. Calif. Acad. Sci. Occ. Papers 132.

Axelrod, Daniel I., and Harry P. Bailey. 1969. Paleo-temperature analysis of Tertiary floras. Palaeogeography, Palaeoclimatology, and Palaeoecology 6: 163-95.

——— 1976. Tertiary vegetation, climate, and altitude of the Rio Grande Depression, New Mexico-Colorado. Paleobiology 2: 235-54.

Ayala, Francisco J. 1972. Competition between species. Amer. Scientist 60: 348-57.

Backeberg, Curt. 1950-51. Results of some twenty years of cactus research. Arranged, edited, and indexed by E. Yale Dawson. Reprinted with corrections, but without change of paging, from Cactus & Succ. Jour. 1950-51: 22: 181-90; 23: 13-20, 45-52, 81-88, 117-24, 149-55, 181-88; 24: 13-22.

———— 1956. Descriptiones cactacearum novarum. Fischer, Jena.

———— 1958-62. Die Cactaceae. 1-6. Fischer, Jena.

———— 1966 (ed. 1), 1970 (ed. 2). Das Kakteen Lexikon. Fischer, Jena.

Bailey, Harry P. 1964. Toward a unified concept of the temperate climate. Geog. Rev. 54: 516-45.

———— 1966. The climate of southern California. Univ. Calif. Press, Berkeley.

Bailey, Irving W. 1960. Comparative anatomy of the leaf-bearing Cactaceae. I. Foliar vasculature of *Pereskia*, *Pereskiopsis*, and *Quiabentia*. Jour. Arnold Arb. 41: 341-56.

———— 1961a. II. Structure and distribution of sclerenchyma in the phloem of *Pereskia*, *Pereskiopsis*, and *Quiabentia*. Jour. Arnold Arb. 42: 144-56.

———— 1961b. III. Form and distribution of crystals in *Pereskia*, *Pereskiopsis*, and *Quiabentia*. Jour. Arnold Arb. 42: 334-46.

———— IV. *See* Bailey and Srivastiva, 1962.

———— V. *See* Srivastiva and Bailey, 1962.

———— 1962. VI. The xylem of *Pereskia sacharosa* and *Pereskia aculeata*. Jour. Arnold Arb. 43: 376-88.

———— 1963a. VII. The xylem of pereskias from Peru and Bolivia. Jour. Arnold Arb. 44: 127-37.

———— 1963b. VIII. The xylem of pereskias from southern Mexico and Central America. Jour. Arnold Arb. 44: 211-21.

———— 1963c. IX. The xylem of *Pereskia grandifolia* and *Pereskia bleo*. Jour. Arnold Arb. 44: 222-31.

———— 1963d. X. The xylem of *Pereskia colombiana*, *Pereskia guamacho*, *Pereskia cubensis*, and *Pereskia portulacifolia*. Jour. Arnold Arb. 44: 390-401.

———— 1964a. XI. The xylem of *Pereskiopsis* and *Quiabentia*. Jour. Arnold Arb. 45: 140-57.

———— 1964b. XII. Preliminary observations upon the structure of the epidermis, stomata, and cuticle. Jour. Arnold Arb. 45: 374-89.

———— 1965a. XIII. The occurrence of water-soluble anisotropic bodies in air-dried and alcohol-dehydrated leaves of *Pereskia* and *Pereskiopsis*. Jour. Arnold Arb. 46: 74-85.

———— 1965b. XIV. Preliminary observations on the vasculature of cotyledons. Jour. Arnold Arb. 46: 445-52.

———— 1966a. XV. Some preliminary observations on the occurrence of "protein bodies." Jour. Arnold Arb. 46: 453-64.

———— 1966b. XVI. The development of water-soluble crystals in dehydrated leaves of *Pereskiopsis*. Jour. Arnold Arb. 47: 273-92.

———— 1968. XVII. Preliminary observations on the problem of transitions from broad to terete leaves. Jour. Arnold Arb. 49: 370-76. (Includes a summary of Bailey's work.)

Bailey, Irving W., and Lalit M. Srivastiva. 1962. IV. The fusiform initials of the cambium and the form and structure of their derivatives. Jour. Arnold Arb. 43: 187-202.

Baldwin, Henry I. 1977. The induced timberline of Mt. Monadnock, New Hampshire. Bull. Torrey Bot. Club 104: 324-33.

Barbour, Michael G., and Jack Major, eds., 1977. Terrestrial vegetation of California. Wiley-Interscience, Somerset, N.J.

Barry, R. G., J. T. Andrews, and M. A. Mahaffy. 1975. Continental ice sheets: conditions for growth. Science 190: 979-81.

Baskin, Jerry M., and Carol C. Baskin. 1973. Pad temperatures of *Opuntia compressa* during daytime in summer. Bull. Torrey Bot. Club 100: 56-59.

Baxter, Edgar M. 1932. Notes on "The Cactaceae." Cactus & Succ. Jour. 4: 281-82, 284.

———— 1935. California cactus. Abbey Garden Press, Pasadena, Calif.

Beard, Eleanor C. 1937. Some chromosome complements in the Cactaceae and a study of meiosis in *Echinocereus papillosus*. Bot. Gaz. 99: 1-21.

Beard, J. S. 1944. Climax vegetation in tropical America. Ecology 25: 127-58.

Beatley, Janice C. 1976. Vascular plants of the Nevada Test Site and central-southern Nevada. Nat. Tech. Inf. Serv., U.S. Dept. of Commerce, Springfield, Va.

Beaty, Chester B. 1978. The causes of glaciation. Amer. Scientist 66: 452-59.

Beauchamp, Mitchel. 1975. Northern limit of *Bergerocactus emoryi* (Engelm.) B. & R. [*Cereus emoryi*]. Cactus & Succ. Jour. 47: 18-19.

Becker, Herman F. 1960. Epitaph ? to *Eopuntia douglassii*. Cactus & Succ. Jour. 32: 28-29.

———— 1969. Fossil plants of the Tertiary Beaverhead Basins in southwestern Montana. Palaeontographica 127: 1-142. *pl. 1-44.*

Behnke, H. D. 1971. Sieve-tube plastids of Magnoliidae and Ranunculidae in relation to systematics. Taxon 20: 723-30.

Behnke, H. D., and B. L. Turner. 1971. On specific sieve-tube plastids in Caryophyllales. Taxon 20: 731-37.

Below, L. E., A. Y. Leung, Jerry L. McLaughlin, and A. G. Paul. *See* McLaughlin.

Bemis, W. P., J. W. Berry, and A. J. Deutschman. 1972. Observations on male sterile Mammillariae. Cactus & Succ. Jour. 44: 256.

Benson, Lyman. 1939. Notes on taxonomic techniques. Torreya 39: 73-75. *f.*

———— 1940/1950/1969. The cacti of Arizona, ed. 1 (with the assistance of J. J. Thornber, A. A. Nichol, and Lucretia Breazeale Hamilton), 1940, Univ. Ariz. Biol. Sci. Bull. 5; ed. 2, 1950, Univ. N. Mex. Press, Albuquerque, and Univ. Ariz. Press, Tucson; ed. 3, 1969. Univ. Ariz. Press.

———— 1941. Taxonomic studies. II. Studies of southwestern cacti. Amer. Jour. Bot. 28: 358-64.

———— 1942. The relationship of *Ranunculus* to the North American floras. Amer. Jour. Bot. 29: 491-500. *pl. 1.*

———— 1943. The goal and methods of systematic botany. Cactus & Succ. Jour. 15: 99-111.

———— 1944. A revision of some Arizona Cactaceae. Proc. Calif. Acad. Sci. 25: 245-68. *pl. 25.*

———— 1945. Nomenclatorial recombinations in *Trifolium* and *Opuntia*. Leafl. West. Bot. 4: 209-10.

———— 1948. A treatise on the North American Ranunculi. Amer. Midl. Nat. 40: 1-261. Suppl. 52: 328-69. 1954.

———— 1950. Permanent plant records. Cactus & Succ. Jour. 22: 115-22.

———— 1951. The Mesa Verde cactus. Leafl. West. Bot. 6: 163.

———— 1953. Relationships of the Ranunculi of the Continental Divide and the Pacific and Eastern forests of North America. Proc. Seventh Internat. Bot. Congress, Stockholm, 1950: 862-63.

———— 1955. The Ranunculi of the Alaskan Arctic Coastal Plain and the Brooks Range. Amer. Midl. Nat. 53: 242-55.

———— 1957a. The *Opuntia pulchella* complex. Cactus & Succ. Jour. 29: 19-21. *3 f.*

———— 1957b, 1979. Plant classification. Eds. 1, 2. D. C. Heath & Co., Lexington, Mass.

———— 1961-62. A revision and amplification of *Pediocactus*—I to IV. Cactus & Succ. Jour. 34: 49-54; 35: 17-19, 57-61, 163-68. *f. 14, 41, 107-8.*

———— 1962. Plant taxonomy, methods and principles. Ronald Press, New York. 1978. Reprinted Wiley, New York.

———— 1966a. Una revisión de *Ancistrocactus*. Cactaceas y Suculentas Méxicanas 11: 3-8, 25-26 (English summary).

———— 1966b. A revision of *Sclerocactus*—I-II. Cactus & Succ. Jour. 38: 50-57. *f. 1-6;* 100-106. *f. 7-9.*

———— 1966c. The objectives and organization of the Cactus and Succulent Society of America. Cactus & Succ. Jour. 38: 191-92.

———— 1968. The complexity of species and the varieties of *Echinocereus pectinatus*. Cactus & Succ. Jour. 40: 119-27. *f. 1-5.*

———— 1969a. The native cacti of California—new names and nomenclatural combinations. Cactus & Succ. Jour. 41: 33.

———— 1969b. The cacti of the United States and Canada—new names and nomenclatural combinations. Cactus & Succ. Jour. 41: 124-28, 185-90, 233-34. *f. 1-4.*

———— 1969c. The native cacti of California. Stanford Univ. Press, Stanford, Calif.

———— 1970a. The Cactaceae. *In* C. L. Lundell and collaborators, Flora of Texas 2: 221-317. *pl. 1-14.* Texas Res. Foundation, Renner. (Also printed separately.)

———— 1970b. Crawling prickly pears. Cactus & Succ. Jour. 42: 89.

———— 1970c. Cactaceae. *In* Donovan S. Correll and Marshall C. Johnston, Manual of the vascular plants of Texas, 1087-1113. Texas Res. Foundation, Renner.

———— 1970d. The rainbow cactus and the Phoenix of long ago. Cactus & Succ. Jour. 42: 172-73.

———— 1974a. New taxa and nomenclatural changes in the Cactaceae. Cactus & Succ. Jour. 46: 79-81.

———— 1974b. Cactales. Encyclopaedia Brittanica. Macropaedia 3: 573-75.

———— 1974-75. The publication date of Wislizenus's memoir of a tour to northern Mexico in 1846 and 1847. Cactus & Succ. Jour. 46: 74; 47: 40-43.

———— 1975. Cacti—bizarre, beautiful, but in danger. Nat. Parks and Conservation Mag. 49: 17-21. Reprinted in Help save our endangered plants, Nat. Parks and Conserv. Assoc., Wash., D.C.

———— 1976a. Nomenclatural recombinations in the cacti of the United States and Canada. Cactus & Succ. Jour. 48: 59.

———— 1976b. Endangered species—heads in the clouds or the sand? Cactus & Succ. Jour. 48: 207-12.

———— 1977a. Preservation of cacti and management of the ecosystem. *In* Extinction is forever. N.Y. Bot. Gard.

———— 1977b. Lectotype or neotype designation for *Mammillaria wilcoxii*. Cactus & Succ. Jour. 49: 34-35.

———— 1977c. How do you preserve an ecosystem? Fremontia, Calif. Native Plant Soc. 5: 3-7.

———— 1977d. Our daily bread and preserving the ecosystem. Cactus & Succ. Jour. 49: 257-60.

———— *See also* Abrams; Correll and Johnston; Hunt and Benson; Lundell; Mitich and Benson; and Woodruff and Benson.

Benson, Lyman, and Robert A. Darrow. 1944. A manual of southwestern desert trees and shrubs. Univ. Ariz. Biol. Sci. Bull. 6.

———— 1954. The trees and shrubs of the southwestern deserts. Univ. N. Mex. Press, Albuquerque, and Univ. Ariz. Press, Tucson. (Ed. 2 of A manual of southwestern desert trees and shrubs, 1944.) Ed. 3, 1981, Univ. Ariz. Press.

Benson, Lyman, and David L. Walkington. 1965. The Southern Californian prickly pears—invasion, adulteration, and trial-by-fire. Ann. Mo. Bot. Gard. 52: 262-73.

———— 1968. Los nopales de California: invasión, adulteración, y prueba de fuego. Cactaceas y Suculentas Méxicanas 13: 27-33, 40-42 (English summary). *f. 16-19.*

Berger, Alwin. 1905. A systematic revision of the genus *Cereus*. Rept. Mo. Bot. Gard. 16: 57-86. *pl. 1-12.*

———— 1926. Die Entwicklungslinien der Kakteen. Fischer, Jena.

———— 1929. Kakteen. Ulner, Stuttgart.

Berger, W. H., and J. S. Kingsley. 1977. Glacial-holocene transition in deep-sea carbonates: selective dissolution and the stable isotope signal. Science 197: 563-66.

Bessey, Charles E. 1914. Stamens and ovules of *Carnegiea gigantea*. Science II. 40: 680.

Billings, W. Dwight. 1945. The plant associations of the Carson Desert region, western Nevada. Butler Univ. Studies, Bot. 7: 89-123.

———— 1973. Arctic and alpine vegetations: similarities, differences, and susceptibility to disturbance. BioScience 23: 697-704.

Billings, W. Dwight, and Harold A. Mooney. 1968. The ecology of arctic and alpine plants. Biol. Rev. 43: 481-529.

Birks, H. J. B., and R. G. West. 1974. Quaternary plant ecology. Halstead (Wiley), New York.

Block, W. 1958. Pharmacological aspects of mescaline. *In* M. Rinkle and H. C. B. Denber (eds.), Chemical concepts of psychosis, 106-19. McDowell, New York.

Bocher, Tyge W. 1950. Distributions of plants in the circumpolar area in relation to ecological and historical factors. Jour. Ecology 39: 376-95.

Boissevain, Charles H., and Carol Davidson. 1940. Colorado cacti. Abbey Garden Press, Pasadena, Calif.

Boke, Norman H. 1941. Zonation in the shoot apices of *Trichocereus spachianus* and *Opuntia cylindrica*. Amer. Jour. Bot. 28: 656-64.

———— 1944. Histogenesis of the leaf and areole in *Opuntia cylindrica*. Amer. Jour. Bot. 31: 299-316.

———— 1951. Histogenesis of the vegetative shoot in *Echinocereus*. Amer. Jour. Bot. 38: 23-38.

———— 1952. Leaf and areole development in *Coryphantha*. Amer. Jour. Bot. 39: 134-45.

———— 1953. Tubercle development in *Mammillaria heyderi*. Amer. Jour. Bot. 40: 239-47.

———— 1954. Organogenesis of the vegetative shoot in *Pereskia*. Amer. Jour. Bot. 41: 619-37.

———— 1955a. Development of the vegetative shoot in *Rhipsalis cassytha* [*baccifera*]. Amer. Jour. Bot. 42: 1-10.

———— 1955b. Dimorphic areoles of *Epithelantha*. Amer. Jour. Bot. 42: 752-53.

———— 1956. Developmental anatomy and the validity of the genus *Bartschella*. Amer. Jour. Bot. 43: 819-27.

———— 1957a. Comparative histogenesis of the areoles in *Homalocephala* and *Echinocactus*. Amer. Jour. Bot. 44: 368-80.

———— 1957b. Structure and development of the shoot in *Toumeya* [*Pediocactus*]. Amer. Jour. Bot. 44: 888-96.

———— 1958. Areole histogenesis in *Mammillaria lasiacantha*. Amer. Jour. Bot. 45: 473-79.

———— 1959. Endomorphic and ectomorphic characters in *Pelecyphora* and *Encephalocarpus*. Amer. Jour. Bot. 46: 197-209.

———— 1960. Anatomy and development in *Solisia*. Amer. Jour. Bot. 47: 59-65.

———— 1961. Structure and development of the shoot in *Dolicothele*. Amer. Jour. Bot. 48: 316-21.

———— 1963a. The genus *Pereskia* in Mexico. Cactus & Succ. Jour. 35: 3-10.

———— 1963b. Anatomy and development of the flower and fruit of *Pereskia pititache*. Amer. Jour. Bot. 50: 843-58.

———— 1964. The cactus gynoecium: a new interpretation. Amer. Jour. Bot. 51: 598-610.

———— 1966. Ontogeny and structure of the flower and fruit of *Pereskia aculeata*. Amer. Jour. Bot. 53: 534-42.

———— 1968. Structure and development of the flower and fruit of *Pereskia diaz-roemeriana*. Amer. Jour. Bot. 55: 1254-60.

———— 1976. Dichotomous branching in *Mammillaria* (Cactaceae). Amer. Jour. Bot. 63: 1380-84.

Boke, Norman H., and Edward F. Anderson. 1970. Structure, development, and taxonomy of the genus *Lophophora* (Cactaceae). Amer. Jour. Bot. 57: 569-78.

Boke, Norman H., and Robert G. Ross. 1978. Fasciation and dichotomous branching in *Echinocereus* (Cactaceae). Amer. Jour. Bot. 65: 522-30.

Borg, John. 1937/1951/1959 (eds. 1-3). Cacti, a gardener's handbook for their identification and cultivation. Macmillan (ed. 1); Blandford Press, London.

Bowden, W. M. 1945. A list of chromosome numbers in higher plants. I. Acanthaceae to Myrtaceae. Amer. Jour. Bot. 32: 81-92.

Braun, E. Lucy. 1938. Deciduous forest climaxes. Ecology 19: 515-22.

———— 1955. The physical geography of the unglaciated eastern United States and its interpretation. Bot. Rev. 21: 297-375.

———— 1956. The development of association and climax concepts: their use in interpretation of the Deciduous Forest. Amer. Jour. Bot. 43: 906-11.

———— 1967. Deciduous forests of eastern North America. Hafner, New York.

Bravo H., Helia. 1937. Las Cactaceas de Mexico. Ed. 1. Mexico City. 1978. Ed. 2, con colaboración de Hernando Sanchez-Mejorada R. (Vol. 1.)

———— 1979. Aspecto sobre la industrialización de los nopales. English translation under: Industrial aspects of prickly pears. Cactaceas y Suculentas Méxicanas 24: 27-31.

Bray, J. R. 1977. Pleistocene volcanism and glacial initiation. Science 197: 251-54.

Breazeale, John M. 1930. Color schemes of cacti. College of Agr. and Agr. Exp. Sta., Univ. Ariz., Tucson.

Brewer, W. H., and Sereno Watson. 1880. Botany. Polypetalae, in Vol. I. (Uniform with the publications of the) Geological Survey of California. Ed. 2 (revised). Boston: Little, Brown. Ed. 1. 1876. Cambridge, Mass.: Welch, Bigelow, and Co., Univ. Press.

Britton, Max E. 1967. Vegetation of the Arctic Tundra. *In* Henry P. Hansen (ed.), Arctic biology, 67-130. Oregon State Univ. Press, Corvallis.

———— (ed.). 1973. Alaskan Arctic Tundra (symposium). Arctic Inst. North America, Wash., D.C.

Britton, Nathaniel Lord, and Addison Brown. 1913. An illustrated flora of the northern United States and Canada, and the British possessions from Newfoundland to the parallel of the southern boundary of Virginia, and from the Atlantic Ocean westward to the 102d meridian. Ed. 2. Scribner's, New York.

Britton, Nathaniel Lord, and Joseph Nelson Rose. 1908a. A new genus of Cactaceae [*Carnegiea*]. Jour. N.Y. Bot. Gard. 9: 185-88.

———— 1908b. A preliminary treatment of the Opuntioideae of North America. Smiths. Misc. Coll. 1786.

———— 1909. The genus *Cereus* and its allies in North America. Contr. U.S. Nat. Herb. 12: 413-37.

———— 1919-23. The Cactaceae. 4 vols. Carnegie Inst. Wash. Publ. 248.

———— 1924. Cactaceae in Paul C. Standley. Trees and shrubs of Mexico. Contr. U.S. Nat. Herb. 23: 855-1012.

Brooks, C. E. P. 1949. Climate through the ages. Ed. 2. McGraw-Hill, New York. Reprinted 1970, Dover, New York.

Brown, Roland W. 1959. Some paleobotanical problematica. Jour. Paleont. 33: 122-24. *pl. 23, f. 3.*

———— 1962. The Paleocene flora of the Rocky Mountains and Great Plains. U.S. Geol. Surv. Prof. Papers 375.

Bruhn, Jan G. 1977. Three men and a drug: peyote research in the 1890's. Cactus & Succ. Jour. Gt. Brit. 39: 27-30.

Bruhn, Jan G., J.-E. Lindgren, B. Holmstedt, and J. M. Adovasio. 1978. Peyote alkaloids: identification in a prehistoric specimen of *Lophophora* from Coahuila, Mexico. Science 199: 1437-38.

Brum, Gilbert D. 1973. Ecology of the saguaro (*Carnegiea gigantea*): Phenology and establishment in marginal populations. Madroño 22: 195-204.

Bryan, E. H., Jr. 1954. The Hawaiian Chain. Bishop Museum, Honolulu.

Bryson, R. A. 1974. A perspective on climate change. Science 184: 753-60.

Buchanan, Frances G. 1931. *Utahia sileri* rediscovered. Desert 3: 75. *f.*

Butzer, Karl W. 1971. Environment and archeology: an ecological approach to prehistory. Ed. 2. Aldine-Atherton, Chicago.

Buxbaum, F. 1944. Untersuchungen zur Morphologie der Kakteenblüte. 1. Teil: Das Gynoecium. Bot. Arch. 45: 190-247.

———— 1950a. Morphology of cacti. Section I. Roots and stems. 1953. Section II. Flower. Abbey Garden Press, Pasadena, Calif.

———— 1950b. Die Phylogenie der nordamerikanischen Echinocactaceen. Trib. Euechinocactineae F. Buxb. Österr. Bot. Zeitschr. 98: 44-104.

———— 1951a. Grundlagen und Methoden einer Eneurung der Systematik der höheren Pflanzen. Springer-Verlag, Vienna.

———— 1951b. Stages and lines of evolution of the Tribe Euechinocactineae. Cactus & Succ. Jour. 23: 193-97.

———— 1953. Morphology of cacti. Section II. Flower. Abbey Garden Press, Pasadena, Calif.

———— 1957. Morphologie der Kakteen. II. Blüte. *In* H. Krainz (ed.), Die Kakteen 1. VIII. Morphologie, 21-30.

———— 1958. The phylogenetic division of the subfamily Cereoideae, Cactaceae. Madroño 14: 177-206.

———— 1959. Die systematische Einteilung. *In* H. Krainz (ed.), Die Kakteen.

———— 1962. Das phylogenetische System der Cactaceae. *In* H. Krainz (ed.), Die Kakteen.

Byles, R. S. 1954-56. A dictionary of genera and subgenera of Cactaceae. Reprinted from Nat. Cactus and Succ. Jour. 9-11: 9: 54-57, 80-83; 10: 11-14, 33-36, 57-60, 82-85; 11: 11-14, 33-36.

Caesalpinius, Andreas. 1583. De plantis libri XVI. Georgium Marecottum, Florentiae.

Cain, Stanley A. 1943. The Tertiary character of the cove hardwood forests of the Great Smoky Mountains National Park. Bull. Torrey Bot. Club 70: 213-35.

———— 1944. Foundations of plant geography. Harper, New York.

Calvin, Ross. 1951. Lieutenant Emory reports: a reprint of W. H. Emory's notes of a military reconnaissance. Univ. N. Mex. Press, Albuquerque.

Camp, W. H. 1947. Distribution patterns in modern plants and the problems of ancient dispersals. Ecological Monographs 17: 123-26, 159-83.

———— 1948. *Rhipsalis*—and plant distribution in the Southern Hemisphere. Jour. N.Y. Bot. Gard. 49: 33-38.

Campbell, Douglas H., and Ira L. Wiggins. 1947. Origins of the flora of California. Stanford Univ. Publ. Biol. Sci. 10: 1-20.

Candolle, Alphonse de. 1855. Geographie botanique raisonée. Paris.

Candolle, Augustin Pyramus de. 1828. Revue de la famille des Cactées. Librairie Agricola de la Maison Rustique, Paris.

Cannon, W. A. 1911. The root habits of desert plants. Carnegie Inst. Wash. Publ. 131.

Carlquist, Sherwin. 1965. Island life. Nat. Hist. Press, Amer. Mus. Nat. Hist., New York.

———— 1966. The biota of long-distance dispersal. I. Quart. Rev. Biol. 41: 247-70. II. Evolution 20: 30-43. III. Brittonia 18: 310-35. IV. Evolution 20: 433-55.

———— 1970. Hawaii: a natural history: geology, climate, native flora and fauna above shoreline. Columbia Univ. Press, Garden City, N.Y.

———— 1974. Island biology. Columbia Univ. Press, Garden City, N.Y.

———— 1975. Ecological strategies of xylem evolution. Univ. Calif. Press, Berkeley and Los Angeles.

Castetter, Edward F., and Prince Pierce. 1967. Cacti of New Mexico. Cactus & Succ. Jour. 39: 60-65.

Castetter, Edward F., Prince Pierce, and Karl H. Schwerin. 1975. A reassessment of the genus *Escobaria* [*Coryphantha*]. Cactus & Succ. Jour. 47: 60-70.

———— 1976. A new cactus species and two new varieties from New Mexico. Cactus & Succ. Jour. 48: 138-39.

———— 1978. *Mammillaria meridiorosei,* a new species from northwest Mexico and the U.S. borderlands. Cactus & Succ. Jour. 50: 176-78.

Chabot, Brian F., and W. Dwight Billings. 1972. Origins and ecology of the Sierran alpine flora and vegetation. Ecological Monographs 42: 163-99.

Champie, Clark. 1974. Cacti and succulents of El Paso. Abbey Garden Press, Santa Barbara, Calif.

Chaney, Ralph W. 1925. A comparative study of the Bridge Creek flora and the modern redwood forest. Carnegie Inst. of Wash. Publ. 349: 1-22.

———— 1936. The succession and distribution of Cenozoic floras around the North Pacific Basin. *In* T. H. Goodspeed (ed.), Essays in geobotany in honor of W. A. Setchell, 55-85.

——— 1938. Paleoecological interpretation of Cenozoic plants in western North America. Bot. Rev. 4: 371-96.

——— 1940. Tertiary floras and continental history. Bull. Geol. Soc. Amer. 51: 649-88.

——— 1944. A fossil cactus from the Eocene of Utah. Amer. Jour. Bot. 31: 507-28, *pl. 1-5, f. 1-6*.

——— 1947. Tertiary centers and migration routes. Ecological Monographs 17: 139-48.

——— 1948. The bearing of living *Metasequoia* on problems of Tertiary paleobotany. Proc. Nat. Acad. Sciences 34: 503-15.

——— 1951. A revision of fossil *Sequoia* and *Taxodium* in western North America based upon the recent discovery of *Metasequoia*. Trans. Amer. Philo. Soc. 40: 171-263.

——— 1952. Conifer dominants in the middle Tertiary of the John Day Basin, Oregon. Paleobotanist 1: 105-13.

Chaney, Ralph W., and Daniel I. Axelrod. 1959. Miocene floras of the Columbia Plateau. Carnegie Inst. Wash. Publ. 617: Part II, 1-134, by Ralph W. Chaney; Part II, Systematic Considerations, 135-267, by Ralph W. Chaney and Daniel I. Axelrod.

Chaney, Ralph W., Carlton Condit, and Daniel I. Axelrod. 1944. Pliocene floras of California and Oregon. Carnegie Inst. Wash. Publ. 533.

Chorinsky, Franziska. 1931. Vergleichend-anatomische Untersuchung der Hargebilde bei Portulacaceen und Cacteen. Österr. Bot. Zeitschr. 80: 308-27.

Clark, Thomas H., and Colin W. Stearn. 1960. The geological evolution of North America. Ronald Press, New York.

Clausen, Jens, David D. Keck, and William M. Hiesey. 1948. Experimental studies on the nature of species III. Environmental responses of climatic races of *Achillea*. Carnegie Inst. Wash. Publ. 581: i-iii, 1-129.

Clements, Frederick E. 1920. Plant indicators. Carnegie Inst. Wash. Publ. 290: 1-388.

Clements, Frederick E., E. V. Martin, and F. L. Long. 1950. Adaptation and origin in the plant world: the role of environment in evolution. Chronica Botanica, Waltham, Mass. Review by Gerald Ownbey, Ecology 33: 431-33. 1952.

Climap Project Members. 1976. The surface of the ice-age Earth. Science 191: 1131-37.

Clokey, Ira W. 1951. Flora of the Charleston Mountains, Clark County, [southern] Nevada. Univ. Calif. Press, Berkeley and Los Angeles.

Clover, Elzada U. 1933. *Astrophytum* in the United States. Desert Pl. Life 5: 20-21.

Conde, L. F. 1975. Anatomical comparisons of five species of *Opuntia* (Cactaceae). Ann. Mo. Bot. Gard. 62: 425-73.

Constance, Lincoln, L. R. Heckard, Kenton L. Chambers, Robert Ornduff, and Peter H. Raven. 1963. Amphitropical relationships in the herbaceous flora

of the Pacific Coast of North and South America. Quart. Rev. Biol. 38: 109-77.

Cooper, W. S. 1922. The broad-leaf sclerophyll vegetation of California. Carnegie Inst. Wash. Publ. 319: 1-124.

——— 1936. The strand and dune flora of the Pacific Coast of North America. *In* T. H. Goodspeed (ed.), Essays in geobotany, 141-87. Univ. Calif. Press, Berkeley.

Correll, Donovan S., and Marshall C. Johnston. 1970. Manual of the vascular plants of Texas. (Cactaceae by Lyman Benson.) Texas Res. Foundation, Renner.

Coulter, John M. 1891-94. Botany of western Texas. A manual of the phanerogams and pteridophytes of western Texas. Contr. U.S. Nat. Herb. 2.

——— 1894. Preliminary revision of the North American species of *Cactus* [*Mammillaria*], *Anhalonium* [*Lophophora*], and *Lophophora*. Contr. U.S. Nat. Herb. 3: 91-132.

——— 1896. Preliminary revision of the North American species of *Echinocactus, Cereus,* and *Opuntia*. Contr. U.S. Nat. Herb. 3: 357-462.

Coulter, John M., and Aven Nelson. 1909. New manual of botany of the central Rocky Mountains (vascular plants). American Book, New York.

Coutant, Mary Witherspoon. 1918. Wound periderm in certain cacti. Bull. Torrey Bot. Club 45: 353-64.

Coville, F. V. 1904. Desert plants as a source of drinking water. Ann. Rept. Smiths. Inst. 1903: 499-505.

Cowper, Denis. 1955. Rediscovery of *Toumeya*. Saguaroland Bull. 9: 105-7.

——— 1956. More about *Toumeya peeblesiana*. Saguaroland Bull. 10: 76, 78.

Craig, Robert T. 1945. The *Mammillaria* handbook. Abbey Garden Press, Pasadena, Calif.

Cronquist, Arthur. 1978. The biota of the Intermountain Region in geohistorical context. Great Basin Naturalist Memoirs 3-15.

Cronquist, Arthur, Arthur H. Holmgren, Noel H. Holmgren, James L. Reveal, and Patricia K. Holmgren. 1972, 1977 (and continuing). Intermountain flora. Vol. 1, Hafner Press, New York; vol. 6, Columbia Univ. Press, Garden City, N.Y.

Cutak, Ladislaus. 1943. The life-saving barrel cactus —myth or fact? Bull. Mo. Bot. Gard. 31: 153-58.

——— 1945. The night-blooming cereus and its allies. Cactus & Succ. Jour. 17 (9): separate inset, 1-15. *f. 1-15*. (Reprinted from Bull. Mo. Bot. Gard. 33 (5): May 1945.)

——— 1946. Is there palatable water in the barrel cactus? Bull. Mo. Bot. Gard. 34: 182-88. *f*.

Dalrymple, Brent G., Eli A. Silver, and Everett D. Jackson. 1973. Origin of the Hawaiian Islands. Amer. Scientist 61: 294-308.

Daubenmire, Rexford F. 1940. Plant succession due to overgrazing in *Agropyron* bunchgrass prairie in southeastern Washington. Ecology 21: 55-64.

——— 1943. Vegetational zonation in the Rocky Mountains. Bot. Rev. 9: 325-94.

——— 1954. Alpine timberlines in the Americas and their interpretation. Butler Univ. Bot. Studies 11: 119-36.

——— 1969. Ecologic plant geography of the Pacific Northwest. Madroño 20: 111-28.

——— 1978. Plant geography, with special reference to North America. Academic Press, New York.

Davis, Ray J. 1952. Flora of Idaho. Wm. C. Brown, Dubuque, Iowa.

Dawson, E. Yale. 1963. How to know the cacti. Wm. C. Brown, Dubuque, Iowa.

——— 1966. Cacti of California. Univ. Calif. Press, Berkeley.

DeCandolle. *See* Candolle.

De Ropp, R. S. 1957. Drugs and the mind. St. Martin's Press, New York.

Dice, Lee R. 1943. The biotic provinces of North America. Univ. Michigan Press, Ann Arbor.

Diers, Lothar. 1961. Der Anteil an Polyploiden in den Vegetationsgürtein der WestKordillere Perus. Zeitschr. Bot. 49: 437-88.

Dilcher, D. L. 1973. A paleoclimatic interpretation of the Eocene floras of southeastern North America. *In* A. Graham (ed.), Vegetation and vegetational history of northern Latin America, 39-59. Elsevier, Amsterdam.

Dingerdissen, J. J., and Jerry L. McLaughlin. *See* McLaughlin.

Div. of Narcotic Drugs, United Nations. 1959. Peyotl. Bull. on Narcotics 11 (2): 16-41.

Dodd, Alan P. 1927. Biological control of prickly pear in Australia. Commonw. Austral. Council Sci. & Indust. Res. Bull. 34.

——— 1940. The biological campaign against prickly pear. Commonw. Prickly Pear Board, Brisbane, Australia.

Dorf, Erling. 1955. Plants and the geologic time scale. Geol. Soc. Amer. Special Papers 62: 575-92.

——— 1959. Climatic changes of the past and present. Contr. Mus. Paleontology, Univ. Michigan 13: 181-210.

——— 1960a. Tertiary fossil forests of Yellowstone National Park, Wyoming. Billings Geol. Soc., Eleventh Annual Field Conference: 253-60.

——— 1960b. Paleobotany. McGraw-Hill Encycl. Science and Tech.: 499-506.

——— 1969. Paleobotanical evidence of Mesozoic and Cenozoic climatic changes. Proc. North American Paleontological Convention, September 1969. Part D: 323-46.

Dort, Wakefield, Jr., and J. Knox Jones (eds.). 1968. Pleistocene and Recent environments of the central Great Plains. Univ. Kansas Dept. Geol. Special Publ. 3. Univ. Kansas Press, Lawrence.

Durham, J. Wyatt. 1950. Cenozoic marine climates of the Pacific Coast. Bull. Geol. Soc. Amer. 61: 1243-64.

Eames, Arthur J. 1961. Morphology of angiosperms. McGraw-Hill, New York.

Earle, W. Hubert. 1962. A new Arizona cactus. Saguaroland Bull. 16: 40-41. *4 photos and cover ill.*

——— 1963. Cacti of the southwest. Daily News, Tempe, Arizona.

Ehleringer, James, Olle Björkman, and Harold A. Mooney. 1976. Leaf pubescence: effects on absorp-tance and photosynthesis in a desert shrub. Science 192: 376-77.

Emiliani, Cesare. 1972. Quaternary paleotemperatures and the duration of the high-temperature intervals. Science 178: 398-401.

Emory, William H. 1848. Notes of a military reconnaissance from Ft. Leavenworth [Kansas] to San Diego, App. 2. As Exec. Doc. 41; Senate Doc. 7, U.S. Govt., and by H. Long and Brother, New York.

——— 1859. Report of the United States and Mexican boundary survey. Cactaceae by George Engelmann. 2 (1): 1-78.

Engelmann, George. 1845/50. Cactaceae. *In* George Engelmann and Asa Gray, Plantae Lindheimerianae. Boston Jour. Nat. Hist. 5: 37-39; 6: 195-209.

——— 1848a. Sketch of the botany of Dr. A. Wislizenus's expedition from Missouri to Santa Fé, Chihuahua, Parras, Saltillo, Monter[r]ey, and Matamoros. *In* A. Wislizenus, Memoir of a tour to northern Mexico in 1846 and 1847. U.S. Senate, Washington.

——— 1848b. Cactaceae of Emory's reconnaissance. *In* Emory, 1848a.

——— 1849. Cactaceae. Plantae Fendlerianae. Mem. Amer. Acad. 4: 49-53.

——— 1852. Notes on the *Cereus giganteus* of southwestern California, and some other Californian Cactaceae. Amer. Jour. Sci. 14: 335-39.

——— 1854. Further notes on *Cereus giganteus* of southeastern California with a short account of another allied species in Sonora. Amer. Jour. Sci. II. 17: 231-35.

——— 1856 (1857, but preprint issued in 1856). Synopsis of the Cactaceae of the territory of the United States and adjacent regions. Proc. Amer. Acad. 3: 259-346.

——— 1859. Cactaceae of the Boundary. *In* Emory, 1859.

——— 1861a. The pulp of the cactus fruit. Trans. Acad. Sci. St. Louis 2: 166-67.

——— 1861b. Cactaceae. *In* Joseph C. Ives, Report upon the Colorado River of the West, explored in 1857 and 1858, 4: Botany, 12-14.

——— 1863. Additions to the Cactus-flora of the territory of the United States. Trans. Acad. Sci. St. Louis 2: 197-204.

——— 1871. Cactaceae. *In* Sereno Watson and Clarence King, Exploration of the Fortieth Parallel, 5: Botany, 115-20.

——— 1876. Cactaceae. *In* J. H. Simpson, Report of exploration across the Great Basin of the Territory of Utah for a direct wagon-route from Camp Floyd to Genoa, in Carson Valley, in 1859, 436-44.

——— 1878. Cactaceae. *In* George M. Wheeler, Report from the United States geographical surveys west of the one hundredth meridian, 6: Botany, 127-235.

Engelmann, George, and John M. Bigelow. 1856 (1857). Description of the Cactaceae. *In* A. W. Whipple, Reports of explorations and surveys for a railroad from the Mississippi River to the Pacific Ocean, 4: 27-58.

England, J., and R. S. Bradley. 1978. Past glacial activity in the Canadian high arctic. Science 200: 265-70.

Epling, Carl, and Harlan Lewis. 1942. The centers of distribution of the chaparral and coastal sage associations. Amer. Midl. Nat. 27: 445-62.

Erdtman, G. 1952. Pollen morphology and plant taxonomy: angiosperms. Almquist & Wiksells, Stockholm.

Evans, D. L., and H. J. Freeland. 1977. Variations in the Earth's orbit: pacemaker of the ice ages? Science 198: 528-29, with a rebuttal by James D. Hays, John Imbrie, and N. J. Shackleton on pp. 529-30.

Evans, Edna H. 1967. They color things red. Pac. Discov. 20: 24-25. *f.*

Everde, J. F., and G. T. James. 1964. Potassium-argon dates and the Tertiary floras of North America. Amer. Jour. Science 262: 945-74.

Ewart, Alfred J. 1910. Prickly pear: a fodder plant for cultivation? Jour. Dept. Agr., Victoria, Australia. Reprint, pp. 1-4.

Felger, Richard S., and Charles H. Lowe. 1967. Clinal variation in the surface-volume relationships of the columnar cactus *Lophocereus schottii* in northwestern Mexico. Ecology 48: 530-36.

Fernald, Merritt Lyndon. 1911. A botanical expedition to Newfoundland and southern Labrador. Rhodora 13: 135-62.

——— 1925. Persistence of plants in unglaciated areas of boreal America. Mem. Amer. Acad. Arts and Sciences 15: 239-342.

——— 1929. Some relationships of the floras of the Northern Hemisphere. Proc. Internat. Congress of Plant Sciences at Ithaca, N.Y. 2: 1487-1507.

——— 1931. Specific segregations and identities in some floras of eastern North America and the Old World. Rhodora 33: 25-63.

——— 1950. Gray's manual of botany. A handbook of the flowering plants and ferns of the central and northeastern United States and adjacent Canada. Ed. 8. American Book, New York; corrected printing, 1970, Van Nostrand Reinhold, Princeton, N.J.

Fischer, Pierre. 1962. Taxonomic relationships of *Opuntia kleiniae* DeCandolle and *Opuntia tetracantha* Toumey. Thesis, Univ. Ariz., Tucson.

——— 1972. Subject: a revision of *Coryphantha vivipara* (the copy available lacking the title page). Thesis, Univ. Calif., Berkeley.

Fischer, R. 1958. Pharmacology and metabolism of mescaline. Rev. Canadienne Biol. 17 (3): 389-405.

Fisher, R. V. 1964. Resurrected Oligocene hills, eastern Oregon. Amer. Jour. Science 262: 713-25.

Flakes, L. A., and E. M. Kemp. 1973. Paleocene continental positions and evolution of climate. *In* D. H. Tarling and S. K. Runcorn, Implications of continental drift to the earth sciences, 535-58. Academic Press, New York.

Flint, Richard Foster. 1977. Glacial and Quaternary geology. Wiley, New York.

Förster, Carl Friedrich. 1846. Handbuch der Cacteenkunde. Wöller, Leipzig. Ed. 2 by Rümpler, 1885.

Fosberg, F. Raymond. 1931a. Remarks on the taxonomy of the Cactaceae and some combinations and names in that family. Bull. So. Calif. Acad. Sci. 30: 50-59.

——— 1931b. The cacti of the Pyramid Peak region, Dona Ana County, New Mexico. Bull. So. Calif. Acad. Sci. 30: 67-73.

——— 1934. The southern California prickly pears. Bull. So. Calif. Acad. Sci. 33: 93-104.

——— 1948. Derivation of the flora of the Hawaiian Islands. *In* E. C. Zimmerman (ed.), Insects of Hawaii, vol. 1. Univ. Hawaii Press, Honolulu.

——— 1958. Vegetation of the islands of Oceania. Study of tropical vegetation, UNESCO, 54-60.

——— 1961. A classification of vegetation for general purposes. Trop. Ecol. 2: 1-28.

——— 1962. Qualitative description of the coral atoll ecosystem. Proc. Ninth Pacific Science Congress, 1957, 4: 61-167.

——— 1966. Restoration of lost and degraded habitats. *In* F. Fraser Darling and J. P. Milton, Future environments of North America. Nat. Hist. Press, Garden City, N.Y.

——— 1967a. Opening remarks: Island Ecosystem Symposium. Micronesia 3: 3-4.

——— 1967b. Some ecological effects of wild and semi-wild exotic species of vascular plants. ICUN Publ. II. 9: 98-109.

——— 1967c. Observations on vegetation patterns and dynamics on Hawaiian and Galapageian volcanoes. Micronesia 3: 129-34.

——— 1967d. Succession and condition of ecosystems. Jour. Indian Bot. Soc. 46: 351-55.

——— 1970a. Island faunas and floras. McGraw-Hill Encycl. Science and Tech.: 309-11.

——— 1970b. The problem of isolation in the lowland tropical rain-forest. Trop. Ecol. 11: 162-68.

——— 1973. Past, present, and future conservation problems of oceanic islands. *In* A. B. Costin and R. H. Groves (eds.), Nature conservation in the Pacific. Australian Nat. Univ. Press.

——— 1974. Phytogeography of atolls and other coral islands. Proc. Second Internat. Coral Reef Symp. I. Great Barrier Reef Committee, Brisbane, Australia.

——— 1976a. Geography, ecology, and biogeography. Ann. Assoc. Amer. Geographers 66: 117-28.

——— 1976b. Coral island vegetation. *In* O. A. Jones and R. Endean (eds.), Biology and geology of coral reefs, 3: Biology, 2, 255-77. Academic Press, New York.

Frank, Gerhardt. 1963. Das Genus *Pediocactus* Britton et Rose. Sukkulentenkunde 7/8: 61-69.

——— 1965. Das Genus *Toumeya*, seine Arten und deren Variabilität. I.O.S. Bull. 2: 84-86.

Franke, Herbert W. 1971. Elektronenrasterbilder von Kakteensamen. Kakt. u. and. Sukk. 22: 15-19. *f. on pp. 16-17.*

Freeman, Thomas P. 1969. The developmental anatomy of *Opuntia basilaris*. I. Embryo, root, transition zone. Amer. Jour. Bot. 56: 1067-74.

——— 1970. The developmental anatomy of *Opuntia basilaris*. II. Apical meristem, leaves, areoles, glochids. Amer. Jour. Bot. 57: 616-22.

Frick, G. A. 1932. Water, water, everywhere! Cactus & Succ. Jour. 4: 242.

Friedrich, Heimo. 1976. Der name Opuntia. Kakt. u. and. Sukk. 10: 218-19.

Ganders, Fred R., and Helen Kennedy. 1978. Gynodioecy in *Mammillaria*. Madroño 25: 234.

Ganz, Martin. 1968. Ovule abortion and fruit proliferation instigated by an insect in *Opuntia macrorhiza* Engelm. Cactus & Succ. Jour. 40: 249-52. *f. 1-6.*

Gascoigne, R. M., E. Ritchie, and D. E. White. 1948 (1949). A survey of anthocyanins in the Australian flora. Jour. Proc. Roy. Soc. N. S. Wales 82: 44-70.

Geyer, Charles A. 1846. Notes on the vegetation and general character of the Missouri and Oregon Territories, made during a botanical journey in the State of Missouri, and across the South Pass of the Rocky Mountains, to the Pacific, during the years 1843 and 1844. London Jour. Bot. 5: Cactaceae on pp. 25-26.

Gibson, Arthur C. 1973. Comparative anatomy of secondary xylem in Cactoideae (Cactaceae). Biotropica 5: 29-65.

——— 1975. Another look at the cactus research of Irving Widmer Bailey. Cactus & Succ. Jour. suppl. vol. 76-85.

——— 1976. Vascular organization in shoots of Cactaceae. I. Development and morphology of primary vasculature in Pereskioideae and Opuntioideae. Amer. Jour. Bot. 63: 414-26.

——— 1977. Vegetative anatomy of *Maihuenia* (Cactaceae) with some theoretical discussions of ontogenetic changes in xylem cell types. Bull. Torrey Bot. Club 104: 35-48.

——— 1978. Wood anatomy of platyopuntias. El Aliso 9: 279-307.

Girard, Victor, and Stanley J. Farwig. 1973. Two forms of *Coryphantha* (*Neobesseya*) *missouriensis* found in Arizona. Cactus & Succ. Jour. 45: 125-31. *f. 1-9.*

Glass, Charles E., and Robert Foster. 1973. The monotypes, Part IV [*Pediocactus paradinei*]. Cactus & Succ. Jour. 45: 286-87. *f. 1.*

——— 1975. The genus *Echinomastus* [*Neolloydia*] in the Chihuahuan Desert. Cactus & Succ. Jour. 47: 218-23.

——— 1977a. Cacti and succulents for the amateur. Blandford Press, London.

——— 1977b. The genus *Thelocactus* in the Chihuahuan Desert. Cactus & Succ. Jour. 49: 213-20, 244-51.

——— 1978. A revision of the genus *Epithelantha*. Cactus & Succ. Jour. 50: 184-87.

Gleason, Henry Allen. 1912. An isolated prairie grove and its phytogeographical significance. Bot. Gazette 53: 38-49.

——— 1913. Relation of forest distribution and prairie fires in the Middle West. Torreya 13: 173-81.

——— 1917. The structure and development of the plant association. Bull. Torrey Bot. Club 44: 463-81.

——— 1923. The vegetational history of the Middle West. Assoc. Amer. Geographer, Annals, 12: 39-85.

——— 1926. The individualistic concept of the plant association. Bull. Torrey Bot. Club 53: 7-26.

——— 1952. The new Britton and Brown illustrated flora of the northeastern United States and adjacent Canada. Vols. 1-3. N.Y. Bot. Gard.

Gleason, Henry Allen, and Arthur Cronquist. 1964. The natural geography of plants. Columbia Univ. Press, New York.

Golley, Frank B. 1977. Ecological succession. Academic Press, New York.

Good, R. D'O. 1964. The geography of flowering plants. Wiley, New York.

Gould, Frank W. 1962. Texas plants—a check-list and ecological summary. Agr. and Mech. College of Texas; Texas Agr. Exp. Sta., College Station.

Grant, Verne. 1979. Character coherence in natural hybrid populations in plants [based partly on *Opuntia*]. Bot. Gaz. 140 (4): 443-48.

Grant, Verne, and Alva Grant. 1954. Generic and taxonomic studies in *Gilia*. VII. The woodland gilias. El Aliso 3: 59-91.

Grant, Verne, and Karen A. Grant. 1971a. Dynamics of clonal microspecies in cholla cactus. Evolution 25: 144-55. *f. 1-5.*

——— 1971b. Natural hybridization between the cholla cactus species, *Opuntia spinosior* and *Opuntia versicolor*. Proc. Nat. Acad. Sci. 68: 1993-95.

——— 1979a. Hybridization and variation in the *Opuntia phaeacantha* group in central Texas. Bot. Gaz. 140 (2): 208-15.

——— 1979b. Systematics of the *Opuntia phaeacantha* group in Texas. Bot. Gaz. 140 (2): 199-207.

Griffiths, David. 1905. The prickly pear and other cacti as stock food. USDA Bur. Plt. Indus. Bull. 74.

——— 1908. The prickly pear as a farm crop. USDA Bur. Plt. Indus. Bull. 124.

——— 1908-12. Illustrated studies in the genus *Opuntia*—I-IV. Rept. Mo. Bot. Gard. 19: 259-72. *pl. 21-28*; 20: 81-95. *pl. 2-13*; 21: 165-73. *pl. 19-28.* 22: 25-36. *pl. 1-17.*

——— 1909. The "spineless" prickly pears. USDA Bur. Plt. Indust. Bull. 140.

——— 1912. The thornless prickly pears. USDA Farm. Bull. 483.

——— 1913. Behavior, under cultural conditions, of species of cacti known as *Opuntia*. Bull. USDA 31.

——— 1914. Reversion in prickly pears. Jour. Hered. 5: 222-25.

——— 1915a. Hardier spineless cactus. Jour. Hered. 6: 182-91.

——— 1915b. Yields of native prickly pear in southern Texas. Bull. USDA 208.

——— 1929. El Nopal como alimento del ganado. Agricultura 55. La Unión Panamericana. Washington, D.C.

Griffiths, David, and R. F. Hare. 1907a. Summary of recent investigations of the value of cacti as stock food. USDA Bur. Plt. Indus. Bull. 102(1).

——— 1907b. The tuna as food for man. USDA Bur. Pl. Indus. Bull. 116.

——— 1908. Prickly pear and other cacti as food for stock. N. Mex. A. & M. Bull. 60.

Griffiths, David, and C. H. Thompson. 1930. Cacti. USDA Circ. 66.

Griggs, Robert F. 1934. The edge of the forest in Alaska and the reason for its position. Ecology 15: 80-95.

Grinnell, Joseph. 1935. A revised life-zone map of California. Univ. Calif. Publ. Zool. 40: 327-30.

Grootes, P. M. 1978. Carbon-14 time scale extended: comparison of chronologies. Science 200: 11-15.

Gulick, John Thomas. 1905. Evolution, racial and habitudinal. Carnegie Inst. Wash., Wash., D.C.

Gutiérrez Carlos, Alfonzo. 1972. Nopalnocheztli. Cactaceas y Suculentas Méxicanas 17: 51-64, 63 (English summary).

Haage, F. A., Jr. 1972. From old letters and documents. Cactus & Succ. Jour. 44: 51-54.

Habermann, Mudr. Vlastimil. 1974. Kaktusy jižní Kalifornie. Svaz Českých Katusářů—Vlastivědný Ústav Olomouc.

Hadley, Neil F. 1972. Desert species and adaptation. Amer. Scientist 60: 338-47.

——— 1975. Environmental physiology of desert organisms. Academic Press, New York.

Halliday, W. E. D. 1937. A forest classification for Canada. Forest Res. Div. Bull. 89: 1-50. Dept. of Resources and Dev., Ottawa.

Halliday, W. E. D., and A. W. A. Brown. 1948. The distribution of some important forest trees in Canada. Ecology 24: 353-73.

Hamilton, W. 1968. Cenozoic climatic change and its cause. Meteorological Monographs 8: 128-33.

Hammond, Allen L. 1971a. Plate tectonics: the geophysics of the Earth's surface. Science 173: 40-41.

——— 1971b. Plate tectonics (II): mountain building and continental geology. Science 173: 133-34.

——— 1976a. Paleoceanography: sea floor clues to earlier environments. Science 191: 168-70, 208.

——— 1976b. Paleoclimate; ice age was cool and dry. Science 191: 455.

Hanks, Sharon L., and David E. Fairbrothers. 1969. Diversity of populations of Opuntia compressa (Salisb.) Macbr. in New Jersey. Bull. Torrey Bot. Club (Torreya) 96: 592-94, 614-42.

Hare, R. F. 1908. Experiments on the digestibility of prickly pear by cattle. N. Mex. A. & M. Bull. 69; USDA Bur. Anim. Indust. Bull. 106.

——— 1911. A study of carbohydrates in the prickly pear and its fruits. N. Mex. A. & M. Bull. 80.

Harrington, H. D. 1954. Manual of the plants of Colorado. Sage Books, Denver.

Harrison, A. T., E. Small, and Harold A. Mooney. 1971. Drought relationships and distribution of two Mediterranean-climate California plant communities. Ecology 52: 869-75.

Haselton, Scott E. 1950. The dawn cactus. Cactus & Succ. Jour. 22: 28-30. f. 11-12.

Hastings, James R. 1961. Precipitation and saguaro growth. Arid Lands Colloquia, 1960-61: 30-38. Univ. Ariz. Press, Tucson.

Hastings, James R., and Stanley M. Alcorn. 1961. Physical determinations of growth and age in giant cactus. Jour. Ariz. Acad. Sci. 2: 32-39.

Hastings, James R., and Raymond M. Turner. 1965. The changing mile. An ecological study of vegetation change with time in the lower mile of an arid and semi-arid region. Univ. Ariz. Press, Tucson.

Hastings, James R., Raymond M. Turner, and D. K. Warren. 1972. An atlas of some plant distributions in the Sonoran Desert. Univ. Ariz. Inst. Atmos. Phys. Tech. Rep. Meteorol. Climatol. Arid Regions 21.

Haworth, Adrian Hardy. 1812. Synopsis plantarum succulentarum. Richard Taylor, London.

——— 1819. Supplementum plantarum succulentarum. J. Harding, London.

Haws, P. G. 1954. The giant cactus forest and its world. Duell, Sloan & Pearce, New York.

Hays, J. D., J. Imbrie, and N. J. Shackleton. 1976. Variations in the Earth's orbit: pacemaker of the ice ages. Science 194: 1121-32.

Heil, Kenneth D. 1979. Three new species of Cactaceae from southeastern Utah. Cactus & Succ. Jour. 51: 25-30.

Henslow, J. S. 1837. Description of two new species of Opuntia with remarks on the structure of the fruit of Rhipsalis. Mag. Zoöl. Bot. 1: 466-69.

Herbert, Charles W. 1969. Papago saguaro harvest. Ariz. Highw. 45: 3-7. f.

Hernandez-X, E., E. H. Crum, W. B. Fox, and A. J. Sharp. 1951. A unique vegetational area in Tamaulipas. Bull. Torrey Bot. Club 78: 458-63.

Hester, J. Pinckney. 1939. New species of cacti. Cactus & Succ. Jour. 10: 179-82.

Heusser, Calvin J. 1967. Pleistocene and postglacial vegetation of Alaska and the Yukon Territory. In Henry P. Hansen (ed.), Arctic biology, 131-52. Oregon State Univ. Press, Corvallis.

Higgins, Ethel Bailey. 1931. Our native cacti. A. T. de la Mare, New York.

Higgins, Vera. 1933. The study of cacti. Blandford, London.

Himwich, Harold E. 1958. Psychopharmacologic drugs. Science 127: 59-72.

Hitchcock, C. Leo, Arthur Cronquist, Marion Ownbey, and J. William Thompson. 1955-69. Vascular plants of the Pacific Northwest. Univ. Washington Press, Seattle.

Hodge, Carle. 1969. Monarch of the desert—saguaro. Ariz. Highw. 45: 6-35. f.

Hodgkins, J. E., S. D. Brown, and J. L. Massingill. 1967. Two new alkaloids in cacti. Tetrahedron Letters 14: 1321-24.

Hoffman, Ralph. 1932. The range of Opuntia prolifera Engelm. Cactus & Succ. Jour. 4: 256.

Hooker, J. D. 1862. Outlines of distribution of arctic plants. Trans. Linnaean Soc. 23: 251-348.

Hopkins, David M. 1959. Cenozoic history of the Bering Land Bridge. Science 129: 1519-28.

——— (ed.). 1967. The Bering Land Bridge. Stanford Univ. Press, Stanford, Calif.

Horich, Clarence K. 1960. Cactus deserts in western Canada. Cactus & Succ. Jour. 32: 160-62.

Horn, E. W. 1913. Prickly pear experiments. Dept. Agr., Bombay. Bull. 58 of 1913.

998   References Cited

Hornemann, K. M. Kelley, J. M. Neal, and Jerry L. McLaughlin. *See* McLaughlin.

Housely, Lucile Kempers. 1974. *Opuntia imbricata* on old Jemez Indian habitation sites. Thesis, Claremont Grad. School, Claremont, Calif.

Hövel, Otto. 1970. Zur Kenntnis der Gattung Schlumbergera Lem. Kakt. u. and. Sukk. 21: 182-86. *f. 1-6.*

Howard, W. L. 1945. Luther Burbank's plant contributions. Coll. Agr. Exp. Sta., Univ. Calif. Bull. 691.

Howden, H. F. 1974. Problems in interpreting dispersal of terrestrial organisms as related to continental drift. Biotropica 6: 1-6.

Howe, R. C., R. L. Richard, Jerry L. McLaughlin, and D. Statz. *See* McLaughlin.

Hull, James C., and Cornelius H. Muller. 1977. The potential for dominance by *Stipa pulchra* in a California grassland. Amer. Midl. Nat. 97: 147-75.

Hultén, Eric. 1937. Outline of the history of the arctic and boreal biota during the Quaternary period. Bokförlags akticbolaget Thule, Stockholm.

——— 1958. The amphi-Atlantic plants. Kungl. Vetenskapsakademiens Handlingar Fjärde Serien. Band 7, Nr. 1. Stockholm.

——— 1963. Phytogeographical connections of the North Atlantic. *In* Löve and Löve (eds.), 1963.

Humphrey, R. R. 1936. Growth habits of barrel cacti. Madroño 3: 348-52.

——— April 1958. The Desert Grassland: a history of vegetational change and an analysis of causes. Bot. Rev. 24: 193-252. Republished by Agr. Exp. Sta., Univ. Arizona, Tucson, December 1958.

——— 1963. Arizona natural vegetation. Arizona Agr. Exp. Stat. Bull. A-45 (map).

Hunt, David R. 1967. Dicotyledones. Cactaceae. *In* Hutchinson, 1967, 427-67.

——— 1971. Schumann and Buxbaum reconciled. The Schumann system of *Mammillaria* classification brought provisionally up-to-date. Cactus & Succ. Jour. Gt. Brit. 33: 53-72.

——— 1976a. Mammillarias in early European literature. (1) Before 1700. Cactus & Succ. Jour. Gt. Brit. 38: 11-14.

——— 1976b. The name game. Cactus & Succ. Jour. Gt. Brit. 38: 17.

——— 1976c. Why not *Chilita*? Cactus & Succ. Jour. Gt. Brit. 38: 57-60.

——— 1978a. Amplification of the genus *Escobaria*. Cactus & Succ. Jour. Gt. Brit. 40: 13.

——— 1978b. Classification of *Mammillaria*. Nat. Cactus & Succ. Jour. 32: 75-81.

Hunt, David R., and Lyman Benson. 1976. The lectotype of *Coryphantha*. Cactus & Succ. Jour. 48: 72.

Hunter, W. D., F. C. Pratt, and J. D. Mitchell. 1912. The principal cactus insects of the United States. USDA Bur. Entom. Bull. 13.

Hutchinson, John. 1967. The genera of flowering plants. (Cactaceae by David R. Hunt.) Clarendon Press, Oxford.

Iltis, Hugh H. 1969. A requiem for the prairie. Prairie Nat. 1: 51-57.

——— 1973. Long-distance dispersal (LDD) within the Arcto-Tertiary Geoflora: eastern North America

as a floristic oceanic archipelago. Abstract of paper presented at First Internat. Congress of Systematic and Evolutionary Biol., Boulder, Colorado.

——— (undated). The Benedict Prairie in Kenosha County, Wisconsin. Wisconsin Chapter of The Nature Conservancy, Proj. 3. (Mimeographed.)

Ivimey-Cook, R. B. 1977. What is a species? Cactus & Succ. Jour. Gt. Brit. 39: 30-32.

Jackson, James P. 1973. Visions of prairie parks. Nat. Parks and Conserv. Mag. 47: 23-26.

Jacobson, H. 1954-55. Handbuch der sukkulenten Pflanzen. 1-3. Fischer, Jena.

Janzen, Daniel I. 1966. Coevolution of mutualism between ants and acacias in Central America. Evolution 20: 249-75.

Jepson, Willis Linn. 1909-1943. A flora of California. (Cactaceae by Samuel Bonsall Parish.) 3 vols. (Issued in parts; vols. 1 & 3 incomplete.) Jepson Herbarium, Dept. Bot., Univ. Calif., Berkeley.

——— 1923-25. A manual of the flowering plants of California. (Cactaceae by Samuel Bonsall Parish.) Assoc. Students Store, Berkeley. Seventh printing, 1970, Univ. Calif. Press, Berkeley and Los Angeles.

Johansen, Donald A. 1933. Recent work on the cytology of the cacti. Cactus & Succ. Jour. 4: 356.

Johnson, Duncan S. 1918. The fruit of *Opuntia fulgida*, a study of perennation and proliferation of the fruits in certain Cactaceae. Carnegie Inst. Wash. Publ. 269.

Johnston, Ivan M. 1940. The floristic significance of shrubs common to the North and South American deserts. Jour. Arnold Arb. 21: 356-63.

——— 1943. Publication dates for botanical parts of the Pacific Railroad Reports. Jour. Arnold Arb. 24: 287-342.

Kaneps, A. K. 1979. Gulf Stream velocity fluctuations during the late Cenozoic. Science 204: 297-301.

Katagiri, Shigeru. 1953. Chromosome numbers and polyploidy in certain Cactaceae. Cactus & Succ. Jour. 25: 141-43.

Kauffmann, N. 1859. Zur Entwicklungsgeschichte der Cacteenstacheln. [Transitions of spines and leaves and of glochids and leaves.] Bull. Soc. Imp. des Nat. de Moscou 32: 585-602.

Kearney, Thomas H., Robert H. Peebles, and collaborators. 1951. Arizona flora. Supplement, 1960. Univ. Calif. Press, Berkeley and Los Angeles.

Keasey, Merritt S., III. 1974. Cactus birds. Pac. Discov. 27: 10-14.

Keller, W. J., and Jerry L. McLaughlin. *See* McLaughlin.

Keller, W. J., Jerry L. McLaughlin, and L. R. Brady. *See* McLaughlin.

Keller, W. J., L. A. Spitznagle, L. R. Brady, and Jerry L. McLaughlin. *See* McLaughlin.

Kellogg, W. W., and S. H. Schneider. 1974. Climate stabilization: for better or for worse? Science 186: 1163-72.

Kelso, Leon. 1954. The sharp point. Cactus & Succ. Jour. 26: 31-32.

Kerr, Richard A. 1978. Climate control: how large a role for orbital variations? Science 201: 144-46.

King, James E., and Thomas R. Van Devender. 1977. Pollen analysis of fossil packrat middens from the Sonoran Desert. Quaternary Res. 8: 191-204.

King, P. B. 1959. The evolution of North America. Princeton Univ. Press, Princeton, N.J.

Kirkpatrick, Bob [Robert H.]. 1971. Micropuntia? Cactus & Succ. Jour. 43: 106-7. *f. 1-2.*

Kladiwa, Leo. 1963. Das *Toumeya*-Problem und die eingezogenen Genera *Navajoa* und *Turbinocarpus.* Sukkulentenkunde 7/8: 42-60.

Klüver, H. 1966. Mescal and mechanisms of hallucinations. Univ. Chicago Press, Chicago.

Kominz, M. A., and N. G. Pisias. 1979. Pleistocene climate: deterministic or stochastic? Science 204: 171-73.

Kruckeberg, Arthur R. 1969. Soil diversity and the distribution of plants, with examples from western North America. Madroño 20: 129-54.

Kuchler, A. W. 1949. Natural vegetation of the world. Map in Goode's School Atlas. Rand-McNally, Chicago.

——— 1964. Potential natural vegetation of the coterminous United States. Amer. Geog. Soc., New York.

——— 1967. Vegetation mapping. Ronald Press, New York.

Kukla, G. J., and R. K. Matthews. 1972. When will the present interglacial end? Science 178: 190-91.

Kurtz, Edwin B., Jr. 1948/49. Pollen grain characters of certain Cactaceae. Bull. Torrey Bot. Club 75: 516-22. *f. 1-9;* Cactus & Succ. Jour. 21: 40-42. *f. 1-8.*

——— 1963. Pollen morphology of the Cactaceae. Grana palynologica 3: 367-72.

Kurtz, Edwin B., Jr., and Stanley S. Alcorn. 1960. Some germination requirements of saguaro cactus seeds. Cactus & Succ. Jour. 32: 72-74.

La Barre, Winston. 1938. The peyote cult. Yale Univ. Publ. in Anthro. no. 19.

——— 1960. Twenty years of peyote studies. Current Anthro. 1: 45-60.

Labouret, J. 1858. Monographie de la famille des Cactées. Librairie Agricole de la Maison Rustique, Paris.

Lanjouw, J., and F. A. Stafleu. 1964. Index Herbariorum. Ed. 5, Part 1 (Regnum Vegetabile 31).

[Lanjouw, J.], F. A. Stafleu et al. 1972. International Code of Botanical Nomenclature. Int. Assoc. Pl. Taxon., Utrecht, Netherlands.

Lanner, Ronald M., and Thomas R. Van Devender. 1974. Morphology of pinyon pine needles from fossil packrat middens in Arizona. Forest Science 20: 207-11.

Lanternari, V. 1965. The religions of the oppressed. Mentor Books, New York.

Larsen, J. A. 1930. Forest types of the northern Rocky Mountains and their climatic controls. Ecology 11: 631-72.

Lawrence, Ned. 1931. Suppose it is spineless. Cactus & Succ. Jour. 2: 242.

Lemaire, Charles. 1838. Cactarum aliquot novarum ac insuetarum in horto Monvilliano cultarum accurata descripto. Paris.

——— 1839. Cactacearum genera nova speciesque novae et omnium in horto Monvilliano cultarum ex affinitatibus naturalibus ordinato nova indexque methodicus. Paris.

——— 1868. Les Cactées. Libraire Agricole de la Maison Rustique, Paris.

Leopold, A. Starker. 1950. Vegetation zones of Mexico. Ecology 31: 507-18.

Leopold, E. B., and H. D. MacGinitie. 1972. Development and affinities of Tertiary floras in the Rocky Mountains. *In* A. Graham (ed.), Floristics and Paleofloristics of Asia and eastern North America, 1-278. Elsevier, Amsterdam.

Leopold, Luna B. 1951. Vegetation of Southwestern watersheds. *In* Nineteenth Cent. Geog. Rev. 41: 295-316.

LeSeur, Hardy. 1945. The ecology of the vegetation of Chihuahua, Mexico, north of parallel twenty-eight. Univ. Texas Publ. 4521: 1-92.

Leuenberger, Beat. 1975. Die Pollenmorphologie der Cactaceae und ihre Bedeutung für Systematik. Diss., Univ. Heidelberg, West Germany.

——— 1976a. Pollen morphology of the Cactaceae. Cactus & Succ. Jour. Gt. Brit. 38: 79-94.

——— 1976b. Die Pollenmorphologie der Cactaceae. J. Cramer, A. R. Gantner Verlag, Vaduz, Liechtenstein.

——— 1978. Type specimens of Cactaceae in the Berlin-Dahlem Herbarium. Cactus & Succ. Jour. Gt. Brit. 40: 101-4.

Leuenberger, Beat, and Rainer Schill. 1974. Epidermal features of some "green mammillarias" (Cactaceae). Cactus & Succ. Jour. 46: 83-85 (with excellent illustrations; scanning electron microscope photographs).

Li, Hui-Lin. 1952. Floristic relationships between eastern Asia and eastern North America. Trans. Amer. Phil. Soc., II. 42: 371-429.

Lindsay, George. 1940. The pitahaya, or organ-pipe cactus. Des. Pl. Life 12: 185-86.

——— 1941. Notes on *Utahia sileri.* Cactus & Succ. Jour. 13: 83-86. *f.*

——— 1952. The use of cactus as stock food. Des. Pl. Life 23: 5-6. *f.*

——— 1955. Some new varieties and nomenclatural changes in *Ferocactus.* Cactus & Succ. Jour. 27: 163-75. *f. 153-61.*

——— 1963a. Cacti of San Diego County [California]. Occ. Papers San Diego Soc. Nat. Hist. 12.

——— 1963b. The genus *Lophocereus.* Cactus & Succ. Jour. 35: 176-92.

Linnaeus, Carolus (Carl von Linné). 1753. Species plantarum. Ed. 1. Holmiae, Laurentius Salvius.

——— 1754. Genera plantarum. Ed. 5. Holmiae, Laurentii Salvii.

Livingston, B. E., and Forrest Shreve. 1931. Climatic areas of the U.S. as related to plant growth. Carnegie Inst. Wash. Publ. 284.

Lockett, H. C., and M. Snow. 1939. Along the Beale Trail, a photographic account of wasted range land.

U.S. Off. Indian Affairs, Educ. Div. Publ., Washington, D.C., 1-56.

Long, Robert W. 1974a. The vegetation of southern Florida. Florida Scientist 37: 33-45.

——— 1974b. Origin of the vascular flora of southern Florida. *In* P. J. Gleason (ed.), Environments of south Florida. Mem. Miami Geol. Soc.

Long, Robert W., and Olga Lakela. 1971a. A flora of tropical Florida. Univ. Miami Press, Coral Gables.

——— 1971b. Geology of southern Florida. *In* Long & Lakela, 1971a, 11-26.

Löve, Askell. 1959. Origin of the arctic flora. McGill Univ. Mus. Publ. 1: 82-95.

Löve, Askell, and Doris Löve (eds.). 1963. North Atlantic biota and their history. Oxford Univ. Press.

——— 1967a. Continental drift and the origin of the arctic-alpine flora. Revue Roumaine de Biologie Série Bot. 12: 163-69.

——— 1967b. The origin of the North Atlantic flora. Dept. Biol. and Inst. for Arctic and Alpine Res., Univ. Colorado, Boulder. Aquilo, Ser. Botanica 6: 52-66.

Löve, Doris. 1962. Plants and Pleistocene—problems of Pleistocene and arctic. McGill Univ. Mus. Publ. 2: 17-39.

——— 1970. Subarctic and subalpine: where and what? Arctic and Alpine Res. 2: 63-73.

Lowe, C., and D. Hinds. 1971. Effect of palo verde (*Cercidium*) trees on the radiation flux at ground level in the Sonoran Desert in winter. Ecology 52: 916-22.

Luchsinger, Arleen Abel. 1965. A revision of *Neobesseya* in the United States and Cuba. Trans. Kans. Acad. Sci. 68: 384-95. *f. 1-2.*

Lumholz, Carl. 1912. New trails in Mexico. Scribner's, New York.

Lundell, Cyrus Longworth, and collaborators. 1942-70. Flora of Texas. Vols. 1-3. (Cactaceae by Lyman Benson.) Texas Res. Foundation, Renner.

Lundstrom, Jan, and Stig Agurell. 1967. Thin-layer chromatography of the peyote [*Lophophora williamsii*] alkaloids. J. Chromatog. 30 (1): 271-72.

Lyons, Gary. 1972. Conservation: a waste of time? Cactus & Succ. Jour. 44: 173-77.

——— 1976. Some new developments in conservation. Cactus & Succ. Jour. 48: 154-62.

——— 1979. The C[actus and] S[ucculent] S[ociety] of A[merica] and conservation: boom or bust? Cactus & Succ. Jour. 51: 9-15.

Mabry, T. J. 1966a. The betacyanins and betaxanthins. *In* T. Swain et al., Comparative phytochemistry. Academic Press, London & New York.

——— 1966b. The betacyanins and betaxanthins. *In* T. J. Mabry, ed., Recent advances in phytochemistry. Meredith, Des Moines.

Mabry, T. J., and A. S. Dreiding. 1967. The betalains. *In* T. J. Mabry, ed., Recent advances in phytochemistry. Meredith, Des Moines.

MacBride, J. Francis. 1950. Natural landscapes of the United States. Chicago Mus. Nat. Hist. Pop. Series, Botany 27.

McCleary, James A., and David L. Walkington. 1964.

Antimicrobial activity in Cactaceae. Bull. Torrey Bot. Club 91: 361-69.

MacDougal, Daniel Tremblay. 1908a. The course of the vegetative seasons in southern Arizona. Plant World 11: 189-201, 217-31, 237-49, 261-70.

——— 1908b. Botanical features of North American deserts. Carnegie Inst. Wash. Publ. 99. Johnson reprint.

——— 1909. The origin of desert floras. *In* V. M. Spaulding (ed.), Distribution and movements of desert plants. Carnegie Inst. Wash. Publ. 113.

——— 1912. North American deserts. Geog. Jour. 39: 105-20.

MacDougal, Daniel T., and E. S. Spalding. 1910. The water-balance of succulent plants. Carnegie Inst. Wash. Publ. 141.

MacGinitie, H. D. 1933. Redwoods and frost. Science 78: 190.

——— 1953. Fossil plants from the Florissant beds, Colorado. Carnegie Inst. Wash. Publ. 599.

Maheshwari, P. 1950. An introduction to the embryology of angiosperms. McGraw-Hill, New York.

Maiden, J. H. 1898. A preliminary study of the prickly pears naturalized in New South Wales. Agr. Gaz. N.S.W. 1-30.

——— 1911-17. The prickly pears of interest to Australians. Agr. Gaz. N.S.W. Misc. Pub. 1430, 1452, 1502, 1561, 1595, 1605, 1679, 1698, 1705, 1719, 1746, 1767, 1823, 1950, 1963, 1975.

Mairn, A. E. M., et al. 1964. Problems in paleoclimatology. Wiley Interscience, New York.

Mann, John. 1969. Cactus-feeding insects and mites. U.S. Nat. Mus. Bull. 256.

Manson, James. 1933. An answer to "Water! water! everywhere!" Cactus & Succ. Jour. 4: 347.

Map of the Dominion of Canada indicating vegetation and forest cover. Nat. Dev. Bur., Dept. Interior, Dom. of Canada, Ottawa.

Marshall, W. Taylor. 1948. Plant of the month. Saguaroland Bull. 2 (no page no.).

——— 1950/53. Arizona's cactuses. Desert Bot. Gard., Phoenix. Ed. 1, 1950; ed. 2, 1953.

——— 1953a. *Toumeya papyracantha* (Eng.) Br. & R. Saguaroland Bull. 7: 51-52.

——— 1953b. *Utahia sileri* (Engelman[n]) Br. & R. Saguaroland Bull. 7: 71.

——— 1955. *Toumeya peeblesiana* (Croizat) W. T. Marshall. Saguaroland Bull. 9: 93-96.

——— 1956a. The barrel cactus as a source of water. Saguaroland Bull. 10: 64-71.

——— 1956b. A new genus of cactuses for Arizona. Saguaroland Bull. 10: 89-91, 107.

Marshall, W. Taylor, and Thor Methven Bock. 1941. Cactaceae. Abbey Garden Press, Pasadena, Calif.

Martin, Paul S., and P. J. Mehringer, Jr. 1965. Pleistocene pollen analysis and biogeography of the Southwest. *In* H. E. Wright, Jr., and David G. Grey (eds.), The Quaternary of the United States. Princeton Univ. Press, Princeton, N.J.

Mason, Herbert L. 1934. The Pleistocene flora of the Tomales Formation. Carnegie Inst. Wash. Publ. 415: 83-180.

———— 1947. Evolution of certain floristic associations in western North America. Ecological Monographs 17: 201-10.

Mauseth, James D. 1976. Cytokinin- and gibberellic-acid induced structure and metabolism of shoot apical meristems in *Opuntia polyacantha*. Amer. Jour. Bot. 63: 1295-1301.

———— 1977a. Cytokinin and gibberelic acid-induced effects on the determination and morphogenesis of leaf primordia in *Opuntia polyacantha* (Cactaceae). Amer. Jour. Bot. 64: 337-46.

———— 1977b. Cactus tissue culture: a potential method of propagation. Cactus & Succ. Jour. 49: 80-81.

———— 1978. An investigation of phylogenetic and ontogenetic variability of shoot apical meristems in the Cactaceae. Amer. Jour. Bot. 65: 326-33.

Mayer-Oakes, W. J. (ed.). 1967. Life, land, and water. Proc. 1966 Conf. on Environmental Studies of the Glacial Lake Agassiz Region. Occ. Papers, Dept. Anthropology, Univ. Manitoba, No. 1. Univ. Manitoba Press, Winnipeg.

Maysilles, James H. 1959. Floral relationships of the pine forests of western Durango, Mexico. Ph.D. thesis, Univ. Michigan, Ann Arbor. 1-165.

McGregor, S. E., Stanley M. Alcorn, Edwin B. Kurtz, Jr., and George D. Butler, Jr. 1959. Bee visitors to saguaro flowers. Jour. Econ. Entom. 52: 1002-4.

McGregor, S. E., Stanley M. Alcorn, and George Olin. 1962. Pollination and pollinating agents in the saguaro. Ecology 43: 259-67.

McKelvey, Susan Delano. 1959. A discussion of the Pacific Railroad Report as issued in the quarto edition. Jour. Arnold Arb. 40: 38-67.

McKenna, M. C. 1972. Possible biological consequences of plate tectonics. BioScience 22: 519-25.

McKenzie, Daniel P. 1972. Plate tectonics and seafloor spreading. Amer. Scientist 60: 425-35.

McLaughlin, Jerry L. 1966- . The cactus alkaloids. (Series of papers, various other authors contributing, commonly with McLaughlin's name last; in order to unify the series, pertinent papers are brought together here by number in the series, regardless of the first-named author):

I. Jerry L. McLaughlin and A. G. Paul. 1966. Identification of n-methylated tyramine derivatives in *Lophophora williamsii*. Lloydia 29: 315-27.

II. 1967. Biosynthesis of hordenine and mescaline in *Lophophora williamsii*. Lloydia 30: 91-99.

III. H. Rosenberg, Jerry L. McLaughlin, and A. G. Paul. 1967. Phenylalanine, DOPA, and DOPA-mine, precursors to mescaline in *Lophophora williamsii*. Lloydia 30: 100-105.

IV. L. E. Below, A. Y. Leung, Jerry L. McLaughlin, and A. G. Paul. 1968. Macromerine from *Coryphantha runyonii*. Jour. Pharm. Sci. 57: 515.

VI. Jerry L. McLaughlin. 1969. Identification of hordenine and n-methyltyramine in *Ariocarpus fissuratus* varieties *fissuratus* and *lloydii*. Lloydia 32: 392-94.

VIII. D. G. Norquist and Jerry L. McLaughlin. 1970. Isolation of n-methyl-3,4-dimethoxy-β-phenethylamine from *Ariocarpus fissuratus* var. *fissuratus*. Jour. Pharm. Sci. 59: 1840-41.

XII. K. M. Kelley Hornemann, J. M. Neal, and Jerry L. McLaughlin. 1972. β-phenethylamine alkaloids in the genus *Coryphantha*. Jour. Pharm. Sci. 61: 41-45.

XIII. W. J. Keller and Jerry L. McLaughlin. 1972. Isolation of (-)-normacromerine from *Coryphantha macromeris* var. *runyonii*. Jour. Pharm. Sci. 61: 147-48.

XV. W. J. Keller, Jerry L. McLaughlin, and L. R. Brady. 1973. β-phenethylamine derivatives from *Coryphantha macromeris* var. *runyonii*. Jour. Pharm. Sci. 62: 408-11.

XVI. P. T. Sato, J. M. Neal, L. R. Brady, and Jerry L. McLaughlin. 1973. Isolation and identification of alkaloids in *Coryphantha ramillosa*. Jour. Pharm. Sci. 62: 411-14.

XX. W. J. Keller, L. A. Spitznagle, L. R. Brady, and Jerry L. McLaughlin. 1973. The biosynthesis of catechol-O-methylated β-hydroxyphenethylamines (normacromerine and macromerine) in *Coryphantha macromeris* var. *runyonii*. Lloydia 36: 397-409.

XXI. J. J. Dingerdissen and Jerry L. McLaughlin. 1973. β-phenethylamines from *Dolichothele sphaerica* [*Mammillaria longimamma* var. *sphaerica*]. Jour. Pharm. Sci. 62: 1663-66.

XXIV. Randall L. Vanderveen, Leslie G. West, and Jerry L. McLaughlin. 1974. N-methyltyramine from *Opuntia clavata*. Phytochem. 13: 866-67.

XXVIII. Richard L. Rainieri and Jerry L. McLaughlin. 1976. β-phenethylamine and tetrahydroisoquinoline alkaloids from the Mexican cactus *Dolichothele longimamma* [*Mammillaria longimamma*, also in Texas]. Jour. Org. Chem. 41: 319-23.

XXXIII. R. C. Howe, R. L. Richard, Jerry L. McLaughlin, and D. Statz. 1977. Crystallization of hordenine HCl from *Coryphantha vivipara* var. *arizonica*. Planta Medica.

———— 1973. Peyote: an introduction. Symp. on Peyote, Houston, Texas. Lloydia 30: 1-8.

McLeod, Malcolm G. 1973. Biosystematics of juicy-fruited prickly pears of Arizona (Cactaceae, *Opuntia*, series Opuntiae). Thesis, Ariz. State Univ., Tempe.

———— 1975. A new hybrid fleshy-fruited prickly-pear in California. Madroño 23: 96-98.

McMillan, A. J. S. 1969. *Zygocactus truncatus* or *Schlumbergera truncata*? A problem in taxonomy. Nat. Cactus & Succ. Jour. 24: 10-12. *f. 1-2.*

Medeiros, Joseph L. 1979. San Luis Island: the last of the Great Valley. Fremontia, Calif. Native Plant Soc. 7: 3-9.

Megata, M. 1941. Eine Liste von Chromosomen bei Kakteen und anderen Sukkulenten. Kyoto Univ., Tokyo.

Melville, R. 1966. Continental drift, Mesozoic continents, and the migrations of the angiosperms. Nature 211: 116-20.

Merriam, C. Hart. 1890. Results of a biological survey of the San Francisco Mountain region and desert of the Little Colorado in Arizona. U.S. Div. Ornith. and Mammal., N. Amer. Fauna 3: 1-34.

——— 1893a. Notes on the distribution of trees and shrubs in the deserts and desert ranges of southern California, northwestern Arizona, and southwestern Utah. N. Amer. Fauna 7: 285-343.

——— 1893b. Notes on the geographical and vertical distribution of cactuses, yuccas, and agave, in the deserts and desert ranges of southern California, southern Nevada, northwestern Arizona, and southwestern Utah. N. Amer. Fauna 7: 345-59.

——— 1893c. The geographical distribution of life in North America, with special reference to Mammalia. Smiths. Inst. Annual Report to July 1891: 365-415.

——— 1894. The geographical distribution of animals and plants in North America. U.S. Dept. Agri. Yearbook 18: 203-14.

——— 1898. Life zones and crop zones in the United States. U.S. Div. Biol. Surv. Bull. 10: 1-79.

Metcalfe, C. R., and L. Chalk. 1950. Anatomy of the dicotyledons. Clarendon Press, Oxford.

Miranda, Faustino, and A. J. Sharp. 1950. Characteristics of the vegetation in certain temperate regions of eastern Mexico. Ecology 31: 313-33.

Mitich, Larry W. 1970. Wyoming native cacti. I & II. Cactus & Succ. Jour. 42: 155-59. *f. 1-6*; 217-21. *f. 7-16.*

——— 1972. The saguaro—a history. Cactus & Succ. Jour. 44: 118-29. *f. 1-13.*

——— 1976. Andrew Halstead Alverson and the California grizzly bear [cactus]. Cactus & Succ. Jour. 48: 171-75, 234-37.

——— 1979. The great Nathaniel Lord Britton. Cactus & Succ. Jour. 51: 118-21.

Mitich, Larry W., and Lyman Benson. 1977. Thomas Nuttall and the cacti of North Dakota. Cactus & Succ. Jour. 49: 1-8.

Mitich, Larry W., and Jan G. Bruhn. 1977. The genus *Ariocarpus*—a bibliography. Cactus & Succ. Jour. 49: 122-27.

Mooney, Harold A., J. Ehleringer, and J. A. Berry. 1976. High photosynthetic capacity of a winter annual in Death Valley. Science 194: 322-24.

Moore, Winifred O. 1967. The *Echinocereus enneacanthus-dubius-stramineus* complex (Cactaceae). Brittonia 19: 77-94.

Moran, Reid. 1953a. Taxonomic studies in the Cactaceae. Gentes Herbarum 8: 316-27.

——— 1953b. Notes on *Schlumbergera, Rhipsalidopsis*, and allied genera. Gentes Herb. 8: 328-45.

——— 1966. The fruit of *Bergerocactus*. Nat. Cactus & Succ. Jour. 21: 30-31. *f. 1-3.*

Munz, Philip A. 1935. A manual of southern California botany. Claremont Colleges, Claremont, Calif.

——— 1959. A California flora. 1-18. Supplement 1968. Univ. Calif. Press, Berkeley.

——— 1974. A flora of southern California. Univ. Calif. Press, Berkeley.

Munz, Philip A., and David D. Keck. 1949. California plant communities. El Aliso 2: 87-105. (Suppl. 2: 199-202. 1950.)

Neff, N., and G. V. Rossi. 1963. Mescaline. Amer. H. Pharm. 135 (9): 319-27.

Newell, R. E. 1974. Changes in poleward energy flux by the atmosphere and ocean as a possible cause for the ice ages. Quaternary Res. 4: 117-27.

Newton, L. E. 1962. George Engelmann, biographical notes and a bibliography. Nat. Cactus & Succ. Jour. 17: 43-45.

Nichol, A. A. 1931. The natural vegetation of Arizona. Univ. Ariz. Coll. Agr., Agri. Exp. Sta. Tech. Bull. 68: 181-222.

Nickerson, Grace P. 1929. *Platyopuntia*: Tuna, nopal, prickly pear, Indian fig. Desert 1: 70.

Niering, W. A., and R. H. Whittaker. 1965. The saguaro problem and grazing in the southwestern national monuments. Nat. Parks Mag. 39: 4-9.

Niering, W. A., R. H. Whittaker, and C. H. Lowe. 1963. The saguaro: a population in relation to environment. Science 142: 15-23. *f. 1-5.*

Norquist, D. G., and Jerry L. McLaughlin. *See* McLaughlin.

Osting, H. J. 1948, 1956. The study of plant communities. W. H. Freeman, San Francisco.

Orpet, E. O. 1929. The *Opuntia* in Australia. Cactus & Succ. Jour. 1: 87, 98.

——— 1939. Spineless *Opuntias* for stock food. Cactus & Succ. Jour. 11: 57.

Parish, S. B. 1930. Vegetation of the Mojave and Colorado deserts of southern California. Ecology 11: 481-99.

Peck, Morton E. 1941. A manual of the higher plants of Oregon. Binfords and Mort, Portland. Reprinted, 1961, Oregon State Univ. Press, Corvallis.

Peebles, Robert H. 1936a. A natural hybrid in the genus *Opuntia*. Cactus & Succ. Jour. 7: 99-101. *f.*

——— 1936b. Large saguaros. Des. Pl. Life 8: 30.

——— 1938. *Toumeya* found in Arizona. Cactus & Succ. Jour. 10: 51. *2 figs.*

——— 1942. Preservation of cactus material. Cactus & Succ. Jour. 14: 3-8, *f. 1-11.*

——— 1943. Watching the saguaro bloom. Des. Pl. Life 15: 55-60.

——— 1947. Saguaro fruit. Des. Pl. Life 19: 89-90.

Petty, F. W. 1935. *Cactoblastis cactorum*. Des. Pl. Life 7: 79-80.

Pfeiffer, Ludovico. 1837. Enumeratio diagnostica cactacearum hucusque cognitarum. Oehmigke, Berlin.

Philbrick, Ralph. 1963. Biosystematic studies of two Pacific Coast opuntias. Thesis, Cornell University, Ithaca, N.Y.

Phillips, Arthur M., III, and Thomas R. Van Devender. 1974. Pleistocene packrat middens from the lower Grand Canyon of Arizona. Jour. Ariz. Acad. Sci. 9: 117-19.

Pickett, Charles H., and W. Dennis Clark. 1979. The function of extrafloral nectaries in *Opuntia acanthocarpa*. Amer. Jour. Bot. 66: 618-25.

Pinkava, Donald J., Lyle A. McGill, Timothy Reeves, and Malcolm G. McLeod. 1977. Chromosome numbers in some cacti of western North America—III. Bull. Torrey Bot. Club 104: 105-10.

Pinkava, Donald J., and Malcolm G. McLeod. 1971. Chromosome numbers in some cacti of western North America. Brittonia 23: 171-76. *f. 1-23.*

Pinkava, Donald J., Malcolm G. McLeod, L. A. McGill, and R. C. Brown. 1973. Chromosome numbers in some cacti of western North America—II. Brittonia 25: 2-9. *f. 1-31.*

Piper, Charles V. 1906. Flora of the state of Washington. Contr. U.S. Nat. Herb. 11.

Poindexter, John. 1951. The cactus spine and related structures. Des. Pl. Life 24: 7-14.

Polunin, Nicholas. 1951. The real Arctic: suggestions for its delimitation, subdivision, and characterization. Jour. Ecol. 39: 308-15.

Porsch, O. 1939. Das Bestäubungsleben der Kakteenblüte. Cactaceae. Jahrb. Deutsche Kakteen-Gesellsch. 1939: 1-147 .

Porsild, A. Erling. 1958. Geographical distribution of some elements in the flora of Canada. Geog. Bull. 11: 57-77.

Prentiss, D. Q., and F. P. Morgan. 1896. Therapeutic uses of mescal buttons (*Anhalonium lewinii*). Therap. Gaz. 3rd ser., 12: 4-11.

Prickly Pear Destruction Commission, Moree. 1927 (Sydney, 1967). [Pest] prickly pear destruction in New South Wales.

Quarterman, Elsie, and Catherine Keever. 1962. Southern mixed hardwood forest: climax in the southeastern coastal plain: U.S.A. Ecol. Monographs 32: 167-85.

Racine, Charles H., and Jerry F. Downhower. 1974. Vegetative and reproductive strategies of *Opuntia* (Cactaceae) in the Galapagos Islands. Biotropica 6: 175-86.

Radford, A. E., Harry E. Ahles, and C. Ritchie Bell. 1968. Manual of the vascular flora of the Carolinas. Univ. North Carolina Press, Chapel Hill.

Rainieri, Richard L., and Jerry L. McLaughlin. *See* McLaughlin.

Rauh, Werner. 1956. Morphologische, entwicklungsgeschichtliche, histogenetische und anatomische Untersuchungen an den Sprossen der Didiereaceen. Akad. Wiss. und Lit., Mainz. Abh. Math.-Nat. Klasse 1956 (6): 345-444.

——— 1961. Weitere Untersuchungen an Didiereaceen. Teil 1 Beitrag zur Kenntnis der Wuchsformen der Didiereaceen, unter besondere Berückssichtigen neuer Arten. S.-B. Heidelb. Akad. Wiss., Math.-Nat. Klasse 1961: 185-300.

——— 1976. The Didiereaceae. Cactus & Succ. Jour. 48: 75.

——— 1977. The xerophytic vegetation of southwestern Madagascar. Cactus & Succ. Jour. 49: 99-103, 155-60, 197-204, 269-73; 50: 11-15, 55-59, 119-21, 159-65, 226-29.

Rauh, Werner, and K. Dittmar. 1970. Weitere Untersuchungen an Didiereaceen. Teil 3. Vergleichendanatomische Untersuchungen an den Sprossachsen und den Dornen der Didiereaceen. S.-B. Heidelb. Akad. Wiss., Math.-Nat. Klasse 1970: 163-246.

Rauh, Werner, and H. Reznik. 1961. Zur Frage der systematischen Stellung der Didiereaceen. Bot. Jahrb. für Systematik, Pflanzengeschichte, and Pflanzengeographie 81: 94-105.

Rauh, Werner, and H.-F. Schölch. 1965. Weitere Untersuchungen an Didiereaceen. Teil 2. Infloreszenz-, blutenmorphologische und embryologische Untersuchungen mit Ausblick auf der systematische Stellung der Didiereaceen. S.-B. Heidelb. Akad. Wiss., Math.-Nat. Klasse 1965: 221-434.

Raunkiaer, C. 1934. The life forms of plants and statistical plant geography: being the collected papers of C. Raunkiaer. Clarendon Press, Oxford.

Raup, Hugh M. 1941. Botanical problems in boreal America. Bot. Rev. 7: 147-248.

Raven, Peter H., and Daniel I. Axelrod. 1974. Angiosperm biogeography and past continental movements. Ann. Mo. Bot. Gard. 61: 539-673.

——— 1978. Origin and relationships of the California flora. Univ. Calif. Publ. Bot. 72.

Reichle, David E. 1970. Analysis of temperate flora ecosystems. Springer-Verlag, New York.

Remski, Sister Marie Fidelis. 1954. Cytological investigations in *Mammillaria* and some associated genera. Bot. Gaz. 116: 163-71.

Rendle, Alfred Barton. 1925, 1930. The classification of flowering plants. Ed. 2, vol. 1. Monocotyledoneae, 1930; vol. 2. Dicotyledoneae, 1925. Cambridge Univ. Press, Cambridge, Eng.

Reveal, James L. 1968. On the names in Fraser's catalogue. Rhodora 70: 25-54.

Richards, P. W. 1952. The tropical rain forest. Cambridge Univ. Press, Cambridge, England. Review by A. G. Tansley in Journal of Ecology 41: 398-99. 1952.

Richmond, Gerald M., et al. 1965. The cordilleran ice sheet of northern Rocky Mountains and related Quaternary history of the Columbia Plateau. *In* Wright & Frey (eds.), 1965.

Riley, Herbert P., and T. R. Bryant. 1959. Preliminary studies in the identification of species by the paper chromatography of fluorescent compounds. Proc. IX Intern. Bot. Congr. 2: 327.

——— 1961. The separation of nine species of the Iridaceae by paper chromatography. Amer. Jour. Bot. 48: 133-37. *f. 1.*

Robinson, Harold. 1973. New combinations in the Cactaceae subfamily Opuntioideae. Phytologia 26: 175-76.

——— 1974. Scanning electron microscope studies of the spines of the Opuntioideae (Cactaceae). Amer. Jour. Bot. 61: 278-83. *f. 1-37.*

Roland-Gosselin, M. R. 1912. Les *Rhipsalis* découvertes en Afrique, sont-ils indigènes? Bull. Bot. Soc. France 59: 97-102. [Are the species of *Rhipsalis* discovered in Africa indigenous? Torreya 13: 151-56. 1913.]

Rosenberg, H., Jerry L. McLaughlin, and A. G. Paul. *See* McLaughlin.

Rouhier, Alexander. 1927. La plante qui fait les yeux émerveillés: le Peyotl (*Echinocactus williamsii* Lem.). [The plant that produces wonderful visions: the peyote.] Paris: Gaston Doin et Cie. [Also as 1927. Le peyotl. Trav. Lab. Mat. Med. Pharm. Fac. Paris 17.]

Rowe, J. S. 1959. Forest regions of Canada. Canada

Dept. Northern Affairs and Nat. Resources, Forestry Branch. Bull. 123. Minister of Northern Affairs and Nat. Resources, Ottawa.

Rowley, Gordon D. 1956. Pierre-Joseph Redouté—"Raphael of the succulents." Cactus & Succ. Jour. Gt. Brit. 18: 91-93.

——— 1958a. The reunion of the genus *Opuntia* Mill. Nat. Cactus & Succ. Jour. 13: 2-6, 25.

——— 1958b. *Astrophytum asterias* Lem. Nat. Cactus & Succ. Jour. 13: 7-8. *f.*

——— 1978a. Phytogeography and the study of succulents. Cactus & Succ. Jour. Gt. Brit. 50: 3-5.

——— 1978b. How big is a saguaro? Cactus & Succ. Jour. 50: 72.

Ruddiman, W. F., and A. McIntyre. 1979. Warmth of the subpolar North Atlantic Ocean during Northern Hemisphere ice-sheet growth. Science 204: 173-75.

Ruggles, W. 1956. Insect heroes [*Cactoblastis*] not welcome in Sydney. Cactus & Succ. Jour. Gt. Brit. 18: 69. (Rept. from Sydney newspaper.)

Sabo, Kathryn. 1978. Assignment: *Ancistrocactus tobuschii*. Cactus & Succ. Jour. 50: 214-15.

Safford, William Edwin. 1909. Cactaceae of northeastern and central Mexico. Rept. Smiths. Inst., 1908. U.S. GPO.

St. John, Harold. 1946. Endemism in the Hawaiian species of *Gunnera* (Haloragidaceae). Hawaiian plant studies, II. Proc. Calif. Acad. Sciences IV 25: 377-420.

Salm-[Reifferscheid]-Dyck, Josef. 1842-49 (1850). Cacteae in horto Dyckensi. 3 vols. Cohen, Bonn. Published 1842, 1845, 1850 (dated 1849).

Sanchez-Mejorada, Hernando R. 1974. Revisión del genero *Peniocereus* (las Cactaceas). Govierno del Estado de Mexico. Direccion de Agricultura y Ganadería. Toluca, Mexico.

——— 1979. The influence of the Mexican War on the discovery of cacti. Cactus & Succ. Jour. 51: 31-35.

Sato, D. 1958. The chromosomes of the Cactaceae. Succ. Jap. 3: 88-91.

Sato, P. T., J. M. Neal, L. R. Brady, and Jerry L. McLaughlin. *See* McLaughlin.

Saville, D. B. O. 1972. Arctic adaptations of plants. Research Branch, Canada Dept. Agri., Monograph 6.

Schelle, Ernst. 1907. Handbuch der Kakteenkultur.

——— 1926. Kakteen. A. Fischer, Tübingen.

Schill, Rainer, Wilhelm Barthlott, and Nesta Ehler. 1973a. Cactus spines under the scanning electron microscope. Cactus & Succ. Jour. 45: 175-85. *f. 1-20.*

——— 1973b. Mikromorphologie der Cactaceen-Dornen. Akad. Wiss. und Lit., Mainz. *In* Kommission bei Franz Steiner Verlag GMBH. Wiesbaden, West Germany.

Schill, Rainer, Wilhelm Barthlott, Nesta Ehler, and Werner Rauh. 1973. Raster-electronen-mikroskopische Untersuchungen an Cactaceen. Akad. Wiss. und Lit., Mainz. *In* Kommission bei Frank Steiner Verlag GMBH. Wiesbaden, West Germany.

Schimper, A. F. W. (transl. W. R. Fisher). 1903. Plant geography upon a physiological basis, 1-839. Reprinted 1960 by Lubrecht & Cramer, Monticello, New York.

Schmidt, Paul. 1969. Hybridization of *Lophophora williamsii* with *Turbinocarpus* and *Mammillaria*. Cactus & Succ. Jour. 41: 265. *f. 1-4.*

Schmutz, Ervin M. 1978. Classified bibliography on native plants of Arizona. Univ. Ariz. Press, Tucson.

Schroeder, R. A., and J. L. Bada. 1973. Glacial-postglacial temperature difference deduced from aspartic acid racemization in fossil bones. Science 182: 479-82.

Schuchert, Charles, and Carl O. Dunbar. 1941. Textbook of geology. Part II. Historical geology. Ed. 4. Wiley, New York.

Schultes, Richard Evans. 1940. The aboriginal therapeutic uses of *Lophophora williamsii*. Cactus & Succ. Jour. 12: 177-81.

Schulz, Ellen D., and Robert Runyon. 1930. Texas cacti. Texas Acad. Sci., San Antonio.

Schumann, Karl. 1898. Gesamtbeschreibung der Kakteen. J. Neumann, Neudamm. (Suppl. 1902.)

Scoggan, H. J. 1950. The flora of Bic and the Gaspé Peninsula, Quebec. Nat. Mus. Canada, Ottawa.

Sellers, E. D. 1965. Physical climatology. Univ. Chicago Press, Chicago.

Senn, Harold A. 1951. A bibliography of Canadian plant geography. IX. 1941-49. Dept. Agr., Ottawa, Publ. 863.

Shantz, Homer L. 1937. The saguaro forest. Nat. Geog. Mag. 71: 519-32.

Shantz, Homer L., and Raphael Zon. 1924. Natural vegetation. *In* Atlas of American Agriculture. U.S. Dept. Agr.

Sharma, H. P. 1954, 1963. Studies in the order Centrospermales. Jour. Ind. Bot. Soc. 33: 98; 42: 19-32, 637-45; Proc. Ind. Acad. Sci. 56B: 269-85.

Sharp, Aaron J. 1946a. A preliminary report on some phytogeographical studies in Mexico and Guatemala. (Abstract.) Amer. Jour. Bot. 33: 844.

——— 1946b. Some fungi common on the highlands of Mexico and Guatemala and eastern United States. (Abstract.) Amer. Jour. Bot. 33: 844.

——— 1950. The relation of the Eocene Wilcox Flora to some modern floras. Evolution 5: 1-5.

——— 1952. Notes on the flora of Mexico: world distribution of the woody dicotyledonous families and the origin of modern vegetation. Jour. Ecology 41: 374-80.

——— 1969. Studies of vegetation in two areas of Mexico. (Review.) Ecology 50 (5): late summer, 1969.

——— 1970. Different ideas concerning the migration of vascular plants and bryophytes from the Old World to the New. ASB Bull. 17: 63.

——— 1971. Epilogue. *In* Perry C. Holt (ed.), The distributional history of the biota of the southern Appalachians. Virginia Polytechnic Inst. and State Univ., Blacksburg. Res. Div. Monograph 2.

Shaw, Elizabeth A. 1976. The genus *Cactus* Linn. Cactus & Succ. Jour. 48: 21-24.

Shelford, Victor E. 1963. The ecology of North America. Univ. Illinois Press, Urbana.

Shreve, Forrest. 1909. The origin of desert floras. *In* V. M. Spaulding (ed.), Distribution and movements of desert plants. Carnegie Inst. Wash. Publ. 113.

——— 1910. The rate of establishment of the giant cactus. Pl. World 13: 235-40.

——— 1911. The influence of low temperature on the distribution of the giant cactus. Pl. World 14: 136-46.

——— 1915. An investigation of the causes of autonomic movements in succulent plants. Pl. World 18: 297-312, 331-43.

——— 1929. Changes in desert vegetation. Ecology 10: 364-73.

——— 1917a. The establishment of desert perennials. Jour. Ecol. 5: 210-16.

——— 1917b. A map of the vegetation of the United States. Geog. Rev. 3: 119-25.

——— 1917c. The physical control of vegetation in rain-forest and desert mountains. Plant World 20: 135-41.

——— 1922. Conditions indirectly affecting vertical [plant] distribution on desert mountains. Ecology 3: 269-74.

——— 1925. Ecological aspects of the deserts of California. Ecology 6: 93-103.

——— 1931a. Physical conditions in sun and shade. Ecology 12: 96-104.

——— 1931b. The cactus and its home. Williams & Wilkins, Baltimore.

——— 1935. The longevity of cacti. Cactus & Succ. Jour. 7: 66-68. *f.*

——— 1941. Forest climatology. Plant World 18: 150-51.

——— 1942. The desert vegetation of North America. Bot. Rev. 8: 195-246.

——— 1944. Rainfall in northern Mexico. Ecology 31: 368-72.

——— 1945. The saguaro (*Cereus giganteus*), cactus camel of Arizona. Nat. Geog. Mag. 88: 695-704.

——— 1951. Vegetation of the Sonoran Desert. Carnegie Inst. Wash. Publ. 591.

Shreve, Forrest, and A. L. Hinckley. 1937. Thirty years of change in desert vegetation. Ecology 18: 463-78.

Shreve, Forrest, and Ira L. Wiggins. 1964. Vegetation and flora of the Sonoran Desert. Stanford Univ. Press, Stanford, Calif. (Includes Shreve, 1951.)

Shurly, E. 1940. A detailed bibliography of *Mammillaria*. Typescript lodged at the Royal Botanic Gardens, Kew, England. 1-5. Copy, Botany Library, Pomona College, Claremont, Calif.

——— 1944. An abridgment of the monograph for mammillarias (typescript). (Abridgment of the 1940 publication, above.) Copies: Royal Botanic Gardens, Kew; Botany Library, Pomona College, Claremont, Calif.

——— 1946. A detailed bibliography of the Coryphanthanae (typescript). 1-2. Copies: Royal Botanic Gardens, Kew; Botany Library, Pomona College, Claremont, Calif.

——— 1956. The black seeds of the genus *Mammillaria*. Cactus & Succ. Jour. Gt. Brit. 18: 123-25.

Sinclair, William. 1928. Prickly pear as stock food and some of its other uses. 1-22. Job Stone, Toowoomba.

Slotkin, J. S. 1956. The peyote religion. Free Press, Glencoe, Ill.

Slotkin, J. S., and D. B. McAllester. 1952. Menomini peyotism. Trans. Amer. Phil. Soc. 42 (4): 565-700.

Small, John Kunkel. 1903/13. Flora of the southeastern United States. Privately printed, New York.

——— 1933. Manual of the southeastern flora. Privately printed, New York.

Smiley, Terah L. 1958. Climate and man in the Southwest. Program in Geochronology Contribution 6. Univ. Arizona, Tucson.

Smythies, J. R. 1963. The mescaline phenomena. Brit. J. Phil. Sci. 3: 339-47.

Snyder, Ernest E., and Dannie J. Weber. 1966. Causative factors of cristation in the Cactaceae. Cactus & Succ. Jour. 38: 26-32.

Solbrig, Otto. 1972. The floristic disjunctions between the "Monte" in Argentina and the "Sonoran Desert" in Mexico and the United States. Ann. Mo. Bot. Gard. 59: 218-23.

Soule, O. H. 1970. George Engelmann: the first man of cacti and a complete scientist. Ann. Mo. Bot. Gard. 57: 135-44.

Spalding, E. S. 1905. Mechanical adjustment of the suaharo (*Cereus giganteus*) to varying quantities of stored water. Bull. Torrey Bot. Club 32: 57-68.

Spaulding, W. Geoffrey, and Thomas R. Van Devender. 1977. Late Pleistocene montane conifers in southeastern Utah. Southwestern Nat. 22: 269-86.

Speirs, D. C. 1978. The evolution of cacti. Cactus & Succ. Jour. 50: 179.

Spencer, J. T. 1955. A cytological study of the Cactaceae of Puerto Rico. Bot. Gaz. 117: 33-37.

Spoehr, H. A. 1919. The carbohydrate economy of cacti. Carnegie Inst. Wash. Publ. 287. Johnson reprint.

Spurr, Stephen H. 1952. Origin of the concept of forest succession. Ecology 33: 426-27.

Srivastiva, Lalit M., and I. W. Bailey. 1962. Comparative anatomy of the leaf-bearing Cactaceae, V. Jour. Arnold Arb. 43: 234-78.

Stafleu, F. A. 1971. Linnaeus and the linnaeans. Regnum Vegetabile 79.

——— 1974. Index herbariorum. Part 1. The herbaria of the world. Ed. 6. Int. Bur. Plant Taxon. & Nomencl., Utrecht, Netherlands.

Standley, Paul C. 1924. The trees and shrubs of Mexico. (Cactaceae by Nathaniel Lord Britton & Joseph Nelson Rose.) Contr. U.S. Nat. Herb. 23: 855-1012.

Stebbins, G. Ledyard, Jr. 1941. Additional evidence for a holarctic dispersal of flowering plants in the Mesozoic era. Proc. Sixth Pacific Science Congress: 649-60.

Stebbins, G. Ledyard, and Jack Major. 1965. Endemism and speciation in the California flora. Ecological Monographs 35: 1-35.

Steenbergh, W. F., and C. H. Lowe. 1969. Critical factors during the first years of life of the saguaro (*Cereus gigantea[us]*) at the Saguaro National Monument. Ecology 50: 825-34.

———— 1976. Ecology of the saguaro. I. The roles of freezing weather on a warm-desert plant population. *In* Research in the parks, U.S. Nat. Park Serv. symp. series, 1: 69-92.

———— 1977. Ecology of the saguaro. II. Reproduction, germination, establishment, growth, and survival of the young plant. U.S. Nat. Park Serv. Scientific Monograph Ser. 8.

Stockwell, William Palmer. 1932. A cactus that reproduces like a date palm. Cactus & Succ. Jour. 3: 187-88.

———— 1935. Chromosome numbers of some of the Cactaceae. Bot. Gaz. 96: 565-70.

Stockwell, William Palmer, and Lucretia Breazeale [Hamilton]. 1933. Arizona cacti. Univ. Ariz. Biol. Sci. Bull. 1.

Stoddart, L. A. 1941. The palouse grassland association in northern Utah. Ecology 22: 158-63.

Stone, Kirk H. 1948. Aerial photographic interpretation of natural vegetation in the Anchorage area. Geog. Rev. 38: 465-74.

Stowe, Lawrence G., and James A. Teeri. 1978. The geographic distribution of C$_4$ species of the Dicotyledon[e]ae in relation to climate. Amer. Nat. 112: 609-23.

Sutton, A., and M. Sutton. 1966. The life of the desert. McGraw-Hill, New York.

Szarek, Stan R., H. B. Johnson, and Irwin P. Ting. 1973. Drought adaptation in *Opuntia basilaris*. Plant Physiol. 52: 539-41.

Szarek, Stan R., and Irwin P. Ting. 1974. Respiration and gas exchange in stem tissue of *Opuntia basilaris*. Plant Physiol. 54: 829-34.

———— 1975. Physiological responses to rainfall in *Opuntia basilaris* (Cactaceae). Amer. Jour. Bot. 62: 602-6.

Tanai, T. 1967. Tertiary floral changes in Japan. *In* Jubilee publication in honour of Prof. Sasa's 60th birthday, 314-34. Hokkaido Univ., Sapporo, Japan.

Tanai, T., and R. Huzioka. 1967. Climatic implications of Tertiary floras of Japan. *In* Geol. Sci., Tertiary correlation and climatic changes in the Pacific, Pap. no. 15. Eleventh Pac. Sci. Congr., Tokyo.

Tate, Joyce L. 1971. Cactus cookbook. Cactus & Succulent Society of America, Santa Barbara, Calif.

Taylor, Dean William. 1977. Floristic relationships along the Cascade-Sierra Axis. Amer. Midl. Nat. 97: 333-49.

Taylor, N. P. 1978. Review of the genus *Escobaria*. Cactus & Succ. Jour. Gt. Brit. 40: 31-37.

———— 1979. Further notes on *Escobaria*. Cactus & Succ. Jour. Gt. Brit. 41: 17-20.

Taylor, R. L., and R. A. Ludwig. 1966. The evolution of Canada's flora. Univ. Toronto Press.

Thackery, Frank A., and A. R. Leding. 1929. The giant cactus of Arizona. Jour. Hered. 20: 401-14.

Thompson, Peter, and Henry P. Schwartz. 1947. Continental Pleistocene climatic variations from speleothem [cavern] age and isotopic data. Science 184: 893-94.

Thornber, J. J. 1910. The grazing ranges of Arizona. Ariz. Agr. Exp. Sta. Bull. 65.

———— 1911. Native cacti as emergency forage plants. Ariz. Agr. Exp. Sta. Bull. 67.

Thorne, Robert F. 1973. Floristic relationships between tropical Africa and tropical America. *In* Tropical forest ecosystems in Africa and South America. Smiths. Inst. Press.

———— 1978. Plate tectonics and angiosperm distribution. Notes Roy. Bot. Gard. Edinburgh 36: 297-315.

Tiagi, Y. D. 1955. Studies in floral morphology. II. Vascular anatomy of the flower of certain species of the Cactaceae. Jour. Ind. Bot. Soc. 34: 408-28.

———— 1957. Studies in floral morphology. III. A contribution to the floral morphology of *Mammillaria tenuis* DC. Jour. Univ. Saugar 6 (2), sec. B: 7-31.

Tichermak, Eric von. 1910. Stachellose Kakteen als Viehfutter. Monats. f. Landwirts. (Repr.) 7 pp.

Tisdale, E. W. 1947. The grasslands of southern interior British Columbia. Ecology 28: 346-82.

Tjaden, W. L. 1966. *Schlumbergera*. Nat. Cactus & Succ. Jour. 21: 84-87. *f.*; 91-93. *f.*

Todd, James D. Thin-layer chromatography analysis of Mexican populations of *Lophophora* (Cactaceae). Lloydia 32: 395-98.

Trapp, Carolyn. 1969. Guide to the cacti of Zion National Park. Zion Nat. Hist. Assn., Zion Nat. Park, Utah.

Trelease, William, and Asa Gray. 1887. The botanical works of George Engelmann, collected for Henry Shaw, Esq. Cambridge Univ. Press, Cambridge, Eng.

Troughton, John H., P. V. Wells, and Harold A. Mooney. 1974. Photosynthetic mechanisms and paleoecology from carbon isotope ratios in ancient specimens of C$_4$ and CAM plants. Science 185: 610-12.

Tsukada, M. 1964. Pollen morphology and identification. II. Cactaceae. Pollen & Spores 6: 45-84.

Turner, Raymond M., Stanley M. Alcorn, and George Olin. 1969. Mortality of transplanted saguaro seedlings. Ecology 50: 835-44.

Turner, Raymond M., Stanley M. Alcorn, George Olin, and John M. Booth. 1966. The influence of shade, soil, and water on saguaro seedling establishment. Bot. Gaz. 127: 95-102. *f. 1-4.*

Turpin, H. W., and George A. Gill. 1928. Insurance against drought. Drought resistant fodders: with special reference to cactus. Union S. Africa Dept. Agr. Bull. 36.

Turrill, W. B. 1951. Some problems of plant range and distribution. Jour. Ecol. 39: 205-27.

Uphof, J. C. (ed. J. J. Thornber). 1916. Cold resistance in spineless cacti. Univ. Ariz. Agr. Exp. Sta. Bull. 79.

U.S. Geological Survey. 1973. The channeled scablands of eastern Washington: the geologic story of the Spokane flood. U.S. Dept. Interior, Sup. of Documents, U.S. Govt. Printing Off., Washington, D.C.

Valentine, D. H. (ed.). 1972. Taxonomy, phytogeography, and evolution. Academic Press, New York.

Vanderveen, Randall L., Leslie G. West, and Jerry L. McLaughlin. *See* McLaughlin.

Van Devender, Thomas R. 1973. Late Pleistocene plants and animals of the Sonoran Desert: a survey of ancient packrat middens in southwestern Arizona. Diss. Abstracts Internat. 34 (11): 1974.

—— 1976. The biota of the hot deserts of North America during the last glaciations. (Abstract.) Dept. Geosciences, Univ. Ariz., Tucson. Meeting Amer. Quaternary Assn. 1-6.

—— 1977. Holocene woodlands in the Southwestern deserts. Science 198: 189-93.

Van Devender, Thomas R., and Benjamin L. Everitt. 1977. The latest Pleistocene and Recent vegetation of the Bishop's Cap, south-central New Mexico [Organ Mts., Dona Ana Co.]. Southw. Nat. 22: 337-52.

Van Devender, Thomas R., and James E. King. 1971. Late Pleistocene vegetational records in western Arizona. Jour. Ariz. Acad. Sci. 6: 240-44.

Van Devender, Thomas R., Paul S. Martin, A. M. Phillips III, and W. G. Spaulding. 1977/1978. Late Pleistocene plant communities in the Guadalupe Mountains, Culberson County, Texas. *In* Roland H. Wauer and D. H. Riskind (eds.), Trans. Symp. on Biol. Resources of the Chihuahuan Desert, U.S. and Mexico. Nat. Park Serv., Washington, D.C.

Van Devender, Thomas R., and James I. Mead. (From undated reprint.) Late Pleistocene and modern plant communities of Shinumo Creek and Peach Springs Wash, lower Grand Canyon, Arizona. Jour. Ariz. Acad. Sci.

Van Devender, Thomas R., and W. G. Spaulding. 1979. Development of vegetation and climate in the southwestern United States. Science 204: 701-10.

Van Devender, Thomas R., W. G. Spaulding, and A. M. Phillips III. 1979. Late Pleistocene plant communities in the Guadalupe Mountains, Culberson County, Texas. *In* H. H. Genoways and R. J. Baker (eds.), Symp. vol., Biol. Investigations in Guadalupe Mts. Nat. Park, Texas. Nat. Park Serv., Washington, D.C.

Van Devender, Thomas R., and Frederick M. Wiseman. 1977. A preliminary chronology of bioenvironmental changes during the Paleoindian Period in the monsoonal Southwest. In E. Johnson (ed.), Paleoindian lifeways. West Texas Mus. Assoc. Mus. Jour. 17: 13-27.

Van Laren, A. J. 1935. Cacti. Abbey Garden Press, Los Angeles.

Van Steenis, C. G. G. J. 1962. The land-bridge theory in botany. Blumea 11: 235-372.

Vasey, George. 1888. Characteristic vegetation of the desert. Bot. Gaz. 13: 258-65.

Walker, Colin C. 1978. Cactus evolution—a plea to curb speculation. Nat. Cactus & Succ. Jour. 33: 58-59.

Walkington, David L. 1966. Morphological and chemical evidence for hybridization of some species of Opuntia occurring in southern California. Thesis, Claremont Grad. School, Claremont, Calif.

—— 1968. The taxonomic history of the southern California prickly pears. Cactus & Succ. Jour. 40: 186-92. *f. 1-7.*

Waring, R. H., and J. F. Franklin. 1979. Evergreen coniferous forests of the Pacific Northwest. Science 204: 1380-86.

Weaver, J. E. 1917. A study of the vegetation of southeastern Washington and adjacent Idaho. Univ. Nebraska Studies 17: 1-133.

Weaver, J. E., and F. W. Albertson. 1956. Grasslands of the Great Plains. Johnson, Lincoln, Nebraska.

Weaver, J. E., and F. E. Clements. 1938. Plant ecology. Ed. 2. McGraw-Hill, New York.

Weber, William A. 1965. Plant geography in the southern Rocky Mountains. *In* Wright & Frey, 1965.

Weedin, James F., and A. Michael Powell. 1978. Chromosome numbers in the Chihuahuan Desert Cactaceae. Amer. Jour. Bot. 65: 531-37.

Weingart, W. 1924. Bau und Funktion von Kakteenstacheln. Zeitschr. für Sukkulentenkunde 1: 155-67.

—— 1932. Kakteenstacheln. Monatschr. Deutsche Kakteengesellschaft, Berlin, 4: 123-28.

Wells, B. W. 1928. Plant communities of North Carolina and their successional relations. Ecology 9: 230-42.

Wells, Philip V. 1966. Late Pleistocene vegetation and degree of pluvial climatic change in the Chihuahuan Desert. Science 153: 970-75.

—— 1970a. Postglacial vegetational history of the Great Plains. Science 167: 1574-82.

—— 1970b. Historical factors controlling vegetation patterns and floristic distributions in the central plains region of North America. *In* Pleistocene and Recent environments of the central Great Plains. Dept. Geol., Univ. Kansas Special Publ. 3.

—— 1976. Postglacial origin of the Chihuahuan Desert less than 11,500 years ago. *In* Roland H. Wauer and D. H. Riskind (eds.), Trans. Symp. on Biol. Resources of the Chihuahuan Desert, U.S. and Mexico. Nat. Park Serv., Washington, D.C.

Wells, Philip V., and Rainer Berger. 1967. Late Pleistocene history of coniferous woodland in the Mohave Desert. Science 155: 1640-47.

Wells, Philip V., and Clive D. Jorgenson. 1964. Pleistocene wood rat middens and climatic change in the Mohave Desert: a record of juniper woodlands. Science 13: 1171-74.

Welsh, Stanley L. 1976. Problems in plant endemism on the Colorado Plateau. Intermountain biogeography, a symposium. Brigham Young Univ., the Intermountain Forest and Range Exp. Sta. of U.S. Forest Serv., Bot. Soc. Amer., and the Biol. Science Section of the Pacific Section of the A.A.A.S. Missoula, Montana, June 1976.

Weniger, Del. 1967. *Opuntia drummondii [pusilla]*— a new record for Texas. Cactus & Succ. Jour. 39: 112-14.

—— 1969. The small-flowered *Echinocerei* of Texas and New Mexico. Cactus & Succ. Jour. 41: 34-43.

—— 1970. Cacti of the Southwest. Univ. of Texas Press, Austin.

Went, Frits W. 1948, 1949. Ecology of desert plants I. Observations on germination in the Joshua Tree Nat. Monument, Calif. Ecology 29: 242-53. II. The effect of rain and temperature on germination and growth. Ecology 30: 1-13.

Whitehead, Jack. 1939. The organ pipe cactus farthest north! Cactus & Succ. Jour. 11: 70-72. *f. 1-2*. See also *ibid.* 10: 122. 1939.

Whitford, H. N., and Roland D. Craig. 1917. A report on the forests of British Columbia (accompanied by map, Climatic Forest Types of British Columbia). Commission on Conservation, Canada. Ottawa.

Whittaker, R. H., and W. A. Niering. 1965. Vegetation of the Santa Catalina Mountains, Arizona: a gradient analysis of the south slope. Ecology 46: 429-52.

Wiggins, Ira L. 1937. Effects of the January freeze upon the pitahaya in Arizona. Cactus & Succ. Jour. 8: 171.

——— 1950. New species and type specimens. Cactus & Succ. Jour. 22: 72-74.

——— 1960. An extraordinary cristate *Lemaireocereus* in Baja California. Cactus & Succ. Jour. 32: 71-72.

——— 1963. The distribution of *Opuntia wrightiana*. Cactus & Succ. Jour. 35: 67-70.

——— *See also* Shreve & Wiggins.

Wilson, J. Tuzo (ed.). 1972. Continents adrift. [Fifteen articles on continental drift and the history of the Earth, published in Scientific American from 1952 to 1972.] W. H. Freeman, San Francisco.

Wislizenus, A. 1848. Memoir of a tour of northern Mexico in 1846 and 1847. U.S. Senate, Washington.

Wolfe, Jack A. 1966. Tertiary plants from the Cook Inlet region, Alaska. U.S. Geol. Surv. Prof. Papers 398-B.

——— 1969. Neogene floristic and vegetational history of the Pacific Northwest. Madroño 20: 83-110.

——— 1971. Tertiary climatic fluctuations and methods of analysis of Tertiary floras. Paleogeography, Paleoclimatology, Paleoecology 9: 27-57.

——— 1972. An interpretation of Alaskan Tertiary floras. *In* A. Graham (ed.), Floristics and paleofloristics of Asia and eastern North America, 201-33. Elsevier, Amsterdam.

——— 1978. A paleobotanical interpretation of Tertiary climates in the Northern Hemisphere. Amer. Scientist 66: 694-703.

Wolfe, Jack A., and David M. Hopkins. 1967. Climatic changes recorded by Tertiary land floras in northwestern North America. *In* K. Hatai, Tertiary correlation and climatic changes in the Pacific. Sendai, Japan.

Wolfe, Jack A., David M. Hopkins, and E. B. Leopold. 1967. Neocene and early Quaternary vegetation of northeastern Eurasia. *In* Hopkins (ed.), 1967.

Wood, Carroll E., Jr. 1971. Some floristic relationships between the southern Appalachians and western North America. Res. Div. Monograph 2. Virginia Polytechnic Inst. and State Univ., Blacksburg.

Woodford, Alfred O. 1924. The Catalina metamorphic facies of the Franciscan Series. Univ. Calif. Publ. Geol. 15: 49-68.

Woodruff, Dorothea, and Lyman Benson. 1976. Changes of status in *Sclerocactus*. Cactus & Succ. Jour. 48: 131-34.

Woods, R. S. 1933. *Opuntia santa-rita*. Cactus & Succ. Jour. 5: 428. *f*.

Woodward, T. E., W. F. Turner, and David Griffiths. 1915. Prickly pears as feed for dairy cows. Jour. Agr. Res. 4: 405-50.

Wooton, E. O., and Paul C. Standley. 1915. Flora of New Mexico. Contr. U.S. Nat. Herb. 19. U.S. Govt. Printing Off., Washington, D.C. Reprinted 1972 by Wheldon & Wesley, Codicote, Herts, England, and Stechert-Hafner Serv. Agency, New York.

Wright, H. E., Jr. 1971. Late Quaternary vegetational history of North America. *In* K. K. Turekian (ed.), The late Cenozoic glacial ages, 425-64. Yale Univ. Press, New Haven, Conn.

Wright, H. E., Jr., and D. G. Frey (eds.). 1965. The Quaternary of the United States. Princeton Univ. Press, Princeton, N.J.

Wright, Ysabel. 1932. *Utahia sileri* in flower. Cactus & Succ. Jour. 4: 213-14. *f*.

Wynne-Edwards, V. C. 1937. Isolated arctic-alpine floras in eastern North America: a discussion of their glacial and Recent history. Trans. Royal Soc. of Canada II (5) 31: 1-26.

——— 1939. Some factors in the isolation of rare alpine plants. Trans. Royal Soc. of Canada III (5) 33: 35-42.

Zimmerman, Allan D. 1978. The relationships of *Cochiseia robbinsorum* Earle. Cactus & Succ. Jour. 50: 293-97.

Zimmerman, Dale A. 1972a. The fruits of *Coryphantha hesteri*. Cactus & Succ. Jour. 44: 85.

——— 1972b. A new species of *Coryphantha* from New Mexico. Cactus & Succ. Jour. 44: 114-16. *f. 1-4*.

——— 1972c. Comments on certain southwestern coryphant[h]as of the subgenus *Escobaria*. Cactus & Succ. Jour. 44: 155-58. *f. 1-5*.

Zimmerman, Dale A., and Allan D. Zimmerman. 1975. *Mammillaria orestera* Benson in New Mexico. Cactus & Succ. Jour. 47: 113-15.

——— 1977. A revision of the United States taxa of the *Mammillaria wrightii* complex with remarks upon the northern Mexican populations. Cactus & Succ. Jour. 49: 23-34, 51-62.

Zimmerman, Elwood C. 1948. Insects of Hawaii. 1-5. Univ. Hawaii Press, Honolulu.

Illustration Credits

Sources for the illustrations used in this volume, including the color plates, are credited in three ways: in most cases the sources are given in the legends for the figures themselves; certain general remarks are given in the Preface and in "Notes on Use of the Text" (p. 251); and the more detailed credits are given below.

Sources of all photographs are given in their legends, with two exceptions: where no source is given, the photograph is by the author; and the words "(See Credits)" in a legend refer the reader to the detailed credits below. The photographs by Homer L. Shantz and Robert H. Peebles are used with the kind permission of Dr. Charles T. Mason, Jr. and the University of Arizona Herbarium. The Griffiths collection is on extended loan to the author by the kind permission of the U.S. National Herbarium, Smithsonian Institution.

The great majority of the line drawings in the book are by Mrs. Lucretia Breazeale Hamilton (see the Preface and "Notes on Use of the Text") or by the author; in both cases the initials on the illustration itself identify the artist (although the two styles would be distinguishable without the initials!), and credit is therefore not repeated in the legend. The few line drawings by others are credited in the legends.

The maps in Part I are by the author. The distribution maps in Part II were prepared by the author and the publisher; the county-line base map for these maps was prepared for the author by Albert P. Burkhardt, the topography was added by the author, and the collection-locality symbols were added to the individual maps by the author (see the Preface and "Notes on Use of the Text"). All photographs and maps by the author appearing herein remain exclusively the property of the author.

Many of the illustrations, chiefly color and black-and-white photographs, have appeared in other published works, and are used here with the kind permission of the publishers. Six of these works are cited frequently, and are therefore given in the legends simply by title. Four are by the author: The Native Cacti of California (Stanford, California: Stanford University Press, 1969); The Cacti of Arizona (Tucson: University of Arizona Press, 1946; ed. 2, 1950; ed. 3, 1969); Plant Taxonomy, Methods and Principles (New York: The Ronald Press Co., 1962); and Plant Classification (Boston: D. C. Heath & Co., 1957). The fifth work often cited, chiefly for the line illustrations by Paulus Roetter, is George Engelmann, "The Cactaceae," in W. H. Emory, Report of the United States and Mexican Boundary Survey, 1859; illustrations courtesy of the Missouri Botanical Garden. The sixth work, finally, is W. Palmer Stockwell and Lucretia Breazeale Hamilton, Arizona Cacti (Tucson: University of Arizona Press, 1933).

Following are the more detailed illustration credits, cited by figure number (those works for which no attribution is cited are by the author):

10. Courtesy of Larry W. Mitich, North Dakota State University of Agriculture and Applied Science, Fargo; Larry W. Mitich & Lyman Benson, Cactus & Succ. Jour. 49: 6. 1977.

11. Courtesy of Larry W. Mitich, North Dakota State University of Agriculture and Applied Science, Fargo; Larry W. Mitich & Lyman Benson, Cactus & Succ. Jour. 49: 3. 1977.

15. Courtesy of Field Museum of Natural History, Chicago; print from the Smithsonian Institution, now at the Hunt Institute for Botanical Documentation, Carnegie-Mellon University, Pittsburgh.

23. Griffiths & Thompson, Cacti, U.S.D.A. Circular 66. 1929.

33. Griffiths & Thompson, Cacti, U.S.D.A. Circular 66. 1929.

36. The electron microscope photographs were made by the Institut für Elektronenmikroskopie, Dr.-Ing. Hermann Klingele, München (D-8 München 22, Adelgundenstr. 8); they were based on the research of Hans Till, Attersee, Oberösterreich.

40. Cactus & Succ. Jour. 21: 55. 1949. Used with permission.

44. Cactus & Succ. Jour. 13: 34. 1941. Used with permission.

50. Cact. y Suc. Méx. 11: 5. 1966. Used with permission.

56. Bull. Torrey Bot. Club 75: 516-22. 1948. Also Cactus & Succ. Jour. 21: 49. 1949; used with permission.

61. (See credit for Fig. 36, above.)

75. Modified from Charles E. Bessey, Ann. Mo. Bot. Gard. 2: 118. f. 1. Used with permission.

100. Evolution 20: 251. f. 1. 1966. Used with permission.

122. Univ. Michigan Contr. Mus. Paleont. 13: 181-210. 1959. Used with permission.

208. Griffiths & Hare, U.S.D.A. Bureau of Plant Industry Bull. 116. pl. 3, f. 1. 1907.

212. Griffiths & Thompson, Cacti, U.S.D.A. Circular 66. 1929.

218. Probably received by David Griffiths indirectly from Luther Burbank. Used with permission of Elizabeth Burbank.

235. Edwards Botanical Register 23 (N. S. 10): pl. 1928. 1837.

270. U.S. Senate Rept. Expl. & Surv. R.R. Route Pacific Ocean. Botany 4: 51. pl. 18, f. 1-3. 1857. Courtesy of the Missouri Botanical Garden.

295. Rept. Mo. Bot. Gard. 22: pl. 7. 1912. Used with permission.

301. Cactus & Succ. Jour. 7: 100. 1936. Used with permission.

303. Cactus & Succ. Jour. 7: 100. 1936. Used with permission.

304. Cactus & Succ. Jour. 7: 100. 1936. Used with permission.

315. Griffiths & Hare, New Mex. Coll. Agric. & Mech. Arts Bull. 60: *pl. 6, f. 2.* 1908.

340. Rept. Mo. Bot. Gard. 19: *pl. 22.* 1908. Also Griffiths & Thompson, U.S.D.A. Circular 66: *pl. 12.* 1930. Used with permission.

463. Rept. Mo. Bot. Gard. 21: *pl. 26.* 1910.

504. Rept. Mo. Bot. Gard. 22: *pl. 9.* 1912.

544. Rept. Mo. Bot. Gard. 22: *pl. 8.* 1912.

545. Rept. Mo. Bot. Gard. 22: *pl. 8.* 1912.

546. Rept. Mo. Bot. Gard. 20: *pl. 4.* 1909.

548. Rept. Mo. Bot. Gard. 20: *pl. 11.* 1909.

552. U.S.D.A. Bur. Pl. Ind. Bull. 262: *pl. 4.* 1912.

553. Griffiths & Hare, N. Mex. Coll. Agric. & Mech. Arts Bull. 60: *pl. 4, f. 2.* 1906.

557. Griffiths & Thompson, U.S.D.A. Circular 66: *pl. 19.* 1930.

558. Martius, Fl. Brasiliensis 4(2): *pl. 61.* 1890.

561. Martius, Fl. Brasiliensis 4(2): *pl. 46.* 1890.

571. Desert Plant Life, March 1926.

572. Desert Plant Life 15: 55-60. 1943.

573. Kearney & Peebles, Arizona Flora, Univ. Calif. Press. 1951, 1960.

580. Natl. Geogr. Mag. 71: 519. 1937.

581. Natl. Geogr. Mag. 71: 519. 1937.

588. Britton & Rose, Cactaceae 2: *pl. 19, f. 1.* 1920.

596. Britton & Rose, Cactaceae 2: *pl. 32, f. 3; pl. 33.* 1920.

597. Illus. Dict. Gardening 1: *f. 408.* 1890.

598. K. Schumann, Gesamtbeschreibung der Kakteen 146. *f. 35.* 1898. (As C. *nycticallis*.)

599. Britton & Rose, Cactaceae 2: *pl. 38, f. 2.* 1920.

604. Britton & Rose, Cactaceae 2: *pl. 30; pl. 32, f. 1.* 1920.

608. Addisonia 16: *pl. 532.* 1931.

618. Nat. Cactus & Succ. Soc. 21: 30-31. *f. 1-3.* 1966.

621. Cactus & Succ. Jour. 13: 195. 1941.

696. Cactus & Succ. Jour. 40: 122. *f. 2.* 1968. Used with permission.

697. Cactus & Succ. Jour. 40: 122. *f. 3.* 1968. Used with permission.

700. Cactus & Succ. Jour. 40: 125. *f. 4.* 1968. Used with permission.

702. Cactus & Succ. Jour. 40: 126. *f. 5.* 1968. Used with permission.

715. Jour. Hered. 25: 326. *f. 12.* 1934.

747. Lyman Benson in C. L. Lundell et al., Fl. Texas. 2: 221-317. *pl. 7.* 1969. Courtesy of Texas Research Foundation.

767. Cactus & Succ. Jour. 38: 55. *f. 4.* 1966. Used with permission.

780. Woodruff & Benson, Cactus & Succ. Jour. 48: 133. *f. 5.* 1976. Used with permission.

793. Cactus & Succ. Jour. 34: 17. *f. 13.* 1962. Used with permission.

799. Kearney & Peebles, Arizona Flora, Univ. Calif. Press. 1951, 1960.

826. Lyman Benson in C. L. Lundell et al., Fl. Texas. 2: *pl. 10.* 1969. Courtesy of Texas Research Foundation.

828. Lyman Benson in C. L. Lundell et al., Fl. Texas. 2: *pl. 11.* 1969. Courtesy of Texas Research Foundation.

843. Lyman Benson in C. L. Lundell et al., Fl. Texas. 2: *pl. 12.* 1969. Courtesy of Texas Research Foundation.

844. Cact. y Suc. Méx. 11: 5. 1966. Used with permission.

General Reference Maps

ATLANTIC OCEAN

GULF OF MEXICO

FLORIDA

ESCAMBIA
SANTA ROSA
OKA-LOOSA
HOLMES
JACKSON
WALTON
WASH-INGTON
GADSDEN
LEON
JEFFERSON
HAMILTON
NASSAU
BAY
CAL-HOUN
MADISON
DUVAL
LIBERTY
WAKULLA
TAYLOR
SUWAN-NEE
COLUMBIA
BAKER
CLAY
GULF
FRANKLIN
LAFAYETTE
UNION
BRAD-FORD
ST. JOHNS
DIXIE
GIL-CHRIST
ALACHUA
PUTNAM
LEVY
FLAGLER
MARION
VOLUSIA
CITRUS
SUMTER
LAKE
SEMINOLE
HERNANDO
ORANGE
BREVARD
PASCO
OSCEOLA
HILLS-BOROUGH
POLK
INDIAN RIVER
PINELLAS
MANATEE
HARDEE
OKEECHOBEE
ST. LUCIE
DE SOTO
HIGH-LANDS
MARTIN
SARASOTA
CHARLOTTE
GLADES
Lake Okeechobee
LEE
HENDRY
PALM BEACH
COLLIER
BROWARD
DADE
MONROE

Pensacola
Tallahassee
Jacksonville
Orlando
Tampa
Miami
Key West

Kilometers 0 50 100
Statute Miles 0 50 100

(A map of Hawaii is on p. 205.)

ARIZONA
1 Fredonia
2 Grand Canyon
3 Oatman
4 Kingman
5 Ashfork
6 Williams
7 Flagstaff
8 Winslow
9 Holbrook
10 St. Johns
11 Quartzsite
12 Wickenburg
13 Prescott
14 Cottonwood
15 Camp Verde
16 Payson
17 Gila Bend
18 Phoenix
19 Casa Grande
20 Florence
21 Superior
22 Globe
23 Safford
24 Morenci
25 Yuma
26 Ajo
27 Tucson
28 Benson
29 Bowie
30 Nogales
31 Fort Huachuca
32 Bisbee
33 Douglas

NEW MEXICO
34 Shiprock
35 Farmington
36 Park View
37 Taos
38 Raton
39 Clayton
40 Gallup
41 Grants
42 Albuquerque
43 Los Alamos
44 Santa Fé
45 Las Vegas
46 Mosquero
47 Santa Rosa
48 Tucumcari
49 Quemado
50 Socorro
51 Mountain Air
52 Fort Sumner
53 Portales
54 Clovis
55 Lordsburg
56 Silver City
57 Hot Springs
58 Carrizozo
59 Roswell
60 Deming
61 Las Cruces
62 Alamogordo
63 Artesia
64 Carlsbad
65 Hobbs

TEXAS
66 Amarillo
67 Lubbock
68 Wichita Falls
69 Odessa
70 Midland
71 Big Spring
72 Abilene
73 Fort Worth
74 Dallas
75 Denton
76 Tyler
77 El Paso
78 Sierra Blanca
79 Van Horn
80 Pecos
81 Candelaria
82 Marfa
83 Fort Davis
84 Alpine
85 Marathon
86 Fort Stockton
87 Presidio
88 Lajitas
89 Sanderson
90 Langtry
91 Sonora
92 San Angelo
93 San Saba
94 Llano
95 Lampasas
96 Temple
97 Waco
98 Bryan
99 Trinity
100 Del Rio
101 Uvalde
102 Kerrville
103 San Antonio
104 New Braunfels
105 Austin
106 La Grange
107 Houston
108 Galveston
109 Beaumont
110 Eagle Pass
111 Tilden
112 Victoria
113 Port Lavaca
114 Laredo
115 Zapata
116 Falfurrias
117 Kingsville
118 Corpus Christi
119 Rio Grande City
120 Edinburg
121 Brownsville

OKLAHOMA
122 Boise City
123 Guymon
124 Beaver
125 Woodward
126 Alva
127 Enid
128 Pawnee
129 Bartlesville
130 Tulsa
131 Clinton
132 Chickasha
133 Oklahoma City
134 Okmulgee
135 Muskogee
136 Mangum
137 Altus
138 Lawton
139 Ardmore
140 Sulphur
141 Ada
142 Atoka
143 McAlester
144 Poteau
145 Hugo

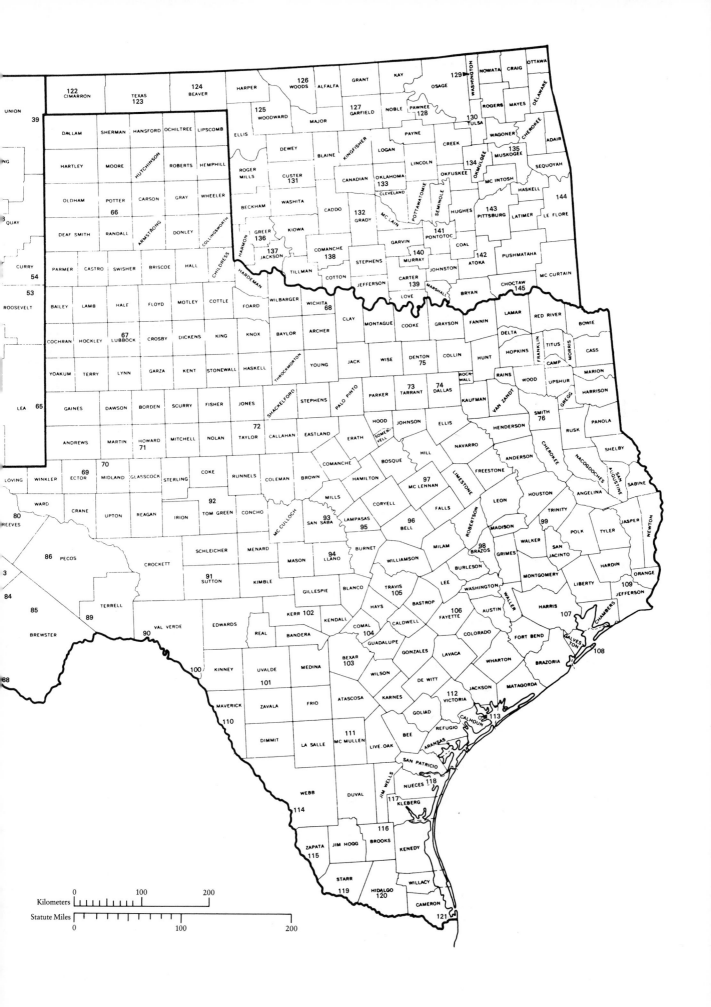

UNION

39

NG

3 QUAY

CURRY
54

53

ROOSEVELT

LEA 65

LOVING WINKLER

WARD

80
REEVES

3

84

88

122
CIMARRON

TEXAS
123

124
BEAVER

DALLAM SHERMAN HANSFORD OCHILTREE LIPSCOMB

HARTLEY MOORE HUTCHINSON ROBERTS HEMPHILL

OLDHAM POTTER
66 CARSON GRAY WHEELER

DEAF SMITH RANDALL ARMSTRONG DONLEY COLLINGSWORTH

PARMER CASTRO SWISHER BRISCOE HALL CHILDRESS

BAILEY LAMB HALE FLOYD MOTLEY COTTLE

COCHRAN HOCKLEY LUBBOCK
67 CROSBY DICKENS KING

YOAKUM TERRY LYNN GARZA KENT STONEWALL

GAINES DAWSON BORDEN SCURRY FISHER JONES

ANDREWS MARTIN HOWARD
71 MITCHELL NOLAN TAYLOR

70

69
ECTOR MIDLAND GLASSCOCK STERLING COKE

CRANE UPTON REAGAN IRION
92

86 PECOS

CROCKETT

85

TERRELL

89

BREWSTER

90 VAL VERDE

HARPER

126
WOODS ALFALFA GRANT KAY

125
WOODWARD MAJOR

127
GARFIELD NOBLE PAWNEE
128

ELLIS DEWEY BLAINE KINGFISHER LOGAN

ROGER
MILLS CUSTER
131 CANADIAN OKLAHOMA
133 CLEVELAND

BECKHAM WASHITA CADDO
132 GRADY MC LAIN

GREER
136 KIOWA COMANCHE
138 STEPHENS GARVIN
140

HARMON
137
JACKSON TILLMAN COTTON JEFFERSON CARTER
139

HARDEMAN WILBARGER WICHITA
68 CLAY MONTAGUE COOKE

FOARD

KNOX BAYLOR ARCHER YOUNG JACK WISE

THROCKMORTON

SHACKELFORD STEPHENS PALO PINTO PARKER

HASKELL

CALLAHAN EASTLAND ERATH SOMER-
VELL HOOD JOHNSON

COMANCHE BOSQUE HILL

COLEMAN BROWN HAMILTON
97
MC LENNAN

MILLS CORYELL

MC CULLOCH SAN SABA
93 LAMPASAS
95 BELL
96

MASON
94
LLANO BURNET WILLIAMSON MILAM

KIMBLE GILLESPIE BLANCO TRAVIS
105 BASTROP

EDWARDS KENDALL HAYS

REAL BANDERA COMAL
104 CALDWELL

KERR 102

KINNEY UVALDE MEDINA

100 GUADALUPE
BEXAR
103 GONZALES

MAVERICK ZAVALA FRIO ATASCOSA WILSON DE WITT

110

DIMMIT LA SALLE
111
MC MULLEN LIVE OAK BEE

WEBB DUVAL JIM WELLS
117

114 SAN PATRICIO

ZAPATA JIM HOGG BROOKS
116 KENEDY

115

STARR
119 HIDALGO
120

WILLACY

CAMERON

121

126

129 NOWATA CRAIG OTTAWA

OSAGE ROGERS MAYES DELAWARE

130
TULSA WAGONER CHEROKEE ADAIR

PAYNE CREEK OKMULGEE
134 MUSKOGEE
135 SEQUOYAH

LINCOLN OKFUSKEE MC INTOSH

POTTAWATOMIE SEMINOLE HUGHES
143
PITTSBURG HASKELL LATIMER LE FLORE
144

PONTOTOC
141 COAL
142 PUSHMATAHA

MURRAY
JOHNSTON ATOKA

LOVE MARSHALL BRYAN CHOCTAW
145 MC CURTAIN

LAMAR RED RIVER

DELTA HOPKINS FRANKLIN TITUS
BOWIE

DENTON
75 COLLIN HUNT
CAMP MORRIS CASS

ROCK-
WALL RAINS WOOD UPSHUR MARION

73
TARRANT
74
DALLAS KAUFMAN VAN ZANDT SMITH
76 GREGG HARRISON

HENDERSON RUSK PANOLA

NAVARRO ANDERSON CHEROKEE SHELBY

FREESTONE HOUSTON NACOGDOCHES SAN AUGUSTINE SABINE

LIMESTONE LEON ANGELINA

ROBERTSON MADISON
99 TRINITY POLK TYLER JASPER NEWTON

BURLESON
98
BRAZOS GRIMES WALKER SAN JACINTO HARDIN

WASHINGTON MONTGOMERY LIBERTY ORANGE
109

LEE AUSTIN WALLER JEFFERSON

106
FAYETTE HARRIS
107 CHAMBERS

COLORADO FORT BEND

LAVACA WHARTON BRAZORIA GALVES-
TON
108

JACKSON MATAGORDA

112
VICTORIA
GOLIAD

CALHOUN
113

REFUGIO

ARANSAS

NUECES
118

KLEBERG

KLAMATH
1

LAKE
2

HARNEY

MALHEUR

OWYHEE

GOODING
LINCOLN
JEROME
3
MINIDOKA
BLAINE
5
POWER
BANNOCK
CARIBOU
6

TWIN
FALLS
CASSIA
ONEIDA
FRANKLIN
7
BEAR
LAKE

LINCOLN
14

SISKIYOU

MODOC
39
Goose Lake

SHASTA

LASSEN

TEHAMA

PLUMAS
40

BUTTE

SIERRA

YUBA

NEVADA

SUTTER

PLACER
Lake Tahoe

YOLO
41

EL DORADO

SOLANO

SACRAMENTO

AMADOR

CONTRA
COSTA

SAN
JOAQUIN
42

CALAVERAS

ALPINE
43

ALA-
MEDA

STANISLAUS

TUOLUMNE

44

SANTA
CLARA
46

MERCED
47

MARIPOSA

SANTA
CRUZ

MADERA
51

SAN BENITO
49
48

FRESNO
54

MONTEREY
50

KINGS

TULARE

SAN LUIS
OBISPO
58

KERN
60
59

64

SANTA BARBARA
61

VENTURA
62
63

65

LOS ANGELES

74

CHANNEL ISLANDS

WASHOE
86
STOREY
92
93
LYON
95
DOUGLAS

Pyramid Lake

PERSHING
87

CHURCHILL
94

MINERAL
96

MONO

ESMERALDA
101

INYO

56
57

STOREY

LANDER

EUREKA
98

97

NYE
100

45

102

SAN BERNARDINO
67
68
70
69
71
72
73
108

66
77

76
75
ORANGE
78
79

RIVERSIDE
85
Salton Sea

SAN DIEGO
81
82
80
83

IMPERIAL
84

HUMBOLDT

ELKO
91
90
89
88

WHITE PINE
99

LINCOLN

103

104
105

CLARK
106
107

BOX ELDER

*Great
Salt Lake*

TOOELE
109

CACHE
110
WEBER
111
MORGAN
DAVIS
112
SALT
LAKE
113

RICH
13
UINTA

SUMMIT

DUCHES
115

*Utah
Lake*
114
WASATCH

UTAH

JUAB
118

MILLARD
117

SANPETE
121
SEVIER
120

CARBO
119

122

EMERY

BEAVER
124

PIUTE

WAYNE
125

IRON
127
128

GARFIELD
129

WASHINGTON
131

KANE
132

SAN

PACIFIC

OCEAN

Kilometers
0   50   100   150

Statute Miles
0   50   100   150

OREGON
1 Klamath Falls
2 Lakeview

IDAHO
3 Twin Falls
4 Burley
5 Pocatello
6 Soda Springs
7 Preston

WYOMING
8 Pinedale
9 Lander
10 Casper
11 Douglas
12 Lusk
13 Evanston
14 Kemmerer
15 Green River
16 Rock Springs
17 Rawlins
18 Hanna
19 Wheatland
20 Torrington
21 Laramie
22 Cheyenne

NEBRASKA
23 Chadron
24 Valentine
25 Scottsbluff
26 Alliance
27 Thedford

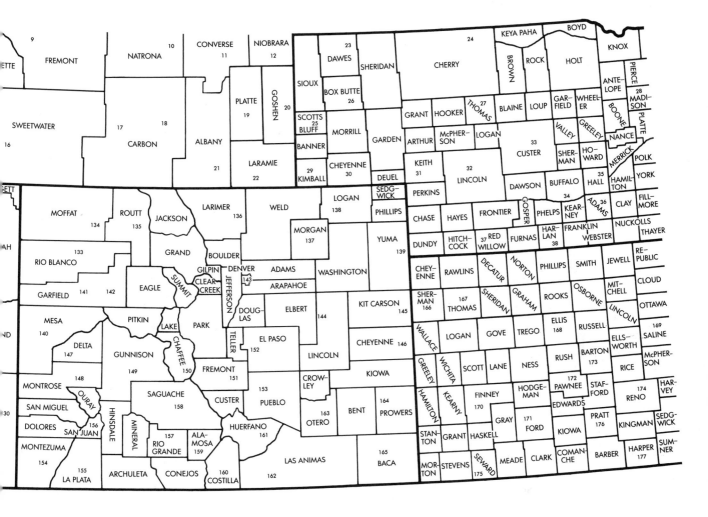

28 Norfolk
29 Kimball
30 Sidney
31 Ogalalla
32 North Platte
33 Broken Bow
34 Kearney
35 Grand Island
36 Hastings
37 McCook
38 Alma

CALIFORNIA
39 Alturas
40 Susanville
41 Sacramento
42 Stockton
43 Bridgeport
44 Leevining
45 Bishop
46 San Jose
47 Merced
48 Salinas
49 Monterey
50 King City
51 Fresno
52 Hanford
53 Visalia
54 Lone Pine
55 Inyokern
56 Death Valley
57 Shoshone

58 San Luis Obispo
59 Taft
60 Bakersfield
61 Lompoc
62 Santa Barbara
63 Ventura
64 Mojave
65 Lancaster
66 Victorville
67 Barstow
68 Baker
69 Ivanpah
70 Ludlow
71 Amboy
72 Goffs
73 Needles
74 Los Angeles
75 Santa Ana
76 Riverside
77 San Bernardino
78 Palm Springs
79 Indio
80 San Diego
81 Escondido
82 Borrego Springs
83 Jacumba
84 El Centro
85 Blythe

NEVADA
86 Gerlach
87 Lovelock

88 Winnemucca
89 Battle Mountain
90 Elko
91 Wells
92 Reno
93 Carson City
94 Fallon
95 Yerington
96 Hawthorne
97 Austin
98 Eureka
99 Ely
100 Tonopah
101 Goldfield
102 Beatty
103 Pioche
104 Moapa
105 Mesquite
106 Las Vegas
107 Boulder City
108 Searchlight

UTAH
109 Wendover
110 Logan
111 Ogden
112 Salt Lake City
113 Tooele
114 Provo
115 Duchesne
116 Vernal
117 Delta

118 Nephi
119 Price
120 Richfield
121 Salina
122 Castle Dale
123 Greenriver
124 Milford
125 Torrey
126 Moab
127 Cedar City
128 Panguitch
129 Escalante
130 Monticello
131 St. George
132 Kanab

COLORADO
133 Meeker
134 Craig
135 Steamboat Springs
136 Fort Collins
137 Fort Morgan
138 Sterling
139 Wray
140 Grand Junction
141 Rifle
142 Glenwood Springs
143 Denver
144 Limon
145 Burlington
146 Cheyenne Wells
147 Delta

148 Montrose
149 Gunnison
150 Salida
151 Cañon City
152 Colorado Springs
153 Pueblo
154 Cortez
155 Durango
156 Silverton
157 Del Norte
158 Saguache
159 Alamosa
160 San Luis
161 Walsenburg
162 Trinidad
163 La Junta
164 Lamar
165 Springfield

KANSAS
166 Goodland
167 Colby
168 Hays
169 Salina
170 Garden City
171 Dodge City
172 Larned
173 Great Bend
174 Hutchinson
175 Liberal
176 Pratt
177 Anthony

Index

A page number in boldface type (**438**) indicates the first page of a major discussion, critical explanation, or key. A page number followed by an "m" (438m) indicates a map of the distribution of a species or its several varieties. A page number in italics (*438*) indicates a black-and-white illustration. Numbers preceded by a "c" (*c87*) indicate illustration numbers (not page numbers) in one of the three color sections (following pp. 468, 596, and 788).

All mentions of botanical names are indexed, but incidental mentions of other subjects are not indexed. Common names of specific cacti are cross-referenced to their botanical names; common names of plants other than cacti are not thus cross-referenced.

Accepted genera, species, and other taxa are not distinguished typographically in the Index from taxa that are not accepted (i.e., synonyms), but the latter are never followed by boldface page numbers. Botanical names appearing in the Documentation (pp. 910-70) are indexed; that section is not otherwise indexed. Personal names are indexed as they appear in the text or in a text reference to a publication; authors of taxa, collectors of specimens, or authors in the References Cited are not indexed. Terms specially defined in the text are indexed; they may also appear in the Glossary (pp. 973-86), but the Glossary itself, along with the rest of the back matter, is not indexed.